THE CHRONOLOGICAL GOSPEL
COMMENTARY

COMBINING THE TESTIMONY OF THE GOSPEL ACCOUNTS
IN A FULLY INTEGRATED
VIEW OF THE LIFE OF JESUS CHRIST

MICHAEL R. HAGERTY

PRIMROSE LANE PUBLISHING

COPYRIGHT © 2007
By Michael R. Hagerty

All rights reserved. No part of this book may be reproduced or transmitted in any form or by any means, electronic or mechanical, including photocopying, recording, or any information storage and retrieval system without permission in writing from the publisher.

Published by Primrose Lane Publishing, Tucson, Arizona

Scripture quoted from *The New American Standard Bible*®,
Copyright © 1960, 1962, 1963, 1968, 1971, 1972, 1973, 1975, 1977, 1995
by THE LOCKMAN FOUNDATION
A Corporation Not for Profit
LA HABRA, CALIFORNIA

All Rights Reserved
Used by permission (www.Lockman.org)

Library of Congress Cataloguing-in-Publication Data
ISBN 978-0-615-45061-2

1 2

PERMISSION TO QUOTE:
The text of the *The New American Standard Bible*® may be quoted and/or reprinted up to and inclusive of two hundred (200) verses without express permission of the Lockman Foundation, provided the verses do not amount to a complete book of the Bible nor do the verses quoted account for more than 10% of the total work in which they are quoted.

Printed in the United States of America

Credits:
Cover image courtesy of FreeDigitalPhotos.net

TABLE OF CONTENTS

Preface v

Introduction vii

CHAPTER 1	His Birth and Kingdom Preaching	9
CHAPTER 2	The Ministry of John the Baptist	55
CHAPTER 3	The Early Disciples	73
CHAPTER 4	Christ's Ministry - Year of Favor	83
CHAPTER 5	His Galilean Ministry	112
CHAPTER 6	The Sermon on the Mount	134
CHAPTER 7	Teaching Through Parables	232
CHAPTER 8	Christ's Ministry – Year of Opposition	265
CHAPTER 9	Working of Miracles	300
CHAPTER 10	Ministering Again in Galilee	329
CHAPTER 11	Conflict with the Pharisees	524
CHAPTER 12	The Olivet Discourse and End Times	557
CHAPTER 13	Last Passover and Passion Week	588
CHAPTER 14	His Arrest and Trial	653
CHAPTER 15	His Crucifixion	685
CHAPTER 16	His Resurrection	702
CHAPTER 17	Final Commission and Ascension	721

Index 747

ACKNOWLEDGEMENTS

To Wayne West, Bill Applegate, and Michael Draper whose encouragement and aggressive optimism were indispensable in getting me beyond mere ideas to success.

To Priscilla for editorial and artistic suggestions and her vantage point as partner, wife, and fellow servant in Christ.

And to our Risen Lord who moves the heart, that the work of our hands may be pleasing to Him.

Preface

Today, commentaries on the New Testament abound. Why then another commentary on the gospels? Pastors, scholars and serious Bible students already have at their disposal a wide array of critical and expository tools for the work of interpretation. But the everyday believer, the lay Christian, whose life is not professionally bound up in the duties of scholar or pastor, often finds the weightier, more critical commentary overwhelming. They frequently need and seldom find a more concise approach to explaining and guiding their understanding of the Scriptures. Seldom are they keenly interested in knowing interpretation 'A' was rejected by Beza, or that Alexandrinus and Emphraemi are the only two uncial manuscripts that leave out the critical wording of a given chapter. As for the New Testament, individual commentaries often lack a consistent purview to all four gospels, making references to the coordinate material a larger task than studying one account.

The *Chronological Gospel Commentary* collapses these inspired accounts into one narrative across them all. Identical information repeated among the gospels is represented once from a selected account. Statements unique to their books are interspersed at their appropriate chronological place. In many ways, this is a harmony of the gospels in a narrative format, without the comparative side-by-side columns for each book, making the text and commentary appreciably more readable, while retaining annotations to each contributing gospel and its verses.

'Chronological' is a bit of a misnomer because there is no universal concord among scholars on the precise order of all events; and there are some issues of harmony where stressing one chronology may appear to undermine another (Ex. the varying accounts of the scene at the tomb of Jesus, Matthew 28:1ff, Mark 16:1ff, John 20:1ff). Thus, any chronology must employ some elements of human interpretation. Bible editions like *The Daily Bible in Chronological Order*, (Harvest House, 1984) are examples of arrangements superintended by careful scholarship.

A commentary should recognize three key objectives:

Understanding. The ease and facility of direct comprehension for its audience by avoiding wherever possible excessively scholastic and intimidating content. Bring the fruit within reach, without compromising the content of truth and knowledge.

Exhortation. Encourage readers to action by emulating the unction and conviction of the Holy Spirit to begin a life that is changed and conformed to the image of Christ.

Application. Provide guidelines and examples that relate to modern life, and reveal helpful insights on the "how-to" of effecting the commands and exhortations of Scripture.

Overview of Features

Chronological Four-Gospel Presentation. All four gospels are collapsed into one running account, benefiting from having events in historical order with all four contributions in one place.

Common Sense in Linguistic Notations. Use of detailed, technical, linguistic analysis helpful to the scholar but less so to the average reader is minimized in accordance with common sense, appearing where it helps one's understanding, curtailed when it is of minor import and value.

Concise, Readable Format. Scripture is broken up into bite-sized sections that can be read devotionally a day at a time if desired. The format avoids a formal, technical apparatus of references to manuscripts and theologians.

Scripture and Commentary in One. Each section presents the pertinent Scripture, followed by verse-by-verse commentary (the reader does not have to jockey Bible and commentary side-by-side).

The NASB Text. The commentary uses the New American Standard Bible®, Copyright © (1995) by permission from the Lockman Foundation.

Introduction

The four Gospels of the New Testament are the written accounts of what originally were verbal sermons and teaching spoken by the apostles as they evangelized and served to administer the various assemblies after the Ascension. Peter's verbal gospel was the first to circulate and became what we have essentially in Mark.

The copies of the gospels we have today do not have signatures or dates. Despite being called *autographs*, we are reasonably confident that the originals did not have them either, because the copying process did not exclude anything that appeared in the original. In later copying, the scribes even preserved little notes written by earlier scribes. It is possible that letters or notes explaining the contents of documents being disseminated may have identified them as coming from the disciples of Jesus, but nothing like that has ever been discovered. So dating the gospels is a matter of deduction from known facts about the period involved, some internal indicators, and the corporate conviction of Christian tradition.

Mark is the first of the written gospels and represents Peter's verbal preaching of the account of Jesus' life. What is amazing is that this account first existed in the memory of a man, so it was memorized and preached virtually the same from place to place. That is a significant accomplishment by today's standards. We have difficulty remembering a few verses, much less a whole gospel, word-for-word. Peter had much to draw on from his firsthand experiences with Jesus, but this had to be redacted down to a finite account. You can imagine the temptation to digress to little stories about how Jesus did such and such. One would wind up with many versions from the same author without some discipline. He needed to and succeeded in concentrating on what the Holy Spirit had in mind.

Mark was composed shortly before 70 A.D., since he does not mention the destruction of Jerusalem (but that is not a necessary proof). We also need to remember that the date of the writing has little to do with the origination of the content in the account. Even if a writer like Matthew or John wrote down their gospels after the destruction of Jerusalem, the content had long been fixed before then in its verbal form. The writing then codified that preaching, rather than being a set of new original works authored later.

Matthew is thought to have written his gospel account around 80 A.D. since it contains so much of Mark. This implies that Mark was "established" if Matthew quotes from it, but the time gap is an estimate. Luke came next and he completes what are called the Synoptics, a term that describes their commonality in using the same material in the majority of passages, and to also serve to separate John's gospel as unique from the other three. Luke also wrote Acts as a companion to his gospel, whose initial purpose seems to have been to better inform a certain Theophilus about things concerning Jesus, and which later won wide acceptance among Christians in general.

John is dated between 85-90 A.D. This is of course an intelligent speculation. Church tradition is one resource that John was written last, primarily due to some disputation over its departure from the common material of the synoptics. It's failure to incorporate much of this common material drew some early suspicion as to its inspiration; concerns which were subsequently laid to rest. In addition, we have the John Rylands fragment, dated around 125-150 A.D. which implies from its discovery in Egypt that John had to have been in circulation long enough to have copies in distant places.

There is also the theory about a source called Q. This is used to explain why Matthew, Mark and Luke have so much information in common. This is not an easy theory to explain and many facets have their good and bad arguments. Q is proposed as an earlier document containing a sort of catalog of the "Sayings of Jesus" and that these three writers used Q in writing there own versions. On the other hand, if we date Matthew on the basis of Mark being in circulation, Q could be simply Mark. Against this explanation is the thinking that if Mark were in fact the exemplar which the others used, their gospels would be quite different since they would desire to have their versions stand out in distinction, or tell the story a bit differently than Mark. Conversely, Q is not proposed as a complete gospel, hence harmony in using it makes sense. While Q is the prevailing theory, nothing definitive can be made either way.

There has been some discussion among Catholics that the Church gave us the Bible, not the other way around. There is a way of understanding this as true, in that the Church settled the issue of what was inspired and what was spurious and did form the final list of the books that formed the canon of the Christian Church. Furthermore, those who wrote the NT were certainly "in the Church," so to some degree the origination of the NT is the work of the Church in that the disciples were part of the Church Jesus established when they wrote.

But from another perspective, the content in the NT, the information, history and teaching, pre-existed the Church as a formal institution. All the events and the memory of those events in the minds of the disciples came first, the formal establishment and administration of the Church coming after the Ascension.

Either way, it would be incorrect to say that the composition of the NT material was a product of the Church in the time of Constantine. Neither Catholic nor Protestant say this.

THE CHRONOLOGICAL GOSPEL COMMENTARY

CHAPTER 1
His Birth and Kingdom Preaching

John 1:1-13
1 In the beginning was the Word, and the Word was with God, and the Word was God. 2 He was in the beginning with God. 3 All things came into being through Him, and apart from Him nothing came into being that has come into being. 4 In Him was life, and the life was the Light of men. 5 The Light shines in the darkness, and the darkness did not comprehend it. 6 There came a man sent from God, whose name was John. 7 He came as a witness, to testify about the Light, so that all might believe through him. 8 He was not the Light, but he came to testify about the Light. 9 There was the true Light which, coming into the world, enlightens every man. 10 He was in the world, and the world was made through Him, and the world did not know Him. 11 He came to His own, and those who were His own did not receive Him. 12 But as many as received Him, to them He gave the right to become children of God, even to those who believe in His name, 13 who were born, not of blood nor of the will of the flesh nor of the will of man, but of God.)

Scripture quotations taken from the New American Standard Bible®,Copyright © 1960, 1962, 1963, 1968, 1971, 1972, 1973,1975, 1977, 1995 by The Lockman Foundation.

(Note: Old Testament quotations in the New Testament are represented in the NASB in caps. Ex: "As He spoke by the mouth of His holy prophets from of old-- Salvation FROM OUR ENEMIES, And FROM THE HAND OF ALL WHO HATE US;)

Commentary

John 1:1, John 1:14
1 In the beginning was the Word, and the Word was with God, and the Word was God.

John goes back further in the narrative than the other gospels, to the place where God was alone with Himself before the present created world; and at this point in time there was the Word, meaning His Word. We later find that this is not just to take us back to the earliest beginning of all things but rather to declare that the Son about whom this account is concerned actually pre-existed the Creation. Christ as Son was there in the beginning. We know this from the later statement that the Word John is talking about became flesh and dwelt among us.

. . and the Word was God. Since we later find out that the Incarnate Son was this Word, we have a formula for declaring that Jesus Christ was God, was deity. What is important here is that 'Word' is being used to describe something that is for us a Person. John is telling us that when you consider God's Word to man, you can consolidate everything He wanted to say to mankind in the Person of Jesus. It is as though God had one simple message – His Son, and the whole Bible is dedicated to the revelation of Him, more figuratively and symbolically in the OT, then vividly in CinemaScope and color in the NT.

Jehovah's Witnesses and other groups that deny the deity of Christ claim that the verse should read *". . and the Word was a god."* This, they claim, is because there is no article here in the Greek and where no article exists, the indefinite article is assumed, hence not "the God" but "a god."

In English, we use either the definite article (the) or the indefinite article (a, an) and in some rare cases no article. Greek does not have an indefinite article (a, an), but assumes it is in use when the definite article is missing. The argument goes, *"if the noun does not use 'the', it must mean 'a' or 'an.'"* But this is not the only grammatical rule in Greek for these cases.

If someone says to you, "a man came to the door today," this assumes you have no prior knowledge of the man – the indefinite article case – in which case you will ask, "What man?" If they say, "*The* man came to the door today," this assumes you already know who the man is – the definite article case.

But if they say, "*Man* came to the door today," you would (with appropriate curiosity) conclude that something like the *essence* of man had come to the door, or mankind came to the door. This will be discussed next, regarding other rules of grammar.

Those translating John 1:1 often let this incomplete story from Greek grammar serve all the needs of understanding the verse, hence : 'theos ein ho logos' equals *"and the word was a god."* But this ignores more in the grammar than the use of the article.

E. C. Colwell discovered an amazing rule from an exhaustive study of Greek usage, which basically said that there are constructions in Greek where the noun can be definite but not use the article 'the.' These are cases where the noun is in front of the verb, called the 'predicate position.' We have a somewhat similar kind of function when we say "*blessed are the poor in spirit*" instead of *the poor in spirit are blessed.* The adjective 'blessed' becomes the subject in front of the verb for emphasis, and it does not need *the* to distinguish it as important.

Colwell's rule also identifies these constructions as actually going further than making the noun merely definite – they convey *essence.* So more than 'the Word is the God', it would convey that the Word was the very essence of God', which is precisely what we have in any responsible translation of the NT.

As we look further at v.14, we find that Jesus Christ was that Word, hence was the very essence of God.

The Import of John 1:49

For those who insist that John 1:1 must be translated *"a god,"* they must engage an inconsistency. In John 1:49, Nathaniel states that Jesus was "the King of Israel."

In the Greek, the construction is exactly the same as in John 1:1, the noun 'basileus' (king) is in the predicate position without the article. If those sponsoring 'a god' wish to insist on it, then they should be consistent at John 1:49 and read "You are *a* king of Israel" which is an assertion even the trinity debunkers would never wish to propose.

What is being said in John is that the Word was the essence of God, which undermines all attempts to make Jesus merely a god. [1]

2 He was in the beginning with God. 3 All things came into being through Him, and apart from Him nothing came into being that has come into being.

John reveals to us that the Son was in the beginning and the very Actor who we see creating in Genesis chapter 1. The mention of all things being made through Him is to exclude the idea that certain things might have come about independent of God.

4 In Him was life, and the life was the Light of men. 5 The Light shines in the darkness, and the darkness did not comprehend it.

That life was in Him means more than biological life. It means fullness of life as intended by the Creator. This was lost at the Fall and Jesus proclaimed that the purpose of His coming was to renew what was lost,

---

[1] Kittel, Theological Dictionary of the New Testament Vol 3, Eerdmans, 1976, pp. 104-108
Robertson, A.T., A Grammar of the Greek New Testament, Broadman, 1934 , p.789ff
Colwell, E.C., A Definite Rule for the Use of the Article in the Greek New Testament p. 20; Daniel Wallace, Greek Grammar Beyond the Basics, Grand Rapids: Zondervan, 1996, 269.

". . that you may have life and that abundantly." This is indicated by the qualifier, *"and the life was the Light of men."*

The relationship of light to life is to highlight an awakening, a distinction from darkness that draws men out into it and toward righteousness. So in this one verse we see telescoped the ideas of the creation of man in innocence, his fall into darkness, the shining of light in that darkness, and the renewal of life by receiving the Light that has always been in Christ first as Creator, then as Savior.

6 There came a man sent from God, whose name was John. 7 He came as a witness, to testify about the Light, so that all might believe through him. 8 He was not the Light, but he came to testify about the Light.

While John the Baptist is chronologically out of place here, his message about Jesus and the Light must accompany what John the Apostle is saying here because these words will not make sense at the point where the Baptist's ministry is described.

"sent from God" is an important phrase because we are given immediate knowledge that John was a messenger commissioned by the Almighty to both reveal and exhort. He is mentioned here in the discussion about beginnings because he adds to the discussion about Light.

In John's Gospel, light is an important theme. It is a useful picture of the state of affairs. Man and his world are in darkness, plagued by man's evil and its consequences. There is an expectation among men for some light from God to shine in that darkness, some glimmer to give one hope that God still exists and has not left man destitute. The Baptist came to bear witness to the light that John the Apostle is now also proclaiming.

John 1:9-13
9 There was the true Light which, coming into the world, enlightens every man. 10 He was in the world, and the world was made through Him, and the world did not know Him. 11 He came to His own, and those who were His own did not receive Him.

Every man? We draw back from this because in our experience we seem to encounter a host of people who give no indication they have been so enlightened. In Romans, this idea is revisited. Paul discloses that God has made Himself known to all men everywhere so that all are without excuse (Rom 1:20). It is the idea that at the judgment no man can claim, "I never knew a thing about you all my life, so how can I be judged?" God will be able to point to that place in time when He revealed Himself inwardly to every man.

And yet surprisingly, we then have *"the world did not know Him."* How does this relate to having the Light enlighten every man? This is simply to say that after the revelation of God to every man, the world tended to forget this experience, primarily because this was subjective, and man became entangled in the practical aspects of living and society. Men learned to get along without God. Thus, God and His Spirit were in the world, yet the world no longer recognized Him, even when the Son was here in person.

That His own did not receive Him seems strange until we realize that one's home town is a place of familiarity and social intimacy and "familiarity breeds contempt." This is simply to say that we get indignant when someone we have known for years begins preaching and exhorting us, as if they've become something special. In Jesus' case he was indeed special, but in ways that are spiritually discerned and this is not always appreciated in all people.

12 But as many as received Him, to them He gave the right to become children of God, even to those who believe in His name, 13 who were born, not of blood nor of the will of the flesh nor of the will of man, but of God.

Many people believe that just being a human being makes them a child of God, since He is our Creator. But the Bible makes it clear that this is not automatic, but involves a right. The bestowal of that right has a prerequisite we must all meet. We must *receive* Him. This means we must not merely acknowledge that Jesus existed, died and rose again, but we must make these facts personal. We must "accept" what He stands for - His message - and the changes in our life He calls all men to make. Separating the mere fact of Christ from what He taught and commanded does not succeed.

It's akin to saying Jesus was a great teacher, a righteous man. You can't say this and ignore the import of His teaching. He doesn't give us that option; and people who do this anyway are simply being superficial. His words are of a nature that one must make a decision about Him one way or the other. We must decide if He was self-deceived or deluded about His message, or if He and His message are the truth about the real world as it is. To decide the former is to reject Him. To decide the latter is to accept Him.

To be *born of God* is declared as distinct from being physically born, and is not achieved by willing it into being. It is not acquired by trying really, really hard. It requires an act of God. So for those who are skeptical about miracles, they have been given the first lesson in Miracles 101. Their being born of God at conversion is the first instance of miracles in their life.

To be born of God is talked about later in John as the second birth, to be born again (3:7). We are born to biological life that begins as dead unto God. We must then be born a second time, but in spiritual terms that make our spirit alive unto God.

Birth means introduction to life and the expectation is to then walk out in it. It is not an experience we have, then put on the shelf and go about our business as before. We have been changed because this birth is of God and has expectations we cannot ignore.

To be born of God means that we are now aware of another world, the one God operates in. Our eyes become open to see that world and it changes how we walk, act, and perceive in the physical world.

John 1:14-18, Luke 1:1-4,

14 And the Word became flesh, and dwelt among us, and we saw His glory, glory as of the only begotten from the Father, full of grace and truth. 15 "For he will be great in the sight of the Lord; and he will drink no wine or liquor, and he will be filled with the Holy Spirit while yet in his mother's womb. 16 For of His fullness we have all received, and grace upon grace. 17 For the Law was given through Moses; grace and truth were realized through Jesus Christ. 18 No one has seen God at any time; the only begotten God who is in the bosom of the Father, He has explained Him." (John 1:14-18.)

1 Inasmuch as many have undertaken to compile an account of the things accomplished among us, 2 just as they were handed down to us by those who from the beginning were eyewitnesses and servants of the word, 3 it seemed fitting for me as well, having investigated everything carefully from the beginning, to write it out for you in consecutive order, most excellent Theophilus; 4 so that you may know the exact truth about the things you have been taught. (Luke 1:1-4.)

The Genealogies of Jesus

Luke 3:23
23 . . being, as was supposed, the son of Joseph, the son of Eli, . .

[76 generations from Joseph back to Adam]

Matthew 1:1-17
1-17 "The record of the genealogy of Jesus the Messiah, the son of David, the son of Abraham, . .

Abraham forward to Joseph, 42 generations

. . . 14 generations from Abraham to David . . .

. . . 14 generations from David to the Babylonian Exile . . .

. . . 14 generations from the Exile to Messiah . . .

Commentary

John 1:14-18
14 And the Word became flesh, and dwelt among us, and we saw His glory, glory as of the only begotten from the Father, full of grace and truth. . . . . 16 For of His fullness we have all received, and grace upon grace.

John mentions actual flesh for two reasons: 1) to proclaim that God purposed that the Son should live among men as a human being and experience all the feelings, pains and thoughts of the human creation; and 2) to repudiate the Gnostic heresy that Jesus was merely a phantom or very effective apparition but never possessed a fleshly body.

The Gnostics didn't disagree that God had the power to do so, but denied God's willingness to contaminate His divine Nature by becoming one with human flesh. Here, John not only puts this idea to rest but also in I John 1:1 where he goes further in saying they actually handled him, which could not have been possible with an apparition.

That Christ was "full of grace and truth" is not to say that all the grace and truth to be had was in Him, since this was also said of Mary at the annunciation. Rather, it aligns with what Jesus declared, "No man comes to the Father but by me."

Grace is something that is being introduced into the backdrop of Judaism. Judaism really didn't have the same concept of grace. The animal sacrifices were a form of grace by alleviating the death of the sinner. But these were tied to the legalism of the Law in which the believer observed things approved and avoided things condemned. In NT Grace, one has a free gift that is totally the work of God on behalf of the believer and is not based on any concept of performance or merit. Man does not participate in the operation of Grace, only in so far as receiving it from God as unmerited favor. This was new to the Old Testament mind.

The importance of its appearance and mention in the Gospels is really what the good news of the gospel is all about. The backdrop of the OT was one of performance before God, the doing of works in the interest of pleasing God; and the perennial disappointment of not meeting the requirements of the Law. There was a sort of corporate sigh among the Jews, a sigh that spoke of the toil, tediousness and inability to permanently fix the problem in man.

The good news of the gospel is that such toil and legalism is over. One has come to forever remedy man's endemic problem once and for all and at last. So Christ was the very fullness of that Grace.

He was the fullness of truth because He was God Incarnate and knows the beginning from the end in all things. He sees all facts and circumstances from every angle possible, perceives accurately every motive and thought. We see this later on with His disciples when He perceives their motives in making certain comments. The same occurred when in the midst of crowds of people or the Pharisees. He knew their thoughts and then spoke such that He cut them to the quick.

In the judgment before Christ, we anticipate that we will not be able to prevaricate or rationalize. He will know the truth about what we did and why, and there will be no arguing or contention about the meaning of actions or words.

But more than this, John is saying that Jesus came to put mankind right with the truth about the world as it really is. There is a realm beyond this physical temporal world of business, family, the tending of crops and the making of money. That realm is far more important to our lives than anything else we presently see. We are born to be related to that realm, so best we encounter it and understand it. That is why His message is about the Kingdom as foremost, not the silly questions man can pose to someone who claims to come down from God.

"grace upon grace" is a way of describing the many graces that comprise Grace overall. The gift of Grace is multi-faceted and its gift goes on surprising us as we live for Him. So beyond the general provision of Grace in salvation, one experiences unmerited favor in so many other areas that it is as though new grace is being piled on grace already received.

17 For the Law was given through Moses; grace and truth were realized through Jesus Christ. 18 No one has seen God at any time; the only begotten God who is in the bosom of the Father, He has explained Him."

Again the contrast between the two periods, which some refer to as dispensations. The period of the Law was characterized by its legalism and its works, with major themes of truth veiled in symbolism, feasts and prophecy. The period of Christ's life and ministry is that of Grace and Truth fully revealed.

It is claimed that Moses saw God hence the shining of his face, and that this is a contradiction to the above. But in Exodus we find that God placed His Hand over Moses as He passed by so that he only saw Him from the backside, consistent with the condition that no man can see God and live. So we learn that the peculiar seeing of God that is inherently dangerous is the seeing of His Face, and in this regard, no man has ever seen it at anytime. Yet God condescended to allow a reflection of Himself to be visible in His only begotten Son, whose appearance and life explained Him to all mankind.

This is what Jesus meant in saying, "He who has seen the Son has seen the Father."

Luke 1:1-4
1 Inasmuch as many have undertaken to compile an account of the things accomplished among us, 2 just as they were handed down to us by those who from the beginning were eyewitnesses and servants of the word, 3 it seemed fitting for me as well, having investigated everything carefully from the beginning, to write it out for you in consecutive order, most excellent Theophilus; 4 so that you may know the exact truth about the things you have been taught.

Luke's account enters here to disclose his purpose in telling the story and to introduce an important element - the credentials of Jesus as Messiah. Since the Gospels declare throughout that Jesus is Israel's long awaited Messiah of prophecy, His pedigree is key to gaining any hearing among the Jews.

That Luke is writing to a Gentile is not out of place because the question of Messiahship is wrapped up in the prophecies of the Jews and there would be an expectation in anyone studying these matters to see those fulfilled.

Luke 3:23-38
23 .. being, as was supposed, the son of Joseph, the son of Eli, ..

... 76 generations - Joseph back to Adam ...

Matthew 1:1-17
1 The record of the genealogy of Jesus the Messiah, the son of David, the son of Abraham:

... 42 generations - Abraham to Messiah ...

We note a major discrepancy - different fathers for Joseph: Eli in one account, Jacob in the other. This has long fed attacks on the reliability of the NT accounts. However, this is explained by simply pointing out that every person has two lineages, through the father and the mother. If Luke is presenting Mary's lineage through David, and Matthew that of Joseph through David, the names will be different, as we see in the lists.

But why then doesn't Luke's genealogy end with Mary instead of Joseph if Eli was her father and not Joseph's? While we see the appearance of women in genealogies, to the Jews it was never customary to have a woman's lineage be formally stated as such, but the man, who is the subject, is instead substituted for the woman's name with the understanding that the father listed is really the man's father-in-law. [2]

Now it seems that this was a lot of tempest in a teapot because everyone would know it was the mother's lineage. But ancient customs do not always comply with the dictates of logic. And you will note that the Jews never voiced complaints about these genealogies or their Davidic connections. Rather, their chief dig was that Jesus appeared as illegitimate, since Mary was with child and Joseph married her as an act of compassion.

The chief point to make here is that on either side, Jesus is connected with David who is key to Messiah's pedigree. Messiah will be the son of David. Any claimant has to prove this. In Jesus' case he gives the Jews both barrels. He is related by blood through Mary and he is related by adoption through Joseph, a perfectly legal means of inheriting a place in a lineage.

To his Jewish detractors, this was unassailable. Even if something might be made of a non-Davidic lineage in some supposed biological father involved in Mary's "indiscretion," Davidic lineage was clearly established in Mary, so the point was moot.

---

[2] Broadus, <u>Commentary on The Gospel of Matthew</u>, Kregel, 1990, p. 6

There are other studies that analyze these lists in comparison to the genealogies in the OT and discuss the discrepancies. But it is always important to bear in mind that Jewish genealogies were never taken as always being required to present a complete and legal record of all ancestors. The official registries among the priests accomplished this. But many other genealogies were redactions or summaries for particular purposes, so names would often be intentionally omitted.

Observations like these and other aspects of Jewish customs have resolved virtually all discrepancies among the various lists.

The Birth of John the Baptist and Jesus

Luke 1:5-25
5 "In the days of Herod, king of Judea, there was a priest named Zacharias, of the division of Abijah; and he had a wife from the daughters of Aaron, and her name was Elizabeth. 6 They were both righteous in the sight of God, walking blamelessly in all the commandments and requirements of the Lord. 7 But they had no child, because Elizabeth was barren, and they were both advanced in years.

8 Now it happened that while he was performing his priestly service before God in the appointed order of his division, 9 according to the custom of the priestly office, he was chosen by lot to enter the temple of the Lord and burn incense. 10 And the whole multitude of the people were in prayer outside at the hour of the incense offering. 11 And an angel of the Lord appeared to him, standing to the right of the altar of incense. 12 Zacharias was troubled when he saw the angel, and fear gripped him. 13 But the angel said to him, "Do not be afraid, Zacharias, for your petition has been heard, and your wife Elizabeth will bear you a son, and you will give him the name John.

14 "You will have joy and gladness, and many will rejoice at his birth. 15 "For he will be great in the sight of the Lord; and he will drink no wine or liquor, and he will be filled with the Holy Spirit while yet in his mother's womb. 16 "And he will turn many of the sons of Israel back to the Lord their God. 17 "It is he who will go as a forerunner before Him in the spirit and power of Elijah, TO TURN THE HEARTS OF THE FATHERS BACK TO THE CHILDREN, and the disobedient to the attitude of the righteous, so as to make ready a people prepared for the Lord."

18 Zacharias said to the angel, "How will I know this for certain? For I am an old man and my wife is advanced in years." 19 The angel answered and said to him, "I am Gabriel, who stands in the presence of God, and I have been sent to speak to you and to bring you this good news. 20 "And behold, you shall be silent and unable to speak until the day when these things take place, because you did not believe my words, which will be fulfilled in their proper time." 21 The people were waiting for Zacharias, and were wondering at his delay in the temple. 22 But when he came out, he was unable to speak to them; and they realized that he had seen a vision in the temple; and he kept making signs to them, and remained mute.

23 When the days of his priestly service were ended, he went back home. 24 After these days Elizabeth his wife became pregnant, and she kept herself in seclusion for five months, saying, 25 "This is the way the Lord has dealt with me in the days when He looked with favor upon me, to take away my disgrace among men."

Commentary

Luke 1:5-11
5 "In the days of Herod, king of Judea, . .

At the close of the OT we find Persia in control of the domains formerly under Babylon, including the land of Israel. Judah has been allowed to return to its homeland from the Exile begun by Nebuchadnezzar in the time of Daniel.

When we open the pages of the NT, we find Rome on the scene, *"Now in those days a decree went out from Caesar Augustus, that a census be taken of all the inhabited earth."*

A further puzzlement in this verse is that we are told that *Herod* was king of Judea, yet this is now a Roman world. What has happened between the close of the Old Testament and the beginning of the New?

Persian rule eventually gave way to the Greeks. At the death of Alexander the Great, the dominions of the Mediterranean, Asia and the East were divided among his generals. Palestine was won back and forth between Macedonian rulers of Egypt and Syria, under Greek rule.

Eventually, the offenses of Greek kings so offended the Jews that they successfully threw off foreign rule in the Maccabaean revolt in the 160's B.C. Judah lived independently for about 70 years, but internal schisms and conflicts over rule eventually resulted in Rome coming in to settle the squabbling, simultaneously making Palestine a Roman province as their fee.

The Romans were very magnanimous when it came to new provinces, especially those that were won without a war. They allowed local rulers to administer these provinces and even maintained designations like "king" (which meant 'client king').

Enter Julius Caesar. While in Egypt, an assassination attempt was made and a man named Antipater managed to save Caesar's life. Antipater's home country was Judaea. He was therefore granted rule over Judaea. Antipater's son was Herod the Great, who inherited rule and also won designation as King from the Senate under Augustus. [3] That is why we find an Idumean ruler named as king over Jewish land and Jewish citizens in an empire where Rome ruled the world.

5 .. there was a priest named Zacharias, of the division of Abijah; and he had a wife from the daughters of Aaron, and her name was Elizabeth. 6 They were both righteous in the sight of God, walking blamelessly in all the commandments and requirements of the Lord. 7 But they had no child, because Elizabeth was barren, and they were both advanced in years.

Zacharias was therefore a Levite, and his branch is given as that of Abijah. The sheer number of Levites throughout Judaea would have been significant, far more than would be needed in the routine services of the Temple. At Passover and the Day of Atonement reinforcements were necessary due to the sheer number of animals brought to the altar, but ordinarily the needs were much smaller than the population of Levites available. To include more of the members of the tribe, a rotation was designed that assigned heads of all the Levite families on a schedule of service that would eventually give all eligible Levites an opportunity to live up to their tribal calling. We enter the story when it had become Zacharias' time to serve.

8 Now it happened that while he was performing his priestly service before God in the appointed order of his division, 9 according to the custom of the priestly office, he was chosen by lot to enter the temple of the Lord and burn incense. 10 And the whole multitude of the people were in prayer outside at the hour of the incense offering. 11 And an angel of the Lord appeared to him, standing to the right of the altar of incense.

The Altar of Incense was located before the veil of the Holy of Holies, i.e. outside in the Most Holy Place of the Temple, according to Moses in Exodus. (The incense described in Hebrews as being inside the Holy of Holies refers to a censor, not the Altar.) The burning coincided with an hour of prayer for the whole citizenry.

That an angel appeared to Zacharias must be combined with the appearance to Mary and the later appearance of angels to the shepherds; and should give to any rational person the notion that something of tremendous moment was unfolding between God and man.

Zacharias fits into the picture as requiring such a visit in that he is the imminent father of John the Baptist, who will be a key figure in the preparation and annunciation of the Messiah. So we see here and later that all the key figures – Mary, Joseph, Zacharias, his wife Elizabeth, the infant John, the shepherds – are all

---

[3] F.F. Bruce, New Testament History, Doubleday, 1969, p. 13

part of the dramatic advent of Messiah and are each attended with special appearances of angels to prepare them for their role.

In Zacharias' case, he had also been praying for a child, despite the barrenness of this wife, Elizabeth. Precedents were available – Abraham and Sarah.

Luke 1:12-18
12 Zacharias was troubled when he saw the angel, and fear gripped him. 13 But the angel said to him, "Do not be afraid, Zacharias, for your petition has been heard, . .

John will be an interesting character. In John's case, no one could say it was all about him. He was about as self-deprecating as one could get. He possessed no permanent dwelling as a home, his clothing was not manufactured or of woven cloth, but was made from the raw materials in nature. His food and living were extremely simple and unrefined. In essence, there was nothing eminent to point to about his person or life, so he was a perfect candidate as a pointer to that One who was greater than him.

16 "And he will turn many of the sons of Israel back to the Lord their God. 17 "It is he who will go as a forerunner before Him in the spirit and power of Elijah, TO TURN THE HEARTS OF THE FATHERS BACK TO THE CHILDREN, and the disobedient to the attitude of the righteous, so as to make ready a people prepared for the Lord."

One has to wonder how John gained a following. His message had to do with personal sin. But Judaism had a procedure for personal sins. You plugged in the infraction against the Law and out came the required sacrifice and retribution. So how would John, with no recognized training, attract people away from the dictates of the Law, to a baptism of repentance?

The Mosaic law was in some respects without much heart. It presented a catalog of offenses. It declared the fee one must pay to remedy the situation – the sacrifice. But there wasn't really a lot of preaching and exhortation unto repentance. You didn't get riveting sermonizing from the Law. Even in the readings in the synagogues, things were rather rote and routine.

But people were not unintelligent. They were all too well aware that something was thematically missing - the kind of unction and urgency in words that would encourage them to change so that they need not find themselves yet again at the Temple the next week.

John's message of repentance filled that gap. John did not purpose to draw people away from the requirements of the Law and Temple. He simply preached a message that filled people with a renewed sense that genuine repentance was ultimately what God was after, not ritual and procedure.

This idea people flocked to. His baptism had no efficacious power as Christian baptism would, but it was an outward act embodying symbolism that served to seal one's conviction and memory of the message. In this, John fulfilled the power of Elijah who was foretold as turning *"the hearts of the disobedient to the attitude of the righteous."*

In so doing, the Gospel states that John prepared a remnant of renewed Jewish believers who would be ready to receive Jesus. All this was being conveyed to Zacharias, who had to be more than overwhelmed.

18 Zacharias said to the angel, "How will I know this for certain? For I am an old man and my wife is advanced in years."

What is interesting here is the similarity to what Mary will later say, yet without the same consequences. Here Zacharias asks for certainty because he is old and his wife is old. Abraham made a similar comment without the same consequences that will come upon Zacharias.

Personally, it is difficult to see something standing out in the words that would explain Zacharias being made dumb, but leave Mary and Abraham without consequences. What we may surmise is that the making of him dumb would serve as a sign more vividly and effectively remembered by the people, something which could be technically linked to his questioning of the prophecy and also serve a higher purpose. Certainly the immediate effect on people around and the even greater effect when he spoke once again at the dedication of Jesus were profound.

Luke 1:24-25
24 After these days Elizabeth his wife became pregnant, and she kept herself in seclusion for five months, saying, 25 "This is the way the Lord has dealt with me in the days when He looked with favor upon me, to take away my disgrace among men."

The disgrace being remedied for Elizabeth by her late pregnancy was the stain of having been barren. Women had few celebrated accomplishments in this society, and childbearing was linked to their femininity and value as a woman. To be barren was to be denied perhaps the only semblance of worth and value in a patriarchal society.

As we shall see, Elizabeth is part of a much greater scene than begetting a child. She shares a wonderful role -to bless the greatest mother in human history.

Luke 1:26-38
26 Now in the sixth month the angel Gabriel was sent from God to a city in Galilee called Nazareth, 27 to a virgin engaged to a man whose name was Joseph, of the descendants of David; and the virgin's name was Mary. 28 And coming in, he said to her, "Greetings, favored one! The Lord is with you."

29 But she was very perplexed at this statement, and kept pondering what kind of salutation this was. 30 The angel said to her, "Do not be afraid, Mary; for you have found favor with God. 31 "And behold, you will conceive in your womb and bear a son, and you shall name Him Jesus. 32 "He will be great and will be called the Son of the Most High; and the Lord God will give Him the throne of His father David; 33 and He will reign over the house of Jacob forever, and His kingdom will have no end."

34 Mary said to the angel, "How can this be, since I am a virgin?" 35 The angel answered and said to her, "The Holy Spirit will come upon you, and the power of the Most High will overshadow you; and for that reason the holy Child shall be called the Son of God. 36 "And behold, even your relative Elizabeth has also conceived a son in her old age; and she who was called barren is now in her sixth month. 37 "For nothing will be impossible with God." 38 And Mary said, "Behold, the bondslave of the Lord; may it be done to me according to your word." And the angel departed from her.

Commentary

Luke 1:26-27
26 Now in the sixth month the angel Gabriel was sent from God to a city in Galilee called Nazareth,

The sixth month would be August-September (the new year began in March-April). This is merely the time of the announcement, not the beginning of Mary's conception. If she conceived sometime in the next two months from when this announcement was made, this would put her delivery in May-June or June-July, which is why a number of commentators place Jesus' real birth closer to summer than winter as we have it today.

Gabriel has been seen earlier in the book of Daniel coming to comfort him about his prayers for Jerusalem (Dan 9:21). Gabriel is traditionally identified as an archangel who seems to be the divine choice for the more significant turns of biblical history. He is remarkable in that he is of tremendous position and mission before God, yet in two of his roles in the Bible he is shown bringing encouragement and comfort to individual persons.

Nazareth. If you were a detail-oriented viewer when seeing the *The Passion of the Christ*, (Icon Productions © 2004) you might have noticed that Nazareth was pronounced, 'en-saret' by the priests in the movie. This was a linguistic slur of the name Nazareth, where the 'Na' simply became the letter N. Then one skipped to 'zareth' in which the 'z' was smoothed down to an 's' and the final 'th' became just a final 't' – 'N-saret.

Nazareth was not a significant town from a purely human perspective. In our frame of reference it would be a few houses by the side of the road, no gas station, grocery store or restaurant (you would need to go into the nearest town for those things). It would have been a group of buildings grouped around a road, with a well. There was obviously a shop or two – Joseph being a carpenter.

For this reason, we see the comment by the Jerusalem leaders, "Can anything good come from Nazareth?" What is profound is that this was the very place chosen by God for the raising of His Son in early life – nothing to boast about, no life in the halls of a palace, not even life inside an important place like Jerusalem. The Savior of mankind grew up in a no-account hollow hardly counting as a village. That is the kind of humbleness we should sit up and notice. It should tell us ahead of time the kinds of things we are to expect from Jesus. Tremendous power in the midst of a gentle humility.

27 to a virgin engaged to a man whose name was Joseph, of the descendants of David; and the virgin's name was Mary.

Liberal battles ensued earlier in the 20th century over the word *alma* for virgin. It can mean young woman, which some believe must accommodate a married young woman, hence the word 'virgin' would not be demanded, and Jesus' birth would not need to be miraculous. It is also asserted that if virgin was intended, there is ready at hand a Hebrew word for that purpose (*bethulah*). But the argument for the virgin birth does not pivot on the point of *alma* vs. *bethulah* alone. The narrative here in the NT makes it clear that virgin was the intent of the prophesy in Isaiah, and the problem faced by Joseph about Mary's disgrace makes it clear this was not a simple case of two married or betrothed partners conceiving a child.

Of course, the liberal side poses that the NT is contrived to make Jesus more than he really was, so making arguments from this narrative are not convincing to them. But as usual, so much depends on one's estimation of what the NT is – a fabrication by clever men, or the very Word of God.

Luke 1:28-34
28 And coming in, he said to her, "Greetings, favored one! The Lord is with you." 29 But she was very perplexed at this statement, and kept pondering what kind of salutation this was.

Much of this is due to the overwhelming experience of having an angel of God appear and speak. The wording here gives the impression that Mary was more concerned about the nature of the greeting than the phenomenon of an angelic appearance, but this is more a matter of the mode of expression with the writer. The pondering included both the fact of the appearing and the greeting. Put simply, she was pondering the whole event and why it was happening.

30 The angel said to her, "Do not be afraid, Mary; for you have found favor with God. 31 "And behold, you will conceive in your womb and bear a son, and you shall name Him Jesus. 32 "He will be great and will be called the Son of the Most High; and the Lord God will give Him the throne of His father David; 33 and He will reign over the house of Jacob forever, and His kingdom will have no end."

We have to reflect here on the tremendously difficult position in which Mary was being placed. She has all the normal expectations of marriage and a family. Everyone who knows her has been caught up in the festivities of her betrothal. Now she is being brought into an arrangement where she will be found with child outside the consummation of her marriage. This was no trivial matter like it is today. She is signing up for public disgrace. She can't explain it by appealing to the angel's visit. Who would really believe her? It would seem contrived and merely a desperate attempt to cover her indiscretion. Socially, this was a no-win situation on all fronts. Her parents and family would be brought into the disgrace, and there was the serious risk of punishment according to Mosaic law.

As Christians far removed, we usually think of this as the lovely story we hear at Christmas time that focuses our minds on the meaning of Christmas and lends that spiritual touch to the craze of shopping and gifts.

We've sanitized the elements of the story, but it is really quite serious and grave.

34 Mary said to the angel, "How can this be, since I am a virgin?"

As above, we can try to compare these words to those of Zacharias to see why he was disciplined for his doubting while Mary wasn't, despite practically the same words. Zacharias says, "How will I know this for certain? For I am an old man and my wife is advanced in years." Mary says. "How can this be, since I am a virgin?" Both are stating their incredulity at the prospect. Both are bringing in their current state as a mitigation.

Some might point out that Zacharias is saying he needs to be more certain, which would be a weakness of faith, since he's being attended by an angel. But Mary is also in the presence of an angel, the miracle of which doesn't seem to bridge the gap either. Mary questions how the birth can come to pass given her situation.

So it's difficult to find some key element differing between the two. That Zacharias mentions the old age of he and his wife might be seen as subjecting him to the same caution the visiting angels gave to Abraham's wife, "But thou didst laugh." But in the end this is a case of trusting the angel to discern the lack of faith in Zacharias which can only be truly seen spiritually. Likewise, the angel perceived no lack of faith in Mary's question.

Luke 1:35
35 The angel answered and said to her, "The Holy Spirit will come upon you, and the power of the Most High will overshadow you; and for that reason the holy Child shall be called the Son of God.

The idea of the Holy Spirit coming upon someone was not foreign. The OT had many precedents where the Spirit was seen to come upon an individual, so this would be perceived as a case of God intervening in a situation that would be impossible otherwise. We don't need to go further and infer that Mary understood how the mechanism would work in impregnating her without intercourse, but frankly, any person of faith can bridge this gap by simply remembering that God is the author of all living things. If He could create Adam from the dust of the ground, it would be no great task to bring life together in a womb by special creation and retain Mary's genetic contribution in the process.

For those who propose that the sin of Adam comes through the flesh, Mary would have to be completely disconnected from genetic contribution, making her merely the incubator of a completely created being in her womb. But few theologians conclude that Adam's sinful nature is transmitted via the flesh, so a genetic contribution in Mary creates no issues.

This tends to speak on the subject of evolution, strangely enough. Christian evolutionists have offered that God simply used evolution as the means of Creation. This has a reasonable ring to it, but it also usually includes a God who is obligated to do everything via "normal" processes – no fiat creation (out of nothing).

So Adam does not come out of the dust of the ground but out of the process of millions of births and genetic variation – making "dust of the ground" merely a poetic device.

But here in the case of Mary, Christian evolutionists cannot propose that Jesus was born through the normal physical union of a man and a woman. The angel is making it clear that Mary will conceive "outside" such a union, meaning a special conception of life requiring God's intervention into the natural order to make it happen.

The import of this is that once you allow God to work in this way, you open the door to special creation and, as such, the commitment to God using evolution because He was committed to not disturbing the natural order of life has less force.

Of greater moment for Mary is the statement that her son will be the Son of God. Faithful Jews were not unacquainted with the idea that Son of God meant Messiah. But the manner of His coming was not as vivid as the simple fact of His coming. So adding to all the things she is being told, she is seeing the completion of the grand picture in reality – that Messiah will come by means of being born into the human race. She is now seeing the very details unfolding of what had been vaguely described up until now, and that she is going to play a critical part.

And note that Mary would not have understood Son of God as merely a son of God. The phrase was a technical term for the Messiah, as witnessed by the vitriol of the Jews against Jesus when He used this term in His ministry.

Luke 1:36-38
36 "And behold, even your relative Elizabeth has also conceived a son in her old age; and she who was called barren is now in her sixth month. 37 "For nothing will be impossible with God." 38 And Mary said, "Behold, the bondslave of the Lord; may it be done to me according to your word." And the angel departed from her.

What strikes us about this is the intimate knowledge angels have of our human lives. The angel is very much aware of what is happening also to Elizabeth. But so much so that the angel mentions the month of her pregnancy. You get the impression of a complete and intimate knowledge of how human pregnancy works, that it is nine months in length, etc. It bolsters our understanding that there are angels who attend the lives of human beings and know the details as much if not better than our close friends. We have every confidence that they know what we're doing right this minute (even as this is being written), they know who's sitting in front of a computer, they know what brand and model it is, and we expect they know the names of the software used; and they know your names, your families, even your avitars and screen names on the internet.

All of which should humble us that God cares that much about what we do that special beings of His own making are given charge of us and our affairs.

The statement that nothing will be impossible with God is to reinforce who is in charge of the universe and who has the power to effect His Will as He wishes. For some critics, this is seen as an all too easy device that saves us from explaining difficulties in an otherwise unbelievable story (a God of the gaps). But when you entertain the possibility of a God like that revealed in the Bible, you get with the package the exercise of power. And that kind of God is going to resolve the impossible with miracles. It is almost as though skeptics seem more willing to accept the idea of God as long as He remains just as trapped and helpless in human and temporal affairs as mankind. Which of course is less credible than simply believing the accounts in the Bible.

Luke 1:39-56
39 Now at this time Mary arose and went in a hurry to the hill country, to a city of Judah, 40 and entered the house of Zacharias and greeted Elizabeth. 41 When Elizabeth heard Mary's greeting, the baby leaped in her womb; and Elizabeth was filled with the Holy Spirit. 42 And she cried out with a loud voice and said, "Blessed are you among women, and blessed is the fruit of your womb! 43 "And how has it happened to me, that the mother of my Lord would come to me? 44 "For behold, when the sound of your greeting reached my ears, the baby leaped in my womb for joy. 45 "And blessed is she who believed that there would be a fulfillment of what had been spoken to her by the Lord."

46 And Mary said: "My soul exalts the Lord, 47 And my spirit has rejoiced in God my Savior. 48 "For He has had regard for the humble state of His bondslave; For behold, from this time on all generations will count me blessed. 49 "For the Mighty One has done great things for me; And holy is His name. 50 "AND HIS MERCY IS UPON GENERATION AFTER GENERATION TOWARD THOSE WHO FEAR HIM. 51 "He has done mighty deeds with His arm; He has scattered those who were proud in the thoughts of their heart. 52 "He has brought down rulers from their thrones, And has exalted those who were humble. 53 "HE HAS FILLED THE HUNGRY WITH GOOD THINGS; And sent away the rich empty-handed. 54 "He has given help to Israel His servant, In remembrance of His mercy, 55 As He spoke to our fathers, To Abraham and his descendants forever." 56 And Mary stayed with her about three months, and then returned to her home.

Commentary

Luke 1:39

39 "Now at this time Mary arose and went in a hurry to the hill country, to a city of Judah, 40 and entered the house of Zacharias and greeted Elizabeth. 41 When Elizabeth heard Mary's greeting, the baby leaped in her womb; and Elizabeth was filled with the Holy Spirit."

This begins a sort of interlude in which we take a slight diversion from moving toward the birth of Jesus and see a glimpse of events during the pregnancy and those that relate to John the Baptist. Elizabeth is described as Mary's relative in Luke 1:36, and many have seen it likely that this meant cousin. The main reason is that they are assumed to be about the same age, since Elizabeth is also at child-bearing age. But we must remember that her husband Zacharias was stricken because of his doubt considering his age and that of his wife. If a cousin, Elizabeth would have to be a considerably older one. So the age difference does bring in the possibility of an aunt-niece relationship.

They are not likely sisters because the Bible readily identifies sisters when that condition exists. In a complete family involving both parents' relations, two people can be related by blood or by the mere fact of marriage. The two need not be blood relations, but could easily be related through the wives of uncles or the husbands of aunts. Not much more than this can be speculated. Since kinswoman or relative are the meanings for the word used (suggenis), blood relation is not mandatory and it is more probable for a relation by family extension.

We find the unborn infant John moving in his mother's womb at the sound of the greeting from Mary. The NT uses the word 'lept' which sounds strange to us because we use that term to mean a jump across a span and there are no spans or places to leap inside a womb. This is simply an old world way of naming the kicking sensation of infants during pregnancy.

However, in this case it was extraordinary because it wound up in Scripture. As we all know, John is to be the forerunner of Christ. His relationship with Him is momentous to all history. That these two unborn infants were brought into close proximity had to be prodigious just on general principles. It would be like unknowingly crossing paths with your future wife or husband years before you meet and fall in love. Heaven notices the crossing of such paths. For these two infants, Heaven surely noticed and it appears there was a spiritual sensing of this importance already in the unborn John.

There are studies that bear out the hypothesis that unborn children experience a sort of 'hearing' in the womb and that events outside have been known to affect them after birth. So there is much to suggest that there is a perception going on before birth. The filling of Elizabeth with the Holy Spirit is meant in the OT sense. There is as yet nothing like the giving of the Spirit to believers that we find inaugurated in the NT.

Yet the Spirit was none the less active in OT times. The filling with the Spirit was viewed as transient and occurred on special occasions when God was doing something momentous with man as His agent.

The filling for Elizabeth seems meant to help her in uttering the proper praise to God and bestowing the appropriate blessing on Mary. We say appropriate because the words that follow do not come from common sense, but from having been given insight from God.

Luke 1:42-45
42 And she cried out with a loud voice and said, "Blessed are you among women, and blessed is the fruit of your womb! 43 "And how has it happened to me, that the mother of my Lord would come to me?
44 "For behold, when the sound of your greeting reached my ears, the baby leaped in my womb for joy.
45 "And blessed is she who believed that there would be a fulfillment of what had been spoken to her by the Lord."

To bless the fruit of a prospective mother's womb is not unnatural or extraordinary. But to call Mary blessed above all women requires knowledge that she didn't ordinarily have, especially considering that this would place her own pregnancy in a lesser light. No doubt about it, this is God working.

Her humility is shown by the joy she has in having the mother of her Lord visit her. So we have much more that Elizabeth has come to know. She knows that Mary's baby is the Messiah (which had to come by revelation in her spirit) and she is intelligent enough to know that this means that Mary carries one who will rightfully be Lord of mankind. Whether Elizabeth comprehends the deity of Messiah or not, it has been made clear in Scripture that Messiah will be at the very least the rightful earthly Lord of God's people. She takes the movement in her womb to signify she has discerned rightly.

It's not clear in v.45 whether Elizabeth is referring to herself as being blessed for believing that she would have a child at her age (a fulfillment of something spoken by the Lord,) or for believing in the fulfillment spoken to her that Messiah would be born of her relative, or that she is referring to Mary's belief in the fulfillment of things spoken to her by the angel.

Luke 1:46-50
46 And Mary said: "My soul exalts the Lord, 47 And my spirit has rejoiced in God my Savior. 48 "For He has had regard for the humble state of His bondslave; For behold, from this time on all generations will count me blessed. 49 "For the Mighty One has done great things for me; And holy is His name.

This begins what Catholics refer to as the Magnificat. Mary now speaks after the words of Elizabeth. One of the major observations is how different this kind of speech is in today's world. No one talks like this, even in serious moments. Our lives are so otherwise oriented today that speaking like this would be considered 'weird' by most people. Now of course this is a unique moment, but in our world, even unique moments don't beget this kind of speech and reflection. (How much the world has changed since those times.)

Mary exalts the Lord, in that she lifts Him up. She gives recognition of His high position, not that her words put Him there, but that her words show Him there, for all people who hear her. We exalt the Lord in our praise. This is to say that we lift God up in the minds of everyone present.

She recognizes that God is Savior, meaning that if she is to be 'saved' from the plight of mankind, it is in God. And she recognizes that God has a plan for that salvation.

Mary is both thrilled and humbled that she was chosen of God, seeing herself as of humble state as men reckon things. She sees herself as bondservant in the manner of Jewish custom – a slave who decides of their own free will to be bound to their master when they can go free if they wish.

Mary is also perceptive of the meaning of everything happening. Despite her humble life and the relative no account surroundings of Judaea in the midst of a world of much more important places and people,

Mary understands that what is happening to her will be recounted to untold generations. What foresight in faith to see that far into the plan. This isn't conceit or an inflated sense of self-importance that can easily come to ordinary people at last getting their day in the sun. This is Mary's understanding that God is at work in a thing of tremendous magnitude and her role as mother will be part of it.

50 "AND HIS MERCY IS UPON GENERATION AFTER GENERATION TOWARD THOSE WHO FEAR HIM.

In this edition of the NASB, all caps in the text mean that an OT passage is being quoted. But we have to be careful in assuming a literal quote verbatim. Here, Mary is quoting Psalms 103:17 *"But the lovingkindness of the LORD is from everlasting to everlasting on those who fear Him, And His righteousness to children's children,"*

As you can see this is not a direct quote but a paraphrase. She is recalling the mercy God shows from generation to generation when He sees awesome respect for His Grace and Glory. The use of caps in our text is to highlight that Mary knows that the idea expressed comes from the Scripture.

God never considers that He has dispensed enough mercy in times past. He treats each generation as new and present and as eligible for His blessings.

Luke 1:51-53
51 "He has done mighty deeds with His arm;

. . *with his arm* is a strange phrase for us. People don't do deeds with their arm so we find this puzzling. The idea is that of an *outstretched* arm, as in the mode of commanding things to be done. In Michelangelo's ceiling in the Sistine Chapel, we see God at the Creation with his arm outstretched, speaking the worlds into being. In the famous statue of Augustus now in the Vatican, we see the emperor posed in a moment of command, with his arm outstretched. This was simply a common piece of body language in ancient times and we see that it comes from an unwitting emulation of God Himself.

. .*He has scattered those who were proud in the thoughts of their heart. 52 "He has brought down rulers from their thrones, And has exalted those who were humble. 53 "HE HAS FILLED THE HUNGRY WITH GOOD THINGS; And sent away the rich empty-handed.*

We have arrived in modern times at a complete 180 in our assessment of similar things today. We are now taught everywhere to feel good about ourselves, that each of us are the best and the greatest, that we can do anything, achieve anything, so go out and "grab the gusto."

But in God's view, we are to recognize our bankruptcy before Him, that all that we are and will be is that which is in Him. So He resists the proud, he brings prideful rulers to an end; they sit no more on their thrones. And quite contrary to today's thinking (and in the past), He lifts up the humble, those of whom the world takes no account.

This is not to say that he exalts them in contrast to the unbelieving world, but He does so in heavenly places, in heavenly affairs. And on occasion, we see someone whose prior ignoble accomplishments transition to great prominence in the world at large (Joseph in Egypt). Men who were virtual unknowns to the world have been raised to world-wide recognition because of their use in God's hands (Billy Graham, Pope John Paul II in modern times).

The utterly opposite outcomes from our normal expectations are noteworthy. The rich will be sent away empty handed, the poor and hungry filled at last. These kinds of wondrous expectations so contrary to those of the world will be possible with the coming of Messiah.

Luke 1:56
56 And Mary stayed with her about three months, and then returned to her home.

A long stay like this also seems out of sorts with our own times. It happens here and there today depending on situations, but in today's world there are a host of inconveniences that make this rather rare. But in ancient times, there were no such modern entanglements and inconveniences, and a stay of three months away from one's home with relatives was very doable and common. It is also a commentary on the disconnectedness of families in general. Then, people easily cohabited with relatives because there was a ready attitude of welcome and support, even if there was no urgent need. Today, it is an imposition to some degree or another and hosting relatives are looking to the exit strategy for all such arrangements, *"When will they be going back home?"*

Luke 1:57-80

57 Now the time had come for Elizabeth to give birth, and she gave birth to a son. 58 Her neighbors and her relatives heard that the Lord had displayed His great mercy toward her; and they were rejoicing with her.
59 And it happened that on the eighth day they came to circumcise the child, and they were going to call him Zacharias, after his father. 60 But his mother answered and said, "No indeed; but he shall be called John." 61 And they said to her, "There is no one among your relatives who is called by that name." 62 And they made signs to his father, as to what he wanted him called. 63 And he asked for a tablet and wrote as follows, "His name is John." And they were all astonished.

64 And at once his mouth was opened and his tongue loosed, and he began to speak in praise of God.
65 Fear came on all those living around them; and all these matters were being talked about in all the hill country of Judea. 66 All who heard them kept them in mind, saying, "What then will this child turn out to be?" For the hand of the Lord was certainly with him.

67 And his father Zacharias was filled with the Holy Spirit, and prophesied, saying: 68 "Blessed be the Lord God of Israel, For He has visited us and accomplished redemption for His people, 69 And has raised up a horn of salvation for us In the house of David His servant-- 70 As He spoke by the mouth of His holy prophets from of old-- 71 Salvation FROM OUR ENEMIES, And FROM THE HAND OF ALL WHO HATE US; 72 To show mercy toward our fathers, And to remember His holy covenant,

73 The oath which He swore to Abraham our father, 74 To grant us that we, being rescued from the hand of our enemies, Might serve Him without fear, 75 In holiness and righteousness before Him all our days.
76 "And you, child, will be called the prophet of the Most High; For you will go on BEFORE THE LORD TO PREPARE HIS WAYS; 77 To give to His people the knowledge of salvation By the forgiveness of their sins, 78 Because of the tender mercy of our God, With which the Sunrise from on high will visit us, 79 TO SHINE UPON THOSE WHO SIT IN DARKNESS AND THE SHADOW OF DEATH, To guide our feet into the way of peace." 80 And the child continued to grow and to become strong in spirit, and he lived in the deserts until the day of his public appearance to Israel.

Commentary

Luke 1:57
57 Now the time had come for Elizabeth to give birth, and she gave birth to a son. . .

The record of John's birth proceeds next. The joy one would expect is extraordinary because it is accompanied by the knowledge that God has shown mercy and how well He cares for those who trust in Him.

Circumcision. An interesting sidebar about circumcision informs us why it was held off until the eighth day. It is now known that vitamin K is essential to the process of clotting in the blood. Vitamin K is not naturally present in our systems until 7 or 8 days after birth. Hence , the commandment to wait until through to the eighth for the cutting away of the flesh. In modern times, we circumcise immediately upon birth. So newborns are given an injection of the vitamin before the procedure. [4]

There was an assumption that the infant was to be named after his father, but Elizabeth intercepted this and directed that he be called John. In Hebrew the name means *Jehovah has been gracious; has shown favor.* This was Elizabeth's prayer of praise back to the Lord. In doing so, the child would forever be a reminder of that blessing and mercy.

That Zacharias was freed to speak once again at this moment was a fulfillment of the words of the angel who smote Zacharias in the Temple. The terminus was to be the "day these things take place." At the birth of John, Zacharias now had the proof at hand against his incredulity. He had learned the lesson that nothing is impossible with God.

Now it can be argued that just the fact of Elizabeth becoming pregnant, the nine months following, and even the moment of actual birth 8 days earlier would have given Zacharias plenty of reasons for revisiting his doubts. But the day of ceremonial commemoration was more appropriate because it was marked by the formalities of registry, naming and circumcision. So it was that the Lord chose this day to free his tongue to the amazement of all.

It says that *fear* also came upon those around. This is not to be ameliorated into what we frequently call awesome respect. Here, there was an element of a foreboding kind of fear, not so much in being afraid of some impending doom, but in having one's heart jump a beat, or one's breath taken away in the wonder of what great and mighty thing may be on the horizon for them and their nation. There were no real precedents of miraculous births inaugurating moments of great change in their past, but people were very prone to read momentous meaning into signs and events like these. So it was not so much a birth per se, but the miraculous circumstances around it that gave people pause.

Luke 1:66-68
66 All who heard them kept them in mind, saying, "What then will this child turn out to be?" For the hand of the Lord was certainly with him. 67 And his father Zacharias was filled with the Holy Spirit, and prophesied, saying: 68 "Blessed be the Lord God of Israel, For He has visited us and accomplished redemption for His people,

It is to be noted that the evaluation of what was happening was to be connected with the redemption of God's people. For most Jews this meant freedom from the oppression of Gentile rule. They longed for this as they had done in the days of Egyptian bondage. It was frankly a grave embarrassment to be called a nation peculiar to the Lord yet be in subjection, to have no real say in your own country.

While a fictional dialog, in DeMille's The Ten Commandments, (Paramount Pictures, 1956) the character of Joshua witnesses to a secular Moses that his God is the Most High God. The Egyptian Moses replies, "If your God is great, why has he left you in bondage?"

While purely fictional, it aptly pictures the kind of reality the Jews in fact felt in those times. So there was a very real expectation in these kinds of circumstances that God would finally bring to pass what He promised His people. Thus we see Zacharias quoting Scripture: *"Salvation from our enemies, And from the hand of all who hate us;"* (Psa 106:10.)

We know from the rest of the story that this characterization of the promise would not be fulfilled despite Zacharias connecting it here. John did herald their Messiah. Messiah did come. But their subjection remained because Messiah came in a way they did not expect; and as such they rejected Him whom they did not recognize.

---

[4] McMillen, S.I., None of These Diseases, Revell, p.93.

Luke 1:74-76
**74 To grant us that we, being rescued from the hand of our enemies, Might serve Him without fear,
75 In holiness and righteousness before Him all our days.**

The tragedy of this prayer is that it was prayed many times but often not fulfilled in God's people. You would think that in the days which were attended by such great miracles as those of the Exodus under Moses, there would be unity and faith and service to the Lord *"in holiness and righteousness before Him."* But such things did not result even then. There was always a mixture of the wicked and selfish among the righteous, that the whole nation could not stand up as a servant.

Never the less, there is the promise in Scripture that that day will come. And despite the rather bad record of his people, Zacharias reiterates his claim on those promises.

76 "And you, child, will be called the prophet of the Most High; For you will go on BEFORE THE LORD TO PREPARE HIS WAYS; . .

Zacharias turns his blessing to his new son and his role as forerunner to the knowledge of salvation. That salvation was viewed among the faithful in two aspects – political salvation from oppression, and spiritual salvation from sin through forgiveness. John was to not only herald the latter expectation, but he was to prepare souls by preaching repentance. There is the inference in the Gospels that the people who flock to Jesus are those who had earlier heard John.

So we have here in the OT economy of things a recognition of the prerequisites to lasting salvation – confession and repentance. This is in contrast to the common belief that just being after Abraham's seed secured these things.

Luke 1:80
80 And the child continued to grow and to become strong in spirit, and he lived in the deserts until the day of his public appearance to Israel.

Strong in spirit. This is a term that is meant to separate those in whom God is working from those who for many reasons are not an active part of His plans and objectives. There is a way in which believers can peacefully abide in the knowledge and faith of God but not be active in what God is doing.

One of the reasons is that we fear how this will upset the lives we've spent so much time arranging and acquiring. We can easily see life as a station in society, an arrival at the comfort we've worked hard to achieve, a place where we have things arranged to our liking. We see our jobs and careers as the means to getting there. So when we "arrive" we are not really ready to hear a message about counting it all as transitory, temporary, and being ready to move off our spot to something God has purposed for us to do.

John is an example of someone not tied to the world or a living to which one can get very accustomed. He lived a life that was ready at any moment to move where God needed him. He had no entanglements.

But John also had no fear of the consequences of standing up for God. He could not have been ignorant or naïve about the trouble he would make for himself in his bold condemnation of Jewish leadership. This is what is meant by the spirit being strong in him. He cared about the message and did not let concerns about what this would do to his life soften it.

In our modern times, it's going to take the same kind of people to bring about change when God once again takes a more direct hand in the human scene. But they will be much harder to find. There are so many more things we must now take into account. *"I can't live in a tent or sleep in the park!"* *"How will I get my medications and see my doctors?"* *"How will we be able to send Erica and Brent to Stanford if I go off on a mission?"*

Now this is not saying that every Christian needs to prepare for the ascetic life, abandon all possessions and be ready to be another John the Baptist. There are many callings and many do not require that kind of sacrifice. Still, someone will need to be that ready because there is and will be the need to make that kind of dent. And for those tasks (and others) the Lord will be looking for those who are *"strong in spirit."*

Matthew 1:18-25
18 Now the birth of Jesus Christ was as follows: when His mother Mary had been betrothed to Joseph, before they came together she was found to be with child by the Holy Spirit. 19 And Joseph her husband, being a righteous man and not wanting to disgrace her, planned to send her away secretly. 20 But when he had considered this, behold, an angel of the Lord appeared to him in a dream, saying, "Joseph, son of David, do not be afraid to take Mary as your wife; for the Child who has been conceived in her is of the Holy Spirit. 21 "She will bear a Son; and you shall call His name Jesus, for He will save His people from their sins."

22 Now all this took place to fulfill what was spoken by the Lord through the prophet: 23 "BEHOLD, THE VIRGIN SHALL BE WITH CHILD AND SHALL BEAR A SON, AND THEY SHALL CALL HIS NAME IMMANUEL," which translated means, "GOD WITH US." 24 And Joseph awoke from his sleep and did as the angel of the Lord commanded him, and took Mary as his wife, 25 but kept her a virgin until she gave birth to a Son;

Commentary

Matthew 1:18
18 Now the birth of Jesus Christ was as follows: when His mother Mary had been betrothed to Joseph, before they came together she was found to be with child by the Holy Spirit.

A very important point for liberals is that this occurred before Joseph and Mary had been physically intimate. So if the liberal has any semblance of value for the testimony of Scripture, he cannot assert that this was a simple case of man and woman conceiving.

We need to clarify that she was (by her husband and parents at least) *found to be with child*. *"By the Holy Spirit"* was not an immediate conclusion, even to Joseph. Found to be with child could be as simple as the observation that she was missing enough of her monthly periods.

In this day and age, it is not a foregone conclusion that men and women abstain from premarital sex. In ancient times, people were not without promiscuity, but in ancient Jewish life this came at an awful price that made two partners think twice. Promiscuity before marriage had a civil penalty regardless of a disinterest in faith. This is simply because among the Jews, the Mosaic Law was the basis of the civil law.

Sex involving unmarried partners was technically distinct from adultery and is what was later distinguished as fornication. But you won't find fornication in the Law. It isn't really employed until the book of Ezekiel, where it is used as an equivalent of harlotry. So in the Law, it was sometimes lumped in with adultery or called uncleanness. But for betrothed couples, it was equivalent to adultery. Here are the pertinent passages:

Deut 22:20-21
20 "But if this thing be true, and the tokens of virginity be not found for the damsel: 21 Then they shall bring out the damsel to the door of her father's house, and the men of her city shall stone her with stones that she die: because she hath wrought folly in Israel, to play the whore in her father's house: so shalt thou put evil away from among you."

The *tokens* of her virginity would have been the lightly bloodied sheets, being her first experience with intercourse. Ordinarily these were given to the parents, but in some cases these were made public to guests for validation.

For anyone suspicious of how the conception took place before the wedding, there would have been no expectation of tokens and instead a jeopardy against the law. Joseph would have known the truth as to any participation of his own. Being that she did not conceive through normal physical relations, her body would have been essentially intact, meaning that tokens would have been expected on her wedding night by those *"in the know"* had there been consummation

This seems oddly embarrassing to us today. In ancient times, there was a gathering after the marriage at the house of the parents. A room had already been arranged (and in many cases was an extension onto the house of one's parents which had been built for the new couple). When time for consummation came during the evening, guests would wish the couple well as they secreted themselves away for the act of consummation. The party would continue which in itself gave the couple the privacy of not being heard. The couple later emerged to the joy of the guests. Sounds bizarre to us, but that was the practice.

What is ironic in Mary's case is that nothing had really occurred to break the sign of her virginity, so their wedding night would actually have produced the tokens looked for. But the Scripture is also clear that Joseph did not have relations with Mary until after the birth of Jesus (Matt 1:24-25). So we have a puzzlement that this was about to become public – a wedding but no tokens, meaning promiscuity. Yet we don't have a statement that tokens were shown, which would at least leave those who were suspicious without vindication that promiscuity was involved.

Depending on Joseph's attitude, her penalty could be as severe as in Deut 22:20 above. (The daughter of a priest would be burned with fire - Lev 21:9.) At the very least, however, she would suffer public disgrace.

Circumstances in each case dictated to what length the husband and the priests would inflict punishment. Much depended on the husband's willingness to marry his betrothed. Times were no longer as they were in the wilderness wanderings and a certain adaptation had crept into the enforcement of the Law by this point in time.

Matthew 1:19-20
19 And Joseph her husband, being a righteous man and not wanting to disgrace her, planned to send her away secretly.

The decision for Joseph was whether he would abandon her to the justice system or arrange for her to escape.
The very fact that he was contemplating the appropriate action indicates that he had been out of the loop up to this point. The only real explanation in his mind had to be that she had been promiscuous. It simply can't be the case that Mary had confided in Joseph about the announcement of the angel, because Joseph would have known his next action.

But this does in the end appear strange because it would seem that Mary would have confided this to Joseph, knowing full well what such a discovery would mean to him and the misunderstanding that would ensue without an explanation. Still, we have no evidence she told him up to this point and her reasons are not made known, and we do have here his state of mind.

But notice here that Joseph has not actually arrived at the conclusion of redeeming her through marriage. He is back at the point of simply trying to spare her the emotional consequences of the Law. Here, disgrace does not rule out being stoned. To be stoned is to bring disgrace on one's remembered reputation.

So we really have a Joseph here who has foregone the hopes of the planned marriage (he must later be supernaturally encouraged to continue with the marriage) and instead is pondering the options of merely sparing his betrothed the public consequences. Sending her away secretly meant that she could not be seized. She would remain guilty but beyond the application of penalties. (It must be born in mind that the priests did not have the means to hunt down fugitives, and women even less so. Nor did they publish public enemy announcements of this nature throughout the country. So escape was a viable option, although how she would live had unpleasant prospects.)

20 But when he had considered this, behold, an angel of the Lord appeared to him in a dream, saying, "Joseph, son of David, do not be afraid to take Mary as your wife; for the Child who has been conceived in her is of the Holy Spirit."

With this announcement, Joseph must now consider how the wedding is to continue. It has been made known that she is with child. What we don't know is how widespread this had become. If it was contained within their families, the wedding could proceed without much consequence. If it was known elsewhere, Joseph would be viewed as the adoptive father of an otherwise fatherless child.

One observation is that during Jesus' ministry, the Jews never brought up any charge about his parentage, which would have been a handy way to discredit him and one they certainly would have employed. Inevitably, it did become known once the gospel accounts began circulating, but there it was proclaimed as a conception by the Holy Spirit. The Pharisees scarcely believed this, but it is interesting that God prevented this charge from being levied.

So it was either a case that only the family knew and the wedding went on as normal without suspicion, or the act of Joseph's compassion overshadowed all such concerns and the Child was accepted as adopted. As earlier, none of this has any impact on Jesus' claim to the lineage of David. The genealogies would not have aroused suspicion since adoption by Joseph would have superseded any issues with some supposed natural father's line. He was linked to David via both Joseph and Mary.

Matthew 1:21
21 "She will bear a Son; and you shall call His name Jesus, for He will save His people from their sins."

Jesus' name was actually 'Yeshua' in Hebrew. It means 'Yahweh is salvation' – ('Ye' is a shortened form of Yahweh when compounded with other words.)

Greek attempted to transliterate this and the result was *Iesous* [pronounced 'yey-soos'] The Greek name was subsequently further transliterated into Latin as 'Iesus', which was also pronounced 'yey-soos.' When Latin letters were anglicized, 'J' was introduced for initial 'I' in names (J was never used in classical Latin), names converted to initial J (Julius Caesar for Iulius Caesar), hence the name became Jesus.

But from first to last, His name meant Yahweh is salvation, written in the Hebrew text as 'the LORD is salvation' where LORD is substituted for the Divine Name.

Matthew 1:22
22 Now all this took place to fulfill what was spoken by the Lord through the prophet: 23 "BEHOLD, THE VIRGIN SHALL BE WITH CHILD AND SHALL BEAR A SON, AND THEY SHALL CALL HIS NAME IMMANUEL," which translated means, "GOD WITH US."

This is quoted from Isaiah 7:14. The context in Isaiah is that of King Ahaz, who fearing an alliance between Assyria and the northern tribes of Israel against him, was in audience with the prophet as to what to do. At first Ahaz feigns not to presume on God for a sign, but Isaiah interprets this as pretense, and declares that the Lord will give the king a sign in spite of him. So it is here that Isaiah speaks the famous words, *"the virgin shall be with child and bear a son."*

Now some have maintained that this was a real miracle that foreshadowed the same miracle that would attend Messiah's birth 750 years later. But this means that Isaiah meant to proclaim the miraculous birth of a child by a real virgin yet in the context and time of Ahaz.

First, at the time of fulfillment, the miraculous circumstances of such a birth are nowhere pointed to. Second, it is the boy's *age* that is the determining indicator. It is when the child comes to know the good from the bad (Isa 7:16) that Ahaz will be free from worry over these kings.

If this was indeed a miraculous birth by a woman who did not have intercourse to become pregnant, this fact was pushed completely into the background and focus was given instead to a specific point in the child's life, which completely disenfranchises the reason for stressing a miraculous birth at the time.

This has caused some to conclude that a virgin did conceive as promised, but in the normal manner of being subsequently impregnated and having a child. So why refer to her as a virgin?

It is thought that when Isaiah spoke these words to Ahaz, there was a court in attendance also, and in the company were women, both concubines and virgins. Isaiah pointed to a particular woman who was at that point in fact a virgin and spoke the prophecy about her. This is indicated by the definite article - 'the.' This means that some specific person known is being pointed out. Otherwise, Isaiah would have used Hebrew form for indicating *"a virgin shall be with child.."* meaning someone not yet known.

By pointing to a particular person, she would be carefully watched and her future child would be observed. The kings did in fact disappear from the scene and this was then checked against the age and moral awareness of the child.

But in Judaism, the verse meant more. This is because Isaiah said more. He connects the child with Messianic claims and prophecies, so the Jews came to understand that this was a double fulfillment – one immediately important to Ahaz, one distant and inevitably important to God's people.

It is interesting that Jesus was never formally named Immanuel. From this announcement up to the actual birth, Joseph would have had time to compare notes with Mary's vision, wherein she received more direct orders about naming him Jesus. The angel's reference to Immanuel actually refers to what others called Him.

Matthew 1:24
24 And Joseph awoke from his sleep and did as the angel of the Lord commanded him, and took Mary as his wife 25 but kept her a virgin until she gave birth to a Son;

That Joseph refrained from sex with Mary is a matter of respect and convenience (there were certain social taboos) but it is important that this statement tends to counter the claim that Joseph and Mary had no relations their whole marriage. The word 'until' has no meaning if there was no change in behavior afterward. If a man remained a bachelor to the end of his life and died in his eighties, it would be misleading to say that he remained a bachelor until his thirties. It would imply that his celibacy changed after thirty.

At the very least, this verse implies by necessity that Joseph and Mary had relations. Whether Mary had other children as a result is open to interpretation.

Luke 2:1-7

1 Now in those days a decree went out from Caesar Augustus, that a census be taken of all the inhabited earth. 2 This was the first census taken while Quirinius was governor of Syria. 3 And everyone was on his way to register for the census, each to his own city. 4 Joseph also went up from Galilee, from the city of Nazareth, to Judea, to the city of David which is called Bethlehem, because he was of the house and family of David, 5 in order to register along with Mary, who was engaged to him, and was with child. 6 While they were there, the days were completed for her to give birth. 7 And she gave birth to her firstborn son; and she wrapped Him in cloths, and laid Him in a manger, because there was no room for them in the inn.

Commentary

Luke 2:1

1 *"Now in those days a decree went out from Caesar Augustus, that a census be taken of all the inhabited earth. 2 This was the first census taken while Quirinius was governor of Syria."*

<u>Caesar Augustus</u>

Augustus was the first and greatest emperor of the Roman Empire. No one later ever equaled his accomplishments or his adept management of the Roman state. In this, he surpassed Julius Caesar, who was certainly of undisputed political prowess and in many ways Augustus' model. But Augustus was able to win and keep the Senate and the people in ways Julius Caesar never managed to achieve.

Despite that greatness, he suffered the fate of all absolute rulers in indulging his personal hatreds and vices. Augustus was more conservative in terms of excesses of power, but he had his faults. One incident involved a man who was in attendance at one of his audiences, and was observed taking notes. The man was ordered to be stabbed on the spot. (Taking notes was despised in such a setting because emperors did not want their words taken down except by approved recorders.) Another man hiding tablets in his toga (mistaken for a sword) was hustled out of the room where the emperor later gouged out the man's eyes.[5]

Some believe mistakenly that Julius Caesar was the first emperor but he was never voted king or emperor by the Senate. In fact it was for these aspirations that he was assassinated by members of the Senate. The Romans had thrown off their kings some 400 years earlier and were proud to now live in a republic.

But wasn't Julius Caesar a dictator? Not after the manner of thinking today – a despot. It was an office or a mode of service to the state for a short period during a crisis. Dictators were expected to lay down their authority when that period ended. Julius declined doing this, to the ire of the Senate, but his abuse of dictatorship was dealt with by assassination. He did not become emperor over the state.

Augustus was Julius' grand-nephew and heir, there being no closer living heirs. His name originally was Octavian and he was related to Caesar through Julius' sister, Julia. Her daughter, Atia, was his mother.

Ironically, Augustus became emperor not many years later, after a period of civil war following the death of Caesar. The Senate's political supremacy was sufficiently weakened by this point in time. Many entertained the idea of solitary rule, given a corrupt and inefficient Senate. Civil wars that poorly attempted to institute this warned of caution at this move, but most people were desperate for change They also had great admiration for Octavian which lessened their fears about despotism. His name was subsequently changed to Augustus.

Here, the cleverness of Augustus is seen at the very start. He formally gave back the government to the Senate as a gesture of good will, retaining the visible forms of their traditions. But everyone knew that in all practical terms he was clearly in charge.

---

[5] Suetonius, <u>Lives of the Twelve Caesars,</u> Vol I, Loeb Classical Library, Harvard Press, 1987, p. 163

The Problem of the Census

Mentioning problem areas can put some people off because in the end God will be found to be true, so worrying technical issues can seem a waste of time. It is however valuable for Christians to at least be exposed to these issues and their resolutions in the interest of talking intelligently in the defense of the faith.

It was common practice among the Romans to take a census about every ten years (some claim it was 14 or even 17 years.) Their primary reason was for assessing taxes based on populations in the provinces. (We can understand why locals despised such announcements.)

There has been much todo over the mention of Quirinius as governor because Josephus identifies him in such a way as to date his census at A.D. 6. This is too late for the birth of Jesus and it creates a conflict because Herod is still alive at this census yet he would have been historically dead ten years by this date.

But there is evidence to suggest that Quirinius was governor twice, or that he was present in Syria earlier and took part in an earlier census on behalf of the emperor. It is believed that Herod delayed the order for a census due to the difficulties among the Jews and that this earlier census, decreed in about 7 B.C. was delayed until 5 B.C. which is correct for the date of Jesus' birth. [6]

It is not a clean resolution because we have to deal with Luke's statement that Quirinius was governor when technically it was another man in the 5 B.C. time frame. But Luke refers to people elsewhere as governor who were not technically governors (Pilate was a procurator.)

Another resolution is that the Greek can be read, *"2 This was the census **before** Quirinius was governor of Syria*

The Christian Calendar

Some may be puzzled at how Jesus can be born in years B.C. which means being born before the year he was born. But this has more to do with how our calendar came to be regulated with respect to Jesus life.

Dionysius Exiguus was a 4th Century monk credited with working out a system of reckoning years according to the life of Christ rather than continuing a calendar based on pagan events, like the years of emperors or the foundation of Rome.

Unfortunately, the documents available to Dionysius were inferior and he placed the date of Christ's birth too late by about 4-5 years. The critical piece of information was the eclipse seen just before Herod's death. In Dionysius' time, there were no astronomical methods for calculating this precisely and he had to go on the inferior testimony of people. We now know that this eclipse was visible at Jerusalem on the night of March 12th, B.C. 4. [7]

Since Jesus birth was about a year prior, we have a date between 4-5 B.C. for his birth. But Dionysius, operating with less reliable data, selected a point five years later and declared that to be the first year "anno domini" – A.D of the Christian calendar.

---

[6] Josephus, Antiquities of the Jews, xviii, 1ff, 26, 102; xvii, 355; BJ, ii,118, 433
F. F. Bruce, New Testament History, Doubleday, 1969, p.32
Turner, Grammatical Insights in the Greek New Testament, Edinburgh, 1966, p.23
P. Schaff, The New Schaff-Herzog Encyclopedia of Religious Knowledge, Vol IX, p. 375
E. Stauffer, Jesus and His Story, SCM Pressm London, 1960, p.31

[7] Anderson, Sir Robert, The Coming Prince, Kregel, 1982, p. 258

The Command to Return to their Place of Birth

Luke 2:3
3 And everyone was on his way to register for the census, each to his own city.

This has been criticized as being quite unnecessary and unsubstantiated. But we actually have records outside the NT to confirm this.

"From the Prefect of Egypt, Gaius Vibius Maximus. Being that the time has come for the house to house census, it is mandatory that all men who are living outside of their districts return to their own homelands, that the census may be carried out . . . " [8]

Luke 2:4-7
4 Joseph also went up from Galilee, from the city of Nazareth, to Judea, to the city of David which is called Bethlehem, because he was of the house and family of David, 5 in order to register along with Mary, who was engaged to him, and was with child.

The decree was interpreted as registry according to one's house, which meant the place associated with one's ancestry, even though and individual might have been born elsewhere. Joseph and Mary were both in the line (house) of David, and David's birthplace was Bethlehem (I Sam 16:1.)

6 While they were there, the days were completed for her to give birth. 7 And she gave birth to her firstborn son; and she wrapped Him in cloths, and laid Him in a manger, because there was no room for them in the inn.

It is interesting that the pageants and plays make much of their going from place to place looking for a room and finally being led to the stable. In fact there are none of these specifics in the gospel accounts. All we are told is that there was no room in the inn. Also, the idea that there was a feast and this was the reason for such overcrowding is not clear here either. The logical reason for there being no room is the census itself, which took several days to complete and required that people stay somewhere locally for an extended period to complete it.

The contrast is profound though. While kings and emperors dined in splendor and were surrounded by royal courts and attendants, another scene was taking place in a small corner of the world, of no account to anyone and seeming of no comparison worth mentioning. In it was the Son of God being born and worshipped by purely ordinary folks and three men of influence, yet attended by mighty angels of tremendous power.

---

[8] Hanson, K.C., Translation of Greek papyrus P.London 904, British Museum. WIPF and Stock Publishers, 1995, 2005. Geisler, <u>Alleged Errors In Luke</u>, Ankerberg Theological Institute, 2005, p. 1

Luke 2:8-20

8 In the same region there were some shepherds staying out in the fields and keeping watch over their flock by night. 9 And an angel of the Lord suddenly stood before them, and the glory of the Lord shone around them; and they were terribly frightened. 10 But the angel said to them, "Do not be afraid; for behold, I bring you good news of great joy which will be for all the people; 11 for today in the city of David there has been born for you a Savior, who is Christ the Lord. 12 "This will be a sign for you: you will find a baby wrapped in cloths and lying in a manger." 13 And suddenly there appeared with the angel a multitude of the heavenly host praising God and saying, 14 "Glory to God in the highest, And on earth peace among men with whom He is pleased."

15 When the angels had gone away from them into heaven, the shepherds began saying to one another, "Let us go straight to Bethlehem then, and see this thing that has happened which the Lord has made known to us." 16 So they came in a hurry and found their way to Mary and Joseph, and the baby as He lay in the manger. 17 When they had seen this, they made known the statement which had been told them about this Child. 18 And all who heard it wondered at the things which were told them by the shepherds.
19 But Mary treasured all these things, pondering them in her heart. 20 The shepherds went back, glorifying and praising God for all that they had heard and seen, just as had been told them.

Commentary

Luke 2:8-10
8 *"In the same region there were some shepherds staying out in the fields and keeping watch over their flock by night. 9 And an angel of the Lord suddenly stood before them, and the glory of the Lord shone around them; and they were terribly frightened. 10 But the angel said to them, "Do not be afraid;"*

The presence of shepherds out in the fields during the night indicates a warmer season of the year rather than the middle of winter. Flocks still had to be pastured in colder seasons but not through the night, unless it was a very mild winter. A December birth for Jesus is not out of the question entirely, but the likelihood is for a warmer season.

The appearance of the angel is accompanied by what is called *"the glory of the Lord"* which here seems to mean light, since it states that it shone around them. Films have tried to picture this but we have to wonder how it really was; certainly something overwhelming. The use of light seems to be an important theme in Scripture, marking moments of revelation from God. The recipient is being given knowledge from above and this is intentionally represented as light from above.

That such a light would come from nowhere and attend the angel's appearance was a profound authentication of the vision. To hallucinate that someone appeared to you and gave you a message might be doubtable later, but the accompaniment of light would be hard to rationalize away.

No doubt they were frightened. Today, young people are almost ready for something like this to happen. There would be less fear and more of "That's cool!" But for unsophisticated ancients, there was genuine fear. Fear of coming face to face with something out of heaven - "Will this be my judgment for a sinful life?" - certainly a fear of the unknown and unexpected.

We have to also realize that the life of the shepherd was extremely quiet. More so than we can usually ever get in the quieter places in a city. It would be so incredibly still, punctuated by the occasional tinkling bells among the sheep. There is a moment very much like this in the opening Nativity scenes from The Greatest Story Ever Told (George Stevens, United Artists, 1965.)

To then have such a break from so contemplative a scene by the shining of a great light, would certainly be startling. Nothing here indicates sound, except the speech of the angel. (So celebrated film music composers would have had nothing to do here, if realism was foremost.)

The angel knows that this will be fearsome and his first words are to allay those fears . .

Luke 2:10-11
". .for behold, I bring you good news of great joy which will be for all the people; 11 for today in the city of David there has been born for you a Savior, who is Christ the Lord."

The good news being announced was that the long awaited Savior, the Anointed One of God has been born unto them. The idea that a Savior was coming goes back into the OT.

In Genesis, at the judgment for their sin, God tells the serpent that there will be enmity between her seed and his, but that her seed will bruise the serpents head (Gen 3:15.) This is incredibly vague by design, but it was the earliest indication that the plan to redeem man from the Fall was already in place.

In Deuteronomy, Moses prophesies to the people that there will come unto them a Prophet from among their people to whom they will hearken (Deut 18:18.) It is this prophet about whom John is asked if he is the fulfillment, *"Art thou that Prophet?"*

But in Isaiah we have a clearer picture that there will come a Savior, and in the form of a new born child *" For unto us a child is born, unto us a son is given: and the government shall be upon his shoulder:"*

That He would be someone to save his people from their sins was less vivid in the OT. We have instead the idea that God would save them from their errors and evil effects, that the Messiah would deliver them from their oppressors and establish a divine Kingdom of His own forever, *"and the government shall be upon his shoulder . . there shall be no end, upon the throne of David, and upon his kingdom, to order it, and to establish . . even for ever."* (Isaiah 9:6.)

But the connection with God's salvation from sin and the coming of Messiah was made to Mary in the naming of Jesus, *"for he shall save his people from their sins."* and this was not a connection the Jews had made, as evident in their disappointment with Jesus in not overthrowing Gentile rule and establishing the kingdom of David's throne.

Luke 2:12-15
12"This will be a sign for you: you will find a baby wrapped in cloths and lying in a manger."

The sign was the finding of the infant in a manger wrapped in cloths. This does not appear to be the kind of sign we might think would be needed – certainly something ala Stephen Spielberg would have been much more spectacular.

But here the sign is more subtle and in many ways more profound. How many children were born in a stable among animal life, animal smells, and animal "belongings?" But even this in itself would not be too extraordinary because everyone knew things were crowded on account of the census. So it might not be too bizarre to have a young couple give birth in a stable under such conditions.

But here it is this fact, coupled with the prediction of the angel. And in the region around Bethlehem, how many situations in a stable would there be? How many would have the child lying in a feeding trough?

But regardless of our own ideas on what would have been a better sign, this one worked extremely well. For you have the shepherds in these next verses proclaiming the message of the angel, having very effectively gotten the confirmation they needed.

13 And suddenly there appeared with the angel a multitude of the heavenly host praising God and saying, 14 "Glory to God in the highest, And on earth peace among men with whom He is pleased."

Now we have sound (compared to the incredibly routine quiet of shepherding.)! One has to wonder the nature of that praise. What was the melody from heaven like? We'll all have to wait and see.

Glory to God must be seen from the perspective of the listener, the beholder. The idea is that of pointing to God and recounting His greatness, righteousness and power. God, in and of Himself, needs no one to point this out to Him. The glorifying of God is meant to be in the presence of man, so that a testimony is made and with the encouragement that man will join the chorus of praise.

15"Let us go straight to Bethlehem then, and see this thing that has happened which the Lord has made known to us." 16 So they came in a hurry and found their way to Mary and Joseph, and the baby as He lay in the manger."

You can imagine the nature of the searching. They were not going from house to house, but were asking about a place with a manger, where a mother and new born child might be. So they are said to have hurried and found their way to Mary and the child.

Luke 2:17-20
17" When they had seen this, they made known the statement which had been told them about this Child. 18 And all who heard it wondered . . . 19 But Mary treasured all these things, . . 20 The shepherds went back, glorifying and praising God . . "

The shepherds then became heralds of the good news, filled with the joy of having connected so readily the prediction of the angel with what they found. But beyond this, this particular sign meant that everything else the angel said must be true – that this child was indeed the Savior expected.

It is understandable that the people are said to have wondered about the things said. Certainly, the ecstatic behavior of the shepherds would add caution to what they were saying. The completely unexpected way in which the Messiah was seen as coming into the world would certainly produce pause and the need to think rather than immediately react. For Mary, she knew the real truth about what was happening, and this she *"treasured"* within her heart.

One might expect from this announcement that the neighboring people would advance the news to all surrounding areas and up to Jerusalem, that the leaders and priests might receive the import of such an announcement. But we don't find this happening. We don't find the nation as a whole receiving this child in any way as their Messiah. The message of the shepherds was more likely taken as just a bizarre event over which time gave way to forgetting such things, especially when the family moved back to Nazareth and nothing came of such things for many years yet to come.

We don't see even the neighbors in Nazareth fawning over the child during his early years, watching and waiting for something extraordinary to happen. They all went on about their business and had to wait some thirty years for the extraordinary.

Luke 2:21-35
21 And when eight days had passed, before His circumcision, His name was then called Jesus, the name given by the angel before He was conceived in the womb. 22 And when the days for their purification according to the law of Moses were completed, they brought Him up to Jerusalem to present Him to the Lord 23 (as it is written in the Law of the Lord, "EVERY firstborn MALE THAT OPENS THE WOMB SHALL BE CALLED HOLY TO THE LORD" , 24 and to offer a sacrifice according to what was said in the Law of the Lord, "A PAIR OF TURTLEDOVES OR TWO YOUNG PIGEONS."

25 And there was a man in Jerusalem whose name was Simeon; and this man was righteous and devout, looking for the consolation of Israel; and the Holy Spirit was upon him. 26 And it had been revealed to him by the Holy Spirit that he would not see death before he had seen the Lord's Christ. 27 And he came in the Spirit into the temple; and when the parents brought in the child Jesus, to carry out for Him the custom of the Law, 28 then he took Him into his arms, and blessed God, and said, 29 "Now Lord, You are releasing Your bond-servant to depart in peace, According to Your word; 30 For my eyes have seen Your salvation, 31 Which You have prepared in the presence of all peoples, 32 A LIGHT OF REVELATION TO THE GENTILES, And the glory of Your people Israel." 33 And His father and mother were amazed at the things which were being said about Him. 34 And Simeon blessed them and said to Mary His mother, "Behold, this Child is appointed for the fall and rise of many in Israel, and for a sign to be opposed-- 35 and a sword will pierce even your own soul--to the end that thoughts from many hearts may be revealed."

Commentary

Luke 2:21-23
21 "And when eight days had passed, before His circumcision, His name was then called Jesus, the name given by the angel before He was conceived in the womb. 22 And when the days for their purification according to the law of Moses were completed, they brought Him up to Jerusalem to present Him to the Lord 23 (as it is written in the Law of the Lord, "EVERY firstborn MALE THAT OPENS THE WOMB SHALL BE CALLED HOLY TO THE LORD" ,

Similar to the birth of John the Baptist, Mary and Joseph waited the specified eight days for Jesus' circumcision and the formal naming of the child. But we see here additional information about the procedure.

Two waiting periods were involved - time for the circumcision procedure, and time until it was lawful to perform the dedication ceremony in the Temple.

In John's circumcision and dedication we may have wrongly given the impression that these occurred in the Temple after the eight days of waiting. But in fact, the circumcision took place in the home. We see the text stating that *"they came to circumcise him,"* so the actual dedication and formal registry happened later as we see explained in the case of Mary.

The second period of waiting is called here *"the days of purification."* Some texts have *"their purification"*. To know which is more accurate we only have to look at the law that is mentioned.

In Leviticus it is stipulated that for women giving birth there is to follow a period of 33 days from her bleeding. This was to purify her for access once again to the Temple precincts and the corporate worship of Israel.

Lev 12:4 *"She will continue in purification from her bleeding for 33 days. She must not touch any holy thing or go into the sanctuary until completing her days of purification."*

Now this may seem strange because the Lord is the one who created the body and its operations, so why penalize His creatures from worship if their bodies are doing what God ordained? Some have offered that this bleeding or ceremonial impurity is the effect of the Fall and as such God's design is no longer in play as perfect and holy. But it is difficult to know how human birth would have taken place without bleeding in the Garden had man not sinned.

But in the end we really can't scrutinize God in this regard. From His standpoint there is now impurity of some sort that requires this time delay; and the faithful who honor God are to observe it.

Another puzzlement is why there would be impurity in Mary's case with the birth of the holiest child ever born? We need to carefully distinguish between following what the Law required and inferring that there was some moral impurity or some tainting of Mary by the birth of Jesus itself.

It is more probable that the connection was with the blood of birth and this was regardless of the holiness of the One born, making it more a ceremonial concern in the Law. (And there simply were no special conditions in the Law for supernatural births of Divine Sons.)

Thus, the dedication in the Temple was 33 days after the actual live birth of Jesus (the two periods of course began together at the birth.)

The Basis of Dedication to the Lord

We need to say a bit more about this dedication and its origin.

In the beginning sections of the Law, God stipulated that the first born of both livestock and man are to be devoted or given to the Lord.

Ex 13:12 *"you shall devote to the LORD the first offspring of every womb, and the first offspring of every beast that you own; the males belong to the LORD."*

In the case of livestock this meant a sacrifice of death, *"you are to break its neck."* But in the case of Israel's firstborn males, the instruction was to redeem them with an animal. This was explained further on as a commemoration or remembrance of how the first born of Egypt were sacrificed to buy the freedom of Israel.

This was explained to children by their fathers, as recorded in Exodus:

Exodus 3:15 *'It came about, when Pharaoh was stubborn about letting us go, that the LORD killed every firstborn in the land of Egypt, both the firstborn of man and the firstborn of beast. Therefore, I sacrifice to the LORD the males, the first offspring of every womb, but every firstborn of my sons I redeem.'*

So the events at the Temple were two-fold: There was the "dedication" according to Exodus above – an offering in place of the consecration of the firstborn, and there was the sin offering which would end Mary's purification process. These in essence coincided at the time of the offering she gave.

The instruction was also that the mother is to give the offering at the door of the tent of meeting, so as not to enter the sanctuary until the offering had been made. In the case of the Temple there was no tent, but there was a door, and it was arranged ahead of time that the priests would be there to receive these offerings in emulation of the tabernacle in the wilderness.

Luke 2:24-27
24 and to offer a sacrifice according to what was said in the Law of the Lord, "A PAIR OF TURTLEDOVES OR TWO YOUNG PIGEONS."

The Law in Exodus stipulated that a lamb was to be brought for the dedication offering that redeemed the male child, and that a pigeon or turtledove could be offered for the sin offering.

Luke 2:36-38, Matthew 2:1-23

36 And there was a prophetess, Anna the daughter of Phanuel, of the tribe of Asher. She was advanced in years and had lived with her husband seven years after her marriage, 37 and then as a widow to the age of eighty-four. She never left the temple, serving night and day with fastings and prayers. 38 At that very moment she came up and began giving thanks to God, and continued to speak of Him to all those who were looking for the redemption of Jerusalem. (Luke 2:36-38)

1 Now after Jesus was born in Bethlehem of Judea in the days of Herod the king, magi from the east arrived in Jerusalem, saying, 2 "Where is He who has been born King of the Jews? For we saw His star in the east and have come to worship Him." 3 When Herod the king heard this, he was troubled, and all Jerusalem with him. 4 Gathering together all the chief priests and scribes of the people, he inquired of them where the Messiah was to be born. 5 They said to him, "In Bethlehem of Judea; for this is what has been written by the prophet: 6 'AND YOU, BETHLEHEM, LAND OF JUDAH, ARE BY NO MEANS LEAST AMONG THE LEADERS OF JUDAH; FOR OUT OF YOU SHALL COME FORTH A RULER WHO WILL SHEPHERD MY PEOPLE ISRAEL.'"

7 Then Herod secretly called the magi and determined from them the exact time the star appeared. 8 And he sent them to Bethlehem and said, "Go and search carefully for the Child; and when you have found Him, report to me, so that I too may come and worship Him." 9 After hearing the king, they went their way; and the star, which they had seen in the east, went on before them until it came and stood over the place where the Child was. 10 When they saw the star, they rejoiced exceedingly with great joy. 11 After coming into the house they saw the Child with Mary His mother; and they fell to the ground and worshiped Him. Then, opening their treasures, they presented to Him gifts of gold, frankincense, and myrrh. 12 And having been warned by God in a dream not to return to Herod, the magi left for their own country by another way. (Matthew 2:1-23)

Commentary

Luke 2:36-38

36 And there was a prophetess, Anna the daughter of Phanuel, of the tribe of Asher. She was advanced in years and had lived with her husband seven years after her marriage, 37 and then as a widow to the age of eighty-four. She never left the temple, serving night and day with fastings and prayers. 38 At that very moment she came up and began giving thanks to God, and continued to speak of Him to all those who were looking for the redemption of Jerusalem.

This section concerning Anna the prophetess really pertains to the end of the section about Simeon. It is provided as another instance of the faithful in Israel, praying expectantly for God to deliver His people from their afflictions and from Gentile rule. Anna comes into the picture as if by a director queuing his actors for their parts in a scene. She comes at the very moment of Simeon's conclusion.

Two things are to be observed here, prophets and the relation of Israel to Gentile kingdoms.

We are still basically in what is called the OT economy. Some call it the OT dispensation. Even though this story is being told in the New Testament and Christ has now come, the real transition will be at the Cross, the Resurrection and the descent of the Spirit.

In that former economy, the faithful were obliged to respect and abide in the dictates of the Law and to look for His voice in those he anointed to speak for Him. Prophecy in the OT was more often connected with *fore*-telling" than forth-telling. In contrast, the NT period has been characterized more with the latter – the delivery of messages and encouragement – rather than predictions about future events. Anna is right at the transition in these modes. She's not predicting times and events as much as describing the One who is to come. So in essence she's giving encouragement (NT style) about a future event (OT style.)

It can be seen in some vantage points that Israel has continually gotten a raw deal in the world. Some of this was their own doing to be sure. There are consequences for disobedience. But in other respects, they seem almost doomed to be under someone's heel. Yet over and over, the remnant of the faithful bring the nation out of those circumstances to endure into the next century and on. So it is here.

The Romans are not necessarily on the scene to punish Israel. The effects of the Babylonian Exile were far-reaching. They returned to their land under Persia, but would never enjoy the complete autonomy and greatness they had under David. From here on they would have some measure of freedom but always as vassals. Greece maintained that condition, as did Rome.

That Anna was praying is an indication of an oppression that seems to have increased since the days of Cyrus and Persia. Greek tyrants like Antiochus IV sparked the Maccabaean revolt. The Romans may have been magnanimous and accommodating in their handling of the provinces, but we must never forget their brutal capacity for cruelty.

This may seem a strange extension, but we see this model carried over in the operations of the Italian mob families. If you are their friend and do them their "services," you are showered with money, houses, cars, etc. You are in the family. But if you cross them, you find your feet in a tub of cement at the bottom of the East River; and that transition can happen virtually overnight. As we reflect on history, we find such things a modern horrifying replay of what was ancient Roman political life. Allies and friends could find soldiers at his home, a knock at the door that left him stabbed or hacked to pieces on his own threshold.

By the time of Jesus, Judea was no longer a free province. It was known for its uprisings and the need to crack down on the winds of rebellion. The presence of crosses throughout Judaea made a powerful statement.

Pilate was notorious for inflaming the Jews by his excessive measures. Josephus describes one incident in the Temple in which Pilate disguised his soldiers as citizens with clubs in their garments and at his signal they clubbed to death dozens of Jews in the precincts of their own temple. Pilate also appropriated Temple funds to build an aqueduct for Jerusalem to the outrage of the populace. Anna's service was one of the few godly responses to these times. As we shall see later, the Gentiles would continue to trod down Jerusalem until *"the times of the Gentiles be fulfilled."*

Matthew 2:1-2
1 "Now after Jesus was born in Bethlehem of Judea in the days of Herod the king, magi from the east arrived in Jerusalem, saying, 2 "Where is He who has been born King of the Jews? For we saw His star in the east and have come to worship Him."

Herod, as described earlier, was the son of Antipater who ingratiated himself to Julius Caesar by saving his life in Egypt. Herod, his son, likewise became known to Caesar's successor, Augustus; and the Herodian family was rather chummy with the imperial family in Rome. Herod Agrippa is actually sent there as a boy to live in the palace and becomes a boyhood friend of Gaius Caligula and the older Claudius - later emperors. (Agrippa was named after Marcus Agrippa, a close friend of Augustus.)

Herod the Great was made king by a decree of the Senate in 37 B.C. You can imagine what his attitude would have been toward men of influence coming from the east to investigate the fulfillment of a kingdom prophecy concerning his own realm. Herod was not a Jew but an Idumaean, and as such had no personal ties to Israel's prophecies.

The Magi are referred to as wise men, but in the sense of astrologers or in some sources, priests. They were not kings, if we stick to Scripture. The word *magi* is from the same word that gives us magician. However, these were not magicians but men who searched the skies and prevailing wisdom for signs and fulfillments.

The Magi are related strictly to Media, Assyria, Babylonia and Persia. They are known in Herodotus to be a caste that provided priests for Persian religious offices.[9] As such they were valued for religious rights, sacrifices, the telling of portents and insights into future events. Astrology and reading the skies for signs would have been integral.

We might then be puzzled why our God would involve men of an idolatrous world to play a part in the story of Christ's birth? We can only surmise by their worshipful behavior that God was declaring His Son to be above all the affairs of men, even their misguided worship of foreign gods.

We must also not infer too much about the religious beliefs of these particular men. They may have been of the Magi, but also such men as God was choosing to be drawn out into the true Light of God. They must have been familiar with the prophecies of the Jews about Messiah but nothing in the available information was telling them of the time. The star was key to attracting their interest.

The Magi are also related to Daniel in that we read that Nebuchadnezzar raised Daniel to be chief over the wise men of Babylon. If the Magi are of that discipline down to NT times, then they would have been familiar with Daniel's prophecies, written in Babylon.

It is not by any means clear how they understood them in relation to our own modern study of them today. But if they were alert enough to follow down the intricacies as we have today and discerned the various decrees concerning the Jews and their return, based on Daniel Chapter 9, they would in fact have been expecting Messiah to come somewhere in the period we have here. The star then would have been the key factor in telling them the precise time.

The names of Balthasar, Melchior and Caspar are legendary without scriptural or patristic support. Balthasar is the Greek equivalent for Belshazzar which might link him to Babylon, but at the time Babylon was a ghost town and subject to Persia. As for three men, we infer this only from the gifts.

The star did not convey information about a king of the Jews. They had acquired this knowledge by their familiarity with the prophecies, perhaps specifically Isaiah 9:6 *"For unto us a child is born.."* Neither can we rule out divine word of knowledge to these men, in that if God intended them to be part of the story, He may have enabled them through His Grace to put the pieces together and know the time was at hand.

It is interesting that before Herod they seem almost to assume that everyone there would know of this event and could simply direct them. They ask where he's to be found, as if all Jerusalem surely knows. As for Herod, mention of a star is serious validation that something legit is taking place, and these are not just wayward vagabonds out on a lark. Herod must, however, be cagey at this juncture if he wishes to intercept and control what is about to happen.

Matthew 2:3-7
3 When Herod the king heard this, he was troubled, . . . 4 Gathering together all the chief priests and scribes . . he inquired of them where the Messiah was to be born. 5 They said to him, "In Bethlehem of Judea; for this is what has been written by the prophet 6 `AND YOU, BETHLEHEM, LAND OF JUDAH,"

The first point of departure was to take a break and huddle with his own advisors about the details of any prophecies. The magi did not state which ones had led them there. As for Herod, it was generally known that Messianic prophecies were peppered throughout the Scriptures, but timings and signs were vague.

This was now not so much a matter of validating any timing involved, but a location. Herod was not questioning their claim that the time had arrived; merely that if it had arrived, the place and circumstances should match prophetic information.

---

[9] Dewald, Waterfield, <u>History of Herodotus</u>, Oxford Univ. Press, 1998, Chapter 1

Someone among his advisors knew his Scripture. He pinpointed Micah 5:2. Bethlehem which was among the smallest in Judah was to be blessed with the birth of the Redeemer.

[It should also be noted that there were no concordances in those days. The men who found this passage would have to have known the running text of these scrolls well enough to know the book and the applicable words by heart.]

The words had to pierce Herod to the quick. Not just a great man, but a "ruler" had been born, and there was already a ruler in his kingdom.

7 Then Herod secretly called the magi and determined from them the exact time the star appeared . . . and said, "Go . . and when you have found Him, report to me, so that I too may come and worship Him

Several things are happening here. Herod inquires about the exact time they first saw the star because he was trying to discern the probable age of the child. This would have revealed for them that he was as clueless about the specifics as they were. But for Herod's purposes, if the magi had been journeying for a couple of years, that would tell him about how old. The same for a few weeks.

Secondly, he intends to use them to mark the child for destruction. He need do no complicated searching or interrogation of the populace with these men here to point the way. He of course throws them off by pretending a desire to worship Him as well.

We can also depend on the fact that such men were not stupid. Here is a king wanting information that will help him welcome his replacement. We are not told how it was that the magi were not watched the whole way with the purpose of taking the child into custody or worse. The other incredible aspect is the continuance of the star. With or without the magi's help, such a light would be an equally efficient way to enable Herod to effect his evil plans. This is further reason for believing the star was supernatural to the magi, but perhaps to no one else.

Matthew 2:9-11
9 After hearing the king, they went their way; and the star, which they had seen in the east, went on before them until it came and stood over the place where the Child was.

The star is said to have been seen in the east, but this refers to where they were when they saw it, not its location in the sky. It would have been in the west if it was to draw them out of the east toward Jerusalem. But if it was very local to them in proximity, it could also have been in the east drawing them across the landscape to the west.

There are some who try to propose planetary alignments to explain the brightness in the sky without resorting to a miraculous light shining down and showing the path. This has many problems that rule it out.

First, these men would know that a celestial light could not pinpoint a location on the earth but indicate merely a direction. There were billions of square miles possible from a light merely in the heavens. So starting out to find a place on earth would be like following Orion.

Second, the light is said to have gone on before them. If you know anything about the distances of the planets and stars, all celestial lights stay fixed as you travel "toward" them (irrespective of their also moving across the sky during the night.) Staying in the same place as you walk or ride toward them might be perceived as moving as you move but all stars behave this way. So one more light would be no different.

Third, we will read later that the star "stood" over the stable to show them the precise location. This just isn't possible with a celestial light, no matter how bright. The light from such a convergence would "stand" over every location on earth. To be described as showing the place, we simply have to have some supernatural coincidence, light emitting from the star in a way that shown down on a specific place.

10 When they saw the star, they rejoiced exceedingly with great joy . . . 11 After coming into the house . . . they fell to the ground and worshiped Him. Then, opening their treasures, they presented to Him gifts of gold, frankincense, and myrrh.

Here the scope of worship changed for His parents. The worship of the local shepherds was one thing. But to have people from far away, outside their own nation worshipping, and completely on their own initiative, was confirmation that the child was indeed all they had been told.

"into the house" This is of great interest because Mary and Joseph are now in a house not the stable. Some have guessed that this might mean some time after the birth in order to have time to arrange for a house. But we must remember that their home is Nazareth not Bethlehem. They had neither the finances or other resources to have two homes.

More likely this was the charity of the locals in Bethlehem, who for many reasons including those of simple compassion, may have offered them room in their home.

The spices are hugely symbolic. Gold was undeniably regal. Frankincense has been variously linked to sacrifice and prayer. Myrrh was used to anoint the dead. That we see these coalescing in a composite image is striking, since we know the middle and the end of the story. But what a point of curiosity and puzzlement these gifts must have been for Joseph and Mary.

Matthew 2:12
12 And having been warned by God in a dream not to return to Herod, the magi left for their own country by another way.

So we see here again the idea that God, despite their relationship to foreign worship, used these men for His own purposes and even spared them the wrath of Herod. This is rather strange when we see His attitude toward other instances of idolatry and "other gods." Again, we are prompted to infer that these men were being called away from their former associations into a newness of light and revelation.

This had to involve a great deal of supernatural intervention because, as above, the star would be a major tip-off if visible to all, and certainly there were resources for having the men followed. That they were able to conduct their mission free and undisturbed, and leave without being arrested is exceptional beyond words. Herod will be left with merely the indicators of an approximate age, no locations except the Bethlehem area. How he deals with this information comes next.

Matthew 2:13-16
13 Now when they had gone, behold, an angel of the Lord appeared to Joseph in a dream and said, "Get up! Take the Child and His mother and flee to Egypt, and remain there until I tell you; for Herod is going to search for the Child to destroy Him." 14 So Joseph got up and took the Child and His mother while it was still night, and left for Egypt. 15 He remained there until the death of Herod. This was to fulfill what had been spoken by the Lord through the prophet: "OUT OF EGYPT I CALLED MY SON."

16 Then when Herod saw that he had been tricked by the magi, he became very enraged, and sent and slew all the male children who were in Bethlehem and all its vicinity, from two years old and under, according to the time which he had determined from the magi. 17 Then what had been spoken through Jeremiah the prophet was fulfilled: 18 "A VOICE WAS HEARD IN RAMAH, WEEPING AND GREAT MOURNING, RACHEL WEEPING FOR HER CHILDREN; AND SHE REFUSED TO BE COMFORTED, BECAUSE THEY WERE NO MORE."

Commentary

Matthew 2:13-14
13 "Now when they had gone, behold, an angel of the Lord appeared to Joseph in a dream and said, "Get up! Take the Child and His mother and flee to Egypt, and remain there until I tell you; for Herod is going to search for the Child to destroy Him."

It would naturally follow that as soon as the Magi left, orders would be given to follow them, locate the Child and do away with Him. We have to realize that in the ancient world, politics was ruthless and brutal without regret. Rulers wielded unimaginable power over wealth and people, so the opportunities to acquire these positions brought out the worst in aspiring candidates. And imperial Rome was modeling this better than anyone. Prospective emperors paved their path to power in blood, even within their own families. Vassal states easily emulated the patterns of their Roman overlords. Gaining office was bad enough. Then began a program of fear and brutality required to maintain your position and intimidate and thwart all those other equally ruthless men who now see you as the obstacle in their own path to power.

Herod was following the way of all rulers of the times. You don't "persuade" contenders to forget their designs, you eliminate them. It was efficient and effective insurance.

Again, it is amazing that the Magi were somehow prevented from leading Herod's men to the site. At least there was enough time for them to visit and worship the Child before Temple troops arrived.

The Lord was already ahead of this plan. As you can see, the timing was rather critical. There was just enough time to receive the magi, then the parents must be told to escape.

Since Herod is said to be about to search – *"Herod is going to search for the Child"* - we must conclude that after being ordered to follow them, Herod's men were frustrated in tracking the Magi to the exact location and were obliged to return without evidence of the Child's death or even a specific location. Herod was then consigned to a search of the area. It was hardly a pleasant moment to be sure.

14 So Joseph got up . . and left for Egypt . . . until the death of Herod. This was to fulfill what had been spoken by the Lord through the prophet: "OUT OF EGYPT I CALLED MY SON."

Egypt is logical for the simple reason that it was the nearest place outside Herod's jurisdiction. The distance to the border would have been about 300 miles. Comparable distances would be: Los Angeles to Las Vegas, New York to Washington D.C., London to just over the border in Scotland. At the slow pace of walking with a donkey, it would take about 6-10 days, depending on delays along the way and how many hours Mary could endure traveling per day.

What is surprising here is that the duration of stay is unknown to them at this juncture, since its end would be the death of Herod. What of their home in Nazareth? How will they pay for things in Egypt?

Here, we must be mindful of the incredible difference in culture between then and now. Getting work in a new locale was much easier than it is today. People were more trusting and reliable, and work did not have the criticality of deadlines and quotas and resumes and competition that jobs do today. There may also have been Divine arrangements ready and waiting in Egypt that would have provided their needs while there.

As for their house, family and friends would be available to watch over their belongings, and someone in Bethlehem could easily have gotten word back to Nazareth. And we must remember that back then one didn't have an ongoing mortgage to pay, insurance, utilities, or forwarding mail to worry about.

The reference to Hosea 11:1 *"When Israel was a child, I loved him, and out of Egypt I called My son."* seems odd because it traditionally applied to Israel in Egypt, called forth in the Exodus.

Israel was new born when it entered Egypt with just the family of Jacob and his sons. There is no hint whatsoever that anything Messianic is intended here or that this would apply to the Christ in some future double fulfillment.

We do have a sort of marker back in Exodus which we can see in hindsight as being related - Ex 4:22:*"Then you will say to Pharaoh: This is what the Lord says: Israel is My firstborn son."* But there would have been no reason for Israel or future generations to identify this as applicable to anyone else but Israel itself. The only warrant we have that these events are a fulfillment is that the New Testament says so.

So while we might be without reason to connect them, we must not argue with God if He does. It may be as simple as God enjoying the design of His Word to the degree that He has hidden meanings that only He appreciates in the things said long ago.

Matthew 2:16
16 Then when Herod saw that he had been tricked by the magi, he became very enraged, and sent and slew all the male children who were in Bethlehem and all its vicinity, from two years old and under, according to the time which he had determined from the magi.

As earlier, we see that the question to the Magi was chiefly to discern the age of the Child. Some have questioned why children two years old and under? If the Magi were seeking a new born, why wouldn't the age be much younger? Again, much depends on how long the men had been seeking the Child, and as we have seen, Jesus was in a house by the time they arrived.
    From our standpoint, the Child couldn't have been too old or his parents would have by then returned to Nazareth. But Herod knew nothing of those details and had to extrapolate from the vague information of the Magi.

Some have also claimed that this proves Jesus was born much earlier (6 B.C.) because Herod died shortly after this event in 4 B.C., hence children at two years old would bring us to B.C. 6. But it is likely that because of the lack of precision, Herod broadened the age bracket, just to be sure. Hence, scholars give 4 – 5 B.C for His birth.

We then have the fulfillment of this horrid event from Jeremiah 31:15, *"A voice was heard in Ramah, weeping . . . Rachel . . . for her children;"*

Ramah was an ancient city in the territory allotted to Benjamin which was the next tribal territory just N of Judah. Ancient Ramah is situated near the Jerusalem Airport. Bethlehem was further south, squarely in Judah, being the city of David. We might find it strange here that a town other than Bethlehem and farther north is mentioned concerning this slaughter, when Bethlehem was the target. The vicinity all around may have had wider application than we might surmise. Remember, Herod was bent on being thorough.
    But there is thematic significance in Ramah. It is the place of Benjamin and Rachel died giving birth to him. Rachel's tomb is actually midway between Ramah and Bethlehem, so it is poignant that she would weep from her grave at the loss of the innocent as far north as her son's home and to the south in Bethlehem.

We might question why God would permit such atrocities and against so innocent a host? We cannot really avoid the conclusion that this was permitted, but we can never go so far as to conclude that it was thereby condoned, or even viewed as a necessary sacrifice.

This is Satan's work through and through, and he had a ready agent in Herod. Men made these decisions not God and they will be held to account not Him. The whole question of why God permitted Satan and Herod to effect their ends without intervening is wrapped up in the whole issue of free will. Men will claim that God did not prevent their evil deeds, but it is men, not God, who conceived such deeds. This will be no argument for freeing them from their willful misuse of personal freedom. Opportunities are one thing. Choices are quite another.

As for the incalculable suffering involved, we can only trust that God simply took them in the midst of their terror, and despite the grief of their parents, these infants would never trade their affectionate place in the arms of God for the earthly life lost to them. We have a glimmer of this deliverance ability from God in Fox's Book of Martyrs. We see the early Fathers suffering the most horrifying deaths in relative peace while continuing their witness until flames snuffed out their voices.

There are accounts of men who in the midst of the flames gave signs to their friends that the ordeal could be victoriously endured, giving hope to those awaiting their own fate. Such accounts put the real matters about these things into perspective. They, and we also, are citizens of another country and death is but a transition to that final home. The means by which it happens are described as incomparable to what lies ahead because, in the end, our lives are bigger, broader, and deeper than what feeble men can do.

When we see them again in our heavenly estate, we will be want in seeing any bitterness, anger or sorrow over the hand dealt to them in the over-arching plan of God?

Matthew 2:19-23, Luke 2:40-52
19 But when Herod died, behold, an angel of the Lord appeared in a dream to Joseph in Egypt, and said, 20 "Get up, take the Child and His mother, and go into the land of Israel; for those who sought the Child's life are dead." 21 So Joseph got up, took the Child and His mother, and came into the land of Israel. 22 But when he heard that Archelaus was reigning over Judea in place of his father Herod, he was afraid to go there. Then after being warned by God in a dream, he left for the regions of Galilee, 23 and came and lived in a city called Nazareth. This was to fulfill what was spoken through the prophets: "He shall be called a Nazarene." (Matthew 2:19-23)

40 The Child continued to grow and become strong, increasing in wisdom; and the grace of God was upon Him. 41 Now His parents went to Jerusalem every year at the Feast of the Passover. 42 And when He became twelve, they went up there according to the custom of the Feast; 43 and as they were returning, after spending the full number of days, the boy Jesus stayed behind in Jerusalem. But His parents were unaware of it, 44 but supposed Him to be in the caravan, and went a day's journey; and they began looking for Him among their relatives and acquaintances. 45 When they did not find Him, they returned to Jerusalem looking for Him.

46 Then, after three days they found Him in the temple, sitting in the midst of the teachers, both listening to them and asking them questions. 47 And all who heard Him were amazed at His understanding and His answers. 48 When they saw Him, they were astonished; and His mother said to Him, "Son, why have You

treated us this way? Behold, Your father and I have been anxiously looking for You." 49 And He said to them, "Why is it that you were looking for Me? Did you not know that I had to be in My Father's house?" 50 But they did not understand the statement which He had made to them. 51 And He went down with them and came to Nazareth, and He continued in subjection to them; and His mother treasured all these things in her heart. 52 And Jesus kept increasing in wisdom and stature, and in favor with God and men.
(Luke 2:40-52)

Commentary

Matthew 2:19-23
" 19 But when Herod died . .

It was not long after this that Herod at long last died. History tells us that he was eaten with disease and that his body was so profuse from noxious oozings near the end of his life that guards sometimes fainted at the odor. He had played the game of king and despot, naïve to its beguiling effects and destructive power. He left the world a great man for his accomplishments, (the refurbishment of the Jerusalem Temple, Masada). But as to character - lower than the dust.

The date is reasonably certain within a month's margin – March – April, B.C. 4. The reason for this degree of certainty is Josephus' mention of an eclipse of the moon just before Herod died.

Two zealot teachers named Jason and Matthias had gathered a band of other radicals and managed to tear down the symbol of Roman authority - the enormous gold eagle over the gate of the Temple. They were caught by Herod's Temple guards and burned alive. Josephus tells us that the eclipse occurred that very night.

From astronomy we know the exact date and even the time – 2 hours 34 min. AM at Jerusalem, in the year 750 A.U.C. (year since the founding of Rome) which is March 12, 4 B.C. [from the tables provided by Johnson, *Eclipses Past and Future*.] [10] *(For more on AUC, see below at Luke 3:1.)*

---

[10] Anderson, Sir Robert, The Coming Prince, Kregel, 1982, p. 258
Johnson, Eclipses Past and Future, Oxford Univ. Press, 1874

We also know from Josephus that Herod died at least seven days before the Passover of that same year, which again astronomy tells us was on April 12. So Herod had to have died somewhere between these two dates in 4 B.C.

22 But when he heard that Archelaus was reigning over Judea in place of his father Herod, he was afraid to go there . . . after being warned by God . . came and lived in a city called Nazareth. . . "He shall be called a Nazarene."

The kingdom of Herod was not bequeathed to a single heir. Herod changed his will several times just before his death and the final version divided the kingdom among four of his sons, Antipas, Archelaus, Philip, and Lysanias. Archelaus received Judaea proper.

Archelaus was exceedingly wicked and completely mismanaged his region to such a degree that a delegation was sent to Rome to depose him. Augustus agreed, but he took this opportunity to install a Roman procurator instead. This series of governors remained over Judaea through to the Jewish revolt and the destruction of Jerusalem in 70 A.D. So you see how it was that we have two key figures during the ministry and death of Jesus, Herod Antipas and Pontius Pilate.

Joseph was duly wary of Archelaus who was a crazed tyrant of unpredictable behavior.

"He shall be called a Nazarene" We really have no OT prophecy that states this. Matthew is quoting something that prophets obviously had spoken about Messiah, but their words appear to be outside the Scripture.

The basis for the connection comes from Isaiah where Messiah is referred to as the *"branch"* of Jesse, (11:1.) The name Nazareth is based on the word *netzer* which means branch. Hence, extra-biblical prophecies arose about Messiah being a netzer which in some versions became "a Nazarene."

But this was somewhat obscure, because the scribes, priests and leaders did not make the connection that Nazareth would be a significant marker for Messiah. In fact, there was a saying among the people, *"Can anything good come from Nazareth?"* (John 1:46.)

By coming to Nazareth in Galilee, they had come under the jurisdiction of Herod Antipas who survives in his place of power well into the adult ministry of John the Baptist and Jesus.

Luke 2:40-41
Luke 2:40 "The Child continued to grow and become strong, increasing in wisdom; and the grace of God was upon Him."

We have incredibly few comments about Jesus' childhood except the one coming next. But it is clear that as He came of age, He demonstrated increasingly the wisdom attending Him as the Son of God.

Grace here is not unmerited favor, as with us. He rightly deserved the favor of His Father in all respects, but the mention of this gives us the idea that there was yet a notable dependency on the blessings of His Father at this point in His life.

41 Now His parents went to Jerusalem every year at the Feast of the Passover. . . "Did you not know that I had to be in My Father's house?"

The Passover was both a night and a period that included the night plus the days following. In its strictest sense it was the night of Nisan 14 in their calendar. But technically, this began the day of the 15th of Nisan because the Jewish day began at 6:00 PM. During the day of the 14th, the Jews would purchase and prepare the things needed for the feast that night as the day approached the changeover to the 15th. This was in strict observance of the procedure done in Egypt during the Plague of the First Born, where the Lord *"passed over"* the houses of those whose doorposts were painted with the blood of the sacrifice.

But Passover came to refer also to the whole week including the Passover night and the six days of the Feast of Unleavened Bread. So it is sometimes referred to as the Feast of Unleavened Bread or elsewhere as the Passover.

The reason for the trip to Jerusalem was that the lamb for the sacrifice and the meal had to be properly inspected, slain by Levites in the Temple, prepared for roasting (usually meaning flayed,) and returned to the family for roasting at home.

The Passover was not technically a sin offering, but it was related figuratively to the sparing of Israel during the judgment of sin. It was a memorial to the deliverance from Egypt. The lamb was slain to provide the blood for marking the doors of Israelite families. The meal was symbolic that a sacrifice had been made to protect them from the death coming on the Egyptians, but also as a pointer to the perfect sacrifice of the Lamb of God who would save His people from their rightful eternal punishment.

Part of this symbolism was in what took place just before this event. Exodus 12 commands that on the 10th of Nisan the family is to acquire the lamb without blemish and keep it until the 14th.

You need to imagine what would take place in this interim. Children and even the adults would become unavoidably attached to it. Then would come the time for slaughter. There would understandably be tears and pleas from the children.

The point to be conveyed was that sin was an awful thing if the sacrifice of such a precious animal was needed to meet the justice of God. And Jesus also was just such a Precious Thing to be abused of men and sacrificed for us.

Luke 2:43
". . the boy Jesus stayed behind in Jerusalem. But His parents were unaware of it, "

We come now to this incident, which seems to put Jesus into an unfavorable light by seemingly not caring about the distress he had caused to his parents. Our first puzzlement is how they could have left without Him. But this is understandable in that they were there with relatives and friends and folks routinely looked out for each other. They also traveled much like a caravan, where people, especially children, could be anywhere along the train of people and belongings in motion. It was assumed that someone had Him in tow and Jesus had been a conscientious and responsible Child.

So we might then question why He would deviate from this and cause His parents worry? When they do find Him, He states that He was about His Father's business. The Greek, *'patayr'* means the affairs of the father, but in reference to looking after the things of the father's house. So the KJV has *"about My Father's business"* but the NASB has *"in My Father's house."*

We have to bear in mind that there are always affairs of Heaven running right alongside the timeline of human affairs. These always must be seen as the pre-eminent activity. Man will have his own circumstances, urgencies and goals that may seem commanding and vexing and of immediate urgency at times, but these cannot invade or usurp the primacy of Heavenly things.

So while Jesus was focusing on what was needed in terms of Heaven, men are called to adjust their attitudes about priorities. Their plans, schedules and urgencies must give way to what is happening on the higher plain.

With no discredit to Mary and Joseph, they were still reeling from the vexing business of trying to find Him and were understandably in no frame of mind to appreciate the above. We can empathize with their worry, but in the end, this is all on the horizontal, and all such things must be put into perspective.

Luke 2:51-52

51 And He went down with them and came to Nazareth, and He continued in subjection to them; and His mother treasured all these things in her heart. 52 And Jesus kept increasing in wisdom and stature, and in favor with God and men.

Jesus' subjection to His parents was not punishment for what His behavior had caused them. It was a return to the conditions under which He had lived all His childhood. He was to demonstrate humility, not grasping arrogance. The lesson for us is that if the Son of God who had rights to everything imaginable submitted Himself to the grossly inferior capacities in His parents, we who have no regal or divine claims whatsoever have even less reason for neglecting the same.

Subjection is a principle more than a behavior. Everyone who is born enters a world where subjection is in every thread of the fabric of life. We get it first from parents. We get it next in school, then in the workplace, then in human society in the form of laws and rules. Young men who leave their parents to make their own decisions and decide to enlist in the service find that they have merely exchanged a little hammer for a much larger one.

Everyone answers to someone, even at the top. We never really get out from under the thumb of someone higher up the chain or of circumstances that obligate us to conform to certain actions. And we find that this is as it was intended, by design. When Jesus met the soldier, he marveled that the man understood the way of authority and subjection.

The President of the United States is at the top where the "buck" supposedly stops, yet he finds he is not an autocrat, but is constrained by the ultimate will of the people and what they elected him to do. He finds that despite his power to act, government is slow and plodding at best.

So we see that Mary came to realize the meaning of her son's words and these added to the treasure building in her heart. That Jesus increased in favor with men is important because it is the purpose of God to draw men to Him and the fullness of life He has planned. His intention is that it be seen for what it is – a wonderful thing, not an arduous thing. A life rightly related to God should attract all but the foolish and the truly evil. People enjoyed being around Jesus. People should likewise enjoy being around His followers.

Christians have lost favor with men of late. Such things are predicted in Scripture, but we can't let that expectation cover those areas of rejection that lie at our own feet. If we are persecuted, we can take some comfort if it is for righteousness sake. But if it's because *we* have the bad attitude, *we* are selfish, *we* lack unconditional love, we cannot trivialize our guilt my making it out as persecution.

Jesus later exhorts us that our works should so shine before men that they glorify God on account of them. This isn't us engineering praise, which is so often the case. It's others outside simply observing our works and drawing the unsolicited conclusion from them that God is great.

A tall order.

CHAPTER 2
The Ministry of John the Baptist

Luke 3:1-6, Matthew 3:4-6. Matthew 3:7. Luke 3:8

1 Now in the fifteenth year of the reign of Tiberius Caesar, when Pontius Pilate was governor of Judea, and Herod was tetrarch of Galilee, and his brother Philip was tetrarch of the region of Ituraea and Trachonitis, and Lysanias was tetrarch of Abilene, 2 in the high priesthood of Annas and Caiaphas, the word of God came to John, the son of Zacharias, in the wilderness. 3 And he came into all the district around the Jordan, preaching a baptism of repentance for the forgiveness of sins; 4 as it is written in the book of the words of Isaiah the prophet, "THE VOICE OF ONE CRYING IN THE WILDERNESS, `MAKE READY THE WAY OF THE LORD, MAKE HIS PATHS STRAIGHT. 5 `EVERY RAVINE WILL BE FILLED, AND EVERY MOUNTAIN AND HILL WILL BE BROUGHT LOW; THE CROOKED WILL BECOME STRAIGHT, AND THE ROUGH ROADS SMOOTH; 6 AND ALL FLESH WILL SEE THE SALVATION OF GOD.' " (Luke 3:1-6)

4 Now John himself had a garment of camel's hair and a leather belt around his waist; and his food was locusts and wild honey. 5 Then Jerusalem was going out to him, and all Judea and all the district around the Jordan; 6 and they were being baptized by him in the Jordan River, as they confessed their sins. (Matthew 3:4-6)

7 But when he saw many of the Pharisees and Sadducees coming for baptism, he said to them, "You brood of vipers, who warned you to flee from the wrath to come? (Matthew 3:7)

8 "Therefore bear fruits in keeping with repentance, and do not begin to say to yourselves, `We have Abraham for our father,' for I say to you that from these stones God is able to raise up children to Abraham. (Luke 3:8)

Commentary

Luke 3:1-2
1 "Now in the fifteenth year of the reign of Tiberius Caesar, when Pontius Pilate was governor of Judea, and Herod was tetrarch of Galilee, ... 2 in the high priesthood of Annas and Caiaphas, the word of God came to John, ... in the wilderness."

"fifteenth year . . "

Interestingly, we can know precisely the very year in our own calendar. In NT times there were three main systems for naming a year. (Our present system of B.C./A.D. was some 300 years away.) In Roman official records, the year was named after the two consuls for the year – *" In the consulship of Marcus Vinicius and Quintus Lucretius"* Also, a year could be named as *anno urbis conditae* – A.U.C. – "year of the city" (i.e. the foundation of Rome.) [11] Or it could be named by the year of the emperor, as we have it here.

We have to keep in mind that in Roman times it was less important to know how many years ago something was than to simply have a "name" for the time. It would be like saying, "In the year the twin towers collapsed, the new library opened in town." In the provinces, however, it was rather difficult to keep track of the consuls, so the AUC method or the emperor's year was used.

The monk, Dionysius, selected the AUC system to discern the year that would become 1 A.D. because it was much easier since it was a running system of years irrespective of who was emperor. But for Luke, the year of the emperor was so much in common parlance, that he uses it here in his gospel.

The accession of Tiberius as emperor on August 19, 14 A.D. was one of the most well-attested dates in the ancient world because it coincided with the death of his predecessor. Augustus had been so incredibly monumental in his affect on the civilized world that his death was a major world event.

There was no accession year system for emperors, so Tiberius' first year would have been the same year he received the principate (became emperor), A.D. 14, and his fifteenth year was A.D. 28. [11]

This is the year John begins his ministry, not necessary the year Jesus began His.

However, the reason for Luke mentioning this year is much more important. It separates the gospel account from mythology or mere stories, and places it within the realm of actual history. In mythology, one doesn't have historical figures of recent times against whose careers and facts the story can be validated. The claims of the gospel accounts were written so as to name names and places that could be verified within the recent memories of the hearers. In many cases, the people were still very much alive and could be asked. This separates the Gospels from myths, which couldn't be validated by anyone.

Tiberius was a step-son by marriage to Augustus. Augustus' second marriage was to Livia to whom Tiberius had been born with her former husband, Tiberius Nero.

". . when Pontius Pilate was governor of Judea, and Herod was tetrarch of Galilee, . . ."

As earlier, the sons of Herod the Great became tetrarchs because they each ruled but one-fourth of the kingdom, and their regions are mentioned here. Pilate was never called 'tetrarch' because he was procurator, not a vassal ruler. A procurator is someone who *curates for* someone else, in this case he conducts political affairs for the emperor.

Pilate is believed to have been appointed by Sejanus, who was Tiberius' right-hand man in Rome, and of tremendous power. Sejanus was notoriously anti-semitic and this may account for Pilate's nettling and harassment of the Jews. [12]

". . in the high priesthood of Annas and Caiaphas"

Caiaphas was officially high priest by appointment, but since his father, Annas, was still living, he is often deferred to somewhat like a co-regent in this office. At His arrest, we see Jesus being first interviewed by Annas before meeting with Caiaphas.

Luke 3:3-4
3 "And he came into all the district around the Jordan, preaching a baptism of repentance for the forgiveness of sins;"

As noted earlier, John did not intend to substitute his baptism for the Temple procedure of burnt offerings. Those who came to him did so because of the preaching and as a sort of ordinance experience that would better recall in their minds and memories their personal commitment to add true repentance to Mosaic ritual. John also did not in any way claim to have the authority to forgive sins, but preached that a repentant heart surely God would not turn away.

---

[11] Hoehner, Chronological Aspects to the Life of Christ, Zondervan, 1977, p. 11
Anderson, The Coming Prince, Kregel, 1982, pp. 95-96

[12] F.F. Bruce, New Testament History, Doubleday, 1969, p. 36

John stayed clear of the cities because it was important to have a place of ministry away from the contentious and argumentative atmosphere he and his followers would have encountered in town. It is truly amazing that this personal preference of John's was incorporated into Isaiah's prophecy concerning him:
"...the voice of one crying in the wilderness,"

We must not infer that John was mindful to fulfill Isaiah, but that Isaiah was picturing what John would do. John was the source of this arrangement. Isaiah looked ahead and proclaimed it.

4 ".. MAKE READY THE WAY OF THE LORD, MAKE HIS PATHS STRAIGHT. 5 'EVERY RAVINE WILL BE FILLED, AND EVERY MOUNTAIN AND HILL WILL BE BROUGHT LOW; THE CROOKED WILL BECOME STRAIGHT, AND THE ROUGH ROADS SMOOTH;

This describes the procedure for welcoming a king. Citizens would clean up unsuitable aspects of their village and the roads approaching them so that the entourage would have level ground, free of boulders and rocks. Dips would be filled in and rises and hills in the way would be leveled. New roadwork might even be done to avoid existing crooked paths. All to make the travel of horses, carts and people as easy as possible.

But this had great figurative meaning to our Lord's coming. On account of His coming, access to Him will be made straight and direct, obstacles will be removed. Valleys and hills picture the stations in life, the lowly and humble compared to the lofty or haughty. These would be brought to the same level playing field before God. Arrogance would be humbled, Poverty of spirit would be lifted.

The aimless paths on which men trod in life would cease to be crooked and meandering, and become straight and clear.

Luke 3:6
6 "and all flesh will see the salvation of God."

This is hyperbole to be sure. It is typically eastern in that it is all embracing when it is clear that the immediate scope is limited, but it is used to convey the grander extent of what the event means. All flesh did not see this salvation then and there at the time, but virtually all flesh has now become acquainted with the story of Christ and the Cross.

And to those whom we might conceive as having never heard or never cared, they will be brought to see that that which they discounted or ignored is the key to their eternal destiny.

Matthew 3:4-8
4 "Now John himself had a garment of camel's hair and a leather belt around his waist; and his food was locusts and wild honey."

This was not a way of life John adopted to be especially odd or bizarre. It was the natural outcome of where he chose to live. To some extent, there may have been Divine intent for John to "stand out" in a way that augmented his ministry, but it was positive not negative or scary. There was definitely no design that he appear as those destitute and possibly dangerous people who strike fear in us today.

5"Then Jerusalem was going out to him, and all Judea and all the district around the Jordan; 6 and they were being baptized by him in the Jordan River, as they confessed their sins."

As said earlier, the Law lacked the piece of the process that enjoined genuine confession and repentance. You could go to the Temple and offer the required sacrifice in a very ritualistic manner without much interaction, counseling or inner contemplation. It could easily be seen as a case of sinning, going to the Temple and paying a sort of spiritual "fee," then on to the things one had to do.

Matthew 3:7-8
7 But when he saw many of the Pharisees and Sadducees coming for baptism, he said to them, "You brood of vipers, who warned you to flee from the wrath to come?

Since Luke presents these words as addressed to the multitudes coming to be baptized, the impression might be that the people at large were addressed. As we see in Matthew 3:7, John spots the Pharisees and Sadducees among the crowd and addresses them as a brood of vipers. John's language had two purposes. 1) to ferret out the cynical and the false, who came merely to observe or even to spy, and 2) to clarify among the penitent what was happening here. This was serious business before the Lord, so don't come to have a nice day in the country, but confront your sins and change your way of living.

Luke 3:8
8 "Therefore bear fruits in keeping with repentance, and do not begin to say to yourselves, `We have Abraham for our father,' for I say to you that from these stones God is able to raise up children to Abraham.

It was necessary to cut asunder all the clever tricks the mind can play on rationalizing our sins. The truly penitent would welcome the message because they were already convicted about themselves.

First he calls them a brood of vipers, meaning they have become crafty as to the consequences of sin. It is as though someone had convinced them that they could somehow escape the wrath to come. These very words are there to let them know that this is a delusion.

He says that they should instead bear the fruits of a real repentance. They should also not hide behind the blessing promised to Abraham. A Jew might rationalize that God will not discard His people because of the promises made, hence, his sins could never have too bad a consequence if he is of Abraham.

The dig is in the statement that God can raise up better children from the stones lying around. Very exhortative stuff. No one got away without conviction. The effect was positive for many, as we shall see next.

Luke 3:9-18

9 "Indeed the axe is already laid at the root of the trees; so every tree that does not bear good fruit is cut down and thrown into the fire." 10 And the crowds were questioning him, saying, "Then what shall we do?" 11 And he would answer and say to them, "The man who has two tunics is to share with him who has none; and he who has food is to do likewise." 12 And some tax collectors also came to be baptized, and they said to him, "Teacher, what shall we do?" 13 And he said to them, "Collect no more than what you have been ordered to." 14 Some soldiers were questioning him, saying, "And what about us, what shall we do?" And he said to them, "Do not take money from anyone by force, or accuse anyone falsely, and be content with your wages." 15 Now while the people were in a state of expectation and all were wondering in their hearts about John, as to whether he was the Christ, 16 John answered and said to them all, "As for me, I baptize you with water; but One is coming who is mightier than I, and I am not fit to untie the thong of His sandals; He will baptize you with the Holy Spirit and fire. 17 "His winnowing fork is in His hand to thoroughly clear His threshing floor, and to gather the wheat into His barn; but He will burn up the chaff with unquenchable fire." 18 So with many other exhortations he preached the gospel to the people.

Commentary

Luke 3:9-10

9 "Indeed the axe is already laid at the root of the trees; so every tree that does not bear good fruit is cut down and thrown into the fire."

John intensifies his exhortation to the crowds by picturing the husbandmen clearing his fields. Trees that have left off bearing fruit are cut down to make a place for new trees that will. And John is telling the crowd that the axe is already laid at the roots, meaning the penalty for not bearing spiritual fruit is at hand. Those who no longer bear fruit will be side-stepped by God in favor of those who will.

Bearing fruit in the Spirit is one of the outpourings of having the new birth. Believers truly converted will not sit idle. But it is a phenomenon of later Christian life that people can adopt indolence and laziness for a variety of reasons; and this we can get used to rather easily. Soon, it's the young people who are supposed to have the verve and vigor, "We've had our day," so we say.

But John is saying that it is a fearful thing to be cast aside by God, to be on the outside looking in on His work of the Kingdom. The people got the message and responded: *"What then shall we do?"*

That is part of what preaching should accomplish and we see it here in the able hands of the Baptist. Preaching should grip us where we are and shake us from our complacency. It should rekindle the desire to not be left behind in God's work. These people do not walk away disgruntled by a "judgmental" preacher. They are pricked in the heart and are running to catch the train leaving the gate. "Help us. What must we do?"

But strangely there are churches today for which such a message is too harsh, too politically incorrect, too alienating. In them, you will never find a message like John's.

There are congregations that, in fact, make it clear they will not tolerate such "pulpiteering."

A mainline denominational church in a large city had a chairman of the board who made it clear to the pastor that the congregation did not need to be taught from the Bible. "They know what it says and don't need their faces rubbed in it week after week." The church has now been through a dozen pastors over the past 30 years and has reduced from a congregation of 800 to scarcely 50 members.

But the people in John's day knew the value of exhortation. They knew something was missing and their hearts told them the malady was with them, somewhere in their own attitudes and life styles. They were ready for this message and John answers them.

Luke 3:11
11 . . . "The man who has two tunics is to share with him who has none; and he who has food is to do likewise" . . tax collectors also came . . . "Teacher, what shall we do?" . . soldiers were questioning him, saying, "And what about us, what shall we do?"

John addresses the plight of the poor around them because that is where the rubber meets the road in Christ-like service. It was and is the chief thing with which our God is concerned regarding service. If we are blessed and another man is destitute, we are to pass along the blessing of God that all might be blessed.

The example of the tunics is amazingly poignant for us in modern times. Few can relate to the impact this exhortation delivered.

A tunic was an outer garment much like a short, unwaisted, straight dress, for both men and women, that covered what we would call crude under garments. Picture a very large potato sack (but of comfortable material) cut open across the bottom and at the top for arm holes and neck. It was of course more stylishly made than a potato sack, but you get the simplicity involved. It was separate from a cloak which was heavier and used only for cold weather or outdoors at night.

And in ancient times in poorer places like Judaea, most folks had basically one or two garments, not a wardrobe of gowns and outfits. They didn't even have what we might call "Sunday best." Your one set of clothes got daily duty throughout the year until they wore out. You were often recognized by what you perennially wore. Your appearance included you and that same old faded tunic.

Picture now what has often been observed in department stores – young girls fretting around rack after rack of clothes, looking for the next addition to a jamb-packed wardrobe of old things they've grown tired of. They have 20-30 times the number of outfits and combinations that most ancients owned at any one time. And they're out shopping for more.

So you can imagine what giving up an extra tunic meant in John's time. It wasn't like taking that occasional trip to Goodwill to offload outdated clothes. It meant going back to one garment from two.

As for the communal living of those times, we are in very different days today. Private ownership, the pursuit of happiness have taken hold and once done are very hard to give up.

Chuck Smith of Calvary Chapel in his early days in Southern California relates how his family regularly opened their home to the hippies of the seventies and his girls literally let their guests take what they wanted from their closets. That would be hard for most folks today who believe that if they've worked hard for what they have, they ought to be allowed to enjoy it.

Luke 3:14
To the tax collectors and soldiers he said, *"Do not take money from anyone by force, or accuse anyone falsely, and be content with your wages."*

Everyone is already aware that Roman officials commonly looked the other way as their agents exacted well-to-do livings from exorbitant practices. Soldiers often used the threat of force or trumped up charges that could land you in a Roman jail in order to extort food, clothing or money.

John is declaring God's view of the poor and destitute, the victims of abuse, and therefore exhorts such men if they desire the good pleasure of God to conduct themselves with compassion. And neither the tax collector nor the soldier could complain that they couldn't do their duty without these measures. It is understandable that the people began to wonder if John was the fulfillment of the One who was promised.

Luke 3:16

16 John answered and said to them all, "As for me, I baptize you with water; but One is coming who is mightier than I, and I am not fit to untie the thong of His sandals; He will baptize you with the Holy Spirit and fire."

John clarifies the nature of his mission and his baptism. He and it are not an end-all to their expectations, but a preparation. Again, John's baptism is with water to indicate its humble and temporary nature. He clearly indicates that the One expected is yet to come that One is of such greater stature and significance that he is unfit to bless Him with the most menial service.

Now we simply have to contrast this with John's tremendous confidence and boldness in his own message. His preaching was unfettered and as radical as you could get in those times. He was fearless and awesome to behold. *(See actor Michael York's portrayal in Jesus of Nazareth,* (Incorporated Television Company, 1977) Yet he readily succumbs and submits to the greatness of the Master soon to be on the scene. A marvelous combination of boldness and humility in the same man. We can appreciate Jesus' words that among those born of woman, there was none greater than John.

So what of the baptism with the Holy Spirit and with fire?

There are several interpretations to be had, each with merit. Those who are of the charismatic movement see this as a reference to the Baptism of the Holy Spirit and the attendant gifts of which Paul speaks. Others believe this refers to the NT institution of believer's baptism which is to be distinguished from John's baptism in that it imparts the indwelling presence of the Spirit and initiates the believer into the Body of Christ.

The latter explanation sounds like more of a fit because the contrast is supposed to be between John's preparatory baptism and the real deal at the coming of Jesus. Also the charismatic meaning of the baptism that bestows gifts was not part of Christian experience until Pentecost, after the Ascension. But the main problem is that this interpretation doesn't explain *"and with fire."*

The charismatic version suffers from the anachronism of referring to the Baptism of the Holy Spirit at such an early stage (which would have left hearers wondering) but it's the only interpretation that adequately explains *"and with fire."* Still, it can also be argued that the idea of believer's baptism and incorporation into the Body of Christ would not be a completely new thing to hearers either.

There's a sort of happy medium. Some formulations of charismatic doctrine offer that the Baptism of the Holy Spirit actually takes place at believer's baptism, as seen by many examples in the post-Pentecost narratives. So these are seen as one and the same, and the mention of "fire" is in reference to the subsequent bestowal and operation in the gifts (pictured as fire above the disciples' heads) which was expected at conversion, not as a separate experience.

But some argue that in the case of the disciples it was separate and that is intended as the model for what goes forward. But in many ways, the disciples are transitional and it may be misplaced for us to conclude a sort of inviolable formula that boxes the Holy Spirit into one and only one mode of operation. Certainly Paul's experiences show it as one and the same with water baptism.

In the end, each must make up their own mind, but it is worth diligent study.

Luke 3:17

17 "His winnowing fork is in His hand . . . to gather the wheat into His barn; but He will burn up the chaff with unquenchable fire."

John definitely has a view toward the dreadful judgment awaiting the unrighteous compared to that of the faithful. Coupled with his emphasis on doing the works of true repentance is the idea that some in the crowd are neglecting the true works because they are not yet of the household of faith and are counting on being subsumed under Abraham's covenant.

But God is to be pictured as having a winnowing fork, with which He will ferret out the unacceptable from the desired product, the chaff from the wheat. The ingenuine, the self-deceived have not escaped God's eye and their destiny is imminent. It is an example from their daily lives that all could comprehend.

There are some today who don't like this kind of message. They react by either rationalizing that they are not of this group, or that John is caught up in primitive mindsets that had yet to be enlightened by progressive views. There is no unquenchable fire because there is no God who would be so unloving and harsh, so the rationalization goes.

But such views are subtly born out of a will that will not be ruled by anyone and a deception that nothing needs to change. But for conservatives, if nothing needs to change then the path to Heaven is wide and accommodating where all that is important is trying to do your best. And frankly, the God who would wink at such arrogance is hardly worth worshipping.

Matthew 3:2, 3:13-17, Luke 3:23
2 "Repent, for the kingdom of heaven is at hand." . . 13 Then Jesus arrived from Galilee at the Jordan coming to John, to be baptized by him. 14 But John tried to prevent Him, saying, "I have need to be baptized by You, and do You come to me?" 15 But Jesus answering said to him, "Permit it at this time; for in this way it is fitting for us to fulfill all righteousness." Then he permitted Him. 16 After being baptized, Jesus came up immediately from the water; and behold, the heavens were opened, and he saw the Spirit of God descending as a dove and lighting on Him, 17 and behold, a voice out of the heavens said, "This is My beloved Son, in whom I am well-pleased." (Matthew 3:2, 3:13-17)

23 When He began His ministry, Jesus Himself was about thirty years of age, (Luke 3:23a)

Commentary

Matthew 3:2
". . the kingdom of heaven is at hand."

We can't ignore that John also had a positive message that was actually a precursor to what Jesus would begin preaching. John preached repentance but for the express reason that *"the Kingdom of Heaven was at hand."* This is something we can't gloss over too quickly.

We often perceive this as a sort of general description of the coming of the Christian life following all that has gone before, the Old Testament and the Law. We are children of the Kingdom in that we accept Christ and this new life is what was being announced. This is partly based on a misunderstanding of what Jesus meant by *"the kingdom of God is within you."*

But there is much more to this expression than this, which makes sense when you think about the fact that the audience hearing this would not have understood an announcement that the Christian life was coming to men. No one knew of any such Christian life nor did they expect it.

What they did expect was the kingdom Daniel talked about in chapter 2, *". . the God of heaven will set up a kingdom which will never be destroyed, and that kingdom will not be left for another people; it will crush and put an end to all these kingdoms, but it will itself endure forever."*

When John and Jesus preached that the kingdom was at hand, there was only one way to understand this for the hearers. It was the political, physical establishment of God 's kingdom on earth. That this was intentional comes from the fact that John and Jesus do not qualify their announcements to make sure that some other kind of kingdom is clearly to be understood. This they do not do and leave the meaning to be understood as it would have been.

To be sure, Jesus will introduce the idea that more was involved, namely that the Kingdom had a spiritual aspect for the inner life, but this was not to be a substitute for the prophetic nature mentioned by Daniel.

Daniel's kingdom was the promise that all the Gentile kingdoms affecting the Jews from Babylon forward would come to an end and be crushed by the coming of God's Kingdom, here on earth, in real time and space.

Some have offered that neither John nor Jesus offered that kingdom as being at hand, primarily because history tells us that such a kingdom did not in fact come. But the reason is not because God had changed His mind about how the Kingdom would come, or because it was always a spiritual kingdom in the hearts of men, but because His people, the Jews, rejected the King of that kingdom. This put in abeyance the political, earthly aspect of its coming but inaugurated the spiritual aspect in the interim.

Jesus genuinely offered the Kingdom to the Jews, as we shall see later in several addresses he makes to them. It is proposed that had Judaism embraced Him as Messiah, the Kingdom promised would have come to be and history would have been entirely different.

We can play hypothetical games about which came first, the offer, the rejection, then the revised plan, or was the revised plan always in view with foreknowledge of the rejection, but the fact remains that a genuine offer was given.

So the Kingdom being preached as at hand had all the full compliments of its prophecy. John and Jesus were declaring that the King was at hand so the Kingdom was at hand and it invited all to become citizens.

We must also take in the whole concept of Heaven being offered. Men pondered whether there was anything beyond the grave. Here Jesus comes as someone who knows. And the expectations of what it would be like would be surpassed in reality. God had provided a place where all the best things have been planned for us. His desire is to finally and eternally bless us. The experiences of Heaven are beyond our ability to comprehend. Even the unbeliever had a secret hope that such was available. In modern people, they may not be keen to accept Jesus as exclusive, but Heaven is the one thing almost everyone expects and hopes to see.

Matthew 3:13-15
13 Then Jesus arrived from Galilee at the Jordan coming to John, to be baptized by him.

As to why Jesus made Galilee his home location of ministry we will learn a bit later. What is of greater moment here is why Jesus came to be baptized at all?

The baptism of John was for repentance. Jesus had nothing needful in this since He had committed no sin. But Jesus came as our Example, to do in the flesh what men are called to do by God.

Now it might be objected that following Christ's example in this baptism wouldn't be the right example, because this baptism wasn't the believer's baptism that later followed in the NT, the one we are to participate in. It might also be more strongly objected that in Catholic doctrine, baptism plays a functional role in actually conveying salvation to the believer, that it is a sine qua non. But Jesus would not be exemplifying this for us because salvation coming to Him was constitutionally unnecessary. It is a mystery we may never adequately explain. But there can be no doubt that His disciples and the early church connected His personal obedience in John's baptism with what believers should emulate and do. Neither were believers historically puzzled by the distinction of Jesus' nature.

It is also important to emphasize that regardless of views that make it symbolic or an ordinance without which one cannot be saved, no believer who is honest with the Scripture can ignore the fact that baptism is something that cannot be ignored or left undone. Whether it is necessary or more a matter of obedience, it cannot be spurned or treated lightly.

But as to the problem of Jesus being a candidate for baptism, John gets the dilemma right off:

14 But John tried to prevent Him, saying, "I have need to be baptized by You, and do You come to me?" 15 But Jesus answering said to him, "Permit it at this time; for in this way it is fitting for us to fulfill all righteousness."

That the situation seemed backward would be clear to anyone sensitive to who Jesus was. But Jesus gave John words that help us explain why He kept the arrangement as it was - *"it is fitting for us . . ."* This is to say, "we have been given the opportunity of pleasing God in doing it this way because it will fulfill all righteousness." Not a detailed answer that fills in all the blanks, but rather an explanation that says it will please God in His own purposes.

We need to be ready for these kinds of answers when what is being asked doesn't seem to fit with our normal expectations. Sometimes the only reason will be that it pleases God and explaining it in detail isn't an option for the present.

In the end, one can't argue that it's okay to be casual about baptism or that it is optional, because if Jesus submitted to it when it was technically not necessary, we have even less an excuse.

This was essentially Jesus' inaugurating event – the formal commencement of His work - and we would rightly expect something extraordinary to accompany it. And this is just what we find.

Matthew 3:16-17
16 After being baptized, Jesus came up immediately from the water; and behold, the heavens were opened, and he saw the Spirit of God descending as a dove and lighting on Him, 17 and behold, a voice out of the heavens said, "This is My beloved Son, in whom I am well-pleased."

It is unclear how much those standing around saw and heard. Matthew here states that He – Jesus – was the one seeing the Spirit descend. But Luke states that the Spirit descended in "bodily form, as a dove" which suggests that this would have been seen by the people.

Also, it's unclear if "this is My beloved Son" was heard by others. By saying "This is . ." we have an expression meant for others, but Mark and Luke have, "Thou art . ." which means an address to Jesus.

We also have the expectation that a voice from heaven declaring such things would seem proof positive of His messiahship so as to eliminate all questions and doubts, something the leaders and priests would have to heed. But this didn't happen, nor was this event later referred to by those defending Him.

But we have to understand that this event was only witnessed by whoever was present on this occasion and there's no indication that the Pharisees and Sadducees were present. Testimonies wouldn't have been taken at face value. It's a bit like telling your neighbors you saw a spacecraft land in your back yard. The larger the claim, the larger the need for corroboration.

The important part of the message is that this was God proclaiming the Person of His Son, and that with Him He was well-pleased. That is the commendation we should all seek for ourselves, that God be well-pleased with us.

We can know this in the basics, in that we are pleasing to God on account of the death of His Son. We are not to gain that pleasure by measuring our performance in works. Paul makes it clear that this approach not only doesn't work, it never worked.

But in another sense there is a striving to please God by obeying and succeeding in those things He bids us do. They are not the basis of our assessment as to salvation, but they are as to our rewards before Him. Some may object that this can place the focus on getting things from God, but Paul does state, *" If any man's work which he has built on remains, he will receive a reward." . . "but each will receive his own reward according to his own labor."* (1 Corinthians 3:14, 3:8) Whether some may wrongly emphasize rewards or not, we are instructed that such things are part of the pleasure of God toward us.

Regrettably, there are some people who care little for (and even resent) the idea that their lives have been designed for one purpose – to please God. But despising it and rejecting it doesn't change its truth. So we really have two choices: if we reject this fact of our existence we will live frustrated lives, bitter and full of disappointment at every turn. Our very faces will reveal the bitter effects of going our own way. But if we accept this fact and respond to it expectantly and with love for it, we find a life of abundance and meaning. And conversely, our faces reflect this to the glory of God.

Luke 3:23
23 When He began His ministry, Jesus Himself was about thirty years of age,

This has been a point of controversy for chronologists whose business is accurately placing Jesus' life and ministry in a real historical context.

For starters, we know that Jesus' ministry begins at the same time or a bit later than John's (but by no means before.) We mentioned earlier that John began in the *"fifteenth year of Tiberius"* which would have been A.D. 28. If Jesus began also that same year or very soon thereafter, he would have been about thirty-one or thirty-two years of age at verse 23 which agrees with *"about thirty years of age."*

[There was no year Zero, hence 4 B.C. to A.D. 28 equals 31 years not 32. This also puts His age at thirty-four or thirty-five at the time of His crucifixion.]

While this seems pretty straightforward, it is not without problems. Other chronological factors to be taken into account are the dates for the officials, Caiaphas and Pilate, and how many Passovers are recorded for Jesus' ministry. Another complication comes into play when scholars try to match up the fulfillment of Daniel's first 69 weeks with the coming of Messiah. Certain ending dates can complicate the timing of when these other events could have occurred. This is merely to say that we can't be rigidly dogmatic about the dates and exact age of Jesus at given points.

Mark 1:12-13, Matthew 4:2-7, Luke 4:5-7, Matthew 4:10, Luke 4:13, Matthew 4:11

12 Immediately the Spirit impelled Him to go out into the wilderness. 13 And He was in the wilderness forty days being tempted by Satan; and He was with the wild beasts, and the angels were ministering to Him. (Mark 1:12-13)

2 And after He had fasted forty days and forty nights, He then became hungry. 3 And the tempter came and said to Him, "If You are the Son of God, command that these stones become bread." 4 But He answered and said, "It is written, `MAN SHALL NOT LIVE ON BREAD ALONE, BUT ON EVERY WORD THAT PROCEEDS OUT OF THE MOUTH OF GOD.' " 5 Then the devil took Him into the holy city and had Him stand on the pinnacle of the temple, 6 and said to Him, "If You are the Son of God, throw Yourself down; for it is written, `HE WILL COMMAND HIS ANGELS CONCERNING YOU'; and `ON their HANDS THEY WILL BEAR YOU UP, SO THAT YOU WILL NOT STRIKE YOUR FOOT AGAINST A STONE.' " 7 Jesus said to him, "On the other hand, it is written, `YOU SHALL NOT PUT THE LORD YOUR GOD TO THE TEST.' " (Matthew 4:2-7)

5 And he led Him up and showed Him all the kingdoms of the world in a moment of time. 6 And the devil said to Him, "I will give You all this domain and its glory; for it has been handed over to me, and I give it to whomever I wish. 7 "Therefore if You worship before me, it shall all be Yours." . . 10 Then Jesus said to him, "Go, Satan! For it is written, `YOU SHALL WORSHIP THE LORD YOUR GOD, AND SERVE HIM ONLY.' "

13 When the devil had finished every temptation, he left Him until an opportune time. . . 11 and behold, angels came and began to minister to Him. (Luke 4:5-7, Matthew 4:10, Luke 4:13, Matthew 4:11)

Commentary

Mark 1:12-13
12 Immediately the Spirit impelled Him to go out into the wilderness.

The Spirit compelled Him that His next task was immediately at hand. In this, Jesus is exemplifying a picture of the life God desires in the child of God who is now governed by the Spirit. We are to be in such intimate communication with his Spirit that we sense the urgency, caution, and inspiration He is conveying to us at any given moment.

In modern times with so many distractions in life, this is seldom really cultivated in Christians today. We are almost forced to concentrate our attention on what's going on at work, getting kids to school or camp, medical bills and insurance claims, term papers, dealing with difficult in-laws, etc. When our head hits the pillow at night we are in no mood to be asked what the Holy Spirit said to us today.

Yet this is the life anticipated by Jesus and the Father. So much of the nettling and vexing in life could be intercepted and dealt with if we were listening first and acting second.

The main problem is that this takes cultivation and patience. We must learn how to sense and comprehend His voice among all the other voices in our lives. And most people just don't have the patience or the time to do this. Plus, there is the reticence of falling into the category of folks who hear things others don't hear. Telling someone that God told you such and such gets a suspicious look these days. So we find ourselves weighing the truth about what God is recommending against the way we wish others to see us.

13 And He was in the wilderness forty days being tempted by Satan;

So it is clear here that the temptation would not be just on the mountain in the three things Satan says to Him at the end of this period. Jesus will be tempted even along the way in terms of the difficulties of privation, those of climbing and scaling the terrain of the mountain, the worries about water, etc. (Not that He would worry, but the temptation is there to worry.)

And we must keep in mind that the Son is condescending to live in a mortal body with all its limitations. Every impediment, the need to rest at intervals, the ache in the muscles would all be temptations to human irritation and anger when He certainly knows how easy this ascent could have been otherwise.

But the question of greater importance is why He was subjected to Satan's temptation at all. Was there really a need? Both persons involved knew the end of the story – that He was the Son of God in whom no sin would be found, that He would be victorious.

Some offer that this was done as another instance of exemplifying how the believer should handle such things, and to show that Jesus had real humanity that could be tempted. The theological issue is the need to combat the idea that Jesus was a phantom, not a real person, or that His contact with spiritual power placed Him outside the realm of an example for us. It was important that the world know *"He was tempted in all things"* such as we.

Another observation is that of Satan and how much he knew or to what degree he was self-deceived. The example-for-us explanation almost makes Satan merely a player in a scene that is more important to others than the players themselves. But if Satan was inwardly self-deceived despite knowing the outcome of his evil labors, then there is need that the scene be played out for real. Satan needed yet another dose of reality about the Person of Jesus as Son of God.

and He was with the wild beasts, and the angels were ministering to Him.

The mention of wild beasts is to highlight the fact that Jesus was really a good distance away from human remedies. It emphasizes the privation of the journey. That the angels ministered to Him should not be understood as feeding Him to withstand the period. This is made clear by His fasting for the forty days. It could easily include the provision of water when needed. Fasting did not exclude water.

But the interesting element of this is the close association with the whole realm of the angels, even in this rather mundane activity of walking out in the wilderness and climbing into the hills. That there was a whole entourage of those beings with whom He had been well-acquainted in His existence before the Incarnation gives us a marvelous picture and expectation of a completely different world just beyond ours, in which God and His angels are regular fixtures.

Matthew 4:2-3
2 And after He had fasted forty days and forty nights, He then became hungry.

Experiences with fasting tell us that the first week is plagued by feelings of hunger, but after five or six days, these pangs go away and we feel comfortable and rather normal. But at or approaching the forty day mark, we begin severe hunger pangs once again, and this is the sign that we are actually beginning to starve to death.

So with Jesus now at this forty day mark, the statement "He was hungry" would be an understatement. The temptation from Satan to eat is now much more than satisfying a raging hunger. It is the key to staving off an imminent death.

3 And the tempter came and said to Him, "If You are the Son of God, command that these stones become bread."

This has the ring of kids at play who invent all kinds of scenarios for super heroes who use their powers to make things happen. Whenever you propose a supernatural personage you open the door in purely human terms to magical characterizations.

But in Satan's case, this is absolutely real stuff. He is well acquainted with divine abilities. This is not a temptation to prove Jesus is really the Son *"If you're the Son of God you should be able to do such and such,"* but more the case of tempting Jesus to use His abilities to satisfy His personal needs, since they are far away from natural means. That He is the Son of God is not being tested. Availing Himself of His powers at the behest of Satan is.

You will note that in all three of these temptations Jesus does not get into philosophical or theological arguments with Satan. He engages in no personal attacks against him. He uses the effective weapon of Scripture, something which Satan cannot deal with. In many ways, this emphasizes the *"living"* aspect of the Word. It actually has functional power against Satan's words compared to mere academic argumentation.

For us, the message is clear. Develop a healthy respect for the power of God's Word and use it.

Matthew 4:4
4 .. "MAN SHALL NOT LIVE ON BREAD ALONE, BUT ON EVERY WORD THAT PROCEEDS OUT OF THE MOUTH OF GOD."

That this Scripture (Deut 8:3) was chosen is certainly spiritually applicable, but for us as limited human beings, we halt a bit in knowing to what degree this can apply in our own lives. Certainly for Jesus, food was secondary to the words of His Father. And in His case, it is clear that every step He took was governed by that intimate communication.

But for us, we see the real need to be concerned about bread and the other necessities of life such that we cannot strike out on a life where physical sustenance will come purely from a spiritual concentration upon God. But there are reasons why this is not what is meant.

Jesus Himself is not adopting a life that excludes any care for the physical needs of His body. He took meals and required sleep like anyone else. Therefore the application of this quoted verse is meant to apply to a situation and situations like it, not as a perpetual thing that forsakes natural sustenance altogether.

It is an emphasis about priorities. We should not let worries about the amenities of life distract us from our dependence on God in every aspect of life. We are to realize that we are made for Him and as such, everything we are and will do is bound up in Him and His Word.

It is by His Word that we even have the food about which we worry and fret. He commanded that nature provide it, so even in this we cannot claim we did it ourselves by planting and harvesting ourselves.

Where the thrust of this verse comes into our lives is in the ease with which we "manage" many aspects of our lives without appeal to God. We leave Him out where it seems to us more practical. Yet He is there nonetheless with a Word for us in every situation, would that we listen and hear it.

Matthew 4:5-7
5 Then the devil took Him into the holy city .. on the pinnacle of the temple . . . "If You are the Son of God, throw Yourself down; for it is written .."

The pinnacle of the Temple can be misunderstood as meaning any precipitous point as in a corner junction of the Temple edifice overlooking the platform and courts below, etc. But "the pinnacle" was a sort of idiomatic term for a particular place in the Temple compound, well-known to local inhabitants. It is still seen today on the SE corner of the wall surrounding the Temple area. It is the sheerest point even today, despite the fact that the wall is Byzantine and doesn't approach the height of the original construction of Herod.

We should be clear also that Satan is not misquoting Scripture. He is quoting Psalms 91:11-12 correctly. But he is misapplying the verse to the situation he has created. He is deceived in thinking that the verse obligates God to invoke this promise in virtually any situation, including contrived ones that purpose to test if this is true.

Now we should be clear about the nature of the temptation. The first was to use power to satisfy urgent physical needs. The second is to use power to attract public attention by employing a trick that would win widespread notoriety, hence gain Him a following much faster than ministering one on one or in smaller crowds.

This is very close to the carnal attitudes we encounter today with respect to the supernatural (which tells us where they came from.) "Do a trick" is a frequent human request. We also see this actually being requested by people later on as Jesus condemns all those who seek signs.

7 On the other hand, it is written, `YOU SHALL NOT PUT THE LORD YOUR GOD TO THE TEST.'

Of interest are Jesus' words, "On the other hand." It is like saying to Satan, "You are quoting Scripture correctly, but you have ignored other verses that comment on its application." He thus quotes Deut 6:16.

Doctrines are not to be built on single quotes. There is a principle that the context of any verse is the entire Bible. That's a tall order, but it is a valid point - that we should take into account all those things Scripture teaches which might have import to what we're reading or teaching. It is part of the exhortation to *"study and show thyself approved."*

In this case, Satan ignored the teaching that the promises of God are not to be used in situations that merely test of the Lord's faithfulness, even if there is a perceived benefit in doing so (the winning of so many souls in such a magnificent display.)

Jesus was adept at putting his finger on what was really happening in Satan's mind. The temptation to win souls took second place to avoiding the repugnance of testing the faithfulness of God.

Luke 4:5-7
5 And he led Him up and showed Him all the kingdoms of the world in a moment of time. . . . Therefore if You worship before me, it shall all be Yours.

Here we see the incredible power Satan in fact possesses. It is popular in some circles to promote the idea that Satan is a sort of benign nemesis who blusters and makes a lot of hay but is easily put back in his place by the authority of the believer. While it is true that we have that authority, we need to be cautious about dumbing down the power he wields.

This is almost a scene from a movie. The kingdoms are "shown," yet this is before the age of the movie screen and projector, before the arrival of the "holodeck." We are not told how Satan made these things visible, but the Scripture states that he did do so and *"in a moment of time"*. There was no "Just let me set this up and plug a few things in."

The temptation here is absolutely direct as to intent. It involves the intermediate temptation of winning all the world for Christ and it implies that Satan had the power over such kingdoms in order to offer them. But the chief aim is that Jesus submit and worship him. This was his aim all along. All the temptations had this ring – that complying with Satan's suggestions was tantamount to coming over to his camp.

But Jesus answers this theme directly, side-stepping any discussion about worlds and kingdoms . .

Matthew 4:10
10 "Go, Satan! For it is written, `YOU SHALL WORSHIP THE LORD YOUR GOD, AND SERVE HIM ONLY.' "

This is a quote from Deut 6:13, 10:20. And it reiterates a principle we sometimes forget – Satan is a *created* being, and as such has all along had the obligation to serve his Creator in obedience and worship. He is not as some propose a dualistic, self-existent, alternate power to God.

So there is just the command to "Go" followed by the reason the conversation is at an end. Very effective and exactly what we would expect from the One who has the upper hand and is ultimately in complete control.

Luke 4:13, Matthew 4:11
13 . . he left Him until an opportune time . . . 11 and behold, angels came and began to minister to Him.

We see here the deep seated self-deception of Satan himself. The contest is considered by no means over between the two. Satan, surprisingly, is not phased by the corrections Jesus makes and the power of the Word against his designs. We say surprisingly because again he knows the end of the story and if he has forgotten, this encounter with Jesus should have been a reminder that he is fighting a losing battle. Yet we see him going off to find a *"more opportune time."* There is only one accounting for this. Utter and total self-deception.

Again we see the angels ministering to him, and in this case this must have included food. And if so, we have to marvel at the wondrous interface these beings have with the temporal world that they can be the conveyors of physical things despite being spirits.

John 1:19-34

19 This is the testimony of John, when the Jews sent to him priests and Levites from Jerusalem to ask him, "Who are you?" 20 And he confessed and did not deny, but confessed, "I am not the Christ." 21 They asked him, "What then? Are you Elijah?" And he said, "I am not." "Are you the Prophet?" And he answered, "No." 22 Then they said to him, "Who are you, so that we may give an answer to those who sent us? What do you say about yourself?" 23 He said, "I am A VOICE OF ONE CRYING IN THE WILDERNESS, 'MAKE STRAIGHT THE WAY OF THE LORD,' as Isaiah the prophet said."

24 Now they had been sent from the Pharisees. 25 They asked him, and said to him, "Why then are you baptizing, if you are not the Christ, nor Elijah, nor the Prophet?" 26 John answered them saying, "I baptize in water, but among you stands One whom you do not know. 27 "It is He who comes after me, the thong of whose sandal I am not worthy to untie." 28 These things took place in Bethany beyond the Jordan, where John was baptizing.

29 The next day he saw Jesus coming to him and said, "Behold, the Lamb of God who takes away the sin of the world! 30 "This is He on behalf of whom I said, 'After me comes a Man who has a higher rank than I, for He existed before me.' 31 "I did not recognize Him, but so that He might be manifested to Israel, I came baptizing in water." 32 John testified saying, "I have seen the Spirit descending as a dove out of heaven, and He remained upon Him. 33 "I did not recognize Him, but He who sent me to baptize in water said to me, 'He upon whom you see the Spirit descending and remaining upon Him, this is the One who baptizes in the Holy Spirit.' 34 "I myself have seen, and have testified that this is the Son of God." (John 1:19-34)

Commentary

John 1:19-21
19 This is the testimony of John, when the Jews sent to him priests and Levites from Jerusalem to ask him, "Who are you?"

It could not have taken long for the Jewish authorities to begin an investigation as to who this bold voice in the Jordan was, and why so many were coming out to see and hear him. *"The Jews"* here means the authorities not the people at large, which would have been the high priest and the officials serving him, but would not necessarily have included Herod's men. There is no doubt that Herod's men also had an interest, since he is later arrested by them, but the statement above would have been in reference to the priests.

That they sent priests and Levites would be for religious reasons, not civil concerns. John was not creating a civil disturbance or undermining public order. He was, however, preaching and baptizing and this necessitated a check as to his conformance with Mosaic law. The Levites were the custodians of all religious practice and interpretations of the Law so this makes perfect sense.

It didn't take long for them to realize that John was preaching "imminence" as to something momentous for Judaism. Someone was being heralded and announced; and John was preaching a message of preparation. So they were quickly prompted to ask if John was himself the One about whom he spake, and if not, what promised prophetic role was he fulfilling?

20 "I am not the Christ."

This means of course they had asked him if he was. The *Christ* does not mean they were asking a uniquely Christian question. The Christ was the Greek term for the Jewish Messiah. Both meant "the Anointed One." That they were asking John if he was this Messiah comes from John's message about judgment – *"His fan is in his hand . . . he will clean his threshing floor and separate the chaff from the wheat."* These were similar to the restoration and judgment pictured of Messiah in the OT.

This is somewhat tricky because there are no OT verses that say exactly what John was saying, put together as he stated. Pieces come from the following references: Isaiah 30:24; 41:16; Jeremiah 15:7 Isaiah 66:24; Jeremiah 7:20. It is John who is connecting them together under inspiration. The Levites knew that several of these were Messianic, so this prompted them to ask about the Christ.

21 "What then? Are you Elijah?" And he said, "I am not." "Are you the Prophet?" And he answered, "No."

Elijah was predicted to come " *"Behold, I am going to send you Elijah the prophet before the coming of the great and terrible day of the LORD."* (Malachi 4:5) This John also denies. It is interesting that they don't ask him about the Messenger of the same book but a chapter earlier, *"Behold, I am going to send My messenger, and he will clear the way before Me."* (3:1) This John would very likely have answered, "Yes!"

The Prophet is in reference to Deut 18:18, *"the Lord thy God shall raise up unto thee a prophet, like unto me, from among thy brethren, and unto Him ye shall hearken."* This had never been fulfilled and was later associated with the Messianic prophecies of Isaiah and others. Again John says no.
Frustrated and unable to link him to traditional personages, they ask, " *"Who are you, so that we may give an answer to those who sent us? What do you say about yourself?"*

John then repeats the most poignant of his messages – the one that answered them directly but left the truth of it to their faith, *"I am a voice of one crying in the wilderness, make straight the way of the Lord."* This was met with puzzlement because all the supposed "messengers" of recollection had been suggested and answered with no.

John 1:25-29
25 "Then why are you baptizing, if you are not the Christ, nor Elijah, nor the Prophet?"

The impetus behind this connection of baptism and the Messiah comes from the OT temple practices in which the priests sprinkled with hyssop and blood, or water, depending on the ordinance, and there is a reference to dipping one's foot in the Jordan (Joshua 3:15.) Hebrews chapter 9 mentions "various baptisms." These were commemorative or restorative in relation to sin or diseases.

But it is a little harder to make a connection between the activity of Messiah and baptisms. The Jews did make this connection, however, most likely by associating John's exhortative message with his baptism. John then clarifies why he baptizes.

26 "I baptize in water, but among you stands One whom you do not know. 27 "It is He who comes after me, the thong of whose sandal I am not worthy to untie."

John's clarification that he baptized using water would not have been especially informative to the Pharisees' question. But as elsewhere he did make the distinction that the One coming after him would baptize differently – with the Holy Spirit and with fire. So he answers them by clarifying his role as herald and preparer, but reminds them that Someone is already among them who is greater.

29 The next day he saw Jesus coming to him and said, "Behold, the Lamb of God who takes away the sin of the world!

John actually says this more than once, as in v.36 below, when he is with Peter's brother Andrew. Here Jesus is coming to John and he announces this about Jesus in faith on the basis of what he witnessed at Jesus' baptism, as we see next.

John 1:33
33 "I did not recognize Him, . . . but He who sent me to baptize in water said to me, `He upon whom you see the Spirit descending and remaining upon Him, this is the One who baptizes in the Holy Spirit.'"

This section will be somewhat confusing and suggests a contradiction. John explains that Jesus is the One he is announcing because he was told ahead of time that the descent of the Spirit upon Him would be the key. But for John, this did not happen until just after the baptism was performed. He says that because he saw this, he is declaring Jesus to be the Son of God.

Now we might be tempted so suppose that being relatives may have forestalled John's ability to see Jesus as Son of God, hence his statement, "I did not recognize Him." Yet we also know that John responded in the womb when Mary and Elizabeth came close to one another. Did John's experience in the womb become fuzzy after years of physical distance between them?

Complicating this explanation is our notice earlier that John did, in fact, recognize Jesus by trying to prevent the baptism, saying that the roles should be reversed, *"It is I who should be baptized by you."* This might be resolved by pointing out that John lived separate from the daily life of Jesus and really did not have a relationship with him, despite family ties, up to the moment when Jesus appeared for baptism.

This arrangement was also important to avoid a charge of collusion – he was baptizing a family member and calling him Messiah. A clever plan of boyhood chums? Rather, John may very well have been using words that intentionally emphasized that he did not recognize him by sight and that it took the Holy Spirit to make the connection.

This still doesn't resolve the issue about when John recognized Jesus – before or after the moment of baptism - but it might be that John somehow perceived in his spirit the descent of the Spirit before the baptism.

CHAPTER 3
The Early Disciples

John 1:35-44

35 Again the next day John was standing with two of his disciples, 36 and he watched Jesus as He walked, and said, "Behold, the Lamb of God!" 37 The two disciples heard him speak, and they followed Jesus. 38 And Jesus turned and saw them following, and said to them, "What do you seek?" They said to Him, "Rabbi (which translated means Teacher), where are You staying?" 39 He said to them, "Come, and you will see." So they came and saw where He was staying; and they stayed with Him that day, for it was about the tenth hour.

40 One of the two who heard John speak and followed Him, was Andrew, Simon Peter's brother. 41 He found first his own brother Simon and said to him, "We have found the Messiah" (which translated means Christ). 42 He brought him to Jesus. Jesus looked at him and said, "You are Simon the son of John; you shall be called Cephas" (which is translated Peter). 43 The next day He purposed to go into Galilee, and He found Philip. And Jesus said to him, "Follow Me." 44 Now Philip was from Bethsaida, of the city of Andrew and Peter. (John 1:35-44)

Commentary

John 1:35-36
35 Again the next day John was standing with two of his disciples . . 36 he watched Jesus as He walked, and said, "Behold, the Lamb of God!" . .

This is the second instance of John seeing Jesus walking, in this case from afar. John again points to Jesus as the Lamb. The Lamb of God sounds strange to someone for the first time. Even as seasoned Christians we tend to just accept it as the language of Scripture. The key is to think like John's hearers, as Old Testament believers.

To the unstudied, lamb of God would have meant the lamb of the burnt offerings, the Passover, the Day of Atonement. Without a more detailed knowledge of messianic passages, most would have received such words with blank looks. How was this to apply to a person?

In John's disciples there would have been preparation by him of the broader meaning. They would have seen the connection of a man being such a Lamb, recalling the expectation of Messiah as a sacrifice, *"All of us like sheep have gone astray, Each of us has turned to his own way; But the LORD has caused the iniquity of us all To fall on Him.*" (Is 53:6.) Even though we are the wayward sheep, He is the substitute for receiving the penalty of our iniquities. He pays the price. He is the Lamb sacrificed. So to point to Jesus as the Lamb of God is to point to the Messiah as He walks off in the distance. The natural reaction to men of faith and expectation is to go after Him. Andrew, the brother of Peter, is one of them.

A bit later, John the Baptist shares with these men that it is necessary that he begin to fade from the scene because Jesus is greater. Remember that John, despite his bold preaching, was a very humble man when it came to his place before God, so his role as preparer for the Christ would necessarily have to diminish when Christ came.

Here he willingly lets his disciples move on to the ministry of Jesus. There is no envy as with rivals. Jesus and John are partners not competitors. It is truly amazing how modern day Christians can take the success and praise of other Christians in a negative way. Some can remember when Chuck Smith of Calvary Chapel first began his meetings. Crowds began attending in the thousands and many were pouring out of local mainline denominations. But the churches were bitter that someone was outshining them and many spiteful things were said about Calvary in those days, even calling it a cult. Those who were there back then can tell you that it was the unadorned gospel and simple worship. Chuck Smith was not even considered dynamic or "polished" in the popular manner people expected, so it was puzzling why so many were going.

Back in the sixties and seventies it was more often the case that preaching was rather mediocre in many churches. Calvary Chapel was being characterized as a threat rather than a praise. Not so with John. He readily stepped back without bitterness. He knew his place and the part he played.

John 1:38-39
38 .. "Rabbi .. where are You staying?" 39 He said to them, "Come, and you will see."

Jesus knew full well the beginning from the end and that in this journey close to John's location He would pick up the first of his disciples. They address Him as Rabbi. This is a term introduced in the NT but the idea of a teacher was not new. You did not have to be formally trained among the Pharisees to be recognized as a teacher. Everyone attended the synagogue and every men had his duty to reading and to sermonize on passages of Scripture. (Jesus does this in the synagogue at Nazareth - a good example of the layperson's duties. – Luke 4:16.)

This meant that the average ancient Jew would be more familiar with Scripture than the average Christian today. Fathers were obligated to teach their children and grandchildren. So it would occasionally fall out that someone not seeking to be a Pharisee might nevertheless acquire special abilities. When these were recognized and appreciated as gifts of God a person not formally trained could be called 'Rabbi.'

Now John's disciples needed no proofs that Jesus was worthy of the designation. What is surprising is that they desired to know where He was staying. This was not a case at all of prying into His personal life. It was the seeking of an opportunity to have more in-depth, alone time with Him, which typically occurred in the places like one's home. It was a desire to sit down in the quietue of a home setting and begin to talk about the important things in life, especially about messianic things.

In Jesus' case, we have no record that He owned a house or any kind of property (which is a bit ironic since He created all things and ultimately owned them by right as Maker.) It's not really reasonable that He took them on this day to the home of his mother because Nazareth was rather far N in the Galilee and He has met them near to John's locale in the region of the Jordan, near Jerusalem (and we have no indication that John wandered as far N as the Sea of Galilee.) The place could have been an arrangement with a relative or friend of the family, but the details are left out and we are to take that as a sign that they are unimportant.

What is of wonderful interest to us is that Jesus was not standoff-ish. Ask your pastor if you can come over and see where he lives some Sunday and see the reaction you get. Many a pastor will consider it rude (we wait to be invited). But Jesus welcomed their company, partly because the general tenor of fellowship and social vulnerability was different back then (people were generally less uppity and private,) and He knew that the time would be taken up with spiritual things. But the purely delightful thing is that Jesus had no qualms about them coming in and seeing the humbleness of His place and His things nor does He feel He is above this or too important to be asked such a thing.

.. they stayed with Him that day, for it was about the tenth hour.

4:00 in the afternoon.
Roman time was broken up into four watches (where we get the name for our wristwatch today) of six hours each, changing at the 12:00 and 6:00 positions. But for the Jews, there were only two divisions of the day – twelve hours of the night (beginning at 6:00 PM) followed by twelve hours of the day, beginning at 6:00 AM (not to be confused with each Jewish day beginning at 6:00 P.M.) So, from 6:00 AM (not counting 6:00) the tenth hour would be 4:00 PM.

The indication was that they therefore stayed overnight since the lateness of the hour made returning the same day inconvenient.

John 1:40-42
40 One of the two . . . was Andrew, Simon Peter's brother. 41 He found Simon and said to him, "We have found the Messiah" . . . He brought him to Jesus.

We learn in v.43 that Peter was from Bethsaida on the N shore of the Sea of Galilee where his trade was fishing as a business, meaning that he did not fish to merely feed his family but fished with nets in order to thereby make a living.

Here we see the difference between the brothers. Peter had decided to follow a practical life in which he made his way in a trade to support his family. This is among the oldest principles of life. We are born and live the early years of our life under the support and care of our parents. But eventually we must leave, follow the pattern of human existence, and strike out our own means to support ourselves in the world and care for our own families.

But Andrew had decided to pursue a more contemplative life at the feet of John, most likely not much respected by his brother. As to Peter's choice we have to keep in mind that life was precarious, just one small step away from poverty or even slavery if you couldn't pay your own way. The lot fell to the eldest to take the reins of support for his parents and family, but it was the responsibility of all males to help as they could. So although we have nothing explicit in Scripture, we might infer an edginess in Peter in which Andrew might be see as "wasting" his life with the Baptist in the wilderness rather than helping his brother keep food on the table.

Nevertheless, Peter is convinced that Andrew is on to something in believing he had found the Messiah. Whether he believed Andrew or not, it was worth it to go and see.

42 . . Jesus looked at him and said, "You are Simon the son of John; you shall be called Cephas" (which is translated Peter).

The nicknaming of Simon is pertinent to the perennial debate about whether it was Peter or his confession that is declared later by Jesus to be the foundation of His Church. But that debate revolves less around linguistics than around the original intent of Peter as a foundation. Was it temporary during the formative years of the Apostolic Church or permanent to the end of the age?

But we should try as much as possible to have a clear view of the linguistics and vocabulary involved, to at least forestall ill-based appeals that might make the vocabulary say more (or less) than it does.

Simon would be a derivative of Simeon, one of the twelve sons of Jacob and a tribe of Israel, a popular name. The idea of nicknaming a person is still in use today and at about the same prevalence as in ancient times. Today it is routine to coin a shorter name for a given name - Bill for William, Nick for Nicholas, Bob for Robert.

But in ancient times it was popular to nickname someone after a peculiar characteristic. James and John were called "sons of thunder." Here Simon is to be called Cephas in Aramaic (pronounced Kepha or Kephas) - a stone. There is no indication that Simon was called Peter before this moment. That the writer uses Peter earlier is anachronistic (speaking in the past using the modern term – like using York when referring to the Roman town of Eboracum).

In terms of pure linguistics there is some ambiguity of usage, but the Catholic meaning has weight – that Cephas and petros mean a larger more imposing rock formation than the smaller stone or pebble. As for Aramaic, Cephas has no OT reference which could be appended since Aramaic is used only in a few sections.

As for the Hebrew of the rest of the OT, we have *'tsoor'*, usually for large masses of rock, and *'eben'* for smaller items. But there are counter-examples. Tsoor can be used for a stone as small as one in the road over which someone could stumble. Conversely, eben has been used for stone covers over wells or pillars (Gen 29:8, 31:5.)

But the meaning intended can also be discerned by paying attention to how the meaning of Cephas was "explained" in reference to Greek when published versions of the Gospels were composed by their authors. Note that Cephas is not simply substituted with a Greek word, which is what a direct translation would have done. Instead, we see the author preserving the Aramaic in the Greek text of the Gospel, then *explaining* how it would be translated into Greek.

Here the author, who knew what Cephas meant in Aramaic, chose *'petros'* in Greek to "explain" what the word meant – *"which is translated Peter"*. The purported suggestion that *petros* meant small stone not a massive rock (so as to later distinguish Peter from his confession) would first need to be supported by Greek usage, regardless of any other concerns. And a search for that usage, i.e. specifically for *'petros,'* will be disappointing. Petros actually has no usage in Greek, except in the NT and only in reference to Peter, the man. This is because the Greek word for rock is really *'petra,'* a feminine form.

But more is gleaned from comparing *'lithos'* to *'petra'* in Greek. Here we find again a little ambiguity but still a trend. Lithos is definitely used for things like pebbles, something someone throws. But it can also be used for large formations – the lithostrotos on which Jesus stood when being condemned in the Praetorium. But it really isn't a case that pebble was intended by petros because it would have been so easy to have supplied lithos, which in most usage would be understood as the small object (if that was the intent.)

The other issue is why *petros* appears instead of *petra*. Here the Catholic answer is as valid as any – the feminine would never be used to nickname a man. And, when we consider that *'petros'* as a masculine form only has use in the NT and in relation to Peter's name, we have to conclude that the change in gender was actually "coined" specifically for Simon by the gospel writers because it doesn't have usage elsewhere in Greek, i.e. there are no other reasons anywhere else where a masculine form of petra would be needed. The feminine form always remains a satisfactory gender when using this word.

But, again, the debate about the primacy of Peter based on Jesus' later words depends much more on the original view of Peter's leadership in Jesus' eyes and those of the early church. It is equally valid that once foundations serve their purpose they give way to focus on the edifice. They become passive not active.

But other Scripture also needs to be taken into consideration when forming interpretations. We have in Paul: *"For no man can lay a foundation other than the one which is laid, which is Jesus Christ"* (I Cor 3:11.) Hence, whatever the Catholic may wish to say about the words of Jesus, the principle meaning must succeed in supporting Christ as the only foundation of His Church, else Paul was mistaken.

The debate goes on and there are ways of looking at key verses differently between groups, but Protestants need to accept that fact that the language does not, in itself, support the typically offered distinction between pebble and rock.

John 1:43-44
43 The next day He purposed to go into Galilee, and He found Philip. And Jesus said to him, "Follow Me." 44 Now Philip was from Bethsaida, of the city of Andrew and Peter.

We must not conclude that Jesus and Andrew were now in Bethsaida, since he meets Peter and then Philip who are from this same town. The reason is that Bethsaida was some 90 miles to the N of Perea and we are told that Andrew found Peter on the day after he left John to follow Jesus *"on the next day."*. You simply can't get all the way north to Bethsaida in a day. The journey was at the very least two or three days.

The more likely explanation is that Peter and Philip were for reasons we are not told in the vicinity of Perea making it easy for Andrew to find his brother and for Jesus to also meet Philip. Perhaps these men were on business in Jerusalem and staying in the area. The scenario would be as follows: The day after leaving John, Andrew finds Peter who was at that time near at hand and introduces him to Jesus. Jesus then purposes to go to Galilee in the north and as he sets out he finds Philip also from Bethsaida but in the vicinity. Following this, Jesus continues on into Galilee where we next see him at the wedding in Cana.

Two things are interesting to observe at this point: 1) the annunciation of Jesus being the Messiah is met with enthusiasm and joy in faithful men, and 2) people who are impressed with Jesus are bringing others to Him – a model for the Christian life.

Some may critique this by pointing out that none of the authorities were acknowledging Jesus as Messiah, only relatively ignorant, simple people who would be uncritically susceptible to enthusiastic excitement. But we have also to keep in mind that the nobility, the Pharisees and the Herodians were profoundly blinded by circumstances of their own making, so the expectation that they ought to be the genuine authentication sought for loses force. It is precisely to those free of sophistication and arrogance - the remnant who awaited the promises of God - that we should look for validation.

Secondly, the activity of bringing people to Jesus has been part of the Christian life for centuries. It is the idea of being so impressed with Him that you want others to know Him also. But the church beyond the life of Jesus has had a greater challenge in this regard. Christians can no longer bring people to Jesus as Andrew did, in the flesh as an objective experience. It is now a spiritually subjective experience, in which faith must span the gap of seeing with one's eyes. Nevertheless, people have been coming very effectively to Jesus ever since. The legions who have joined the ranks of the Church throughout history are proof of this has not been an impediment.

But the impetus for bringing is still the same – being so impressed with the Person of Jesus that we want others to know Him also. The world does not understand this zeal and misinterprets it as trying to dominate their culture with one's private religion. But we will learn in the upcoming dialog with Nicodemus that people are going to misunderstand because they lack the gift of the spirit that comes with being born again.

John 1:45-51, John 2:1-12
45 Philip found Nathanael and said to him, "We have found Him of whom Moses in the Law and also the Prophets wrote--Jesus of Nazareth, the son of Joseph." 46 Nathanael said to him, "Can any good thing come out of Nazareth?" Philip said to him, "Come and see." 47 Jesus saw Nathanael coming to Him, and said of him, "Behold, an Israelite indeed, in whom there is no deceit!" 48 Nathanael said to Him, "How do You know me?" Jesus answered and said to him, "Before Philip called you, when you were under the fig tree, I saw you." 49 Nathanael answered Him, "Rabbi, You are the Son of God; You are the King of Israel." 50 Jesus answered and said to him, "Because I said to you that I saw you under the fig tree, do you believe? You will see greater things than these." 51 And He said to him, "Truly, truly, I say to you, you will see the heavens opened and the angels of God ascending and descending on the Son of Man." (John 1:45-51)

1 On the third day there was a wedding in Cana of Galilee, and the mother of Jesus was there; 2 and both Jesus and His disciples were invited to the wedding. 3 When the wine ran out, the mother of Jesus said to Him, "They have no wine." 4 And Jesus said to her, "Woman, what does that have to do with us? My hour has not yet come." 5 His mother said to the servants, "Whatever He says to you, do it." 6 Now there were six stone waterpots set there for the Jewish custom of purification, containing twenty or thirty gallons each. 7 Jesus said to them, "Fill the waterpots with water." So they filled them up to the brim. 8 And He said to them, "Draw some out now and take it to the headwaiter." So they took it to him. 9 When the headwaiter tasted the water which had become wine, and did not know where it came from (but the servants who had drawn the water knew), the headwaiter called the bridegroom, 10 and said to him, "Every man serves the good wine first, and when the people have drunk freely, then he serves the poorer wine; but you have kept the good wine until now." 11 This beginning of His signs Jesus did in Cana of Galilee, and manifested His glory, and His disciples believed in Him. 12 After this He went down to Capernaum, He and His mother and His brothers and His disciples; and they stayed there a few days. (John 2:1-12)

Commentary

John 1:45-47
45 Philip found Nathanael . . . "We have found Him of whom Moses in the Law and also the Prophets wrote--Jesus of Nazareth . . Nathanael said to him, "Can any good thing come out of Nazareth?"

"of whom Moses . . wrote"

Philip is referring to Deuteronomy 18:15 in which a Prophet is to rise from among God's people. This came rather early to be understood as Messianic. Philip had concluded in his meeting with Jesus that He fulfilled not only Moses but the other Messianic prophecies as well.

Now this is somewhat difficult because there was a definite political aspect to Messiah that was customarily more emphasized in these times (and a reason for disappointment in the leaders with respect to Jesus as Messiah). Jesus could not have provided indicators in this regard for Philip because He made it clear that He was not fulfilling this aspect. (This will be made clearer when we get to the synagogue in Nazareth where Jesus reads from Isaiah – Luke 4:17ff.) So Philip had to have been especially keen on seeing Messiah fulfilled in the peaceful attributes that marked Israel's Messiah – proclaiming freedom to captives, healing the lame, etc.)

Matthew 2:23
Philip makes a point of mentioning Nazareth and we see that Nathaniel essentially asks why this could ever be significant. This implies that Philip is stressing it, as in *Jesus of <u>Nazareth</u>*! When we were discussing Joseph settling in Nazareth after returning from Egypt, Matthew states that this fulfilled what was said – that He would be called a Nazarene.

Search as we might in the OT, we cannot find a statement to this effect applying to Israel's Messiah. The only reference is that of Isaiah 11:1, *"Then a shoot will grow from the stump of Jesse, and a branch from his roots will bear fruit."* Nazareth was named after the idea of an insignificant twig in mind – *netzer* – and both Matthew and Philip have picked up on this as being Messianic. Some two thousand years later, we find it hard to see this as the light of understanding suddenly coming on. But to those closer to these prophecies and full-fledged Jews, we must defer to their insight.

Nathaniel's quip – *"Can anything good come from Nazareth?"* – was a byword among the Jews, here a derogatory jibe. It would be said in the mouth of a less informed Jew, compared to Philip, who saw the connection to Messiah.

47 Jesus saw Nathanael coming . . and said . . "Behold, an Israelite indeed, in whom there is no deceit!" Nathanael said . . "How do You know me?" . . . "Rabbi, You are the Son of God; You are the King of Israel."

Notice that Jesus does not call Nathaniel a Jew, but an Israelite. This is the more ancient and native term for the people of God. 'Jew' is short for a citizen of Judah, meaning the half-nation from the dividing of former Israel into two nations in the OT. After the death of Solomon, ten tribes split into Israel in the N and Judah and Benjamin in the S (called collectively Judah). After the Assyrian captivity, Judah (and Benjamin) remained the only lasting representative of what was once united Israel. They too were judged by Babylon, but returned under Nehemiah. As such they remained the only continuing nation, even in Jesus' time.

But Jesus prefers to harken back to their true origin. God's people may now be reduced to Judah, but they are still essentially seen in the Father's eyes as Israel – the people "governed by God."

That Nathaniel was without guile means that he was not typical of men in those days who often made their way in the world by adopting a sort of cynical and clever way to secure some measure of living among cheats and connivers. In many ways they had to become such men to survive. To adopt a life not based on deceiving people in order to make your living was notable.

This does not mean that Nathaniel was a well-educated, well-versed Jewish believer, as we saw above in taking up the common phrase about Nazareth.

His acknowledgement of Jesus as King of Israel is based in part on Philip's testimony but also on something that just happened. He asks how Jesus knows him and Jesus answers that He saw Nathaniel under a tree *before* Philip brought him.

Now there's nothing significant about noticing someone under a tree as you're approaching a particular place. This is not an extraordinary thing to recall. What impressed Nathaniel was not that Jesus saw him earlier, but that He knew that Nathaniel was a man without guile without "knowing" him in the normal sense. You don't get that by observing a man merely standing under a tree.

Nathaniel puts the pieces together – this and Philip's testimony – and quickly concludes Jesus is this King. As we said earlier in John 1:1 (*"and the Word was God"*), the Greek construction shows essence – the Word was the very *essence* of God. (The noun for 'king' is in the predicate postion and without the article.) So we have exactly the same Greek construction, hence the technical rendering would be: *"You are the essence of kingship over Israel"*, which would be equivalent to calling Jesus the Messiah.

John 1:48-51
Jesus answered and said to him, "Because I said to you that I saw you under the fig tree, do you believe? You will see greater things than these." 51 And He said to him, "Truly, truly, I say to you, you will see the heavens opened and the angels of God ascending and descending on the Son of Man."

Jesus then proceeds to give this man and everyone standing around an incredible blessing, perfectly in line with someone coming as the real deal, the genuine Messiah. He comments that knowing Nathaniel from just seeing him under the tree will be paltry compared to what they are yet to see.

"angels ascending and descending." We are somewhat perplexed here because there is no event where this is seen in Jesus ministry. The baptism was the closest thing and that was now past. The Transfiguration was the next closest, but Nathaniel would not be present, nor would the others, except Peter. So when would Nathaniel and the others addressed see the angels ascending and descending on the Son of Man?

This phrase comes from Genesis where Jacob saw this very image in a dream. The object on which the angels moved was a ladder into Heaven. When we begin to entertain the possibility of a connection, we can see Jesus' words applying to Himself as being the "Ladder" – the only true and permanent Way of access between Heaven and earth, and that His work and ministry would occasion a host of angelic business to and from.

This may seem to some like a stretch, so we might ask what other purpose the vision had for Jacob? What did it actually inform him about?

He was being shown a picture of access between earth and Heaven. He did not understand its meaning clearly at all, did not relate it to any particular event in his life or surroundings, but took it as a gift of revelation, a touch of God given to him, about something pertaining to earth and Heaven. We can see now that Jacob was being given insight - that God was establishing a channel of access between man and God; and the history that would unfold was a long preparation for it. But its ultimate fulfillment (which Jacob could not fully perceive at the time) was Jesus, the Son, coming to earth and finally putting in place the very means for personal access by every man.

As for Nathaniel, the key is *"upon the Son of Man."* As an observer and follower of Jesus, he would see the light of Heaven coming upon Jesus in the form of His power, authority and instruction. Heaven will have been opened for man to perceive directly in the Person of Christ. It is as though Heaven was shining a light and it was focused on Jesus wherever He went.

John 2:1-5
1 On the third day there was a wedding in Cana of Galilee, and the mother of Jesus was there; 2 and both Jesus and His disciples were invited to the wedding.

Now a change of scene, and the main reason Jesus was going into Galilee. *"On the third day"* might sound like a Bible discrepancy if taken to mean the third in the series of days mentioned earlier, *"the next day . ."* *'the next day" . . "the third day . ."* This would not give Jesus and his small group time to journey N to Cana, a two to three day journey.

But this really should be taken as according to custom, which would mean *"the third day since the last events mentioned."* If taken this way, 'on the third day' would mean after three days since the dialog with Nathaniel. Plenty of time to walk to Cana.

3 When the wine ran out, the mother of Jesus said to Him, "They have no wine." 4 And Jesus said to her, "Woman, what does that have to do with us? My hour has not yet come." 5 His mother said to the servants, "Whatever He says to you, do it."

Some have inferred impertinence on Jesus' part, especially in the KJV, which has: *"Woman what have I to do with thee?"* Even in both renderings we pull back from someone addressing their mother as "Woman" which seems impersonal at the very least.

But this was not out of custom at all in these times, as evidenced by Mary not taking offense and simply saying, "do whatever he tells you."

But why would Mary approach her son to remedy the problem at all? Jesus was not a wine merchant, had no access to stores of wine from which he could remedy the situation. But it is clear from Jesus' response that Mary was requesting a more extraordinary remedy at her son's disposal. This certainly means a miracle of some sort.

Despite extra-biblical legends of Jesus performing miracles as a child, there is no indication that Mary was accustomed to miracles in the life of her son and therefore knew He could fix this problem by performing one. This is clear from Jesus' words that His time had not yet come, which strongly suggests that Jesus specifically avoided supernatural displays until the moment for which He was born had arrived. So our expectation from these words is that Mary would not have a reference to past miracles as the basis for her request.

Nevertheless, she is asking for some sort a miraculous remedy regardless. This can easily be explained in reference to her knowledge of who her son really was. He is now an adult and has obviously left home to begin his ministry. So the miracles attendant with the *Son of God* would be, in her mind, now enabled, if held in abeyance before.

Jesus' words are meant to simply say, *"what business is the supply of wine to me when my business if of the Kingdom, not entertainment?"* And when we understand that the chief object of the devil's temptations was to get Him to use His powers for personal reasons, we see that this comment is certainly apropos.

"My hour has not yet come." is an idiomatic phrase that did not mean a task occupying just an hour, but the commencement of an event of any duration. It was timed in the sense of beginning at an appointed time. We see here that Jesus was on a divine schedule, that certain things had to come about at appointed times and this was to be diligently kept. One of those events was the riding into Jerusalem on the foal of an ass. Harold Hoehner in *Chronological Aspects Of The Life of Christ*, proposes that the precise end of the 69 weeks of Daniel's prophecy is the Triumphal Entry of Jesus into Jerusalem, to the very day, from the decree to rebuild Jerusalem. [13]

The theory is complicated but has considerable merit. And surprisingly this is corroborated in the statement of Jesus to those who scolded Him to keep the people quiet, *"If these are silenced, even the very stones will cry out . . knowing the Day of thy Visitation."* (Luke 19:40-44.) It is as though Jesus was saying that even nature knew what day this was. But as to Cana, some distance before the rigidly timed Triumphal Entry, we see Mary being a typical Jewish mother, ignoring her son's words, and proceeding as though her request will be granted – *"do whatever he tells you."*

Now this seems to run counter to everything just said. If it was not Jesus time, as he clearly states, then why did He comply and perform the miracle anyway? Perhaps something in her son's demeanor helped her know that He was not totally opposed. Or perhaps the Father made it known to His Son that now was the moment to begin his role as Messiah and Son of God before all men. The latter seems problematic since Jesus was not deficient in knowledge of such things, but we also have His statement that the day and the hour of His Second Coming were restricted from Him, known only to the Father.

John 2:6
6 Now there were six stone waterpots set there for the Jewish custom of purification, containing twenty or thirty gallons each . . .

This has been the source of many bitter arguments – whether Jesus made real wine or merely a sort of grape juice or watered down wine used for normal meals. The problem deals with why Jesus would make any substance so clearly related to human vice – are we not to avoid all associations with evil?

It is true that routine home meals, especially among the poorer folks, used watered down wine, or in some cases a form of juice from grapes. But we have here not a routine meal in a home, but a festive occasion

---

[13] Anderson, The Coming Prince, Kregel, 1982, pp. 127
Hoehner, Chronological Aspects to the Life of Christ, Zondervan, 1977, p. 137

where the real stuff was expected, much like champagne at weddings today. (Back then there were no Shirley Temples.)

The other indicator that this was not grape juice or otherwise non-intoxicating is in the host's remarks. *But you have kept the good wine until now."* As some may have heard in relation to this account, it was the practice of hosts, in order to have some semblance of financial relief in hosting large parties, to put out the best wine first, then when guests were sufficiently inebriated, to bring out the cheaper libation. But this host marvels that the best wine has come at the end. This can only mean that Jesus had actually produced the intoxicating variety that guests expect at the beginning. Despite the horror that fundamentalists try to avoid, the custom cannot be overlooked or distorted to serve one's theological dispositions.

Still, we do have to ask why, in ethical or moral terms, Jesus would do this, when such drink has been the medium through which so much unhappiness has resulted? We can offer two observations: 1) the view of wine, even for children, was different in NT times. It was a necessary substitute for an often deplorable water and was not axiomatically associated with immorality as we think of it today, and 2) the source of the vice is not in the substance but in the abuse of the substance, which is in the will of the individual not in the molecules of the wine. Even in Jesus day, when wine was viewed differently, drunkenness was a moral sin not contamination from a sinful substance.

Paul tells us to shun the very appearance of evil. We can see this as not having even the opportunity of a bottle of wine in our homes. But if we apply this to other things like the abuse of sexual desire, we must ask: are we to shun our marital relations because they can always lead to some sexual sin if viewed in carnal terms?

We are given the gifts of God in nature and man is always obligated to know how to partake of such things without abusing them or employing them for evil purposes. We are not to use sexual permission in marriage to rape our wives. Neither are we to be drunk with wine.

John 2:11-12
11 This beginning of His signs Jesus did in Cana of Galilee, and manifested His glory, and His disciples believed in Him. 12 After this He went down to Capernaum, He and His mother and His brothers and His disciples; and they stayed there a few days.

Whatever Jesus' words to Mary as to His time not yet come, Scripture declared this act to be the beginning of His signs of authentication as Messiah and a help to his disciples deepening their belief that He was the Christ. We can delve no deeper nor scrutinize further this declaration than at its simple face value, since the Scripture cannot be broken. Whatever our observations, Scripture declares the nature of the miracle.

"went down to Capernaum"

Capernaum was basically due east from Cana at the very top, center of the Sea of Galilee. It was by no means lower, as toward the S, which is the normal meaning of "going down." What is meant here is elevation. Capernaum and the shores of Galilee would have been at a lower elevation than Cana, so it is perfectly logical to say one is going down when traveling to Capernaum. The same is the meaning of "going up to Jerusalem" when referring to the walk from Bethany, which was to the west not to the north.

CHAPTER 4
Christ's Ministry - Year of Favor

John 2:13-25
13 The Passover of the Jews was near, and Jesus went up to Jerusalem. 14 And He found in the temple those who were selling oxen and sheep and doves, and the money changers seated at their tables. 15 And He made a scourge of cords, and drove them all out of the temple, with the sheep and the oxen; and He poured out the coins of the money changers and overturned their tables; 16 and to those who were selling the doves He said, "Take these things away; stop making My Father's house a place of business." 17 His disciples remembered that it was written, "ZEAL FOR YOUR HOUSE WILL CONSUME ME."

18 The Jews then said to Him, "What sign do You show us as your authority for doing these things?" 19 Jesus answered them, "Destroy this temple, and in three days I will raise it up." 20 The Jews then said, "It took forty-six years to build this temple, and will You raise it up in three days?" 21 But He was speaking of the temple of His body. 22 So when He was raised from the dead, His disciples remembered that He said this; and they believed the Scripture and the word which Jesus had spoken. 23 Now when He was in Jerusalem at the Passover, during the feast, many believed in His name, observing His signs which He was doing. 24 But Jesus, on His part, was not entrusting Himself to them, for He knew all men, 25 and because He did not need anyone to testify concerning man, for He Himself knew what was in man. (John 2:13-25)

Commentary

John 2:13
13 The Passover of the Jews was near, and Jesus went up to Jerusalem.

The Passover was one of the most important and diligently kept feasts in Judaism, being integral to their remembrance of the exodus from Egypt, one of the most dramatic and spectacular miracles in all of history. It also began the progress of feasts for each year.

But more than this, the observance was an express command of God. It was inextricably tied to the setting of the new year, a very important designation for all the feasts, but critical to the Passover because it was to be performed on a specific day of the first month and was to coincide with the full moon. The exact day of the Passover was the evening of the 14th day of the first month of the new year.

The 14th was therefore "regulated" from whatever day was chosen as New Year's day each year, and that was always selected by an observance of the new moon. When the 12th month was at an end, the priests began looking at the evening skies for the first sign of the new moon in order to declare which day would be the first day of the new year (and it was "declared" not calculated or reckoned, which came much later.)

Now everyone knows the new moon can't really be observed because it is completely dark in the evening sky; and the Jews had no means of deriving the true new moon astronomically. So they had to look for the first appearance of the moon's thin sickle on its disk. Astronomically, this is 18 hours old from the true new moon. But it could be the case that overcast prevented this observance for several days. In such cases, the priests waited no more than 2 days to declare the first day of the month.

(This did not create the problem of beginning the next year late, because, again, there was an observation to fix New Year's Day.) [14]

---

[14] Anderson, The Coming Prince, Kregel, 1982, p. 99n

From this day, the 14th was fixed by simply following the days of the month (i.e. no attempt was made to observe the full moon in order to set Passover, and in almost all cases the 14th and the new moon coincided.)

The Passover evening also began the Feast of Unleavened Bread which lasted a week. The Passover mentioned here is the first of the Passovers we use to determine the duration of Christ's ministry.

"went up to Jerusalem"

Jesus is at Cana in the north, so this is another case of "going up" or "going down" having reference to elevation, not going north or south. Jerusalem would be down if meaning south, but in this reference up, because it meant Jerusalem was at a higher elevation.

John 2:14-17
14 And He found in the temple those who were selling oxen and sheep and doves, and the money changers seated at their tables.

The idea of selling animals for sacrifice was a realistic expectation from the OT. The Jew was required to bring animals of a certain quality only - "without blemish". It was not feasible that everyone had such candidates at home, so the idea of having to buy a suitable animal was not an offense of the commandment.

The problem was that this business was being conducted within the Temple precincts, and the priests and leaders of Israel had adopted a system that required payment only in Temple shekels, which could only be acquired at the Temple. This not only involved some profiteering at the expense of worshipers but created noticeable congestion around tables and booths. The constant din of haggling over exchange rates wholly distracted from the business of the Temple which was meditation and prayer.

The booths and tables would have been in the Court of the Gentiles, prior to entrance into the holier precincts, and most likely under the shelter of the colonnades around its perimeter.

16 And He made a scourge of cords . . . stop making My Father's house a place of business." . . 17. . "ZEAL FOR YOUR HOUSE WILL CONSUME ME."

Peace loving people everywhere recoil from this show of violence on Jesus' part, especially when combined with the loss of money which was not a trivial thing in these times. An overturned table might be the loss of literally months of earnings in but a moment. Birds let loose would have to be acquired all over again. So there are some who have a great deal of difficulty accepting Jesus' behavior here when it could have been handled differently.

Thankfully, our Lord does not consult man about the best way to do things. You can imagine the long drawn out arguments, the rationalizations, and ensnared discussions that would have ensued if Jesus had tried to "negotiate" with these men. We must give Jesus the benefit of the doubt that this was the only way to correct the offense and the only way to make it indelibly clear.

Other gospels have, "My house shall be a house of prayer." It is amazing that his disciples were men who could recall Psalms 69:9 from memory and see its application to this very scene. We must remember that they did not have Bibles at the ready or concordances. Their memories of synagogue readings and discussions with their elders were all they had for remembrance. And we can assume that the Holy Spirit brought these things to their mind.

John 2:18-21
18 The Jews then said to Him, "What sign do You show us as your authority for doing these things?"

Such a serious act like disrupting what was considered lawful business, causing loss of property and money, would certainly prompt a question like this one. It would be like saying today, "What do you think you're doing?" which is really a question about one's authority to act. It is interesting that they ask for a sign. The reason is that inquiring into the claim that He was a Rabbi or a teacher would not have settled the matter. Such persons do not have this measure of authority by reason of their talent or position. He was proscribing a practice allowed by the highest authorities in the city. So a sign of exceptional authority was in view.

Here would be a perfect time to do something movie fans would expect – levitate persons or objects, cause lightning to strike, etc. But these would easily be associated with witchcraft, especially if those offended wanted good reason to discredit Him and resume their business.

19 "Destroy this temple, and in three days I will raise it up." 20 The Jews then said, "It took forty-six years to build this temple, and will You raise it up in three days?"

Jesus on occasion does not give people the answer they are expecting. Here, he is answering them after the manner of a spectacular sign, but it has no practical value. The Temple would basically have to be destroyed to test His claim, and no one was going to do that any time soon. So in their perception of the context it was an empty statement. But of course Jesus was talking about something completely different, so in essence He did not give them what they expected, or at least in terms they could understand.

But interestingly, we have a time marker here that needs to be checked against known history. Herod began the refurbishment of the second Temple in 18 B.C. This older second temple had stood for over four hundred years since its building by Zerubbabel. Forty-six years of Herod's new work would bring us to A.D. 29 (remember no year zero.) So we are in the right time frame with historical validation in perfect accord. In actuality, Herod's Temple was finally completed in 65, which means it stood complete for a mere five years before being destroyed down to its foundations by the Romans in A.D. 70.

That said, how then are we to take the comment, *"It took forty-six years to build this temple"* when it actually took eighty-two? The temple proper, the actual sanctuary, was begun and completed first and its immediately surrounding courts. These were finished within the time period mentioned. Even still, these first constructions had not just being completed in the very year these men were speaking, but had been finished for some time. [15]

So. the better understanding of this statement is that the temple "had been in construction" for the past forty-six years (and was still continuing.) Either way, this was meant to show ridicule and incredulity at Jesus' claim – that it was a fantastic claim with no means of proof.

21 But He was speaking of the temple of His body. So when He was raised from the dead, His disciples remembered that He said this; and they believed the Scripture and the word which Jesus had spoken.

We don't relate to this kind of an answer because people just don't talk this way today. We are very logical and common-sensical, and to speak in parodies or symbolism is generally lost on folks today. If He was talking about His own body, why not come out and say so, or choose another example?

But we are learning here that Jesus is tremendously complex, as we might expect. He is ahead of us by leaps and bounds and His meanings are sometimes only made clear after many discussions and much thinking.

In this case, being specific that He meant His body would have sent men off into avenues of planning that might prematurely have put Jesus in mortal jeopardy in order to prove His claim. In the above He has given them all something to think about and an opportunity to explain more to His followers in private.

---

[15] Hoehner, <u>Chronological Aspects to the Life of Christ</u>, Zondervan, 1977, pp. 38-43

But we are also very much aware that Jesus does openly drop hints about the far-reaching plans of God and what's happening on the grander scale, regardless of who may understand such things. It's a way of declaring the facts of what's happening from the Kingdom of Heaven's point of view. Notice Jesus with Pilate later on when He says that if He were coming as the kind of King Pilate meant, then would His followers fight. Yet this was spoken to a man who hadn't the slightest idea of its meaning.

John 2:23-25
23 .. during the feast, many believed in His name, observing His signs which He was doing.

Jesus later denigrates those who seek for a sign, yet we see him here accommodating people, that their belief is thereby helped. In these cases, He is using his abilities to heal and help his brethren. In the other case, they are seeking a sign as a first principle for accepting Him. But here, it is more likely that the people already believed in Him and were seeking healing, pure and simple.

24 But Jesus, on His part, was not entrusting Himself to them, for He knew all men, 25 and because He did not need anyone to testify concerning man, for He Himself knew what was in man.

An odd verse indeed. This is speaking of the people who are believing in Him on account of the things they received and witnessed. But entrusting Himself to them means to become subject to them, as in joining them, becoming one of their group of friends, joining in with their activities and life. But people who are easily convinced by signs and wonders are often susceptible to unpleasant behavior.

There are certain kinds of people who when they rub elbows with celebrities often lose their sense of decorum and try to exploit their newfound privilege or do silly or even brazen things. Jesus desired to avoid all that. He did not entrust Himself to them *"because He knew what was in man."* Yet no one could say He was stuffy or aloof. He came to serve, but He did not belong to anyone but the Father.

John 3:1-16
1 Now there was a man of the Pharisees, named Nicodemus, a ruler of the Jews; 2 this man came to Jesus by night and said to Him, "Rabbi, we know that You have come from God as a teacher; for no one can do these signs that You do unless God is with him." 3 Jesus answered and said to him, "Truly, truly, I say to you, unless one is born again he cannot see the kingdom of God." 4 Nicodemus said to Him, "How can a man be born when he is old? He cannot enter a second time into his mother's womb and be born, can he?" 5 Jesus answered, "Truly, truly, I say to you, unless one is born of water and the Spirit he cannot enter into the kingdom of God. 6 "That which is born of the flesh is flesh, and that which is born of the Spirit is spirit. 7 "Do not be amazed that I said to you, `You must be born again.' 8 "The wind blows where it wishes and you hear the sound of it, but do not know where it comes from and where it is going; so is everyone who is born of the Spirit."

9 Nicodemus said to Him, "How can these things be?" 10 Jesus answered and said to him, "Are you the teacher of Israel and do not understand these things? 11 "Truly, truly, I say to you, we speak of what we know and testify of what we have seen, and you do not accept our testimony. 12 "If I told you earthly things and you do not believe, how will you believe if I tell you heavenly things? 13 "No one has ascended into heaven, but He who descended from heaven: the Son of Man. 14 "As Moses lifted up the serpent in the wilderness, even so must the Son of Man be lifted up; 15 so that whoever believes will in Him have eternal life. 16 "For God so loved the world, that He gave His only begotten Son, that whoever believes in Him shall not perish, but have eternal life. (John 3:1-16)

Commentary

John 3:1
1 Now there was a man of the Pharisees, named Nicodemus, a ruler of the Jews; this man came to Jesus by night

The Pharisees were one of two religious parties in the Judaism of Jesus' day. The Pharisees and Sadducees were the religious conservatives and liberals, respectively.

'Pharisee' comes possibly from *'perusim'* – "separate ones," or from *'parosim'* – "specifiers." The Sadducees are believed to have been named after a priest named Zadok, but it is unclear whether this was the Zadok of David's day or later. These parties seem to have arisen after the Maccabaean revolt (167-142 B.C.). [16]

The Pharisees came from the middle class, hence their more conservative beliefs. They held to a more stringent, strict adherence to the Law of Moses and burdened the people with rather tight practical ordinances such as how much weight one could carry on the Sabbath without it being considered work, what distances constituted a legal Sabbath-day's journey. We see them questioning Jesus as his disciples are gleaning grain for food on the Sabbath.

The Sadducees were predominantly from the aristocracy or the noble families, hence their more liberal views. They did not believe in doctrines like the Resurrection which becomes an issue Paul takes advantage of later in the NT. These parties traded dominance back and forth over many decades, depending on the times and the ability of its members to hold influence.

"named Nicodemus"

To become a Pharisee required study and then recognition by the existing body in order to be added to its membership. This also would qualify Nicodemus as a "teacher of Israel" because much of the qualification was based on knowing the OT.

That he was seeking Jesus out might have meant that he had been delegated by the Pharisees to gain a better understanding of who this man was, but this is forestalled by the statement *"this man came to Jesus by night"* which would indicate he wished to avoid notice and came for personal reasons. Certainly the dialog turns into a very personal discussion.

Nicodemus comes as an example of many people seeking the Kingdom. We will see a bit later a man coming to Jesus asking what he must do to inherit eternal life. There were those believers who desired the right things and came to think in themselves that despite all the precepts of the Law, there has to be something more. In this way, Nicodemus is not much different than the Gentile who looks about his world and even evaluates the religion of his people, but says there has to be more to the God who is out there. And so Nicodemus comes with this in mind, to interview the man whose notoriety as one blessed of God with unique insight is seen as a source of answering this question, "Is there more?"

John 3:2-5
2 and said to Him, "Rabbi, we know that You have come from God as a teacher; for no one can do these signs that You do unless God is with him."

Giving compliments at the beginning of a meeting of this kind is Eastern etiquette. But this would also be a good sign that this is not an adversarial encounter. To say *"you have come from God"* is qualified with "as a teacher," so this would not be an admission by Nicodemus that Jesus was Son of God, but that he was gifted. Ordinarily, there would be a denigration of looking to signs, but in this case Nicodemus is mentioning them as a mark that Jesus is blessed of God. This, Jesus does not upbraid.

3 Jesus answered and said to him, "Truly, truly, I say to you, unless one is born again he cannot see the kingdom of God."

Again, we see a case of Jesus cutting to the heart of the matter in another man's business. There is no waiting to see what Nicodemus is here to ask, but He begins immediately to address a subject Nicodemus actually needs to hear. This is not about an intellectual curiosity or inquiry, it is about Nicodemus and the truth about his own faith.

---

[16] Tenney, <u>Zondervan Pictorial Encyclopedia of the Bible</u>, Vol 4, Zondervan, 1976, p.745, Vol 5, p. 211

Here the objective is *"seeing the Kingdom of God."* This was a desire of every faithful Jew, so Nicodemus will be keen on this statement. But the key is in something to which Nicodemus cannot relate at all – being born again.

As we see, he could not relate to this from his training as a Pharisee and teacher. There simply was no such concept in the OT. There was much familiarity with the operation of God's Spirit upon men, but this was never couched in terms of being born. All that Nicodemus could comprehend in this was that he must repeat the event of his own birth, and thusly he replies:

4 "How can a man be born when he is old? He cannot enter a second time into his mother's womb and be born, can he?"

It is not a case of inferring that his first birth was defective and he must go back to the beginning again, but that he understood Jesus correctly to mean that the birth must be done a second time – an additional birth. But Jesus was fully aware that he would misunderstand and was ready to explain.

5 Jesus answered, "Truly, truly, I say to you, unless one is born of water and the Spirit he cannot enter into the kingdom of God.

We traditionally explain that water means natural birth and the second birth is spiritual. But it has always bothered some folks that natural birth is described as from water, especially when saying "born of woman" would be much more direct. But from God's point of view, natural birth was fully designed to involve the watery incubation of the womb, which for nine months has as its most prominent feature, water. It is even the breaking of that water which signifies that birth is imminent. It is this birth that is distinguished from the second birth, which Jesus later explains is spiritual.

Also, Pentecostals and charismatic believers have tried to make this a case for distinguishing the two baptisms – believer's baptism and the baptism of the Holy Spirit. But the clarification Jesus gives rules this interpretation improper. But also, if we rely on the NT as a guide to these events, we see more often than not that the baptism of the Holy Spirit occurs simultaneously with believer's baptism (Acts 10:44-48.)

Jesus goes on to explain what He means . .

John 3:6-12
6 "That which is born of the flesh is flesh, and that which is born of the Spirit is spirit. . . . "The wind blows where it wishes and you hear the sound of it, but do not know where it comes from and where it is going; so is everyone who is born of the Spirit."

Here Jesus clearly states that the birth by water is the birth to fleshly existence – the birth as a human being. But He here discloses to Nicodemus that there is another birth possible – one that is *"of the Spirit."* This is entirely new. He is introducing two unique classes of things – the way of the flesh, the mind, and intelligence, and the way of the Spirit. This is an important point in understanding what He explains next. Like the wind, with respect to the Spirit, one can see its effects but not know much about its origins or operation. In other aspects of life, man can figure out why things are happening and even harness certain powers and forces to his advantage.

But the spiritual realm is not understood in the same manner or with the same faculties. If you try to use those pertaining to the flesh you will be confounded and perplexed. This happens to be the scene played out in many churches today when the Spirit begins to move among its members. Those who are used to explaining everything in rational terms are at a complete loss to explain what is happening, and often reject it because it is calling on a capacity they do not see in themselves, and this can be intimidating.

9 Nicodemus said to Him, "How can these things be?" 10 Jesus answered and said to him, "Are you the teacher of Israel and do not understand these things?

That Nicodemus asks this question, means that he is trying to do the above – trying to understand the way of the Spirit using rational approaches to understanding. Jesus questions him that in all his training as a teacher, he has somehow failed to understand the difference between these two great principles, between these two great worlds? He is leading ever more powerfully to the conclusion that the Spirit must be understood *spiritually.*

11 "Truly, truly, I say to you, we speak of what we know and testify of what we have seen, and you do not accept our testimony. 12 "If I told you earthly things and you do not believe, how will you believe if I tell you heavenly things?"

This is not easily understood because we must ask when Jesus spoke of earthly things? We don't see him teaching people the better techniques of planting and harvesting, how to build an irrigation system for one's field, or a better roof for one's house. He hasn't taught on the principles of creative and dynamic investing, social organization, or the secrets of herbs and medicines for better health. So when did Jesus speak of earthly things? Wasn't everything Jesus taught spiritual in nature?

The key is His statement that He and his disciples have taught what they *"know and have seen."* This would mean that what had been taught about earthly things and earthly relationships also falls within the things Jesus had come to teach His disciples. By the earthly things is meant the more practical aspects of their spiritual teaching in general, spiritual truths on a horizontal plane.

We do see Jesus teaching men about one's relationship to his neighbor (the good Samaritan), what happens if a man steals your coat, should the Jews pay taxes to the Romans, does one have a responsibility to give if one is poor (the widow's mite)? With respect to investing, He did teach that one should do so to realize gain, not merely to safeguarding the principle.

There must have been some degree of disinterest or disagreement about these practical matters among the people, including those whom Nicodemus represented, because Jesus tells him that if He has spoken of these things (which can be valued by using human reason) and they do not believe, how can Nicodemus believe the more spiritual things, the truly heavenly things?

John 3:13-16
13 No one has ascended into heaven, but He who descended from heaven: the Son of Man."

We are prompted to ask how this statement fits with the foregoing? But Jesus is clarifying that man, in and of himself, is not capable of ascending into Heaven for inquiry and learning. Only the One who has come down to visit man is capable of that. So it is in Nicodemus' best interest to seek all understanding from that One while He is present.

It's a nice way of saying, "Pay attention, Nicodemus, I come from God and I'm telling you the secret to the abundant life."

14 "As Moses lifted up the serpent in the wilderness, even so must the Son of Man be lifted up; 15 so that whoever believes will in Him have eternal life."

Again, this seems to be a disconnected utterance, but it fits well with what Jesus is telling Nicodemus about the very source of the information he's receiving. And the subject at hand is being born in the Spirit, being able to see the Kingdom of God. This is the subject of salvation, about which the Jew had considerable expectation.

Jesus is telling Nicodemus that not only is He the key to the information he is getting at the moment, but Jesus is the very key that makes that information possible. The preamble to this point is the incident of Moses in the wilderness (Num 21:9). Moses raised the brazen serpent as a sign toward which the faithful should look and be healed of the judgment of the serpents. The lifting up of Jesus is in reference to the Cross, not only as a means for salvation and eternal life, but as a sign toward which the faithful will look, the very symbol of salvation. To Nicodemus, this meant that the Man he was talking to was the very key to his own salvation and that of the entire world.

John 3:16
16 "For God so loved the world, that He gave His only begotten Son, that whoever believes in Him shall not perish, but have eternal life."

Here is the first representation of the "remedy" aspect of the Gospel. It speaks of a ransom. This was something understood by the Jew. It was done perennially in the Temple sacrifices – some other living thing was sacrificed to ransom man from the penalty of his own sins.

But the idea that God would give His Son as that ransom, as that sacrifice, was not as clear. Messiah had by this time become the *political* remedy and conquering hero for the Jews. The idea that He would suffer and actually become the object of wrath in appeasing a God angry with sin had been moved into the background. But notice here that Jesus prefaces this concept with a picture of the love of God. It is His love for the world that constrains Him to make this arrangement with His own Son.

"only begotten"

We are to here remember the case of Abraham and Isaac. Isaac was not the only begotten, but he was the only real expectation of Abraham in the promise with Sarah. When Isaac was born, the technical primacy of Ishmael (what man had wrought) could not invade the joy of fulfillment in what God had promised. Yet, it was this son of the promise whom Abraham was now being asked to sacrifice.

When Abraham lifted the knife, God then spoke and his hand was stayed – *"I see your faith, in not withholding your son."* In contrast, who spoke when Christ was placed on the Cross? Who said, "I see your faith, come down, all is well?" With God's own Son, it had to be played out as planned, the death had to come, the payment made. How much richer then is God's giving up of His Son?

". . that whoever believes in Him shall not perish, but have eternal life."

This is not as exclusively phrased as will be later formulated ("he who does not have the son, hath not the life." – I John 5:12), but it sets the condition which other world religions regard as arrogance in the extreme. It is a claim that there is only one Way, and all others are false.

In our modern world, and even in the ancient one, there was and is a magnanimity that grants legitimacy to various religions, and that all are seeking the same object in their own unique way. So the claim of exclusivity is very unpopular and not in the spirit of diversity and acceptance. This kind of thing also follows from democratic ideas which are more about what is fair than about absolute right and wrong.

Nevertheless, this remains the eternal truth of the Gospel – that the God of the Bible is the only God Who is there, that Christ has come and eternal life is in Him alone.

As to 'perishing,' the proper presentation of the Gospel must have the presupposition that all men are perishing. More and more people are less and less convinced of this in modern times. It is a point that must be re-won when witnessing to the lost.

One of the great difficulties is in getting an individual to acknowledge that their personal behavior and actions have placed them in the category of the perishing, that Someone is that angry with them to mete out such a destiny. But the truth of this point is rooted in absolute truths, which the modern world is quickly learning to abandon as a category of things.

But beyond personal sin, one must embrace universal sin, because there will always be the belief that one's personal life is surely an exception to the hideous deeds of more reprobate persons. *"We're certainly no Hitler, and we abhor gross and outrageous behavior, so God will take this into account when judging us."* So, this message must include the concept that all are guilty in Adam's sin and as such, without remedy. All are perishing. And the important point is that there *is* a Remedy. The purpose of witnessing is to give people a reason to reach for it.

John 3:17-36
17 "For God did not send the Son into the world to judge the world, but that the world might be saved through Him. 18 "He who believes in Him is not judged; he who does not believe has been judged already, because he has not believed in the name of the only begotten Son of God. 19 "This is the judgment, that the Light has come into the world, and men loved the darkness rather than the Light, for their deeds were evil. 20 "For everyone who does evil hates the Light, and does not come to the Light for fear that his deeds will be exposed. 21 "But he who practices the truth comes to the Light, so that his deeds may be manifested as having been wrought in God."

22 After these things Jesus and His disciples came into the land of Judea, and there He was spending time with them and baptizing. 23 John also was baptizing in Aenon near Salim, because there was much water there; and people were coming and were being baptized-- 24 for John had not yet been thrown into prison. 25 Therefore there arose a discussion on the part of John's disciples with a Jew about purification. 26 And they came to John and said to him, "Rabbi, He who was with you beyond the Jordan, to whom you have testified, behold, He is baptizing and all are coming to Him."

27 John answered and said, "A man can receive nothing unless it has been given him from heaven. 28 "You yourselves are my witnesses that I said, `I am not the Christ,' but, `I have been sent ahead of Him.' 29 "He who has the bride is the bridegroom; but the friend of the bridegroom, who stands and hears him, rejoices greatly because of the bridegroom's voice. So this joy of mine has been made full. 30 "He must increase, but I must decrease. 31 "He who comes from above is above all, he who is of the earth is from the earth and speaks of the earth. He who comes from heaven is above all. 32 "What He has seen and heard, of that He testifies; and no one receives His testimony. 33 "He who has received His testimony has set his seal to this, that God is true. 34 "For He whom God has sent speaks the words of God; for He gives the Spirit without measure. 35 "The Father loves the Son and has given all things into His hand. 36 "He who believes in the Son has eternal life; but he who does not obey the Son will not see life, but the wrath of God abides on him." (John 3:17-36)

Commentary

John 3:17-18
17 *"For God did not send the Son into the world to judge the world,"*

A righteous God visiting the created world necessarily implies judgment in a Judaistic sense because Judaism was a works-based approach where an assessment in terms of reward and punishment was implied. (This was not the intent of the Law from God's perspective, as Paul later reveals in Romans and Galatians.)

So John gets this notion out of the way in the business of Christ coming into the world. It is that the world might be saved, not that it be brought to accountability. This is one of the most profound and rather realistic aspects of the entire story of the Bible. It is realistic in that it is fully expected from the kind of restorative God revealed in the OT. Most people think of the OT God as angry, exacting and ready to judge. But so much in Israel's history reveals an intelligent, compassionate God who has a perfect plan for man's life, and is full of patience and longsuffering in spite of man's refusal to give him worship and obedience. It makes perfect sense that such a God would further endeavor to visit man to more clearly convey His love in the best terms possible, as opposed to being aloof, condescending and remote.

That the world might be saved through God's own Son is a perfect image of that love and contrary to the world's view of accountability. The world would never conclude that the lawgivers, kings and monarchs would effect an arrangement in which evil-doers would be redeemed from their due punishment by an arrangement that made the king's innocent son pay the price.

That is why the whole story of salvation is so authentic. Man would never conceive something like this. The myths of Greco-Roman antiquity all have man getting the just desserts of his deeds. Such an arrangement bears the mark of being genuine because only a God working on principles separate from his creatures could establish such a remedy.

18 ". . . He who believes in Him is not judged; he who does not believe has been judged already . ."

Freedom from impending judgment is declared to be in Christ. But this is not saying that such a judgment was merely a myth, a mistaken notion of man. The second part declares that he who does not have the Son is *"judged already."* At the very least this means that all men without Christ have committed sins worthy of judgment and have no other means of avoiding it. This is a truth about the world, the way things simply are. God is just and will not let offenses go unpunished, except within the Grace He alone provides.

There is, however, a more complicated explanation as to why those without Christ are condemned already – that all men come into the world under judgment until they gain the Son (*" Behold, I was brought forth in iniquity, And in sin my mother conceived me."* Psalms 51:5).

This is very difficult because it sets up the idea that man is born into judgment without his cognitive awareness. He is indicted before he takes breath. This all bears on the subject of original sin, which did not get much discussion until Augustine. Yet so much of Paul in Romans is explained by this concept.

There is good reason to be repulsed by the notion of coming into the world without our consent and being condemned on the basis of someone else's prior act. This is not a topic for beginners or for those less studied in NT theology. Conversely, it isn't a subject that can easily be dismissed or tritely swept under the carpet.

Suffice it to say that whether the more complicated issue of original sin applies or the inevitable principle that all men will sin cognitively, man without Christ faces a foreboding destiny.

What is important here is the positive part of the principle – that man need not *remain* judged. This is the essence of the "good news" of the Gospel. What the Law could not do because of the weakness of man, is now available in Christ. The "sigh" of the OT believer at the desperation in meeting the dictates of the Law was met with the joy of incredible relief, that all of its requirements are now met in Christ and the believer need only *"have"* Him. Good news indeed!

To "have" the Son would have been puzzling for an OT believer. There was no concept in Judaism of "acquiring" or possessing Messiah, except in the sense of having Him present among His people. Here, it is clear to Nicodemus that the inner freedom of being relieved of judgment depended on actually possessing Messiah in some sense yet unknown. Jesus was conveying what would later be explained in more detail – that possessing Christ is made possible by receiving the Spirit, who communicates the presence of Christ in the human heart.

This is reiterated by Jesus in *"He who has the Son has the Father."* It follows that the three Persons reciprocate each other, hence he who has the Spirit has the Son, etc.

John 3:19-23
19 "This is the judgment, that the Light has come into the world, and men loved the darkness rather than the Light, for their deeds were evil.

Turning again to the subject of judgment, Jesus declares the basis for all final judgment. Light has come into the world not only in Christ's coming but in ages past, and man is responsible. God was not slack in revealing Himself and his Word to mankind from the beginning. That revelation came and with respect to it, man can be brought to account.

Some will object that if this means the revelation in the Bible, there are hosts of people who have lived and died who have never heard or known of the Bible. How can these be held responsible for its light? Paul answers this by showing that God's light came in two other forms besides His written word: revelation of His handiwork in nature, and the personal revelation of Himself to every man in their hearts (Rom 1:18-20.)

The judgment before God of the unbeliever will not be a long set of arguments outlining all the things a person has done wrong. It will simply be a case of looking for them in the Lamb's Book of Life. When the name does not appear, the question as to why will be answered with, *"You loved the darkness rather than the light because your deeds were evil."* It will be an answer that will stop all mouths, because it will ring true at the very core. All other arguments will be a waste of time.

The mention of their deeds being evil is the very reason they did not wish to come to the Light. It would mean exposure and confrontation with one's acts and attitudes and when such deeds are loved and enjoyed, they cannot bear the Light of truth.

20 *"For everyone who does evil hates the Light, and does not come to the Light for fear that his deeds will be exposed. 21 "But he who practices the truth comes to the Light, so that his deeds may be manifested as having been wrought in God."*

Here, two completely opposite attitudes. One based on evil deeds and the other based on the desire to please God with deeds that practice the truth. This is endemic of the consummate evil doer, that he seeks in all things to avoid exposure. This means that he is aware that the Light exists, that it is wholly opposite and can expose. But his heart is sold to evil and the fear of giving it up prevents him from acknowledging that something is wrong with the way of evil compared to the way things are supposed to be.

But this can also apply to the Christian who falls into sin. While indulging it and knowing it to be wrong, he fears the Light with respect to the exposure of his sins to others. He may even become cynical about the goodness of those who love the Light and rationalize the duplicity of his own allegiances. But true believers will come to see their folly and recognize the goodness of the Light they know to be true, and the former state will not become permanent.

22 *After these things Jesus and His disciples came into the land of Judea, and . . with them and baptizing. 23 John also was baptizing in Aenon near Salim . . for John had not yet been thrown into prison.*

The scene now changes. Jesus has left Nicodemus and it is presumably several days later. He is journeying out in the Judaean countryside. Aenon near Salim is about two-thirds of the way to the Sea of Galilee, and is near the Jordan. So Jesus would be at the Jordan itself, but near these towns. We find Jesus and His disciples baptizing near to where John is also baptizing. This is mentioned for thematic reasons - to set the stage for distinguishing between John's ministry and that of Christ.

John 3:25-29
25 *Therefore there arose a discussion . . . "He who was with you beyond the Jordan, . . .is baptizing and all are coming to Him." 27 John answered and said, "A man can receive nothing unless it has been given him from heaven."*

John's disciples appear to be concerned that someone else, even if it be the Christ whom John identified, is now drawing considerable people to Him. The comment is borne out of the natural inclination to think that one's work is unique, and if a calling of God, specially blessed. Competition can be seen as threatening from a carnal point of view but also as puzzling from a spiritual view in that one realizes he may be out of touch with what God is doing. Notice John's reply. He reminds them that nothing substantial in God's eyes can be done unless it be first granted in Heaven. This is a message for all ministers who seek service to God.

Many churches invent programs and activities they believe critical to some objective which agrees with the encouragements of Scripture but seem to bear limited fruit for all the money and time spent. What is lacking is the bidding and urging of God. This is never seen until after the fact because the bidding and urging of God are often only seen in the highest, most generic form – *"Go and make disciples of all men ."* But the specific means may be purely man-made. Having God in the general call to service is not the same as having God in the details.

Some churches have no business being on television because God was never in the decision to make TV the means for a particular church to reach unbelievers. It may be wasting more of God's money than doing something much more effective (and less expensive), like training its members to be witnesses for personal evangelism. For John's disciples, they are pointed toward the fruit of Jesus' ministry and that it could not be possible without the blessing of Heaven.

29 "He who has the bride is the bridegroom; but the friend of the bridegroom, who stands and hears him, rejoices greatly because of the bridegroom's voice. So this joy of mine has been made full.

John explains that his role was herald, not the main event. The example from the marriage ceremony is important and very descriptive. The bride and bridegroom are the focus of the whole event. The friend has his part, but he must give way to what the moment is about – the joining of bride and bridegroom and the joy of that union. So John is saying that as Preparer, the focus may have been on him for his part, but it must now be on the main event which is what Christ is doing and will do.

The mention of the bridegroom's voice is from the Jewish custom in which the bridegroom is separate from the bride's party and her attendants. But at a designated time the bridegroom and his party come to the place of the wedding, usually the parents' home. As he approaches from a distance, he shouts that he is near so that those within can rejoice that the wedding proper is now ready to proceed. The friends who are with the bridegroom naturally hear his voice and rejoice for the same reasons.

John 3:30-32
30 "He must increase, but I must decrease. 31 "He who comes from above is above all, he who is of the earth is from the earth and speaks of the earth."

In concert with all John has said, he summarizes everything in one poignant phrase, "I must decrease." To be from above is of the highest order of all things. This is to recognize that the world is created and for a purpose. Men can ignore that purpose but its truth is not changed. All that will become of the earth and all the material things we see and use today is dependent on the plan of God for the consummation of all things.

What is of fascinating interest is that even today, despite all our technology and the harnessing of many powers, the forces of nature can put man back to the most basic of life's concerns in a moment of time. We are suddenly brought face to face with the precarious nature of those things we depend on most and how easily it can all be undone. If simple nature can do that, the powers that rule in Heaven are of much greater aspect and deserve all the more our respect.

32 "What He has seen and heard, of that He testifies; and no one receives His testimony.

Christ testified of what He had seen and heard in Heaven. He knew the way of things in Heaven, the Grand Plan, and the way of the earth. This again is exactly what we would expect from someone coming from Heaven – to explain the most urgent of things, the very things important in Heaven and what is needful on earth.

But John says that no one receives His testimony. This is the general observation concerning God over the centuries. He spoke through his prophets but the majority of people were not listening. In terms of the general revelation mentioned by Paul in Romans, the people of the earth have had that knowledge, but turned it into selfish things, or other gods of wood and stone. The existence of hundreds of other religions is testimony that the world has not received the testimony of God, preferring other testimonies of their own making.

John 3:33
33 "He who has received His testimony has set his seal to this, that God is true.

The seal mentioned here is the result of receiving the testimony of God. It is a resultant effect of the receiving process. We acquire the knowledge that God is true – that He is really there, not merely something we must strive to perpetuate in our own minds.

Philosophers of the 17th and 18th centuries dealt with the problem of knowledge and how man can actually know that something exists or that our knowledge represents reality. Some men introduced the novelty of doubt about the certainty of what is claimed to be real (Descartes, Locke.) Others built on that thinking to further distinguish knowledge by experience from knowledge that is evident in itself, and particularly whether knowledge that cannot be shown to be either, i.e. faith, is knowledge at all? (Kant, Hume.)

So it is popular to spoof faith as conveying no true knowledge because it is subjective, cannot be transferred as truth to someone else (unless they have the same experience) and cannot be verified like other forms of knowledge. So when the believers say they know that God exists, this is nonsense to the philosopher or the scientist because it is based on faith, which is outside the realm of recognized means (which is what the term *metaphysics* means).

But the Bible claims that knowledge can be conveyed by faith, and more reliably than man can claim for secular disciplines. The reason this is not convincing to the unbeliever is that it takes faith to experience the reality of that knowledge, *"Faith is the substance of things hoped for, the evidence of things not seen."* So those who receive His testimony acquire knowledge that serves as a seal, validating the truths spoken.

John 3:34-35
34 "For He whom God has sent speaks the words of God; for He gives the Spirit without measure.

The unlimited Spirit here given is meant to distinguish Christ from all other human agents who receive the Spirit in part. In Him there is no measured anointing, no limited degree. You get unrestrained access to the truth unfiltered by the limitations of human frailties.

35 "The Father loves the Son . . He who believes in the Son has eternal life; but he who does not . . . the wrath of God abides on him."

That all things have been given under His authority is to authenticate His teaching, the truths of which He speaks and His work as being supremely effective. He is in charge of all things and thereby His words have all authority and power.

This is in contrast to what man may say but not be able to do. The greatest people in the world promise many things but may or may not deliver. The President of the United States in his State of the Union address promises every year that wrongs will be fixed and things that ought to be done will be accomplished. He has the greatest powers and resources at his disposal. Yet every year we find that not everything he promised, though in sincere earnest, was at his disposal to make happen.

With Jesus, we can be assured that all He promises, all He predicts, all He wills to do will be accomplished because He has at His disposal power and might and will unspeakable and full of glory.

John 4:1-16
1 Therefore when the Lord knew that the Pharisees had heard that Jesus was making and baptizing more disciples than John 2 (although Jesus Himself was not baptizing, but His disciples were), 3 He left Judea and went away again into Galilee. 4 And He had to pass through Samaria. 5 So He came to a city of Samaria called Sychar, near the parcel of ground that Jacob gave to his son Joseph; 6 and Jacob's well was there. So Jesus, being wearied from His journey, was sitting thus by the well. It was about the sixth hour.

There came a woman of Samaria to draw water. Jesus said to her, "Give Me a drink." 8 For His disciples had gone away into the city to buy food. 9 Therefore the Samaritan woman said to Him, "How is it that You, being a Jew, ask me for a drink since I am a Samaritan woman?" (For Jews have no dealings with Samaritans.) 10 Jesus answered and said to her, "If you knew the gift of God, and who it is who says to you, `Give Me a drink,' you would have asked Him, and He would have given you living water." 11 She said to Him, "Sir, You have nothing to draw with and the well is deep; where then do You get that living water? 12 "You are not greater than our father Jacob, are You, who gave us the well, and drank of it himself and his sons and his cattle?"

13 Jesus answered and said to her, "Everyone who drinks of this water will thirst again; 14 but whoever drinks of the water that I will give him shall never thirst; but the water that I will give him will become in him a well of water springing up to eternal life." 15 The woman said to Him, "Sir, give me this water, so I will not be thirsty nor come all the way here to draw." 16 He said to her, "Go, call your husband and come here."

Commentary

John 4:1-7
1 Therefore when the Lord knew that the Pharisees had heard that Jesus was . . baptizing more disciples than John . . . 3 He left Judea and went away again into Galilee.

We must never conclude that Jesus was at anytime afraid of the Pharisees themselves, or what they might do to Him. This was purely a matter of timing. Jesus did not wish to provoke them to acting earlier than the appointed time. He therefore left for another journey into Galilee.

We also learn that Jesus was baptizing with His disciples. But John feels strong about clarifying that Jesus Himself did not perform baptisms, but delegated His disciples to baptize. This is not a proof text that Jesus had a low opinion of baptism or that it was optional, as some churches teach. (Their argument would be that if baptism was essential to salvation, Jesus would never cast any aspersions in His own behavior about baptizing.)

But the reason Jesus did not personally baptize is on another plane. He did not want to create a division among his followers on the basis of who baptized whom. We can understand that persons baptized by Jesus might turn this into an advantage, *"But I was baptized by Jesus"* and this could easily be avoided by delegating.

Whether one teaches that baptism is essential for salvation or an act of obedience to the Lord's command separate from what is needed to be saved, no conservative NT church can neglect it. The end result of any and all arguments is that all must be baptized if they wish to be obedient to the Lord.

4 And He had to pass through Samaria. 5 So He came to a city of Samaria called Sychar, near the parcel of ground that Jacob gave to his son Joseph; and Jacob's well was there.

Samaria was one of the northern cities that had come to be repopulated since the carrying away of the northern tribes into Assyria in the 8th century B.C. Ironically, it had again for the second time become a city in opposition to the primacy of Jerusalem and its Temple.

In the period between the testaments, a faction developed that rejected Jerusalem and traditional Judaism and separated themselves in Samaria. The result was a distinct rift between Jew and Samaritan that remained in Jesus' day.

Interestingly, the Jewish-Samaritan issue was very similar to the Christian-Mormon issue today. Mormons separated themselves from historic, traditional Christianity, seeing it as an abomination. They have separate and unique Scriptures, a separate worship and priesthood. In many ways they exemplify better the tenets of Christianity than many Christians do. But ironically, they had for a time a strange view of marriage and continue in a different view of the deity of Christ that contradicted traditional views.

Similarly, the Samaritans despised traditional Judaism, held apart unique sections of OT Scripture, set up a separate temple and priesthood, were exemplified by Jesus as having a better sense of charity (the Good Samaritan), yet also, had a strange view of marriage whereby they inter-married among themselves to the degree that they suffer in present times from idiocy and other side-effects.

Samaria proper was W of the road on the way that led to the Sea of Galilee. The key cities were Shechem and the city of Samaria. Sychar was a smaller town just E of Shechem.

Jacob had arranged land rights for his twelve sons. In the conquest of the land under Joshua, Joseph was given the area that became Samaria, settled at various times between the half tribes of Ephraim and Manasseh. Jacob had dug wells at Shechem and Sychar. (If one of the two sites with a well is legitimate as Sychar, we may in fact be able to look at the very well mentioned in this story.) The well at Sychar was exceptionally deep due to its water table sitting on a basalt formation some 50 meters below the surface.

6 . . So Jesus, being wearied . . . was sitting thus by the well. . . about the sixth hour. There came a woman of Samaria to draw water. 7 . . Jesus said to her, "Give Me a drink."

We have here in the hands of Jesus Himself a tremendously valuable lesson with respect to witnessing. It involves a frequently dreaded situation we all face – our eventual confrontation with certain individuals who are ready to foment a full course of justifications as to why their lives don't have to change; and who need little provocation to add, "Don't judge me or you'll get both barrels!" We are easily perplexed because we are caught between the unction that such persons need Christ, but we find ourselves at a complete loss as to how to begin without creating a train wreck.

This situation is precisely the one Jesus faces here with the woman at the well. We need to observe carefully how He deals with it, to the effect that her life is in fact successfully and permanently changed. We need to first observe who this woman is and the circumstances of her life. For starters, she has three strikes against her at the very outset. She is a Samaritan. She is a woman; and she is of low reputation in that she practices serial monogamy outside the legitimacy of marriage.

Ordinarily, the stigma of these factors would cow most people into the kind of person who spoke seldom in public and stayed at home as much as possible to avoid social interaction. But here, we find a woman who is outspoken, opinionated and confrontational, even after she learns that Jesus is a man of considerable wisdom and savvy. This suggests that she has come to justify within herself her chosen way of life, her moral attitudes and a view that she is as good as anybody else.

Some expositors have gone a bit farther to infer that she may be approaching Jesus as a new chapter in her string of "arrangements", since this kind of behavior is characteristic of a flirtatious and forward manner. The lesson here from Jesus is that the very worst thing a Christian can do in these circumstances is to begin with a judgmental approach or even the mere hint that your only reason for talking to them is to bring them out of their sinful life.

Observe Jesus. He avoids this tack until the moment is right and the way has been prepared. It's not that He is afraid. He simply knows what is expedient and what isn't. Instead, He begins with a discussion about what she is there to do. He takes advantage of the symbol of water to open a discussion about the things that satisfy. He wants her to see the difference between earthly satisfactions (hence, why her life has come to be what it is) and the satisfaction of things from above. Take off the veneers, the blustering, the masks, and all men everywhere have a place in the heart where they yearn for this kind of satisfaction.

Notice that Jesus does not begin weakly, but in a manner that is daring (to get her attention) while not being judgmental - *"Give me a drink."* The text explains that this is because His disciples had gone away to buy food, but we see that Jesus had more serious intentions.

John 4:9-12
9 "How is it that You, being a Jew, ask me for a drink since I am a Samaritan" (For Jews have no dealings with Samaritans.)

The tack worked in so far as it caught her attention immediately. She is surprised first that a Jew would talk to her, but also that He has had the boldness to order her to bring up a drink. It has served to take the focus off the obvious and in fact she is able to bring up herself the negative factors that separate her from the Jews - a sign of a complete lack of intimidation from Jesus. She feels free enough to mention the very things that would ordinarily provoke denigrating words.

10 . . . Jesus answered . . "If you knew the gift of God, and who it is who says to you, `Give Me a drink,' you would have asked Him, and He would have given you living water."

But Jesus side steps her question and moves her focus to the extraordinary circumstances in which she finds herself at this very moment. He explains that there is a "gift" in play - one that if appreciated would alleviate her concerns about the strangeness of the circumstances. He is in essence answering her by announcing that she is being visited by someone extraordinary.

"the gift of God"

The gift is not something known to her or understood as obvious between the two of them. It is Jesus Himself as Messiah. This is surely a gift in that she has the rare opportunity of speaking to the Savior of God's people and the whole world. If this were known to her, she would instead be asking for the kind of water that eternally satisfies. But this is all unfortunately lost on her at first.

11 "Sir, You have nothing to draw with and the well is deep; where then do You get that living water?
12 "You are not greater than our father Jacob, are You, who gave us the well, and drank of it himself and his sons and his cattle?"

She chooses to skip over further inquiry about who Jesus is and is much more intrigued with the mention of living water. But she misunderstands this as a means of relieving her daily chore. However, she quickly discerns that He can't be referring to the well and its drudgery because He lacks any means, which is all the more poignant given its depth. But more than this, the water in this well is used by everyone and, as such, it has yet to be perceived as "living water."

She entertains the notion that if He is talking in such terms, He might be great enough to turn this common water into something miraculous. She poses this in a sort of incredulous question – *"You're not greater than our father Jacob who gave us this well are you?"* It sounds like an expression of incredulity, but in essence it is one that contains expectation and hope that He might be able to make good on His claim.

John 4:13
13 "Everyone who drinks of this water will thirst again; 14 but whoever drinks of the water that I will give him shall never thirst; . . . a well of water springing up to eternal life."

As we've seen before, Jesus does not answer her question in her own terms but uses the question to make further, deeper disclosure about the subject He is really addressing. First, He clarifies that He does not mean the water in the well. *"Everyone who drinks this water will thirst again."*

The analogy is that everyone who seeks to satisfy some human, purely horizontal need will thirst for it again. This is the way of human existence. We think that if we can just have such-and-such we will never ask for another thing again, our lives will be so full of the happiness of having it that we can live devoid to all future wants and desires. But it never happens. We get that certain thing and we merely move to a new plateau of wants and desires, new horizons stretch out before us, and our list of wants remains just as before. Such is the way of earthly desires. While we can't live without some aspect of earthly needs and wants, there is a water – a supply for living – that does satisfy completely and finally. And it is not meagerly dispensed, but *"springs up to eternal life."*

Is Jesus teaching that the water of eternal life will, if properly sought, supplant all earthly thirsts? Experience tells us no. We will still need a better car, a better home, a better job. Instead, it is a lesson about the difference. We are to understand the weakness and entrapment of earthly satisfactions and add to our life the satisfaction of that which is from above. The former are necessary evils, the latter is a necessary good.

A minister once came to a Christian couple who were experiencing oppression and even worrisome experiences in their house. He noticed on the wall in the entryway an arrangement of pictures representing prominent figures in world religions, with Jesus arranged as merely one of many. There were baghwans, Hindu personages, representations of Mohammed, etc.

He suggested that this may be the source of their problem. It was for him a sign that the couple was still looking for that which would satisfy their spiritual quest for the truth. But it must be made clear that Jesus is not merely one of many legitimate paths. When someone finds Jesus, the search comes to an end. Neither would it do to simply arrange Jesus above all the others.

The only right arrangement was to take the others completely away and leave Jesus alone on the wall. For them the search needed to come to an end. Searching for truth in other options was never going to satisfy. Making Jesus the One and True Lord would.

John 4:15-16
15 "Sir, give me this water, so I will not be thirsty nor come all the way here to draw." 16 . . "Go, call your husband and come here."

She has yet to gain His meaning - understandable from the few words He has actually spoken. But she realizes that He is serious about giving her something in line with His words, so she asks, *"Give me this water."*

Jesus then speaks at a completely oblique angle to the discussion. *"Go, call your husband."* This is meant to bring the example of the two waters to bear on the subject of her way of life and the kind of satisfaction it provides. Her life was one of using men, not at its lowest modality as a prostitute, but on a rung slightly higher, with some strongly rationalized sense of respectability. She had lived with men without marrying them, but had purposed to live as man and wife, monogamously. But the end of all such relationships is boredom and the inevitable search for the next live-in opportunity. She would never be able to get the concept of living water until she came to see the waste this kind of life begets. As for living water, she needed to be able to reach for it. And she would never do that by continuing to legitimize her present state.
   Now in Jewish social life, this arrangement was no more acceptable than prostitution. She was probably just as ostracized socially. Judaism at the time of Jesus did not rigorously exercise the Mosaic Law about fornication. Her life would not be classed as adulterous because her mates were not living with her while otherwise married, and she herself was not otherwise legitimately married. In these times, even some cases of outright adultery were overlooked (the woman about to be stoned had lived for some time in her practice without the Law being invoked.)

But the key to her understanding the truth about the living water of which Jesus speaks is wrapped up in the truth about her lifestyle. This must be settled first. In other words, she cannot acquire the living water and then begin thinking about changing her present life later. Spiritual life comes only when we abandon all legitimacy and trust in our former life. We must first agree and confess that our former way of life is wrong. We will see next how she responds . .

John 4:17-38
17 The woman answered and said, "I have no husband." Jesus said to her, "You have correctly said, `I have no husband'; 18 for you have had five husbands, and the one whom you now have is not your husband; this you have said truly." 19 The woman said to Him, "Sir, I perceive that You are a prophet. 20 "Our fathers worshiped in this mountain, and you people say that in Jerusalem is the place where men ought to worship."

21 Jesus said to her, "Woman, believe Me, an hour is coming when neither in this mountain nor in Jerusalem will you worship the Father. 22 "You worship what you do not know; we worship what we know, for salvation is from the Jews. 23 "But an hour is coming, and now is, when the true worshipers will worship the Father in spirit and truth; for such people the Father seeks to be His worshipers. 24 "God is spirit, and those who worship Him must worship in spirit and truth." 25 The woman said to Him, "I know that Messiah is coming (He who is called Christ); when that One comes, He will declare all things to us." 26 Jesus said to her, "I who speak to you am He."

27 At this point His disciples came, and they were amazed that He had been speaking with a woman, yet no one said, "What do You seek?" or, "Why do You speak with her?" 28 So the woman left her waterpot, and went into the city and said to the men, 29 "Come, see a man who told me all the things that I have done; this is not the Christ, is it?" 30 They went out of the city, and were coming to Him. 31 Meanwhile the disciples were urging Him, saying, "Rabbi, eat." 32 But He said to them, "I have food to eat that you do not know about." 33 So the disciples were saying to one another, "No one brought Him anything to eat, did he?" 34 Jesus said to them, "My food is to do the will of Him who sent Me and to accomplish His work.

35 "Do you not say, `There are yet four months, and then comes the harvest'? Behold, I say to you, lift up your eyes and look on the fields, that they are white for harvest. 36 "Already he who reaps is receiving wages and is gathering fruit for life eternal; so that he who sows and he who reaps may rejoice together. 37 "For in this case the saying is true, `One sows and another reaps.' 38 "I sent you to reap that for which you have not labored; others have labored and you have entered into their labor." (John 4:17-38)

Commentary

John 4:17-19
17 The woman answered and said, "I have no husband." . . . Jesus said . . "You have correctly said, `I have no husband'; 18 for you have had five husbands, . ."

We learn that this was a setup designed specifically to get her to verbalize her state of living. It is not a setup in the negative connotation of taking advantage of her. It is simply a means of getting her to begin talking about her lifestyle. Jesus has first gained "permission" to do this by all the foregoing.

People have gates that guard their willingness to disclose personal things in their lives and we must knock at those gates with kindness and compassion, seeking permission to enter. Jesus spoke of things that intrigued her, He was a man of exceptional presentation and curiosity; and He has also put her at ease - He was not the kind of person who would take advantage of her. The gate had been opened.

Jesus further compliments her in being forthright and truthful; rather than deceptive or clever. But having gained some measure of permission to invade her private life, He now places His finger on the spot that is critical. *"you have had five husbands, and the one you have now is not your own."* This might seem technically incorrect. It is doubtful that she was ever married in her other relationships (though this is not ruled out) but she is nevertheless not married now. Yet Jesus says the husband she has now is not her own, meaning he does not belong to her in a legal sense. (This does not mean the man belongs to someone else, as in being married, because this would be adultery and she is not described as a woman in adultery.)

But this technicality is not the basis for testing Jesus' words. God perceives the condition of marriage is valid whether civil union is involved or not. But this is not to mean people can disregard civil legalities. It means that if a man and woman lie together in sexual union, they have become man and wife in the eyes of God. Hence, Jesus identified six such unions for her, therefore six husbands.

19 "Sir, I perceive that You are a prophet.

Her tone has now immediately changed. Whatever dallying she might have pursued in this discussion, she now realizes that she is in the presence of someone with divine insight. He could not have known this about her by acquaintance (He is an unknown person to her and her community.)

Prophecy has two modes: *fore*-telling (predicting the future – the meaning we normally think of), and *forth*-telling (speaking as the voice of God's in things recent or current.) When we study prophecy in the OT we find that a considerable amount of material is of the forth telling variety. God often decries the current condition of His people and calls them to repentance and faith.

Her statement here and those following are a way of giving space to this revelation, a sort of diversion for the moment that will reduce the pressure of this disclosure. She must know that He is bound to say more, so she moves the discussion to the subject of who He is and the role He is playing. It is not a question for clarification, it is a declaration. This leads her (conveniently) to shift the emphasis away from her personal life and onto subjects that pretend an interest in a higher order – who has the proper worship among our two peoples? And it is the kind of thing you would want to ask anyone blessed with insight from God.

John 4:20-23
20 "Our fathers worshiped in this mountain, and you people say that in Jerusalem is the place where men ought to worship."

"On this mountain" means Mt. Gerizim. Sychar was in the valley between Mt. Ebal to the N and Mt. Gerizim to the S. The Samaritans had chosen Mt. Gerizim as their rival against Mt. Moriah. A temple (later destroyed by Hadrian) was constructed on its summit to counter the Temple at Jerusalem.

21 ".. Woman,.. an hour is coming when neither in this mountain nor in Jerusalem will you worship the Father. 22 "You worship what you do not know .. for salvation is from the Jews.

The formality of where and how worship was best performed was coming to an end. It had been rigorously commanded in days of old and the Jews were faithful to keep it. The Samaritans were just as diligent to the idea that proper worship ought to be maintained, they just differed as to details. But Jesus was announcing that the new life was about to come into the world, in which worship would no longer be as it was, but in every man's heart, in every place.

This is a hint to the coming of the Holy Spirit to indwell men's hearts and make a sanctuary therein. This would make Mt. Moriah or Mt. Gerizim, Jerusalem or Samaria, in fact any particular temple, obsolete. We see this clearly in the ripping of the Temple curtain at the time of Jesus Crucifixion.

"what you do not know .. salvation is of the Jews"

This does to death the idea of independent movements apart from the will of God. Despite their desire to purify and restore religion, they had no calling from God to separate themselves. Theirs was different than a reform of Judaism. The Samaritans had built something independent not restored. They would not have been able to arrange for official Levites to run the temple services so were obliged to use half-breed mixtures from that tribe.

All of this was misplaced according to Jesus - "You worship what you do not know." The Jews at least worshiped on the basis of revealed knowledge – that salvation is of the Jews. This is important because all religion must conform to the plan of God. God is planning the salvation of the world through His Son, and that in fulfillment to prophecy. When you move away from that heritage, you move out from under God's plan and the means by which He will bring it to completion. Salvation is of the Jews and this cannot be changed, else all of prophecy is mistaken.

23 "But an hour is coming, and now is, when the true worshipers will worship the Father . ."

This might sound like a contradiction to all the foregoing. Why emphasize the Jews if a new phase of worship is coming? The new phase cannot be divorced from its roots. It is only possible by means of what God did with His people. Christ is the key to this new worship, but Christ is nevertheless of the Jews. The mention of the new hour coming is that this woman and all the world must come back to the promises of God in Judaism, now fulfilled in Christ.

It is as though there are two trains at the station, the right one and the wrong one. Some folks get on the wrong train, some get on the right one. When the right one begins to leave the gate, folks left on the wrong train soon realize the train they should have taken. Those who don't wish to be left behind run to get on board. That is what Jesus is saying. Something is about to change. The correct train (the religion of God's peculiar people) is about to leave the station. Get on board now, or you may find yourself standing in the station on the wrong train.

John 4:24-26
23 ". . in spirit and truth; for such people the Father seeks to be His worshipers. 24 "God is spirit, and those who worship Him must worship in spirit and truth."

"in spirit and truth" will be explained below. Here Jesus declares whom the Father seeks.

The new worship is to be in spirit and in truth. The Father will be looking for that kind of worshiper. The reason is actually something that had been true from time immemorial. *"God is Spirit"* Not God is *a* spirit, but *is* Spirit.

God is incorporeal. He exists in His essence in spirit form. That is why we use the word 'spiritual' - we are talking about things that pertain to Him as spirit. Jesus is teaching that if God is Spirit, we cannot relate to Him in merely physical terms, nor with merely of the faculties by which we communicate in the world. This includes the rational things, like human thoughts and the limits of human reason. *"My ways are not your ways, saith the Lord."*

We are to worship God with those means and capacities that *can* communicate with Him as Spirit. We are given such means in Christ. Every person who has ever lived was born with a spiritual component, but it came into the world dead unto God. It could not perceive rightly the things of God. *"But a natural man does not accept the things of the Spirit of God, for they are foolishness to him; . . . because they are spiritually appraised."* I Cor 2:14) In Christ, our spirits are made alive toward God and we are able to *"compare spiritual things with spiritual."* These are those whom the Father seeks, those who are ready to be made alive in their spirits.

"The woman said to Him, "I know that Messiah is coming . . . when that One comes, He will declare all things to us." It is clear that she has now become overwhelmed. And we can understand why. Jesus has introduced something that is not only brand new but rather deep in terms of the operations of God. Rather than engage a subject for which she is ill-suited and certainly unprepared, she leans on the promise of Messiah, who will straighten out all such things when He comes, *"He will declare all things to us."*

Now Jesus has her in the right place. All the foregoing (the talk about living water, the way of her present life, the correct places of worship, the promise of something new) she has chosen cleverly to subsume under one enigmatic and distant topic: the coming of Messiah. And, ironically, to whom is she now talking?

26 "I who speak to you am He."

Jesus is rather careful to whom He reveals His identify. He is concerned about timing, but in cases where timing is not threatened, He often reveals Himself as Messiah. We will find this repeated again later in the tender case of the boy thrown out of the synagogue (John chapter 9.) What is so amazing here is that the genuine article is in front of her. For us, we are hearing His personal admission of identity as the King of Glory, the Creator of the universe, the real and genuine Savior of mankind.

The Divine Majesty that walked the courts of that very Heaven that is really there has actually and truly come to earth to dwell among men. And here, in ways not bombastic or spectacular, He quietly reveals this to one person alone and without fanfare.

In these cases, they go and announce this to others. But as humanity will often have it, the testimony of no-account persons is often discounted as below the noise. They seldom rise to a level that alarms the authorities. And for a time, this is to Jesus' advantage.

John 4:27-32
27 At this point His disciples came, . . . yet no one said, "What do You seek?" or, "Why do You speak with her?"

In accordance with custom, His disciples are surprised that He is talking with a Samaritan, but we read that they were stopped from questioning Him about it. This is to say that by this time they had learned that the unexpected had a certain reasoning and usefulness in Jesus. He makes no mistakes, never takes the wrong path, never wonders which way is the correct way, never mistakenly talks to the wrong people. Hence, no one said, "What are you doing."

28 So the woman left her waterpot, and went into the city and said to the men, "Come, see a man who told me all the things that I have done; this is not the Christ, is it?" They went out of the city, and were coming to Him.

John is careful to mention that the woman leaves her waterpot behind. She is so transformed by this encounter that the task for which she came is now far out of mind and all she can think of is telling others of this man at the well. This is the spirit and unction that Christians are to have in their daily lives. We are to have such an encounter with the Master that we can think of nothing but telling others about it.

Think for a moment that you have just received a windfall of a billion dollars, free and clear. (You've won the lottery, or inherited from a relative.) How long would it take you to tell others? As time passes, would you not still be thinking of ways to weave the news of your windfall into the conversation? We find this easy to realize with respect to money or things, getting married or having children. But meeting Christ in our hearts, connecting with the Savior, gaining eternal life – these we can somehow come to regard as unexceptional, even mundane, as we continue to live our lives.

Contrast now the difference between this woman and Nicodemus. Both were given revelations about the new life. Both had extraordinary aspects to their meeting with Jesus. Nicodemus was sophisticated, learned and wealthy. We know nothing more of what he did with his encounter with Jesus, except that he appears again to help with His burial. But the woman at the well is of no account socially, most likely shunned and ostracized (albeit of her own doing.) Yet her transformation is noted in Scripture; along with the fruit of it. The people of the city were coming out to Him. This helps us understand why Jesus came not to the nobles and the rich, but to the lowly. That is where the fruit was to be found.

32 "I have food to eat that you do not know about." . . "My food is to do the will of Him who sent Me and to accomplish His work.

The disciples are reminded that it is considerably past the noontime meal and He has not eaten. Unlike many of us who faint at the thought of going long without our lunch, Jesus had no critical concerns about taking or missing a meal. His food was the work of the Father. We marvel that He could be this absorbed in fulfilling that work, that physical needs were secondary.

Most of us have had those moments when we are so excited about a project and we're enjoying the work so much that time flies and we suddenly realize that our missed lunch was three hours ago. We truly did not notice.

The Meaning of Disciple

A disciple in ancient times was similar to what we find in the account of Socrates and his students. Men sat at the feet of their teacher and then adopted his way of life, his philosophy, making his things their own. Such was Plato, who is more famous than Socrates.

In the ministry of Jesus, his disciples were to do the same. It was a choice to take on His teaching and way of looking at the world and things above, and to adopt His manner of ministry and life. If we likewise desire to be His disciples, we may question the necessity of donning a cloak and sandals, but we cannot be fuzzy about making His teaching and purpose our own. The Son's mission to mankind was to do the will of His Father.

Later we hear Jesus say, *"I am doing those things I see the Father doing."* (John 5:19.) This must also be the mission of those who choose to follow Him. This means at the very least we must first know what the Father is doing, that we may emulate Him. That's a hard one for many people. It takes discernment in the spiritual plane, and many folks have difficulty just discerning things in the earthly plane. It is something all Christians need to cultivate. It will not come by magic. We need to exercise this ability just as the disciples of Socrates set out on a course of exercising their understanding of his philosophy and mode of speech. The disciples of Jesus came to be called "little Christs" which is what *christianos* means. They got that designation because people heard them and saw them doing the same things that Christ had done.

John 4:35-38
35 "Do you not say, `There are yet four months, and then comes the harvest'? Behold, I say to you, lift up your eyes and look on the fields, that they are white for harvest.

Jesus is asking them to use the powers of reasoning that God gave them and to combine this with the spiritual enlightening they are receiving from God as they walk with Him. On the earthly plane they can tell when harvest is nigh because they see the tell-tale signs. If they use spiritual sight, they will realize that the harvest of human souls in not merely close to its time, but the time has come. The fields are white for harvest. The spiritual insight needed to see this was the knowledge that men everywhere were more than ready to hear the good news of Christ's Gospel. All that was needed was someone to go, for someone to begin speaking. Does this mean every person was ready? We know the answer is no because of those who resisted Him and put Him to death. But it did mean that there were sufficient who were ripe and ready for harvest, and these would become the Church waiting to be born.

It is possible that Jesus in fact pointed toward the crowds of those now coming out to see Him. *"See the fields white for the harvest"* Whether every man ready to believe or not, there were those among them who would, and these were enough to be seen as a harvest ready for reaping.

36 "he who reaps is receiving wages . . fruit for life eternal . . he who sows and he who reaps may rejoice together. . . 37 "'. . One sows and another reaps.'"

Notice what constitutes the fruit for life eternal. It is the souls of those who are harvested. When we ask what materials are building the Kingdom of Heaven, we find that it is being built with the souls of people. They are the building blocks. The streets of gold and the River of Life have no meaning if no one lives there. That this reaping is already occurring is meant to apply to their own work with Jesus. The quotation *One sows and another reaps"* is not a scriptural quotation but an adage from the simple observance of life.

38 "I sent you to reap that for which you have not labored; others have labored and you have entered into their labor."

The point about one sowing and another reaping is explained in respect to their own context. They are collecting the harvest but they did not labor to plant it. They are reaping what someone going before them sowed. This is somewhat obscure because we don't see others in the OT sowing work that is similar to that of Jesus. We also have as a predecessor the four hundred years of the inter-testimental period, for which we have no Scriptural information at all.

But we can see the nature of that work in the ministry of John the Baptist. At the very least we have recognizable, preparatory work in him that paved the way for the harvest of Jesus and His disciples. In earlier times of the OT period, the prophets spoke to the remnant of Judah and we can easily believe that had Jesus come then, there would likewise in those times have been an audience ready to hear Him and receive Him.

In our own application, we are to see ourselves as co-laborers with other Christians. We will seldom if ever be the whole show in any one person's life. We will simply be one of many who contribute to the salvation of that one soul. And it is to this teaching that Paul addresses his dissertation about the body with many members (I Corinthians chapters 12-14.)

John 4:39-54, Luke 4:14-20, Luke 4 14-30

39 From that city many of the Samaritans believed in Him because of the word of the woman who testified, "He told me all the things that I have done." 40 So when the Samaritans came to Jesus, they were asking Him to stay with them; and He stayed there two days. 41 Many more believed because of His word; 42 and they were saying to the woman, "It is no longer because of what you said that we believe, for we have heard for ourselves and know that this One is indeed the Savior of the world."

43 After the two days He went forth from there into Galilee. 44 For Jesus Himself testified that a prophet has no honor in his own country. 45 So when He came to Galilee, the Galileans received Him, having seen all the things that He did in Jerusalem at the feast; for they themselves also went to the feast.

46 Therefore He came again to Cana of Galilee where He had made the water wine. And there was a royal official whose son was sick at Capernaum. 47 When he heard that Jesus had come out of Judea into Galilee, he went to Him and was imploring Him to come down and heal his son; for he was at the point of death. 48 So Jesus said to him, "Unless you people see signs and wonders, you simply will not believe."

49 The royal official said to Him, "Sir, come down before my child dies." 50 Jesus said to him, "Go; your son lives." The man believed the word that Jesus spoke to him and started off. 51 As he was now going down, his slaves met him, saying that his son was living. 52 So he inquired of them the hour when he began to get better. Then they said to him, "Yesterday at the seventh hour the fever left him." 53 So the father knew that it was at that hour in which Jesus said to him, "Your son lives"; and he himself believed and his whole household. 54 This is again a second sign that Jesus performed when He had come out of Judea into Galilee. (John 4:39-54)

14 And Jesus returned to Galilee in the power of the Spirit, and news about Him spread through all the surrounding district. 15 And He began teaching in their synagogues and was praised by all. 16 And He came to Nazareth, where He had been brought up; and as was His custom, He entered the synagogue on the Sabbath, and stood up to read. 17 And the book of the prophet Isaiah was handed to Him. And He opened the book and found the place where it was written, 18 "THE SPIRIT OF THE LORD IS UPON ME, BECAUSE HE ANOINTED ME TO PREACH THE GOSPEL TO THE POOR. HE HAS SENT ME TO PROCLAIM RELEASE TO THE CAPTIVES, AND RECOVERY OF SIGHT TO THE BLIND, TO SET FREE THOSE WHO ARE OPPRESSED, 19 TO PROCLAIM THE FAVORABLE YEAR OF THE LORD." 20 And He closed the book, gave it back to the attendant and sat down; and the eyes of all in the synagogue were fixed on Him. (Luke 4:14-20)

21 And He began to say to them, "Today this Scripture has been fulfilled in your hearing." 22 And all were speaking well of Him, and wondering at the gracious words which were falling from His lips; and they were saying, "Is this not Joseph's son?"

23 And He said to them, "No doubt you will quote this proverb to Me, `Physician, heal yourself! Whatever we heard was done at Capernaum, do here in your hometown as well.' " 24 And He said, "Truly I say to you, no prophet is welcome in his hometown. 25 "But I say to you in truth, there were many widows in Israel in the days of Elijah, when the sky was shut up for three years and six months, when a great famine came over all the land; 26 and yet Elijah was sent to none of them, but only to Zarephath, in the land of Sidon, to a woman who was a widow. 27 "And there were many lepers in Israel in the time of Elisha the prophet; and none of them was cleansed, but only Naaman the Syrian." 28 And all the people in the synagogue were filled with rage as they heard these things; 29 and they got up and drove Him out of the city, and led Him to the brow of the hill on which their city had been built, in order to throw Him down the cliff. 30 But passing through their midst, He went His way. (Luke 4 14-30)

Commentary

John 4:39-45
39 .. many of the Samaritans believed ... because of the word of the woman ... were asking Him to stay .. 42 "It is no longer because of what you said that we believe, for we have heard for ourselves and know that this One is indeed the Savior of the world."

Notice the success of this witness. We see the kind of profound change that comes from a transformed life. This is real power in the spoken word. This is genuine transformation by the Spirit, the kind of change we long to see today. The key is not in practiced, fancy words, well-prepared ahead of time, but in knowing what the Spirit is doing and responding to it. The difference between success and merely mediocre results is in knowing the right things to say and how to convey them. This does not come by practicing sound bites. It comes by listening and discerning the Spirit's voice as we encounter another person needing Christ.

Jesus remains in Sychar for two days because they compelled him to do so. A simple conversation at the well had resulted in the conversion of a whole town. And we must note that they are not riding on the coat tails of the woman's experience. It is not like the visions and holy sightings, where one person experiences and everyone else wraps their faith around the place and the witness.[17] The people themselves have now affirmed the things of God having heard the wonders of them personally.

43 After the two days He went . . into Galilee. . . 44 a prophet has no honor in his own country. . 45 . .the Galileans received Him, having seen all the things that He did in Jerusalem at the feast

Jesus now continues the journey he began – to go into Galilee. The citizens there welcomed Him, having heard and seen what He did at the feast. The feast here means the Passover where He had cleansed the Temple. Many of those who were at that scene are now back in Galilee and have heard he is coming. But in the midst of this journey, Jesus explains that a prophet is without honor in his own country.

His own country could mean the whole land, Galilee and Judaea. But we see here that He is welcomed in many places in the Galilee. This is then a reference to what is about to take place in Nazareth, his home town.

John 4:46-54
46 He came again to Cana . . there was a royal official whose son was sick at Capernaum. . . . 47 he went to Him and was imploring Him to come down and heal his son . . 48 "Unless you people see signs and wonders, you simply will not believe." . . 50 "Go; your son lives." . . 51 As he was now going down, his slaves met him, saying that his son was living. . . 53 the father knew that it was at that hour in which Jesus said . . . 54 This is again a second sign that Jesus performed when He had come out of Judea into Galilee.

Jesus stops at Cana instead of going to Nazareth first, as was the case on His last trip. An official had come from Capernaum about his son, which, ironically, will actually be Jesus' resting place in this excursion into the region. But this man has no knowledge of that and his son's condition makes the meeting with Jesus urgent.

"Unless you people see signs and wonders . ."

This seems a very rough answer to someone in such need. We see all the evidence of his faith in Jesus to do what he asks. He has also come in person rather than sending servants, leaving his son in the care of others, not knowing even if he still lived. Why would Jesus characterize his plea as among those who seek signs and wonders in order to believe? Several commentaries suggest that Jesus was not unbraiding him about what he demonstrated in his faith, but in what he lacked. Jesus perceived the "manner" in which this man expected the miracle to be performed and this placed him among those who look for some sign that a miracle will be performed.

---

[17] Catholic miracles of Mary's appearance at Lourdes, France (1858); Fatima, Portugal (1917)

The man expected Jesus to return with him to Capernaum and there perform some visible mannerism, some sign or supernatural work that would give him the added faith that his son would be made well, even if only to be there and lay on hands. This is very subtle for us to comprehend because the man obviously had faith that Jesus could heal. But to some degree the proof was not yet in the pudding, and the man needed Jesus to be present in his home that this level of faith would be made complete.

This was a pattern of expectation among lesser divines. They would speak incantations, raise hands and shake, quaver the voice and do other signs designed more to impress than to heal. Hence, Jesus, in the man's mind, must come and do His thing. That was the key to the man's assurance.

Now this alone was not such a grave mis-step of faith. The man was exercising what he normally expected based on experience. But Jesus was, in fact, using this instance to also introduce something extraordinary, not only for this man to see but for all those watching. He would heal this man from a distance, never seeing him or touching him in person.

This is the element in the man's faith that was lacking, which Jesus wished to expand in him. It was also the kind of faith He wanted all of God's people to begin believing and using. The faith to heal by word alone.

"Go, your son lives."

We don't know how reluctantly the man may have moved next, whether his face was mixed with expressions half of faith, half of wonder or even some disbelief. But he did leave for home and encountered his servants with the news. The connection of the times - the hour between 1:00 and 2:00 PM - might be seen as a sign which bolstered his faith, but it was not of the same class as those things Jesus decried. The sign given the father was a validation after the miracle, not the kind of sign sought before a miracle that men might have a reason to believe.

Luke 4:14-16
14 And Jesus returned to Galilee in the power of the Spirit, . . . 15 And He began teaching in their synagogues . . . 16 And He came to Nazareth, where He had been brought up; and as was His custom,

The repetition here is to emphasize that Jesus was moving and directed by the Spirit. He is therefore precisely where He ought to be at all times. That the power of the Spirit is mentioned is key because it means that the Son has suspended the use of His own powers while in the flesh so that when and where He must act with power He meets the Spirit who joins Him and empowers Him. He is not, as in human operations, out doing His own work and expecting the Spirit to be called when needed. They are working in concert, hence, power is dispensed in the right place at the right time.

As He moves E from Cana, news of Him spreads and He is attracting crowds along the way. We must be careful in assuming that all such people are becoming His followers or "Christians" in the NT sense of the word. Many are merely curious as to what He might do. To be sure, He and His disciples are making genuine followers along the way, but the proof of how many remain and how many fall back into the woodwork of their daily lives is to be seen later.

"teaching in their synogogues"

The synagogue system is not seen in the closing pages of the OT. It simple appears in place and well established as we open the gospels. The synagogue was a place of spiritual learning and worship, but not a place of formal offerings and compliance with the feasts. Jews everywhere were expected to make the journey to Jerusalem at the appointed times; and for other offerings (Mary bringing the sin offering after the birth of Jesus.)

This necessarily brings up the case of Jews too far away to make such a journey. It is to some degree considered part of their 6th century punishment that they had been dispersed such that they could not participate in the Temple ordinances. Jewish leaders of the times and historians in our own times explain this variously as a case of making the best of one's limitations. There was no temple in Rome, Macedonia or Asia Minor that those Jews of the diaspora might use. According to strict OT ordinances they were not being compliant in their distant homes. (That they were in distant homes was never intended. They were there because of their sins.) The best they could do was meet in places like synagogues and continue to read and study their scriptures. And the synagogue had come to Judaea but not as an alternative to the Temple.

Jesus then arrives in Nazareth, attends the synagogue there and is given a scroll. This procedure is part of the synagogue practice. Each man in the community is given a turn to read a portion of Scripture which a leader assigns him and then he is expected to add commentary.

Luke 4:17-21
16 .. He entered the synagogue on the Sabbath, and stood up to read. 17 And the book of the prophet Isaiah was handed to Him.

This means that since He was unexpected, He was no doubt taking the place of another man whose turn it was to read that day. This often happened when guests came, as a gesture that honored them. As above, the passage is assigned to Him from the elder of the synagogue, but we will soon see this was no human coincidence.

**18 .. "THE SPIRIT OF THE LORD IS UPON ME, BECAUSE HE ANOINTED ME TO PREACH THE GOSPEL TO THE POOR. HE HAS SENT ME TO PROCLAIM RELEASE TO THE CAPTIVES, AND RECOVERY OF SIGHT TO THE BLIND, TO SET FREE THOSE WHO ARE OPPRESSED,
19 TO PROCLAIM THE FAVORABLE YEAR OF THE LORD." . . 20 And He closed the book, gave it back to the attendant and sat down;**

The reader had the privilege of selecting the precise passage from what was handed to him. Jesus chose this section from Isaiah 61:1, and we can see why. This was Messianic and everyone in the place knew it quite well. Each of these phrases – preaching to the poor, release to captives and the oppressed, healing to the blind – were taken as earmarks of Messiah, so one claiming to do these things was saying something extremely serious.

He then closes the book precisely at the juncture between the declaration of the peaceful mission of Messiah and that of His future judgment. (In our terms, between first advent prophecies and those judgmental aspects of His Second Coming.) The place stopped was just before: *"And the day of vengeance of our God;"* Everyone was now ready for His commentary.

20 .. and the eyes of all in the synagogue were fixed on Him.

To those listening, the passage was taken as a whole and not split up (they knew of no first and second comings.) So it is understandable that their keenness to listen had no expectation of the sermon about to come from the Reader. They had no doubt heard the claims about His messiahship, if only in rumor. So they were poised all the more to hear what insights (or declarations) this man would make.

21 And He began to say to them, "Today this Scripture has been fulfilled in your hearing."

This is not a statement which began with, "If you can receive it" which would mean this was merely a picture of the fulfillment. He was claiming the actual fulfillment and it was obvious He meant He Himself.

Luke 4:22-28
22 And all were speaking well of Him, and wondering at the gracious words which were falling from His lips; and they were saying, "Is this not Joseph's son?"

No doubt He said more which is not specifically recorded here because John tells us that as he was speaking they wondered at the words falling from his lips – the present participle – which meant the action was continuing into the present. We are, however, surprised that they did not rise immediately in indignation, that a man would be so bold as to claim to be their Messiah. But it should be noted that in prophecy someone was to come; and it would be a man; and such a one would make similar claims. So it was not a case of the village braggart boasting the claim.

The news of His works had preceded His arrival such that there was a delayed reaction (you did not want to be in opposition to the real Messiah, so it would be best to wait and take this further.) Jesus, however, gives them cause in his next words.

23 ". . you will quote this proverb to Me, `Physician, heal yourself! . . . do here in your hometown as well.' " 24 And He said, "Truly I say to you, no prophet is welcome in his hometown.

Much of our understanding of this upbraiding must come from our confidence that Jesus was reading their hearts. To cry to the physician to heal himself usually meant to care for your own family as well as you serve others. So Nazareth was calling for Him to do the same things done from Cana and effected in Capernaum (the man with the son.)

But it is not the desire for healing but the spirit in which it is being requested. His is virtually being ordered. The offense is that Jesus was there to offer new life, that they become citizens of the Kingdom He is announcing; and they see Him merely as a magician who can fix their many problems. They have not as yet treated Him as unwelcome at this juncture, though He repeats the saying, a prophet is not welcome in his hometown. This is, rather, an anticipation of what is about to happen.

25 " many widows in Israel in the days of Elijah . . . 26 yet Elijah was sent to none of them, but . . . Zarephath, . . 27 many lepers in Israel . . . and none of them was cleansed, but only Naaman . . " 28 And all the people in the synagogue were filled with rage as they heard these thin

This was to them an insult in that He was identifying them with those unworthy of healing in the times of Elijah and Elisha. The lesson which they knew from the OT was that these were passed over because they lacked the faith needed. What was interfering with their faith in Him was their knowledge of His life in Nazareth. "Is this not Joseph's son?" It is one of the voices in the mix of praise and doubt that says, "We know you, and you come to us as Messiah?"

But note the transition. *All* the people rose up in rage. How easy it was to move from compliments and praise to words of anger. The mettle of their faith is now seen for what it was. There is an adage that remains today, "Familiarity breeds contempt" and it applied here in Nazareth as well as it does today.

Luke 4:29
29 . . and they got up and drove Him out of the city, and led Him to the brow of the hill . . in order to throw Him down the cliff. But passing through their midst, He went His way.

Nazareth is built on a significant rise above the plain and on one side of this promontory there still exists a very sharp drop to the surrounding countryside. So, the movement of the crowd would not require carrying Him in custody up some distant hill where He could be thrown off. The escarpment was very near at hand. (*"out of the city"* does not here mean some distance – the town was extremely small. So this would be but a few minutes away at best.)

But again, Jesus is on a divinely appointed plan and nothing man or the devil might try to do could alter it. How He escaped is not told, and we are amazed because all had their eyes fixed on him and would certainly see or feel any physical attempt to do this (they didn't all walk casually over to the cliff, but had Him well in hand.) This is certainly a case of supernatural power, being in their grasp one minute and nowhere to be found the next.

This is the first case of what we might ineptly term failure on Jesus' part. He certainly left with nothing accomplished, save the revelation about the passage from Isaiah. His good witness and works had born the fruit of hatred and violence. But failure is only appreciable where there is an expectation of success. As for Nazareth, there clearly was none. Jesus had long before predicting the outcome to His disciples.

CHAPTER 5
His Galilean Ministry

Luke 3:19,20, Matthew 4:12-22, Luke 5:1-11
19 But when Herod the tetrarch was reprimanded by [John] because of Herodias, his brother's wife, and because of all the wicked things which Herod had done, 20 Herod also added this to them all: he locked John up in prison. (Luke 3:19,20)

12 Now when Jesus heard that John had been taken into custody, He withdrew into Galilee; 13 and leaving Nazareth, He came and settled in Capernaum, which is by the sea, in the region of Zebulun and Naphtali. 14 This was to fulfill what was spoken through Isaiah the prophet: 15 "THE LAND OF ZEBULUN AND THE LAND OF NAPHTALI, BY THE WAY OF THE SEA, BEYOND THE JORDAN, GALILEE OF THE GENTILES -- 16 "THE PEOPLE WHO WERE SITTING IN DARKNESS SAW A GREAT LIGHT, AND THOSE WHO WERE SITTING IN THE LAND AND SHADOW OF DEATH, UPON THEM A LIGHT DAWNED." 17 From that time Jesus began to preach and say, "Repent, for the kingdom of heaven is at hand."

18 Now as Jesus was walking by the Sea of Galilee, He saw two brothers, Simon who was called Peter, and Andrew his brother, casting a net into the sea; for they were fishermen. 19 And He said to them, "Follow Me, and I will make you fishers of men." 20 Immediately they left their nets and followed Him. 21 Going on from there He saw two other brothers, James the son of Zebedee, and John his brother, in the boat with Zebedee their father, mending their nets; and He called them. 22 Immediately they left the boat and their father, and followed Him. (Matthew 4:12-22)

1 Now it happened that while the crowd was pressing around Him and listening to the word of God, He was standing by the lake of Gennesaret; 2 and He saw two boats lying at the edge of the lake; but the fishermen had gotten out of them and were washing their nets. 3 And He got into one of the boats, which was Simon's, and asked him to put out a little way from the land. And He sat down and began teaching the people from the boat.

4 When He had finished speaking, He said to Simon, "Put out into the deep water and let down your nets for a catch." 5 Simon answered and said, "Master, we worked hard all night and caught nothing, but I will do as You say and let down the nets." 6 When they had done this, they enclosed a great quantity of fish, and their nets began to break; 7 so they signaled to their partners in the other boat for them to come and help them. And they came and filled both of the boats, so that they began to sink.

8 But when Simon Peter saw that, he fell down at Jesus' feet, saying, "Go away from me Lord, for I am a sinful man, O Lord!" 9 For amazement had seized him and all his companions because of the catch of fish which they had taken; 10 and so also were James and John, sons of Zebedee, who were partners with Simon.

And Jesus said to Simon, "Do not fear, from now on you will be catching men." 11 When they had brought their boats to land, they left everything and followed Him. (Luke 5:1-11)

Commentary

Luke 3:19
19 But when Herod the tetrarch was reprimanded by [John] because of Herodias . . he locked John up in prison.

We return briefly to the closing events in John the Baptist's ministry.

The Herod here is Antipas, whose realm was Galilee. He lived in Jerusalem but had palaces and fortresses in other locations. Josephus tells us that John was put into the prison at Machaerus on the E side of the Dead Sea. Machaerus was one of three fortresses built by Herod the Great, Masada and the Herodium being the other two. *(For more on tetrarchies, see above at Luke 3:1-6)*

Herodias had been married to Philip, Antipas' brother, when she left him for Antipas. She lived with him at first, but they eventually married. The Herods often emulated the patterns of the Roman nobility, who routinely forced people to divorce so they could form new unions. (Tiberius was forced by Augustus to divorce his first wife Vipsania and marry the emperor's daughter Julia.)[18] The Herods took this as license to do likewise in satisfying their own ambitions and desires.

John, as mentioned earlier, was a humble man, but rather bold in his preaching, and careless about his own life in the interest of saying the truth. We do not see the direct excoriation of Herod in John's preaching as shown in the NT. It may have been in response to questions from the Herodians in general at the Jordan, or it may have been in sermons that decried the times and the condition of Israel under its oppressors.

John accuses the tetrarch of adultery in unlawfully putting away his former wife and stealing away that of his brother's, for lust. But the apostle states here that the Baptist reprimanded Antipas for other deeds he had done. This was of course actionable speech, so it was only a matter of time that he was arrested. John was kept here for some time, as a sort of curiosity. We derive this conclusion from Herod being reluctant to put him to death.

Matthew 4:12-16
12 When Jesus heard that John had been taken into custody, He withdrew into Galilee; 13 and leaving Nazareth, He came and settled in Capernaum, which is by the sea, in the region of Zebulun and Naphtali. 14 This was to fulfill what was spoken through Isaiah the prophet:

Again, Jesus was not running for fear, but avoiding the untimely precipitation of events that would upset the time table He was faithfully keeping.

"withdrew into Galilee" - Wasn't he already in Galilee by being in Nazareth? He was indeed. But this reference is not to the region, but to the sea itself, specifically the town of Capernaum on its N shore.

15 "THE LAND OF ZEBULUN AND THE LAND OF NAPHTALI, BY THE WAY OF THE SEA, BEYOND THE JORDAN, GALILEE OF THE GENTILES –

The mention of Zebulun and Naphtali is critical because it here fulfills a prophecy. (Zebulun and Naphtali were sons of Jacob and therefore tribes of Israel.) As northern tribes, they had been long since taken off the land (8th century) and had intermingled with other Near Eastern nations. The area mentioned was predominantly Gentile because these cities and the area around the Sea of Galilee came to be populated with Gentiles due to the area being a key passageway for journeys between the Mediterranean and the East, between northern kingdoms and Egypt.

16 "THE PEOPLE WHO WERE SITTING IN DARKNESS SAW A GREAT LIGHT, AND THOSE WHO WERE SITTING IN THE LAND AND SHADOW OF DEATH, UPON THEM A LIGHT DAWNED."

Israel from of old was encouraged to be a light unto all nations. The covenant of Genesis 12:3 promised Abraham that all the nations of the earth were to be blessed by his offspring. But Israel had neglected this by cloistering themselves within their land and even despising the Gentile with many ordinances regarding defilement. They made provision that Gentiles could come to Jerusalem (they even had a court of the Gentiles in the Temple) but they did not generally evangelize. Isaiah was prophesying that this promise to Abraham was still standing and would be eventually accomplished.

The fulfillment is now accomplished here in Jesus who was now walking in the Galilee of the Nations, among those in need of light, and essentially completing what Israel had left undone for centuries.

---

[18] Suetonius, Lives of the Twelve Caesars, Loeb Classics, Harvard Press, London (1951), p. 303

Matthew 4:17-19
17 From that time Jesus began to preach and say, "Repent, for the kingdom of heaven is at hand."

This is John's preparatory message and Jesus picks it up also. This is not because He owes this to John, but because both men were caught up in what God was now doing. He was inaugurating the Kingdom of God as now being present and at hand.

We cannot minimize this emphasis or rationalize it into just another term for the new life of God in the hearts of men. The Kingdom here means the one Daniel prophesied – the Kingdom that was to come and crush all those preceding it. This means that in this announcement, something linked to Daniel is meant. We are confused by this because we do not see Jesus accomplishing any of this in His first advent. He also deliberately closed the book of Isaiah so as to highlight His peaceful mission only.

But this does not undermine His offer of the Kingdom to the Jews as their Messiah in accordance with Daniel. The offer is not verbalized, except in the simple presentation of Him as their Messiah. The Kingdom is being offered in the act of offering Himself as their King. They must accept Him as King for the Kingdom to become physical fact. This they reject. And the result is that the political and physical aspects of this Kingdom are postponed to His Second Coming. You will note that Jesus leaves off preaching about the Kingdom of Heaven being at hand when opposition to His offer is entrenched beyond hope.

18 Now as Jesus was walking by the Sea of Galilee, He saw two brothers, Simon . . and Andrew his brother . . 19 "Follow Me, and I will make you fishers of men."

This seems a bit disjointed since Simon and Andrew have been traveling with Jesus since their meeting back in Perea where Jesus also picked up Philip and Nathaniel. Some time has transpired after Jesus' arrival in Capernaum. Matthew's Gospel is an independent account, so he introduces Simon and Andrew in this manner. But as we have seen, John's account shows clearly that this was not their first meeting with Him.

Simon, now being in Capernaum, has had time to return to his fishing trade, and Andrew is with him, having left behind his period with the Baptist.

"Follow Me"- Again, we are puzzled at this calling so late in the order of events, since they had been following Him from Perea to Galilee, then to Jerusalem, to Sychar, and again into Galilee. This is not explained merely by Matthew's account being separate from John's, because it is a quote of Jesus that must be coordinated with the information in John's gospel.

Jesus is here calling them away from their trade for permanent, full-time ministry. As to the contradiction of having already "followed" up to this point, they were essentially on a brief diversion with Him, but had by no means abandoned their trades or made arrangements to transfer their duties permanently to someone else. (Simon is said to be from Bethsaida, but he had boats also in Capernaum.)

"fishers of men"- Jesus chooses a figure with which they can all relate. We can't press the analogy too far. They are not to catch men for food - there is no parallel here to ensnaring prey. But they will cast their nets, and they will learn its related "trade." But the catch will be men not fish.

But even here, they did not immediately follow. Perhaps some additional time was needed to make arrangements. We conclude this because there is another call to follow a bit later which states that they immediately did so; and there is the intervening event we see next of Jesus teaching from Simon's boat and the miraculous draught of fish.

Luke 5:1-11
1 Now it happened that while the crowd was pressing around Him . . 3 He got into one of the boats, which was Simon's, and asked him to put out a little way from the land. And He sat down and began teaching the people from the boat.

Gennesaret is another name for the Sea of Galilee. "Now it happened that" is a phrase that introduces the element of a time gap. Some unknown interval has transpired from his calling the disciples and the events that follow here. While Jesus continued to teach in and around the shoreline, his notoriety was so widespread that he had become the focus of anyone needing miracles and healing.

"the crowd was pressing around Him."

We have to keep in mind that people were largely without any health care. They were wholly deprived of the kinds of treatment and medications we have today. Ailments went largely untreated. People suffered immeasurably from things we normally treat off the shelf at a drug store. So when someone came along who could cure by his touch, the crowds weren't merely exuberant welcoming committees, but terribly desperate people fierce to touch Him in the hope of transferring to themselves some lasting relief from all their miseries.

To extricate Himself from them, Jesus asks Simon to take Him out in his boat. Luke mentions that the fishermen had gotten out and were mending their nets. Whether Simon was still among them or these were the men who were now working Simon's trade on his behalf, Simon himself takes personal command of his boat and rows Jesus out just enough to quiet the people and permit an atmosphere of teaching.

4 . . "Put out into the deep water and let down your nets for a catch." . . 5 "Master, we worked hard all night and caught nothing . . 6 they enclosed a great quantity of fish, . . .8 "Go away from me Lord, for I am a sinful man, O Lord!" For amazement had seized him and all his companions . . .10 and so also were James and John, sons of Zebedee, who were partners with Simon.

After the teaching, Jesus bids them go out for a catch (the other disciples were obviously present.) This was not a matter of exercising their trade but to teach them more about who He was.

The miraculous draught had a profound and humbling effect on Simon. *"Go away from me Lord, for I am a sinful man.* In the presence of someone with this much power, Simon came abruptly face to face with his own unworthiness. It was an overwhelming awareness of who Jesus was and that he did not deserve to be in His presence. As Christians we can easily relate. If Jesus were to appear in our homes, we would be instantly reminded of how we have lived our lives, the sins in which we now stumble and our unworthiness before our Lord and Savior.

Simon cannot bear the gaze of his Lord, for he knows himself, his attitudes and his own sins. We also have here the introduction of James and John, the sons of Zebedee. So the party of the disciples numbers six: Simon, Andrew, Philip, Nathaniel, James and John.

10 . . And Jesus said to Simon, "Do not fear, from now on you will be catching men." When they had brought their boats to land, they left everything and followed Him.

That they immediately left their nets has rational sense only if they were prepared and ready to do so. This can only mean prior contact with Jesus, prior preparation that there would be such a call. The notion that many have held in ignorance – that at their first encountering of Jesus they abruptly abandoned their whole livelihood and followed him - is against common sense. This then is their effective call to ministry, the one that sets them permanently on a new road.

Mark 1:21-38
21 They went into Capernaum; and immediately on the Sabbath He entered the synagogue and began to teach. 22 They were amazed at His teaching; for He was teaching them as one having authority, and not as the scribes.

23 Just then there was a man in their synagogue with an unclean spirit; and he cried out, 24 saying, "What business do we have with each other, Jesus of Nazareth? Have You come to destroy us? I know who You are--the Holy One of God!" 25 And Jesus rebuked him, saying, "Be quiet, and come out of him!" 26 Throwing him into convulsions, the unclean spirit cried out with a loud voice and came out of him. 27 They were all amazed, so that they debated among themselves, saying, "What is this? A new teaching with authority! He commands even the unclean spirits, and they obey Him."

28 Immediately the news about Him spread everywhere into all the surrounding district of Galilee. 29 And immediately after they came out of the synagogue, they came into the house of Simon and Andrew, with James and John. 30 Now Simon's mother-in-law was lying sick with a fever; and immediately they spoke to Jesus about her. 31 And He came to her and raised her up, taking her by the hand, and the fever left her, and she waited on them.

32 When evening came, after the sun had set, they began bringing to Him all who were ill and those who were demon-possessed. 33 And the whole city had gathered at the door. 34 And He healed many who were ill with various diseases, and cast out many demons; and He was not permitting the demons to speak, because they knew who He was.

35 In the early morning, while it was still dark, Jesus got up, left the house, and went away to a secluded place, and was praying there. 36 Simon and his companions searched for Him; 37 they found Him, and said to Him, "Everyone is looking for You." 38 He said to them, "Let us go somewhere else to the towns nearby, so that I may preach there also; for that is what I came for." (Mark 1:21-38)

Commentary

Mark 1:21-22
21 They went into Capernaum; and immediately on the Sabbath He entered the synagogue and began to teach. 22 They were amazed at His teaching; for He was teaching them as one having authority, and not as the scribes.

We must remember that the only places of worship were Jewish, and since Jesus would challenge the Judaism that prevailed it seems strange that He had a welcome in the synagogue. But this is Jesus' year of favor. He is appreciated for His wisdom. He also has yet to confront the Pharisees of Jerusalem.

But what is important is that Jesus did not begin a competitive movement outside Judaism. He began by working within its structure, honoring the essential goodness of its provisions in Scripture but enlarging the originally intended meaning which at this point had been distorted by the ever-increasing architecture of the priesthood and leading authorities. We will see an example of this wisdom as to the original intent of God later in His teaching about divorce. To the technicality of the Law He adds wisdom - *"But from the beginning it was not so."* - and proceeds to explain the heart of God in giving the Law as it was.

"not as the scribes"

Two things are to be observed. First, the scribes did not teach like Jesus was teaching. Second, the people knew its nature well enough that all John had to say was *not as the scribes.* What is puzzling at first is that there is set up here a supposed contrast - Jesus with authority, the scribes without authority.

But this seems contradictory because the scribes were in fact the recognized authority in the Scriptures. It was the scribes who knew the passage in Micah to inform Herod that Christ would be born in Bethlehem. But this comparison is more about the kind of authority perceived between the two, not a case of one having it and the others not having it. The scribes accrued to themselves authority by virtue of the rather wooden memorization of the Bible and their role as walking concordances of Scripture. They knew the Scripture by rote, and this made for an authority without much heart or real understanding. The scribes could get you to a passage that addressed a certain subject, but they could not expound to an appreciable depth on its meaning.

This was more the role of the rabbi. But even here, rabbis would often take on the more academic posture of quoting other notable rabbis rather than interpreting the scriptures from their own inner knowledge and wisdom. (Not that this was non-existent, but the pattern was as above.) The film *Yentl* (Barwood Films, 1984) provides an excellent portrayal of scriptural study among students being trained for rabbinical service. They don't argue with their opponents by citing supporting scriptures for their views. They spend all their time citing Rabbis Ben Yosef, or Hillel, which their opponent counters by citing Rabbis Ben Ioudah, or Shimmai.

Jesus taught differently. He not only "explained" the Scripture but what was behind the Scripture. He proved his interpretations using Scripture to interpret Scripture. But the key was His insight into the meaning. And this lent to His audience sensing that He knew what He was talking about. The scribes seldom went out on limbs to claim they knew the true meaning of anything.

Mark 1:23-27
23 .. there was a man in their synagogue with an unclean spirit; . . .24 "What business do we have with each other, Jesus of Nazareth? Have You come to destroy us? I know who You are--the Holy One of God!"

The verse doesn't mention more than one spirit, which seems contradictory to the use of the third person plural. But this coincides with the idea that demonic spirits are in league with each other and often speak as a collective. We see this again in Mark 5 where we hear the unclean spirit reply *"my name is Legion, for we are many."* What is interesting here is that these spirits know who Jesus is. The people could not ignore the vindication of authority this conveyed to Jesus Himself. Full-fledged demons were acknowledging His ability to destroy them. If there were some who still entertained doubts, this bizarre interjection from the realm of evil had to have made every person present a believer.

There is little to be found in messianic prophesies that deals with Messiah's command over demons. So the demons' fear of destruction alone would not necessarily have bolstered the people's faith in Him as Messiah, per se. But they say more.

They continue by saying that they know who He is – *"the Holy One of God."* This is by no means a simple generic phrase for someone blessed of God. It is a clear messianic title, known in Judaism to apply to Messiah. What is ironic here is that demons had no problem acknowledging this, but the people of God would, to the extent that they "crucified the Lord of Glory."

25 "Be quiet, and come out of him!"

Notice the lack of long-winded incantations. These are simple, straightforward words. The demons were in the man. The command was simply that they come out. These are not magic words that man must now take as a formula to speak precisely as Jesus spoke. The words only had power because of the One speaking them, not the other way 'round. For those in ministry today, gifted with the ability to cast out demons, it is the authority imbued from God, not the words spoken. We are to be agents of God, not magicians.

Notice the following reaction from the people. The focus was on His authority not His power.

27 . . "What is this? A new teaching with authority! He commands even the unclean spirits, and they obey Him."

We're bound to pay attention to the words of a man who can command this kind of power because it requires real authority over such things and that authority then extends to all other things. What is important here for all believers is that we are not in precarious dread of some day coming up against demons with whom we must fend for ourselves. With faith in Christ we gain the protection of His authority over the demonic world, such that they must obey His authority and power.

Mark 1:28-31
28 And immediately after they came out of the synagogue, they came into the house of Simon and Andrew, with James and John. 30 Now Simon's mother-in-law was lying sick with a fever; and immediately they spoke to Jesus about her.

The house of Simon and Andrew was near the synagogue. That Simon's mother-in-law was in his home was almost un-noteworthy to John's readers. It is less likely that the mother was there merely because she was sick. But more likely she had come to live with them in her senior years, which was customary and without the sense of inconvenience we perceive today in the disconnected families of modern times.

That Simon was married, being the future progenitor of the Church's celibate popes, is not really a major problem for Catholics, in that the administration of the Church is viewed as a living thing that continues to be informed by revelation. Hence, Peter can have been married, but the Lord can also later make the priesthood and the Papacy a celibate office. Protestants have no need to explain the above because they reject the normative Tradition of the Catholic Church beyond the Bible. And in Scripture they see no call to celibacy for priests and popes.

What is compassionate about this event is that Jesus did not exclude his disciples from the working of His grace and power. The disciples were caught up in ministering to others. But when the needs became personal, Jesus' love and grace were just as readily available to bless them also.

31 And He came to her and raised her up, taking her by the hand, and the fever left her, and she waited on them.

In the cases of Jesus healing and casting out demons, the cures were whole and complete, with nothing lacking. People did not receive partial or temporary cures but were wholly delivered. There are some faith healers today who cover their inadequacies by encouraging a sort of "follow-up" period in which the sufferer is to diligently "claim" their healing despite what are termed "tricks of the devil." The fault for not being completely healed is therefore now with the believer not the healer. (Even in the gift of medicine, which is wonderful and praiseworthy, everyone has experienced that recovery is a slow process. We often need rest to recover fully from medical treatments and sometimes repeated treatments.)

But this is not what we find in the work of Jesus. We see here that not only was the mother made well, but no resting period was needed to recover from her ordeal. She was ready to get up and serve in the amenities of drink and food, so much so that it was hard to imagine that just moments ago she was incapacitated in her sufferings.

Mark 1:32-38
32 When evening came, after the sun had set, they began bringing to Him all who were ill and those who were demon-possessed. 34 . . and [He] cast out many demons; and . . was not permitting the demons to speak, because they knew who He was.

As earlier stated, a high percentage of activity in any town or village routinely dealt with various states of ill health. Doctors and crude hospital settings left much to be desired and sometimes left the patient worse than before. Understandably, this aspect of Jesus' healing power became the most significant reason for people flocking to Him. We see scenes today of food relief trucks being swamped by people waiting for hours or even days to get food. What has riveted their attention on a certain location is the prospect of food, nothing more. So in many of these scenes, the crowds are there predominantly to get healed.

Interestingly, here is it said that Jesus prevents them from making Him known. Yet in the synagogue this was permitted. The key factor is the degree in which a scene is private or public. The more public and mixed a crowd is, the more cautious Jesus is about tripping the wire that will turn on the authorities prematurely.

35 In the early morning, . . Jesus got up, left the house, and went away to a secluded place, . . . 37 they found Him, and said to Him, "Everyone is looking for You." 38 He said to them, "Let us go somewhere else . . that I may preach there also; for that is what I came for."

The need for Jesus to set Himself apart is, in fact, a window into His humanity and the giving up of His immediate intimacy within the Trinity. He was made to endure the limitations of being human. This did not mean that He was deficient in the knowledge He could receive, but only that the mode of receiving it would need to change. The Son must now pray and listen with the faculties of human kind. Setting Himself apart was a necessary part of that seeking and hearing.

It was necessary to be undistracted, even from the comments and talk from his disciples. Concentration was needed to hear the voice of His Father, not because the mechanism for doing so in Him was defective or unreliable, but because as a human being He could now be distracted by so many earthly and human sources. This is also something we must take as an example to follow. Quick and efficient is the popular mode today, but it won't really do in this realm. Every believer needs some place where they can spend time alone, without distractions, to seek and listen for God's guidance and instruction. We often talk about the joy of "alone time" at a retreat, but then leave it in the mountains when we return to the scurry of normal life.

In this verse we can safely surmise that Jesus had become aware that the time had come to move on in the unfolding plan of the Father. He separated Himself to solidify His understanding of what He was sensing and to get a clear view of where He was to be next. He comes from this prayer time fully purposed. He immediately announces their need to go further into other towns, and rather abruptly so, despite the words of His disciples that there remained still more seeking Him where they presently were.

"for that is what I came for"

Knowledge is to precede judgment. The world was genuinely guilty and worthy of judgment. There were untold crimes that had long awaited final justice against their perpetrators. But Jesus came to first shed light in this darkness, that those who might would repent. So Grace in the work of the Son preceded the due penalty of divine judgment and it must have its course of mercy among men.

Matthew 4:23-25, Mark 1:40-45, Luke 5:17, Mark 2:2-12

23 Jesus was going throughout all Galilee, teaching in their synagogues and proclaiming the gospel of the kingdom, and healing every kind of disease and every kind of sickness among the people. 24 The news about Him spread throughout all Syria; and they brought to Him all who were ill, those suffering with various diseases and pains, demoniacs, epileptics, paralytics; and He healed them. 25 Large crowds followed Him from Galilee and the Decapolis and Jerusalem and Judea and from beyond the Jordan. (Matthew 4:23-25)

40 And a leper came to Jesus, beseeching Him and falling on his knees before Him, and saying, "If You are willing, You can make me clean." 41 Moved with compassion, Jesus stretched out His hand and touched him, and said to him, "I am willing; be cleansed." 42 Immediately the leprosy left him and he was cleansed. 43 And He sternly warned him and immediately sent him away, 44 and He said to him, "See that you say nothing to anyone; but go, show yourself to the priest and offer for your cleansing what Moses commanded, as a testimony to them." 45 But he went out and began to proclaim it freely and to spread the news around, to such an extent that Jesus could no longer publicly enter a city, but stayed out in unpopulated areas; and they were coming to Him from everywhere. (Mark 1:40-45)

When He had come back to Capernaum several days afterward, it was heard that He was at home. (Mark 2:1) 17 One day He was teaching; and there were some Pharisees and teachers of the law sitting there, who had come from every village of Galilee and Judea and from Jerusalem; and the power of the Lord was present for Him to perform healing. (Luke 5:17)

2 And many were gathered together, so that there was no longer room, not even near the door; and He was speaking the word to them. 3 And they came, bringing to Him a paralytic, carried by four men. 4 Being unable to get to Him because of the crowd, they removed the roof above Him; and when they had dug an opening, they let down the pallet on which the paralytic was lying. 5 And Jesus seeing their faith said to the paralytic, " Son, your sins are forgiven." 6 But some of the scribes were sitting there and reasoning in their hearts, 7 "Why does this man speak that way? He is blaspheming; who can forgive sins but God alone?" 8 Immediately Jesus, aware in His spirit that they were reasoning that way within themselves, said to them, "Why are you reasoning about these things in your hearts? 9 "Which is easier, to say to the paralytic, `Your sins are forgiven'; or to say, `Get up, and pick up your pallet and walk'? 10 "But so that you may know that the Son of Man has authority on earth to forgive sins"--He said to the paralytic, 11 "I say to you, get up, pick up your pallet and go home." 12 And he got up and immediately picked up the pallet and went out in the sight of everyone, so that they were all amazed and were glorifying God, saying, "We have never seen anything like this." (Mark 2:2-12)

Commentary

Matthew 4:23-25
23 Jesus was going throughout all Galilee, teaching . . . proclaiming the gospel of the kingdom, and healing every kind of disease . .24 news about Him spread throughout all Syria; . . 25 Large crowds followed Him from Galilee and the Decapolis and Jerusalem and Judea and from beyond the Jordan.

This is the fullest statement describing His year of popularity. He remained in Galilee, healing and teaching. And all his meetings among the people were marked by the dispensation of widespread healing. We can see Him moving among the crowds, touching hundreds in succession as He moved, not needing even to stop and listen to each request. Just touching and laying hands on person after person. That news reached all of Syria is notable because this was a large region N of Palestine. The Decapolis was the name for the ten cities across the Jordan in the area of Hippos, Pella and Gadara.

Healing of this type and magnitude is viewed by some churches as a power and gift not retained into the present age. It is part of a general view that the gifts of the Holy Spirit mentioned by Paul in I Corinthians were temporary in nature and faded out in the early centuries after the deaths of the Apostles. Yet we read of events of miraculous healing and of the other gifts in I Corinthians still today. Some churches affirm these as having never been retracted by God, others see this phenomena as a delusion among ignorant believers.

Jesus stated that His followers would do greater things than He Himself had done because He was returning to the Father. There is no time limit on this statement. In Paul, some gifts like prophecy and tongues seem to have an implication of coming to an end, but the condition is *"when the Perfect shall come,"* and this is variously understood. We may recoil from some of the approaches and styles of the tele-evangelists and their healing ministries, but amid the obvious chicanery of some there can be seen authenticated instances of divine healing. The key, as in Jesus use' of healing, is being at all times within the will of the Father.

Mark 1:40-45
40 And a leper came to Jesus, beseeching Him and falling on his knees before Him, and saying, "If You are willing, You can make me clean."

This man's request is noteworthy and we see in just a moment that Jesus was moved with compassion. The man is not merely grabbing at Jesus to get his healing. He is not shouting or demanding, as so many must have been doing.

He clearly recognizes that God is not a Person to be ordered about. He is obliged to appeal to God's Will and it is his earnest hope that God will look compassionately on his need. This is humility before one's God. And you can almost see the smile of tenderhearted compassion on Jesus' face as he hears this request.

41 Moved with compassion, Jesus stretched out His hand and touched him, and said to him, "I am willing; be cleansed." . . . 43 And He sternly warned him . . 44 "See that you say nothing . . but go . . to the priest and offer for your cleansing what Moses commanded, as a testimony to them."

We might ask why Jesus warned this man so cautiously but did not do so with the throngs of others mentioned above? As before, the key is the potential for an untimely alarm to the authorities in Jerusalem. (However, this seems contradicted in the next scene where the Pharisees are present.)

In the case of this man, he had leprosy and this required an additional procedure subsequent to the healing – that he go to the Temple and offer the required sacrifice signaling the end of his impurity. Leviticus 14:1ff *"On the eighth day he must take two unblemished male lambs, an unblemished year-old ewe lamb, a grain offering of three quarts of fine flour mixed with olive oil, and one-third of a quart of olive oil. The priest who performs the cleansing will place the person who is to be cleansed, together with these offerings, before the Lord at the entrance . ."*

45 But he went out and began to proclaim it freely . . . to such an extent that Jesus could no longer publicly enter a city, but stayed out in unpopulated areas . .

Too much can be made about an absolute strictness with which Jesus tried to avoid premature notoriety. It is obvious here that those warned did not contain themselves, and Jesus surely knew this would happen. So the criticality of doing so is not so much indicated as is His preference to do what He could to minimize it.

But notice here that the testimonies were having such an effect that in order to frustrate any potential ill-effects, He is now obliged to stay out in rural areas. This would at least give the authorities more to think about (it would take a bit more effort now to formally confront Him.) But more casual confrontations were still possible as we see next.

Luke 5:17
17 When He had come back to Capernaum . . He was teaching; and there were some Pharisees and teachers of the law . .

The Pharisees and teachers did not all live in Jerusalem. It was only a matter of time that members of this group would begin to attend his gatherings, to listen in as observers for any evidence of false teaching or procedure. This kind of pessimism was a matter of habit associated with healers and holy men who attracted crowds, primarily because there had been charlatans in the past (the 'Egyptian' of Acts 21:38), and it was the duty of the authorities to nip such nuisances in the bud.

That there were Pharisees directly from Jerusalem was to some degree ominous, since these would be most likely to have an immediate influence with the Jerusalem authorities. Again we read that the "power of the Lord" was key to His ability to perform healing. This sounds strange because we later hear Jesus say, *"All authority and power has been given to me."* But it is always the case that the wielding of authority and power are subject to the Father, and even Jesus submits to this. He does not do according to His own will but that of the Father only.

Mark 3:2-5
2 And many were gathered together, so that there was no longer room, not even near the door; and He was speaking the word to them.

We cannot begin to imagine the quality and depth of these sermons. You simply cannot have it any better than to hear truths falling from the lips of Jesus. He knew how to create an atmosphere that riveted your attention on every word. There was no dozing off in these settings. No mental diversions that anticipated that later lunch with friends.

3 And they came, bringing .. a paralytic .. unable to get to Him . . . they removed the roof above Him; .. let down the pallet on which the paralytic was lying. 5 And Jesus seeing their faith said to the paralytic, " Son, your sins are forgiven."

Jesus honored these extraordinary measures because it was a case of someone with exceptional need being deprived because of the crowds. Their ingenuity was a mark of determined faith, *"And Jesus seeing their faith.."*

But Jesus was to do more than merely heal the man. He first proclaimed his sins forgiven of God. We are not to conclude that his sins were the cause of his paralysis. In another case, Jesus raises the question of whose sins might be considered the cause of an infirmity, after which he explains they had no relation to it at all. Jesus was, in fact, introducing another amazing aspect of His coming – that He would be the key to the forgiveness of sins.

To the Pharisees present, the reaction was predictable. But we must not be unduly hard on them over their concern about blasphemy, which was truly a serious issue. Today, we would be likely to take action against a teacher who regularly blasphemed in the presence of our young children. But rather than speak out in the midst of what might prove a spectacular healing, they keep their concerns about blasphemy to themselves.

Herein was yet another opportunity for Him to demonstrate more of His powers and abilities. He hears them, despite their being discrete.

Mark 2:8-12
8 .. "Why are you reasoning about these things in your hearts?" 9 "Which is easier, to say to the paralytic, `Your sins are forgiven'; or to say, `Get up, and pick up your pallet and walk'?"

He demonstrates that He knows what they are thinking. As such, He addresses the means by which they ought to assess blasphemy. Ordinarily, blasphemy in this context would mean mere human beings pronouncing the forgiveness of sins. This is God's realm or at the very least requires the concurrence of God.

But so also does healing. There was never an example in Jewish history of someone healing of their own power. It had always signaled a person who was in touch with the power of God. But the authority to heal was precisely the same authority required to speak for God. Jesus was simply asking them to include this factor in their assessment of whether blasphemy had in fact occurred. So Jesus connected the authority to forgive with the authority to heal and then proceeded to heal the paralytic man. But Jesus said much more in this action.

10 ". . So that you may know that the Son of Man has authority on earth to forgive sins"

'Son of Man' is a technical term in Judaism for the Messiah. It was first used in the Psalms to describe the figure of Messiah, then in Daniel when he was describing the One who approached the Ancient of Days (Psalms 8:4, Daniel 7:13.)

For those listening with the intent to trap Him, He had just given them ample evidence. The difference between merely letting news of His messiahship filter up to the Pharisees and this utterance is that Jesus was here in control of how this was conveyed. He had prefaced this claim by discussing the means of telling when true authority was in play. His claim to be Messiah was connected to His authority to heal, and for this they were now divinely accountable. To anyone who was capable of conviction, this should have given them some pause (the operative word being 'capable of conviction.')

What is interesting is that Mark and the others do not continue with any consequences immediately developing from this encounter.

12 . . "We have never seen anything like this."

Paralysis was and remains today a tough order for faith healers to contemplate. It is so comprehensive and involves so many associated conditions besides nerve damage (atrophies, etc.) It was among the toughest of expectations for cure imaginable. So it is not surprising that they react with these words. But to the Master and Creator of the human body, this is no impediment; no major task for Him who created the world out of nothing.

Mark 2:13-14, Luke 5:29, Matthew 9:11-13, Luke 5:32-39

13 And He went out again by the seashore; and all the people were coming to Him, and He was teaching them. 14 As He passed by, He saw Levi the son of Alphaeus sitting in the tax booth, and He said to him, "Follow Me!" And he got up and followed Him. (Mark 2:13-14)

29 And Levi gave a big reception for Him in his house; and there was a great crowd of tax collectors and other people who were reclining at the table with them. (Luke 5:29)

11 When the Pharisees saw this, they said to His disciples, "Why is your Teacher eating with the tax collectors and sinners?" 12 But when Jesus heard this, He said, "It is not those who are healthy who need a physician, but those who are sick. 13 "But go and learn what this means: `I DESIRE COMPASSION, AND NOT SACRIFICE,' (Matthew 9:11-13)

32 "I have not come to call the righteous but sinners to repentance." 33 And they said to Him, "The disciples of John often fast and offer prayers, the disciples of the Pharisees also do the same, but Yours eat and drink." 34 And Jesus said to them, "You cannot make the attendants of the bridegroom fast while the bridegroom is with them, can you? 35 "But the days will come; and when the bridegroom is taken away from them, then they will fast in those days." 36 And He was also telling them a parable: "No one tears a piece of cloth from a new garment and puts it on an old garment; otherwise he will both tear the new, and the piece from the new will not match the old. 37 "And no one puts new wine into old wineskins; otherwise the new wine will burst the skins and it will be spilled out, and the skins will be ruined. 38 "But new wine must be put into fresh wineskins. 39 "And no one, after drinking old wine wishes for new; for he says, `The old is good enough.'" (Luke 5:32-39)

Commentary

Mark 2:13-14

13 And He went out again by the seashore; . . . 14 He saw Levi the son of Alphaeus . . . "Follow Me!" And he got up and followed Him.

On all occasions of the disciples being called, it is not the case that He came upon them out of the blue, said "Follow me," and they then dropped everything and began following Him. As with Peter and Andrew, earlier, we saw that He had prior familiarity with them and the final call was after their having gotten to know what He was about. We have no record of Jesus and Levi getting to know each other prior to this call, but the pattern has been established, and it would have been as strange back then as it would be today for someone to abruptly leave their responsibilities.

The mention of Levi as the son of Alphaeus has generated much discussion, even among the early church fathers, as did the alternate name, Matthew. This would ordinarily mean that Matthew was the brother of James, son of Alphaeus. This has been problematic because among the disciples, the gospel writers have been keen to mention men as brothers (Simon and Andrew, James and John.) Hence, some have proposed that James and Levi had different fathers with the same name.

Still others have proposed that there were two different tax collectors among Jesus' disciples – Matthew and Levi. The problem here is that this would make for thirteen apostles, not twelve, and in the lists of the apostles, Matthew only is mentioned.

Mark 2:13-14, Matthew 9:11-13
29 And Levi gave a big reception for Him in his house, behold, many tax collectors and sinners came and were dining with Jesus . . 11 "Why is your Teacher eating with the tax collectors and sinners?" . .12 "It is not those who are healthy who need a physician, but those who are sick. . .13 . . `I DESIRE COMPASSION, AND NOT SACRIFICE,' "

We learn from Mark that the house was that of Levi and that he had invited many from his class of friends. This setting is interesting because Jesus is their guest, but He implies through His analogies that those hosting Him are sinners or the sick in need of a physician.

It is a wonder that the tax collector had any friends to invite. It's reasonable he would have other tax collectors as friends. As for the others, we must assume that in the interest of having at least some friends he did not treat everyone despicably.

Reclining at table was both an eastern custom and one adopted in Greco-Roman culture. We are not to conclude that this meant lying flat on one's stomach, trying to eat. Rather, pillows and such arranged to support a reclined position but with the torso more upright to allow food to be taken down.

How the Pharisees came to be there is not stated. But it is likely they were gathered at the door or the window openings along with the crowd of onlookers. Being an observer close enough to speak to those inside was just the way of things in villages and towns. When something happened in a home, those nearby came to look, invited or not.

As noted above, the Pharisees would have been the conservatives of the day, and as such they would have shunned associations with the ungodly. To befriend such people was to neglect the responsibility to tell them they must first repent. That Jesus was known as a rabbi, He would be expected to do likewise. That their conservative position was extreme is shown by their haste in concluding that merely eating with such people condoned their lifestyles. This meant that paying attention to what Jesus was teaching would have been eclipsed by their preoccupation with outward appearances – *"Why do you eat with tax collectors and sinners?"*

Luke 5:32-33
"It is not those who are healthy . . but those who are sick. . . 32 for I did not come to call the righteous, but sinners."

Ordinarily, this would be insulting. We aren't told the reaction of each person there. It is likely that some did find this offensive. But there is no outburst recorded, no complaint verbalized about Jesus' comments. There are a couple of reasons why this occurred as it did.

First, in the ancient world there was among common people more ready recognition of one's sinful life in certain classes of people. Upstanding citizens would be horrified to have themselves characterized in this way, but the lower classes did not have that level of sophistication. The prostitute knew what she was and her primary justification was her desperateness to make a living. She did not argue with society (as they do today) that her profession was as good as anyone else's. The same applied to the tax collector.

Second, Jesus represented hope for those who knew themselves and desired to climb out of the life they now lived. This is to say that when Jesus implied that those present were the sinners He had come to save, the majority were intensely interested, knew themselves, and would not have disagreed. Jesus here quotes to the Pharisees a compilation between Hosea 6:6 and Exodus 33:19. But He does not merely quote it. He asks that they go and learn its meaning. As such, He disengaged Himself and rather pointed to Scripture as their accuser. They need only study such passages to see their error.

"I have not come to call the righteous but sinners to repentance."

It is not that Jesus did not come for the righteous, but that He did not come to bring them to repentance. His work on the Cross was just as needful for the righteous, but the prior call to repentance was for the sinner. Neither did this mean that the righteous did not sin or that only those who never sinned were the righteous. It is to designate that with respect to sin wherever it may be found, He came to call men away from it, not to condemn or judge them on account of it.

33 And they said to Him, "The disciples of John often fast and offer prayers, the disciples of the Pharisees also do the same, but Yours eat and drink."

This begins the sort of checking/entrapment approach which will characterize the Pharisees from here forward. The Pharisees could discredit a man in two ways: 1) by showing that his teaching or practice was in conflict with Scripture, or 2) by showing that he was in conflict with them as the religious leaders of Israel. They knew full well that their particular view of prayer and fasting could not be found specifically in Scripture, so their question was not about Jesus' attitude toward Scripture itself.

To reject them as the custodians of God's truth for His people, however, was to reject God's chosen. This included the tradition of how the scriptures were to be applied. They had by now observed that He had not strictly follow these traditions. So their question is not aimed at entrapping Him about a particular scripture, but about His attitude toward them. Jesus must either agree that they have the correct view, making Him and His disciples contrary in practice, or He must deny their view, making Him disrespectful of their position.

Jesus takes the latter option, but not to deny them their position outright, but rather to show that their interpretation here is too narrow.

Do Matthew and Luke Present a Discrepancy?

Their accounts seem to raise an apparent discrepancy. Here, the Pharisees and Scribes are asking this question as part of their ongoing dialog with Jesus, whereas Matthew has the disciples of John asking this question. Also, these versions do not discuss the same aspects of the old and new cloth.

The key is in Mark's rendition of this account. Mark states that both the Pharisees and John's disciples asked this question, *" John's disciples and the Pharisees were fasting; and they came and said to Him,"* The dilemma of who really asked the question can be resolved if we consider that both parties asked the question more or less consecutively. Perhaps John's disciples asked first, then the Pharisees repeated the question, as in:

Disciples of John: *"We fast and the disciples of the Pharisee's fast, but why do your disciples not fast?"*

Pharisees: *"Yes, the disciples of John fast, and the disciples of the Pharisees also, but why do your . ."*

Luke presents the Pharisees' question while Matthew presents the question from the disciples of John. This is the classic case of having more than one component comprising a condition, but no discrepancy if you choose to mention only one. In the formula A+B it is possible to say A, or B by themselves because A is true and B is true. They are true, but simply incomplete. But you cannot say A and B are true followed by A is true but not B.

So, as long as the gospel writers did not say *"only John's disciples asked,"* or *only* the Pharisees asked, there is no discrepancy.

But we might ask why the disciples of John seemed here aligned with the Pharisees in questioning Jesus. It is possible that these are those disciples of the Baptist who encountered the arrival of Jesus with some indignation. He was, after all, stealing away some of their party; and John was talking about decreasing while Jesus increased. It is reasonable that some took this badly and may have taken up an adversarial position which fueled the occasion to test Jesus. This would place them more on the side of the Pharisees than with their friends among the disciples of Jesus.

Luke 5:34-35
34 "You cannot make the attendants of the bridegroom fast while the bridegroom is with them, can you? 35 "But the days will come . . when the bridegroom is taken away from them, then they will fast in those days."

Ultra-conservatives tend to see things as black and white and often wrapped up in an emphasis on certain things at the expense of balance. This is not to say that the preferred mode of understanding is to always look for compromise. Here, Jesus doesn't deny the appropriateness of fasting and praying, He simply denies that it should be practiced as they have come to see it. But He doesn't pit Himself against them, group against group. He simply explains why their view is too narrow. In essence, He reasons with them. And He uses analogies with which they are very familiar.

As we learned above in John the Baptist's case, the friends of the bridegroom are not cloistered and contemplative when the groom is with them, but rejoice and enter into the festivities of the wedding scene. This is not a picture of fasting and prayer. For the Pharisees this would produce some overworking of the analogy: how is Jesus of Nazareth to be seen as the bridegroom and in such a way that His disciples are His attendants?

The intended Bride is Israel herself, but this is a conclusion they would hardly make themselves, and Jesus did not help them with more explanation. So the analogy for them is simply that there are appropriate times for all things, including the occasions for fasting and praying, and if so, it is allowable to behave differently at other times.

The rub comes in with respect to the model for prayer and fasting which both the Pharisees and John's disciples have adopted. But since there were no scriptures that could be marshaled to support their traditional view, they couldn't argue. What is subtle here is that while comparison to Jesus and his disciples is readily understood (the attendants do not fast when they are with the bridegroom), there is no ready parallel to fasting when the bridegroom is taken away. The custom of the wedding feast did not have this feature.

But for John's disciples, there was instant recognition ready at hand. They were at that very moment fasting because John was now in prison. Their bridegroom had been taken away and they were now fasting. Jesus was here hinting at the future moment when He too will be taken away in the Crucifixion and the tomb, and then his disciples would fast and pray.

Jesus continues this aspect in the very next analogy.

Luke 5:36-39
36 "No one tears a piece of cloth from a new garment and puts it on an old garment; . . 37 no one puts new wine into old wineskins; . . 39 And no one, after drinking old wine wishes for new; for he says, `The old is good enough."'

The analogy is about what happens when something new is brought into contact with something old (the new cloth on old garments, new wine in old wineskins.) He is picturing the New Covenant coming into contact with the Old - the new life in Christ against the Old Testament and the Law. The garment is pictured as needing repair. But merely adding new patches to it is not adequate or helpful. The new patches will pull the old fabric when they shrink from being washed. The suggestion here is that what is really needed is a whole new garment. The same is said for the wineskin. When putting new wine into an old wineskin, the freshness of the wine may test the old cracks and weaknesses to the point of bursting, and all is lost. Again, what is really needed is new wineskins.

The application is that the faith Jesus is talking about is not something meant to be pressed and fitted into the OT forms and patterns. Instead they are arriving as something new, something that takes the baton forward. This can be seen as a strong argument for casting away absolutes. Liberalism might be seen as a case of simply being adult, by seeking out that which is new and disconnecting from old traditions. But there is a difference between shedding the forms in which wisdom was conveyed and the wisdom itself.

The other observation is that Jesus is the one inaugurating what is new. This is not an endorsement that man is now equally fit to shed old traditions wherever they be found and inaugurate new ones.

The Two Versions of The Parable

Luke's version, above, emphasizes that new and old things don't match and the outcome is worse because the new must be torn into pieces in order to make patches. Matthew and Mark emphasize the ill effects of adding new cloth to the old, since the new cloth will make the old garment worse by shrinking – *"But no one puts a patch of unshrunk cloth on an old garment; for the patch pulls away from the garment, and a worse tear results."*

Again, this may be resolved by proposing that Jesus may have said both things in His reply. He may have first explained that the new must be torn to provide material for the patch and the net result would be a noticeable mismatch. He may then have added that if the new is unshrunk when added, it will then also tear the old garment when washed. And again, Luke chooses to represent one part of this teaching while Matthew and Mark emphasize the other.

"And no one, after drinking old wine wishes for new; for he says, `The old is good enough.'"

This is an odd addition. Since the emphasis has been on new vessels to accommodate new wine it seems counter to his point to mention that someone who has drunk the old wine does not wish for the new. The best explanation is that this identifies people who are complacent in the old things and are therefore not looking for something new. With respect to new things, there will always be two groups: those who are looking for them, and those who want to maintain things as they are.

The Pharisees would be of the latter group, and more from a selfish point of view, being the principal party in Jerusalem.

Matthew 12:1-8, Mark 2:27, Matthew 12:9-10, Mark 3:4, Matthew 12:11-12, Mark 3:5-6, Matthew 12:15-21
1 At that time Jesus went through the grainfields on the Sabbath, and His disciples became hungry and began to pick the heads of grain and eat. 2 But when the Pharisees saw this, they said to Him, "Look, Your disciples do what is not lawful to do on a Sabbath." 3 But He said to them, "Have you not read what David did when he became hungry, he and his companions, 4 how he entered the house of God, and they ate the consecrated bread, which was not lawful for him to eat nor for those with him, but for the priests alone? 5 "Or have you not read in the Law, that on the Sabbath the priests in the temple break the Sabbath and are innocent? 6 "But I say to you that something greater than the temple is here. 7 "But if you had known what this means, 'I DESIRE COMPASSION, AND NOT A SACRIFICE,' you would not have condemned the innocent. 8 "For the Son of Man is Lord of the Sabbath." (Matthew 12:1-8)

27 Jesus said to them, "The Sabbath was made for man, and not man for the Sabbath. (Mark 2:27)

9 Departing from there, He went into their synagogue. 10 And a man was there whose hand was withered. And they questioned Jesus, asking, "Is it lawful to heal on the Sabbath?"--so that they might accuse Him. (Matthew 12:9-10)

4 And He said to them, "Is it lawful to do good or to do harm on the Sabbath, to save a life or to kill?" But they kept silent. (Mark 3:4)

11 And He said to them, "What man is there among you who has a sheep, and if it falls into a pit on the Sabbath, will he not take hold of it and lift it out? 12 "How much more valuable then is a man than a sheep! So then, it is lawful to do good on the Sabbath." (Matthew 12:11-12)

5 After looking around at them with anger, grieved at their hardness of heart, He said to the man, "Stretch out your hand." And he stretched it out, and his hand was restored. 6 The Pharisees went out and immediately began conspiring with the Herodians against Him, as to how they might destroy Him. (Mark 3:5-6)

15 But Jesus, aware of this, withdrew from there. Many followed Him, and He healed them all, 16 and warned them not to tell who He was. 17 This was to fulfill what was spoken through Isaiah the prophet: 18 "BEHOLD, MY SERVANT WHOM I HAVE CHOSEN; MY BELOVED IN WHOM MY SOUL is WELL -PLEASED; I WILL PUT MY SPIRIT UPON HIM, AND HE SHALL PROCLAIM JUSTICE TO THE GENTILES. 19 "HE WILL NOT QUARREL, NOR CRY OUT; NOR WILL ANYONE HEAR HIS VOICE IN THE STREETS. 20 "A BATTERED REED HE WILL NOT BREAK OFF, AND A SMOLDERING WICK HE WILL NOT PUT OUT, UNTIL HE LEADS JUSTICE TO VICTORY. 21 "AND IN HIS NAME THE GENTILES WILL HOPE." (Matthew 12:15-21)

Commentary

Matthew 12:1-5
1 At that time Jesus went through the grainfields on the Sabbath, . . His disciples . . began to pick the heads of grain and eat. . . 2 the Pharisees . . said to Him, "Look, Your disciples do what is not lawful to do on a Sabbath."

This opens into plain sight the minutia with which the Pharisees wrestled in order to micro-manage the dictates of the Law. The OT states that it is not lawful to do work on the Sabbath. This is not a simple thing to interpret, and it may not mean what we mean by work in American culture. The word is *melachah* and it is variously translated depending on how orthodox you are as a Jew. It is first used in relation to God's work creating the world and life, therefore to some Jews it means any kind of creative work by man. Ironically, this prohibited work on building a synagogue for example, but allowed the rabbi to conduct services. But it simultaneously prohibited work in secular employment or manual labor in one's field.

The rabbis chose as a model all the activities associated with building a sanctuary and these then became prohibited. The list expanded to include just about everything, because so many activities could be considered supportive to such a task.[19] Strangely, they expanded to include reaping crops and even things

---
[19] Ginsberg, The Sabbath in the Classical Kabballah, State University New York Press, (1989), p.64

like writing letters on a page or lighting a candle. This is the framework of intricate, divergent application in which Jesus is now addressed by the Pharisees.

Pointing out that his disciples were doing something unlawful is notable for two reasons. They were somewhat hesitant at this stage to accuse Jesus directly because of the undisputed wisdom He demonstrated. So they directed their charge against His disciples (which indirectly pointed back to Him as their teacher). Secondly, we see the degree of laxity that had developed with respect to Sabbath laws by this time, since they do not pursue the punishment called for in the Law.

As for the Law and the Sabbath, it was understood since the earliest times that works of pity and mercy were not prohibited, and certainly one had to eat on the Sabbath. But for the legalistic Jew, preparing the food was work, so it was exhorted that they prepare it the day before or be obliged to fast.

3 "Have you not read what David did when he became hungry . . 4 and they ate the consecrated bread, which was not lawful for him to eat

Jesus answers their charge by simply asking them to keep things in proper perspective. They are complaining about the minor work required to retrieve grain and to eat it (which outside their extra-biblical machinations was permitted), but they make no historic objections and accept as legal David's entering into the sanctuary and partaking of the holiest form of food in their faith. This was meant to show that their duplicitous behavior disqualified them from dictating the terms of the Law.

5 "Or have you not read in the Law, that on the Sabbath the priests in the temple break the Sabbath and are innocent?

Again, He cites a legal act of work to which they all will concur. The priests were exempt from the prohibition. But as is now His pattern, He says more that will eventually be used against Him.

[gutter/margin: Matthew 12:6-8]
6 "But I say to you that something greater than the temple is here.

By this He means His own presence. Messiah is greater than the Temple and His very presence and the work He is doing supersedes the importance of those things made sacred in the Temple.

7 "But if you had known what this means, 'I DESIRE COMPASSION, AND NOT A SACRIFICE,' you would not have condemned the innocent. 8 "For the Son of Man is Lord of the Sabbath."

Here is a lesson on the interpretive tool called the Analogy of Scripture - Scripture interprets Scripture. [20]Jesus has just put His finger on a verse that controls the meaning of the Sabbath laws. A verse the Pharisees were too blind to see. It is not merely a text from the Scripture but a direct quote from God as to what He desires.

This is what comes of legalism. One gets wrapped around the axle in trying to micro-manage something God has commanded and one can no longer see the import of other verses. Here also Jesus puts Himself in further jeopardy with the Pharisees by applying "Son of Man" to Himself. But this is now secondary. His point is that Messiah has command over how the Sabbath is to be observed. This means that even if the old dispensation concerning the Sabbath was just as the Pharisees interpreted it, Messiah has the power to introduce a new dispensation in which the old regulations are now to make way for the new.

---

[20] Ramm, <u>Protestant Biblical Interpretation</u>, Baker, (1970), p.36

Mark 2:27
27 "The Sabbath was made for man, and not man for the Sabbath.

The purpose of stating this is to reiterate the intention of God in instituting the Sabbath. It was not made for God but for man. It was not of such a magnitude that man should be considered made specifically to obey its superiority over him – the case of man made for the Sabbath. As such, man is expected to observe the strict charges concerning it, but not at the expense of mercy, health, and charity with respect to human life, therefore man is to observe it but not be ruled by it.

Matthew 12:9-10
9 . . He went into their synagogue. 10 And a man was there whose hand was withered. . . "Is it lawful to heal on the Sabbath?"-- . . that they might accuse Him.

At this juncture, we now see the Pharisees no longer following Him so as to glean from His wisdom, but to trick Him into actionable speech or deeds. To the Jew it was only permissible to render first aid or care that would prevent a man from dying of injuries or wounds. To heal a withered hand would be prohibited because such an act could easily wait until after the Sabbath. This they found as a perfect trap, because the very case before Jesus was surely an act of mercy, but one that could wait.

Mark 3:4
4 And He said to them, "Is it lawful to do good or to do harm on the Sabbath, to save a life or to kill?" But they kept silent.

Those setting the trap now find themselves in one of their own. They know they can't answer in favor of good because this must be qualified if they wish to be faithful to their tradition. They also know full well they cannot publicly recommend the doing of harm by proscribing all work. So they say nothing.

Matthew 12:11-12
11 And He said to them, "What man is there among you who has a sheep, and if it falls into a pit on the Sabbath, will he not take hold of it and lift it out? 12 "How much more valuable then is a man than a sheep!

Rather than engaging in a theological discussion about the interpretation of terms, Jesus cleverly takes advantage of the ambiguity in their own practice of such things. He appeals to what they all know they would do in the case of a sheep in the pit. Ironically, in their own ambiguity they had actually discovered the true spirit of the Sabbath by way of necessity. But here also Jesus drives the nail in the coffin. Why would they do such things for the lowly sheep but in their legalism leave man to suffer.

Mark 3:-6
5 After looking around at them with anger, grieved at their hardness of heart,

We all fear this look on Jesus' face. We all have moments of hardness of heart, and lapses of sin. But we trust and hope that all our failings will be met with the gentle expression of understanding and compassion on the face of Jesus – one that does not condone but encourages restoration.

The key is in the heart. Are we grieved at our failings, are we struggling but determined to repent? These will not be met with anger. But the Pharisees were in no wise grieved or looking to repent. They were full of self-justification, pride and arrogance.

"Stretch out your hand!" . . and it was restored to normal, like the other. . . . 6 . . and [they] conspired against Him, as to how they might destroy Him.

The command conveys to everyone present that He has every intention of proceeding with the healing. What is so incredibly telling is that they then became eye witnesses to the miracle. They saw before their very eyes the hand become normal, yet went out from this scene to devise ways to destroy Him. It pictures how incredibly small their faith was. It had become merely a system of managing ordinances, not much different than the role of a building inspector today, whose job is to make sure you haven't violated code. This was their life, their little empire of importance. So much so that God was no longer recognizable among them. He would come but they would not be moved.

.. with the Herodians

Mark 3:6 includes mention of the Herodians. These were the sycophants, administrators, officials, and the nobility allied with Antipas, essentially anyone friendly to the heirs of Herod the Great. But why include this class in the machinations of the Pharisees?

Despite Herodian rule as tetrarchs, Rome reserved the right of capital punishment in non-free provinces. In coming to the decision that Jesus must be done away with, the Pharisees must now tread the maze of Roman red-tape in getting a man sentenced. Pilate must be called in from Caesarea. They would need the influence of Herod.

(The outline and details of this plan is seen at the arrest of Jesus.)

Matthew 12:15-17
15 But Jesus, aware of this, withdrew from there. Many followed Him, and He healed them all, 16 and warned them not to tell who He was.

This seems odd, since Jesus has by now made several undeniably bold statements in the presence of those who can do Him the most harm. But we must always be cautioned that Jesus is managing these circumstances in perfect accord with his Father. He is treading with great skill the ridge between witnessing to the truth and preventing premature arrest.

One of His frequent means for frustrating His enemies is to move His location. In a small region like Galilee, this seems hardly effective. But it had the singular effect of at least removing Himself from the immediate atmosphere of contention. And often the heat of an issue will dissipate somewhat when things return to normal and one has regular duties to which one must return.

17 This was to fulfill what was spoken through Isaiah the prophet:

We have here one of the most beautiful and tender pictures of Messiah to be had in the Bible. It is a picture of the Father declaring His delight as He reveals His Son, *"Behold My Servant, . . My Beloved in Whom My soul delights."*

proclaiming justice to the Gentiles.

We must remember that to a very large extent, the Law and the ways of Judaism remained isolated from the Gentiles. There is a hint that the Law was applicable to the Gentiles, but we do not see God enforcing the stipulations of the Mosaic Law on the nations. They are held instead to the Law once written on their hearts, the Law that prevailed even in God's people before the Mosaic Law – the age of conscience in the time of Abraham.

But the nations without the written code of God were permitted to exercise their free will to adhere to or deviate from that original revelation. Hence, we see nations with quite different laws, even those that offend the God of Israel, yet curiously embracing commonality in many areas with the Law of God. All nations had laws against theft, murder, and adultery.

To proclaim justice to the nations is as though they at long last will hear again the righteousness of God, so long drummed out of their hearing by other voices. The last verse states that the Gentiles will come to hope in His Name.

"He will not quarrel . . nor will anyone hear His voice in the streets."

This begins a soliloquy on the gentleness of the Messiah, despite His promised victory of the enemies of God's people. He will not be the kind of person who is quarrelsome or contentious. He will not stand in the street and make Himself the object of attention by loud proclamations.

Matthew 12:20
20 . . a battered reed He will not break, a smoking wick He will not quench

Here is perhaps the most delicate of attitudes and behavior ever pictured. His walk will be so gentle that were He to pass by a reed bent over and ready to break off, the brush of the air from His stride would not sever it. The gentleness of His stride will not completely put out a wick that is smoldering – literally smoking in the ebb of extinguished flame. Such gentleness will endure until He comes again to lead in victory.

CHAPTER 6
The Sermon on the Mount

Mark 3:7-12, Luke 6:12-19

7 Jesus withdrew to the sea with His disciples; and a great multitude from Galilee followed; and also from Judea, 8 and from Jerusalem, and from Idumea, and beyond the Jordan, and the vicinity of Tyre and Sidon, a great number of people heard of all that He was doing and came to Him.

9 And He told His disciples that a boat should stand ready for Him because of the crowd, so that they would not crowd Him; 10 for He had healed many, with the result that all those who had afflictions pressed around Him in order to touch Him. 11 Whenever the unclean spirits saw Him, they would fall down before Him and shout, "You are the Son of God!" 12 And He earnestly warned them not to tell who He was. (Mark 3:7-12)

12 It was at this time that He went off to the mountain to pray, and He spent the whole night in prayer to God. 13 And when day came, He called His disciples to Him and chose twelve of them, whom He also named as apostles: 14 Simon, whom He also named Peter, and Andrew his brother; and James and John; and Philip and Bartholomew; 15 and Matthew and Thomas; James the son of Alphaeus, and Simon who was called the Zealot; 16 Judas the son of James, and Judas Iscariot, who became a traitor. 17 Jesus came down with them and stood on a level place; and there was a large crowd of His disciples, and a great throng of people from all Judea and Jerusalem and the coastal region of Tyre and Sidon, 18 who had come to hear Him and to be healed of their diseases; and those who were troubled with unclean spirits were being cured. 19 And all the people were trying to touch Him, for power was coming from Him and healing them all. (Luke 6:12-19)

Commentary

Mark 3:7-11
7 Jesus withdrew to the sea .. and a great multitude from Galilee followed;

Jesus now returns to the shoreline.

In terms of location, it is doubtful the authorities did not know where Jesus was generally at any given moment. They didn't have cell phones to keep the Jerusalem leadership informed, but if they had wanted to capture Him, they had only to know the general area and to follow the crowds. The key element that kept them at bay for a time was His immense popularity among the people and the people's general dislike for the Pharisees in general.

To strike when crowds of people were being literally healed in the hundreds would be political suicide unless they could pin down some sort of sorcery or witchcraft for which they could then be seen as the guardians of the ancient faith. We see that even in the plans for the arrest when they had the charges at the ready, they took consideration of the people's reaction and decided to act at night.

The news of Him was now widespread and this on account of the permanent nature and generosity of His healings. People were not just made to feel slightly better for a few days. They were not trained to exercise a mind-over-matter healing where everything depended on their ability to "claim" their healing. This was the real deal, the genuine article. Something half good or temporary would have been found out rather soon and disaffection would have soon caught up with the original news of His work. So this is a real testimony to the genuineness of His healing power.

9 And He told His disciples that a boat should stand ready . . . 10 for He had healed many, [that they] pressed around Him in order to touch Him. . .11 the unclean spirits .. would fall down before Him and shout, "You are the Son of God!"

We cannot adequately appreciate this scene without having been there. As explained earlier, the teaching would draw many who were thirsty for the truth, but the primary reason the multitude followed Him was that He might relieve the desperate plight of maladies and illnesses that had long ago taken the joy out of their faces and replaced it with fretting, bitterness and just plain suffering.

Here the gospels portray this desperation at its fever pitch. Jesus must now plan for contingencies that would protect His very person against the pressure from the crowds. There is a scene from *The Greatest Story Ever Told* (George Stevens, United Artists 1965) which rather ably conveys this desperateness and near danger. The crowd presses Him toward the edge of the water such that He must walk out on a narrow platform with His eyes out to the sea. Crowding the end of the platform are hundreds of people shouting with hands outstretched that He might touch them. The combination of the action, the setting and music make for a powerful demonstration of just Who He had come to be in their eyes. (Worth seeing.)

The Gospels add to this account what the unclean spirits proclaimed at His presence. These would be spirits inhabiting the bodies of people given over to their influence. Yet in the presence of Jesus, they are revealed as to what they are. They separate themselves as to speak on their own, such that the person possessed is but a passive vessel, merely rendering their speech in natural terms.

But notice the utter command Jesus has over them. They do not utter blasphemous words, they do not sow verbal seeds of doubt among the people. They don't venture the kind of dialog in which Satan engaged Jesus on the Mount of Temptation. It is as though they are "forced" to proclaim the very truth concerning Him. And that meant command. Command over the very forces of evil. This could only have added to His wonder in the people's minds. They were familiar with the signs of possession. For such demons to be compelled to admit the truth, being bound from doing otherwise, was effective beyond measure.

Now combine all of this into the completed scene and we have hundreds of people gathered and following every move of but one single Person; the clamour of voices, the arms and hands stretched out to Him for but a single touch, the demons themselves giving voice to His majesty and authentic deity, the need for Him to even separate Himself from the press of the crowd. It is overwhelming to just imagine. It had to be inspiring and humbling to witness in person.

We are prompted to almost utter those prior words Simon Peter, "Lord, depart from me, for I am a sinful man."

Luke 6:12
12 It was at this time that He went off to the mountain to pray, and He spent the whole night in prayer to God.

This is something to which in practice few people can relate. We have no difficulty understanding the "alone time" concept of being separate from the distractions of life; we even long for it frequently. But the idea of a whole night in prayer taxes our capacities in today's world. We are easily bored with the plenitude and variety of entertainments available to the average person. While we can appreciate the break that solace and a peaceful setting of undefiled nature would provide, some may find themselves with nothing more to say after the first twenty minutes.

They will have cycled through all their loved ones and friends, all those altruistic concerns like praying for our leaders and our nation, and for those hungry and hurting in the world. But then they may become silent while thinking of more to say and feel. They will begin to pay more attention to the rustling of the leaves or the chirping of the birds, or the babbling of a brook, and begin to ask themselves how long is enough in pleasing God with the service of prayer?

Jesus' prayer was strikingly dissimilar to the descriptions above. It is proper to surmise that He would have spent the time praying intensely for each man who would walk with Him, not just in general, but with the insight He had as to each man's gifts and failings. He would pray for direction from His Father as to where He should be and what He should do. He would be praying for insight to see the workings of the evil one in thwarting His plans and for the continued power from the Father to upset the hold of unclean spirits on men, and to discharge them to their judgment and destiny.

When we think about prayer being a dialog in a relationship, we can begin to see how it can very naturally fill hours of time, much as we were ready to do and did with our youthful infatuations and those we eventually came to cherish when falling in love. Time did not matter, nor did we think about having talked too much or for too long. It's a secular analogy, but a relationship of love has parallels wherever it may be found and in whatever context, even the spiritual. It is the behavior of devotion, plain and simple.

Luke 6:13
13 And when day came, He called His disciples to Him and chose twelve of them, whom He also named as apostles:

We can see that some aspect of His all-night prayer must have concerned whom He would call to complete the number of His closest disciples. The number twelve can be taken down several paths of numerology and imagery, some perhaps valid, some rather speculative and fanciful. Later in the Gospels we hear Jesus proclaim, *" you also shall sit upon twelve thrones, judging the twelve tribes of Israel."* (Matthew 19:28) Also, in the Revelation we see these thrones and crowns.

So aside from the numerology or symbolism that 'twelve' might convey, their number is at the very least intended to align with the number of the historic tribes; and perhaps that number was itself inaugurated on the basis of divine symbolism and the meaning of numbers.

"whom He also names as apostles"

The word *apostolos* means one who is sent, usually with a message, but can include the idea of a mission. The idea that it meant someone with authority was something added by its special NT association with the Twelve and the unquestioned authority these had over the churches. But authority as a connotation was really not part of the original term. So the term carries with it both the idea of being *called* and of subsequently being *sent*.

There are many people running today, but God hasn't sent them. We all are expected to take the exhortations from Scripture and preach the Gospel to those whom God desires to save. But the calling to full-time, dedicated ministry is something not all people receive. Some, with minds of their own, are not willing to wait for that calling or may even doubt it will ever come. Desiring ministry anyway, they take matters into their own hands and then work and strive to strike out a ministry for themselves under the guise that they are doing all for God according to His general exhortation that we "Go." The result can be an array of ministries and tent meetings that look more like man than the true calling of God.

To some degree, the focus in the Catholic Church that bases its worship and work on preserving the authentic callings of the holy Apostles is sincerely elemental to a NT faith. The recent revival in Protestant churches to return to the faith of the New Testament church is meant with similar sincerity, at least in recognizing the germinal value of the historic apostolic callings. But the same principle applies – wherever men abandon secular life for full-time service, they must do so because they are called. And such men, and those who receive them, should test the genuineness of that calling.

Luke 6:14-16
14 Simon, whom He also named Peter, and Andrew his brother; and James and John; and Philip and Bartholomew; 15 and Matthew and Thomas; James the son of Alphaeus, and Simon who was called the Zealot; 16 Judas the son of James, and Judas Iscariot, who became a traitor.

These are familiar to us when we read them, but only the names of a few seem to stick more tenaciously in our memory. We note there are three James mentioned, two of which are apostles. James, the brother of John, the son of Zebedee, and James the son of Alphaeus. These are not to be confused with the James here said to be the father of Judas or with the later James, the half-brother of the Lord, not listed here among the apostles (Matthew 13:55.)

We also see two named Judas (pronounced 'youdas'). The first Judas is said here and in Acts to be the son of James (separate from the two apostles.) He cannot be the author of the Epistle of Jude because there the author clearly states he is the *brother* of James. Some have therefore attributed the Jude of the epistle to be the half-brother of Jesus. Since Jesus also had a half–brother named James (Matthew 13:55), this would make Jude of the epistle the brother also of James (as stated there.)

The main difficulty with this identification is that the church has historically attributed the Epistle of Jude to the apostle. But that cannot succeed without resolving the two designations, *"son of James"* and *"brother of James."* Here, Judas the apostle (not Iscariot) is also called Thaddeus (Mark 3:18), the full name being Lebbeus Thaddeus.

The names we hardly hear anything about elsewhere are Bartholomew, James the son of Alphaeus (James the less), Simon the Zealot, and Judas the son of James, discussed above. We have no informed explanation why the NT does not give equal time to these four. Philip receives mention again in Acts with regard to the Ethiopian eunuch. As for the James, son of Zebedee, he is martyred early in the Acts and is subsequently overshadowed by James, the Lord's brother, overseer of the Jerusalem church and the writer of *James*.

What is of interest to almost everyone is that the betrayer was among those deliberately chosen. Some see this as a case of predestined purpose. Jesus had to die for the sins of the world. He therefore had to be put to death at the hands of men. Betrayal was not the only means, but certain a means of accomplishing this. As to why betrayal and not simply the devious ends of his detractors, is the subject of many sermons and papers.

Perhaps the best accounting is that Jesus wished to show that His love and calling to service are extended to all, even at the risk of rejection and jeopardy against His own purposes. It is to show the pure, untainted, unbiased love of God to all regardless of love, doubt or ill towards Him, that He may be found unassailable in mercy and grace in the day of judgment.

Much philosophically has been ventured on the enigma of Judas Iscariot. The pop musical *Jesus Christ Superstar* [21] attempted to bring all such philosophizing into focus by making Judas the trapped and predestined hero.

Some have offered that Judas will have an argument against God in the day of judgment, in that he can claim he fulfilled the promises of God – Jesus had to die for the sins of the world and he was the key to making that happen.

The counterexample comes from the OT, where we see God using Babylon and Assyria to inflict a well-deserved punishment on His people. But He then judges Assyria and Babylon for their role. This is seen as gross contradiction in the hands of a fickle God. It is a mystery that is wrapped up in the will to do evil and the Lord taking advantage of that will in order to use a tool for punishment, useful to His own ends. But the

---

[21] Stage play – Andrew Lloyd-Weber, MCA, Inc.1971; motion picture - Universal Pictures, 1973

tool may not claim special pleading, because their heart was evil to begin with. Such will be the case with Judas.

Luke 6:17-19
17 Jesus came down with them . . . and a great throng of people from all Judea and Jerusalem and the coastal region of Tyre and Sidon, . .18 had come to hear Him and to be healed of their diseases . . 19 for power was coming from Him and healing them all.

Again, He resumes His ministry of teaching and healing, but now with the full compliment of His apostles. The keynote here in people's rush to see Him is that *"power was coming from Him . ."* Some have offered that this is merely a way of explaining that Jesus was calling down power that came directly from Heaven to the individual. But there are reasons to interpret this as explaining the channeling of power through the very Person of Jesus Himself. This is not meant to be a scientific description, but the words are clear that power was coming from Him, that He was a functional part of the channeling of such power.

It was once observed in a healing service of the late seventies that light was seen transferring from the healer to the recipient, like salvos from a cannon. It is anecdotal to be sure, but it does align marvelously with the statement we have here in the Gospels.

On the other hand, we are not to devise an interpretation that is so mechanical that Jesus must receive a sort of "allotment" of power which He held locally in Himself, dispensed as He wished, then refilled through prayer. It is a power of the Father, given by the Father through the Son. It is a divine chain of blessing but not to the extent that we must today always seek a healer or we are without remedy. As Jesus is today at the righthand of the Father and likewise in our hearts, He still remains that functional key, laying hold of the Father and the believer in marvelous union, that the channeling of such power remains a hope to every believer.

Matthew 5:1-8
1 When Jesus saw the crowds, He went up on the mountain; and after He sat down, His disciples came to Him. 2 He opened His mouth and began to teach them, saying, 3 "Blessed are the poor in spirit, for theirs is the kingdom of heaven. 4 "Blessed are those who mourn, for they shall be comforted. 5 "Blessed are the gentle, for they shall inherit the earth. 6 "Blessed are those who hunger and thirst for righteousness, for they shall be satisfied. 7 "Blessed are the merciful, for they shall receive mercy. 8 "Blessed are the pure in heart, for they shall see God. (Matthew 5:1-8)

Commentary

Matthew 5:1
1 When Jesus saw the crowds, He went up on the mountain; and after He sat down, His disciples came to Him. 2 He opened His mouth and began to teach them, saying,"

Matthew is the only writer who provides the complete details of the Sermon on the Mount. Mark 3 and John 6 mention that He went up with His disciples, but they include none of what was spoken. Luke presents a redacted version of some things taught here.

The location of this sermon is not as some suppose on the Mount of Olives, but farther N near Capernaum on what has come to be called the Mount of the Beatitudes. It was called Mt. Eremos in ancient times (though its name is not mentioned in the Gospels) and is situated within the four mile gap between Capernaum and Tabgha, on the NW side of the Sea of Galilee. That it could hold the numbers implied by the Gospels is evidenced by its continued use in modern times. Recently in 2000, a Catholic conference of 100,000 visitors was planned for the Pope's visit.

Most people assume the sermon was intended and addressed to the crowd. But the sermon was actually addressed directly to the disciples in the hearing of the crowd. The text states that He withdrew with His disciples, having seen the crowds, and then began to teach them. Having said that, we cannot push this distinction so far as to rule out any consideration or engagement of the crowds at all. The withdrawal of Jesus and the Twelve would not have stopped those who were following Him. Those fit enough for the easy grade to the top would certainly have gathered to hear and see more. So it is very likely that Jesus did not ignore them and may have raised His voice sufficiently to permit the audience to hear. But we should be clear that the content was meant at least initially for the disciples.

The Beatitudes

The NT does not specifically call this sermon the Beatitudes. It has come to mean this because of the repetitive use of "Blessed are . ." Beatify is our English word for the connotation of 'blessed' in the Gk word *makarioi*, hence the English name of this section of teaching

The Beatitudes are a list of blessed states. This is one of Jesus' early, formal sermons and it is designed to answer one of the most important questions man may ask. Given a God of righteousness and justice, *"How then can I please God?"* For Someone to come from God and speaking to mankind, this would be a question of the first order. And so it is an answer of the first order.

If one wished to do so – to be rightly related to the Creator of the Universe – here is provided those states of blessedness that please Him. Contrary to "go and do," the exhortation is to go and *be*.

Matthew 5:3
3 "Blessed are the poor in spirit, for theirs is the kingdom of heaven."

Makarioi means to call blessed, to esteem fortunate, to count happy. From this word the sermon is called the Beatitudes. Makarios, or beatify, has nothing to do with our word 'beauty,' since it is an inward state of being, not a quality of outward appearance.

"the poor in spirit"

This does not mean the poor, per se (the financially destitute), but it can mean them if they have the quality intended by this phrase. The poor in spirit are those who are downtrodden in their hearts, having their human spirit weakened by the circumstances of life and the abuses of their fellow man. God is quick to send promise that He cares for these sincerely and compassionately. But how is this a recommendation of how to be?

In life there seem always to be two great classes: there are those who rule and those who are ruled; those who lead and take charge, and those who follow There are those who bully and those who cower; the oppressor class, the victim class (Marx), and those who are strong, those who are weak.

Observe a team-meeting at work. You will see those who dominate the meeting and those who may also contribute but are largely passive. Even in simple conversations, there is usually one person dominating or controlling the conversation and someone else more passive.

In ancient times, these distinctions were much more acute. There were always those individuals who constantly looked for any opportunity to dominate or demonstrate their importance over others and very often if they could not achieve it in formal ways, they resorted to dominating the unfortunate and the meek in the midst of crude and pitiful conditions that made up neighborhood life.

Jesus does not here state that the physical conditions which made them downtrodden will surely be taken away. He does not promise wealth to those who are financially poor. He promises the Kingdom of Heaven to be their compensation.

This helps us to focus on the full condition being described. It is not those who are destitute and bitter, those who are in poverty and angry, those who think they deserve something but have been denied. It is rather those who are humble in their circumstances, who acknowledge they are unworthy to "claim" or expect wealth and position in life. They are similar to the meek in that they are satisfied to take the lesser places in life, to know who they are in comparison to an Almighty God, yet who trust that He will care for them and compensate them in the currency of His Kingdom.

Matthew 5:4-5
4 "Blessed are those who mourn, for they shall be comforted."

This is not a broad promise to all persons everywhere who mourn, whether with faith or without. We see the truth of this today in that many mourn and are often not comforted. People eventually get over the loss of a loved one but this is not what is meant.

Mourning for a loved one, as believers or not, indicates we have bonded and cared for another person in ways that are generally commendable to God. But this can be completely secular without regard for God, drawing purely from those things in which all men still bear a resemblance to God in their natures. It can be felt and experienced without reference to faith. Such people can remain uncomforted because the comfort here promised is only found in God. So it is a promise of a comfort otherwise lacking in a godless life, but also a call to be people of faith, that the comfort truly adequate for our need can be given.

Now this should not be taken as a rule that God will rigidly refuse such comfort unless they be of faith. It may be that God's provision in this way will be the key to bringing them to salvation and restoration in Him. But the idea is the same – He is the key to the comfort we need, for outside Him no such comfort is assured.

As to the nature of the comfort itself, it is not an unconditional assurance that their loved one will be in Heaven. God does not suspend the requirements He established for salvation in the presence of desperate and tragic mourning. It is rather a comfort that conveys Divine understanding of the feelings and pain being felt and that making oneself right with God is the key to all happiness in life. It is the focus on the larger picture of what is taking place in life, that there is life and death. That there must be an expectant hope that all the Why's can somehow be answered in the arms of Someone who understands more deeply than any human friend can.

5 "Blessed are the gentle, for they shall inherit the earth."

This is the better rendering of the more familiar *Blessed are the meek . ."* The reason for the change in modern versions is the negative connotation that 'meek' conveys as to timid or fearful, or in more extreme senses - quislings. This was, of course, never the intended meaning. The word here means those who prefer the gentler way, the kinder approach, who are not brash or arrogant, haughty or bullish.

That they shall inherit the earth is in some ways prophetic and rather well aligned with apocalyptic literature like the Revelation. For we see the future of our world being given over to those who are citizens of the Kingdom of Heaven, now come to earth. Those who have been last in life will be first in the Kingdom. It is not so much meant as a reward but as an outcome of the path they have chosen. They have become part of that company who were chosen all along to inherit the earth when the time of His restitution of all things comes to pass.

Matthew 5:6-8
6 "Blessed are those who hunger and thirst for righteousness, for they shall be satisfied."

This is the attitude and orientation of the one who desires God and wishes to be made right with Him. He seeks to live his life according to the user guide of the Creator. He recognizes the eternal value of God's ways and standards and he thirsts after them to hear more and more and to become ever closer to them in all he does. The idea is that there can be a love for the righteousness of God, that sees it as so totally right and applicable to life – the way life was intended to be lived - and so one thirsts for more understanding of it.

Such a person is promised the satisfaction they seek because they are seeking the very thing constituting the reason they were in fact made – to know Him and to be like Him in fellowship and love. The exhortation here is to seek this hunger and thirst for one's life, as opposed to accepting the counterfeits and substitutes of tarnished righteousness which the world offers more expediently.

7 "Blessed are the merciful, for they shall receive mercy."

It is almost an axiom in life that those who complain about the lack of compassion, consideration and mercy they receive at the hands of others have the same behavior in these things. Those clamouring the loudest in their demands for mercy are usually those who have given little of it themselves. It is almost as though they recognize their plight as a proper judgment and they fear it because it is so true and (if they were honest) just.

If we seek the mercy of God we must demonstrate it in our actions and attitudes, for it is an offense to withhold it in arrogance or pride and then plead for it in our own case. It is the sign of supreme self-centeredness (we give nothing and expect everything), and this God will not reward.

Now we may complain that God's mercy is fine, but the mercy from others (even if a means) is a precarious thing. So are we not still in jeopardy of mercilessness? Here is where faith proves itself as the answer to all things. If God is sovereign, the acts of men in relation to His people are clearly in His hands and mercy even from unbelievers can be included in His promise above.

8 "Blessed are the pure in heart, for they shall see God."

To be pure in heart is to return one's heart to the way God made it in the beginning. We learn to deviate from this state by learning the ways of men, beginning even with our own parents. Far too soon, even infants learn the opportunities that satisfy wrong motives and the heart soon becomes something different, on its way to needing the salvation all men will need if they are to return to the purity of heart that is in God alone. The promise of seeing God is again not so much a reward as a state of blessedness that comes with the condition. To be pure in heart is to see the things of God and His mind and heart as they are.

Matthew 5:9-12, Luke 6:21
9 "Blessed are the peacemakers, for they shall be called sons of God. 10 "Blessed are those who have been persecuted for the sake of righteousness, for theirs is the kingdom of heaven. 11 "Blessed are you when people insult you and persecute you, and falsely say all kinds of evil against you because of Me. 12 "Rejoice and be glad, for your reward in heaven is great; for in the same way they persecuted the prophets who were before you. (Matthew 5:9-12)

Blessed are you who hunger now, for you shall be satisfied. Blessed are you who weep now, for you shall laugh. (Luke 6:21)

Commentary

Matthew 5:9
9 "Blessed are the peacemakers, for they shall be called sons of God."

Despite the scenes of violence in the OT, the God of the Bible is a God of peace. This seems like a glib contradiction but the principle of promulgating peace cannot be separated from a principle of justice. This is simply because all men do not cooperate with peace. There is always a need to correct, curtail, and even summarily judge those who act against peace. This does not undermine God's desire and preference for peace. The call for peace means that in the world there will be conflict, whether it be a simple argument between two people or the violence of war. Hence, there is a need from the divine point of view for peace *makers*.

The peacemaker is someone who reminds combatants that peace is always the alternative, but more than this it is a real alternative, and one that serves both parties better than conflict. In the heat of conflict, this may be seldom heeded. So the peacemaker must also have the cleverness to adeptly intercept the conflict and diffuse the fiercest emotions to an agreeable stand-off that permits each side to think more on the issues at hand and the consequences.

In fierce and angry conflicts, nothing seems more important than doing harm to one's opponent. So altruistic interjections about the fellowship of man and what benefits society will fall on deaf ears. But that's the secular approach to peacemaking. The peacemaker here in the Beatitudes is one who brings the God of Heaven into the discussion. It is often a more effective remedy to remind combatants that such a conflict is wrong because it offends God.

From the mouth of someone who exudes powerful confidence that can be enough to cause people to stop and think about their actions. Parents, in arguing with their kids about the rules, often resort to "Because I say so!" This is rather hard for kids to understand, especially when they are being taught at school that relativism and a world free of absolutes is the mode of day. In such cases, parents would do better by simply saying, "Because it pleases God."

We need to remind ourselves that the connection kids might have to God does not critically depend on us as parents. If we read Romans correctly, God is very capable of making Himself known to our children independently. We can therefore with confidence appeal to the pleasing or displeasing of God as an effective argument for why there are rules. (But this only works if, as parents, we have made sure the rules we establish at home are godly ones.)

But in all areas of life, we as followers of Christ need to look for opportunities to convey peace between people in our immediate view, and from a larger view, the restoration of peace between all men and God.

"they shall be called the sons of God."

Sons of God, because such are those born of Him. To be born of God is to take on the Father's attitudes and desires, to want what He wants. And let us be clear – God wants peace among men and with Himself more than any human institution past or future. So much so that He gave His Son to be a sacrifice to effect that peace. And what better than that which by making things right on the inside.

Paul states that we at last have peace with God (in contrast to the enmity that prevailed) because of what has been done in Christ (Romans 5:1). Those, therefore, who are in Christ as children of God cannot separate themselves from His role in the institution of peace.

Matthew 5:10
10 "Blessed are those who have been persecuted for the sake of righteousness, for theirs is the kingdom of heaven."

Persecution is seldom perceived as a blessing. But it's not saying "happy" are those. Blessedness is not simply the state of being happy, but rather the state of being *called* blessed, *esteemed* fortunate, or *counted* as happy. It is an attitude from the perspective of God not necessarily always the inner perspective of the believer. So it is not concomitant that we perceive blessed feelings when being persecuted, but that we comprehend how this pleases God.

Men are not eager to experience this (although it was reported in the Roman persecutions that some Christians actually leapt into the flames or the claws of wild beasts, that their martyrdom be accomplished all the more quickly.)

In distant times, people were by nature more altruistic about sacrificing their lives for others. At a time of the Me and X generations, people are thinking more about what's in it for them. Altruistic principles are everywhere in doubt. *"Why give up my life so that someone else can go on enjoying theirs? Why do it if I won't be around to enjoy the benefit?"*

So, the only genuinely effective reason for suffering for a good cause is persecution for *righteousness'* sake. It is the only one in which the victim sees a benefit beyond their act. Because righteousness carries its benefit beyond this life into the next that they have some hope of spiritually sharing in it.

But it is also the most enigmatic because it involves persecution for having done what is right. Most people understand incurring the wrath and anger of others for their own selfishness, failures or missteps. Like it or not, we at least understand it because we know that we messed up and there are consequences. But we don't understand nor do we accept without complaint a suffering or persecution for doing the right thing. And we can easily blow our promise of blessing by fighting back or exhibiting anger or rage at being misjudged.

Now it must be hurriedly reiterated that sacrifice and suffering cannot be purely secular and count for something simply because it defends righteousness. There is an attitude among quasi-believers and even outright non-believers that what is done philanthropically for God will benefit them in the likelihood there is such a thing as the Judgment. But this is a mistaken conclusion. It is God who sees the heart and whether it is done by faith, and we know from Scripture that all things done without faith are ultimately for naught. *"[it] did not profit them, because it was not united by faith"* (Hebrews 4:2)

"theirs is the kingdom of heaven"

This was also said of the poor in spirit. We must avoid making these into functional formulas – possession of the kingdom belongs only to those who are poor in spirit or who have been persecuted. In general terms, the end of the blessed states is the same for all who aspire to them. All such persons will inherit eternal life in Christ , will enjoy the benefits of the kingdom. But it would be a bit boring to repeat this from beatitude to beatitude. And there are in some cases additional blessings to be highlighted: *"they shall see God."* . . . *"they shall be called the sons of God."*

Matthew 5:11
11 "Blessed are you when people insult you and persecute you, and falsely say all kinds of evil against you because of Me."

This is similar to that just said above, but adds *"because of Me."* It is profoundly predictive that the righteousness on account of which we will be persecuted will be directly related to the Person of Christ. This is again enigmatic because who is more loving, gentle, compassionate and a better friend than Jesus? What can the world have against Him compared to everyone else?

But it is the message associated with Jesus that offends and subjects us to persecution. This is very important because we often count as persecution the anger and hatred of people for things that are in fact our own fault or our mistake. This is not persecution on account of Jesus. If we snub our neighbor and he gives us trouble we can't call it part and parcel with suffering for our faith.

Jesus brings peace and the answers to life, but He also brings an implied and even voiced condemnation of the life without God. You get Jesus but at the cost of having to first hate and abandon your present life. This, many people are not willing to do and resent being asked.

Hence, anyone who loves his life as it is will find Jesus an embarrassment, a fly in the ointment, a jab in the ribs that reminds them that something has to change. And a ready justification for those who wish to mollify the conviction of those reminders is to persecute this kind of life. To treat it as just an abnormal distortion of the Christian life and label such preachers as just being "out of it." When Christians first became subjects of persecution in Rome they were called *"haters of mankind"* by the citizens [22] certainly a strange appellation, since Christians were taught to love their neighbors as themselves.

The reason is made clearer when we observe the life Christians tacitly condemn by their abstainance. They were basically party poopers in Roman eyes, when we consider that the more popular evening activities involved frolicking, hedonistic escapades and orgies. So Christians became known as people who hated the enjoyments of life, indeed appearing to hate the very society of man.

Today, it is virtually the same but without the ordeal of the arena. Interestingly, during the protests at abortion clinics making the news in Southern California in the late 1980's, some abortion advocates were heard to shout, *"Bring back the lions!"* – a chilling indicator of how hatred for Christ could one day repeat history.

Matthew 5:12
12 "Rejoice and be glad, for your reward in heaven is great; for in the same way they persecuted the prophets who were before you."

As above, our reward may never be earthly, and in the case of an untimely death, certainly never. But we are promised a heavenly reward, which is not to focus on the getting of rewards, but on the knowledge that we have pleased God greatly for service well done.

There is also an added comfort – that we are to count ourselves in the company of a great collection of saints who have gone before, including the prophets. In our world today, we seem far removed from the seriousness and the magnitude of accomplishments which the prophets of old represent to the faith. It would be arrogance to glibly share their spotlight. But Jesus proclaims that those who are persecuted on account of their relationship to Him are esteemed by God Himself as among the same company.

Luke 6:21
21 "Blessed are you who hunger now, for you shall be satisfied. Blessed are you who weep now, for you shall laugh."

Luke presents a more summarized view of the same beatitude above (Matt 5:6). He mentions hungering for righteousness as simply hungering and promises a hunger that will be satisfied. But we must take the whole witness of the Gospels into account to understand parallel statements, and in Matthew Jesus clarifies that it is the hunger after righteousness that will be satisfied.

But is there any justification for a promise about physical hunger? In a general way, Christians can look back on their lives thus far and see the provision of God. Has a Christian ever been hungry and not satisfied? Everyone certainly knows of real cases. But moments of hunger are not in view. A life routinely supplied by God's care and provision is the context, if it be pressed to include physical hunger and the providence of God.

"for you shall laugh"

This does not mean in general that the children of God will laugh *in their mourning*. It means that those who mourn and believe that life will be forever overshadowed by the sad reminder of their loss, will laugh *again* and be able to one day again see the beauty and blessing of life.

---

[22] Tacitus, Annals, xv, ch. 44, Penguin Classics, 1956

Jesus then moves to a series of woes, which are designed to stand in contrast to the blessed states.

Luke 6:24-29, Matthew 5:38-39, Matthew 5:41, Luke 6:30-36
24 "But woe to you who are rich, for you are receiving your comfort in full. 25 "Woe to you who are well-fed now, for you shall be hungry. Woe to you who laugh now, for you shall mourn and weep. 26 "Woe to you when all men speak well of you, for their fathers used to treat the false prophets in the same way. 27 "But I say to you who hear, love your enemies, do good to those who hate you, 28 bless those who curse you, pray for those who mistreat you. 29 "Whoever hits you on the cheek, offer him the other also; . . - 38 "You have heard that it was said, `AN EYE FOR AN EYE, AND A TOOTH FOR A TOOTH.' 39 "But I say to you, do not resist an evil person; . . - 29 and whoever takes away your coat, do not withhold your shirt from him either. . . - 41 "Whoever forces you to go one mile, go with him two. . . - 30 "Give to everyone who asks of you, and whoever takes away what is yours, do not demand it back. 31 "Treat others the same way you want them to treat you.

32 "If you love those who love you, what credit is that to you? For even sinners love those who love them. 33 "If you do good to those who do good to you, what credit is that to you? For even sinners do the same. 34 "If you lend to those from whom you expect to receive, what credit is that to you? Even sinners lend to sinners in order to receive back the same amount. 35 "But love your enemies, and do good, and lend, expecting nothing in return; and your reward will be great, and you will be sons of the Most High; for He Himself is kind to ungrateful and evil men. 36 "Be merciful, just as your Father is merciful. (Luke 6:24-29a, Matthew 5:38, Luke 6:29b, Matthew 5:41, Luke 6:30-36)

Commentary

Luke 6:24
24 "But woe to you who are rich, for you are receiving your comfort in full."

Following the beatitudes there is a complete change in tone, one that might seem to break the wonderful spirit of the foregoing. But it is just as much an obligation for one coming from Heaven to tell us about what is wrong and to be avoided as to tell what is encouraged for righteousness. What is interesting here is that this is not a surprise to people living in these times. It is, however, for some folks today because so many are on the path of optimism and have long since regarded things like judgment to be ancient myths. But for the ancients, even the unrighteous knew of an impending, ominous day when men would be judged for their acts. Such thoughts are peppered throughout secular classical literature. [23]

So it was requisite that Christ confirm what had been in fact laid in the heart of all men about the justice of God. These are warnings that serve to call men back to faith if they are now infrequently inspired by the goodness of what is right. And there is always a curious mixture of obedience and disobedience in everyone. The woes take away any sense of being glib or careless about one's life, even if inspired toward righteousness.

The rich are not those who simply have money, per se, regardless of how it was acquired. It is directed to those whose wealth has affected how they perceive themselves to be because of it. It is not to those who simply have money but to those who count themselves with their money as among the rich. To these He says they have their comfort in full. This is elsewhere stated as *"they have their reward."* (Matthew 6:2)

This is couched then in terms of the expected reward. We can choose an eternal reward or an earthly one. When men play the riches card they are telling God they desire the immediacy of reward in earthly terms they can enjoy here and now and that they have little patience to wait. They are also telling God that they cannot count on an eternity promised, so they are choosing something that is certain, the here and now. Jesus simply says that they have exchanged what could be an eternal reward for an earthly one.

---

[23] Plato, Dialogues, Timaeus 24e-25a; Epictetus, Golden Sayings, LX

This is not the case with godly people who happen to be wealthy. It is possible to please God in the possession of wealth so long as it does not possess the soul. The test is in being able to give it away or abandon it when the time comes. However hard that is to do can be a sign of how much our heart may have changed.

Luke 6:25-26
25 "Woe to you who are well-fed now, for you shall be hungry. Woe to you who laugh now, for you shall mourn and weep."

Sounds like the call for a grim and austere life where no one laughs or enjoys a good meal. This is actually a continuation of the disparagement of the rich. As rich, they take pride in being well-fed. With so many in abject misery and desperately in need of a good meal, taking any pride in one's ability to set a good table would be shameful in God's eyes. To cast this to the wind and grasp for whatever pleasures may be had, earns one the immediacy of his reward. But none later. It is like the son who demands his inheritance before the proper time. There is none to be had when the time comes.

But again it is a question of attitude and balance. Having a feast at a wedding is not the same as taking pride in one's wealth as a lifestyle. It's not clear what *"you shall be hungry"* means in reality. Will their riches soon come to naught and they inevitably feel those pangs of hunger they so tritely disregard? Or will they experience the awakening of their need for God, hunger after Him, but all too late?

In the coming Kingdom, Christ declared that all the injustices will be righted, the crooked shall be made straight, the high made low. So there may indeed have been some at the time of Jesus who would see ruin and hunger in the physical sense, and certainly all who are selfish and evil will see their need for God, but be denied. And also in the millennial kingdom many offenses will be reversed in the lives of real people and real circumstances in those days.

26 "Woe to you when all men speak well of you, for their fathers used to treat the false prophets in the same way."

This almost anticipates that the test for doing well in God's eyes is to be despised in men's eyes. But this is directed at particular cases. We are to be wary of praise from men who are not of faith, who are carnal in their outlook, who seek to advance man without much concern for God. If we get praise from such people we need to be asking if it is because we are furthering their world view, appealing to their humanistic goals, or is it because they are made to see the light of God and the truth of the Gospel? Jesus elsewhere says that our works ought to be such that others who see those works praise God because of them. (Matthew 5:16) The key is the praise is directed to God not to us.

A reminder for those who are listening (and for those of us familiar with the accounts of the OT) is to note that praise historically accorded false prophets and the denigration of those who were true. Those who tickled the ears were acclaimed, those who proscribed and denounced evil were vilified or killed. Such is the warning also for us.

Luke 6:27-28, Matthew 5:43-44
27 "But I say to you who hear, love your enemies, do good to those who hate you, 28 bless those who curse you, pray for those who mistreat you."

Jesus takes this opportunity to talk about our attitude toward those who mistreat us. It is a corollary to the praise from evil men for false prophecies. When we speak the truth, we will beget enemies and suffering. This is also a return to more positive attitudes but in this case about suffering at the hands of evil men. We are to have an attitude toward them and suffering that is opposite to nature.

In this day and age, especially in free societies, it is all about what is fair. Affronts are many times nothing more than the sense that something done to us was not deserved, or we were in some way denied freedom from mistreatment that others are enjoying, that we've been singled out for the opposite. We also harbor a resentment that if we don't retaliate we are letting the perpetrator get away with it and actually giving them impetus to do more harm. There are some dependencies here. If we are afforded legal recourse in matters that the state protects on our behalf, we have leave to pursue them if it is without vengeance, spite or hatred. But even in these proceedings we are to demonstrate love for our enemies. The reason for this is two fold.

First, it disarms our enemies because it takes away the potency, the pay off, of doing something in retribution. Many acts of evil against us are perceived as retaliation against something they perceive we are doing or have done. When we demonstrate love, we take away at least some of the rationale for their actions. Love can cause one to rethink if they've been too quick to judge. Love can show signs of true regret and remorse.

It is a proven principle that things go better for people who confess their wrongs than for those who are belligerent or arrogant about their innocence. It's much harder to come down hard on someone who admits their wrong and is asking for forgiveness. But enemies can rage even hotter when they see arrogance and feel the need to show us reality - *"We'll teach him a thing or two!"*

Second, loving and doing good to one's enemies is God's actual and very real position. For all men – they are born at enmity with God. For all men - God blesses us whether we be good or evil. He reaches out in love whether we are the least sinner or the vilest. If we say we desire to be like God in all we do, we must face the fact that we must emulate Him in this regard.

Luke 6:29a, Matthew 5:39
29 "Whoever hits you on the cheek, offer him the other also;

His audience needs a specific example to drive the point home. It is not that they don't understand His words, but sometimes a vivid, specific example will make the point clearer than generalizing can.

Then as today, if you strike someone there is an immediate emotional need to retaliate. This is as true for women as it is for men. True, there are some who are weak or cowardly and might just run for fear of more violence, but within them is the desire to retaliate none the less. But no one entertains the idea of giving the bully an opportunity to do it again.

But let's be clear: this is not a case of inviting the next blow just for the sake of it or of showing how much we can take. It is a case of demonstrating a spiritual *will* to not retaliate in kind. It is a matter of showing to the offender that we carry a tremendous power within, one that he does not possess. To not strike is to show that we have made a choice and we have the power to effect that choice.

In the film *Schindler's List*, (Amblin Entertainment, 1993), Schindler, suggests to the commandant of the camp that he show the greater power in himself by choosing *not* to shoot prisoners for target practice. Killing was easy. Choosing to not kill was much harder and a greater challenge, and therefore a greater show of strength (which happens to be a biblical principle.) Though temporarily tried, it couldn't be sustained because the man in question lacked the spiritual power Jesus was talking about. But the principle within the sphere of the Christian life is true.

Matthew 5:38-39
38 "You have heard that it was said, `AN EYE FOR AN EYE, AND A TOOTH FOR A TOOTH.'   39 "But I say to you, do not resist an evil person;

This is the old economy – retaliation in kind, according to Mosaic law. It was not based on grace and love which were difficult principles to incorporate into the law during the primitive period in man's social history. (Some might argue that not much has changed.) But this does not prevent Jesus from inaugurating how Christians are to act despite that system set up to embrace the race of men, chosen or Gentile.

The civil law may have its exaction of penalties, but for believers, we are to act differently – to not exact the retaliatory action due. In fact, we are not to resist the evil person in general. This does not mean we are to enable them to do more evil, but we are not to pick up the same weapons of attack with which they are abusing us. We are to show that we do not resort to the world's means to settle our differences.

Luke 6:29b
29 .. Whoever takes away your coat, do not withhold your shirt from him either."

In the spirit of showing the opposite attitude from the world, love exhibits care for the man who steals to meet his need. From God's perspective, the man needs help to meet his needs, not anger. We are not only showing that we are not going to retaliate but we that we see the need that caused him to resort to stealing and we are ready to help him in it.

Matthew 5:41
41 "Whoever forces you to go one mile, go with him two.

This ancient custom is by now familiar to many of us. Soldiers could compel a citizen to carry their equipment through a town and back on to the road to give them rest. In this application, Jesus is introducing the idea, *"The first mile was obligatory, but the second mile is on me. It's me helping you because I want to."*

Matthew 5:45
Matthew adds to the material cited in Luke by presenting the following to clarify how we emulate God in these actions: *"for He causes His sun to rise on the evil and the good, and sends rain on the righteous and the unrighteous."*

Two observations. First, we emulate God in that we add to the general providence He provides for both the evil man and the good one irrespective of their acts.

Second, note that it is spoken of as *His* sun. God is the ultimate owner of the materials and forces in the universe. He is owner by virtue of being maker. If we created through our own mastery and ability a robot in our garage, we would not think of the robot as now owning itself, even though it was built to do things without our manipulating its parts. It remains ours by virtue of our creating it.

Thus all things of the material world are not ours to buy and sell or to own and keep. We are custodians at best and this should change our attitude about the things we think we own.

Luke 6:30, Matthew 5:42
30 "Give to everyone who asks of you, and whoever takes away what is yours, do not demand it back.

This addresses more the giving of alms to the needy than the willingness to lend items to neighbors. This is a sore subject with people today, especially with professional beggars on the medians and corners of our streets. Spoiling our compassion are the typical sob stories about needing bus fare to get to some distant city.

But we see here no layout of qualifications – *"give to everyone provided they have legitimate plights of woe."* To be sure, we have to balance this with being good stewards and not enabling someone else's sin, but this has to come from knowledge not suspicion. Lacking that, we are to give in the spirit of charity and helpfulness.

Many of the homeless who beg on the streets are legitimately needy on a daily basis for food and some money for amenities. That they adopt a sob story that isn't true to better ensure a compassionate response shouldn't really restrict the giver. Very few feel they can be frank and simply say, "I'm just plain broke and I need the money." So, while not throwing out obvious caution, we ought to give people some modicum of slack on just how truthful their story has to be.

That someone may take our money and buy liquor is not something we can control with certainty. Encountering them in front of the liquor store is. But it is not completely out of the question that they might just as likely buy a long-deprived hot meal or some Tylenol. Again, it is a case of how much direct knowledge we have. If it's clear they will buy booze, we have to be responsible which may mean no to money but yes to buying them lunch at the corner restaurant. In the end, God judges you for your spirit of charity and the recipient for his use of the gift. Christ merely asks that we be ready to give in body and attitude.

"whoever takes away"

In an age where ownership and the acquisition of things is part of society, this is hard. It means essentially that if someone borrows something from you and chooses not to return it, you are to consider it a gift to them, meaning that you purpose that it be a further blessing.

It's hard to desire to bless someone who is taking advantage of you. But this, again, is precisely God's position with us, so we are asked to emulate Him. We receive and take for granted (without the idea of return) the common blessings of life, yet God continues His providence over the world because He loves us and wants to bless us despite our attitudes.

So let's be clear about the principle involved: it's about winning one's neighbor to Christ, not about enforcing what's fair and making sure people know who owns what. This is extremely hard to live out in practice, but it is part of seeing ourselves as stewards not owners of the things we have. It is also difficult when it concerns fairly expensive things that will be hard to replace.

We must sometimes wonder if God passes us by in His search for people He can use because He knows that if He takes hold of us, up will come a host of mesh and wires, pipes, and conduit that would make an efficient and clean break extremely messy. It's an attitude and way of life Jesus had, but it comes at the sacrifice of many of the things we've grown to regard as necessary for happiness.

Luke 6:31-33, Matthew 5:46-47
31 "Treat others the same way you want them to treat you. 32 If you love those who love you, what credit is that to you? For even sinners love those who love them. 33 If you do good to those who do good to you, what credit is that to you? For even sinners do the same."

Here then is the exposition of the Golden Rule. This is a two-fold approach to behavior that is based on the idea of blessing others who mistreat us. What hits us strongly is that, in terms of retaliation, our behavior is not to be a recompense for how others treat us – we aren't to justify our reactions on the basis that someone else did the same to us.

In terms of blessing others, the key to assessing the right action or response is in the qualifier, worded in terms of our own likes and wants. Note it is less about how to pick good gifts and more about treating others well. The problem is in figuring out how they would want to be treated. Truly intimate knowledge of that kind is available for only a few people in our lives.

But for the many others, Jesus states that there is a ready guide right inside each of us that will tell us the answer. We merely have to ask how we would like to be treated and in that assessment we will have a reasonably accurate view of what they would like also. And this works simply because all men are basically the same in general terms. All people appreciate being respected, loved, listened to. This won't work well for the perverted or misguided, whose cravings we could hardly encourage. But then we must remember that the test is not what they will want specifically, but what we and most of mankind would want generally. This is not about some specific thing that will indulge one's lusts, but about being respected, loved, and valued.

The statements that then follow seem odd because they break from treating everyone well to blessing our enemies. But this is in line with our enemies expectation of wanting, despite the contradiction of their evil, to be treated decently. It focuses on who are to be the objects of our good treatment, which may be counter to our normal inclinations.

We are to bless them also and if we are in doubt about how, look to those things we would want done to us. This is because at bottom, even our enemy wants good treatment, and may in fact be the way he is because of the lack of it. The important point being stressed is that the reward is weighted toward the hardness of the act, not the act per se. There is no expectation of reward for blessing those who love us, because this is no more remarkable than the behavior of sinners. We are called to show the extraordinary not the mundane, and in so doing, we draw men to an extraordinary God.

Luke 6:35-36
35 ". . and your reward will be great, and you will be sons of the Most High; for He Himself is kind to ungrateful and evil men."

All along the focus has been on what pleases God. To mention that our reward is great in Heaven keeps that theme in focus. This again is hard because we are constantly asking for good things here and now. Some have gotten very few good things at all and to now hear that they must be Heavenly-minded in terms of reward can be overwhelming. The problem with receiving much of Jesus' teaching is that we realize we've been beguiled by all the wrong things and we're not sure we can make the transition to Heavenly ones. Seeing results here and now, having the ready sense of accomplishment, feeling the thrill of winning right now are hard to give up. But that is part of being Heavenly-minded. It is also a fact about the way things are with God. The longer we put off getting accustomed to it the harder it will be.

The last exhortation of v.33 is one of the chief themes of this section – doing the truly hard things that are opposite to nature. These are commanded because it is what God Himself is like, what He Himself experiences, and if we desire to be like Him we must do likewise - *"Be merciful, just as your Father is merciful."*

Matthew 5:13-20
13 "You are the salt of the earth; but if the salt has become tasteless, how can it be made salty again? It is no longer good for anything, except to be thrown out and trampled under foot by men. 14 "You are the light of the world. A city set on a hill cannot be hidden; 15 nor does anyone light a lamp and put it under a basket, but on the lampstand, and it gives light to all who are in the house. 16 "Let your light shine before men in such a way that they may see your good works, and glorify your Father who is in heaven. 17 "Do not think that I came to abolish the Law or the Prophets; I did not come to abolish but to fulfill. 18 "For truly I say to you, until heaven and earth pass away, not the smallest letter or stroke shall pass from the Law until all is accomplished. 19 "Whoever then annuls one of the least of these commandments, and teaches others to do the same, shall be called least in the kingdom of heaven; but whoever keeps and teaches them, he shall be called great in the kingdom of heaven. 20 "For I say to you that unless your righteousness surpasses that of the scribes and Pharisees, you will not enter the kingdom of heaven. (Matthew 5:13-20)

Commentary

Matthew 5:13-14
13 "You are the salt of the earth . ."

Salt in ancient times was universally regarded as a very good thing. In modern times it can be a menace to the machines and technology of man. But in ancient times it was hardly ever seen this way. It preserved foods that would otherwise jeopardize life in an ancient environment. It made it possible to survive despite the lack of modern conveniences.

Jesus here picks up on the preservative aspect of salt in relation to the church. Some see this in Thessalonians were Paul says that the evil one must prevail for a time until that which hinders is taken out of the way (2 Thess 2:7) The use of the masculine pronoun creates difficulty in seeing this as the church, but it is equally difficult to propose that the Holy Spirit is the *"one"* to be taken out of the way, since He is directly involved thereafter in the salvation of many who come to Christ. But the idea is planted that what is of God serves to restrain or to preserve against rampant evil that would otherwise prevail.

But Jesus turns to the subject of the salt losing its potency, its savor. Now it is no longer good for its purpose. It preserves no food. It must be turned out to its other use which was rather ignoble. Spent salt was used to keep roads serviceable by killing out plants and weeds on roads that had to be left unattended for long periods and were beyond immediate forms of maintenance. So it had become in fact only valuable as a chemical.

The question is asked by Jesus, how can it become salty again since salt is its own unique entity (its essence is in itself and no other)? There is nothing it can be combined with to restore its salty nature. Mixing it with newer salt actually dilutes that source rather than restoring what was lost. Hence, the parallel aspect in Christians as they live in the world cannot be counterfeited in the world, as Jannes and Jambres did in pharaoh's court (Ex 7:11). One must come back to the Lord and be made new. As such, we get nowhere asking God to merely refurbish our sinful self. He must make all things new in us.

14 "You are the light of the world."

The concept of light in darkness is a major theme in John's Gospel. It is necessary to repeat because men are to be convinced that they live in darkness that it may kindle their desire to move toward the light. The darkness is seen as man's path, living according to his own wits, according to his own sense of what is valuable and true. It is self-centered, which is today what humanism is all about. It leads to destruction – *"there is a way that seemeth right unto man, but the end thereof is destruction."* (Proverbs 14:12.)

Cities, especially those on hills, gave hope to the weary traveler. (You can endure almost anything if you see a light at the end of the tunnel.) Putting one's light under a bushel is the point of the analogy and while we ponder why people would shy away from telling others the wondrous news of salvation in Christ, we answer it almost immediately in the fear of rejection and persecution that may come with witnessing.

It is not the wariness or fear that is meant here, but the effect - to stay quiet and out of sight. There are folks who fear confrontation and ridicule so desperately that they make considerable effort to blend into the woodwork at the office or in the neighborhood or at school, in dread fear that someone will discover them. We might question their faith, but this is hardly our right to judge. Jesus asks us to contemplate what this condition means. *"Who would put their light under a bushel?"* The foolishness and ineffectiveness of this posture is being highlighted, which means if we are doing this we ought to think about what we're about, what we are called to do and if being a Christian is what we really desire?

The proper place for our lamp can be scary for some, placed on a lampstand out in the middle of the room where it gives light to the whole house. This is not a sheepish, timid analogy, but a strong, intentional frame of mind. To be a light and know full well that it will be seen by all.

Matthew 5:16-17
16 Let your light shine before men in such a way that they may see your good works, and glorify your Father who is in heaven."

We must notice first off that this is unsolicited glorifying. We are not pushing or engineering men into praising God. This comes unsolicited from their own hearts and their own conclusions. This is meant to apply to man in general, not believers exclusively, which would in that case be rather easy to achieve. It is the idea that the men do not normally give God glory but are willing to do so by seeing the works. They are also not praising God for us. They are praising Him for the works they see. Which means that the works are genuine and their value is appreciated independently. They stand on their own.

That's a tall order. Today we see Christian work as a sort of choreographed thing, needing the accompaniment of preaching or some encouraging emphasis in word or music to complete the connection.

Here Jesus is saying they are to look simply at the works without our commentary and connect the dots. They are to see enough to prompt genuine praise of God.

17 Do not think that I came to abolish the Law or the Prophets; I did not come to abolish but to fulfill."

Sooner or later Jesus was going to have to address His relationship to the Law, because the authorities were already noting what they believed to be departures from strict ordinances. So Jesus sets the record straight that He did not come to override the Law with His own teaching, but instead to fulfill it.

Now to the intelligent hearer this meant two things. First, that He saw the Law as good and righteous. Second, that He intended to fulfill it. A more positive statement could not have been made. But as with all things, Jesus teaches something unexpected, contrary to tradition. There was a sense they would understand about fulfilling the Law which simply meant obeying the requirements of the Law. But it would be rare if even probable at all to hear someone talking about fulfilling the Law, per se.

In prophecy, one purpose is to predict. Fulfillment means that there is a distantly connected piece that validates what is promised. Once that occurs, the prophecy is completed, fulfilled. It has served its purpose. This sense of fulfillment was not related to the Law because the Law was seen as permanent, never going away, never having completed its job. Yet we see the idea of completion illustrated in Paul. *"for the Law was our schoolmaster to bring us to Christ."* (Gal 3:24). Once done, it has accomplished, in an individual, its purpose. But it is not done away with altogether because there are always new students, those who need the schoolmaster to continue to bring its students to Christ.

But what Jesus is talking about here is fulfilling the very purpose of the Law which was to get men right with God. And He was doing this where no other could.

Matthew 5:18-19
18 "For truly I say to you, until heaven and earth pass away, not the smallest letter or stroke shall pass from the Law until all is accomplished."

Here Jesus affirms that in terms of the Law, its precepts are eternal down to the gnat's eyelash.

The original has the terms *iota* and *keraia*. The former is the name of a Greek letter, the latter is the Greek equivalent of the name for Hebrew's smallest pen strokes or marks, called horns. It is likely that Jesus, speaking Aramaic, used the name for the smallest letter (*yod*) followed by the name commonly coined for the marks (*keh-ren* - horn). The tiny distinctive end marks on Hebrew letters were called horns, and they distinguished letters with similar strokes from each other (ת , ה, מ , ב).

In translating this speech into Greek, the writer must have perceived that his readers would not relate to *yod* or to its equivalent in Greek (upsilon) as the smallest of letters, which would frustrate the point being made. Instead, he chose to substitute the same concept in Greek, which was to employ the name of Greek's smallest letter, iota (*ι*).

But when he came to 'horn,' it was clear that Greek had nothing equivalent in concept (Greek had no horn-like embellishments). It may very well have seemed that the clearest course was to simply translate Hebrew's word for horn into the Greek equivalent – *keraia*.

When it came to English, the KJV rather crudely referred to the letter iota as a mere jot, and the horns as a "tittle." In the NASB we find restored the original ideas of 'smallest letter or stroke.'

Jesus was saying in metaphorical language that the Law was so permanent in its righteousness, that not even those marks associated with its transcription would pass away. Paul in his great treatise on Law and Grace, reiterates that the Law is righteous and good (Romans 7:12)

But if Jesus did not come to annul the Law then it is still binding. And if it is still binding, from what are we said to be free? We are free from the use of the Law to establish right standing before God. The Law tells us what perfect righteousness is, but it cannot help us achieve that righteousness by trying to follow it.

It condemns every attempt, because we are made weak by it. We are freed from this aspect of the Law in that our righteousness before God is now accomplished in Christ.

19 "Whoever then annuls one of the least of these commandments, and teaches others to do the same, shall be called least in the kingdom of heaven; but whoever keeps and teaches them, he shall be called great in the kingdom of heaven."

To annul is to take on the attitude that a commandment is no longer valid or applicable, and more so in following through by ignoring it as archaic and of no personal import. This attitude usually doesn't stop with oneself. The pride that makes this decision must be shared, people must be made aware of this "enlightened" wisdom, and so this annulling is "taught" to others, leading them also astray.

We wouldn't expect such people to be anywhere in the Kingdom of Heaven, so why the thought that they have the least respectable position there? In some contexts, the Kingdom of Heaven includes all living persons as the created beings of God. The Kingdom is therefore sometimes pictured as the grand play in which God and mankind have their roles and the story unfolds as it has.

In perhaps another sense, those who do such things may in fact be believers who have become deceived or are in error, and their place in the Kingdom is not removed entirely, but they suffer the ignominy of having led people astray in their error.

Matthew 5:20
20 "For I say to you that unless your righteousness surpasses that of the scribes and Pharisees, you will not enter the kingdom of heaven."

This is one of the hardest sayings we can find and for these hearers, even more so because they were under the OT economy that listened to the teachers of the Law and regarded diligent compliance a life long challenge. The Pharisees, despite their sectarian errors and hearts of stone, were diligent in the extreme as to the dictates of practicing the Law. They were the ultra-conservatives of their day. Folks may have had doubts about their party in this or that issue, but everyone concurred that the Pharisee knew more than anyone else all the requirements of the Law in behavior and deed.

It would be enough to tell people that every person must meet the righteousness described by the Pharisee. But to tell people they must exceed this standard was overwhelming. But the intent was to create the hardest scenario that could be imagined. It was intentional on Jesus' part to portray the most arduous arrangement perceivable. Why? Because the hearer would eventually cry out, "Who can be saved?" and would fall on the mercy of God. Such a man would be where God wanted him, bankrupt and helpless to fulfill it.

We see this pictured in the case of the two men in the Temple, the one a Pharisee, busily recounting all his successes before God, and the other a tax collector feeling so wretched that he could not lift his eyes toward Heaven. He asked that God be merciful to him, a sinner. (Luke 18:3) That is the heart in which men are to come to Christ, not justifying this or that, or minimizing their wrongs and emphasizing their good, but bankrupt and ready for the mercy of God.

Matthew 5:21-48

21 "You have heard that the ancients were told, `YOU SHALL NOT COMMIT MURDER' and `Whoever commits murder shall be liable to the court.' 22 "But I say to you that everyone who is angry with his brother shall be guilty before the court; and whoever says to his brother, ` You good-for-nothing,' shall be guilty before the supreme court; and whoever says, `You fool,' shall be guilty enough to go into the fiery hell."

23 "Therefore if you are presenting your offering at the altar, and there remember that your brother has something against you, 24 leave your offering there before the altar and go; first be reconciled to your brother, and then come and present your offering. 25 "Make friends quickly with your opponent at law while you are with him on the way, so that your opponent may not hand you over to the judge, and the judge to the officer, and you be thrown into prison. 26 "Truly I say to you, you will not come out of there until you have paid up the last cent."

27 "You have heard that it was said, `YOU SHALL NOT COMMIT ADULTERY'; 28 but I say to you that everyone who looks at a woman with lust for her has already committed adultery with her in his heart. 29 "If your right eye makes you stumble, tear it out and throw it from you; for it is better for you to lose one of the parts of your body, than for your whole body to be thrown into hell. 30 "If your right hand makes you stumble, cut it off and throw it from you; for it is better for you to lose one of the parts of your body, than for your whole body to go into hell."

31 "It was said, `WHOEVER SENDS HIS WIFE AWAY, LET HIM GIVE HER A CERTIFICATE OF DIVORCE'; 32 but I say to you that everyone who divorces his wife, except for the reason of unchastity, makes her commit adultery; and whoever marries a divorced woman commits adultery."

33 "Again, you have heard that the ancients were told, `YOU SHALL NOT MAKE FALSE VOWS, BUT SHALL FULFILL YOUR VOWS TO THE LORD.' 34 "But I say to you, make no oath at all, either by heaven, for it is the throne of God, 35 or by the earth, for it is the footstool of His feet, or by Jerusalem, for it is THE CITY OF THE GREAT KING. 36 "Nor shall you make an oath by your head, for you cannot make one hair white or black. 37 "But let your statement be, `Yes, yes' or `No, no'; anything beyond these is of evil."

38 "You have heard that it was said, `AN EYE FOR AN EYE, AND A TOOTH FOR A TOOTH.' 39 "But I say to you, do not resist an evil person; but whoever slaps you on your right cheek, turn the other to him also. 40 "If anyone wants to sue you and take your shirt, let him have your coat also. 41 "Whoever forces you to go one mile, go with him two. 42 "Give to him who asks of you, and do not turn away from him who wants to borrow from you."

43 "You have heard that it was said, `YOU SHALL LOVE YOUR NEIGHBOR and hate your enemy.' 44 "But I say to you, love your enemies and pray for those who persecute you, 45 so that you may be sons of your Father who is in heaven; for He causes His sun to rise on the evil and the good, and sends rain on the righteous and the unrighteous. 46 "For if you love those who love you, what reward do you have? Do not even the tax collectors do the same? 47 "If you greet only your brothers, what more are you doing than others? Do not even the Gentiles do the same? 48 "Therefore you are to be perfect, as your heavenly Father is perfect." (Matthew 5:21-48)

Commentary

Matthew 5:21-24
21 " `YOU SHALL NOT COMMIT MURDER' . . . 22 and whoever says to his brother, ` You good-for-nothing,' .. and whoever says, `You fool,' shall be guilty enough to go into the fiery hell."

We can get wrapped up too tightly in trying to analyze why merely calling a man a fool makes us as guilty as if we had committed murder. The courts of human government would never so prosecute. And in God's eyes we would be reticent to conclude that telling a man he is good for nothing would count as seriously as murdering the man. But all such things are to be placed in the context of sin, and sin separates us from God. So a man who does not advance to murder is just as separated and worthy of judgment as the man who murders, therefore what is the point in talking about the degree of wrong?

So here it is not that the courts ought to be condemning men for calling others fools, but that the Supreme Court of God sees all the actions of men in sin as sin in His economy, hence we are worthy of condemnation. (Not a popular acknowledgment today.)

The primary takeaway from this lesson is that one cannot hide behind the safety of having at least not murdered. God looks at the thoughts and the motives of behavior and sees enough to condemn us when measured against His standards of righteousness. In this Jesus is not easing up on the Law, He is making it more rigorous than before. It was difficult to keep, now it is impossible if the thoughts are to be judged also.

23 ". . if you are presenting your offering . . and . . your brother has something against you, 24 leave your offering . . first be reconciled to your brother, and then come and present your offering."

This is not the case of remembering that *you* have something against someone else, but that he or she has something against you. This would mean that he has complained to you about it, or others have made it known that so-and-so is upset with something you've done. Jesus here presents God's view about what is preferred.

What is an offering? Is it something God needs and therefore is sanctified as inviolate? The purpose of man giving offerings is to either commemorate the goodness of God or to meet the demands regarding sin and forgiveness. It is done in order to say something to man rather than to fill some need in God. But to make offering for one sin while another one remains unresolved is not efficacious, neither is the case of offering something for a sin, but making no restitution to the one offended. God would rather see a brother restored through repentance and forgiveness than seeing the sacrifice on the altar.

And we see that this is not something completely new. Saul was told by Samuel that his disobedience was more important to God than making offerings to Him - *"to obey is better than sacrifice."* (I Samuel 15:22)

Matthew 5:25-28
25 "Make friends quickly with your opponent at law . ."

Ancient life included provisions similar to those today in which an injured person could sue us for damages. So the context here is established guilt on our part, not defense of ourselves as innocent. This is directed at the awareness of being guilty but preferring to take our chances in court; and perhaps if we are fortunate enough to hire a clever lawyer, we might get off. Yet as children of God, we are to recognize our guilt (the thing we normally try to hide), and seek reconciliation outside the legal means.

Now here the court is not the divine court, as above, but the earthly court, primarily because the agent handing us over happens to be our opponent. This is to say that we play a precarious game with misbehavior and the risks of being let off or not (and their consequences). But if we are guilty, the likelihood is greater that we will be found so and all our moves to avoid responsibility may very well end us up in jail.

". . *the last penny*" This merely emphasizes that our cleverness will not relieve our paying our full debt before the law and we will find that it would have been better to be honest and to have sued for peace. It focuses attention on our being pro-active about our responsibilities as citizens To avoid the very mistakes that would land us in court, we ought to be all the more circumspect.

27 "YOU SHALL NOT COMMIT ADULTERY;. . .28 but I say to you that everyone who looks at a woman with lust for her has already committed adultery with her in his heart."

This is framed from the view of men looking at women, but it applies to both sexes looking at the other (or even their own) with lust.

We have to bear in mind that Jesus as Creator is fully aware that it is He who created human sexual response. Yet we find Him proscribing it with rigorous conditions. This is not because He made a mistake in the Creation, but that man has abused the gift of God and where abuse persists, correction and even abrogation are necessary.

So we find Jesus laying down a more rigorous obedience to the Law than the Pharisees ever dreamed. It is not enough to be pure in deed, but people must be pure in their thought. To do so would actually exceed the practice of the Pharisees which Jesus had already taught was necessary if one wished to approach by works. This is not about the initial tempting thought (we are all fallen and impure thoughts are going to arise within us.) It is about entertaining such thoughts. It is not that such thoughts appear, but that they remain.

Temptation is going to bring the thought into consciousness; it is not sin when it does. But to dwell and indulge the thought, to let it possess us, this is where sin is conceived. So the notice of a beautiful woman or handsome man is an event. The lingering thought of being with them moves the initial thought to lust. We are not responsible for the first (except to avoid situations known for their temptations) but we are wholly responsible for the second.

Now this is of course not limited to adultery, but applies to fornication (illicit sex between the unmarried) and to all other forms of lust in which we indulge the desire to have something forbidden or that steals our heart away from God.

Matthew 5:29-32
29 "If your right eye makes you stumble, tear it out and throw it from you; for it is better for you to lose one of the parts of your body, than for your whole body to be thrown into hell. 30 "If your right hand makes you stumble, cut it off and throw it from you; for it is better for you to lose one of the parts of your body, than for your whole body to go into hell."

Many have tried to resolve the difficulty of these verses by explaining that Jesus never intended anyone to cut off parts of their body, that He was just talking in hyperbole. But it is more the case that the eye and the hand do not actually cause us to sin, so there would be no occasion to literally do what He says. That is not the same as saying He never intended it literally. If it were to be discovered that our eye or hand caused us to sin, separating them from us would be the proper step to preserving us against judgment.

'Stumble' is an interesting word and is used in this sense uniquely in the NT. To sin is to stumble, as on a path. The stumbling takes our eyes off the goal ahead of us and retards our progress in that we must now pick ourselves up, or even nurture our wounds before continuing. In the NT the stumbling can also picture the case of quitting the path altogether, and looking for easier ones.

As it happens, sin occurs in the human heart. So to follow Jesus' command, we must excise our selfish, corrupted heart. In doing so we must come to the only Physician who knows how, and He will not only take away the old heart but is ready with a new one, one that desires righteousness, and desires the practice and effecting of love.

32 . . " . . but I say to you that everyone who divorces his wife, except for the reason of unchastity, makes her commit adultery; and whoever marries a divorced woman commits adultery."

Very hard words in modern times, where divorce is accommodated as one of society's frequently applied remedies for our mistakes. This is covered again in Matthew 19. The verse quoted here is Deut 24:1-3. This will come up later in reference to why Jesus' new teaching is right if Moses permitted divorce. Here Jesus conveys the heart of God, how He sees the marriage bond and how serious it is when it is broken.

First, there is an exception – that of unchastity. Interestingly, the other Gospels leave this qualification out. But the rule of interpretation is that the harder verses interpret the weaker. More information is considered harder than less information, in that it is more complete and has more stipulation, therefore it rules the more vague. To make the shortened versions rule the interpretation would be to actually eliminate information, which is never the intent of biblical interpretation.

The word is *'porneia'* from which we get our word pornography. (This is one case where the NASB has chosen a weaker, vaguer word when much stronger words were available.) Porneia can be translated as adultery, fornication, homosexuality, lesbianism, intercourse with animals, sexual intercourse with close relatives, and sexual intercourse with a divorced man or woman. So it is basically any form of illicit sexual activity. Whether this is something that occurred prior to marriage or is committed while in the state of marriage, the act serves as a basis for dissolving the marriage if the offended party wishes it. But it does not forestall the offended partner from forgiving his wife or husband and remaining married.

But beyond the exception, we have the hardest words of the teaching. They apply more to remarriage after divorce than to the act of divorce itself. For a husband to simply divorce his wife because she no longer pleases him, actually occasions the likelihood that she will commit adultery. This is because she will inevitably remarry and when that occurs, her bond to the first husband is still considered valid (since the grounds for divorce were not met), hence she is committing adultery, not so much for being married again, but for having relations with someone else. And the man who divorces his wife is in the same condition if he remarries.

But the sin extends further. The man who marries the divorced woman will join her in her act of adultery as will the woman who marries the husband who divorced his first wife. So the adultery spreads fourfold from but one act of divorce based on mere discontent.

The import of this becomes clearer in I Corinthians - if they divorce they are to remain single, or else be reconciled to each other (7:11). However, one condition will undo this restriction for the party that waits – the remarriage of the partners. This is because a new union makes reconciliation of the first union biblically impossible, as described below from Deuteronomy.

But we need a word about the legalism involved here. We cannot assuage the harshness of the command, but we are not to use these verses to make those who have divorced and remarried in fear of their souls, or worse, try to undo the subsequent remarriages and restore what was lost.

In the end, sin is sin and our response is to confess it as sin. But what action we take in terms of remedy or restoration depends on how far things have gone. We must observe the prohibitions in Moses: *"4 then her former husband who sent her away is not allowed to take her again to be his wife, since she has been defiled; for that is an abomination before the LORD, "* (Deut 24:4)

Jesus does not discuss the problem of abuse that could make necessary a divorce for protection's sake. In I Corinthians, Paul deals with the case of the unbelieving husband who is content to live with the believing spouse. She is not to divorce or consider her marriage illegitimate because the man is not a believer (I Cor 7:15).

Some argue that ill-treatment by a believing partner who is oblivious or uncaring about their sin is the same as acting as an unbeliever, and further that such behavior hardly qualifies as desiring to live with the spouse in anything resembling marriage. As such, the wife might think herself free to leave according to the biblical terms of I Corinthians, in that her husband's behavior is not conducive to remaining as man and wife.

The problem with this approach and interpretation is that it ignores the restorative resource we have in God. Choosing abandonment by making hasty assessments of our spouses can be easily abused and divorce can become rampant among Christians at the very moment when God desires to show Himself stronger than the world.

Matthew 5:33-37
33 "Again, you have heard . . `you shall not make false vows, but shall fulfill your vows to the Lord.' . . 34 make no oath at all, . . 37 "But let your statement be, `Yes, yes' or `No, no'; anything beyond these is of evil.

The subject of oaths was a common problem because the things sworn to were ever increasing; were simultaneously becoming unreliable phrases. One had to swear by more and more important things to engender confidence that one meant what one promised.

Oaths were used instead of legal documents in ancient times, so folks were accustomed to evaluating the sincerity and reliability of things said verbally. In Abraham's day, men did the seemingly odd thing of putting their hand under the other man's thigh to signify an oath (Gen 24:2). (This was not as embarrassing an act as we might surmise. It was not much different than two men today sitting and talking, then gripping a man's leg or knee when making an urgent point.)

This gesture and the invoking of an oath came into being precisely because men came to weaken their simple yes's and no's. They needed some added gesture to let the other man know they meant business. Today, oaths have been abandoned as binding agreements in preference for written contracts because men no longer honor their words. They have become clever about wiggling out of things they've merely said.

In the courts, proof of oral contracts can be binding but hard to prove. Spoken oaths still prevail for witnesses. They can do so because there is someone taking down such depositions in writing and the laws against perjury are ready at hand to be enforced. But Jesus is commanding that we go back to the original idea – one that did not need an oath or a gesture or a contract to assure others we would do as we said. We are to let yes be yes and our no be no.

Now this change cannot happen overnight for any one of us. Society will not be anxious to return to this standard. Jesus is recommending we ought to in essence "re-train" the society around us at least, such that men come again to regard our word as our bond. With respect to us as individuals, they need only hear us say, "Yes" to be assured we will be good to our word. This is tough because modern circumstances can so easily interfere with our ability to guarantee our word. Just meeting on time can be complicated by unforeseen traffic conditions. But the new attitude recommended includes actually changing our habits and how we prepare to ensure commitments. We leave extra early to make sure we're on time, we ask a couple dozen more questions to avoid misunderstandings that might prompt us to renege. We say no to other things so our yes's can remain assured and achievable. All of which translate to our being more diligent, more inconvenienced, more circumspect than the "no biggie" attitudes by which we are so used to living.

"anything beyond these comes from evil."

This is a serious challenge in today's society. People do not believe in absolutes, so they view all things as transitory, true for now, but open to change. You will find with each generation in history an increasing tendency to qualify decision points, words that give people exit or bowing out strategies. Folks may give their word but there will always be extenuating circumstances. In fact, we are rearing ever newer generations ever more adept and ingenious in converting purely routine events into "emergencies" that others will be counted on to accept. And they will meet irritation and anger with reminders that they really didn't promise. This is the new and deliberate strategy of the post-modern mind, the voice of the Me Generation. Promises are really more like probabilities. It is a world of *definitely* – maybe.

To do as Jesus recommends will create genuine fear in many people who despise the discipline of thinking and reasoning, and always live on the cusp of spontaneity and excitement. They haven't the knowledge at their disposal for making the right decision, so they decide by trial and error, all under the presupposition that anything can be undone or redone. We don't see this in Jesus at all. He is able to give an answer and stick with it. If we are to be like Him, we need to learn to cultivate this attitude and capacity.

Matthew 5:48
48 "Therefore you are to be perfect, as your heavenly Father is perfect.

This is a command, not a suggestion, which means we are expected to do as commanded. We are to be perfect, and the measure is the perfection that belongs to God - to anyone hearing this, a profound impossibility. And that was actually intentional and deliberate by design.

We are meant to think of the sheer impossibility of becoming that perfect - in the flesh, in our own strength. The fact that we cannot do so does not take away the command or mean that it was rhetorical.

In the OT, God said that the soul that sins it shall die. He did not rescind the command just because He didn't want all men to die, or seeing that they have gone right ahead and sinned, and must die. He provided a substitutionary process of animal sacrifices, which He viewed as a temporary means of postponing the personal penalty for sin. Animal sacrifices were, however, not an effectual substitute. Meaning they were not regarded as the sacrifice *in place of* man's own penalty due. They were an accepted means of *postponement*. They appeased God that He would wait to settle affairs until later. Hence, the idea of a last judgment and the accounting of deeds done in the flesh.

Likewise here, in Jesus and the NT, we find that man's inability to perform perfectly before God does not cause God to rescind the standard of perfection required. It is to be met by someone else on our behalf.

Here, it *is* an effectual sacrifice - one that completes our obligation, nothing postponed.

So we see that the commandment is valid and remains in effect regardless of the impossibility of man fulfilling it, and this causes us to fall on the mercy of God, who has already made provision for that mercy without nullifying the needs of justice. Christ both meets the needs of justice (that someone must pay with their lives) and the needs of mercy (that men may continue to live not only here and now but in the life to come.)

Matthew 6:1-13
"Beware of practicing your righteousness before men to be noticed by them; otherwise you have no reward with your Father who is in heaven. 2 "So when you give to the poor, do not sound a trumpet before you, as the hypocrites do in the synagogues and in the streets, so that they may be honored by men. Truly I say to you, they have their reward in full.

3 "But when you give to the poor, do not let your left hand know what your right hand is doing, 4 so that your giving will be in secret; and your Father who sees what is done in secret will reward you. 5 "When you pray, you are not to be like the hypocrites; for they love to stand and pray in the synagogues and on the street corners so that they may be seen by men. Truly I say to you, they have their reward in full. 6 "But you, when you pray, go into your inner room, close your door and pray to your Father who is in secret, and your Father who sees what is done in secret will reward you.

7 "And when you are praying, do not use meaningless repetition as the Gentiles do, for they suppose that they will be heard for their many words. 8 "So do not be like them; for your Father knows what you need before you ask Him. 9 "Pray, then, in this way: `Our Father who is in heaven, Hallowed be Your name. 10 `Your kingdom come. Your will be done, On earth as it is in heaven. 11 `Give us this day our daily bread. 12 `And forgive us our debts, as we also have forgiven our debtors. 13 `And do not lead us into temptation, but deliver us from evil. ' (Matthew 6:1-13)

Commentary

Matthew 6:1-4
1 "Beware of practicing your righteousness before men to be noticed by them; otherwise you have no reward with your Father who is in heaven.

Now it would seem that the practice of righteousness before men is precisely what we are to do in order to draw all men unto Christ. He has just said previously that we are to let our light so shine that others may see our works and glorify God.

But this is about practicing so as to be noticed by them, meaning to build up one's pride in himself. When He says that we have no reward with the Father, it is because we have sought an earthly reward (to be thought highly of by men) and so we have received it. So it is a principle we should take note of: we can seek earthly rewards or heavenly ones, but not the former as equal to the latter. We may receive both, but we are to seek one in preference to the other.

In churches today it is so very easy to get involved so as to be seen as someone special, someone in authority, or someone with influence. This is made evident when there is disdain or the lack of interest in doing something alone, without people around to notice.

C.S. Lewis' commented notably concerning heaven – *"there will be surprises."* Not only as to who is saved and who isn't but as to what was done for God and what was done for self.

3 "But when you give to the poor, do not let your left hand know what your right hand is doing, 4 so that your giving will be in secret;

"left hand . . right hand" This is just an idiomatic phrase for keeping things very discrete. The business in your right hand is so private that even the left hand of your body does not know about it, (which is technically and biologically inaccurate because hands do not know. But it was meant metaphorically.)
The intent is that we do everything to be sure that our giving is in secret so as to forestall any credit coming to us.

The KJV has *"will reward you **openly**"* but 'openly' does not appear in the Greek text, hence the NASB version - 'will reward you.'

It is to mark that we work for our Invisible Father and are content that only He sees the work done.

Now this is a true wonder of His grace and love, because it is enough to be His children and citizens of His Kingdom. To work should not engender in us any view towards reward. We ought to be glad to do them for our loving Father. But His love is such that He delights in giving us gifts in recognition of what we have done, and in this He shows the excellence of His nature in unexpected blessings.

Matthew 6:5-6
5 "When you pray,.. not.. like the hypocrites;.. I say to you, they have their reward in full. 6 "But.. go into your inner room . . . and pray to your Father who is in secret, and your Father. . . will reward you

The word *hypocrite* comes from Greek drama, meaning the actor pretends or plays a part while not being the person in the part themselves. We are therefore hypocrites when we put forward the pretense of another person to be seen by others. Much of this has also to do with our self image, and today there are many who cannot bear that others see who they really are. In society it is easy to emulate someone else and pretend very effectively to be that person.

The actor Cary Grant, had a rather low self esteem in his youth and when acting came his way, he adopted Cary Grant as his persona. He said that he played him so well that he became Cary Grant in real life. He did not mean that the transformation worked. He meant that he became very adept at always being "on." [24]

We are not to use prayer as a vehicle for our own public aggrandisement, - to advance the image we want others to see. Some folks know how to pray very eloquently in public but have a meager private prayer life. What is striking about this teaching is its validation that God sees in secret. We sometimes attribute vision to physical presence. If no one is here so no one is seeing. Part of the conscience we are to have as Christians is being ever mindful that God not only sees our actions and hears our inner thoughts, but knows their motives.

The atheist dismisses this as so much bunk because the very scene of hearing all the voices in the world and all their motives at the same time is beyond comprehension, and for some just plain nonsense. But of course the problem is in trying to bring God down into the confines of human understanding, to make Him conform to the limits of what men can do. He is in fact beyond all comprehension, a being so unlike His creatures that we make a grave mistake in assuming He is just like us.

"inner room . . close the door"

Some call this "alone time" with God, but whatever we choose to call it, it is needful that we have both a place and the time to be alone. This is a tall order when you're raising a family of little ones. It's a difficult thing even for a new couple because being private can be misunderstood by our wives and husbands.

The view that has helped many is the idea that God is very willing to make an appointment we set with Him and ourselves. Once made, He will be waiting there faithfully for us. That we forget Him and go on about our lives should prick our consciences and get us to fixing whatever interruptions and cares prevent us from getting back to meeting with Him as planned.

So the encouragement is to make that appointment. Make it with Him and with yourself and keep it. He promises that those who seek Him will be rewarded.

---

[24] McCann, Cary Grant: A Class Apart, Columbia University Press, (1998), p.235

Matthew 6:7-8
7 ".. do not use meaningless repetition as the Gentiles do, . . . 8 .. for your Father knows what you need before you ask Him."

The *Gentiles* here means those of Gentile religions. The examples would be the Greeks and the Romans, but also historically the Assyrians, the Babylonians and the Persians. His hearers would know this almost firsthand, for they were the living descendents of folks who were exiles among such people, who heard on a daily basis the kind of prayers being offered. Repetition was the mode of day in these prayers, to pray the same prayer over and over. This is characteristic of the Muslim prayers repeatedly called from minarets and loudspeakers today. Repetition is primitively viewed as "catching" the attention of the Almighty.

But Jesus explains that this kind of repetition is not needed because the Father already knows what we need before we ask. So it is not to be a case of attracting His otherwise busy attention to our insignificant human lives. It is to be personal and based on a knowledge that He is already listening.

Now this will seem to be soon contradicted when we get to the teaching on praying earnestly, as in the case of knocking incessantly at the door until the one inside opens to us. But we will see there that the context is to demonstrate our earnestness and sincerity in what we ask, not to arouse a sluggish God from the ease of His rest.

"not with many words"

To pray like this means we must think about what we will pray, and at least organize our thoughts. We are not to memorize a speech, or practice eloquence before the Lord, but are to be precise, specific and orderly. The idea is that simplicity is best, not a flurry of words. To be simple we need to understand the basic elements of what we wish to say and not just ramble on. But most importantly, we are not to waste time with fluff and flurry.

Have you ever noticed how some folks when praying in a group will end up telling a story as they pray about some need? It winds up being more of a communication horizontally to those listening not a vertical prayer to God. That's what God desires, that we pray vertically not horizontally.

(Now it should be understood that the intentions of people praying are thoughtful and they wish to inform as they pray, but such a prayer has many times gotten out of hand to the degree that one almost feels that prayer has somehow ceased for the moment and sharing is now taking place. Believers just need to be more mindful of the One to whom they are praying.)

"knows what you need before you ask"

Some see this as a reason to question why prayer is needed at all? If He knows what I need, why doesn't He provide it straightway and dispense with what now seems a charade?

The answer is simply that this is a relationship. And as such, we each have our responsibilities in that relationship. It is not that God is stingy. It is that the act of asking and praising bring objectivity to something rather subjective. We are putting into real words something that is felt or believed or hoped for. And this solidifies its reality for us.

But more than this, it involves us. To say "God knows so let Him provide" is terribly one-way-ish. – *'Let me go about my business and let God do His thing with respect to me'*. That's not a relationship. Try it with your wife or husband and see what happens.

What should amaze us is that God is not so aloof, so "other" from us that He cannot be approached or spoken to. He is a God who has arranged the communications line between us. We should feel privileged that we can speak to the Creator of the universe, the Living God.

Matthew 6:9-11
9 "Pray, then, in this way: `Our Father who is in heaven,"

It is another wonder of His grace toward us that He gave us a model of prayer. When you think about someone coming from Heaven to explain how things are in reality with God, among the expected questions an interview with such a person is the question of how we are to pray to the God who is really there, the God of Reality? So He not only has given some instruction about what to do and what to avoid, but He goes even further and says, *"Here's an example."*

Now this was not to be the one and only legitimate, officialized prayer. Is it a model of what prayer should comprise and the spirit in which it should be prayed.

"Our Father . . "

Note that we are not to begin immediately with our needs. We are to begin with an acknowledgment. That God is not merely a Father, but ours. We are saying two things here: that He is our *Father* and that He is *our* Father. We are declaring to Him that we see Him like an earthly father, giving us life, leading us in His experience about the world. Teaching us, guiding us, and protecting us as a father does for his family.

We are also declaring that we claim Him as our own. He is not just "around" so to speak, to be called to when needed. He is our own Father, not merely the Father of all.

"Hallowed be Your name"

We declare here something He already knows perfectly well. But it is important that we restate this when we pray because we are creatures that can easily forget this and become too familiar with God that we lose that sense of awesome respect. He is above all other things Holy.

Hallowed means 'set apart' but we have come to associate it with a category of things so set apart as to be fundamentally different from humanity. Holiness for us seems to necessitate bringing in His righteousness and His justice, such that we approach Him with some caution, not brazenly or irreverently.

10 "Your Kingdom come"

We are to acknowledge frequently that God's chief purpose is that His Kingdom come on earth. It is to say that all that He is and all that He wills should be made manifest here and now on earth as well as in Heaven. It is as though the earth is an incomplete piece of a larger picture waiting to be set into its place that the whole theme can now be enjoyed. The earth is "connected" with God's plans for His Kingdom and it has always been the desire that they be united. That is why Jesus and the Baptist proclaimed that it was "at hand." It was being offered so as to complete the picture, the divine concept of unity with God in all things.

It is a genuine mystery (as Paul states) that the earth has remained separate, the incomplete piece throughout the life of man on the earth. But that mystery is wrapped up in the free will of man in the context of love for man. And that means that the ideal must wait while what is real is worked out in Grace.

11 "Give us this day our daily bread"

Now we may come and petition. And by daily bread we mean all the sustenance of life. Man has instead learned to regard the getting of food and provisions for life the work of his own hands. He does not see God delivering food directly to his door, so he concludes that God has abdicated this responsibility simply because we must do the heavy lifting, it seems.

But in terms of heavy lifting, consider how difficult providing for one's family would be if you had to make the crops actually grow; if you had to move the seasons into place? Now we can say that the seasons occur by our revolution around the sun, but why do plants respond differently because of that distance? That process is quite out of our control in terms of the biological and botanical principles involved. We know all about them, but we can take no credit for their being there in the first place. So who has done the biggest job, God or us?

And even in the ability to get gain and employment such that we can provide for our families, has He not enabled us and gifted us with those capacities and made others to see that our contributions are worth the hiring?

We owe Him everything pertaining to our lives, the tangible and the intangible, and we are to pray to Him as Provider. But we need to observe that this is a daily thing.

The outlook on provisions is day by day, not a six-month plan or a three-year outlook. It is not that He is limited to what can be provided in a day, but that we are not to see Him as the Supermarket in the Sky, "so think big when you ask." He wants us to think daily about our needs from Him, that He is willing to be there on a daily basis and that He likewise does not treat us as wholesale, big box recipients with whom He only wishes to be bothered once a month.

Matthew 6:12-13
12 "Forgive us our debts . ."

This part of the petition is moral in nature rather than practical. We are to keep our accounts with Him current. This means frequently praying that He forgive us our sins. But note that these are characterized not so much as sins but as things "owed" – debts.

When a man sins, he incurs a debt. What is that debt? It is his life. *"the soul that sins, it shall die"* Ezekiel 18:4 We see this in secular images like Blind Justice carrying scales, where crimes are balanced by puinishment. It is reminiscent of the divine institution that sin is a debt that must be offset by a payment. When we sin against our fellow man, we sin against God and therefore owe Him a payment as much as we owe the one injured.

But notice there is a conditional clause *"as we forgive our debtors."* We are to be forgiven while practicing forgiveness to others who are in our debt. This will be made clear by the parable of the man who was forgiven the debt of talents.

And we will see next an expansion on this principle in terms of our actions in relation to God's.

13 "Lead us not into temptation . . "

Some have questioned why this is necessary if God does not tempt us to sin? *Let no one say when he is tempted, 'I am being tempted by God';* James 1:13

This is among the most difficult verses to explain in the NT because every attempt to explain away its contradictions seems to present more. If we say it means that we pray not to be subject to the kinds of things Job suffered by the permission of God, how can this be avoided by this prayer if He wills it? If we say that this is a prayer about our own propensities – may we not lead ourselves into places and circumstances – we are prone to ask why it doesn't say this?

We might offer that in the course of our being led by God we may have to be exposed to things that would tempt us and we are asking that He not lead us thusly. But if He is leading us, He knows what He is doing, and whatever may tempt us is not His doing anyway.

So its understanding seems to defy all our feeble attempts. We are left with these truths: in some sense we can't explain why He wants us to pray not to be led, and that is to be balanced with another truth – that He tempts no one.

"But deliver us from evil"

A note will tell most Bible readers that this is better understood as the evil "one." The reason for this is the presence of the definite article- 'the' - which expresses the idea of something specific and in the knowledge of the hearer.

But this is not a prayer for deliverance from a particular evil that all know about, which would be the meaning: *"deliver us from **the** evil."* So we are obliged to shift the point of reference to the only other specific evil known, which is Satan.

As to deliverance, we need to have confidence that we will be surely delivered by One who has power over all circumstances and events.

There was once told a story of a woman who was set upon by thugs who meant to do her physical harm as well as rob her. She cried out, *"Lord help! Your property is in danger!"*. The men left in what she described as mortal fear, as having seen something too horrible to contemplate.

We cannot pray this as a magic word to avoid all suffering and persecution in life. We are promised a dose of persecution, and Jesus led the example of suffering at the hands of evil. But we can be thankful that those moments are occasional. And as such there will be many more moments when our prayer for protection is in perfect accord with His will for us.

We will surely not survive our call to be a martyr, but this does not preclude all prayers for protection until then.

Matthew 6:13
"For thine is the kingdom, and the power, and the glory, for ever. Amen."

This doxology is not represented in the NASB or the NIV. The reason is that it is not considered part of the original text. It is lacking in all the most ancient manuscripts; it is not present in the Old Latin or the Vulgate. It has also gone unmentioned by the earliest Latin fathers.

This shows the value of textual criticism and its service to Christian faith. It is no doubt a doxology of good intentions, and its sentiments are biblically supported elsewhere in concept at least. But the business of textual criticism is to be clear on what was written in the originals, not what someone added in a moment of religious fervency.

So while we might not let go of it easily, we are first called to be honest with respect to the Bible because it is the objective reference for our faith.

Matthew 6:14-23
"14 "For if you forgive others for their transgressions, your heavenly Father will also forgive you. 15 "But if you do not forgive others, then your Father will not forgive your transgressions. 16 "Whenever you fast, do not put on a gloomy face as the hypocrites do, for they neglect their appearance so that they will be noticed by men when they are fasting. Truly I say to you, they have their reward in full. 17 "But you, when you fast, anoint your head and wash your face 18 so that your fasting will not be noticed by men, but by your Father who is in secret; and your Father who sees what is done in secret will reward you. 19 "Do not store up for yourselves treasures on earth, where moth and rust destroy, and where thieves break in and steal. 20 "But store up for yourselves treasures in heaven, where neither moth nor rust destroys, and where thieves do not break in or steal; 21 for where your treasure is, there your heart will be also."

22 "The eye is the lamp of the body; so then if your eye is clear, your whole body will be full of light.   23 "But if your eye is bad, your whole body will be full of darkness. If then the light that is in you is darkness, how great is the darkness! (Matthew 6:14-23)

Commentary

Matthew 6:14-15
14 "if you forgive others . . . your heavenly Father will also forgive you. 15 But if you do not . . . then your Father will not forgive your transgressions.

We must be careful here to not enter once again into a salvation earned by works or one's performance in the sight of God. It can be inferred that this is precisely what is being recommended - forgive in order that you be forgiven of God; His forgiveness then being tied to our own acts toward others.

But Paul soundly repudiates the idea that blessings or a right standing before God are conditional on how well we do in actions and works.

We need to understand this verse in the same manner that we understand 1 John –

"The one who says, "I have come to know Him," and does not keep His commandments, is a liar, and the truth is not in him;" 1 John 2:4. *"The one who says he is in the Light and yet hates his brother is in the darkness until now."* "2: *If anyone loves the world, the love of the Father is not in him."* 2:15

Is it the case that the minute we cease to keep His commandments, we become a liar and devoid of the Truth? Is it true that should we come in a certain instance to hate a brother, we are deceived about living in the light and in fact must acknowledge that we live in darkness? Is it true that if we love any aspect of the world, the love of the Father ceases to be in us?

We are to understand 1 John as dealing with conditions, not instances of sin. These are life attitudes that beget the darkness and lack of love. It is teaching that if we have the attitude that keeping His commandments is optional or unnecessary we make ourselves a liar. It is the readiness to hate as a normal response to adversity that puts us in darkness rather than in the Light. It is the double-mindedness that legitimizes the ways of the world while purporting to be His followers that inhibits the love of the Father living in us, not that we happen to have a favorite movie, love to go out dancing or enjoy a Starbucks every morning.

But if our life is purposed to do the opposite of these things, yet we stumble, we should not conclude that we have been deceived all along that the truth was ever in us, because we can acknowledge our love for the truth, despite not being perfect to fulfill all righteousness.

So likewise here also. It is a life or a mode of behavior that is unforgiving, that prefers vengeance and "teaching others the wrong they've done us" that disqualifies us from depending on the Grace of God's forgiveness. We will later see this in the parable of the man who's debt was forgiven and goes out and threatens harm to his own debtors if things owed to him are not repaid.

This understanding should also settle the issue of whether this is another unpardonable sin – not forgiving others, - to be added to the blasphemy of the Holy Spirit. If it is understood as above, an individual instance of unforgiveness would not be in the same class as blasphemy of the Holy Spirit, but a life of unforgiveness could be seen as resisting the influence and normative power of the Holy Spirit, and therefore rather close to the condition that qualifies as the blasphemy.

And in individual cases, our act of unforgiveness, while not jeopardizing our salvation, might bring consequences that express God's attitude toward our sin and that all is not well between us and Him. It prompts us to keep short accounts with the Lord.

Matthew 6:16-20
16 "Whenever you fast, do not put on a gloomy face as the hypocrites do . . they have their reward in full. . . 17 anoint your head and wash your face . . 18 and your Father who sees what is done in secret will reward you."

Those who made a show of fasting were much like the actors on a stage, there to play a part which had little to do with their real lives. Spiritual hypocrites had no real intention of living by their faith, but wished to be seen as devout and holy men.

Now it would seem that such hypocrisy would be inwardly known and as with all charades and the effort to keep up appearances would become sheer drudgery and be eventually abandoned. That, in fact, was often the case. Hypocrites often simply gave up.

As for the others, we must keep in mind the tremendous advantage play acting in this kind of society gained for an individual. The classes in society were much more distinct. The rich were extremely so, and the poor also extremely so. There were very few in the middle. So life was a constant struggle to avoid the stain of the lower class, and this generating any number of desperate moves and machinations to gain the admiration of others.

To put on gloom or even the feigning of agony in prayer, and doing it publicly, would hopefully cause others to say, "What a saint so-and-so is. Look how he agonizes in prayer." But Jesus recommends that we arrange our appearance as one in whom all things are well and free of trouble. We are to have our hair shining with the anointing of oil and our face fresh and washed as though we are attending a social affair in good spirits, full of energy and joy. Our personal appearance and public persona is to be such that we are *not* noticed. And we are further to be satisfied with being only seen in secret by God.

19 "Do not store up for yourselves treasures on earth, . . 20 But store up for yourselves treasures in heaven, where neither moth nor rust destroys, and where thieves do not break in or steal;

The acquisition of material possessions was constantly fueled by the observance everywhere of the plight of the poor. It was an effort to be as separate from them as possible and of course to eek out any enjoyment one could gain. Today we seldom see the kinds of people the truly destitute poor comprise. The homeless who beg or solicit on the medians are surprisingly removed from the destitute poor of ancient times. Many of the homeless show in their appearance that they have some access to the means of personal hygiene, laundry and medical services.

We only occasionally see those one or two who have been sleeping out in the elements, clothes caked with grim, sweat and dust, skin ravaged by time and the heat, and whose hair is something out of prehistoric times. But such persons were commonly seen in ancient times and their state all the more routinely feared. The getting of things was the sign of preferable standing in society, even if monetarily one had nothing that approached the upper classes.

It is a wonder that anyone appreciated the alternative being offered – seek treasures rather in Heaven. These were perceived as intangibles, rendering nothing of immediate value, and for many the dictates of the here and now were the only focus that mattered. It's a bit like asking a child who is crazed with the idea of having the latest version of *Nintendo* to consider putting the money aside for college.

To help the transition in thinking, Jesus reminds His audience of the fate of earthly treasures. No sooner do we get them than they begin a steady path to despoilment. They must ever be cleaned and polished, and even that process serves to rub away their glory and they begin to acquire the telltale stains of having been used. And there is always the principle of obsolescence. Walk through a junk yard on the outskirts of town and see the end of what were once shiney new models in showrooms, whose appearance caught the eye and turned one's head. Now they are faded, moth-eaten, pealing and rusted, and the dream of no one anymore.

In contrast, the things of Heaven are free from such corruptions. But more than this, they are the things that will appoint and adorn a much longer period than our lives will ever measure – eternity future. We are to "invest" in those things that will serve to furnish and dress our eternal dwelling places.

There was an anecdote that circulated a few years back about a wealthy woman and her maid, both of whom were Christians. The woman had amassed a considerable fortune that she used to ensure a life of ease and luxury for herself. Her maid was just the opposite, making many personal sacrifices with considerably less income so that others might be blessed.

The maid died and later the woman herself. When the woman was being escorted to her home in heaven, she noticed the wonderful mansions along the way, and then one of particular beauty and grandeur. The angel explained that this was the house of her maid, at which the woman imagined the veritable palace that must be awaiting her. As they continued, the houses got smaller and less stately, until they turned onto the last of several streets to a little modest home of unimposing aspect. "Here we are" said the angel.

"There must be some mistake," said the woman. "My maid received that glorious mansion and I am to live here?" The angel replied, "Your maid spent her whole life sending us the materials of love, faith and self-sacrifice, such that we had plenty with which to build her that beautiful home. But as for you, these are all the materials you sent us."

We must never forget that the kingdom is to be built of the souls of men and the good works done to show the love of God toward all men. These are its building blocks and they will translate into the stuff with which Christ "prepares a place for us."

Matthew 6:21-22
21 "for where your treasure is, there your heart will be also."

It is a principle of life that our heart follows the things we come to value. It wraps itself around such things and provides the energy and time that our devotion requires. The trouble with man is that the objects of devotion can be earthly and carnal, many of which are fueled by their immediate promises of gratification. So our heart readily goes out after them.

Jesus is saying that what we value determines where our heart will be. So be very sure that what we value is long-lasting, eternal and eternally valuable. If we wrap our hearts around the temporal, it will disappoint us because it will not last and our heart will be despondent at the loss, seeking another patron on which it can spend its energy.

In life, we often find that our job is a thing we must do, but our passion often lies elsewhere. We can be so-so at work in terms of energy, interest and the willingness to spend extra time. But when it comes to our passion, no expenditure is too great. Jesus is saying, "Make the things of Heaven that passion and you will be rewarded in ways that will never disappoint because they will be eternal."

22 *"The eye is the lamp of the body . ."*

This is in what is called phenomenal language – the language of appearances. It is not meant to convey that as light enters the eye there is a reflection that spreads through its inner parts. It is describing how we perceive the effect of light coming into our eyes. Our bodies are comprised of many processes, the majority of which do their work completely blind. "Seeing", per se, is not a necessity for their operation in any sense imaginable. How they sense the presence of amino acids or hemoglobin has nothing to do with seeing.

But we as sentient creatures see. As we look out into the world beyond our skin, that world is characterized by what we take for granted and seldom think about – the presence of light everywhere that enables us to know where we are and what we are doing. Light is not necessary for us in sensing our own being, but we immediately become used to it being the key to performing all the functions in life. As such, it lights up every experience.

It naturally follows that if our eyes are not clear, if they obstruct the getting of light, we perceive our selves and our bodies as filled with gloom and murk. In the case of the blind, all is darkness and life is a matter of groping in that darkness, which we can learn to deal with, but the learning is never characterized as finally coming into the light.

Jesus then transitions the context. If the light we need for life is gone, the resulting blindness and its darkness is profoundly complete. But there is another form of light, the light of the soul, that can be perceived irrespective of the physical. And if this light is lacking and we are in that kind of darkness, how much more profound it is than physical darkness.

This is something that mankind overlooks in his busy-ness to enjoy life as long as it lasts. Man can be fully healthy in vision and sight but be in complete darkness as to his soul. Christ's message and that of the Gospel is to rekindle the awareness of the darkness rationalized away so long ago, but which plagues every aspect of living.

Matthew 6:24-34

24 "No one can serve two masters; for either he will hate the one and love the other, or he will be devoted to one and despise the other. You cannot serve God and wealth. 25 "For this reason I say to you, do not be worried about your life, as to what you will eat or what you will drink; nor for your body, as to what you will put on. Is not life more than food, and the body more than clothing? 26 "Look at the birds of the air, that they do not sow, nor reap nor gather into barns, and yet your heavenly Father feeds them. Are you not worth much more than they? 27 "And who of you by being worried can add a single hour to his life? 28 "And why are you worried about clothing?

Observe how the lilies of the field grow; they do not toil nor do they spin, 29 yet I say to you that not even Solomon in all his glory clothed himself like one of these. 30 "But if God so clothes the grass of the field, which is alive today and tomorrow is thrown into the furnace, will He not much more clothe you? You of little faith! 31 "Do not worry then, saying, `What will we eat?' or `What will we drink?' or `What will we wear for clothing?' 32 "For the Gentiles eagerly seek all these things; for your heavenly Father knows that you need all these things. 33 "But seek first His kingdom and His righteousness, and all these things will be added to you. 34 "So do not worry about tomorrow; for tomorrow will care for itself. Each day has enough trouble of its own." (Matthew 6:24-34)

Commentary

24 "No one can serve two masters;.."

It is a principle in life that we follow someone or something. Even those who are leaders, who enjoy command, who dominate the scene have someone or something they admire, someone they are emulating, some principle that drives them forward. Even those who are so low in self-esteem as to have no motivation or drive to achieve are still vulnerable to anyone who pays attention to them. They adopt them easily as someone to whom they give allegiance and deference, who will help them climb out of the misery of their so-called life. They are busy in their inner life dreaming of being someone else.

These are all allegiances that can captivate and inspire. They give people tangible expectations of achieving the things they want or crave for themselves. And in that sense they can be seen as having a master.

The reason this is important is because when religious tenets of faith come along, there is a propensity to *manage* these rather than exchanging one for the other. We want both not either/or. And that is because we are told constantly that we can have both. But Jesus is telling us that this is a deception. Our allegiances cannot be split between two masters. And we need to be clear that this is not about the more trivial goals we might have for ourselves. It is about major world views, the things we decide to follow, to which we will willingly give our time and energy. One master we can acquire from the world, the other we acquire through faith.

He is telling us that while we might see things running swimmingly at first, there will always come a conflict where one allegiance demands its right over the other and we are then in the dilemma of choosing. And when we choose, we have come to love one and despise the other, especially if the conflict involves sacrifice.

The other reason this will be especially hard to receive today is because we are so busy following the intoxicating formula of "Me first." We are told almost daily that we are the "masters of our own destiny" – an interesting choice of words, since the subject here is masters.

This modern mantra is perceived as a deliberate shaking off of the old master of a bygone age, who expected conformity and dictated absolutes. So it's understandable that when the NT comes along and recommends that we return to the one way, one truth idea, there are going to be objections and a reaction of disdain.

On the other side, we are not to understand this as meaning that we are not to be in the world at all. Some see the choice as a case of giving up any and all expectations in the world for Christ. We need to be clear that He does not want us so heavenly minded that we are of no earthly good. He has chosen us especially *because* we are agents in the world. We are to have families and careers that support them. We are to contribute to the society in which we live. But we need to always bear in mind that our behavior in these roles is to be governed by Him not by the dictates of the world.

Allow a digression to illustrate this point. In I Samuel chaper 17, David is volunteering to fight Goliath. There are plenty around him to remind him that his stature and capacities are inadequate to the task compared with those of Goliath. "Goliath is a seasoned veteran of battle, you are just a boy."

To many, these comments are a case of bringing reality into the picture. And this is what secular leaders' are always looking for and glad to find - someone with some sense in their head so as to acquaint dreamers with the facts of the real world. "Battle-hardened strength against total weakness. Who do you think is going to win?"

But David was told not to look at the external properties of the battle, what men see and heed first. The strength of a man is not in what is on the outside, but what is on the inside. He saw beyond the physical properties to what God had in view.

So David lived very much in the world. He stepped out on a very real plane and faced a very real adversary. But David's world view was entirely different. It was not about what he would do and what Goliath would do. It was about what God was doing.

Matthew 6:24b
24 .. "You cannot serve God and wealth."

The tone of this teaching is directed to those things that call for our divided allegiance. Even after we become aligned with God's Kingdom - we make our choice – the world can beckon us to itself in the interest of stealing us away again. We can be on our way in the ship with a clear direction ahead, but the Sirens of other masters can call to us from the shore. [25]

Wealth is first and foremost a pursuit. It is not simply being rich, it is the desire to remain rich and to become richer and richer. It is mentioned by Jesus because it is so intoxicating. It is the reason why people with no self control will pump salvo after salvo of nickels into slot machines hoping the next spin will turn them into winners. And if not, then the next spin, or the next after that.

But the primary reason wealth is posed as opposite to serving God is because once acquired it can beguile the owner into the deception that enough money will solve everything, will fix every problem in life. And that is the role God wants us to see in Him. He wants us to see Him as the only true source of supply for all we need. And His competitor is money because money is so immediate and so efficient. Once infected, man will face the dilemma that he cannot serve both.

Matthew 6:25-26
25 "For this reason I say to you, do not be worried about your life, as to what you will eat or what you will drink; nor for your body, as to what you will put on. Is not life more than food, and the body more than clothing?"

The worry about what we will eat, drink or wear is in a different context for most of us today. It is usually a case of adding variety and quality but seldom about having or not having. In ancient times, however, it was very much about having or not having. Variety and fashion were only concerns for the rich. So when Jesus said, *"Don't worry about what you will eat or wear"* these were more vital concerns than we think about

---

[25] In mythology the Sirens were women who called out the names of passing sailors from the shore in alluring tones to distract them from their course.

today. This dichotomy of the rich vs. the poor can produce two very opposite views about God and His provision. The poor may be prone to assume He is too busy with weightier matters than to worry about the trivialities of what one family or another has to eat or wear.

Jesus answers this by bringing in a proper sense of perspective – if He takes care of the lilies of the field. If life and the body are more than food or raiment, then because of these things God will not abandon their basic needs. It is not because He values food and clothing, but because He values life and the body He has given us.

The rich on the other hand will develop a different attitude. They are bent on acquisition and the next new thing. As such, they may have a distorted view of God's provision. Either they expect God to "bless" them in their efforts to keep up with the Jones's, or they may disdain the call to return from materialism to simplicity. Jesus words about life and body being the more important things can either bring them to their senses or move them further into self-centeredness.

To both, He still says: you are not to worry about these things, whether it be in terms of basic provisions, or in terms of the latest fashions. Trusting in God will bring both to a common ground in Him – the poor up from their lack, the rich down from their excess; both appreciating what is important: the life and body God has given all men.

But the question may still arise, *"Yes, but will He provide for me? Will He be moved to care for things as insignificant as those that apply to one life?"* Jesus answers this by an observation in life

26 "Look at the birds of the air, that they do not sow, nor reap nor gather into barns, and yet your heavenly Father feeds them. Are you not worth much more than they?

It is a true wonder that the birds are able to meet their needs without the industry and planning man finds so necessary. They can be seen by the cynical as merely at the whim of nature to fend for themselves or die, but God has built into nature enough to satisfy their needs.

They don't hoard against some future day of lack. They have innate confidence that all they will need to eat for every day will be available every day, so they return home with nothing but themselves and they start out the next day with nothing but themselves.

That is what is meant by our heavenly Father feeding them.

Yes, there are those who will try to make exceptions the rule and point out that many animals die due to changes in their habitats that eliminate necessities for life. As with all things in the Bible, God is talking about the general state of things, not the rarities of nature.

And the point, of course, is in the last line: *"Are you not more important than they?"*

This will satisfy the humble, but shame the materialistic. The humble will be renewed with confidence that God will not abandon them for weightier matters. The rich will entertain disdain for the call to be satisfied with one's daily bread, but its truth will be undeniable.

Matthew 6:26
26 ". . the lilies of the field . . they do not toil nor do they spin, . . not even Solomon in all his glory clothed himself like one of these. But if God so clothes the grass of the field, . . will He not much more clothe you?

Another example from nature is needed because it must be made clear that in the case of the birds and even more so with the lilies, they are without capacity to provide for themselves, they are wholly dependent. In the case of the lilies, two additional observations are added: their beauty from God surpasses what the richest man can provide for himself, and despite these things, they are subsequently thrown into the fire when the season has passed or the land needs to be cleared.

To highlight their raw beauty, the colors in nature or so pure as to be unmatched by the artificial means of human fabrication. The reds, the yellows, the blues are of such extraordinary purity and depth, the whites so incredibly pure, as to always stand out far and away from what man can make. The mention of their being burned is to highlight the irony of their arbitrary nature, despite their beauty. Their existence is that precarious; and as such we might conclude an incredible waste of effort in pouring such quality into things that can so easily become mere disposable debris. This, even more than the case of the birds, rivets our attention on how much greater we are in God's eyes. And if so, our expectations must accord with the difference.

Matthew 6:27-34
27 "And who of you by being worried can add a single hour to his life?"

This is paralleled in Luke 12:12:25. A textual difficulty arises here in the NASB translation. The phrase *"can add a single hour to his life"* is not in the Greek text. Consistently here and in Luke 12:25 we have in the Greek *"can add to his stature one cubit."* In fact there are no variants in the manuscripts that would substantiate a different rendering as we have here. Ironically, the Received Text of the KJV happens to support the best Greek texts.

However, the study of these verses presented what translators perceived as a problem in consistency. Adding what would amount to eighteen inches to one's stature was not a small amount, and takes the analogy completely out of the context of Jesus' teaching. It was therefore thought by editors of the NASB that the meaning is better rendered *an hour to one's life.* The NIV also follows this rationale, while the American Standard Version (1901) preserves the Greek original.

Hence, this constitutes one of the rare cases where translators' license deviated from a rigidly faithful representation of the text. [26]

We are totally dependent on God and there are things we simply cannot change or improve no matter how much effort we muster. All things are in His hands. Better that we get on board with His plan for our lives if we are to be satisfied and full in this life.

30 ".. You of little faith!"

Jesus adds this rejoinder, which seems harsh, but was so endemic in those comprising His audience. It was so incredibly common to forsake faith in God's provision at this level of life, and to miss the lessons available in the things mentioned above. It is not a case of not having faith, but of having a faith too small.

33 "But seek first His kingdom and His righteousness, and all these things will be added to you."

We seldom believe this in practice. It is fine as an academic acknowledgement, but we leave behind the sound of these words in the sanctuary and proceed out into our daily lives as though we must face reality and make certain things happen by our own efforts. We may have the notion that this works for the special cases – the saints or those called to full-time service. But the average person often thinks that if they don't make it happen, it won't.

The key to this verse is in what *all these things* means. First, we need to get it straight that this is not a formula for getting all the things we ever wanted. It is talking about the things we need, not the things we want. But it can include things we want if they be in accord with the things He wants.

---

[26] Alford, Greek Testament, Vol I, Part I, Guardian Press (1976), p.67

In other words, whether we have needs or wants, if they are about His Kingdom, then seeking that Kingdom and His righteousness will give us the assurance they will be provided. This is terribly hard for people caught up in materialism. Because it may mean that He will not add unto us the Thomasville dining room set that will make all our neighbors green with envy.

This exhortation asks us to focus on our orientation in life, - is it around the right things or the selfish things. The formula works when the heart is in the right place. This is expanded in James where the apostle writes, *"Ye ask, and receive not, because ye ask amiss, that ye may consume it upon your lusts."*

34 "So do not worry about tomorrow; for tomorrow will care for itself. Each day has enough trouble of its own."

This will of course drive schedulers and planners mad, since their whole mode of day is in looking ahead and contemplating contingencies for future eventualities. It is in practical terms decidedly unavoidable. We wouldn't be able to plan for our children's education if we didn't look beyond today's needs. But Jesus is talking about worry, not wisdom. We may have plans, but the outcome of those plans is beyond our control. Even the best plans go awry when the time comes. There is always some factor we didn't expect, some twist that defeats our plan.

The thrust of this is that we concentrate on the day at hand, in the understanding that we will do well just handling its cares and issues, than to also worry about the next day.

We need to avoid a legalism here that would enforce no thoughts about what is planned for tomorrow or next week. That would be hard to dismiss from our minds. But again, it is talking about worry. Are we fretting, are we stressing about all possible eventualities? Worry is a clear sign that we are not walking by faith, nor with the confidence that God walks with us.

Find a passage where Jesus worried. Ever notice that Jesus never ran in the Gospels? Absolutely nothing took Him by surprise because He knew that His heavenly Father was there in the midst of all He was doing, and whatever lies or fears might be thrown at Him about the "urgencies" of the moment (as in Lazarus), He knew who was in control.

Luke 6:37-42, Matthew 7:6
37 "Do not judge, and you will not be judged; and do not condemn, and you will not be condemned; pardon, and you will be pardoned. 38 "Give, and it will be given to you. They will pour into your lap a good measure-- pressed down, shaken together, and running over. For by your standard of measure it will be measured to you in return." 39 And He also spoke a parable to them: "A blind man cannot guide a blind man, can he? Will they not both fall into a pit?

40 "A pupil is not above his teacher; but everyone, after he has been fully trained, will be like his teacher. 41 "Why do you look at the speck that is in your brother's eye, but do not notice the log that is in your own eye? 42 "Or how can you say to your brother, `Brother, let me take out the speck that is in your eye,' when you yourself do not see the log that is in your own eye? You hypocrite, first take the log out of your own eye, and then you will see clearly to take out the speck that is in your brother's eye." (Luke 6:37-42)

"Do not give what is holy to dogs, and do not throw your pearls before swine, or they will trample them under their feet, and turn and tear you to pieces." (Matthew 7:6)

Commentary

Luke 6:37
37 "Do not judge, and you will not be judged; and do not condemn, and you will not be condemned; pardon, and you will be pardoned."

Other versions have, *"lest you be judged."* The idea is that of avoiding judgment of oneself by purposing not to judge. Judging and condemning are cautioned because they are the reserve of God Himself, who judges with perfect wisdom, a complete knowledge of the facts, and with justice.

This is among the most misused verses of the Bible and is ready at hand in the mouth of the unbeliever to fend off evangelistic attempts to convert him – *"who are you to judge me?"* But evangelism infers a necessary judgment – the unbeliever is without Christ, without salvation, condemned, so despite our desire to avoid the appearance of judgment, there is always one in play by default. Hence, the unbeliever quotes this verse to avert having to account for himself before God, but especially before Christians. And often it is just a ruse to preserve their way of life.

The key to this teaching is *"and you will not be judged."* If God has given wisdom and foreknowledge to judge, then what fear has the believer in proclaiming it? The judgment to be avoided is that of God, and if we judge with God's insight, He is the one to whom we will answer. And if it was according to His bidding there will be no judgment to fear.

The sting comes in when we take to ourselves the role of judge without warrant. Assessing other people's state, worthiness or place before God purely on our own. This is delicate because we can easily deceive ourselves that our assessment is God's own.

Another related failing is our propensity in general human affairs to draw conclusions in haste. We hear just enough to arouse suspicions and then proceed to make a complete case without hearing all the facts. Then when more of the facts are made known, we cover our embarrassment by contorting the interpretation of the facts so that our initial judgment can stand without retraction. All of that sort of thing is of evil and selfishness. Hence Jesus says there is judgment waiting in the wings for us.

Condemnation is in the same context because so much of judging is condemnatory. To condemn is God's prerogative. It is His Kingdom, not ours. He sets the rules as to who gets in. Condemnation is more serious than judging in that it is more final, more teleological (matters concerning the final outcome of things) and no man can say he knows such things. So while a person is certainly acting outside the righteousness of God and openly curses God, his ultimate end cannot be known, whether he will be saved or not.

Someone could have looked at Paul while he still breathed threats against Christians and made a "final" assessment of his life and would of course have been dead wrong.

A positive exhortation is recommended - *"pardon and you will be pardoned."* It is akin to showing mercy if we wish mercy to be shown to us. The principle is not a formula for how to get into God's good graces. Salvation is still the requirement, but it is meant to show that we can't practice mercy and pardon opposite to God's will in these things and then expect mercy to be shown to us.

Luke 6:38
38 "Give, and it will be given to you."

This can be seen the wrong way – if you want to have things given to you, give. That shouldn't be our reason. Rather, it is a way of explaining why we may not be receiving. We don't possess a giving attitude in disposition or deed.

There are some folks who always see themselves as being on the receiving end of other people's charity, but never as the giver. They want always to get but not often to give, or if so, begrudgingly. The truer spirit is to give without expectation of reward or return in kind. It is taking joy of one's life that others are blessed that is the preferred attitude. And if we take the opposite, Jesus is saying that when we begin to ask why we are not receiving, we have our answer.

"They will pour into your lap a good measure--pressed down, shaken together, and running over."

When we give with the right spirit, we will find that our Lord is not slack in blessing us back. This is the measure of His goodness. We ought to be fully satisfied that others are blessed. Yet He loves us so much He cannot withhold a return of blessing. It is not something He owes us. It is something He simply wishes to give back in His love for us and our obedience.

'They' means the agencies of His blessing back to us. God very seldom acts personally in the world, but always through his creation. He "arranges" the persons and affairs that will minister the blessings.

"pressed down, shaken together, running over" are customary terms from the times. When measuring out quantities, especially things like grain, the seller could easily get away selling less quantity for the same price by simply filling the bushel and collecting the cash.

The conscientious seller would pour in a portion, shake the grain to get rid of pockets of air, then press it down. Then add more, doing the same until the bushel represented true value for the money paid. That is what characterizes the blessing of God. Not given stingily or miserly, but of the truest value, with generosity.

"For by your standard of measure it will be measured to you in return."

If you are cheap and miserly, your rewards will be the same. God is simply saying that we cannot have double-standards between others and ourselves.

Luke 6:39-41
39 And He also spoke a parable to them: "A blind man cannot guide a blind man, can he? Will they not both fall into a pit?"

The train of thought is still about judgment but the emphasis is now about humility as the basis for not judging. It is a matter of knowing our place among other men.

The guide and the one guided are at different places. The one who is blind cannot think of himself more highly than his circumstances. He is dependent on those who can see, so he must face his dependency as it is. He must accept his place and the fact that there are those with sight while he has none.

40 "A pupil is not above his teacher; but everyone, after he has been fully trained, will be like his teacher."

Likewise, a pupil must defer to his teacher. The teacher has been trained and he has yet to be trained. He must not consider himself above his teacher, but know his place.

This is not a justification for class discrimination – that some people are better than others. The question is not about superiority or inferiority of person, but about roles and places in society. Some people translate this into the same thing as discrimination about personal worth because if a person only gets menial jobs while others get the lucrative ones, they are less inclined to write it off as a matter of roles.

What complicates this is that capabilities can be tied to social prejudice. The person of social prejudice doesn't get the best education, hence they are suited only for the more menial jobs. It is the vicious cycle that modern societies face today in poverty and discrimination.

But the fact remains that no matter how compassionate we are, some folks are not suited for certain roles because of things that have nothing to do with class designations. Some people can wish to be executives at large corporations, but they have to face the fact that they don't have the acumen, experience and character to do what executives have to do.

The better example is teachers. There are some who have the gift and some who no matter how much they study and learn simply don't. It's not a commentary on their worth. It's a commentary on the roles for which they are best suited.

41 "Why do you look at the speck that is in your brother's eye, but do not notice the log that is in your own eye?"

It is popular to interpret this from the perspective of the optometrist. A speck in someone else's eye looks like a log in ours because it is immediately in front of the lens of our eye. This is possibly the meaning and the ancients certainly understood how our perspective is changed by the proximity of things.

But there is also merit in Jesus using this metaphor to observe that we often pick on relatively minor issues in others and overlook much larger issues in ourselves. A person can complain that so-and-so is a womanizer, but overlook the miserable way they treat their wife and kids.

Luke 6:42
42 ".. first take the log out of your own eye, and then you will see clearly to take out the speck that is in your brother's eye."

We are first to be without reproach ourselves if we are to point out the faults of others. Jesus exemplified this in the incident with the Magdalene - *"He who is without sin cast the first stone."* This is to say that if we spent time cleaning out our own logs we would have much less time available to look at other people's faults. But note here – He does say, *"then you will see clearly to take out the speck.."* He is not saying we are never to presume to take out the speck. He is saying don't be a hypocrite while doing it.

Taking out the speck in our brother's eye is not a contradiction to our call to avoid judging. The taking out is to be a work of aid and help, not judging. It involves the idea of pointing out a defect, but it is in the interest of helping not discriminating. If we see our brother having trouble in personally managing his finances, we can point this out (point to the speck) in offering to help him get control of things. It isn't a case of judging him, but it does involve the frankness to observe that he's struggling. But it would do no good if we were terrible ourselves in personal finances, or in some other visible area like morals or personal responsibility.

Matthew 7:6
6 "Do not give what is holy to dogs, and do not throw your pearls before swine, or they will trample them under their feet, and turn and tear you to pieces."

These are not words we expect from someone as tender-hearted as our Lord. They seem harsh and extremely judgmental – that there are persons to be characterized as dogs or swine.

But this is a caution about giving our energies and time in spiritual matters to people who have no care for them and who show no evidence that they have any intention of taking things seriously.

This is subtle because all unbelievers in some sense do not care for the things of God, else they would be believers. But this is talking about that class of people who are bent on ridiculing God, making jokes of serious things and are ready to bait believers so that they can humiliate them.

In the excellent Sixties's film *Charly* (ABC Pictures Corp., 1968), Charly is mentally handicapped and works at a bakery. His co-workers pose as "friends" but it is quickly apparent that they only do so to find opportunities to make fun of him and get the whole place laughing. Motives can often be other than they appear (that is the moral gained from *Othello* – that man is foolish to think things are always as they appear). Once this sort of thing is apparent, we are to move on to more productive efforts.

In a debate with evolutionists it soon became apparent to the creationist that the only real interest his opponents had was to entertain him long enough to find an opportunity to put down Christian faith. They were not interested in looking at evolution honestly, but more at spoofing religion.

Once that becomes known in any circumstance, continued efforts are a waste of time. They are a waste because there are others God has prepared for the gospel who are ready to receive it and if we are tied up in pointless conversations, we are unavailable for the wrong reasons. And if we should find ourselves unavailable (as will happen on occasion) it ought to be for the right reasons.

"tear you to pieces"

In the case of the evolutionists, they did in fact become vicious and it was later discovered that their viciousness was actually a sort of conspired objective, enjoyed on many previous occasions with prior victims.

The other key reason is the discredit it brings in the eyes of others respecting God. This is not completely avoidable and we are going to make mistakes. But our caution is not only to conserve our time and energies, but to be caring about the reputation of God and our Savior, that we not contribute unwittingly to a besmirching of His character before the world.

So we are to be careful. We may not have the ability to see the condition before getting into it, but once we do, we need to act accordingly.

Matthew 7:7-29

7 "Ask, and it will be given to you; seek, and you will find; knock, and it will be opened to you. 8 "For everyone who asks receives, and he who seeks finds, and to him who knocks it will be opened. 9 "Or what man is there among you who, when his son asks for a loaf, will give him a stone? 10 "Or if he asks for a fish, he will not give him a snake, will he? 11 "If you then, being evil, know how to give good gifts to your children, how much more will your Father who is in heaven give what is good to those who ask Him!"

12 "In everything, therefore, treat people the same way you want them to treat you, for this is the Law and the Prophets." 13 "Enter through the narrow gate; for the gate is wide and the way is broad that leads to destruction, and there are many who enter through it. 14 "For the gate is small and the way is narrow that leads to life, and there are few who find it."

15 "Beware of the false prophets, who come to you in sheep's clothing, but inwardly are ravenous wolves. 16 "You will know them by their fruits. Grapes are not gathered from thorn bushes nor figs from thistles, are they? 17 "So every good tree bears good fruit, but the bad tree bears bad fruit. 18 "A good tree cannot produce bad fruit, nor can a bad tree produce good fruit. 19 "Every tree that does not bear good fruit is cut down and thrown into the fire. 20 "So then, you will know them by their fruits."

21 "Not everyone who says to Me, `Lord, Lord,' will enter the kingdom of heaven, but he who does the will of My Father who is in heaven will enter. 22 "Many will say to Me on that day, `Lord, Lord, did we not prophesy in Your name, and in Your name cast out demons, and in Your name perform many miracles?' 23 "And then I will declare to them, `I never knew you; DEPART FROM ME, YOU WHO PRACTICE LAWLESSNESS.'"

24 "Therefore everyone who hears these words of Mine and acts on them, may be compared to a wise man who built his house on the rock. 25 "And the rain fell, and the floods came, and the winds blew and slammed against that house; and yet it did not fall, for it had been founded on the rock. 26 "Everyone who hears these words of Mine and does not act on them, will be like a foolish man who built his house on the sand. 27 "The rain fell, and the floods came, and the winds blew and slammed against that house; and it fell--and great was its fall." 28 When Jesus had finished these words, the crowds were amazed at His teaching; 29 for He was teaching them as one having authority, and not as their scribes." (Matthew 7:7-29)

Commentary

Matthew 7:12
7 "Ask, and it will be given to you; seek, and you will find; knock, and it will be opened to you. . . ."

This is not an invitation to ask without discernment. James makes it clear that we can ask in error for the wrong things and with the wrong motives. What Jesus is conveying is the general concept that God is not a miser who gingerly hands out provisions and then only if they really, really qualify.

Jesus wishes the generosity of the Father to be known. The beginning of the right heart is to seek the Father and this implies that we seek Him to adore Him, and to serve Him. That is an attitude that should not focus on getting but on giving, making our wills conform to His, not His to ours.

8 "For everyone who asks receives, and he who seeks finds, and to him who knocks it will be opened."

Again, this is the general case, not absolutely every case fully guaranteed. We will find it generally and routinely to be true that we receive what we ask for, we find what we are looking for, that doors are opened when knocked.

The key is in asking, seeking the things of God; knocking on the doors pertaining to the work of the Kingdom. This is the meaning because Jesus elsewhere says, *"Seek the Kingdom of God and His righteousness and all these things will be added unto you."* To bring this point home, Jesus asks them to refer to common sense in their own experience, in order to see there the character of God's love –

9 "Or what man is there among you who, when his son asks for a loaf, will give him a stone? 10 "Or if he asks for a fish, he will not give him a snake, will he?

No one listening could deny this, whether they did it well themselves or not. It is contrary to nature to give our children some evil thing when being asked for something good.

Surprisingly, people did think this negatively about God. They attributed their calamities and woes to a God who tested them, tried their mettle or punished them through mishaps. So they more often than not saw Him as someone who cared little for their wishes in comparison to His pre-eminent needs which were usually arduous and difficult.

Jesus is speaking from firsthand knowledge of having been with His Father. He knows the truth to be different.

11 "If you then, being evil, know how to give good gifts to your children, . ."

The goodness we attribute to our own selves is at the very least applicable also to a perfect God. The creature cannot be greater in something than the Creator. And in this we see God excelling mankind because He gives good gifts when they are not deserved and in spite of our disobedience.

Man has low tolerance for mistakes in others. We give a person a few mistakes and then we write them off in the forgiveness department. We harbor bitterness to the degree that we withhold love until they recognize our hurt. With God there is justice to be sure, but it is tempered by longsuffering – the very quality we are short on.

12 "In everything, therefore, treat people the same way you want them to treat you, for this is the Law and the Prophets.

As earlier, Jesus is relying on a principle we have right inside us for telling what will bless the other person. We don't have to have detailed knowledge about the special wants and wishes of all our fellow men. We can look within and ask what would bless us and be close to the mark for anyone else. But, of course, this means that category of blessings we share in common: the desire for respect, consideration, compassion, acceptance and love. It is not a guide to things like DVD players, hot wheels, digital cameras, etc.

That this is the Law and the Prophets is an idiomatic way of saying this is the message of God. It is one of the main points in what He has to say to us. Love your fellow man as you love yourself. When we look at the Law of Moses, we see a predominance of ordinances on how to rightly behave toward our neighbor. God certainly wants our love (the vertical) but He quickly turns it toward the horizontal.

It can be said that He is as concerned about our love toward one another as He is about our love for Him. We must do both and we kid ourselves when we think we can do the one and not the other.

Matthew 7:13-15
13 "Enter through the narrow gate; for the gate is wide and the way is broad that leads to destruction."

In an Internet forum, liberal Christians believed the complete opposite of what we have above - that the way of salvation was much wider than the narrow limits Christians often proclaim. For liberals it was a call to open the minds and boundaries of narrow thinking (which is what liberalism means) but it was at the sacrifice of the truth as proclaimed here by Jesus.

Man is always looking for the easiest way to get things accomplished and when something desirable is also hard you can bet man will find a way to ameliorate the difficulty by clever philosophizing. What is insidious is the fact that such people don't see that they have turned 180 degrees in their opinions.

It's not that God wished to make things hard just because it pleased Him. It is because man has fallen so far from that which righteousness actually is, that the true path now seems narrow and hard. It is in fact narrow because it can't include man's digressions and liberalizations. It's hard because it now runs against the grain to which man has become so accustomed. It is also hard because man lost in the Fall that capacity to easily meet the needs of righteousness.

So that all are clear, Jesus is also dis-authenticating the broad path. It is not merely a less beneficial path, or a less virtuous path. It is a path leading to destruction. It leads to destruction because it eliminates the urgency of man to do what he must do. It permits man to keep hiding from the thing he is trying to avoid – confrontation with his sin. That is why it is destructive.

In Michelangelo's *Last Judgment*, we see a man with his head in his hands, staring out into the reality of a judgment just received. He is at last acquainted with the truth he has been avoiding all his life and he knows what awaits him. It is so opposite to his expectations as to be stupefying. *"for the gate is small and few there are who enter in."*

15 *"Beware of the false prophets, who come to you in sheep's clothing, but inwardly are ravenous wolves."*

In God's universal grace He respects human freedom. This includes the freedom to be false and to deceive oneself. It also includes the permission to let Satan take advantage of human freedom and human nature in combination. So while God sends prophets to speak the truth, there will be counterfeits. And not obvious ones but rather cleverly disguised charlatans. They come appearing as the sheep. What many do not realize, is that they are really being seen as victims, as prey. The wolf has one object in mind – to destroy and devour.

There are two forms of false prophets: those who are truly agents of the devil and those who have lent themselves to self-deception. The latter don't see themselves as desiring to destroy. They see themselves as desiring to better inform, to instruct more wisely. But in distracting believers away from the truth, they are naïve to their use by Satan and the destructive influence they wield. So it amounts to the same result in both cases – destruction and devouring.

The very next question from the listener would be, "How are we to tell the difference?"

16 *"You will know them by their fruits. Grapes are not gathered from thorn bushes*

By fruit is meant spiritual fruit that glorifies God. False teachers and prophets will have success. They will have crowds of followers, monetary prosperity and even impressive facilities and amenities. But when you pop the hood, when you probe in more detail, you will find people who are back-stabbers, thieves who fleece the flock, and all sorts of people who evidence their lack of love and Christ-likeness the minute things don't go their way. Smiling faces quickly turn to anger.*"Grapes are not gathered from thorn bushes."*

However, the "knowing" part implies knowledge of what the genuine article is, so as to differentiate it. So this knowing is not in the unbeliever but in those who believe but may be prone to deception. Just as it takes a little bit of experience to recognize the species of plant or bush and the expectation about its fruit, so the Christian must have the basics of what is to be expected from the Christian life. Those who do not have this discernment are those in greatest jeopardy.

19 "Every tree that does not bear good fruit is cut down and thrown into the fire."

The lesson is about knowing their fruits. The point of talking about plants being cut down and thrown into the fire is to emphasize that this necessarily requires knowledge of the fruit expected, else one would invoke an action arbitrarily harsh without that knowledge. It is to say that if you are able to make so harsh and final a decision about a living thing, you must have the knowledge to do so. The same will be true of false prophets and workers of deception.

Jesus is also saying that bearing bad fruit will not be rewarded. He even hints here that bearing bad fruit will cause God to simply bypass you and use someone else. That may be preferable for the present, but it won't be in the judgment before Christ.

This is not teaching that should we bear bad fruit we have transitioned to the fate of the wicked and the fires of Hell. It is an expression of continued action. If you persistently bear bad fruit you are evidencing that you have none of the saving life in you and there is only one destiny ahead.

This is a worrisome warning. But let's understand this in the context provided. On in v.20 Jesus says, *"so then, you will know . ."* This is called the subjunctive in Greek and it connects things joined by purpose. Another way of saying it is "in order that." So all the foregoing is purposed to help us know. It is both a condemnation of the truly wicked, and a warning to those of faith that if they bear bad fruit in a situation, they are emulated or resembling those whose destiny is the fire.

21 "Not everyone who says to Me, `Lord, Lord,' will enter the kingdom of heaven, but he who does the will of My Father who is in heaven will enter.

It seems incongruent that someone not desiring to do the will of the Father would cry out, "Lord, Lord." But the heart is deceitfully wicked. Man can cry out for the Lord *on his own terms*. He can be double-minded in wanting the best of both worlds, his own will realized, and heaven in the bargain. So it will be a case that people unfit for the Kingdom will nonetheless cry out for it.

In some pictures along this line, it is a case of realizing too late, and then crying out to be saved from impending judgment. The parable of the Ten Virgins will later be seen as an example. Those who were careless for the things of preparation are now knocking at the door to be let in also.

The very nature of the Kingdom implies a King, a Lord over the Kingdom who sets the rules. It follows that one should ask the requirements of citizenry of the King if one desires to enter in.

But man loses this analogy when it comes to spiritual things, because it is always possible that God has no requirements, that He is generous enough to welcome everyone as citizens, hence worry about requirements is easily postponed or even exempted.

In contrast, the Kingdom of Heaven is about the King and no matter how magnanimous we want things to be, you can't divorce the Kingdom from the King, and the NT discloses the kinds of things the King expects of His citizens.

Matthew 7:22-24
22 "Many will say to Me on that day, `Lord, Lord, did we not prophesy in Your name, . . . 23 "And then I will declare to them, `I never knew you; depart from me you who practice lawlessness.'"

This is a difficult verse to embrace because we see people doing the works of God, yet are being told they were never known of God.

First, God does know them, else He is not omniscient. This is a knowing of them as children of faith. It is very close to the knowing of one's wife, but more like the knowing of his family members. It is an intimate knowing, the kind that comes from fellowship with God.

But how then do such non-knowing persons do miracles in His name? It would be hard to infer Satan because he would not enable miracles in God's name.

This is a case of God honoring His name where it is invoked but not justifying the person who uses it. We have the example of Balaam who did bless Israel, even though God knew his double-minded weakness for gain. King Saul was acting clearly against the will of the Lord, yet sat prophesying among the prophets (I Sam 10:10ff)

Judas was among those who cast out demons, and yet was himself the *"son of perdition"*. The Church Father, Origen, said that in his time the name of Christ was so frequently used to cast out spiritis that sometimes it worked when used by wicked Christians.

The idea here is that when the judgment before Christ comes, we will stand with all our motives revealed for what they were. We may have helped someone become saved, but we never took the path ourselves. We may prefer ourselves a certain way, but God will see the truth. It is a warning that we are not to use circumstances as the guide to discerning our acceptance before God, but we are to pursue Him and what true righteousness entails. That is being sure as opposed to being lazy.

They work iniquity and lawlessness because they seek to use God as a tool or a magic spell, with the intent of aggrandizing themselves. They have fallen happenstance on a phenomenon – that God will on occasion honor His name – and they see themselves as its operators.

24 "Therefore everyone who hears . . . and acts . . may be compared to a wise man who built his house on the rock."

This is a key verse for those who emphasize works over faith. It is not just the hearing but it is the doing. That doing is involved cannot be denied because here it is clearly demarcated from hearing alone. Those against works being conditional understand this to be comparing hearing and acting, not believing and acting. Many understand that believing is next after hearing and it includes the necessary stuff to ensure that actions will follow faith.

Certainly one point is common to all: following through in action from what is believed builds a stronger inner faith that can withstand much more than hearing without action. Hearing without action suggests no faith to trust and believe. In such a case, tribulation would cause abandonment, a running away to any haven one can find.

The example of a foundation upon a rock is clear to the audience. Faith must be founded in things that are substantial, real and enduring, else it is not worth much - just an idea whose time may come and go. To be a foundation for life, its truths must be unmovable. But strangely, people believe in things, even Christianity, without discerning this aspect, without really knowing that the foundation is secure or why.

The result is disaster and homelessness in adversity.

Matthew 7:26-29
26 ". . like a foolish man"

His house is described as being built on sand because it so aptly pictures the unstable nature and shifting base that ignorant or frivolous faith is like. There are people who perennially travel from religion to religion, around the cornucopia of ideologies, aimlessly seeking comfort rather than truth. They can't find truth because they haven't taken the time to ask how it will be known from falsehood. So what is popular today is replaced by something else when the infatuation subsides. James describes this as being tossed to and fro by every wind, or adrift on the waves wherever they may lead.

28 When Jesus had finished these words, the crowds were amazed at His teaching; 29 for He was teaching them as one having authority, and not as their scribes.

The people listening are now brought back into focus and we are told of their amazement at His teaching. We have to realize that as 21st century people, we take Christ's teaching as familiar words we've all heard many times before.

But for the folks here listening, this kind of exposition about the will of God and His expectations about righteousness were new in their arrangement and depth. Such things were there in the OT, but had not been put together or explained in these terms so clearly.

What Jesus taught made sense. It was not esoteric or eclectic, reserved for the doctors and rabbis. It made sense because Jesus appealed in many cases to their own sense of logic and reason. They were finding that many of the truths of God were just like life and nature in reality. It was beginning to click that the reason they made sense was because there was one Author of both - the spiritual and the natural orders.

Luke 7:1-9, Matthew 8:5-13, Luke 7:10
1 When He had completed all His discourse in the hearing of the people, He went to Capernaum. 2 And a centurion's slave, who was highly regarded by him, was sick and about to die. 3 When he heard about Jesus, he sent some Jewish elders asking Him to come and save the life of his slave. 4 When they came to Jesus, they earnestly implored Him, saying, "He is worthy for You to grant this to him; 5 for he loves our nation and it was he who built us our synagogue."

6 Now Jesus started on His way with them; and when He was not far from the house, the centurion sent friends, saying to Him, "Lord, do not trouble Yourself further, for I am not worthy for You to come under my roof; 7 for this reason I did not even consider myself worthy to come to You, but just say the word, and my servant will be healed. 8 "For I also am a man placed under authority, with soldiers under me; and I say to this one, `Go!' and he goes, and to another, `Come!' and he comes, and to my slave, `Do this!' and he does it." 9 Now when Jesus heard this, He marveled at him, and turned and said to the crowd that was following Him, "I say to you, not even in Israel have I found such great faith." (Luke 7:1-9)

"I say to you that many will come from east and west, and recline at the table with Abraham, Isaac and Jacob in the kingdom of heaven; 12 but the sons of the kingdom will be cast out into the outer darkness; in that place there will be weeping and gnashing of teeth." 13 And Jesus said to the centurion, "Go; it shall be done for you as you have believed." And the servant was healed that very moment." (Matt 8:5-13)

When those who had been sent returned to the house, they found the slave in good health. (Luke 7:10)

Commentary

Luke 7:2-5
2 And a centurion's slave, who was highly regarded by him, was sick and about to die.

We are reminded about the scene of this discourse when the narrative tells us that Jesus now went to Capernaum. He had been all this time speaking on the Mount of the Beatitudes.

The scene along the way involving the centurion and his slave is among the most interesting incidents in Jesus' ministry because it gives us insight in relations between Romans and Jews we usually don't think about and it is an episode that demonstrates great principles of faith and authority.

Military service in Roman times was a minimum of ten years on active duty. It often went to fifteen or twenty years and quite often was all spent in the same location. So soldiers were understandably irritable and belligerent by having to live in desolate or inhospitable places for such long periods. Many often lost property and families back in Italy because their wives grew tired of waiting for their retirement. In many cases, however, men could arrange for their families to live with them and these families very often became members of the societies in which they served.

A centurion was over a sub-group of 100 men in a legion of between 3,000 to 6,000 men. The Romans did not station a full legion at Jerusalem, but placed one instead at Caesarea and elsewhere as in Syria. These troops were called into Jerusalem at the feasts because these were by past experience times of unrest. At other times a smaller contingent called a cohort was permanently there.

In the case of this centurion, he had become part of the community and was of such a friendly disposition toward the Jews that he built the local synagogue. So we learn by this that the Roman military was not always true to its stereotype. Its ranks were diverse, filled with both reprobate men and men of good character and kindness.

Likewise, slavery was not always the demoralizing life of misery we think of in these times. People came into slavery for various reasons. Crimes against persons or the state could bring a person into slavery as a judgment. Sheer poverty made people prey to traders who could overtake them and make money selling them to buyers of slave labor. Captives of war were automatically part of the slave market.

But many people who were slaves were in fact grateful that they were under the provision and protection of a master because they had no resources to live otherwise. Much depended on the beneficence and kindness of masters, and we have ample evidence that such people existed. Here, the centurion's slave is loved by his master. The slave was thought of more as a member of the household staff than a slave.

The character of the centurion is not something he himself uses as a bargaining chip with Jesus. It is rather the Jews themselves who argue his case to Jesus. In fact, we learn that the centurion did not petition Jesus in person at all, but sent friends.

As Jesus starts His way to the man's home, the centurion learns that Jesus is coming and sends friends to speak for him.

Luke 7:6-8
6 "Lord, do not trouble Yourself further, for I am not worthy for You to come under my roof;

These are the words of the centurion in the testimony of his friends on his behalf. Three things are happening in the centurion's statements to Jesus:

"for I am not worthy"

The centurion is a man of position in the military. He is similar to a captain. The next rank above him is tribune. He serves in the most powerful army on earth. For him to say he is unworthy is a major expression of humility. This is key to opening the blessed grace of God toward him.

7 ". . just say the word"

He is also a man who understands faith in the supernatural and he recognizes power from God. He understands this so well that he knows Jesus need not come to his home to do His good work. He believes that Jesus can heal by word alone.

8 "For I also am a man placed under authority"

He understands the principle of authority, that authority is key to the exercise of power. This man serves in a powerful army, yet that power is possible only because its resources are all under authority. He gets things done because those under him obey his authority. He sees Jesus as one who has command over the supernatural. Just as he can say, "do this" and it is done, he knows that Jesus can do the same.

But notice how he says this. He doesn't merely say, "I'm a man who gives orders and they are done." He says, "I am a man ***under*** authority." His ability to give orders is based on he himself being under someone else's authority in which he is similarly obedient.

What he is recognizing is that life does not work with everyone doing whatever they wish, guided by their own independent authority. It is designed to work with all men being under some form of control and discipline. We begin with our parents. Outside our home we come under the authority of our teachers. We leave home only to come under the authority of our boss and the authorities that govern society. If we become an executive, we have someone higher up over us. When we become the head of the company, we are under the authority of the stockholders.

It is the way life is and it works. All of these things are key to the man getting the desire of his heart from Jesus.

Luke 7:9-13
9 Now when Jesus heard this, He marveled at him,

He marvels because He has not seen such faith anywhere in Israel. It is a faith that incorporates humility - not a strong suit for the Jews. The faith to heal by word – often thought by them to need physical presence, signs, and authority – was by no means esteemed by their local rulers, the Herodians, much less by the Romans.

"I say to you that many will come from east and west, . .

Jesus then uses this instance of faith to upbraid Israel for having the opposite example. He pictures the great supper in heaven where those present will dine with the key saints of Israel's foundation, Abraham, Isaac and Jacob, who's name was changed to Israel.

There will be those who come to dine but they will be cast out. They are described as the *"sons of the kingdom."* This is odd because we have the idea that only believers are the sons of the kingdom. And our idea of salvation and heavenly reward entertains no idea that those subject to being cast out could even approach the supper.

This is an allegorical picture, not a picture of the reality of things as they will be. It is used to generally describe the expectations of Jews in the heavenly estate – they expect to sup with the greats of their past. But some will be allowed and some will be cast out These are those of the physical lineage of Abraham – Abraham's seed – who will not be citizens of the kingdom. Paul says not all who are the seed of Abraham are of the faith of Abraham, (Galatians 3:7) John the Baptist upbraided the Pharisees by exhorting them to do the works of repentance if they wished to claim descent from Abraham. (Luke 3:8)

So those who are thrown into outer darkness where there will be gnashing of teeth are those of Israel who claim righteousness and the expectation of dining with the saints, but have not the faith exemplified by this Gentile centurion - *13 And the servant was healed that very moment. . . 10 When those who had been sent returned to the house, they found the slave in good health.* (Matthew 8:13, Luke 7:10)

We can understand how Jesus came to be hated.

Luke 7:11-28, Matthew 11:2-15, Luke 7:29-30

11 Soon afterwards He went to a city called Nain; and His disciples were going along with Him, accompanied by a large crowd. 12 Now as He approached the gate of the city, a dead man was being carried out, the only son of his mother, and she was a widow; and a sizeable crowd from the city was with her. 13 When the Lord saw her, He felt compassion for her, and said to her, "Do not weep." 14 And He came up and touched the coffin; and the bearers came to a halt. And He said, "Young man, I say to you, arise!" 15 The dead man sat up and began to speak. And Jesus gave him back to his mother. 16 Fear gripped them all, and they began glorifying God, saying, "A great prophet has arisen among us!" and, "God has visited His people!" 17 This report concerning Him went out all over Judea and in all the surrounding district.

18 The disciples of John reported to him about all these things. 19 Summoning two of his disciples, John sent them to the Lord, saying, "Are You the Expected One, or do we look for someone else?" 20 When the men came to Him, they said, "John the Baptist has sent us to You, to ask, `Are You the Expected One, or do we look for someone else?' " 21 At that very time He cured many people of diseases and afflictions and evil spirits; and He gave sight to many who were blind. 22 And He answered and said to them, "Go and report to John what you have seen and heard: the BLIND RECEIVE SIGHT, the lame walk, the lepers are cleansed, and the deaf hear, the dead are raised up, the POOR HAVE THE GOSPEL PREACHED TO THEM. 23 "Blessed is he who does not take offense at Me."

24 When the messengers of John had left, He began to speak to the crowds about John, "What did you go out into the wilderness to see? A reed shaken by the wind? 25 "But what did you go out to see? A man dressed in soft clothing? Those who are splendidly clothed and live in luxury are found in royal palaces! 26 "But what did you go out to see? A prophet? Yes, I say to you, and one who is more than a prophet. 27 "This is the one about whom it is written, `BEHOLD, I SEND MY MESSENGER AHEAD OF YOU, WHO WILL PREPARE YOUR WAY BEFORE YOU.' 28 "I say to you, among those born of women there is no one greater than John; yet he who is least in the kingdom of God is greater than he." (Luke 7:11-28)

12 "From the days of John the Baptist until now the kingdom of heaven suffers violence, and violent men take it by force. 13 "For all the prophets and the Law prophesied until John. 14 "And if you are willing to accept it, John himself is Elijah who was to come. 15 "He who has ears to hear, let him hear" (Matthew 11:12-15)

29 When all the people and the tax collectors heard this, they acknowledged God's justice, having been baptized with the baptism of John. 30 But the Pharisees and the lawyers rejected God's purpose for themselves, not having been baptized by John. (Luke 7:29-30)

Commentary

Luke 7:11-13-16
11 He went to a city called Nain; . . 12 . . a dead man was being carried out, . .

Jesus is now about to demonstrate that He was not a mere magician as Janis and Jambres were in Pharaoh's court, but was in touch with unfathomable power. Miracles of healing could always be explained away as they are today – the person wasn't as sick as they appeared; they just needed some "mind over matter" encouragement.

But death was a barrier that no one had crossed and come back. It was irreversibly permanent. When our loved ones die, it is the reality that they are in fact gone from all the places we used to see them and not somewhere hiding that brings home that they are gone indeed. This miracle was not going to be done in private. There was a considerable crowd who could then validate what they were about to see. In a private setting like that of the daughter of Jairus, there could be some doubt that magic may have been used instead, or that she was only in a coma.

13 He felt compassion for her,

We at first need to appreciate the situation of this mother. This was her only child. Due to the inferred age of her son (he was a man) in addition to the fact that she was a widow, the opportunity to have perhaps another child was long past and she faced a life not only without her son, but without the traditional hopes of how she would be taken care of. This death was inordinately tragic.

As believers familiar with this passage on many occasions, we accept the story uncritically and the additional questions skeptics like to probe seldom arise – why did He not have compassion on all the others?

We have to face the truth that though Jesus had the power He did not heal everyone, which can be seen in the atheist's eyes as a breach of moral responsibility. But the argument must then be pursued back to its logical ends – why is there any evil or sickness in the world if God is all powerful and all loving? Clearly it is His will that we deal with adversity rather than being perpetually freed from it. C.S. Lewis deals with this in *The Problem of Pain*.(MacMillan, Oxford, 1962) It is ultimately the necessity of having some contrast in life from which to appreciate blessing. God is more interested in showing the world what the believer can do by faith in the midst of adversity than making it easy to be happy with all misfortunes removed.

So then why did Jesus heal any at all?

This is truly a mystery with God. He prefers strength in adversity by faith, but extends grace in healing here and there by the pleasure of His will. The healing acts of Jesus did have one important purpose – to demonstrate power. And the conclusion is that He got it from the Almighty. But these acts were also demonstrations of real not feigned compassion for the plight of those suffering. So it is a mystery.

As such, we are prevented from forming a systematic understanding, a set of formulas, in predicting what He will do, which keeps us ever in a mode of faith rather than axiomatic expectation.

15 The dead man sat up and began to speak . . . 16 Fear gripped them all, and they began glorifying God, saying, "A great prophet has arisen among us!" and, "God has visited His people!"

This is the object in the mind of Christ – that they glorify His Father. The scene of the dead man sitting up, getting out of his bed and walking home with his amazed mother is beyond comprehension. Resuscitations in medical terms have always merely brought people back into some form of consciousness, but back also to the frailty of their weak and ailing condition; not to the state of sitting up, speaking and being given to his relatives to take home.

a great prophet

Today we would conclude a faith healer not a prophet. But in ancient times there were no faith healers with healing ministries. If healing did take place it was usually in the hands of a prophet of God (Elisha and the son of the starving woman – 2 Kings 4:18)

Luke 7:18-23
18 The disciples of John reported to him about all these things. 19 Summoning two of his disciples, John sent them to the Lord, saying, "Are You the Expected One, or do we look for someone else?"

As the report of this is spread (v.17) news arrives from his own disciples to John in prison.

The question asked by John. "are you the expected one?" seems so out of place for a man like John who was seen earlier to have figured things out by faith and had confirmation in the vision of the dove that Jesus was this person indeed.

We must remember that John was human despite his faith. Deprivation and misery in an ancient prison could cause any man to wonder if he had heard God correctly about certain things. Thoughts about his whole ministry and calling would certainly be reviewed in his mind in the face of his sufferings; and the place of his kinsman, Jesus. He was not in prison because of his association with or declarations about Jesus. He was there because of his charges against Antipas and Herodias.

But that Jesus was roaming free and still preaching and he was in prison may have spawned a desire to confirm who Jesus was, not from doubt but from a desire to renew that he had at least been right about that. So his disciples convey his question to Jesus, who interestingly does not comment in any way that this is a problem in John's faith.

22 "Go and report to John what you have seen and heard: the BLIND RECEIVE SIGHT, the lame walk, the lepers are cleansed, and the deaf hear, the dead are raised up, the POOR HAVE THE GOSPEL PREACHED TO THEM."

Jesus provides Messianic markers from the OT in answering John. Isaiah 35:5 and 61:1 were clearly known to the Jews as earmarks of Messiah when He comes. The deaf are also mentioned in 35:5 but since they are not quoted as specifically written, the NASB does not show them as a direct OT quote.

Isaiah 61:1 comes from an unquestioned Messianic passage. The poor are there called the afflicted. Jesus did not vaunt himself to John but allowed Scripture to affirm Him.

23 "Blessed is he who does not take offense at Me."

This seems strange here because John would not have taken offense at Jesus. But John's words in terms of confirmation are often ironically the words of those who are skeptical and in some way find Jesus an offense to their own lives and wills.

As to offense at all, we find that we can view Jesus from two discrete vantage points that often do not intersect in our minds. He is lovely, tender-hearted, caring, and merciful. But He is also one with a hard doctrine and tough expectations. He says He represents the Father's love for you and me, but He also said that if we love family more than Him we can't be His disciple.

So there is an attraction to His love and a recoiling from His sense of the commitment, and this can cause men to be offended.

Luke 7:24-28
24 .. "What did you go out into the wilderness to see? A reed shaken by the wind? 25 "But what did you go out to see? A man dressed in soft clothing? Those who are splendidly clothed and live in luxury are found in royal palaces!"

The expressions here are difficult in helping us understand the point being made. Jesus is essentially asking what they expected to see when they went out to John?

They did not travel the considerable distance on foot to see merely a reed shaking in the wind. If so, they ought not to complain when something extraordinary was seen. They did not come to see a man dressed as though he lived in comfort in town or in his palace. They should not be surprised that they saw the odd look and appearance of John. It added to the curiosity that brought them out to see him.

Then he focuses in on the problem of why some did not engage the message of John –

26 "But what did you go out to see? A prophet? Yes, I say to you, and one who is more than a prophet."

A prophet was someone to rally behind and also someone from which to hide. Jesus now focuses on their desire to see a real prophet but their naivite at possibly being the target of his prophecies.

27 "This is the one about whom it is written, `BEHOLD, I SEND MY MESSENGER . . 28 . . among those born of women there is no one greater than John;"

Jesus confirms that John's own claim for the role of Messenger was right as rain. He was dead on - the very one pictured hundreds of years earlier in prophecy. *"No one greater"* is not technically true because it must be tempered with Jesus Himself, who was born of woman but certainly greater than John.

But barring that case, is John in truth greater than any other human being? We would have to include Abraham, and Moses. In terms of thought is he greater than Socrates and Aristotle? In terms of accomplishments, greater than Alexander or Caesar? When we think of this crudely dressed, itinerant preacher we have to wonder how this could be true? But as great as all those other men are, they pale in comparison to what Jesus came to do. His work exceeds in scope and power anything done by those men, including parting the sea.

Hence, the forerunner, the herald, shares in the greatness of the one announced because he had to do this by faith not by sight. So to have that kind of faith and commitment is extraordinary.

". . yet he who is least in the kingdom of God is greater than he."

Interestingly, in terms of the kingdom, anyone who comes into it is considered greater than John. This means simply that his joys and experiences in the Kingdom will be far greater than those of any achievements on earth, so any citizen is of greater station and place than those of human efforts.

We can begin here to understand why the first words of both John and Jesus were the good news of the "kingdom." It was of such importance and the populating of it with the souls of men so important that it was issue No. 1 in all they did.

Matthew 11:12-15
12 "From the days of John the Baptist until now the kingdom of heaven suffers violence, and violent men take it by force."

This is among the most difficult verses in Jesus' teaching because it associates words we would never see as belonging together at all – acquiring the kingdom by violent men and by force.

The verse is explained by commentators as referring to the spiritual fervor that men exercised toward the announcement of the presence of the kingdom and their desire to rush into it. This is not exactly a clear answer to the imagery seen.

But in other ways, we can see some of this in the revivals of modern times. The Great Awakening of the recent past was marked by many episodes of spiritual ecstasy and physical excitement. In the film, *Hallelujah* (King Vidor, MGM) from the 20's, the blacks portray the ecstatic moments of revival that are often described as the fearful things evangelicals never want occurring in their churches.

Jesus may be teaching here that among those desiring the kingdom there are some who are notably strong in spirit and stand out as almost too strong in their zeal. And there is insight in that Jesus is pointing to John *as an example* of what He's saying. John was of that nature. In Franco Zeferelli's *Jesus of Nazareth*, (Incorporated Television Company, 1977), the actor Michael York plays the Baptist and in a way that recalls the fierceness of his spirit in the Lord. A good example of perhaps what Jesus means here.

13 "For all the prophets and the Law prophesied until John. 14 "And if you are willing to accept it, John himself is Elijah who was to come. 15 "He who has ears to hear, let him hear"

Jesus is not saying that John *was* Elijah who is to come, as in Malachi 4:5. The phrase *"If you are willing to receive it"* is an indicator provided by the speaker that an analogy is in play. We are not to take the words literally but as an analogy. John is an image or a reflection of the coming of Elijah again.

Luke 7:29-30
29 having been baptized with the baptism of John. . . 30 . . not having been baptized by John

It is not that the baptism of John performed the kind of spiritual enlightening that comes with Christian baptism – John's baptism did not save. But the repentant heart of those coming to be baptized opened them to such insights, to be able to see the truths of which John spoke.

The Pharisees are not rejecting because they lack something imparted by the baptism, but because they were unrepentant in the first place, and God resists the proud. It is not impossible that divine wisdom was part of the gift received by those at John's baptism, but we don't have knowledge enough to say.

Luke 7:31-50
31 "To what then shall I compare the men of this generation, and what are they like? 32 "They are like children who sit in the market place and call to one another, and they say, `We played the flute for you, and you did not dance; we sang a dirge, and you did not weep.' 33 "For John the Baptist has come eating no bread and drinking no wine, and you say, `He has a demon!' 34 "The Son of Man has come eating and drinking, and you say, `Behold, a gluttonous man and a drunkard, a friend of tax collectors and sinners!' 35 "Yet wisdom is vindicated by all her children."

36 Now one of the Pharisees was requesting Him to dine with him, and He entered the Pharisee's house and reclined at the table. 37 And there was a woman in the city who was a sinner; and when she learned that He was reclining at the table in the Pharisee's house, she brought an alabaster vial of perfume, 38 and standing behind Him at His feet, weeping, she began to wet His feet with her tears, and kept wiping them with the hair of her head, and kissing His feet and anointing them with the perfume.

39 Now when the Pharisee who had invited Him saw this, he said to himself, "If this man were a prophet He would know who and what sort of person this woman is who is touching Him, that she is a sinner." 40 And Jesus answered him, "Simon, I have something to say to you." And he replied, "Say it, Teacher." 41 "A moneylender had two debtors: one owed five hundred denarii, and the other fifty. 42 "When they were unable to repay, he graciously forgave them both. So which of them will love him more?" 43 Simon answered and said, "I suppose the one whom he forgave more." And He said to him, "You have judged correctly."

44 Turning toward the woman, He said to Simon, "Do you see this woman? I entered your house; you gave Me no water for My feet, but she has wet My feet with her tears and wiped them with her hair. 45 "You gave Me no kiss; but she, since the time I came in, has not ceased to kiss My feet. 46 "You did not anoint My head with oil, but she anointed My feet with perfume. 47 "For this reason I say to you, her sins, which are many, have been forgiven, for she loved much; but he who is forgiven little, loves little." 48 Then He said to her, "Your sins have been forgiven."

49 Those who were reclining at the table with Him began to say to themselves, "Who is this man who even forgives sins?" 50 And He said to the woman, "Your faith has saved you; go in peace."
(Luke 7:31-50)

Commentary

After commending John the Baptist, Jesus then characterizes the generation of Jews to which He has come.

Luke 7:31-33
31 "To what then shall I compare the men of this generation, and what are they like?

In almost every age, the advancing generations are often characterized disparagingly for not continuing to value the standards of their predecessors. In biblical times, there was less of the generational changes we see today, but there were seasons when indolence and disregard were heightened. In the time of the Baptist, Judaism had become ritualistic, while a small remnant were truer children of faith. These responded to John's message. The former saw him as a curiosity.

In all events, for the Son of God to so characterize one's generation was a grave matter, because we know Him to have supreme and final judgment in His hands.

32 ". . they say, `We played the flute for you, and you did not dance; we sang a dirge, and you did not weep.'"

This is described elsewhere by Paul as receiving the prophecies and advice that tickled their ears. *"For the time will come when they will not endure sound doctrine; but wanting to have their ears tickled, they will accumulate for themselves teachers in accordance to their own desires"* (2 Tim 4:4)

In modern churches today, it is surprising how congregations deal similarly with their ministers. There are churches that dictate what the people will tolerate from the pulpit. There are some churches that have actually told their pastor they no longer needed to be instructed from the Bible – that they knew the Bible and preferred topics on social and community issues instead.

Threats of leaving the church and their sizable donations with them often cower men into complacent professors lecturing on interesting topics. But John was not a "play along" type. He had his own message and cared little about what comfortable people wanted to hear.

33 "For John the Baptist has come eating no bread and drinking no wine, and you say, `He has a demon!'

In other words, if he is not going to sing to our tune, we will vilify him as having a demon. This does two things. It hides their indolence behind the charge that he is too strange to be entertained, and it ensures that no one of their class will continue to take him seriously, being poisoned by demonic influence. Jesus then opens the sore wider by showing how they have applied this to Him also. Public embarrassment is clearly imminent.

Luke 7:34-36
34 "The Son of Man has come eating and drinking, and you say, `Behold, a gluttonous man and a drunkard, a friend of tax collectors and sinners!'

Jesus was certainly neither of these things. But because He enjoyed dining and drinking at table with those He met, the offended crowds had something on which to pounce that would turn other hearts away from Him and also mollify His stinging words about their hypocrisy.

It was a play on their part that depended on the principle that a little knowledge is dangerous. It played into the hands of people who only knew a few things about Jesus, who could be manipulated into believing that there was more to Him than was being portrayed. A friend of tax collectors and sinners was meant to convey association with their life style not that He merely condescended to speak to them.

In these charges, it was a matter of taking appearances and working them into defamations of character. This is repeated today when the world wishes to defame Christians, not for their good deeds, but for their message and intolerance.

35 "Yet wisdom is vindicated by all her children."

This sounds like an existing adage Jesus' is employing but it is not identified as such in commentaries specifically. It may be that something like this was known in contemplative cultures; it's hard to conceive as being totally brand new. Whether new or old, Jesus is making its most famous and memorable use here.

The idea is that wisdom is personified as getting children whenever they emulate and acquire her. Vindication means to be shown to be correct or free of a charge. It is like the word acquit. The undeclared charge is that something is being falsely proclaimed as wisdom. The vindication is in the consistency of all those who live by the wisdom and who show it to be true by its application to life. Wisdom is an abstract idea but its purpose is to be lived out in real life. Those who succeed in demonstrating this are vindicating it as a wisdom that works.

Why does Jesus say this in response to what people are saying about Him? The charges are based on superficial awareness not real knowledge of Him. Whether He is wise despite distorted appearances can be proven by hearing Him and applying what He says to one's life.

36 Now one of the Pharisees was requesting Him to dine with him, and He entered the Pharisee's house and reclined at the table.

We learn in a moment that the Pharisee was a man named Simon. He is not by any evidence being cynical or merely entertaining in his invitation, so we are inclined to conclude he is friendly and curious toward

Jesus. He is not a follower, but sees the merit and extraordinary nature of Jesus' doctrine. Being schooled, he is keen for a more serious doctrinal interchange and in a setting well suited for unintimidating discourse.

The scene is sometimes assumed to involve a triclinium – a three-sided Roman table with adjoining furnishings for reclining while eating. But we don't know how formal this dinner was, how many other guests were there or how wealthy Simon was. Smaller reclining arrangements were known than a full triclinium. It would fit the occasion and it can be assumed that the Pharisee's friends were included.

To be sure, here in the Gospel account the guests reclined. Some picture this with guests lying on one side. But where many guests are present and there is meant to be dialog between everyone, lying on one side would limit you to the person turned to face you, and your back would be to most everyone else. Turning your head to speak to others would be rather uncomfortable.

In imperial Roman dining, the more noble guests had pillows and arrangements for lying at an angle on their backs and being fed by servants. That would not be the case here. It is more likely that where group interaction was desired, people reclined on their stomachs. Also the legs and feet did not lay out flat but were inclined somewhat downward away from the table by mats so designed.

Luke 7:37-39
37 And there was a woman in the city who was a sinner . . she brought an alabaster vial of perfume, 38 and standing behind Him at His feet, weeping, she began to wet His feet with her tears"

We are first surprised that a woman of her station enters and gets this far without being intercepted and put out. However, what she does is actually part of the arrangement for the dinner. There were servants who came along behind and washed the feet of the guests as they reclined. However, we need to observe that in Simon's case this had not been arranged for, since Jesus makes a point of this later. In general however, her specific identity would have been easily missed in the busy work of serving the table.

The stereotypical portrayal of this is with Jesus sitting up and her approaching face to face, then anointing His feet. But in reality His feet would have been out behind Him as she came to them. And we see Jesus turning in order to observe her.

The identity of this woman is difficult. John says that Mary of Bethany was the one who came and anointed Jesus' feet, and used her hair. But the woman here is a sinner and Mary of Bethany had no such reputation. Some have inferred the Magdalene, but Jesus has not yet met her and when He does, she does not appear to know Him already. So this is an unnamed woman, meaning there were at least two anointings of similar description.

But the host soon discovers she is an intruder.

39 he said to himself, "If this man were a prophet He would know who and what sort of person this woman is who is touching Him, that she is a sinner."

What is not obvious but extremely interesting is that Simon says this to himself which means that the author did not get the man's thoughts into this narrative by hearing him say it. Jesus was really the only one in the room who would have known what he was thinking. John then would have to have gotten this from Jesus or by inspiration from the Holy Spirit at the time he wrote.

We need to be careful about judging the Pharisee too harshly about his concern. He is expressing proper Mosaic legal concerns about defilement. These are not man-made minutia over which he had unwarranted concern. If a woman was involved in carnal sins she was defiled. *[if] a man lie with her carnally, . . and she be defiled,* Numbers 5:13

To come in contact with someone defiled (or an uncleanness), transmitted defilement to that person. *Or if he touches human uncleanness, of whatever sort his uncleanness may be with which he becomes unclean, and it is hidden from him, and then he comes to know it, he will be guilty.* Lev 5:3.

For Jesus to allow her to touch Him meant ceremonial uncleanness was transmitted to Him, about which He ought to be very concerned.

Luke 7:40-50

40 And Jesus answered him, "Simon, I have something to say to you." And he replied, "Say it, Teacher."

Notice that Jesus does not come right out and speak the man's thoughts in public which would have directly offended his host.

Instead, Jesus introduces a new line of talk with his host. *"I have something to tell you."* He is going to relate a parable that will indirectly make the point about judging and compassion.

41 "A moneylender had two debtors: one owed five hundred denarii, and the other fifty. . . 42 he graciously forgave them both. So which of them will love him more?"

It is simple to conclude greater gratitude and love for greater debts forgiven. But this will now be used to pinpoint what Simon was doing in respect to the woman and all such sinners in general.

44 Turning toward the woman, He said to Simon, "Do you see this woman? I entered your house; you gave Me no water for My feet, but she has wet My feet with her tears and wiped them with her hair.

He asks at first that Simon observe the woman, to set the application at the forefront. This is ultimately going to be about the woman and how her act will instruct everyone present.

But Jesus immediately shifts to what Simon has neglected doing. This is to make the woman's deed stand out clearly and unmistakably. He doesn't just say, "Look at what she is doing." He contrasts what she is doing to what Simon did not do. Furthermore, he is the host and she is uninvited - neither guest nor servant.

47 "For this reason I say to you, her sins, which are many, have been forgiven, for she loved much; but he who is forgiven little, loves little."

We are at first puzzled why this distinction is made because if Simon has fewer sins, how is this a detriment? How should a person with greater sins and a worse reputation be a lesson to a man who is of good reputation and for the right reasons – has personal piety?

The lesson is about the *potential* the woman represents compared to Simon's own piety and legitimate concern for the Law. There is a potential here in his home to convert sins into tremendous love and that is a reason to set aside judgment in favor of compassion. Yes the Law is valid as to the condition of the woman. Yes, it is correct to not ignore or condone sin. But Jesus is showing the attitude of the Father. Jesus loves the sinner. He desires to forgive not condemn; to lift them out of sin toward righteousness. And so should Simon.

Then Jesus does something very edgy. Something that could alienate Simon from any further lessons.

48 . . "Your sins have been forgiven." . . . 49 "Who is this man who even forgives sins?" . . . 50 "Your faith has saved you; go in peace."

Simon has not seen Jesus yet as Messiah and the dinner is not a sign that he is entertaining this. He is certainly interested in hearing more from Jesus on an intimate level without crowds of people present. But Simon is still a Pharisee and bound to the conservative rigidity of that order. To forgive sins is seen in his eyes as blasphemous because only God can do this, meaning the claimant is taking God's position.

Simon does not rend his clothes, which tells us that he is notably conflicted, knowing full well what his response ought to be, yet restrained by the unmistakable heavenly signs of his Guest.

Several ask the obvious question, *"who is he that forgives sins?"* but we are not told whether this precipitated into immediate action by the authorities. There were plenty of witnesses but nothing immediately comes of it. No doubt this later served as circumstantial evidence that furthered the plans of the Sanhedrin, but it is interesting that this is not offered as evidence of His actionable behavior.

Jesus then leaves this scene and begins an active tour of cities and preaching.

Luke 8:1-3, Matthew 12:22-30
1 Soon afterwards, He began going around from one city and village to another, proclaiming and preaching the kingdom of God. The twelve were with Him, 2 and also some women who had been healed of evil spirits and sicknesses: Mary who was called Magdalene, from whom seven demons had gone out, 3 and Joanna the wife of Chuza, Herod's steward, and Susanna, and many others who were contributing to their support out of their private means. (Luke 8:1-3)

22 Then a demon-possessed man who was blind and mute was brought to Jesus, and He healed him, so that the mute man spoke and saw. 23 All the crowds were amazed, and were saying, "This man cannot be the Son of David, can he?" 24 But when the Pharisees heard this, they said, "This man casts out demons only by Beelzebul the ruler of the demons." 25 And knowing their thoughts Jesus said to them, "Any kingdom divided against itself is laid waste; and any city or house divided against itself will not stand. 26 "If Satan casts out Satan, he is divided against himself; how then will his kingdom stand? 27 "If I by Beelzebul cast out demons, by whom do your sons cast them out? For this reason they will be your judges. 28 "But if I cast out demons by the Spirit of God, then the kingdom of God has come upon you. 29 "Or how can anyone enter the strong man's house and carry off his property, unless he first binds the strong man? And then he will plunder his house. 30 "He who is not with Me is against Me; and he who does not gather with Me scatters. (Matthew 12:22-30)

Commentary

Luke 8:1-2
1 Soon afterwards, He began going around from one city and village to another,

From Capernaum, Jesus is now taking a tour of the adjoining towns and villages. The ancients called some of these "cities," despite the sizes of other cities like Jerusalem, Rome or Athens; so the idea included a scope we're not used to in modern times.

Again, the message of Jesus was the proclamation of the Kingdom of God, and we need to reiterate that its existence was not a new thing in the ears of His audience. They may have had scant understanding of it. They may not have been able to expound on it in any detail. But there was a general expectation among the majority about its eventuality. Jesus was now saying it was at hand. This drew at the very least a curiosity. The Twelve were with Him as He traveled.

2 and also some women . . . Mary who was called Magdalene, from whom seven demons had gone out, . . Herod's steward, and Susanna, and many others who were contributing to their support out of their private means.

We see here a picture of how Jesus and the disciples made ends meet as they ministered away from their normal means of support. People recognized their itinerant mode and were quickened by God to give compassionately and in the spirit of helps.

It is not a case that Jesus would have been destitute had no one supported them. We see Him later providing tax money in the mouth of a fish. So producing the things needed was never an issue. But He chose not to employ supernatural methods and instead make opportunities for others to enter into the blessing of the work of God.

Some view this negatively – Jesus and his men were placing extra burdens on the people by occasioning sacrifice from people already in various states of need. But it is really an expression of love from God, because He is inviting them to receive blessing, not to add strain by sacrificial giving. We have every confidence that those who gave were in no wise made more destitute and would find their state improved because of their acts of charity. It is again the principle that God loves the giver and returns blessing in contrast to the pagan systems for which giving was a one-way street.

We are introduced to Mary Magdalene and some find this out of chronological sequence because they assume she is the woman caught in adultery to whom Jesus says, "Go and sin no more." This is often the portrayal in films. But the woman is not identified in that later incident. And while she was earlier demonic, that event took place in Jerusalem, while Magdalene is here in the Galilee.

'Magdalene' was not her family name or cognomen. It was an epithet – something that characterized a person, like John the Baptist or the Gadarene demoniac. It may come from her association with the region of Magdala, or it may come from the Hebrew for 'curled hair' – an epithet for an adulterer.

We are told that the women she is with were delivered from evil spirits and Mary is notable in having seven cast out. This is mentioned as though it is a very well understood phenomena. From our perspective in modern times, it is something of the ancient past or of more recent colonial times, but never-the-less dismissed as part of a more ignorant and superstitious age. But Jesus does not attribute it to mental illness as do modern, "enlightened" people. He teaches that the devil and demon possession are very real.

Our assumption here is that these exorcisms occurred earlier when Jesus was previously in Galilee. They show their gratitude in their giving whenever He visits their area.

Another note is the person of Susanna, related to Herod's household staff. The gospel is not specific in its appeal. It speaks to all persons regardless of stations in life. We see later the very wife of Pilate being favorably disposed toward Jesus in so much as she was personally affected about His nature in a worrisome dream.

Matthew 12:22-23
22 Then a demon-possessed man who was blind and mute was brought to Jesus, and He healed him, so that the mute man spoke and saw. 23 All the crowds were amazed, and were saying, "This man cannot be the Son of David, can he?"

We see in Jesus' workings of miracles truly extraordinary events. He is not merely healing withered hands or making cripples walk. He was correcting conditions so beyond normal remedies to which the afflicted were resigned to their fate, as a man in prison merely awaiting his inevitable death in chains.

We can't begin to imagine what life would be like being blind and unable to speak. For those who were mute, they could use their hands to gesture and convey needs and words to others. But sight would be indispensable. You had to see to control and validate your gestures. You had to see to evaluate the effectiveness or lack thereof in others.

So to be also blind would be a physical indictment of unimaginable despair and frustration, total dependence on others, and constant disappointment in misunderstandings because one could not communicate.

The bitterness in this, knowing that all those around you had their faculties in tact while you were being denied them, could easily shake a fist toward heaven. You may not be a tool of any use to the devil, but keeping you in your hatred of God and compensating by various demonic pleasures ensured that you would be one more soul the Almighty would not get.

But the devil overlooked the Jesus factor. Into this scene steps Jesus to upset all the devil's plans. All three conditions were remedied in a single moment. He was freed from the demons that plagued him and both his sight and voice were now available for Godly purposes. His life of service to Satan was now a season past. A new life was now opened before Him, one he had never been able to know before.

The wording of the witnesses to this event is noteworthy. They do not say, *"This man is the Son of David."* – the positive form. Instead, they are voicing the negative form - *"This man cannot be the Son of David, can he?"* - which first actually poses the doubts and skepticism circulating around.

This is simply a form that affirms the positive but does so from an assumption in the negative. It's like saying, "Darth Vader can't be Luke's father, can he?" It's an acknowledgment that he is, but from incredulity.

Jesus later helps people with this decision point by saying, *"though you do not believe Me, believe the works, so that you may know and understand that the Father is in Me, and I in the Father." (John 10:38)*

Matthew 12:24-25
24 But when the Pharisees heard this, they said, "This man casts out demons only by Beelzebul the ruler of the demons."

The local Pharisees are now stuck. They cannot deny miracles are being performed. They cannot deny these are marks of Messiah's coming. They cannot deny relatively ignorant people are connecting the dots. But they are loath to authenticate any of this because it will mean the disenfranchisement of their whole system, agreement with John's cutting indictments against them, and that Jesus' doctrine is in fact right. There is only one avenue of escape: attribute these things to the only other power that works supernaturally – the devil.

Beelzebul is alternatively named Beelzebub in some translations. It is a window into the very real appreciation that ancients had for demonic forces, in having incidents of the past where the names of demons actually became known and that there was a hierarchy.

We must be cautious in assuming that the Bible is itself stating a direct fact that such a demon with this name exists. This is always presented as the beliefs of the people being quoted. But we can draw the probability of its reality from the lack of correction from Jesus – He engages them about Beelzebul as though the name is real. We also have considerable confidence from circumstantial facts - that demons speak through their hosts, and that the name could have reasonably become known that way.

25 And knowing their thoughts Jesus said to them, "Any kingdom divided against itself is laid waste . . "

Jesus doesn't here deny the existence of Beelzebul or that the demon would be an alternate explanation of supernatural events. He simply asks them to look at the logic attending these events, which ought to inform them which is right. If Satan is the author of the power they see, and he is the one who created the circumstances needing the application of that power, Satan would be working against himself.

Where there is division in a kingdom, a conquerer has an advantage for laying it waste. Division means the undermining of its purposes, and here Satan casting out himself is contradictory. It is like a person building a house part of the day and tearing it down for the remainder. The utter silliness of this proposition in the ears of the people and the Pharisees themselves exposes them as simply reaching. It posits them as actually working against the will of God, whom they claim to be serving. The embarrassment of being exposed as self-serving is now rampant, and yet there follows another instance that furthers their hatred.

Matthew 12:29-30

29 "Or how can anyone enter the strong man's house and carry off his property, unless he first binds the strong man? And then he will plunder his house.

Jesus extends this with another analogy. It is needful to nail down the necessity that Satan had to bind himself in the explanation of the Pharisees by pointing out that you can't enter to plunder a man's goods if you have nothing in your plans that involves immobilizing him first. Since Satan would not do this, the only explanation left is that it is of God.

30 "He who is not with Me is against Me; and he who does not gather with Me scatters.

This is the principle piece of logic that is inescapable about Jesus in all ages. We can develop clever explanations and coping strategies that make this all merely a philosophy up for consideration - great words from a great teacher. Apply them or not as you see fit.

But Jesus gives no such option. He forces a decision by proclaiming that indolence or postponement after specific knowledge is a decision, not a postponement. One cannot deceive themselves by being neutral, therefore safe by not overtly rejecting. Those who will claim they never cognitively rejected Christ will be told that they did so by not accepting Him. To postpone acceptance is rejection, and the horror of this is that there will be no clever arguments entertained. This will be the fact of the matter.

This seems harsh, but this is not philosophy where issues are merely academic. Life is precarious, always on the verge of being cut short by calamity. One's eternal destiny is but a fatal accident away. No matter what our rationalizations, all men face a day in Court to account for their lives. That will become the sudden reality, no matter what a person may choose to believe or ignore. It can be remedied to the good by engaging Christ for who He is and how He affects that date in Court.

Matthew 12:31-32, Mark 3:28-30, Matt 12:33-37, Mark 3:21, Matthew 12:38-42
"Therefore I say to you, any sin and blasphemy shall be forgiven people, but blasphemy against the Spirit shall not be forgiven. 32 "Whoever speaks a word against the Son of Man, it shall be forgiven him; but whoever speaks against the Holy Spirit, it shall not be forgiven him, either in this age or in the age to come (Matthew 12:31-32) . . because they were saying, "He has an unclean spirit." (Mark 3:28-30)

33 "Either make the tree good and its fruit good, or make the tree bad and its fruit bad; for the tree is known by its fruit. 34 "You brood of vipers, how can you, being evil, speak what is good? For the mouth speaks out of that which fills the heart. 35 "The good man brings out of his good treasure what is good; and the evil man brings out of his evil treasure what is evil. 36 "But I tell you that every careless word that people speak, they shall give an accounting for it in the day of judgment. 37 "For by your words you will be justified, and by your words you will be condemned." (Matt 12:33-37)

21 When His own people heard of this, they went out to take custody of Him; for they were saying, "He has lost His senses." (Mark 3:21)

38 Then some of the scribes and Pharisees said to Him, "Teacher, we want to see a sign from You." 39 But He answered and said to them, "An evil and adulterous generation craves for a sign; and yet no sign will be given to it but the sign of Jonah the prophet; 40 for just as JONAH WAS THREE DAYS AND THREE NIGHTS IN THE BELLY OF THE SEA MONSTER, so will the Son of Man be three days and three nights in the heart of the earth. 41 "The men of Nineveh will stand up with this generation at the judgment, and will condemn it because they repented at the preaching of Jonah; and behold, something greater than Jonah is here. 42 "The Queen of the South will rise up with this generation at the judgment and will condemn it, because she came from the ends of the earth to hear the wisdom of Solomon; and behold, something greater than Solomon is here. (Matthew 12:38-42)

Commentary

Matthew 12:31-32
31 ". . any sin and blasphemy shall be forgiven people, but blasphemy against the Spirit shall not be forgiven. . . 32 Whoever speaks a word against the Son of Man . . . whoever speaks against the Holy Spirit, it shall not be forgiven him

The subject has been commitment or rejection regarding Jesus – *"He who is not with Me is against Me"* and it has also been about the illogic that His works are those of Satan. This gives Jesus cause to introduce a very important related subject that carries an awful indictment. It is extremely important that people realize what trite dismissals of His doctrine can mean to their eternal destiny, especially rationalizations of a certain type.

Jesus now discusses the concept of blasphemy against the Spirit.

Normally, we think of blasphemy as taking the Lord's name in vane – to reference it or use it irreverently as to drag it into unholy situations. But there is a meaning that also entails resistance so grievous that one attributes the works of God to the devil. The state of mind that would do this is so deceived, so deviant from real truth as to permanently grieve God.

The Holy Spirit in His work among all believers is to bear witness in the human heart as to the things of God. He is there to convince in the inner soul. Miracles, the teaching of the Word, the recognition of its truth as real, not imaginary or mere opinions, is a work God fully intended to accompany what the atheist or the agnostic accounts as mere claims. The believer has the advantage that the *"Spirit has born witness with their spirit, that these are the things of God."*

People will resist this witness – we all did to a certain extent as unbelievers. But eventually we could not resist the overwhelming witness and confirmation His Spirit brought to such things.

So the person who is so entrenched in their own estimation of truth, who perpetually resists the witness of the Holy Spirit, can serve to grieve Him to the place where there is no forgiveness remaining for Him.

This is an unpopular teaching because we don't like to entertain the idea that God's patience can run out. But the characteristic of this resistance is that one has actually twisted reality so thoroughly as to call the wonder of God's work the doings of the devil. Such misapprehension, such defective comprehension as that, is said here to be beyond forgiveness.

Though a fictional story, in the film *The Robe* (Twentieth-Century Fox, 1954), the character of Peter performs a healing while excluding a pagan doctor from observing. When the doctor enters and sees the patient restored and well, his first response is "sorcery."

Nothing is said here about the believer needing to be the policeman of this condition. It is very possible to discern that someone has reached such a point, but about final judgments we are warned to not act as final judge. The facts may be clear before us and we may be expected to use caution in getting ensnared with such people, but the assessment that they are in that class is reserved for God alone.

The reason is in the words, "or in the age to come." We simply do not have a purview into that age to know every case so as to know who will be there and who will not, who will receive forgiveness at God's hand in that time and place and who will not.

But the verse must have some meaning for the listener, since it does no practical good to instruct about something which only God can discern.

It is simply to be aware of where God's energy is to be best spent in us, and to watch for the limits of what we are to do. At some point in some people's lives, we must give them over to God as judge and turn our attention to those who have been prepared and are "ripe for the harvest."

Matthew 12:33-35
33 "Either make the tree good and its fruit good, or make the tree bad and its fruit bad; for the tree is known by its fruit."

In the form of an imperative, this sounds like something man is said to have done or now does - *"make a tree"*. But this is merely a hypothetical about created things for various purposes. In truth, bad trees are so because of the Fall. God did not create them to be bad. So it is more to highlight that there are circumstances that account for why good trees are good and bad trees are bad yet these may not be known. So the key for the observer is in the resulting fruit. In agriculture we never really know the difference until the fruit is seen.

This is tagged on to the discussion about the Blasphemy of the Holy Spirit because their condition will be evident in what they produce. In this case, the fruit is their open declaration of demonic sources with respect to divine works.

4 "You brood of vipers, how can you, being evil, speak what is good? For the mouth speaks out of that which fills the heart.

A brood conveys the process of rearing and nurturing to the preparation of their work. They are not isolated persons but a company of similar minds that feed and reinforce one another. One has the picture of a hundred meetings were Christ's teaching and work was discussed and the ways to discount it or undo it.

The analogy of the tree is applied in the incredulity of how good could come from hearts of evil similarly to how good fruit could come from a tree prepared to produce bad. Jesus elsewhere says that it is not what goes in that defiles a man but what comes out (Matt 15:11.) What comes out is "produced" by the heart, so the heart must have been already stained and tinctured with evil before such words came forth.

This is complete with respect to the Jewish authorities, but it can also be partial in us, His servants. We can let a part of our hearts be stained and polluted by evil and we find then to our surprise that we can speak rather evil things despite being His child. It is because our hearts can be compartmentalized and we can from time to time not be wholly committed in heart and mind.

35 "The good man brings out of his good treasure what is good; and the evil man brings out of his evil treasure what is evil.

We must allow that this is not always a case of "through and through" in believers. Believers are to some extent a mixture of both as they travel the path of sanctification. But the teaching is nevertheless true. The treasures within us produce according to their nature.

But the thrust of Jesus words are to characterize the general proneness of men in terms of good and evil. There are men who are prone to good from the heart and those who are opposite, and these are seen as treasures out of which men draw the contents.

Matthew 12:36-37
36 "But I tell you that every careless word that people speak, they shall give an accounting for it in the day of judgment. 37 "For by your words you will be justified, and by your words you will be condemned."

This haunts believers and unbelievers alike – that all we say, even the flighty careless things we didn't mean are going to come back to haunt us as we stand before God. Some proceed to dismiss this eventuality by dismissing God, or at least His judgment.

Of course this is hard to do considering the person of Jesus, since His authority to say what's what in that Day is vindicated in His Resurrection.

Does this have application to the Christian? Are we to be brought forward to give an account of our words, having been saved and beyond the judgment of God.?

This also sounds a great deal like works if by our words we are to be justified or condemned.

But that is really the key to understanding the application and the audience. The words that will affect condemnation or justification to the greatest extent are those spoken in accepting Him as Lord or rejecting Him. And if we have words on file that recount our acceptance, we are justified.

So is there yet a fear of every idle word being accounted for? If the context is right as in the above, every idle word is to let the audience know that in the case of unbelief, every idle word will count, but in the case of belief, every idle word has been forgiven.

Christians often have the fear that all their secret sins and the "words" associated with them will be laid bear and recited in one great public accounting in which all our loved ones and friends will see at last who we really were. The Lord's compassion comforts us that this will be private.We must also remember that the most important words are those that said, "I'm a sinner and I accept your sacrifice as payment for my sins and I wish to serve you all the days of my life." Those are the words Jesus will recite for the believer, followed by" "Enter into My Heaven rest, thou good and faithful servant."

Mark 3:21
21 When His own people heard of this, they went out to take custody of Him; for they were saying, "He has lost His senses."

"His own people" means certain of those from His home town of Nazareth, or it may mean certain of His relatives. The words most likely to have caused this reaction would have been, *" Whoever speaks a word against the Son of Man it shall not be forgiven him."*

Without faith, words like this from someone you have known on a socially intimate basis is rather intolerable. Notice that they are not willing to go so far as to label Him a deceiver, but that He has lost his senses –a sort of backhanded kindness that He was not responsible for this teaching.

Matthew 12:38
38 Then some of the scribes and Pharisees said to Him, "Teacher, we want to see a sign from You."

The Pharisees did not have a ready excuse of intimate knowledge from living in His village. They must resort to trickery and subterfuge that may eventually expose Him to the people for what they suspect Him to be. Ordinarily, this would seem to be just the thing that would turn skeptics into men of faith. We are somewhat programmed to think this way. Even fantasy films convey the idea that boys with special powers prove themselves to the dropped jaws of all their jeering friends by performing some stupefying feat at which all prior doubters back away in utter awe.

But we must not be fooled that the request of the Pharisees is for an honest test that will release for them the faith to accept Him as genuine. His claims are far too radical and deleterious to their system for that to be even possible. The request for a sign is to provide a means for attributing sorcery, or worse; and to then fully discount Him in the eyes of the people over whom they would be seen as protectors.

This of course Jesus perceives.

Matthew 12:39-40
39 . . "An evil and adulterous generation craves for a sign; and yet no sign will be given to it but the sign of Jonah . . . 40 three days and and three nights in the belly of the sea monster. . so will the Son of Man be three days and three nights in the heart of the earth.

We are prone to take some exception with Jesus because we are people who value miracles and Jesus did say elsewhere that we are to believe the works that He does as evidence needed for faith. This is because we are drawing the conclusion that the corollary is also in play, "those who seek for a sign are an evil and adulterous generation." Much depends on the beginning motive.

Those who seek a sign to vindicate belief over against doubt have a heart turned toward God. Those who seek a sign to discredit and spoof have the opposite. Jesus is saying that an indication that tells us we have before us an evil generation is the insistence on signs. He also calls them an adulterous generation, which seems strange because adultery is a specific sin and the Pharisees as a generation were not all guilty of cheating on their wives.

Of course, Jesus is here referring to the OT idea that unbelief was as adultery with God because it is never just unbelief, but putting something up instead of God, even if it be oneself - something on which we pour out affection and allegiance. For the Pharisees it was their place and system of leadership.

"no sign but that of the prophet Jonah"

What was Jonah's sign? It would be the one given to Nineveh (we are helped by Jesus telling us this much in a moment.) A sign is an outward symbol or something seen externally as opposed to something perceived intellectually or by contemplation.

Consider the "appearance" of Jonah to the Ninevites. He had been vomited up on the shore having spent three days and nights in the corrosive environment of the creature's stomach. Ordinarily, the vapors and chemicals would suffocate prey and begin the decomposition done by the stomach. But Jonah's survival is a testament to God's purpose – he was to be taken in but not be ultimately harmed.

Even so, it is reasonable that his clothes, hair and skin would have suffered from the effects of his peptic environment. He would have been deposited on the shore virtually bleached white from head to toe. It is also less likely that enough people would have been right there to have seen his arrival on shore which did not necessarily have to include the stereotypical representation of the beast coming up onto dry land so as to be seen.

So the sign would be less likely the facts of his experience and arrival, but instead his very bizarre appearance from its effects. And what was the sign purposed to do? To add an unforgettable visual aid to Jonah's message which was "Repent."

This was John's very message to the Pharisees. *"Do then the works befitting repentance."* The Pharisees asked for a sign and Jesus proclaims that the only meaningful sign apropos to their condition was that of Jonah to Nineveh.

This was, of course, a major slap in the face since the Ninevites were Gentiles and they repented, becoming then among the people of God – the ones *with* the message no longer the targets of the message.

But the reason for selecting Jonah is made clearer.

40 ". . so will the Son of Man be three days and three nights in the heart of the earth."

This is actually the real sign to be given them. The sign of Jonah is to say merely that the sign they will be given is like that of Jonah – a sign that is meant to move them to repent.

But in the fulfillment no such sign like that of Jonah is seen, at least as visibly shocking and full of impending doom as that of Jonah.

The sign is the Resurrection following what would be the very well known duration of time wherein He would have been considered "buried" in the tomb.

How is this a sign in the same class as Jonah's experience and message? Jonah's appearing to the Ninevites as he did was enough to cause them to repent, including their king.

The Resurrection and its report throughout all the region would be a sufficient event that would hold them all accountable to God for their belief or rejection. It would become the decision point that could not be avoided.

Where the analogy ends is that Nineveh repented. The leaders of Israel did not.

Matthew 12:41-42
41 "The men of Nineveh will stand up with this generation at the judgment, and will condemn it because they repented at the preaching of Jonah; and behold, something greater than Jonah is here.

Not to be taken as a commentary on the consciousness and activity of the dead, but rather an eastern mode of figurative speech that also personified things like the earth opening her mouth to receive the blood of righteous Abel or the bodies of sinners in judgment, or the rocks and hills giving voice.

It is to say that Nineveh at least repented at the message given and as such can be pictured as being called to testify about the hardened hearts of the Jews. This was again a considerable slap because it is a Gentile nation giving witness against the people of God.

The reason is clearly stated, *"something greater than Jonah is here."* Those to whom greater light has been given, greater accountability is assessed.

42 "The Queen of the South will rise up with this generation .. "

Another stinging rebuke from the Gentile world. She who was not of the house of God recognized the wisdom and blessing of God on His people, yet the very people of His choosing could now no longer recognize God's wisdom speaking and working in their very midst.

Again, all the more condemnatory because *"something greater than Solomon is here."*

Matthew 12:43-45, Luke 11:27-28, Matthew 12:46-50, Luke 11:33-36

43 "Now when the unclean spirit goes out of a man, it passes through waterless places seeking rest, and does not find it. 44 "Then it says, `I will return to my house from which I came'; and when it comes, it finds it unoccupied, swept, and put in order. 45 "Then it goes and takes along with it seven other spirits more wicked than itself, and they go in and live there; and the last state of that man becomes worse than the first. That is the way it will also be with this evil generation." (Matt 12:43-45)

27 While Jesus was saying these things, one of the women in the crowd raised her voice and said to Him, "Blessed is the womb that bore You and the breasts at which You nursed." 28 But He said, "On the contrary, blessed are those who hear the word of God and observe it." (Luke 11:27-28)

46 While He was still speaking to the crowds, behold, His mother and brothers were standing outside, seeking to speak to Him. 47 Someone said to Him, "Behold, Your mother and Your brothers are standing outside seeking to speak to You." 48 But Jesus answered the one who was telling Him and said, "Who is My mother and who are My brothers?" 49 And stretching out His hand toward His disciples, He said, "Behold My mother and My brothers! 50 "For whoever does the will of My Father who is in heaven, he is My brother and sister and mother." (Matthew 12:46-50)

33 "No one, after lighting a lamp, puts it away in a cellar nor under a basket, but on the lampstand, so that those who enter may see the light. 34 "The eye is the lamp of your body; when your eye is clear, your whole body also is full of light; but when it is bad, your body also is full of darkness. 35 "Then watch out that the light in you is not darkness. 36 "If therefore your whole body is full of light, with no dark part in it, it will be wholly illumined, as when the lamp illumines you with its rays." (Luke 11:33-36)

Commentary

Matthew 12:43-45
43 "Now when the unclean spirit goes out of a man, it passes through waterless places seeking rest, and does not find it.

No matter how modern man chooses to explain away demons as beliefs of ignorant times, the character and integrity of Jesus makes their reality unavoidable. Jesus in no way treats them as fictions or myths. This passage is a good example of just how straightforward their real existence actually is.

This comes from seeing how Jesus, without a hint of chagrin, describes in matter-of-fact terms their habits and modes of operation. The case is of a demon that gives up on its host, then goes to seek rest. We might be tempted to conclude that it has become exhausted in its expending of energy to control and possess a human being so as to eventually seek rest. But we find in a moment that it finds no rest and returns, which is antithetical to a state of exhaustion, because why return to the condition that sapped its resources?

Rather, we are to understand "seeking rest" as seeking a new home – a new soul – and that the wandering typifies a state of restlessness, and rest that of a home. The idea of a wasteland simply means it finds no candidates. (We might wonder why it left in the first place if this is the result. But we aren't told the reason, except to conclude that it may be by a casting out or that it gets the gumption to try something new.)

The pressure to be comfortably at rest again in a new host is overwhelming.

44 "Then it says, `I will return to my house from which I came'; and when it comes, it finds it unoccupied, swept, and put in order.

The restlessness with no other prospects causes the demon to view its last home as the best thing remaining.

The idea that it finds the place *"unoccupied, swept and in order"* means that when the individual was delivered, he did not fill his soul with something else, i.e. a faith in God. His soul remains "unoccupied." Nor is another demon now there. This is to say that no lesson was learned in his deliverance, he is dull to the need to put the right things in its place.

45 "Then it goes and takes along with it seven other spirits more wicked than itself, and they go in and live there; and the last state of that man becomes worse than the first.

An empty soul is not a safe soul. It cannot take comfort or confidence in the freedom it now has, while taking no spiritual action to ensure it never happens again. This is the case of individuals who are simply not in tune with the larger spiritual issues of life, who see life as largely practical and may even consider religion sort of silly or mere nonsense.

There is a rationalization even in modern times that religion is a crutch for people of weak constitutions, who can't think for themselves and are prone to follow others who can talk a good line. In the case here of possession, one would think the person would now be keen to spiritual realities and abandon their cynicism. But people are varied in terms of motivations and it is often the case that when the crisis is over, they do not learn the lesson, but return to what is easiest, our same old ways.

Here, the demon invites others to take up residence and the next state of the man is noticeably worse. That is essentially what exorcism is about in the hands of the clergy – to be sure to replace possession with Christian faith.

". . That is the way it will also be with this evil generation."

This is a declaration about the future. This evil generation is endemic such that it will be found still living in the days when Christ comes to judge the world. As things get worse, people without a godly focus will have exchanged their fewer possessions for ever worse ones, such that their condemnation will not be merely a shame, but a necessity.

This generation is filled with rejection of the Truth. So will that later one be.

Luke 11:27-28
27 "Blessed is the womb that bore . . .28 "On the contrary, blessed are those who hear the word of God and observe it."

Some might take this as a denigration of His mother's role in birthing and nursing Him. But it is a matter of showing the immense contrast in terms of what blesses. The woman is not being upbraided for choosing something so little to praise. She has listened to His teaching and recognizes the incredible rightness in it that she bursts into praise.

But Jesus wishes to make sure that the wrong conclusion from that praise is not drawn – that the truly blessed are those called to special service for God. Mary's role was extremely rare, so rare as to be of little application to anyone else in humanity, since how likely is it that someone would bare another man of the nature of Jesus?

So for Jesus, it is all important that in the subject of "blessedness," the focus be on the hearing and doing of God's Word. What makes this blessed is that His Word has worked its way into the life, it constrains the life to do the righteousness, and frankly, if no one ever does the righteousness taught, its teaching would be in vain.

That is, of course, the rub that atheists and reprobate people everywhere quickly discern. That this is not recreational philosophy, but a way of life meant to be lived out in actions and thoughts. The atheist and debunker will have none of this, so he spoofs the doctrine wherever he can.

Matthew 12:46-50
46 While He was still speaking to the crowds, behold, His mother and brothers were standing outside, seeking to speak to Him.

For Catholics, this verse presents a difficulty to be managed in defending Immaculate Conception, because that doctrine not only proclaims Mary's innocence at Jesus birth, but her perpetual sinlessness, which sexual relations would have made untenable in the Catholic mind. Hence, Jesus cannot have actual brothers by Mary and Joseph.

Much of this treatment comes from Catholic Tradition, which can only be taken at face value as it's proclaimed, without use of the typical historical processes for validating facts. It has the advantage of being believed back to within centuries of the apostles, but Protestants reject it because of its conflict with Scripture on the universal application of sin to all mankind and the lack of a specific expression in anything that could be attributed directly to the apostles themselves.

For Catholics, *brothers* are translated *cousins*, relying on the alternate meaning of *'adelphoi'* as kin. The main support for retaining 'brothers' is that there are two clearly different words for brother and cousin – *'adelphos'* and *'suggenes.'* Admittedly this distinction is blurred in Aramaic, but the writing of the Greek versions of the Gospels is widely held to have been a "new" work not merely a case of mechanically translating pre-existing Aramaic language into Greek.

The writer therefore had at his disposal all the clarity available in Greek, so as to better translate the intent known in the mind of those words that were by nature less precise. The men with Mary were either known in fact to be real brothers or to be real cousins. So the writer had no hindrances whatsoever in choosing the appropriate word. Since he chose 'adelphoi' we are compelled by simple logic to conclude he intended that as the meaning. He certainly knew the real facts.

48 "Who is My mother and who are My brothers?" 49 And stretching out His hand toward His disciples, He said, "Behold My mother and My brothers! . . . 50 whoever does the will of My Father . . . he is My brother and sister and mother."

These and similar words are often attributed to a sort of coldness in Jesus that cares only for His mission and denigrates the natural affections we develop for family and friends. Jesus previously said publicly to His mother, *"Woman, what have I to do with thee?"*

Understanding Jesus there and here would have readily come from being there to see His expressions in person and to see how He treated His family members. We must draw our conclusions from His tender manner elsewhere and the upholding of the love of God in all things.

In eastern manner and thought, things mentioned are often used as launching pads for teaching valuable truths, and are often couched in terms whose comparison with the things used may attribute denigration, but are clearly understood as being tools in the hands of the speaker.

Jesus' wishes to introduce the novel notion that those who follow Him are as much His family as His natural kin because they and He are one in His Father, Who makes all believers co-heirs, therefore the family of God.

It is notable that, contrary to liberalism and the social gospel peddlers, Jesus does not point to all in the room. That is what the liberal would have Jesus do. But Jesus limits this designation to those who are both hearers and doers – His own disciples.

Also of note is that the state of His disciples is hardly that of perfection. They are not perfect doers of His Word, yet are called His family members because their hearts are inclined to do it.

Luke 11:33-35
33 "No one, after lighting a lamp, puts it away in a cellar nor under a basket, but on the lampstand, so that those who enter may see the light. 34 "The eye is the lamp of your body . ."

Here we have a repetition of what He taught on the Mount of the Beatitudes (see Matthew 6:22), but here He emphasizes more the purpose of the light in relation to the individual and the world. In the Sermon on the Mount, the emphasis was on inner light compared to inner darkness.

Here it is about the light we are to shine out into the world. There are others in darkness and our light is to shine so as to draw men out from darkness.

There are folks who often adopt the mode or style of living that is not verbal in witness. They are in dreadful fear of speaking up about saving faith or mentioning Christ in a social or public setting.

To some extent, Christ questions the genuineness of one's salvation if they are embarrassed to confess Him – *"neither will I confess him before My Father."* But we have to be as sensitive as the all-knowing Christ in allowing for the reality that some people are so desperately wounded in their own self image and confidence that forcing them into public witness may be in fact detrimental until those issues are healed.

In no way is a natural hindrance to become a permanent excuse. Those who love the Lord and are genuinely saved will have a new natural desire to witness of the gift and hope they've found.

It is a matter of love for the lost that must get us eventually over our natural fears and on to the work of evangelism.

So we are to put our lamp deliberately in public view. "Deliberate" brings to mind an anecdote of an opposite analogy, but a good example just the same. When we go to the dentist, he says, "Open, please." But to open means deliberate consent, and we feel neither. It means we have resolved to take this seriously and let happen all that is necessary. To put our lamp deliberately out in public view means we are resolved to give ourselves an exposure that is clear and unmistakable. We are willing to be known as Christians rather than simply blending in with all sorts of other "good" people.

35 "Then watch out that the light in you is not darkness.

This sounds like a logical contradiction because light in us cannot be darkness. But it can be in terms of what the world sees, just as putting a light in the cellar does nothing for the darkness in the house.

We are to be watchful because the devil is staying up nights thinking of ways to get our light hidden and out of the way, hence of no effect. And he is clever to not come all of a sudden with suggestions obviously contrary to God. Instead, he comes with slight variations, full of perfectly good reasoning that take us slightly off the mark. And gradually he woos us away from what we are called to do. So we are to be watchful for those temptations, but also generally observant that our light has not unwittingly become hidden.

Luke 11:37-54

37 Now when He had spoken, a Pharisee asked Him to have lunch with him; and He went in, and reclined at the table. 38 When the Pharisee saw it, he was surprised that He had not first ceremonially washed before the meal. 39 But the Lord said to him, "Now you Pharisees clean the outside of the cup and of the platter; but inside of you, you are full of robbery and wickedness. 40 "You foolish ones, did not He who made the outside make the inside also? 41 "But give that which is within as charity, and then all things are clean for you.

42 "But woe to you Pharisees! For you pay tithe of mint and rue and every kind of garden herb, and yet disregard justice and the love of God; but these are the things you should have done without neglecting the others. 43 "Woe to you Pharisees! For you love the chief seats in the synagogues and the respectful greetings in the market places. 44 "Woe to you! For you are like concealed tombs, and the people who walk over them are unaware of it."

45 One of the lawyers said to Him in reply, "Teacher, when You say this, You insult us too." 46 But He said, "Woe to you lawyers as well! For you weigh men down with burdens hard to bear, while you yourselves will not even touch the burdens with one of your fingers. 47 "Woe to you! For you build the tombs of the prophets, and it was your fathers who killed them. 48 "So you are witnesses and approve the deeds of your fathers; because it was they who killed them, and you build their tombs. 49 "For this reason also the wisdom of God said, `I will send to them prophets and apostles, and some of them they will kill and some they will persecute, 50 so that the blood of all the prophets, shed since the foundation of the world, may be charged against this generation, 51 from the blood of Abel to the blood of Zechariah, who was killed between the altar and the house of God; yes, I tell you, it shall be charged against this generation.'

52 "Woe to you lawyers! For you have taken away the key of knowledge; you yourselves did not enter, and you hindered those who were entering." 53 When He left there, the scribes and the Pharisees began to be very hostile and to question Him closely on many subjects, 54 plotting against Him to catch Him in something He might say. (Luke 11:37-54)

Commentary

Luke 11:37-39
37 . . a Pharisee asked Him to have lunch with him; . . . he was surprised that He had not first ceremonially washed before the meal.

This first appears as though Jesus is disrespecting a ceremonial law that the Pharisee is doing obediently, but about which Jesus is being casual.

Put simply, there was no law that the Jews were required to wash before eating. There were a number of specific commands to wash in respect to offerings in the temple or as ceremonial cleansings after having touched something that defiled a person. But nothing was required before eating a meal.

So what we have is a case of tradition mandated by the leaders of Judaism and they had been entrusted with the oracles of God.

This is how referential authority can slip. A body of men can introduce a ritual or a law on the basis that they are doing so to preserve a biblical precept (ceremonial cleanliness) and it eventually becomes indistinct from the received Law in the mind of later generations.

39 . . the Lord said to him, "Now you Pharisees clean the outside of the cup and of the platter; but inside of you, you are full of robbery and wickedness.

Most folks would consider this politically incorrect and rude to one's host. Jesus is paying back the invitation to dine with a cutting indictment.

But we have to keep in mind that, like John before Him, Jesus is not under obligation to let the mores and customs of men interfere with what He came to do. If it means becoming unpopular, so be it. Jesus will not be confined by the common need to be popular at all costs.

Now Jesus is *not* telling the Pharisee that outward cleanliness in ceremonial washings was in general a mistake and that inner cleanliness was what was meant in the Law all along. The Law did call for outward cleansings.

Jesus is merely pointing out that despite there being no law in this case, the Pharisees in general spent considerable effort on the outer cleanliness but paid little attention to the inner soul.

full of robbery

It seems incongruent that such a disciplined group like the Pharisees could be charged with robbery. But this would have been the getting of money through processes couched in legal terms. In the Third Reich, Hitler took great pains to couch all his actions as perfectly legal for the betterment of German society and state. He was not viewed as a lawbreaker until later when men were forced to compare his actions to the general precepts of universal morality.

For the Pharisees, one method would be confiscation of property associated with indictments of individuals who were in conflict with the Sanhedrin. Part of their remuneration would be the forfeit of their property to the commonwealth for their crimes.

Another means would have been extortion as a prerequisite to lending certain services or protections that would not have been given on their merits alone.

The Pharisees are unique in national affairs because they were both religious and civil leaders, often called "rulers of the Jews" in those who comprised the Sanhedrin. Rulers eventually resort to the foibles of ruling – techniques and procedures that employ "efficiency" under the guise of some greater interest.

. . wickedness . .

There was to some extent a real wickedness in the Pharisees, despite their posing as the custodians of the faith. This seems overly harsh for such a conservative religious order, but there is one fruit that proves this to be true – their rejection of the divine truth that was in Jesus.

No matter what your religious energy might be, if you cannot recognize the One coming from the God you claim to serve, you have missed the mark along the way and your life must be characterized as opposite to that truth, which is basically what wickedness means.

We must also keep ever in mind that these men purposed in their hearts to do away with Jesus. They actually conceived it as right and dutiful to put Him to death. Such plans and their justifications can only come from evil.

Luke 11:40-44

40 "You foolish ones, did not He who made the outside make the inside also? 41 But give that which is within as charity, and then all things are clean for you

They are called foolish for not discerning this – that God made both the inside and the outside. This seems a strange way to answer because the idea expressed is not direct but requires some contemplation. The idea is that the Pharisees are busy worrying about the outside in terms of defilements on the basis that God made the outside of the body and wishes it to be holy and clean, hence, their neglect of the inside suggests that the inner man was not made to be clean also.

This He calls foolishness. It is foolishness because the slightest contemplation about the way man works would have clarified that evil is born out of the heart.

"give that which is within as charity"

This is to say that if you do all things out of love, the worry about defilements will be set back into its proper proportion and many things formerly only illegal by human ordinances will actually disappear when love is the aim. If love were preferred, things like proper work on the Sabbath, or whether it was necessary to wash before eating would be seen correctly rather than legalistically.

42 "But woe to you . . you pay tithe of mint . . . yet disregard justice and the love of God;

The Greek for tithe is *'apodekatoo'* – pronounced *apo-deka-**tah**-oh* and it meant the giving of one tenth.

Tithing concerned first fruits of things produced. The man in his field was to give a tithe of the best portion to the Lord of what he harvested. The Pharisees wished to be seen as ahead of the pack in religious obedience, so they tithed also on exotic things ordinarily out of the mainstream and in remarkably small quantities, so as to be seen as exemplars of faithfulness to the Law.

Jesus is saying that they spend considerable energy making sure their tithe is seen as exhaustively compliant, but they disregard the precepts of justice and love.

but these are the things you should have done without neglecting the others.

Jesus is not saying these things were wrong.. He is telling them that their diligence is commendable, but not at the expense of the more worthy duties.

43 "Woe to you . . For you love the chief seats in the synagogues . . . 44 Woe to you! For you are like concealed tombs . . "

Leadership and positions of authority have their perks. Those who strive to rule often do so purely for the rewards and aggrandisements that come with the job. People in federal public office often betray that their reasons for running and staying in office are more about a house in the Hamptons than about serving the public. Actual service seems like a necessary nuisance in achieving their personal goals.

Having chief seats would be small potatoes in today's estimation of perks, but in ancient times one's outward appearance of importance and status was a functional component of wielding all the more authority over the masses. One's place in public events and worship was something "seen" by all, so a great deal of fretting and energy was spent making sure one was seen. In many cases, being seen was making up for a prior life of being unnoticed.

In the Zefferelli film *Brother Sun, Sister Moon* (Paramount, 1973), the bishop of the town is seen working with the magistrates on a parade of dignitaries including the visiting emperor. The magistrates have designed a plan for who will be where in the procession, and the bishop immediately protests that his own position will be completely out of sight.

Where people were "seen" made a statement of their importance, and in these times, being important was the aim of life.

"For you are like concealed tombs, and the people who walk over them are unaware of it."

The point is to say that people are unaware (or even reminded) of the corruption of the body taking place in the tomb. This is similar to the "whited sepulchers" analogy He makes elsewhere. The corruption within is concealed from view, so the outside gives the impression of purity.

Again, this focuses the indictment on their principle that what is "seen" is all important while neglecting true purity and cleanliness inside.

Luke 11:45-47
45 One of the lawyers said to Him in reply, "Teacher, when You say this, You insult us too."

So it is clear that an insult is in play. Jesus is actually indicting those to whom He is a guest.

Jesus did not address lawyers by using the general term 'Pharisees.' It was not necessary to be a Pharisee in order to be a lawyer. But what was the Law thus adjudicated by these lawyers? The Mosaic Law; which meant that lawyers were joined at the hip with the Scribes and Pharisees. So they perceived the insult also, even though aimed at the ruling class.

46 But He said, "Woe to you lawyers as well! For you weigh men down with burdens hard to bear, while you yourselves will not even touch the burdens with one of your fingers.

There are lessons here for modern lawyers as well. For these in the verse, the burdens hard to bear were the legal entanglements with which the poor client had to comply in order to be represented or secure confidence in the outcome. In many cases, this involved paying for witnesses in one's favor. It also, as now, involved lining the pockets of your counsel with cash.

Not even touching these burdens meant that they had loop holes for themselves when the time came. Lawyers also served to assist in the enforcement of the Law among the citizenry in the practice of giving legal advice about prospective actions. Clients would be counseled to follow overly burdensome procedures to ensure legality.

Today, there are additional things that introduce what we might see as "burdens." The legal profession is all about winning, as opposed to letting justice prevail. It is about working the nooks and crannies of generally written laws so that one "wins" purely on technicalities, irrespective of the patent guilt of their clients.

The result is the creation of more law to cover the misuse or even the outright travesties of clever adjudicating.

47 "Woe to you! For you build the tombs of the prophets, and it was your fathers who killed them."

It is strange how magnanimous evil people can become when their enemies are out of the way. In Roman society, enemies of the ruling class were often celebrated with honorary funerals paid for by the very people who engineered their downfall.

In some cases, this was done to cast off any suspicions about their being involved – you couldn't be connected with murder if you are honoring them. In other cases, it was simply a way of rejoicing about them being in the grave instead of the fly in your ointment.

All of this dissertation is speaking about hypocrisy.

Luke 11:49-51
49 ". . `I will send to them prophets and apostles, and some of them they will kill and some they will persecute, 50 so that the blood of all the prophets, . . may be charged against this generation, 51 from the blood of Abel to the blood of Zechariah,

Jesus appears to state that it was for this reason that prophets were sent – that men would manifest the evil described.

First, this does not mean that God wished His servants to be persecuted or killed. He sent them to His people that they have a point of accountability for their wickedness. If evil is to be judged, it must have a reference point in the call to righteousness. It must have a backdrop against which it stands out and is seen for what it is. God certainly knew they were evil men. But it was necessary that someone preach righteousness to them such that in the day of judgment, God can point to their accountability.

As for the servants He used, one could infer that they were being used as a sort of sacrificial fodder. But from their vantage point, the call to righteousness has its own merit all by itself. It is always a reason for being. And if the call is genuine, then there is a genuine expectation of repentance. (Jonah is a good example.)

"so that the blood of the prophets . . . may be charged against this generation."

It is as though there is a credit and debit system in place. When evil is done, it is "charged" to one's account. How realistic this is does not mollify the concept that records of deeds are being kept and will be the case against the person at the Judgment. The use of "so that" is a subjunctive expression in Greek and is used to indicate purpose or intent. A is done so that B may result.

Again, we cannot escape the idea that God did send these men with a purpose that includes their persecution and death. But the moral sting of this is eliminated by the analysis above of the need for accountability and that declaring righteousness carries its own justification.

"from the blood of Abel to the blood of Zechariah"

Why was Abel's blood shed? Because his deeds of righteousness were intolerable witnesses to the deeds of his brother. Cain wished so desperately to be accepted on his own terms before God, that he came to assess that his brother could no longer live, else he would remain a perpetual indictment against him.

The career of Zechariah is rather brief in Chronicles compared to his book of prophesy (2 Chr 24:20-21.) There we learn of the plot to do away with him. That the "altar and the house of God" are mentioned is to highlight that these holy precincts held no conviction against their deed. He was of priestly lineage, so it is possible that Jesus' mention of the location makes this deed all the more ignominious if Zechariah was in the midst of temple duties.

The tomb of Zechariah is seen today near the SE corner of the Temple compound. It is distinguished by its square low tower and pyramid roof.

'yes, I tell you, it shall be charged against this generation.'

The deeds were done by their forefathers, but Jesus is assuring them that the charge will be laid at their feet also because they have precisely the same heart as their fathers. They approve of what their fathers did.

In all reality, some of the very men present at this dinner will be among those who call for His death in the night session of the Sanhedrin at Jesus' arrest and trial.

Luke 11:52-54
52 "Woe to you lawyers! For you have taken away the key of knowledge; you yourselves did not enter, and you hindered those who were entering."

Another indictment against the work of the lawyers of the day – that they hid from their clients and the people in general the key to the knowledge of true righteousness in that they sustained the traditional righteousness of the ruling class in its stead.

The height of the indictment is that they spent all their energies defining the righteousness with which the people must comply, yet with respect to true righteousness had no intention of following it either.

53 When He left there, the scribes and the Pharisees began to be very hostile and to question Him closely on many subjects, 54 plotting against Him to catch Him in something He might say.

The reaction is not surprising. An innocent invitation to dinner has turned into an adversarial confrontation of the highest order. Their whole function in society is being thrashed, and in very judgmental terms.

Notice that the truth of His words are out of the picture entirely. No one is musing His thoughts or taking time to evaluate themselves by them. He has offended virtually everyone, and the only thing acutely in the foreground now is how to recover, how to retaliate.

They are not looking for evidences of His truth. They are looking for anything they can hang on Him that will further their case to have Him done away with.

Luke 12:1-8
1 Under these circumstances, after so many thousands of people had gathered together that they were stepping on one another, He began saying to His disciples first of all, " Beware of the leaven of the Pharisees, which is hypocrisy. 2 "But there is nothing covered up that will not be revealed, and hidden that will not be known. 3 "Accordingly, whatever you have said in the dark will be heard in the light, and what you have whispered in the inner rooms will be proclaimed upon the housetops. 4 "I say to you, My friends, do not be afraid of those who kill the body and after that have no more that they can do. 5 "But I will warn you whom to fear: fear the One who, after He has killed, has authority to cast into hell; yes, I tell you, fear Him!

6 "Are not five sparrows sold for two cents? Yet not one of them is forgotten before God. 7 "Indeed, the very hairs of your head are all numbered. Do not fear; you are more valuable than many sparrows. (Luke 12:1-8)

Commentary

Luke 12:1
1 Under these circumstances, after so many thousands of people had gathered . . . He began saying . . . " Beware of the leaven of the Pharisees, which is hypocrisy.

The dinner had turned into something the host and his fellow Pharisees reacted to with spite. They had extended a friendly gesture and Jesus had returned the favor with criticism and derogation. But there is a pervasive quality to truth – it must be told. But it was not received as such. That is the delusion of self-deception – it works out how we are not in the wrong even though we are wrong.

This begins Jesus time of disfavor with the authorities. They had not been warm to Him prior to this and had even tried to trick Him on occasion. But here He has actually spoken out publicly and in a derogatory tone.

We see Jesus now beginning to warn His followers about the Pharisees, which will be seen as divisive, but necessary.

The scene here changes away from the house of the Pharisee to the general condition surrounding Jesus thereafter. The crowds are measured now in hundreds and with such a clamoring to see and hear Him that people were being injured.

There is no indication that anyone was killed or gravely injured, which may help explain why we have no mention that Jesus took note of this but rather begins teaching despite the circumstances. It is also possible that certain of His followers took some measure of control to forestall serious injuries.

The leaven of the Pharisees is an idiomatic phrase that plays on the nature of yeast to spread throughout an entire lump of dough. Two features are visible: the pervasive nature of yeast and that it takes time to be fully effected (the reason the Israelites were instructed to not wait for the normal rising of bread but to eat it unleavened.)

The leaven of the Pharisees was their deception about true righteousness and the imposition of human traditions in place of it; yet all very logically and rationally worked out. They preached the right message but added extra burdens not called for by God (the washing of hands before a meal); and they themselves had worked out ways to avoid certain of those burdens personally (or did only as much as was necessary for show) - *"listen to what they teach you, but do not follow their example."*

The analogy of time in leaven is that they had become what they were over a long time, which wooed the unsuspecting inch by inch into acceptance and even justification. They were the religious leaders of the nation and their long-standing reputations seemed impenetrable monoliths of authority.

In the Frank Capra film, *Mr. Smith Goes to Washington* (Columbia Pictures, 1939), Smith comes against the corruption with the simplicity of the "founding" principles and moral precepts. And he faces down very well-known faces in Congress, people who were giants.

The Pharisees now being addressed were of such notoriety. Many were staring directly at Jesus as He spoke. You can imagine doing this today in the U.S. Senate, putting forth moral indictments with men like the notable senators and congressmen of today staring back at you but a few feet away. It is a commitment to truth despite the consequences, something we ordinary folks think twice about.

. . hypocrisy

'hypocrite' comes from the Greek word for play acting or pretending. There is a capacity in all of us to go through the motions of a rightly-indicated behavior, though our heart is not sincere in it. To some it seems strange that a person desiring to do good, especially Christian good, would rationalize this kind of thing within themselves, but the cases involved almost always have to do with very strong, emotional dysfunctions that are hard to control and often battle against doing what one knows is right. Paul describes this in Romans chapter 7 as the warring between flesh and spirit. There it is in relation to righteousness and sin, and here it is very much the same but differently oriented. Here we actually come to do the right thing for fear of the stigma or embarrassment in neglecting it. So we act out the right behavior to avoid the judgment of others. That is hypocrisy.

It is what the world is eager to point to - the man who claims to be in Christ but slips up and betrays that he is less changed by Christ than expected. That is the foible of hypocrisy – we slip up and fail somewhere along the line in keeping up appearances and the false façade. Then others see the real us, and our witness for Christ is thereby damaged.

In the case of the Pharisees, it was all about show and their public persona, but behind closed doors they were as wicked and deceitful as the unreligious man.

Luke 12:2-5
2 "But there is nothing covered up that will not be revealed, . . . 3 whatever you have said in the dark will be heard in the light, and what you have whispered in the inner rooms will be proclaimed upon the housetops.

Perfectly horrifying declarations, and words every person including Christians hope will somehow not be true. For we all have secret sins about which we are embarrassed, even if now under the control of the Spirit. Certainly the things over which we slip and stumble we don't want shouted from the rooftops.

First, this is not a picture of how we will be reconciled about our works and rewards in Heaven – that those attending Christ's throne will uncaringly announce on loudspeakers our most embarrassing moments in the flesh.

It is rather a prediction concerning those who adopt the view that there will be no consequences for things done in secret, or even this disbelief that God sees in secret. This has a two-fold aspect.

First, persistent sin that is casually disregarded has a way of making its way into public view. Televangelist troubles of 1990's are painful examples. The corporate fraud of recent times is an example in the secular world.

The key here is a disbelief in the unrighteousness of one's actions, a lack of concern that things need to be made right with the Lord and neglect in prayer for the power to repent. The Lord is gracious and longsuffering, but eventually the cup of toleration fills and the Lord may engineer or at least allow natural circumstances to create opportunities for exposure.

It is a sober warning for those who treat sin lightly as though God looks the other way in all but the most serious issues.

The second aspect is eternal judgment. For the truly wicked, there is a sort of public disclosure of one's sins that is made the case for punishment. Some believe that there will be no long drawn out arguing about the unfairness of things or the like, and that the bare facts of what one has done with Christ will be the only indictment - one with which the sinner won't be able to disagree.

But we do see in Christ's parable of the judgment that there is discussion about what was not done unto Him – *"Ye did it not unto Me"* – which leaves some room for a recounting of the sins of life.

For the Christian believer, the debt owed from our sins has been paid. It is no longer then a case of accounting for them in terms of worthiness. It may not even be a case of having to account personally for them in terms of rewards (Paul merely talks about the things of no eternal worth burning up on entry.) So for believers, we should take comfort that Jesus is not going to callously expose us to the rest of faithful Christendom, based on the words here.

4 ". . . do not be afraid of those who kill the body . . 5 . . fear the One who, after He has killed, has authority to cast into hell; yes, I tell you, fear Him!"

The idea continues here respecting accountability, namely clarifying to Whom we should be the more fearful of accounting for ourselves. If their sins will find them out, the sinner ought to fear the one who will expose them truly, and apply the more enduring punishment for them.

The comparison with those who merely can kill is important for two reasons. First, those who can kill cannot affect harm on the soul. This is a message for the believer. The world will threaten death and suffering for the faith (the persecutions) but can do nothing against the soul to determine the outcome one way or the other. Having no further power beyond this is the point.

Second, God does have power beyond physical death, to wreak eternal punishment on the soul. This is a message for the unbeliever, and a warning to take things seriously when considering what lies beyond the grave.

"Yes, I tell you fear Him!"

An exclamation is seen here in the language. This indicates that the fate of the soul, the pains to be suffered, are dreadful enough as to be avoided at all costs. It is like saying, "You don't even want to think about going there." We are not told the scientific description of Hell and its torments except in the pictures of hell fire, intense heat, thirst and privation. We can extrapolate from the rich man's plight that someone at least should send word to his brothers to avoid the place.

Some have considerable difficulty picturing the God of love designing the torments that plague Hell as a punishment He personally inflicts. Many try to characterize it as a place where the greater harm is done by its inhabitants to themselves and others with no need of any help from God. But to some degree we must bring God into the picture as Creator of the place and its physical conditions, since it is described as a place "prepared" for the devil and his angels.

This rubs us wrong because of our preference for the loveliness of God and His kindness and care for all the living.

But reality is often quite different than our preferences and the Bible must be taken in its whole witness. God has prepared a place and the circumstances for the wicked, and Jesus spent a great deal of time warning people about it.

Love cannot be simultaneously unjust. Justice requires punishment. The disconnection of these is a defining feature of corruption – that the unjust go unpunished. So, like it or not, punishment is in the equation. Our objective is to avoid it and turn our heads rather toward the rewards of Heaven awaiting the righteous.

Luke 12:6-7
6 "Are not five sparrows sold for two cents? Yet not one of them is forgotten before God."

The price of sparrows is mentioned only to highlight that their worth in human terms is rather small. Despite this, they are still known by God. Their families and offspring are known, the day of their births are known.

" "Indeed, the very hairs of your head are all numbered."

Some have come to regard this as hyperbole only to make a point – God is concerned about every detail. Yet there is nothing to prevent us concluding that His knowledge of us includes the numbering of our hairs, as in 13,206. It is preceded by "Indeed" which was a way of preparing the hearer for a declaration of truth as facts.

7 Do not fear; you are more valuable than many sparrows.

We would all agree that mankind with all his capacities and potential to achieve is of more value. Still there are some who believe all life is valued the same in God's eyes – that life is life wherever it is found.

But nature teaches us that there are different values for things, that the communal idea of absolute equality of all things is not realistic. The fact that certain animals actually bear by design thousands of offspring to offset immediate losses to predators, suggests that not all life is valued the same, else there is moral culpability in creating a world in which 90% of those born are directly eaten. God created the food chain and some individuals seem to come into life only to supply it. It is a great enigma in which we shrink back from attributing callousness to God. Much can be attributed to the effects of the Fall. But this is to say the truths of the world are there nonetheless.

However we work out the explanations, we must at least face squarely the words of Jesus, that with respect to men, they are more valuable than sparrows.

Luke 12:8-23
8 "And I say to you, everyone who confesses Me before men, the Son of Man will confess him also before the angels of God; 9 but he who denies Me before men will be denied before the angels of God. 10 "And everyone who speaks a word against the Son of Man, it will be forgiven him; but he who blasphemes against the Holy Spirit, it will not be forgiven him.

11 "When they bring you before the synagogues and the rulers and the authorities, do not worry about how or what you are to speak in your defense, or what you are to say; 12 for the Holy Spirit will teach you in that very hour what you ought to say." 13 Someone in the crowd said to Him, "Teacher, tell my brother to divide the family inheritance with me." 14 But He said to him, "Man, who appointed Me a judge or arbitrator over you?" 15 Then He said to them, "Beware, and be on your guard against every form of greed; for not even when one has an abundance does his life consist of his possessions." 16 And He told them a parable, saying, "The land of a rich man was very productive. 17 "And he began reasoning to himself, saying, `What shall I do, since I have no place to store my crops?' 18 "Then he said, `This is what I will do: I will tear down my barns and build larger ones, and there I will store all my grain and my goods. 19 `And I will say to my soul, "Soul, you have many goods laid up for many years to come; take your ease, eat, drink and be merry."' 20 "But God said to him, `You fool! This very night your soul is required of you; and now who will own what you have prepared?' 21 "So is the man who stores up treasure for himself, and is not rich toward God." 22 And He said to His disciples, "For this reason I say to you, do not worry about your life, as to what you will eat; nor for your body, as to what you will put on. 23 "For life is more than food, and the body more than clothing. (Luke 12:8-23)

Commentary

Luke 12:8-10
8 ". . everyone who confesses Me before men, the Son of Man will confess him also before the angels of God;"

Jesus is here putting faith where the rubber meets the road. Christianity is not to be a recreational philosophy, an academic exercise. We are not to study it, appreciate its tenets, but put the book back on the shelf when we are called away to the affairs of our "real life."

We are to allow the principles of Christ's teaching to *change* our lives, to set us on a new course, to put into practice what has been taught. That means bringing His teaching to bear on all the aspects of our former life so as to make it our new life. We are to stand up and be noticed for the change in us. We are not to hide within the woodwork so that no one will suspect we are any different than before. The new life is not meant to be held in private, something we do in the safety of our homes or in our churches, yet kept clearly away from the rest.

This teaching is a corollary. It has a positive statement and a corresponding negative statement. He who confesses Me, I will confess. He who denies Me, I will deny. This brings up the subject of public witness and the very real fear many people have of speaking out about their faith. The transformation of the soul from death to life is not something that is to be appreciated privately and kept to oneself. With the new life and the indwelling of the Spirit comes an eagerness to tell others, to make the experience available to others.

On the one hand, it is the sharing of a wonderful experience, full of inner joy, freedom and love. On the other, it is a repudiation of self and a proscribing of carnality. So it will be variously received, hence the range of reactions. Some favorable and glad, some angry and persecutorial. It is the former we prefer. We would have no difficulty witnessing if that were always the case. We fear the latter in a society where well-being is so dependent on getting along with diverse people of diverse values. We think twice today about witnessing because the consequences have the potential of so radically changing the security of our livelihood. Witnessing in some parts of the world means being set upon and killed. Elsewhere it can mean losing your job or the acceptance of neighbors and friends.

Against this Jesus says, "Fear not him who can only kill the body . . but Him who can kill body and soul in Hell." Unfortunately, many live in a society where appropriating that teaching is very hard to contemplate.

To whatever extent we are given opportunity, the Christian needs to be fruitful in public witness. It is not a case that one instance comdemns – Jesus is not saying one denial begets denial of us before the Father. It is a condition that routinely shrinks from exposure. It is an indication of a lack of transformation. And as such, we are most likely in a condition that Christ would not have affirmed in the first place.

10 "And everyone who speaks a word against the Son of Man, it will be forgiven him; but he who blasphemes against the Holy Spirit, it will not be forgiven him.

This was spoken of earlier under Matthew 12:31, above. Blasphemy is to offend God in speech or to besmirch His name or His person by casting unfavorable light or denigration on Him. It is associated in recent times with the use of profanity, but that is really only an instance of blasphemy, not blasphemy defined.

In the NT, it usually means resisting the work of the Holy Spirit to the degree that one finally and irrevocably offends God. A telltale sign is the attribution of the works of God to Satan. It is interesting that the indictment does not include speaking against Christ. This is explained as Christ in the flesh. When a man speaks to another person, he cannot reach within and influence the other man's ability to see the truths spoken. Jesus had all power, but He chose to leave the realization of truth to His hearers, so that they be accountable.

It is the role of the Holy Spirit to bear witness to the human spirit that the truths of God are being spoken, that something very right is being heard. If a person resists this witness, the penalty is considered the more damning because it is the most intimate kind of awareness one can have. To resist that continually is to be outside the house of faith.

Luke 12:11-13
11 "When they bring you before . . . the rulers and the authorities, do not worry about how or what you are to speak . . . 12 for the Holy Spirit will teach you in that very hour what you ought to say."

The exact circumstances don't occur for us very often if at all. Few of us are asked to speak to our civic or national leaders. Even here, when the occasion arises, we prepare our words ahead of time so as not to embarrass ourselves in public speaking.

This is not as much an admonition about public speaking in general as a case of defending ourselves in adversarial circumstances, where charges are in play against us. It is describing the lack of opportunity to prepare, not the neglect of all preparations per se. When we are hauled before magistrates we are in a state of confusion and stress that prevents contemplation. We can be put in a situation where we've simply had no time to think about the best answers to give.

Jesus is saying that in those circumstances be without fear or anxiety, the Holy Spirit will give us the words at the proper time.

This is not derogation against proper preparation for a sermon or Bible study. We need to think through our material and apply all the skills we have in our possession to helping the hearers grasp the message clearly and effectively – because we have the opportunity and the time.

Still, it is interesting that there are some preachers and teachers who have so close a relationship with the Holy Spirit that they can speak extemporaneously without notes and deliver powerful sermons that demonstrate they have been alone with God.

But it is not something that can be merely emulated without the prerequisite – intimacy with the Holy Spirit.

13 "Teacher, tell my brother to divide the family inheritance with me."

We come now upon a situation in which a person's approach to Jesus is purely on the basis of authority and respect. He has not taken time to contemplate Jesus' message or His approach to the things of man and the things of God. To this man, Jesus is merely someone to whom his brother will have to listen. Jesus is a means to an end – the effecting of an outcome he desires concerning their inheritance.

It is an odd and rather out of place question. It is the kind of thing we find in modern times when a person totally unacquainted with Christianity asks an off-the-wall question that simply reveals how completely the person has heretofore lived without care for the things of God.

Jesus' response is one that doesn't really dignify the ignorance of the question. He doesn't take the question seriously and begin to discern who is in the right. Instead He questions the propriety of the question itself, as if to shine a light on the obtuse nature of the man's whole approach.

He asks, *"Who made me the judge of these affairs?"* It is to highlight that judging such things is not what He is about – that His purpose and message are on a completely different plane. It also shows that the man's approach is completely materialistic and self-centered, focusing on what he is to get in his inheritance.

Within seconds, Jesus then speaks about greed. In a matter of moments He has put his finger on the root of the difficulty. For the man, it is not whether the brother is being fair, it is all about what the man can get, hence greed.

Luke 12:16-23
16 "The land of a rich man was very productive.

Now comes a parable to illustrate the liabilities of entertaining greed. The rich man is concerned with how he will further house his wealth, how he will be able to sustain his well being and the blessings of his riches. He does so without worry about the precariousness of life, as though a long life is unquestionably secure. The only cares are how to enjoy life for the longest period possible.

We find God calling him a fool and threatening the demand of his life that very night. (Contemplate how unprepared we would be for sudden and immediate death.) This is not a matter of spite or some capricious whim. God has a timetable for every life and a deadline at which time that life will be called for its return to God. God is sovereign over this and the interjection of God is to tell the man that Someone else rules the circumstances he thinks are so secure.

The lesson is: what then becomes of this wealth? What has his greed rendered in the end? It has not prepared him for what is now ahead. He is suddenly and prematurely ***done***.

"So is the man who stores up treasure for himself, and is not rich toward God."

Riches are all relative to one's environment. Earthly riches are dependent on one's continuity on earth. Heavenly riches are dependent on Heaven's continuity and one's longevity in it. The earthly frame of reference is temporary with loss as the only ultimate outcome. The Heavenly frame of reference is eternal where riches are permanently eternal.

Jesus' point is that to miss this distinction, to miss out on ensuring one is a citizen of the Heavenly kingdom is all the more grievous for the greedy because they will lose their earthly wealth by the sheer nature of things and miss out on an eternal wealth that lasts forever.

Now to be clear, Heaven is not to be sought materialistically or as a better source of material wealth than earthly riches. It is to appreciate the spiritual riches rather than the materialistic ones, to see that they are far more satisfying. That they are also eternally durable is icing on the cake.

22 And He said to His disciples, "For this reason I say to you, do not worry about your life, as to what you will eat; nor for your body, as to what you will put on. 23 "For life is more than food, and the body more than clothing.

He then turns to His disciples to bring home the message in this for them. It is a warning that the spiritual is the better possession.

The opposite is what the world teaches in every commercial and in every TV show and film. Even Christians are succored in to this message of prosperity in doctrines like being a "King's kid." "He is the King and He wants us to live like princes and princesses." It is man's twisting of theology to somehow have greed and Christ together. The disciples are to prefer the other values that living comprises. It signals that life for an apostle would be spartan and lean compared to the world.

Think about Jesus Himself. When He left the earth at the Resurrection, what possessions did He leave behind that needed to be arranged for? Literally nothing. He had no furniture, no closets of clothes, no carts, horses, oxen. No home to sell, no debts to resolve. He was able to leave for Heaven with no unfinished business left behind. A life that was completely fulfilled without the acquisition of things.

Luke 12:24-40
24 "Consider the ravens, for they neither sow nor reap; they have no storeroom nor barn, and yet God feeds them; how much more valuable you are than the birds! 25 "And which of you by worrying can add a single hour to his life's span? 26 "If then you cannot do even a very little thing, why do you worry about other matters? 27 "Consider the lilies, how they grow: they neither toil nor spin; but I tell you, not even Solomon in all his glory clothed himself like one of these. 28 "But if God so clothes the grass in the field, which is alive today and tomorrow is thrown into the furnace, how much more will He clothe you? You men of little faith! 29 "And do not seek what you will eat and what you will drink, and do not keep worrying. 30 "For all these things the nations of the world eagerly seek; but your Father knows that you need these things. 31 "But seek His kingdom, and these things will be added to you. 32 "Do not be afraid, little flock, for your Father has chosen gladly to give you the kingdom.

33 "Sell your possessions and give to charity; make yourselves money belts which do not wear out, an unfailing treasure in heaven, where no thief comes near nor moth destroys. 34 "For where your treasure is, there your heart will be also. 35 "Be dressed in readiness, and keep your lamps lit. 36 "Be like men who are waiting for their master when he returns from the wedding feast, so that they may immediately open the door to him when he comes and knocks. 37 "Blessed are those slaves whom the master will find on the alert when he comes; truly I say to you, that he will gird himself to serve, and have them recline at the table, and will come up and wait on them. 38 "Whether he comes in the second watch, or even in the third, and finds them so, blessed are those slaves. 39 "But be sure of this, that if the head of the house had known at what hour the thief was coming, he would not have allowed his house to be broken into. 40 "You too, be ready; or the Son of Man is coming at an hour that you do not expect." (Luke 12:24-40)

Commentary

Luke 12:24-28
24 "Consider the ravens, .. how much more valuable you are than the birds! .. 25 And which of you by worrying can add a single hour to his life's span? .. 27 Consider the lilies, how they grow: .. not even Solomon in all his glory clothed himself like one of these. .. 28 how much more will He clothe you? You men of little faith!

Jesus repeats some of His Sermon on the Mount in this new setting (see also Matthew 6:28, above.) His comment about adding a single hour to one's life points to the idea that there is a clock ticking out a predefined duration for each individual's life, something God has determined ahead of time, which worry or effort on our part cannot alter.

We see an excerption for bargaining with God in the person of Hezekiah, who asked for additional years and was given them (I Kings 20:1.) But we don't argue from the exceptions, but the general rule.

There are some who disagree that because of this condition, men have no basis for any worry at all. When a project at work has millions of dollars at stake and there is suspicion that derelicts are at the helm, some believe there are justifications for that kind of worry. When bellicose countries invite themselves unwelcomed into the nuclear family, the free world worries justifiably.

The reason Jesus brings life span into the picture is that if our day of death is fixed, nothing fatal can happen to us before then, and no preparations can avoid it when it comes. We can be on a cruise and the ship is going down, but if it isn't our time, nothing about the awful plight of circumstances around us is gojng to take us before then. If it is our time, we must be resigned to it in God's overall plan for us. In either case, there is no basis for worry because we will either live or be brought to rest in Jesus.

Where the rub comes in is in the intermediate conditions – living but paralyzed, living for months with difficult pain or privation. We naturally fear these conditions because they are not only arduous but we see them as robbing us of precious time to enjoy the life we have left.

That, of course, is a set of circumstances of our own doing. Our expectations our life can be our own or they can be God's. When we look at John the Baptist, Paul, Jesus, we see men who gave up those expectations and took on whatever was asked of them, including suffering. They did not view it as cheating them out of the enjoyments they would have had otherwise.

This is very hard for us because we fear that we are miles away from the same mettle that formed these servants of God, and life teaches us that, more than in those days, the pleasures and comforts of life are everywhere to be had and expected.

In terms of this immediate lesson, it was to address the disciples and their immediate concerns about food, clothing, and shelter. In these things, a ready example was available for the viewing in creatures of lesser value.

"You men of little faith."

This seems unduly harsh, but it is meant to apply more to the whole condition of worry, especially about the immediate things mentioned. It is not going to be the case that food and raiment are going to fall into their laps on general principles. It is through faith in the Father's ability to provide that these things will be given them. They worry about these things because they are looking at the horizontal picture and they don't see that approach free of pitfalls and dilemmas that are inherently plagued by the fickle nature of man. It is specifically because they are looking along the horizontal that worry naturally arises.

In the vertical plane, there is all manner of hope and expectation from a God who owns all things and if they are about His business, His love and compassion will secure the needs of each day – *"your Father knows that you need these things."*

All of their concerns in this regard and in the major issues of martyrdom and service are handled by faith.

Luke 12:31-34
31 "But seek His kingdom, and these things will be added to you. 32 "Do not be afraid, little flock, for your Father has chosen gladly to give you the kingdom.

Some view this as a magic formula for getting the things in life they have always envied. But of course it is conditional on something that would axiomatically forestall their expectations about self-aggrandizement –

the preference for the things of the Kingdom. It simply is not possible to truly seek the things of God's kingdom and continue in wishing for wealth and possessions.

Now to be sure, there are folks who do this very thing all the time – they are faithful church members and desire to serve Christ, and they also wish they were living in the plush homes up the hill and driving the expensive cars. But it is always a case double-mindedness and that means to some extent they are not seeking the best things of the kingdom.

It really is an inverse reciprocal relationship. The degree to which we seek the Kingdom and its righteousness determines the degree to which we seek earthly pleasures. The more the Kingdom, the less the world; the less the Kingdom, the more the world.

Interestingly, in the midst of this teaching, they might still harbor doubt that the principle will really work, if in fact they are not seen as in the right place with the right motives. We are always doing a critique of ourselves – are we working with a truly right attitude of heart, are we being selfish to some extent and will that interfere with God's provision?

Jesus then gives them great encouragement. He assures them that His Father is actually "glad" in having chosen them. No recalcitrance, no regrets or second thoughts, but gladness.

33 "Sell your possessions and give to charity; make yourselves money belts which do not wear out, an unfailing treasure in heaven, where no thief comes near nor moth destroys.

This is by no means an admonition to be prepared for the earthly bounty God will bring their way. It is not recommending strong money belts in anticipation of all the wealth God is planning to add to them for their service.

He is talking about the riches of Heaven. The money belt that doesn't wear out is a metaphor for that which will hold the *"unfailing treasure in heaven."* They must by needs be concerned about the earthly matter of keeping whatever monies they have protected and conserved as they walk and minister. But this is merely practical and actually involves a certain amount of nuisance. Their focus is to be on the heavenly riches related directly to spiritual service and spiritual reward. These are of such a nature that moth and dust are not merely ineffective, they have no meaningful application at all.

34 "For where your treasure is, there your heart will be also.

The heart (not the organ but the seat of emotion and will) is a mystery within us. We recognize its operation and its effects, and psychologists spend lifetimes trying to analyze it professionally and clinically. But we are left to its slavery nonetheless, we follow its effects whether they be in its joy and exhilaration, or in its hatred or anticipation for a touch of evil. Men are made with this capacity – to have hearts that move them to acts and to states of mind.

Take a moment to think about the young girl or boy forced to visit their aunt and uncle, who soon become those dull, familiar lumps of humanity from the sheer boredom of every minute. Then suddenly the whole scene changes when something about which they are majorly passionate appears. The girl learns there's a stable and horse riding just over the hill, or the boy learns the basement as just been redone as a game room, chock full of all his favorite electronic challenges. It is amazing how our attitudes change when our heart is fed with its delights and desires. What we "treasure" is actually what our hearts desire to have.

When Jesus says, *"there will your heart be also"* He is not saying there is this thing called a treasure and your heart goes out after it. He is saying that the thing treasured and the passions of the heart are one and the same. Find your treasure and you will have found your heart.

But this is spoken in a tone that anticipates the possibility of change. What is the point of disclosing this condition if it is immutable, an uncompromising fact of life?

He is, in fact, introducing the idea that the heart and its treasures not only can be changed but ought to be. We learn elsewhere that our hearts are not self-sustaining entities unto themselves but actually serve masters; and this can change. We learn that these masters are two: the self or God. And marvelously we have the power to choose who will rule.

Now at this juncture, it seems very hard to imagine a person deliberately changing what their hearts passionately treasure and have the heart comply willingly. In the human plane, our expectations would be absolutely correct. In and of ourselves, we are already poisoned with treasures long since firmly set in place.

So it is a work of God that actually changes what the heart treasures. It is God's doing in the Spirit that moves a person away from the world's treasures and makes us into someone who, through an act of "conversion," can a moment later be transformed into someone who values heavenly things more.

Luke 12:35-37
35 "Be dressed in readiness, and keep your lamps lit. 36 "Be like men who are waiting for their master when he returns . . . 37 "Blessed are those slaves whom the master will find on the alert . . he will gird himself to serve, and have them recline at the table, and will come up and wait on them.

This is a more obscure teaching only in that it is not taught frequently from our pulpits and is often skipped over in sermons.

It is all about attitude of service. We can serve begrudgingly or with alertness and attentiveness to do the best in what we do.

Charles Colson wrote a book a few years back, *Why America Doesn't Work*.[27] In it he discusses what has gone wrong in the American work ethic and why we are headed for becoming a third world nation as we farm away the work that used to make our name renown in the world.

Today there are any number of factors that erode a person's attitude in the work place, some coming from their employers. But for several decades now, each generation of young people working has been less motivated to do good work, more interested in how much time off is available or how little one can do and still get paid.

In just about any major department store you will have difficulty finding employees in a section who actually know important details of the products they sell. And if you indicate that you expected them to know, they tell you they're not getting paid enough to care about knowing.

In contrast, their counterparts in prior decades got relatively the same wage, but took pride in knowing their product lines, in helping the customer pick out the truly suitable item, and could tell you about new products the store would be selling. They knew when replenishments were due for an item and whether their pricing was comparable to other stores. Why? Because they simply took an interest. They considered knowing this information worthwhile.

Today, you get a blank look or dismay at the prospect of having to go ask that rare person in the store who might know. You're question is interrupting the only thing they seem trained to do, keeping up a steady rhythm at the register.

The picture of the master who rewards the alert and faithful slave was not drawn from routine human affairs. It was somewhat of a hyperbole by drawing in the attitude of God to those who serve Him as described. He will desire to share His table with us and even take the role of serving us. In the earthly realm, there were master and slave relationships very close to this but also rather rare.

---

[27] W Pub Group, (1992)

It is sometimes easy to infer that good attitudes are only expected in heavenly service because there are none of the stresses and disappointments of secular service in them. But Jesus is also admonishing us to have this attitude in our earthly duties of service, the attitudes we demonstrate to our employers and co-workers. In this we are to stand out, and standing out against the backdrop of normal expectations is an important theme in Christian life.

But there is a second theme in this teaching – that of watchfulness and preparedness. The good slave also anticipates his master's arrival and is ready.

Luke 12:38-40]
38 "Whether he comes in the second watch, or even in the third, . . 39 "But . . if the head of the house had known at what hour the thief was coming, he would not have allowed his house to be broken into.

The good servant is alert and does not say the hour has now passed for continued diligence. How then was he at the door when his master did return? He remained continually ready at all times. He did not seek to know how he could split up the time between his own affairs and those of his master. This is now completely foreign to our work ethic today.

Jesus then shifts slightly to view things as the head of the house. This man's concern would be to protect his home, his possessions and his family. Certainly anyone with a responsible nature would make added preparations if it were known when a thief were coming.

But in the earlier case of the slave, he did not know which hour. In the case of Jesus coming again, we do not know which hour. Yet there is a call nonetheless to be ready, which means being ready at all times.

"You too, be ready; for the Son of Man is coming at an hour that you do not expect."

How does the Christian make themselves ready for that coming? One preparation is to break our hindering connections to the world. How many of us would hesitate in a call to service because the entanglements in normal life have us bound to where we are and what we must keep doing?

Another preparation is in keeping our accounts short with the Lord. Are we clean and free of the "ought" between us and Him.

Third, are we ready with a witness when the time comes? Are we attentive to the signs of the times? When God reaches down once again to shake the earth and call men to repentance before His final judgment, will we be ready to speak to the lost, the confused and the desperate?

We may not feel ready in all those areas, but Jesus is asking all believers in this time of relative peace to contemplate what readiness means in anticipation of His coming again.

Luke 12:41-59
41 Peter said, "Lord, are You addressing this parable to us, or to everyone else as well?" 42 And the Lord said, "Who then is the faithful and sensible steward, whom his master will put in charge of his servants, to give them their rations at the proper time? 43 "Blessed is that slave whom his master finds so doing when he comes. 44 "Truly I say to you that he will put him in charge of all his possessions.

45 "But if that slave says in his heart, `My master will be a long time in coming,' and begins to beat the slaves, both men and women, and to eat and drink and get drunk; 46 the master of that slave will come on a day when he does not expect him and at an hour he does not know, and will cut him in pieces, and assign him a place with the unbelievers. 47 "And that slave who knew his master's will and did not get ready or act in accord with his will, will receive many lashes, 48 but the one who did not know it, and committed deeds worthy of a flogging, will receive but few. From everyone who has been given much, much will be required; and to whom they entrusted much, of him they will ask all the more.

49 "I have come to cast fire upon the earth; and how I wish it were already kindled! 50 "But I have a baptism to undergo, and how distressed I am until it is accomplished! 51 "Do you suppose that I came to grant peace on earth? I tell you, no, but rather division; 52 for from now on five members in one household will be divided, three against two and two against three. 53 "They will be divided, father against son and son against father, mother against daughter and daughter against mother, mother-in-law against daughter-in-law and daughter-in-law against mother-in-law."

54 And He was also saying to the crowds, "When you see a cloud rising in the west, immediately you say, `A shower is coming,' and so it turns out. 55 "And when you see a south wind blowing, you say, `It will be a hot day,' and it turns out that way. 56 "You hypocrites! You know how to analyze the appearance of the earth and the sky, but why do you not analyze this present time? 57 "And why do you not even on your own initiative judge what is right? 58 "For while you are going with your opponent to appear before the magistrate, on your way there make an effort to settle with him, so that he may not drag you before the judge, and the judge turn you over to the officer, and the officer throw you into prison. 59 "I say to you, you will not get out of there until you have paid the very last cent." (Luke 12:41-59)

Commentary

Luke 12:41-45
41 "Lord, are You addressing this parable to us, or to everyone else as well?"

The reason for this question is due to the severity of the warning Christ has given. He has laid out some sobering exhortations about being found doing the master's will when he returns and the inability to discern that time.

The natural question is whether this exhortation is being given just to the disciples – the Twelve – or to all who will come to believe in Him? It is a parable because the characters involved are not meant to point to any particular real persons, and the situation is not some particular situation that has taken place. The characters are created in the mind of the teller and are placed in the situation described for the purpose of teaching a lesson.

(The parable of the man with the vineyard and the tower did not describe some specific man who had the vineyard, but was drawn from the general yet very real circumstances of men with vineyards and towers.)

Jesus does not answer them directly here, but He does answer this question when the teaching is repeated in Mark 13:37. There He definitely says, *"What I say I say to all."* As we read the rest of what Jesus says, we understand that the exhortation is for all people to whom the truth has been revealed and that there is a difference in accountability between those who have heard and those who have not. That would apply to everyone not just the apostles.

42 "Who then is the faithful and sensible steward, whom his master will put in charge of his servants . . . 45 But if the slave . . . begins to beat the slaves, both men and women, and to eat and drink and get drunk; "

Here we have the same theme repeated as before – the man found doing his master's will shall be rewarded with greater responsibilities and blessings.

But Jesus explains more on the corollary condition. It is not just a case of being indolent or unwatchful, but a case of taking advantage of the master's delay to act irresponsibly. Here the slave takes unwarranted authority unto himself and wreaks private vengeance or anger on those he has come to despise, or for the purpose of vaunting himself over them.

He also is careless in indulging his vices to a degree he would not get away with were the master at home. The irony is that he forgets that the master may return when unexpected. Hence, the evil of this state of mind.

This is actually quite prevalent today in the modern work force. There are folks out there who will take strict advantage of their boss's absence to do any number of things that wouldn't fly were he around. There is a mentality that says, "I'm not busting my butt when no one's around." It's a mentality that believes that doing as little as possible while still getting paid is a good thing.

We've all seen situations whether fictional or real in which the boss shows up and the beer bottles and lounge chairs go flying as men quickly cover up their lax behavior and try to assume again their serious, professional faces.

It may not be eating and getting drunk like the slave in the parable, but it's spending half the day talking to your friends on the phone, extended lunches, or internet surfing. After all, who's around to care?

In terms of spiritual things, Christians can become lazy and indolent in their spiritual lives also. We can begin to leave off praying, become lax in daily devotionals and reading, adopt the practicality of the world because it seems easier than the harder things of the Spirit. And the world helps us along more than it did in ancient times. There are a host of things and technologies ready to make life easier and allow us to get along just fine without God being called upon every hour.

So we are easily lulled into a false sense of security, helped all the more by our impression that our Master delays His next coming. We look outside our homes and we see a world getting along rather well, certainly no visible signs of being on the verge of the Second Coming, at least this week, this month.

Most in society know about the presence of spiritual light available in Christianity. Most know right from wrong and that those assessments are very closely aligned with the truths of the Bible. But many pretend that there will be loopholes or that somehow it will end up different. So they act and live carelessly. They say to themselves, "This or that is a small thing with God." Hence, they justify their own version of righteousness and set for themselves standards of their own making.

Luke 12:46-48
46 the master of that slave will come on a day when he does not expect him and at an hour he does not know, and will cut him in pieces, and assign him a place with the unbelievers.

Here the slave is a picture of both the practical conditions described (the master will come and punish him) and of end times when Christ comes again. Those found being careless about their spiritual lives will be judged and categorized quite opposite to their self-delusions about their end.

"cut him in pieces" is being applied more to the slave in the parable than to the parables extended audience. Masters did deal harshly and even cruelly with their slaves.

But we don't often associate Christ's Second Coming with Him literally cutting people in pieces. The sword that proceeds out of His mouth (Rev 1:16) is called the Word of God, which ameliorates the notion of a slaughter in favor of a final judgment where people are sent to their final destiny.

However, there is slaughter by the sword in the end times battles against those amassed to fight against righteousness. There is true bloodshed and carnage. So we can say that to some extent the indictment of cutting to pieces and of a destiny among unbelievers is appropriate for haters of God in the extension of this parable.

47 " . . will receive many lashes, . . . 48 will receive but few. From everyone who has been given much, much will be required; and to whom they entrusted much, of him they will ask all the more.

Knowledge is the key to accountability. Jesus is in fact allowing for the case of those who did not know the truth. The slave who acted similarly but did not know the right behavior expected of him will receive fewer lashes.

Note that he is not set apart with no punishment at all on account of his ignorance. He is lashed for the part of common sense he should have obeyed. This is often a taunt from the atheist – "Will God still judge those wholly ignorant of Jerusalem and a place called Calvary?" It is a taunt that expects *no* penalty at all for ignorance about specifics.

This ignores that God has placed knowledge both morally and spiritually in nature – the nature around us and the nature within us. It tells of things of God and we can perceive them. Regarding them, all men are without excuse (Romans, Ch 1). So the ignorant slave is lashed for those things to which he should have been obedient by common sense, through common moral conscience.

Yet there is mercy in Jesus' words. He recognizes the difference in accountability. He also prays this specifically in the case of those putting Him to death, *"Father forgive them for they know not what they do."*

Luke 12:49-51
49 "I have come to cast fire upon the earth; and how I wish it were already kindled!

A truly enigmatic statement. In its raw reading, we would conclude that Jesus is actually eager to bring final judgment on the world. Yet we know He doesn't intend this meaning from His manner of speech in the synagogue in Nazareth, where He deliberately closed the scroll before the very sentence of the Lord's fiery judgment (Luke 4:20, Isaiah 61:2).

Jesus also promises that there is coming a baptism with the Holy Spirit and with fire. But that is less in mind here because he describes the divisions that are waiting in the wings, divisions that are contrary to the peace expected.

50 "But I have a baptism to undergo, and how distressed I am until it is accomplished! 51 "Do you suppose that I came to grant peace on earth? I tell you, no, but rather division;

The whole counsel of God is always important in any strain of teaching we might envision. There are those who choose to stress the peaceloving nature of Jesus and often forget this statement – *"I came not to grant peace but division."*

Peace in the heart, yes - that ends the enmity between us and God. But not peace with evil men who will continue to resist righteousness. Not even peace among friends and family. It is a peace that ends the war with God, but a peace that stands against unrighteousness and thereby divides.

"But I have a baptism to undergo, and how distressed I am until it is accomplished!

A baptism is also an idiomatic expression for an anointing – a call to accomplish a purpose. We know that Jesus did not undergo another ceremonial baptism like that of John. Here He means the baptism of His passion - a term we use to group all the events of His suffering and death. It is not just a baptism to suffering, but a baptism to suffering that is bound up in what He has come to accomplish. He is not merely to die as a matyr or a sacrifice (a lamb), but as one who takes away the sins of the world. That is not just a transaction made peaceably between God and Son. It is a violent fulfillment of a covenant, one that requires a bloody death.

The distress is a way of describing all the anticipation leading up to the moment of fulfillment. It is both a recognition that it will not be easy, but also an anticipation that with the pangs of suffering, the end result is at hand. It is likened to the pain of childbirth. A woman dreads that pain, but has another sense of relief that the end of all the discomfort of nine months is now here and the joy of a child is near at hand.

Luke 12:53-56
53 "They will be divided, father against son and son against father, mother against daughter and daughter against mother, mother-in-law against daughter-in-law and daughter-in-law against mother-in-law."

Jesus predicts that those divided against the Kingdom will be the members of one's own household. In Judaism, this is more obvious because Jesus would be seen as a blasphemer worthy of death in calling Himself God, and association with Him would be tantamount to abandoning the faith of their fathers.

Fathers proclaiming they no longer have sons would be common.

In non-Jewish settings in modern times, it is not rare that children becoming Christians create divisions for parents and siblings. This would be the case in unchristian households. It brings an unwelcome light of moral judgment on everyone's lifestyle and values. People don't like being convicted by force and they will often react not with awakening and gratitude but with bitterness and polarization.

54 "When you see a cloud rising in the west, . . . 55 And when you see a south wind blowing . . 56 You know how to analyze the appearance of the earth and the sky, but why do you not analyze this present time?

This is what is part of the recognition that ours is a reasonable faith. We do not believe in a mystery religion, wrapped up in secret knowledge available only to initiates or an elite group of savants. It is filled with matters of common sense, the common sense God put into the creation of man by design. We are meant to look around, take stock and figure things out.

Jesus is simply saying that the signs of what is happening in the Kingdom are as readily available to them as the signs in the weather.

What then was expected of them? That they see the travail of man trying to be righteous. That they see the utter failure of man to do this on his own. That they appreciate the cry of the soul for an everlasting remedy. That they recognize the truth of that remedy walking among them.

And more pertinent to the parable just spoken, that they recognize that much is at stake in not being ready.

Luke 12:57-59
57 "And why do you not even on your own initiative judge what is right?

Are we not told by the same Master to "judge not?" If we study the complete teaching, we will remember that He said not to judge *lest* we be judged, and that with the judgment we make we will ourselves be judged.

Therefore to judge what is right is to have no fear of the same judgment coming back upon us.

But it is important here to recognize that this judgment is characterized as of their own initiative. It is within them, and they can exercise it by their will. This is more on the common sense nature of the righteousness of God. To the man who is disposed to that righteousness, God's way of doing things, of looking at things, is amazingly right. It has merit that is apparent.

To the man who is oppositely disposed, he has poisoned himself from what would ordinarily be common sense. Liberal Christianity is a poison in intellectualism that has disabled the use of that common sense. The truths of God no longer make sense as they should. Hence, they can no longer judge "on their own initiative" what is right.

59 " you will not get out of there until you have paid the very last cent."

This is often confusing because it is addressed to His disciples and all believers. Is there then an expectation of being sued and found legitimately guilty such that hard payment is exacted?

Jesus is teaching that there can come an attitude of self-righteousness even among His believers that ignores truth. We may indeed defraud our fellow man and justify it or rationalize it away.

Jesus says that instead of being obstinate and arrogant or presumptuous about our being right, make an effort to hear our accusers and be ready to receive truths opposite to our arrogance that clarify how we really act.

Otherwise, to remain obstinate and self-righteous, we may find ourselves in prison for just reasons, not because of persecution.

Witness Jim Bakker of the recent past. He held out until the very last in doing no wrong, until he was tearfully led away in handcuffs while the world filmed it for TV news.

CHAPTER 7
Teaching Through Parables

Luke 13:1-17
1 Now on the same occasion there were some present who reported to Him about the Galileans whose blood Pilate had mixed with their sacrifices. 2 And Jesus said to them, "Do you suppose that these Galileans were greater sinners than all other Galileans because they suffered this fate? 3 "I tell you, no, but unless you repent, you will all likewise perish.

4 "Or do you suppose that those eighteen on whom the tower in Siloam fell and killed them were worse culprits than all the men who live in Jerusalem? 5 "I tell you, no, but unless you repent, you will all likewise perish."

6 And He began telling this parable: "A man had a fig tree which had been planted in his vineyard; and he came looking for fruit on it and did not find any. 7 "And he said to the vineyard-keeper, `Behold, for three years I have come looking for fruit on this fig tree without finding any. Cut it down! Why does it even use up the ground?' 8 "And he answered and said to him, `Let it alone, sir, for this year too, until I dig around it and put in fertilizer; 9 and if it bears fruit next year, fine; but if not, cut it down.' "

10 And He was teaching in one of the synagogues on the Sabbath. 11 And there was a woman who for eighteen years had had a sickness caused by a spirit; and she was bent double, and could not straighten up at all. 12 When Jesus saw her, He called her over and said to her, "Woman, you are freed from your sickness." 13 And He laid His hands on her; and immediately she was made erect again and began glorifying God.

14 But the synagogue official, indignant because Jesus had healed on the Sabbath, began saying to the crowd in response, "There are six days in which work should be done; so come during them and get healed, and not on the Sabbath day." 15 But the Lord answered him and said, "You hypocrites, does not each of you on the Sabbath untie his ox or his donkey from the stall and lead him away to water him? 16 "And this woman, a daughter of Abraham as she is, whom Satan has bound for eighteen long years, should she not have been released from this bond on the Sabbath day?" 17 As He said this, all His opponents were being humiliated; and the entire crowd was rejoicing over all the glorious things being done by Him. (Luke 13:1-17)

Commentary

Luke 13:1
"Do you suppose that these Galileans were greater sinners than all other Galileans because they suffered this fate? . . .

While Jesus was teaching the material discussed in the last chapter, Pilate had arranged an incident that would deliver a message to insurgents and troublemakers. Some believe that a certain Judas Gaulonita (called *Judas the Galilean* in Acts) had been recently troubling Pilate with spurts of insurgency against Roman rule, and that the incident being reported to Jesus was related. Judas as leader was beyond Pilate's reach, and it is inferred that certain Galileans having come to Jerusalem for worship were part of this faction.

Pilate had on another occasion conceived a plan that disguised certain of his soldiers in local garb with hidden clubs, and at the right moment gave a signal from his tribunal for attack. This was in response to the uproar the Jews caused over robbing Temple funds to pay for his aqueduct. *(see further in Josephus.)*[28]

Though not said, the access of soldiers into the temple court would have needed similar disguises. In this case, swords were used instead of clubs. These men were murdered, perhaps at the very moment their offerings were being slain in the outer court – *"whose blood Pilate mixed with their sacrifices."*

---

[28] Antiquities, xviii,.3.2, Baker Book House, (1974)

It was anticipated that by Jesus being a Galilean, he would have some reaction or comment. Perhaps the one reporting was a zealot and expected that this incident might move Jesus to invoke His powers in ways they wholly lacked.

Jesus, instead, uses this incident (and another one he mentions in a moment) to teach a lesson about sin and temporal calamities. In other words, He will take no action that would feed the zealots' cause, because that was not His purpose in this advent.

Jesus asks if the men murdered *deserved* their fate on account of more notable sins? Being in a band of rebels and malcontents, it is reasonable that such men were less devout, less inclined to peace, and as such, incurred God's disfavor more than others.

If rulers were God's instrument of preserving society by judging evil doers, were these men then more guilty of sins, being malefactors in their ruler's eyes?

Before completing the teaching, He adds another example.

Luke 13:4
"Or do you suppose that those eighteen on whom the tower in Siloam fell and killed them were worse culprits than all the men who live in Jerusalem?

The tower is said to be *in* Siloam as opposed to the tower *of* Siloam, but the distinction is moot. Siloam is a pre-Israelite settlement that became part of the City of David and the location for the pool of Siloam and its tower.

The City of David is a little spit of land that juts out like the southward extension of Florida, and is located in the lower southeast extremity of Jerusalem. It juts out on a ridge just below the southeast corner of the Temple compound, with the valley of Kidron and the Mount of Olives to the east, the Tyropoeon Valley on the west. There was an ancient wall encompassing this area, with the pool of Siloam at its SE extremity (inside), and a tower near the same location at the SE corner.

The tower joined the converging walls and obviously had an interior exposure as well as an exterior one that met with a sheer decent down the adjoining valley. It is this tower that collapsed killing some eighteen persons. We are not told when this occurred by any historians of the times. But it was recent enough to be referred to in brief.

In the 1920's remains of the base of the tower were found but not identified as such, later to be identified as the tower.

Here is a reference to background information, although the author makes some conclusions about the Temple not widely accepted by most scholars. [29]

Again, Jesus asks if this calamity was in response to greater sins in these men than in others.

"I tell you, no, but unless you repent, you will all likewise perish."

Jesus definitely says, "No." This was to correct the well-established notion that calamity was a sign of sin, while blessing was a sign of favor. Job's counselors take this tack in explaining his misfortunes. Jesus also corrects this idea in the case of the man born blind. *"Who sinned, this man or his parents?"* (John 9:3ff)

---

[29] Tenney, Zondervan Pictorial Encyclopedia, Vol 5, p. 427, Zondervan, (1974)

But Jesus denounces this idea because sin is sin, and without faith, all men are guilty. Also, calamaties are not linked to punishments for sin (the case of the man born blind). There are no gradations of sins in terms of eternal life. The least sinner will perish without faith as surely as the most grievous.

These are very harsh words to hear in an audience for whom performance in relation to the Law was critical in their eyes. It was also a wake-up call for those who had rationalized their acts and behavior to the extent that repentance was no longer a process to keep current. There were justifications and rationalizations in rampant fashion among the people in general, in part because of the promises given to Abraham, and they were Abraham's seed.

Jesus therefore uses these occasions to explain that if they were counting themselves blessed to have not been so judged of God, they are in for a rude awakening at the Last Judgment. To this end, Jesus further talks about the fruits of repentance, things God is expecting to see in faithful men, and what happens to those who neglect them. (The same message incidentally that John had for the Pharisees.)

Luke 13:6
"A man had a fig tree which had been planted in his vineyard; and he came looking for fruit on it and did not find any.

Ancient and modern people can relate to this example. Trees that don't produce are just wasting space in our gardens and yards. We conclude that something is amiss and quite beyond our ability to remedy – it's just a bad tree - so out it comes.

Note here that there is a note of patience and longsuffering. The owner gives three years of grace for the tree to produce, just in case it is a matter of conditions having nothing to do with the tree itself.

But when frustration has reached its limit the keeper encourages the owner to wait one more year. The purpose in telling this aspect is to highlight the longsuffering of God, that He is open to letting love run its full course. It is even a matter of giving extra grace in improving the conditions for recovery (the moat and fertilizer.)

In the case of Abraham and the three angels, he bargains them down to just ten righteous souls in the city for which they agree not to destroy it. That's love at work, and far beyond what human patience would entertain.

But it is a lesson for us to not postpone things. God may be longsuffering but the frailty and precariousness of life may not live to an equal length. While we're postponing and counting on God's patience and love, we may be cut short. Today is the day of our salvation, not when we get around to it in the freedom of God's longsuffering.

Luke 13:10
there was a woman who for eighteen years had had a sickness caused by a spirit;

We here have insight into the power of demons to inflict physical calamities on their hosts. Somehow in her life she became open to this influence and the result was the debilitating condition she was now in. We must remind ourselves that the devil is called the *destroyer*, and our end state is never going to be better than our first.

Note here also that Jesus does not first insist on some profession of faith, as is considered necessary in some Christian ministries. He does not invoke a promise that she will serve God if He delivers her. He simply lays hands on her, the demon is dispersed, and she is made well.

This is not to say that exorcized people are to be left in carnal freedom from their maladies. Jesus' teaching on the wandering demon who returns to his former place is a warning against that. (Matthew 12:44) Her subsequent glorifying of God cuts away any notion that she was merely delivered but not converted.

But the synagogue official [said] . . "There are six days in which work should be done; so come during them and get healed, and not on the Sabbath day."

Here is Judaistic legalism in action. The miracle is ameliorated in this man's eyes because he is steeped in the legalism of his faith. It is a blindness because it has rendered him unable to recognize a true work of God, of which even common sense would have informed him.

His was in fear that God had been disobeyed and to ignore it made him complicit. Hence, he was compelled to speak out. It was a sign of how desperately locked into legalism he was. The form of religion had become more important than the religion itself. A lesson for some Christian churches as well.

Luke 13:15
"hypocrites . . each of you on the Sabbath unties his ox . . and leads him away to water him? . . should she not have been released from this bond on the Sabbath day?"

Should not all bonds be given the same grace? And in her case, was her binding the more needful than watering an ox? That is why Jesus called them hypocrites, because they considered the work to assist an ox or a donkey a nit but freeing a woman from demonic possession was beyond the pale.

They were also hypocrites because they knew in their consciences that Jesus' work was more needful and glorified the use of the Sabbath more, but because it was being done by Jesus, their need to vilify him gave them an opportunity to invoke "the Law" as a means to discredit Him, even though they had rationalized exceptions for themselves.

What glory to God is there in watering your livestock compared to restoring a woman to God? Isn't the Sabbath more appropriately used if the resultant glory to God is greater?

. . all His opponents were being humiliated; and the entire crowd was rejoicing over all the glorious things being done by Him.

A clear polarization is seen here between the entire crowd and His opponents. The crowd was not dull in seeing the hypocrisy of their leaders. There was resentment not only at this but in their having to submit to their dictates.

And the explanation of Jesus made such good sense that the unsophisticated people could easily see the love of God in contrast to the wooden religion of the Pharisees. They are said to rejoice not so much over the humiliation of their leaders, but over the winning out of God's truth over them. They rejoiced over things that evidenced God's glory. And the difference was so striking, they could not keep silent.

Matthew 13:1-23
1 That day Jesus went out of the house and was sitting by the sea. 2 And large crowds gathered to Him, so He got into a boat and sat down, and the whole crowd was standing on the beach. 3 And He spoke many things to them in parables, saying, "Behold, the sower went out to sow; 4 and as he sowed, some seeds fell beside the road, and the birds came and ate them up. 5 "Others fell on the rocky places, where they did not have much soil; and immediately they sprang up, because they had no depth of soil. 6 "But when the sun had risen, they were scorched; and because they had no root, they withered away. 7 "Others fell among the thorns, and the thorns came up and choked them out. 8 "And others fell on the good soil and yielded a crop, some a hundredfold, some sixty, and some thirty. 9 "He who has ears, let him hear."

10 And the disciples came and said to Him, "Why do You speak to them in parables?" 11 Jesus answered them, "To you it has been granted to know the mysteries of the kingdom of heaven, but to them it has not been granted. 12 "For whoever has, to him more shall be given, and he will have an abundance; but whoever does not have, even what he has shall be taken away from him. 13 "Therefore I speak to them in parables; because while seeing they do not see, and while hearing they do not hear, nor do they understand.

14 "In their case the prophecy of Isaiah is being fulfilled, which says, `YOU WILL KEEP ON HEARING, BUT WILL NOT UNDERSTAND; YOU WILL KEEP ON SEEING, BUT WILL NOT PERCEIVE; 15 FOR THE HEART OF THIS PEOPLE HAS BECOME DULL, WITH THEIR EARS THEY SCARCELY HEAR, AND THEY HAVE CLOSED THEIR EYES, OTHERWISE THEY WOULD SEE WITH THEIR EYES, HEAR WITH THEIR EARS, AND UNDERSTAND WITH THEIR HEART AND RETURN, AND I WOULD HEAL THEM.' 16 "But blessed are your eyes, because they see; and your ears, because they hear. 17 "For truly I say to you that many prophets and righteous men desired to see what you see, and did not see it, and to hear what you hear, and did not hear it.

18 "Hear then the parable of the sower. 19 "When anyone hears the word of the kingdom and does not understand it, the evil one comes and snatches away what has been sown in his heart. This is the one on whom seed was sown beside the road. 20 "The one on whom seed was sown on the rocky places, this is the man who hears the word and immediately receives it with joy; 21 yet he has no firm root in himself, but is only temporary, and when affliction or persecution arises because of the word, immediately he falls away. 22 "And the one on whom seed was sown among the thorns, this is the man who hears the word, and the worry of the world and the deceitfulness of wealth choke the word, and it becomes unfruitful. 23 "And the one on whom seed was sown on the good soil, this is the man who hears the word and understands it; who indeed bears fruit and brings forth, some a hundredfold, some sixty, and some thirty." (Matthew 13:1-23)

Commentary

Matthew 13:1-9
That day Jesus went out . . And large crowds gathered to Him, so He got into a boat and sat down, and the whole crowd was standing on the beach.

Jesus is still in and around Capernaum in all the foregoing narrative so we're not puzzled by the proximity of the sea. He is about to tell one of his most famous parables, filled with application and meaning applicable to all ages to come.

Again, the purpose of getting into a boat is to enforce respect for His person and to make way for a sort of pulpit more visible to all than had he remained on the shore.

Two things of a different class will be learned in this teaching. The giving of and the explaining of the parables, and why Jesus uses parables in contrast to straightforward teaching.

The presentation has a deliberate order.

The Parable of the Sower and the Soils (*to all without explanation*)
The explanation of why Jesus uses parables (*to the disciples only*)
The explanation of the Parable of the Sower (*to the disciples only*)
The Parable of the Wheat and the Tares (*to all without explanation*)
The Parable of the Mustard Seed (*to all without explanation*)
The Parable of the Leaven (*to all without explanation*)
The explanation of the Wheat and the Tares (*to the disciples only*)
Parables to the Disciples:
(the Lamp, the Growing Seed, the Treasure, the Pearl, the Draught of Fishes)

The scene is paradoxical because of the unknown proximity of the disciples in relation to the people. There are definite changes where Jesus purposes to speak only to the disciples and not to the people, yet the people nearest them would certainly have overheard.

They could have been with Him in the boat or out in adjoining boats where He could then turn to them and address them more privately, but v.10 describes them as "coming" to Him to ask a question.

"Behold, the sower went out to sow;

A ready example for what Jesus wished to teach about the Word and its fruit was available in the sowing of seed. There is the sower who does the work of casting the seed and has the expectation of good results. There are the various conditions of the ground that can't be avoided in the action of casting out seed – the seed is broadly cast for ease and economy of effort. There are then the various yields. A perfect tool for describing the various types of men who receive the Word.

The various soils include that beside the road, that on rocky places, that among thorns, and the good soil.

We'll leave the interpretation until after Jesus answers the disciples question about why He teaches in parables.

Matthew 13:10-17
10 And the disciples came and said to Him, "Why do You speak to them in parables?"

The scene is best pictured as Jesus speaking from the boat to the crowd which included the disciples in the foreground. He gives the first parable, then perhaps gave the crowd a moment to think about it. In this small interim, the disciples may have then approached the boat, gathered around Him in the shallow water and asked this question, which Jesus then addresses just to them, out of the hearing of the crowd.

"To you it has been granted to know the mysteries of the kingdom of heaven, but to them it has not been granted.

This separation for the disciples, and the indictment from Isaiah spoken in a moment about people with hardness of heart is a reason why we must have some means of seeing the disciples being physically separated. When Jesus adds the explanation of the parable, if the people were ready at hand, this would negate the above statement and what follows immediately here.

Even still, His words seem very unlike the Jesus we prefer in our minds. That God would withhold teaching about His Kingdom seems out of sorts with the whole idea of casting seed broadly, and out of sorts with Jesus' openness and availability to all who sought Him.

But the idea here is not about withholding information, per se, but about keeping the direct explanation of meaning at a distance, and for a reason. The crowd is mixed. There are those truly seeking, and there are those who have no intention of believing. There are those with open hearts and those with closed ones.

The use of a parable is to draw out those who are truly seeking by getting them to think about what has been said and its application. But to those with hardened hearts, they will merely shake their heads in confusion and call it just so much story telling.

"For whoever has, to him more shall be given, and he will have an abundance; but whoever does not have, even what he has shall be taken away from him.

This sounds opposite to our version of human nature. We would want to give to the person who has not, not to those who already have.

But the lesson here is about the openness of the heart. Those who have been open will already have received things from the Lord, and to those the Lord desires to continue giving. To those who are not open, they will not have such things, and to them not only does the Lord desire to not give but to take away. This was reiterated earlier in Jesus' exhortation to not cast our pearls before swine.

The critic will say this is nonsense because He has just said the person does not have, so how can things be taken away? What is being spoken of here is the general revelation compared to special revelation. They lack those instances of special revelation (didactic teaching) and none will be given to them henceforth either. But they do have the witness of the general revelation which Paul discusses in the first chapters of Romans. Jesus is saying that in their hardness of heart, even the effect of that revelation will be taken from them; will be made to have no real effect.

"Therefore I speak to them in parables; because while seeing they do not see, and while hearing they do not hear, nor do they understand.

It is a case with such people that they see the miracles and the acts of God but they do not thereby believe, they do not walk out in that faith, they do not change.

The same in hearing; they hear the sounds, they recognize the words, but they don't get the meaning.

Now it would seem that the answer is in more adequate and detailed explanations, not in the mystery of parables. But there is a reason why Jesus chooses the obscure instead of the more explanatory with this class of people.

"In their case the prophecy of Isaiah is being fulfilled, which says, `YOU WILL KEEP ON HEARING, BUT WILL NOT UNDERSTAND; YOU WILL KEEP ON SEEING, BUT WILL NOT PERCEIVE; . . . WITH THEIR EARS THEY SCARCELY HEAR, AND THEY HAVE CLOSED THEIR EYES, OTHERWISE THEY WOULD SEE WITH THEIR EYES, HEAR WITH THEIR EARS, AND UNDERSTAND WITH THEIR HEART AND RETURN, AND I WOULD HEAL THEM.'

This is perhaps the most difficult verse in the NT. It conveys the idea that God deliberately wishes to avoid a condition whereby such people would turn and be healed.

We often explain the hardening of hearts by God (e.g. Pharaoh) as God furthering the hardness that they themselves have chosen. It is an explanation that takes the sting out of God deliberately barring people from the truth that would save them. They did this to themselves, so God is letting them have their way.

But here we have the opportunity of "turning" in the offing. We see described the actual potential of turning away from their hardness, not the resolute determination to further their hardness.

Those who do not believe in the Calvinist idea of predestination for the wicked are very much without an explanation for this passage. It can't be explained away as simply their own hardness, because it is the opportunity of returning that is considered objectionable to God. And since predestination is not an explanation, there is no resolution at hand.

This verse only gains meaning within a predestination context, in which there are those who are made as vessels of wrath (Romans 9:22) and preaching that would effect a turning has been decreed otherwise.

Some may argue that if predestined then why the concern that they would turn because they are predestined not to. But reformed expositors explain that the statement from Isaiah is a poetic way of saying this very thing. It is meant in the hypothetic sense not the real sense.

Still, neither explanation is completely suitable and it remains one of the most puzzling verses in the Bible.

"But blessed are your eyes, because they see; and your ears, because they hear. For truly I say to you that many prophets and righteous men desired to see what you see, and did not see it, and to hear what you hear, and did not hear it.

In contrast, His disciples are of a unique class. They are not only like those in the crowd whose faith would draw them out through curiosity, introspection and contemplation, but they are blessed to receive the more insightful teaching of Jesus and to see the Gospel in action in everything they did with Him.

This, Jesus identifies as the very things the righteous men of old would have coveted.

Now He explains to them the meaning of the parable.

We find that each of the soils represent types of people and their conditions on whom the seed of the Word is said to be "sown."

The Seed Beside the Road

Matthew 13:18
"When anyone hears the word of the kingdom and does not understand it, the evil one comes and snatches away what has been sown in his heart.

The evil one is seen in the birds who come to snatch it away. We are not told in the parable itself that the soil does not "understand" the seed sown, only that the birds come and take it.

But it is the condition that they can snatch it away that tells the story. The word has not been studied, sought after for its meaning and remains as it is "beside the road."

Satan steals away the Word from us by distracting us away from its urgency and importance so that we leave it for another day, and soon that other day becomes years and we forget what was given to us. It is therefore metaphorically snatched away, but gone nonetheless.

The Seed On Rocky Ground

". . this is the man who hears the word and immediately receives it with joy; yet he has no firm root in himself, but is only temporary, and when affliction or persecution arises because of the word, immediately he falls away.

This describes a large segment of people in churches today. Church attendance is a social activity that adds respectability in the thinking of many people. There is even a provocation to think more seriously in things said in sermons, people leave services with a high sense of invigoration and moral purpose, but it proves to be temporary.

There is no real change in the inner soul, no transformation that brings enabling power and understanding within. The test is in times of affliction or persecution. The old self quickly shows itself as unchanged and carnal reactions and attitudes play out as they always have.

In terms of affliction and persecution, if one sees church as a sort of club or as an intriguing philosophy, a person will think twice about putting their well being or their lives on the line for it.

He falls away from the Word to his former self, the self that has remained unchanged all along.

The Seed Among Thorns

Matthew 13:22
". . this is the man who hears the word, and the worry of the world and the deceitfulness of wealth choke the word, and it becomes unfruitful.

Somewhat like the man who lets the seed sit by the roadside, the Word becomes neglected or of no lasting effect due to the concerns of life.

This is a frequent circumstance in churches today. People hear the Word preached as though they are in an almost surreal inner sanctum of holiness – the beauty of the church setting, the music, the nicely dressed congregation, only to go out into the real world and ask, "How does this relate?"

We leave the sanctuary and are soon out in traffic where the news or the secular sounds from the radio are playing. We see the billboards, the dismal familiarity of store fronts along our route, reminders about work the next day, the commercial jet out in the distance.

We are vividly reminded that this is the real world and we can sometimes ponder what meaning the sermon just heard has in it? When we get home the same patterns of living resume, kids chattering and reminding us of events and schedules we must keep, the laundry still waiting to be done, etc.

But more than these things, our whole outlook on life and our current values and goals can overwhelm us by our own doing. How will we survive the coming years and retirement? Where are we on that plan to get the big job and the big salary? Where are we in enjoying to the max the one and only life we have?

Those concerns can put the Word on the backburner or present such urgencies that the Word is choked out of the discussion, the planning, and the meaning of life.

The Seed In the Good Soil
\
Matthew 13:23
". . this is the man who hears the word and understands it; who indeed bears fruit and brings forth, some a hundredfold, some sixty, and some thirty."

Understanding comes from a thirst to know. Very few things come as a snap to our understanding. We have to pursue them to grasp their deeper meaning. That is the heart of the person Jesus earlier described as the one who thirsts after righteousness. It is not just a desire for knowledge, but knowledge put into practice. The promise here is that those who seek and acquire understanding will yield fruit by default.

It is interesting that the yields are variously described, allowing for some being less than a hundredfold. It is not a case of allowing for half or third best efforts. It is a case of all being best efforts, but the fruit being limited by other conditions. Paul did not have fruit in some towns to a hundredfold, not due to his not trying his best, but to the conditions in those to whom he ministered.

So what is the point of mentioning these conditions? Can we move from one type of soil to the good soil? The implication is yes. In each case, it is the will of the individual that determined the condition of their soil and the results. But wills can be changed and we are exhorted here to seek the place where our soil is ready for the seed, ready to seek the understanding of what is planted and ready to work out the reality of its meaning in the bearing of its fruit.

Matthew 13:24-43, Mark 4:21-29, Matthew 13:44-52

24 Jesus presented another parable to them, saying, "The kingdom of heaven may be compared to a man who sowed good seed in his field. 25 "But while his men were sleeping, his enemy came and sowed tares among the wheat, and went away. 26 "But when the wheat sprouted and bore grain, then the tares became evident also. 27 "The slaves of the landowner came and said to him, `Sir, did you not sow good seed in your field? How then does it have tares?' 28 "And he said to them, `An enemy has done this!' The slaves said to him, `Do you want us, then, to go and gather them up?' 29 "But he said, `No; for while you are gathering up the tares, you may uproot the wheat with them. 30 `Allow both to grow together until the harvest; and in the time of the harvest I will say to the reapers, "First gather up the tares and bind them in bundles to burn them up; but gather the wheat into my barn."

31 He presented another parable to them, saying, "The kingdom of heaven is like a mustard seed, which a man took and sowed in his field; 32 and this is smaller than all other seeds, but when it is full grown, it is larger than the garden plants and becomes a tree, so that the birds of the air come and nest in its branches."

33 He spoke another parable to them, "The kingdom of heaven is like leaven, which a woman took and hid in three pecks of flour until it was all leavened."

34 All these things Jesus spoke to the crowds in parables, and He did not speak to them without a parable. 35 This was to fulfill what was spoken through the prophet: "I WILL OPEN MY MOUTH IN PARABLES; I WILL UTTER THINGS HIDDEN SINCE THE FOUNDATION OF THE WORLD."

36 Then He left the crowds and went into the house. And His disciples came to Him and said, "Explain to us the parable of the tares of the field." 37 And He said, "The one who sows the good seed is the Son of Man, 38 and the field is the world; and as for the good seed, these are the sons of the kingdom; and the tares are the sons of the evil one; 39 and the enemy who sowed them is the devil, and the harvest is the end of the age; and the reapers are angels. 40 "So just as the tares are gathered up and burned with fire, so shall it be at the end of the age. 41 "The Son of Man will send forth His angels, and they will gather out of His kingdom all stumbling blocks, and those who commit lawlessness, 42 and will throw them into the furnace of fire; in that place there will be weeping and gnashing of teeth. 43 "Then THE RIGHTEOUS WILL SHINE FORTH AS THE SUN in the kingdom of their Father. He who has ears, let him hear. (Matthew 13:24-43)

1 And He was saying to them, "A lamp is not brought to be put under a basket, is it, or under a bed? Is it not brought to be put on the lampstand? 22 "For nothing is hidden, except to be revealed; nor has anything been secret, but that it would come to light. 23 "If anyone has ears to hear, let him hear." 24 And He was saying to them, "Take care what you listen to. By your standard of measure it will be measured to you; and more will be given you besides. 25 "For whoever has, to him more shall be given; and whoever does not have, even what he has shall be taken away from him." (Mark 4:21-25)

26 And He was saying, "The kingdom of God is like a man who casts seed upon the soil; 27 and he goes to bed at night and gets up by day, and the seed sprouts and grows--how, he himself does not know. 28 "The soil produces crops by itself; first the blade, then the head, then the mature grain in the head. 29 "But when the crop permits, he immediately puts in the sickle, because the harvest has come." (Mark 4:26-29)

44 "The kingdom of heaven is like a treasure hidden in the field, which a man found and hid again; and from joy over it he goes and sells all that he has and buys that field. (Matthew 13:44)

45 "Again, the kingdom of heaven is like a merchant seeking fine pearls, 46 and upon finding one pearl of great value, he went and sold all that he had and bought it. (Matthew 13:45-46)

47 "Again, the kingdom of heaven is like a dragnet cast into the sea, and gathering fish of every kind; 48 and when it was filled, they drew it up on the beach; and they sat down and gathered the good fish into containers, but the bad they threw away. 49 "So it will be at the end of the age; the angels will come forth and take out the wicked from among the righteous, 50 and will throw them into the furnace of fire; in that place there will be weeping and gnashing of teeth.

51 "Have you understood all these things?" They said to Him, "Yes." 52 And Jesus said to them, "Therefore every scribe who has become a disciple of the kingdom of heaven is like a head of a household, who brings out of his treasure things new and old." (Matthew 13:47-52)

Commentary

Matthew 13:24
"The kingdom of heaven may be compared to a man who sowed good seed in his field. But .. his enemy came and sowed tares among the wheat. . . Allow both to grow together until the harvest; 'First gather up the tares and bind them in bundles to burn them up; but gather the wheat into my barn.'"

Jesus has at some point now turned back to the crowd as evident from Matthew 13:34-36 below. He will speak three more parables to them and then will take the disciples into the house and continue speaking to them in private.

The Parable of the Tares is purposed to teach about an enigmatic aspect of the Kingdom of heaven, which we often simply relate as a parable about the Church. But it is more than the Church in that believer's faith has historically been more than the physical institution of the Church. It is about the true citizens of the Kingdom which will be comprised of OT saints as well as the NT Church.

The enigmatic aspect is its physicality in the world and that it will not be a place populated only with believers, nor will it be uniform in beliefs. i.e., its physical assembly will also contain at any given time representatives of the enemy.

The good seed are those believers who initiate the church and populate it at first. Satan then proceeds to infiltrate his agents into it. This is possible because the door is basically open to all. One need not become faithfully united to merely attend services, although in these early times it would have been hard to remain so.

In today's churches, an individual can remain in hiding about their own lack of faith for years and never be asked to leave. We don't scrutinize attendees. It is also possible in some churches to become a member having never really become saved in the NT sense. Some membership classes are extremely vague in asking a verbal commitment from prospective members. All that really counts is that someone has taken the membership class.

As for acting the role of tares, many such people don't do anything particularly active in disrupting the church, except perhaps at home in relation to their believing spouses.

But some damage can occur from the example such people exhibit in their away-from-church lives. They can lead unsuspecting and naïve Christians to think that a certain amount of moral license is winked at by God.

Other areas of trouble occur when such people are naively elected to responsible lay positions in the church and become roadblocks to spiritual initiatives by seeing these things only from a practical or business perspective. Many a board of trustees in longstanding churches might be properly called "the board of crustees" due to their miserly and controlling posture and their continual preference for running the church like a business.

Another area of trouble occurs when the church goes through a spiritual crisis - a new pastor comes on the scene who actually preaches a full and conservative Gospel. Many a "Save Our Church" committee has been formed by the tares living in the midst of believers.

'Do you want us, then, to go and gather them up?'

The natural human response is to do a housecleaning. But Jesus indicates that this is not the will of the Father, which may seem strange because it appears to feed the liberal mindset that such things are too harsh, while God is anything but liberally minded.

The problem is in how that would be effected. How would the church ferret out the true tares of the enemy without doing a whole lot of judging. That would actually become more divisive than the problems the tares might create – *lest ye take up the wheat with the tares."*

It is ultimately God's business and Jesus is saying He will take care of these matters at the Judgment.

It is also a statement that the Holy Spirit is more than capable of preserving churches from long lasting effects from the tares, so long as the majority of people are true believers and trust in Him.

That some churches have died or become secularized is almost always due to the population balance shifting more to the tares than to believers. In liberalism it is actually not unheard of for a church to begin more as a club than as a representative of Christ's body.

Matthew 13:31
"The kingdom of heaven is like a mustard seed,.. smaller than all other seeds, but when it is full grown, it is larger than the garden plants and becomes a tree, so that the birds of the air come and nest in its branches."

He spoke another parable to them, "The kingdom of heaven is like leaven, which a woman took and hid in three pecks of flour until it was all leavened."

Then next two parables present the idea of the Kingdom being something very small, but growing, to have a tremendously large effect, uncharacteristic of its initial size. This points to the future of the Kingdom in Christ's Church.

It is a miracle of nature that the mustard seed can become its end result. It is no longer seen this way in our knowledge of how DNA can develop the structures of a living organism. It is now merely a matter of building blocks.

But the point is not taken from the science but from the aspect of appearance. In the mind of the ancients it was an incredibly small thing becoming something very noticeable.

The birds coming to nest is a picture of the seed become so significant that it serves as a resting place for the birds. The Church begun by a small band of simple men has become a haven for those in need of spiritual rest from the weariness of a life attempted by oneself.

Yeast also serves this analogy in being but a small compound that needs very little mechanical action to raise the whole mass of dough.

Christ's Church will begin not only with a very few members, but with people of no account from a worldly point of view. They are not an institution of noted scholars, not a renowned center of business and trade, not a league of noble generals with pedigrees of battle honors and victories.

They come from a nation known for knowledge and business acumen, but these are mere fishermen, simply provincials. Yet what was begun in them became so great as to inherit the remains of a decadent empire, to replace its temples with churches, and to change the notoriety of its chief city – Rome - from being known as a pagan capital to an ecclesiastical one. So influential was Christianity that even the manner of reckoning time past and future was forever changed to reflect the Christ it preached.

There is now hardly a place in the known world that has not heard the name of Jesus or been told of His death and Resurrection.

Matthew 13:34
All these things Jesus spoke to the crowds in parables, and He did not speak to them without a parable. This was to fulfill what was spoken through the prophet: "I WILL OPEN MY MOUTH IN PARABLES; I WILL UTTER THINGS HIDDEN SINCE THE FOUNDATION OF THE WORLD."

This completes the things Jesus desired in this gathering to address to the people at large. This does not mean that for all crowds everywhere He only spoke in parables. It is saying that in the things He spoke to this crowd on this occasion, He spoke only in the form of a succession of parables. And it is by extension a note about the general mode of teaching to the mixed public.

The OT quotation is from Psalm 78:2, which is a general statement from God in the midst of statements of worship by His people. He will speak to them in parables, they will teach the things of God to their children.

There are two ideas expressed here: the notion of parables which are not clear dissertations of truth, and the revelation of hidden things. These seem antithetical. Parables, as explained earlier, do hide truths to some extent in that their immediate device is an analogy or a figure of the real thing being taught. The Kingdom is not leaven itself, but what the Kingdom is like is learned by focusing on what leaven does.

This doesn't make a contradiction. Things are being revealed that were previously hidden. That the means requires introspection and contemplation does not negate that revelation is occurring.

Matthew 13:36
Then He left the crowds and went into the house. And His disciples came to Him and said, "Explain to us the parable of the tares of the field."

Jesus now gathers His disciples for more direct teaching and to give them the interpretive skills involved in using parables. This follows His previous statement that this kind of teaching is restricted from the general crowd and reserved for His true followers.

From a practical standpoint and considering the difficulties of having the disciples and the people in such close proximity, a change needed to be made from the boat to the house.

It is understandable that the disciples would pick things up at the very next parable after that of the sower. He had explained that parable out in the boat. All things said thereafter needed similar understanding. So they begin with the Parable of the Tares.

And He said, "The one who sows the good seed is the Son of Man, and the field is the world; the harvest is the end of the age; and the reapers are angels.

What we are getting here is the relationship of the elements of the parable to real, actual things. Not only is the parable being explained, but information about the reality of the world and its future is being told.

We are told that the sower is Jesus Himself, the implication being that the seed is the Word of His Father being spoken and preached to men. That the field is the world might be seen as limited to the small area of real estate on which Jesus walked, since this was the only place at present where His Word was being "cast."

But if this is about the Kingdom and if we also take Paul's later words in Romans to heart, the world is the world, the planet, in that the Son has been involved in the preaching of God's righteousness to all people in both the general and special revelation since the beginning.

If those outside the revelation in Judaism are also accountable, then the word has been preached, the seed cast, elsewhere than Israel.

We get here also a confirmation that the last Judgment is not a myth, but there is to be a harvest at the end of the age to which all men will be assessed as to their response to the revelation given. It also teaches that there is a present age, meaning there were and may be other ages.

In *Lord of the Rings*,[30] there is a statement that the age of hobbits and elves is coming to an end and the age of man is now approaching. Tolkien meant this deliberately to mirror the biblical idea that man now lives in an age that will come to an end and transition to another age, that of the Kingdom of God.

It seems the stuff of myths and fables, but it is actually based on the real design of God for the world that really is. There are ages, and we are living in but one. And though we know little if anything about the grand scheme of all ages, we are to focus on how life in this age is to prepare us for the one to come.

The writer of Hebrews says we are citizens of another country and that as true citizens we know that we are in a distant land for a short time and long to be in our own country. That is the heart and hope of all believers, the hope that sustains us everyday in its promises.

The identity of the good seed and the tares is obvious, especially when the tares are linked to the enemy. We shouldn't be confused that the comparison is not between good seed and bad seed, per se, but between good seed and the grown results of the bad seed sown. The good seed does not exclude the result (the fruit of the good seed in believers.)

"and the enemy who sowed them is the devil,"

There are Christians who dismiss the idea of a real devil as latent superstition from an ignorant age; which would work, had it not been voiced in the mouth of Jesus. We can dismiss the inculcation of superstition on the part of unenlightened ancient people, but it is immeasurably difficult to maintain this when dealing with Jesus. We have someone here whose wisdom cannot be denied, even by the unbeliever. Even for those who deny a real Jesus, whoever (in their mind) was the source of the things said by Jesus, that person was certainly not ignorant, nor a victim of the superstitions of his times.

That such a person acknowledged the reality of the devil is significant for the unbeliever because to dismiss it as superstition runs counter to all the wisdom and extraordinary insight of everything else. In other words, it all hangs or falls together, and it is difficult even for the unbeliever to dismiss it all.

For the believer, we can also fall into the fog of not acknowledging the reality of Satan and his menacing in our lives. We can readily follow the logic of the world and attribute such things to the facts of the world in which we live, the way of life, which does not suddenly change because we have become Christians. It's the troubles of the life, not spiritual warfare.

So we adopt an approach to life that ceases to pray against the work of Satan as though that is to some degree sort of "silly," nor do we pray to have the power to resist him that he would flee from us, as was commended in the NT. We fall into Satan's most insidious lie – that he doesn't really exist and all the talk about Him can be explained otherwise.

But Jesus makes it clear he is real and that a significant part of our new life will be forced into a confrontation with him.

---

[30] Tolkien, The Return of the King. Houghton-Mifflin, New York, (1966)

"So just as the tares are gathered up and burned with fire, so shall it be at the end of the age."

Again, more reality checks about the truth of the end of the age and the very real nature of a final judgment, especially for the wicked.

Men can dismiss this as superstition, ignoring the illogic of the above, and choose to live as though such things will never happen. But the risk that they are wrong is a matter about which men would not wish to be wrong. This is a major witnessing point in evangelism.

It was more crudely expressed in the hell-fire and damnation sermons of past eras (Jonathan Edwards, *Sinners in the Hands of an Angry God*). And despite our abandonment of such rhetoric for more seeker sensitive speech, the idea remains cogent that the consequences of being wrong are a risk that needs to be thought out more seriously than blithely taking the word of recreational philosophers who think they have rationalized it away. Those philosophers will hardly stand and defend us at the Judgment, should it prove to be real.

Matthew 13:41
"The Son of Man will send forth His angels, and they will gather out of His kingdom all stumbling blocks, and those who commit lawlessness,

Here too we see the clear endorsement of the reality of angels, who have many duties, but have this one also – that they know and will be able to discern true believers from the tares. They will be able to gather the tares out and prepare them for judgment.

This ought to be harrowing for the unbeliever to contemplate, because the assessment of who is a tare is in the hands of beings who carry the capacities associated with extraordinary powers and intimate acquaintance with the Almighty and Righteous God. Human rationalizations will pale in comparison to the knowledge of the angels. How can our own philosophizing be compared to their razor-sharp acumen?

All the more reason for any man to investigate how he may ensure he is on the right side of that assessment while he has time and breath remaining.

in that place there will be weeping and gnashing of teeth.

It is often a case that postponement of reality results in almost a convulsive crying when that reality hits a person square in the face. All the self-deception vanishes and the consequences of so vigorously ignoring all the warning signs and having entertained so grave a mistake about reality come crashing in. There will be a grievous weeping by those who realize that not only were they completely wrong and foolish, but they face now a perpetual everlasting destiny.

The gnashing of teeth is the response of the recalcitrant disbeliever but it reveals that the basis was all along a hatred of God. This is the person who always had a bone to pick with God in life, whose philosophy of life was somehow better than God's and was bitter that God's way of things won out by the mere superiority of arms - God exerting his greater power to insist on His own way.

This prevails in other aspects of everyday life. In politics, there may be real truths from the opposing party but because precisely because it is the other party, there is wholesale rejection. And when the other party actually wins victories, there is a sort of gnashing of teeth in contrast to honest praise based on recognized merit. What one gets is just more hatred that the other side is winning.

In Hell, there will be the same but heightened beyond measure. It will be a hatred that the side of righteousness has won out and the results are eternal and everlasting.

"Then THE RIGHTEOUS WILL SHINE FORTH AS THE SUN in the kingdom of their Father. He who has ears, let him hear.

Jesus pulls in a reference to Daniel 12:3 about the state of the everlasting Kingdom and that of the righteous. The comparison is meant to be completely striking and completely opposite in characterization. The wicked will be gnashing their teeth, not humbled by the truth at last, and the righteous will be shining in the comfort and pleasure of the blessings of God.

"he who has ears, let him hear" is a special phrase used by Jesus to indicate that the meaning is not obvious nor caught by everyone. It is a truth out there for the seeker to find, but not obvious to everyone. If you have ears that seek and thirst after righteousness, you will hear these words and they will take root in you. If not, they will be obscure and without comprehension.

Mark 4:21-25
"A lamp is not brought to be put under a basket, is it, or under a bed? . . . For nothing is hidden, except to be revealed; nor has anything been secret, but that it would come to light.

This is a brief parable about the light of a lamp, very similar to previous teaching in the Sermon on the Mount. It is stated in brief because the disciples are familiar with it already. Jesus adds more to it in this rendition than before.

In Mark, this is preceded with *"and He was saying to them"* and this helps us to discern that Jesus is not speaking to the crowds again but continuing to speak to the disciples in the house.

Jesus adds here a repeat of another earlier teaching – that things thought to be secret will be brought to the light. The light of righteousness is a light that is so clean as to bring ultimate visibility to all truth and falsehood simultaneously. Falsehood is revealed because righteousness stands out so brightly in its rays.

The infectious work of the cockroach out on the countertop in the middle of the night is brought to an end when we turn on the light.

"Take care what you listen to. By your standard of measure it will be measured to you; and more will be given you besides. "For whoever has, to him more shall be given . . "

To take care means to give attention to, in contrast to being wary.

"by your standard of measure. ." is a teaching about capacities and the enlarging of capacities. God knows what we can absorb at any given place in our lives and He expertly arranges knowledge and teaching to come our way that speaks within the capacity. We are certainly exposed to teaching beyond this, but we are also exposed to teaching within it, and that is what we are to consider and study.

Very often folks get frustrated that there is too much to learn, and too much beyond their ability to amass and comprehend. So some people just forsake study altogether – *"The Bible is just too complicated for me, I'm just not a Bible scholar."* But they ignore the things they can understand, which if they hadn't, they would have found God expanding their capacities so that more and more things would begin to sense and come clear. *"by your standard of measure it will be measured to you; and more will be given you besides.*

This prompts a reiteration of the teaching that to those who have will be given more, and from those who have not, even what they have will be lost.

Mark 4:26
"The kingdom of God is like a man who casts seed upon the soil . . The soil produces crops by itself; first the blade, then the head, then the mature grain in the head."

The growing seed is both a teaching on the process of maturity and, on the nature of the harvest, is related to the Kingdom.

With respect to personal growth, there is a process of growth in the Word of God, and there are limits of expectation related to it. Like the crop, ancient man could not explain how the seed sprouted, only that it did. How God enlarges the maturity and capacity for the things of God is a mystery also, but nonetheless the results are things we clearly see.

Patience is being enjoined as we grow. We should delight in the fact that we are being made to grow, rather than complaining that we do not know as much as so-and-so.

With respect to the harvest of the Kingdom, again the path to harvest is not immediate. Not all seeds immediately become harvestable grain, but the sower must exercise patience and husbandry in waiting out the time of harvest.

The planting of the Word, the nurturing of it through patience and longsuffering in its preachers and the preparation toward the harvest of God are facts in the Kingdom of God. Some come at the first planting of the seeds, but others need patience in becoming ready for the harvest of God.

When the crop permits . . " means that God does not strong-arm believers into the Kingdom. He is instead patient to let the believer establish the truth in their own hearts, He reaps because the believer has given permission in his own will to be harvested.

(Predestinarians will take issue with this in that God makes them ready by sovereign election to grace, not by anything they do themselves. But this is why there is controversy. There are verses that leave the readiness accountable to the individual.)

Matthew 13:44
"The kingdom of heaven is like a treasure hidden in the field, which a man found and hid again; and from joy over it he goes and sells all that he has and buys that field.

"Again, the kingdom of heaven is like a merchant seeking fine pearls, and upon finding one pearl of great value, he went and sold all that he had and bought it.

. . is like. . . It should be noted that these parables are not definitions for the Kingdom in toto, but aspects of it being described, or in some cases the same aspect being described from different perspectives (the mustard seed and the leaven.)

These analogies are a little difficult for moderns to relate. Why not simply take the treasure home and hide it in his own field? The idea is that the man goes through the proper procedures to own the field and its treasure, rather than just stealing it. (The pearl is in a merchant's shop not out in a field. It must be purchased not stolen.)

We don't relate to this in modern times because upon finding a million dollars in a suitcase in a field, it will certainly just as quickly wind up in the trunk of our car with no concerns about who it belongs to.

However, stealing in ancient times was just as readily understood as taking those things one knew didn't belong to them, as it is today. So to avoid impropriety, the right thing to do was to buy the field legally. The added parable of the pearl makes it clear that legal acquisition is deemed necessary by the finder.

In this application, the prize in the field – the gift of eternal life – is so valued that it is worth selling all that one owns to secure it. It is the recognition that its acquisition comes at a price and we are more than willing to pay it.

This is not to be taken as a doctrine that one can pay their way into the Kingdom. It is an analogy that one is to be willing to give up all prior earthly possessions to gain eternal ones. This is the substance of the man with many riches, to whom Jesus said, *"Go and sell all that you have and give the money to the poor, then come and follow Me."*

"Again, the kingdom of heaven is like a dragnet cast into the sea, . . So it will be at the end of the age; the angels will come forth and take out the wicked from among the righteous,

The analogy to the culling out of fish at the end of the day is not to be taken too tightly feature for feature. For example, we know that the wicked will not accompany the righteous through the Pearly Gates to then undergo the scrutiny of the angels and be sent packing.

The idea is that we are to learn about the Kingdom in the picture, of sorting out the bad fish from the good, and that there is a qualification for being treated with value in the harvest. Also the fishermen value the good fish but have no care for the bad ones.

Yet in the strict analogy, both fish die. The good fish do not technically receive any better reward for being chosen because they merely end up as someone's dinner. Hence, the analogy is to be limited merely to the idea that all humanity is gathered at the end, and there will be decisions, like those of the fishermen on the shore amidst their nets, to ferret out the good from the bad. I.e. not all will have the same end before God.

The call is to those who are unsure. If you see that there is going to be an assessment, and this is what the Kingdom is like, you had better seek what it will take to be found a good fish in the end.

Matthew 13:51
"Have you understood all these things?" They said to Him, "Yes."

This is not perfunctory. Jesus was ready to explain more had there been doubts or confusion remaining.

After two thousand years, we find it still difficult to answer yes for ourselves as the disciples did. We can attribute their yes as God having opened their understanding and to the excellent speech of Jesus.

In asking this, Jesus is also asking if they are getting the hang of the parable method as a tool. Are they seeing how the obscure can be used to picture the specific?

"Therefore every scribe who has become a disciple of the kingdom of heaven is like a head of a household, who brings out of his treasure things new and old."

This seems odd to us in modern times because our idea of a scribe is limited to a particular activity. In Judaism, the scribes were the natural choice for teachers because they had to know the Scriptures so well to be able to copy them and reference them in national affairs. It was a scribe who informed Herod that the Messiah was to come from Bethlehem.

So this has the effect of Jesus calling the men who have now learned His teaching "scribes," which they would take as a great compliment, meaning they were considered skilled to teach the truths of God.

In this also, the scribe was like a head of household whose responsibility it was to teach his family. He was to study and learn so as to bring out of his own treasury of knowledge things of old as well as new applications in life's ongoing challenges. But they are more than heads of households, who would not have had the expertise of the scribes, in that they were now both.

Matt 8:18-21, Luke 9:60-62, Mark 4:35-41
18 Now when Jesus saw a crowd around Him, He gave orders to depart to the other side of the sea. 19 Then a scribe came and said to Him, "Teacher, I will follow You wherever You go." 20 Jesus said to him, "The foxes have holes and the birds of the air have nests, but the Son of Man has nowhere to lay His head." 21 Another of the disciples said to Him, "Lord, permit me first to go and bury my father." (Matt 8:18-21)

60 But He said to him, "Allow the dead to bury their own dead; but as for you, go and proclaim everywhere the kingdom of God." 61 Another also said, "I will follow You, Lord; but first permit me to say good-bye to those at home." 62 But Jesus said to him, "No one, after putting his hand to the plow and looking back, is fit for the kingdom of God." (Luke 9:60-62)

35 On that day, when evening came, He said to them, "Let us go over to the other side." 36 Leaving the crowd, they took Him along with them in the boat, just as He was; and other boats were with Him. 37 And there arose a fierce gale of wind, and the waves were breaking over the boat so much that the boat was already filling up. 38 Jesus Himself was in the stern, asleep on the cushion; and they woke Him and said to Him, "Teacher, do You not care that we are perishing?" 39 And He got up and rebuked the wind and said to the sea, "Hush, be still." And the wind died down and it became perfectly calm. 40 And He said to them, "Why are you afraid? Do you still have no faith?" 41 They became very much afraid and said to one another, "Who then is this, that even the wind and the sea obey Him?" (Mark 4:35-41)

Commentary

Mark 8:18-21
"The foxes have holes and the birds of the air have nests, but the Son of Man has nowhere to lay His head."

The scene has changed again such that Jesus has noticed a crowd gathering around Him. It is most likely a separate event from the foregoing because we last saw Him in the house teaching, but now crowds are gathered around Him suggesting He was now outside again.

He orders His disciples to row across the sea of Galilee, and we come to know later that this was over to the E shore on a SE heading from Capernaum because we find them entering the country of the Gerasenes.

Before departing, three men approach Him about their calling to follow Him. The first here is a scribe of the Jews who expresses a fealty Jesus sees as premature - *"I will follow you wherever you go."* Jesus may appear to be inordinately negative or pessimistic, but He is really acting in love toward this man by reminding him what the cost of his statement will mean.

"foxes have holes and the birds of the air have nests, but the Son of Man has nowhere to lay His head" is a warning that following will involve significant privation and denial of the things he is most likely very used to as a scribe. He would have been a man reasonably well-paid for his services, commensurate with his education in the Scriptures.

We aren't told whether the man thought twice and changed his mind or became more resolute and followed, but the statement is there for all followers of Jesus to contemplate – that following might mean a calling to privation and austerity. What will we do when that decision needs to be made?

Another of the disciples said to Him, "Lord, permit me first to go and bury my father."

The second man is in a similar position. Having heard what Jesus just said to the scribe, he now contemplates how to extricate himself from his personal affairs in order to be available to follow. His case, he thinks, enjoins compassion. Surely Jesus will be accommodating.

Even believers find Jesus' reply as just barely on the good side of being callous. *"Allow the dead to bury their own dead;"*

The first point of departure is to not agonize over the details of who will bury the man's father and what Jesus meant by the dead burying the dead. The chief point is to highlight how people treat calls to service. In our modern world, Christian service can be regarded as just one of many activities.

For the man here, Jesus is essentially saying, *"This is not a recreational excursion."* Many today might say, *"Let me do X and I'll catch up with you at noon."* Jesus is saying, "Get a grip. Comprehend the magnitude of what is being set before you." Here we have the most important person who has ever lived inviting a man to the work of the Kingdom - the one work that can set the destiny of human souls – and we're worried about when we'll get back to cleaning out the garage or who's going to coach the team if we leave?

Now the case of the man's dead father is not in the same class, but the lesson about opportunity and availability is just as valid.

Who are then the dead who will bury the dead? First, it can't mean the absurd – the actual dead called to bury other dead. Instead, it is those who live in the world yet remain unenlightened to the faith of the Kingdom and are spiritually dead. They exist but they do not live in the sense that Jesus taught – *"I came that you may have life and that abundantly."*

To leave the dead to be buried by the dead is to leave the dead to be buried by those whose realm is the world and the affairs of the world, who are alive biologically but dead spiritually.

Were those of the man's family and friends among this dead? The statement is a commentary on the state of humanity and a parody on the difference between existence and true life. So the individual state of the man's own family is not in focus as much as the state of mankind.

Taking care of the burial of one's father was part of the parental respect all Judaism instilled in its citizens. It was part of honoring father and mother. So how did Jesus come to say such things to a man in mourning?

It may have been customary that burial was integral to showing respect, but from God's point of view, one is honoring the empty vessel. The soul is not there. So honoring a corpse was not honoring the person in any real sense, only in some customary sense.

We also have no purview about the rest of his family. Were there brothers or friends who could easily take care of the physical arrangements?

Even with these explanations, it seems harsh and uncaring to have the son leave in the very midst of funeral preparations on what would seem a rather selfish and indulgent quest.

We shouldn't draw large scale normative teaching about funerals and ministry from Jesus' words. Each case must be judged on its own merits. Had there been absolutely no one to bury the father, and had the family been destitute, Jesus' may have had different things to say.

This man is different from the scribe in that with the scribe we get caution about considering the cost, but no exhortation to follow and leave earthly affairs behind. This man gets an exhortation, that despite the emotional needs of the moment, he must choose – *" but as for you, go and proclaim everywhere the kingdom of God."*

The point needing to be made is that Satan and our flesh will be resourceful in finding many excuses for serving God, many of which make perfect sense on the human plane. But we are to be Godly-minded, concerned about the things of the Kingdom, and that will mean misunderstandings from those in the world about commitments and earthly allegiances.

In the end we must choose and be ready to accept the earthly consequences of our choice for God. Nothing could be more poignant in that tension than the case of the man needing to bury his father. But if a choice was exhorted there, it will certainly be exhorted in all the lesser cases life can imagine.

The lesson for today's postmodern man is bound up in our being regularly accustomed to getting by all rules. There is always an exception available if our case is pleaded. People do wrong things but there are always folks around to decry the need to be harsh with the consequences. Jesus is teaching that some things are absolute and not to be compromised, and unfortunately compromise is a major value today.

Luke 9:60-62
Another also said, ". . first permit me to say good-bye to those at home." . . . "No one, after putting his hand to the plow and looking back, is fit for the kingdom of God."

This man's case is less urgent and perhaps best seen as exemplifying the common rationalizations we can conjure up for not doing what we're supposed to do.

As for not looking back, we are reminded of Lot's wife, who was judged to the ultimate degree for looking back. Many criticize God for strict, puritanical execution of judgment in a case of understandable curiosity. But Lot's wife did not look back in curiosity. She looked back longingly on the destruction of that to which she had become attached. She held affection for the place being destroyed, and God wished there to be a clean break and a look forward, not forever back.

That is why Jesus added that no one doing so *"is fit for the kingdom of God."*

Mark 4:35
"Let us go over to the other side."

At evening, Jesus now moves to begin the journey across the sea in earnest. The disciples are said have taken Him "just as He was" into the boat. We have no details, but perhaps the sheer magnitude of all the foregoing now showed itself in His face and body and the disciples clearly saw the need to take Him under their own assistance into the boat. In the next scene on the sea He is fast asleep at the height of the storm which implies exhaustion.

And there arose a fierce gale of wind,

The bodily rest of which Jesus took advantage was not arbitrary, but as in all things pertaining to His life, was meant even in this detail to accomplish a higher purpose. He is "unavailable" in the presence of a severe storm, and the disciples are about to learn a lesson about Him, the power He commanded, and the things expected of their own faith.

The storm is sometimes pictured like those on the Atlantic or in the North Sea, of huge aspect, with thunder and lightning and the like. As we see here more closely, it was predominantly fierce winds.

Such unpredictable gales were and remain a common feature on the Sea of Galilee. On land we have something similar in severe bursts and windsheers that have downed aircraft in unexpected moments of disaster.

Wind is the key factor in exciting water into waves and for the type of craft they managed, the boat was easily overwhelmed, despite the manpower on board.

and they woke Him and said to Him, "Teacher, do You not care that we are perishing?"

Considering that these men were able and experienced handlers of boats in general, this particular storm must have been extraordinary, and necessarily so, since the specific lesson to test their faith would not have been learned by the ordinary challenges they routinely faced in their trade.

And He got up and rebuked the wind and said to the sea, "Hush, be still." And the wind died down and it became perfectly calm.

To have been there and seen such power would have been overwhelming. Men even today have little effect on harnessing the forces of nature. We are left to try to apply technology or our meager use of power to lessen the effects. We could set off a nuclear weapon in the midst of a monster hurricane and perhaps change some aspect of its course or severity, but at what lasting effect, except to introduce the world to an even worse disaster.

Here we have Jesus who occupied the coordinates in space of a mere man, speaking words, and the forces of nature are harnessed and comply. We have in the boat a Person who was in touch with incredible, inconceivable power.

For these men, the miracle was unmistakable. It could not be rationalized away. Storms and gales came suddenly but did not leave suddenly. To see nature come to rest at the mere speaking of words put them all in both fear and awe.

A moment like this is seen in fifties film, *The Day the Earth Stood Still* (Twentieth Century Fox, 1951) in which the visitor threatens the destruction of the earth should its inhabitants refuse to meet and hear his warning. A professor he has befriended asks incredulously, "Such power exists?" The visitor answers, "I assure you such power exists."

The disciples too are seeing for themselves that such power exists. It enriches our faith that this was not science fiction, but reality - the Lord whom we serve, for whom nothing is impossible in heaven and earth.

Mark 4:40-41
"Why are you afraid? Do you still have no faith?"

Jesus was not this naïve on any conceivable account. It is a rhetorical question and He fully understands why they are afraid. But Jesus did not accommodate their natural fears though He knew whence they came. The question is so incredibly against nature that it just has to contain an extraordinary truth about to be revealed. Asking why they are afraid is a means of introducing them to the great lesson. It is so irrational it commands their interest.

Yet all He offers beyond this is another question - *"Do you still have no faith?"* But that was enough. That was complete and fully adequate because He has been teaching them that with faith they can move mountains, with faith they can change the worst sinner into a victorious servant of God. With faith they wrench Satan from his grip on the human soul and deliver people from the despairing indictment of permanent disease and deformities.

They became very much afraid and said to one another, "Who then is this, that even the wind and the sea obey Him?"

Despite the best intentions of our Lord, they prove to be yet unperfected in their faith. They proceed to do precisely what He exhorted them not to do – they become very much afraid indeed. But now with an added wariness. They must add to their natural fear of all that is happening among the heavens and on the sea the overwhelming revelation of Who was with them in the boat and what power this One wielded.

The kids of our modern age would be prompted to say, "Cool," having long since gotten over the surprise of the spectacular in countless episodes at the movies. But the fear most strongly felt now by the disciples was the fact that they and their lives were now intimate with such a Person and if He can do such things, what forebodings are ahead in their weaknesses and inadequacies? There is always that dread of what might happen if we were to run afoul of someone with that much power.

We find Peter on seeing the early miracles of Jesus saying, *"Get away from me for I am a sinful man."*

Mark 5:1-20
1 They came to the other side of the sea, into the country of the Gerasenes. 2 When He got out of the boat, immediately a man from the tombs with an unclean spirit met Him, 3 and he had his dwelling among the tombs. And no one was able to bind him anymore, even with a chain; 4 because he had often been bound with shackles and chains, and the chains had been torn apart by him and the shackles broken in pieces, and no one was strong enough to subdue him.

5 Constantly, night and day, he was screaming among the tombs and in the mountains, and gashing himself with stones. 6 Seeing Jesus from a distance, he ran up and bowed down before Him; 7 and shouting with a loud voice, he said, "What business do we have with each other, Jesus, Son of the Most High God? I implore You by God, do not torment me!" 8 For He had been saying to him, "Come out of the man, you unclean spirit!" 9 And He was asking him, "What is your name?" And he said to Him, "My name is Legion; for we are many." 10 And he began to implore Him earnestly not to send them out of the country.

11 Now there was a large herd of swine feeding nearby on the mountain. 12 The demons implored Him, saying, "Send us into the swine so that we may enter them." 13 Jesus gave them permission. And coming out, the unclean spirits entered the swine; and the herd rushed down the steep bank into the sea, about two thousand of them; and they were drowned in the sea.

14 Their herdsmen ran away and reported it in the city and in the country. And the people came to see what it was that had happened. 15 They came to Jesus and observed the man who had been demon-possessed sitting down, clothed and in his right mind, the very man who had had the "legion"; and they became frightened. 16 Those who had seen it described to them how it had happened to the demon-possessed man, and all about the swine. 17 And they began to implore Him to leave their region. 18 As He was getting into the boat, the man who had been demon-possessed was imploring Him that he might accompany Him. 19 And He did not let him, but He said to him, "Go home to your people and report to them what great things the Lord has done for you, and how He had mercy on you." 20 And he went away and began to proclaim in Decapolis what great things Jesus had done for him; and everyone was amazed. (Mark 5:1-20)

Commentary

Mark 5:1
They came to the other side of the sea, into the country of the Gerasenes.

We have here an account that presents difficulties as to its details and has fueled charges that the Bible contains evident errors.

Matthew differs from Mark and Luke as to the name for the region to which Jesus arrives from the journey across the sea, Matthew has Gadarenes, Mark and Luke have Gerasenes.

A town's point of reference was always (even if vaguely) somewhat beyond its dwellings and streets, so people living in proximity to a town were associated with it.

Somewhat near the area of this account there were two towns, Gadera and Gerasa, cities of the Decapolis. But each of these was inland by many miles. Neither was the sea nearby, so neither did they also have a steep ravine down to the sea. But the Gospels state He arrived in *"the country of the . ."*, rather than in the towns of the Gadarenes or Gerasenes.

Thompson, the biblical archaeologist (c. 1859) mentions the existence of a "region" on the coast between Gadera and Gerasa that has cave tombs (the demoniacs we soon meet) and a steep ravine just as the accounts describe.[31] The location is such that an association with either town is reasonable.

So Matthew may have been among those had a habit of referring to the area as Gadarene, while Mark here was among those calling it Gerasene territory. This would hardly be an error, if it was up to the individual as to how he saw the connection inland.

Later in the early Fathers, Origen documented the application of the term Gergesenes for this area, hence a third name sometimes seen in commentaries (Gergesenes is not in any NT text.)

Since there was no city called Gergesa, many believe that Origen had come upon a variation of Geresene, in which the Aramaic sound of the 'r' comes out almost like 'rg' in pronunciation. Hence Gerasenes would sound like Gergesenes.

immediately a man from the tombs with an unclean spirit met Him, and he had his dwelling among the tombs.

Having settled the problem of the two towns, we are immediately presented with another apparent discrepancy – the single demoniac compared to Matthew's mention that there were two.

Gleason Archer in his text on Bible discrepancies,[32] offers a common explanation used in other cases like this – if there were two then there was at least one, hence this is not an error. It is a case of emphasis not precision. Some have joined this reconciliation by posing that one of the men may have been reclusive and may have hidden at the sight of Jesus and the others.

But in Matthew it is clear that both men are outspoken and both present obstacles to normal traffic on the path by the tombs. Even with Jesus, one is not intimidated compared to the other and they both speak – *"they cried out, saying, "What business do we have with each other, Son of God? Have You come here to torment us before the time?"* (Matthew 8:29)

Thus, the reasons why Mark and Luke focused on one of these men and did not mention the other are puzzling, but not a fundamental difficulty. That reasons are not given or apparent does not rule out that reasons existed.

An example is available in Lafayette's visit to the United States. One account mentions him alone, the other mentions both him and his son. These are not considered discrepancies but historical privilege.

Mark 5:4
and the chains had been torn apart by him and the shackles broken in pieces, and no one was strong enough to subdue him.

We have here the picture of what powers can be imparted by demons to their hosts. There are those who believe that the powers of evil are purely spiritual and there is no physical connection between them and us, that possession is a metaphor for the spiritual influence only.

But here we see superhuman abilities in contact with physical stuff, like chains. Hence, we need to take demonic possession more seriously than some folks choose to characterize.

It is also to be noted that the man was not just a little off his rocker, but was such a nuisance as to occasion many attempts to restrain him.

---

[31] Thompson, The Bible and Archaeology, Eerdmans, (1972)
[32] Archer, Encyclopedia of Bible Difficulties, Zondervan, (1982), p. 324

There have been documented accounts of grown men being thrown across the room by mere children in operations of exorcism.

and gashing himself with stones.

There are some folks who are rather cavalier about joining forces with the devil or in looking forward to the pranks and mayhem they can effect in Hell. They relish the indulgence of unbridled pleasure they can have in this life and the next.

But the deception is in failing to acknowledge that the devil is called the destroyer. His aim is to ruin and destroy the individual. Here we see the state of the man as not enjoying the pleasures of hedonistic life, but of attempts to destroy himself by gashings with stones. He is in the very act of living out Satan's end plan – his utter and complete destruction.

Mark 5:7
"What business do we have with each other, Jesus, Son of the Most High God? I implore You by God, do not torment me!"

Mark states that he (singular) ran up and speaks but later the man speaks in the plural. Such is the state of men so possessed. The demarcation line between self identity and that of demons is thin. One can switch between persons of speech because possession is so enmeshed.

What is of course the most striking is the immediate recognition of the Person of the Son by a man He who of himself had not met Jesus. But those within him had.

You can imagine the effect this had on those standing around. To be recognized and feared by demons was to be seen as more than a mere man. It was to be someone accessible to the world beyond.

For He had been saying to him, "Come out of the man, you unclean spirit!"

The imperfect tense here means repeated past action continuing into the present. It is similar to *"he kept on saying . ."*

We get from this that Jesus did not speak the command only once, but was continuing to speak it so as to overcome the fierce grip in which the man was being held.

"What is your name?" And he said to Him, "My name is Legion; for we are many."

The command to give forth their names is seen by many as a validation that one has acquired the authority of God to exorcize. But it is not a formulaic conditional to being effective. However, it is seen by many as an effective validation that divine authority is in play.

It is interesting that so many had come to reside in the man. We don't know the prior state of the man that allowed this to happen. Jesus earlier taught that if a man keeps his inner self clean and swept but nonetheless empty in terms of spiritual life, he is open to Satan and the states that can inevitably result.

This is the precarious position of those who are content to leave God alone and who expect Him to leave them alone. Atheists buy into the idea that by jettisoning God, all supernatural foolishness is banished to the realm of myth and fantasy. They are not prepared for the other side of the supernatural in whom they can be easily seduced by the introductory pleasures of possession.

And he began to implore Him earnestly not to send them out of the country . . . "Send us into the swine so that we may enter them."

Again we find this curious mix between third person singular and plural, he and them. *He* implores that *they* not be sent.

Why they fear being sent out of the region is not discernable, although Luke adds the detail that it is fear of the abyss. It may refer to their fear of becoming disembodied spirits and the unknown agony such a state imposes. This may account for their desire to go into the swine.

The fact that the swine subsequently perish seems contradictory to their request since they lose their hosts regardless. But this may be explained by their being perhaps wholly ignorant of the crazed end effect this will cause, while Jesus knows precisely the impending outcome.

It is not cogent that their path to other sinister tasks is less agonizing and more in line with their usual habits if by way of the swine than as disembodied spirits, because Jesus accommodates them and it would be incongruent for Him to accommodate them in any respect.

"that we may enter them." is a sobering statement. It brings into very sharp focus that there is a real world of demons who seek to enter men, that these are facts of reality, these things really do occur. That should be sobering for the unbeliever who reads this account.

The result is more immediate than they had anticipated. Their ignorance may have been due to the difference between possession of human beings vs. animals. It is likely that their request was not informed of how differently animals would respond to their presence. It's a bit like saying, "Get me away from all this. Send me aboard the Titanic I beg you."

The reaction of those standing around was mixed. There was amazement that the man was in his right mind, but there was fear mixed with resentment that not only was a host of demons now unleashed, but that it also occasioned a loss to their business (they were herdsmen.)

Mark 5:14-17 And they began to implore Him to leave their region. . . the man who had been demon-possessed was imploring Him that he might accompany Him. . . "Go home to your people and report to them what great things the Lord has done for you, and how He had mercy on you."

Jesus was not a man moved by fear of other men. His decision to leave was no doubt based on the knowledge that nothing more would be fruitful under the circumstances.

Despite the man's desire to join them, He directs him to share his story with his own people.

It is interesting that Jesus does not command him to tell others about what *He* had done for him, but what God had done. This was in perfect accord with His repeated statements that He was here to do the will of His Father, not His own will.

As the man goes, it seems reasonable that there were those in his home town in similar or other need and yet Jesus does not travel with him to heal them. There is the issue of the fierce imploring of the people just mentioned, but also there is the general case that Jesus did not heal everyone everywhere He went.

Healing and the grace of God is to be a matter of faith, not a matter of having Jesus being physically present to effect it. And if by faith, all that is really needed to engender that faith is the testimony of those touched and healed. God is visiting His people with miracles hence now is the time to let faith do its work.

So healing key people and sending them as seeds of faith for the rest is the business of Jesus.

Mark 5:21-43

21 When Jesus had crossed over again in the boat to the other side, a large crowd gathered around Him; and so He stayed by the seashore. 22 One of the synagogue officials named Jairus came up, and on seeing Him, fell at His feet 23 and implored Him earnestly, saying, "My little daughter is at the point of death; please come and lay Your hands on her, so that she will get well and live." 24 And He went off with him; and a large crowd was following Him and pressing in on Him.

25 A woman who had had a hemorrhage for twelve years, 26 and had endured much at the hands of many physicians, and had spent all that she had and was not helped at all, but rather had grown worse-- 27 after hearing about Jesus, she came up in the crowd behind Him and touched His cloak. 28 For she thought, "If I just touch His garments, I will get well." 29 Immediately the flow of her blood was dried up; and she felt in her body that she was healed of her affliction. 30 Immediately Jesus, perceiving in Himself that the power proceeding from Him had gone forth, turned around in the crowd and said, "Who touched My garments?" 31 And His disciples said to Him, "You see the crowd pressing in on You, and You say, `Who touched Me?' " 32 And He looked around to see the woman who had done this. 33 But the woman fearing and trembling, aware of what had happened to her, came and fell down before Him and told Him the whole truth. 34 And He said to her, "Daughter, your faith has made you well; go in peace and be healed of your affliction."

35 While He was still speaking, they came from the house of the synagogue official, saying, "Your daughter has died; why trouble the Teacher anymore?" 36 But Jesus, overhearing what was being spoken, said to the synagogue official, "Do not be afraid any longer, only believe." 37 And He allowed no one to accompany Him, except Peter and James and John the brother of James. 38 They came to the house of the synagogue official; and He saw a commotion, and people loudly weeping and wailing. 39 And entering in, He said to them, "Why make a commotion and weep? The child has not died, but is asleep." 40 They began laughing at Him. But putting them all out, He took along the child's father and mother and His own companions, and entered the room where the child was. 41 Taking the child by the hand, He said to her, "Talitha kumi!" (which translated means, "Little girl, I say to you, get up!") . 42 Immediately the girl got up and began to walk, for she was twelve years old. And immediately they were completely astounded. 43 And He gave them strict orders that no one should know about this, and He said that something should be given her to eat.
(Mark 5:21-43)

Commentary

Mark 5:21
When Jesus had crossed over again . . one of the synagogue officials named Jairus came up, . . "please come and lay Your hands on her, so that she will get well and live."

Jesus returns to the precincts of Capernaum from which He had gone over to the country of the Gerasenes. The synagogue is notably the one to which Jesus' Galilean ministry would be associated. It's 4th century buildings have been partially re-erected but the remains of the synagogue of Jesus' day are still below ground level.

"Official of the synagogue" does not tell us his position or duties. Officials were not the rabbis of the synagogue, but consecrated men who assisted in various duties conducted there. For example, the caring for and unveiling of the Torah for readings by worshipers would be an official duty, as would the carrying of first fruits on behalf of local worshippers to Jerusalem. Assistance at weddings and funerals would be included. However Jewish sources correct the idea that the officials were the elders. Those would have been yet another class of persons distinct from the congregation of worshippers.

Now the man Jairus would have been under some conviction to adopt the attitude of the Pharisees, represented locally by the rabbis and elders in his area. Yet he risks his position because of the desperate plight of his daughter and the presence of Someone who could guarantee healing.

We can argue theology and doctrines through all their various rabbit trails, but when real genuine need comes to the fore, the basic expressions of the heart take over and sweep all philosophizing off the table.

The request is made in the hearing of the crowd and the sight-seers among them are true to form in desiring to be on the scene for another miracle.

Mark 5:25
A woman who had had a hemorrhage for twelve years,

On the way to the home of Jairus, we have this almost out-of-place interjection of the woman with the hemorrhage. It is of course completely in context if we allow that the walk to Jairus' house could easily involve intervening events, but we are initially surprised by the lack of preliminary words that would help us see it as a parenthetic.

We have to take a moment to appreciate her condition and situation. It is not much different from the poor person in pre-Medicare America. Having limited resources and having to do without the necessities of life to afford whatever care one could get, it would be the utter depth of despair to realize that the physicians paid for with precious funds were either quacks or incompetent. Even if the best in their field, having become worse by them would be a depression considered unbearable by many today. It accounts for many who take their lives.

We highlight this to make it more vivid that Jesus is bringing real and genuine healing to some of the worst conditions of life - diseases and situations that spell a life sentence of abject misery in the souls of human beings.

People often criticize Christians in that they do not seem to address the most urgent needs around them, but opt for church programs, fellowship dinners and Bible studies that do little to directly help the needy. Here we see Jesus, a Dignitary from Heaven of the highest order, coming to earth, and rather than meeting with all the other notable men of high order, He comes immediately to the most needy and begins to relieve their suffering.

It is similar to the cries of the children in bondage that had come up to the Lord in the days of the Exodus. He says there that He surely has heard their cries and the first commandment of action to Moses was to begin the work that would relieve them.

We are given the privilege of actually hearing her thoughts. She has the faith that by only touching His garments, she could be healed. It is a sign of humbleness and certainly a low self-esteem that she did not consider herself worthy to have Him even stop and lay hands on her. In the midst of that lowliness came an extraordinary faith that her healing could be had by merely grasping His garment.

This certainly occasioned the proliferation of relics as touch points of miracles, even among Protestant faith healers who advertise holy water and handkerchiefs or merely placing one's hand on the radio. It is a distorted corruption of the faith that heals into a thing that heals and it only takes a careful re-acquaintance with this woman's account to see the error of it.

Mark 5:30
"Who touched My garments?"

Preceding this is the immediate knowledge that power had gone out from Him. Now this is curious because we would have thought that such power was in the total command and control of Christ and could not be dispensed without His intention. Meaning He would have to have known to whom it was given for it to be given.

In contrast, it is also not warranted to conclude that His healing power was a mechanism, like the bare ends of an electric cable, ready, with or without consent, to discharge its effects. It is more likely that the power He had to heal was directly related to His intimacy with His Father, that He was doing what the Father was doing, and in the case of the woman, the Father met her faith with genuine power through the Son that did not require Jesus' personal touch and will as the catalyst.

He certainly was involved enough to know that power had gone forth. This is an amazing window into the power Jesus held. It was true spiritual power acting so strongly and effectively as to take on the qualities of mechanical exchange – as something sensed as coursing through Him and exiting.

"You see the crowd pressing in on You, and You say, 'Who touched Me?'"

This is one of the lighter and almost comical interjections we have in the NT. With so many bodies in close contact, the question would be seen as incredible. It is also fascinating because this kind of incredulity gives us a personal continuity right back into the midst of the apostles, since we find ourselves saying this very kind of thing and in this very same manner in the here and now of modern life. It's like finding a modern expression cropping up in ancient times.

We certainly know better, but it helps us to understand that the apostles and the people of these distant times were not all that dissimilar to us.

Of course, what Jesus was asking was not who had touched Him per se, but who had touched Him to cause that kind of power to be dispensed?

"Daughter, your faith has made you well; go in peace and be healed of your affliction."

The woman's appearance and behavior were obvious, though these would not have been ultimately needed for Jesus to discover her.

We can only imagine the components that made up her fear and trembling. The healing alone would cause anyone to be in awe. Physical trembling would naturally attend the physical changes in her body. But there is also the awareness that she has immediately become the focus of public gaze, and she has also now effected the very thing she did not feel worthy enough to seek – the interruption and delay of Jesus on His path to divinely appointed ends in order to care for someone as lowly as her.

To everyone with low self-image, we have here a lesson of tremendous hope. Not only are you never too lowly for Jesus' touch, but you are in just the right place to exercise extraordinary faith. This lowly woman, immersed in the life-long echoes of self-deprecation, sounding their message in endless reprises, has found a high place of honor by being remembered down through the ages as a woman of exceptional faith. Nothing most of us have done in our own life could hope to count enough to have the equivalent distinction of being remembered in Scripture, yet we are tempted to deceive ourselves into thinking that we are somehow better off socially, financially, and physically than this woman.

Jesus makes it plain that it is not His garment nor even Him personally that has effected the healing, but her faith. Certainly, Jesus and the power He possessed was involved, but none could be accessed without her faith. This brings hope to all those who have come to live after His ascension and the passing of His apostles – that faith seen by the Father will open the outpouring of His grace.

Mark 5:35
they came from the house of the synagogue official, saying, "Your daughter has died; why trouble the Teacher anymore?"

We have here almost the screenplay for a movie. The apostle is telling the story *as the events unfold*, even to the detail of how one event overlaps into the next. We get back to the subject of this section by hearing of the arrival of people coming from Jairus' house in the midst of Jesus' conversation with the woman. That is exactly how things happen in real life. Events do not wait for their proper cue to come on stage, they occur in total disregard for other events. They have no obligation to be polite and wait their turn. This is the mark of genuine eyewitness testimony.

For Jairus, this had to be a moment not only of complete despair but perhaps even of some anger. Had Jesus not been delayed, He might have arrived in time to save the man's daughter. The woman had been healed but she was not dying. His daughter was on the verge of death and is now gone. Where is the vindication of simple priorities?

To those announcing the news, the case is closed. She is dead. They entertain no expectation that something can yet be done. They have not yet come to appreciate the ability of Jesus to remedy the impossible.

"Do not be afraid any longer, only believe."

In the midst of whatever feeling the man might have had, the most important thing to convey was that this was not the end of the story. Death had not had the final say.

This is what faith needs to engender in us - that life, the world, the machinations of the devil do not have the final say concerning us. *"All things are possible through Him who strengthens us."*

Mark 5:38
and He saw a commotion, and people loudly weeping and wailing.

Whether the girl was in fact dead or had become unconscious as to appear dead to the physicians methods of testing life made no difference to the friends and neighbors.. We find that it is the latter because Jesus explains she is not actually dead.

But to the mourners, she had all the signs, and things were in progress according to custom. In Jewish life, mourners were actually paid to weep and wail for the deceased, but in this case there was plenty of reason to shed genuine tears.

"The child has not died, but is asleep." We have no reason to conclude that Jesus was deceiving them, so it is safe to conclude that she had lapsed into a state that defied the imperfect techniques of determining remaining life.

"talitha kumi!"

Some versions have "talitha kum" but the word for arise is pronounced "koo-mee."

He has put out all the scoffers and ridiculers and included Peter, James and John, and the father and mother.

We learn by the provision of the translation of the Aramaic He spoke that talitha was not her name but his address to her as "little girl." It is also a rather loose translation into English because the words, "I say to you" are not represented in the Greek text. It is *"Little girl, get up."*

Immediately the girl got up and began to walk,

Again we are shown the utter thoroughness of Jesus' healing power. She is not brought to the state of having just had surgery and is in recovery where her ability to get up and walk might be weeks away. It is as though she has been remade from the beginning with damaged parts made new and in perfect working order.

for she was twelve years old seems to have no purpose in qualifying the description of her recovery. Her youth would have had nothing practically to do with her healing, since the woman had been made perfectly well also, having lost her youth. We shouldn't conclude that this is superfluous, but we are at a loss to know why it was added.

Mark 5:43
And He gave them strict orders that no one should know about this, and He said that something should be given her to eat.

His business is not yet complete. He must curtail any premature signaling to the Jewish authorities, which would be difficult with the crowd eventually seeing the results. Yet there was secrecy as to what actually happened in the room and His statement that she was merely sleeping did not necessitate an accounting that she had been raised from the dead.

For Him to also make sure she was given food shows His personal care for her beyond what would be expected. It is a tenderness and sensitivity that recognized all her needs, even though He certainly knew that this could be easily deduced by her parents.

Matthew 9:27-34
27 As Jesus went on from there, two blind men followed Him, crying out, "Have mercy on us, Son of David!" 28 When He entered the house, the blind men came up to Him, and Jesus said to them, "Do you believe that I am able to do this?" They said to Him, "Yes, Lord." 29 Then He touched their eyes, saying, "It shall be done to you according to your faith." 30 And their eyes were opened. And Jesus sternly warned them: "See that no one knows about this!" 31 But they went out and spread the news about Him throughout all that land.

32 As they were going out, a mute, demon-possessed man was brought to Him. 33 After the demon was cast out, the mute man spoke; and the crowds were amazed, and were saying, "Nothing like this has ever been seen in Israel." 34 But the Pharisees were saying, "He casts out the demons by the ruler of the demons." (Matthew 9:27-34)

Commentary

Matthew 9:27
two blind men followed Him, crying out, "Have mercy on us, Son of David!"

We are not told specifically where Jesus was going after leaving the house of Jairus, but He is followed by two blind men who implore Him to deliver them also. That they were blind means the account of what had just happened was being related to them by others and they were able to summon help to assist them in following Him. They were there like everyone else for the miracle anticipated with Jairus' daughter. Now filled with more faith than ever, it was their turn to seek the Master.

"Son of David" is an OT technical term for the Messiah, which would have marked these men as ideologically complicit in promoting Jesus in the eyes of the authorities. But they are not taken to task, simply because the authorities could not arrest and arraign every person with wild ideas.

The reason the Gospel distinguishes these men is not only because they possessed the faith to be healed, but because their faith went further in concluding that this was their nation's true Messiah as well. It means they were acquainted with His biblical qualifications, and that they believed God even when their leaders had long since given up such expectations in their own lifetimes.

"Do you believe that I am able to do this?"

It is not clear if the house is their own or someone else's, but it is in this house that they come to Him. His question seems superfluous since they have already asked for healing. But there is a certain formality of faith expression that Jesus is eliciting, a profession that is not left vaguely assumed but is made publicly patent for all to hear.

We must remember that in this crowd it is not like a biblical screen epic where all the actors are swooning in spiritual rapture, ala Cecil B. DeMille. There are folks standing around on the periphery with arms folded and skeptical countenances. If you asked them, the answer might be testy or argumentative; at the very least hesitant. But these men are being asked to show that it is a simple faith that is being looked for, a faith uncomplicated by sophisticated theologizing. Then men reply with a simple, "Yes Lord."

Another remarkable thing about these men is that they are wholly unaccustomed to the Jesus factor, yet have faith. Modern Christians don't note much surprise at men answering Jesus in this way. Were He to ask them, the answer is a no-brainer - the truth being so obvious. But we're completely accustomed to the reality and work of Jesus. He is not a foreigner to us, or a social oddity whom we contemplate with some wariness.

In these men's lives, Jesus was understandably too new, too abruptly injected into the normal course of human affairs, with little time to get used to Him as men normally build confidence. This is the very reason some stand aloof and skeptical. Yet these men set all that aside and see the visitation of God for what it is.

Healing and the petitioner's attitude in prayer are the most enigmatic things about divine healing one may attempt to understand. There are churches that teach that healing is almost a formula modeled after events like these and should be resurrected from the doldrums of complacency in modern times. Others are happy to leave it as a rare occurance at God's will but not something to actively pursue as a ministry. Still others teach that there is no circumstance possible in which it is not God's will to heal the sick, therefore the explanation to why some are not healed is due to some impediment to faith.

The latter is not without biblical support. Jesus criticized the disciples for not having faith to understand certain truths or to perform certain miracles. But the formulas for success all have their points of failure. People who don't seem to have much faith at all or certainly not very commendable attitudes are healed and folks with all the faith and loving hearts in the world are left in their sufferings.

But there is no doubt that faith in the petitioner or the one praying for the infirmed is pointed out by Jesus as the essential key. What we learn from experience is that God's will to heal is also a factor.

Jesus here in the gospels has a green light from the Father to heal and to thereby draw men close to the Kingdom. His will do heal is almost axiomatic.

In the modern church age, the will of the Father is still key but not assumed to be desired in all cases, as in a mechanism that provides healing. This is legitimately deduced by certain powerful works of His grace in people whom He has chosen not to heal but to make His Name great in their weaknesses. It is hard to believe someone like Joni Eareckson[33] does not wish to be delivered from her paraplegic condition (it is simply naïve to say this has never been a thought.) But she has come to so cherish what God has done with her in ministry by not choosing to heal that if asked to choose between a normal physical life without her ministry or her current condition with her ministry, the decision is clear and unmistakable.

Matthew 9:29
Then He touched their eyes, saying, "It shall be done to you according to your faith." And their eyes were opened.

Those of us with sight fail to adequately appreciate its restoration from darkness. The author remembers once visiting a blind Christian brother at his home for the first time. It was late when arriving, and as we talked, the house just kept getting darker and darker until you could barely make him out in the room. It became then and there a point of appreciation for what being blind meant. His darkness was so normal that the thought of turning on lights just wasn't part of his routine. That is a darkness so complete as to give us pause to think.

---

[33] Joni Eareckson-Tada, has remained permanently paralyzed from a swimming accident in 1967.

A moment before, these men were steeped in darkness, groping and ever learning to "see" by other means. A moment later, the time it took to merely touch their eyes, the entire visible world was theirs again. Again, Jesus was not healing corns on the feet, but serious and very real conditions that had enslaved people to prisons of misery and disability.

"See that no one knows about this!"

We have come to see this as the least obeyed command Jesus ever gave. We wonder why at this juncture Jesus bothers. Much of the explanation is wrapped up in the accountability to speak His desire whether men respected it or not. Jesus sincerely does wish them to be publicly cautious about their healing. But He is also not responsible for men's actions and He does not curtail His exhortations just because He knows full well they will do the exact opposite. His purpose is to speak His will and let all men heed it or not to their own accountability.

That doesn't mean Jesus pretended to be naïve. It means that He was already at three while other men were still back at one, and while the commandment was necessary, He has already taken man's reactions into account. His death and the manner of it were already known to Him. Rejection and disobedience were factored in.

Matthew 9:32
a mute, demon-possessed man was brought to Him.

Here continues the turning point in the attitude of the authorities that puts them into the category of blaspheming the Holy Spirit.

It is not clear whether the muteness was caused by the demon or if the demon was maintaining the enslavement that nature had bestowed. But two miracles resulted – the man was delivered from Satan and he was made to speak.

Hence the prompting to say, *"Nothing like this has ever been seen in Israel."*

But the Pharisees were saying, "He casts out the demons by the ruler of the demons."

Here is the reaction from the hardened heart. So cold and dead to the things of God, so used to the humanization of religion that God is effectively banished from their scene, these men have the dilemma of how to account for what they have seen with their own eyes.

Their self-deception has disabled them from the most obvious dictates of logic. The only semblance of pitiful reason left to them is to point toward the only supernatural power remaining a candidate – the work of that evil one. Yet it escapes them completely that to attribute the casting out of demons to the ruler of the demons is to have Satan cast out Satan, which utterly fails to register in any way as absurd. Such is the effect of bitterness and hatred on God's gift of reason.

Jesus had previously made this same observation to the embarrassment of their comrades a bit earlier at Matthew 12:22 above.

CHAPTER 8
Christ's Ministry – Year of Opposition

John 5:1-23
After these things there was a feast of the Jews, and Jesus went up to Jerusalem. 2 Now there is in Jerusalem by the sheep gate a pool, which is called in Hebrew Bethesda, having five porticoes. 3 In these lay a multitude of those who were sick, blind, lame, and withered, waiting for the moving of the waters; 4 for an angel of the Lord went down at certain seasons into the pool and stirred up the water; whoever then first, after the stirring up of the water, stepped in was made well from whatever disease with which he was afflicted.

5 A man was there who had been ill for thirty-eight years. 6 When Jesus saw him lying there, and knew that he had already been a long time in that condition, He said to him, "Do you wish to get well?" 7 The sick man answered Him, "Sir, I have no man to put me into the pool when the water is stirred up, but while I am coming, another steps down before me." 8 Jesus said to him, "Get up, pick up your pallet and walk." 9 Immediately the man became well, and picked up his pallet and began to walk. Now it was the Sabbath on that day.

10 So the Jews were saying to the man who was cured, "It is the Sabbath, and it is not permissible for you to carry your pallet." 11 But he answered them, "He who made me well was the one who said to me, `Pick up your pallet and walk.'" 12 They asked him, "Who is the man who said to you, `Pick up your pallet and walk'?" 13 But the man who was healed did not know who it was, for Jesus had slipped away while there was a crowd in that place.

14 Afterward Jesus found him in the temple and said to him, "Behold, you have become well; do not sin anymore, so that nothing worse happens to you." 15 The man went away, and told the Jews that it was Jesus who had made him well. 16 For this reason the Jews were persecuting Jesus, because He was doing these things on the Sabbath. 17 But He answered them, "My Father is working until now, and I Myself am working."

18 For this reason therefore the Jews were seeking all the more to kill Him, because He not only was breaking the Sabbath, but also was calling God His own Father, making Himself equal with God. 19 Therefore Jesus answered and was saying to them, "Truly, truly, I say to you, the Son can do nothing of Himself, unless it is something He sees the Father doing; for whatever the Father does, these things the Son also does in like manner. 20 "For the Father loves the Son, and shows Him all things that He Himself is doing; and the Father will show Him greater works than these, so that you will marvel. 21 "For just as the Father raises the dead and gives them life, even so the Son also gives life to whom He wishes. 22 "For not even the Father judges anyone, but He has given all judgment to the Son, 23 so that all will honor the Son even as they honor the Father. He who does not honor the Son does not honor the Father who sent Him. (John 5:1-23)

Commentary

John 5:1
After these things there was a feast of the Jews, and Jesus went up to Jerusalem.

This account appears here in our chronology much later than its early position in John because it occurs in Jerusalem, and we have just seen all the forgoing work and ministry of Jesus occurring in the Galilee.

The feast is not identified and we have no information about the season that might lend a clue. We do find out that the healing of the man at the pool takes place on the Sabbath, but this does not obligate us to a feast like the Passover. (Besides, there are three Passovers mentioned elsewhere in John, to which a fourth cannot be reasonably added.)

Now there is in Jerusalem by the sheep gate a pool, which is called in Hebrew Bethesda, having five porticoes.

The sheep gate is that mentioned by Nehemiah (3:1.) At the time of Jesus, sheep were slaughtered within the temple precincts, therefore the sheep for those feasts were conveyed through this gate in preparation.

The location of this gate and the pool is problematic, since archaeologists have located it variously on the north, east and south sides of the Temple. The best of these is that on the N, which is also called Stephen's gate, near St. Anne's Church. The best basis for this is that Nehemiah is traditionally said to have commenced his work on the N side of the Temple and worked his way around the complex. The Sheep Gate was the first accomplishment, per Neh 3:1. The remains of the pool have not been found, but it's suggested reconstruction along with the gate can be seen on the N side of the now famous model of the city in Jerusalem.

The porches mentioned were actually 'porticos' (Gk. *'stoa'*) rather than our idea of a front stoop. They were slabs of stone surrounding the pool over which a set of arched openings from supporting columns was arranged

The pool is alternately called Bezetha and Bethsaida, but Bethesda is closer to the Hebrew *beth chesda*. In Hebrew, the 'ch' sound is a harsh guttural for our 'h.' To anglicize it would render *beth hesda*.

waiting for the moving of the waters;

It is likely that the porticos were in fact built because of this very phenomenon. They provided a ready place for people to slip into the water considering their various conditions.

What is of keen interest is that God had made such an arrangement – that an angel would disturb the water at set times and that this would be the means of Him dispensing grace to the sick. If He was inclined to heal, why not simply do so and avoid the disappointments of trying to be first, healing but one person at a time?

We are of course without warrant to judge the Almighty. That He has the power to heal and all are not healed is simply a fact in the Bible for which He offers no explanation, except that such things come by faith. Faith is necessary for healing but faith does not obligate healing. That healing is available at all is a blessing, considering the alternative. So we are encouraged to see it as such instead of asking why there isn't more.

Interesting here also is the interface between spirit and material substance, that an incorporial thing can have a corporial effect on the water.

John 5:5
A man was there who had been ill for thirty-eight years. Jesus saw . . and knew

This particular man had been disadvantaged by the desperate selfishness of others who had always been able to get in before him, which means he had personally been present and witnessed a number of stirrings over the years. His condition obviously made him perennially slower and no one had proven to be compassionate enough to let him have his moment at their expense.

"Jesus .. knew" We here have insight into the intimate knowledge God has of our everyday affairs. He is not unaware of our trials and struggles, our disappointments and frustrations with the simple business of living. He knew the thirty-eight years of affliction personally and intimately.

"Do you wish to get well?"

Again, we have Jesus asking the obvious, but for the purpose of engendering that moment in time where faith is clearly the subject in view to enact the grace required. The man does not answer with a direct, "Yes Lord" but it is understood by his explanation that he cannot get into the water fast enough.

Some have complained that this man could have arranged for others to assist him with getting in first, but this is not as simple as it sounds. The coordination to move another person is always more cumbersome than a person who can move by themselves. And the others at the pool would certainly anticipate the meaning of these arrangements and act accordingly.

So in the end it's the problem of desperate selfishness which illness can create in the sick - a desperation that sees no one else but themselves and their needs.

John 5:8
"Get up, pick up your pallet and walk."

Jesus here bypasses the whole arrangement with the waters, and simply heals the man directly. The man's patience in not giving up hope in his thirty-eight years of trial and error is rewarded by a healing that dispenses with the need for the pool and its miracle entirely.

He is made so well that he can be told to carry his pallet. His *pallet* was the wooden platform on which he was accustomed to sit to avoid constant contact with the streets and other surfaces. It would have been the equivalent of a chair, which despite not being terribly comfortable, was essentially a means of not having to sit on the ground.

So the Jews were saying to the man who was cured, "It is the Sabbath, and it is not permissible for you to carry your pallet."

Here is where legalism reveals its Achilles heel. It has no room for compassion and love. The Jews who legislated the Law were technocrats (and hypocrites in the bargain.) They found it easy to recite the dictates of the Law from the antiseptic environment of academia. It mattered little that the person addressed was in misery or full of the joy of the Lord. The Law was the Law. And of course it was the Law for everyone else. Let their own lives come to misery or complication and the exemptions became rampant.

The specific issue was the doing of work on the Sabbath; and carrying a pallet exceeded the small exertions that constituted unlawful Sabbath work.

John 5:12
"Who is the man who said to you, `Pick up your pallet and walk'?"

It is his explanation that he was commanded to do so that gains their attention to discover precisely whom? That person will have committed the greater sin.

Interestingly, we learn that Jesus had not revealed His name nor was the man yet acquainted with His notoriety. Perhaps by design, the man could not therefore feed this mini-inquisition of the Jews, which turned out initially to be a rather more effective alternative to simply commanding him to tell no one.

But this was short lived as we see in a moment.

". . do not sin anymore, so that nothing worse happens to you." The man went away, and told the Jews that it was Jesus who had made him well.

This conversation is later in the temple when Jesus comes upon the man and commends his good health. This verse is often used to justify affliction as a penalty for sin. Job's counselors certainly believed in this principle.

We can't avoid the conclusion that affliction can be the temporal result of sin, but we must avoid the idea that all affliction is a sign of the displeasure of God. Jesus in another incident will ask whether the young man born blind sinned or his parents? His answer is neither, but that he was made blind for this very moment of glorifying God.

So it is not 'either/or' and certain conditions have nothing to do with sin. In this man's case, there is a valid connection between his physical condition (or the threat of worse) and his spiritual condition. So we are not entitled to walk away freely with the idea that God will not visit us with afflictions in relation to our sins. Pain and suffering are sometimes described as the body's language for telling us something is physically amiss. It is reasonable and according to experience that God would use those signals for spiritual issues also. It certainly commands our attention like nothing else.

The man, now knowing Jesus as the healer, *"told the Jews that it was Jesus who had made him well."* We mustn't infer that he desired to get Jesus in trouble, but rather to complete the full witness to these same men of what God had done. It is born out of a naivite that all God-fearing men will rejoice at the visitation of God.

John 5:18
For this reason the Jews were persecuting Jesus, because He was doing these things on the Sabbath.

Not physical persecution as with Christians in Rome, but a frequent exchange of vitriol and accusations, and the testing by questions to entrap Him. The other forms of this persecution would have been their public denunciations among the people and their secret planning to find ways to do away with Him.

As for their direct acts of persecution, we seeing their most notorious example in the following. They ask him why He did what was unlawful on the Sabbath.

"My Father is working until now, and I Myself am working."

We wonder how this would be a direct answer to their charge? But He is explaining that the same God who gave them the Sabbath is working His will also in the very acts they are criticizing. How can the lawgiver be criticized when demonstrating what true obedience to the command means?

This cuts them with a double-edged sword. They are cut one way by the sheer force of the evident miracle performed, which they must somehow now struggle to explain or acknowledge. They are cut the other way by Him calling God his own Father – *because He not only was breaking the Sabbath, but also was calling God His own Father, making Himself equal with God.*

This was more than just calling Himself a member of God's chosen nation – a son of God. The Jews understood this to mean blasphemy in their frame of reference because despite Scripture calling all men of faith "sons," a Jew hesitated to speak this of himself as a point of personal bragging because it came so close to the technical phrase "Son of God" which meant equality with God. The same applied to Daniel's term "Son of Man." These were technical terms for the Messiah or someone blessed with the deity of God.

"Truly, truly, I say to you, the Son can do nothing of Himself, unless it is something He sees the Father doing;

Here, Jesus opens up publicly about the intimate relationship the Son has with the Father. It is an explanation of everything Jesus is doing and a vindication of His work. It is not work done of Himself but has the very mark of the Father through and through, something true believers will recognize.

And it is born entirely out of love from the Father to the Son.

John 5:20
"For the Father loves the Son, and shows Him all things that He Himself is doing; and the Father will show Him greater works than these, so that you will marvel.

We almost get the idea of a viewing screen in which Jesus sees the Father out ahead of Him doing a work, and Jesus then emulates it like a son emulates his father in a building project out in the garage. We can get too mechanical in this characterization by pondering how God is doing the work first, yet the healing is not effected until Jesus performs it. But much of our dilemma comes from implying too much western specificity in eastern phrases - *"I do what I see my father doing"* can simply be an ancient way of saying He is doing what He foresees the father doing in Him. It does not necessitate that the Father must physically do something first before the Son.

Much of this conceptualization is bound up in perceiving the future. Jesus, in essence, sees ahead of time the will and desire of the Father working in the Son and when He says that these are the things the Son is doing, He means that He is living out the actuality of what His foreknowledge sees.

This plays into our feeble attempts to understand predestination and foreknowledge. It can be asked if the future determines what is predestined or does what is predestined determine the future?

In terms of sheer logical (not temporal) order, His predestining logically occurs first by an act of His sovereign will because His will is independent of time. The effecting of His will is then available to be seen by His foreknowledge. He sees then what He previously decreed.

The reason for this order theologically is that if one truly sees the future, foreknowledge cannot exclude knowledge of the things predestined, so predestination cannot follow foreknowledge but must precede it. Foreknowledge sees what the future is, but predestination determines what comprises that which is seen.

Whether we grasp this fully or even correctly does not undermine the facts being conveyed – that Jesus is in someway seeing ahead the things the Father wills to do and they are described as present (He does what the Father *is* doing not what He will do); and Jesus is accomplishing those very same things.

"For just as the Father raises the dead and gives them life, even so the Son also gives life to whom He wishes.

Jesus is here attributing things to Himself that have been long understood as clearly belonging exclusively to God. The power to give life and to judge. He is also so bold as to say that the Father does no judging that is not now in the hands of the Son.

The time has come for Jesus to confront traditional Judaism head on, and the dialog that begins here is a commencement of that thrust.

John 5:23
He who does not honor the Son does not honor the Father who sent Him.

This is the chief rub of the Christian message then as now. We must accept Jesus if we desire to honor God. For the Jews, it came down to their tradition and the person of Jesus. For people today, it comes down to Jesus against all other contenders. But the indictment is clear: he who does not honor the Son does not honor the Father.

That is why the Gospel is unpopular today, because it is intolerant and narrow in its exclusivity. We find this unpopular because democracy and humanistic philosophies have taught us that things ought to be fair and equitable for all. Telling the other religions they are illegitimate has been banished from today's vocabulary. The truth of it is, of course, wrapped up in the integrity of the claimant, which is why the Resurrection is so key to the Gospel account. Paul says that without it we are of all people most to be pitied. (I Cor 15:19)

John 5:24-36
24 "Truly, truly, I say to you, he who hears My word, and believes Him who sent Me, has eternal life, and does not come into judgment, but has passed out of death into life. 25 "Truly, truly, I say to you, an hour is coming and now is, when the dead will hear the voice of the Son of God, and those who hear will live. 26 "For just as the Father has life in Himself, even so He gave to the Son also to have life in Himself; 27 and He gave Him authority to execute judgment, because He is the Son of Man. 28 "Do not marvel at this; for an hour is coming, in which all who are in the tombs will hear His voice, 29 and will come forth; those who did the good deeds to a resurrection of life, those who committed the evil deeds to a resurrection of judgment.

30 "I can do nothing on My own initiative. As I hear, I judge; and My judgment is just, because I do not seek My own will, but the will of Him who sent Me. 31 "If I alone testify about Myself, My testimony is not true. 32 "There is another who testifies of Me, and I know that the testimony which He gives about Me is true. 33 "You have sent to John, and he has testified to the truth. 34 "But the testimony which I receive is not from man, but I say these things so that you may be saved. 35 "He was the lamp that was burning and was shining and you were willing to rejoice for a while in his light. 36 "But the testimony which I have is greater than the testimony of John; for the works which the Father has given Me to accomplish--the very works that I do--testify about Me, that the Father has sent Me. (John 5:24-36)

Commentary

John 5:24
24 " he who hears My word, and believes Him who sent Me, has eternal life, and does not come into judgment, but has passed out of death into life.

Job asked, *"If a man dies, will he live again?"* (Job 14:14) The question of what happens after death has pervaded all human history but was given the most promise in Israel, where some evidence of life after death was made known from time to time.

While we may question what the witch of Endor conjured up to appear as Samuel, the idea that men had an existence beyond the grave was evident. The concept of Sheol or Hades had been long since traditional by Jacob's time, David spoke of going to his dead infant son, and Elisha saw Elijah taken up by the chariot to that place of abode in the next life.

Still, each man might question what their personal fate would be after death, not certain that theirs was as sure as the saints of old. In the time of Jesus it was a wait and see affair. Men were bound to the Law and its judgments. They could only strive to keep it and hope their efforts moved the heart of God to kindness and mercy.

Here, Jesus comes to them and says, *"he who hears My word and believes . .has eternal life . . not judgment . . but has passed from death to life."*

Yet His work on the Cross had not yet been effected, and it is clear that by it were all men to be saved who believe in its efficacy to pay the penalty due for all sin. So how does Jesus proclaim that men who believe have eternal life at the moment He speaks and are not to come to judgment?

The Cross was the means of forgiving sin and without its work we cannot enter Heaven, for nothing unclean may enter there, and being unforgiven of sin keeps one unclean.

But faith is the ingredient that actually saves and it can be seen apart from the work of the Cross in terms of function. Post Calvary, one must believe in the sacrifice of the Cross as a point of faith, but one can also believe in Christ, without specific reference to the Cross, i.e. as Son of God; as He who brings spiritual union with the Father. This is not a preference to ignore the Cross (for Christ can't be separated from it) but it is a faith that can come to love Him as Son independent of understanding the Cross. It is to love the Son because He is the Son. Axiomatically, all would come to also embrace the importance of the Cross.

When Christ taught and healed people and commended faith and acknowledgement of the coming Kingdom, He did so without reference to the Cross. When He told people their faith had saved them, the Cross was nowhere in their immediate view. Their faith in Him, what He could do and who the Father was served all the needs that freed them from bondage.

The *process* would include both the exercise of faith and the work of the Cross to satisfy the demands of the Law. The Cross was inevitable, so focus on faith in His words did not nullify the need for the Cross. It was decreed to occur. It was therefore more a matter of timing. Faith prior to the Cross was always viewed by the Father as being benefited and completed by the impending work of the Cross. But it may not have been functionally in focus for believers.

What is important however in these words to His hearers was that assurance of participation in the life to come was a done deal if they simply believed sincerely in his words and on the One who sent Him. Gone are all the worries about one's score card with the Law. Gone is the anxiety that one might be self-deceived and end up in eternal misery on some unforeseen technicality.

The power of this declaration was in Jesus' character and persona as a man come from God. The miracles attested to His having at the very least an "in" with God and a command over God's powers. Combine this with the incomparable wisdom of His teaching and you gain a tremendous confidence that if anyone knew the truth about the getting of eternal life, it would be this man.

This is the essence of the "good news" of the Gospel – that God has visited men and opened a way into Heaven for faithful men that relieves the perennial predicament with the Law.

He adds that such a person will *bypass* the judgment all men feared and the transition is characterized as a simple change *"out of death into life."* Like moving from one room into the next.

This was a completely radical idea, but intriguingly welcome. Jesus was breaking all the molds, but in a way that did not repulse but rather drew men toward God.

John 5:25
"Truly, truly, I say to you, an hour is coming and now is, when the dead will hear the voice of the Son of God, and those who hear will live.

This had a clever double meaning. To the everyday, unsophisticated, mundane person it would have meant that those in the grave would hear the voice and come to life – a promise of the resurrection. That this was not the only meaning should not be construed as being unintended at all. It is true that the dead shall hear the voice at Christ's coming and shall rise (I Thess 4:16)

But it is also true that those dead in their sins and in the legalism of the Law would hear Christ's earthly voice and come to newness of life.

"For just as the Father has life in Himself, even so He gave to the Son also to have life in Himself;

Here we have a little window into the self-sustaining essence of God Himself – the uncaused cause. We may regress as much as we wish in the cause and effect analysis of the world but we eventually must posit an uncaused cause – something for which there is no prior cause to effect its existence.

The Father is here described as having life in Himself, meaning no other gave it to Him. Likewise, the Father made the Son.

Now this seems to be contradictory because life in the Son is said to be *"given"* by the Father, so it would be dependent on that giving. Yet our doctrine of the Trinity explains that the Son is eternal with the Father, so it is not possible to say there was a point when the Son did not have life and was subsequently given life by the Father. So the very fact that the Scripture here says that life was given cannot be forced to mean dependence. It is a non-technical, non-analytical way of describing of the intense unity with Father and Son, that if the Father has life in Himself, so also does the Son.

John 5:27
and He gave Him authority to execute judgment, because He is the Son of Man.

That authority is bound up in Him being Messiah – the anointed one of Daniel's prophecies. Messiah is to come and make all things right between man and God, to restore that which was lost. Isaiah's prophecies are full of this idea that when He comes He will make the crooked paths straight.

John the Baptist cited Isaiah in terms of judgment when he quoted, *"His fan is in His hand, and He will thoroughly clear His threshing floor;"* (Isaiah 41:6)

" for an hour is coming, in which all who are in the tombs will hear His voice, . . . those who did the good deeds to a resurrection of life, those who committed the evil deeds to a resurrection of judgment.

So Jesus does reinforce the plain sense idea of the resurrection by predicting the assurance of the two great destinies.

Some have concluded a doctrine of works for determining which, but we need to understand the mode of speech being employed before making specific doctrine from these words.

First, it is very general; a case of describing as simply as possible the two great classes and their destinies. The just will rise to life and the evil to judgment. The mention of "deeds" is included to clarify that these ends are the individual's own doing, something for which he is responsible. So there are two resurrections – one to life and one to death, and they have a relationship to the deeds of righteousness or deeds of evil, respectively.

But we read elsewhere that the good deeds that bring a resurrection unto life cannot be had without faith in Christ, that nothing lastingly good can be seen as such without Him. So an attitude that one can work good deeds that beget a resurrection to life while ignoring Christ is forestalled.

In contrast, while salvation is by grace through faith and not of works, this does not preclude a judgment based on works. There will, in fact, be a resurrection unto such a judgment for the wicked, who have rejected grace and preferred to take their chances with God according to their deeds.

We hear this routinely among friends and acquaintances – *"I'm a good person in both my family and in society. God will weigh the good against the bad and I see myself going to Heaven."*

Those who prefer this as the basis for their own judgment will be accommodated.

John 5:30
"I can do nothing on My own initiative. As I hear, I judge; and My judgment is just, because I do not seek My own will, but the will of Him who sent Me.

Here we have absolute unity and subjection combined. There is an independence implied – that He could work on His own initiative if He desired it. But He prefers the will of His Father.

We have no real example of this in family life today. Even though a young child may have his father as his hero and mentor, he does not desire to only think and will the things of his dad. He has an independent life that merely mixes in with his love and adoration of his dad, so it is hard for us to relate completely with what Jesus is telling us about His Father.

Much is wrapped up in our inability to understand the Trinity and the depth of the interpersonal relationships between Father, Son and Holy Spirit.

We can learn and apply as much as possible by seeing this as the model of unity and aspiring to it. There is a phrase popular today: "WWJD – *what would Jesus do?*" It's a catch word and as such may have its day and join the fate of other catch words, but it captures the idea here and elsewhere that we are to take our personal thoughts captive and compare them to the will of God for our lives.

To merely ask what God might think about X is something many Christians fail to do in everyday life. Many people accept jobs, choose their mates and invest money without this consideration at all and wonder why life is not fulfilling or is filled with troubles.

The rub will always come in the statement: "do not seek your own will." It is the most natural outcome in life to have our desires and make plans for our lives. Everyone else is busy doing this and expects us to be doing the same. The bulk of conversation is about the progress and assessment of those very things. To resent being asked to give up all such things and submit rather to those things desired of God is endemic to the flesh. To prefer only the things of the Father is endemic to the life in the Spirit. Hence, the enmity between flesh and Spirit, the war between man and God.

John 5:31
"If I alone testify about Myself, My testimony is not true. 32 "There is another who testifies of Me, and I know that the testimony which He gives about Me is true.

It is hard to embrace the idea that Jesus could testify on His own and it not be true. It gives us some insight into the complex nature of the incarnation. He is not referring to anything substantive in His relationship as Son. That is an intimacy that could never be threatened by independence.

He is rather referring to that mysterious mixture of humanity and divinity described in creeds as "fully man and fully God." He was tempted as we are, so He was also tempted to work and speak on His own authority apart from that of His Father.

The other who testifies of Him is both His Father and John the Baptist. In essence this is the same testimony, for John was speaking the self-same testimony.

You have sent to John, and he has testified to the truth. 34 "But the testimony which I receive is not from man, but I say these things so that you may be saved.

This may appear denigrating to John's testimony but it is said to contrast the very different natures between John and Christ. John was a man through and through, Jesus the incarnated Son of God. This is to contrast the men and their sources.

When the people went to John they were receiving witness through a man with all his limitations and incapacities. John rightly quoted from the prophets, again other men blessed of God. But no one attributed to him a self-contained authority.

When coming to Jesus, they are not receiving from a mere man, but from the Son of God, whose intimacy with God cannot be compared. With Jesus, they distinguished Him as a man having authority. This is because Jesus did not quote OT men as the routine basis for His own teaching, but presented new insights not taught before; and those coming from His Father.

John 5:35-36
"He was the lamp . . "But the testimony which I have is greater than the testimony of John;

This is not condescending. John himself knew the difference - *"I must decrease, He must increase."* Jesus points to the works to distinguish Himself from being characterized as just another John the Baptist. Remember He is addressing the Pharisees who are challenging His authority, especially to re-interpret the Sabbath.

Jesus is appealing to them to consider the nature of the works, and that a greater Person than John is here.

John 5:37-47
37 "And the Father who sent Me, He has testified of Me. You have neither heard His voice at any time nor seen His form. 38 "You do not have His word abiding in you, for you do not believe Him whom He sent. 39 " You search the Scriptures because you think that in them you have eternal life; it is these that testify about Me; 40 and you are unwilling to come to Me so that you may have life. 41 "I do not receive glory from men; 42 but I know you, that you do not have the love of God in yourselves. 43 "I have come in My Father's name, and you do not receive Me; if another comes in his own name, you will receive him. 44 "How can you believe, when you receive glory from one another and you do not seek the glory that is from the one and only God? 45 "Do not think that I will accuse you before the Father; the one who accuses you is Moses, in whom you have set your hope. 46 "For if you believed Moses, you would believe Me, for he wrote about Me. 47 "But if you do not believe his writings, how will you believe My words?" (John 5:37-47)

Commentary

"And the Father who sent Me, He has testified of Me. You have neither heard His voice at any time nor seen His form.

Jesus now turns deliberately critical of their spiritual failings. Rather than positive phrases of faith and love we find Him saying things like, *"You haven't heard . . you don't believe . . you don't have . . . you are unwilling."*

For some this is uncharacteristic of love. We often complain back to those who adopt similarly frank words that they are being negative in a culture where that is now gloomish and antiquated. There are even psychologists today who would criticize Jesus for repeatedly and inappropriately using the "you" word, signifying verboten accusatory remarks.

It is a fact that people fall into two great camps, the optimists and the pessimists, each decrying the outlook of the other. But here we find Jesus having a balance of both. There is a time for encouragement and a time for chastisement. A time for fun and a time for the unfun aspects of hard work. On the human plane, we abuse the balance and so there are whole movements to do away with the negative side altogether without taking into consideration that it is still needful.

We have only to look at what a child becomes after being raised by parents who believe that saying "No" is injurious and harmful. We have only to look elsewhere at our education system where making sure little Johnny feels good about himself is more important than whether Johnny acquires the hard and sometimes unpleasant discipline of actually learning something. Rather than studying what Einstein thought or learned, kids are taught to investigate how Einstein felt [34] And primarily because one would have to say no to something that was more fun.

"And the Father who sent Me, He has testified of

He begins with a statement of who is really validating His words and work. It is a call to examine and contemplate the evidence which the Father has condescended to include with the message of righteousness.

How has the Father actually testified of Jesus, that they could he held accountable for it?

From first to last, everything about Jesus was exceptional – the kinds of things which separately might be explained away, but together were impossible to rationalize as coincidence.

His birth was extraordinary, being accompanied by claims of manifestations of angels to shepherds. Magi attended the days near his birth with gifts unsolicited by his parents or any dignitary sending word to far off places. The scribes connected the dots for Herod that being born in Bethlehem had import to prophetic circumstances.

His connection with John's ministry at the Jordan and the fulfillment of those prophecies, followed by the unending reports of miracles, were testimonies in language that ignorant and intelligent people could easily comprehend, that He was of God.

The sheer wisdom of His teaching, despite it being out of sorts with their convolution of it, would have been inwardly recognized as true, though desperately feared of being given any credence.

Paul talks about God having made Himself known to every man, even to those who lived without exposure to the special revelation of His Word. It is that same witness that has occurred in every man who encountered Jesus. The Spirit testified, "This man is of Me" and some let it come out in audible speech while others were checked by the practiced sophistication of man's thinking which said, "But he is not of our party."

"You have neither heard His voice at any time nor seen His form."

He begins his rebuke with the facts about what they think they have heard. If Paul is true, then God did speak to them. But part of hearing is recognition and He is here saying, more than the act of perception, they have not heard - being so hardened as not to even recognize. It is really about recognition which is brought forward by adding mention of not recognizing the form of God in their midst. As men of faith they ought to be able to recognize God among them, but they are hardened by their tradition to see God only in those forms they have determined for themselves.

So this does not nullify Paul but emphasizes that by their own choice they have come to no longer recognize His voice or His form of appearance.

"You do not have His word abiding in you, for you do not believe Him whom He sent.

Faith is more than believing *in* God. It must also *believe* God, as in believe what He says. Believing in our parents is not the same as believing them. To not believe God is what makes it impossible for that Word to live in them.

This is important for Christians – that the Word lives in us. It can be approached academically, where it is viewed as Christian literature, or even as just so many platitudes or nice words spoken in the reverberant ambiance of a comfortable and ornately adorned sanctuary. But for it to live in us (abide), it must be taken

---

[34] Sykes, <u>Dumbing Down Our Kids,</u> St. Martin's Press, New York, (1995), p. 39

into the life as a rule of action, self-control and purpose. It must be consulted and made to constrain what we do and think and believe. This, the Pharisees, had long since rationalized away.

You search the Scriptures because you think that in them you have eternal life; it is these that testify about Me;

It is like saying, "What good does it do to master the Scriptures if when God comes down to men you cannot recognize Him?" Their motives were right – to seek the truth about eternal life. But with all things there is more to searching than accumulating the facts. It is the seeking and getting of the wisdom between the facts that gives them meaning and understanding.

Had they done this, they would have understood that the Law was designed to make the soul bankrupt of itself in meeting the needs of that perennial predicament of obedience. It was designed to drive the soul to the mercy of God. And in that plea come all the Scriptures that proclaim that God had made ready a sacrifice eternally complete and thoroughly satisfying in the person of one who would come in the anointing of prophecies and promises foretold, who would give His life as a ransom.

There they would have found the secret to acquiring eternal life in the Kingdom by being ready to recognize its King. This is why Jesus connected so profoundly the Kingdom to the King and the failure of the Jews in having one without the other.

"and you are unwilling to come to Me so that you may have life."

At first this seems like a tall order for people who were not expecting Him nor that He would be the key to that life. But He has just stated that such things were revealed in the Scriptures, had they been listening and seeking with the openness to God that is commended of all men.

This holding them accountable for the revelation which was made known seems a bit harsh for us now that the NT has come, because for them this meant the Old Testament, and in it such things were more latent than patent, more figurative and metaphoric than in plain speak.

But there were those in ages past who got it. Jesus said of Abraham that he *"rejoiced to see day and he saw it . ."* (John 8:56). That means that Abraham could see in the revelation thus far given the truths that would have to await many thousands of years to be realized.

It is reasoned that the moment to which Jesus refers is that moment when Abraham raised the knife over his son Isaac so as to render him fit as a blood sacrifice. He had earlier been given the insight to say, *"God will provide Himself the sacrifice"*, a piece of wording that did not refer to Isaac as the victim. When we consider the lamb then caught in the thicket as a substitute, the fact that this sacrifice occurred within sight of Mt. Moriah, perhaps within sight the future place of Christ's Cross, this makes his understanding of how God would reconcile the world to Himself all the more vivid. Hence, Jesus says rightly that Abraham saw it and rejoiced.

These were testimonies that the Jews read over and over and were expected to likewise "get."

Instead they are filled with the self-righteousness of an engineered system of their own making. We can only imagine the indignation and inner rage at being told that they must "come" to a man whom they despised and repudiated, even more, to regard Him and the One who has the key to granting the eternal life they sought. This would have been almost intolerable, and certainly fueled their desire to destroy Him.

"I do not receive glory from men; but I know you, that you do not have the love of God in yourselves.

The "but" here is almost a "because", as in: *"I do not receive glory from men;* **because** *I know you, that you do not have the love of God in yourselves.* Without this, it is difficult to connect the two sentences – why not receiving glory from men is connected with the fact that he knows them.

Men are called to glorify God and by extension the Son. It is not that this imparts Heavenly glory as in light, majesty, radiance, beauty and holiness to Him, but that it points other men to the proclamation of these qualities. Men glorify God by proclaiming the things of God that catch other men's attention and promote the same in them. The essence of His glory is part of Him innately by being the Son of the Father.

So here, Jesus is saying that He does not receive the glory men seek to have from each other – *"glory from men"* – because He knows men (and these men in particular) that they do not have that which would allow them to bestow the glory He would receive, namely, they lack the love of God in the first place.

"I have come in My Father's name, and you do not receive Me; if another comes in his own name, you will receive h

– an ironic contrast when dealing with the people of God. They ought to receive someone coming in the Father's name and not him who would come in his own. But they have it precisely backwards – that their authentication is in a man's name, as in the great rabbis and schools of interpretation like Hillel or Shammai. These they heed with real solemnity and authority. But a man coming in the name of God is eyed with suspicion.

Now today this is rather expected, since we are almost immediately put on guard by someone claiming to be the messenger of God. And justifiably so from the many charlatans and quacks that have led so many of the gullible astray. In Jesus' time, this was more of an anomaly due to the presence of a much tighter scrutiny by officials. This is to say that charlatans with the deliberate intent to deceive would know ahead of time their chances of success, whereas today the freedom to deceive unchecked is accepted as just a phenomenon of our free society.

"How can you believe, when you receive glory from one another and you do not seek the glory that is from the one and only God?

This is perhaps the oldest statement of the "good ol' boy" principle we could find. Power in ancient life, as now, was all about gamesmanship and less about altruistic principles of making one's nation great or serving its people. It is part of the corruption that power begets. We become less philanthropic and more intrigued by how much more power and wealth we can get by craft and sheer knack. It becomes a game because it becomes an issue of who wins – more specifically, "How can I win?" This includes having the right friends and benefactors – *"you receive glory from one another."*

Judaism had fallen into this deception but was blinded by the covering of being proclaimed the chosen of God. The system had subtely come to own them in their zeal to serve God. Where humility and modesty would have normally checked greed and power-mongering, it was being done to further the will and purposes of God, so all too soon the ends began to justify the means.

For Jesus to make this statement was to almost clap one's hands in a crowd, so as to alert everyone that the original motives and goals are here not there – that we should be seeking the approval of God and all the requirements that includes.

And isn't this the way of Satan in deceiving us, by degrees; until we wake up and find we are at odds with God and have failed to notice the change?

"Do not think that I will accuse you before the Father; the one who accuses you is Moses, in whom you have set your hope.

The chief claim of the Jews is that they purpose to follow Moses, which was commanded of God in Scripture. And they cannot be criticized for having this as their aim; they are not out of line and they are counting on Jesus not daring to deny this either. In this they believe they have their key trump card, ready for use at the proper time.

Jesus anticipates this. It was tried with John the Baptist, but using the case of Abraham. It failed to be effective there because John took it a step further and charged them that they ought to bear the fruits worthy of being his offspring.

Here Jesus makes the same point with Moses and for more important reasons. First, the Jews confronting Jesus were not claiming their relationship with Abraham, but their relationship with Moses This is because doctrinally Abraham spoke little that would serve their needs as pertaining to Pharisaism. But keeping Moses was the very essence of the Pharisee and furthermore had the commandment to do according to Moses more than to do according to Abraham.

But worry about engaging this argument does not bother Jesus because Moses and all the OT had been purposed to prepare for the Son and to uphold the truths of God which He not only knew but fully embodied. How then could Moses be a threat or a rebuke? In fact, in Moses were the necessary things that would have taught them to expect Him – *"For the Lord thy God shall raise up out of the midst of thee a prophet, like unto Me from among thy brethren. And unto him ye shall hearken." (Deut 18:15)*

It is interesting that when Jesus was questioned by the Jews early on, they asked if he was *that prophet* (John 1:21), meaning the one spoken of by Moses.

Hence, the rebuke, *"For if you believed Moses, you would believe Me, for he wrote about Me."*

"But if you do not believe his writings, how will you believe My words?"

Here is of course the fundamental problem. It is not a case of not reverencing or knowing the words of Moses; these they knew better than any race on earth. But they did not believe them so as to be constrained by them.

There was a recent article in a Bible college magazine on the "D" word becoming the new dirty word among Christians – meaning D for doctrine. It discussed the emphasis on orthodoxy over the last century and the neglect of *orthopraxy* – the putting into practice what orthodoxy teaches.

It was the same with the Jews of Jesus' day. It was their failure to put into life the words of Moses that disabled them from believing His words.

Mark 6:1-6a, Matt 9:35-38, Matthew 10:1-4, Mark 6:7, Matthew 10:5-14

Jesus went out from there and came into His hometown; and His disciples followed Him. 2 When the Sabbath came, He began to teach in the synagogue; and the many listeners were astonished, saying, "Where did this man get these things, and what is this wisdom given to Him, and such miracles as these performed by His hands? 3 "Is not this the carpenter, the son of Mary, and brother of James and Joses and Judas and Simon? Are not His sisters here with us?" And they took offense at Him. 4 Jesus said to them, "A prophet is not without honor except in his hometown and among his own relatives and in his own household." 5 And He could do no miracle there except that He laid His hands on a few sick people and healed them. 6 And He wondered at their unbelief. And He was going around the villages teaching. (Mark 6:1-6a)

35 Jesus was going through all the cities and villages, teaching in their synagogues and proclaiming the gospel of the kingdom, and healing every kind of disease and every kind of sickness. 36 Seeing the people, He felt compassion for them, because they were distressed and dispirited like sheep without a shepherd. 37 Then He said to His disciples, "The harvest is plentiful, but the workers are few. 38 "Therefore beseech the Lord of the harvest to send out workers into His harvest." (Matt 9:35-38)

1 Jesus summoned His twelve disciples and gave them authority over unclean spirits, to cast them out, and to heal every kind of disease and every kind of sickness. 2 Now the names of the twelve apostles are these: The first, Simon, who is called Peter, and Andrew his brother; and James the son of Zebedee, and John his brother; 3 Philip and Bartholomew; Thomas and Matthew the tax collector; James the son of Alphaeus, and Thaddaeus; 4 Simon the Zealot, and Judas Iscariot, the one who betrayed Him. (Matthew 10:1-4)

7 And He . . . began to send them out in pairs, . . (Mark 6:7)

5 These twelve Jesus sent out after instructing them: "Do not go in the way of the Gentiles, and do not enter any city of the Samaritans; 6 but rather go to the lost sheep of the house of Israel. 7 "And as you go, preach, saying, `The kingdom of heaven is at hand.' 8 "Heal the sick, raise the dead, cleanse the lepers, cast out demons. Freely you received, freely give. 9 "Do not acquire gold, or silver, or copper for your money belts, 10 or a bag for your journey, or even two coats, or sandals, or a staff; for the worker is worthy of his support. 11 "And whatever city or village you enter, inquire who is worthy in it, and stay at his house until you leave that city. 12 "As you enter the house, give it your greeting. 13 "If the house is worthy, give it your blessing of peace. But if it is not worthy, take back your blessing of peace. 14 "Whoever does not receive you, nor heed your words, as you go out of that house or that city, shake the dust off your feet. (Matthew 10:5-14)

Commentary

Jesus went out from there and came into His hometown;

This is another instance of Jesus returning to Nazareth only to be met with disbelief and the derision that comes from familiarity. Then as now, exhortation, preaching and rebuke are tolerated in only one direction – elder, priest or rabbi to citizen, grandparents to parents and parents to children. But it is never tolerated from children to parents or from sibling to sibling. In general society it is not tolerated from peer to peer unless the position is duly earned. Jesus was called a rabbi but He attended not an hour of formal rabbinical training. It was here more a title of respect which depended on the disposition of the beholder. Others saw his equivalency as rabbi without reference to some specific training, but those who knew Him could not give grace to its informality. Nor could they look past it and see that He was rabbi by virtue of wisdom from above.

Now the people of Nazareth were not reacting because they possessed a local knowledge of His wayward past. It was not a list of sins which prevented the acknowledgement. It was a general attitude of contempt at His righteousness, something which society has a difficult time accepting in general.

Jesus would have been a model child and teen. He would have been the son every parent would have wished for. But as in the case of Abel, this would be like shining a bright light on everyone else's attitudes and failings. The people of Nazareth were merely joining Cain in their desire to have Him out of their midst.

Are not His sisters here with us?"

The Greek for *'sister'* is the feminine of adelphos – *'adelphe.'* It is not limited to mean only a real sibling of a blood parent. Here are the alternate meanings of *adelphos:*

1. a brother, whether born of the same two parents or only of the same father or mother
2. having the same national ancestor, belonging to the same people, or countryman
3. any fellow or man
4. a fellow believer, united to another by the bond of affection
5. an associate in employment or office
6. brethren in Christ (his brothers by blood, all men, apostles, Christians, as those who are exalted to the same heavenly place

With Greek alternate meanings, there is a tendency to use a lexicon to select the meaning closest to one's liking, under the guise that one can say it is after all a meaning according to the lexicon.

But alternate lexical meanings are not entered as merely optional equivalents of choice – choose #1 or #2 – it matters not. Each alternate has a history of use and therefore a paradigm of use, which means that certain conditions were observed in usage that determined that an alternate needs to stand out from the predominant meaning. Thus it follows that to employ it, one must therefore see the same conditions in the given text that occasioned the development of the alternate in the first place. (The word 'escalate' is an example in English, meaning rather different things in a war campaign than in a department store.)

Many of these conditions have to do with prepositions or prepositional phrases that take certain forms of the words they modify and change the usage. Other factors are the aspects of grammar (but more predominantly of context).

Now someone might wish to question why research can't still be considered open ended, such that the case to which they earnestly desire the alternate to apply ought to be added to the evidence, (i.e. why can't it be that yet another context has been discovered in which the alternate applies)?

Simply put – so much time has now transpired between the originals and the present day in the study of usage that all the cases and instances that serve to define alternate meanings have for several centuries been exhaustively known. Given enough time, it boils down to there being a finite set of examples, plain and simple.

Much of this is due to the fixed nature of the Koine Greek, having long since ceased as a developing language. Its forms and usage have stood still for centuries, meaning there's a fixed amount of information to explore and that's it. This allows scholars to explore all the known usages and contexts that would dictate primary and alternate meanings.

For this reason, lexicons now publish the alternates with both confidence and finality, such that translators and students have very little occasion to conduct long, technical forms of research to ferret out subtle intricacies of usage.

That is what the apparatus in a Greek text and the technical data in a lexicon represent.

As for *adelphe*, all the meanings above are determined by context, meaning it will be clear that a national ancestor or a person's relative or a sister in Christ is alternately intended rather than a blood sibling because the context makes it clear that a literal sister could not be meant.

And the rule of interpretation does not require that you prove the context for the *primary* meaning. Rather, because of its predominance, the primary meaning is always indicated by the absence of any special contexts for alternates. The rule is: "If the plain sense makes sense, seek no other."

While it is true that certain contexts make it odd that Jesus' brethren are called His brethren and not the children of Mary when they are seen with her, there are perfectly adequate explanations for why the author chose the identification with Jesus rather than His mother that do no violence whatsoever to the customs or logic of the times. But it needs to be observed that much of the necessity to see such persons as kin rather than as literal siblings is due to the commitment of Catholics to the doctrine of Immaculate Conception. This will, as a result, be strongly objected to and claimed as rightly demanded from the text itself.

Whether this is actually true or not is tested by removing the doctrine as an assumption to see if the verses which now stand without it still demand a translation as kin rather than siblings. And when this is done, we may find some vagary as to which must be meant to the elimination of the other, but we do find conspicuous the obvious lack of a *demand* for 'relative.'

Jesus was .. teaching in their synagogues .. and healing .. He felt compassion for them, because they were distressed and dispirited like sheep without a shepherd.

It is strange that these people lived as citizens of the people chosen of God, the people to whom the "oracles of God were entrusted" yet they were like sheep without a shepherd.

Much of this is due fundamentally the general illiteracy and lack of formal education among the poorest classes. Philip was able to recall the OT predictions about Messiah and apply them to Jesus without running first to the synagogue to make sure. There were many others like Philip who could connect the dots; and some who even with this knowledge had issues of over-sophistication that complicated their acceptance of Jesus. But the masses of the poor would certainly outnumber this class in terms of large amounts of knowledge. They might be familiar with Scripture but not well-read of Scripture.

In addition to this, however, was the need for leadership among God's people. As everyone knows, there can be knowledge of what Scripture says, but a lack of what it means or how it is to be applied. The leadership of Judah was busy aggrandizing themselves, building their little fiefdoms and suzeraincies, to make adequate service for the needs of spiritual direction for the common people.

In Medieval times, significant numbers of Catholics in Europe are recorded as having became disenchanted with the clergy and hierarchy of the Holy Church who had become bywords of disappointment and disillusionment in their deportment and conduct. It was equally a time like that here in Mark in which the people were filled with distress and dispiritedness, having shepherds in name but lacking the leadership and care of shepherds in practice.

This condition Jesus senses and feels intensely, enough to get mentioned here in the Gospel. It moves Him to compassion, that the meeting of such needs was long overdue This awareness was vindicated by the response He got from people everywhere. He was followed because He was at last bringing water into a spiritual wasteland. It was an indictment against the authorities and priests since it was clear the people were not getting it from them.

For us as modern Christians, we need to be asking the same questions and having the same expectations. Are we adrift in our churches without a shepherd? Do we have shepherds in name only or do we have shepherds who care for the flock?

"The harvest is plentiful, but the workers are few.

Christians need to embrace this idea – that the world is a field set for harvest. We tend to think that the world is the world, and if it wishes to be left alone we ought to accommodate it. We will not *impose* the will of Christ. The world has the right to its own purposes.

But God has a different view. People have been created for a purpose and despite their independence and freedom to neglect it, God can treat and regard His creation according to his own programs as He wishes. People are made for fellowship with Him and He violates nothing by invoking His will to convert men into citizens of His Kingdom.

So there is a harvest and there is a need to send out workers, whose mission has precedence over any human goal. The workers are few because there are few who are willing to be on the front lines where the battle is taking place. There are few who desire to confront the world in the interest of reaping. Which means there are more who are complacent, who are busy striking an acceptable balance with the world and have adopted a sort of peaceful co-existence that is mutually beneficial. The exhortation to prayer is that this situation will be changed, that God will send out men in greater numbers.

Now at first glance this seems odd because if God is the key to the sending, then why does He need prayer to urge Him to further action? If He needs X number of workers, why not send X number of workers?

But what is meant here is the work of the Lord to change the disposition of the heart, such that the worker now desires to go. And where challenges between God and the will of man are concerned, prayer is encouraged as the means to break such impasses.

There are any number of places whose living conditions can mollify the desire to go, not only to minister but to live. Work among the homeless or in those places where rampant diseases and social depression make for misery at every turn is not the kind of thing one asks for on purpose. We think that those who go there do so out of a sense of duty, but we fail to realize that God has been in their hearts ahead of time to give them the desire.

This is absolutely critical to ministry because the sense of duty is simply not enough to sustain a ministry of sacrifice in constantly unpleasant circumstances. The worker has to have a love for the work, a desire to be there. That is what gets them to uproot their families, get the support, buy the plane tickets and actually move there.

Jesus summoned His twelve disciples and gave them authority over unclean spirits

Here the Protestant must concur with the Catholic that Jesus is setting up the Apostles to continue what He has begun, that this whole arrangement is not merely temporary, a flash in the pan, a capricious visitation from the gods, but rather a permanent invasion meant to change the world forever.

We cannot dilute the giving of authority to these men. Paul calls them the foundation stones of the Church (Eph 2:20.) We would not be here as Christians today had this not been done. It was meant to be conducted beyond Christ's earthly ministry and beyond the lives of these men. The authority here is specific to disease and illness, and the casting out of demons. But we later find Jesus giving them a general authority – *"whatever you bind will be bound, whatever you loose will be loosed."*

There is of course a difference of opinion as to whom the extension of this authority was meant to apply – to these men and their successors or to these men as representing all believers after the statement of Peter, *"You are a kingdom of priests . . a royal priesthood."*

"Now the names of the twelve apostles are these: . . ."

(see previously at Luke 6:12 ff)

And He . . . began to send them out in pairs, and gave them authority over the unclean spirits;

We aren't told why sending them in pairs was necessary beyond what we can surmise practically. A man by himself is more vulnerable. Two men form a union that adds weight to their testimony and forestalls a charge of fanaticism.

But functionally it would be a good working arrangement. One may pray while the other works. Or where earnest prayer is needed, two praying has doubled the influence of one.

The authority over unclean spirits opens the door to understanding the way of the powers that live beyond our world. There are demons, yet Christ has authority over them. Men may pray that someone be delivered, but the guarantee of success is bound up in the principle of authority Christ holds. These are very real powers and the disciples happen to be in the company of the One who holds the key to controlling them.

Picture the act of a private citizen who goes to a hostile foreign country to negotiate a peace. Without the backing of his government, his words will be treated as nice sentiments but not as anything truly effective or substantial. He has no authority to act and therefore no power. Despite the liberality of their evil, demons are ultimately subject to God, and Jesus is God's Son. Note the spirits who gave the sons of Sceva a licking for presuming too much on themselves, for acting in spite of the authority given from Christ. (Acts 19:13ff)

"Do not go in the way of the Gentiles, and do not enter any city of the Samaritans; but rather go to the lost sheep of the house of Israel."

This seems somewhat out of sorts with a worldwide concern for salvation that ought to extend to all nations. It is not a case of convenience – they could only go and do so much. The Samaritans were not in New Jersey after all.

The key to this commandment has to do with the overarching plan for the Kingdom of God, which involved the Jews most necessarily and thematically. The King was come to offer the Kingdom to its first citizens of promise – the Jews. There was a need to present the offer and to hold them accountable for their response. This was primary in a Kingdom sense, so it became primary in every practical sense. They were to finish the work among the Jews first, then go to the Gentiles.

This is because, like no other people on the face of the earth, they were key to the establishment of His Kingdom and could not be simply lumped into the general category of people needing salvation. They are called lost sheep despite having the most diligent and vigorous leaders who ensured the ancient code continued to live in present times. But they had become lost because they had lost sight of the God behind the code. It had become perfunctory mechanics, not the relationship begun in Eden where Adam and God walked and talked in the garden.

"And as you go, preach, saying, `The kingdom of heaven is at hand.'

Notice the key message. It is not "God has a wonderful plan for your life." Rather it is "the kingdom of heaven is at hand." This is a continuation of what John preached, and what Jesus first preached to gain His first hearing among the people. It is the overriding message God desired to get across from the start and it is brought back in periodically to remind us that this is the key to all that is happening.

God has prepared a Kingdom. It is now come in the visitation of its King, and men must be made fit for its citizenship.

"Freely you received, freely give."

This is an exhortation to not turn the ministry into a profit-making enterprise. They are not even to seek wages for the work. They did not pay money to be taught by Jesus, it was given freely. They must not make others pay just to hear their teaching or receive their services.

for the worker is worthy of his support.

They are not to make preliminary provisions for their work or the traveling expenses this will necessarily involve. No bag for petty cash, not even extra clothing.

Now it seems contradictory to then indicate that they can depend on support because of the work they do, especially knowing that the support would certainly come from the people to whom they ministered (there was no Baptist Convention or "Gospel Missions Worldwide" to support them along the way. It would come largely from the people to whom they were sent. We find this in the women who are seen to be giving to the work of Jesus whenever He visited their town (Luke 8:1-3.)

But this is not soliciting pay for services. It is a matter of prompting through the Holy Spirit and the moving of the heart. Even our government honors the donations made to churches as not counting for revenue, because it is optional, the services of the church can be had without giving, and what is received is a matter of benevolent disposition, not a fee for services rendered.

The arrangement that is being set up is one of blessing for minister and recipient. The minister is not to commercialize his ministry. Yet there is need for his support. The recipients are to be the hand of God caring for the minister and receiving yet a further blessing from participating in His work.

"And whatever city or village you enter, inquire who is worthy in it, and stay at his house until you leave that city.

It was important that they be wise about the hospitality extended to them. People can be hospitable but not necessarily worthy roommates. College dorm experiences are good examples of how this can go awry.

Now the Apostles were certainly not aimless, naïve college students who were ripe pickings for fast-talking, dominant acquaintances. But it was a matter of avoiding what can be thoughtfully avoided using a little common sense. Coming back after a day of ministry to familial strife, casual morals, or religious contentiousness is taxing and counter-productive when the need of the moment is rest and good fellowship.

Also, the "worthy" in a community were generally the most respected and heeded members, so a certain amount of protection attended their hospitality.

give it your blessing of peace. . . . take back your blessing of peace . . shake the dust off your feet.

Despite the exhortation, there were bound to be mistakes in judgment causing them to wind up in the troublesome situations they desired to avoid. It is an acknowledgement that despite our magical view of New Testament times, the Apostles did not walk in constant communication with the Holy Spirit, telling them which corner to turn and which street to now take.

That is the very reason they are being told here what to do if their discernment fails them. They are to stand for righteousness and not cave in to the circumstances that moderns would consider no biggie today.

Where intransigence and obstinency persist they are to retract the blessing first given when they arrived. Was this necessary? Logic would say no, since God would not have been obligated to bless purely on the basis of the disciples naïve pronouncements.

It is more likely a declaration for the benefit of the hosts. It is being made known that their behavior is out of favor with the work of God and their expectations from the earlier pronouncement are now null and void.

"shake off the dust from your feet"

This is odd to hear from the mouth of Jesus because it is a visible gesture of insult that expresses disgust. It is in the same class but not as vulgar as modern gestures are today. It was perceived as unfavorably as modern gestures are today, but it did not convey the vulgarity of sexual innuendos that modern gestures are deliberately designed to do.

Here the insult is in extending one's disgust in the company of another to such a degree that carrying away the very dust from their home on one's feet is objectionable.

Again, there is no functional necessity. Dust is dust. It has no moral qualities. But it is a statement to the hosts of the ill favor they hold with God for their attitudes and actions.

Matthew 10:16-23
16 "Behold, I send you out as sheep in the midst of wolves; so be shrewd as serpents and innocent as doves. 17 "But beware of men, for they will hand you over to the courts and scourge you in their synagogues; 18 and you will even be brought before governors and kings for My sake, as a testimony to them and to the Gentiles. 19 "But when they hand you over, do not worry about how or what you are to say; for it will be given you in that hour what you are to say. 20 "For it is not you who speak, but it is the Spirit of your Father who speaks in you.

21 "Brother will betray brother to death, and a father his child; and children will rise up against parents and cause them to be put to death. 22 "You will be hated by all because of My name, but it is the one who has endured to the end who will be saved. 23 "But whenever they persecute you in one city, flee to the next; for truly I say to you, you will not finish going through the cities of Israel until the Son of Man comes.
(Matthew 10:16-23)

Commentary

". . sheep in the midst of wolves; . . be shrewd as serpents and innocent as doves.

This is actually the opposite of the adage. It is usually the wolf among the sheep.

There here is a sobering fact about the gospel and the world. It is going to be a hostile conflict. There will certainly be many who are ripe for salvation, who are already seeking its truth and will welcome it with a ready and open heart. But there will be others of a different disposition, those who are sold to the world and the way of the world.

The gospel is bound to cause trouble because the philosophy and attitude of the world is so opposite to it. When these two meet, there will be a fight, plain and simple. The world is not going to give up what it loves and cherishes.

If we lift ourselves up to a high vantage point over the early history of the Church, we see the action/reaction view more clearly. Jesus came and preached the good news of salvation and the coming of Messiah. The reaction was ridicule, persecution and crucifixion. The disciples of Jesus get converted and change from carnality to walking in the Spirit. We then see the backlash of the world, epitomized in ancient Rome, rendering its opinion of the gospel by trying to stamp its "wickedness" out of the empire. It is the action of the gospel and the subsequent reaction of the world.

Thus, Jesus prepares them for the real environment into which they will be thrust. They will be sheep among wolves, as opposed to wolves among sheep.

" shrewd as serpents and innocent as doves."

This is a great combination because it offsets the disadvantages of each while gaining their strengths. The serpent is crafty and shrewd, but these are employed to what we might consider evil ends – the killing of prey. The dove is the image of gentleness and meekness, hence innocence, but it has a disadvantage in vulnerability and supposed gullibility.

When combined, we gain the shrewdness of the serpent to offset the vulnerability of the dove, and the innocence of the dove to offset the intimidation, aggressiveness and violence of the serpent.

Too often these are either/or decisions in Christians. Being too much like doves we are taken advantage of, tricked or fooled by our enemies, or considered out of touch with reality. Being too much like serpents, we bluster and manipulate our way into places of power that tend to make us not much different from the secular world – the church is then run like a business.

When in balance like the above, we begin to see how marvelously similar we are to Jesus.

"*. . for they will hand you over to the courts . . you will even be brought before governors and kings for My sake,*"

The sheer scope of the effect on the world is clarified. It will extend to kings and governors. This makes it clear that the principles they have been taught are huge not small, major not minor, far-reaching not parochial.

This is the expectation from the world and its slavery to sin. Satan as master will not blithely relinquish his citizens to the truth. The result will be that the soldiers of the faith will be handed over to the courts and tribunals, that the world may be rid of them.

But Jesus adds that this is for the purpose of giving a witness to magistrates and the Gentiles in general. One might question how effective that witness has been if it results in the hatred and evil comprising death and persecution. This doesn't sound like *MasteringEffective Witnessing 101*.

It is instead how the persecution is endured and the extent to which it is suffered that comprises the most powerful aspect of the witness. There is the gospel content to be sure, but there is the added unction that this is a way of life worth dying for in the interest of others.

Certainly, the sight of Stephen's stoning had a lasting effect on Saul. And whether governors or emperors are changed or not, they are made accountable more than simple preaching or the general revelation could ever have done.

do not worry about how or what you are to say; for it will be given you in that hour what you are to say.

As earlier commented, we would be inclined to make arduous preparation for such encounters to ensure our words are not lost in the mind by sheer nervousness and that our speech is such that we not lose such a rare opportunity to get everything said.

But it is precisely for this reason that Jesus exhorts them to not plan ahead. It would be man's idea of what was important and in these moments it must be God's purpose for the hour, who knows the very words that will have the greatest effect.

There is an old adage – "Give a project to man and he will surely screw it up." It shows how completely other we are compared to God and His omniscience.

Picture instead that you had been given the opportunity to speak to a man like Yasser Arafat (while he was alive and kicking.) You are given a choice from God: you can go as yourself, or Christ can take your human form and go instead. In terms of simple effectiveness, which would you welcome? The call to let God speak in you is very similar to option two.

Now for the disciples, we need to keep in mind that for them their appearance before magistrates and the synagogues would seldom have been peacefully scheduled audiences. They would likely be hurried affairs, occasioned by arrests and being seized in haste by the authorities. So for them, there would routinely be little time to think about preparing words. You could be arrested and within twenty minutes find yourself standing before a tribunal.

Now the rub for modern Christians is more about discerning the voice of God and our lack of any reasonable confidence that we would even hear much less comprehend it. We are not accustomed to hearing voices in this age of the Church, and there is a widespread stigma imposed on those who claim they do.

So this exhortation is met with some apprehension and even fear. A lot has to do with our letting our limitations in ordinary situations dictate the likelihood of our proficiency in urgent ones. We don't routinely hear the voice of God in a way that we could cite exact words heard, so we are doubtful this capability will be available in an emergency.

But it is important to note that many capacities come to us from God "at the moment" not necessarily ahead of time. Consider the martyrs and their need to endure the flames and the violence of wild beasts. They had no more capacity to do those things ahead of time than we do. They were not special Christians because they lived in the first century. They had the same doubts and fears as all of us today. But they were given the ability and grace to endure when the time came, and this is evident by the peaceful manner in which they endured their sufferings.

If someone puts their hand over the heat of a barbeque and holds it there until the pain really registers, they will ask themself how anyone could endure that peacefully. Yet you are not in the position of witnessing for the faith through death while standing in front of your barbeque. So we have no idea how well or how badly we will do in the real circumstances. And God assures us that He will supply all the grace we need to be the right witness when the time comes.

"For it is not you who speak, but it is the Spirit of your Father who speaks in you.

Again, it will not be a case of being sure we have superhuman discernment. God is more than able to overcome our human limitations and get His message through to us clearly and unmistakably. And in the end, we ought to desire that it be His words rather than our own. We will sincerely want the Father to be speaking, if this is our one chance to meet so profound an opportunity.

But we cannot overlook the need to do all we can to remain close and intimate with His Spirit while we live in peace and safety. Let's face it, the person who has ignored God most of his life and not cultivated the sense of God's presence and influence in their lives has a slim basis for profound expectations from God. As with all things, we must be obedient to do our part, and God will be faithful to do His part.

"Brother will betray brother to death, and a father his child

These words would be puzzling because there were no ready paradigms for this in their immediate experience. But this was to be literally lived out in the Roman persecutions, when informers were rewarded for turning in their neighbors. In the case of family members, there came to be a sort of twisted logic that to turn in Christianized members of your own family deflected any suspicions that you might be of the same evil and secured that you were *caesaris amicus* – friend of Caesar. It was the intense urgency to preserve oneself against the disaffection that Christianity would inevitably occasion that gave birth to this behavior.

This later created the problem of dealing with the 'lapsed' – those who had compromised to preserve their lives. The added problem of discerning whether informing was part of their sin complicated the assessment of their worthiness for reinstatement.

"You will be hated by all because of My name,

It is here important to stress that it not because of religious belief in general, but on account of His Name. Sadly, there are people who call themselves Christian but are flatly embarrassed when someone injects the name of Jesus too frequently into conversation. Such people are labeled fanatics or outspoken beyond what social etiquette dictates as acceptable.

It is questionable whether suffering for "religion" counts equally with suffering for a clear association with Jesus as Lord. While that may be hard to answer definitively, we cannot avoid the words above which certainly establish the expectation that our suffering is to be *"because of My name."*

but it is the one who has endured to the end who will be saved.

Some use this as a support for faith plus works as the key in securing salvation. The implication is that if one has faith and does not endure, one will not be saved. This can be seen as supporting the "fall from Grace" doctrine, because if we can't fall, why the exhortation?

Others see it not as a conditional but as a statement of fact - what true believers will in fact do because they have the faith that saves. It is like saying, "believers love because they are Christians" compared to "believers are Christians because they love."

There is also the reasoning that if one is assured of salvation, the means God will use are just as assured as the acts of endurance. So the exhortation to endure is not contradictory to that assurance but is the assured means for it.

"But whenever they persecute you in one city, flee to the next

Now this sounds opposite to the encouragement to make a stand for the gospel, namely to not escape persecution by fleeing to safety. But whether one stays and dies or whether one moves on and extends their witness is a matter of personal conviction. Not all testimonies are to be seen as calls to martyrdom.

Much of this depends on the attitudes of the persecutors. Are they presenting a life or death decision point or are they simply beating you to dissuade you? In Paul's case, he faced no official, capital indictments until the appropriate time, and did in fact move to the next town, all in the perfect plan of God. God simply had a set number of things to accomplish through Paul and until then, it would be persecution but not martyrdom.

". . you will not finish going through the cities of Israel until the Son of Man comes."

This is one of the more problematic verses in the NT because it involves a time-based prediction and an expected result. It can be variously understood: a) the Son of Man will come before His disciples finish preaching in all the cities of Israel, and b), the program of witnessing will never be finished up to the coming of the Son of Man, i.e. witnessing will be an open ended task through to the day of His appearing.

Since Christ did not come again in their lifetimes it is hard to press the first meaning as the one intended. Support for the second meaning is seen in the unique use of the word *"until"* instead of the word *"before"* Until is more a description of the length of time whereas *before* indicates a conditional. "You must hit the ball until you hear the bell" - a statement of duration, how long. "You must keep attending the class before getting a certificate" indicates a conditional. Since *until* was used instead of *before*, the second meaning is further supported.

Matthew 10:24-39

24 "A disciple is not above his teacher, nor a slave above his master. 25 "It is enough for the disciple that he become like his teacher, and the slave like his master. If they have called the head of the house Beelzebul, how much more will they malign the members of his household! 26 "Therefore do not fear them, for there is nothing concealed that will not be revealed, or hidden that will not be known. 27 "What I tell you in the darkness, speak in the light; and what you hear whispered in your ear, proclaim upon the housetops.

28 "Do not fear those who kill the body but are unable to kill the soul; but rather fear Him who is able to destroy both soul and body in hell. 29 "Are not two sparrows sold for a cent? And yet not one of them will fall to the ground apart from your Father. 30 "But the very hairs of your head are all numbered. 31 "So do not fear; you are more valuable than many sparrows. 32 "Therefore everyone who confesses Me before men, I will also confess him before My Father who is in heaven. 33 "But whoever denies Me before men, I will also deny him before My Father who is in heaven.

34 "Do not think that I came to bring peace on the earth; I did not come to bring peace, but a sword. 35 "For I came to SET A MAN AGAINST HIS FATHER, AND A DAUGHTER AGAINST HER MOTHER, AND A DAUGHTER-IN-LAW AGAINST HER MOTHER-IN-LAW; 36 and A MAN'S ENEMIES WILL BE THE MEMBERS OF HIS HOUSEHOLD. 37 "He who loves father or mother more than Me is not worthy of Me; and he who loves son or daughter more than Me is not worthy of Me. 38 "And he who does not take his cross and follow after Me is not worthy of Me. 39 "He who has found his life will lose it, and he who has lost his life for My sake will find it.
(Matthew 10:24-39)

Commentary

"A disciple is not above his teacher . . It is enough for the disciple that he become like his teacher . . If they have called the head of the house Beelzebul, how much more will they malign the members of his household! "Therefore do not fear them,

The key statement to understand is *"do not fear them."* The statements before this are to assist them in not being afraid. The fear being highlighted is that of persecution because they are His disciples.

"a disciple is not above his teacher, as slave not above his mast" In the literal sense, this suggests that they needed to be checked against thinking they were above Jesus in some way that would lessen, remove, or engage better the potential of persecution. But that is virtually impossible to imagine in such men as these.

Rather, Jesus here clarifies that it is expected that when maligning the master of a household, his malefactors are going to encounter a person of more grave aspect and there is more to consider in terms of what one will get back in retaliation or contentiousness, i.e. it will be a harder move than to attack merely the members of the household or slaves. *"how much more will they malign the members of his household."*

It is better to infer that Jesus has chosen an idiom that drives home the equality of expectations applicable to them as His followers, - *"it is enough for the disciple to become like his master"* - without inferring they had high-minded attitudes. It is addressing an attitude, fear or misapprehension that because they are not men of the caliber of Jesus, their persecutions might be taken as too personal, too much the result of their weakness and failings. In this sense the words, *"is not above his master"* are taken to mean *"is not set apart from his master"* If they are coming to be like Him, suffering like Him will be a sign of identification not a sign of inferiority or failing. So expect the same things.

As to not being afraid in expecting the same, knowing the reason and the probability ahead of time does serve to lessen one's fears, not that being persecuted will carry no fears at all.

for there is nothing concealed that will not be revealed, or hidden that will not be known.

A postamble to not being afraid is added – that all things will eventually be made known, as in coming to the light of judgment. People often suffer misdeeds, persecutions and abuse thinking that no one cares, no one even notices, never will there be a day of recompense. Easing the fears about such things can come in the knowledge that the perpetrators and enemies of God will be held to account and the very deeds will be played back in the light of day for all to see.

Ultimate victory can be a form of comfort while enduring otherwise intolerable things.

"What I tell you in the darkness, speak in the light; and what you hear whispered in your ear, proclaim upon the housetops."

God is the ultimate Judge who will bring to light all things men have thought hidden and forgotten. It is a picture of the future judgment as to works to which the wicked will be brought.

Yet this is now being extended as a command to the disciples. It is a picture of two things of importance. They will be the instruments of declaring truths about things hidden, good or bad, including the errors of men's hearts, as the more immediate means of effecting God's judgment in the here and now (some things will be judged before that great day of Judgment.) It is also an insight into the way of personal revelation from God to man – God will tell us in secret, as a whisper in the ear, and we are to then proclaim it publicly in preaching and witnessing.

In the case of revealing the deeds of men, we see this in John the Baptist, who shouted out right in public the misdeeds and sins of Herod and Herodias. What was being done in secret was now being shouted out loud. The disciples are being told they are to expect to be used similarly.

In terms of revealing truths that need to be preached, we are reminded of Elijah's experience in seeking the voice of the Lord. It did not come in the wind, or the earthquake or the fire, but in the still small voice. (I Kings 19:12.)

So the general idea being conveyed is that truth will be spoken quietly and secretly to the servants of God, and be it a revelation of evil thoughts or a declaration of spiritual truths, it will be in turn shouted from the housetops by His chosen.

"Do not fear those who kill the body but are unable to kill the soul; but rather fear Him who is able to destroy both soul and body in hell.

Man deduced rather early on that to threaten death was the most effective means of getting people to do one's bidding. When you think about revolutions and insurrections, they involve the use of weapons that threaten death. Because the ends are viewed as so high, men see the most powerful means for getting compliance as essential. Because the stakes of life are so high, the vast majority of the victimized yield.

A brutal dictator uses the power to kill because he knows his victims are in dread fear of death. It is resorted to immediately not inevitably because it is so efficient.

In war, arms of deadly force are employed because it is perceived that the only way to get the other side to give up is to actually point weapons at people and start firing. It is saying, "I'm going to threaten something so terrible that you will be forced to sit up and take notice. That is how wars begin. Sadly, it is not effective at ending them quickly.

Jesus' exhortation about not fearing those who can only destroy the body is tough to embrace when the flames are upon us with searing heat. But this is largely because many people have not experienced the truth that the spiritual is really of greater power than the physical.

It is a great message of the Bible that the most important operations in the universe are on the plane of the spiritual. We tend to think in order of importance that there is first the plane of the physical, then the plane of our thoughts, philosophies and ideologies, then the plane of the spiritual. And we tend to think of the abstract and the spiritual as sort of expendable to the urgency of the physical. If we are in major pain, we have little patience for mere thoughts about altruistic ideas and golden principles that do nothing to stop the agony of the moment. Many have come to believe that the spiritual is nice, but seldom works in the sense of invading the physical realm.

But the Bible teaches that everything is ultimately related to the spiritual because everything has its origin in God, who is Spirit. Why the universe is the way it is, why our body is desperately ill at the moment, why our marriage is a nightmare are all related to man's orientation to the spiritual world that is God, all in all. His power to heal where doctors have no clue is a spiritual thing. The state of our marriage is due to our not abiding in the spiritual truths that are in God and are essential to His being. The state of the world is directly related to how men incline (or not) their hearts toward Him.

Our very creation is based on things decided, decreed and executed first in the spiritual realm. We are here for a purpose and intended to be returned to that realm when all is done. So when men threaten the loss of life, they are under the false belief that they are ending our "being", our existence. But they have no such power, because what we are truly lives beyond the flesh and the destiny of that is in the hands of the Almighty.

"Are not two sparrows sold for a cent? And yet not one of them will fall to the ground apart from your Father. 30 "But the very hairs of your head are all numbered.

As earlier in the gospels, the statement is to highlight the small amount of money one needs for buying two sparrows – a valuation in men's eyes. Yet God cares for them and knows all their mishaps in detail. So much more does He value and care for us.

This has far-reaching implications for our general attitude toward the things that happen to us. We are to force into consciousness the recognition that nothing has befallen us that God does not know, that God has not permitted. It is common to believe that the world and the events of our lives are spinning quite apart from God, purely on their own; and that God is there like the call to 911, to hastily arrive at the merry-go-round gone off its track, and fix it aright again.

We can often fail to abide in the notion that God has permitted all that we experience to happen, that it is all seen ahead of time and does not take Him by surprise. This should prompt us to cease asking why this is happening to us (as though it is a violation of a better plan) but rather "what are God's purposes for me in this?"

"everyone who confesses . . I will also confess . . whoever denies . . I will also deny him before My Father who is in heaven.

This has been used by Satan to discourage and defeat many Christians. It is compared with I John 4:3, "And every spirit that confesseth not that Jesus Christ is come in the flesh is not of God:" such that we are in dread fear that if we shrink back from a challenge to witness or we will be denied by Christ.

In so many of these cases, it is a matter of continual action not a matter of pointed action. It is not an incident of denial, but a life of denial. This is not to minimize the seriousness of not confessing Christ. It is to ask whether the act signifies endemic denial or overwhelming circumstances in a life otherwise living in faith.

The condition of the 'lapsed' – those who denied Christ to avoid persecution in Rome – dealt with this very issue. Is there to be compassion on those whose human fears could not be assuaged, or is any flinching in human fear to be deemed a sign of a defective or ingenuine faith?

Under no circumstances are we to conclude that when the time comes we can rely on the compassion of others to understand our cowardice. The believer is here enjoined to consider very seriously what denial or a failure to confess will beget before the throne of God. The compassion argument is circumstantial, meaning there is always some possibility remaining that the more rigorous meaning about any instance might in fact be the intent.

Do not think that I came to bring peace on the earth; I did not come to bring peace, but a sword.

For those who know the end of the story, this cannot be taken literally to mean no peace was intended of any kind but only a real sword. The reason is found in two key passages: Luke 4:17-21 – Jesus closed the scroll at the very point where the prophecy about Messiah turned to vengeance and judgment; and John 18:36 – "If My kingdom were of this world, then My servants would be fighting so that I would not be handed over to the Jews;"

Here it is made plain that the particular role of Messiah that would include a sword and a judgment for having exhausted the means of peace was not His for the present. Had He spoken in future tense - "think not that I will come" or "I will not come to bring peace," we would have justification to maintain literal understandings.

Being past tense verbs, we must seek to understand in what sense this can remain true but not literally so. And he supplies the way by His next statements:

"For I came to SET A MAN AGAINST HIS FATHER, AND A DAUGHTER AGAINST HER MOTHER, AND A DAUGHTER-IN-LAW AGAINST HER MOTHER-IN-LAW; and A MAN'S ENEMIES WILL BE THE MEMBERS OF HIS HOUSEHOLD.

So we see that the division exemplified by a sword, and the breaking of the peace are the polarizations, estrangements and alienations that will accompany the preaching of the gospel, even to the dividing of family members.

Now some may object that this is completely antithetical to God's high view of the family and it is hard to reconcile a deliberate purpose to disrupt it. But it is not an assault on the institution of the family. In fact, the gospel is the key to renewing harmony and love lost within the family. It is very much like the ignorant, backwards jungle dweller, whose daughter has come to know that the medicine of the white man will cure her father, but he not only refuses it but threatens to disown her if she does not renounce her connection with the "foreign devils."

The quote is from Micah 7:6. Micah is speaking of the conditions that exist during Judah's dark period under the reign of Ahaz, one of its worst kings. He is lamenting these same conditions, but in the present, not the future. Instead of "to set a man against his father", Micah states that a man *is* against his own father, as are daughters against their mothers, etc.

It is a case where, had Jesus not connected the texts, we would not have applied them to Him by virtue of how they appear in Micah. This was not a messianic verse seen by the Jews as marking Messiah for identification. Jesus is exercising His authority over the Word to make the connections as He deems them applicable.

In the case of Micah, the strife and estrangements were due to the desperation of the times and the attendant acts of self-preservation. Desperate times test the validity and allegiances to principles. Those who did not embrace them genuinely abandoned them quickly to save their hides.

"He who loves father or mother more than Me is not worthy of Me; and he who loves son or daughter more than Me is not worthy of Me.

There are some who believe that Jesus would never go this far – to separate affection between Himself and the family. For some, having a family was so much the heartfelt goal in young life, and the acquiring of it so rewarding, that some parents believe God will understand if we prefer the order of family, God, and country.

Much of this has to do with one's attitude about who God is and perhaps some underdeveloped notions of his nature and needs. We can come to think that our little boy or little girl is very real and tangible and much more helpless and needful of our love, help and support, and that God is ultimately in need of nothing in any substantive way, so why usurp the needs of the helpless for the needs of the One who is perfectly complete?

But again, this is a case of the spiritual plane being the ultimate base for all existence and life - the run rules on all things created. To neglect this or to opt for substitutes conceived by our limited reasoning is contrary to it and a recipe for trouble and unhappiness.

We can take considerable comfort that God is not asking for a sacrifice, a permanent exchange of child for God. It is a matter of establishing the necessary priorities about eternal things, which will outlast the short time we live with our families by light years of time. When we consider the sheer duration of eternity, it will be the main thing we do in all our existence. It will be infinitely more frequent and repeated in its experiences than the unbroken line of heartbeats that have comprised the continuum of our lives since birth.

It is again to focus attention on why we were made, to what purpose were we born? No joys and exhilarations can deflect our long range view of that purpose, that ultimate destiny.

And he who does not take his cross and follow after Me is not worthy of Me. "He who has found his life will lose it, and he who has lost his life for My sake will find it.

Again we must distinguish between incidents in which we fail to take up our cross and a life that stands back from doing so. Most literally, the cross would mean the willingness to die for the faith. But in daily practical terms, there are two senses in which we can apply it: 1) the willingness to bear the consequences of our association with the gospel, and 2) our need to put our former life to the death in the interest of walking in the newness of life.

In all senses, following after Jesus has ramifications. They may culminate in a sacrifice of death (the early Christians in Rome sometimes met their fate in a matter of a hours after converting), or it may result in ridicule among friends, or persecution. But it is the willingness to pay the price, to accept the consequences that are embodied in the believer's cross. It is also the willingness to jettison sins and old habits that keep us from a full life in Him – to put old things to death.

The sobering aspect of this is that Jesus connects this with being worthy of Him. It is a statement that one is dead serious about the life in Jesus - being more important than merely living. Try as we might to water this down into palatable doctrine, this is a truth we must face and determine to do in our calling to follow Him.

"He who has found his life will lose it, and he who has lost his life for My sake will find it.

To find life means the experience of coming to know one's life, to set goals and begin the process of achieving those goals. We come into this world without a clue as to what we are to become or achieve. In our secular existence, we learn that life presents a wide variety of possible goals, possible ways of life and through parents and friends we choose one and begin to pursue it.

As we become successful and the choice we've made begins to click, we have the sense that we have "arrived." We are on the path to making a life for ourselves that is now separate from our parents. It is our life and no one else's. This is the one who has "found his life."

But Jesus says that such a person will lose that life by default. It is going to happen by the surety that all men die. Things slow down and the ride is eventually over. All achieving is at an end.

Think of the great projects and campaigns that the ancients strove to achieve. The Rome built by Augustus is just plain gone. The inner skeletons of its existance are all that can be seen. All the drawings, the plans, the funding, the contractors, the laborers that went into the refurbishment of Rome have been torn down and used for other purposes. It's not only over, it's been over for more than a millennium.

But the one who gives up that life and those expectations created for the self and does so for Christ's sake, will find not only life, but the meaning of life. When we come to live as we were made to live, our former, lesser, dreams become much like old clothes, the ones we are suddenly surprised to find in the attic and can't believe we used to wear.

Matthew 10:40-42, Matthew 11:1, Luke 9:6-9, Mark 6:17-29

40 "He who receives you receives Me, and he who receives Me receives Him who sent Me. 41 "He who receives a prophet in the name of a prophet shall receive a prophet's reward; and he who receives a righteous man in the name of a righteous man shall receive a righteous man's reward. 42 "And whoever in the name of a disciple gives to one of these little ones even a cup of cold water to drink, truly I say to you, he shall not lose his reward." (Matthew 10:40-42)

When Jesus had finished giving instructions to His twelve disciples, He departed from there to teach and preach in their cities. (Matthew 11:1)

Departing, they began going throughout the villages, preaching the gospel and healing everywhere. (Luke 9:6)

Now Herod the tetrarch heard of all that was happening; and he was greatly perplexed, because it was said by some that John had risen from the dead, 8 and by some that Elijah had appeared, and by others that one of the prophets of old had risen again. 9 Herod said, "I myself had John beheaded; but who is this man about whom I hear such things?" And he kept trying to see Him. (Luke 9:7-9)

For Herod himself had sent and had John arrested and bound in prison on account of Herodias, the wife of his brother Philip, because he had married her. 18 For John had been saying to Herod, "It is not lawful for you to have your brother's wife." 19 Herodias had a grudge against him and wanted to put him to death and could not do so; 20 for Herod was afraid of John, knowing that he was a righteous and holy man, and he kept him safe. And when he heard him, he was very perplexed; but he used to enjoy listening to him.

21 A strategic day came when Herod on his birthday gave a banquet for his lords and military commanders and the leading men of Galilee; 22 and when the daughter of Herodias herself came in and danced, she pleased Herod and his dinner guests; and the king said to the girl, "Ask me for whatever you want and I will give it to you." 23 And he swore to her, "Whatever you ask of me, I will give it to you; up to half of my kingdom." 24 And she went out and said to her mother, "What shall I ask for?" And she said, "The head of John the Baptist." 25 Immediately she came in a hurry to the king and asked, saying, "I want you to give me at once the head of John the Baptist on a platter." 26 And although the king was very sorry, yet because of his oaths and because of his dinner guests, he was unwilling to refuse her.

27 Immediately the king sent an executioner and commanded him to bring back his head. And he went and had him beheaded in the prison, 28 and brought his head on a platter, and gave it to the girl; and the girl gave it to her mother. 29 When his disciples heard about this, they came and took away his body and laid it in a tomb. (Mark 6:17-29)

Commentary

"He who receives you receives Me

On the heels of the discussion about allegiances, Jesus has been predicting the divisions that would ensue on account of the Gospel, He then connects their acceptance or rejection by others with the acceptance and rejection of Him as Son of God.

This idea of representative associations does not mean that the disciples had carte blanche to act independently of their Lord. It is a case of "as they act." It is doing so in His spirit and power that those who receive them receive the Master also. We need to also distinguish between personality or technical issues of conflict and a conflict over the ministry they presented. Arguing over a bill for provisions did not mean the proprietor was rejecting Christ. The relationship being applied is in respect to the conduct of the spiritual teaching and service of their ministry.

Now this aspect was very necessary because it is clear that Jesus' physical presence in the world was limited, that He would leave behind His disciples to continue what was begun, and there had to be some form of acknowledgement that things done by others would be regarded as done by the Son who was absent. The disciples would now be the ones physically present, but they would be connected with the spiritual presence of Christ, who would make connection with the spiritual presence of the Father. To receive the disciples' message is to receive Christ's message is to receive the Father's message.

"He who receives a prophet in the name of a prophet . . . he who receives a righteous man in the name of a righteous man . ."

This doublet of the idea is a matter of doing something *in the spirit of* honored or revered persons of the same class. It is a case of receiving a prophet because he is a prophet of God, and doing so in the name of some great prophet. Receiving them into your home, your town or your affairs in the name of Elijah would be a way of showing extraordinary recognition of the gift of God in them.

Likewise, one could receive a righteous person on account of his righteousness and in the name of someone heralded as righteous, like Abraham.

It carries with it the idea that one would not deliberately abuse this connection, that before taking the phrase one would consider the obligation of invoking such a name.

It was largely a matter of reputation and integrity in the community. If you carelessly invoked Moses in matters of the slightest importance, and especially if you bungled things or your hospitality ended up poorly given, your reputation suffered and you were seen as treating the honored person lightly or even casting them in bad light by your actions. So doing something in the name of a prophet or a righteous man involved serious thinking.

But this is not to be confused with the prohibition against oaths. It was not a case of saying "By Elijah, I receive you and give you nourishment." It was a case of saying, "In the name of Elijah, here is water and food and rest." It is to say you honor God as exemplified by His saints.

The connection for the disciples is that there will be people who will receive them because of their connection to Jesus, and this is not contrary to custom.

In all such cases, the reward was the expectation that God would not fail to reward such a person (the one receiving the prophet.) However, the reward is qualified as the "prophets' reward" which would mean less materialistic and more spiritual. It was readily understood as meaning the same blessings the prophets looks forward to in eternal life with God.

Neither is it a works righteousness. It is not the key to acquiring eternal life, but is a statement that those who otherwise have the faith that will bring them eternal life will see rewards for this kind of service as will the prophets and the righteous of old.

"truly I say to you, he shall not lose his reward."

He departed from there to teach and preach in their cities.

These are specifically the cities of His own disciples, namely the Twelve. We later see Bethsaida being one of them – the home town of Peter and Philip.

They preached and healed "everywhere." This is the expectant hope of all who seek healing – that God will heal as broadly and as completely as possible that an individual may have the hope of being included and that it be thoroughly good.

This, we see in Jesus and the disciples. He touches an incredible number of people wherever He goes and the healings are not partial, but thoroughly restorative. People are made completely well, not merely moved to the recovery room.

'Everywhere' is of course hyperbole. In some cases, the Scripture states that all were healed in a certain place, but in the case of crowds in the thousands, we might rationally conclude that not all could get close enough to be touched. Yet, the Scripture doesn't state that during these sessions, some left without being healed, so our supposition is purely based on practical considerations, which have no bearing on the expectations we might have shortly when we get to the feeding of the crowd in the next few verses.

Now Herod the tetrarch heard of all that was happening; and he was greatly perplexed, because it was said by some that John had risen from the dead,

The Herod here is Antipas, who had been given the Galilee, but confirmed more easily by his perplexity over word that John the Baptist has risen, John being imprisoned by Antipas, Antipas being the one who had Herodias.

(As earlier described, a tetrarch is a one-fourth ruler in what was formerly a single realm. There were four sons who divided the unified holdings of Herod the Great. But by Jesus' time there were only three – those of Antipas, Philip, Lysanius. The fourth, that of Archelaus, was forfeit to Rome under Pontius Pilate.)

The notoriety of Jesus was now unavoidable and we can understand why. You have now a region with a tetrarch and Jewish officials, in which a massive crowd in the thousands is seen almost daily; and in the midst, a constantly moving mass of humanity surrounding a person walking among them. It was an event of major proportion happening under the nose of the authorities.

If aliens were to have hovered over the skies of Giza in Egypt five thousand years ago, they would have noticed a flurry of humanity in huge numbers concentrated on a single point in the landscape – a pyramid. It would have registered as an extraordinary event suggesting great importance.

Similarly here, there is a flurry of activity and importance happening in Judaism's land, on its hills, in its towns. It is not merely a picnic or a lunch on the hillside, but a man in the midst of a work of God. The sheer numbers make it a thing the authorities cannot ignore.

Herod is perplexed of the rumor that John has risen. It would be surprising to learn if Herod even believed in an afterlife. But the reality of what was being reported would certainly have caused him to wonder if the subject had been heretofore treated too glibly.

The reason is told in what we moderns have come to term as a "flashback." In fact, none of the gospels recount the event in the present, but tell of it after the fact.

We are told that John's death is an event of the past and to understand Herod's fears we are sent back to precipitating events. He had ordered John killed at the whim of a girl and her mother. But more than this, Herod had entertained some appreciation for John and had purposed to keep him safe (v.20.) So the killing of John was perceived even by Herod as something full of bad omens and foreboding.

Now he finds that John is reported to have come back from the dead – perhaps for some form of redress?

and by some that Elijah had appeared, and by others that one of the prophets of old had risen again.

Elijah was promised to appear in Malachi 4:5 *Behold, I am going to send you Elijah the prophet before the coming of the great and terrible day of the LORD*

The prophecy of Moses in Deuteronomy 18:18 was not yet fulfilled. Some may have reasoned that the coming of "that Prophet" would be in the rising and reappearance of a former one.

Herod said, "I myself had John beheaded; but who is this man about whom I hear such things?" And he kept trying to see Him.

"But who is this man?" does not mean he had by now dismissed all rumors about John. He simply has not followed the rumor far enough to conclude there is but one person of consideration – that John himself has come back to life. His fears tell us that his curiosity is in finding out if John has indeed come back, and to do that he must look into the man walking around in his kingdom.

on account of Herodias, the wife of his brother Philip,

Here then is the flashback in detail. We have no background in the Bible regarding Herodias, so we must appeal to the historian Josephus who wrote some 50 years after these events.

Herodias was a close relative in the Herodian family (her name is a giveaway.) She was the daughter of one of Herod the Great's sons, but married one of his other son's, Philip (her uncle), then married another of the sons, Antipas (another uncle.) Salome was her daughter by Philip, hence the legendary attraction Antipas had for Salome was not for his own daughter but certainly incestuous, being his grand-niece. At her level in the genealogy, Herodias was sister to Herod Agrippa who figures in the book of Acts. (The Agrippa of Paul was this man's son, Agrippa II.)

on account of Herodias, John had proclaimed her mock marriage to Antipas illegal in Jewish law. It is even doubtful if it was fully legal in Roman law – there seems to have been a divorce from Antipas' first wife, but we see no formal divorce from Philip and are inclined to believe Herodias simply came to live with Antipas, then married him.

Herodias had a grudge against him

This is an understatement par excellence, since we see her rage and hatred in seeking attempts at his death and in coaxing her daughter for the head of the Baptist. John was like the Washington Post of his day, exposing the sin repeatedly to the populace, and even while in prison, his voice would have echoed through the halls to every guard and official the embarrassment of her sin.

That she could not do away with him on her own is bound up primarily in needing the approval of Antipas, which means that she had not developed the kind of behind-the-scenes machinery of her own that someone like Livia Augusta had engineered behind the thrones of Augustus and Tiberius in Rome.

Nor was her power sufficient for acting and apologizing later, as was often the way with stronger queens.

for Herod was afraid of John, . . but he used to enjoy listening to him.

This is not to say that Herod was inclined toward the truth of what John preached, but men, especially men of learning, can take an entertaining interest in profundity. John was amazingly self-confident in his stand, so very assured of his place in God's plan; and this held the fascination of Herod. Because around him were sycophants and quislings who were as ambivalent as the shifting of the wind.

We aren't told if 'listening' meant discussions in which the prophet explained the truths of God, or that Herod merely enjoyed hearing the sound of his prophesying and praying in prison. It is likely that some dialog around interesting questions may have occurred, but we have no reason to infer that Herod "sat at the feet" of the prophet while he preached and taught.

A strategic day came

This is the fullest rendition in the gospels and we learn here of the setup arranged for Herod by means of the dance on his birthday and the predictability of him granting a reward. The location is the palace with its prison out near the Jordan at Machaerus, not the famous palace in Jerusalem.

The gospels don't state specifically that the dance was an arrangement through the cunning of her mother against the Baptist. But here Mark opens with, *"a strategic day came"* which can only mean strategic for Herodias. Thus, the dance is rightly included as part of her scheme and not merely a circumstance she saw and took advantage of.

She would play on Herod's evident interest in the younger member of the package he had appropriated from Philip. He would be ready to reward Salome for a dance Herodias would make certain he enjoyed.

The tragedy of power and indulgence is that the latter makes one drunk to the voice of wisdom otherwise keenly available in matters of state. Herod is so thoroughly unhinged that he promises up to the half of his kingdom. The trap needs only the trigger to be sprung. Salome need only ask for the right thing.

Everything comes crashing in on Herod as he realizes that he must grant her wish, that his wife has finally won against his longstanding recalcitrance, that in the end John couldn't have remained unpunished and Antipas is a pitable prisoner of his own lasciviousness.

And although the king was very sorry, yet because of his oaths and because of his dinner guests, he was unwilling to refuse her.

and brought his head on a platter, and gave it to the girl; and the girl gave it to her mother.

We should note that the girl gains nothing in this arrangement - she was after all offered real and very tanglible wealth and possessions (not that we should feel sorry for her.) But it is clear that this is Herodias' arrangement and her victory, in that the head will go from executioner to daughter to mother.

When his disciples heard about this, they came and took away his body and laid it in a tomb.

The grave, of course, remains unknown from antiquity. That his disciples could come into the vicinity of the prison and palace officials, and Herod himself, and not be arrested for their association (as was threatened in the precincts of the inquisitions of Jesus) indicates that John was not perceived as a movement, but as an itinerant preacher, a loner. His disciples would have been seen as his friends, and even criminals had the right to be buried by their friends.

This ends the career of John. We reel back from the idea that we have here a man who did such profound work and was called the greatest among those born of woman, yet his earthly reward was the dungeon, and with it the prospect and then the reality of a slicing stroke from the executioners blade; to have one's head fall into the muck and mire of a prison floor; having been created a precious son of the living God, but treated as befitting animals at the slaughter.

The carnal world will see this as a waste because the material world is all there is and if we end badly in it we end badly for all time. But that is where the good news of the New Testament stands out against the false religions and ideologies of the world – that this is not the end of the story, but the gateway to what awaits us beyond.

But let us be clear. There is a great battle going on in high places and to stand for righteousness is to gain the attention of the combatants and bring that battle down into our lives. To one degree or another we will suffer the hatred of that enemy. Thankfully, it is a battle whose outcome and victory are already known for those who are of faith.

CHAPTER 9
Working of Miracles

Mark 6:30-31, 37, Luke 9:10-11, Mark 6:33-35, John 6:3-14
30 The apostles gathered together with Jesus; and they reported to Him all that they had done and taught. 31 And He said to them, "Come away by yourselves to a secluded place and rest a while." (For there were many people coming and going, and they did not even have time to eat.) -- Taking them with Him, He withdrew by Himself to a city called Bethsaida. -- 33 The people saw them going, and many recognized them and ran there together on foot from all the cities, and got there ahead of them. 34 When Jesus went ashore, He saw a large crowd, and He felt compassion for them because they were like sheep without a shepherd; -- 3 Then Jesus went up on the mountain, and there He sat down with His disciples. -- and He began to teach them many things. -- and welcoming them, He began speaking to them about the kingdom of God and curing those who had need of healing. -- Now the Passover, the feast of the Jews, was near. (Mark 6:30-31, Luke 9:10, Mark 6:33-34, John 6:3, Luke 9:11, John 6:4)

35 When it was already quite late, His disciples came to Him and said, "This place is desolate and it is already quite late; 36 send them away so that they may go into the surrounding countryside and villages and buy themselves something to eat." (Mark 6:35)

5 Therefore Jesus, lifting up His eyes and seeing that a large crowd was coming to Him, said to Philip, "Where are we to buy bread, so that these may eat?" 6 This He was saying to test him, for He Himself knew what He was intending to do. (John 6:4-6)

And they said to Him, "Shall we go and spend two hundred denarii on bread and give them something to eat?" (Mark 6:37)

7 Philip answered Him, "Two hundred denarii worth of bread is not sufficient for them, for everyone to receive a little." 8 One of His disciples, Andrew, Simon Peter's brother, said to Him, 9 "There is a lad here who has five barley loaves and two fish, but what are these for so many people?" 10 Jesus said, "Have the people sit down." Now there was much grass in the place. So the men sat down, in number about five thousand. 11 Jesus then took the loaves, and having given thanks, He distributed to those who were seated; -- and He kept giving them to the disciples to set before them; -- likewise also of the fish as much as they wanted. (John 6:7-11a, Mark 6:41, John 6:11b)

12 When they were filled, He said to His disciples, "Gather up the leftover fragments so that nothing will be lost." 13 So they gathered them up, and filled twelve baskets with fragments from the five barley loaves which were left over by those who had eaten. 14 Therefore when the people saw the sign which He had performed, they said, "This is truly the Prophet who is to come into the world." (John 6:12-14)

Commentary

The apostles gathered together with Jesus; and they reported to Him all that they had done and taught. And He said to them, "Come away by yourselves..

We see here the manner in which Jesus mentored the disciples. He gave them instruction to a certain level and then it was up to them to go and try it firsthand, learning the way of it by doing. Returning with accounts of how they did, the discussion and training went further.

We can imagine Jesus correcting all the little pitfalls and misfires as they reported things that went well and things not so well. We can see Him instructing them on how to avoid vacuous arguments and pointless discussions, what statements would have been simpler and more concise. How to avoid side trails and get to the heart of the matter with people.

He desires that they now get away in seclusion for rest, which is enigmatic because He certainly knows what is about to take place – that the people are going to meet Him at His arrival and make seclusion impossible. We wonder if Jesus is here entertaining some form of deception in suggesting seclusion when He knew it would be the complete opposite?

For those who know the future, there is a certain aspect of deception involved by default. It is more a case letting the future play out as it will, rather than heading off the future by means of one's knowledge of it. Jesus can know that there will be no seclusion yet offer it to the disciples, in that He is not obliged to disclose all He knows simply because He knows it. And the wrong of deception is in causing injury in the withholding of all the facts. None of this was involved here.

It is perfectly true that they had come to a point where rest and seclusion were in order. Making this suggestion was to establish in them in making provision for it in their ministries.

Taking them with Him, He withdrew by Himself to a city called Bethsaida.

As above, Jesus was working in the cities of the disciples, of which Bethsaida figured prominently. We find in a moment that He is not aiming at the town but for a mountain or hillside in the vicinity (John 6:3)

The people saw them going,

To clarify the scene, Jesus and the men are taking a boat (Mark 6:32) and some of the people choose to run all the way around the lake front to Bethsaida such that they may arrive ahead of Him.

This seems odd because the straightest and shortest course would be across the lake, making the road around certainly longer. But boat travel is not necessarily swift depending on conditions. The boat was made to be powered by a sail or by oars, so the small voyage could have been rather slow and lightly powered if winds were noticeably slight. It may indeed have been a very casual sailing, more like a drifting across, compared to the steady run being conducted around the lake.

When Jesus went ashore, He saw a large crowd, and He felt compassion for them because they were like sheep without a shepherd;

The plans for seclusion were now lost, but we don't see this received with disappointment. It says Jesus had compassion for them. This is the mark of one who is like Christ, to put aside personal wishes and prefer the needs of others.

sheep without a shepherd is repeated over in Matthew 9:36 on a different occasion. This is not a discrepancy because it is not a case of reporting some actual fact that is occurring, but rather, this is an observation by the disciples of what Jesus felt, not being tied to any specific event, and each author chooses when to mention it.

Then Jesus went up on the mountain, . . began to teach them many things . . and welcoming them, He began speaking to them about the kingdom of God and curing those who had need of healing.

The combination of the gospels is a bit difficult because each is stressing different aspects of this scene. Jesus takes to a hillside nearby and sits down with His disciples to continue teaching and instructing them. But there are hundreds of people with them and as it says, these "he welcomed" and cured those in need of healing.

Now the Passover, the feast of the Jews, was near.

This is the third Passover mentioned in Jesus ministry which might obligate us to a 4-year ministry, since there is yet the Passover of His passion, except that the first Passover occurred when He was a child and visited the Temple with His parents (Luke 2.)

So the Passover here is the third in his earthly life, but the second since He began His ministry, the first being just after the miracle at Cana (John 2.)

His disciples came to Him and said, ". . send them away so that they may go into the surrounding countryside and villages and buy themselves something to eat."

The response of the disciples was conditioned on the lateness of the hour and their location having no ready means of provisions nearby. The logical thing to do was to send people on their way, back to their own homes for food and drink.

[He] said to Philip, "Where are we to buy bread, so that these may eat?"

Jesus heads off this suggestion by asking Philip where they can buy what is needed? He certainly knows where and whether that is even feasible, but the point is to get the disciples thinking about the need to take care of this right where they stand, not by sending the people home. *This He was saying to test him, for He Himself knew what He was intending to do.* (John 6:4-6)

Shall we go and spend two hundred denarii on bread?

The question is not asking what Jesus then desires they first go and do, but one of incredulity – "are you expecting us to go and buy bread for all these with two hundred denarii?"

This is indicated by Philip's immediate observation, *" Two hundred denarii worth of bread is not sufficient"*

Two hundred denarii was the equivalent of 200 days wages. A day's wage was enough to buy more than bread, but if used to buy bread only would probably purchase 15-20 loaves, if that. Two hundred denarii would therefore feed roughly between two and four thousand people, and only with bread. Hence, not enough to feed five thousand.

"There is a lad here who has five barley loaves and two fish

This observation by Andrew is meant to double the effect of Philip's comment on the inadequacy of the situation. Together, these are like saying, "How would we buy the necessary food with the money we presently have, and here in our midst is but a boys lunch!"

Jesus said, "Have the people sit down."

It is the precise setting for the miracle intended and what his disciples have now spoken that necessitate its execution –not enough food on hand, nor enough money to buy it.

By telling them to order the people to sit down, Jesus is telling them this is about to be taken care of by Him and by the powers available to Him. We are told the number is five thousand persons, to be distinguished from the later event of the four thousand (Matthew 15:38.)

The differences are in the details, the five thousand involved five loaves and two fish, the four thousand involved seven loaves and *"a few fish"*. The five thousand yielded twelve baskets left over, the four thousand, seven. Both are done in the Galilee and on mountain or hill sides.

Some have concluded that because the events have details not too far off from each other, that this is one event reported somewhat differently in John than in the synoptics. But we are prevented by the fact that Jesus references them later as two events, *"Do you not yet understand or remember the five loaves of the five thousand, and how many baskets full you picked up? "Or the seven loaves of the four thousand, and how many large baskets full you picked up?* (Matthew 16:9-10)

One puzzling aspect is why in Matthew's account the disciples later broach the same concerns about provisions, having learned already in the case of the five thousand? It is a question we cannot really explain, except to appeal to their humanity.

He distributed to those who were seated; -- and He kept giving them to the disciples to set before them;

While it says *"he distributed"* we see that it was through His disciples. The gospel writers do not show how this specifically occurred. How, for example, did the twelve baskets get into the picture from the five loaves and two fish? Jesus gave thanks for the bread and fish, but then a multiplication would have to have take place that necessitated the baskets.

Perhaps the fish and loaves were in a single basket which when taken around among the people became filled. But it says that *He kept giving them to the disciples to set before them* which implies that other baskets were asked for, filled and returned for refilling until all were fed.

We have no report in these accounts of what had to have been seen in an around Jesus – an empty basket being miraculously filled with bread and fish, then another empty basket receiving the same, over and over. Films have portrayed this as having the baskets sent out and remaining filled despite people taking from them. But this is precluded by the statement that Jesus continually gave them for distribution which implies an emptying and a filling process.

also of the fish as much as they wanted.

Like healing, Jesus does things beyond expectations. It was not just enough fish that men had one apiece, but that they had as much as they wanted. Taking two or three did not present a problem of having enough for others. It was all taken into account, as much as was desired was made available.

"Gather up the leftover fragments so that nothing will be lost."

Losing nothing in excess did not mean collecting for the additional consumption of the people present, since they were now filled. We must infer that the remainder was given to others on the way back into town or distributed to the poor That there were twelve baskets and not some other number implies these were each of the ones used by the Twelve to distribute, but this doesn't explain the corresponding miracle when only seven baskets remained.

"This is truly the Prophet who is to come into the world."

There was much of the miraculous to praise. For those in the outlying areas, they could simply observe that all were getting fed when no means was seen anywhere to account for it. They would also have witnessed the abundance of food as the basket came near. For those near to Jesus, they would have additionally seen the empty baskets being filled out of thin air. Hence no shortage of reasons for proclaiming that the Prophet had come.

This would be that foretold in Deuteronomy 18:15-18 *The LORD thy God will raise up unto thee a Prophet from the midst of thee, of thy brethren, like unto me; unto him ye shall hearken; . . 18"I will raise up a prophet from among their countrymen like you, and I will put My words in his mouth, and he shall speak to them all that I command him. "*

Now this prophecy says nothing about miracles that would identify his arrival for the people. Yet the words *like you* v.18, suggest that this Prophet will employ miracles of huge aspect as did Moses. Certainly, this event was large enough in scope as to occasion the connection.

What is important here is the connection to the great principles of God among His people in the provision of hope in the midst of trials. Israel understood from its history that it would be under many trials and persecutions. In the midst of this was the hope of deliverance and restoration in the coming of "that Prophet" and in the promises concerning Messiah.

With Jesus, they see after so long a dearth of spiritual hope a renewed expectation that the time has at last come and they have been blessed to now see it, for which they cannot keep back the words, *"This is truly the Prophet who is to come into the world."*

Mark 6:45-52, John 6:17a, Matthew 14:28-31,33, John 6:21

45 Immediately Jesus made His disciples get into the boat and go ahead of Him to the other side to Bethsaida, while He Himself was sending the crowd away. 46 After bidding them farewell, -- so Jesus, perceiving that they were intending to come and take Him by force to make Him king, withdrew again to the mountain by Himself alone. (Mark 6:45-46, John 6:15)

16 Now when evening came, His disciples went down to the sea, 17 and after getting into a boat, they started to cross the sea to Capernaum. It had already become dark, and Jesus had not yet come to them. (John 6:16-17a)

47 When it was evening, the boat was in the middle of the sea, and He was alone on the land. 48 Seeing them straining at the oars, for the wind was against them, at about the fourth watch of the night He came to them, walking on the sea; and He intended to pass by them. 49 But when they saw Him walking on the sea, they supposed that it was a ghost, and cried out; 50 for they all saw Him and were terrified. But immediately He spoke with them and said to them, "Take courage; it is I, do not be afraid." (Mark 6:47-50)

28 Peter said to Him, "Lord, if it is You, command me to come to You on the water." 29 And He said, "Come!" And Peter got out of the boat, and walked on the water and came toward Jesus. 30 But seeing the wind, he became frightened, and beginning to sink, he cried out, "Lord, save me!" 31 Immediately Jesus stretched out His hand and took hold of him, and said to him, "You of little faith, why did you doubt?" (Matt 14:28-31)

21 So they were willing to receive Him into the boat, (John 6:21)

51 Then He got into the boat with them, and the wind stopped; and they were utterly astonished, 52 for they had not gained any insight from the incident of the loaves, but their heart was hardened. -- And [they] . . worshiped Him, saying, "You are certainly God's Son!" -- and immediately the boat was at the land to which they were going. (Mark 6:51,52, Matthew 14:33, John 6:21)

Commentary

Immediately Jesus made His disciples get into the boat and go ahead of Him to the other side to Bethsaida,

This is a little confusing because in the previous section they had already sailed to Bethsaida, near the scene of the feeding of the five thousand, and they are now being asked to sail over to Bethsaida, despite being already in its vicinity.

Many scholars have suggested that there were two Bethsaidas, one called Bethsaida Julias on the eastern shore of the lake, and another called Bethsaida of Galilee at the entry point of the Jordan and closer to Capernaum. Also, John distinguishes Philip as being from Bethsaida of Galilee, which wouldn't be a necessary qualification if there were just one (John 12:21.)

So we have the feeding of the five thousand taking place near Bethsaida Julias, on a mountain, and the disciples then being ordered to take the boat over to Bethsaida of Galilee, which was virtually next door to Capernaum. John's reference to the journey as starting out to cross to Capernaum (6:17) would agree with another Bethsaida associated closely with Capernaum, such that an author could refer to the journey either way.

We must also bear in mind that Peter had boats in both Capernaum and Bethsaida which would be easier to manage if Bethsaida were the town next door rather than the one further east. We also have external reference in Josephus who says that his jurisdiction was in the Bethsaida of Gaulonitis, an area never referred to as in Galilee.

After bidding them farewell, . . perceiving that they were intending to come and take Him by force to make Him king, withdrew again to the mountain by Himself alone.

It is clear that these events have now stirred some to conclude his messiahship and the fulfillment of prophecies to the degree that they would seize Him so as to make Him king. This is, in fact, what was expected to happen from His early preaching that the Kingdom was now at hand. But this was now ironically out of the question, since the authorities were rejecting Him, and their acknowledgment was key. An amateurish attempt to set Him up as king would end very badly for all concerned. He was now well on His way to the truer plan between Him and the Father, by which the rejected king must be killed and return again.

Jesus therefore sends the disciples back to Capernaum (a direction we soon see them to have understood) and He dismisses the crowd so as to make a firm and decided escape from them to pray.

We might think that Jesus was praying for the special power He would need in preparation for the miracle on the sea. But its clear from his concerns about premature reactions that His aim is to intensify the spiritual unity with the Father, understandably limited by the flesh, and which will renew the purposes ahead of Him in every decision and action according to plan. Thus, we need to renew our attitude toward prayer in that even Jesus regularly appealed to it to overcome the limits of His incarnation.

Now when evening came, His disciples went down to the sea, and after getting into a boat, they started to cross the sea to Capernaum. It had already become dark, and Jesus had not yet come to them.

Here we see that the disciples understood they were to return further to Capernaum not just to Bethsaida. Jesus had not returned by evening and they assumed His present plans did not include joining them on the return journey. As to being puzzled or dismayed, they had been given their orders and they knew Him to be someone who knew the meaning of His own words. The fact that He had separated from them meant they were on their own at this point and waiting for Him was not part of the order.

He came to them, walking on the sea;

Now they are forced to use the oars because the sail was of no use with the wind against them. The "fourth watch" is a Roman term, by which is meant the hours between 3:00 – 6:00 AM. Watches were sets of three-hour divisions through the night – this being the last before beginning the corresponding watches of the day.

If they started out at evening and it was now about the fourth watch (just before or just after 3:00 AM) they would have been at their rowing for some six hours or more and not yet arrived at their destination. In fact, from John's gospel we learn that they had sailed but 25-30 furlongs (4 miles) (6:19), which is just over half the distance across the lake itself.

Again, if Bethsaida Julias was their starting point and Capernaum is just over midway on the N shore, the distance is not a necessary discrepancy at all, and they were no doubt almost there when they see Jesus on the water. This also accounts for the statement that after Jesus got into the boat they found themselves at their destination.

they supposed that it was a ghost, and cried out; for they all saw Him and were terrified.

It states that He intended to pass by them, which would indicate He was looking ahead, not at the men in the boat; all of which would have added to the initial dread of what they saw.

We must keep in mind that these conditions - the darkness, the wind and the difficulty in making progress - were all occasions for setting the mind ill at ease. The natural fear of not knowing what's out there and having the wind whistling against you in the darkness can cause one to entertain fears that constantly have to be checked and reality re-clarified.

Now, while trying to succeed in conquering their childish fears, they see what they cannot perceive otherwise as a ghost. So we quite understand they *were terrified.*

We wonder what purpose Jesus would have had in this arrangement or in posing Himself on the water as He did? It is more than just walking on it, but also in His manner, so as to pass by them. It is clear that Jesus desires at certain moments to make it clear to them that He is "other" than mere human flesh – that He is Incarnate Son of God – and that His command and use of nature can express themselves in strange contrast to their expectations. He is providing a vision, austere as it may be, of who He is.

They cry out and He breaks His forward gaze and begins speaking to them. They recognize His voice and enough is said beyond what is recorded - (*He spoke with them*) - that Peter becomes calm enough to make a request -

"Lord, if it is You, command me to come to You on the water."

We are left to surmise if this is a desire in Peter to acquire this special ability for himself (imagine being able to say, "I walked on water also"), or if Peter's exuberance is so overwhelming that he earnestly desires to be with Jesus. It is a bold request either way, but it has to be based in a faith that Jesus could make this happen. It is raw, unadulterated faith, rooted in the simplicity that Jesus can do anything, as He is now demonstrating, hence, to ask this is only a matter of will, not power.

"Come!"

We might expect, like a censuring parent, that Jesus would not entertain this request since it seemed too much like mere caprice or a desire for something akin to magic. But surprisingly He invites Peter to come on out. It is here that we are reminded of Jesus' later statement to them in their preparation for ministering after His ascension, *"Greater things shall ye do because I go to the Father."* (John 14:12.)

Jesus is deliberately interested in them repeating and excelling in His own miracles and works. He expects this and unbraids them for their lack of faith when they meet with a lesser success. We must embrace the reality and the intent that we are not to always be appropriately less in power and capacity, but rather equal in availing ourselves of all that is necessary to the furtherance of the Gospel.

Beckoning Peter to come and participate in the same miracle is genuine and intended. It is only his own weakness in faith that is criticized, not that the attempt itself was foolish from the start.

But seeing the wind, he became frightened, and beginning to sink, he cried out, "Lord, save me!"

Many lessons and sermons have been spoken on the extension of this event to our own lives. We are given the analogy that to take our eyes off Jesus is to precipitate failure. We cannot denigrate this as a misappropriation of the lesson. It is true that Peter's failing was only in being distracted by the wind, which surely brought him back to the human question, "What do I think I'm trying to do?"

Now this realization came after a sufficient time of him walking indeed as far out as where Jesus was, because Jesus is close enough to reach out and grab him when the distraction had its effect. So Peter was able to get that far on faith, a considerable confidence that this cannot be rationalized as a sort of ancient, ignorant way of explaining that Peter never walked at all and sank almost immediately, hence Jesus did not intend that man repeat such a miracle.

"Lord, save me!"

Much also can be made of this statement, in many analogies to the desperate cry of the soul when it realizes it is going down for the count. When we truly see our condition and have cast off all sophistication, we are ready to cry, "Save me, Lord." For Peter, he meant, "Keep me from drowning" but we can't resist the extension. It is verse with one meaning, but many applications.

"You of little faith, why did you doubt?"

This perplexes us because it presents the idea that success is conditioned upon eradicating all doubts and we find that near impossible to do completely. If we have even one doubt are we then disabled from the successful outcome of the works God bids us do?

There can be no doubt in the NT that faith is the key to the power, the discernment and the gifts of God. We cannot operate in them without it. The key here with Peter and with us is not if there are any doubts whatsoever, but whether our faith is characterized as great or little, strong or weak. It is not like leaven which leavens the whole lump, but which is in control. Is faith in control or is fear and weakness?

In the disciples, they are here often described as having little faith, which is understandable in these formative moments as they learn the way of faith and how it is engaged with God. But with this is the intent that it not remain so, hence we are not entitled to beg off with God because, after all, even the disciples were weak in faith.

Some have criticized Jesus in being too hard because He certainly knew they would not have His own degree of faith, so complaining seems too idealistic. But it is a valid method of inspiration toward greater things to clarify that the reason for failure is in little or in weak faith. It is meant to engender an appeal for greater faith, and that is the key to it coming about.

So they were willing to receive Him into the boat,

This is the logical place to include the parallel words from John. Having seen all these things and been thereby comforted, they were willing to have Him come into the boat with them.

and they were utterly astonished, . . but their heart was hardened. . . [they] . . worshiped Him, saying, "You are certainly God's Son!"

This is an odd combination from the gospels because it sets up an apparent contradiction. If they were astonished because their hearts were hardened, how is it that they then worship with the declaration that He is God's Son?

We are also not told the reason they had become hardened over the loaves. In a later discussion, there is some consternation that Jesus has criticized them for not having brought bread, and while this might be seen as a reason for an attitude toward Jesus (they may have seen Him as overly critical) none of this was part of the feeding of the five thousand earlier.

We are only told that the hardness was the cause of their not gaining insight about the miracle. Perhaps some understanding is to be had in Jesus' later questioning if they had understood the meaning of the two feedings and the basketsful left over – " *"Do you not yet understand or remember the five loaves of the five thousand, and how many baskets full you picked up? "Or the seven loaves of the four thousand, and how many large baskets full you picked up? "How is it that you do not understand that I did not speak to you concerning bread?* " Matthew 16:8.

This was in relation to the charge to beware of the leaven of the Pharisees at which they thought He was criticizing them that they had not brought bread. In general, the hardness here is not a matter of being offended with Jesus or that He was too harsh or critical, but that it is referring to whatever impediment prevented them from seeing the truths in these things. (This will be discussed further at Mark chapter 8.)

Astonishment is understood because the miracle would not fit with whatever stumblings produced their hardness of heart (or their inability to get the message) in all the foregoing. But that this resulted in praise is more difficult to understand. The key is in the tenses.

Some might infer that because they were hardened, they remained hardened even despite the miracle. But it is the miracle that is for the moment re-confirming the truth against their rationalizations or whatever is hindering their understanding. So they are able to transition from hardness to faith because of the extraordinary nature of this miracle.

and immediately the boat was at the land to which they were going.

This is to say that they were nigh to the destination at the point of seeing the vision – Jesus also being able to see them struggling from the shore. In the course of events wherein Peter walks and Jesus then enters the boat, the boat continued to move on its course (perhaps some men still rowed, despite the events with Peter and Jesus) and they were able to see their destination when the winds were stilled.

Mark 6:51-56, John 6:22-40
53 When they had crossed over they came to land at Gennesaret, and moored to the shore. 54 When they got out of the boat, immediately the people recognized Him, 55 and ran about that whole country and began to carry here and there on their pallets those who were sick, to the place they heard He was. 56 Wherever He entered villages, or cities, or countryside, they were laying the sick in the market places, and imploring Him that they might just touch the fringe of His cloak; and as many as touched it were being cured.
(Mark 6:51-56)

The next day the crowd that stood on the other side of the sea saw that there was no other small boat there, except one, and that Jesus had not entered with His disciples into the boat, but that His disciples had gone away alone. 23 There came other small boats from Tiberias near to the place where they ate the bread after the Lord had given thanks. 24 So when the crowd saw that Jesus was not there, nor His disciples, they themselves got into the small boats, and came to Capernaum seeking Jesus.

25 When they found Him on the other side of the sea, they said to Him, "Rabbi, when did You get here?" 26 Jesus answered them and said, "Truly, truly, I say to you, you seek Me, not because you saw signs, but because you ate of the loaves and were filled. 27 "Do not work for the food which perishes, but for the food which endures to eternal life, which the Son of Man will give to you, for on Him the Father, God, has set His seal."

28 Therefore they said to Him, "What shall we do, so that we may work the works of God?" 29 Jesus answered and said to them, "This is the work of God, that you believe in Him whom He has sent." 30 So they said to Him, "What then do You do for a sign, so that we may see, and believe You? What work do You perform? 31 "Our fathers ate the manna in the wilderness; as it is written, `HE GAVE THEM BREAD OUT OF HEAVEN TO EAT.' "

32 Jesus then said to them, "Truly, truly, I say to you, it is not Moses who has given you the bread out of heaven, but it is My Father who gives you the true bread out of heaven. 33 "For the bread of God is that which comes down out of heaven, and gives life to the world." 34 Then they said to Him, "Lord, always give us this bread." 35 Jesus said to them, "I am the bread of life; he who comes to Me will not hunger, and he who believes in Me will never thirst.

36 "But I said to you that you have seen Me, and yet do not believe. 37 "All that the Father gives Me will come to Me, and the one who comes to Me I will certainly not cast out. 38 "For I have come down from heaven, not to do My own will, but the will of Him who sent Me. 39 "This is the will of Him who sent Me, that of all that He has given Me I lose nothing, but raise it up on the last day. 40 "For this is the will of My Father, that everyone who beholds the Son and believes in Him will have eternal life, and I Myself will raise him up on the last day." (John 6:22-40)

Commentary

When they had crossed over they came to land at Gennesaret, and moored to the shore.

Again, we meet with a few more confusing geographical terms. Gennesaret is a town just west of Capernaum. It is also the name for the small plain in which Capernaum sits, and is used as another name for the Sea of Galilee. *they came to land at Gennesaret* might be reasoned as coming to shore at Capernaum which is also at the plain of Gennesaret, but this would be an odd stretch of wording because saying, "at Gennesaret" would usually be understood as at the town, since there was one. And since there was also the town of Capernaum, saying *at Gennesaret* when one meant Capernaum would be totally misleading. So we must take the words more literally to mean that they did arrive at Gennesaret.

Thus it happens that across all these accounts we have them being ordered by Jesus to sail to Bethsaida, which they understood to really mean a return to Capernaum, yet they ended up in Gennesaret a bit further west of Capernaum.

This is probably due to their struggle against the wind having set them a bit off course, causing them to travel further west than intended.

immediately the people recognized Him, . . . Wherever He entered villages, or cities, or countryside, they were laying the sick in the market places

It states that the people began immediately to carry the infirmed to Him. The utterly desperate conditions of people in these times made healing *the* primary draw of the crowds to Jesus. We tend to think of folks as somehow being holier in biblical times and that they came to Jesus for predominantly spiritual reasons. But many came just to get healed because the times were so desperate. So we are going to see huge crowds wherever Jesus goes, but we need to accommodate more utilitarian reasons on their part than we might otherwise conclude.

What is of interest is that Jesus does not hold back healing on this basis. We don't see Him holding counseling sessions with each candidate to screen only those with the best spiritual purposes. The healing was very broad.

that they might just touch the fringe of His cloak; and as many as touched it were being cured.

God honored this method, though it be seen as creating a sort of magical interface for healing. We recoil from charlatans on the radio who promise to send a healing cloth for a donation, but this has precedent in the NT (the cloth, not the donation), both here and in Paul who sent a handkerchiefs (Acts 19:12.)

God honors things that release faith, though they may seem strange to us. Reason would question if such people really had the faith to be healed or were simply taking advantage of a mechanism that worked, but that is for God to tell. What God sees in each human heart, man cannot scrutinize.

So when the crowd saw that Jesus was not there, nor His disciples, they themselves got into the small boats, and came to Capernaum seeking Jesus.

The scene now shifts back to the place of the feeding of the five thousand and the crowds left behind when the disciples left for Capernaum. These people noticed that Jesus had not gone with them (they did not know about His appearance on the sea and having joined the disciples again.)

They observe that there is a single boat, most likely left by the disciples for Jesus, since they were leaving without Him. They are gathered at the scene of the miracle in the hope that Jesus would reappear from His seclusion and use the boat to return across the sea.

Word of the miracle has now spread to Tiberias, midway down the western side of the sea so that the residents have now taken boats and arrived also in search of Jesus. All eventually discern that He is not on that side of the lake any longer and they head for Capernaum.

So despite landing at Gennesaret, He has worked His way back into Capernaum.

"Rabbi, when did You get here?"

This is quite understandably the very first question. The unused boat would mean He had walked around the north rim back to Capernaum and someone would surely have seen Him.

He deliberately does not answer their question but begins to address why they came seeking Him.

you seek Me, not because you saw signs, but because you ate of the loaves and were filled.

There is a reason for this response. How He came to return to Capernaum would be wrapped up in His spiritual power, the miracle of it, etc. But He unbraids them that they are not seeking Him because of the signs and wonders seen at the feeding, but merely because they ate and were filled. In other words, they did not value the miraculous aspect more than the sheer fact that they had gotten plenty to eat on that day.

This seems hard to understand since we can't see how the miracle of it could be ignored. But it is a feature of fallen humanity that it can rationalize away the supernatural in preference for the materialistic.

That they did not value the signs done that day made them unfit to appreciate or even believe how He had gotten from Bethsaida to Capernaum. It is an insightful way of saying why He is not going to tell them.

This attitude of theirs is made clearer by the following –

"Do not work for the food which perishes, but for the food which endures to eternal life, which the Son of Man will give to you, for on Him the Father, God, has set His seal."

Their concerns were for the stomach and how to satisfy its needs. Jesus was merely a benefactor for daily bread.

The contrast with what He was offering was between the perishable nature of food and the imperishable nature of spiritual food. What good does it do to be filled in the stomach while empty in spirit? The focus is also on eternal life, what preparations are being made for it? What He is offering is designed to last into eternal life.

He follows by adding that He can provide that kind of food. It is not a mere lesson by a rabbi after which one might wonder how to acquire it, but He is a complete package – He explains what is needed and has the ability to provide it.

This He says He can do because He is specially commissioned by the Father - *"On Him . . He has set His seal"*. This is an understatement for the benefit of the people. He is in truth more than a mere agent of the Father, having permission to act for Him. He is deity and in touch with its powers.

This is thought to express a vague reference to the limits of His incarnation in which He has given up or suspended use of His powers except as the Father wills, so that He may be the example for us, having suffered the limitations of human existence. So He uses terms like this to express His authority in terms the people can readily understand without prompting a whole theological discussion of the Trinity, that few would be able to grasp much less readily believe. However the biblical response to the *kenosis* explanation does not allow Him to be divested of divine power, but rather that He chose not to avail Himself of it.

What shall we do, so that we may work the works of God?

Again, they ask a somewhat ignorant question. It is also similarly utilitarian. "Okay, we shouldn't just seek the needs of our stomachs, so tell us what to do in performing the works of God."

It is a utilitarian question because it merely seeks to fix the problem highlighted. It does not ask nor expect that there is a relationship to be had as a prerequisite. Spirituality is cast in terms of service, things to do.

This is partly due to Jesus' stress on *"Do not work . . but rather work . ."* This is understood by them as service, the execution of tasks - that satisfying the spiritual is in doing things.

"This is the work of God, that you believe in Him whom He has sent."

Jesus explains that it begins with an attitude toward God, a belief that includes Him whom the Father has sent. Spiritual food is not about doing works but about becoming a child of God, being like the Father, born of Him.

"What then do You do for a sign, so that we may see, and believe You? What work do You perform? 31 "Our fathers ate the manna in the wilderness;

They are learning, to a small degree. They did not value the miracle of the feeding and the sign it conveyed, but they have come His way towards at least valuing a sign, that they might believe Him, as He states they must do. They even bolster their request by recounting the kind of sign they take great stock in – the giving of manna in the wilderness.

This is ironic because Jesus had just repeated a smaller instance of that miracle in the feeding of the five thousand and they did not discern its importance. Perhaps it was because it was not seen as "coming down from Heaven" and how it came to appear was confused by the activity of serving and managing the baskets. Perhaps this is why they chose this miracle for contrast – because Jesus had fed five thousand in an afternoon, while their God had fed a half-million souls for forty years.

But to return the irony, Jesus can use it to show their error.

it is not Moses who has given you the bread out of heaven, but it is My Father who gives you the true bread out of heaven.

This is the core of the issue – recognizing God Himself at work rather than merely His servants. The manna was God's gift and had they enlarged their perception and knowledge of God in learning about it, they would have seen a similar gift given at the feeding on the mountain side, provided by the same Hand. As long as they focused on Moses as giver, they would not see the connection.

who gives you the true bread out of heaven.

There is an enticement or a hook at the end of this statement – the true bread out of heaven. It is there to prompt them to wonder what this is. It is also stated as something that is happening to them right now - *"who gives you [present tense] the true bread."*

Jesus wishes that the two be distinguished – there is the bread of Moses out of Heaven and there is a true bread. The one they understand (the manna). The other they see as clearly not the same as Moses' bread, yet to what does it refer?

"For the bread of God is that which comes down out of heaven, and gives life to the world."

Another clue. It also comes down out of Heaven and gives life not just to certain men, but to the world. Moses' manna did not give life to the world. Jesus on the other hand claims to have come from the Father and He has been preaching about the eternal life in the Kingdom since Day One.

"Lord, always give us this bread."

We should not infer by *Lord* that they recognize Him as Lord of Heaven. It is a title given out of respect and honor, in this case for Jesus as rabbi.

It is difficult here to know if they are again being utilitarian and wishing to simply be permanent beneficiaries of such a blessing, or if they have become truly enlightened and opened to their spiritual need.

That John is presenting it as their response without further need of admonition by Jesus indicates that he sees it as the latter – a genuine enlightenment to the truth that Jesus is proclaiming.

I am the bread of life; he who comes to Me will not hunger, and he who believes in Me will never thirst.

It could be restated as, *"I am the bread of eternal life."* He never meant Himself as the food that sustains the biological machine, though He is key to its creation and supply. His focus is not on the eighty years or so of earthly, biological life (life as *bios*), but on life as *zoe*.

All men are made for that life, though they settle for the earthly span of existence. Those who sense this and yearn for it are now called to come to Him, that the eternal hunger of the soul to be right with the world and its Creator will be eternally satisfied. The thirst for righteousness will be eternally filled.

What does it mean to come to Him? It is to recognize the eternal hunger within, that He is the supply and to move to Him while simultaneously moving away from our former life. This is mirrored in the physical actions of the apostles who left their nets and that way of life and came to Him. There was nothing sinful about their former work, but they had to abandon it in order to follow Him.

For those of us who are not called to full-time ministry as they were, we must repeat the other abandonment they also experienced – the giving up of life's hold on us and we on it, in terms of ultimate allegiances. It is an abandonment of our way and the notion that our thoughts are just as good as His. To come to Him is to leave something else, and not temporarily but permanently.

"But I said to you that you have seen Me, and yet do not believe.

Here is a clarification about the coming. It is in response to a calling. It is not the coming per se, but the coming in answer to a call – *"No one can come to Me unless the Father draw him."*

Those who have seen Him (meaning Him and His works) yet do not believe are demonstrating that they have come to Him on their own terms, not in response to the calling of the Father.

All that the Father gives Me will come to Me, and the one who comes to Me I will certainly not cast out.

We learn here that the Father is directly involved in giving believers to His Son. In a moment this will be expanded to mean that no one can come unless drawn (John 6:44.) But once drawn or "given", there is then a principle in play that such will come, and of those, Jesus will not reject any.

That does not mean the ones who have come never leave, just that if they do, it is not because they have been rejected by Christ. It is an assurance for those whose heart is pure and sincere, that they have a security in the Father and in His Son that nothing from Heaven will interfere with their coming or cast them out.

This is the will of Him who sent Me, that of all that He has given Me I lose nothing, but raise it up on the last day.

It is the Father's will that none are lost, but it may not be man's will to remain found. Hence, we are to ponder how this could be characterized as having lost nothing? Whether of God's doing or man's, those who abandon the faith are lost.

This is better explained in the predestinarian model in which the elect are certain to be saved and those who abandon the faith were not part of those who were given. There are some also who distinguish between "drawn" and "given", the latter being the elect, the others outside the elect.

More insight can be gained by noticing the neuter in *raise it* up on the last day. This would seem to be a reference to the Body of Christ, and if so, it is the Body as a whole that is seen as given and not lost.

". . everyone who beholds the Son and believes in Him will have eternal life, and I Myself will raise him up on the last day."

We have tremendous confidence in this, that our belief in Him secures us into eternal life and it is Christ who will personally raise us. This is to mean that the raising is a matter between Him and us, not a process by which He raises as a disinterested party. If we as individuals are raised, He has given word that it be done respecting us as an individual, not as merely a member of a class of those who will be raised. It means He takes a personal interest in raising us.

This joins with the other assurances that we are secure in our salvation:

Therefore there is now no condemnation for those who are in Christ Jesus. (Romans 8:1)

For by grace you have been saved through faith; and that not of yourselves, it is the gift of God; (Eph 2:28)

Let us draw near with a sincere heart in full assurance of faith, having our hearts sprinkled clean from an evil conscience and our bodies washed with pure water. (Hebrews 10:22)

That you may stand perfect and fully assured in all the will of God. (Col 4:12)

John 6:41-59
41 Therefore the Jews were grumbling about Him, because He said, "I am the bread that came down out of heaven." 42 They were saying, "Is not this Jesus, the son of Joseph, whose father and mother we know? How does He now say, `I have come down out of heaven'?" 43 Jesus answered and said to them, "Do not grumble among yourselves. 44 "No one can come to Me unless the Father who sent Me draws him; and I will raise him up on the last day. 45 "It is written in the prophets, `AND THEY SHALL ALL BE TAUGHT OF GOD.'

Everyone who has heard and learned from the Father, comes to Me. 46 "Not that anyone has seen the Father, except the One who is from God; He has seen the Father.

47 "Truly, truly, I say to you, he who believes has eternal life. 48 "I am the bread of life. 49 "Your fathers ate the manna in the wilderness, and they died. 50 "This is the bread which comes down out of heaven, so that one may eat of it and not die. 51 "I am the living bread that came down out of heaven; if anyone eats of this bread, he will live forever; and the bread also which I will give for the life of the world is My flesh." 52 Then the Jews began to argue with one another, saying, "How can this man give us His flesh to eat?"

53 So Jesus said to them, "Truly, truly, I say to you, unless you eat the flesh of the Son of Man and drink His blood, you have no life in yourselves. 54 "He who eats My flesh and drinks My blood has eternal life, and I will raise him up on the last day. 55 "For My flesh is true food, and My blood is true drink. 56 "He who eats My flesh and drinks My blood abides in Me, and I in him. 57 "As the living Father sent Me, and I live because of the Father, so he who eats Me, he also will live because of Me. 58 "This is the bread which came down out of heaven; not as the fathers ate and died; he who eats this bread will live forever." 59 These things He said in the synagogue as He taught in Capernaum. (John 6:41-59)

Commentary

Therefore the Jews were grumbling about Him

We should take grumbling to mean they were decidedly upset and indignant, not merely pondering what he meant.. They were upset with His words about being the better bread that comes down from Heaven, making Himself not only to be better than Moses, but to be divine, since He is claiming that He Himself came down, as opposed to His words and wisdom.

We will see this same word (*'gogguzo'*) used of the disciples in a moment, but we won't attribute the same attitudes behind it.

The mention of the grumblings of the Jews is to highlight that Jesus' teaching has finally amalgamated as a systematic and deliberately opposing approach to their way of managing and living Judaism. It is a call to return to the simplistic truths of God and His statutes. It gets behind the statutes and pictures the heart of God in them; and this is something that has long since been lost in the Pharisees and learned Jews of the time. It has become formalized to the place that ritual and legality have replaced knowing the heart of God. We saw this a while back in the stooped woman made miserable by a demon. The Pharisee could not see the miracle Jesus had just performed but had his eyes focused instead on the legal issue of the moment – *"There are six days in which we may labor. This ought to have been done on one of those days, not the Sabbath!"* (Luke 13:11.)

"Is not this Jesus, the son of Joseph, whose father and mother we know? How does He now say, `I have come down out of heaven'?"

This will be the constant taunt in this locale – *"we know this man – He is merely Joseph and Mary's son of Nazareth."* It is the ancient condition of *familiarity breeds contempt.* Yet we are not in Nazareth but in Capernaum.

It must be understood that these towns and this whole region are very close knit. Now Nazareth is a good twenty miles from Capernaum, but the upper lake region was frequented by inland residents for all kinds of reasons throughout the year. It is also likely that some folks with not much to do except create trouble were following Jesus to various places, partly to see what He would do next and partly to "re-educate" gullible people.

The chief complaint of disbelief was the breach of logic, the incongruency, that someone whom they knew to be born of human parents in a perfectly natural way could be someone come down from Heaven, and that this someone was Jesus, with whose life and family several were familiar.

It is the unexpectedness that the Incarnation would take place as it did, even though several messianic passages predicted not a Messiah descending supernaturally from Heaven, but one born of woman *"a virgin shall conceive and bear a son."*

"Do not grumble among yourselves. 44 "No one can come to Me unless the Father who sent Me draws him; and I will raise him up on the last day.

Interestingly, Jesus does not launch into a dissertation on those very Scriptures which would have vindicated the mode and manner of His coming. Instead, He appeals to the way He is to be accepted by men in this first advent. Men are to be *drawn*, and that by His Father.

Among the Jews there were all kinds of people, but those that mattered most in the advance of the Kingdom were those who were looking for it, who were ready for the message of the King when He arrived.

This creates a theological problem of how to account for the lost. If getting saved depends on the Father drawing them to His Son, are those who neglect the Son not drawn, hence are there some drawn and some not drawn? If all are drawn but can be lost (the Arminian position), then why claim that none whom the Father gives Him will be lost? But if only those who cannot be lost are drawn (the Calvinist position) then the claim is not incongruent

There are no immediate resolutions to these questions, but this is nevertheless part of the path all must travel towards an understanding of Scripture.

This is an answer to their grumbling in that their ability to see the truth of who He is and whether His teaching is from above will depend on how open they are personally to the testimony of the Father – to the fact that the Father is drawing men to Him.

So as they grumble, He is asking them to examine the basis for it. Is it based in a legalistic system or is it based in a knowledge of what their God is doing? They have always assumed these are one and the same. Jesus is challenging them to examine whether this is true or mistaken.

And here He has said something so profound that the incredulity of it has stunned them from following up with further criticisms of His audacity. He will raise them up in the last day. This claimed an incredible authority and intimacy with the very power and private reserve of God. Now, the very promise of life after death is in His hands by the will of the Father.

"It is written in the prophets, `AND THEY SHALL ALL BE TAUGHT OF GOD.'

Then comes the OT quotation – Isaiah 51:13, Jeremiah 31:34 – as a reminder of very basic truths they seem to have dispensed with long ago.

With Judaism and with early Christianity in the Catholic Church, the subject of how one is to be taught the things of God came to be a subject of importance and legislation. Along with this is the reason to believe the things of God in general. Why are we to believe these things and how is that belief to come about?

For Judaism, it devolved into a dissertation about the history of God's people and their being entrusted with the truths of God, substantiated by miracles in its political, social and religious life. In Catholicism it came to revolve around the evidences that the Church was given the authority to represent Christ on earth and was bequeathed the truths of the New Covenant as His custodian and promulgator.

But Jesus' use of these OT prophecies is to hearken back to what God intended in the beginning – that men would come to know Him by means of Him and Him alone. This is what Paul means in Romans when he teaches that God has made Himself known to every living person, such that all are without excuse (Romans 1:19ff.)

" All your sons will be taught by the Lord" (Is 51:13.) Here was the intent of God – that they come to know Him not through the lesson plan but through a relationship with the living God. The way to knowing God will not be horizontal but vertical – *"No longer will a man teach his neighbor, or a man his brother, saying, 'Know the Lord,' because they will all know me,"* (Jeremiah 31:34.)

Today, this is viewed with some hesitancy because it has resulted in so many divergent interpretations. Catholicism's solution has been to centralize teaching and the teaching authority - if man will not be unified by perception in the same Spirit, he must be unified in an objective teaching.

Jesus' reference here is not to the whole of biblical study and understanding, else the writing of the Bible was largely a wasted effort. It is about the essentials of knowing God, how that is to be effected. In Judaism, the history and traditions of the Jews as God's people could be easily misinterpreted as the essence of knowing their God – it could easily become a substitute for the inner relationship and knowing intended. In the early Church, the sacraments, the rituals, the catechism, the bequeathed authority could easily become the substitute.

Jesus was saying, let man do what we will, the basics are embodied in a man alone with God where he communes with Him. The truths are true because God reveals their truth to him, not because of their associations with intermediate authority, their longevity or attending history. They are verified as true inside the human heart by the witness of the Spirit that these are the truths of God.

This is not to disparage the need for objective learning and the need to check against the spurious and the creative.

"Everyone who has heard and learned from the Father, comes to Me."

This is the key rejoinder against His detractors. Truth and wisdom vindicate themselves. They are recognized by those who have been with the Father and learned from Him. The reason these grumble at Him is because they have not so learned.

"Not that anyone has seen the Father, except the One who is from God; He has seen the Father. "Truly, truly, I say to you, he who believes has eternal life.

This seems a bit odd as interjected here for clarification. It was said to ensure folks not get the wrong impression that to learn from the Father would be to sit down and see Him across the table and be instructed as a teacher instructs his pupil. His hearers know perfectly well that this is forbidden all men – *"No man hath seen God and lived"* – and Jesus certainly knows this is not what He meant. Still, He adds this to remove any doubt that He might be teaching it, primarily because the Jews are already sharp to note that Jesus has radical teachings and the phrase *"contrary to the Law of Moses"* is frequently employed concerning Him.

"I am the bread of life. . . "This is the bread which comes down out of heaven, so that one may eat of it and not die.

More than the claim to be the bread of life eternal, Jesus must deal with the comparison that is going to be made with the manna provided through Moses. This is important because the Jews are not going to tolerate any man who might claim superiority to what Moses did.

Cleverly, the most effective approach is to point out the most obvious distinction – men ate Moses' bread and nevertheless died. It's intent was temporal, earthly, biological. But that is not the total sum of what comprises life. Life was meant to be abundant, and in terms of the spirit. And in that regard, Moses' bread had no efficacy.

He is now come to bring down that spiritual food that sustains one unto eternal living – a living that never sees death, never perishes.

This is the ancient question of Job – *"If a man die, shall he live on?"* The Jews would have answered Yes, but all the connective tissue in between, how that is to be worked out, was cloaked in vagaries and speculations.

Now, Jesus is stepping onto the scene and talking about the very means by which that is to be had, so He rightly proclaims *"I am the bread of life – [all that you seek in this regard is now present with you.]"*

We have to extend some compassion to the Jews because this is entirely brand new in terms of detail. To eat bread that enables a person to live forever is not a vivid picture in the Hebrew Scriptures. Further missing is the idea soon elaborated – that He is that food, that they must partake of Him as that bread. Even His disciples say in a moment – *"this is a difficult saying, who can understand it?"*

This is in fact brand new to everyone involved. No one has ever spoken like this or drawn these parallels before. It is a complete change in thinking about how life in the spirit is to be communicated. There is an eating of flesh and a drinking of blood that are to be essential, and people simply never saw this even hinted in the OT. Yet the way Jesus is speaking, the unquestioned authority with which He has spoken up to now and the miracles attending His teaching are preventing people from just dismissing Him as a madman. Something is enigmatically true in all this, but it is beyond their comprehension. Hence, there are many scratching their heads and many with flummoxed looks as they all question what in the world He is now teaching?

"and the bread also which I will give for the life of the world is My flesh."

Note, it is not His life that is given as bread, but His flesh. One cannot eat "life," but one can see an analogy of partaking of flesh in the course of eating food for sustenance.

Now the Jews had absolutely no way of knowing that Jesus was referring to His Crucifixion in which His very flesh was offered as a sacrifice. We see this after the fact because *"give for the life of the world,"* recalls the Cross.

But for the Jews, they initially make the connection that this is not metaphorical but real. By His tone of voice and mode of expression, they get the idea right readily that Jesus means they must eat His flesh.

"How can this man give us His flesh to eat?"

Some choose to regard this as a fault of the Jews in misunderstanding His intent and taking things too literally. They rely on the ignorance of the audience to forestall any notion that this would be literal, hence, it must be completely symbolic and metaphorical in meaning.

But notice Jesus' reply -

"Truly, truly, I say to you, unless you eat the flesh of the Son of Man and drink His blood, you have no life in yourselves.

If they were taking this too literally, Jesus does not help them away from it by what He says above. He could be counted on to make the more metaphorical and allegorical speech known in phrases like, *"If you can receive it,"* meaning there is a special, non-obvious meaning in play. He doesn't do that here.

We must be clear to keep the distinction from Moses in the foreground. The manna was material and temporal, eaten by the mouth and consumed in the stomach. It was physical, earthly, biological. The bread of life Christ is talking about is all about the spirit and life eternal. *That which is flesh is flesh, that which is spirit is spirit."* The bread of life is to be taken in as food, not by the mouth (which would have linked it to Moses' bread) but by the spirit.

He says if you do not *"you have no life in yourselves."* It is clear He does not mean the physical life sustained by the manna, but He means eternal life – you have no eternal life in you. And eternal life is all about the spirit, not about the flesh.

"He who eats My flesh and drinks My blood has eternal life, and I will raise him up on the last day.

Can this refer to the Eucharist as Catholics claim? If that was the intent, then the ceremony - the taking of the elements in the sacrament - would be seen as bestowing salvation unto eternal life (which some Catholics believe is in fact its very purpose.)

However, Protestants stress that the NT makes it plain that eternal life is secured through faith. Faith is an exercise of the spirit. And if we are to be faithful to the distinction made between Christ's bread and the manna of Moses, then Christ's bread is about spiritual things not physical things.

Therefore, the bread is spiritual food and the partaking of it is via one's spirit. It is union with Christ and thereby union with the Father, which is the primary idea later enjoined in the word *"communion"* associated with this sacrament in both Catholicism and Protestantism.

"For My flesh is true food, and My blood is true drink. "He who eats My flesh and drinks My blood abides in Me, and I in him.

Here is the chief Catholic argument that the bread is His Flesh in substance. True food would seem to remove all doubt that something more than the merely symbolic is being discussed. One cannot entertain true food in a symbol. Hence, the bread must be flesh.

But again, we must maintain the separation that is already clear between Moses and Christ – physical vs. spiritual. If this is an intended distinction, there is no expectation that true food must mean material food.

Christ's flesh is true food in the same sense that eternal life is true life. Eternal life is being contrasted with physical life, the former being superior and wholly other. The true food is being contrasted with physical food, the former being superior and wholly other.

It is also interesting to observe that the identifications go in one direction only – flesh toward bread of life, not bread toward flesh. It is the flesh that is that bread of life, not the bread that is that flesh. Some may say this is quibbling about things that have mutually equality by sheer logic. But this is not a syllogism. It is a means of describing spiritual things in human language.

It is true in logic that if A=B, then B=A. But in theological terms this is not always true. Take the Trinity. We would expect the logic: if A=B and C=B then A=C. It would be true that the Son = God and the Spirit = God. But it is not true that the Son = the Spirit. The bare logic can break down in theological systems, depending on the ideas involved (i.e. there is more to the theology than raw principles of logic.)

So it is possible to conclude that Christ's flesh is the bread of life and that the bread of life is Christ's flesh, but also exclude that it is necessary that any bread consecrated as *portraying* the bread of life must by necessity be Christ's flesh.

Against this the Catholic argument would offer that Jesus clearly said, *"This is my body given for you."* while handing them physical bread.

Of the Catholic doctrines to which Protestants take exception, the Catholic understanding manages to preserve more literally the plain sense of the teaching than do Protestants. Catholics may be said to take the application too far into the physical realm, but Protestants routinely take the application too far toward the symbolic realm.

There can be no doubt that Jesus here intended an eating of His flesh to be understood. It is also clear that there is a very valid contrast being maintained between the physical and the spiritual, between manna and the bread of life, between Moses and Christ.

"He who eats My flesh and drinks My blood abides in Me, and I in him.

And how do we abide in Him? Is it not in a spiritual operation of the heart, soul and spirit? Some see this as meaning that the eating and drinking are the spiritual partaking of Him in the realm of the spirit. Others believe the early Church had it more correctly - that abiding meant obedience in one's participation and enjoyment of the Holy Eucharist.

"As the living Father sent Me, and I live because of the Father, so he who eats Me, he also will live because of Me.

One of the chief supports for the idea that some aspect of this teaching had to be spiritual not physical, (hence metaphor and or symbol must have some role), is that this idea of "eating Christ" was spoken some time before the first institution of the Eucharist, and those hearing it would not have had any means to understand that the fulfillment was intended for the sacrament.

Jesus says, *"he who eats Me, will live forever"* which was a categorical statement about eating the whole of Christ. It would have been understood crudely as cannibalism (which incidentally the pagans logically attributed to early Christians.) There has to be some message in this to the audience at hand, not some secret message that would have to wait for the Upper Room.

As the people pondered what He meant by "he who eats Me," they would be thrown into a perfectly normal alternative mode of thinking –that this must be spiritual talk, some form of metaphor. Thus their initial literalism that asked the question "how can we eat his flesh?" is forced to rethink this as metaphor or allegory on account of Him saying not merely to eat His flesh but to eat Him. Since we don't see any instance of this being fulfilled literally it means that, even for Catholics, some move toward the allegorical is necessary.

The alternative to literalism is to understand that to eat Christ is to take Him in *as* one takes in food. As physical food is assimilated in a way that imparts its properties and nutrients throughout the whole body, so Christ is to be taken in and allowed to impart His effect on the whole inner constitution of the soul. What we believe, think and feel are to be conditioned by the taking in of Christ.

This is what formed the basis of the phrase, "to receive Christ." It is to take Him in.

not as the fathers ate and died;

The question is whether the emphasis is on *"not as the Fathers ate"* (favoring the Protestant view) or on *not as the Fathers died.* (favoring the Catholic view)? The best rendering has it applying to both and to separate the application is unnatural to language.

So it is clear that there is to be a distinction between what the Fathers did in that their eating did not preserved them to eternal life, whereas the bread of life does, but also a distinction that the new eating and the new food is not as it was with the Fathers, i.e. physical and transitory.

John 6:60-71
60 Therefore many of His disciples, when they heard this said, "This is a difficult statement; who can listen to it?" 61 But Jesus, conscious that His disciples grumbled at this, said to them, "Does this cause you to stumble? 62 "What then if you see the Son of Man ascending to where He was before? 63 "It is the Spirit who gives life; the flesh profits nothing; the words that I have spoken to you are spirit and are life. 64 "But there are some of you who do not believe." For Jesus knew from the beginning who they were who did not believe, and who it was that would betray Him.

65 And He was saying, "For this reason I have said to you, that no one can come to Me unless it has been granted him from the Father." 66 As a result of this many of His disciples withdrew and were not walking with Him anymore. 67 So Jesus said to the twelve, "You do not want to go away also, do you?" 68 Simon Peter answered Him, "Lord, to whom shall we go? You have words of eternal life. 69 "We have believed and have come to know that You are the Holy One of God." 70 Jesus answered them, "Did I Myself not choose you, the twelve, and yet one of you is a devil?" 71 Now He meant Judas the son of Simon Iscariot, for he, one of the twelve, was going to betray Him. (John 6:60-71)

Commentary

"This is a difficult statement; who can listen to it?"

The "statement" is the teaching that closed the previous section – *"Truly, truly, I say to you, unless you eat the flesh of the Son of Man and drink His blood, you have no life in yourselves."* . . *"he who eats Me, he also will live because of Me."* In their minds the difficulty is two-fold: *1) – how to conceive of "eating" Jesus, and 2) – how to understand it if the meaning is otherwise?*

All of Jesus' words were very emphatic, and He repeated the difficult part in several ways, so that no one could say they misheard or didn't get the emphasis. Jesus is, in truth, talking in some sense or another about partaking of Him after the manner in which men consume food. Nor does He explain this as He did with the Parable of the Sower. He leaves the comprehension of this for another time – at the Last Supper.

His disciples grumbled at this,

We will find out in a moment that the disciples here do not mean just the Twelve, but a larger group of followers who were indeed walking with Him to learn of Him and His teaching.

This grumbling is the same word used of the Jews who met Jesus at Bethsaida as they came ashore and objected to His statements there, but because these are disciples, we must not attribute the same content as was in the mouths of His detractors. Here, it is a case of being given a very enigmatic teaching, hard to comprehend, but also having the possibility of meaning something they would abhor in reality – the eating of the flesh of their Master. Those who had not been more intimately trained would have been less able to give Jesus the benefit of the doubt that whatever the meaning, He could not have intended something abhorrent or perverted.

"What then if you see the Son of Man ascending to where He was before? "It is the Spirit who gives life; the flesh profits nothing; the words that I have spoken to you are spirit and are life.

He asked them, *"Does this cause you to stumble?"* To stumble in this ancient frame of reference could mean to have a set back in one's beliefs or understanding, to trip over a concept or doctrine, and it could extend to the meaning that a person doubts their beliefs as a result. But stumbling does not necessarily include falling way into unbelief or rejection.

Paul's use of it in Romans explained how one's behavior toward certain foods could cause a brother to fall into sin (Rom 14:15-21), but the context about food specifically does not include the brother abandoning Christ as a result, although other stumblings in this same section do.

We see that some of these folks do walk away, which they may very well have been prepared to do on other accounts. But the state of not understanding things and entertaining doubts is not necessarily a stumbling that gives up the faith.

"What then if you see the Son of Man ascending to where He was before?

As an answer Jesus simply points to what their response might be if He were to ascend to His place in Heaven before the Incarnation? The answer has to do with how we tend to rationalize extraordinary things into more palatable reasoning.

If He were to ascend in their very presence, what would become of this? Would they take it as a vindication of all that He was or would they rationalize it away as a hallucination in the presence of intimidating polemics from the Pharisees?

"It is the Spirit who gives life; the flesh profits nothing; the words that I have spoken to you are spirit and are life.

Who He is and what He teaches must be verified in the Holy Spirit as an inner witness. Similar to the disciples of Socrates, they are to own the principles taught, to make them their own teaching, to know them and encourage them in others. But Socrates never made this kind of statement – *He who eats me will also live.* The truth of that statement cannot come from the horizontal, but must come from above. To understand what He meant, one must be in touch with the Holy Spirit who, despite our rational inability to understand, confirms that such things are the truths of God. We are to *own* them whether we understand them or not.

So the same Spirit who would confirm that an ascension vindicates Christ is the same Spirit that will confirm, despite the failure of human reason, that something about Jesus' teaching is the very truth of God. This is what spells the difference between those who walk away and those who stay. Those who stay overcome their rational incredulity and give Jesus the benefit of the doubt.

"But there are some of you who do not believe."

For some, the rational was all-important, and this teaching was devoid of all sense and reason on the human plane. If they had doubts before, they are doubled now and the only recourse is to return to their former sane life where things made much more sense before Jesus came along.

"For this reason I have said to you, that no one can come to Me unless it has been granted him from the Father."

This is a spiritual coming not a physical one. Those following who then turn away had come physically but had not come spiritually.

This is a teaching best understood in the Reformed (Calvinist) interpretation, because only the elect are called by the Father. In the Arminian position, there is a tendency to teach that all men are called of the Father to come to Christ and so the calling is universal.

But here the point is about those walking away being distinguished as to this calling. It is suggesting that they are abandoning Jesus because they were not called. Furthermore, the universal call idea must deal with people who fall away after accepting Christ (in the Arminian terms of accepting Him) because one may question why God would call people whom He knew would abandon their faith?

Arminians explain that the calling is separate from the obedience, and those who fall away are called but did not choose to endure in obedience. This seems a good explanation were it not for Jesus' teaching earlier on in which He states that none that the Father gives Him will He lose (John 6:39.)

As a result of this many of His disciples withdrew and were not walking with Him anymore.

It is these words that signal their departure. They not only did not get an explanation of what this enigmatic eating was all about, but they have been told that the source of their inability is related to whether they were even called by the Father to come and be His disciples.

The true believer is not going to accept this conclusion because he will have an inner witness that verifies his having been called. The result will be to stay with Jesus and seek understanding.

The doubter and the tenuous follower will not accept this either but will take it as an insult, putting him in a class whom the Father did not deign to call. This person will abandon Christ to return to that form of religious life in which he had other assurances of God's blessing. In other words, *"If I stay with this man I will have to deal with his opinion of my rejection by God, but if I return to the Pharisees, I can abide in all my old expectations about God's favor."* Or he may abandon faith altogether, believing he might do better on his own.

In churches of more recent times, some Calvinists went to the extreme of identifying the non-elect from the elect and this had the same effect as we see above. People simply walked away from the church or went to churches that rejected Calvin.

In the case of Jesus, it was a matter of separating the sheep from the goats, in that true believers would be spurred on to ensure their calling and more understanding, while false believers or the merely inquisitive would be repelled.

"You do not want to go away also, do you?"

Somewhat rhetorical from Jesus' point of view, knowing their hearts, but an answer the disciples needed to verbalize for themselves. They had to be as perplexed about it as anyone else, yet their faith needed to be brought into the foreground, that it be seen as the key to giving Jesus and the Father the benefit of the doubt, that despite complete inability, they were in the midst of divine truth.

"Lord, to whom shall we go? You have words of eternal life.

Here they speak out all the import of what has been said above. Despite the patently obvious confusion over this enigmatic teaching, they are nonetheless undeterred in following Him. They affirm it must somehow be true because He has the words of eternal life. That is faith overruling reason. It is something every believer then and now must face in the evaluation of truth. When reason fails us, are we willing to let faith secure the truth, or are we insisting that all truths must submit to the dictates of reason?

"We have believed and have come to know that You are the Holy One of God."

This is what Jesus meant about ascending to Heaven. It is the same faith assuring them of who Jesus is that is assuring them about the truth of the bread from Heaven. It is what keeps believers in the faith despite whatever contradictions atheists and Bible debunkers might pose.

Jesus answered them, "Did I Myself not choose you, the twelve, and yet one of you is a devil?"

This is a statement reiterating the mastery of Jesus over all the affairs of His own ministry and those of the world in which He walks. He knows the beginning from the end, the truth from the lie, faith from unbelief. He has chosen them all well, even to the choosing of His betrayer.

John gives us a clue for the future in preparation for what Judas will do. It's primary purpose is to disclose a betrayer while not leaving a more specific statement that would produce intrigue against the others.

Jesus knew that Judas would betray Him, yet He chose him among His twelve intimate disciples. This is what makes the Gospel story harder to conceive as a man-made conception. Men would never have had Jesus picking a man He knew would be His betrayer.

It is a mystery as to the exact purpose, since arrest and crucifixion could have come from almost anywhere outside His followers. Perhaps it was to demonstrate that truth does not necessarily win men to righteousness. The sin of the heart can explain away the purest truth when one is determined to have his own way.

Mark 7:1-13, Matthew 15:10-20, Mark 7:16, Mark 7:19

The Pharisees and some of the scribes gathered around Him when they had come from Jerusalem, 2 and had seen that some of His disciples were eating their bread with impure hands, that is, unwashed. 3 (For the Pharisees and all the Jews do not eat unless they carefully wash their hands, thus observing the traditions of the elders; 4 and when they come from the market place, they do not eat unless they cleanse themselves; and there are many other things which they have received in order to observe, such as the washing of cups and pitchers and copper pots.) 5 The Pharisees and the scribes asked Him, "Why do Your disciples not walk according to the tradition of the elders, but eat their bread with impure hands?"

6 And He said to them, "Rightly did Isaiah prophesy of you hypocrites, as it is written: `THIS PEOPLE HONORS ME WITH THEIR LIPS, BUT THEIR HEART IS FAR AWAY FROM ME. 7 `BUT IN VAIN DO THEY WORSHIP ME, TEACHING AS DOCTRINES THE PRECEPTS OF MEN.' 8 "Neglecting the commandment of God, you hold to the tradition of men."

9 He was also saying to them, "You are experts at setting aside the commandment of God in order to keep your tradition. 10 "For Moses said, `HONOR YOUR FATHER AND YOUR MOTHER'; and, `HE WHO SPEAKS EVIL OF FATHER OR MOTHER, IS TO BE PUT TO DEATH'; 11 but you say, `If a man says to his father or his mother, whatever I have that would help you is Corban (that is to say, given to God),' 12 you no longer permit him to do anything for his father or his mother; 13 thus invalidating the word of God by your tradition which you have handed down; and you do many things such as that." (Mark 7:1-13)

After Jesus called the crowd to Him, He said to them, "Hear and understand. 11 "It is not what enters into the mouth that defiles the man, but what proceeds out of the mouth, this defiles the man." 12 Then the disciples came and said to Him, "Do You know that the Pharisees were offended when they heard this statement?" 13 But He answered and said, "Every plant which My heavenly Father did not plant shall be uprooted. 14 "Let them alone; they are blind guides of the blind. And if a blind man guides a blind man, both will fall into a pit." 15 Peter said to Him, "Explain the parable to us." 16 Jesus said, "Are you still lacking in understanding also? 17 "Do you not understand that everything that goes into the mouth passes into the stomach, and is eliminated? 18 "But the things that proceed out of the mouth come from the heart, and those defile the man. 19 "For out of the heart come evil thoughts, murders, adulteries, fornications, thefts, false witness, slanders. 20 "These are the things which defile the man; but to eat with unwashed hands does not defile the man." -- If anyone has ears to hear, let him hear." (Matthew 15:10-20, Mark 7:16)

Commentary

The Pharisees and some of the scribes gathered around Him

The scene and the time has now changed, since the topic is now distinct from the foregoing and it is apparent from the Pharisees complaint that the disciples are eating a meal.

These Pharisees are said to have come from Jerusalem. They include some of the scribes who were no doubt along to check out the accuracy of Jesus' use of Scripture. As said in an earlier section, the Pharisees were very conservative believers in Judaism, but they did not personally have a good mastery over the content of the Scriptures. They knew the key verses that informed them as to their duties and the daily life of the Jews. But finding key verses of prophesy, especially the many diverse references to Messiah, was not their specialty, being rather the preserve of the scribes.

The subject of washing before eating was discussed earlier in the episode at the Pharisees home (Luke 11:38.) There was no OT law or ordinance about such washings, although it was legally prescribed to be concerned about defilements.

This observance of washing was rather part of the traditions of the elders, which constituted something similar to Catholic tradition – a sort of commentary in both teaching and practice, deemed to be a sacred interpretation of what God meant in Scripture.

Yet we see what kind of respect Jesus had for such things in the license He gave to His disciples. It is a lesson for us that men can embellish the Word, adding reasonings and ordinances that God did not intend, all in the name of defending His Word. Jesus is here making it clear that this sort of thing can go awry in the hands of imperfect men.

and when they come from the market place, . .

The reason for this practice was due to contact with Gentiles and things Gentiles had touched. Even devout Jews may have been careless about hygiene and in the marketplace one is exposed to any number of random contacts among a multitude of unknown circumstances.

Leviticus charged the people to observe things that made them unclean and the remedy was washing in a bath and waiting until evening to be clean again (22:4), but this had to do with access to holy gifts, not to ordinary food. But an observation soon came about that to touch food in the home while unclean made the food unclean for the others. The conclusion was to wash when taking food at all. But if uncleanness was actually inferred and if one was invoking the law about washings to ordinary food, they were not being consistent in also waiting until evening for it to pass.

"Why do Your disciples not walk according to the tradition of the elders, but eat their bread with impure hands?"

This is deliberately phrased to put Jesus at a disadvantage in front of the people. It simultaneously reiterated for the people that the Pharisees were doing their sworn duty – to protect and preserve the traditions of Judaism as its custodians.

"Rightly did Isaiah prophesy of you hypocrites,

First, we are brought to appreciate the recognition Christ had for men like Isaiah. Jesus honors his ordination of God and that he fulfilled his purpose despite his martyrdom at the hands of those who hated him and his message. We see here that Jesus regards him as a co-herald of the faith, a citizen of the heavenly realm, well-known of Christ and the Father.

Despite these being the most conservative and rigidly obedient folks in Judaism, it is ironic that their hypocrisy needs to be addressed. But how were these men hypocrites? Were they not upholding more rigidly than any a strict adherence to the Law?

But it was a matter of appearances only. They did not care to apply the Law to their own personal lives but engaged in the business of making it a burden for the people at large. But how is this related to their tradition? Again, isn't the tradition focused on service to God?

To decide to go further than the revealed Word is to have a lower view of the revealed Word. It is a sense of daring that no truly devout person would take, primarily because intimacy with the Word of God begets an ever-increasing need for humility. The more we expose ourselves to the Word, the more we come to know that in us alone dwells no good thing.

So to propagate precepts of men alongside the Scripture, as having equal or even greater weight, is to reveal one's lack of humility, one's arrogance, and therefore one's hypocrisy.

'THIS PEOPLE HONORS ME WITH THEIR LIPS, BUT THEIR HEART IS FAR AWAY FROM ME. 7 'BUT IN VAIN DO THEY WORSHIP ME, TEACHING AS DOCTRINES THE PRECEPTS OF MEN.'

The quote is from Isaiah 29:13. These leaders of the Jews could equally quote OT reference that proved their obedience to the teachings of Moses, yet Jesus distinguishes between merely mouthing their recognition of God and the condition of their heart.

In fact, it is the condition of the heart that produced what they called the "traditions of the elders." It is man's propensity to improve on things, even if spoken by God. Men in every age have ever been unsatisfied with the role of mere listener, of mere student to someone else's teaching. They must in some way be co-teacher, even with God Almighty. Add to this the distinction of being entrusted with the oracles of God, and the Jews were ripe for taking divine teaching farther than intended.

All of this was done in the name of protecting and observing God's word. But it was done to such a degree that the line between man's teaching and God's revelation became blurred. And because so many of the Jews were illiterate, the freedom to do this unchecked became a way of life.

We are not to conclude that the Talmud or the Midrash were in view here as documents, since these were not compiled until several centuries later. But the unwritten or verbal forms that comprised these later documents certainly were current in Jesus' day. The Talmud was oriented around procedures and ordinances, including injunctions on the conduct of daily affairs, based on OT teaching. The Mishnah was the first section of the Talmud. The Midrash was a set of commentaries, dealing with the interpretation of OT books.

To be sure, there were many other more serious examples of human precepts legislated upon the people, but this one (eating with unwashed hands) served so very well because it so clearly exemplified teaching that had no corresponding injunction from the Scripture. It was truly exemplary of meeting Isaiah's rebuke – that precepts of men were being taught as doctrines.

"Neglecting the commandment of God, you hold to the tradition of men."

There are some who charge that the Church followed Judaism's bad example by likewise developing a Christian tradition alongside the NT. There are similarities to be sure, but this equation is rejected at least for the reason that the Jewish traditions resulted in rejecting Christ, whereas Christian traditions uphold Him.

Much can be said for the Catholic claim that the Church's tradition came directly from the hands of Christ to His apostles and thus to His Church, so it is not to be compared with the tradition of the Jews. It is perfectly reasonable to expect that many conversations ensued outside the material in the NT pertaining to how formal teaching was to be understood and taught. If all that Christ ever said to the disciples in three years of ministry is what is found in the Gospels, it would have to have been one of the quietest of periods in their whole lives. We can read all His teaching in a matter of a few hours.

We expect more to have been said and both Protestant and Catholic have a genuine interest in knowing that material before venturing explanations of their own. Still, there must be a demarcation line between the revealed truths of God and human precepts. Claiming also to be the means of Grace in the world and promulgating error, even knowingly, erodes trust and arouses suspicion and cynicism.

This is simply a fact because we have before us a patent case of abuse in this regard, against which we are exhorted to not make the same mistake in Christ's Church. This is especially appropriate considering that both peoples – the Jews and the Church - had the mandate to preserve and maintain the truths of God. Both have had the temptation and the opportunity to go further in their zeal and privilege to make more of God's Word than intended.

Whether the Church will hear the same indictment Jesus gave to the Pharisees is a matter for each person to assess for themselves with the aid of history's record, biased or unbiased as it may be.

setting aside the commandment of God in order to keep your tradition.

Do you get the idea that Jesus is rather upset with their handling of Judaism and the Word of His Father? We see injustice and hypocrisy in our own society and we wish we had the means to confront judges and lawmakers with their private manipulation of the system. It is a burning issue that plagues our very assessment of these offices.

So in Jesus, we have an intimate awareness of just how far these men had gone.

He adds to their crimes by citing cases of actually setting aside commandments of God to keep their own traditions intact. The example is the principle of *'Corban'* which was simply a phrase that identified something being dedicated for the use of God alone.

We see this clearly exampled in the life of Samuel, being given over by his mother Hannah into the house of Eli the priest, to be raised up in the service of God. The purpose of Corban was to interject a warning when something given to God (person or thing) was about to be used for a secular purpose. But this was to be handled with some application of reason and common sense.

As with all such mechanisms, man will find a way to abuse it. Men soon discovered a clever way to get out from under parental demands, by dedicating themselves to the Temple or some other form of religious service, which the priests and leaders accepted. That Jewish tradition permitted such loopholes without the scrutiny against evil-mindedness is the case Jesus now makes. It is a proof of how wrong-minded one can become by letting tradition dictate behavior.

The evil was more acutely seen in children trying to get out of the expenses and inconveniences of caring for aging parents, paying for funeral services, and assuming the payment of their debts. But it also promoted taking a free ride in the home and shirking perfectly normal responsibilities.

"It is not what enters into the mouth that defiles the man, but what proceeds out of the mouth, this defiles the man."

As an extension of his rebuke of the Pharisees, Jesus felt the need to teach the positive side of this issue to the people at large. The negative message was just given – that the Pharisees were imposing the words of man over the word of God. There was also a need for the positive message that explained what the truth was concerning defilements.

That things taken in as food did not defile seemed contrary to the Law of Moses in which a number of animals were forbidden as things that defiled a person – made them unclean. So how is it that Jesus now controverts this by saying that things taken in as food do not defile?

First, we must recognize that the food in the discussion was not the forbidden, unclean things in the Law. The Jews were complaining about not having washed before eating *permitted* foods. How were these then unclean? By contamination among Gentiles or unkempt handlers.

As we search the Mosaic Law we find no specific references to contamination or uncleanness occasioned by simple contact with a Gentile. There are plenty of references to forms of human uncleanness, having to do with diseases, sexual impurity, or idolatry. But nothing proscribes touching a Gentile because of uncleanness.

What ensued in Jewish tradition is the idea that the Gentile practiced all sorts of sinful deeds and thus his person was stained by them and may very well represent contacts with sexual impurity or unclean animals. (We note the priests at Jesus' trial before Pilate not being willing to enter the Praetorium that they might remain undefiled for the feast. They had not touched Pilate, but there was fear that simply being in the offices of Gentile authorities could bring them into contact with something an unclean person may have touched.)

But precautions to this extent were not actually seen in the Law. It was a matter of direct contact with unclean things, not fear of all the potential exposures.

Jesus was in essence saying, *"You spend all your time worrying needlessly about whether a Gentile might have contaminated your food, yet you pay no attention to the defilement that can come from your hearts and proceeds out of your own mouths."*

"Do You know that the Pharisees were offended when they heard this statement?"

This is one of the few references to the disciples cautioning Jesus about His speech. It must have come after a noticeable upset among the Pharisees and perhaps words from them that He was worthy of proscription and judgment by the authorities.

He has now furthered the case against Himself and the disciples are wondering if this was His intent. Feeding this concern is their background in knowing the power and authority of the Pharisees, but also in this particular case, that they had something to the case they were presenting against Jesus – that there were legitimate concerns about defilements in the Law and it may have not seemed overboard to use extra precautions, as in washings.

However, true contaminations of the types they feared among the Gentiles would not have been dealt with simply by washings. In many cases, fasting and waiting seven days before being pronounced clean again was in order.

Jesus, like John before Him, is at this juncture unconcerned about the consequences of speaking the truth. Where before He had some concerns at key moments about premature exposure to the authorities, He is less concerned now.

Rather than a great lesson on defilements and their interpretation, He chooses to disclose the root or the issue - the heart and spiritual blindness - because these are the true motives behind the anger of the Jews.

"Every plant which My heavenly Father did not plant shall be uprooted . . . they are blind guides of the blind.

He uses the analogy that there can be plantings not intended by the Father. The inference is that of the Parable of the Sower – that the enemy came and sowed them. This does not mean the enemy created the Pharisees as human beings, but that he had taken over their hearts that they no longer saw the truths of God clearly.

Technically, all plants are planted by the Father (if this means creation). But as people come under Satan's influence, they become as one "sown" by the evil one.

These will be uprooted in the judgment, but also in temporal life, in that God in His sovereign love has replaced the bad with the good. But their chief mischief is that being blind they presume to lead the blind.

This bears on the innocent and the naïve who are led astray by such men through clever talk and the persuasiveness of learned words. We see this elsewhere in Jesus' teaching that it would be better that a millstone were tied around their neck and they be drowned in the sea for having led the innocent astray.

It also opens the door to some thought that in the Judgment, persons thus led astray may be dealt with differently than persons deliberately contrary to the things of God.

"Let them alone . . " is a form of resignation about their fate, not that Jesus or anyone else was ready to do something about them. It is to say that their end is already prepared, it is only a matter of their coming to it. Their blindness will cause them to stumble and indeed ultimately stumble to an ultimately ignoble end.

Peter now asks for an explanation about the things that defile. *"Explain the parable to us."*

"Do you not understand that everything that goes into the mouth passes into the stomach, . . "But the things that proceed out of the mouth come from the heart, and those defile the man.

He first expresses His incredulity that they have not understood the difference. The reason things going in do not defile is that they are dealt with in the stomach and their impurities are eliminated from the body.

Again, this pertains to foods permitted in the Law. It is a bit of biology in play more than spiritual law. The concerns about unclean things in the OT were predominantly about disease and infections by associations with animals that were prone to carry them or who as food could become unpleasant to the system.

The laws pertained to visible or knowable things. Complete cleanliness was not possible for permitted foods either, with flies and air-borne contaminants, etc. But in general these were accommodated in the design of the stomach and the digestive system. Many potentially harmful elements from the external world are dealt with in the acids of the stomach and toxins are routinely eliminated. This is what Jesus meant by pointing out the operation of the stomach. Many of the silly things the Jews had people fretting over were things ordinarily taken care of by digestion.

The other principle is that the mouth speaks what the heart has conceived. So in the opposite direction from going in the mouth, things coming out are of greater concern. We speak hateful things because our heart is first filled with hatred. We speak words of jealousy and envy because our hearts are covetous. *"For out of the heart come evil thoughts, murders, adulteries, fornications, thefts, false witness, slanders. 20 "These are the things which defile the man;*

As we look at this list we can clearly see that each one involves conditions of the heart that have their expression in outward actions. Murder is born of hatred. Adultery and fornication are born of lust. Theft is born of covetousness. Lying is born of love of self, to protect it from consequences. Slanderings are born of pride and the desire to keep others below oneself.

If anyone has ears to hear, let him hear.

After speaking these things, He caps these statements with this familiar phrase. It is an idiomatic phrase that suggests the meaning is not obvious and one is encouraged to ponder it. But more specifically one is encouraged to seek God for its wisdom.

It is to point out that one must be *inclined* to hear if one wishes to actually hear. In the teaching about defilement (what goes in does not defile), there is an additional comment from the parallel in Mark 7:19 *(Thus He declared all foods clean.)*

CHAPTER 10
Ministering Again in Galilee

John 7:1, Matthew 15:21, Mark 7:24, Matthew 15:22-28

After these things Jesus was walking in Galilee, for He was unwilling to walk in Judea because the Jews were seeking to kill Him. (John 7:1)

21 Jesus went away from there, and withdrew into the district of Tyre and Sidon. -- And when He had entered a house, He wanted no one to know of it; yet He could not escape notice. -- 22 And a Canaanite woman from that region came out and began to cry out, saying, "Have mercy on me, Lord, Son of David; my daughter is cruelly demon-possessed." 23 But He did not answer her a word. And His disciples came and implored Him, saying, "Send her away, because she keeps shouting at us." 24 But He answered and said, "I was sent only to the lost sheep of the house of Israel." 25 But she came and began to bow down before Him, saying, "Lord, help me!" 26 And He answered and said, "It is not good to take the children's bread and throw it to the dogs." 27 But she said, "Yes, Lord; but even the dogs feed on the crumbs which fall from their masters' table." 28 Then Jesus said to her, "O woman, your faith is great; it shall be done for you as you wish." And her daughter was healed at once. (Matthew 15:21, Mark 7:24, Matthew 15:22-28)

Commentary

This was a radical move in Judaism, since there were very strict laws still on the books respecting defilements from certain foods. This gives some justification to the doctrinal approach called "dispensationalism." It is the idea that certain modes of operation between God and man changed at strategic points through time.

We cannot ignore that the Gospel writer is divinely discerning a major change in the believer's relationship to forbidden foods. These foods defiled men from participating in the Temple services and feasts. But these were soon to be superseded by Christ's sacrifice on the Cross, so the ceremonial aspect of uncleanness was being replaced, hence, the concern about defilements from food was no longer valid.

We see in Acts a similar repetition of this concept in the vision upon the sheet shown to Peter in which God declares, *"What I call clean you must not call unclean."* Certainly, it was being employed as an analogy that permitted him to minister to the Gentiles (the unclean), but the fact that unclean animals were being depicted as now clean cannot be ignored because if all the old restrictions were still in effect, it would be misleading to undermine them in an analogy.

After these things Jesus was walking in Galilee,

We aren't told the exact location, but the reason for remaining in Galilee is because of the notoriety He now had among the Jerusalem Pharisees who were more populous in Judea. While He is now more open and candid in His teaching, He is also still on a divine timetable and He did not wish to precipitate premature arrest by being careless about His locale.

It might be wondered why He felt safer in Galilee which was Herod's realm, Herod being partial to those who sought to seize Him? But Herod was considerably less religious than secular and it would take a civil or criminal offense to move him to action regarding Jesus. Thus far Jesus was no such person in his mind.

and withdrew into the district of Tyre and Sidon

Tyre and Sidon are on the coast about 25 miles apart, so Jesus has journeyed west from the Sea of Galilee toward the coastline of the Mediterranean. Tyre is very old, founded 2700 years before Christ when this area was originally part of Phoenica and was one of their key ports. (It is today part of Lebanon.) Nebuchadnezzar did not succeed in capturing Tyre. Alexander however did, about three hundred years later.

Tyre existed as two precincts - a mainland city and an island city just off shore. When Alexander had conquered the mainland city, a considerable number of people and troops had retreated to the island. The causeway out to the island still seen today was built by Alexander to gain access to it and finish his war against Tyre.

Sidon is perhaps the oldest city in the middle east, but was less notable historically. It remains extant today with its name still intact among the major cities in modern Lebanon.

And when He had entered a house, He wanted no one to know of it; yet He could not escape notice.

This is an odd note because we are aware of Jesus power to effect what He wishes, so if He wished to be secret, it should not have been thwarted. But this is really a window into the mystery of His incarnation, in that He is in some way also subject to the limitations and frustrations which are part and parcel to humanity. Where the line is drawn between sovereignty and failing to have expectations met is not clean and distinct.

And a Canaanite woman from that region came out and began to cry out,

Elsewhere she is called a Greek and a Syrophoenician (Mark 7:26.) This designation links her back to the Canaanites and especially the curse on Canaan because of his father's action in the time of Noah (Gen 9:22-25.) The result was that Syrophoencians were a shunned and despised class.

"Have mercy on me, Lord, Son of David; my daughter is cruelly demon-possessed."

Ordinarily this would be attributed to the curse of long ago. Cursed people become open game for the likes of Satan. Jesus does not answer her, which we learn later was merely a pretense with a purpose.

She is not only a shunned person but had become a nuisance in shouting out at Jesus and his disciples, hence their request, *"Send her away, because she keeps shouting at us."* Our knowledge of Jesus with the woman in the house of the Pharisee should tell us that there are no "shunned" people in Jesus world view. Yet he answers in a completely opposite manner:

"I was sent only to the lost sheep of the house of Israel."

This would be a denigrating statement because it suggests that only certain people are to be blessed and all others are to be excluded. This statement conditions how we are to understand the enigmatic statement that comes next.

The woman comes and bows down, determined to secure help from Jesus. But He merely furthers the suggestion of discrimination . .

"It is not good to take the children's bread and throw it to the dogs."

There is no way to water this down into politically correct speech that is not discriminatory in some sense. But the discrimination is not between Canaanites and Jews but between children and non-children of the Kingdom. It is similar to the earlier warning to not cast pearls before swine. One must invest the truth in those who are ready to receive it.

At first glance, it appears that Jesus is discriminating against this woman by suggesting she is among the dogs to whom it would be an offense to give food intended for the children. Left alone and final, this would have conveyed the idea that being of the wrong class, she was not to receive His blessing. But she responds with a clever rejoinder -

"Yes, Lord; but even the dogs feed on the crumbs which fall from their masters' table."

Here is a woman that will not take no for an answer. She knows the curse, but she also believes that somewhere in the midst of the curse there is mercy, because she knows He is a God who both curses and blesses.

This response and Jesus acknowledgement of it helps us understand a different tone in Jesus' words than merely discriminatory remarks. He is teaching that the Word of God and its blessings are intended as food for *all* the faithful, but they are first given to the chosen people – the Jews. So they are not given without qualification to the Gentiles, i.e. the Jews are the divine conduit of blessing to the world – *"In your seed all the nations of the earth shall be blessed." Gen 22:18.*

So it is a case that food is not given directly to the Gentiles, but while given to the Jews, its abundance will spill over to be gleaned by the Gentiles, whoever shall desire it - hence the picture of the dogs desiring what is on the table and waiting eagerly for whatever falls from it.

The dogs are not shunned. Neither are the Gentiles to be shunned. But the dogs are not allowed up on the table to take directly the food for the children, nor is it to be "served" to them as it is to the children. Likewise, the Gentiles are not the chosen people, nor are they entrusted with the oracles of God, yet they are intended to receive their benefits.

"O woman, your faith is great; it shall be done for you as you wish." And her daughter was healed at once.

Jesus sees that she perceives this mode of dispensation of grace, that she has not become embittered that the Jews are privileged , and desires whatever God is willing to give out of the overflow.

So we see that much of this was a sort of staged engagement for drawing out the woman's faith. We readily see this in the sheer character and compassion of Jesus' words – *"O woman, your faith is great; it shall be done for you as you wish."*

It's not merely "woman" but "O' woman." It is like saying "Oh dearest soul." He has found a jewel of faith where it would ordinarily be unexpected and pervaded by bitterness. She has found the secret that unlocked the pouring forth of grace and healing. It worked and deliverance for her daughter was granted.

We demand the things of God that were given to others yet we fail to grasp the secret, which is a determined faith.

Matthew 15:29-31, Mark 8:1-10, Matthew 16:1-4, Mark 8:13, Mark 8:14, Matthew 16:6-7, Mark 8:17-21, Mark 8:22-26

29 Departing from there, Jesus went along by the Sea of Galilee, and having gone up on the mountain, He was sitting there. 30 And large crowds came to Him, bringing with them those who were lame, crippled, blind, mute, and many others, and they laid them down at His feet; and He healed them. 31 So the crowd marveled as they saw the mute speaking, the crippled restored, and the lame walking, and the blind seeing; and they glorified the God of Israel. (Matthew 15:29-39)

1 In those days, when there was again a large crowd and they had nothing to eat, Jesus called His disciples and said to them, 2 "I feel compassion for the people because they have remained with Me now three days and have nothing to eat. 3 "If I send them away hungry to their homes, they will faint on the way; and some of them have come from a great distance." 4 And His disciples answered Him, "Where will anyone be able to find enough bread here in this desolate place to satisfy these people?" 5 And He was asking them, "How many loaves do you have?" And they said, "Seven." 6 And He directed the people to sit down on the ground; and taking the seven loaves, He gave thanks and broke them, and started giving them to His disciples to serve to them, and they served them to the people. 7 They also had a few small fish; and after He had blessed them, He ordered these to be served as well. 8 And they ate and were satisfied; and they picked up seven large baskets full of what was left over of the broken pieces. 9 About four thousand were there; and He sent them away. 10 And immediately He entered the boat with His disciples and came to the district of Dalmanutha. (Mark 8:1-10)

1 The Pharisees and Sadducees came up, and testing Jesus, they asked Him to show them a sign from heaven. 2 But He replied to them, "When it is evening, you say, `It will be fair weather, for the sky is red.' 3 "And in the morning, `There will be a storm today, for the sky is red and threatening.' Do you know how to discern the appearance of the sky, but cannot discern the signs of the times? 4 "An evil and adulterous generation seeks after a sign; and a sign will not be given it, except the sign of Jonah." -- Leaving them, He again embarked and went away to the other side. (Matthew 16:1-4, Mark 8:13)

14 And they had forgotten to take bread, and did not have more than one loaf in the boat with them. -- And Jesus said to them, "Watch out and beware of the leaven of the Pharisees and Sadducees." (and of Herod – Mark) They began to discuss this among themselves, saying, "He said that because we did not bring any bread." -- 17 And Jesus, aware of this, said to them, "Why do you discuss the fact that you have no bread? Do you not yet see or understand? Do you have a hardened heart? 18 "HAVING EYES, DO YOU NOT SEE? AND HAVING EARS, DO YOU NOT HEAR ? And do you not remember, 19 when I broke the five loaves for the five thousand, how many baskets full of broken pieces you picked up?" They said to Him, "Twelve." 20 "When I broke the seven for the four thousand, how many large baskets full of broken pieces did you pick up?" And they said to Him, "Seven." 21 And He was saying to them, "Do you not yet understand?" (Mark 8:14, Matthew 16:6-7, Mark 8:17-21)

22 And they came to Bethsaida. And they brought a blind man to Jesus and implored Him to touch him. 23 Taking the blind man by the hand, He brought him out of the village; and after spitting on his eyes and laying His hands on him, He asked him, "Do you see anything?" 24 And he looked up and said, "I see men, for I see them like trees, walking around." 25 Then again He laid His hands on his eyes; and he looked intently and was restored, and began to see everything clearly. 26 And He sent him to his home, saying, "Do not even enter the village." (Mark 8:22-26)

Commentary

Departing from there, Jesus went along by the Sea of Galilee

We are getting the picture of what might appear to be a haphazard tour in and around the Galilee region. He is in Capernaum, then over to the eastern shore for the feeding of the five thousand, then back to Capernaum, then up to the NW to Tyre and Sidon, then back over along the shores of the Sea of Galilee. We might expect a tour that was more organized – that took in all the places in the vicinity and moved on, etc.

But this haphazard route served at least to take predictability away from the authorities in their desire to keep tabs on His whereabouts. He could not be expected to show up in adjacent towns but might simply disappear only to show up days later at the opposite end of the Galilee. He could easily leave at night with no word left behind where He was going.

and having gone up on the mountain, He was sitting there. 30 And large crowds came to Him, bringing with them those who were lame, crippled, blind,

There is nothing to indicate that this mountain is the same as that for the feeding of the five thousand earlier. It is a similar set of conditions – he goes up and sits down, the people come to Him with the sick and disabled. He feeds them in the same manner. But the location is not known to be the same.

and he healed them

For men, despite this being a divine gift, it can become an old theme in which our excitement and exuberance can wane with yet another healing service. It can become somewhat rote and even mundane. But with Jesus we don't see Him tiring of dispensing this blessing to the crowds.

One observation we should make is the incredible number of people who must have been sick or in need just in this small area of the world in this time frame. All through Jesus' ministry of some three years, virtually everywhere He went, there were people lined up to be healed. It helps us understand the sheer magnitude of people who ordinarily suffered in these times. For it to be constant, there had to be an incalculable number of sick people everywhere.

Still, we never hear Him say, "No, not today."

So the crowd marveled as they saw the mute speaking, the crippled restored,

As before, what is unique from faith healers today is that Jesus was healing some of the most devastating conditions known, and to such a degree of completeness that people began immediately doing the things they were hindered from doing. There was no recuperative period, no time of continuing to "claim" one's healing.

This kind of transformation and healing was so extraordinary as to evoke praise to God at the very sight of it.

"I feel compassion for the people because they have remained with Me now three days and have nothing to eat.

The Gospel says, "in those days" which we might take as an introduction to a different and far removed scene, but the rest of this section indicates that it is the same scene with the crowd that gathered on the mountainside for healing.

It has been three days. We are not to infer that there was no food in all that time, but that it had run out and the people were in need of something to eat. It might also be wondered that after that long a stay, wouldn't most have been ready to return home? But it is the sheer magnetism of His presence and the ongoing healing that kept them there. And perhaps word had spread about the event of the five thousand in Bethsaida Julia, so expectations were high that He would take care of things here also.

"If I send them away hungry to their homes, they will faint on the way;

Here we have a more specific reason why they yet remained – whether near or far, it was now doubtful that the majority could return home without fainting on the journey. Being distracted by the miracles, they had simply stayed too long.

"Where will anyone be able to find enough bread here in this desolate place to satisfy these people?"

This seems so odd to us, since the memory of the five thousand under identical circumstances was not too far back in time. But it is relayed as though that was not useful to them at all. We know they could recall it because in a moment Jesus reminds them. Yet, here at this point they seem to have not learned what would be expected.

Nor do we get any impression that they are saying this with tongue-in-cheek with a sort of smile on the face, as in *Now where I wonder would we possibly find enough food for all these people?"*

"How many loaves do you have?"

The seven loaves and a few fish distinguish this from being just a different accounting of the event with the five thousand. We also have Jesus' lesson a bit later where He asks them to consider both events and their outcomes.

How these were multiplied physically in the miracle we are again not told, but following the manner and mode of work done in the earlier event it is a safe assumption that the disciples likewise took baskets out to the people, then brought them back for refilling. The miracle of having them fill up again must have been seen visibly by those closest to Him.

Again, there was excess left over, a testimony that God does not do things stingily or just barely, but abundantly.

And immediately He entered the boat with His disciples and came to the district of Dalmanutha.

This region is wholly unknown today with nothing corresponding to it in modern times. In contrast to the earlier event, Jesus leaves with His disciples and they arrive together.

The Pharisees and Sadducees came up, and testing Jesus,

Wherever the location, the Pharisees where near at hand and His arrival was anticipated. Again, the Pharisees might be characterized as the fundamentalist conservative party, whereas the Sadducees would have been the more liberal, but also more theologically adept party.

They ask Him to show them a sign, specifically a sign from Heaven. This is asked from the vantage point of how one is to know true things? We infer this from Jesus answer – *"When it is evening, you say, `It will be fair weather, for the sky is red.'*

There are many truths, some made obvious through common sense, some through experience in observing the ways of the earth and the world, others by revelation. Jesus is teaching here that all truth is united in its congruency and in having its source in the Father. Truth makes sense whether in practical things or in spiritual.

Jesus is appealing to how they have already come to recognize truths and is expecting them to put things together about other essential questions using the same gifts of God.

Do you know how to discern the appearance of the sky, but cannot discern the signs of the times?

What were the signs of the times He expected them to also discern? The coming of the Kingdom. This is not a case of having special divine knowledge, as a savant might have in the secular or occultic frame of reference. The events of Messiah's coming and with Him the age of the Kingdom were all predicted in sufficient detail that they should have recognized His coming from Scripture alone.

This had already been partly applied in King Herod's time. The scribes advised the king that the Christ was to come from Bethlehem. Isaiah foretold the very words John preached in the wilderness and everyone knew that John identified Jesus as the one for whom he was forerunner. Isaiah also foretold of the healing ministry of the Christ. Messianic passages were plentiful. So why did they not recognize Him?

Their system of interpretation had long been oriented around protecting their system of authority. Add to this that with any theological system, one is prone to emphasize certain things in preference to others. The Jews were looking for a deliverer – a conquering hero over their oppressors. They looked to the warrior king of the prophesies, not the gentle healer, not the man from that place called Nazareth.

What Jesus is doing here is to put His finger on this very difficulty, this particular ineptitude. They were not complete in their study of coming things and because of it they missed the essentials that would have pinpointed Jesus as the very man.

When people use the term "signs of the times" it is meant to convey the idea of major change. It identifies a wave of revolution and change that parts company with the past and looks ahead to a notably different future. In every way that is precisely what is taking place in Jesus' first advent. He is putting an end to the slavery of the Law, He is executing the one, all-sufficient sacrifice after which no more are required, He is inaugurating the age of the indwelling Spirit.

When we consider that this is being spoken to the Pharisees and leaders of the Jews, it has an even greater sting. They above all others ought to have been on the ball, and they have been found lacking and slack concerning so momentous an event.

"An evil and adulterous generation seeks after a sign;

This is a bit confusing because Jesus elsewhere exhorts the Pharisees to consider His works if they have issues with Him personally - *though you do not believe Me, believe the works, so that you may know and understand that the Father is in Me, and I in the Father."* (John 10:38.) So it seems contradictory to then condemn folks for seeking a sign.

But in the case of these men, He knows their hearts – that they are putting up the requirement for signs because they are already ill-disposed to accept Him on any terms. They have a heart that will readily rationalize away such miracles as the work of Satan (which their party had already actually done elsewhere in their encounters with Jesus. – Mark 3:22ff)

But why the accusation of adultery? It is doubtful the Pharisees as a generation were known for cheating on their wives. Adultery is being used as in the prophets – being the wife of the Lord, yet going out after other gods. Even here we are puzzled how such a rigorously conservative group as the Pharisees could be charged with idolatry.

Jesus understood their system through and through. He knew each and every motive of their hearts and that they had cleverly fashioned a form of Judaism to suit them and their order. They had in essence made up a form of religion that competed with the true faith of Israel and was leading many astray in its legalism. They also had selfish motives and intentions which is a valid form of substituting something one loves more for God.

It had devolved to the point that they no longer recognized the genuine works of God and they were ready to blithely attribute such things to Satan. So in a very real way they were being unfaithful to God as a wife might be unfaithful to her husband.

and a sign will not be given it, except the sign of Jonah."

'kai' in Greek can also mean but, as in *"but a sign will not be given it, except the sign of Jonah."* This is a better translation because Jesus has just rebuked them for seeking a sign, then says *but* a sign will be given.

What was the sign of Jonah? As we read the OT story, we find no mention of a sign Jonah performed for the Ninevites. He simply preached repentance and its power had the effect of turning the whole city.

It has been proposed that the sign was Jonah himself as he approached Nineveh. Having been three days in the stomach of the creature, his appearance would have been anything but normal, in fact quite bizarre. His clothes would have been bleached white, as was his skin and hair, even his eyebrows. This would have been the visible sign.

Add to this his message of impending destruction and you have a powerful witness to the effecting of repentance.

The sign of Jonah for the Pharisees was the proclamation of repentance with destruction waiting in the wings. This was John's message. He even included the threat that the winnowing fork was ready to separate the chaff and Master's the fan was in his hand ready to whip up the flames to burn them away. The axe was already being laid at the root of the tree.

In very real terms, this impending destruction was close at hand - the destruction of Jerusalem during the imminent war of the Jews against imperial Rome.

Jesus was telling these men that if they were in this frame of mind and spirit, there was only one sign appropriate for them – the sign that conveyed impending destruction lest they repent.

Leaving them, He again embarked and went away to the other side.

We later find Him approaching Bethsaida, so we must assume He is on the eastern side of the Galilee and the embarkation by boat is a return to the vicinity of Capernaum-Bethsaida.

they had forgotten to take bread, . . "Watch out and beware of the leaven of the Pharisees and Sadducees.

This highlights the infancy period the disciples had entered and the difficulties with which they often struggled in getting His meaning.

Some have suggested that the disciples here understood Jesus to be talking about the getting of bread when they arrived, and to not seek it from the Pharisees. They had not secured provisions at their embarkation point and would be in immediate need to get them after they arrived. They therefore understood Jesus to be warning them to not seek such supplies from the Pharisees – the leaven in their bread was to be avoided. So we can see them replying, *"He said that because we did not bring any bread."*

Others see this as a perception that Jesus was being subtle in pointing out that they had forgotten to bring bread on board and was using this phrase to gently rebuke them for their forgetfulness, as in – *"He mentioned 'leaven' to remind us that we forgot the bread."*

In either perception, Jesus was doing neither of these, but was actually continuing a lesson about what had just happened back on the land – His encounter with the Pharisees and what they should know about future encounters.

But first He must correct their misdirection about His meaning.

"Why do you discuss the fact that you have no bread?

Whichever of the two understandings they had above, it was clear the disciples had in mind that He was talking about physical bread, namely food. So Jesus rightly asks, *"Why are you talking about bread?"*

He then reminds them that if bread was His concern, they ought to have learned what is possible concerning the lack of food from the feeding of the five thousand and then the four thousand?

"do you not remember, when I broke the five loaves for the five thousand, how many baskets full of broken pieces you picked up?"

We must also take note that He is not completely casual in this upbraiding. He recites Isaiah's taunt (Is 6:10), *having eyes, you do not see; having ears you do not hear."* This is carefully done, because the passage from Isaiah also includes the indictment that their ears are stopped lest they turn and repent, and He does not wish to make that application to His disciples.

He also recasts this quote in the form of a question, "do you not see? . . do you not hear?" which is not an exact quote of Isaiah. But it often happens that OT passages are paraphrased or revised slightly to fit into the context and tenses of the point of application. This is not a case of fiddling with Scripture to one's own ends, and we are talking about Scripture in the hands of the Son of God.

As for His actual intent, the *'leaven'* of the Pharisees is a symbol of their hidden wickedness, as leaven is hidden in a lump of dough and its effects spread to the whole lump. There is a righteousness in their teaching, but a deception in their application and especially in their example. They are clever in their use of religious law and precept and the disciples are at present no match for these men. Christ's exhortation is to stay clear of them.

And they came to Bethsaida. And they brought a blind man to Jesus

This is a somewhat unique healing because Jesus must employ laying on hands a second time to effect a complete healing.

Of first note, Jesus separates the man from the business in the village. He wants this to be private. We have no direct understanding of the purpose for spitting on the man's eyes. Elsewhere, He is said to spit on His fingers and apply them to the person. This may simply have been a touch point for the release of faith, something indicative of a medium through which the healing would be conveyed, and this may have been helpful to the man in his own faith.

"I see men, for I see them like trees, walking around." Then again He laid His hands on his eyes; and he looked intently and was restored, and began to see everything clearly.

We are bereft of any explanation as to why the first laying on of hands did not work completely. It does not lie in some ineffectiveness with Jesus, so we are inclined to assume that the process of partial restoration, testing the sight thus far, and then completing the healing was intended for the man himself – something Jesus understood about him that occasioned this approach.

The Chronological Gospel Commentary – The Four Gospels

Matthew 16:13-23
13 Now when Jesus came into the district of Caesarea Philippi, He was asking His disciples, "Who do people say that the Son of Man is?" 14 And they said, "Some say John the Baptist; and others, Elijah; but still others, Jeremiah, or one of the prophets." 15 He said to them, "But who do you say that I am?" 16 Simon Peter answered, "You are the Christ, the Son of the living God." 17 And Jesus said to him, "Blessed are you, Simon Barjona, because flesh and blood did not reveal this to you, but My Father who is in heaven.

18 "I also say to you that you are Peter, and upon this rock I will build My church; and the gates of Hades will not prevail against it. 19 "I will give you the keys of the kingdom of heaven; and whatever you bind on earth shall have been bound in heaven, and whatever you loose on earth shall have been loosed in heaven." 20 Then He warned the disciples that they should tell no one that He was the Christ. 21 From that time Jesus began to show His disciples that He must go to Jerusalem, and suffer many things from the elders and chief priests and scribes, and be killed, and be raised up on the third day. 22 Peter took Him aside and began to rebuke Him, saying, "God forbid it, Lord! This shall never happen to You." 23 But He turned and said to Peter, "Get behind Me, Satan! You are a stumbling block to Me; for you are not setting your mind on God's interests, but man's." (Matthew 16:13-23)

Commentary

Caesarea Philippi . . "Who do people say that the Son of Man is?"

Caesarea Philippi was the capital city built by Herod Philip for his tetrarchy of Ituraea and Trachonitis. This was an area considerably N and NE of the Sea of Galilee, almost into Syria. Caesarea Philippi was at the base of Mt. Hermon, approximately center between these areas. It's name combined to honor both Augustus and Herod Philip. The area today is known as Banias or Paneas, after the Roman god, Pan. It is noted for a beautiful spring and waterfall associated with the god. The spring served as one of the sources for the Jordan.

It is time now for the Twelve to solidify the reality of who Jesus is. Their doubts were accommodated during the early travels and events, but they and Jesus are making the turn toward the final events of His ministry and the turnover of Kingdom business to them. They must all be united in who He really is.

Several continue to speculate.

"Some say John the Baptist; and others, Elijah; but still others, Jeremiah, or one of the prophets."

Note that these men are answering Jesus' question about what "others" are saying (which was the question) but none have offered their own convictions.

The mention of John the Baptist is reminiscent of what Antipas himself had come to wonder about Jesus – that John had come back to life, being so powerful a spokesman for God. That some of the disciples mention this is an indication that this was more than a stray idea here or there. 'Elijah' was a candidate because the people and their leaders were aware of the great prophecy in Malachi – *"Behold, I will send you Elijah the prophet before the coming of the great and terrible day of the LORD.* (4:5)

There was no expectation of Jeremiah returning but this may have been bound up in the idea that the prophet of Moses was yet to come, and perhaps it would be the reappearance of someone like Jeremiah (see Luke 9:8.) With reports of what others think out of the way, Jesus now asks them what they themselves think.

"But who do you say that I am?"

They must now put all the facts and teaching together. They can no longer be just observers, but must turn observation into faith, into profession. This is challenging because regardless of what they have seen, there is always some measure of doubt. There is always the bare fact that the one speaking to them is merely a man. But is there enough to go beyond this and believe that He is the Son of God, the Messiah? The Holy Spirit was not slow to fill at least one man with the courage to say what others might not be ready to say,

Simon Peter answered, "You are the Christ, the Son of the living God."

Peter has often been characterized as the less educated, less refined of the disciples, with men like Philip and Andrew being more contemplative, Peter being a more pragmatic man. It is not they who jump up and make this declaration, which might indicate that the contemplative life can sometimes encourage hesitation. But Peter is a man whose boldness is both a benefit and an embarrassment at times. His boldness will cut off the ear of the priest's adjutant and it also serves him well here in bridging the gap of actual, certain knowledge with faith.

Jesus recognizes this very thing . .

"Blessed are you, Simon Barjona, because flesh and blood did not reveal this to you, but My Father who is in heaven.

Barjona was not his last name, but was a designation that he was the son ('bar') of Jonas. Jesus points out that Peter had not come to this conclusion through normal human reason or the faculties he was given as a man, but that this only could come to him by the agency of God. It is exactly the same for all believers in all times. Reason will not argue the case completely. Each must come to the realization that this is the truth and that realization is enabled by the Holy Spirit.

We must also properly conclude that God is setting Peter forward in the group so as to lead them by the very fact that God only enabled Peter to so speak and proclaim, i.e. none of the others were similarly moved to speak also. Others surely followed Peter's profession, but the enabling to speak out first was given to one man, and this needs to be honestly acknowledged by all believers, despite our denominational differences.

"I also say to you that you are Peter, and upon this rock I will build My church;

We cannot ignore that Jesus is focusing on Peter. The Protestant preference to bypass Peter and point to his faith is hard to square with the picture the language is conveying.

Now as to *'this rock'*, battles have been waged for centuries. *'This'* is what is called a demonstrative pronoun. It is used to point to something when we don't know what it is called or don't wish to use its name. We say, "take this over to the business office" instead of, "take this cash-flow balance report over to the business office." But we also use 'this' in combination with its name in order to designate a particular thing among other things – this house, that tree, etc. That is how *'this'* is being used here in Matthew. It is *this* rock, meaning something known to the hearers and being separated from other things.

'rock' is the Greek word 'petra' which is the feminine form of 'petros' with which Peter has been nicknamed. Together, *'this rock'* is being used to point to something already known in the scene. Whether this is Peter himself or something else is not clear merely from the language.

Protestant interpreters have picked up on the change in gender as indicative that Peter the man is not in view as the foundation of Christ's Church, but rather Peter's faith, hence the faith of all believers. Others note the play on words between petra and petros as purposely moving from something ordinary to something very large – petros meaning a manageable stone and petra meaning a massive rock. Catholic apologists stress that the two words were all along intended to be petra . . petra, i.e. *thou art Petra and upon this petra I will build . .*", but because the first part was meant to point to the man Peter, the masculine was used.

It should be noted that Petros . . petros would have yielded a confusing manner of speech similar to *thou art Peter and upon this Peter I will build . .*" which has two problems: it uses an awkward repetition which would have been remedied by *thou art Peter and upon you shall I build . .",* and it would drop the benefit of the feminine form which more often suggests a massive rock. Much of this argumentation is speculative at best, meaning that each side of the argument depends on an assumption about what was intended. Was *petra .. petra* the idea or was the play on words the idea?

Catholics also reference the Aramaic as an indicator, noting that there is no gender issue with 'cepha' and that it is but one word for both stone and massive rock. But there are in fact other words in Aramaic that distinguish between these, however in favor of the Catholic appeal, 'cepha' is used interchangeably for stone and massive rock.

One observation of importance is that regardless of the usage in Aramaic, when it came time to write in Greek, the authors were obligated to choose the right words, and their choices indicate something about their intent, irrespective of the inequities between languages.

As for the Protestant interpretation that the rock is Christ, this would have created a confused image, since Christ as builder would also seen as the rock used to build. The key is in how far one can press the primacy of Peter, even if all can come to agree that Peter is truly being singled out as leader. In a moment, Jesus will declare that Peter has the "keys" and the binding and loosing authority. But how much can we conclude from this bestowal?

Does the rest of the NT support the idea that Peter alone is being given this authority? The keys are only mentioned in relation to Peter. But the power to bind and loose follow so closely and thematically that they are hard to see as separated. In Matthew 18:18 we see Jesus giving the same authority to all present which included others besides the Twelve.

Mark and Luke actually leave out these critical statements (Mark 8:27ff, Luke 9:18ff) which is hard to reconcile with the significance Catholics place on this teaching. Just a bit later we see them arguing over who will be greatest (Mark 9:34, 46.) For them to so argue about this (regardless of the silliness in doing so), it is evident they had not come away from the declaration of Christ about the rock with the idea that Peter was that rock.

In Galatians, Paul refers not to the pillar of the Church but to the *pillars*. This is definitely in keeping with the idea of a foundation, but in naming them he puts James first and Peter second. (Gal 2:9.) This would likewise indicate that His disciples did not have a clear understanding from Christ's words that Peter was the rock.

As for Peter himself, we must add Peter's own instruction in his letters (I Peter 2:5ff), which in reference to *'petros'*, he calls all believers living stones for building the very thing mentioned above by Christ. He further calls all believers a royal priesthood. Paul teaches in many places the believer's authority before God as an individual without human mediation.

Did the early Church agree in common that these verses established the primacy of Peter? Chrystostom comments on this passage, *"On this rock; that is, on the faith of his confession . ."* Elsewhere he is seen to reiterate this understanding and never any other to the extent that he says, *"He did not say 'upon Peter' for it was not upon man, but upon his faith."* Chrysostom was joined by several respected contemporaries: Gregory of Nyssa, Isadore of Pelusium, the Latin Father Hilary, by later Greek Fathers – Theodoret, Theophanes, Theophylact, and John of Damascus. Against these were Origen, Cyprian, Basil, Gregory Naz., Ambrose, Jerome, Cyril, and Alexander.)

One can argue which group was the better to interpret these passages, but one thing is clearly evident from these facts – the doctrine about Peter's primacy can not have come nor was it clarified or solidified from the Deposit of Faith in the Tradition, else all these respected men would have held its view in common. Meaning, that the traditional teaching from the Apostles themselves was vague enough to leave room for debate, which means the interpretation of Christ's teaching was not clearly understood as what Catholics have historically taught.

In summary, if Peter was in fact here being designated in his role as pope for Christ's Church, having unique authority over the rest, the disciples do not appear to act or behave consistent to it. They, including Peter, did not write consistent to it, and the traditional teaching that became the unwritten foundation of teaching for the Holy Church did not make this understanding universally clear, as evident from the ability to question it by respected theologians and doctors.

and the gates of Hades will not prevail against it."

Catholics see this as an endorsement of the Catholic Church specifically because the Church Peter began became the Roman Catholic Church. Protestants see it as a surety to Christ's Church wherever it is found, Protestant or Catholic. Much depends on what prevails against what in this sentence.

At a general level, there are two senses in which this can be understood – the active sense in which the gates of Hell will not succeed in their assault on the Church, and the passive sense in which the gates will not prevail in resisting the overpowering of the Church.

'katischusousin' can mean to prevail against or to overpower. The NASB has *and will not overpower it."* but it admits of the alternate reading, *shall not prove stronger than it* which would support the passive sense above. On the surface, churches are free to choose the sense that supports their doctrinal commitments.

But one should note that there is no case in biblical usage in which gates are used in the aggressive sense of coming out to wage an assault.

When we pay closer attention to the text itself, the Greek words used, the parts of speech and the case endings used, we see a possible preference for one sense over the other.

If the verse is to mean *shall not overpower it*, then the word *'it' – (auteis)* would need to be a direct object of the verb (i.e. in the accusative case.) But this word is in the genitive case, meaning 'of it', and it is also in the feminine gender, meaning *'of her.* If the meaning is 'to overpower', then the sentence would result in, *shall not overpower of her*, which is poor grammar.

But if the meaning is *to prevail against*, then the rendering would be more like, *shall not prevail of her,* or more properly *not prevail against her*, meaning the Gates not prevailing against a conquering Church.

Secondly, *'hell'* is really Hades in the text, and these are not synonymous. Hades is viewed as holding both the wicked and the righteous until judgment, as shown by the parable of Lazarus and the rich man, in which a gulf is fixed between the two camps. In this sense then, both the righteous (the Church) and the wicked go through Hades' gates, but when Christ comes, He will call for his Church and these gates will not prevail in holding it captive.

"I will give you the keys of the kingdom of heaven;

This is not repeated to the others, but the binding and loosing authority is so tied to these keys that when the binding authority is repeated as given also to all the apostles, the gift of the keys would be hard to exclude.

This is, of course, a major point for Catholics and appears in their imagery and emblemage of both Peter and that of the Pope. It is a primary basis for papal authority – he uniquely holds the keys given to Peter.

and whatever you bind on earth shall have been bound in heaven, and whatever you loose on earth shall have been loosed in heaven."

There can be no doubt that this is special authority being bestowed from God and exclusive (it is not granted to other faiths, even Judaism.) But this cannot be limited to Peter and his successors because Matthew 18:18 repeats this bestowal upon all the apostles.

Here the verb is in the 1st person singular – 'deiseis' – but in Matthew 18:18 the verb is in the 2nd person plural – *whatever you(pl.) bind* 'deicheite.'

We see this taking effect in Peter's ministry as he deals with Ananias and Sapphira early in Acts (5:1). But we also see this in practice in Paul who summarily judges a man as delivered to Satan for the destruction of the body that his soul be preserved to eternal life (I Cor 5:5).

The question of whether such authority lasted beyond the apostles is divided on Catholic and Protestant lines. The Catholic sees this maintained in the succession from Peter. The Protestant sees it as operating until the deaths of the apostles but not being maintained by all believers beyond them.

Then He warned the disciples that they should tell no one that He was the Christ.

Understandably, this declaration was to be wisely held by His disciples and not used carelessly to precipitate action against His timetable. The warning was also related to the admission because His Messiahship was not to be that expected by the Jews – there would need to be explanations for which the timing was wholly premature.

that He must go to Jerusalem, and suffer many things from the elders and chief priests

Very shortly thereafter the subject turns the corner to the facts about Jesus' passion. It is interesting that the mention of rising after three days gets completely lost in the emotion of Peter over the impending tragedy. This proves too much for Peter to embrace and understand - *"God forbid it, Lord! This shall never happen to You."*

We ourselves can be very understanding and accommodating that Peter is simply wishing no harm would come to Jesus, especially what he knows would be a criminal's punishment.

But Jesus sees more to this than we do.

"Get behind Me, Satan! You are a stumbling block to Me; for you are not setting your mind on God's interests, but man's."

This is supportive of why Protestants reject the idea that the 'rock' is Peter himself, because the faith within a particular man can be varying and wavering, as seen here. The Catholic, however, can accommodate weakness in faith in Peter and his successors but not see this as affecting the bestowal of authority to the office.

Christ's declaration of Peter's faith is still echoing in the ear when we hear this rebuke. We almost want to do a double-take to be sure we're hearing this correctly.

Certainly more is here than the simple words of Peter's concern. Perhaps the tone of voice or the reading of the heart. But Jesus must be perceiving that if uncorrected, Peter would do much that might work against the plan of God. It is necessary that Christ die. Peter must embrace this as the plan, and something forceful was needed to get this point to him.

Satan is here personified in his influence among men. Peter has in no wise sold himself to the devil. But rather it is like Paul's statement that whatever is not of faith is sin and plays into Satan's purposes.

In very real terms, Satan was intently interested in thwarting Christ's saving work, which despite our seeing that work in His ministry and healing, is first and foremost embodied in the Cross. Salvation is in the Cross and Peter is here, albeit unintentionally, moving to protect Jesus from it. So we can see a proper reference to Satan, even though it would not be our own immediate response.

This understanding is further validated in Jesus' additional words, *"you are not setting your mind on the things of God."*

Mark 8:34-38, Mark 9:1

34 And He summoned the crowd with His disciples, and said to them, "If anyone wishes to come after Me, he must deny himself, and take up his cross and follow Me. 35 "For whoever wishes to save his life will lose it, but whoever loses his life for My sake and the gospel's will save it. 36 "For what does it profit a man to gain the whole world, and forfeit his soul? 37 "For what will a man give in exchange for his soul? 38 "For whoever is ashamed of Me and My words in this adulterous and sinful generation, the Son of Man will also be ashamed of him when He comes in the glory of His Father with the holy angels." (Mark 8:34-38)

1 And Jesus was saying to them, "Truly I say to you, there are some of those who are standing here who will not taste death until they see the kingdom of God after it has come with power." (Mark 9:1)

Commentary

"If anyone wishes to come after Me, he must deny himself, and take up his cross and follow Me.

We may have assumed that the dialog with the disciples about Jesus being Messiah was private, but we see here that there were people present but at a distance. The teaching that followed the former dialog is now intended for both His disciples and the crowd, which He summons to come nearer.

To come after or follow Jesus had a prerequisite – the denial of self. This was not a requirement to simply by unselfish, to adopt a better view that preferred others over self. It was a requirement about which we learn more in Paul's writings – to deny the essence of the self without Christ, that that entity can no longer exist for itself.

Self here means the idea of independent being, separate and discrete from God. Man since the Fall had acquired for himself a way of being that worked out a means of succeeding in life by oneself or in cooperation with others who were likewise independent. Society was like men on a raft adrift in an uncertain sea, who must cooperate with each other and work to draft a plan to survive. It is a sense of being that does not include God or dependency on Him.

That is the self that must be denied, the idea that one has the wherewithal to make it by themselves. That is the person who does not need God, who defies dependency on something other than oneself.

This is a very unpopular message today, because everywhere in America the new order dictates that the self is the chief thing for any person and the standards of others are either arbitrary or inconsistent or untrue. Much of the promotion of self these days is in fact due to society's misperception of the biblical idea of humility, that one must submit to God and God's representatives – the Church. Society had enough of that approach over centuries of abuse and in the 60's and 70's began to elevate self as just as valid as any posed absolutes. 'Victorian' is a byword for self-deprecation and cowing to social norms and mores. The "Revolution" of the sixties was a statement that society had had enough of that.

The result has been the new approach that 'celebrates' mere participation compared to substantive achievement and 'authenticates' people in their choices without imposing moral judgments. Thus, it is harder in the latest generations to convince people to give up a self that has been promoted for decades.

"his cross . ."

Notice, He does not say "My cross." We might conclude that each must take up his own cross, not the cross of Christ. But to take up one's own cross would mean that one must stand for one's own values to the point of death, and while noble, it would not be a case of following Christ, per se.

The thrust here is clearly that of identifying with Christ's own Cross, to be willing to stand as He stood for righteousness, not preferring self as the bar that evaluates obedience.

It is the believer's cross in the sense that they must take up their own instance of Christ's cross, not to die for the sins of the world, but to be willing to die for righteousness' sake. It is to identify with and die for the things with which He was identified and bore His Cross.

Whether that comes to physical persecution and martyrdom or whether it means being willing to suffer persecution from others and society, it all counts for the denial of self and the willingness to accept in one's person the consequences of standing for God's righteousness.

How does this play out in a modern society like ours? We have mortgages, SUVs, careers in business, health care, education, science and industry. Simple acceptance in society means neighborhood events, keeping our kids up with the latest in clothes, entertainment and being fair-minded in society's sense of the word.

We have certain commitments that can't be avoided without standing out as weird, prudish or unsociable.

We must face the choice of whether society's right of passage is more important than the Bible and, if not, to be willing to accept the social consequences for taking our stand. The Romans called Christians "haters of mankind" because they did not go along with the leisure activities in which pagans indulged to ease themselves of the unpleasant effects of daily life.

We may be called "puritanical" or "legalistic," but in the end our assessment by the Lord will not include how well we pleased society and avoided its persecutions.

"whoever wishes to save his life will lose it, . .

To save one's life means to save it by one's own efforts, independent of the criteria established for saving it. It is a myth that one can work out their own means to secure a life after the grave. Life after death is not simply "out there" for the having and there are many paths to it. It has one path, one set of requirements because it is under the sovereignty of the God who makes such a life possible. He sets the rules and to ignore them is foolishness and self-deception.

To lose one's life does not mean that if we are self-centered and self-seeking we are precipitating a premature death. It is not an axiom that to be selfish hastens the surety of an immediate or imminent demise. It is to say that in the end one will lose all that one has sought and worked to gain. This idea of loss or waste is seldom entertained. Even though one can conceive of death as ending their efforts, in the working of it one puts off that idea and considers both achievement and effort worth the doing for as long as it lasts. Some have a misinformed notion of some kind of inevitable continuity beyond the earthly life. Few actually follow through with the existentialists in viewing life as meaningless, where effort and enjoyment are merely bare, impersonal facts that come to no real purpose or conclusion.

For the atheists and existentialists, God will apprise them of what they will be missing. For the misguided believers who trusted in some kind of afterlife, there will be the revelation that the life they hoped for has been lost.

"but whoever loses his life for My sake and the gospel's will save it."

To lose one's plans for life is what Jesus is talking about, not to die or be martyred. It is to give up one's own aspirations, one's own plans for their life, and accept God's purpose for them.

Joni Earickson was a young girl of seventeen, full of typical plans for a happy life, marriage and children. She was paralyzed from the neck down in a diving accident and this has remained permanent to the present. She must be helped with bathroom activity, she has to be turned every half hour to avoid bed sores, her mobility is confined to what she can do from a wheelchair. For her, this is reality for the rest of that life for which she had quite different plans.

God has used her in ways no one else could have accomplished quite like her. She now sees her life as something God planned for her, but she had a great struggle giving up her claims to a life she wished and desired. We can envision her asking, "Why didn't I get the life my friends expected and got?"

To save one's life in this way focuses on the larger meaning of life. It is to secure that kind of life for which Life was created. It is the life we will live for an incomparable time compared to the earthly one, such that for its sheer length, life will have no other meaning than the heavenly one.

That is what Jesus is drawing all men to consider. That is the advertisement in what He is teaching. To live eternally and in a life much more fulfilling than anything we accomplished here and now.

"For what does it profit a man to gain the whole world, and forfeit his soul?

This is meant to focus attention on the outcome which many are ignoring or may not even believe – that one could lose his soul for eternity. What profit then is there in all the effort of earthly life, only to lose the eternal one?

Now this verse does not mention eternal life. In fact, the later mention of heavenly things below involves Heaven coming to earth in judgment, not the believer going into eternal life.

But the soul has always been viewed as that which lives on after death, so the implication is obvious that eternal life is to be connected with the state of the soul.

We are also further puzzled by the statement that the soul is "lost," when it is clear that the soul of the wicked also lives on after death, but to a different end.

The loss of the soul is first in contrast to the keeping of the soul in relation to Heaven. To not be a soul in Heaven is to have a soul that isn't worth claiming as having "kept." But it also has a second sense that actually dictates a nature to such a soul that is equivalent to having all along been lost. There is a destruction of the soul promised for the wicked. How long they continue after death is hardly relevant if the final end is absolute annihilation and destruction. If the soul will eventually be completely destroyed in the Lake of Fire, then talking about it living beyond the grave for a season (albeit a very long season) has little moment.

The condition Jesus describes (discovering the truth about the keeping or losing of one's soul) is effectively pictured in Michelangelo's *Last Judgment*, in the Sistine Chapel. There, all manner of men receive the final verdict concerning life. We cannot help but recall the words, *"What does it profit a man to gain the whole world..."*

In that Judgment, all the efforts and philanthropy, all the philosophical rationalizations that sounded so right in casting such worries to the wind will be of no avail. The truth they confidently explained away is now in front of them and all they might lean on from their past life is useless. *"The thing I feared most has come upon me."*

"For what will a man give in exchange for his soul?

Not the buying back of the soul for oneself, but to redeem the soul back from destruction and condemnation.

This picture follows very naturally from the former scene of facing the loss of the soul in the Judgment. Those caught in this dilemma will immediately resort to bargaining. They will search and appeal for something they can offer to change the state of their soul.

But Jesus states that when that time comes, the time for mounting up things of equivalent value has expired. Nor does the NT retain any hope that some thing could ever be offered, as in a bargain. No earthly thing, no earthly effort or work will be recognized as legal tender, because the worth of the soul is measured in spiritual achievements, and all of those are under the judgment and assessment of God, the very One now judging. We will have had one life in which to engage those things. Once done, the opportunities to achieve them are gone.

Hence, the picture is one of desperation. The soul before judgment is looking about for things to offer for redeeming the soul, and nothing is found.

"whoever is ashamed of Me . . the Son of Man will also be ashamed of him . ."

Sobering words we hope will never be said of us.

There is a difference between being fearful of confrontation and those encounters for which one is ill-prepared or inadequate. Many Christians can witness very effectively, but may not have the ability, personality or capacities to engage an adept and polished atheist. The NT discourages us from casting our pearls before swine and to avoid contentious arguments that are fruitless and will only lead people away from the truth. But Christians can be placed in situations not of their own choosing in which a stand for Christ is needed, but they feel out-gunned by the superior techniques and abilities of others. This is not a case of being ashamed, but simply being fearful of not being effective or of giving fuel to the haters of God.

The person being described here by Jesus is the person who is actually ashamed of what Christ and Christianity represent. How can one be a Christian and feel this way? The teaching is virtually saying that one's Christianity is in doubt if such an attitude prevails and is never overcome by confident faith. To this Christ says He will be ashamed of such a person in the Judgment.

We live in a world that is ever emboldening itself against Christian teaching and values. It can present exhortations to get with the program society dictates or suffer the consequences. When someone holds that as a chief value, the teaching of Jesus, even the mention of His name, becomes an embarrassment with which some wish not to be associated. As such, it declares the truth about our decision for Christ, whether it was an exercise like getting a merit badge in the Scouts, or a life-changing event.

There are some Christians in certain churches who will actually defend society's view that mentioning Jesus is inappropriate in public. Some folks contemplate the embarrassment and shame in turning a "successful" secular party into a church service by mentioning Jesus Christ in earshot of all the guests. Whether the embarrassment is in realizing one shouldn't have been there in the first place or in being ashamed of Jesus anywhere outside the walls of a church must be assessed individually against the witness of the NT.

What Jesus is teaching is that true shame will be recompensed before the Father, so count the cost.

in this adulterous and sinful generation,

He used this designation to highlight the conflicts that will naturally come as a believer promulgates revolutionary ideas in a world that does not want to be reformed. The challenge of being bold or ashamed is heightened by the presence of an evil generation that will take special interest in arranging such tests.

there are some of those who are standing here who will not taste death until they see the kingdom of God after it has come with power.

This is a difficult verse because it is clear that the disciples all lived and died without the Kingdom coming to earth in fulfillment of OT promises. We are helped in understanding this better by seeing that what follows (the Transfiguration) is what is meant, but the terminology seems for us too strong to permit that event as its fulfillment.

Part of the problem is in placing too much stress on *after it has come with power* such that it obligates a meaning of end times and the Second Coming. But we saw with the early preaching of John and Jesus that the Kingdom was at hand even though the events attributed to the Second Coming were nowhere in view. In some very real way the Kingdom was at hand, and here also in some very real way some of those present will see the Kingdom coming in power.

Some have chosen to see the fulfillment in the Day of Pentecost, which was the first filling of the Kingdom with its citizens in such massive numbers, and on account of a profound display of power in spiritual gifts.

Still others see the fulfillment in the destruction of Jerusalem which finally broke the connection to the old covenant and the age of the new, which embodied one's entrance into citizenry in the Kingdom.

But despite the force of the terminology, it is not by mere chance that the Transfiguration is recounted next. If we follow the deliberateness of the Gospel writers, the close proximity of these accounts, especially with an expectation of fulfillment left hanging at the end of Mark chapter 8, we cannot overlook the applicability of the Transfiguration.

In the Pentecost and the destruction of Jerusalem, the King is not visibly present. In the Transfiguration, not only is Christ present and shown in His Heavenly role, but continuity of the Kingdom back into the OT to include its saints is represented in Moses and Eljjah.

Mathew 17:1-13

1 Six days later Jesus took with Him Peter and James and John his brother, and led them up on a high mountain by themselves. 2 And He was transfigured before them; and His face shone like the sun, and His garments became as white as light. 3 And behold, Moses and Elijah appeared to them, talking with Him.

4 Peter said to Jesus, "Lord, it is good for us to be here; if You wish, I will make three tabernacles here, one for You, and one for Moses, and one for Elijah." 5 While he was still speaking, a bright cloud overshadowed them, and behold, a voice out of the cloud said, "This is My beloved Son, with whom I am well-pleased; listen to Him!" 6 When the disciples heard this, they fell face down to the ground and were terrified. 7 And Jesus came to them and touched them and said, "Get up, and do not be afraid." 8 And lifting up their eyes, they saw no one except Jesus Himself alone.

9 As they were coming down from the mountain, Jesus commanded them, saying, "Tell the vision to no one until the Son of Man has risen from the dead." 10 And His disciples asked Him, "Why then do the scribes say that Elijah must come first?" 11 And He answered and said, "Elijah is coming and will restore all things; 12 but I say to you that Elijah already came, and they did not recognize him, but did to him whatever they wished. So also the Son of Man is going to suffer at their hands." 13 Then the disciples understood that He had spoken to them about John the Baptist. (Mathew 17:1-13)

Commentary

Six days later Jesus took with Him Peter and James and John his brother,

Peter, James and John are hereafter singled out as what might be called the inner circle among the Twelve. The idea of an inner circle is distasteful to some because it smacks of favoritism, which seems uncharacteristic of the universal, impartial love of Jesus. But this criticism comes more from our democratic ideology where all things must be fair to all concerned, equal opportunity, etc.

But in practical terms, many aspects of life, even in modern democracies, require delegation to some and not others. Everyone cannot be chief executive officer. All players cannot be captain of a team. The necessities of leadership and the very idea that fewer decision makers is better than many, dictates that authority must be delegated to individuals, and that separates them necessarily from the rest. In our case here, we know of no one outside this group complaining.

James here is not the Lord's brother but the son of Zebedee by mention of his brother John.

and led them up on a high mountain by themselves.

The mount of the Transfiguration is not clearly identified today, even though visitors to the Galilee are pointed to a traditional location. There are two candidates:

Mount Hermon. This is the more popular candidate, even though less traditional, because it is the highest in the area and it is in close proximity to where Jesus was just teaching - Caesarea Philippi,

Mount Tabor. The traditional site. However, it is relatively low in elevation and in the middle of a densely populated area even in ancient times. Also, Nain is situated on its summit and the account here suggests an unpopulated area.

And He was transfigured before them;

We are often surprised by the Bible's relatively bland statements about events of tremendous aspect. The sheer enormity of what was taking place, Jesus being changed in physical appearance, personages from Israel's past appearing and clouds and glory attending the whole scene is summed up in *He was transfigured before them.* And this by men who had the closest intimacy with the men who witnessed it, having heard firsthand their experience recounted.

We are not told how the transfiguration was performed, what powers obtained, etc. The Bible does not convey this information, as if scientific scrutiny were an obligation. It simply reports the events as facts. The parting of the sea for Moses is not described in the terms of physics but simply reported as by a strong east wind.

What was the purpose in having Jesus transfigured? All along these men were engaging what in their human eyes was a man, in body the same as any other man. They had come to the revelation of asserting His Messiahship, but His real nature, the way He existed truly in the Kingdom of His Father was not adequately seen in His human form.

To solidify who He was and that He had an existence and form prior to His earthly life that would resume after its end, they needed to see Him as He really was – the Son of God.

and His face shone like the sun, and His garments became as white as light.

He remained anthropomorphic (of human form) because His face and garments are mentioned. There is no indication from Scripture that His existence as deity and as Son necessitated some bizarre form beyond man's imagination. In essence, His form would be incorporial as Son, since He taught that God is Spirit. What happened in the Incarnation is an epiphany, an appearance in a form man can comprehend. But we must conclude that this was very near the Heavenly form since it was being disclosed to them and it would be odd to pose yet another accommodating appearance.

That His face shone is reminiscent of Daniel's prayers and visions, *"and cause thy face to shine upon thy sanctuary . . (and) his face as the appearance of lightning."* (Dan 9:17, 10:6)

We see this more clearly in the vision John sees in the Revelation, *"and His face was like the sun shining in its strength."* (Rev 1:16)

And behold, Moses and Elijah appeared to them, talking with Him.

Did Moses and Elijah actually appear from their graves? There is no definitive doctrine that those who sleep in the Lord cannot be called to appear, but the finality of death as being the end of earthly works seems to mitigate against it. Where did they get their bodily forms if their originals were now gone to dust? Of course, anything is possible with God, and He is the author of the body.

We can be helpfully informed from Samuel where we hear of Saul's request of the witch of Endor to bring up Samuel. Her utter shock at the appearance of Samuel indicates that she had all along intended some other apparition or trick of her own divination. She knew Samuel's appearance was not her own work but that of Almighty God.

There simply is not enough information to form a doctrine that God would never do such a thing, hence, we cannot dismiss that Moses and Elijah were the very persons present, as opposed to mere representations.

Why these figures? Moses was the greatest of the OT saints, surpassing Abraham in notoriety primarily because of the deeds done by him and the giving of the Law. Abraham was father of the race and a major exemplar of faith, but his achievements did not compare in Jewish eyes to those of Moses. The Jews claimed lineage by Abraham, but they claimed Moses as the rule of their religious life. Of any who could represent the old covenant, Moses stands out from the rest.

In addition to this, an even stronger reason for having Moses present is the dangling prediction of the Prophet to come. What more befitting arrangement than to have the predictor present at the moment of fulfillment?

Elijah was the most renown among the prophets. He did not write. Isaiah and Jeremiah are each of imposing length in the OT canon. Isaiah stands out for his many references to Messiah. But Elijah is predicted as coming again before the great day of the Lord. Perhaps this is the reason for his selection.

The appearance of these two with Jesus is to state emphatically that the entire revelation of God is bound up in one truth – the OT points to Christ and Christ has come. It is as though the whole message of God is rolled up in one vision. If there was any doubt about the authentication of Jesus in the larger plan of God over all time, these men drive that authentication home. If there was any doubt whether Moses would have seen Jesus as Messiah and the Prophet to come, there is no doubt now.

"Lord, . . . I will make three tabernacles here, one for You, and one for Moses, and one for Elijah."

This is the human response. Mark adds that Peter did not know how to speak because of his fear. This accounts for the strange suggestion that they needed booths either for shade, comfort or veneration.

For a vision like this, it was thought that preparations must be made for what comes next. Tabernacles may have come from the idea of the feast of Succoth or Tabernacles., in which the Jews who came to the Temple lived in little booths or tents and entertained guests. It may have occurred in Peter's muddled mind that to entertain and enjoy their heavenly guests, such structures were expected.

We should resist the idea that Peter intended shrines or places of worship.

In the midst of these words, God interrupts the scene and speaks from the cloud.

"This is My beloved Son, with whom I am well-pleased; listen to Him!"

It is as though the Father is cutting short the prattle of man's ideas and putting everyone present on the right footing. This was an earlier pronouncement from Heaven that the disciples were not present to hear, being not yet chosen at the time of Jesus' baptism. To have the key figures of authority and power present with Jesus and God speaking audibly in the midst of it all, declaring the authenticity and genuineness of Jesus as Son was an overwhelming experience.

We see next that they fell face down and were terrified.

The command to listen to Him was to signal the end of the old dispensation in which the Law and the Prophets comprised the normative teaching for God's people. That form of witness was now being subsumed in the Person of the Son, such that all listening for the voice of God, all subsequent revelation, was in Him.

"Get up, and do not be afraid."

In many such appearances that stupefy and intimidate mankind, the first words to the people from deity or messengers is *"Be not afraid."* This was said to Mary at the annunciation. It is understandable in ancient times, considering the superstitions of the times that men might easily slip into irrational fears. These words were intended to set one's mind immediately at ease that the unexplainable was coming from God and He meant no harm, but blessing.

As quickly as the vision appeared, it disappeared and Jesus was alone with them. The manner in which reality in the spiritual realm can fade in and out of the temporal one intrigues us all. We are tempted to say, "Just like in the movies!" when in truth the novels and the movies can trace their ideas back to what people had been reading in the Bible for generations.

"Tell the vision to no one until the Son of Man has risen from the dead."

The reason for this caution is largely practical. We might think it would have been an excellent thing to announce and thereby further authenticate Jesus among the people, but Jesus knew that such things would actually be difficult to take seriously. Here is the mark of the godly. Mere man would have used it otherwise.

There is an interesting scene in *The Bishop's Wife* (1947), in which the bishop asks the angel to simply create the planned cathedral out of thin air. It would certainly save work and money, and would gain believers all the more. The angel asked, "How would you explain it?"

We can be counted on in many circumstances to have naïve expectations of how people will respond. In this case, not only would the disciples be laughed at in claiming to have seen Moses and Elijah, but the claim for Jesus' participation would be seen as self-serving, as contrived to enlarge the company of followers. It would also be fuel to His enemies who would use it to prove to the people that He was deranged or mad.

Interestingly, He permits this disclosure to be done after the resurrection. Then, of course, there would be other evidence that He was who He said He was.

"Why then do the scribes say that Elijah must come first?"

The reason for this question is in response to the caution to keep this quiet. In their minds, the greatest authentication is to announce the appearance of Elijah, since that was key to the coming of Messiah. Now they had seen Elijah. This would surely establish Jesus in indisputable terms.

"Elijah is coming and will restore all things; 12 but I say to you that Elijah already came,

This sounds like double-talk. Elijah is coming and has already come. This is explained in terms of double-fulfillments and also in terms of foreshadowing or types. There are instances in which persons are pre-figurements of an event that will actually be properly fulfilled later. Joseph is traditionally called a type of Christ in that he was sold into slavery by his brethren – Jesus was betrayed by His own. Joseph was tempted but did not yield. Joseph rose from his prison to authority and power. Joseph's brethren were restored to the one they had rejected – the Jews will one day embrace Christ.

Elijah is predicted before the great and terrible Day of the Lord. This is generally understood to mean the Day of His wrath, but it is clear the Jews revised the expectation to an appearance at the coming of Messiah who would be the instrument of that Judgment.

So Elijah is yet to come because the Day of Judgment is yet to come, even in Jesus' day, since He did not come then to judge.

Still, He declares Elijah has already come. The tone of His speech tells them that He is not referring to the just-witnessed vision, but to an event in history. He adds that the people did not recognize him and did as they pleased to him. He further adds that the persecution and death that happened to this Elijah, He will similarly suffer.

Then the disciples understood that He had spoken to them about John the Baptist.

The key is *"at their hands."* It suggests the very same people. Who then was the Elijah already come, who suffered at the hands of their present leaders? John is the only candidate. He came before as an announcer and preparer, and this is seen as the role of the Elijah of Messiah's coming.

Elsewhere Jesus says, *"If you can receive it, this is Elijah who was to come."* (Matt 11:14) The phrase "if you can receive it" or "if you can accept it" is a technical phrase or idiomatic expression that introduces the idea that what follows would not normally be deduced. It is a special mode of speech, asking the hearer to entertain a figure or an analogy.

He is basically stating that John is not literally the Elijah to come but the pre-figuration or type of that Elijah. This should not be construed as nullifying all expectation that Elijah is yet to come in end times.

Mark 9:14-28, Matthew 17:20-27, Mark 9:30-32

14 When they came back to the disciples, they saw a large crowd around them, and some scribes arguing with them. 15 Immediately, when the entire crowd saw Him, they were amazed and began running up to greet Him. 16 And He asked them, "What are you discussing with them?" 17 And one of the crowd answered Him, "Teacher, I brought You my son, possessed with a spirit which makes him mute; 18 and whenever it seizes him, it slams him to the ground and he foams at the mouth, and grinds his teeth and stiffens out. I told Your disciples to cast it out, and they could not do it."

19 And He answered them and said, "O unbelieving generation, how long shall I be with you? How long shall I put up with you? Bring him to Me!" 20 They brought the boy to Him. When he saw Him, immediately the spirit threw him into a convulsion, and falling to the ground, he began rolling around and foaming at the mouth. 21 And He asked his father, "How long has this been happening to him?" And he said, "From childhood. 22 "It has often thrown him both into the fire and into the water to destroy him. But if You can do anything, take pity on us and help us!" 23 And Jesus said to him, " `If You can?' All things are possible to him who believes." 24 Immediately the boy's father cried out and said, "I do believe; help my unbelief."

25 When Jesus saw that a crowd was rapidly gathering, He rebuked the unclean spirit, saying to it, "You deaf and mute spirit, I command you, come out of him and do not enter him again." 26 After crying out and throwing him into terrible convulsions, it came out; and the boy became so much like a corpse that most of them said, "He is dead!" 27 But Jesus took him by the hand and raised him; and he got up. 28 When He came into the house, His disciples began questioning Him privately, "Why could we not drive it out?" (Mark 9:14-28)

20 And He said to them, "Because of the littleness of your faith; for truly I say to you, if you have faith the size of a mustard seed, you will say to this mountain, `Move from here to there,' and it will move; and nothing will be impossible to you. 21 But this kind does not go out except by prayer and fasting." (Matthew 17:20-21)

30 From there they went out and began to go through Galilee, and He did not want anyone to know about it. 31 For He was teaching His disciples and telling them, "The Son of Man is to be delivered into the hands of men, and they will kill Him; and when He has been killed, He will rise three days later." 32 But they did not understand this statement, and they were afraid to ask Him. (Mark 9:30-32)

22 And while they were gathering together in Galilee, Jesus said to them, "The Son of Man is going to be delivered into the hands of men; 23 and they will kill Him, and He will be raised on the third day." And they were deeply grieved. 24 When they came to Capernaum, those who collected the two-drachma tax came to Peter and said, "Does your teacher not pay the two-drachma tax?" 25 He said, "Yes." And when he came into the house, Jesus spoke to him first, saying, "What do you think, Simon? From whom do the kings of the earth collect customs or poll-tax, from their sons or from strangers?" 26 When Peter said, "From strangers," Jesus said to him, "Then the sons are exempt. 27 "However, so that we do not offend them, go to the sea and throw in a hook, and take the first fish that comes up; and when you open its mouth, you will find a shekel. Take that and give it to them for you and Me." (Matthew 17:22-27)

Commentary

When they came back to the disciples,

During the time when Peter James and John were witnessing the transfiguration further up the mountain, the rest of the disciples were dealing with a situation in the crowd that had gathered below. A man had brought his son to be delivered of an evil spirit. The disciples made an attempt to cast it out but to no avail.

This lack of similar power in the disciples was now causing much discussion between the people and the disciples. It is as though they were asking, *"What's the problem here? Jesus is able to cast out demons. Why can you not do the same?"* The disciples are caught in the dilemma of trying to explain it.

On seeing Jesus, the crowd abandons the disciples and flocks to Him.

"Teacher, I brought You my son, possessed with a spirit which makes him mute;

Ordinarily, this would not necessarily be attributed to an evil spirit, except that the father explains, *"whenever it seizes him, it slams him to the ground and he foams at the mouth, and grinds his teeth and stiffens out."*

To all, this was clear evidence of a demon. We should note that demonic activity was not viewed with skepticism or cynicism as it is today.

"O unbelieving generation, how long shall I be with you? How long shall I put up with you?

At first this sounds like a rebuke for having asked Jesus to free the boy, as in *"How long must I be troubled by people like you?"* But this is not the meaning, simply because any request to be free from a demon is a blessed thing, since it returns the person to the service of God. Regardless of the manner in which the person arrived at their plight, seeking deliverance is the most right thing one can do.

The rebuke concerns the conditions among these people that provided fertile ground for such wickedness to be planted. When we encounter demon possession, the first thought is how has the person come to such a place? What went wrong in their choices that led them to this condition? It is the indolence and neglect of spiritual things, the living of life without much concern for God or taking Him into the soul that leaves one vulnerable to another master.

Demon possession does not happen without consent. Demons don't pounce on a man and take possession of him against his will. They cleverly and adeptly gain permission. This is the generation over which Jesus mourns and cries out in dismay.

In a moment the father explains that this has been happening since childhood. One must question the ignorance of training and instruction that must have prevailed to allow someone so young to be taken. Yet we see in modern times how permissive parents allow their children to indulge even demonic interests in the respected privacy of their rooms, with rationalizations and excuses for not acting.

immediately the spirit threw him into a convulsion, and falling to the ground,

We have here great insight into the operations of that world beyond the temporal. There is the world of demons who have purpose and intent, a plan of action, a mission. Yet in that other world, they know and fear the Son of God, for in God's universe of all things there is sovereignty and mastery in Him alone. That they are allowed to exist is a mystery, yet the truth we know about God is consistently portrayed in His not letting absolute power get out of His hands.

At the mere presence of Jesus, the demons make themselves known. When did such beings know Him so as to tremble? In that world that exists ever as real as this one, in which such beings have clear knowledge of the way of things, and who is really in absolute command.

The reason for the convulsions and flailing is the beginning of a fight – *"we wrestle not against flesh and blood but against principalities and powers."* The demons are not going to go quietly or without a fuss. It is in part to show what fierce power they have over their host and to take especially forceful hold on him in defense.

to destroy him.

People glibly quip that they relish a life with Satan as their lord. He at least is ready to feed all their selfish wants. There is no moralizing or caution against wanton pleasure.

What people don't realize until too late is Satan's hidden plan to destroy them. The purpose of possession is to steal away a soul that could be won for Christ. But that is not the end. Death is then the aim, because once dead, all opportunity to serve God is lost. There is only one destiny – to continue in Satan's service (if evil spirits can come from the disembodied of the wicked) or at least to be counted in the host of the unrighteous forever. So destruction is the aim, not a life of pleasure.

Here we see Satan desiring to destroy the boy physically so as to have him eternally, foiled up to now by friends and family.

But if You can do anything, take pity on us and help us!"

In this request is the hint of unbelief. The father is not completely certain, especially with the poor performance of the disciples.

Jesus first addresses what is needed – faith. In reply, Jesus repeats, *"If you can?"* It is a statement of incredulity in the man's request. He then instructs the man that all things are possible by means of belief.

"I do believe; help my unbelief."

Here is the most honest prayer in the Bible. In an instant the man re-assesses the Person in front of him, His character, deportment, His authoritative and confident tone, the expression on His face. He rekindles his confidence enough to say, *"I do believe"* but he adds the reality of what he knows about himself. He knows there is unbelief there also - *"help my unbelief!"* - but he does not wish it to be an impediment. He now wants that too to be dealt with by Jesus.

Help my unbelief is the greatest prayer we can pray because it acknowledges our need to believe and our weakness in believing on our own. It acknowledges that God is the author of faith and as such can turn unbelief into faith.

I command you, come out of him and do not enter him again."

The command to come out is accompanied by the command to not enter again. It is to assure parent and child that they must not be in fear of the demon overriding Christ's work after He is gone. We are hesitant to conclude that this is a hands off command for any future oppression. Man can invite such powers within, and this command does not preclude that. But it does assure them that they have nothing to fear from this demon if they fill the void with the Spirit of God.

and the boy became so much like a corpse

A trick of the demon as a last fling of defiance upon leaving. To make the boy appear dead might cause all to infer that Jesus' work had proved fatal. Think of the trouble this would have caused. The father could have complained that at least before he had his son alive.

Jesus foils this deception by raising him up to consciousness and a new life.

"Why could we not drive it out?"

The next scene is the very natural inquiry by the disciples as to why things transpired as they did? Why, if they were empowered, did they fail?

We come here to appreciate the need to match power with degrees of circumstances and conditions. Things are not usually simplistic, though first steps will be. Learning cannot embrace everything at once, like trying to drink from a fire hose. They were introduced to healing and deliverance but as with all courses on how to do things, there is always the "advanced" course.

"Because of the littleness of your faith;

Two conditions needed to be addressed. The quantity of faith and the fervency of the faith one has. Lest they (or we) conclude that success is based on how much faith one has (that failure means the need for more faith) Jesus explains that faith of the smallest order can do impossible things. *"you will say to this mountain .. and it will move."* So it is not the quantity of faith that is critical.

If not, then it must be the fervency in the faith one has. We sometimes mis-state our condition as not having enough faith, when it is really a case of not leaning on the faith we already have.

When Jesus says, *"Because of the littleness of your faith"* as an answer to their query, He does not mean quantity but littleness in terms of dependence, in terms of fervency. This cannot be otherwise, due to His mention of the mustard seed. If it was quantity of faith, the mustard seed analogy is completely out of place as a clarification.

On the other side of the issue, quantity does come into play in the Christian life in the sense that God is the bestower of our faith and as Paul states, He dispenses it in measure as He wills *" as God has allotted to each a measure of faith."* (Romans 12:3) We are not to necessarily pray so as to acquire more than God has allotted, neither are we are to assume that we receive only one dose and God will not increase it as He wishes when the need arises. It is His doing not ours. Whatever He gives us, we are expected to use it to the fullest.

As for the moving of mountains, some have dismissed this as merely literary hyperbole, with no intention of literal fulfillment. This is seldom a device in Jesus' teaching. His words are most often meant to be taken literally.

So can the believer move a mountain? Prayer is to be in accord with God's purposes, not a mechanism for getting what we want. So it might be reliably said that if God wishes us to move a mountain by speaking it in faith, the mountain will surely be moved. We simply have no occasion when such a feat would be called for. This does not justify an interpretation that Jesus never intended us to conclude that a mountain could ever be actually moved.

But this kind does not go out except by prayer and fasting."

Here is the instruction on the use of faith, no matter how small. Faith is not to be used as a magic word, in which a simple unimpassioned pronouncement is all that is needed. In the case of demons especially, there will be a stubbornness to move at the first command. They possess a craftiness that is brazen enough to hope that by resistance, the believer will become despondent and leave off of any further pursuit.

Sincerity and fervency are needed in some cases and prayer and fasting are stated as the appointed means for unleashing the requisite power. Some might see this as somewhat silly because God is in full charge of His own power and can dispense it anytime, anywhere. There are no prerequisites, simply His own decision to do so. So what is actually added by fasting?

As in all things between God and man, the arrangement of things and the stipulation of requirements is more for man's benefit than God's. Our interaction with God is a relationship not an arrangement. We are to come to know Him better through working the deeds of righteousness, and we are to learn more about ourselves. One of those lessons is sincerity and fervency.

In the later teaching about the woman knocking at the neighbor's door for bread, it is her fervency that moves the man to open to her. Some see God as reluctant or miserly in handing out blessings. On the contrary, we believe God desires to bless. So why require incessant appeals and knockings? To solidify the experience of being fervent and determined.

"The Son of Man is to be delivered into the hands of men, and they will kill Him; and when He has been killed, He will rise three days later."

They continue throughout the Galilee and Jesus returns to the subject of His passion and death. This is the same subject Peter could not accept earlier at Caesarea Philippi. Here it is reiterated, but Peter has learned his lesson.

Despite this teaching (now the second instance) we will later find the disciples despondent and confused when it actually occurs. Perhaps the embracing of it was so incongruous and emotionally troubling that it never took completely in these early preparatory statements. Hence, *But they did not understand this statement, and they were afraid to ask Him.*

We need to fully understand the absolutely devoted attitudes these men had to their Master. Jesus was so lovable a person to be with, their association with Him was incomparable. They quite naturally wished it to go on and on. An end to such things was not even a thought. So while they had learned that challenging or questioning such a picture was unwise, emotionally they suppressed it to the degree that it was always received with befuddlement and as such, they were disoriented and despondent when the events played out in reality.

Also, in these preparatory statements, the idea of rising again in three days was something the disciples had to be reminded of. It will not be seen as an obvious expectation stemming from moments like these.

Some have questioned why Jesus would willingly embrace this outcome, if it was the work of evil men? He had the power and wisdom to side-step this, to sovereignly prevent it. What, after all, could mere men do to Him?

But we learn, of course, that His death was actually part of the overall plan. It was necessary that a permanent sacrifice be made for the sins of the world, one that would not have to be repeated, as in the Mosaic economy. He was the only candidate, so a death must take place.

To offend the Romans would not suffice because it would never be for the right reasons. In their eyes He would only be crucified for sedition or claiming a realm that belonged to the emperor. But to be killed by the Jews carried all the significance of the claim to be God and Messiah. It would be a death based on claims about His true essence, something the Romans would never take seriously enough, as seen in Pilate's initial response.

"Does your teacher not pay the two-drachma tax?"

The scene has now changed to Capernaum and some time after the above discourse. The collector's of the taxes were not diligent enough in general to know if every citizen had paid taxes, including newcomers and visitors. They had registers, but the population did not stay static, making the lists only helpful for permanent residents.

But Jesus and His men would have had notoriety in this area and any alert tax collector would be prompted to inquire whether such men as these had paid the tax? Their records showed no such payment, so the official approaches Peter not with the exhortation, *"You need to clear your accounts with us."* but with a question that assumes there is an avoidance taking place. It is the equivalent of *"Why does your teacher not pay?"*

What was this tax? It is here called the di-drachma tax or the two-drachma tax, but we learn through OT study that this was the Temple tax, originally the tax to support the Tabernacle. We find this in Moses command from Exodus 30:11. It is stipulated there as a half sheckel, but in Greek coinage two drachmas were roughly equivalent. In regions inconvenient to Jerusalem, one could not exchange or acquire the sheckel, which was by now no longer the coinage of Judaism, but used in the Temple only. So the Greek coin was accepted.

This is not to be confused with tribute money for Rome. Tribute money was an indemnity on a conquered people, paid to the victors as a perennial punishment.

He said, "Yes."

It is unclear whether Peter was answering, "Yes, he pays it" or "Yes, he does not pay it." Technically, a yes answer to the official's question posed in the negative would be to agree with the proposition – that the teacher does not pay. Either way, we learn that Jesus intends to comply with the tax.

"What do you think, Simon? From whom do the kings of the earth collect customs or poll-tax, from their sons or from strangers?"

Before just complying, Jesus wishes to set the record straight about the truth of the obligation. This is a Jewish tax, commanded of His Father back in Moses' time. Thus, it was not a heathen tax about which the Jew could harbor resentment. But Jesus wishes to clarify whether an injunction like this applies to Him or not?

He asks if kings in general tax their own families or do they tax the subjects of their realms, i.e. strangers as opposed to kin?

Peter answers with the reply of common sense. "Strangers." In everyone's mind it ought to be jelling that Jesus is the Son, therefore family - not a stranger.

Jesus replies, *". . then the sons are exempt.,* meaning He has no obligation to pay a tax levied by His own Father, if the son is considered by common sense to be exempt.

We shouldn't be confused by the term poll-tax as deflecting us away from the temple tax. In ancient times, the poll tax was a per-capita tax on each individual, based on the latest census. It was a means of paying for government, despite the wealth of monarchs because kings were loath to support all the needs of government by themselves and deplete their personal wealth.

In the U.S., the poll tax came to be associated with permission to vote. But neither of these meanings is intended here. This is the Temple tax related to Exodus 30:11.

"However, so that we do not offend them,

The "however" of this verse makes it clear that Jesus did not expect the people or the official to understand this distinction, so He makes provision for Peter to acquire the needed money. Were this a tribute payment, perhaps His words would have been different. Perhaps He would not have seen the need to go through the motions to show obedience.

There would be enough charges against Him when the time came. No need to add to them unnecessarily.

when you open its mouth, you will find a shekel

This is a miracle in keeping with Christ as Lord, owning all that comprises creation. Ownership inheres by default in the one who creates. It is not bestowed but obtains de facto. Jesus owns every coin the Jews mistakenly think belongs to them, whether Greek, Roman or Jewish.

We are not to join the liberals who naturalize everything by explaining it was just a fish that happened to swallow a coin inadvertently tossed earlier into the sea. We are left with the incredible luck of Peter catching it first off. It was rather the creation of the coin out of nothing and making it to appear in the mouth of the fish first caught by Peter.

It is also a reminder that in terms of outright ownership, we own no single thing. It is all the Lord's material and property. We are at best temporary custodians.

Take that and give it to them for you and Me.

That a full sheckel was provided confirms that this was the Temple tax, since it is for two persons, a half sheckel each.

We aren't told why Jesus arranges for only Himself and Peter. They all shared a purse in common, so it was not a case of favoring Peter and leaving the rest to fend for themselves. It was more a case of the lesson involved about sovereignty, honor to His Father in an ordinance, and the fact that the question of the official created the opportunity to teach.

Mark 9:33-35, Luke 9:47-48, Mark 9:42, Matthew 18:3-4, 10-11
33 They came to Capernaum; and when He was in the house, He began to question them, "What were you discussing on the way?" 34 But they kept silent, for on the way they had discussed with one another which of them was the greatest. 35 Sitting down, He called the twelve and said to them, "If anyone wants to be first, he shall be last of all and servant of all." (Mark 9:33-35)

47 But Jesus, knowing what they were thinking in their heart, took a child and stood him by His side, 48 and said to them, "Whoever receives this child in My name receives Me, and whoever receives Me receives Him who sent Me; --- and whoever receives Me does not receive Me, but Him who sent Me." . . . 42 "Whoever causes one of these little ones who believe to stumble, it would be better for him if, with a heavy millstone hung around his neck, he had been cast into the sea. --- for the one who is least among all of you, this is the one who is great." (Luke 9:47-48, Mark 9:42)

3 and said, "Truly I say to you, unless you are converted and become like children, you will not enter the kingdom of heaven. 4 "Whoever then humbles himself as this child, he is the greatest in the kingdom of heaven. --- 10 "See that you do not despise one of these little ones, for I say to you that their angels in heaven continually see the face of My Father who is in heaven. 11 For the Son of Man has come to save that which was lost.] (Matthew 18:3-4, 10-11)

Commentary

They came to Capernaum; .. "What were you discussing on the way?"

On the way back to Capernaum, the disciples had been discussing who was the greatest among them. This is a matter of the carnal values still in them having a run in the yard. Man is prone, despite closeness with Jesus, to lapse into earthly considerations and valuations. It is a slip back toward what they were all used to – the way the world sees things. Not ignorant of this conversation, Jesus asks them about this discussion.

This is not a case of Jesus not knowing and having to ask, nor is it a case of Jesus pretending not to know. It is a common way of joining a discussion even if you know what the subject is about and have overheard some or most of it. It is a way of adding yourself to the discussion.

Since we know the topic, we can assume Jesus is engaging it in order to set them aright about such questions, rather than for philosophical reasons.

But they kept silent, for on the way they had discussed with one another which of them was the greatest.

A perfectly understandable response. The very presence of Jesus into the center of this discussion caused each man to face the silliness and self-serving nature of it. They had learned this much from being with Jesus, that humility was high on the list of character qualities, and this discussion was the complete opposite. It was an resurgence of their carnal natures into divine things and this embarrassed them into silence. We can imagine the looks on their faces.

Sitting down, . . . "If anyone wants to be first, he shall be last of all and servant of all."

Notice that He does not upbraid them or criticize them directly for such talk. Instead, He engages the topic seriously. It is not a sin to desire to excel in the things of God, to pursue greatness in those achievements. He assumes this is their aim (whether true or not), and if so, they need to know how it is acquired.

It is the exact opposite of common sense. To be first one must choose to be last. To be master, one must choose to be a servant.

This is simply because the Kingdom is where humility and love are the prime qualities, serving others is among the greatest values. So to be great is to be humble, selfless, prefer others before self and prefer service to being served.

Jesus . . took a child and stood him by His side, . . "Whoever receives this child in My name receives Me, and whoever receives Me receives Him who sent Me;

It states that He knew their hearts and thoughts. This dictated the need for an example. Since children were present, He saw an excellent way to make His point.

He did not at first say *whoever receives Me as this child* but rather whoever receives this child. Grown men were being asked to receive and accept the child, meaning as a companion, as a person, as someone worthy of sincere address and dialog.

This meant a humility that required one to drop the sophistication and pragmatism that had been acquired into adulthood. It takes humility and simplicity to engage a child as a person with sincerity, without condescension. In fact, most children dislike adults who speak down to them. They recognize that the adult is merely holding their sophistication and snobbery in suspension.

To receive a child in Christ's name was to accept him in the same love Jesus had for children. Children represented the unsullied view out into the world, the readiness to believe and trust. It was the closest thing to the pre-Fall condition of Adam, and Jesus is here pointing to them as exemplars of how men ought to return to that simplicity and trusting character.

To be able to receive a child in the same attitude that Jesus accepted them was to embrace Jesus' world view, His values and thoughts of higher things. It was to receive Him also.

and whoever receives Me does not receive Me, but Him who sent Me."

Immediately, this sounds like double-talk - the one who receives Him does not receive Him. To those who refuse to give God the benefit of the doubt, this saying is just more evidence of a hopelessly confused message. But the wording is in a form meant to highlight that the receiving is not limited but includes much more.

The receiving of Jesus is not of Jesus *only*, but His Father also. So there are three persons being received in one act: the child, and by that attitude the Son, and by union with the Father, the Father also.

"Whoever causes one of these little ones who believe to stumble, it would be better for him if, with a heavy millstone hung around his neck, he had been cast into the sea.

A statement mirrored in the other Gospels, it is both highlighting the value of a child on heavenly terms, and giving ominous warning of the seriousness with which misleading such a one is taken.

Why the severity? Because we are dealing with unadulterated innocence and trust, and to take advantage of that to one's private benefit is grossly offensive to God. This is one of the main themes in Dickens' *Oliver Twist*. An innocent boy is taken advantage of and he is continually contrasted with those boys who have long since been beguiled into losing their innocence. Our present day society has learned how to extend this kind of abuse in unspeakable ways.

To cause them to stumble is to place oneself as an obstacle in the right way before them, to hinder their progress toward the better goal. To steal a reference to another film, Disney's *Pinocchio* is another vivid example. He is taken off the path of duty by scoundrels and then educated in the arts of deceit and trickery.

for the one who is least among all of you, this is the one who is great."

Here Jesus is furthering the word "receive" to mean "become like." Children are routinely assessed as the least considerable members of society. They are not appealed to in matters of importance domestically or politically. So to become like them is to become least in secular valuations. Yet the reward is in being considered great in the Kingdom.

"Truly I say to you, unless you are converted and become like children, you will not enter the kingdom of heaven.

But He did not leave well enough alone. He pressed the point further by actually setting this as a criteria for entrance into Heaven. If one was ill-disposed to the humility involved in becoming like a child, they must think again, because such a heart is the qualification for Heaven.

Here Jesus is not asking men to become silly, aimless, and empty-headed. The focus is on the key words *"be converted"*. Conversion has a prerequisite of trust and children trust because they have not yet acquired the cynicism and distrust of adult life. So it is both a childlike trust that makes one ready for conversion, and a conversion that enables a continued attitude of childlike trust that is in view – *Whoever then humbles himself as this child, he is the greatest in the kingdom of heaven.*

for I say to you that their angels in heaven continually see the face of My Father who is in heaven.

This is a verse that helps to establish the sanctification of children in the state of innocence. This is inferred by the assigning of angels to their care. Note that the picture chosen is not their presence around children as protection, but that of such angels before God's face. It is to highlight that nothing occupies their urgency more than comprehending God on the behalf of their charges.

Of course, we get from this the idea of guardian angels. But it is unclear how long or to what limit these angels remain. Most attribute the age of accountability as the moment when each man is on his own with respect to his duties and choices.

For the Son of Man has come to save that which was lost.

It's somewhat puzzling why this statement is made on the heels of the discussion about children and greatness? The overall theme is about entering into Heaven and the attitude of the heart that enables such grace to be given. The coming of Jesus must be seen against the backdrop of all that has gone before, all the way back to Eden, where something was lost. Man fell.

Since then the territory of human souls is seen as lost to Heaven and gain to the prince of the power of the air. Jesus' coming was to regain what was lost, to restore man to his heavenly destiny and citizenship.

The connection with the humility and trust of a child is pre-Fall Eden. That was the state of man before the beguilement. That is what was lost.

Luke 17:7-10, Matthew 18:12-14, 18:7, Mark 9:43-50
7 "Which of you, having a slave plowing or tending sheep, will say to him when he has come in from the field, `Come immediately and sit down to eat'? 8 "But will he not say to him, `Prepare something for me to eat, and properly clothe yourself and serve me while I eat and drink; and afterward you may eat and drink'? 9 "He does not thank the slave because he did the things which were commanded, does he? 10 "So you too, when you do all the things which are commanded you, say, `We are unworthy slaves; we have done only that which we ought to have done.' " (Luke 17:7-10)

12 "What do you think? If any man has a hundred sheep, and one of them has gone astray, does he not leave the ninety-nine on the mountains and go and search for the one that is straying? 13 "If it turns out that he finds it, truly I say to you, he rejoices over it more than over the ninety-nine which have not gone astray. 14 "So it is not the will of your Father who is in heaven that one of these little ones perish. . . . 7 "Woe to the world because of its stumbling blocks! For it is inevitable that stumbling blocks come; but woe to that man through whom the stumbling block comes! (Matthew 18:12-14, 18:7)

43 "If your hand causes you to stumble, cut it off; it is better for you to enter life crippled, than, having your two hands, to go into hell, into the unquenchable fire, 44 where THEIR WORM DOES NOT DIE, AND THE FIRE IS NOT QUENCHED.] 45 "If your foot causes you to stumble, cut it off; it is better for you to enter life lame, than, having your two feet, to be cast into hell, 46 where THEIR WORM DOES NOT DIE, AND THE FIRE IS NOT QUENCHED.] 47 "If your eye causes you to stumble, throw it out; it is better for you to enter the kingdom of God with one eye, than, having two eyes, to be cast into hell, 48 where THEIR WORM DOES NOT DIE, AND THE FIRE IS NOT QUENCHED. 49 "For everyone will be salted with fire. 50 "Salt is good; but if the salt becomes unsalty, with what will you make it salty again? Have salt in yourselves, and be at peace with one another." (Mark 9:43-50)

Commentary

"Which of you, having a slave plowing or tending sheep, will say to him when he has come in from the field, `Come immediately and sit down to eat'?

Part of the humility lesson turns to a different aspect. One can get the impression that by doing the things of God, even being close to the Son of God, one has an angle with God or an edge on which one can rely.

Jesus introduces this idea by appealing to common sense in everyday life. Servants who do what they are told cannot expect to sit down with the master at his table like a guest or a member of his family and partake of dinner - *"will [he] say to him, 'Come . . and sit down to eat'?"*

Instead, the master will treat him as a servant, expecting him to do his duties in serving the dinner, not partake of it. The result is that when they are done serving, they have not bettered their stand with the master but remain the servants they always were.

So the lesson here is that the disciples not build themselves up in their own minds to say they are something because they walk with the Son of God.

Why was this injected here? Because they had been talking about who would be the greatest, and that whole subject was only possible in their minds because they had been chosen by Jesus and were being trained to serve the needs of God.

So do we then discount all works as having no impression on God whatsoever? In terms of an appeal, they do not. We cannot point to our works, even those clearly commanded of Him, and expect them to make up for the condition of our hearts.

Where works come into play in God's economy is in blessings and rewards, not state or status. Whether rewarded or not, we are to do works because they benefit the purposes of the Father, not because they mount up an appeal for us to be weighed in the balance against our lives. They are to be done because they are the righteousness of God. All other things that attach to them are icing on the cake, but never the motivation.

If any man has a hundred sheep, and one of them has gone astray, does he not leave the ninety-nine on the mountains and go and search for the one that is straying?

This too, seems difficult to see as pertaining to the same context. But this will be made clear in a moment.

The analogy from sheep herding is very appropriate because experience tells us that sheep are always prone to wander. Some cases are known in which a sheep without guidance can wander away to a place of no food and water and simply die of starvation, without the sense to go back the way it came.

So the idea of leaving the ninety-nine is immediately troublesome, because one would, in the real world, truly risk losing the whole herd on account of the one. For this reason we must not stretch the analogy farther than intended. It is simply meant to convey the difference in attitude over the one lost sheep compared to all the rest who had not chosen to wander.

We are not to ponder what happened to the ninety-nine while the shepherd was away, but focus on the confidence the shepherd had over those that had not strayed such that he could focus his attention on getting the lost one back. He does this to point back to the beginning – the case of innocent children – but in a different way.

Earlier, the child was an example of trusting, unsophisticated faith. The child was there an example not of infants or small children, but of people of all ages of the right kind of faith. But here the sheep has strayed. The child is now less an example of the right kind of faith and more a transition to the vulnerability of a child who has gotten lost.

Jesus is now making the analogy about the child as a child, and once lost, the shepherd is willing to leave the herd to regain it. It is not about a child who has drifted from the faith, but one who in being vulnerable has simply gotten lost.

That this is the meaning here at the end of this teaching we get from his next words – *"So it is not the will of your Father who is in heaven that one of these little ones perish."* This is a return to the subject of the actual child being used as an analogy. Those sitting around are keen about the attitude of God toward children. Despite the lesson being offered, what does God think about them as children? He wraps up His lesson by returning full-circle to the child and the Father's care for him.

"Woe to the world because of its stumbling blocks! For it is inevitable that stumbling blocks come; but woe to that man through whom the stumbling block comes!

Whether it be a child or that soul who trusts freely and generously, stumbling blocks are a fact of life. They will join the evidence that will mount up to condemn the world and its ways. But the warning to those sitting around Him is simple – don't be one of them. Don't be the one by whom temptation comes.

We cannot stop temptations everywhere in the world, but we can take responsibility for our own actions.

"If your hand causes you to stumble, cut it off; . . . "If your eye causes you to stumble, throw it out;

Virtually everyone is quick to state that Jesus never intended anyone to cut off their hand or pluck out their eye. But we do this for the wrong reason – that the members or organs of the body are not the source of sin, so they would never need to be cut away and cast off. Sin is conceived in the heart, we reply. All quite true.

But this is not mere hyperbole. Jesus is deadly serious. A life of sin will certainly be the issue of getting into heaven. It is the condition remaining in an unrepentant life. Hence, if it could be shown that your hand or eye caused you to continually sin as a way of life, it would in fact be better to rid yourself of them to stop the stumbling. (Stumbling here meaning sin.)

The difference in making this admission is that the cutting off aspect is not completely tongue-in-cheek. It would be called for if it were true, which means it is in fact called for wherever it happens to be true. And where is the seat and source of sin in our lives? Is it not in the heart? Which is to say we are to cut out our carnal hearts, and throw them from us. Elsewhere we find that God is in the business of giving us new hearts, made new by His saving grace.

This is one of the most difficult aspects of the conversion and salvation message of the Gospel. People want to make God merely another activity or dimension of their old life, which for the most part they wish to leave as is. The Gospel asks for a repudiation of the old life and the old heart. We are to abandon them, not add God and church and religion to them. It is to be a thorough remake in which the old house is torn down. That is the part of the true Gospel that many reject. It is too costly, too self-deprecating, too invasive.

44 where THEIR WORM DOES NOT DIE, AND THE FIRE IS NOT QUENCHED.
46 where THEIR WORM DOES NOT DIE, ...
48 where THEIR WORM DOES NOT DIE, ...

vv. 44 and 46 do not have this OT quote in the earliest manuscripts, but because a number of later ones contain it, the editors of the NASB did not remove it on that basis alone. The NIV did remove the quote in v.44 and all of v.46 on this basis. It is retained in v. 48.

The reference is to Isaiah 66:24, which is a post-millennial context – the coming of the new heaven and the new earth after world conflict in the last great battle with evil. Isaiah states that in the aftermath, the worms of the dead will not die but live to devour eternally, and the fires of the place will not be quenched. This seems contradictory to the context of a new heaven and new earth, since the dead, their worms, and the fire would be of the old order.

But since the saints of the new world can go out and see the dead (66:24), there is an understanding that the place of destruction is still available to be seen. Perhaps a place will remain set apart in this new order where a visible reminder will remain of the fate of the haters of God.

We see some of this in the parable of Lazarus, where the righteous and the wicked are able to see across to each other.

That Jesus here picks up on this reference in the context He is teaching means that this cannot be about the actual people of battle in end times but represents the fate of all the wicked.

"For everyone will be salted with fire.

Here we have a somewhat confusing mixture of metaphors. We will be salted with fire, and we must ensure a saltiness for ourselves. Much may be made clearer if we were acquainted more with the idiomatic or customary uses involved. These are not entirely clear.

That everyone will be salted with fire means believers as well. For the unbeliever, it will be a judgment by works alone, which of course will be their undoing. But the hint here is that the works will be tested by fire, such that gems and precious stones will survive but wood, hay and stubble will be consumed. For the wicked, all will be of the latter category.

For the believer, the testing by fire will be about rewards, not salvation. *". . each man's work will become evident; for the day will show it because it is to be revealed with fire, and the fire itself will test the quality of each man's work. If any man's work which he has built on it remains, he will receive a reward. "* (I Cor 3:13-14)

"if the salt becomes unsalty, with what will you make it salty again? Have salt in yourselves, and be at peace with one another."

Here the subject shifts to the salt by which we are to be called the salt of the earth (Matt 5:13.) It is as though the mention of being salted by fire has reminded the Lord to reiterate the teaching about salt in the believer's life.

Throughout this context the real subject is genuine faith, service, and humility. Our genuineness, our authentic Christianity will be tested by fire. To live an authentic, genuine and fruitful life, we must be the salt of the earth, hence the exhortation to maintain our saltiness.

How does the believer act on Jesus' exhortation to remain salty? To be salty is to be effective for the purpose intended. Salt is for preserving foods. That does not mean that the saltiness of the Christian is only in relation to preserving goodness in the world. It is only a metaphor. The subject is effectiveness in general, not preservatives specifically.

We remain effective by being open to the voice of the Holy Spirit, to hear Him and be ready. It is to keep our faith from waning or being overwhelmed by the affairs and concerns of the world.

This is to say that the fervency and employment of our faith is in our hands. We are responsible for maintaining it, by worship, devotion, prayer, study of God's Word, service and fellowship. These are activities of the Christian life, not the Christian life itself; but they provide the opportunities to avail ourselves of the spiritual means for life and growth.

Have salt in yourselves means refresh your supply. No one expects the same quantity of salt to be used over and over for a lifetime. When we salt beef, we could perhaps sweep it off and use it again. But experience will tell us the limits of doing this and we will realize the need for fresh salt. That is our job – to maintain our supply and its effect on us.

"be at peace with one another."

One of the key ways to express our saltiness in society is to be at peace with each other. It will strain and test all our spiritual resources to do this one thing, hence it will test our mettle (how salty we really are.)

Mark 9:38-41, Matthew 18:21,22, Luke 17:3,4

38 John said to Him, "Teacher, we saw someone casting out demons in Your name, and we tried to prevent him because he was not following us." 39 But Jesus said, "Do not hinder him, for there is no one who will perform a miracle in My name, and be able soon afterward to speak evil of Me. 40 "For he who is not against us is for us. 41 "For whoever gives you a cup of water to drink because of your name as followers of Christ, truly I say to you, he will not lose his reward. (Mark 9:38-41)

15 "If your brother sins, go and show him his fault in private; if he listens to you, you have won your brother. 16 "But if he does not listen to you, take one or two more with you, so that BY THE MOUTH OF TWO OR THREE WITNESSES EVERY FACT MAY BE CONFIRMED. 17 "If he refuses to listen to them, tell it to the church; and if he refuses to listen even to the church, let him be to you as a Gentile and a tax collector.

18 "Truly I say to you, whatever you bind on earth shall have been bound in heaven; and whatever you loose on earth shall have been loosed in heaven. 19 "Again I say to you, that if two of you agree on earth about anything that they may ask, it shall be done for them by My Father who is in heaven. 20 "For where two or three have gathered together in My name, I am there in their midst."

Then Peter came and said to Him, "Lord, how often shall my brother sin against me and I forgive him? Up to seven times?" Jesus said to him, "I do not say to you, up to seven times, but up to seventy times seven." (Matthew 18:21,22)

"Be on your guard! If your brother sins, rebuke him; and if he repents, forgive him. And if he sins against you seven times a day, and returns to you seven times and says 'I repent,' forgive him." (Luke 17:3,4)

Commentary

"Teacher, we saw someone casting out demons in Your name,

We come to the subject of who is authorized to work in the Lord's name. Even at this early stage with Jesus still discipling the Twelve, there are others outside this intimate company also working.

We are not told the man's name or how or where he came into contact with Jesus. We can only infer that he took the message of the Lord to heart, was changed by it, and felt the call of the Father to preach the message of the Kingdom like his Master. There can be no question that the disciples had formed the impression that the only authorized workers were those that followed in their company; and that Jesus repudiated this requirement.

Does this disenfranchise the apostles as that authority through which the church would be administered and taught? Does the history of what happened (centralization around the apostles and their successors only) inform us about the legitimacy of other men?

The presence of the other man did not disenfranchise those designated to hold authority in the Church. The other man was not challenging or claiming equal authority. He did not have the close intimate contact and training given directly from the hand of Jesus. On the other hand, his work was not censured for not being under the supervision of Jesus or the authority being given to the Twelve, and he did have sufficient authority to effect the casting out of demons.

Protestants view this narrative as supporting the idea that believers are independent in their relationship to Christ and need no intervening human authority to authenticate and authorize Christian work.

The Catholic view is that work and teaching must not deviate from the faith taught to the apostles by Christ; and a normative succession of authority was established to ensure it.

To the Catholics' favor, some uniformity of doctrine had to be instituted to prevent private factions and disunity about matters of belief. These occurred anyway, but the argument is that there was at least a standard rule to which one could appeal.

To the Protestants' favor, there is the unmistakable distinction that the man worked separately, ergo an authorization to work that does not seek prior apostolic approval.

Certainly for both Protestants and Catholics alike, whoever works will be judged against the teaching of Christ. So the issue is not separate vs. centrally-controlled teaching, but adherence to the faith of Jesus and the Twelve. The reason the man is not censured is that he is preaching the same Gospel – " *"Do not hinder him, for there is no one who will perform a miracle in My name, and be able soon afterward to speak evil of Me.* "

Were he to be teaching contrary, citing the inferred accommodation of his independence would have little bearing. Which is to say that despite any man's independence, conformity to the faith of the apostles obtains into the future – " *"For he who is not against us is for us.* "

The problem, of course, is exacerbated by the historic criticisms of Catholicism in this role. Does conformity continue if Catholicism ceases to represent that seminal faith? May a man work independent of Catholic authority but not independent of that original, incipient apostolic authority? That is of course the main issue in the Reformation, and remains in debate as to which side settled the question satisfactorily.

We are asked to be conformed to the doctrines of the faith, not to the Church as an institution. The Church is never seen in the NT as the direct object of faith, it is not an entity toward which one has faith. We are to exercise faith in the same faith explained by Jesus, meaning we are to join the host of those who believe what He believed. Hence, the Church as the corporate body of believers is unavoidable in faith, but it is never the object of that faith.

for there is no one who will perform a miracle in My name, and be able soon afterward to speak evil of Me.

We are here reminded of Saul among the prophets (I Sam 10:11) who was said to be prophesying, yet was rejected of the Lord. While the OT does not explicitly state that Saul died with his lot among the wicked and condemned, he died an unrighteous man's death and his sins were stated as the reason. Yet irrespective of this, he did prophesy and he did live to speak evil thereafter.

That this is not a contradiction is the fact that OT examples are not forwardly conditional on NT principles. The new life Jesus was inaugurating was not constrained by how men acted in the old economy. Jesus is here talking about the present and future, and in that new life, no man would be able to do a miracle in His name and then speak evil of Him,

"For he who is not against us is for us.

This is the spirit of love and acceptance for all who do the work of Christ. We must assume that it was maintained in the apostles after the Ascension. But in later centuries, the Church soon established that it was impossible to be *"for Christ and the apostles"* while being separate from the Holy Church, the truth of which depends on earthly and divine Churches being one and the same.

"For whoever gives you a cup of water to drink because of your name as followers of Christ, truly I say to you, he will not lose his reward.

(see earlier at Matthew 10:41)

"If your brother sins ,

The brother here is a member of the Church, since the matter has the final recourse of an appeal to the church, excluding the idea of brothers in the family or merely in society. This lays to rest that believers who are described by Paul as free from the law of sin (Rom 8:2) ought never to sin again. The words of Jesus here anticipate this very thing.

Jesus here is establishing the way of righteousness in addressing someone else's sin. This is not a contradiction of Jesus later teaching - *"he who is without sin cast the first stone."* That teaching dealt with condemnation, not rebuke. This procedure is about the manner of bringing someone's sin to their attention for repentance sake.

go and show him his fault in private;

The first step is an act of love, in that we choose not to gossip or backbite but approach the offender personally with respect for his or her privacy. It is the step that most avoids personal embarrassment – *" if he listens to you, you have won your brother. "*

But if he does not listen to you, take one or two more with you

Realizing obstinancy, the next step again strives to maintain love. It is not an immediate proclamation to all the Church, but to expand the audience of those privy to the issue by just a few. There are two reasons for this: a) one is continuing to respect the privacy of the offender, b) in the presence of resistance, corroboration is needed to forestall a useless contest of contraries ("Did too!" "Did not!")

BY THE MOUTH OF TWO OR THREE WITNESSES EVERY FACT MAY BE CONFIRMED

This reiterates what was an OT adage from Scripture – Deut 19:5. It's presence in the law was precisely for the reason stated above, to forestall a contest between contraries. A person noting the presence of witnesses knew they could not deny a recounting of things later.

"If he refuses to listen to them, . . . and if he refuses to listen even to the church

Finally, if resistance is sustained, the matter is made fully public. This was meant more for the effect of the threat itself, being that most conscientious people knowing this eventuality, would come clean or simply leave the Church. Still, the case for the one holding out to the bitter end must be accounted for.

Listening to the church indicates that the matter is presented in a manner whereby the church can register its approval or disapproval. To listen to the church implies the church speaking on the matter, not merely the elders. The result is expulsion from the fellowship of the local church, but as the church became many assemblies, a notification must have been sent to other churches advising them of the judgment, that the person would not simply join another fellowship unrepentant.

This came to be the process of excommunication in the Catholic Church, which carried not merely the denial of fellowship, but the denial of communion (the Eucharist) which meant condemnation if unrepentant, since it was deemed that outside the Church there was no salvation.

In its seminal concept as in the gospels here, the idea was not vindictive but restorative. It was to bring the offender to their senses by deprivation of the community and sacraments of the Church.

"and if he refuses to listen even to the church, let him be to you as a Gentile and a tax collector."

As to the harshness charged against the Catholic procedure, we should note the rather harsh words of our Lord – *" let him be to you as a Gentile and a tax collector. "* Gentile here means someone without faith in a general sense (the Gentiles were otherwise regarded as a field rich unto harvest.) Here Gentile is being used idiomatically to mean the unrighteous of the nations who knew not God.

Similarly, tax collector was a metaphor for a person totally sold to the world and its ways. It does not designate a death knell of judgment on such a person, since Jesus had a tax collector among His followers.

Interesting is the fact that the man writing these words was that tax collector.

The general idea is that if a man is truly a believer, he will be reformed by the manner by which other believers now regard him. This is often misunderstood and misapplied in the priggish and aloof behavior of Christians toward unbelievers that characterized earlier periods of later Christian times. Shunning the unbeliever in preference to ministering to him is not the idea.

In the case here, love and exhortation were tried. Recalcitrance has a limit with regard to tolerance. This is not a justification for intolerance and avoidance of the unbeliever who has yet to receive Christ and needs the witness of preaching.

Historically, however, it is hard to understand the biblical justification for adding persecution and execution to the statement, *"let him be to you as a Gentile and a tax collector "*. Much of this came about in relation to the state being the agent of punishment and that crimes against the Church were eventually viewed as capital crimes against the state. But if going to the extreme of taking such a person's life was abhorrent to the Church, it certainly had the power and influence to intervene.

Again, in fairness to Catholicism, the errors in rationale that justified the persecutions on both sides have long since been seen for their ignorance and misalignment with the purposes of God, and today excommunication has returned largely to the restorative concept Jesus has explained above.

whatever you bind on earth shall have been bound in heaven;

Here we have a repetition of what was spoken directly to Peter (v. 16:19.) There, the personal pronoun was second person singular – meaning *"to you, Peter."* Here the personal pronouns are second person plural - *"to you all"*.

The use of pronouns prevents us from being dogmatic either way in making the addressees the whole group of His followers, or just the Twelve (there were more than the Twelve present as evident from v. 18:2.) It could mean just the Twelve or all present as representing all believers.

Protestants who criticize exclusive apostolic authority will press this to mean a binding authority given to all believers. But it is difficult to see this meaning played out in practice in the early Church. We don't see the individual Christian believer exercising this bind and loosing role, whereas we do see it clearly in the work and ministry of the apostles and the bishops who succeeded them.

Still, some would point to the very example a moment ago in the man casting out demons. He is certainly exercising the power to bind and loose, yet he is clearly not of the Twelve.

A Protestant explanation is that the believer's authority has historically waned because of the devolving manner of teaching in the early centuries, which emphasized apostolic applicability over and against individual authority. But in Protestant churches where the concept is being revived, we are puzzled to know what specific things the individual believer would bind or loose? In some churches this is clearly seen in things like exorcism, which is a gift not restricted to the clergy. But this can't be the only sense, and we don't see any churches teaching that individual believers bind and loose in terms of salvation, i.e. to bind meaning to restrict or bar from access, to loose meaning to declare as saved, nor do they individually make other judgments in the church that exemplify these, although there is some sense in which the collective of believers in a church might do this *(see also below at "if two of you agree.")*

Other Protestants see this as a power and authority given to the elders in any church – that decisiveness and authority must exist and be a mirror of divine decisions for the Church to function as Christ intended.

Catholicism has a weighty argument that they alone preserve a succession of ordination from the original men who received this from Christ. Protestants cannot deny the historicity of institutional succession, but question the truth of spiritual succession, i.e. human, material succession does not infer divine, spiritual succession.

shall have been bound in heaven;

Something must be said to highlight the specific wording used. It is not that whatever they choose to bind, Heaven will be forced to endorse, but their binding and loosing will have been preceded by knowledge of what Heaven desires. Hence, the wording, *"shall have been bound . ."* – passive past tense, instead of *"shall be bound."*

"Again I say to you, that if two of you agree on earth about anything that they may ask, it shall be done for them by My Father who is in heaven.

Can two believers pray that some benefactor gift them each a million dollars? We know from James that to pray amiss is to upset the principle of confidence in prayer (James 4:3.) And this must be kept in association with the context in which it appears – the binding and loosing authority being delegated.

Jesus is exemplifying how the binding and loosing will be effected – by an agreement among them. The Father will never paint Himself into a corner to be subject to the will of man. Likewise, the promise above is conditional on the servants agreeing on things ordained of God, things that pertain to the advancement of His Kingdom.

Even here, we see Peter not able to exercise this promise in relation to his own death. He would not have been able to pray, even in agreement with another apostle, that he be spared such an end among the haters of God. Of course, we have his own testimony that he accepted the prophesy of Jesus concerning his death, so he would not have sought such a prayer. But this does highlight that simple agreement, per se, is not a mechanism.

"For where two or three have gathered together in My name, I am there in their midst."

This is perhaps one of the strongest verses supporting the idea that legitimate faith and service to Christ is not to be constrained within the bounds of a particular institution. For centuries Catholics were taught and believed that salvation could not occur outside the Catholic Church. In its plain sense, the above opens the context to Christians at large in the world, irrespective of denominations. Nor does the statement imply that salvation can occur outside a broader definition of Christ's Church (in His name must have some constraining influence.) But it is hard to press that "in His name" must mean and can only mean within a particular fellowship of Churches.

This goes for Protestant churches who promulgate that genuine salvation can only be had in their confession of faith.

In fairness to the Catholic view, the verse can be seen as focusing on the presence of Jesus in the midst of the smallest group of believers, not on the independence of place or situation. An understanding that the context intended was the Church Christ established specifically with the apostles is not unreasonable or particularly forced.

The confidence in this verse is the thing to be emphasized. One does not need the formal environment of the church building or the presence of an ordained priest for Christ to be present in their midst. This was characteristic of the attitudes of the old economy. The OT was all about intermediaries, authorized go-betweens who grasped God with one hand and the believer with the other.

Access to the risen Lord is now unfettered, aptly symbolized in the rending of the Temple curtain which had represented more than anything else the inaccessibility of the believer directly. Here, things are announced as changed. The believer can create an instance of the church itself – believers accompanied by the presence of the risen Lord – in but a small group of two or three.

Historically, in terms of appearance and formality, the Church emphasized the opposite mode, whereby everything related to Christ's presence required mediation or at least the presence of ordained clergy. This is certainly hard to square with the clarity and simplicity of the above.

"Lord, how often shall my brother sin against me and I forgive him?

Within the context of dealing with a brother who has sinned, it was natural to wonder how one should deal with repeated offenses, or cases where repentance did not seem evident. Peter is able to foresee this eventuality and broaches what would in due course inevitably arise.

"up to seven times" should not be construed with too strict a numerological significance. Peter did not mean *"unto the perfect number of times?"* Seven would have rather been regarded as a "sufficient" number of times. It was hardly the number of purely human toleration (we are normally exasperated by the third repetition.) 'Seven' would have come from Peter's understanding of traditional and rabbinic interpretation, gained many times in the expositions provided in the synagogue.

"Be on your guard! If your brother sins, rebuke him; and if he repents, forgive him.

First, there is no direct answer immediately, but a reiteration of the need to rebuke in conjunction with forgiveness. In some cases, the offender may volunteer confession, in which case a rebuke is unnecessary. But the idea is that there is a confrontation either at the hands of the Holy Spirit or through Christian agency which makes the sin clear and unmistakable. This is to be followed by repentance and forgiveness.

Note that Jesus does actually make repentance the condition of bestowing forgiveness. The idea is that some discernment is to be in play, that we not forgive willy-nilly or too casually.

Conversely, we are not to invoke exacting qualifications on what constitutes complete repentance. That the believer will do this imperfectly is the very point of the question at hand. Jesus commends repeated forgiveness, even beyond traditional limits, so *"if he repents"* cannot mean completely and perfectly, with never another incident again.

We are to look for sincerity and a will to repent. But the truth that repentance has occurred will have to be proven over time, and since that cannot be foreseen, forgiveness can't be withheld until it is, else there would be no occasion for wondering how many times.

The main purpose in this teaching is to handle those very real cases in which the struggles with sin are not easily accomplished; and being glib about this reality or applying a legalistic process will have the opposite effect.

"I do not say to you, up to seven times, but up to seventy times seven.

Now the question is answered directly. 'Seventy times seven' is again not a numerological dictum that adds special meaning. It's purpose is to simply name a number that is markedly beyond the human limits of toleration. The math was simple – 490 times. It was not meant as the real limit, as in 490 not 491 times. It was simply to put man over the edge in what was expected. No one would have by nature the patience to endure 490 offenses in an individual. Might as well say, *"Forgive unendingly."* which is of course the real meaning,

We are not to place limits. Why? Because God doesn't place limits, a character about His grace upon which we constantly rely. No one would wish to see God exercising forgiveness to us in the manner men do. Our condemnation would have been a done deal long ago.

And if we are to be like Him, we must exercise the same unlimitedness He exercises toward us, in which we trust over and over in our lives.

Does this open the door for abuse, whereby we are taken advantage in our generosity? Certainly yes. But always with this process, we need to be reminded of the conditional – *"if he repents."* While this can't mean getting things completely perfect in short order, it neither means abandoning any and all concerns about sincerity.

As we exercise the unlimited patience of God toward forgiveness, we are duty bound to disciple the offender into examining whether he knows what repentance means. Forgiveness is not carte blanch. Honest attempts at repentance followed by future stumblings is not the same as a carelessness to repent at all.

Matthew 18:23-35
23 "For this reason the kingdom of heaven may be compared to a king who wished to settle accounts with his slaves. 24 "When he had begun to settle them, one who owed him ten thousand talents was brought to him. 25 "But since he did not have the means to repay, his lord commanded him to be sold, along with his wife and children and all that he had, and repayment to be made. 26 "So the slave fell to the ground and prostrated himself before him, saying, `Have patience with me and I will repay you everything.' 27 "And the lord of that slave felt compassion and released him and forgave him the debt.

28 "But that slave went out and found one of his fellow slaves who owed him a hundred denarii; and he seized him and began to choke him, saying, `Pay back what you owe.' 29 "So his fellow slave fell to the ground and began to plead with him, saying, `Have patience with me and I will repay you.' 30 "But he was unwilling and went and threw him in prison until he should pay back what was owed.

31 "So when his fellow slaves saw what had happened, they were deeply grieved and came and reported to their lord all that had happened. 32 "Then summoning him, his lord said to him, `You wicked slave, I forgave you all that debt because you pleaded with me. 33 `Should you not also have had mercy on your fellow slave, in the same way that I had mercy on you?' 34 "And his lord, moved with anger, handed him over to the torturers until he should repay all that was owed him. 35 "My heavenly Father will also do the same to you, if each of you does not forgive his brother from your heart." (Matthew 18:23-35)

Commentary

" the kingdom of heaven may be compared to a king who wished to settle accounts with his slaves."

A very real obligation to announcing the Kingdom, especially a Kingdom that will have aspects not seen in the OT, is to offer explanations and analogies to what the Kingdom is like. So we see Jesus regularly providing pictures of that Kingdom in the form of parables or metaphors.

Here, the subject is about how equitable mercy, gratitude and thankfulness will be in the Kingdom, hence how we ought to act as its citizens.

one who owed him ten thousand talents was brought to him.

A talent was a Greco-Roman monetary unit and a unit of weight. It had origins in Babylonian and pre-Roman Jewish systems. In Jewish terms it was equivalent to 3000 shekels, while in Roman and Greek terms it was equal to 6000 denarii or drachmas, respectively. Modern equivalents cannot be made precisely because a number of factors are not standard – the value and revaluing of the denarius at different periods. Do we relate the ancient day's wage to minimum wage today or higher?

Both the Greek drachma and the Roman denarius are said to be equal to a penny in modern coinage, primarily because a penny in old English usage was a day's wage, hence the King James Version employing the word 'penny.'

But since the penny no longer represents a day's wage in modern times, it is a misleading reference for us today. For example, 6000 pennies would be $60.00 for the talent. This is an accurate equivalency if you maintain reference to the coin itself. But inflation would make this almost 10,000 times less valuable in our minds than its value in ancient times.

In our story, were we to use English money back in ancient times. 10,000 talents would mean the slave owed the king about $600,000 – a sizeable sum, but also misleading in terms of the value the hearers would have registered. It is much the same as trying to relate today's nickel to the 1930's.

Better to evaluate it in terms of equivalent purchasing power. A penny was an entire day's wage. But is this minimum wage or skilled labor? Skilled labor today means someone in a professional trade. Very few people in ancient times were in skilled labor trades. The contractor would be, but his laborers wouldn't.

For the workers hired into the field in Jesus' parable, we have basic manual labor, which would not be skilled per se. So it might be reasonable to equate the denarius for a day's wage to unskilled manual labor, perhaps twice the minimum wage today.

In that sense, it would be equivalent to approximately $120, based on an average hourly rate of about $15 an hour. This would make our talent in this story about $720,000 (not $60.00). Scholars equate the talent in Alexander's time to about $600,000.[35] So the amount owed here – 10,000 talents - would be about $7,200,000,000. Other commentaries relate it to $7,500,000.

Other equivalencies remind us that David provided 3,000 talents for the Temple, so the servant here owed over three times the amount David contributed (I Chron 29:4).[36]

This may seem a ridiculous amount for a servant to owe his king, but the idea is to represent a contrast, and this is a parable. It's a sort of Old World way of saying *gazillions*.

The lack of consistent conversions into modern money is problematic, but more puzzling is how a slave could owe a king this much money? But the word for slave also means servant, which could mean anyone in service to the king, an officer of the court, a regent, etc. Perhaps the debt refers to secret embezzlement of royal (and therefore sizeable) resources, now discovered and brought to account.

In other terms, indebtedness was sometimes translated into labor owed the master in terms of years, etc. As pure labor, the debt owed would be about 164,000 years of work. But monetary debt is the meaning maintained throughout, also for the servant under this man.

We must keep in mind that figuring out how the debt could be owed by a slave is not the point of the picture. It was obviously a hyperbole presented for effect. It is equivalent to saying, *"he owed an incalculable debt which would have indentured him for the whole of his life."*

"So the slave fell to the ground and prostrated himself before him, saying, `Have patience with me and I will repay you everything.'"

The king had demanded full payment to avoid abject slavery for the man and his family. This helps us understand that the service to the king was not as a condemned slave because that kind of slavery was now being threatened.

This is a story of how humility and respect begot compassion in the master. The debtor did not wrangle about the amount or the situation being unfair. There was no question about his debt. He was appealing for mercy and patience in his misfortunes. This moved the king to not only agree but further to actually relieve the entire debt.

---

[35] Keyne Cheshire, Alexander the Great, Cambridge University Press (2009) p 185
[36] Broadus, Commentary on Matthew, Kregel 1990 p 391

Again, we have to wonder how any debt that great could be forgiven? Two observations here:

1) The offenses of debtors were often exaggerated into general terms of valuation – like 10,000 talents – when no actual monetary debt was owed or approached that much; it was more an emotional compensation for a grave offense – *"Your offenses are worth 10,000 talents."*

2) The lesson is in the fact that compassion should have no limits based on the amount owed. This is certainly how God views things. We owe Him an incalculable debt in terms of sins committed, yet His compassion is ready to forgive them no matter how many or how grave – " *"And the lord of that slave felt compassion and released him and forgave him the debt."*

"But that slave went out and found one of his fellow slaves who owed him a hundred denarii; and he seized him and began to choke him, saying, `Pay back what you owe.'"

Declining to do the calculation, we get the picture of the profoundly smaller debt.

We immediately recoil from the slave's behavior. He shows no sign of gratitude and thanksgiving, but uses the opportunity to think more highly of himself than before too highly, in that he has become superior and tyrannical.

This is a feature of fallen human existence, that man can use the goodness done to him for evil purposes. Man makes the mistake of turning the incredible relief of mercy into an inference that one has worked his way out of his dilemma, ergo, he has proven how much better he is than the average man. This leads to pride, arrogance and intolerance.

But he was unwilling and went and threw him in prison until he should pay back what was owed.

This, despite the same pleading he himself had made. It does not still ring in his ears or bring him to humility. Perhaps he knows himself too well - that all men are liars and will say anything to acquire mercy.

His crime is that he does not pass along the mercy and forgiveness given him for his own debts.

"So when his fellow slaves saw what had happened, they were deeply grieved and came and reported to their lord all that had happened.

Note they were able to be grieved because they were as yet uncorrupted by the false sense of good fortune affecting their fellow servant. The outrage must be reported. We see common sense and customary judgment taking hold. It is not acceptable, even in secular society, to show this kind of disrespect for mercy and forgiveness, to not pass on mercy as a sign of gratitude and its associated humility.

"And his lord, moved with anger, handed him over to the torturers until he should repay all that was owed him.

The reason given is clear – *" I forgave you all that debt because you pleaded with me."* It is a lesson that even secular society knows as true – that gratitude ought to follow mercy.

The folly in the man's thinking caused him to be worse off than when owing the debt. Before he was threatened with being sold (transferred) to another owner who would not treat him as well. Now he is in prison as a criminal where one is aggressively punished in sufferings and tortures.

The former was a penalty for not paying his debt, but only offered more uncomfortable service, not direct punishment. The latter applied immediate suffering.

The Chronological Gospel Commentary – The Four Gospels

"My heavenly Father will also do the same to you, if each of you does not forgive his brother from your heart."

An ominous warning that has caused many to lose sleep through the ages. We must be sure to keep the context and the details in focus, or else we will turn our God into a petulant tyrant who can change His mind about us whenever we falter.

We must keep in mind that it is true that if we follow the servant's example above, we can expect appropriate punishment and delivery to the place assigned for the wicked. But a frame of mind and a heart such as this is surely not a way of life in a regenerate person, one born again from above. We will surely commit the sin of not passing along mercy and forgiveness here and there, and, yes, it can always be contrasted against the immense and generous forgiveness of God for all our sins. But the key is in having the attitudes and arrogance of the servant, the forgetting about who we are and what God has done for us.

The warning is intended that we not let ourselves become the servant in the story. Were we to abandon Christ to that degree, or were it the case that we had Him in name only and acted as above, we can surely expect the outcome Jesus predicts.

John 7:2-24
2 Now the feast of the Jews, the Feast of Booths, was near. 3 Therefore His brothers said to Him, "Leave here and go into Judea, so that Your disciples also may see Your works which You are doing. 4 "For no one does anything in secret when he himself seeks to be known publicly. If You do these things, show Yourself to the world." 5 For not even His brothers were believing in Him. 6 So Jesus said to them, "My time is not yet here, but your time is always opportune. 7 "The world cannot hate you, but it hates Me because I testify of it, that its deeds are evil. 8 "Go up to the feast yourselves; I do not go up to this feast because My time has not yet fully come."

9 Having said these things to them, He stayed in Galilee. 10 But when His brothers had gone up to the feast, then He Himself also went up, not publicly, but as if, in secret. 11 So the Jews were seeking Him at the feast and were saying, "Where is He?" 12 There was much grumbling among the crowds concerning Him; some were saying, "He is a good man"; others were saying, "No, on the contrary, He leads the people astray." 13 Yet no one was speaking openly of Him for fear of the Jews.

14 But when it was now the midst of the feast Jesus went up into the temple, and began to teach. 15 The Jews then were astonished, saying, "How has this man become learned, having never been educated?" 16 So Jesus answered them and said, "My teaching is not Mine, but His who sent Me. 17 "If anyone is willing to do His will, he will know of the teaching, whether it is of God or whether I speak from Myself. 18 "He who speaks from himself seeks his own glory; but He who is seeking the glory of the One who sent Him, He is true, and there is no unrighteousness in Him. 19 "Did not Moses give you the Law, and yet none of you carries out the Law? Why do you seek to kill Me?"

20 The crowd answered, "You have a demon! Who seeks to kill You?" 21 Jesus answered them, "I did one deed, and you all marvel. 22 "For this reason Moses has given you circumcision (not because it is from Moses, but from the fathers), and on the Sabbath you circumcise a man. 23 "If a man receives circumcision on the Sabbath so that the Law of Moses will not be broken, are you angry with Me because I made an entire man well on the Sabbath? 24 "Do not judge according to appearance, but judge with righteous judgment." (John 7:2-24)

Commentary

Now the feast of the Jews, the Feast of Booths, was near

The Feast of Booths is also called the Feast of Tabernacles and the Feast of Ingathering. In Hebrew it is called *Sukkot*, pronounced soo-kote. It is meant to commemorate the aspect of the wilderness wanderings in which Israel dwelt in tents. There is a place called Succoth near Goshen related to the going out of Israel from Egypt. It was their first stopping place on the journey and their first arrangement along the road for cooking and relaxation from travel. (Ex 12:37)

After Israel was in the land there was no "journey", per se, so a pilgrimage to the Temple in Jerusalem was incorporated. The people then set up temporary dwellings in and around the Temple area where they rested and entertained guests. (this is thought to be a basis for Peter suggesting booths for the personages visible with Jesus at the Transfiguration.) Today, Jews actually build make-shift dwellings (boxes) outside their homes and move into them during the feast.

"Leave here and go into Judea, so that Your disciples also may see Your works which You are doing.

His brothers are speaking from a secular frame of mind – it is reasonable to now make an appearance in the holy city and quit this remote area where things go largely unnoticed. By itself, *"go into Judea'* would not mean Jerusalem except we have the mention of the feast.

"your disciples" does not mean the Twelve, but those believers in Jerusalem who are impressed with Him and would desire to see Him work among them instead of so far away in Galilee – " *"For no one does anything in secret when he himself seeks to be known publicly."*

If You do these things, show Yourself to the world."

This was Satan's temptation on the mountain. Do something that will catch everyone's attention – like hurling yourself from the Temple and being rescued by your Father. It reveals the unbelieving nature of his brothers – not an unnatural reaction of siblings. We have to assume that James and Jude are among them at this point, not yet coming to accept Him as Messiah.

But Jesus recognizes where this is coming from -

"My time is not yet here, but your time is always opportune.

This was both an exhortation to good things and a rub. It has a real truth that it is positive – *you are not hindered by my timeline, so opportunities to do the work of the Father are abundant for you* – and it has a somewhat cynical tone – *. . but then you would have to believe in the message the Father is sending* which highlights how hypocritically they are acting to be concerned that works are seen by his followers in the neglected city.

It is a two-fold opportunity – to preach the message instead of Him doing so, but to also come to faith, an opportunity to believe in Him. This is both embarrassing and anti-climactic. He is making each brother feel the discomfort of their doubts and He is turning their expectations of seeing miracles over to them to do, hardly a satisfying alternative in their minds.

"The world cannot hate you, but it hates Me because I testify of it, that its deeds are evil.

This comment shines a light on their disbelief. The world cannot hate them because they are not yet identified with Him. It is *not* to be understood as the contrast between Christ and His followers, because He elsewhere clearly states that the world will in fact hate them because it hates Him (John 15:18).

It is not that the world is consciously sold to sin and the ways of evil through and through, but that it is comfortable with the pleasures of sin and wickedness while seeing life with some focus on doing right . This is a real and very hard deception. One is not preaching against a coven of Satanic practices, but what the everyday man considers normal for himself, his friends around him, and society. To upset this, to say that one's life and that of his neighbors is all wrong, is to invite hatred.

Jesus came to testify that all of that has to change to please God. People don't like being told that the life they have crafted from all their experiences and natural gleanings has been misguided.

"Go up to the feast yourselves; I do not go up to this feast because My time has not yet fully come."

We have to be cautious here of taking a meaning that puts Jesus in a prevaricating situation. He has stated He will not go up, yet in the next verses does go up. The refusal is to be understood as a refusal on their terms, not an outright declaration that He will not go at all. We get this from the qualifier *"because my time is not yet fully come"*, which is telling us that going on their terms would violate this. When we do see Him going anyway, there is again a qualifier – *in secret, not publicly.*

Yet we need to discern this further because when He later arrives, He does not remain secret, but publicly teaches right under the noses of the authorities. What is being avoided and controlled by Jesus is the idea of making a spectacle, of entering in a sort of entourage with lots of commotion, pomp and circumstance. He is not to go up as the great healer, or amid a declaration that "Here is the Son of God!" We will see that His purpose will be to teach, and in a way that will pit Him against the leaders of the Jews – a notably different purpose than His brothers sought.

So the Jews were seeking Him at the feast and were saying, "Where is He?"

The Jews seeking Him were mixed. Some were among the authorities who fully expected an opportunity to seize Him in Jerusalem because He would be obligated to come in obedience to the requirements of the feast. Perhaps this had been the reason Jesus was left alone for a season – they knew the coming feast would bring Him to them. Others were seeking Him for the reasons His brothers indicated, to gain more teaching and truth from Him and, of course, miracles. Hence, the question from both groups, *"Where is He?"*

That this was the principle topic at the feast tells of how much effect He has now had on the whole area in His work and teaching. It is as though the feast was secondary and encountering Jesus was now center-stage.

"He is a good man"; . . . "No, on the contrary, He leads the people astray."

Notice that no one was saying He was Messiah. We shouldn't infer that those saying He was good had tacit or loose affinity with Him. It was far too dangerous at this point in time to verbalize His messiahship. The contrast above is to highlight the two camps – those who believed in Him and those who were hardened.

"He leads the people astray" is a commentary on how the Jews saw His truth. This is the sort of thing we say of cults that try to draw people away into something misguided, leader-focused, and doctrinally false to true religion. Ironically, Christianity is Christ-focused and it does ask for a departure from historic practices. But it could not be characterized as deviant, since it promulgated the fulfillment of the old, not its repudiation – *"I came not to destroy the Law and the Prophets but to fulfill."*

Yet no one was speaking openly of Him for fear of the Jews.

As above, all these comments were made in close quarters among friends of people in close proximity. No one was standing on a platform and making a speech or a sermon about Him.

This comments on the tentative nature of people's faith at this point. One can have very sincere belief, but because it is new, and especially because it is radical, one may recoil from putting one's livelihood and life in jeopardy on account of it.

It is strange that the Jews (meaning the Jewish leaders) are the objects of fear. They should be embracing Him. But the leaders are charged with protecting the historic faith and with measures that cause a man to sit up and take notice. Their scrutiny had a formidable power with which their words or accusations could ruin a man in society. This is the strangest irony – that the very persons who were expected to be open to the work of God are striking fear toward accepting it.

But when it was now the midst of the feast Jesus went up into the temple, and began to teach.

This is a common form of repetition. Jesus was already said to have gone up, but as the account continues, the author returns to the subject of Him going up, this time in more detail.

in the midst of the feast does not mean in the middle of the same day His brothers went up. The feast was a seven-day affair. *In the midst* means on a day in the middle of that week.

He appears in the Temple, here meaning the outer courts, not the sanctuary, where people often gathered in large numbers to hear people speak, enjoy the company of other worshippers and in general be among the surroundings of the Temple precincts.

and began to teach. This was not forbidden for laymen nor only the preserve of the Pharisees. It was not performed lightly because regardless of the relative freedom to do so, one drew the immediately attention of Jewish leaders.

Jesus now does this very thing, with a purpose. We will see that His teaching is to bring to culmination the nature of His Person, not by brash declaration, but by appealing to the logic of God's revelation, their own expectations from common sense, and the exercise of true faith.

"How has this man become learned, having never been educated?"

We are not told the content of His teaching on this occasion, and there are no parallel accounts that give insight. The rest of this section deals primarily with everyone's reaction to what He taught and the manner of it.

The astonishment was like that met earlier in Galilee, where it was commented that He taught as one having authority, not like the scribes. To recall, the scribes did not teach on their own authority but appealed to rabbis, scholars and doctors of their historic past.

Jesus was doing something out of the ordinary. He was explaining the meaning of Scripture and the meaning of true faith in His own words, and He was not quoting or citing the men of the past as authorities for His points. In classic teaching, the teacher studied so as to support each of his key points and conclusions from prior divines of great reputation. Teaching thus became more a matter of concatenating former treatises in old and even creative ways, but one stayed within the received material. One did not venture into independent thought. The idea of originality at the personal level was extraordinary and reserved for those who were rarely appointed to be added to the host of seers and guides.

"having never been educated" is not to be construed that Jesus spoke with the telltale signs of the uneducated. They are not commenting on a crude manner or poor modes of expression. They were observing that He had all the refinements of a superb education, yet no one could recall His having enrolled or attended formal schools.

"My teaching is not Mine, but His who sent Me.

This is to reply *"What formal teaching does one need if they speak directly the words of the Father?"* It was a piece of logic no one could deny. Their God would surpass any human ability, making education superfluous. Yet, the rub was in accepting His speech as that of God.

To the dispassionate mind, this kind of statement makes complete sense for someone come from God. They would not speak for themselves as messenger, but for the One sending them. They would be in the background while the work, message and Sender would be in the foreground.

not Mine is somewhat enigmatic, because nothing would be His anyway that wouldn't be the Father's also. So there is really no such thing as Mine distinct from the Godhead. Jesus would not have a message separately and secretly squirreled away independently as His own.

"If anyone is willing to do His will, he will know of the teaching, whether it is of God or whether I speak from Myself.

This was not only the test they were to apply to Him back then in the time of His appearing, but it is the test we are to apply today in assessing the truths of God.

This implies that there is a sense by which one can judge and identify it rightly. In fact, there is such a sense mentioned by Paul, - *because that which is known about God is evident within them; for God made it evident to them. 20 For since the creation of the world His invisible attributes, His eternal power and divine nature, have been clearly seen, being understood through what has been made, so that they are without excuse.* (Romans 1:19-20)

This is a revelation against which all men will be held accountable. Man cannot say, *"I never knew you at all my whole life."* God will be able to point to the place and time in which He made Himself known to every individual.

It is that revelation to which future revelations are compared, so that the man of righteousness says within his heart, "This is right, this is true." In fact, *"I've heard this before."* He recognizes it in relation to the first revelation.

Now to be sure, the revelation Paul speaks of is in no way as complete as the Scripture. But it has the same character, it speaks with the same voice, which is recognized from then on.

But men are capable of sealing off the testimony of that first revelation, such that some may not recognize it immediately. Still, here is Jesus saying that its import is not so far off that it can't be appealed to for validation. To His detractors He commends that if they are willing, they will know the teaching and that it is of God.

In modern times, we have become sophisticated in pretending that the truth is far from us, so every man is on his own to discover it without judgment as to which is right above all others. But all men know the truth of God, according to Paul, so everything else is just self-deception and avoidance, about which modern man has become exceeding clever and adept.

"He who speaks from himself seeks his own glory;

Here is an appeal to simple logic. The self-seeker glorifies himself. This could be pointed to in innumerable instances from their past. But they would be hard-pressed to deny that Jesus had continually pointed to the Father, giving Him glory in every teaching, in every miracle. When you have found that kind of person, *"he is true, and there is no unrighteousness in him. "*

"Did not Moses give you the Law, and yet none of you carries out the Law?

There are two things being said here. Moses gave them the Law yet they have found clever ways to avoid many of its precepts. Nor was it a case of following most and slipping on but a few. Jesus made it clear that to slip on one nullified the obedience to all the rest, (James 2:10) (We can assume that Jesus taught this for His brother to have conveyed it in his epistle.) So it was right to say *none of you carries out the Law.*

Secondly, the Law was designed that none would carry it out perfectly, hence all being guilty by it continually. It was all along too high a standard for the efforts of man. It required the perfect obedience of the Son to fit the needs of fulfilling all righteousness, dying for the world, rather than His own sins.

"Why do you seek to kill Me?"

This conclusion bounds out into the forefront from the prior sentence. *"If none of you can keep the Law on numerous counts, why do you seek to kill me for disobeying one law – that of the Sabbath?"*

First, they were hardly qualified to assess obedience, and thereby assess the severity of disobedience. If they could be self-deceived into exempting themselves, they were hardly qualified to levy exacting punishments.

But second, they could claim direct commandments to proscribe and punish breaches against the Law despite their own weaknesses. Jesus answers this also by conveying that if disobedience brings death, why are they not all under the same sentence? And if they can exercise some compassion for themselves and their fellow leaders, why not toward Him?

This, of course, is what Jesus teaches in the parable of the two men at the Temple (Luke 18:10.) The man who is looked down on by the Pharisee as full of ineptitude toward the Law went home more righteous because he admitted his sins and fell on the mercy of God. That is what Jesus expected from men of God. Mercy and compassion. The same which they freely exercised with respect to themselves.

That he asks this also indicates that their designs were well known. But even without this, it would not be too far-fetched an assumption based on the nature of Jesus' own claims and what penalties these carried.

The crowd answered, "You have a demon! Who seeks to kill You?"

Here, a clever ploy of which men have availed themselves for centuries – to conceal proof of motive behind a lack of substantive evidence. We say, *"I never called you an idiot to your face."* But we gave so many indications by our actions and manner that saying the words would have added nothing more.

The Jews were hiding behind the technical fact that no bench warrant was ever issued, no public denunciation by the high priest was made that a man could point to on record. And it also serves as another opportunity to characterize Jesus as possessed – *"You have a demon"*, which was a colloquial way of saying, *"You're deranged. You're nuts."*

This is a more serious charge than we might think, but Jesus does not over-react. Instead, He brings simple logic back into the scene -

"I did one deed, and you all marvel.

The deed in question seems to be the healing of someone on the Sabbath. The only two records prior to this are the man with the withered hand (Luke 6:7) and the woman with the sickness (Luke 13:16.) Since Jesus next refers to the man, it must be the former.

As to "one deed," Jesus is pointing out that He has done many things over which they took lesser notice, but this one they pick on because it suits their purposes.

"For this reason Moses has given you circumcision

Much of this whole dialog is to highlight their inconsistencies. They are acting legalistically and with rigid interpretation, but they are not being consistent. The case of circumcision on the Sabbath is an example. The circumcision is not the circumcision itself, (which began with Abraham not Moses – Gen 17:10), but circumcision permitted on a Sabbath day when work was proscribed.

"If a man receives circumcision on the Sabbath so that the Law of Moses will not be broken, are you angry with Me because I made an entire man well on the Sabbath?

The law of the Sabbath was adjusted to accommodate the law to circumcise on the eighth day, *"that the Law be not broken."* And if the law of the Sabbath could be accommodated for a matter bearing more on ceremony than on immediate health, why not the case of a man being made whole? It was a case that ritual (circumcision) had now become more important than works of health and healing, hence, they could justify the ritual being accommodated but not the other. Legalism had extinguished compassion.

"Do not judge according to appearance, but judge with righteous judgment."

This is simply a call to look below the surface at the deeper significance, meaning and intent of a thing in order to judge it correctly. That is why we are cautioned against judging because probing the truth to all its depth is not done hastily but with patience and compassion.

It is said St. Augustine was much more understanding, compassionate and merciful toward sinners than many of his fellow bishops, primarily because he had come to the Lord from a life of unrelenting sin and knew the agony of trying to restrain it. The truth of a person's motives in sin need discernment instead of hasty judgment.

Another meaning for this teaching is to avoid form criticism - appearances. There is a recent adage popular today: *"if it walks like a duck and it quacks like a duck, it must be a duck."* This is form criticism as opposed to getting at things by reviewing each case by its own merits and facts – "do not judge according to *appearance."*

But the teaching goes beyond acquiring all the facts. We are to judge with righteous judgment, meaning that by which God would judge. That requires an acquaintance with what God is saying, how God is assessing, and in general, men do not wait for that kind of discernment, nor are they well-practiced in it.

John 7:25-39
25 So some of the people of Jerusalem were saying, "Is this not the man whom they are seeking to kill? 26 "Look, He is speaking publicly, and they are saying nothing to Him. The rulers do not really know that this is the Christ, do they? 27 "However, we know where this man is from; but whenever the Christ may come, no one knows where He is from." 28 Then Jesus cried out in the temple, teaching and saying, "You both know Me and know where I am from; and I have not come of Myself, but He who sent Me is true, whom you do not know. 29 "I know Him, because I am from Him, and He sent Me." 30 So they were seeking to seize Him; and no man laid his hand on Him, because His hour had not yet come.

31 But many of the crowd believed in Him; and they were saying, "When the Christ comes, He will not perform more signs than those which this man has, will He?" 32 The Pharisees heard the crowd muttering these things about Him, and the chief priests and the Pharisees sent officers to seize Him. 33 Therefore Jesus said, "For a little while longer I am with you, then I go to Him who sent Me. 34 "You will seek Me, and will not find Me; and where I am, you cannot come." 35 The Jews then said to one another, "Where does this man intend to go that we will not find Him? He is not intending to go to the Dispersion among the Greeks, and teach the Greeks, is He? 36 "What is this statement that He said, `You will seek Me, and will not find Me; and where I am, you cannot come'?"

37 Now on the last day, the great day of the feast, Jesus stood and cried out, saying, "If anyone is thirsty, let him come to Me and drink. 38 "He who believes in Me, as the Scripture said, `From his innermost being will flow rivers of living water.' " 39 But this He spoke of the Spirit, whom those who believed in Him were to receive; for the Spirit was not yet given, because Jesus was not yet glorified. (John 7:25-39)

Commentary

The whole question of expectations for someone coming down from heaven is in play here. Jesus came down in the midst of a very real set of circumstances – the actual ones happening at the time – not some mystical scene disconnected with reality. The Pharisees were powerful and clever. His coming would naturally engage them, just as walking into Congress and making claims would get an immediate reaction from very real lawmakers. So here with Jesus there is bound to be trouble.

So some of the people of Jerusalem were saying, "Is this not the man whom they are seeking to kill?

Some of those hearing Jesus within the Temple court soon recognized Him as the very man the authorities were seeking to kill. This means quite clearly that rumors had spread of this intent, and since the people themselves would not have originated such ideas, the plan must have been based in real comments, albeit unofficial, in which officials let slip their intent to be rid of Him.

It is difficult to imagine religious people committed to a God of love and peace entertaining the thought of taking a person's life. It is a violence unbecoming of a people of faith and we as Christians today would be horrified at the suggestion that the best way to deal with so-and-so is to kill him. Yet this was clearly entertained as a resolution for the Jesus issue.

Helping us to understand how men of faith could arrive at such a conclusion are the many injunctions in the OT for putting a man to death for infractions of the Law – *"Bring the one who has cursed outside the camp, and let all who heard him lay their hands on his head; then let all the congregation stone him.* (Lev 24:14.) So there was divinely sanctioned precedent for capital punishment of people committing a certain level of offense against the Law.

But the case against Jesus was not straightforward. What had angered the Jews into a persecutorial mode was the claim to be Son of Man and His work on the Sabbath. The former depended on the testimony of witnesses, but finding consistent recollections in detail would be problematic.

So while they would have been more inflamed by the blasphemy of messianic claim, they chose the Sabbath laws as more defensible. But while these were technically punishable by death (the man who gathered sticks on the Sabbath in Moses' day) the Jews, in practice, did not routinely execute people in these times for Sabbath violations. This is why the plan to kill Him was not official but couched in rumors. The case was not quite full enough to eliminate suspicion that this was just personal animosity rather than legal infraction.

"Look, He is speaking publicly, and they are saying nothing to Him. The rulers do not really know that this is the Christ, do they?

That the former was the state of things with the Pharisees is evident by the above observation by the people. He was speaking right out in the open and the authorities were taking no action. Indeed, they would have been part of the very crowd hearing Him speak. As it was, they were entertaining His sermon to glean more evidence that He was worthy of death within the Law.

The statement, *"the rulers do not really know . ."* is rhetorical. It is more a statement of incredulity than a surmising of facts.

"However, we know where this man is from; but whenever the Christ may come, no one knows where He is from."

The incredulity is now seen as coming from His detractors and doubters among the people. They are astonished that the rulers have not taken action, and now reiterate the reasoning by which they are comforted that He could not be the Messiah.

The Christ was not seen in the OT as being from anywhere recognizable, excepting his place of birth (which for them ironically was not a fact that connected any dots.) No OT reference indicated His home as being Nazareth, and the statement He would be a Nazarene required a somewhat esoteric interpretation of Isaiah.

That Jesus was clearly known as local, having ordinary upbringing in a town well known but of questionable notoriety made the reasoning all the more valid in their mind. This could not be the Messiah.

"You both know Me and know where I am from;"

Here, He does not mean Nazareth. This would have played into the reasoning by which they were rejecting Him. He meant that they knew His true Person and origin by virtue of His teaching and works. Were He to have meant "from Nazareth" He would have connected *"I have not come of Myself"* by using *"but"* – as in: *"you know where of I come (Nazareth) but I come not of Myself."* The use of *and* indicates that both where He comes from and it being not of Himself are in the same context.

Yet this has the appearance of contradiction, because we find Him accusing them of <u>not</u> knowing the Father who sent Him. This was said to highlight the inner witness of God that He was the Christ (the part they knew) and their simultaneous rejection of that witness, in keeping with lives that do not really know the Father (that which they didn't know.)

The facts are in front of them (that which they know) but the belief about their meaning is lacking. They know Christ who is patently in their presence as the Christ, but they don't know, latently, the One who sent Him.

"I know Him, because I am from Him, and He sent Me."

This is precisely the expectation of Messiah come from God. He will represent the God of their fathers, not Himself alone. He will be seen as *"coming from Him"* and sent by Him. He is not to simply appear, but He is to come to fulfill a purpose. Meaning He comes as one sent,.a perfect fulfillment of these expectations.

So they were seeking to seize Him;

The facts were undeniable, yet He represented a rebuke to their carefully crafted version of Judaism. The fact that He Himself was so true made the bearing of His indictments that much more intolerable. It is like the video tape in court that reveals the evil character and intentions of the accused to public view. It is undeniably true and thereby unendurable.

Yet their hatred could have no success because the Father was ultimately sovereign over these affairs and the time table decreed for such things would not be violated – *His hour had not yet come."*

But many of the crowd believed in Him; and they were saying,..

Now, those of His followers and supporters counter with different reasoning. When Messiah does come (assuming the mind of His detractors) would that One go beyond the signs Jesus had performed? It was a logic that could not be denied. Jesus had authenticated Himself by miracles and signs in a manner no less fulfilling than their expectations would be on any account.

and the Pharisees sent officers to seize Him

Despite their reluctance to arrest Jesus on less than conclusive evidence, the above comments must have been accompanied by tumult and loud verbal conflict, such that the whole peace of the Temple court was disrupted, and to the fault of whom? The teacher from Galilee. Whatever the reasons, the Pharisees believed the opportunity to seize Him had been thrust unexpectedly in front of them, like eventualities we do not expect that obligate us to think on our feet and adjust our time table for acting.

The officers would not be Roman troops, but Temple police. These were available in a sort of matrix of authority that came ultimately from Herod, but gave such men over to the immediate needs of the Sanhedrin. They were very much like the city guards in Rome proper who were truly trained soldiers but whose duties were more like local police.

sent officers indicates that the Pharisees were standing apart, hanging back in the porticos or colonnades surrounding the court, and gave orders that sent the officers to the scene of the discord. But this took some time, since we see considerable dialog continuing.

"For a little while longer I am with you, then I go to Him who sent Me. 34 "You will seek Me, and will not find Me; and where I am, you cannot come."

Knowing of these orders and seeing the arrangements being made to get the police involved, Jesus takes this opportunity to engage His impending end and return to the Father. The preparations for this arrest are simply a foretaste of that moment when He would be seized in fact, tried and crucified; the precipitation of events by which He would leave this world to return to the former.

This is an amazing window into the sheer scope of Christ's nature. He existed from time immemorial, was known as the Beloved in Heaven, covenanted with the Father to be born into the earthly scene, accomplish His divine ends, then return to that same continuum of eternal existence and divine essence once again. This puts to rest any notion of a mere spiritual takeover of some elect human person who would teach, heal and die, becoming essentially as the dust when the crucifixion was complete. The pre-incarnate Christ, the earthly Jesus and the glorified Christ are one and the same in continuity and Person. That His incarnate life has continuity to the rest is seen in the statements that He now continues forever to bear the marks of His passion while seated at the righthand of the Father (John 20:27, Acts 1:11.)

" You will seek Me, and will not find Me; and where I am, you cannot come."

This was two-fold but directed primarily at the Pharisees. His detractors would seek His body for proof against the claim of resurrection and not find Him, nor would they be able to come where He truly was.

In a related application, His followers, hearing the reports that He was not in the tomb, would seek Him and find after the Ascension that He was no longer in the earthly realm. Nor could they in this age come to His heavenly estate.

"Where does this man intend to go . . to the Dispersion among the Greeks, and teach the Greeks,"

Such is the mind at odds with the things of God. Since He was a mere man, He could only go where mortals may go – some place among the nations.

The Dispersion was a technical term for the condition in which Jews were forced to leave their traditional homeland and live among the nations. This first occurred with the Assyrian captivity of the 8th century in which the N tribes of Israel were taken to Assyria, later to disperse among the nations, never to return until end times. It occurred for Judah in the S under Nebuchadnezzar when its citizens were taken to Babylon (586 B.C.) This forced deportation among the nations came to be called the Dispersion.

There was, however, also a voluntary dispersion taking place among Hellenized Jews since the time Greece ruled over the Holy Land. They did not become Greek (Hellenic) but Greek-like (Hellenistic.) Here, many of the more liberal Jews appreciated the Western culture of the Greeks above their own and adopted that lifestyle and culture for their own. This is why Greek had become the lingua franca even in places like Judea, when Latin was the language of their conquerors.

"among the Greeks . . to teach the Greeks" The most logical place apart from the Levant was Greece. Asia Minor was too close at hand, as was Syria or Egypt.

But of course this was completely off the mark of what Jesus meant.

Now on the last day, . . "If anyone is thirsty, let him come to Me and drink.

To anyone who had paid the least attention to the character and thrust of Jesus' teaching, they would know He meant spiritual drink and the thirst was one after righteousness before God.

That there was an audience appreciative of the idea of thirst is indicative of the condition which ritual and liturgy incur at the sacrifice of spiritual satisfaction. Here is a people at large in the Temple, from many regions of the province, having been under the tutelage of the Pharisees and Scribes, yet needful and able to recognize a thirst within their souls.

It is essentially the same thirst that modern man perceives. We are made for fellowship and union with God, and a life without these is conscious of the God-shaped whole inside, aching to be filled and made complete.

It is the inner yearning that has spawned all the religions of the world in feeble man-made attempts to seek that filling, that spiritual completion. Satan has been quick to distract and deflect whole masses of people into false religions that are pursued without ultimate satisfaction by traditional, familial or culture obligation. This is why certain of the sensitive and introspective in these religions can be wooed away to Christ. They continued to perceive in their former practice no lasting, complete satisfaction that ever quenched the thirst Jesus speaks of here.

"Let him come to Me and drink." stands out in contrast to most intermediatory, rite-based religions in which the worshipper faces obstacles or requirements and no guarantee of acceptance. Jesus says, "Let him come" meaning there are no restrictions or pre-requisites. Just come and drink.

From his innermost being will flow rivers of living water.' "

Drinking and satisfying thirst was readily understandable, but now something else is added that one could not have conceived. Rivers of living water will flow out into the world. The believer will become the source not merely the recipient. This is not meant in the sense that the believer replaces Christ or the Holy Spirit as spiritual source. It means he becomes the conduit of the Holy Spirit's life to others, the means through which it is disseminated. But the new idea is that the waters of life are not just taken in but flow out, as from a well.

This is a powerful image because it contrasts with the depressing image the people were now quite used to – a spiritually dry ground, dusty through centuries of lifeless repetition and ritual.

The contrast was striking because water easily related to life, strength, vitality, and refreshment like a well-watered plant. Coming from a pool or a lake, we see supple skin and a look of vitality. It's very figure in a land where water was precious had a drawing power like nothing else. Jesus couples this with belief, because belief connects man to the spiritual plane; and although the most ethereal and intangible, it remained in devout people's minds as the most powerful of all forces.

But this He spoke of the Spirit, whom those who believed in Him were to receive; for the Spirit was not yet given, because Jesus was not yet glorified.

This clarification is added by John to ensure that its dispensation was deliberately associated with the descent of the Spirit after the Ascension of Christ, i.e. that Jesus was not purposed by the Father to be the immediate means.

The rivers were not physical but spiritual - the flowings of spiritual life. This inner reception of Spirit and subsequent flowing was a transition whose demarcation point would be Pentecost. And Pentecost was not to take place until Jesus had ascended.

In truth, everything about our spiritual life in this age relates back to the coming of the Spirit at Pentecost. Our ability to comprehend His Word, to remember it when needed, our use of spiritual gifts, the indwelling presence of the Spirit are all forward running results of the event at Pentecost. Ergo, John's need to connect these promises of Jesus with the means by which God would effect them.

John 7:40-53
40 Some of the people therefore, when they heard these words, were saying, "This certainly is the Prophet." 41 Others were saying, "This is the Christ." Still others were saying, "Surely the Christ is not going to come from Galilee, is He? 42 "Has not the Scripture said that the Christ comes from the descendants of David, and from Bethlehem, the village where David was?" 43 So a division occurred in the crowd because of Him. 44 Some of them wanted to seize Him, but no one laid hands on Him.

45 The officers then came to the chief priests and Pharisees, and they said to them, "Why did you not bring Him?" 46 The officers answered, "Never has a man spoken the way this man speaks." 47 The Pharisees then answered them, "You have not also been led astray, have you? 48 "No one of the rulers or Pharisees has believed in Him, has he? 49 "But this crowd which does not know the Law is accursed." 50 Nicodemus (he who came to Him before, being one of them) said to them, 51 "Our Law does not judge a man unless it first hears from him and knows what he is doing, does it?" 52 They answered him, "You are not also from Galilee, are you? Search, and see that no prophet arises out of Galilee." 53 Everyone went to his home. (John 7:40-53)

Commentary

"This certainly is the Prophet." . . "This is the Christ." . . "Surely the Christ is not going to come from Galilee, is He?

Several questions begin to be asked among the people. Some are identifying the man they are hearing with the Prophet predicted by Moses (Deut 18:18), some with the Messiah. Others who are more studied in the Scripture are pondering the details of the prophecies. These may have been members of the Pharisees among the crowd or members of the Scribes (who would know the details of Scripture and references better than the Pharisees.) Or it may have been very learned people in the crowd.

The issue was Messiah's place of origin. Nothing stated anything about Galilee and Jesus' Galilean origin was the most known thing about Him. But it was Bethlehem from which Messiah would spring.

Clearly, the story of His birth was not widely known. We think this odd because everyone today knows this story quite well. But we must remember that the means that would make this widely known were not yet composed or disseminated. His birth was some thirty years before and while its details and circumstances were extraordinary and noticed by those local to Joseph and Mary, His birth did not become a sacred story passed along with Him wherever He went. The virgin birth aspect was not recognized by anyone beyond His parents and their families and it is not known how much of that was believed by all members.

It did not in any way catch the attention of Jerusalem so as to be relayed over and over as another chapter in the miraculous history of Israel. Even Zacharias' prophesy and proclamation was a vague and distant memory. By this time in Jesus' life, the events in Bethlehem were not only not known as miraculous, but it was doubtful they were known at all. Had they been known, the very question, *"Has not the Scripture said that the Christ comes from the descendants of David, and from Bethlehem, the village where David was?"* would have rung an immediate bell.

What should strike everyone about this verse is the sheer irony involved, the marvelous irony in God and His plan for salvation. You have His detractors asking the very question that proved He was Messiah, but in ignorance. You want to jump into the scene and shout, *"Bingo, you've got it!"* or *"Hello! Jesus **was** born in Bethlehem.*

This is one of those "cosmic" moments when the planets seem to be aligned for some unknown reason, like being told that long before you were married you once sat down in a seat your future wife just vacated and you didn't know it.

The people here were virtually inches away from the truth and didn't know it.

So a division occurred in the crowd because of Him. Some of them wanted to seize Him, but no one laid hands on Him.

What is at the same time puzzling is why Jesus or any of His disciples did not set the record straight by telling of His birth in Bethlehem? Instead, the crowd is left in a state of division over who he was and what should be done with Him.

We must assume it was perceived by Jesus as making no difference toward any move to accept Him formally and corporately. Settling His place of birth still left the issue of accepting His message. Besides, when enough people in a crowd are bent on a certain outcome, technicalities fall by the wayside, even a technicality as momentous as this.

"Why did you not bring Him?"

Another piece of wonderful irony. The officers who return empty handed to the Pharisees explain, " *"Never has a man spoken the way this man speaks."*"

So bound to an evil mind are these Pharisees that they completely miss the import of these officers coming under Jesus' influence and power. It utterly fails to succeed in speaking to the error of their own hearts, but instead they cling to the deception that Jesus has beguiled them – " *"You have not also been led astray, have you?"* It is not a case of truth being told, but a case of leading men astray. They are so far from the truth that they can no longer recognize it.

And we in modern times cannot recoil in surprise at such willfulness. So many in churches today will cling to false doctrines and traditional beliefs that when the true doctrine is proclaimed it is rejected as a misinterpretation that desires to lead people astray. This folly of the Pharisees has been replayed endless times in the history of the Church.

In a positive vein, we should each strive to so speak the things of God that the truth of it is similarly commended. Yes, the officers were praising Jesus and we should not seek to be personally praised. But it is also clear the content and the manner of the teaching were the substance appreciated. It was not the assessment of a man but the assessment of a message that had reached their hearts.

Preachers and teachers should be striving in all their training, study, prayer and devotions to repeat this effect in their own lives. If following Jesus means being like Him, we ought to desire to say the things He said so that they beget the same profundity about truths made known. There are a thousand ways to say things, each perfectly fit for their occasion. Desiring to hear the words, "I've never heard it put quite so well" is not prideful or self-seeking if it results in a heart turned toward God.

"No one of the rulers or Pharisees has believed in Him, has he?

This is an attempt by men challenged at the root of their professional existence to defend their place and reputations. Their whole way of life and their standing in the community is in the dock, being scrutinized and challenged for its worthiness. Notice that they do not challenge the report of the officers. They couldn't. They appeal instead to the persuasive power of numbers and authority. This is always the desperate appeal when pushed against the wall theologically or doctrinally. It is not how righteous and defensible the doctrine is, but how many have believed it for so long.

None of the Pharisees? They are conveniently ignoring Nicodemus. But interestingly, in a moment we will see that he is present and actually speaks up at this very juncture.

49 "But this crowd which does not know the Law is accursed."

Here we see an uncovering of their evil mind and the extent of their desperation. They attack the hearts of the people themselves. They do not merely call them ignorant, which many of them plainly were, but accursed. Everyone else is to be blamed but they themselves. Jesus is the trouble maker, the officers are fools and the crowd are ignorant cattle fit only to be cursed.

What was happening in truth was that the Law as interpreted by the Pharisees was being re-examined and re-explained in a manner that exposed their manipulations of it. The people actually knew rather well the law of the Sabbath, but they were beginning to question whether it had been taught to them in proper balance with grace and mercy. Jesus was accused of breaking the Sabbath laws, but how could a man speaking like this be guilty? Something had to be missing in the Pharisees' view of the Law for this to be the case.

So the Pharisees must reach for the only argument left – *"You simply don't understand the Law like we do."*

Nicodemus . . said to them, 51 "Our Law does not judge a man unless it first hears from him and knows what he is doing, does it?"

For men defending their better understanding of the Law, they are laid low by the words of Nicodemus. It was more than giving him a hearing. That part had been presently accomplished. It was the fair assessment of his defense that must be added.

In Jesus' case, He had defended all His action with Scripture or an interpretation that got behind the letter and had revealed the spirit of the word. In no instance had Jesus stated, *"I don't care what the Law says"* or *"There are reasons why it doesn't apply to Me."* He always explained how He was working in accordance with its intent.

We can only imagine the faces of the Pharisees hearing this rebuttal. Not only was their argument now false that all the rulers were unanimous against Him, but they were being shown by one of their own that they were fudging the laws about evidence and judgment to meet their own ends. The word 'livid' comes to mind.

"You are not also from Galilee, are you? Search, and see that no prophet arises out of Galilee."

Two digs are set back upon Nicodemus. They are not suggesting he was born in Galilee (which would not have made much of a point) but rather that He is talking as though he has come with Jesus out of Galilee. They are rhetorically asking if he is not among the company with Jesus.

The second statement is their hip-pocket fix to the predicament, saved to be reiterated when things got to an impasse. Jesus is from Galilee and no prophet, less so the very Messiah, comes from Galilee. This served to end the discussion, such that all departed and went to their homes. We can be sure that this culmination of events spawned a search among the Pharisees for more incriminating evidence that could not be turned against them. From this point forward there will be more intense watching and listening to gain such evidence, and there were many more meetings of the Sanhedrin to plot and craft an effective case.

We see the results of this planning in the trial before Caiaphas, that they have produced witnesses to His statements against the Temple and those that appeared to be against Caesar, and that they have contingencies in case these fail. All of these machinations can be seen to have proceeded from this event in the Temple.

John 8:1-21
1 But Jesus went to the Mount of Olives. 2 Early in the morning He came again into the temple, and all the people were coming to Him; and He sat down and began to teach them. 3 The scribes and the Pharisees brought a woman caught in adultery, and having set her in the center of the court, 4 they said to Him, "Teacher, this woman has been caught in adultery, in the very act. 5 "Now in the Law Moses commanded us to stone such women; what then do You say?" 6 They were saying this, testing Him, so that they might have grounds for accusing Him. But Jesus stooped down and with His finger wrote on the ground. 7 But when they persisted in asking Him, He straightened up, and said to them, "He who is without sin among you, let him be the first to throw a stone at her."

8 Again He stooped down and wrote on the ground. 9 When they heard it, they began to go out one by one, beginning with the older ones, and He was left alone, and the woman, where she was, in the center of the court. 10 Straightening up, Jesus said to her, "Woman, where are they? Did no one condemn you?" 11 She said, "No one, Lord." And Jesus said, "I do not condemn you, either. Go. From now on sin no more."

12 Then Jesus again spoke to them, saying, "I am the Light of the world; he who follows Me will not walk in the darkness, but will have the Light of life." 13 So the Pharisees said to Him, "You are testifying about Yourself; Your testimony is not true." 14 Jesus answered and said to them, "Even if I testify about Myself, My testimony is true, for I know where I came from and where I am going; but you do not know where I come from or where I am going. 15 "You judge according to the flesh; I am not judging anyone. 16 "But even if I do judge, My judgment is true; for I am not alone in it, but I and the Father who sent Me. 17 "Even in your law it has been written that the testimony of two men is true. 18 "I am He who testifies about Myself, and the Father who sent Me testifies about Me."

19 So they were saying to Him, "Where is Your Father?" Jesus answered, "You know neither Me nor My Father; if you knew Me, you would know My Father also." 20 These words He spoke in the treasury, as He taught in the temple; and no one seized Him, because His hour had not yet come. 21 Then He said again to them, "I go away, and you will seek Me, and will die in your sin; where I am going, you cannot come."
(John 8:1-21)

Commentary

But Jesus went to the Mount of Olives. Early in the morning He came again into the temple,...

This recounts the major confrontation Jesus is about to have with the Pharisees. It is a milestone of tremendous magnitude in light of the issues addressed and the introduction of what the Pharisees would see as outright blasphemy.

But first Jesus goes to the Mount of Olives. This is in contrast to the last verse of chapter 7 where the people are seen going out to their homes. Jesus is going to the mount to pray and for a moment of intense union with the Father in preparation for the next day's confrontation.

He comes again to the Temple courts and begins to teach the people who have gathered around Him. We have no mention of His disciples, so it is unclear that they are present, yet the recording of this level of detail requires that some of them had to be present.

The scribes and the Pharisees brought a woman caught in adultery, and having set her in the center of the court,...

The scribes and Pharisees would be the proper authorities to bring a case against the woman. They constituted members of the council that ruled Jewish religious law and affairs. The disposition of her case in terms of punishment was another matter. The first order of business was her guilt.

However, this was a bit rhetorical. They certainly did not need Jesus' opinion on her guilt. They had caught her in the very act. The approach to Jesus had ulterior motives. They knew Him to be one who reinterpreted the traditions and laws of Judaism. This was to be a chief element in their case against Him. They anticipated an opportunity to capture more evidence by asking His opinion about the woman.

Adultery does not necessitate that the woman was married and therefore committed the act in respect against her husband. She could be called an adulterer if her male partner was married but she was unmarried. In other words, both partners are adulterers even if only one is married.

Neither is this an act of fornication (*pornea*) between two unmarried people, sometimes thought incorrectly to be classed under the general heading of adultery. The word here is *'moicheia* which was consistently applied to cases where one partner was married.

"Now in the Law Moses commanded us to stone such women; what then do You say?"

Technically, the Jews did not have permission from the Roman authority for capital punishment. This was not rigidly enforced and there were exceptions in which the Romans found it expedient to look the other way – the case of Herod Antipas with John the Baptist. They risked harsh treatment or imprisonment for violating this restriction too often or in cases of significance in Roman eyes. (This is a reason but not the only reason why they sought permission in Jesus' case, because He was a person of notoriety in the area.)

Here, they are apparently ready to ignore the proscription and take their chances that Pilate would do nothing.

As for the framing of the question, the use of *"what then do you say?"* is a signal about their motives. 'Then' is deliberately used to suggest that Jesus' opinion would be different. *"The Law says such-and-such, BUT what do you say?"*

And of course John tells us directly that they were in fact testing Him – *They were saying this, testing Him, so that they might have grounds for accusing Him.*

Notice that Jesus does not engage the legal and philosophical issues with them, but acts quite unexpectedly

But Jesus stooped down and with His finger wrote on the ground.

That there was ground in which one could write indicates that this part of the court had an earthen floor not concrete or stone. We can assume that the colonnaded porticos around the perimeter were paved. But the center floor must have been open ground. (It is also possible that if it was paved, Jesus was near a section left unpaved.)

This is the only instance of Jesus ever writing something, and of course its content is completely unknown. Everything is left to conjecture, which we will entertain in a moment when He does this again.

"He who is without sin among you, let him be the first to throw a stone at her."

The Law did not stipulate that accusers be guiltless, nor that those punishing the condemned be guiltless. But there was in the Law a call to consider just before punishment one's righteousness in making the accusation. *the hand of the witnesses must be first upon him (the accused)* (Deu. 17:7). This meant that the accuser could not secure the judgment of the court and then let others take on the odium of punishing the offender. The very accusers must throw the first stone. The purpose was to cause the accuser to think about the outcome of false accusation that might thereby kill the innocent. It was a call to evaluate the risk against one's reputation if things were later discovered contrary to the facts known.

Jesus use of this phrase was to recall the stipulations of Deuteronomy.

Now in this case, the woman's guilt was beyond doubt. There was no fear of being careless in terms of Deut 17:7. But Jesus had added something. *"Let him who is without sin . ."* While technically not stipulated, there was always a sense that compassion was the higher law. But this was not a case that risked killing the innocent. But by adding this, Jesus was questioning the rush to have punishment carried out. Where was compassion in all of this, especially being knowledgeable of their own sins?

They are somewhat stupefied by this question. They are pondering two things: why this question makes any difference, and how to answer Him? Their legalistic nature is saying this makes no difference, but their hearts are twinged with the suggestion that self-assessment ought to enter in to how they are handling things.

While they ponder this question, He again writes in the ground.

Again He stooped down and wrote on the ground.

The better conjectures about this act suggest that, based on the reaction of the accusers, Jesus must have been writing down instances of sin, each of which some member of the party was guilty. Some see it as Jesus writing each of their names next to the sin they had committed. Whether this explanation or the former, they cease their prosecution and slip away, one by one.

The writing of sins of which these accusers were guilty would be quite intimidating and even if not exposing their names, the capability of Jesus' to make things personally embarrassing would be impetus enough to make oneself scarce.

Any other explanation creates additional problems and expectations of turmoil in the crowd. According to Matthew Henry in his commentary on John, there were ancient adages, one of which seems to have been *"The earth accuses the earth, but the judgment is mine."* Were He to have written this, it is doubtful the accusers would have simply slipped away one by one, but rather they would have raised a ruckus that He was claiming for Himself the judgment of God. Hence, if we cannot resist conjecture where the Bible is deliberately silent, the writing of sins seems the best candidate.

beginning with the older ones

An interesting feature of the account. Certainly the younger are more reckless, less disciplined morally. But the younger men have less of a sophisticated sense of reputation at stake. The older men would have households and businesses and the pecking order to consider.

and He was left alone, and the woman, . . "Woman, where are they? Did no one condemn you?"

Some have offered that this was Mary Magdalene and many films have portrayed it as such. But the woman here is nowhere identified with the Magdalene, not to mention the specific reference that that Mary had seven spirits cast out by Jesus (Mark 16:9), which was not done here.

Jesus points to the lack of accusers and the absence of their condemnation but we are not to suppose that Jesus was winking at her adultery, as might appeal to the more liberal brethren. It was not the lack of guilt but the lack of condemnation He was pointing out – *" I do not condemn you, either."* This did not mean *"I don't find you guilty either."*

We must be clear that Jesus is rescinding the right to exercise what the Law provided. It is not that punishment could not have been executed, but that the accuser has the right to plead for mercy with respect to judgment.

The husband against his wife's adultery, might plead that punishment be stayed if he is willing to forgive her and encourage a sincere repentance.

This mercy is clear in what Jesus said next -

"Go. From now on sin no more."

That is the exhortation made to every believer who comes to saving faith. Salvation is not merely an event along the continuum of a life that is otherwise unchanged. Repentance is the doorway to salvation, but it is not momentary. We are to begin a new life in which the old things are passed away. They do not go away on their own accord, but must be pushed away. That is what repentance means. That is what this woman is being asked to do – to go on from here with a determination to not sin.

Paul describes this as being freed from the law of sin and death (Roman 8:2). We know that despite this declaration of fact, Christians will sin. The key is that they have abandoned a life of sin, a condonation of sin as normal.

He further describes our former life as a slavery to sin, in which sin calls and we run out to it having no real power to resist (Romans 7:23,25). But that slavery was broken at salvation (Romans 8:21). We need not obey the call of sin (I Cor 10:13). Where we did not have a choice, we do now. Where we did not have capacity, we do now. So Christ can say with complete confidence, *"Go and sin no more"* because we have been freed from its slavery.

Then Jesus again spoke to them, saying, "I am the Light of the world; he who follows Me will not walk in the darkness, but will have the Light of life."

We find that not all the Pharisees left, only the accusers of the woman. Thus, Jesus begins teaching again. He makes the bold claim He is the Light of the world. The Jews did not miss the analogy to divinity.

Before considering their reaction, we need to amplify His use of light and darkness. The sinful world of unrighteousness is a world in darkness, not by decree, but by choice – *and this is the judgment, that men loved darkness rather than light.(John 3:19.)* It is dark despite men being able to see, despite being able to be enlightened on the horizontal plane, because true light – the kind that makes one truly alive – is on the vertical plane and is spiritual, not ethical or philosophical.

But proclaiming that there is such a light implies that there are those who desire to leave the darkness and come into the Light. The announcement makes no sense if this were not so. That is the salvation and newness of life being offered. That is what the offer of citizenship in the coming Kingdom is all about; living not just now but forever in that marvelous Light.

"You are testifying about Yourself; Your testimony is not true."

This is to say that Jesus is claiming glory for Himself as a mere mortal man, and He is wrong in doing so – *"your testimony is not true."* But the untruth they are talking about is more than the wrongness of claiming this for oneself. It is all about His teaching, especially His re-interpretation of the Law, His violation of their understanding of its precepts and their obligation to recast His works as coming from another source of power.

Again the discussion returns to the subjects discussed the previous evening.

"Even if I testify about Myself, My testimony is true, for I know where I came from and where I am going;

He acknowledges their point about the propriety of making claims for oneself – *"Even if I am . ."* but He now asks them to consider if all instances of this are forbidden. Certainly, Messiah will be able to assert things about himself without a charge of conceit, because they will be true. There is no error or liability in proclaiming what is actually true.

We need to pause for a moment to appreciate *"where I come from and where I am going."* In college, especially in philosophy, even secular education exposes students to the question of the meaning of life. The classic questions for essay are: *Who am I? Why am I here? Where am I going?"* The chief difficulty creating all the trials, strife, wars, hatred, unhappiness, confusion and emptiness in the world can be related to how people have answered those questions. Satan is ready and waiting to answer these for us and many are beguiled. Others live as though lost without a compass, adrift on an unknown sea of ideas and disappointing answers.

Jesus could rightly answer those questions as they ought to be answered for everyone else. We all come from the Father who is the giver of life, we are here to do His will, hence we ought both to know where we are going in earthly life and that we are ultimately on our way into His eternal Kingdom. No longer lost. No longer wooed by empty answers and dead end streets. No longer groping in the darkness but walking in the Light.

Of the opposite were the Pharisees – *" but you do not know where I come from or where I am going."* They were the custodians of the oracles of God yet did not know from where Jesus had come.

"You judge according to the flesh; I am not judging anyone.

The line between reason and faith is subtle and we can often be deceived by it. We regard human reason as the gift of God, but we then elevate it as the prime truth detector and therein we stumble. It is the Achilles' Heel of evolutionary theory – that all of life can be reduced to knowable, explainable processes. It is reason being given complete charge of all knowledge and all reality. In that world, there is no room for God and faith. In fact, philosophy came to call it metaphysics – beyond physics, meaning the unknowable, the unverifiable.

Jesus is accusing these men of reducing true religion to what can be managed in the mind and with reason. They have conceived alongside the Scripture a whole corpus of man-made explanations and practicum that eventually were appealed to more than the Scripture itself – *neglecting the commandment of God you hold the tradition of men."* (Mark 7:8.)

I am not judging anyone.

A perplexing statement, because Jesus has stated His opinion of them on several occasions. In this discourse He has judged them as not knowing the Father from whom He comes. He later will call them whited sepulchers. So what sense can He mean not judging them?

There are two senses subtly intended. First, they were judging Him according to the flesh, but He was not judging any man in this manner. This seems an odd interpretation until we realize that their whole frame of reference for judgment was carnally based *"you judge according to the flesh"*, so Jesus' replied within the only frame of reference they knew. *"I judge no man as you judge."*

A second sense is also valid as a parallel theme. Jesus did not come to ultimately judge the living and the dead in His first advent. This is the reason for closing the scroll of Isaiah where He did – just prior to the prophet's statements about judgment and the day of vengeance (Luke 4:18ff, Isaiah 61:2.) By claiming to judge no man, He was reiterating that all men were still under the grace of God as to their end, and still had time to ensure their inheritance in the Kingdom.

"But even if I do judge, My judgment is true; for I am not alone in it, but I and the Father who sent Me.

Jesus recognizes that these men are going to find His statement perplexing in light of His many prior statements about them. Neither can He count on them understanding the subtlety of His meaning, so He entertains their connotation that He is denying having judged them. He therefore qualifies His statement by clarifying that if He has judged them in their frame of reference, it was not without the Father's concurrence, nor was it false as they are doing with Him.

This should also qualify all our fears about violating Jesus' commandment that we not judge, *"lest we be judged."* (Matthew 7:1.) If we judge with God's judgment we have no fear of the consequences from God. The rub is in knowing the mind of God when we see the need to judge.

"Even in your law it has been written that the testimony of two men is true.

This could be seen as somewhat glib or tongue in cheek. After all, anyone could claim they have the Father's testimony to add to their own. The second Witness cannot be interrogated. But in this case His Father was in fact the other witness and if the principle applied to men why not to God?

The issue would be whether that second Witness could be seen as agreeing. And this hinged on their ability to comprehend the work of God in the life of His Son. It was again an indictment on their condition – *"You have the precept about witnesses, but you lack the ability to discern their testimony."*

the Father who sent Me testifies about Me."

To what could they have related such a testimony? Jesus is saying the Father is testifying. They are pondering Where? When?

And in this they are bereft because all the answers are readily available to them in their own Scriptures – God has not veiled that testimony in secret. God is also testifying in the human heart, theirs of which is hardened.

"Where is Your Father?"

This is asked cynically as in, *"Where is your **true** father?"* Jesus returns them to the answer they will not admit, *"You know neither Me nor My Father; if you knew Me, you would know My Father also."*

These words He spoke in the treasury

The treasury was not the place of money changers, but rather a store house for donations made for the Temple upkeep and operation. Articles on the layout of the Temple put it in the Women's Court, which would not have been where the first confrontations took place with the Pharisees but outside that area one step further removed away from the sanctuary. If this is true, then Jesus had moved with the Pharisees during the course of their encounter to this court. However, other scholars indicate that the exact location is not clear (Dr. Barry Smith, Religious Studies, Atlantic Baptist University, c. 2004.)

"I go away, and you will seek Me, and will die in your sin; where I am going, you cannot come."

Addressed to the Pharisees, this meant that they would seek to verify His death when rumors began about His resurrection. Such an investigation would result in their passing around the story that His disciples had stolen away His body to make the resurrection look genuine.

His prediction that they would die in their sin was conditioned on them remaining as they were. *"Continue to reject me and you will die in your sin."*

John 8:22-38

22 So the Jews were saying, "Surely He will not kill Himself, will He, since He says, `Where I am going, you cannot come'?" 23 And He was saying to them, "You are from below, I am from above; you are of this world, I am not of this world. 24 "Therefore I said to you that you will die in your sins; for unless you believe that I am He, you will die in your sins." 25 So they were saying to Him, "Who are You?" Jesus said to them, "What have I been saying to you from the beginning? 26 "I have many things to speak and to judge concerning you, but He who sent Me is true; and the things which I heard from Him, these I speak to the world." 27 They did not realize that He had been speaking to them about the Father.

28 So Jesus said, "When you lift up the Son of Man, then you will know that I am He, and I do nothing on My own initiative, but I speak these things as the Father taught Me. 29 "And He who sent Me is with Me; He has not left Me alone, for I always do the things that are pleasing to Him." 30 As He spoke these things, many came to believe in Him.

31 So Jesus was saying to those Jews who had believed Him, "If you continue in My word, then you are truly disciples of Mine; 32 and you will know the truth, and the truth will make you free." 33 They answered Him, "We are Abraham's descendants and have never yet been enslaved to anyone; how is it that You say, `You will become free'?" 34 Jesus answered them, "Truly, truly, I say to you, everyone who commits sin is the slave of sin. 35 "The slave does not remain in the house forever; the son does remain forever. 36 "So if the Son makes you free, you will be free indeed. 37 "I know that you are Abraham's descendants; yet you seek to kill Me, because My word has no place in you. 38 "I speak the things which I have seen with My Father; therefore you also do the things which you heard from your father."

39 They answered and said to Him, "Abraham is our father." Jesus said to them, "If you are Abraham's children, do the deeds of Abraham. (John 8:22-38)

Commentary

So the Jews were saying, "Surely He will not kill Himself, will He

We see here the unfortunate effect that obstinancy has on spiritual perception. The Jews were very used to figure and analogy, to metaphor. They were not generally in the mode of the Greeks who looked at things very analytically. Yet here they are without understanding of what Jesus means and are loath to conclude that He means to return to the Father, to Heaven. So they are obliged to seek the meaning in purely practical terms. Jesus must mean He plans to kill Himself and thereby go to a place they cannot come – *"Where I am going, you cannot come"*

But Jesus brings them back to those claims they find intolerable -

"You are from below, I am from above; you are of this world, I am not of this world.

You can almost see their expressions – *"We're going back to that again."* But Jesus can do no more than proclaim what is true. He is not responsible for the attitudes and mode of thinking that makes this incredible. He has no obligation to accommodate their state of mind and soft pedal the Son of God discussion.

". . not of this world." This is hard to reconcile with any theory that makes Jesus merely a man on whom God dispensed special grace and wisdom – that the man Jesus became the Christ. He proclaims that He, as they see Him, is from first to last of another realm. He pre-existed in that realm and will return to it.

If Christians are to identify with Christ, we must think in terms of other worldliness also. We are to be other-world-minded. We should take notice of the William Walker hymn that sings *"This world is not my home, I'm just a passing through."* We, like Christ, as fellow citizens of the Kingdom beyond. We are destined for it and in terms of time it will be more of what our life is about than here on earth.

This realization should constrain us in our ties to this world, what allegiances, contracts and covenants we make in it.

". . from above," has given rise to Heaven being in the sky, and this notion preceded Jesus' teaching. We tend to think analytically as to boundaries and such. The great master painters pictured Heaven as an invisible world among the clouds, with angels and key personages floating in the skies above the affairs of men.

Paul talked about going to the third heaven (2 Cor 12:2), which in more analytical terms would mean beyond the boundary of the stars. But Paul was not establishing a scientific cosmology, implying distances, directions and boundaries.

We see Heaven close at hand to the earthly scene in stories like Job, where Satan's dialog with God implies proximity and visibility to Job's condition. We are more inclined to see Heaven as a dimension of existence rather than a place beyond certain physical boundaries in the universe.

We further see Heaven and Earth in close proximity in the Revelation where the New Jerusalem is seen descending. *"Down out of heaven"* certainly conveys direction and implies the sky, but it would be difficult in any model to see it coming from anywhere else.

So to some extent it is proper to refer to Heaven as above us, but in better terms "beyond us." And beyond us means away from the earth, so anywhere away from the earth is technically "up."

"Therefore I said to you that you will die in your sins; for unless you believe that I am He, you will die in your sins."

Here He clarifies that He was not making a categorical judgment upon them but a conditional one. We do not go beyond the proscription about judging when we surmise that any person who continues a life of sin will not be saved. Paul reiterates this in 1 Corinthians – *Or do you not know that the unrighteous will not inherit the kingdom of God? Do not be deceived; neither fornicators, nor idolaters, nor adulterers, nor effeminate, nor homosexuals, nor thieves, nor the covetous, nor drunkards, nor revilers, nor swindlers, will inherit the kingdom of God. (I Cor 6:9.)*

"Who are You?"

Perhaps the most poignant question in the Bible. He has said so much that is enigmatic, so much that runs counter to their expectations, that they are thrown back to the most basic question, *"Who then are you?"* Some may see it as a command, to fess up to who He is and what He is about.

This of course is the key question every person will be asked in relation to eternal life. "Who is Christ and what have you done in relation to Him?" All men must settle this question one way or the other and thereby settle their destiny one way or the other. It is unfathomable the incredible number of people who will be astounded to realize that the entire future of their existence beyond the grave will come down to this assessment. The question they have been avoiding all their lives will be the cornerstone on which all hinges.

The Pharisees are asking this question on the earthly plane – they seek to know if He is the Prophet or Elijah or a charlatan. They have no capacity to discern who He is spiritually, yet that is the plane on which His nature truly exists. Who He is depends for its very essence on the spiritual plane and their bankruptcy in it is the reason they are forced to ask it on the human plane.

"What have I been saying to you from the beginning?

All the evidence for this discernment has already been given. This they have refused to heed, and Jesus has no obligation to meet any recalcitrant demands for something more. Were they to simply go back over His testimony, His teaching and His works and see them with eyes open to the work of the Father, they would see how fitting these things were to the simple expectations of logic and reason. He has acted and taught exactly as one coming from God.

"I have many things to speak and to judge concerning you,

Jesus lets them know He could say plenty concerning the condition of their hearts and their actions both public and secret, but He gives them grace in this by pointing to the things He is bid to speak from the Father only – *"and the things which I heard from Him, these I speak to the world."*

Even in this they are slow of hearing and perceiving, *They did not realize that He had been speaking to them about the Father.*

"When you lift up the Son of Man, then you will know that I am He

Jesus gives them a point of verification about His nature. They will not acknowledge Him now, but when He is lifted up, they will then know the truth of which He speaks. They will come to realize He was of the Father as He said.

This is a reference of course to the Crucifixion. But in that event, we don't see them acknowledging this as He predicts. In truth, many actually did, but were loath to admit it publicly. There were many rationalizations overlaid upon truthful assent. And if the time frame is not critical, there is the prophecy in Isaiah reiterated in the Revelation, that they will look upon Him whom they have pierced (Rev 1:7.) At that point the men standing before Jesus will be long dead, but there is a sense that at the Crucifixion and in the Revelation these men will both see at the Cross and in the Judgment the One they have put to death as being the true Son of God.

So Jesus is essentially telling them that if they don't acknowledge Him now, the Cross will force them to see it, and if not even then, they will be compelled at the Judgment.

He has not left Me alone, for I always do the things that are pleasing to Him."

Here are the words of total devotion and love of the Father. We see the intimacy of that right relationship between Father and Son, the Father does not abandon the Son, the Son is not left alone in the world. And the Son has no desire other than to do what is pleasing to the Father. It is not slavery but complete devotion and a desire to remain in the goodness of it.

That is what the Christian believer is challenged to seek also, that they come to a place where pleasing the Father in Heaven is all the mind conceives and wishes. That is the child who emulates being born of God.

This testimony was so true, so like one who had been with the Father that many in the company of the Pharisees *came to believe in Him.* For some, everything suddenly came together in both memory, heart, and mind. These last words brought everything into focus, all His actions, teachings and claims, and their faith was free now to be released and embraced beyond all their former doubts.

Not all were thus freed in their faith, but to those who were He turns and speaks -

"If you continue in My word, then you are truly disciples of Mine; and you will know the truth, and the truth will make you free."

Freedom through belief was something every one in Judaism would understand. Even the most diligent follower of the Law knew the toil of doing so, of being ever watchful of infringements and stumblings, the myriad of ordinances both God-ordained and man-made. What man would not yearn for some sense of final freedom, not from faith, but from the drudgery of human obedience in faith?

There was everywhere an innate hope that faith would come to a state where obedience and satisfaction before God was automatic, fulfilled by nature, no longer by effort. We can only imagine that when Jesus mentioned 'freedom,' every eye was filled with wonderment as to whether that possibility had now come.

These who believed were given this hope, having set aside the doubts the others still retained.

"If you continue in My word, then you are truly disciples of Mine;

Believers cannot simply believe in Him and leave it at that. They must live by His words, by His instruction and teaching, and take on His way of life as their own. In ancient times this was more readily understood, even among pagans (Socrates.) To be a disciple, one adopts the life, philosophy and thinking of the master.

In modern times, this is less clearly the expectation. Christians in some churches can get away with mere spiritual assent in a purely academic mode, making little effort to change other aspects of life in a desire to emulate Christ. But that is treating Christ as an interesting subject, not a way of life.

How do we continue in His Word? This is the primary reason for the Gospels and the rest of the New Testament. That we have an objective point of reference for knowing and continually being reminded of what His Word contains. Our responsibility first as disciples is to know the content of His Word. To continue in it is to live its precepts in daily life, that His teaching constrains our decision making, our attitudes toward circumstances and other people, and that we embrace a calling upon our life to accomplish something intended by God for the building of His Kingdom.

We should get used to the questions: *"What now God?"*, in the present, and *"What next God?"* for the future.

But there is also the idea of perseverance in Jesus' words here – *"If you continue . ."* It is not a following in our youth and letting that carry us into old age. It is a continuum of abiding. We can't let the lunch we had when we turned twenty serve for the rest of our lives. We likewise can't let the zeal of our beginning life as a Christian serve for spiritual sustenance all the rest of our lives.

The unbelieving Pharisees reply -

"We are Abraham's descendants and have never yet been enslaved to anyone; how is it that You say, `You will become free'?"

Technically, this was being disproved at the very moment by the presence of a Roman procurator. Before that, the Greek generals who inherited Alexander's empire jockeyed Palestine between them. Before that, Babylon then Persia took their turns subjugating the Jews. In fact, since the exile, the Jews have been perennially enslaved.

What they mean here is that they have *survived* what earthly kingdoms had done to them. The promises to Abraham have been kept and they are alive and viable as a nation and a faith even to the present, despite their many trials. They are appealing to the covenants God made concerning them and they are throwing this back at Jesus' proclamation of freedom. In essence, to survive is to be unscathed by what men may do, and in that sense free from them.

But Jesus reminds them that there is another slavery they are ignoring, one that has nothing to do with political slavery -

"Truly, truly, I say to you, everyone who commits sin is the slave of sin.

Slavery to sin is a new way of looking at the predicament of man. Paul expounds on this in Romans. The slavery Jesus is talking about and the freedom from it is in relation to sin's power. This is also the slavery from which every Jew wishes to be free. It is the reality of slavery that makes the Law so arduous and so tiresome in its repetitions. Endless sacrifices for endless sinning.

To bring in Paul's later theology, without Christ man is a slave to sin because he has within him no power to break its bondage over the life. It calls and we must run to it. Jesus is here describing that kind of slavery and the promise of freedom from it.

"The slave does not remain in the house forever; the son does remain forever.

The object of moment is *"abiding in the house."* A slave does not have perpetual rights to be forever connected to the house. They can be sold or given to another because they are not considered members of the family. The son, however, has perpetual guarantees.

Now how does this observation apply here with the Pharisees? Slavery to sin and slavery to the Law are being equated with societal slavery. By turning the Law into a legalistic drudgery, they have become slaves, and as such they have ceased being sons.

What is being declared here is that Jesus has come to break that bondage for anyone who wishes to return to sonship in God.

This is what He means by the following -

"So if the Son makes you free, you will be free indeed.

If a slave, then freedom is again acquired by an act of a freeperson (in the analogy, a son.) And if the son emancipates the slave He is as free as any law could make him.

In spiritual terms, Christ alone can declare us free from the bondage of sin, and that of the Law. The Jews hearing this are at a juncture where things are on the verge of major dispensational change. The old covenant is soon to be over and the new is at the gates. The new is represented by the Son and if He makes them free they are free indeed.

But this means abandonment of the old for the new, and this is of course the fundamental issue preventing them from coming in. They repeat that they are Abraham's descendents and they are loath to give this up.

"I know that you are Abraham's descendants; yet you seek to kill Me, because My word has no place in you.

This next statement is perfectly placed. If they are Abraham's descendents, why are they seeking to kill someone of whom Abraham would approve, being equally dedicated to the Father. We learn later in Paul that the covenant of faith given to Abraham was not abrogated when the covenant of Moses came along – *the Law, which came four hundred and thirty years later, does not invalidate a covenant previously ratified by God, so as to nullify the promise.* (Gal 3:17.)

If Abraham and Christ are united, then the desire to kill Jesus vacates any claim to be Abraham's descendents.

"I speak the things which I have seen with My Father; therefore you also do the things which you heard from your father."

This entire dialog is like a film heading for its denouement – the resolution of all plot lines and themes. The central issue that is creating all the problem is verbalized in their own question, "Who are you?" Every question on their part, every answer on His part, then the next question, etc. are all headed toward a zenith in which this issue will again be brought forward as key.

In this reply above, He now clearly and succinctly contrasts the two allegiances in play. He does the things of the Father, and they are listening to another father. This is axiomatic from the previous statements. If they are seeking to kill Him and He is of the Father, they must have another father for whom they work.

This of course is a direct attack for which serious consequences could ensue. But they engage Him for the sake of everyone listening.

They answered and said to Him, "Abraham is our father."

This could not be denied from a genealogical standpoint. They were indeed his descendents in the flesh. It is meant to stop His mouth on any further rejoinders because all Jews everywhere had to acknowledge the authority of Abrahamic descent. This was also the comeback given to John at the Jordan. And we see that Jesus will give an identical reply.

"If you are Abraham's children, do the deeds of Abraham.

Claiming to be a son by birth does not make one a son by character or spirit. Billy Graham's son, Franklin, was undeniably Billy's son, but for many years was in rebellion against his father's calling and life. In terms of faith, He did not become his son in truth until he embraced his father's faith. And faith is the subject here, not lineage, and not secular, familial relations.

What were the deeds of Abraham? To walk with a trust and faith in God that was willing to do the opposite to what human nature prescribed. To be obedient against the dictates of reason. It was not an obedience for obedience's sake. It was obedience to what he had heard.

Abraham did not let the incredulity and seemingly almost pagan request for sacrifice deter his knowledge of what he had *heard.* He could have asked, *"Did God send me through the agony of waiting for a son into my eighties, only to offer him as a bullock for a sweet smelling savor?"* Instead, he raised the knife.

Again, this was not obedience apart from God's voice. It was obedience to God's voice. The Jews had come to an obedience apart from God. Doing the deeds of Abraham meant that they ought to have been stayed on the presence and voice of God, not the letter of the Law. Without this, one makes himself blind to a change in dispensations. And that is the very thing taking place here.

Next, we will see the climax of this confrontation and the most powerful of Jesus' claims to be Son of God.

John 8:40-59

"But as it is, you are seeking to kill Me, a man who has told you the truth, which I heard from God; this Abraham did not do. 41 "You are doing the deeds of your father." They said to Him, "We were not born of fornication; we have one Father: God." 42 Jesus said to them, "If God were your Father, you would love Me, for I proceeded forth and have come from God, for I have not even come on My own initiative, but He sent Me. 43 "Why do you not understand what I am saying? It is because you cannot hear My word. 44 "You are of your father the devil, and you want to do the desires of your father. He was a murderer from the beginning, and does not stand in the truth because there is no truth in him. Whenever he speaks a lie, he speaks from his own nature, for he is a liar and the father of lies. 45 "But because I speak the truth, you do not believe Me. 46 "Which one of you convicts Me of sin? If I speak truth, why do you not believe Me? 47 "He who is of God hears the words of God; for this reason you do not hear them, because you are not of God."

48 The Jews answered and said to Him, "Do we not say rightly that You are a Samaritan and have a demon?" 49 Jesus answered, "I do not have a demon; but I honor My Father, and you dishonor Me. 50 "But I do not seek My glory; there is One who seeks and judges. 51 "Truly, truly, I say to you, if anyone keeps My word he will never see death." 52 The Jews said to Him, "Now we know that You have a demon. Abraham died, and the prophets also; and You say, `If anyone keeps My word, he will never taste of death.' 53 "Surely You are not greater than our father Abraham, who died? The prophets died too; whom do You make Yourself out to be?"

54 Jesus answered, "If I glorify Myself, My glory is nothing; it is My Father who glorifies Me, of whom you say, `He is our God'; 55 and you have not come to know Him, but I know Him; and if I say that I do not know Him, I will be a liar like you, but I do know Him and keep His word. 56 "Your father Abraham rejoiced to see My day, and he saw it and was glad." 57 So the Jews said to Him, "You are not yet fifty years old, and have You seen Abraham?" 58 Jesus said to them, "Truly, truly, I say to you, before Abraham was born, I AM." 59 Therefore they picked up stones to throw at Him, but Jesus hid Himself and went out of the temple.

Commentary

"But as it is, you are seeking to kill Me, a man who has told you the truth, which I heard from God; this Abraham did not do.

To support His claim that they are in league with another father, Jesus appeals to His having told them the truth and yet they seek to kill Him.

Truth for most people is limited to truth about certain things. We can't know the truth about everything so we settle for enough truth to make life meaningful and enjoyable. At some point people get beyond the practical truths and on to the more philosophical ones, wherein the meaning and truth about the reality of the world becomes a question, i.e. what is the real state of affairs concerning the world?

Without discipline and order, people attempt to answer that question as best they can on their own, often rather poorly. In many cases, it becomes easier to save time and just follow the adept and persuasive philosophizing of others who appear to have gotten there ahead of them. Depending on locale and culture, one can adopt any of a thousand explanations on the truth of reality, hence you get the mundane to the downright silly; the genuinely weird and twisted to the rational and rather nicely thought out.

The history of philosophy will help one to see the progress of these explanations, and it will help one see something else - no one has succeeded in an explanation that encompasses all reality in a unified theory that ends all speculation.

Jesus offers the opportunity to ask Someone who is in the know. Man cannot possibly be in all the critical places at the right times to garner and perceive all angles of facts, including motives and thoughts. Did

Roosevelt want a war to end the Depression? Those thoughts can never be known to the satisfaction needed for reality. But Someone else was there to know, in fact, there in all places, and in all times.

Where the rub comes in is in knowing that truth first – that He exists and that He knows.

The Bible says that this kind of truth is not veridical nor scientific but spiritual – *But a natural man does not accept the things of the Spirit of God, for they are foolishness to him; and he cannot understand them, because they are spiritually appraised.* I Cor 2:14. (We see again how the spiritual plane is the most powerful and the most meaningful of all dimensions.)

Hence, the secret to obtaining that knowledge is to respond to the call of God in the human heart and to be rightly related to Him.

To the dispassionate mind, Jesus has provided abundant contributions to the assessment of whether His truth is the Truth about reality – the way things really are. He was miraculously born, His birth was attended by the announcements of angels, He possessed wisdom whose accounting could not be attributed to human education, His baptism was accompanied by a declaration from Heaven that He was the Son of God, His power to heal was incomparable and beyond scientific explanation, His truths were recognized in people already possessed of a faith visited upon them by one and the same God. Despite the horrors of His scourging and the Cross He remained stayed on the grace it would provide for salvation. He predicted His resurrection and its accomplishment was witnessed to by over five hundred people, and the promise of the indwelling Spirit at His resurrection has been experienced by all who embrace saving faith.

His death and resurrection answered all the essential questions about human existence, sin and evil, and life beyond the grave – a life already anticipated in other religions, though distorted and corrupted.

For the honest seeker of the truth about reality, that is a bucketful of things to consider, and unlike anything other religions have to offer. Ironically, the Jews were closest to that truth in terms of opportunity and privilege, but so far away in genuine faith.

"We were not born of fornication; we have one Father: God."

When Jesus stated that they were doing the deeds of their father, they knew what He meant. Since He was aligning with the God of their fathers, He could only be pointing to Satan with regard to them.

While Jesus wasn't accusing them of that, this may be a dig at His own birth. But they are also defending against an illicit devotion to what is unholy. They were not children of Satan in the sense of loving and reveling in the evil of that alliance. They claimed allegiance to the same Father Christ claims to be from.

The Jews did not relate to God as Father, but they are employing the term Jesus is using in contrasting Himself with them. They are accused of having another father. So their denial is in the same terms, *"No, not that other father but the Father of whom you speak."*

If God were your Father, you would love Me

This is so axiomatic. It is ironic that the people see it, but the leaders of the Jews are blind to it. The people connect Jesus easily to the simpler God of love they have come to perceive despite the Pharisees. The latter are caught up in the legalism of the exacting God of the OT.

This had to cut them deeply, because all around them were those who saw the connection by means of love between God and Jesus.

Why do you not understand what I am saying? It is because you cannot hear My word.

A rhetorical question as seen by His immediate answer to it. How should they have heard His word? Paul explains that the opening of the ear is the Lord's doing in the presence of faith. The natural man cannot hear it or understand it.

If ever we needed an historical example of the kind of person Paul describes in 1 Corinthians chapter 2, it would be these Pharisees.

A danger sign for Christians who let the world crowd out the vitality of their faith is this test respecting the hearing of His Word. Does it now fall on deaf ears? Are truths once understood now a mystery? These would be signs we are out of His will and not in His Way of faith.

You are of your father the devil, and you want to do the desires of your father.

Here is the great deception. These men do not cognitively know they are being used by the devil. They made no conscious pact with him. They have no cognitive desire to serve Satan's bidding. Is Jesus therefore exaggerating? Is He over the mark in this indictment? Men who serve Satan certainly do not think of themselves as serving God.

Yet selfishness, greed, and arrogance are human attitudes Satan can use to thwart the plans of God. And what better subjects than those in the visible service of God? By wanting to do their own will, they play into the hands of one who can make their will serve his own.

He was a murderer from the beginning, and does not stand in the truth because there is no truth in him.

From the beginning? Yes, in the murder of Abel by his brother. He has always been out to destroy the righteous, and that plan has now taken root in the Pharisees.

Satan deceives further in hiding the fact that he stands not in the truth by substituting a truth that makes sense on the human plane. Evolution makes sense at a high level because if you don't ask too many questions, the idea that God used raw, unaided nature to serve His ends has an appeal. The appeal that science and religion are really not at odds is philanthropic, magnanimous, conciliatory. But if it is not true in the details, it does no good to believe it in the general.

The explanation that the Red Sea was the marshy area called the Sea of Reeds and the way through the sea was merely a brisk wind blowing back relatively shallow waters has an appeal that sheds the need for undue supernaturalism. So we are beguiled to take away the miracle in the interest of demythologizing the Bible. All along unaware that there is no truth in the new propositions to begin with.

for he is a liar and the father of lies.

Lying is commensurate with a heart that desires evil. It is necessary to deceive people into doing what you want, because telling them outright will not succeed, wherein is the basis of Satan's role as father of lies? In his initial fall from Heaven.

Satan's fall was the result of desiring to be like the most high (Isaiah 14:12-14.) This reveals that angels have the capacity to will separately from God. Satan desired what was outside God's will - to be equal to Him. Frustration in not having his way produced rebellion, and to have a company fall with him means convincing others that God was unsuitable to be served, and therein was deception and the distortion of the truth born.

In the garden, this ability was seen as already perfected. He knew what to say that would appear reasonable and cogent, with just enough hook to catch interest – the notion that God was keeping certain truths from them. Then more lies upon the first lies. Satan poses as one who knows better the things that go on with God. Better follow his guidance rather than be taken advantage of.

What is deceptive is that he always begins with a measure of truth. Jesus says whenever he speaks a lie he does so from his own nature, meaning that his motives are to deceive, to thwart, to destroy. Therefore he counts on us being fuzzy about where his truthtelling ends and his lying begins.

"But because I speak the truth, you do not believe Me."

When people come to believe the half-truth or even the lie as the truth, over time and without challenges they become accustomed to it. They come to be at home with it and consider it an attribute of what is normal.

When Copernicus and Galileo presented their novel notions of the cosmos, it wasn't their possession of more accurate science that caused bishops and cardinals to reject their findings, but the accustomed nature of the old view. Men in the Church were simply too accustomed to geocentrism and anything else was unthinkable.

The Jews were so used to the idea that Messiah would come in a particular manner and that God's revelation was slow and gradual not radical and revolutionary, that when Jesus spoke the real truth, they were virtually programmed to not believe Him.

Which one of you convicts Me of sin?

With the Jews it was more than intense personal dislike for Jesus and what He stood for. He did in truth violate their rendition of the Law. All their prior actions against people on that basis had worked. The precedents had been successful.

But Jesus knows that He has not violated the intent of any law. He therefore challenges them to bring the law forward (which is the point of asking who convicts Him of sin?)

This is clever tactics, because now an individual must take ownership of the charge. He cannot hide behind the opinion of the collective. This is the deception of the collective having argumentative power. Collectives are always made up of individuals and it is often merely an impression that what a spokesman claims as everyone else's view is in fact everyone's view. In so many cases, it is really the view of the loudest and most intimidating member, which is the very old concept of a gang, members of which are essentially authenticating the personal desires of a strong man. The gang is often just a louder voice for the will of their leader.

If I speak truth, why do you not believe Me?

Notice that this question is repeated many times. Jesus' purpose in doing so is to bring His listeners over and over to the bar of assessing what truth is and whether they are risking the consequences of opposing it.

This is often a tool of the devil and evil men in general who take advantage of an individual's inability to discern the truth for themselves. They play on people's fear of making a mistake. No one desires through ignorance to be on the opposite side of the truth. It is used in many creative scams that trick people into thinking that if they don't act, they will lose something extremely valuable, like their retirement.

But in the hands of Jesus, this is no scam. The cleverness of the Jews is in fact the scam – beguiling the people at large that righteousness is according to their interpretation. And the irony is that it did not destroy people as popular scams do today. They could fool people and get away with it for centuries because one was dealing with the abstract – matters of faith for which the acid test came at the end when no one could come back and warn the living.

But the real truth about the way things actually are has a way of vindicating itself to people of faith. Those not part of the machinery were still free enough to see the truth when it came. That others could not should have been a call to self-examination.

In contrast to the scam, Jesus was in fact asking men to consider the consequences of being on the opposite side of God. But He did not play on the inability of people to discern truth. This, in addition to genuine compassion, was the reason for the miracles, that it be not just the effectual smooth talking of a learned man, but teaching that came with evident power from above.

Thus He is able to say, *"He who is of God hears the words of God; for this reason you do not hear them, because you are not of God."*

To be told you are not of God must have been sobering coming from a man like Jesus, who even if His theology was not liked, had the very apparent endorsement of God to do what He did. A man with that commendation from above might be absolutely right about who is of God and who isn't. Very sobering.

This cuts them to the quick so completely that their hatred cannot be restrained. They seek words that will openly discredit Him and turn His truth into deception

"Do we not say rightly that You are a Samaritan and have a demon?"

When dealing with the woman of Samaria we noted that the Samaritans had taken the brazen step of departing from historic and traditional Judaism to the degree that they honored a different mountain than Moriah and a revised Torah (the Samaritan Pentateuch.)

This is a clever move on their part because in terms of form, at a high level of observation, Jesus is acting like a Samaritan in coaxing believers away from their traditions and promulgating what could appear as a revisionist faith. If He gained a following, He would effect a similar breaking away, a schism, that could be classed as more Samaritan infiltration and disruption.

It is not concomitant that demonic entanglement was part of the Samaritan schism. They're simply adding it to His actionable practices. Jesus elsewhere connects this with blasphemy against the Holy Spirit, which has helped to define this term as attributing to Satan the works of God (Matthew 12:31.)

Jesus answered, "I do not have a demon; but I honor My Father, and you dishonor Me.

Spoken as a resultant clause, not as two acts side by side. He honors God and thereby their response is to dishonor Him. This is to avoid the disconnection of one from the other. They cannot claim to join Him in honoring the same God He honors, but take exception with Jesus himself. If they search His words carefully, they cannot separate Him from the former because they would have to identify how He had dishonored the Father.

They could try to point to His working contrary to Moses, but they could not deny He gave glory in everything to God, not to Himself. If an analysis of His teaching were honestly done, He would be seen as glorifying not denigrating, edifying not tearing down, helping people use their faith not distracting people from their faith.

there is One who seeks and judges.

Here is a reminder that the true test of all things is God not man. How were the Jews to know if they were in the favorable judgment of God? Through obedience and spiritual awareness. They had unfortunately lost fervency in the latter. To spiritually discern takes freshness and vitality, maintained over and over in the life. They had given this aspect up long ago. They were left with but one test – the dictates of the Law and their performance in relation to it.

In the later evangelical churches this was repeated with respect to being filled with the Spirit. Embarrassed by the charismatic movement and needing an explanation that assured their members that all was well despite the claims that something extraordinary accompanied the filling, they offered the explanation that to be filled was basically to renew one's commitment to Christ, to revive one's fervor to serve Him. But as to spiritual gifts, no expectation of these was to be regarding as normal.

It was a way of explaining away what had been lost and recasting what was expected in terms of what now remained – *"Let's just explain being filled in terms that are not much different from what everyone is already doing. No need to "seek" anything."*

The problem was that this was not NT teaching. It was rationalization on a grand scale that minimized that unction to do what the Bible suggested. The NT does put forth the expectation of gifts with the filling and gives no indication that these were intentionally designed as temporary.

The Jews had done the same in terms of conviction. Your standing was no longer spiritually discerned but assessed in terms of statistical obedience to the Law.

"Truly, truly, I say to you, if anyone keeps My word he will never see death."

Considering the mix of the crowd He has around Him, Jesus is saying all the wrong things. But all bets are now off, so why not spell things out fully?

To grant eternal life was tantamount to calling oneself God. It was not entirely new. They had heard Him pronounce sins forgiven (Mark 2:5), but now He was granting eternal life on the basis of belief in Himself.

This confirmed their thoughts that He was deranged and that by way of demons -

"Now we know that You have a demon. Abraham died, and the prophets also; and You say, `If anyone keeps My word, he will never taste of death.'

Their proof is that the great fathers and prophets were surely men who kept God's word, yet they all tasted death.

There was nothing special in the idea of 'tasting' death. It was simply a picture-based way of describing experience. They key was in the different understandings for life and death.

This is again a ploy. There were two understandings of life and death – temporal and eternal - and the Jews were not ignorant of the latter as some might suppose. The unbiased mind would have easily switched to the eternal meaning, since it would have been common sense that Abraham and the prophets had died in the natural sense.

But the Jews wish to make Jesus look ridiculous and simultaneously side-step any further engagement of the eternal claims He was making. So they deliberately pose as having understood Him to mean physical death which any rational man would dismiss as wrongheaded.

To extend the ridiculous characterization they tempt Jesus to compare Himself with Abraham. If Abraham could not avoid temporal death - *"whom do you make yourself out to be?"*

The trap has now been laid for Jesus to claim that He is greater than Abraham. By this He would surely be vilified by all sincere Jews and the Pharisees would have succeeded in disconnecting Him from His followers and returning them to their own fold.

". . it is My Father who glorifies Me, . . Your father Abraham rejoiced to see My day, and he saw it and was glad."

Jesus is not in the least unaware of their designs and, contrary to our expectations, has every intention of taking the bait. He reiterates that He glorifies the Father and the Father Him, that to do otherwise would be to join their fellowship of liars.

He then proceeds to do exactly what they had hoped. He states that the Abraham they so revere foresaw His own day and rejoiced in it. This was tantamount to Abraham acknowledging the larger greatness of Jesus day, making Abraham the lesser and Jesus the greater.

Before getting to the Jews' reaction, we need to ask when Abraham saw this and rejoiced?

There is no OT passage that ever states this acknowledgement in these terms. No event is recorded in which Abraham is seen to acknowledge the coming of the Son of God and thereby rejoiced in the future plan of God. However, many students and scholars agree that there is an event of rejoicing connected with sacrifice, a son, a lamb, and a mountain wherein Abraham could have been given such insight.

In the sacrifice of Isaac, Abraham would see two important things beyond the simple truths of faith and obedience. Abraham, in being willing to give his son, would have understood what it meant for God to give up a son of promise as a fit sacrifice according to the dictates of a larger love for the whole world. He would have identified with the pain of it.

Abraham would further have seen the saving hand of God effected through obedience in faith that then saved his son from death. He would have seen firsthand the promise of a substitute in the ram caught in the thicket. And he would have had to have noticed the unique form of his wording to Isaac, " *"God will provide for Himself the lamb for the burnt offering, my son."* (Genesis 22:7-8 .) And can we avoid seeing the significance that this sacrifice was set in the very vicinity of that hill upon which the Son of God would die?

Now in this latter analogy, God provided no substitute for Jesus' sacrifice. No ram caught in the thicket for Jesus on the Cross. But for Abraham to rejoice in Jesus' day, he would have to have seen that future uninterrupted sacrifice as that which ended all sacrifices; and that was something worth rejoicing indeed. So in his own act, Abraham would have seen two things: the use of the son for the sacrifice, and the idea of grace in providing a substitute for the one rightly to have died.

Despite mere conjecture, it is irresistible to not avoid the conclusion that this was the moment of which Christ was speaking. The Jews now reply -

"You are not yet fifty years old, and have You seen Abraham?"

They show controlled restraint, in part because they are side tracked by what this new comment implies. They are temporarily thrown off from completing their diatribe over the comment about not tasting death. They must first deal with the claim of contemporary existence with Abraham. For Abraham to see Jesus' day meant that Jesus lived during Abraham's lifetime and that the patriarch lived long enough to see a day of glory somewhere in that ancient past concerning him.

They had no basis for concluding that Abraham could have looked ahead to the present day in this much detail. First, it was not Abraham but God who stated large-scoped things about Abraham's seed. They saw no prophetic office in Abraham of this kind of scope and scale.

Second, to entertain this was to admit Jesus had the endorsement. Hence, they are forced to ask Him to explain his age in light of the longevity required, as we see above.

"Truly, truly, I say to you, before Abraham was born, I AM."

We would have expected *"I was"*, not I am. But we see in a moment that the Jews understood it just as He worded it.

There is only one other place where I AM is used to express other time frames than the present - the burning bush out of which God gave His Name to Moses (Exodus 3:14.) What was spoken is understood by the Jews to be an "explanation" of the Name, not the Name itself. The actual Name is now universally agreed to have been *Yahweh'*, being the closest use of potential vowels for filling in the consonants used in the text. Yahweh is a form extending from the verb *'haya'* - "to be" - which is thematically and linguistically consistent with the idea: I AM THAT I AM or I AM WHO I AM. Thus, we have the idea that in all time frames – past, present and future – God simply IS.

In Exodus 3:14, Moses is not given the Name itself in this particular text, but we see him employing it in his subsequent writings, so the assumption is that the Name was given at the same time but that dialog was not recorded. (That Moses had used the four-consonant designation for the Divine Name[37] earlier in the Hebrew text before this revelation is merely anachronistic – the accounts were written after Moses already knew the Name and was employing it.)

We are also reminded that the idea of Christ being in the past, present and future reiterates this I AM connection. We have it in Hebrews – *Christ the same yesterday today and forever* (Hebrew 13) and in the Revelation – *"I am the Alpha and the Omega," says the Lord God, "who is and who was and who is to come, the Almighty."* (Rev 1:8.)

Nor is this an interpreter's stretch that Jesus was employing this terminology from Exodus, as is clearly evident in the immediate reaction of the Jews.

Therefore they picked up stones to throw at Him, but Jesus hid Himself and went out of the temple.

It would be safe to say that trying to make His charge that they sought to kill Him a mere figment of His imagination was now abandoned. They could not now resist anymore their true desires to have Him done to death.

---

[37] The encounter related in Exodus 3:14 gave to Moses the personal name of God, that Moses would convey to the people in their anticipated question, *"What is His name?"* For fear of its profanation among the Gentiles, the Jews later deliberated obliterated this name in the text by failing to pass on the vowels known to be used in the four consonants – YHWH - representing His name. When the Masoretes produced their edition of the Scriptures in order to finally document the vowels used in throughout the Hebrew text (they had been preserved only in tradition), they did not know the vowels for the Divine Name. They substituted the vowels for *adonai*, which is why our English translations use LORD where the consonants appear in the original.

John 9:1-41
1 As He passed by, He saw a man blind from birth. 2 And His disciples asked Him, "Rabbi, who sinned, this man or his parents, that he would be born blind?" 3 Jesus answered, "It was neither that this man sinned, nor his parents; but it was so that the works of God might be displayed in him. 4 "We must work the works of Him who sent Me as long as it is day; night is coming when no one can work. 5 "While I am in the world, I am the Light of the world." 6 When He had said this, He spat on the ground, and made clay of the spittle, and applied the clay to his eyes, 7 and said to him, "Go, wash in the pool of Siloam" (which is translated, Sent). So he went away and washed, and came back seeing.

8 Therefore the neighbors, and those who previously saw him as a beggar, were saying, "Is not this the one who used to sit and beg?" 9 Others were saying, "This is he," still others were saying, "No, but he is like him." He kept saying, "I am the one." 10 So they were saying to him, "How then were your eyes opened?" 11 He answered, "The man who is called Jesus made clay, and anointed my eyes, and said to me, `Go to Siloam and wash'; so I went away and washed, and I received sight." 12 They said to him, "Where is He?" He said, "I do not know."

13 They brought to the Pharisees the man who was formerly blind. 14 Now it was a Sabbath on the day when Jesus made the clay and opened his eyes. 15 Then the Pharisees also were asking him again how he received his sight. And he said to them, "He applied clay to my eyes, and I washed, and I see." 16 Therefore some of the Pharisees were saying, "This man is not from God, because He does not keep the Sabbath." But others were saying, "How can a man who is a sinner perform such signs?" And there was a division among them. 17 So they said to the blind man again, "What do you say about Him, since He opened your eyes?" And he said, "He is a prophet."

18 The Jews then did not believe it of him, that he had been blind and had received sight, until they called the parents of the very one who had received his sight, 19 and questioned them, saying, "Is this your son, who you say was born blind? Then how does he now see?" 20 His parents answered them and said, "We know that this is our son, and that he was born blind; 21 but how he now sees, we do not know; or who opened his eyes, we do not know. Ask him; he is of age, he will speak for himself." 22 His parents said this because they were afraid of the Jews; for the Jews had already agreed that if anyone confessed Him to be Christ, he was to be put out of the synagogue. 23 For this reason his parents said, "He is of age; ask him."

24 So a second time they called the man who had been blind, and said to him, "Give glory to God; we know that this man is a sinner." 25 He then answered, "Whether He is a sinner, I do not know; one thing I do know, that though I was blind, now I see." 26 So they said to him, "What did He do to you? How did He open your eyes?" 27 He answered them, "I told you already and you did not listen; why do you want to hear it again? You do not want to become His disciples too, do you?" 28 They reviled him and said, "You are His disciple, but we are disciples of Moses. 29 "We know that God has spoken to Moses, but as for this man, we do not know where He is from." 30 The man answered and said to them, "Well, here is an amazing thing, that you do not know where He is from, and yet He opened my eyes.

31 "We know that God does not hear sinners; but if anyone is God-fearing and does His will, He hears him. 32 "Since the beginning of time it has never been heard that anyone opened the eyes of a person born blind. 33 "If this man were not from God, He could do nothing." 34 They answered him, "You were born entirely in sins, and are you teaching us?" So they put him out. 35 Jesus heard that they had put him out, and finding him, He said, "Do you believe in the Son of Man?" 36 He answered, "Who is He, Lord, that I may believe in Him?" 37 Jesus said to him, "You have both seen Him, and He is the one who is talking with you." 38 And he said, "Lord, I believe." And he worshiped Him. 39 And Jesus said, "For judgment I came into this world, so that those who do not see may see, and that those who see may become blind."

40 Those of the Pharisees who were with Him heard these things and said to Him, "We are not blind too, are we?" 41 Jesus said to them, "If you were blind, you would have no sin; but since you say, `We see,' your sin remains."

Commentary

We have here one of the most tender moments in the Bible, between Jesus and the young man born blind. Having the burden of a life without sight, His gift of healing becomes an instance of more abuse. He is thrown out of the synagogue for chiding the Pharisees about not knowing better who could have healed him with such power. Jesus does not leave Him despondent and sorrowful, but gives him yet another gift – the revelation that he sits in the presence of Messiah.

As He passed by,

We are tempted to ask, "passed by what?" But this is a colloquial phrase meant to describe in indefinite terms the general condition of moving beyond the present scene to that of the next. In the last scene, the Jews are picking up stones to kill Him, and it is said that He *hid Himself and went out of the temple.*

How this specifically happened we don't know, nor did the writer consider it important to describe in detail. There was a tumult at His last and extraordinary statement ("I AM"), so we are to naturally infer that in the confusion He was able to slip out of the crowd. But this is harder than it might seem. Jesus would certainly have remained discernable in an angry crowd, and those closest would have taken hold of Him. We are not to assume that they became so caught up in their furor that they lost sight of Him. He would have been the keen target of their insults and fist waving. Attempting to merely slip out of this crowd would have been more difficult than the typical Hollywood adventure film portrays.

We must therefore attribute some supernatural means involved in His escape.

He saw a man blind from birth.

We cannot imagine this ourselves. To be blind from birth means a world made up of inferences about the true appearance of things. Even the human body would not be fully appreciated as a whole picture, being perceived always only in parts at a time. The beauty of sunrises and sunsets, the shade from a tree, the majesty of the distant mountains were all unknown.

His state was regarded variously, as we learn in Job, and often attributed as an indictment for sin.

"Rabbi, who sinned, this man or his parents, that he would be born blind?"

We are not to conclude that because Jesus contradicts their inference then sin must never be the cause of physical maladies. We see Him saying earlier the very opposite – *Afterward Jesus . . said unto him, "Behold, thou art made whole: sin no more, lest a worse thing come unto thee."* (John 5:14)

So while sin might be a cause, it's not a principle that it is always the cause. Physical conditions can be used by God to get our attention about sin. They signal to us that the good life we desire is being interfered with by something that needs our attention, and perhaps that something is our moral or spiritual failing.

"It was neither that this man sinned, nor his parents; but it was so that the works of God might be displayed in him."

On the one hand, we see this as very positive – to be chosen of God to show His glory in us. On the other hand, we recoil from so long a period of deprivation and suffering merely to serve the needs of glory. The latter is of course carnal. It is based on the sense of one's right to the conditions of their life.

Paul explains this quite well in Romans, *Or does not the potter have a right over the clay, to make from the same lump one vessel for honorable use and another for common use?* (Romans 9:21.)

We are to infer from Jesus' words that for both parents and son, the blindness was a work of glory waiting in the wings for just this very moment. The boy was born a dozen or more years ago, destined for this place in time where his life and that of Jesus coincided – *" so that the works of God might be displayed in him. "*

So it is not that God exercised His right to do as He pleased with expendable creatures, but that He had all along the intention of a glorious outcome, one that blessed both the boy and the world around him.

"We must work the works of Him who sent Me as long as it is day; night is coming when no one can work.

A bit enigmatic. It might seem fatalistic in that after Jesus leaves, no one will be able to work in the darkness that will ensue. But this is not the sense meant and the history of the church is just the opposite. Also He will later say, *". . greater works than these he will do; because I go to the Father."* (John 14:12)

Instead, this expression is meant to convey the contrast between opportunities present and later gone. He is here now, and He works while opportunity to work (light) is at hand. This explains the urgency of even working on the Sabbath. But it also conveys that opportunities come and go, and when they are gone (the night), one cannot work as when the time was right.

For Jesus and the young man, He has just talked about God's purposes. Here is an opportunity in His path to so work. Now is the time, not later. *"While I am in the world, I am the Light of the world."*

In terms of personal application, we must regard seriously the lack of control over our time of death, which comes down to much the same idea – that opportunities will be given us to work, but later they will be gone. Therefore do the work of God when it is at hand, for there will come a time when it will be too late. It will be night and we can no longer work.

He spat on the ground, and made clay of the spittle, and applied the clay to his eyes,

Why this medium is used we cannot say. There was nothing magical about the mixture, except that it contained the holiest of spittle in all the universe. It is here used as a touch point of faith - for the release of faith. Men sometimes benefit from some physical point of contact, something more than bare faith. Earlier, in the case of the woman in the crowd, touching His garment was just such a touch point. Later we see Paul sending handkerchiefs to the sick.

This has been the subject of ridicule in the hands of tele-evangelists and faith healers, but it is not the principle but the abuse of the principle that should bring caution and skepticism.

"Go, wash in the pool of Siloam"

We have to wonder how he would know the way to the pool? We have to assume that he had assistance. While knowing the way by his other senses, enhanced to make up for his blindness, might have given him the path, we see in a moment that his life was characterized not by mobility but by restriction. He had sat and begged.

Siloam is familiar to us from the earlier mention of its tower. Both tower and pools were located on the southeast spit of land jutting out from the Temple mount, sometimes called Ophel, or the old city or the City of David.

There are two pools known to have existed in the vicinity. The upper pool was known from early Christian centuries and was refurbished in the 5th century. It is a virtual square pool surrounded today by city buildings and a mosque.

The lower pool was recently discovered in late 2004 and announced in 2005. It has three sets of steps separated by landings.

So he went away and washed, and came back seeing.

Notice that Jesus did not need to be present to effect the healing work. As the man went, the work was accomplished merely with the man's faith and the will and power of God.

It is hard to imagine what his feelings must have been to suddenly see a world he had not seen so directly before. Colors would have been completely unknown and thrust upon his senses for the first time. He would at last now see the faces of his own parents, family and friends, the neighborhood buildings and finally the face of Jesus.

"Is not this the one who used to sit and beg?"

Here we are made to recall the substance and form of his life. Despite the resourcefulness we see in the blind today, in ancient times they did not make their way around in society quite as easily. Many were resigned to a life of being set down at the beginning of the day in one's familiar spot, being seldom spoken to, and waiting hour after hour merely for the sound of a coin dropping into the begging bowl.

He would have been a fixture on the landscape of the neighborhood, the one you see at this particular corner, etc. There was confusion among the locals as to whether it was him or someone who only looked like him. But he kept saying, *"I am the one."*

He wished to be deliberately known as the very one, because such a great thing had happened to him. In fact it was essential that his former state be acknowledged, that a miracle not be rationalized into something ordinary, as in, *"He's just an ordinary boy, not the beggar."*

"How then were your eyes opened?"

So first we have the local people questioning him immediately about the details. He will later be taken to the Pharisees who would be seen as more capable of discerning a hoax from the real thing.

Here, the man has no hesitation in mentioning Jesus' name - *"The man who is called Jesus made clay, and anointed my eyes,*

They brought to the Pharisees the man who was formerly blind.

This was done for a couple of reasons readily apparent. The man did not know where Jesus was at the moment, which meant the affair could not be further scrutinized by those around. Further, this had happened on the Sabbath.

"This man is not from God, because He does not keep the Sabbath."

The issue at hand was whether this was a work of God and what was to be thought of the healer?

The formula for the Pharisees was simple – the man of God does not violate the Sabbath. He cannot be of God. It was a simple case of vaunting authority to settle the matter, and in the presence of no one who could rebut this, they hoped this would aid the disaffection of people from the person of Jesus and His popularity.

But even without Jesus present, this was not as easy as they thought. The sheer logic of the situation could not be avoided, and that didn't take Jesus being on the scene for it to be rightly assessed.

"How can a man who is a sinner perform such signs?" And there was a division among them.

You can't argue with that kind of logic. In effect, the excellent teaching the Pharisees had managed among the people was coming back at them. While it might be questioned whether a good man was working a miracle of God or not, it was certain that a sinner would not have the blessing of God needed to effect one.

The division was over those who could not let go of that logic and those who easily took the word of the Pharisees despite the machinations that logic might introduce.

Getting nowhere, they resort to asking the man who was there -

"He is a prophet."

Note that not everyone in Jerusalem knew Jesus as a claimant to be Messiah. Nor does the man call Jesus a healer or miracle worker. These were seldom in use at the time.

Prophet was not a clear fit either since few prophecies were attended by healings. Most resorted to the old term *'prophet'* because they were the closest thing to a man gifted of God. And to some degree the man's response is one of ignorance and being put on the spot.

This did no substantive good and furthered their disbelief that a miracle had actually occurred. In essence, they were suspecting some kind of gag or trick was being played – *The Jews then did not believe it of him, that he had been blind*

"Is this your son, who you say was born blind? Then how does he now see?"

The purpose of asking the parents was two-fold - to ferret out a better explanation for how he now sees (perhaps this was a temporary condition explainable in natural terms), but also in the hope in discovering a gag if his parents were to scold their son for wasting everyone's time on a prank.

"We know that this is our son, . . . but how he now sees, . . . or who opened his eyes, we do not know. . . . His parents said this because they were afraid of the Jews;

Was this a lie from fear? They imply that they were not present when Jesus found their son for they would have known at least Jesus' name, as was evident with the son. We learn that their words were guarded because confessing Jesus as the Christ was actionable with the Pharisees.

Nor does the question of the Pharisees here in the text ask them to verify if "Jesus" did the healing. So we might wonder how they came to fear the association of Jesus in this affair?

It's unlikely that they came to know this from their son, because if they had, they would hardly be subsequently gone from the scene, needing to be called by the authorities. It may be very likely that those going to get them informed them of the details as they were brought.

In this fear, the parents try to deflect the threat of trouble - *"Ask him; he is of age, he will speak for himself."* This is not a cowardly means of shifting the focus to someone else. It was a case of letting the innocence of their son and his simple testimony dissipate the scene as much a possible. His youth and the general astonishment over what had happened all served to blur the details. (Would we be able to wax well with journalistic precision if minute by minute absolutely everything meeting our eyes was being seen for the very first time?) The hope in the parents was that this would dismiss the inquiry as not worth the time and effort.

So a second time they called the man who had been blind, and said to him, "Give glory to God; we know that this man is a sinner."

This was powerful and clever wording. It reminded the young man to consider on which side the glory of God was better served, and this would engender some fear and trembling, to not make this kind of mistake.

They were also reminding him that his Healer was considered a sinner by the authorities. All of this was meant to constrain his reply.

"Whether He is a sinner, I do not know; one thing I do know, that though I was blind, now I see."

Again, a simplicity that could not be argued with. The young man was in no position to validate a state of sin (he had to take their word for it.) But again the facts could not be ignored. Either God empowered sinful men to work His will, or the Pharisees were wrong about Jesus. The young man is clever enough to leave that discernment to them. He avoids this judgment and stays with the apparent facts.

It was a divinely supervised discourse in that it returned the assessment of Jesus as sinner back to those charging Him. They gained no additional vindication for their judgment, hence they must continue to own for themselves their hatred and rejection of Him.

Not satisfied with this, they return to an inquiry of exactly what took place.

"I told you already and you did not listen; why do you want to hear it again? You do not want to become His disciples too, do you?"

They have clearly underestimated the young man they are engaging. He is only apprised of limited facts. His entire connection with Jesus was while he was yet blind.

But the man has a new boldness, despite the intimidating presence of the Pharisees. He chides them that they've not been listening which is a criticism most people would never entertain. Yet he adds more to their disgust and dismay – that they are acting like those who wish to become His disciples.

"You are His disciple, but we are disciples of Moses . . but as for this man, we do not know where He is from."

Again, the imposition of the great hammer that will settle right from wrong. It is the age-old weapon of intimidation by class distinction. All the key words for that intimidation are used – "you" and "we" are employed. Moses, an unquestioned authority, is pitted against the enigma of who Jesus is?

Ironically, this admission will be their undoing in the simple analysis of an unsophisticated young man who has just experienced simple faith at work.

"Well, here is an amazing thing, that you do not know where He is from, and yet He opened my eyes.

The unanswerable logic of applied faith is impenetrable. Everything this young man says is about observation and truth, no philosophizing or speculation.

It comments immediately on the efficacy of their holy offices. If they are in the know in matters of the nation's faith, it ought not to be the case that someone can open the eyes of the blind and they be completely in the dark to explain it.

But he says more, revealing the training in Judaism he has received despite his disability.

"We know that God does not hear sinners; . . Since the beginning of time it has never been heard that anyone opened the eyes of a person born blind. . . If . . not from God, He could do nothing."

"We know" conveys something that corporate Israel has learned from Scripture and the teaching of the elders – a principle that is now coming back on them. Nor has the history of healings been so extraordinary as to effect the kind of thing that has just happened.

It is both the extraordinary nature of the work and the claim that this man is a sinner that make the point so strongly. If a sinner, a lesser work or a "re-explanation" of the work might be rationalized. But with this kind of miracle, the sinner aspect refuses association in the mind.

"You were born entirely in sins, and are you teaching us?"

Even the Pharisees know this logic to be true, but to entertain the young man's inference is unthinkable. They resort to simple condemnation as an excuse to dismiss everything he has said. The sinful state of Jesus has its complications, but one thing they know – the young man's maladies are a clear indication of his sins, hence he has no place from which to teach them.

So they put him out.

This would indicate that he is at least thirteen years of age, since entrance into the synagogue was for adults only, and thirteen was the demarcation point. The bar-mitzvah was the right of passage to participation in the activities in the synagogue.

To be put out of the synagogue was tantamount to a disaffection with the nation and the faith. It is equivalent to what excommunication became in the Catholic Church – deprivation from the elements and formal worship of the faith. It put you into the category of vandals and thieves who never darkened the door of the synagogue.

So this was a serious outcome, and the very reason the parents were noticeably wary. We don't know if the ban extended to his parents.

Jesus heard that they had put him out, and finding him, He said, "Do you believe in the Son of Man?"

Here we see Jesus as personal Savior rather than generically as Savior. In the Gospel accounts we often see the large scene and the need for Jesus to stay aloof from too intimate a contact with the people at large. He preaches in large settings, heals among hundreds of people and confronts the authorities in settings that place the individual person into the background.

But here we see the very tender heart of Jesus focused on the life of just one person. News of the Pharisees summary action eventually spread to the attention of Jesus where He was. We wonder about Jesus needing to wait for the news, knowing all things as He often demonstrated. For whatever the reason, the timing of His return to the young man was set to be triggered off the natural process that conveyed local news.

We see further that He went to find him. Our Savior and Lord left what He was doing to find this young man. It is a living rendition of the lesson of the lost sheep, for whom the shepherd left the ninety and nine to retrieve the one lost (Luke 15:4.)

He knows the circumstances. He is not there to argue with the injustice and haste of the authorities. He will make no move to restore the young man to the synagogue. Instead, He will change the whole point of worship and faith for this young man, such that the synagogue is no longer an issue. There was little hope that the authorities would change their ruling, so why not do away with the chief factor – the criticality of the synagogue itself. Why worry about being ostracized if the whole importance of the synagogue is replaced with something greater?

Hence, the beginning question was not about the incident or the authorities, but about the Son of Man.

"Who is He, Lord, that I may believe in Him?"

Here we have a man open to the things of God. There is no sophistication, no qualifications fueled from an adult skepticism. He is ready to believe if shown.

Jesus said to him, "You have both seen Him, and He is the one who is talking with you."

We can only imagine the effect of this revelation in conjunction with everything this young man has experienced. He has been healed by a man of great wonderment. He has been introduced to a radically different world and experiences never known so beautifully and explicitly before. And now he has the added blessing of being in the very presence of Messiah, him being the very Man who healed Him.

What worries need he have about excommunication if he has met and talked with Messiah? Whatever the future holds, it cannot be worrisome if Messiah has become personally part of his life. His response is overwhelming – *"Lord, I believe." And he worshiped Him.*

"For judgment I came into this world, so that those who do not see may see, and that those who see may become blind."

At first, this appears contradictory to Jesus' earlier statement that He judges no man. How does He then come into the world "for judgment?"

In moral and ethical judgment but not for final judgment. Neither He nor we can avoid the spiritual discernment of righteousness and evil. His preaching came to demarcate this distinction in much clearer ways than had been provided in the past (the Law did not cover lust as equivalent to adultery, hatred equal to murder, etc.)

We recoil a bit from the intent that those who see shall become blind. If they see, why would they be made blind? It was a false seeing, not a true seeing. They saw on their terms, within their pre-conceived framework only. As such the truth they needed to see was far from them.

By Jesus declaring that truth in their midst, He effectively made them blind. They became suddenly acquainted with the blindness they had all along.

Apparently, the Pharisees were in ear shot of this, meaning they had followed Jesus back to the young man, or perhaps gathered round when Jesus appeared in the vicinity again.

They now respond to what they just heard -

"We are not blind too, are we?"

Jesus had spoken about the blind in general. The natural question was whether He included the custodians of the faith and the Scriptures in that group?

Jesus said to them, "If you were blind, you would have no sin; but since you say, `We see,' your sin remains."

A perfect reply. It is all up to how much one knows. If one is ignorant, then willful sin cannot be charged. But they wish to be known as those that see, and they say, "we see." So it is a Catch-22. They are loath to admit they don't see, even though that would be the means of extending grace on account of ignorance. It is their undoing because they are now responsible if they in fact see. And if responsible, their sin is not dismissed from ignorance.

Jesus is not here addressing original sin in Adam, but cognitive sin based on the knowledge of what is right and wrong. Regardless of the applicability of original sin to their general condemnation and need of salvation, to sin in the presence of knowledge vacates any appeal to blindness as a call for mercy.

John 10:1-21

1 "Truly, truly, I say to you, he who does not enter by the door into the fold of the sheep, but climbs up some other way, he is a thief and a robber. 2 "But he who enters by the door is a shepherd of the sheep. 3 "To him the doorkeeper opens, and the sheep hear his voice, and he calls his own sheep by name and leads them out.

4 "When he puts forth all his own, he goes ahead of them, and the sheep follow him because they know his voice. 5 "A stranger they simply will not follow, but will flee from him, because they do not know the voice of strangers." 6 This figure of speech Jesus spoke to them, but they did not understand what those things were which He had been saying to them.

7 So Jesus said to them again, "Truly, truly, I say to you, I am the door of the sheep. 8 "All who came before Me are thieves and robbers, but the sheep did not hear them. 9 "I am the door; if anyone enters through Me, he will be saved, and will go in and out and find pasture. 10 "The thief comes only to steal and kill and destroy; I came that they may have life, and have it abundantly. 11 "I am the good shepherd; the good shepherd lays down His life for the sheep. 12 "He who is a hired hand, and not a shepherd, who is not the owner of the sheep, sees the wolf coming, and leaves the sheep and flees, and the wolf snatches them and scatters them. 13 "He flees because he is a hired hand and is not concerned about the sheep.

14 "I am the good shepherd, and I know My own and My own know Me, 15 even as the Father knows Me and I know the Father; and I lay down My life for the sheep. 16 "I have other sheep, which are not of this fold; I must bring them also, and they will hear My voice; and they will become one flock with one shepherd. 17 "For this reason the Father loves Me, because I lay down My life so that I may take it again. 18 "No one has taken it away from Me, but I lay it down on My own initiative. I have authority to lay it down, and I have authority to take it up again. This commandment I received from My Father."

19 A division occurred again among the Jews because of these words. 20 Many of them were saying, "He has a demon and is insane. Why do you listen to Him?" 21 Others were saying, "These are not the sayings of one demon-possessed. A demon cannot open the eyes of the blind, can he?"

Commentary

We begin here a shift in subject whereby Jesus introduces the analogy of sheep and the shepherd as a simile to the relationship of the Lord to believers and theirs to Him.

"Truly, truly, I say to you, he who does not enter by the door . . . he is a thief and a robber.

This is an analogy straight out of their common practice as herdsmen. Not all were thus employed but it was so common a scene that the general public were very familiar with the habits of both sheep and shepherd.

A fold of sheep was both a term for a close grouping of sheep and for the enclosure in which sheep were kept when not out in the fields. Here it means the latter because there is reference to the door.

There are many obvious things here, but the ideas being contrasted are openness in relation to rightful ownership compared to fear and stealth in relation to thievery. The thief is known for his mode of entry, as is the shepherd for his.

"Some other way" is meant to highlight the inaccessibility to the right way, how "other" his way must be.

Jesus describes the negative condition first so as to set the tone of the discussion – to beware. It is a discourse on telling the difference. One could hope to know the false by mastering the awareness of the good, but this does not always take into account the cleverness of the false.

"But he who enters by the door is a shepherd of the sheep."

The reason this is set as an identifier is that the shepherd has nothing to fear out in the open. He can come through the door because he has no evil motives to hide. All he does he does freely in the open.

"To him the doorkeeper opens, and the sheep hear his voice, and he calls his own sheep by name and leads them out.

Doorkeeper here means the gatekeeper, which does not mean the shepherd has so much wealth that he can hire someone merely to open and close the gate, but merely that his partners in the work might open the gate for him as they begin each of their shared duties. Whether family or hired help, the point is that they recognize him because he has one thing the thief does not have – demonstrated commitment to the care of the sheep.

Beyond this is the necessity to have the sheep's concurrence in being led. The key is the voice. It is well known by experience that a stranger approaching a pen will cause the sheep to immediately move away to the opposite end. The ordinary means of recognition is not present and the natural timidly and fear in sheep operates by design. *" A stranger they simply will not follow, but will flee from him, because they do not know the voice . . "*

And in the voice is the use of the names. So it is the sound of the voice as it forms recognized patterns of the names.

In preparation for the believer, the expectation is that we are to become accustomed to the sound of the voice and very used to the things the voice speaks.

Now for some, this borders on an expectation of mysticism where the believer is to hear as the mystic hears. But it need not be to this degree of physicality at all. The majority of believers hear in the heart. They sense in that inner ear the direction and fellowship of the Lord. It is the awareness of His presence and the sense of knowing what is expected that serves the target of the analogy here.

the sheep follow him . . When he puts forth all his own, he goes ahead of them, and the sheep follow him

We might expect as with all animals that freedom from confinement would occasion immediate escape. But not so with sheep if accustomed to the care of the shepherd. This takes a conditioning process, since from the wild (or if newly purchased from someone else) the shepherd himself is a stranger. So the trust is cultivated and once gained, no fear of escape is warranted.

Now the picture might be taken too far so as to imply that the shepherd could, in effect, walk out in front with no thought to the rear whatsoever. In Jesus' earlier example of the ninety and nine, the emphasis was on the propensity to stray. So while the shepherd can lead by walking ahead, this does not imply that his attention and actions to the rear are unnecessary. In fact, a dog or two have been ready and efficient means of keeping strays in line.

But the point is that it is not like herding ostriches, where gaining even a few dozen yards would be a major accomplishment. The sheep generally follow, and that easily by means of something as simple as the human voice.

but they did not understand what those things were which He had been saying to them.

'figure of speech' is the word in Greek for parable – *'paroim* So the writer is telling us that Jesus did intend this to mean more than animal husbandry. We are used to seeing this in hindsight, so it is easy to draw in the application. But the disciples are just beginning, not to mention that the key to the hearing – the gift of the Holy Spirit – had not yet been given.

He is describing the state of things when He leaves. This is important because during His ministry it was easy to fall back on His very real, very audible voice and His actual presence for all the guidance they needed. But this could not be permanent; and if not, then cultivating the skill of hearing without Him being present was needed.

I am the door of the sheep. "All who came before Me are thieves and robbers,

It is interesting that He does not identify here with the shepherd of the sheep, but rather with the door. The door is the opening of opportunity to pasture and nourishment. As Messiah and Savior, Jesus has an essential role as a doorway or gate through which man gains access to the spiritual nourishment longed for in every soul. The Temple curtain will be rent, opening access formerly barred.

It is not that He shouldn't be seen as the shepherd, but that here He prefers to be seen as the Door.

"All who came before" is hyperbole meant to apply to those immediately before Him, as in the present leaders, but might extend to centuries past. But we should not understand Him to include Abraham, Moses, David, the prophets, etc. These were hardly thieves and robbers.

He is speaking of all persons who have come in the manner of the analogy, with ulterior motives other than the true care of the house of faith. We learn further from His additional indictments that the Pharisees are meant because of the motives underlying their service and the selfishness and personal gain behind it.

but the sheep did not hear them.

But they did hear them, especially if the Pharisees are to be charged with leading people astray.

In this case, observing the analogy of the sheep and its context is extremely helpful. The sheep recognize their own shepherd but not that of a stranger. If the sheep of one shepherd were to be sold and mixed in with the sheep of a stranger, these last would not recognize (hear) the voice of their new caretaker. They would be the "odd men out."

This is the teaching being described with respect to believers. Those who had come to know the voice of God in faith came under new caretakers. These they viewed with skepticism and caution. These also flocked to Jesus at His coming because they recognized Him as the voice of God, their true Shepherd.

This introduces that notion of the Remnant, the faithful in all ages. They seek true righteousness and as such come to recognize it and thirst after it. When the false comes along, they react accordingly.

if anyone enters through Me, he will be saved, and will go in and out and find pasture.

Here we find why Jesus identified with the door instead of the shepherd. The door is the way out to find pasture, the door is the path to salvation.

This lays aside the notion that Christianity is a spectator sport. One takes in nourishment for the activity of living. Nourishment and doing go hand in hand. Receiving only and giving nothing is not the life intended.

"The thief comes only to steal and kill and destroy; I came that they may have life, and have it abundantly.

Again the intent of the thief is contrasted. It is not a care for the sheep but rather to have and to destroy. It is difficult to believe that there are those even in the Church itself who are sold to the enemy and desire to undermine the Church of the New Testament, preferring instead the church of their own making. What is desperately sad is the deception that such people believe they are serving the needs of truth and therefore the needs of God. It is the deception that respects God but despises the Church.

In contrast, Jesus came to bring life not destruction. This is the first mention of an abundant life. It was described figuratively at the well with the woman of Sycchar to whom He described a life as a river of living water.

We note that Jesus does nothing partially or half way. His healing is complete and full. His death will be fully satisfactory as the payment for sin. And the life He offers is not just an addition to life already in place, but a life that will be lived abundantly. Abundant means 'plenty to go around,' nothing lacking. It is the life intended by the Father for all who believe. It is paradise regained, Adam returning to life before the Fall.

But He now changes the discussion to something more enigmatic.

"I am the good shepherd; the good shepherd lays down His life for the sheep."

Here the analogy disconnects from living practice, in that shepherds were never seen dying for their herd. But we see next in the comparison with the hired hand, that the true shepherd was willing to put his life in danger for the safety of the sheep. This aspect of shepherding Jesus borrows to show that He will go further – to actually sacrifice Himself on their behalf.

"He who is a hired hand, . . . sees the wolf coming, and leaves the sheep and flees, and the wolf snatches them and scatters them.

This is an extremely effective way to inject again the idea of actual death in the case of their own Shepherd. The hired hand fears for his own life and considers the sheep as expendable to his own safety. The end is that he is saved and the sheep are lost.

Jesus doesn't break completely from the analogy in order to speak of His death, but leans on the shepherd's willingness to risk life and limb to save his sheep. He is willing to stand between them and the wolves. The ordinary shepherd will risk (within limits) his life for the sheep because his role is to care for them. But when eternal life is at stake, the True Shepherd will risk all, that the sheep might be saved.

I know My own and My own know Me,

This is the true relationship of the believer and the Son. We have no fear of Christ saying to us, "I never knew you." nor is He ever without the knowledge that His own know Him.

This is a kind of knowing that the rationalistic humanist rejects because he cannot accept that real knowledge can come by faith. It is metaphysics, which specifically means beyond those validating means which verify that knowing has occurred.

But the Bible proclaims that God sets the rules for how knowing occurs and by what means, not man. The fact that faith doesn't bring knowledge that can be verified in a laboratory does not mean faith cannot convey knowledge otherwise. It's truth can be just as real as New York City. It simply can't be conveyed to others like the truth of New York City. It must instead be perceived in each sole individually.

The truth that is in Christ is not transferable to the next person by witnessing, else salvation would be largely a matter of fact, like New York City is a fact. Instead, that truth must be experienced internally in the soul, for which witnessing leads the individual to perceive it. We all share a common faith not because we got it from each other, but because we each got it from the same Lord and God who unites us in that one truth.

"I have other sheep, which are not of this fold; . . . and they will become one flock with one shepherd.

This verse is often used to justify the diversity of Christianity apart from NT apostolic tradition where "not of this fold" is understood to mean not of the disciples Jesus is teaching. This meaning gains support from the earlier verse in which Jesus condoned the work of a man not walking with them (Mark 9:38ff.)

Others, such as Mormons, see the verse pointing to their own future coming as separate from the Catholic-Protestant traditions.

The question is whether *'this fold'* is meant to describe the apostles or Christianity within Judaism. If the former, then Protestantism was anticipated. If the latter, then the Gentiles were intended.

The best rendering is the latter for the following reasons. Schism would not be so benignly characterized, and the qualifier of unity *"they will become one flock"* certainly does not characterize the relationship between Catholics and Protestants, even yet.

The Mormon meaning is likewise ruled out for similar reasons – since it began on the basis that current Christianity was an abomination, which is not an argument for unity but for replacement.

That the Gentiles were in view is clear from other verses in the NT (Matt 4:16, Acts 10:11, Rom 11:12ff.)

because I lay down My life so that I may take it again.

This is the first real reference in this subject to the hope of His Resurrection. Talk thus far had been about His death and their despondency and confusion was notable if final and absolute.

Note that the life is not given again from without, but He Himself takes it again. It is to say that the Son would survive the death of Jesus as man, yet be present to take up again His physical life, because He would live outside the events of His death and burial. And He speaks of this being possible because of His authority to do so.

"No one has taken it away from Me, but I lay it down on My own initiative.

Here we gain insight that the death of Christ was not a misfortune that the Father had to fix. It was not an inevitability because of man's evil ways. It was part of the plan – to lay down His life willingly. There was a transaction between Father and Son in which the Son agreed to die.

This is necessary in redemption because redemption means the payment due is paid by someone else. And in seeking someone else, no living man could pay it because, having sins, they could only pay for their own; and this was not the desire of God. Justice demanded man pay with his own life but love sought salvation through the sacrifice of another.

The incarnate Son was the only means whereby a perfect, sinless sacrifice could die for the sins of others.

Now to some extent this explanation seems silly to the atheist. If God was disposed to let man off, why not do so and avoid having an innocent man die. If the reason an innocent man must die is because of the rules, change the rules.

But irreverent men cannot comprehend the needs of divine justice. They think only in utilitarian terms – get the job done, do the practical thing.

This commandment I received from My Father."

This completes the picture of the transaction - the covenant - made between Father and Son. He agrees willingly and the Father, by commandment, gives the Son authority (including all power) to take it up again. [38]

We are not to infer that if the Son needed a commandment He was in some way less than God. Communication within the Godhead is comprised of decrees, or expressions of divine will. They are words of agreement between Persons, but man is not to take them as commands given from the superior to the inferior.

Note that He is not given this of the Father after the death, but received it before the present. It is a dialog that had already occurred between Father and Son.

A division occurred again among the Jews because of these words.

We are reminded that Jesus is actually speaking such enigmatic words to a mixed crowd. To His detractors it is evidence of more madness. To those now drawn closer to Him these words are combined with the event that had just happened – the healing of the blind man. Though they may not understand Him, He has *"opened the eyes of the blind"* and since demons do not do this, neither can the words be those of demons.

Luke 9:51-56, Luke 17:11-19
51 When the days were approaching for His ascension, He was determined to go to Jerusalem; 52 and He sent messengers on ahead of Him, and they went and entered a village of the Samaritans to make arrangements for Him. 53 But they did not receive Him, because He was traveling toward Jerusalem. 54 When His disciples James and John saw this, they said, "Lord, do You want us to command fire to come down from heaven and consume them?" 55 But He turned and rebuked them, [and said, "You do not know what kind of spirit you are of; 56 for the Son of Man did not come to destroy men's lives, but to save them."] And they went on to another village. (Luke 9:51-56)

11 While He was on the way to Jerusalem, He was passing between Samaria and Galilee. 12 As He entered a village, ten leprous men who stood at a distance met Him; 13 and they raised their voices, saying, "Jesus, Master, have mercy on us!" 14 When He saw them, He said to them, "Go and show yourselves to the priests." And as they were going, they were cleansed. 15 Now one of them, when he saw that he had been healed, turned back, glorifying God with a loud voice, 16 and he fell on his face at His feet, giving thanks to Him. And he was a Samaritan. 17 Then Jesus answered and said, "Were there not ten cleansed? But the nine--where are they? 18 "Was no one found who returned to give glory to God, except this foreigner?" 19 And He said to him, "Stand up and go; your faith has made you well."

Commentary

When the days were approaching for His ascension, He was determined to go to Jerusalem;

The scene has now changed and an unknown time period has elapsed. His last scene was in fact in Jerusalem in the Temple and then with the man born blind. But He is here described as coming from Samaria into Galilee on His way back to Jerusalem, yet we see no account of His subsequent journey that far north before this point.

---

[38] Berkhof, Systematic Theology, Eerdmans, 1976 p. 283

We marvel that a man would willingly purpose to begin the process of his persecution and death. And even more in that Jesus certainly knew the intensity of the scourging and the pain of the Cross ahead of Him. We've seen the intensity portrayed in films like *The Passion Of The Christ*. [39] Were mortal man to have mustered some semblance of courage and entered into a noble agreement to suffer for so high a cause, we might find as the first blows come we are reeling with hands raised to stop and renegotiate the agreement.

Not so with our Lord. He knew more realistically than we what was ahead, yet *determined to go to Jerusalem.*

We see that while the path included the Cross, the focus was on the Ascension. It was the unerring truth that deliverance and glory were assured on the other side that served the needs of His Passion. It was the completed work not the cost that moved Him. So great and momentous was the plan of salvation and His willingness to be the suffering component in its plan.

and He sent messengers on ahead of Him, . . . a village of the Samaritans . . But they did not receive Him

The path to Jerusalem necessarily passed through villages occupied by Samaritans. It is because they knew of His intent to go up to Jerusalem that they withdrew hospitality. We can assume the news of His encounter with the woman of Samaria was now known, but His intent to authenticate Judaism by going to the city turned sentiments against Him.

"Lord, do You want us to command fire to come down from heaven and consume them?"

We see here the immaturity yet in the disciples and the glibness with which they make such a suggestion. They were talking about the deaths of real people. It was a case of newly found powers causing them to lose their sense of compassion. This can happen when office and the powers of office take too much of the stage in one's life. It becomes all about operating in the miracles and consequences can become expendable things we treat tritely or glibly.

We shouldn't attribute callousness to them, but more an immaturity that is pre-occupied with the powers available.

"You do not know what kind of spirit you are of;"

He treats them with compassion, understanding and grace (we would have expected, "You dunderheads!")

There are two misunderstandings they entertain with respect to spirit. They are not aware of the fleshly spirit that has overtaken their sense of compassion – *"You know not the kind of spirit you are presently of."* The have thought too highly of themselves and their powers. It is a spirit that will turn godly intentions to carnal ends.

But they are also not knowing of the Spirit by which such powers are made available to them – *"You know not of the Spirit in Whom such powers always fulfill the purposes of God."*

"for the Son of Man did not come to destroy men's lives, but to save them."

This is the state of affairs which should constrain all of their motives, thoughts and actions.

It is not that Jesus' was never meant to ever come as the Destroyer of the wicked. We see Him in this role in the Revelation. It is that He is not in that role now, in His first coming to announce the imminence of the Kingdom.

---

[39] Icon Productions, Tweniteth Century Fox, © 2004

Even in His ascended state beside the Father, He does not mete out destruction. The world is under this grace even now, until the Day of the Lord, when conditions will be otherwise. So the emphasis in Him is to "save" - the mind of which we should be also.

His reaction is not to condemn these Samaritans but to move on *to another village.* That is our mode of operation also. If men will not hear us, don't wrangle with them or inundate them with philosophical discussion. Move on to seek out those who are ready for the Gospel.

This was exemplified in an experience of Chuck Smith (Calvary Chapel, California) where he attended an evening cook out at the beach. Some college students chided him about Christian faith with the intent of embroiling him in philosophical arguments. Chuck simply side-stepped this and explained how once he was wandering to find the truth, but when he met Jesus he received complete peace. He both found the truth and was found by it. He was now at peace.

It was an argument with which they could not contend, and while subjective to Chuck, it had an appeal, as it does in every honest seeker.

But had they not responded, Chuck would simply have moved on to seek out those who were ready for that peace.

As He entered a village, ten leprous men who stood at a distance met Him;

They stood at a distance as was expected, unless deranged or ill-possessed of social mores. The leper was a source of defilement for any Jew, and as such, their compassion for others dictated that whether they received compassion or not themselves, they were duty-bound to not spread their disease to clean persons. The leper was to stand apart and to announce that he was a leper when people approached.

How they met him is not described in detail except to say that they came close enough for dialog.

they raised their voices, saying, "Jesus, Master, have mercy on us!"

So they had heard of Him enough to regard Him as Master. The Greek has *'epistates'* which means superintendent or overseer, much as lord is used in the secular sense.

They raised their voices which would indicate that their initial call was at a distance. The call for mercy was the only recourse open to them. Medicine was of no use, nor would the disease simply go away on its own. It was a death sentence unless healed by divine intervention.

Mercy is invoked because the call to God's healing for them must necessarily choose not to hold their sins against them as a conditional. So it was not *"have compassion on our plight"* but *"have mercy in spite of our unworthiness."* Mercy is a word about guilt and punishment, not about empathy for one's condition.

"Go and show yourselves to the priests." And as they were going, they were cleansed.

Jesus intends to put in the hands of the Pharisees more evidence that He is not in league with the devil. They are about to see another instance of deliverance to a faithful life from an unspeakable evil.

Note that they were not healed first. No formal exercise of laying on of hands, no miracle coming upon them at His touch. They are to go in faith with nothing yet changed and on the way they will be cleansed.

This is incredible power that does not need a mechanism or an avenue of dispensation, such as touch, to be effected. It can be willed and nature complies.

Now one of them, . . turned back, glorifying God with a loud voice,

One of the ten has the sense of gratitude a person of faith and humility would perceive in such a moment. It takes humility because one must have the notion that this is undeserved, hence, thanks is in order. The others lacked this. They were glad to be relieved of their malady, but in some sense it was regarded as some new found deservedness, as the final rectifying of a huge mistake.

What is remarkable is that this one man is also a Samaritan in whom some degree of arrogance and pride was a matter of circumstance.

"Was no one found who returned to give glory to God, except this foreigner?"

The wording is an indictment against the others and may indicate that they were Jews. But even if not, it is his attitude that condemns the rest of stubborn Judaism, who refused to acknowledge the truth of God in their midst. It takes a foreigner to demonstrate gratitude and thanksgiving.

"Stand up and go; your faith has made you well."

Does this mean that the others were in fact not healed since Jesus now pronounces it so? The Scripture does say they were healed as they went. So we are to treat what is said to the one man as a confirmation not a condition. The others were healed unconditionally, but it will not count to their record of faith.

Should Jesus have healed the others knowing of their ingratitude? We have the NT teaching that *His rain falls on the just and the unjust.* (Matthew 5:45.) There is a difference between knowing ahead of time there will be a sin of omission, and knowing ahead of time there will be a deliberate sin.

The healing despite ingratitude is not a case of enabling evil. It will instead be used to show God's mercy at the Judgment – *"You were shown mercy but were ungrateful."*

But if we have certainty or great likelihood that a gift will be used for evil, we have a responsibility first to God and the advance of righteousness. The beggar in the parking lot or on the median is sometimes hard to judge in this regard. It is not the hard luck story but the sense of flimflam that we need to discern (even the legitimate have a hard luck story.)

A good example is the scene in *Falling Down* [40] with Michael Douglas, where a homeless person asks for a handout and throws the lunch offered to him on the ground, demanding money. He chases Douglas and resorts to things like, "Just give me your money!" To comply would not be mercy but an enabling of evil.

---

[40] Warner Bros. 1993

Luke 10:1-24, Matthew 11:20-27

1 Now after this the Lord appointed seventy others, and sent them in pairs ahead of Him to every city and place where He Himself was going to come. 2 And He was saying to them, "The harvest is plentiful, but the laborers are few; therefore beseech the Lord of the harvest to send out laborers into His harvest. 3 "Go; behold, I send you out as lambs in the midst of wolves. 4 "Carry no money belt, no bag, no shoes; and greet no one on the way. 5 "Whatever house you enter, first say, `Peace be to this house.' 6 "If a man of peace is there, your peace will rest on him; but if not, it will return to you. 7 "Stay in that house, eating and drinking what they give you; for the laborer is worthy of his wages. Do not keep moving from house to house. 8 "Whatever city you enter and they receive you, eat what is set before you; 9 and heal those in it who are sick, and say to them, `The kingdom of God has come near to you.'

10 "But whatever city you enter and they do not receive you, go out into its streets and say, 11 `Even the dust of your city which clings to our feet we wipe off in protest against you; yet be sure of this, that the kingdom of God has come near.' 12 "I say to you, it will be more tolerable in that day for Sodom than for that city. 13 "Woe to you, Chorazin! Woe to you, Bethsaida! For if the miracles had been performed in Tyre and Sidon which occurred in you, they would have repented long ago, sitting in sackcloth and ashes. 14 "But it will be more tolerable for Tyre and Sidon in the judgment than for you. 15 "And you, Capernaum, will not be exalted to heaven, will you? You will be brought down to Hades! 16 "The one who listens to you listens to Me, and the one who rejects you rejects Me; and he who rejects Me rejects the One who sent Me."

17 The seventy returned with joy, saying, "Lord, even the demons are subject to us in Your name." 18 And He said to them, "I was watching Satan fall from heaven like lightning. 19 "Behold, I have given you authority to tread on serpents and scorpions, and over all the power of the enemy, and nothing will injure you. 20 "Nevertheless do not rejoice in this, that the spirits are subject to you, but rejoice that your names are recorded in heaven."

21 At that very time He rejoiced greatly in the Holy Spirit, and said, "I praise You, O Father, Lord of heaven and earth, that You have hidden these things from the wise and intelligent and have revealed them to infants. Yes, Father, for this way was well-pleasing in Your sight. 22 "All things have been handed over to Me by My Father, and no one knows who the Son is except the Father, and who the Father is except the Son, and anyone to whom the Son wills to reveal Him." 23 Turning to the disciples, He said privately, "Blessed are the eyes which see the things you see, 24 for I say to you, that many prophets and kings wished to see the things which you see, and did not see them, and to hear the things which you hear, and did not hear them."

Commentary

Now after this the Lord appointed seventy others,

The appointment of the seventy is a subject of lesser exposition in part because so much focus is on the Twelve, but also because not much more information is given than we have here.

What we do learn about this is that some seventy other persons had become followers to the degree of faith and commitment that they were available to be sent to the work in assigned towns. Getting things started in ministry is the hardest part of any work. It is a matter of breaking folks away from their current expectations and wishes to something new, and that must be based on a genuine belief that captures the significance and desire of the work to be done.

So we see here the long term effect of all the preaching and miracles – the beginning of a self-motivated Christian community, not merely a man and his disciples walking about. To have seventy such persons available and dedicated would be an encouragement to anyone in ministry. And these are not just congregants in a church somewhere, acting gracious and expectant with the new minister. These are people ready to walk out with instructions to do the work of the Gospel.

and sent them in pairs

Partly for protection and for companionship, but also for effectiveness. The weaker man can benefit from observing the stronger one. The less eloquent can learn from the verbally adept. The shy can learn from the gregarious.

But also the one can pray while the other ministers, the one can add support and insight to the witness of the other. In church visitation programs, often a new Christian is taken out with an experienced Christian to observe and learn the skills of approaching unchurched people, answering questions and giving encouragement in joining the house of faith.

to every city and place where He Himself was going to come.

The places were those along the path toward Jerusalem. We see that they go but they weren't intended to stay until He arrived, since we see them returning with their reports. They were acting much like heralds and forerunners, but this included preaching and miracles.

"The harvest is plentiful, but the laborers are few;

This is the goal, the objective of the work – a reaping and gathering in of a living harvest of souls. This is connected with the preaching of the Kingdom. The gathering is for its citizens, those who will occupy it and live in it. So the sea of humanity before them is seen as a harvest where one by one the citizens are acquired in faith.

The laborers are few because the work is yet new, but also because the world is used to its present path and change is not welcomed by everyone. It takes a catching sight of the new thing happening and enough excitement about it to abandon one's former life, or enough of it to be available for its purposes.

Hence, He appeals to the prayer, *"therefore beseech the Lord of the harvest to send out laborers into His harvest."*

This tells us also that people are ready to be gathered in harvest. The time of harvest implies that the grain is visible in the plant, the fruit is on the vine or on the branches. There has been a preparation of the soul that makes the person ready to hear and run toward the newness of faith. Jesus is saying that such a preparation has been made by the Father and there is a need for workers to go and gather.

Nor was this restricted to the beginning days of Christ's Church. In every age since, God has and is similarly preparing hearts to receive Him, to long for Him; such that when the worker in the Gospel comes along they are ready to believe.

We look at the world as an impossible place for harvesting believers. Everywhere is the advertisement of carnal interests and lusts, the human struggle to have and have more. But among them are those whom God is preparing for faith. So the harvest is ever ready at every hour.

The application of this prayer and call is that we embrace the need to be gatherers as well as church members. Beseeching the Lord for laborers means that we should also be ready to join them ourselves.

"Go; behold, I send you out as lambs in the midst of wolves.

We often find this quote away from the context of the seventy and infer that it was something said only to the apostles, since the instructions are so specific. But as we see here it is said to the larger body of workers.

To be sent out as lambs in the midst of wolves would appear precarious and fatalistic, in that the means of predation and slaughter are readily seen (no herdsmen would send his lambs to pasture with a pack of wolves already in the field.)

But this is spiritual language about a spiritual battle. It is not about flesh and blood, but about *principalities and powers in high places* – heavenly places. And in a spiritual battle, being on the side of the source of all spiritual power assuages all worry about being lambs.

The wolves are those who vaunt self or who work for the enemy. The Christian is thrown off by the bluster and fuss of the wolves about them, but the issues are about higher powers – spiritual matters not worldly ones. And the lamb can win that battle despite all appearances contrary.

"Carry no money belt, no bag, no shoes; and greet no one on the way.

There is to be some haste in getting to their destinations, such that they are to avoid greetings and conversation along the way. But the lack of provisions is not also for reasons of haste but because hospitality is expected (and is anticipated as "prepared for") such that they will not need to bring such things with them.

"If a man of peace is there, your peace will rest on him; but if not, it will return to you.

Realistic preparation for mixed reactions is part of ministry. The worker is to approach with a blessing of peace rather than skepticism. The approach of peace will be a test case for discerning demeanor and temperament. Peace will be reciprocated in kind among the peaceable, but an occasion for conflict among the ill-tempered. We have all witnessed contestable outbursts like *"Peace!. Is it peace that God allowed X to happen to me and ruin my life?"* For some, the mere mention of divine peace will bring confrontation and anger, for others a welcome to safety and care.

it will return to you

Not as a reciprocation of peace, but as a ball returning to the thrower from a wall. It returns intact, not taken in or received. Not returned on the initiation of the receiver.

"Stay in that house, .. Do not keep moving from house to house.

The purpose here is to show proper gratitude. To eat and partake and then move on conveys the idea of fleecing the flock. They are to show that they value this relationship and the gifts given by staying with their hosts.

"Whatever city you enter and they receive you .. "But whatever city you enter and they do not receive you, .. "

Healing and blessing are not absolutely unconditional, but have at least the prerequisite of need and openness. We don't see God ready to heal the man with arm's folded in anger against Him.

The Lord desires to heal but so many are not disposed to receive it. Whether it be anger at God or anger at one's fellow man, the heart becomes the chief stumbling block to all manner of blessings ready to be given.

The focus here is on doing the work that is appointed and to avoid the circumstances that will hinder it.

`Even the dust of your city which clings to our feet we wipe off in protest against you;

Rather strong language. It would be clearly insulting and we don't attribute this kind of reaction to our Lord. Yet we are reminded that He called the Pharisees "whited sepulchers" and a "brood of vipers" (Matt 23:27, 33.) So our Lord was not shy of insults when appropriate; however these were not insults out of meanness but as judgments, which He had authority to declare.

To wipe off the dust is to say that even that would retain a disgusting contact with the town and its people. The town is so reprehensible that you don't want to take even its dust with you.

This was not something Jesus newly invented for these occasions. It was a colloquial expression already in place. Thus, the people receiving it would know it to be a condemnation of them and their town.

The modern church would regard this as too harsh today. It would not be compassionate, certainly closing the door to remediation. But rejection of the goodness of the Gospel is a sign of commiseration with the evil one. Men ought to recognize and desire true goodness wherever it be found. It should be a haven of rest amid the struggles of life. But if rejected, one is signaling their allegiance to the other master, leaving the judgment pronounced as the best answer.

'yet be sure of this, that the kingdom of God has come near.'

This is purposely added, as with the case of the good reception, to both work fear and doubt about one's place against God, and to show that the arm of God's mercy is extended still.

In the last days of Jerusalem's downfall by the Babylonians, Jeremiah prophesied that the Lord was still stretching forth mercy to them to repent (Jer 26:3, 27:5)

"I say to you, it will be more tolerable in that day for Sodom than for that city.

Why more tolerable than for Sodom? Sodom committed more heinous acts than resisting the Gospel it would seem.

It is because Sodom did so in the vacancy of Gospel truth, not in ignorance of righteousness, but lacking the clear preaching of the good news as was being done now. Sodom will surely be punished, but these towns more so because truth unlike any before was preached in them and they would not have it.

"Woe to you, Chorazin! Woe to you, Bethsaida!

Chorazin, Bethsaida and Capernaum did not have sins of notoriety, like Babylon or Rome; but rather these cities had received the most exposure to Christ's work and ministry, they had the greater opportunities, and where these exist, greater expectation and accountability exists (Matthew 11:20)

But note, even the effectiveness of Jesus Himself did not win everyone. We should not berate ourselves unnecessarily in our own failures if He experienced it also. It was not ineffectiveness but the incredible bondage of hardened hearts.

sitting in sackcloth and ashes

These were long established traditional signs of repentance. One dressed in deliberately uncomfortable garments (sackcloth is rough and itchy) and ashes were dirty, making your appearance full of smudges and spots, as a person diseased by their sins.

more tolerable for Tyre and Sidon

In these places He had cast out demons. So these are named as places where evil resided, yet they responded to the Gospel. Whereas in Chorazin, Bethsaida and Capernaum, they were not notable for sins, but apparently did not respond in as great a number.

It is ironic that there is more fruit among the truly wicked than among the good men of a community. Those who see themselves as already good are not in need of a saving message, and resent the suggestion, compared to those who know what they are and what they need.

So we have here a justification for some belief about conditions and circumstances entering into different levels of accountability. We will not all be judged the same, so comparisons are illusory and misleading. Each man will be judged on the amount of light received and the opportunities given.

What is halting about this is that Capernaum was His town of choice, His home base. Yet He is able to prophesy, *" And you, Capernaum, will not be exalted to heaven, will you? You will be brought down to Hades! "*

The seventy returned with joy, saying, "Lord, even the demons are subject to us in Your name."

So while staying in one place and not moving from house to house was commanded, the intent was for a prescribed amount of time and then to return. This is not contradictory to His command to remain in one place. That command was to avoid a charge of ingratitude. But to leave the town altogether when the time came would not be so regarded.

They return with completely positive stories of success and wonder. Today we merely hope that such would return as successful. Too often today we almost anticipate a measure of failure or inadequacy. This is in part because in many places the church has become lax in its relationship with the empowering work of the Holy Spirit. Many rely on what might be characterized as largely secular approaches to ministry, and these carry all the vagaries and precariousness of secular ways.

But the message here is that there is success available to those wholly given to the work and who seek the Spirit's enabling.

With respect to the demons being subject to them, He adds an observation from eternity past -

"I was watching Satan fall from heaven like lightning.

We have no direct account of this in the Bible, but a number of references to it having occurred.

Again the word of the LORD came to me saying, 12 "Son of man, take up a lamentation over the king of Tyre [Satan] . . "You were in Eden, the garden of God; Every precious stone was your covering . . On the day that you were created They were prepared. . . You were on the holy mountain of God; You walked in the midst of the stones of fire. 15 "You were blameless in your ways From the day you were created Until unrighteousness was found in you. . . Therefore I have cast you as profane from the mountain of God. And I have destroyed you, . . I cast you to the ground; I put you before kings, That they may see you. (Ezek 28:11-17.)

Jesus is saying that He was there to witness this event. It is meant as an encouragement that a power exists under which Satan must yield; and they are in possession of it – *"Behold, I have given you authority to tread on serpents and scorpions, and over all the power of the enemy . ."*

This is hyperbole – not meant to be a magic trick they would perform in public to gain a hearing. The serpent and the scorpion were figurative of the agents of evil, as He then adds, *"and over all the power of the enemy"*

"Nevertheless do not rejoice in this, that the spirits are subject to you, but rejoice that your names are recorded in heaven."

We can take the wrong impression from the exact words in this statement which might elude us from the idiomatic sense being employed. The wording is for comparison, not for making a choice between the two.

Again, all things are to be viewed in perspective and in relation to one another. It is not a command to not rejoice *at all* in their command over spirits, but to not make it so notable as to lessen the weight of a greater rejoicing – that they were counted as citizens of Heaven. It is a command to keep things always in the right perspective, to give things their appropriate weight.

"I praise You, O Father, Lord of heaven and earth, that You have hidden these things from the wise and intelligent and have revealed them to infants.

Jesus takes a moment to declare public praise for the work being done. It is out in the open, among all present. He speaks to His Father as one would speak to their earthly father, without embarrassment at bringing Heaven into the picture. For Jesus, there is no demarcation line between earthly and spiritual communication.

Note that He is said to rejoice in the Holy Spirit, as opposed to 'in His Father.' It is one of the few places where we see Christ's relationship with the Third Person shown in this way. And it proclaims the marvelous state of agreement among the Persons of the Godhead.

Here we also see the deliberate decision to *not* use the religiously literate and intelligent people already available but to begin work among the unsophisticated, among infants in the faith. They lack the haughty arrogance that knowledge can bring. They have an honesty and simplicity that will help the reception of the Gospel, not hinder it.

This is not a denigration of wisdom and intelligence, per se. We are not better off shedding our learning and becoming dullards for Jesus. The intelligent are here representative not of excellence in knowledge but of the misuse and mis-effect of knowledge. When knowledge is purely for the getting, it ceases to be divinely useful.

no one knows who the Son is except the Father, and who the Father is except the Son, and anyone to whom the Son wills to reveal Him."

This is the exclusiveness that the world rejects. That knowledge of the true and living God is contained in one relationship and one alone. It is a reciprocal exclusive knowledge. The Father is only known fully and rightly in the Son and vice versa. This is not to say that the OT saints believed falsely or inadequately. But they did believe latently. This means that God was in representation rather than in personal intimacy. Abraham and Moses talked with God intimately, but the rest saw God intermediately through their representation. It was mediatorial.

Now, God is among them face to face. He can be addressed and answers can be had. There can be seen an expression on the face to add meaning to what is said. The life can be observed firsthand, not by inference.

This ultimately makes even rational sense, in that there is a propensity in man to see religious truth as singular not multiplicitous. The "many pathways to God" approach is popular but almost always viewed as a compromise to the ideal. Truth is always "the" truth about a thing, not many truths, so choose one. It is either true that New York City exists or it isn't. We don't have the luxury of many different truths about that. Likewise there is an expectation that there is one real truth out there about God, judgment and righteousness. That is an ideal that is here proclaimed as in fact real.

"Blessed are the eyes which see the things you see,

This implies the Twelve, not the whole assembly of the seventy. Certainly the things said seem applicable to them all, but the point of mentioning the turning to the disciples has no meaning if all are meant, since addressing all then turning to speak to all makes no sense.

In our world of spectacular sights, we don't relate to the events of the Gospel ministry as being the most longed for of sights to see. But in the context of Israel's history and the unfolding story of God's grace to men we are better able to see it. These are the most important subjects man can entertain. There is prophecy in the past, therefore anticipation of fulfillment in the future. The goodness of that fulfillment occupied the hearts of faithful men and kings of old. They did in fact long for that day when the resolution of all things would come – " *21 Because the creature itself also shall be delivered from the bondage of corruption into the glorious liberty of the children of God. 22 For we know that the whole creation groaneth and travaileth in pain together until now. 23 And not only [they], but ourselves also, which have the firstfruits of the Spirit, even we ourselves groan within ourselves, waiting for the adoption, [to wit], the redemption of our body."* (Romans 8:21-23)

Matthew 11:28-30, Luke 10:25-37

28 "Come to Me, all who are weary and heavy-laden, and I will give you rest. 29 "Take My yoke upon you and learn from Me, for I am gentle and humble in heart, and YOU WILL FIND REST FOR YOUR SOULS. 30 "For My yoke is easy and My burden is light." (Matthew 11:28-30)

25 And a lawyer stood up and put Him to the test, saying, "Teacher, what shall I do to inherit eternal life?" 26 And He said to him, "What is written in the Law? How does it read to you?" 27 And he answered, "YOU SHALL LOVE THE LORD YOUR GOD WITH ALL YOUR HEART, AND WITH ALL YOUR SOUL, AND WITH ALL YOUR STRENGTH, AND WITH ALL YOUR MIND; AND YOUR NEIGHBOR AS YOURSELF." 28 And He said to him, "You have answered correctly; DO THIS AND YOU WILL LIVE."

29 But wishing to justify himself, he said to Jesus, "And who is my neighbor?" 30 Jesus replied and said, "A man was going down from Jerusalem to Jericho, and fell among robbers, and they stripped him and beat him, and went away leaving him half dead. 31 "And by chance a priest was going down on that road, and when he saw him, he passed by on the other side. 32 "Likewise a Levite also, when he came to the place and saw him, passed by on the other side. 33 "But a Samaritan, who was on a journey, came upon him; and when he saw him, he felt compassion, 34 and came to him and bandaged up his wounds, pouring oil and wine on them; and he put him on his own beast, and brought him to an inn and took care of him. 35 "On the next day he took out two denarii and gave them to the innkeeper and said, `Take care of him; and whatever more you spend, when I return I will repay you.' 36 "Which of these three do you think proved to be a neighbor to the man who fell into the robbers' hands?" 37 And he said, "The one who showed mercy toward him." Then Jesus said to him, "Go and do the same." (Luke 10:25-37)

Commentary

"Come to Me, all who are weary and heavy-laden, and I will give you rest.

The most immediate context for heavy-laden is the requirements imposed by the Law as legislated by the Pharisees. We see this clearly in Jesus' indictment elsewhere – *" For you weigh men down with burdens hard to bear, while you yourselves will not even touch the burdens with one of your fingers."* (Luke 11:46)

So the common person of Judaism was ready to hear a message of rest and an easy yoke. The yoke was the binding bar that teamed oxen abreast for plowing or for driving heavy loads. A hard yoke is one that staggers or halts the team because of hard ground and a stuck plow or an uphill grade that causes labored, uneven progress.

The easy yoke is the task that the animals can perform by simply walking ahead. Picturing man at the yoke, it is a task that he can manage in his own strength, without stress and sweat and without the need for the whip. That is the yoke that Israel longed for.

Now Christianity is not generally considered easy but rather hard to live, so the idea of an easy yoke seems puzzling. But man has the propensity to overload his own sense of duty and that of others. This was historic practice in the medieval church (as also in recent times) - emphasizing a whole architecture of the believer's works toward the acquisition of a genuine salvation. As such, it could be realistically questioned whether the Lord's yoke was easy or not?

The Church was careful not to teach that salvation was works based, but rather since works were enjoined and considered indispensable to genuine faith, believers burdens, penance, temporal expurgations and the like became associated with the assurance of salvation.

This, Jesus rebuked in the Jewish idea of works righteousness according to the Law. This aspect Jesus declared now to be lightened and made easy to bear.

From the modern believer's perspective, what the Lord gives man to do and to work, in general, is easy, manageable, within his abilities. Moses was an example, though we think of his work in major proportions and a tremendous challenge. But in terms of abilities, physical labors, complex problems to solve, Moses did not have to acquire special training, political adeptness, or problem solving skills. He offered what he had and God supplied the rest.

So in terms of the burden, its importance was weighty indeed, but the stress upon Moses to personally resolve the challenges was less than we think. We don't see Moses stressing over the burden (except by misperception.) In truth, what God gave him to do was manageable and he proved this in his life.

". . and I will give you rest." But to be sure, the concept here is rest from overburdened labors, undue stress and anguish, not from all burdens whatsoever.

"Take My yoke upon you and learn from Me, . . . For My yoke is easy and My burden is light."

For each of us, it's the same principle. God gives us manageable things we can do with our present resources and talents. If we are complaining that it's too tough, it may be because we've added things God did not direct or command.

It is to be characteristic of the Christian worker that he is not stressed, not running to meet the needs of his burdens. He is at peace with God in charge and he is in the right place and the right time with sufficient time and abilities to get the job done. Jesus did not run anywhere in His ministry.

"Teacher, what shall I do to inherit eternal life?"

So it is clear that eternal life was not new in the NT. Job spoke a similar question, *"If a man die shall he live on"* (Job 14:14.) It is also clear that the answer was not heretofore understood with definiteness. Seeking answers as to the requirements was still poignant.

A man of God like Jesus was by reputation alone a candidate for such a question. Jesus represented an opportunity to weed out misconceptions, validate others and bring needed clarity.

But it was a formulaic question. It was posed in the framework of things to do not attitudes to be.

"What is written in the Law? How does it read to you?"

Jesus refers to answers already made available in the OT, despite what learned men had done to confuse them. A lawyer was by definition acquainted with the Law because Jewish civil laws were largely OT Mosaic Law. And the subject was eternal life, so Jesus was not asking him to comment on purely civil laws outside religious matters.

Ordinarily, the scribes and rabbis were the interpreters, but there was an expectation that the lawyer would have a personal opinion on what the OT said on the subject. In doing so, Jesus was asking that he not spout the party line, but give an assessment from the heart and mind.

The man quotes the V'ahavta which follows immediately after the shema – *"Thou shalt love the Lord thy God with all your heart . ."*

Do this and you shall live."

Jesus confirms he has understood correctly. Notice that there is no reference to the works of the Law for righteousness' sake. It is a set of relational precepts about the attitude of the heart and following through with actions that involve the whole strength and the whole mind.

". . shall live." But the man is already living. Nor is this a promise that he will live to a ripe old age, nor a promise that he will be immortal in the flesh. It is all about the question, *"if a man die, will he live on?"* Jesus' promise answers the question – he will gain eternal life.

We absolutely must appreciate the question. The idea of oblivion after earthly life ends was and is not logical. What we perceive about life within us suggests an ongoing awareness that should not end. We cannot conceive of becoming nothing without thought, utterly non-existent. So the idea that death does not end our awareness, our acts of knowing, is common across humanity and the logical extension of the quality, intricacy and depth of awareness, and the character of life.

God has always been the criterion by which such a blessing is to be granted – that we be rightly related to God who is the owner and architect of Heaven. It is what He says that gets us in. And He asks that we be both rightly related to Him and to our neighbor.

But wishing to justify himself, he said to Jesus, "And who is my neighbor?"

Notice that his question is characterized as justifying himself. About what? The part about the neighbor.

It is clear by the very question that he hasn't met this qualification with all his neighbors therefore the question now arises as to who Jesus means to include, in the hopes that not everyone will count, especially those to whom he has not so acted. That is a move to justify, to see if the appropriate exemptions will gain him still the eternal life he seeks.

Jesus replied and said, "A man was going down from Jerusalem.."

Jesus does not launch into a philosophical discussion about practicalities or limitations, but tells a story that will illustrate those who will be considered our neighbors – i.e. He doesn't give a list but provides the principle that will identify our neighbors.

Note, it is not a beggar or destitute man whom society was used to spurning and avoiding. Just giving such a person their eye would occasion unwanted attention and appeals when many were interested in just getting on with their business.

But this man in not one of that class. He is an ordinary citizen by lack of any denigrating descriptions. He simply meets with foul play, making all the subsequent avoidances the more reprehensible. His passers by are so prejudiced against inconvenience, they ignore a man they might otherwise have addressed civilly.

"And by chance a priest was going down on that road, and when he saw him, he passed by on the other side."

The priest is the first of the examples because compassion is all the more expected from him. Yet he chooses not only to leave off any attentions but passes on the opposite side of the road, distancing himself as far as possible from the inconvenience in his way.

The plight of the needy can be messy. The solutions are hardly ever simple. People who might help unfortunately learn this and it cautions them next time around.

But the unfortunate seldom have the ability to arrange their trials for convenience. Life for all of us is precarious. We are just inches away from disasters and calamities that could make us homeless or destitute.

Losing one's job at age 55 with most of one's savings tied up for retirement would be devastating because getting hired at a comparable salary is remote (getting hired at all is remote.) And using up one's retirement to live means inevitably leaning on the provisions of the state. So a simple matter like getting laid off can, in a matter of a few months, affect the rest on your life. Getting a chronic disease that has exorbitantly expensive treatment can exhaust all the financial preparedness of a lifetime.

Fixing bad water connections for a poor person's washer may cause the equally decrepit washer to reveal all its latent failings when renewed water pressure is applied. Fixing the leak in the roof may reveal massive termite and water damage that translates to a whole new roof. Life can be messy. And few are willing to dive in and help to the real extent needed.

Of all the sources for help, the priest or minister have the greatest expectation for the simple reason that they are full time in that ministry. They are dedicated to that purpose, as opposed to other men who have secular jobs and duties that divide their time.

The image is designed with a purpose – to show what the priesthood has become by this point in time. It is just another profession with self-perpetuating needs oriented inward not outward.

The priest was focused on what was at the end of his journey –even if it was merely the rest and relaxation he felt due him after a full day of duties in the city.

Christianity has not remedied this dysfunction in some church circles. There are plenty of ministers who look perfectly horrified at the thought of a messy resolution to certain situations of need.

"Likewise a Levite also, when he came to the place and saw him, passed by on the other side.

Technically, the Levite was also in the same class as the priests (they were drawn from his tribe), but here this man is distinguished as a member but not serving as priest. There were at any given time far too many Levites to serve the finite manpower needs of the Temple services. So this man is cleverly identified in the story to exemplify someone who did not have the full time obligations of serving the needs of the people, yet had the traditional obligation to be of that character. As a Levite he still represented the tribe set aside for temple service.

True to form, he too emulates his priestly brother.

"But a Samaritan, who was on a journey, came upon him; and when he saw him, he felt compassion,

This is also expertly contrived in the story – to show by embarrassment what ought to have been done. It takes a Samaritan to show the Jew what compassion is all about.

Now by contrived we don't mean made up with some degree of malice to deceive. It is being composed to exemplify very real conditions of the heart that actually exist, and in this way it is much like a parable. On the other hand it is not impossible that the Son of God in times past observed the very thing being described on hundreds of occasions.

For this reason, the mention of the Samaritan is to heap burning coals upon Jewish heads. Not only is he of the wrong class and regarded with disdain, but he does the very things commanded of a compassionate heart.

His generosity does not end when arriving at the inn, but extends to the man's care after he leaves for his own business – *"whatever you spend, I will return and repay you."*

"Go and do the same."

The first question might then remain in the form, "Are we then expected to care for all the destitute on all the roads of the world?" It would be just the right question to forestall the exhortation on the basis of sheer scope.

But the Samaritan was not praised because he had helped every man, just the man in his path.

Luke 10:38-42, Luke 11:1-13
38 Now as they were traveling along, He entered a village; and a woman named Martha welcomed Him into her home. 39 She had a sister called Mary, who was seated at the Lord's feet, listening to His word. 40 But Martha was distracted with all her preparations; and she came up to Him and said, "Lord, do You not care that my sister has left me to do all the serving alone? Then tell her to help me." 41 But the Lord answered and said to her, "Martha, Martha, you are worried and bothered about so many things; 42 but only one thing is necessary, for Mary has chosen the good part, which shall not be taken away from her." (Luke 10:38-42)

1 It happened that while Jesus was praying in a certain place, after He had finished, one of His disciples said to Him, "Lord, teach us to pray just as John also taught his disciples." 2 And He said to them, "When you pray, say: ` Father, hallowed be Your name. Your kingdom come. 3 `Give us each day our daily bread. 4 `And forgive us our sins, For we ourselves also forgive everyone who is indebted to us. And lead us not into temptation.' " 5 Then He said to them, "Suppose one of you has a friend, and goes to him at midnight and says to him, `Friend, lend me three loaves; 6 for a friend of mine has come to me from a journey, and I have nothing to set before him'; 7 and from inside he answers and says, `Do not bother me; the door has already been shut and my children and I are in bed; I cannot get up and give you anything.' 8 "I tell you, even though he will not get up and give him anything because he is his friend, yet because of his persistence he will get up and give him as much as he needs. 9 "So I say to you, ask, and it will be given to you; seek, and you will find; knock, and it will be opened to you. 10 "For everyone who asks, receives; and he who seeks, finds; and to him who knocks, it will be opened. 11 "Now suppose one of you fathers is asked by his son for a fish; he will not give him a snake instead of a fish, will he? 12 "Or if he is asked for an egg, he will not give him a scorpion, will he? 13 "If you then, being evil, know how to give good gifts to your children, how much more will your heavenly Father give the Holy Spirit to those who ask Him?" (Luke 11:1-13)

Commentary

Now as they were traveling along, He entered a village; and a woman named Martha welcomed Him into her home.

Jesus is now near Jerusalem because the home of Martha and Mary was in Bethany which could literally be seen afar off from the walls of the city. This is our first introduction to this family, that also features Lazarus whom Jesus will raise from the dead.

This narrative tells of the first meeting among many to come. Bethany and this home are a convenient and welcome resting place on the Sabbath, away from the precincts of Jerusalem.

She had a sister called Mary, who was seated at the Lord's feet, listening to His word.

We will later learn that this was Lazarus' house and domestic duties for entertaining were clearly those of the women. So for Mary to sit and listen to Jesus set her apart from the expectations of custom which Jesus is always curious to honor when it comes to the things of God.

This is the position of believers – at the feet of the Master, not talking but listening. Today, this is unsatisfactory for some. There is a certain arrogance and presuming among ministers in our present day that is very unlike the scene before us. Some wish to do all the talking and none of the listening, and one senses that ministry was created as a vehicle for them and their talents. It causes one to doubt how much time if any they spend sitting at His feet and just listening.

To listen is to yearn for knowledge and wisdom from above, to be educated about spiritual things and have their enigmas and paradoxes explained. With Jesus they were not technical dissertations but wisdom for living, attitudes and actions.

But Martha was distracted with all her preparations;. . do You not care that my sister has left me to do all the serving alone? Then tell her to help me."

There is a busyness with duties and chores that can get the best of us and become an enterprise unto itself. We can get so wrapped around the axle in the details of a thing that we lose the perspective of where such things fit into the larger picture at hand. The city superintendent who suddenly has only half the men he needs for putting up street decorations for Christmas may fret and fume on the mistaken belief that Christmas just can't be had if the decorations don't get up.

In our scene here, someone had to serve the needs of the guests. But was it critical? Not really. Can we picture Jesus being terse or petulant if nothing was prepared until later?

But the lack of recognition of the better choice by Mary indicates there is perhaps more than a concern for who is doing all the work. There are some workers in the church who are less spiritually and more practically minded, often in purely secular ways. They can organize work details at the church, balance the books and financial statements, volunteer in the kitchen for the church socials, but they take their leave of mid-week Bible studies and prayer meetings. They often find reasons for slipping out of the church service to do something "important."

Such persons often adopt a rather bossy, officious manner and sometimes show disdain when the spiritual ignores the practical, as in the case of Mary choosing to listen rather than help.

Whether these were actually the inner attitudes of our Martha here we should not judge too hastily; but she does, in her external actions, exemplify that class of busy church people so described.

"Martha, Martha, you are worried and bothered about so many things;

All perhaps with a good purpose in mind, but worry and fussing are indications of an overemphasis on things of a minor nature. We have this propensity to lose our sense of proportion –what is really important and what is supportive or even expendable.

Think of the minister who, before preaching his well-prepared message, asks for testimonies. A member stands only to take up half his sermon time with a truly urgent need. The degree to which the minister is surrendered to the Lord's purposes is measured by how many times he looks at his watch and frets over how he will ever get to his sermon.

The Lord is telling Martha that in the large scheme of God's concerns, the business of the kitchen is not worth the worry she is expending. There is a greater thing happening here - *" only one thing is necessary, for Mary has chosen the good part, which shall not be taken away from her."*

"Lord, teach us to pray just as John also taught his disciples."

This subject would did come up before (Matt 6:7), but we should not assume that Jesus gave no training on prayer whatsoever until now. This request is really more about personal, devotional prayer between the individual and God.

In ritualistic Judaism, prayer was treated as applicable to situations. One could pick up models for certain kinds of prayers and one observed public prayer in the synagogue, but there was always a question as to how one should approach God intimately.

The disciples observed Jesus on many occasions taking Himself apart to pray alone, yet the content and manner of this might have been considered too personal or too forward for questions.

But the occasion presented itself that they ventured the question, and they found Jesus very accommodating.

"When you pray, say: ` Father, hallowed be Your name. Your kingdom come. 3 `Give us each day our daily bread. 4 `And forgive us our sins, For we ourselves also forgive everyone who is indebted to us. And lead us not into temptation.' "

Luke presents a shorter version than that here in Matthew Ch 6. That it is different is not a discrepancy but a proof that the prayer was not meant to be a formula to be said exactly as it was given, but rather a model of the things one should include.

Matthew 6 (earlier) has the following:

Our Father who is in heaven, Hallowed be Your name. 10 `Your kingdom come. Your will be done, On earth as it is in heaven. 11 `Give us this day our daily bread. 12 `And forgive us our debts, as we also have forgiven our debtors. (Matthew 6:9-12)

So Matthew adds "Your will be done on earth as it is in Heaven" and also "but deliver us from evil."

The text for the KJV also added the phrase "For thine is the kingdom, and the power, and the glory, for ever. Amen." but this is not in any of the manuscripts before the 2nd century. It is however in the majority of all manuscripts taken together, but this proves a point demonstrated some time ago by Westcott and Hort [41] – that the majority text [42] is no longer considered the most reliable witness to the originals. The King James Bible used the majority text as its source.

Our Father who is in heaven

Prayer is to be personal with God. We are encouraged to call Him "Father", rather than the less intimate "God." That should signal the many God seekers that the Christian life is different from all other religious life in that man and God are son and Father.

One of the tell tale signs that a person lacks that personal relationship is in their choice of words. "Getting closer to God" is preferred to "Giving my life to Jesus," It's not "My walk in the Spirit" but rather "My life with God." These all indicate a sort of generic Christianity that prefers to be religious but not terribly personal.

Jesus is teaching here that we ought at the very outset of prayer to regard ourselves as speaking to our Father.

---

[41] Westcott and Hort developed an approach to discerning which manuscripts were closest to the orignals by organizing manuscripts by their historical traditions, each of which had less or more authority based on their variant readings.

[42] The Majority Text was a composite of all the readings found in the majority of manuscripts, rejecting those with fewer occurances.

Hallowed be Your name.

The first words are to be those of praise, not petition.

The Greek word used is the imperative from *'hagiazo'* – to make holy, which must be understood uniquely, because the Name is already holy, irrespective of man. This is an ancient form of speech that uses a command to represent an appeal. So it is not "Let your Name be made holy," but that it be regarded as holy among men.

To take the Lord's name in vain was to bring it into ignoble and dishonorable circumstances, to use it as a curse. So while the word 'God' and the word 'damn' are legitimate words in some contexts (the Bible uses them in many places without jeopardy), in combination with other connections the intention results in a use objectionable to God.

In all things we are to honor and sanctify His Name, whether this be the generic title God or the name of His Son or the ancient names used by Moses.

`Your kingdom come. Your will be done, On earth as it is in heaven.

We are to be ever Kingdom-minded, in that we see ourselves as citizens of a far off kingdom that is coming ever nearer in patent fact while it exists in latent fact in the hearts of believers. Jesus offered a very real kingdom, not an imaginary, philosophical or metaphorical one. That Kingdom would have been established as real, political, and earthly, had the Jews accepted Him as Messiah.

That they did not meant merely the postponement of its coming, not as a mishappened coming. Hence, we are to pray always for its coming – the picture of which we see in books like Daniel and the Revelation.

As we pray for the coming of this Kingdom we are also to pray for the effecting of God's own will. In anticipation of that Kingdom, we are to pray that His will be manifested in all things. It is to be on earth, not merely in Heaven. Liberals prefer this to be in the hearts of believers, not in physical form. But this is born out of a low view of Scripture, especially prophecy, which they believe always pointed to the spiritual and was simply misunderstood by ancient minds as literal.

Conservative arguments are numerous and effective in preserving a literal view of the Kingdom, despite the contemplative, introspective benefits of the spiritual view.

`Give us this day our daily bread.

Here then is the first petition – our desire for sustenance. It recognizes first, by the word 'give' that He is to be the source of supply. This, the carnal and pragmatic man does not understand. Man now gets food by his own efforts in the field, by planting and harvesting, and by saving new seed for the next year. It is a system that works quite well whether we pray to God or not. Hence, praying for it seems like just so much going through the motions.

But man forgets where the process came from and what sustains it to continue working. There is a hidden dependency on all the factors that make the process even possible. Photosynthesis must continue to operate. What can man really do to guarantee that? He chooses to depend on such processes replicating themselves by the sheer chemistry of new generations, but nothing guarantees against the next generation of seeds and plants simply ceasing to so operate.

It is also 'daily.' We pray for the day, not the whole month or the year. That is not because the system is precarious, but because the reminder about dependency is to be daily.

`And forgive us our debts, as we also have forgiven our debtors.

The first petition was practical and biological. The next is spiritual and moral. We are to be mindful of our sins and that there is but One who forgives sins. We are to keep short accounts with God.

Sins are described as "debts" because we become obligated to God in terms of a transaction. By sinning something now becomes owed by us unto God.

The raw justice of God demands that thing be the life – *"the soul that sinneth it shall die."* (Ezekiel 18:4.) Man is to forfeit his whole life if he sins. That is why when God in His grace arranged a way that man could still live, something else had to die. It is an economy we cannot explain about God. This is the way the scales are rebalanced in His system of things; and to ignore His system of things is utter folly.

In the old covenant, what was owed was a sacrifice. In the new covenant, what is owed now is a confession (but still also a sacrifice, a petition regarding the blood of Christ, and repentance. But there is a conditional spelled out in the words "as we forgive" or "For we also forgive."

Our request for forgiveness is in the midst of our practice of forgiving. We shouldn't neglect the parable of the man with great debt, who did not reciprocate its being forgiven when it came to a debt owed to him.

And do not lead us into temptation, but deliver us from evil.

One of the more difficult verses in the NT. It is difficult because God is not to be seen as leading us into temptations (James 1:13.) Temptations here mean temptings toward evil, not merely the gumption to do a particular thing. So if God would never tempt us, how could it ever be appropriate to ask Him not to?

For this reason, many commentaries completely skip this section without comment. Others pose this as a way of saying, "Ensure, O God, that we are not led into temptation." But the verb is not meant as passive "that we be not brought into" but is active imperative – "that you not bring us into." So linguistically, this remains difficult.

Perhaps some relief can be had in that God, while not actively leading us, does oversee all the affairs concerning us, and in this regard it is right to ask that our own ways not be allowed to take us by the ways of temptation. In this way, "lead us not" means "permit us not to be led" which involves God in the address, but does not obligate God as the one leading.

"`Friend, lend me three loaves; . ."

The time is also appropriate to discuss the urgency of prayer. We have now its basic form, but there is always the question about how much and how many times we are to pray, especially for the same thing.

Some have the notion that a strong faith need only pray once and let faith have its working effect. To do otherwise is to show lack of faith. But Jesus here enjoins repetition for urgency's sake.

The finality of the friend's condition in his bed with children tucked in is carefully included. We are to feel the futility of the situation. The time for appeal has come and gone and we must inconvenience our neighbor just when we are depending on his good nature and generosity.

The rising of the neighbor at the persistence of the petitioner can attribute more than intended to God. He is not the reluctant neighbor who will be fussing and fuming as He opens the door to us. The urgency is a lesson in the exercise of faith. Is this a whim or is it faith? To lengthen the process of appeal and petition, we consult our motives and the truth about what we ask. We learn thereby and know better what to ask and how to ask next time.

So we ought to be cautious of the warrior of faith who might convince us that once is enough for the truly faithful man. Jesus has instructed us that we be persistent, and not leave off until we secure what we need from God.

Will this then work for a new Lexus? The petitioning process will work to clarify to the sensitive heart the propriety in the things we ask for, as James teaches us that we don't receive because we ask amis (James 4:3.)

"So I say to you, ask, and it will be given to you; seek, and you will find; knock, and it will be opened to you.

The understanding is always that such petitioning is in regard to the will of God and the work of the Kingdom. The things given will not be selfish but those things needed to meet the needs of the work. That will necessarily include food, clothing, shelter, learning, skills and talents, and money. What is to be sought is the wisdom of God, the answers to our questions about Heavenly truths, not the personal means to wealth and power. The doors that will opened are the opportunities to minister and serve, not the private pathways to self-aggrandizements and position.

If we are complaining that nothing is being given to us, we are not finding what we seek, and doors are not opening for us, it's time to examine our motive and desires, our goals and objectives. Are we seeking for ourselves or for His Kingdom?

"Now suppose one of you fathers is asked by his son for a fish; he will not give him a snake instead of a fish, will he?

Another aspect of asking and receiving is fulfillment in relation to expectation. While a Jewish audience, there were notions floating about from Greek mythology. The common picture of the gods was one of caprice and prankishness, which devout Jews would never have embraced, but the more illiterate and impressionable might. If there was any question about whether God might give the opposite of a son's desire, Jesus settles this.

In similarity to this idea, we sometimes have the notion that God wants our lives to be arduous and filled with trials that our character be the more readily and strongly built, fitted all the better for His service. Hence, there is the idea that what God gives back for our petitions is less than exciting, certainly not what we expected.

While this is true to a certain extent, it is not a case of God deliberately choosing to be a killjoy. Jesus here instructs us that like an earthly father, God desires to delight us in His provision for us. He will not trick us as the heathen conception of the gods, but has as much enjoyment in granting our hearts desires as does the earthly father. In fact, more so.

But notice that the "more so" is qualified. Jesus clearly says the willingness of the Heavenly Father is greater with respect to giving them the Holy Spirit. Our responsibility in asking is to have desires of the heart that are pleasing to Him and to seek the gift of the Holy Spirit and His ongoing gifts of spiritual character and empowerment.

John 10:22-42

22 At that time the Feast of the Dedication took place at Jerusalem; 23 it was winter, and Jesus was walking in the temple in the portico of Solomon. 24 The Jews then gathered around Him, and were saying to Him, "How long will You keep us in suspense? If You are the Christ, tell us plainly." 25 Jesus answered them, "I told you, and you do not believe; the works that I do in My Father's name, these testify of Me. 26 "But you do not believe because you are not of My sheep. 27 "My sheep hear My voice, and I know them, and they follow Me; 28 and I give eternal life to them, and they will never perish; and no one will snatch them out of My hand. 29 " My Father, who has given them to Me, is greater than all; and no one is able to snatch them out of the Father's hand. 30 "I and the Father are one."

31 The Jews picked up stones again to stone Him. 32 Jesus answered them, "I showed you many good works from the Father; for which of them are you stoning Me?" 33 The Jews answered Him, "For a good work we do not stone You, but for blasphemy; and because You, being a man, make Yourself out to be God." 34 Jesus answered them, "Has it not been written in your Law, `I SAID, YOU ARE GODS'? 35 "If he called them gods, to whom the word of God came (and the Scripture cannot be broken), 36 do you say of Him, whom the Father sanctified and sent into the world, `You are blaspheming,' because I said, `I am the Son of God'? 37 "If I do not do the works of My Father, do not believe Me; 38 but if I do them, though you do not believe Me, believe the works, so that you may know and understand that the Father is in Me, and I in the Father."

39 Therefore they were seeking again to seize Him, and He eluded their grasp. 40 And He went away again beyond the Jordan to the place where John was first baptizing, and He was staying there. 41 Many came to Him and were saying, "While John performed no sign, yet everything John said about this man was true." 42 Many believed in Him there.

Commentary

At that time the Feast of the Dedication took place at Jerusalem;

"Dedication" is the Hanukkah of the Jews today, also called the Feast of Lights and began on the 25th of Kislev (Nov-Dec.) Families kindled lights accumulated one by one for each of the seven days of the feast.

This is one of the rare verses when the time of year is also mentioned, but this would easily have been discernable from the timing of the feast.

in the portico of Solomon.

This area was on the southern part of the outer enclosure called the Court of the Gentiles. It was a richly colonnaded hall with a second story of columns supporting a higher ceiling than the other porticos in the complex. In artists' reconstructions, it's roof is seen above the outer walls.

Because Jesus is walking in this section of the Temple, there are notable members of the Jewish authorities there also, and these approach Jesus for a definitive answer on his messiahship.

"How long will You keep us in suspense? If You are the Christ, tell us plainly."

Jesus had answered this already but not in terms they wanted, terms that could be actionable if worded in specific ways. He had said He was of the Father and came as the bread of life, that He was the Son, both Son of Man and Son of God. Yet these were ambiguous because if arrested, He might claim that these were meant in ordinary usage – He was a son born of the family of man, He was a son as a servant of God, therefore a son as the faithful can be sons.

No doubt they believed He meant otherwise, for which they desired to do Him harm, but how to avoid His cleverness at trial was worrying them.

So the direct question, "Are you the Christ, tell us plainly." No metaphors, no mincing words.

"I told you, and you do not believe; the works that I do in My Father's name, these testify of Me.

We must also realize that they were essentially asking Him to indemnify Himself and play directly into their hands. Of course, He does not coalesce and gives them instead the same testimony previously given.

This is not subterfuge or deception on His part. Messiahship is more than technical requirements. It takes spiritual awareness if He is to be the spiritual Savior of the nation, and this they have demonstrated they lack, and in fact, are loath to entertain.

Notice the witness of OT prophecy concerning the spiritual aspect of His coming:

The Spirit of the LORD will rest on Him, The spirit of wisdom and understanding, The spirit of counsel and strength, The spirit of knowledge and the fear of the LORD. (Isa 11:2)

And He will be the stability of your times, A wealth of salvation, wisdom and knowledge; The fear of the LORD is his treasure. (Isa 33:6)

Clearly they rejected this in Him, so why belabor proofs against which they are already ill-disposed.

How did His works testify of Him? It is not just the miraculous aspect. If so, Jannes and Jambres would have been able to convince people they were of the same God as Moses. The "testimony" is that of the Holy Spirit speaking to man's spirit that these are the things of God – *The Spirit Himself testifies with our spirit that we are children of God,* (Rom 8:16.)

Now the reference in Romans is about the knowledge that we are His children, but the work of the Spirit with our own spirit extends to many other spiritual proofs, one of which was that Jesus was the Christ.

"But you do not believe because you are not of My sheep.

Class distinction? Exclusive club? In fact, yes. Man in his carnal and self-centered ways is being contrasted with the children of the Father. The latter see themselves as sheep when the Shepherd comes to lead them. But this distinction was not new with Jesus. There has always been a distinction between the remnant of God, who are looking for Him in all things, ready to believe, thirsting after righteousness. And there have always been the other class – the ones who are earthly-minded, caring about self and what is theirs. Is it exclusive? Yes, in that the unrighteous are excluded.

The rub of clubishness is that it is eclectic and snobbish. But the sheepfold of Jesus is open to all who are willing. It is not Jesus choosing His favorites for His team, it is us determining whether we will join or have nothing to do with Him.

The Pharisees made their choice and this bars them from further knowledge and right belief - *but to them it is not given, lest they turn and I should heal them.* (Matthew 13:15.) Their disbelief is also characteristic of the modern man's view of the world. In Christ all knowledge is in right proportion and we are at peace with God and our view of the world. We gain this by being His. We miss this by choosing otherwise, and the result is that we make the best of the world by our own wits and therein is the awful history of mankind in one sentence.

"My sheep hear My voice, and I know them, and they follow Me;

This is not the physical voice by which the disciples recognized Jesus. They hear His voice in the inner self, where the soul perceives. There is a testimony from God there and either an assent or a denial there also.

But this is something that must be cultivated by frequent exposure. The occasional Christian is not going to get this. Consider the relative who calls maybe once every couple of years and when he does, he just begins talking as though we know who he is from the sound of his voice. We are usually racking our brains to remember which of our many distant memories he represents.

But friends who call regularly need no announcement of who they are. We're very used to the sound and timbre of their voice and the acknowledgement is instantaneous.

The difference is frequency of contact and a cultivation of friendship. That is what God desires in us. He was called the *"friend of Abraham"* which almost seems flip when applied to deity, but those are God's words about the relationship, not man's.

We are known of Him, Jesus says. This means that the same Person who died on the Cross, who before that ministered and healed, who walked on the sea, who was there to create all the elements and forces of the universe, knows us. This is Creation. This is what it was all meant to be. God is a Person and He created other persons that there would be fellowship among them.

So it follows that He is not an aloof God, threatening punishments if not obeyed, or removed and apart like Zeus at Olympus; but He is interested in knowing us and having a relationship that is meaningful and worth the giving up of His Son.

and I give eternal life to them, and they will never perish; and no one will snatch them out of My hand.

Eternal life was something actually more precious than the gold of kings. Pharaohs, kings and emperors coveted the hoarding of gold and precious objects, but they all sought eternality as the ultimate object of desire. The Pharoahs prepared for it in the furnishings and security of their tombs and adjacent temples. Emperors ensured their deification by having themselves so declared even before their deaths. It's importance is unmistakable in the history of man, and the longing for it seems part of the created nature since Eden.

Doesn't it make amazing sense that One coming from God would then talk about acquiring the ultimate goal before all men's eyes – eternal life? And He here has the boldness to say that He can grant it to whom He chooses.

"they will never perish . ."

Which is to mean awareness and perception of self in existence, not precluding a physical perishing, since all believers of past ages have died. What we consider living is the sum total of experiences and awareness moment by moment. Our life is a continuum of that awareness, and no one really accepts the idea that it will one day just cease, that we will become nothing, consigned to oblivion - not in a new place to be but completely without being at all.

That is the promise of Jesus to those who are His.

"no one will snatch them . ."

Which indicates that there will be those who will try. There will be attacks and sorties to get us back into our former state. But we are to consider ourselves safe and without fear that the cart may be upset and we be thrown out on a whim. Nor can someone else steal us back again. This is marvelous confidence against the devil. Though he desire to sift us like wheat, nothing he can do will undo that state of belonging to Christ.

The Jews picked up stones again to stone Him.

He is not arrested because again this means a trial before the Sanhedrin, and while they all hated Him and His teaching, one needed charges that would stick and pass scrutiny. These they did not have ready and arranged, and their experiences in seeking witnesses yielded ambiguity.

He has not said expressly, "I am your God" nor has He said, "I am Messiah." He has spoken positively and encouragingly about eternal life, about hearing the voice of the Shepherd; and His statement that He had the power to give it to them might be seen as merely the words of a deranged person, not someone trying to undermine the faith of Israel.

But His words were personally intolerable, and lacking the readiness of a formal trial some ventured to short circuit the process by doing away with Him and facing the consequences later.

"I showed you many good works from the Father; for which of them are you stoning Me?"

Jesus knows full well that they are not upset with His works but with His claims which they consider blasphemous. But they have come to call it blasphemy because they have not discerned the nature of His deeds. His mention of the works despite knowing that blasphemy is the issue is to get them to once again engage their incongruent logic – can a man be blasphemous who does the things this man does?

It is an irony because they are coming against Him knowing the works, and to get their focus back on the import of the works He asks them to name the work. Which of course they are loath to do because it would undermine the force of any charge of blasphemy, so they resort to isolating the issue to blasphemy – *"For a good work we do not stone You, but for blasphemy; and because You, being a man, make Yourself out to be God."*

Again, it would seem that this could be taken to the Council, but the technicalities of the case are complicating this move.

It is also supreme irony in that there was agreement between Son and Father that the Son would die. But none would have expected that it would come by way of the Jews killing their own Messiah.

"Has it not been written in your Law, `I SAID, YOU ARE GODS'?

The verse quotes Isaiah 82:6 where the prophet quotes God saying to the people that they are gods (meaning they have the blessing of divine privilege and the oracles of God) yet they will nonetheless be judged in their disobedience.

This is clever use of Scripture. It does not directly apply to their claims because He above all knows that in His claims He means more than this verse proves.

It is rather a case of throwing a monkey wrench into their already frenetic machinations – the notion that there were precedents for men being called gods. It is just another jab that will slow down their wicked plans against Him; because it forebodes the precariousness of a case that might be formed against Him. Things can be variously interpreted, and if so, where are the definitive charges that He has acted deserving of death?

Nothing would be more embarrassing than to have their case thrown out on ambiguities.

And here is that ambiguity laid bare for them to consider – If God called them gods to whom merely the word of God came, *"do you say of Him, whom the Father sanctified and sent into the world, `You are blaspheming,' because I said, `I am the Son of God'?* Christ had more reason to be so called than did Isaiah's audience, yet they wink at the former case and are enraged at the present one.

"If I do not do the works of My Father, do not believe Me;

Here Jesus acknowledges that faith and its evidences should be consistent. He fully agrees that one claiming to come from God should do works that are seen as from the Father. He acknowledges the right of suspended belief where this fails – *"Feel justified in not believing, if the works are false."*

But there is a corollary – if they are of the Father, then belief ought to follow.

but if I do them, though you do not believe Me, believe the works, so that you may know and understand that the Father is in Me, and I in the Father."

Notice the generous grace in this offer. If they have an issue with Him being the source of the claim, then take the works by themselves and prove that God is in their midst and He is whom He says He is.

Therefore they were seeking again to seize Him, and He eluded their grasp.

The sheer logic of this is unmistakable and dictates they ought to be doing things commensurate with being servants of God. Their abhorrence merely sheds unwanted light on their condition and this becomes intolerable, especially in public where their humiliation is all the more embarrassing.

Hatred and rage vacate all semblance of reason. They forsake their cautions and premonitions and whether they desire to seize Him for arrest or to do immediate violence, all is blurred by the heat of their emotions. Yet again he eludes them.

We hear next of His return to the Jordan where John has ministered and the people profess their belief in Him by reason of John's endorsements and predictions concerning Him.

This is deliberately added on the heels of the former to contrast the two responses. It is still the same today. Walk on to a university campus and you can expect laughter and reviling. Walk among the common, the poor and unsophisticated and there will be a harvesting of thirsty souls.

The souls out at the Jordan hungered and thirsted after righteousness and were blessed. The learned and influential of the holy city had long ago abandoned it.

John 13:22-35

22 And He was passing through from one city and village to another, teaching, and proceeding on His way to Jerusalem. 23 And someone said to Him, "Lord, are there just a few who are being saved?" And He said to them, 24 "Strive to enter through the narrow door; for many, I tell you, will seek to enter and will not be able. 25 "Once the head of the house gets up and shuts the door, and you begin to stand outside and knock on the door, saying, `Lord, open up to us!' then He will answer and say to you, `I do not know where you are from.' 26 "Then you will begin to say, `We ate and drank in Your presence, and You taught in our streets'; 27 and He will say, `I tell you, I do not know where you are from; DEPART FROM ME, ALL YOU EVILDOERS.'

28 "In that place there will be weeping and gnashing of teeth when you see Abraham and Isaac and Jacob and all the prophets in the kingdom of God, but yourselves being thrown out. 29 "And they will come from east and west and from north and south, and will recline at the table in the kingdom of God. 30 "And behold, some are last who will be first and some are first who will be last."

31 Just at that time some Pharisees approached, saying to Him, "Go away, leave here, for Herod wants to kill You." 32 And He said to them, "Go and tell that fox, `Behold, I cast out demons and perform cures today and tomorrow, and the third day I reach My goal.' 33 "Nevertheless I must journey on today and tomorrow and the next day; for it cannot be that a prophet would perish outside of Jerusalem. 34 "O Jerusalem, Jerusalem, the city that kills the prophets and stones those sent to her! How often I wanted to gather your children together, just as a hen gathers her brood under her wings, and you would not have it! 35 "Behold, your house is left to you desolate; and I say to you, you will not see Me until the time comes when you say, `BLESSED IS HE WHO COMES IN THE NAME OF THE LORD !' "

Commentary

"Lord, are there just a few who are being saved?"

Among those who followed Jesus, we find a person who has been listening and thinking. Whether to the words of Jesus or the things life itself teaches, this person had come to the conclusion that one needed to be saved from their current condition and the way was not easy. As such, few there were who found it and remained on its path.

So this insightful person asks so as to confirm - were there, in fact, few being saved?

"Strive to enter through the narrow door;

This is not then the wide and open path as many think today. The path to righteousness is not found in that wide panoply of options, all leading to the same place, as liberal religionists and free thinkers would have us believe.

Jesus is here telling us that the truth about faith and religion is narrow, one way and specific. This is incredibly unpopular today, especially in liberal America where democracy has spilled over into religion to ensure that all is fair and non-judgmental. Stand up and say it is one way against all others and you will be vilified as narrow minded, too fundamental, and even fanatical.

This is, of course, why Jesus was hated by the Jewish authorities. He was so narrow in this that despite having things in common with His own contemporary Judaism, He found exceptions even in this from which He set Himself apart.

On the one hand, people today loath the idea that one faith would stand up and disenfranchise everyone else for their own brand of religion. On the other hand, people by nature do actually want simplistic, definite answers to hugely thematic questions.

That the door is narrow, one must take adequately in store. The way will be hard for getting through it, so anticipate it and prepare accordingly. The picture is one of extra effort and perhaps some discomfort to contort our shapes to fit through.

It is wholly contrary to expectations. We imagine a large beautiful city and a large magnificent gate of entrance. No one pictures that the way in will be a little hole hammered out in the wall, around on some insignificant side.

But if the goal is to get through, then one takes this into account and sees how he can manage it. But it will be the determination to get through that will help one figure out how to accomplish it.

Now the question might arise why God designed things this way? Why not make the path as broad as possible? Anything else seems eclectic - "only the best get to be saved."

But it is designed this way to prove the sincerity and honesty of the seeking and to weed out the insincere and self-centered seekers who have ulterior motives, as seen in the next phrase.

for many, I tell you, will seek to enter and will not be able.

In contrast, there will be those who want everything to be easy and of minimal effort. Seeing not only the narrowness of the door but the difficulty of people struggling at its opening to get through will cause many to say, "Forget it."

There is also the notion here (brought in from the other idea that it is a narrow path as well as the door) that many will not have the diligence, patience and stamina for the rigors of the narrow path. People often make up their minds in life about how much hassle they are going to suffer in their pursuit of happiness and comfort, and things that cross that line are abandoned before starting.

These are often little contracts we make with ourselves that prevent us from doing the harder but more valuable and enduring things. They have a firm idea of how much comfort and ease they want in life and when something threatens it, they regard it as stealing precious time and opportunity. Such are the lookie loo's who window shop Christianity but end up going elsewhere when conviction and follow through are required.

"Once the head of the house gets up and shuts the door,

A somewhat puzzling analogy, which western minds often see as adding nothing to the teaching.

The picture here is in relation to the narrow door just mentioned. It is a scene in which there is a master who teaches all who pass by and linger to hear the master's words. Also implied is that there are two classes of listeners – those who have taken what is taught and are applying it, and others who still come by in curiosity, wishing to hear something novel, but who treat the whole thing like so much entertainment. *(There were such as these with respect to John of whom Jesus asked, "Whom did you go out to see? A reed shaken by the wind?" and elsewhere "You piped and he did not dance.")*

But the master eventually gets up and puts an end to the teaching, goes in and closes the door. Those outside stand and knock to be let in or to appeal to him for more teaching.

But the answer from inside will be -

`I do not know where you are from

Now if Christ is the Master in the analogy, then He surely knows all about them. But He is saying that He does not know them as God intended – a true fellowship between each. (One cannot have an intimate relationship that is one-sided.)

There is an objection to this reply.

`*We ate and drank in Your presence, and You taught in our streets*';

Meaning, we have shown some interest, showed friendliness, heard your teaching. Why treat us thusly?

There are those in churches today who are everyone's friend and helper and desire their help and friendship to be, in a philanthropic way, useful to the church's mission and goals, but who have none of Christ's life in them. It is horizontal effort often characterized by the retention of noticeably carnal attitudes and approaches or suggestions.

They mistakenly count such support and effort in "buying" them bargaining power with God in the day of Judgment. But Jesus knows the inner soul and all its motive and allegiances.

Depart from Me, all you evildoers.'

The addition of this rebuff is not well accepted as in character with a loving a patient Lord who would not *"quench a smoking flax"*. Our liberal brethren will charge that this is a mistaken Christianity, distorted by more primitive and ignorant men, taken far afield from the original intent of Christ. "He would never reject those asking to be taught." Hence, they teach that the door must always be open to inquiry. We note that this approach extends into liberal politics where harsh, punitive remedies to national and international crises are obfuscated in favor or humanitarian offers of the "one more chance at diplomacy" alternative. In the end, we find ourselves only fooled by evil men who count on our magnanimity to buy more time in avoiding an inevitable accountability for evil plans and subterfuge.

In the end, we are really obliged to trust in Jesus' assessment of their motives and heart, which liberal people are always loath to do. It would give Jesus too much authority which undermines the liberal platform of not offending anyone. Every person must have some good in them and it must therefore be the fault of culture, parents or circumstances that cause them to make wrong decisions. This is of course mistaken.

"In that place there will be weeping and gnashing of teeth when you see .. yourselves being thrown out.

Again, this flies in the face of the liberal agenda which prefers to see all men being welcomed into the blessings of the Kingdom and none thrown out. For this reason, liberal theologians and ministers reject this kind of Christ, and since that kind of Christ is portrayed in the NT, something must have gone wrong in the transmission of it to modern times, that it contain such objectionable speech in the mouth of a loving Lord.

But it really boils down to the fact that evil men cannot equally co-habit the Kingdom of God with the righteous, else the death of Christ was a thorough waste and completely unnecessary. And once that admission is made, even if by the sheer morality alone, one must then embrace that some will be thrown out while others accepted, so we are at the unpleasant place nonetheless.

And while the rub may come with ordinary human beings thinking too glibly that they have the capacity to say whom, we should really have no problem, if at this bare position at least, allowing the Son of God to have such capacity and authority.

"And they will come from east and west and from north and south, and will recline at the table

Here is described the great Supper, which John later describes as the Marriage Supper of the Lamb in the Revelation (19:9). *"from east and west . ."* is merely a poetic way of indicating "from everywhere", meaning that the guests are innumerable and from every place, which also indicates a prediction that faith will have been promulgated and believed in every place.

If the cultural analogy is to hold then we have a scene in which the bridegroom and bride are the ones honored at a dinner prepared by family and friends in honor of their marriage – the equivalent to both the rehearsal dinner and post-ceremony reception in today's terms. But the guests who are the subject in Jesus' teaching here are those invited, not the bride herself.

This would appear then to separate believers into classes – those who are considered the bride and those who are merely guests, which creates a problem because there ought to be but one class of all believers – no distinctions – as Paul teaches, *"neither Jew nor Greek, neither slave nor free."*

Can it be that invited guests to the marriage supper are not members of the Kingdom? But if not, how are they set apart as mere guests, when elsewhere we hear that believers as part of the Church are His bride? We read in Revelation Chapter 21 that the new Jerusalem is the bride and it features both a reference to the twelve tribes of Israel and the twelve apostles, making it a reference to the whole company of all believers.

But some interpret this teaching of Jesus as a very general reference to the enjoyment *all* have at a marriage supper with a de-emphasis on who are guests and who is the bride. It is a blessed day and a blessed time and all are privileged to be in the whole company.

Others interpret this as a very real distinction between the Church from all other believers in Christ, where the distinction is made acute in the Rapture (which takes the Church out of the earthly scene and those who come to Christ thereafter are believers but do not constitute what formerly was instituted as the Church.) Much of this is promoted by the idea that a return to Israel as God's servants necessitates a view of the two groups, united in the same Christ, but not in the same historic or dispensational roles.

But we must take notice that Jesus does not expound on the detailed features in the analogy which tells us that they should not be made more important here than intended. Instead, Jesus moves on to emphasize the different expectations and outcomes in this event. Those who were first in their earthly pursuits may be found to be last in their heavenly place, as those who thought very lowly of themselves on earth will find themselves honored.

And this of course plays into the who attitude of the teaching at hand – that men are permitted whatever attitudes and assessments they may choose, but only those of faith and humility will count.

"Go away, leave here, for Herod wants to kill You."

That the Pharisees are warning him is puzzling and we are hesitant to attribute real care to them. Some see it as a ruse to get Him all the quicker to Jerusalem proposing that Herod was threatening Him while in Galilee. But we have just seen earlier that He was far from Galilee at this time and as near to Jerusalem as any would want.

Others see it as a case of wishing to upset His plans and bring the nettling complication of dodging Herod into the picture, such that He might be ineffective where He was and perhaps elsewhere also.

Still others see these men as among those who secretly admire Jesus and warn Him out of genuine concern, e.g. Nicodemus, Joseph of Aramathea.

We have nothing in Scripture representing such a threat from Antipas but against this being a sort of trick we have Jesus' reply back to Herod, which takes the threat as something real (He had the knowledge to know for certain, and if it were merely a lie of the Pharisees we wouldn't expect a reply to Herod at all.)

Furthering the idea that this might be a lie is the inference that Herod would not have issued the threat since Jesus was no longer in the Galilee, but we find that merely being a Galilean and in Jerusalem was sufficient for Herod to want Him bought to him.

Again, Jesus' serious straightforward reply gives us every reason to conclude that Herod did so order whether Scripture records this or not.

"Go and tell that fox, `Behold, I cast out demons and perform cures today and tomorrow, and the third day I reach My goal.'

"that fox" here tells us that Herod is to get an answer and that means Herod had done what the Pharisees announced.

We are not to conclude that Jesus is three days away from the Crucifixion because we have all the teaching in between and the journey back into Perea from where the sisters of Lazarus call Him to heal their dying brother.

There are two statements of similar nature made: *"I cast out and cure today, tomorrow and the third day I reach my goal."* but also technically in contradiction, *" I must journey on today and tomorrow and the next day;"* which seems to preclude reaching one's goal on the third day.

In fact, this must be seen more in the line of His answer to Herod. Despite the threat, He has work yet to do today, tomorrow and on the third day, all of which have in Him achieving what He must do (reaching His goal.) It is a statement back to Herod that His own goals cannot be affected or disrupted and He intends to meet the needs of the purposes set before Him.

As to the contradiction that He will journey on the same third day in which He would reach His goal is only apparent. Journey to a place and completing the work intended are not mutually exclusive – do one or do the other. Certainly both may be done.

All of which is to stress even more that the intent of these statements is to announce that His work will not be hindered if both journeying and completion are involved.

Making this all the more an answer to Herod is the following -

for it cannot be that a prophet would perish outside of Jerusalem.

This would ordinarily sound as though Jesus intended to confine His work to Jerusalem, but since we know it will take him considerably east, it is a statement of huge confidence – that nothing Herod can do will interfere with that work nor cause Him to be taken or killed outside the city.

As to some kind of "principle" that prophets are not to die outside the city, there is nothing establishing this as a law or precept. It is rather the witness of history that the Jews have done to death earlier prophets near or in the city. Zechariah was so murdered in the course of his activity at the altar.

"O Jerusalem, Jerusalem, the city that kills the prophets and stones those sent to her!

This is again is a supreme irony of the Jews as the people of God. The killing of messengers of God by heathen nations is understandable, since like Pharaoh, they would repeat, "I do not know your God." But for Israel to have done so would never have been imagined.

How often I wanted to gather your children together, just as a hen gathers her brood under her wings, and you would not have it!

Here then is what the human institution of religion begets, when men take light of it and turn into something self-centered for personal gain. They reject the truth in the name of religion.

We see here also the tender heart of the same God who had revealed Himself to them with promises and covenants He fully intended to keep, but eventually they would desire to have none of. The hen protecting the brood is a picture of protection. The chicks are those so seeking and ready to run under the mother's wings.

It is not that the wayward had gotten too far out by mistake, but that they despised the very idea of submission and their own need. It is the bane of many forms of "organized" religion in which man sees better how to manage the house of God, as if God is an absentee landlord leaving them completely in charge. The Pharisees could not be approached with the reality of God if it challenged their own place and authority. Even miracles did not gain their attention.

"Behold, your house is left to you desolate; and I say to you, you will not see Me until the time comes when you say, `BLESSED IS HE WHO COMES IN THE NAME OF THE LORD !' "

This anticipates the Crucifixion, after which neither the Jewish authorities or the nation as a whole saw Jesus again. Desolation applied to both their house and to their land. It referred primarily to the departure of God from them as a people. It was not an abandonment of them as a people, but a departure of His presence. The same occurred in the chapters 8-11 of Ezekiel when he saw the Lord lift up in His glory and ascend resolutely from the temple and into Heaven.

Neither were put into effect immediately after the Crucifixion, but the rending of the curtain in the Temple was a visible sign of the departure of God. Certainly the ensuing judgments at the hands of the Romans, the leveling of the city and the land's decline into desolation are a fulfillment. That Israel remains today without the means to fulfill the OT prescriptions for sacrifice, especially the Day of Atonement and the sin offerings is and indication that these are no longer honored nor would they be received.

until the time comes when you say, `BLESSED IS HE WHO COMES IN THE NAME OF THE LORD'

A quote from Psalm 118:26, Jesus connects the blessing associated with all who come to honor and worship the true and living God with the terminus of the indictment. It is to say that blessing and fullness in the Lord are connected to one's desire to worship God as He is. This the Jews who are present cannot fulfill in any way by rejecting so precious a One as now sent to them.

Luke 14:1-33

1 It happened that when He went into the house of one of the leaders of the Pharisees on the Sabbath to eat bread, they were watching Him closely. 2 And there in front of Him was a man suffering from dropsy. 3 And Jesus answered and spoke to the lawyers and Pharisees, saying, "Is it lawful to heal on the Sabbath, or not?" 4 But they kept silent. And He took hold of him and healed him, and sent him away. 5 And He said to them, "Which one of you will have a son or an ox fall into a well, and will not immediately pull him out on a Sabbath day?" 6 And they could make no reply to this.

7 And He began speaking a parable to the invited guests when He noticed how they had been picking out the places of honor at the table, saying to them, 8 "When you are invited by someone to a wedding feast, do not take the place of honor, for someone more distinguished than you may have been invited by him, 9 and he who invited you both will come and say to you, `Give your place to this man,' and then in disgrace you proceed to occupy the last place. 10 "But when you are invited, go and recline at the last place, so that when the one who has invited you comes, he may say to you, `Friend, move up higher'; then you will have honor in the sight of all who are at the table with you. 11 "For everyone who exalts himself will be humbled, and he who humbles himself will be exalted."

12 And He also went on to say to the one who had invited Him, "When you give a luncheon or a dinner, do not invite your friends or your brothers or your relatives or rich neighbors, otherwise they may also invite you in return and that will be your repayment. 13 "But when you give a reception, invite the poor, the crippled, the lame, the blind, 14 and you will be blessed, since they do not have the means to repay you; for you will be repaid at the resurrection of the righteous."

15 When one of those who were reclining at the table with Him heard this, he said to Him, "Blessed is everyone who will eat bread in the kingdom of God!" 16 But He said to him, "A man was giving a big dinner, and he invited many; 17 and at the dinner hour he sent his slave to say to those who had been invited, `Come; for everything is ready now.' 18 "But they all alike began to make excuses. The first one said to him, `I have bought a piece of land and I need to go out and look at it; please consider me excused.' 19 "Another one said, `I have bought five yoke of oxen, and I am going to try them out; please consider me excused.' 20 "Another one said, `I have married a wife, and for that reason I cannot come.'

21 "And the slave came back and reported this to his master. Then the head of the household became angry and said to his slave, `Go out at once into the streets and lanes of the city and bring in here the poor and crippled and blind and lame.' 22 "And the slave said, `Master, what you commanded has been done, and still there is room.' 23 "And the master said to the slave, `Go out into the highways and along the hedges, and compel them to come in, so that my house may be filled. 24 `For I tell you, none of those men who were invited shall taste of my dinner.' "

Now large crowds were going along with Him; and He turned and said to them, 26 "If anyone comes to Me, and does not hate his own father and mother and wife and children and brothers and sisters, yes, and even his own life, he cannot be My disciple. 27 "Whoever does not carry his own cross and come after Me cannot be My disciple. 28 "For which one of you, when he wants to build a tower, does not first sit down and calculate the cost to see if he has enough to complete it? 29 "Otherwise, when he has laid a foundation and is not able to finish, all who observe it begin to ridicule him, 30 saying, `This man began to build and was not able to finish.' 31 "Or what king, when he sets out to meet another king in battle, will not first sit down and consider whether he is strong enough with ten thousand men to encounter the one coming against him with twenty thousand? 32 "Or else, while the other is still far away, he sends a delegation and asks for terms of peace. 33 "So then, none of you can be My disciple who does not give up all his own possessions.

Commentary

It happened that when He went into the house of one of the leaders of the Pharisees

We have another instance of a major contention against Jesus by the Jewish leaders – His lack of deference to the laws about the Sabbath. The Pharisee would certainly not be among those who tried on more than one occasion to stone Him (John 8:59, 10:31.) He would not necessarily have to be a follower since others of his friends *"were watching Him closely."*

Suffice it to say that there is enough friendliness toward Him to invite Him in for enjoyment and rest on the Sabbath. We might see it to be formal, but the meal is simple in keeping with the occasion.

And there in front of Him was a man suffering from dropsy.

This would not be a poor person of the streets, but is one of the guests who had the condition. Dropsy was what we call edema today - a swelling from excessive accumulation of fluid in tissue. The most common places were in the feet and ankles, which Jesus would have seen as the man either washed or arranged himself at table. It can be painful but is more often very inconvenient and embarrassing.

Jesus knows perfectly well the hearts and minds of those attending and takes the opportunity with this man to again show who He was and to teach the lesson of the Sabbath law.

"Is it lawful to heal on the Sabbath, or not?"

Ordinarily not a controversial question. For the Pharisees it would always be no.

The controversy here is that with Jesus they are presented with the monkey wrench of doing a work of God that would help a man's condition, and the dilemma of how this could be wrong on a day that honored the God who would be effecting the healing? But if God is the author of the Sabbath law, why not easily wait until the following day? As we will see, it is the most fundamental fact that it is not against the day and its law to render grace to heal. Such was not forbidden of the Father.

They are again forced to be silent because they cannot deny the legitimacy of both precepts, yet they are in contradiction. They are searching for the reasoning that would justify their law while also pondering the seemingly impossible suggestion that their law has been misunderstood from the beginning.

He answers this for them by demonstrating the patent good which could not be denied by anyone present - *And He took hold of him and healed him, and sent him away.*

"Which one of you will have a son or an ox fall into a well, and will not immediately pull him out on a Sabbath day?"

As before, Jesus reiterates what was probably secretly practiced and rationalized on innumerable occasions. So all the fuss about the Sabbath was formal and public but not privately followed to the same degree. Jesus was not here authenticating the private indulgence of infractions, but teaching that the law had been taken too far.

He noticed how they had been picking out the places of honor at the table

The Pharisees were a religious order but like any society of leaders who rule, there comes about a pecking order and a sense of who is more important than another. It plays into an arrogance and haughtiness that soon characterizes one's service. Soon, everything one does is tainted by how it will affect one's position among others.

Jesus knows this all too well and He observes it even here in how they enter the house and engineer themselves to the desired places at table. It would not have been a scramble for seats, since men knew their relative places, but order and closeness to the host would have caused some elbowing and rudeness among the higher privileged.

". . do not take the place of honor, . . But . . go and recline at the last place,

Love prefers the honor of the other person as a preference over self. It is not grasping but feeling OK with being last. The issue with grasping and engineering oneself to be first is more than denigration of others, but a certain lack of trust in the provision of God. It is the belief that one must get or be deprived, as if the getting is always up to oneself. It is saying, "I must get because I cannot count on God giving."

But in terms of sheer honor, the grasping act is blinded by its ambition to the risk of the complete opposite – embarrassment. In the words of Jesus we have the amazing simplicity of how true and legitimate honor is effected – to be invited to it from a place of humility. To toot one's own horn is never as rewarding as having others toot theirs about you.

Now we can imagine what men will now do with such a teaching. They will now sit deliberately in the last places, and perhaps even begin to fight over them in anticipation of being called to the higher seats of honor. But this is hardly humility.

Humility here means an attitude of the heart that is at peace and at home in the last place. Being called to the place of honor is unexpected and surprising. And as for surprises, Jesus adds the following -

"For everyone who exalts himself will be humbled, and he who humbles himself will be exalted."

The world does not understand this. It is backwards to the whole concept of achievement and reward. Those who strive to do well and make a difference ought to be recognized over those who are indolent, so we are taught.

The principle is very similar to rewards, but in terms related to God's standards not man's. He who strives to have his reward from men is seen as having gotten all due rewards. None remain in Heaven to give. But in respect to humility and honor it is a case of just recompense, the reaping of seeds sown.

The humble and lowly will be rewarded with honor and exaltation. It is a compensation for things suffered. Those grasping and clamoring for honor will be made lowly because all their actions in life have disrespected the values of God and others. They will be last as in sense of least. Those more like God will now have places of honor, those less like him will be humbled and given the opposite of the expectations.

Where total selfishness and godlessness prevail, the humility is manifested in not being among the righteous at all. It is the shock that those routinely despised in life for not achieving great things are found to be the most honored, while the selfish and conniving are sent to perdition.

"When you give a luncheon or a dinner, do not invite your friends

Driving this home is another example opposite to expectations and reason. Note the phrase *"otherwise, they will invite you in return . ."* It is a thing to be avoided, not anticipated. It is as though the eventuality will spoil the desired outcome. This is the aspect that is contrary to human nature – that we would see it as negative.

"But when you give a reception, invite the poor, the crippled, the lame, the blind,

Two things form the blessing involved. First , the poor have few if any of the opportunities for such an invitation, so to invite them is to bless them in something they seldom if ever enjoy.

But secondly, it is a blessing for us in that we have done it knowing there is no repayment in store – *"and you will be blessed, since they do not have the means to repay you; "*

This recommendation will have a sobering effect on most people.

The distinction about repayment is here aligned with concerns for self. These are the very things that prevent us from doing them are they not? "What will the neighbors think of us now?" It is a forsaking of how one wishes to be seen that halts us in our tracks.

And that is why this teaching is in keeping with the earlier one just given on humility.

for you will be repaid at the resurrection of the righteous."

For many, the waiting for this is unsatisfactory. It will not only be too long a wait but will be in a form unappreciated by fleshly expectations and appetites. The deception in this is the lack of true proportion respecting eternity. We see our lives out ahead of us as a very long span, despite statistics, and we think only in terms of the here and now. But when we transition to eternity, the sheer size of that dimension will make earthly life but a flash in the pan.

What we have to do in eternity will become what life is and so much so that what has gone before will have no moment at all. Take the young man who is sentenced to life in prison. He looked at life before as defined by fun with his buddies, pizza and beer, school, cars, girls. Now his life is the cell block, the sound of iron doors, mechanisms, the smell of prison chow, the hollering and the dispositions of guards and inmates. All that was lived, enjoyed and hoped before is gone. This is what now defines his life.

Alternatively, Heaven will be a replacement of the opposite kind. Its peace, love, light, beauty and fellowship will come to "define" life and living. The sooner we look to its rewards and systems of value the better.

"Blessed is everyone who will eat bread in the kingdom of God!"

A statement of truth and of faith. No one nor Jesus take exception to it, although Jesus' next words indicate that the man and others hearing it might need instruction on just which class of persons will be so blessed in the end.

"A man was giving a big dinner, and he invited many; . . . "But they all alike began to make excuses."

We are not to try and figure out which man and what dinner. As a parable, a fictional story was completely acceptable as long as it fit within reality, using facets and features with which men could relate. The subject here is not common daily affairs but those of heaven, yet the principles are all easily recognized and understood. There will be those finding excuses for attending, as happens in life.

We should take notice that the reasons are what some might call "lame." One can look at his land anytime, it need not interfere with a dinner. Who tries out his team of oxen at dinner time? And do newly married persons not dine? All of which is a subtle indication of certain disregard for the host and his invitation. These are the excuses for which one reaches when we haven't the stomach for simply saying, "I don't care to attend."

This forms the basis also for the host's outrage at being snubbed – *". . Then the head of the household became angry"*

`*Go out at once into the streets and lanes of the city and bring in here the poor and crippled and blind and lame.' . . . and compel them to come in, so that my house may be filled.*

We might question how this is compensation for being snubbed? One is giving up one of the chief anticipations of a dinner party – the association with the influential and the rich. To invite such as are now described would turn the event into something quite different than expected. The whole scene is now characterized by the ill-manners of the poor amid the settings of fine table cloths and utensils.

But the focus here is on the good will of the host – that he be able to expend his generosity on others. So if the haughty and uppity care not to receive it, he will seek those who will appreciate it.

This is an apt picture of the Kingdom in response to the Pharisee's comment of praise. God seeks those on whom He may dispense His generosity and blessing. And He calls those gladly who will appreciate it, irrespective of class or social position.

It is also a lesson that those whom men look to as something to be noticed have, ironically, no respect for Heavenly things of value. Now the Pharisees existed on the basis of religious values, yet they can be related to the excuses in the parable because they believed that simply their place and position would secure them to eat bread in the Kingdom. They can be related to those disdaining the dinner invitation because they have so disdained the true things of God as taught by Jesus.

So it is certainly true that those so eating will be blessed, but these men are in for a surprise about who will be invited and taste of that table. " `For I tell you, none of those men who were invited shall taste of my dinner.' "

"If anyone comes to Me, and does not hate his own father and mother and wife and children and brothers and sisters, yes, and even his own life, he cannot be My disciple.

The scene is now outside and Jesus feels the need to address the reasons people ought to have for following Him. It is reasonable to expect that many were following Him as entertainment, some in anticipation of miracles, and others to hear His truths spoken. But Jesus was here to gain followers who would take the mission forward. He is not a spectacle but a transformation to a changed life.

He speaks in almost rude and disrespectful terms to get their attention. Familial love was not to be denigrated in Jewish society. It was not only key but an essential way of life. This they got not just from themselves but from their God – *"honor thy father and mother that thy days be long on the earth."*

The honor of God above these institutions was also understood, but Jewish life seldom put this to the test in practical, real ways; so it was normal to think of absolute preference for God in the abstract and absolute preference for parents in reality.

Complicating this further was that Jesus was here enjoining the allegiance due God. But He is not calling for them to worship Him but to the conditions of being His disciple. Discipleship was to be taken seriously, and we have here many people who are following after Him who are engaging all too casually the commitments at stake.

Does following Christ then and today entail the hatred of father and mother? The word hatred (*miseo*) cannot be linguistically weakened to mean "less preferred." Disappointingly, it's normal usage is for attitudes of detestation and the kind of hatred we normally associate with the term. It is rather the rule of the analogy of faith that tells us it cannot be commending outright detestation of our parents in order to follow Christ. And we have the closing summary of Jesus as to clarify this as well.

That rule obliges us to conclude that it is a case of comparative allegiance. It is much like the case of the man who wishes to postpone his following in order to bury his father. Jesus does not ask him to denigrate his father, but to make a choice as to which is more important.

Some see this very distinction in the case of Esau and Jacob – *"Esau have I hated."* It is brought into focus by Paul in Romans when discussing election (9:13). There the context is not divine, condemnatory hatred, but the choices of God as to His servants. God chose Jacob and did not choose Esau. But all would agree He continued to love both sons of Isaac.

Furthermore, to hate one's life, per se, will have poor effectiveness as a disciple. Hence, it is a case of preference, who rules, who leads, that is in question. We are to hate the rule and selfishness of our life in its ability to distract us from service to God.

"cannot be My disciple."

This is not a return to legalism – get rid of all of self and others beforehand, then be My disciple. It is the attitude of the heart and the will to act accordingly. How much we have succeeded in setting our lives in their proper place is not the condition, but that we will to do so. It is a call to a decision, not fanaticism.

"For which one of you, when he wants to build a tower, does not first sit down and calculate the cost

This is a call to assess the cost of discipleship. Today we can be distracted by the indoor activities of Church life and imperfectly assess the costs that becoming a Christian will incur. Often, standing up for Jesus in public, taking the righteous stand among friends is not in the bargain, and the proof is that when these occasions arise, we think it is someone else's duty – someone we say is "called" to do such things.

So like any project we wish to succeed and whose results we want to endure, we must count the cost ahead of time as we do with our earthly projects. Good planning anticipates what is needed so that all is provided to meet with success.

Christian discipleship is not anticipated in material terms but in spiritual. Virtually all the things needed are immaterial, in the realm of the Spirit, conveyed between God and our souls. It is more than spiritual equipping. It is the will to use it, and that will to be separated from the allegiances of the world.

all who observe it begin to ridicule him,

As in the case of the person who cannot finish his project for poor planning, the Christian who takes on discipleship with little or no intent to count its cost, soon faces the ridicule of others, not for his stand for Christ, but for his lack of a stand, for his ineffectiveness.

The atheist will chide us for two reasons: the message and its power, but also when we give him more ammunition against the truth of Christianity in our own ineffectiveness.

"So then, none of you can be My disciple who does not give up all his own possessions.

Here then is the summary that sets the tone and the meaning. It is our allegiance to things and people that must be dealt with in discipleship. Whom do we run after when they call?

Luke 14:33-35, Luke 15:1-32

33 "So then, none of you can be My disciple who does not give up all his own possessions. 34 "Therefore, salt is good; but if even salt has become tasteless, with what will it be seasoned? 35 "It is useless either for the soil or for the manure pile; it is thrown out. He who has ears to hear, let him hear." (Luke 14:33-35)

1 Now all the tax collectors and the sinners were coming near Him to listen to Him. 2 Both the Pharisees and the scribes began to grumble, saying, "This man receives sinners and eats with them." 3 So He told them this parable, saying, 4 "What man among you, if he has a hundred sheep and has lost one of them, does not leave the ninety-nine in the open pasture and go after the one which is lost until he finds it? 5 "When he has found it, he lays it on his shoulders, rejoicing. 6 "And when he comes home, he calls together his friends and his neighbors, saying to them, `Rejoice with me, for I have found my sheep which was lost!' 7 "I tell you that in the same way, there will be more joy in heaven over one sinner who repents than over ninety-nine righteous persons who need no repentance.

8 "Or what woman, if she has ten silver coins and loses one coin, does not light a lamp and sweep the house and search carefully until she finds it? 9 "When she has found it, she calls together her friends and neighbors, saying, `Rejoice with me, for I have found the coin which I had lost!' 10 "In the same way, I tell you, there is joy in the presence of the angels of God over one sinner who repents."

1 And He said, "A man had two sons. 12 "The younger of them said to his father, `Father, give me the share of the estate that falls to me.' So he divided his wealth between them. 13 "And not many days later, the younger son gathered everything together and went on a journey into a distant country, and there he squandered his estate with loose living. 14 "Now when he had spent everything, a severe famine occurred in that country, and he began to be impoverished.

15 "So he went and hired himself out to one of the citizens of that country, and he sent him into his fields to feed swine. 16 "And he would have gladly filled his stomach with the pods that the swine were eating, and no one was giving anything to him. 17 "But when he came to his senses, he said, `How many of my father's hired men have more than enough bread, but I am dying here with hunger! 18 `I will get up and go to my father, and will say to him, "Father, I have sinned against heaven, and in your sight; 19 I am no longer worthy to be called your son; make me as one of your hired men."'

20 "So he got up and came to his father. But while he was still a long way off, his father saw him and felt compassion for him, and ran and embraced him and kissed him. 21 "And the son said to him, `Father, I have sinned against heaven and in your sight; I am no longer worthy to be called your son.' 22 "But the father said to his slaves, `Quickly bring out the best robe and put it on him, and put a ring on his hand and sandals on his feet; 23 and bring the fattened calf, kill it, and let us eat and celebrate; 24 for this son of mine was dead and has come to life again; he was lost and has been found.' And they began to celebrate.

25 "Now his older son was in the field, and when he came and approached the house, he heard music and dancing. 26 "And he summoned one of the servants and began inquiring what these things could be. 27 "And he said to him, `Your brother has come, and your father has killed the fattened calf because he has received him back safe and sound.' 28 "But he became angry and was not willing to go in; and his father came out and began pleading with him. 29 "But he answered and said to his father, `Look! For so many years I have been serving you and I have never neglected a command of yours; and yet you have never given me a young goat, so that I might celebrate with my friends; 30 but when this son of yours came, who has devoured your wealth with prostitutes, you killed the fattened calf for him.' 31 "And he said to him, `Son, you have always been with me, and all that is mine is yours. 32 `But we had to celebrate and rejoice, for this brother of yours was dead and has begun to live, and was lost and has been found.' " (Luke 15:1-32)

Commentary

"So then, none of you can be My disciple who does not give up all his own possessions.

The Christian may rightly ask if he is to have no possessions at all and live homeless and dependent on society? With Jesus, hyperbole is often used to focus attention on the theme. He obviously accepts the clothing with which the disciples are dressed. They have money among their band for various needs. Some have boats and hardware associated with their trade still back in their hometowns. Peter has a least a wife, if not children, and the possessions that meet their needs.

Jesus is not talking about the possessions themselves but our perceived right to those possessions. Do we own them or do they own us? If giving something we own to the poor is prevented by our right to have it, or our need to keep it, then it is getting in the way. Better not to have had anything of this sort in the first place. Jesus exemplified this best in His exhortation *"and whoever takes away your coat, do not withhold your shirt from him either."*

We are to be custodians of the things we own, not possessors. This is very hard in this day and age because necessities make the difference between a life of comfort and one of misery. The Lord does not disdain such things, only our fear of being without them, many of which are unnecessary in the larger scope of who we are to be in Him.

He follows this with *"Therefore, salt is good; but if even salt has become tasteless, with what will it be seasoned?"*

This is not in reference to things, but in reference to us as owning things, such that we become useless, as salt can come to be of no further use. So is the man who is tied to his possessions and cannot be used.

"This man receives sinners and eats with them."

The Jews were always enjoined to reach out to the sinner that he might be brought in to the house of faith – *"Let the wicked forsake his way And the unrighteous man his thoughts; And let him return to the LORD, And He will have compassion on him, And to our God, For He will abundantly pardon."* (Isaiah 55:7)

Instead, the Jews were accustomed to set the rules of compliance within the Law and let the unrighteous make their own beds. The unrighteous were to be avoided, not won to the faith. They were seen as those that defiled the righteous, not those in need of purification from their defilements.

This sets the stage for why Jesus replies with the analogies that follow -

"What man among you, . . . does not leave the ninety-nine . . and go after the one which is lost until he finds it?

We ponder how this can speak to the issue of why He is associating with sinners. Occasions like this were very aptly portrayed in Zefferelli's television mini-series, *Jesus of Nazareth* [43], where Jesus is seen at the home of the tax collector amid a scene we would never associate with a minister. Seated all around and throughout the room are men and women dressed in the garb of worldly life, including women of the oldest profession. Yet they are intrigued and intently listening to every word.

This is to be contrasted with the other scenes in the Gospels where Jesus attends the very proper and righteous tables of the Pharisees, who disdain His teaching, while the prostitutes, tax collectors and those prone to too much wine are taking in all He says and receiving their conviction with humility.

So what does the finding of one's sheep have to do with the situation in which the Jews find Jesus?

"When he has found it, he lays it on his shoulders, rejoicing. . . . he calls together his friends and his neighbors, saying to them, `Rejoice with me, for I have found my sheep which was lost!'

Jesus came to save the lost. Is it any small wonder that the next few parables are therefore about things lost and then found, and the rejoicing that results.

---

[43] © Incorporated Television Company, 1977

If you have come to save the lost, it follows that you be found among them in order to speak to them. That is precisely where we find Jesus throughout His ministry – among that very real mix of the faithful and the lost. He brings healing to the faithful and light to the lost.

The sheep that became lost and was found are those with whom He sits They are lost and He has found them. But where is the rejoicing of the friends? Certainly not in the Pharisees where it ought to be found. But rather in the angels, as He concludes at the end – *"I tell you that in the same way, there will be more rejoicing in heaven over one sinner who repents than over ninety-nine righteous persons who need no repentance."*

Reiterating this theme is sorely needed, hence He adds the parables of the lost coin and the prodigal son.

"A man had two sons.

What could be more potent than what nature teaches right within the family itself? Then as now it so often comes out that we have a compliant son or daughter and then a strong-willed one. How many lessons in life await us in this arrangement.

give me the share of the estate that falls to me.'

More in ancient times than now, there was an arrangement whereby the son could ask and get his inheritance ahead of time. Now this assumes a wealthy family with financial assets stored up in addition to property. (The father does not sell a portion of his property, but rather, the son receives money.) In poorer families without a monetary "nest egg" this would have been out of the question, because the father would have had to sell his property and home while still living.

Today, few parents save up and set aside their posthumous gifts to their children. This benefit comes instead from the division of assets and insurance.

But in ancient times, the overall wealth of the father was viewed at any given point in time as being owed to the children in shares. So a wealthy father could give up whatever portion could be calculated at the time.

So he divided his wealth between them.

This suggests that the other son received his also, which is possible, but it is also likely that the term "between them" simply means a calculation that took into account what was due the other son.

there he squandered his estate with loose living.

Here we have another avenue of teaching available in the parable, off the main point, but of value. With the word "squandered" comes a whole train of precipitating thoughts about the attitudes that would enable such squandering. There are some who grow up expecting much more than life delivers, always envious of what others have and feeling deprived of opportunities to enjoy all of the best things available. So when money comes their way, they make up for lost time and are soon bankrupt.

'Loose living' conveys a disregard for the precepts and values taught by the father, a world view that is selfish and always waiting to indulge one's appetites and wants.

a severe famine occurred in that country, and he began to be impoverished.

True to experience, nature often compounds our indiscretion at the worst possible moment. Not only is he out of money but the times turn desperate all around. The purpose of this is to aggravate his desperation by having no one available for charity.

And he would have gladly filled his stomach with the pods that the swine were eating, and no one was giving anything to him.

The fruits of carelessness are never anticipated. This is simply because to do so is to steal precious joy and excitement from the exhilaration of the moment. It's like giving a child $100.00 and exhorting him to put half away for a rainy day. He is already spending every dime in his mind and the thought of making half virtually unusable is a downer against all the prospects of enjoyment now reeling in his head.

For our prodigal son here, he has come to such a state that the food of the swine appears desirable, yet not even this was given to him. And why? Because he cared little for using his new found wealth wisely and responsibly. And nature found a way of rewarding him for this attitude.

"But when he came to his senses,

It is our hope for every wayward child, that such circumstances will bring them to their senses. For those where some flicker of the light of God remains, this can still occur. But for many, the circumstances end up producing bitterness and hatred for the right way, because it speaks against those desires still in control, whose lesson has not yet and may never be learned.

But for the benefit of God's revelation to man, the effects of nature and circumstances are in fact used of God to bring us to our senses, and our failure to heed them does not nullify the principle. That God so arranges the affairs of nature and mankind will be made to speak as evidence in the Judgment.

"Father, I have sinned against heaven, and in your sight;

Notice that sin against heaven comes first. He recognizes the large issues at play in these circumstances. This is the heart that can be moved by God. The heart that is purely horizontal, purely practical and rationalistic sees none of this. "It is the 'fickle finger of fate', nothing more." And here one is using that term loosely because "fate" is to them no more a living and willing principle than the supposed myth that God lives and wills. It is more "the odds" or the pure statistics that account for things in this frame of mind.

I am no longer worthy to be called your son; make me as one of your hired men."'

Sin is often two-fold in its affect. It is always against God, but also against man. So repentance must involve both. As we receive the forgiveness of God, He turns us toward the one we have offended and says, "Make things right with them, also."

The son has come to full humility in counting himself no longer worthy to be called his father's son. So many today never get to this place. Mistakes merely occasion the search for an escape hatch, an easy rescue. They count on the love of parents to provide a safe, non-judgmental haven from their mis-steps. A place where they can pick up again where they left off, largely unscathed.

But the son here considers that what he has done disqualifies him from special pleadings, privileges and the grace due a son, because he has trampled on sonship itself. Instead, he is left only to value the lowly place of a hired hand, who ironically now has it better than he does.

his father saw him [afar off] and felt compassion for him, and ran and embraced him and kissed him.

Here we come upon the major lesson in this context. It is not the things we can learn from the folly of the strong-willed child and how he comes to his senses (although that lesson is to be had also.) But rather, because of the context here with Jesus, it is all about losing, finding and rejoicing. It is about the forgetting of past sins and hurts, because the son has returned to properly love the father and count as precious what he disregarded before.

Now to be frank about reality, not all fathers would respond in this way. Many would hold the hurt and bitterness of their sons actions, and in some cases, repentance does not mend the irretrievable damage done. But it is for this reason that the actions of the father are characterized as they are.

We are expected to repent before God (we cannot be flip and careless in accounting for our sins.) But unlike the earthly failings of men, we are not to regard God as withholding His joy until we "prove" how sorry we really are. This is a human corruption, based largely on man's inability to forget hurts and offenses and the need to see proper compensation for mis-steps and hurts.

The father runs at the very sight of his son, without pre-conditions being met. There is no bitterness that will make the son pay dearly for his offenses.

That is the point with Jesus. Once true repentance is realized, God rejoices with no conditionals on how clean one must become to be embraced again. It is a ready rejoicing over the finding of the lost. All the parables and examples convey this so readily that we have no basis for stressing any other point. *"' he was lost and has been found.' And they began to celebrate. "*

"Now his older son was in the field, . . . he heard music and dancing.

Here we find that the lesson, despite its positive encouragement, comes with a negative indictment. It encourages the appropriation of the right attitude of the father but now highlights the wrong attitude of the other son (which will speak directly to the Pharisees who, like him, are not so glad about the finding of the lost.)

"`For so many years I have been serving you and I have never neglected a command of yours; "

The other son's focus was on his service and the expectations that come with obedience. What was vividly before him was the difference in service and dedication and that to honor his brother was to disenfranchise his own dedication. "If my brother's indolence and squandering can be rewarded, have not all my efforts above his been a waste? What did my striving harder and more faithfully achieve in the end?" He has clearly misunderstood the fattened calf as a reward for his brother.

This is the piece of the parable aimed at the Pharisees. Like the brother, they were saying, "look at our faithfulness and diligence to do the Lord's will, and see with whom Jesus chooses to associate! We have been faithful, yet this Jesus says there is more rejoicing over these sinners than for us." So like the brother, it is all about comparative rewards for comparative service.

But look at the father's words of explanation –

`But we had to celebrate and rejoice, for this brother of yours was dead and has begun to live, and was lost and has been found.' "

None of these words say the celebration is about service and faithfulness, but that someone thought to be dead is found alive. This is the difference between the son's focus and that of the father. It is also the focus of the Heavenly Father concerning the lost. It is not about performance but about life and death, about being lost and being found.

Luke 16:1-31

1 Now He was also saying to the disciples, "There was a rich man who had a manager, and this manager was reported to him as squandering his possessions. 2 "And he called him and said to him, `What is this I hear about you? Give an accounting of your management, for you can no longer be manager.' 3 "The manager said to himself, `What shall I do, since my master is taking the management away from me? I am not strong enough to dig; I am ashamed to beg. 4 `I know what I shall do, so that when I am removed from the management people will welcome me into their homes.'

5 "And he summoned each one of his master's debtors, and he began saying to the first, `How much do you owe my master?' 6 "And he said, `A hundred measures of oil.' And he said to him, `Take your bill, and sit down quickly and write fifty.' 7 "Then he said to another, `And how much do you owe?' And he said, `A hundred measures of wheat.' He said to him, `Take your bill, and write eighty.' 8 "And his master praised the unrighteous manager because he had acted shrewdly; for the sons of this age are more shrewd in relation to their own kind than the sons of light.

9 "And I say to you, make friends for yourselves by means of the wealth of unrighteousness, so that when it fails, they will receive you into the eternal dwellings. 10 "He who is faithful in a very little thing is faithful also in much; and he who is unrighteous in a very little thing is unrighteous also in much. 11 "Therefore if you have not been faithful in the use of unrighteous wealth, who will entrust the true riches to you? 12 "And if you have not been faithful in the use of that which is another's, who will give you that which is your own? 13 "No servant can serve two masters; for either he will hate the one and love the other, or else he will be devoted to one and despise the other. You cannot serve God and wealth."

14 Now the Pharisees, who were lovers of money, were listening to all these things and were scoffing at Him. 15 And He said to them, "You are those who justify yourselves in the sight of men, but God knows your hearts; for that which is highly esteemed among men is detestable in the sight of God. 16 "The Law and the Prophets were proclaimed until John; since that time the gospel of the kingdom of God has been preached, and everyone is forcing his way into it. 17 "But it is easier for heaven and earth to pass away than for one stroke of a letter of the Law to fail. 18 "Everyone who divorces his wife and marries another commits adultery, and he who marries one who is divorced from a husband commits adultery.

19 "Now there was a rich man, and he habitually dressed in purple and fine linen, joyously living in splendor every day. 20 "And a poor man named Lazarus was laid at his gate, covered with sores, 21 and longing to be fed with the crumbs which were falling from the rich man's table; besides, even the dogs were coming and licking his sores. 22 "Now the poor man died and was carried away by the angels to Abraham's bosom; and the rich man also died and was buried. 23 "In Hades he lifted up his eyes, being in torment, and saw Abraham far away and Lazarus in his bosom.

24 "And he cried out and said, `Father Abraham, have mercy on me, and send Lazarus so that he may dip the tip of his finger in water and cool off my tongue, for I am in agony in this flame.' 25 "But Abraham said, `Child, remember that during your life you received your good things, and likewise Lazarus bad things; but now he is being comforted here, and you are in agony. 26 `And besides all this, between us and you there is a great chasm fixed, so that those who wish to come over from here to you will not be able, and that none may cross over from there to us.' 27 "And he said, `Then I beg you, father, that you send him to my father's house-- 28 for I have five brothers--in order that he may warn them, so that they will not also come to this place of torment.' 29 "But Abraham said, `They have Moses and the Prophets; let them hear them.' 30 "But he said, `No, father Abraham, but if someone goes to them from the dead, they will repent!' 31 "But he said to him, `If they do not listen to Moses and the Prophets, they will not be persuaded even if someone rises from the dead.' " (Luke 16:1-31)

Commentary

"There was a rich man who had a manager,

This parable is among the most obscure and confusing because at first glance it appears to be recommending that one make friends with the world, especially the mammon of the world, and this is so contrary to the teaching of Jesus elsewhere – *"You cannot love God and mammon."*

To understand its proper teaching, let's look at its elements.

and this manager was reported to him as squandering his possessions.

This manager is about to be fired for mismanaging his master's funds. He is given a space of time to make an accounting and in this time he thinks about how he can remedy the situation or minimize the effects this will have to his future livelihood. " *`I know what I shall do, so that when I am removed from the management people will welcome me into their homes."*

`How much do you owe my master?'.. `Take your bill, and sit down quickly and write fifty.'

This he does with succeeding debtors of his master in various discounts. Now this is by no means beneficial to his master, since the master will receive less than is owed. The manager thereby increases his risk of further angering his master. So why do this at all? Why not take his discharge and his master's anger as they are without further exacerbation?

It is expressly because he cannot find other work that will suit his limitations or pride – *"I cannot dig and I will not beg."* So he must apply ingenuity to make a way for himself when the discharge is effected. But If he has friends who owe him a favor, they may help him in opportunities otherwise unaccommodated.

So if he is going to get fired anyway, at the sacrifice of further enmity with his master why not devise some means of surviving it, even if at the last hour. The discounts will please the debtors and make them friends with some obligation to reciprocate.

Nevertheless, we don't expect the following ..

"And his master praised the unrighteous manager because he had acted shrewdly;

He has just been cheated out of money owed. Has not this manager once again lived up to that intolerable ineptitude that justifies dismissal? How is there any room for praise?

He is not praised for the impact of his scheme on the master, but on his shrewdness to take care, even if late, for his welfare in the light of his pending plight. It is the quick thinking, even if for selfish reasons, that is praised.

We may also be overlooking the fact that the debts have now been recovered where they had before remained unpaid; and most people are happy to get most of what is owed than a perennial postponement and no income at all.

Jesus now brings this application to spiritual things, but again in a very enigmatic way.

for the sons of this age are more shrewd in relation to their own kind than the sons of light.

This is to say that the praise from the master is in accordance with his own estimation of shrewdness, as he would measure it, being in the world. The manager appealed to a solution that might not have been fully righteous, but spoke in the language of that wisdom the master understood.

This is also to say that both master and manager were not dealing fairly with their debtors, indicated by a comparison with the "son's of light." As such, the deal finally struck may have in actuality been more commendable because it ended up charging a fairer debt owed than before.

9 "And I say to you, make friends for yourselves by means of the wealth of unrighteousness, so that when it fails, they will receive you into the eternal dwellings.

Now the tougher part of the exhortation from Jesus. It appears to recommend that we make friends on the basis of unrighteous wealth. We know Jesus to not condone this, so there must be something we're missing.

It can be seen as applying to the whole of life in general and the hope of eternal life thereafter – *eternal dwellings*. The "friends" would be a figure of the rewards of good works related to wealth. Wealth is ordinarily characterized as unrighteousness because of the usual means by which it is acquired, the effect it has on our allegiances and values and the change in friendships that can result, not to mention the worries attendant with any substantial wealth.

So to use wealth for good purposes builds up security for eternal habitation. The manager may have ended up blessing the debtors and forcing the master to actually levy a more just debt.

Another variation on this same explanation is that the "friends" are the works themselves in relation to the unrighteousness of wealth, that are personified as those who will testify on our behalf at the Judgment.

'When it fails' is seen as any collapse of the system by reason of famine or catastrophe or by reason of one's death when all money ceases to benefit the holder.

"He who is faithful in a very little thing is faithful also in much; and he who is unrighteous in a very little thing is unrighteous also in much.

Thus follows similarly enigmatic teaching about degrees of faithfulness. It is not to say that by fulfilling the righteousness of a small thing, one automatically fulfills the righteousness of larger things. But the attitude of being faithful will, in general, serve a person equally well in larger issues. It is the principle not the degree.

The corollary helps to set this more clearly. To be unrighteous in small things usually extends to larger things when the opportunity arises. Thus, we tend to refuse our trust of someone who is unprincipled in minor areas involving simple ethics when larger issues of trust are called for – *" "Therefore if you have not been faithful in the use of unrighteous wealth, who will entrust the true riches to you?"*

Hence, the attitudes found in the small things extend to the large, whether of evil or good.

"And if you have not been faithful in the use of that which is another's, who will give you that which is your own?

The older principle was that we ought to respect other people's affairs and possessions more than our own. This was based on our lack of intrinsic right to upset another persons affairs. They entertained properly the expectation to exercise control over their own things, since they and not others owned them. (Oddly, this is not the view today in some people who often feel they have no obligation to respect other people's property.)

Here, the principle is applied to business and apprenticeship. The apprentice works with the vision of having his own business some day. He may get it by way of retirement of the owner, or by starting his own with opportunities and perhaps even starter money loaned to him by others.

But he must gain the confidence of others, and here Jesus tells us that that is built up in the smaller things not the larger ones.

"No servant can serve two masters; for either he will hate the one and love the other, or else he will be devoted to one and despise the other.

There are modern contexts in which we don't see this as precisely applicable. Many work two jobs and show equal respect for each boss. But in ancient times, things were a bit different. Employers expected total commitment and allegiance from their employees, so if it were a case that a man worked for two masters, there would be a real conflict of interest, creating a situation where he had to choose. And in such cases, he will inevitably choose the one he likes.

Even in the modern context, if one was forced to give up the second job, he would decide which on the basis of the one he is more devoted to.

But Jesus is also talking about allegiances in general, and in relation to God and the world. Then as now, there are ideologies calling to us for affection and commitment. Our desire to have it all often creates the dilemma of obligating ourselves to more than one, and for a season nothing seems to be in conflict. But eventually conflict arises and we must choose.

Jesus is teaching that when that time comes, one must understand their choices. And in truth it is better to not indulge situations where a choice must be made.

You cannot serve God and wealth."

Wealth is being pitted against God in the sense of a contest for allegiance. Some object that it is not money but the love of money, but this can serve as a deception because it is so often the case that wealth engenders all the worst habits and attitudes, so trying to separate them is often moot.

Certainly by wealth Jesus does mean our attitude toward it and this is rightly pitted against God who is wholly otherwise. Many people have acquired wealth and used it not only wisely but effectively and generously toward the work of God. So we do need to be cautious in painting the situation with too broad a brush. But the import of Jesus' words is that in general, man is possessed by his wealth such that he cannot serve both God and money.

The reason for this general dictum is that wealth creates demands which would otherwise not be present. Everyone will have their hand out for a donation to their cause, relatives will appeal to familial bonds in helping them out of their personal plights. The desire to preserve your capital will present commitments to track and pursue investments, all of which steal time and attention that would otherwise not be necessary.

One will frequently and regularly arrive at moments which must decide whether answering the urgent calls of finance and money management should have precedence over the things of God.

Now the Pharisees, who were lovers of money, were listening to all these things and were scoffing at Him.

This is the reaction of many when they are caught dead to rights. The accusation is too pointed and the best recovery is to scoff and distract its import by setting up an appearance that all such things are nonsense.

This was no doubt aided by the fact that all possessions of money cannot be generalized completely, so it can't be as black and white as Jesus makes it to be.

But Jesus sees through this as self-justification -

"You are those who justify yourselves in the sight of men, but God knows your hearts;

This is the root of the issue that prevents them from hearing sound teaching. They have exchanged justification before God for their own, which is the only path available when one is bent on having things their own way. It becomes no longer God's Word, but our special insight as to what is God's word and what isn't.

Virtually every self-styled prophet and "revealer" of divine truths adopts a stance that criticizes Scripture as corrupted and substitutes their own ideas of reform for the path toward truth. The Jews were never so radical as to become cultic, but they did contrive a Judaism for themselves that no longer represented the true heart of God.

Jesus calls them back to that seminal will and heart of God by telling them that the God of their fathers was still alive and ever present to judging their hearts.

for that which is highly esteemed among men is detestable in the sight of God.

And here was one chief self-deception – they had been beguiled by what men valued and these were filthy rags in God's eyes.

Now there are many who will object that it can't be universally absolute because so many things man has thought, written and accomplished have provided unquestionable good to society. As common in these teachings, this is spoken about the general case, not every possible specific case. It is generally true that what men hold as valuable are most generally detestable in comparison to what God values. Men are generally selfish, and even when they are gracious and kind it can often be with ulterior motives. (Many people obey the speed limit not because they believe in the rule of law, but because they wish to avoid the consequences of getting caught.)

"The Law and the Prophets were proclaimed until John; since that time the gospel of the kingdom of God has been preached,

Clearly this is a change in dispensations – the Law and the Prophets, now the Gospel. This introduces the idea that God is not woodenly rigid in His approach to man over time but had an unfolding plan which revealed truth in stages, and when such milestones arrived, changes in approach came with them.

So this is not to establish a flexibility with God, dictated by man's social circumstances, but dictated by God's unfolding plan. From Adam to Moses, it was an age of conscience without written law as to divine things. From Moses to Christ it was an age of Law because conscience was weak in self-deception without something objective in hand. The Law spelled out specifically what the conscience failed to do when combined with the heart of man. From Christ onward, it was the Gospel of the kingdom which was a gospel of grace in contrast to works. Such a grace was enabled by the death of Christ as the one effective sacrifice for sin, and the giving of the Holy Spirit, whereby the conscience could be moved by the spirit toward righteousness and away from sin.

and everyone is forcing his way into it.

This is an odd phrase to add because we don't think of faith as a forceful thing on our part, but often a peaceful, contemplative experience. What Jesus is highlighting is the reaction of the many to the Gospel that frees them from the law of sin and death, and in the cultural context of the Jews, from the slavery associated with the Law. As such, we see more vividly people grasping at the salvation and healing of Jesus because it so contrasted with the drudgery of their current lives.

It can be said in those truly genuine evangelistic meetings that once people recognize their need and decide to get saved, they move very definitely toward it, not hesitantly. This will also be vividly seen on the Day of Pentecost when five thousand are saved in one day.

We also have the life of one like John the Baptist who took the way of salvation in a deliberate fashion that begot boldness and a carelessness about consequences from evil men.

"But it is easier for heaven and earth to pass away than for one stroke of a letter of the Law to fail.

So that there are no misunderstandings about the validity of the former dispensation, Jesus clarifies that the Law is not done away with in its truth, merely as to its means. It is still true that adultery is sinful. Murder has in no wise ceased now to be wrong. But the approach to God is now to be by means of the Gospel of the Kingdom and its King.

The contradiction is resolved in that Christ fulfills the Law in Himself *"Think not that I came to destroy the Law, but to fulfill it."* So with Paul, we say in unison that the Law is righteous and good, but the way to fulfilling it is in Christ through grace.

To reiterate the continuation of the validity of the Law, He states a precept that continues as before -

"Everyone who divorces his wife and marries another commits adultery, and he who marries one who is divorced from a husband commits adultery.

This precept of the Law is still just as binding as before, despite the statement that the Law has been superseded by the Gospel. What the Law stipulates we must do to meet the needs of righteousness is still valid, according to Jesus. What has changed is the means by which we fulfill them. The Law is said to be fulfilled for us on our behalf by Christ – *"who is the end of the Law for all who believe."* (Rom 10:4.)

Now as to the precept itself, we must avail ourselves of the full counsel of Jesus teaching on this, whereby in Matthew 19:9 Jesus adds, "except for marital uncleanness," which some versions translate as fornication or adultery.

This was a very hard saying because the Jews, despite their rigidity with the Law, fully exercised Moses exception that they could put away their wives through a writ of divorce. So not only did this renew conviction about having divorced illegally, but for those remarrying there was triple the sin in making oneself an adulterer along with one's new spouse. (It is still being married in God's eyes that causes relations in another marriage to be adultery for both parties.)

Despite modern societies having their laws originally founded on the laws of the Bible, almost all have accommodated divorce and remarriage without any need for justification at all. A few centuries back, Protestant secular laws still stipulated adultery as the sine qua non which would grant divorce. In decades prior to the sixties, one at least had to prove the conditions that mandated divorce. Now virtually everywhere we have no-fault divorce for irreconcilable differences, the irreconcilability of which no one has to prove.

For Christians who desire to return to the biblical standard, many are shocked to find that the Bible is not as magnanimous as society, and have a tough time accepting these precepts in practice. Many who are otherwise conservative are willing to ironically join the liberals in this particular by calling such rules too antiquated.

We later see Paul expand on this in I Corinthians, chapter 7.

Jesus then tells a parable to highlight the legitimacy and validity of the precepts in the Law -

"Now there was a rich man, . . . And a poor man named Lazarus . . "

In addition to the point of the lesson, we also see a window into the very real plight of the poor. Few of us can identify with the condition of having absolutely nothing. We go home to our refrigerators with the confidence that the things we expect to find will be there. We never anticipate what the poor would get – an open door with nothing inside, not even cold air.

Picture the reality that no paycheck or wage is available anymore to change things tomorrow or the next day. Picture yourself hungry and nothing on the shelves, in the freezer or the fridge; every speck of food long since eaten or spoiled and thrown out. You are then obliged to do what we see others doing, begging for the compassion of others to bestow generosity and kindness. And all the while the pain of hunger.

So here we have Lazarus, dreaming of the remote possibility of merely eating the small crumbs falling from the table. In a scene in the film *Hombre*[44], an Indian riding in a coach with a refined white couple is rudely asked if Indians actually eat dog. He asks if she was ever hungry? "Not a sittin' down to supper hungry, but the kind where you can feel the raw insides of your stomach rubbing against each other? You get that hungry, you'll eat it. And lick your plate."

---

[44] 20th Century-Fox, (1967)

"Now the poor man died and was carried away by the angels to Abraham's bosom; and the rich man also died and was buried.

That Lazarus was carried away by angels helps us understand the state of the righteous dead compared to the lost. The parable is not meant to be taken literally in all its details but as far as essentials upon which we can rely, it establishes that a consciousness continues after death, that at this precise transition we suddenly see the angelic world, that we are taken to the next place beyond death, and that we have enough of our senses intact to experience the comfort of whatever might correspond to Abraham's bosom.

As in the passage of Peter's confession, where we discussed theories of Hades holding both the righteous and the lost, here we have a distinction – that the righteous go to Abraham's bosom and the dead go to Hades, as the rich man is now seen to do. Contrasting this is the statement of Jacob who in grieving about the loss of his son Joseph exclaimed that this would bring his grey hairs down to Sheol, which for all intents and purposes was equivalent to Hades.

So many understand this to be a demarcation within Hades wherein the righteous who receive comfort are said to be in Abraham's bosom, or later to be present with Christ, and the lost are in what remains of Hades. But for the record, much of this is just speculation since the Bible offers few details which would help explain things further.

Important now is the dialog between Abraham and the rich man, who in this parable are in close enough proximity as to see and hear each other.

`Father Abraham, have mercy on me, and send Lazarus so that he may dip the tip of his finger in water and cool off my tongue, for I am in agony in this flame.'

We have the impression that the dead will change their attitude when confronted with realities of their state after death. But it is also believed that such persons will enlarge and deepen their hatreds in life, seeing that they are lost and have nothing more to lose.

For the rich man, he has not quite advanced to heights of corruption, seeing that he later wishes to warn his brothers about such a fate, but he has not changed his arrogance and high-mindedness. He still believes he can order such a person as Lazarus to serve his needs. He still sees such people as instruments rather than people, and he is not convicted into more humility by the scene of Abraham comforting him whom he saw only as a beggar.

His personal agony is the only thing of moment. How to get relief. We see this so frequently in our ever more self-centered society. People have focus only on self, where self needs to go, what self needs to get, and everyone else are mere objects around which one must navigate in the course of getting there. Traffic is an excellent place to see such attitudes and behavior in action.

" `Child, . . you received your good things, and likewise Lazarus bad things; but now he is being comforted here, and you are in agony.'"

Here we find some basis for the notion of recompense or compensation for things suffered in earthly life. Some wince at this in that if we do any good in this life it would seem we are then stealing rewards from the next. This of course is not the meaning intended.

The rich man did no good with an eye to pleasing God, so the only reward he will receive is what he has already received in the world – *"you received good things. . ."* As for recompense, that is another matter, depending on the evil held over to his account. But this addresses merely his expectation of reward beyond the grave, of which there is none.

For Lazarus, the picture is one of compensation, not recompense. His achievements are few in material terms, but he obviously looked to Heaven in enough faith that his sufferings are deemed worthy of compensation in terms of a long awaited comfort.

'Agony' Many people retreat from this horrifying prospect and place their trust in their idea of a loving God who would never mete out such a fate upon any person. It is a view of God that leaves out justice, for in justice there cannot be laxity with respect to punishment due. That is precisely why God could not just forgive all mankind for their sins, but required payment, despite His love, and why it was absolutely necessary to sacrifice animals as a substitute and eventually offer His Son as everlasting substitute. Justice must be served, despite love, as much as a parent must punish his child even though he loves him. In the case of man's salvation the eternal stakes were much higher.

We can see this in our own circumstances, even though we wish it not so concerning God. We can be very liberal when it comes to our own punishment. We look furtively and anxiously that special considerations will somehow let us off. But when the tables are turned and we have been hurt or abused, we do not tolerate a judge who merely slaps the hand of the offender and applies a weak-kneed warning, "Try very hard not to do that again."

"This is not justice!", we shout. Neither is it in God's economy of things. But the beauty is that God has arranged a way that we can in fact be let off while justice is also served. His Son died in our place to pay the price justly owed by us, that we not die but live.

The sheer fixity of the rule of justice is forced into the parable by the statement, `*between us and you there is a great chasm fixed, so that those who wish to come over from here to you will not be able, and that none may cross over from there to us.'*

There is no remedy for the rich man's plight. The time for arranging for that is over. Which ought to be a sobering thought for us and the unbeliever because there are no second chances, no opportunities to fix things if they be seen as having gone awry.

`Then I beg you, father, that you send him to my father's house-- for I have five brothers--in order that he may warn them,

Still issuing orders, but there is at least here a note of compassion for the lost which is now a bit too late. Such compassion is ridiculed and spoofed in the earthly life. There are those who are so brazen and cavalier as to now glibly welcome Hell as the end to their lives – until they get there.

We have here the negative urgency to speak the Gospel, but we ordinarily are encouraged to do so positively – speaking the blessings that one can enjoy in eternal life. Either way, it is a focus on telling something with which we are emotionally engaged. Were we to come back from a vision of Hell, we would begin telling neighbors and citizens as a warning. Were we to come back from a vision of Heaven, we would be likewise compelled to tell others of its wonders. We seem to have no difficulty in risking wariness from others when announcing to everyone we've won the lottery. But witnessing of the love of God in Christ and the free gift of salvation from death and destruction seem less to shout about for some.

"But Abraham said, `They have Moses and the Prophets; let them hear them.'

Ordinarily we would expect a request that would evangelize the lost would be granted. So we are surprised that Abraham is not moved by the nature of such a request. But he has the wisdom of God and His Lord's mind such that he can see how very much has already been given and how sufficient it is to the salvation of men's souls. Moses did not speak vividly and definitively about Christ, but he was the means of that grace that sufficiently awaited Christ, and the remnant of all prior ages saw this and were saved by it.

The rich man is not impressed, as he does not see how Moses was urgent enough now that he sees the awful aspect and reality of his fate.

but if someone goes to them from the dead, they will repent!'

This is secular thinking with respect to the efficacy of signs and wonders. "Show us a sign" is the frequent request as a criteria for belief when all the while men are prepared to explain it away, because to assent to it is to be expected to change. Abraham knows this, hence his reply –

'If they do not listen to Moses and the Prophets, they will not be persuaded even if someone rises from the dead.'"

This is hard for us to imagine because we are raised on films, make believe and how the magic of spectacle can impress. But when dealing with humility before God, confession and repentance, we forget the other mitigating factor – the will of the self and its desire to keep its own way.

This is what engages rationalization as a defense mechanism. Like Scrooge and the ghost of Marley, that appearance of Christ - merely a bad bowl of soup.

The point of this parable, in addition to its internal informativeness, is to reiterate how efficacious the Law is in its essence. It can still draw men to a righteousness and if viewed with the right heart will lead them to Christ and His Gospel. So says Paul, *"the law was our schoolmaster leading us to Christ."* (Gal 3:24.)

Luke 17:20-37
20 Now having been questioned by the Pharisees as to when the kingdom of God was coming, He answered them and said, "The kingdom of God is not coming with signs to be observed; 21 nor will they say, `Look, here it is!' or, `There it is!' For behold, the kingdom of God is in your midst." 22 And He said to the disciples, "The days will come when you will long to see one of the days of the Son of Man, and you will not see it. 23 "They will say to you, `Look there! Look here!' Do not go away, and do not run after them. 24 "For just like the lightning, when it flashes out of one part of the sky, shines to the other part of the sky, so will the Son of Man be in His day. 25 "But first He must suffer many things and be rejected by this generation.

26 "And just as it happened in the days of Noah, so it will be also in the days of the Son of Man: 27 they were eating, they were drinking, they were marrying, they were being given in marriage, until the day that Noah entered the ark, and the flood came and destroyed them all. 28 "It was the same as happened in the days of Lot: they were eating, they were drinking, they were buying, they were selling, they were planting, they were building; 29 but on the day that Lot went out from Sodom it rained fire and brimstone from heaven and destroyed them all.

30 "It will be just the same on the day that the Son of Man is revealed. 31 "On that day, the one who is on the housetop and whose goods are in the house must not go down to take them out; and likewise the one who is in the field must not turn back. 32 "Remember Lot's wife. 33 "Whoever seeks to keep his life will lose it, and whoever loses his life will preserve it. 34 "I tell you, on that night there will be two in one bed; one will be taken and the other will be left. 35 "There will be two women grinding at the same place; one will be taken and the other will be left. 36 Two men will be in the field; one will be taken and the other will be left."] 37 And answering they said to Him, "Where, Lord?" And He said to them, "Where the body is, there also the vultures will be gathered." (Luke 17:20-37)

Commentary

"The kingdom of God is not coming with signs to be observed; nor will they say, `Look, here it is!' or, `There it is!'

Now this might be considered contradictory because Daniel provided signs of the times for the coming Kingdom –

"So you are to know and discern that from the issuing of a decree to restore and rebuild Jerusalem until Messiah the Prince there will be seven weeks and sixty-two weeks;" (9:25)

"and the people of the prince who is to come will destroy the city and the sanctuary. And its end will come with a flood; even to the end there will be war; desolations are determined." (9:26)

"And he will make a firm covenant with the many for one week, but in the middle of the week he will put a stop to sacrifice and grain offering;"

To understand His words here, which have the expectation of being immediate and imminent, we need to appreciate that there is one Kingdom coming, but there is more than one opportunity presented for its inauguration. Jesus is, on the one hand, offering the coming Kingdom here and now to the chosen people, He being their king in their very midst. And on the other hand, knowing in advance their rejection, He will speak in terms of a kingdom that must await many other events on the world stage.

The words in Daniel, above, are those based on the postponement of its coming due to Israel's rejection. They are future time markers, not in the calendar, but as descriptions of future events, with durations in *terminus a quo, terminus ad quem* format (the point from which and the point toward which.) There is an expectation of a covenant of seven years, and there is an expectation of a prince who will come and defile the sanctuary.

But Jesus is talking about signs which men will not be able to point to, which would be puzzling in light of the clear knowledge of what exists in prophesy.

What is important here is to notice the tense of the verb for *"the kingdom of God is not coming . ."* We have here the present tense *(erchomai)* not future. The Kingdom is not to be expected *in the present* with signs to be looked for. Were He to say, "the Kingdom *will not* come with signs" there would be a conflict with what Daniel provides in Scripture.

Jesus is therefore talking about a Kingdom that is ready to come right then and there, in the present. And we have no reason to think that it is some other kingdom than that prophesied of old.

Now this sounds just as confusing as simply proposing Jesus was in conflict with Daniel. How can the Kingdom be presently coming and also coming in the future?

The answer is wrapped up in the expectation that Jesus was to come twice as Messiah. We refer to these as First and Second Advent. That He was not accepted by the Jews makes no difference in Him being Messiah in every real sense at His first advent. And He will clearly be Messiah at His second coming.

To enable this understanding, He adds this comment -

For behold, the kingdom of God is in your midst."

First, this is an often mistranslated or misinterpreted verse, made to say the Kingdom of God is within each of us, meaning within all believing hearts. Many, many people prefer this meaning and despite the following explanation, many will not be moved from it for any amount of money.

But when we understand the setting and all the foregoing, who are those asking the question, and the business about signs, we really must entertain that having the Kingdom in one's heart could not be intended, if only for the simple reason that it is being said to the Pharisees, in whom the Kingdom was not (i.e how could He have said the Kingdom was within them?) And if He meant that it is within all true believers, there would be no point in saying this to the Pharisees when it was within another class of people altogether.)

'entos' does mean *within* in normal usage and can mean *in the middle*. Linguistically, there is nothing that demands 'in the midst' as the alternative. But context does, and clearly forbids the normal usage here[45].
The relation of this statement with the foregoing is also of extreme importance in understanding it correctly. The subject is signs. And with respect to that, none are to be looked for because the "King" of that Kingdom is standing in their very presence. Where the King is, there also is His Kingdom.

---

[45] NIV margin note, Alford, Greek Testament, Vol 1, Guardian, Grand Rapids (1976) p.609

". . you will long to see one of the days of the Son of Man, and you will not see it. 'Look there! Look here!' Do not go away, and do not run after them."

This introduces the notion that He will not always be with them and they will yearn for even one of those days to be lived again or that such days return in the future. Jesus does not forestall any expectation that He would return but warns them that His return will not be announced ahead of time. So should someone do so, it will be false – *" do not run after them."*

Such is the folly of so many groups who take their congregations to remote places to wait for the appearance of the Lord on a specific day. Our Lord's words have been proven true over and over by the day passing with no such appearance. And the gullibility of followers is even more foolish in their willingness to entertain second and third attempts at the same prophecies.

"For just like the lightning, when it flashes out of one part of the sky, shines to the other part of the sky, so will the Son of Man be in His day.

It will be sudden, and unexpected, but nonetheless far-reaching in its visibility. Such are the words elsewhere of it being like a thief in the night, which comes upon a household unexpectedly, without warning (1 Thess 5:12.)

As for Daniel's expectations, these are general as to time, not specific to a day or hour. We are to be aware that the times are near, perhaps even very near; that nothing holds back the fulfillment, yet still taken suddenly by the day of the appearance itself.

"But first He must suffer many things and be rejected by this generation.

Adequately clear is the phenomenon of two comings in Scripture, made additionally plain also by this statement. Isaiah pictures the two advents often telescoped together in one view, but whose enigma is resolved only by the proposition of two comings. Jesus read just such a passage from chapter 61 in the synagogue, yet stopped reading just before the portion dealing with the events of God's vengeance. This required that He stop mid-sentence, which shows the deliberateness of the recitation. There was a point to be made, else why not speak at least the whole sentence?

Isaiah portrayed the career of the 'anointed one' as freeing the captives, healing the brokenhearted and proclaiming the day of vengeance, all in one view. Yet these have now been separated by two thousand years of human history. It is as though Isaiah was looking across the mountain tops only, not seeing the valleys in between, which was sufficient for his view, but not the whole story.

In Daniel, we see prophesy about the coming of Messiah the Prince, but then Messiah being "cut off, but not for himself" (9:27). Yet he also prophesied about the stone cut without hands, coming and breaking all the former empires of man. So also in Daniel one has the enigma of the coming of Messiah as not singular, but dual.

Jesus affirms this here by disclosing the conditions of His next coming, and the necessity that in this present coming, He must suffer at the hands of the present generation.

"And just as it happened in the days of Noah, so it will be also in the days of the Son of Man:

A prediction that despite man's progress on other levels, he will be morally unchanged, and much the same as he was when Noah was chosen at the great Flood. And what was their character then? *"they were eating, they were drinking, they were marrying, they were being given in marriage"* – in essence, living their own lives quite apart from any concerns about God, His righteousness or the penalties of sin. Each man doing what was right in his own eyes.

Today, this plays quite well in our post-modern world. We are at last experiencing the delayed effect of the 18th century philosophers like Hegel, who argued for a unity that avoided the traditional "black and white" appeal to truth and falsity. Truth now depended on how things joined in the middle, which led the way to situational ethics. Hence, lying was not "absolutely" wrong in all circumstances, but the truer absolute about lying depended on blending the validity of the negative circumstances also. This he referred to as 'synthesis."[46]

Today, it is popular to justify anyone's view as equally good and decry the notion that all ideas must measure up against absolute values. So man's view is as good as God's, and may even be more informed, since God seems not to bother with the details. We have now a world in which all things depend on circumstances. Truth is the good that is right in our own eyes.

So in the next coming, it will be as in the days of Noah, judgment coming almost on the heels of the last laugh.

As a side-bar, we cannot escape notice that Jesus took the story of Noah as fact. Today, it is for many people merely a fable from an ignorant and fable-prone past. But regardless of our machinations over difficulties with the physics of the earth and our knowledge of biology, Jesus puts His stamp of approval on the account, and we are then obliged to do likewise if we desire to be His disciple. Which simply means that something is missing in man's assessment of things, which we have learned is not hard to imagine in any case.

"It was the same as happened in the days of Lot:

The repetition of the situation with Sodom and Gomorrah continues to tell the outcome of sin that reaches an intolerable state with a righteous God. Man sinned before the Flood and was judged. Men of Sodom sinned so desperately that they too were judged. The culmination of God's patience with all mankind since the Flood is coming, and its day will be like those of the past –people reveling in their sin, who will be startled into reality by the Day of Vengeance.

"On that day, the one who is on the housetop . . must not go down . . likewise the one who is in the field must not turn back. "Remember Lot's wife.

The warning is about urgency and being ready to separate from a world about to be judged. The man on the rooftop is not to think he has time to gather his belongings, The one in the field is not to think about returning to his house.

The sin of Lot's wife was not that she looked back in curiosity about God's destructive power, but that she longed for what was being destroyed. The man on the housetop or in the field is not to value his trappings in the life of the world soon to be judged.

It is much like the man today who if asked to flee but will be concerned about his HDTV, or the woman her jewelry and fine china.

This also brings up the issue of believers and the rapture, who are not expected to be present when judgment suddenly comes to a sinful world.

---

[46] Schaeffer, The Christian View of Philosophy and Culture, Crossway Books, (1982), p.14

"Whoever seeks to keep his life will lose it, and whoever loses his life will preserve it.

This sounds immediately contradictory. If a man seeks to keep his life, has it and is less likely to lose it. More enigmatic is the idea that if one loses his life it is preserved.

But Jesus is talking about our attitude toward our lives, especially the one that includes ownership.

We all develop a sense of ownership for our life, evidenced by our irritation with people who try to run it for us. This is, in fact, the chief deception about democracy combined with free enterprise. It protects us in worship and faith, but it promotes independence and the love of life for its own sake – that we are the masters of our own fate.

Jesus on the other hand asks that we give up the rights that government or society might extend to us, that we become governed by God. Hence, the more we try to keep our lives for our own selves, the more we have lost that life in the end. The more we give up our right to our lives, the more we find the true life we were meant to live, and in the end, eternal life also.

This comes into play on a daily basis, not merely in the context of salvation. We will be routinely faced with situations where we are free and even obligated in the world's eyes to exercise our right of revenge, or payback or justice. Yet we may be asked of God to suspend our claim of that right, and do the thing most worthy of love, grace or mercy. The woman may have the right to divorce her husband for adultery, but she may be asked of God to forgive him, not claim that right, and continue to love him toward restoration.

" there will be two in one bed; one will be taken and the other will be left. . . two women grinding at the same place; one will be taken and the other will be left.

Many have used this as a picture of the rapture, or the gathering of God's elect out of the world at the end of the age, and there is no question that the words easily picture this. But the context is judgment. And if this means the judgment that comes at the end of the thousand year reign, we have the faithful living among the wicked of that age. So the one taken could just as easily mean the one taken in judgment and the righteous being left to remain.

This is also made clearer by His ending remark -

And answering they said to Him, "Where, Lord?" And He said to them, "Where the body is, there also the vultures will be gathered."

This answer has been used to support both ideas that the body is of those taken for salvation or of those taken to judgment, the former case being about eagles not vultures, hence some translations have *"where the body is the eagles will be gathered."*

In fact, the Greek *'aetos'* is routinely translated 'eagle.' But context always determines the meaning of any word and one must ask what meaning there could be to eagles gathering to accompany the body of believers? Remember, this an answer to the question "Where Lord.", meaning where will the ones taken be, since there would be little concern about "where" if applied to those who remain where they are. And we have no picture anywhere else of such a gathering with eagles in relation to the gathering unto the Lord or to those protected during the tribulation.

But if the context is judgment, and the body is the carcass and the birds are vultures, the gathering of them is most definitely an answer to "where" just as the circling of vultures signals the location of the carrion on which they feed.

All of which is to say, plug in a meaning that those taken are taken in salvation, and one begets enigma in Jesus' answer about either eagles or vultures. Plug in a meaning that those taken are taken in judgment and no enigma remains at all, because *'aetos'* can easily be understood as vultures instead of eagles.

Luke 18:1-14, Matthew 20:1-16
1 Now He was telling them a parable to show that at all times they ought to pray and not to lose heart, 2 saying, "In a certain city there was a judge who did not fear God and did not respect man. 3 "There was a widow in that city, and she kept coming to him, saying, 'Give me legal protection from my opponent.' 4 "For a while he was unwilling; but afterward he said to himself, 'Even though I do not fear God nor respect man, 5 yet because this widow bothers me, I will give her legal protection, otherwise by continually coming she will wear me out.' " 6 And the Lord said, "Hear what the unrighteous judge said; 7 now, will not God bring about justice for His elect who cry to Him day and night, and will He delay long over them? 8 "I tell you that He will bring about justice for them quickly. However, when the Son of Man comes, will He find faith on the earth?"

9 And He also told this parable to some people who trusted in themselves that they were righteous, and viewed others with contempt: 10 "Two men went up into the temple to pray, one a Pharisee and the other a tax collector. 11 "The Pharisee stood and was praying this to himself: 'God, I thank You that I am not like other people: swindlers, unjust, adulterers, or even like this tax collector. 12 'I fast twice a week; I pay tithes of all that I get.' 13 "But the tax collector, standing some distance away, was even unwilling to lift up his eyes to heaven, but was beating his breast, saying, 'God, be merciful to me, the sinner!' 14 "I tell you, this man went to his house justified rather than the other; for everyone who exalts himself will be humbled, but he who humbles himself will be exalted." (Luke 18:1-14)

1 "For the kingdom of heaven is like a landowner who went out early in the morning to hire laborers for his vineyard. 2 "When he had agreed with the laborers for a denarius for the day, he sent them into his vineyard. 3 "And he went out about the third hour and saw others standing idle in the market place; 4 and to those he said, 'You also go into the vineyard, and whatever is right I will give you.' And so they went. 5 "Again he went out about the sixth and the ninth hour, and did the same thing.

6 "And about the eleventh hour he went out and found others standing around; and he said to them, 'Why have you been standing here idle all day long?' 7 "They said to him, 'Because no one hired us.' He said to them, 'You go into the vineyard too.' 8 "When evening came, the owner of the vineyard said to his foreman, 'Call the laborers and pay them their wages, beginning with the last group to the first.' 9 "When those hired about the eleventh hour came, each one received a denarius. 10 "When those hired first came, they thought that they would receive more; but each of them also received a denarius.

11 "When they received it, they grumbled at the landowner, 12 saying, 'These last men have worked only one hour, and you have made them equal to us who have borne the burden and the scorching heat of the day.' 13 "But he answered and said to one of them, 'Friend, I am doing you no wrong; did you not agree with me for a denarius? 14 'Take what is yours and go, but I wish to give to this last man the same as to you. 15 'Is it not lawful for me to do what I wish with what is my own? Or is your eye envious because I am generous?' 16 "So the last shall be first, and the first last." (Matthew 20:1-16)

Commentary

there was a judge who did not fear God and did not respect man

Despite all that God had done among His people, there existed men who did not care about God and had equal disrespect for everyone else. Times were hard and without the comfort of God, men who made such choices became cynical, bitter and resentful of life in general. Still, this man was a judge, which meant that above everything else at least the law had merit, even if all men were inept at obeying it.

Today, as then, men come into life who will not respond to the message of God no matter who or how effective the preaching may be. It just does not click and they go to their grave with a bitter and wasted life behind them. Millions have perished in this manner through history. It is an enigma because we want to believe that every person can be reached with the right message and approach. Yet Paul states that some are as vessels fitted for destruction (Romans 9) which let us in on the reality that there will be those who will never turn to God.

"There was a widow in that city, and she kept coming to him, saying, `Give me legal protection from my opponent.'

The setting conveys that previous attempts were turned down by this judge over and over, yet the woman was persistent. It is hard to entertain that a judge would exercise his office on a personal basis or let emotions or attitudes about life affect his judgment. In ancient times more than now, people were in fact purely at the mercy of the judge's disposition.

The woman is of another cloth. She knows her case to be worthy and does not take the prior judgments as final. This also comments on a state of affairs that permitted her to these appeals, in other words, the judge did not refuse to continue seeing her, knowing his prior rulings.

because this widow bothers me, I will give her legal protection, otherwise by continually coming she will wear me out.'"

This indicates that the case was not a matter of obvious, or clear legal facts, which left the door open for a change in his ruling. But he relents not so much on the merits but on the desire to have her inconvenience out of the way.

This is subtle, because the law is the law and he could just as easily have refused any further audiences. So we can assume that his statement about being worn out is but a mask for not caring much for the merits of her case.

"Hear what the unrighteous judge said; 7 now, will not God bring about justice

i.e. not what follows, but what the judge is related to have just said in the story. We must be careful here to not put these words actually in the mouth of the judge in the parable. Jesus is saying that the judge "conveys" this to us in his actions, hence, "listen more to what is said by what he did." Followed immediately by the application of contrast – *will God not bring about justice?*

"His elect" becomes one of the early references to this idea in Jesus' teaching. the more of which is reserved for Paul to teach in his epistles. The idea of an elect is one of choosing. To be elect is to be chosen, and this necessarily means some are not chosen. Certainly to offer that all are elect by default destroys the notion of electing anyone. What does it offer as a distinction if all are elect?

We recoil from this in that we prefer God to be fair in His actions and choices, and no one wishes to entertain themselves as being unelected or not chosen by God. How this works in God's view of things and how we ought to understand will depend on our further study in Paul's epistles to the Romans and the Ephesians.

As for this teaching, God is seen as bringing about justice for His elect who show their persistence in repeated petitions.

and will He delay long over them?

A rhetorical question that expects a no answer. We might object that there is some delay by the phrase *"who cry to Him day and night."* For some, this conveys an unacceptable idea of God – one who must be rousted from his recalcitrance to give gifts and comfort.

As in the example of the neighbor seeking bread late at night, God waits to see sincerity in contradistinction to flip and careless requests. Sincerity is solidified by persistence and not being answered at the first prayer. We will think more about the righteousness of our petition the more we repeat it. The insincere and selfish will fall away, the genuine and worthy will remain.

"I tell you that He will bring about justice for them quickly

We might immediately complain here that God does not as a rule answer quickly, and for many, He seems to come at the very last minute when we are almost at the point of exasperation.

A great deal of this sort of thing is the experience of people who also pray too late and expect God to jump at their needs. Where was the prayer before we got into this mess?

All of which is to say that prayer is to be an expression of faith, and faith ought to be operating before we get into trouble, not finally prompted on the occasion of troubles.

For those who are walking in faith, God will be seen to bring in justice at just the right time. That this is the backdrop of this teaching is seen in Jesus' next statement -

However, when the Son of Man comes, will He find faith on the earth?"

The "however" means the foregoing idea or principle is conditioned on a stipulation. *"Will He find faith on the earth"* implies He is looking for faith, and in relation to the principle of petitions, His swift justice expects to have seen faith in the formula.

And He also told this parable to some people who trusted in themselves

The writer prepares us for the purpose behind the next parable – to speak to all those who trust in themselves and their deeds before God. Why did this need to be said ahead of time?

Judaism would be the backdrop of all the early followers of Jesus, and the Jews very easily came away in their Judaism with the idea that one's performance in relation to the Law was key to their acceptance before God. No doubt they had a basis for this in the Mosaic writings, which clearly pictured *"do this and live, do the other and be cursed."*

Yet if one studied all the laws and then also paid attention to Jesus' more stringent understanding of them – a man's thoughts were just as much a violation as his actions – one would come away with complete frustration at the impossibility of meeting its needs at all. And that is precisely where Jesus and the Father wish men to be in relation both to the Law and to Him.

"Two men went up into the temple to pray, one a Pharisee and the other a tax collector.

The setting is deliberate. We have the man who would be praised most highly in his attempts to fulfill the Law, and a man who would be considered least likely to fulfill it by the very nature of his profession. The expectation would be that the lesson was to emulate the Pharisee and continue to vilify the publican.

This is helped by what the Pharisee is heard to say -

`I fast twice a week; I pay tithes of all that I get.'

Obedience is a virtuous thing, hence, there is anticipation that the Pharisee will be honored in this teaching. But just before this, the Pharisee is seen to say something else -

`God, I thank You that I am not like other people: swindlers, unjust, adulterers, or even like this tax collector.

Immediately for us we would find this a signal of pride which we have learned God does not respect. But for the ancient Jews, this was actually approved. For them, pride in the things of God was not a wrongful pride, because it had God's Law as its aim.

But here, the pride has another component – that of condescension, which closeness to God does not foster. He is thankful that he is not like those of the disreputable classes.

Now initially, we have much to thank God for in this regard, but this means we are grateful to God for His lifting us away from such states, not so that we can look down on them, but so we may be grateful for His grace. The Pharisee is going beyond gratitude to condescension. And this means he is not inclined to reach down to help the sinner come to where he now is.

Furthermore, in recounting his successes in the Law he is breaking the law then and there, because boasting and judging are violations of loving God with all one's heart and one's neighbor as oneself. It is to forget the admission of Isaiah – *"In sin did my mother conceive me."*

Now the contrast in the attitude of the tax collector –

"But the tax collector, standing some distance away, was even unwilling to lift up his eyes to heaven,

We might ask why a man of despicable profession would care? As often happens in life, we take on our career before we come to our senses about faith and righteousness, and when we do, we may consider it our duty to make a godly thing out of a worldly thing, or at the very least to make the best of something we cannot easily change (there were no job search agencies in those days.) Perhaps the tax collector became one of the few honest men in the vicinity, and used his office to ease the odium of taxes rather than exacerbate it.

Nonetheless, his attitude is one of complete honesty and humility before God. He knows his sins and perhaps also his weakness in not being able to change all the ugly aspects of his life and living. Unlike the Pharisee, he not only does not try to list his accomplishments, for which there had to be some, but rather sees himself as unworthy to even look toward heaven. It would be far too brazen.

For today's generations, this is opposite to popular thinking. We are taught that there is worth in self "as we are" and we are not to succumb to the message that we need more to be acceptable.

In churches, it is popular to emphasize, "We accept you just as you are" which is fine. But then we adopt preaching and ministry that backs away from confrontation and offense about change. The result is that we end up "staying" as we are.

but was beating his breast, saying, `God, be merciful to me, the sinner!'

The very attitude we are to have after confronting the awesome aspect of the Law. The Law was expressly built to convey *complete* righteousness which is a tall order for man, so tall as to cause man to fall on the mercy of God. This is the heart that is then prepared for the role of the Son of God – to fix finally and completely man's ineptitude before a fully righteous Law.

"I tell you, this man went to his house justified rather than the other;

So it is not the man's performance before the Law but his humility before the Law that justified him. From this the Pharisee was far removed, as are all such persons then and now who think themselves someone of whom God should take notice because of their works.

for everyone who exalts himself will be humbled, but he who humbles himself will be exalted."

The Pharisee and all like him will be humbled in the day of judgment, finding their attitudes have heaped more accountable sin on the pile, while the humble will occupy the places of honor the Pharisee falsely assumed would be his.

Another parable is given with the same lesson about expectations due from efforts in comparison to human expectations about others -

1 "For the kingdom of heaven is like a landowner who went out early in the morning to hire laborers for his vineyard.

The succession of groups hired carries the expectation of differences in compensation because of the human expectation that more work in comparison to others will beget more wages. When this turns out not to be the case, there is a reminder of the agreement each made with the landowner.

Now in practical terms, this might seem of little consequence. The landowner will still be seen as unscrupulous by hanging on the terms of an agreement which people would not have known would be unfairly applied against what custom dictates. In other words, had the landowner announced ahead of time his policy toward others, the contract may have been reconsidered.

This explanation is important because this is going to be attributed to God, whom we would not want to accuse of unfairness or miserly practice.

But the lesson is about generosity not miserliness. Much of this assessment depends on whether a denarius was a fair wage or a stingy one. History informs us that it was the unquestioned compensation for a full day's labor. So the subject now is clearly one of greed.

The laborers are not concerned about having reluctantly agreed for less, but about being deprived of the landowner's exceptional generosity, exampled by what he was willing to pay those working but a few hours.

But so this can be applied also to God, Jesus reminds His listeners that there was a fair agreement that no one would consider unjust – a denarius for a day's labor.

`Is it not lawful for me to do what I wish with what is my own? Or is your eye envious because I am generous?'

No one can ultimately complain if an owner does as he pleases with his own affairs, as long as it is not against what is customarily equitable or unethical.

Notice also that the landowner identifies what is really at stake. Their envious eyes are on the additional gain which his generosity opens up as an opportunity.

The lesson in terms of divine actions is that we are not to criticize God for how He deals with others in comparison to us, because not only is He sovereign and all wise, but if He has dealt with us equitably and justly, we are not deprived but blessed. And in the end, we are to be happy being the least in the Kingdom if only to be there at all. Every other concern comes of greed and that has no place in such a glorious realm.

A modern parable once spoken described a little town where one day a man who had come into some money began to make up little letters with money in them which he distributed to people in town. Each week they all looked forward to their little letter.

But eventually the man exhausted the money he had set aside for gifts and the letters stopped. The people began then to complain that there were no more letters and they had been depending on them for their living.

The man replied that gifts are the blessing of the gift-giver and under his authority to give or not. As such, they should enjoy the blessing as it lasted, but to expect it continually would cease to make it a gift and now an obligation.

It was their false expectation that turned the gift into an obligation. So it is with God. We have no means to obligate God to bless us. That He does we should receive with thanksgiving as long as He will is to give.

"So the last shall be first, and the first last."

This is not a mere supposition or possible outcome, but is stated as an assured fact of the future. Those who were grasping in life so as to be first *will* have had their reward, there being none expected in heaven for such motives, hence the end of the line, the last place if there at all.

For those who were abused and deprived while others pushed in to be first, they will be compensated for their suffering and lack by finding themselves finally first – a reward at last, and more valuable than the earthly ones denied.

John 11:1-54
1 Now a certain man was sick, Lazarus of Bethany, the village of Mary and her sister Martha. 2 It was the Mary who anointed the Lord with ointment, and wiped His feet with her hair, whose brother Lazarus was sick. 3 So the sisters sent word to Him, saying, "Lord, behold, he whom You love is sick." 4 But when Jesus heard this, He said, "This sickness is not to end in death, but for the glory of God, so that the Son of God may be glorified by it." 5 Now Jesus loved Martha and her sister and Lazarus. 6 So when He heard that he was sick, He then stayed two days longer in the place where He was.

7 Then after this He said to the disciples, "Let us go to Judea again." 8 The disciples said to Him, "Rabbi, the Jews were just now seeking to stone You, and are You going there again?" 9 Jesus answered, "Are there not twelve hours in the day? If anyone walks in the day, he does not stumble, because he sees the light of this world. 10 "But if anyone walks in the night, he stumbles, because the light is not in him." 11 This He said, and after that He said to them, "Our friend Lazarus has fallen asleep; but I go, so that I may awaken him out of sleep." 12 The disciples then said to Him, "Lord, if he has fallen asleep, he will recover." 13 Now Jesus had spoken of his death, but they thought that He was speaking of literal sleep. 14 So Jesus then said to them plainly, "Lazarus is dead, 15 and I am glad for your sakes that I was not there, so that you may believe; but let us go to him."

16 Therefore Thomas, who is called Didymus, said to his fellow disciples, "Let us also go, so that we may die with Him." 17 So when Jesus came, He found that he had already been in the tomb four days. 18 Now Bethany was near Jerusalem, about two miles off; 19 and many of the Jews had come to Martha and Mary, to console them concerning their brother. 20 Martha therefore, when she heard that Jesus was coming, went to meet Him, but Mary stayed at the house. 21 Martha then said to Jesus, "Lord, if You had been here, my brother would not have died. 22 "Even now I know that whatever You ask of God, God will give You." 23 Jesus said to her, "Your brother will rise again." 24 Martha said to Him, "I know that he will rise again in the resurrection on the last day." 25 Jesus said to her, "I am the resurrection and the life; he who believes in Me will live even if he dies, 26 and everyone who lives and believes in Me will never die. Do you believe this?" 27 She said to Him, "Yes, Lord; I have believed that You are the Christ, the Son of God, even He who comes into the world."

28 When she had said this, she went away and called Mary her sister, saying secretly, "The Teacher is here and is calling for you." 29 And when she heard it, she got up quickly and was coming to Him. 30 Now Jesus had not yet come into the village, but was still in the place where Martha met Him. 31 Then the Jews who were with her in the house, and consoling her, when they saw that Mary got up quickly and went out, they followed her, supposing that she was going to the tomb to weep there.

32 Therefore, when Mary came where Jesus was, she saw Him, and fell at His feet, saying to Him, "Lord, if You had been here, my brother would not have died." 33 When Jesus therefore saw her weeping, and the Jews who came with her also weeping, He was deeply moved in spirit and was troubled, 34 and said, "Where have you laid him?" They said to Him, "Lord, come and see." 35 Jesus wept. 36 So the Jews were saying, "See how He loved him!" 37 But some of them said, "Could not this man, who opened the eyes of the blind man, have kept this man also from dying?"

38 So Jesus, again being deeply moved within, came to the tomb. Now it was a cave, and a stone was lying against it. 39 Jesus said, "Remove the stone." Martha, the sister of the deceased, said to Him, "Lord, by this time there will be a stench, for he has been dead four days." 40 Jesus said to her, "Did I not say to you that

if you believe, you will see the glory of God?" 41 So they removed the stone. Then Jesus raised His eyes, and said, "Father, I thank You that You have heard Me. 42 "I knew that You always hear Me; but because of the people standing around I said it, so that they may believe that You sent Me." 43 When He had said these things, He cried out with a loud voice, "Lazarus, come forth." 44 The man who had died came forth, bound hand and foot with wrappings, and his face was wrapped around with a cloth. Jesus said to them, "Unbind him, and let him go." 45 Therefore many of the Jews who came to Mary, and saw what He had done, believed in Him.

46 But some of them went to the Pharisees and told them the things which Jesus had done. 47 Therefore the chief priests and the Pharisees convened a council, and were saying, "What are we doing? For this man is performing many signs. 48 "If we let Him go on like this, all men will believe in Him, and the Romans will come and take away both our place and our nation." 49 But one of them, Caiaphas, who was high priest that year, said to them, "You know nothing at all, 50 nor do you take into account that it is expedient for you that one man die for the people, and that the whole nation not perish." 51 Now he did not say this on his own initiative, but being high priest that year, he prophesied that Jesus was going to die for the nation, 52 and not for the nation only, but in order that He might also gather together into one the children of God who are scattered abroad. 53 So from that day on they planned together to kill Him. 54 Therefore Jesus no longer continued to walk publicly among the Jews, but went away from there to the country near the wilderness, into a city called Ephraim; and there He stayed with the disciples. (John 11:1-54)

Commentary

Now a certain man was sick, Lazarus of Bethany, the village of Mary and her sister Martha.

We mentioned Bethany, Mary, Martha and Lazarus earlier, but Lazarus was not a character in earlier references. Jesus visited Bethany where Mary was seen listening to Jesus instead of helping her sister Martha, but we did not hear about Lazarus in the narrative.

Now John introduces him formally and reminds us to whom he is connected. Lazarus and the women are brother and sisters, living in what most probably was their home as children, their parents unexplainably gone. The home would now be Lazarus' property in a legal sense, even if an older sister existed.

It was the Mary who anointed the Lord with ointment, and wiped His feet with her hair, whose brother Lazarus was sick.

This is to tie the family together and give the reader a familiar context for the names. But this is anachronistic. The incident of Mary anointing Jesus with the ointment has not occurred yet. John is aware that the story of her doing so is known in verbal tradition by this time and from the other gospels. It is much like saying, "This is the Mary you are all familiar with for anointing Jesus' feet." (even though he had yet to tell the account himself.)

The reason this must be seen as anachronistic is that when the account is told of Mary anointing Jesus (John chapter 12) there is mention of Lazarus as having been raised. So the anointing took place after the raising which John has now before us.

"Lord, behold, he whom You love is sick."

We learn later that Jesus was about four day's distance away, yet the sisters were able to discern where and send word. The message is specially worded so that their appeal to His love would bring Him all the more immediately. That is also the expectation John wishes to convey. A friend, especially a friend who can heal, ought to come immediately to take care of those He loves.

We are now poised for the rather unexpected response from Jesus, which becomes the more important theme to be conveyed.

"This sickness is not to end in death, but for the glory of God, so that the Son of God may be glorified by it."

Lazarus will in fact be dead by the time Jesus gets there. How then is the sickness not unto death (Gk: *toward death*? Since Jesus mentions that this is for the glory of God, we have the expectation that a miracle is in store and in such a case, the finality of death as terminating our sojourn on earth need not be final.

Now some wince at the use of a man in this way for the glory of God. Lazarus was allowed to fall ill and to such a degree of ill feeling that he dies. We recoil at the notion that man's well being and life itself is expendable so that God may get glory.

Most fear less the actual moment of death than the act of dying. While some may not know what lies beyond death, the moment itself when soul leaves body is not dreaded as much as the things we might experience and suffer in the process of dying.

But this is man's carnal view of things, including God's nature. It is not a case of God needing as much glory as He can get, hence, all men are expendable to it. It is an opportunity to demonstrate resurrection to a people in need of hope about eternal life. It is the need to show that power exists that can undo the finality of death.

We might take up Lazarus' complaint that he must suffer for such a demonstration, but we don't find him in fact complaining, that we can see. We are also not privy to what comforts God provided Lazarus in his ordeal that made all things bearable and worth the inconveniences.

Now Jesus loved Martha and her sister and Lazarus.

This love was not based on a lifetime of friendship with them. He had lived most of His life far away from Bethany. His love came from but those few occasions of meeting and visiting when He came to Jerusalem.

This is the nature of the Christian in emulating Christ – to find love quickly in the heart without the traditional and customary pre-requisites of earning it through time. Man has the habit of reserving "love" for those special relationships that have proven worthy. We love those who are lovable, and withhold it from those who, in our estimation, aren't. Even genuine love of parents, compared to dutiful love, has a certain pre-requisite in children. Parents must meet the lovable criteria to be loved in truth, else receive a sort of obligatory love in spite.

This, of course, is a human failing and one that Christianity is meant to change. Were we to have walked along with Jesus as did the disciples, we would have been continually surprised at the many people we might have shunned or avoided or wished were elsewhere, to whom Jesus showed sincere love.

For our own selves, we certainly count on His unconditional love for us, that He will overlook the ugly and unpleasant things others see, perhaps justifiably, and remain that haven of acceptance for us.

The purpose in highlighting Jesus' love for this family is to shut away the notion that Jesus was impersonal when it came to the glory of the Father – that people and feelings were expendable to those purposes. He loved them, and that means He felt their worry and later their pain of loss and the full import of wanting their brother made well.

So when He heard that he was sick, He then stayed two days longer in the place where He was.

And on the heels of that acknowledgment we have an unexpected response – he sits down and waits. Why not at least begin the journey back? We have noted that Jesus did not run to remedy urgencies. The purpose in this reaction is to make certain for all who are with the family, that Lazarus was in fact dead.

There is a miracle in the making and it is vital that Lazarus' condition not be rationalized away on suppositions that he might have merely swooned, where he might be living though barely detectable. Further, we do not see Him hurrying back when He does get up to go. He is always at His own pace, never in the wrong place in Heaven's order of things.

"Let us go to Judea again."

The narrative says, "after this," so we are to infer some additional time, not merely after He spoke. And we find that the band is now seemingly concerned with other matters – *"Rabbi, the Jews were just now seeking to stone You, and are You going there again?"* It is almost as though the Lazarus affair is out of mind. And further we have discussion and teaching on the wisdom of going into Judea.

"Are there not twelve hours in the day? If anyone walks in the day, he does not stumble, because he sees the light of this world.

The subject is providing about opportunity to be snared again by the authorities. At first, we don't see how the above answers that fear. But it is to highlight the things upon which men are to rely as contrasted to that on which the wicked depend.

It is a simple principle that men who work in the daylight rely on the light to see their way and know the duties they are about, and avoid things that might stumble them. Men who work or operate at night very naturally are prone to stumble on things that can't be seen clearly.

The wicked are also accustomed to operating at night to be out of notice by the authorities. The righteous and upright man depends on the light for his living and duties, the wicked despise the light and depend rather on the darkness to cover their deeds.

Now Jesus ends this statement with the phrase, *"because the light is not in him."* which should signal us that this is more than practical wisdom, since the light of day is not "within" a man but lights his external world. That He mentions this means that He is also talking about the Light upon which men should rely spiritually, and if done, what fear have we in where we are bid to go and when?

"Our friend Lazarus has fallen asleep; but I go, so that I may awaken him out of sleep."

This is a term not yet used in the New Testament for death, so we understand the disciples misunderstanding that He meant Lazarus was in slumber.

That we know the real meaning helps us see that John is preparing us for the phenomenon of resurrection. Jesus is saying, "Lazarus has died and I must go and awaken him out of death." But the concept is so extraordinary that Jesus couches it in deliberate ambiguity, not to deceive them but to make the event all the more powerful.

but they thought that He was speaking of literal sleep. The Greek has "speaking of the repose of sleep," so we don't have as close a literal rendering in the NASB as elsewhere. The idea is accurately conveyed but the words are not precisely rendered.

He also comments on why He delayed in setting out for Bethany . .

"Lazarus is dead, and I am glad for your sakes that I was not there, so that you may believe; but let us go to him."

It is more an announcement, not a presumption based on time. Jesus knows that Lazarus has died by virtue of His deity. It was necessary that Lazarus be good and dead when He arrived – *for their sakes* – that they and all others may believe.

Therefore Thomas, who is called Didymus, said to his fellow disciples, "Let us also go, so that we may die with Him."

Didymus meant "twin.' This is the apostle, as we have no knowledge of another Thomas in the same band. He can be counted on to be slow to conclude what others readily run to in faith. He is not recalcitrant, simply one of those who likes to be surer than others who may run or conclude uncritically.

Thomas' statement is in line with the cautions of the other disciples already mentioned –"why go into Judea if they seek to take you?" He is continuing that frame of mind by concluding, "If He must go into Judea and we must follow, then let us go that we may die with Him." So it is not a skepticism about who Jesus was or what his own duty was, (he does say, "let us go") but an expression of not knowing the purpose or understanding Jesus' answer.

"Lord, if You had been here, my brother would not have died.

People resort to cause and effect when major events adversely affect their lives. Things happen because of other things that happen, and this can often create a need to assess accountability. Emotions and this desire to account for why cause Martha (and later even Mary) to express some mild disappointment – that Lazarus' dying is due in part to Jesus' delay.

Frustration and bitterness can often seek to find the circumstances one can blame for their difficulties because entertaining that no one is to blame is to admit that this is one's life, and one is doomed to continue to draw the unlucky straw. So explanations that have some rationality but send the focus away from self are often desperately sought.

To Martha's credit are the next words, that indicate she is not railing against Jesus but disappointed, and this turns to hope and expectation because she must now see in His eyes the acknowledgment of her sorrow and grief – *"Even now I know that whatever You ask of God, God will give You."*

"Your brother will rise again."

This is almost unexpected, even though wished for, due to her response - *"I know that he will rise again in the resurrection on the last day."* One almost can see a look toward Jesus out of the corner of her eye, wondering if there is more than this only in what Jesus meant?

This gives us clear warrant for understanding that there was an OT Jewish belief in life after death and that it would come at the culmination of all things – *in the last day*. Some try to argue that this was wholly lacking in any concise terms in Judaism and was only introduced as an expectant hope in the NT. So we have not only a resurrection concept but a clear eschatological (end times) concept in place by this time.

And now of course the setup has been made complete for the most profound statement in the gospels -

"I am the resurrection and the life; he who believes in Me will live even if he dies, and everyone who lives and believes in Me will never die.

Anyone in earshot of this statement would have gasped, even if politely, because no man was expected to claim this. Resurrection was solely in the purview of Almighty God to grant and effect. He was not saying that He was identical to the resurrection, as He was to His messiahship – events and persons are not veridically identical things.

He is, however, saying that He is resurrection personified, in that He is the gateway by which it is attained. It is somewhat like saying that Microsoft® is in the building when Bill Gates is in attendance at the seminar. He personifies his company because he can make decisions that will be put into living practice.

For everyone who believes in Jesus, He has the power to make resurrection a personal reality.

And just so we are certain, He does not mean immortality in the flesh. *"even if he dies"* means a life unaffected by a physical death that takes place. It does not mean a life that suspends the expectation of physical death.

But what does it mean to "believe in Him?" Certainly, it doesn't mean to merely believe that He existed. Believing in something can be made to be that simple in some people's mind, as in to believe Plato existed. But to "believe in" Plato normally carries the idea that you embrace his thinking and his approach to the world, especially because Plato is all about philosophy and one cannot believe in Plato and exclude it.

So with Jesus. We cannot merely believe He lived and taught, nor can we have a sort of mushy, vague expectation that if we are simply kind-hearted toward Him, He will work things out for us in the end. All that He was and continues to be is about the new life and citizenry in the Kingdom of His Father. To acknowledge Him but set aside His purpose and reason for coming is to reject Him.

But further than this, we have the command that we *believe Jesus*, meaning that we accept what He said, taught and commanded us to do.

But we must note the magnitude of the promise here – we will *"never die."* That is so extraordinary to not be taken lightly. Absolutely everyone encounters this question – *"if I die, will I live on?"* Does awareness and life continue beyond this realm of existence? Here is not a vague surmising, but a definite answer in the most blunt and clear terms possible. *We will "never die."*

This is something the other religions cannot claim. Buddhism and Hinduism and the other eastern religions offer a vague "oneness" with the universe, that does not disclose anything concerning "awareness." No one really knows what "oneness" means to the individual after death.

Islam promises eternal life, but the path is precarious and dependent on good works. One does not have anything close to the formula that "belief on someone = eternal life." Nor does it have the validity of that claim vindicated in something as powerful as a demonstration of the resurrection.

Do you believe this?"

To reiterate that it is more than belief that Jesus simply is, Christ asks Martha whether she "believes" what He has just said. This is all the more critical when we realize that Martha did not have the centuries of tacit belief in this very thing. She was exposed to this idea for the first time. She must assess the magnitude of the statement, against what her Judaistic faith was telling her, and she must assess the man Jesus, as to His reliability in saying so. All of this is being required as she contemplates how to answer. And we can expect that she desires to answer truthfully, not to accommodate Jesus or dispel the pressure of the confrontation.

And all of these elements are in her answer -

"Yes, Lord; I have believed that You are the Christ, the Son of God, even He who comes into the world."

She affirms her belief that Jesus is who He says He is. She affirms His reliability in talking about who gets resurrected in asserting He is both Messiah and Son of God. (Can it be that someone who has these attributes has no authority over access to resurrection?)

Therefore, when Mary came where Jesus was, . . . "Lord, if You had been here, my brother would not have died."

The realities and emotions of death have overwhelmed Mary also, that she shifts some of the nebulous blame on the "fates" to Jesus, in not coming sooner. He is not callous or unemotional, but we find Him easily able to join their grief, knowing as He does that Lazarus will be restored to them - *He was deeply moved in spirit and was troubled,* We cannot know definitively what 'troubled' means, whether He was grieved at their impious innuendos about His delay, or that this is just a colloquial term for sharing their grief.

It says His 'spirit' was moved, as in compassion, which gives us a window into the connectivity the Spirit has directly to our emotions and feelings. It is not a mere acknowledgment of our feelings but being moved by them.

There are three terms that represent stages of involvement in another person's grief or hurt. Sympathy says, "I can understand what you're going through." Empathy says, "I understand because I've been there myself." Compassion says the most, "I understand, I've been there, and here – here's a helping hand to ease your grief."

The original idea of being 'moved' was to be moved out of one's place to provide help. Today it doesn't mean much more than sympathy. But certainly in Jesus, it would have been full compassion – a compassion that is now walking up the rocky areas behind the home to the family tombs.

Mary does not have the benefit of Jesus' encouragement about the resurrection given to Martha. Instead, Jesus chooses to comfort her by action. He prepares to go to the tomb itself that the demonstration which will glorify God may soon be a comfort to everyone. Therein is compassion at work.

"Where have you laid him?" They said to Him, "Lord, come and see." Jesus wept.

He must go to the tomb itself, which confirmed the very reality of what Jesus was about to do. This was action now to bolster the words spoken. You have to actually go to the tomb if you promise that one who now lies dead in it will live again.

On arrival, Jesus weeps. We find this hard to understand, since normally grieving is over the loss, or the dread of where the loved one is presently and the things being experienced. None of these would be a cause of weeping, since He knew that Lazarus would be brought back, hence no loss, and He certainly knew that Lazarus was in no torment or grief among the supposed toils of the dead. So we remain puzzled as to what could be the basis for this weeping?

We must be mindful that there is at all times a marvelously unexplainable convergence of the Divine and the human in Jesus. On the cross, He says, "I thirst" knowing more surely than anyone that soon He will be beyond all caring about such things.

Yet there is a sort of compliance with the dictates of His human form that are deemed needed for visibility, so He desires a drink at the cross, and can weep according to the same emotions as those who are mourning. It is a necessary duality in His nature and response, despite the singularity perceived in the sheer logic involved.

We are also reminded of Isaiah's characterization – *"he was a man of sorrows, and acquainted with grief"* (Isa. 53:3.)

Soon we learn the purpose -

"See how He loved him!" But some of them said, "Could not this man, who opened the eyes of the blind man, have kept this man also from dying?"

Two reactions from two views of the situation. The compassionate noticed His love whether they understood his delay or not. Others could not avoid the critique over the failed expectation – that a man who had such power ought not to have been without action. The one is able to bridge the paradox by faith and love, the other is stuck on the paradox by a preoccupation with earthly assessments.

"Remove the stone"* . . . *"Lord, by this time there will be a stench"

The rubber at last meets the road. Removing the stone removes all doubt about the fully serious claim. Access to the dead body is ultimate reality. Ethereal ideas that Lazarus will be alive in the hearts of those who loved him (a typical liberal re-explanation of such miracles) are now impossible, in fact banished. We're talking about involving the real, albeit very dead, Lazarus in whatever is about to take place.

We can contemplate from afar the strength to suffer at the stake – until very real and searing flame is applied to very real and tender flesh. Then and there we come to realize that whether we like it or not we are now quite committed.

Martha, despite her hopes and expectations and the faith she has just pronounced, is jerked back into reality – "surely by this time he stinketh." It is a statement that brings in the incredulity of our fleshly mind as to how a corpse beginning to decompose has tissues suitable for life even if raised? It is a convergence of all the misinformation and ignorance in general about resurrection specifics – how the body participates in the miracle, etc. She is expressing what ignorance limits her from understanding- that if resurrection is possible, certainly reconstituting the elements of the body is not a pick-breaker.

Jesus does not upbraid her, but reminds her of what she affirmed as her belief. He asks her to put that now into practice – *"Did I not say to you that if you believe, you will see the glory of God?"*

We are to be doers of the Word not "knowers" of the Word. His word to us is for use, not merely knowledge. This is the difference between people who read the Bible for information and those who read it for living. The former approach it without any commitment to be changed by it, the latter look forward to how they might be changed by it.

"Father, I thank You that You have heard Me.

We have here a very interesting distinction between what Jesus knows to be true and what Jesus is obliged to do on account of others. He speaks His thanks for being heard. Yet He knows by the intimacy between Himself and the Father that He is heard as he prays.

So He follows this immediately with an explanation that is meant to answer the quandary that being thankful for hearing will evoke. Does the Father not hear Him always? Is He on His own at times, hence a genuine thanks when He comes to know the Father is listening?

This He forestalls by, " *"I knew that You always hear Me; but because of the people standing around I said it, so that they may believe that You sent Me."*

Of importance is the obligation to conclude that prayers about this have already been uttered, for which He now thanks the Father. He has paved the way toward the miracle through intimacy with the Father. It is this communication for which He is thankful.

"Lazarus, come forth."

Some have observed in many a sermon that it is good that He said, *"Lazarus"* come forth, since had He said merely *"Come forth"* the whole hillside would have risen with the dead.

It is of course the will behind the words, not the magic in the words, that would have accomplished what was specifically intended.

The man who had died came forth, bound hand and foot with wrappings, and his face was wrapped around with a cloth.

The miracle did not go so far as to put Lazarus into fine clothes and out of his wrappings. It is as though He wished to avoid any fantastic rendition of the miracle as men are prone to tell fables. It could not be claimed that Lazarus, adorned in precious garments, floated out of his bonds to stand again with his sisters. No. He was resurrected just enough as concerns the body and the mind, but reality was retained so far as to keep him entangled by his former bindings. It is life being restored in the reality of a real world, not a fantasy that suspends reality.

Therefore many of the Jews who came to Mary, and saw what He had done, believed in Him.

and saw what He had done . .

Jesus was now walking away and there in broad daylight stood the effects, being viewed by all. Lazarus was standing at the mouth of the tomb for all to see, clearly alive and ready to be unbound. The raw facts before them made one profound statement – *"See now what I can do?"*

But some of them went to the Pharisees

It is hard to imagine that the Pharisees would not become privy to this event. The report would be one thing. Validation by visiting Bethany would be another. We aren't told that they investigated the facts, but it is likely that they did, since we hear some of them saying, *"this man is performing many signs. If we let Him go on like this, all men will believe in Him . . "* There is genuine concern that the sheer nature of the signs will make for division and a kind of unrest that will attract the Roman authority. Such concerns would not be as serious if they took the report as embellishment or fabrication.

and the Romans will come and take away both our place and our nation."

This was not supposition but had precedence. In the time of Macedonian rule by the Seleucids, Antiochus IV deposed the rightful high priest and placed someone of his choosing to serve. The ephod of the high priest had been confiscated on the superstition that it gave the priests magical powers by which they wielded national authority. Nothing prevented the extension that the Romans might do likewise – *"and take away . . our place . ."*

But one of them, Caiaphas, who was high priest that year,

Caiaphas was high priest in place of his father, Annas, who was still living but retired. We later see Jesus after His arrest sent first to Anna out of respect.

The high priestly office among the Pharisaic party was a mixture of OT ordinance and modern evolution of secular rule. In concept, there was no such thing as secular rule, since the source of all important law was Moses and the nation lived by the Law of the Torah. But neither was there an OT conception of the Sanhedrin over which the high priest presided. It was a council brought about by necessity, extending the idea of the elders of Israel in ages past, yet more formally convened and established.

To ensure compliance with Mosaic Law, the high priest presided and essentially declared the final decisions of the council, and like the OT model was the single person to which all deferred.

"You know nothing at all, nor do you take into account that it is expedient for you that one man die for the people, and that the whole nation not perish."

Typical of people in dominant positions, everyone else knows less than the person in charge, who must continually assess the "real" truth in all matters and straighten out the bunk and ineptitude from the wisdom needed.

The reference to the necessity that a man die for the nation is not a reference to an OT precept or prophesy. We learn in the next verse that Caiaphas prophesied this earlier (hence, his jab that they have not taken this into account.) We must not conclude that such a prophecy was necessarily of God.

There are two possibilities: a) that Caiaphas prophesied in the flesh that a man's death would spare the nation, b) that Caiaphas was unwittingly used of God to prophesy about Christ's death which was necessary for the nation to be saved. There is a certain irony in the latter. And if so, it would not count with the Lord in the judgment – *"did we not prophesy in your name? . . Depart from me ye workers of iniquity."* (Matthew 7:22.

So from that day on they planned together to kill Him.

Whatever the lack of some specific OT precedence for this salvatory death, the rest of the Pharisees take it as sufficient reason to seek His death with newfound justification. Perhaps it was reminiscent of the whole sacrificial system by which the nation was yearly spared the punishment of God in the offering made on the Day of Atonement. The lack of horrific recoil at the suggestion of human sacrifice may inform us of the shallow base in Scripture generally prevalent in the Pharisees. Remember that the Scribes were the most literate in the Scripture, the Pharisee much less so.

Therefore Jesus no longer continued to walk publicly among the Jews,

This sounds contradictory to the same concern voiced by the disciples at the beginning of this section. The relaxing of caution and the taking up again of caution is dependent always on the will of the Father. It is not a universal precept once invoked. Jesus is under complete guidance by His Father, and there were times when the Father directed Him to avoid the Jews and the city, and other times when the way was curiously clear to go in and speak or work.

into a city called Ephraim; and there He stayed with the disciples.

Some confusion can exist over the duplicate references using Ephraim in the Bible. Ephraim was first a half-tribe of Joseph, sharing with Manasseh. In the conquest, the tribe of Ephraim received a portion of land to the north of Judah. In the civil war, Israel centered its ten tribes away from Judah and around the city of Samaria, but prophets often referred to Samaria as Ephraim in deference to the tribe and the lot of land nearby given by Joshua.

In Jesus' day, there was a small town of no account called Ephraim, which may have had connections back to the time before the Assyrian Captivity of the northern tribes, but was not of much aspect or importance in New Testament times.

Matthew 19:3-12, Mark 10:2-27, Matthew 19:27-30
3 Some Pharisees came to Jesus, testing Him and asking, "Is it lawful for a man to divorce his wife for any reason at all?" 4 And He answered and said, "Have you not read that He who created them from the beginning MADE THEM MALE AND FEMALE, 5 and said, `FOR THIS REASON A MAN SHALL LEAVE HIS FATHER AND MOTHER AND BE JOINED TO HIS WIFE, AND THE TWO SHALL BECOME ONE FLESH'? 6 "So they are no longer two, but one flesh. What therefore God has joined together, let no man separate." 7 They said to Him, "Why then did Moses command to GIVE HER A CERTIFICATE OF DIVORCE AND SEND her AWAY ?"

8 He said to them, "Because of your hardness of heart Moses permitted you to divorce your wives; but from the beginning it has not been this way. 9 "And I say to you, whoever divorces his wife, except for immorality, and marries another woman commits adultery." (Matthew 19:3-9)   10 In the house the disciples began questioning Him about this again. 11 And He said to them, "Whoever divorces his wife and marries another woman commits adultery against her; 12 and if she herself divorces her husband and marries another man, she is committing adultery." (Mark 10:10-12)

10 The disciples said to Him, "If the relationship of the man with his wife is like this, it is better not to marry." 11 But He said to them, "Not all men can accept this statement, but only those to whom it has been given. 12 "For there are eunuchs who were born that way from their mother's womb; and there are eunuchs who were made eunuchs by men; and there are also eunuchs who made themselves eunuchs for the sake of the kingdom of heaven. He who is able to accept this, let him accept it." (Matthew 19:10-12)

13 And they were bringing children to Him so that He might touch them; but the disciples rebuked them. 14 But when Jesus saw this, He was indignant and said to them, "Permit the children to come to Me; do not hinder them; for the kingdom of God belongs to such as these. 15 "Truly I say to you, whoever does not receive the kingdom of God like a child will not enter it at all." 16 And He took them in His arms and began blessing them, laying His hands on them.

17 As He was setting out on a journey, a man ran up to Him and knelt before Him, and asked Him, "Good Teacher, what shall I do to inherit eternal life?" 18 And Jesus said to him, "Why do you call Me good? No one is good except God alone. 19 "You know the commandments, `DO NOT MURDER, DO NOT COMMIT ADULTERY, DO NOT STEAL, DO NOT BEAR FALSE WITNESS, Do not defraud, HONOR YOUR FATHER AND MOTHER.' " 20 And he said to Him, "Teacher, I have kept all these things from my youth up." 21 Looking at him, Jesus felt a love for him and said to him, "One thing you lack: go and sell all you possess and give to the poor, and you will have treasure in heaven; and come, follow Me." 22 But at these words he was saddened, and he went away grieving, for he was one who owned much property.

23 And Jesus, looking around, said to His disciples, "How hard it will be for those who are wealthy to enter the kingdom of God!" 24 The disciples were amazed at His words. But Jesus answered again and said to them, "Children, how hard it is to enter the kingdom of God! 25 "It is easier for a camel to go through the eye of a needle than for a rich man to enter the kingdom of God." 26 They were even more astonished and said to Him, "Then who can be saved?" 27 Looking at them, Jesus said, "With people it is impossible, but not with God; for all things are possible with God." (Mark 10:13-27)

27 Then Peter said to Him, "Behold, we have left everything and followed You; what then will there be for us?" 28 And Jesus said to them, "Truly I say to you, that you who have followed Me, in the regeneration when the Son of Man will sit on His glorious throne, you also shall sit upon twelve thrones, judging the twelve tribes of Israel. 29 "And everyone who has left houses or brothers or sisters or father or mother or children or farms for My name's sake, will receive many times as much, and will inherit eternal life. 30 "But many who are first will be last; and the last, first. (Matthew 19:27-30)

Commentary

"Is it lawful for a man to divorce his wife for any reason at all?"

It says they came testing Him. The reason the test was conceivable is that there was a perception in the Law that Moses made provision for divorce. Whether this is actually true remains to be seen when they quote the pertinent section below.

Again, the Pharisees are delighted to have yet another opportunity in which Jesus is made to pit Himself against Moses. All they need do is stand back and let the anticipated reaction among the people do its work. But Jesus goes back to basics and reiterates what marriage was intended to be –

"Have you not read that He who created them from the beginning MADE THEM MALE AND FEMALE, . . .

The distinctiveness between male and female was to be unified in marriage – *"the two shall become one flesh;"* thus creating a bond that is to be protected – *"What therefore God has joined together, let no man separate."*

This sets the stage that divorce for any reason was not the intent, but rather marriage was to be seen as a union meant to be kept in place, not broken for trite reasons.

"Why then did Moses command to GIVE HER A CERTIFICATE OF DIVORCE AND SEND her AWAY ?"

Here is their trump card, the verse[47] they were itching to employ that would trap Jesus into repudiating Moses. He must either contradict Himself and His noted strong teaching about divorce elsewhere, or contradict Moses. They have Him just where they want Him. He cannot win on any account, so they think.

This is very tricky because we find in the Law a provision by Moses for this very thing – *if a man's wife find no favor in his eyes . . . if a second husband hate her . . let them write a bill of divorcement.* Moses appears to be accommodating divorces for less than adultery by also stipulating the abomination of a wife returning to her first husband after a second divorce.

---

[47] Deut 24:1-4

But Jesus refers to this as Moses "suffering" their writs of divorce, which is not the same thing as a positive directive at all.

Now there were the cases of uncleanness found after marriage which meant a case of defrauding - the woman who lay with a man while betrothed to another. But the strictness of the Law provided that she be stoned, not divorced. Divorce may well have been an option when circumstances deemed death too severe a judgment. But this is not the question they put to Jesus. It is the case of divorce "for any reason."

But more importantly, the Hebrew does not support the reading they give to Deuteronomy 24:1-4. It does not say "give her a certificate of divorce" i.e. a command, but rather what happens if a man chooses to do so civilly when he finds some unseemly thing and writes her a bill of divorce.

Here is the raw Hebrew: *"if not she is finding grace in his eyes, that he finds in her a nakedness of thing, and he writes for her a scroll of divorce . ."*[48] Nothing in the text hints that the issuing of the writ was in compliance with a command of Moses in such cases.

The whole context was about remarrying the first husband after subsequent marriages and the abhorrence with which God viewed this.[49]

As to divorce for any reason, there were actually precedents in the opposite direction. Other areas of the Law forbade a man divorcing his wife all his life under certain conditions – the case of falsely charging unchastity to get out of a marriage Deut 22:19 19 *"and they shall fine him a hundred shekels of silver and give it to the girl's father, because he publicly defamed a virgin of Israel. And she shall remain his wife; he cannot divorce her all his days."*

It is a classic case of the Jews taking "inference" and legislating it as binding law. If Moses while discussing some other problem makes no comment on the propriety of divorces, there is seen then an inference that divorce was permitted.

But this ignores the lack of a precept. It also ignores elsewhere the statement, *"For I hate divorce,"* says *the Lord.* Malachi 2:16.) Now the subject is Israel's spiritual divorce as the wife of God, but is it conceivable that He could hate it here and have no concern about it in civil life?

So the test is to see if Jesus will contradict the inference Moses appears to give, and which was certainly the practice in traditional history since Moses, without objection.

Jesus avoids the entanglement over interpretations and readings and chooses to take them back to the heart of God. Laws were written to express the heart, mind and will of God. Discover these and you will have found the basis for any law.

"Because of your hardness of heart Moses permitted you to divorce your wives; but from the beginning it has not been this way.

First, the verse is re-explained to them for what it really was – accommodation. Moses "suffered" their divorces because of the hardness of their hearts. Meaning, he did not condemn them but acquiesced to them. This is not the same as an express command, as the Jews were here implying.

Now the heart of God – *"but from the beginning it was not so."* God intended marriage to be a lifetime bond, a union so invasive that it was described in Genesis as a union of flesh. That is the true heart of God. Once perceived, the idea of divorcing one's wife because she burned the food ought to stand out as just plain perversion.

---

[48] Westminster Leningrad Codex
[49] Kiel, Delitzsch <u>Old Testament Commentary</u>, Vol 1, Eerdmans, (1975) p417

"And I say to you, whoever divorces his wife, except for immorality, and marries another woman commits adultery."

This is God's view of the thing. A man and wife are to do all they can to honor the marriage bond, not look for loopholes. They are to consider the seriousness of the results of improper divorce – they become adulterers in marrying again.

The exception for immorality is lacking in the other parallel references, (Mark 10:11, Luke 16:18.) The rule of interpretation is that the stronger verses rule the weaker ones. In this case, Matthew is more complete (stronger), so it rules Mark and Luke, preventing them from being the paradigm over Matthew. In other words, Mark having no exceptions stated cannot be pushed so strongly as to nullify the conditionals that in fact exist in Matthew.

The disciples said to Him, "If the relationship of the man with his wife is like this, it is better not to marry."

The natural conclusion is that there are whole scores of marriages all around them that ought not to have taken place and which, if the rule Jesus just stated were applied, would consign men and women to much misery. The implication is that if man cannot rely on divorce as an escape route should things go badly, he needs to be very sure of the happiness that can be had in a desired marriage, or be resigned to wait until it is assured. It also implies that there is need for a commitment to make it work, since unforeseen troubles are a part of life.

Jesus does not countermand this conclusion.

But He said to them, "Not all men can accept this statement, but only those to whom it has been given.

Which sounds like marriage is but for the few who are thusly gifted. But He is not saying that marriage is for the select few, but rather, the acceptance of these conditions is for those who have asked and gained the ability to receive it. This kind of commitment comes from above. It is an understanding not all partners have. To that extent, it will work or not. Men who understand it will get on well in marriage. Those that don't will have troubles or end up committing the sins described.

We find this expanded on in perfect agreement in Paul's advice about marriage (I Cor chapter 7.) There Paul describes in more detail the behavior intended – that if the couple separate, let them remain single, etc.

"For . . . there are also eunuchs who made themselves eunuchs for the sake of the kingdom of heaven. He who is able to accept this, let him accept it."

Which is to say that what seems hard is a matter of fact, yet there are those who embrace it for the glory of God.

Now there is need to address the condition of modern Christians who with each decade are becoming more and more the routine victims of divorce. From this teaching, one can come away with a conviction that may stifle their approach to God and future service. If we have divorced for unbiblical reasons, have we now something to repent of and is it hindering our relationship with God? Is there hope and acceptance for that increasing number of people who have been divorced?

First, we must recognize that what is being described above is nothing more than sin, and like all sins, "we have an advocate with the Father" in the operation of confession and forgiveness. Once done, restoration and repentance depend on where we are and where our former mate is. We are expected to repent to the degree that we can. Breaking up our current marriage and remarrying our first spouse is, as seen above, not possible.

Repentance then becomes what we can do, and that might very well include a change in our feelings and attitude toward others, including the conditions now playing in our present life.

What might influence our spiritual life before a God who feels this way about divorce is an attitude that is lax or accommodating, which considers it "no biggie, it happens all the time."

Healing and forgiveness can come by acknowledgement and confession. Restoration and new service can come with commitments to change our part in how things went wrong, especially if there is risk that life will repeat itself.

"Permit the children to come to Me; do not hinder them; for the kingdom of God belongs to such as these.

Earlier in Matthew, Jesus used a small child to exemplify the humility needed for the citizen of the Kingdom. And some point out that this does not establish that children are saved, but merely that their trusting natures exemplify what was being taught.

But here we have another treatment of the same subject by Jesus wherein He teaches that the kingdom is their possession. This is more than inferring their salvation from the mention of their angels, or their being an example (Matt 18:2.)

What is it about the small child that grants them this privilege? Is it not their utter lack of sophistication and trusting in the care and protection others will provide?

Erick Erickson's version of Maslow's Hierarchy of Needs[50] describes the first level as that of trust vs. non-trust. It is that stage where infants learn that they can trust to be taken care of when discomfort or need arises. Once realized, this remains with an individual through life, conditioning the degree to which they trust or not. Most succeed in at least this level, and for this reason, Jesus singles them out as exemplary of the Kingdom.

We are to trust God regarding His goodness toward us. It is the sophisticated mind that conceives of complications – will God's desire for me be what I want for myself? The child is not at that point of independence that they will no longer take the hand of their father to go willingly and trustingly where he leads.

So serious is this attitude to be in us that Jesus adds, *"Truly I say to you, whoever does not receive the kingdom of God like a child will not enter it at all."*

"Good Teacher, what shall I do to inherit eternal life?"

The approach is immediately defective to some degree – he calls Him merely a good teacher. This man has heard about Jesus, but has yet to understand who Jesus is. He naturally has questions about eternal life, and here now is a man of extraordinary insight. The opportunity to learn what the real criteria might be cannot be let by.

The man is also approaching the whole subject on the basis, held by all around, that the criteria will be in something one does. On that score, there is no doubt that what the Law stipulates is impossible for anyone to meet perfectly. So perhaps he can get a "revised" sine qua non from Jesus, a cut to the chase as to what will in truth ensure eternal life.

---

[50] Maslow, in Theory of Human Motivation, Psychology Review Vol 50, 1943

"Why do you call Me good? No one is good except God alone.

Jesus prefaces His answer with this well-placed question, which actually does come first because the man called Him good before asking his question. It is a question as an answer. Ordinarily, this would be a nit not worth the focus. Calling someone a good teacher was done all the time and was hardly seen as the basis for analysis.

The reason Jesus pays preliminary attention to it is to use it to make a point. It is to pick up on the words and use them to help the man conclude even more than he asked. Asking him why he calls Him good when there is only One who can rightly be called good will force the man to consider who Jesus then is.

We might expect the man to say, "Oh no, I didn't intend that." But Jesus is in truth asking him to consider who He is and then re-assess that answer.

Now, the subject of what meets the needs of eternal life -

"You know the commandments, `do not murder, do not commit adultery, do not steal, do not bear false witness, do not defraud, honor your father and mother.' "

These are not all, but are cited to represent them all. Note that murder is used to clarify "kill," so that we establish, against the critic, that the Bible does allow for the legal taking of life.

Now if Jesus' point will be that it is not the degree of success in the Law, why cite these precepts? It is to put the man in the right position to hear what will get him into heaven. He must first face where his obedience fits in; and in order to do that, there must be an accounting.

"Teacher, I have kept all these things from my youth up."

Here is a diligent man. And there is no indication that he did this out of pridefulness or the need to show off. Without qualification, we can assume he took the injunctions of the OT seriously and wished to please God. This is expressly why the very next verse tells us that Jesus felt love for him. It is on the heels of this accounting that Jesus sees a man who did such things honestly and with a good heart.

But as with all mechanisms for righteousness, there is a focus on the mechanism and not on the changes that are supposed to take place in the heart.

"One thing you lack: go and sell all you possess and give to the poor, and you will have treasure in heaven; and come, follow Me."

First, He was not establishing that he must adopt the life style of His disciples – to abandon their possessions and walk after Him wherever He goes. There were many believers in Jesus who did not walk with Him as the disciples did.

Rather, his missing element is that he has possessions and is attached to them. It is one thing to follow the dictates of the written Law. It is another to follow the leading of God should He call. To do the former but have an impediment for doing the latter is a hindrance of greater importance than slipping here or there with respect to the Law.

God did not impose the Law that it be observed in a vacuum, but that it be lived. And the living of it meant being ready to do the will of the Lawgiver. We say we are Jesus' disciples, but if He were to bid us go to another country to live and attempt to pull us up from our surroundings, up would come a whole network of pipes and wires and interconnections to the world, from which the idea of extrication seems hopeless. Are we in fact too tied to the affairs of everyday living that we are no longer usable?

"But at these words he was saddened, and he went away grieving, for he was one who owned much property."

We live in a culture where there is a path toward fitting in with society, whose right of passage is the acquisition of certain essentials – like a respectable home, a late model car, kids in the latest fads and fashions, etc. We spend much of our early life getting along our path to be able to afford such things. So when we do get them, we are not open to giving them up in order to be more readily available to God. We have "earned" them through a long path of sacrifice and hard work.

Yet this is the attitude that prevents us from being pliable and useful. To meet the needs elsewhere, someone needs to leave where they presently are and what they have, and go. To meet a need tonight, someone needs to set aside the movie they were looking forward to watching. Are these things to be done only by those few who managed somehow never to have needed things?

"How hard it will be for those who are wealthy to enter the kingdom of God!"

There is a power that wealth exerts on us. We think this analytically silly, because inanimate things don't wield power. But this is just another way of talking about our own willingness to be changed by the feelings that come with having wealth. We acquire wealth for two reasons: to enjoy things that are desirable (and usually too expensive for everyone else), and to impress others, which is an added pleasure to merely enjoying the things themselves.

Enjoyments we can afford will always have limits and will also be tarnished somewhat by the knowledge that what we have almost everyone else has also. Wealth is the seeking of that which is exceptional. This is the primary reason why the wealthy are so snobbish. They have run the gamut of the ordinary. They are now running the gamut of the extraordinary, and spending huge sums to get that next exhilarating experience from the next exotic thing. That is why the Ming vase is precious, because to have something so rare is to be above the crowd.

For the wealthy, there will be the look back at all the achievements respecting wealth and things that will prevent the humility and openness to the kingdom. The wealthy will always be evaluating what they must give up, rather than what they will gain.

"It is easier for a camel to go through the eye of a needle than for a rich man to enter the kingdom of God."

The picture says it all. We have trouble getting a mere thread to go through it.

There is some discussion on the closeness in Greek to the word for 'rope' and that for 'camel' and that perhaps the use of camel was a mistranslation in later copies. There is no help from textual criticism, since the manuscripts are said to have had the change to camel by the time those used to validate the text were executed.

Some have noted a spurious reference to the 'Needle's Eye' which was supposedly a narrow pass on a mountain road in which there was a hole in the rock large enough for a man to pass but an animal like a camel had to be unloaded and made to scooch through on its knees. The other supposed reference is to a hole in the city wall of a similar nature (Hasting's Dictionary of the Bible, 1901)

While this is chock full of good sermon material about how much humbling it takes for the camel to get through, there is just nothing archaeological, geological or historical to support such a place having existed.

And the idea to be conveyed is the impossibility of passage, not the feasibility of passage if one makes exceptional effort.

"Then who can be saved?"

Since the subject was only about the rich, this seems a strange question. But it is picking up on the general problems of possessions in general, and the other classes would be perceived as having issues about ownership also. Left unresolved, most people would be without remedy if their possessions prevented them. Jesus then adds that God was not satisfied to let things stand, While it might be impossible as depends on man alone, *"all things are possible with God."*

This is the key to all our challenges. We assess them in human terms and faint in anticipation. But adding the God factor always changes any situation. This the atheist and the humanist are not willing to allow. All must be assessed in terms of unaided nature and man alone by himself. Hence, the miraculous is always something naturally explainable or is superstition, but not reality. For them, man reforming himself by association with God is merely man finding at last the resources that were there all along.

The problem of course is that many things cannot be resolved or fixed by purely human efforts and at some point the intervention of God must be brought in to account for the results.

For the Christian, it will always be a case of how much of self is trying to remain in control and how much of God is being allowed in.

"Behold, we have left everything and followed You; what then will there be for us?"

Peter can be counted on to voice those emotions still tied to the flesh. He is no doubt a changed man for having walked with Jesus. But he expresses without much reserve what others may have been thinking. Having the basics in life seems natural if not necessary. And all are thinking about how permanent this itinerant life style is going to be. There is also the idea of how their ministries are to evolve. Are they to remain completely without for the duration, or are there earthly rewards or at least some improvements ahead?

But the way Jesus is talking, Peter concludes that He is suggesting they give up all such expectations.

"Truly I say to you, that you who have followed Me, in the regeneration when the Son of Man will sit on His glorious throne, you also shall sit upon twelve thrones, judging the twelve tribes of Israel.

Contrary to the theme of austerity, Jesus does talk in terms of things and position about their future. But it is the heavenly future. There is certainly the risk that heads will get bigger with this expectation of prominence, but life with the coming Holy Spirit will teach them over and over the lessons of earthly service and humility.

"And everyone who has left houses or brothers or sisters . . "

Jesus is conscientious to let them know that He acknowledges their sacrifices. He is also intimately knowledgeable that He and His Father will not be slack in giving rewards to those who have served. Being obedient to God is its own justification. It need not be enticed by the prospect of reward. The righteous ought to desire to please God with obedience.

God could look at it just that way – that obedience is justification enough for the work. Yet He goes further and has stored up compensations for all, and not mere stipends, but things worth many times what was given up for the work.

And they are to be comforted with a repeat of the earlier principle - *"many who are first will be last; and the last, first,"* meaning that if they are denied while on earth, there is compensation in Heaven.

Mark 10:32-34, Luke 18:31, 34, Matthew 20:20-23, Mark 10:35-45

32 They were on the road going up to Jerusalem, and Jesus was walking on ahead of them; and they were amazed, and those who followed were fearful. And again He took the twelve aside and began to tell them what was going to happen to Him, 33 saying, "Behold, we are going up to Jerusalem, and the Son of Man will be delivered to the chief priests and the scribes; and they will condemn Him to death and will hand Him over to the Gentiles. 34 "They will mock Him and spit on Him, and scourge Him and kill Him, and three days later He will rise again." (Mark 10:32-34)

31 Then He took the twelve aside and said to them, "Behold, we are going up to Jerusalem, and all things which are written through the prophets about the Son of Man will be accomplished. 34 But the disciples understood none of these things, and the meaning of this statement was hidden from them, and they did not comprehend the things that were said. (Luke 18:31, 34)

20 Then the mother of the sons of Zebedee came to Jesus with her sons, bowing down and making a request of Him. 21 And He said to her, "What do you wish?" She said to Him, "Command that in Your kingdom these two sons of mine may sit one on Your right and one on Your left." 22 But Jesus answered, "You do not know what you are asking. Are you able to drink the cup that I am about to drink?" They said to Him, "We are able." 23 He said to them, "My cup you shall drink; but to sit on My right and on My left, this is not Mine to give, but it is for those for whom it has been prepared by My Father." (Matthew 20:20-23)

35 James and John, the two sons of Zebedee, came up to Jesus, saying, "Teacher, we want You to do for us whatever we ask of You." 36 And He said to them, "What do you want Me to do for you?" 37 They said to Him, "Grant that we may sit, one on Your right and one on Your left, in Your glory." 38 But Jesus said to them, "You do not know what you are asking. Are you able to drink the cup that I drink, or to be baptized with the baptism with which I am baptized?" 39 They said to Him, "We are able."

And Jesus said to them, "The cup that I drink you shall drink; and you shall be baptized with the baptism with which I am baptized. 40 "But to sit on My right or on My left, this is not Mine to give; but it is for those for whom it has been prepared." 41 Hearing this, the ten began to feel indignant with James and John. 42 Calling them to Himself, Jesus said to them, "You know that those who are recognized as rulers of the Gentiles lord it over them; and their great men exercise authority over them. 43 "But it is not this way among you, but whoever wishes to become great among you shall be your servant; 44 and whoever wishes to be first among you shall be slave of all. 45 "For even the Son of Man did not come to be served, but to serve, and to give His life a ransom for many." (Mark 10:35-45)

Commentary

"Behold, we are going up to Jerusalem, and the Son of Man will be delivered to the chief priests and the scribes

The narrative says that some among the disciples following Him were "fearful." This is understandable from the previous section, since Jesus had just talked about what a commitment to walk in His ministry would mean. Some had even voiced how they had given up all to follow Him, being perplexed that this was somehow not yet enough. He now adds something even more ominous into the contract.

The time is approaching when He will actually submit to His enemies and be taken by them. This will be hard for His followers to understand because in practical terms, this undoes the effects of His ministry. If He is to be condemned as a criminal in the eyes of the Law, it would appear to nullify His teaching as it would now be seen as truly contrary to the faith of their fathers.

What is less understood at this point is the role Jesus is to play in the Sacrifice that will end all sacrifices. Yes, He came to enlighten and call all men to the Kingdom of His Father But He came to perform a function as well, one needed in compliance with the intent of the Law and the divine plan of God – *" and they will condemn Him to death and will hand Him over to the Gentiles."*

So, even His foreknowledge that the Romans would be engaged as the instrument of His death was proclaimed. Some might say this was no prophecy since this was Roman provincial procedure in non-free regions like Judea. But the death sentence for Jewish offenses was not always carried out by the Romans themselves, Their permission to do so was however essential.

"They will mock Him and spit on Him, and scourge Him and kill Him, and three days later He will rise again."

All the essential elements of His execution are foretold here. Interestingly, the writer does not comment on their reaction to the resurrection in three days. It is as though this passes clearly over their heads.

These are thoroughly discouraging predictions. That such a One as He would be mocked and made the laughing stock by evil men was inconceivable. His innocence and spiritual strength could not be that callously disrespected. How could any hatred rise to such a degree that some would spit on Him?

Not everyone would be personally familiar with the actual savagery of scourging. Much depended on whether you had ever witnessed one at the hands of the Romans, and only the grotesquely curious flocked to such scenes. They were also usually conducted in the fortress of Antonia whose courtyard was not in general public view.

As portrayed in the film *The Passion of the Christ* (Icon Productions © 2004), it was hardly a lighter affair than the act of execution itself might be. We cannot imagine anyone submitting to it willingly. Jesus knew the path to the Cross went by way of the scourging post. Twenty lashes with the flagrum would be beyond what some men could stand. To have received that many and then realize in the case of forty that the ordeal was only half over is hard to imagine.

It would be understandable that an enigmatic capper about the resurrection might not have been equally taken in mind amid the troubling descriptions just given.

"Behold, we are going up to Jerusalem, and all things which are written through the prophets about the Son of Man will be accomplished.

The "things" referred to were those about His passion. Isaiah had written extensively about the suffering of Messiah, such that chapter 53 became known as the Suffering Servant passage – *"He was despised and forsaken of men, A man of sorrows and acquainted with grief; And like one from whom men hide their face He was despised, . . . we ourselves esteemed Him stricken, Smitten of God, and afflicted . . He was pierced through for our transgressions, He was crushed for our iniquities; . . . And by His scourging we are healed . . . He was oppressed and He was afflicted, Yet He did not open His mouth; Like a lamb that is led to slaughter, And like a sheep that is silent before its shearers, So He did not open His mouth."*

Daniel later prophesied that Messiah would come and be "cut off, but not for himself."

This was, of course, that aspect of Messiah His followers had not entertained.

But the disciples understood none of these things, and the meaning of this statement was hidden from them, and they did not comprehend the things that were said.

It is difficult to be dogmatic that God deliberately withheld this understanding, since the words "were hidden from them" could easily apply as the effects of their not having understanding of it in themselves. There appear no indicators that would explain why God would sovereignly prevent their understanding.

More than likely, much was to depend on how they related all their experiences to the written word in the days following His ascension. The full gospel message would begin to be formed and articulated thereafter and that would include bringing in understanding from the OT, wherein they would see the connections to the purposes of God predicted there. Such an understanding comes best by a purposed and dedicated study, which would have to wait until these events concluded.

Then the mother of the sons of Zebedee came to Jesus with her sons

This would be the mother of James and John, who were of the inner circle with Peter. There was already an observed speciality for these three. The Transfiguration had excluded the others in preference to them. Their mother would have seen this preference which would have been the occasion for an expectation born out of purely human thinking.

"Command that in Your kingdom these two sons of mine may sit one on Your right and one on Your left."

Here is a pious woman who has no issues with her sons giving up their familial responsibilities to follow Jesus. She is more than supportive as evidenced by her request. She acknowledges their work to the extent that she desires preferential reward for it.

This is a case of association providing occasion for dropping normal propriety and caution and being too familiar with someone of notoriety and importance. It is like the minister who comes to dinner. Some may venture to drop respectful address, slap him on the back as a good ol' boy, and even make jokes at his expense, all because the appearance of familiarity tends to relax formalities and with it the proper modicum of respect.

Here, their mother ventures such daring because the way seems to have been paved by familiarity.

"You do not know what you are asking. Are you able to drink the cup that I am about to drink?"

At first it would seem that this rejoinder would stop the whole issue in its tracks and end all such talk. The sons themselves ask (Mark 10:35), and offer, *"we are able,"* but they have yet to see what it will mean. They have not witnessed the scourging and the agony of the cross. They are like young bucks itching to get into the war and do some fighting, until it comes upon them and their courage runs out the bottom of their feet.

Note that Jesus does not correct their naïve exuberance.

"My cup you shall drink;

It is a very subtle transition. Why ask if they are able if He knows they will in fact drink? The question lets us know that He sees their naivite. But He also knows that this naiveté will turn into maturity and courage, and one day they will in fact taste of His cup.

So to answer the mother's question, He must turn to the real principles that will be at play in making this determination – *". . but to sit on My right and on My left, this is not Mine to give, but it is for those for whom it has been prepared by My Father."*

This is the real answer. The former was for the benefit of the sons more than to immediately answer their mother.

The parallel in Mark 10:35-39 represents the sons asking instead of the mother. But it may very well have been that the mother asked, and the sons reiterated saying, "Yes, grant us that we may sit . ." Mark chose to leave out the mother's question and include that of the sons, since it would have been repetitious.

If Mark was written and available by the time Matthew was produced and Mark already had the question of the sons, Matthew may have chosen to present the excluded feature that the mother had actually asked first.

None of this undermines the authenticity of the two accounts.

Hearing this, the ten began to feel indignant with James and John.

We can clearly imagine how this very public encounter was received by the other ten disciples. Nothing much has changed since those days – men continue to be indignant at the grasping attempts of those they see as their peers. It is insulting in the sense that they perceive a precipitating attitude that sees them as having no stake of equivalent merit.

To forestall this, Jesus avoids the problem of having to take sides, which would only ensure more divisiveness.

"You know that those who are recognized as rulers of the Gentiles lord it over them; and their great men exercise authority over them. "But it is not this way among you,"

"Lord it over them" means that rulers take care to remind others of their position and often abuse their authority to ensure that recognition. It is a carnal treatment of authority and in a very real sense, the issue between the disciples is revolving around the same kind of carnality.

He reminds them that it is not to be this way among them. Virtually everything they do will be foreign to the natural expectations of men and their own natural selves. This is simply because man has gone so far astray from the original intent of God in the creation that the new life is deliberately arranged to set such things at odds and to re-focus man on the original idea.

" but whoever wishes to become great among you shall be your servant; and whoever wishes to be first among you shall be slave of all.

These are completely foreign conclusions in logic. The servant and the slave are the lowest echelons of society, attended by no conceptions of greatness that anyone could conceive.

But here, service is the way to greatness. And this is explained in terms of love and compassion which obligate men to constantly put themselves second and prefer the betterment of others. So it follows that the attitudes of a servant and a slave are more honored than earthly greatness.

It might seem that any path to personal greatness would be discouraged, since the attitude of a servant bars such aspirations. But in terms of the Kingdom, aggressiveness to do the will of the Father is encouraged. Such was John the Baptist, whose fervor and aggressive nature was commemorated by Jesus as great in the Kingdom.

So it is ironic that humility and the renouncing of earthly greatness is to end up rewarded with greatness in the Kingdom

But there is another reason – the need to emulate what the Son came to do -

"For even the Son of Man did not come to be served, but to serve, and to give His life a ransom for many."

Ordinarily, even the Jews would have seen their conquering Messiah as one who was to be served. They would surely have arranged for him to stay in the most luxurious of surroundings, they would have donated staffs of people to care for his needs, and formulate an architecture of agents to do his every bidding. He would be a king and that translated to being served.

This will come to an emotional head when Jesus deigns to wash the disciples' feet. Peter will recoil at the very idea. For Jesus to be seen in so lowly a role of servant will be repugnant.

The idea of a "ransom" is metaphorically conveyed in the OT. The Jews clearly understood that the animals sacrificed for sins were taking the punishment they rightly deserved, that they may live to serve the Lord and not die.

But the idea that Messiah would serve in that role, as a ransom, went promptly into the background in their handling of prophecies and the OT in general. This is the primary reason why knowledgeable men like the disciples, and notable men among the Jews could not put these ideas together respecting Israel's Messiah, and why the disciples seemed dumb struck when such words were spoken.

Ransom is an excellent word here, because it speaks of a redemption. Redemption is not simply paying for something one desires. It is a payment that re-establishes what has been lost. When someone is kidnapped, redemption is to pay to have the loved one restored to the family. The "ransom" is the money paid to effect the redemption. And that is precisely why ransom is employed here.

There is no kidnapping involved, but man has just the same become "lost" to the Kingdom by his rebellion and self will. Some might aver that there is a kidnapping in that men who are lost are gained by the devil.

This comes with consequences – the loss of citizenship in the Kingdom and the impending punishment for sin. Man can be redeemed from this condition back into the Kingdom by the paying of a ransom. That redemption was *always* in Christ's sacrifice, even for OT people. But in OT times, men could not wait for the "fullness of time" by which Messiah was to come. In the interim, God established that animal sacrifices would postpone the accounting for their sins until that Day when Christ would pay the price from time past to all times future. They therefore "pointed" to Christ's death, not being efficacious in and of themselves – *" For it is impossible for the blood of bulls and goats to take away sins"* (Hebrews 10:4)

This is extremely important in the message of the Gospel. It is often soft-peddled in the interest of attracting believers to the loving aspects of the new life in Christ. But the Gospel was meant to announce a fix to man's dilemma, man's problem. Solving the issue of sin and the law of sin in mortal flesh was key to what Jesus came to do. The Cross is surely about love, but not man's love for his fellow man, not man living peaceably with other men. It was about God's love for man that He was willing to send His Son to fix man's endemic problem – to lift debilitating sin out and away from the relationship between God and man.

If we fail to preach this and believers fail to grasp this, we create a church filled with people who are accepted "as they are," but who might very likely remain as they are.

Luke 19:1-10, Mark 10:46-52, Luke 18:43

1 He entered Jericho and was passing through. 2 And there was a man called by the name of Zaccheus; he was a chief tax collector and he was rich. 3 Zaccheus was trying to see who Jesus was, and was unable because of the crowd, for he was small in stature. 4 So he ran on ahead and climbed up into a sycamore tree in order to see Him, for He was about to pass through that way. 5 When Jesus came to the place, He looked up and said to him, "Zaccheus, hurry and come down, for today I must stay at your house." 6 And he hurried and came down and received Him gladly. 7 When they saw it, they all began to grumble, saying, "He has gone to be the guest of a man who is a sinner." 8 Zaccheus stopped and said to the Lord, "Behold, Lord, half of my possessions I will give to the poor, and if I have defrauded anyone of anything, I will give back four times as much." 9 And Jesus said to him, "Today salvation has come to this house, because he, too, is a son of Abraham. 10 "For the Son of Man has come to seek and to save that which was lost." (Luke 19:1-10) .

46 Then they came to Jericho. And as He was leaving Jericho with His disciples and a large crowd, a blind beggar named Bartimaeus, the son of Timaeus, was sitting by the road. 47 When he heard that it was Jesus the Nazarene, he began to cry out and say, "Jesus, Son of David, have mercy on me!" 48 Many were sternly telling him to be quiet, but he kept crying out all the more, "Son of David, have mercy on me!" 49 And Jesus stopped and said, "Call him here." So they called the blind man, saying to him, "Take courage, stand up! He is calling for you." 50 Throwing aside his cloak, he jumped up and came to Jesus. 51 And answering him, Jesus said, "What do you want Me to do for you?" And the blind man said to Him, " Rabboni, I want to regain my sight!" 52 And Jesus said to him, "Go; your faith has made you well." Immediately he regained his sight and began following Him on the road (Mark 10:46-52) , glorifying God. And all the people, when the saw it, glorified God also (Luke 18:43)

Commentary

And there was a man called by the name of Zaccheus; he was a chief tax collector and he was rich

The comment that he was rich serves to highlight the manner in which tax collectors made their living. The Romans either paid no stipend at all to tax collectors, or it was pitably meager. The expectation was that the man would extort whatever additional funds were needed for his living above the levy being laid. Some might ask why the Romans, knowing this, did not take the extra as well? It was simply a matter of business. Who would work for what would then amount to nothing?

Yet this tax collector is interested in Jesus, perhaps having come to a sense of compassion that his riches had come on the backs of his neighbors and friends and the fruits of that were hardly enjoyable if one was virtually alone in society.

"Zaccheus, hurry and come down, for today I must stay at your house."

Being short and having climbed a tree to see, Zaccheus would have had no expectations of a personal encounter. So we can imagine his surprise when Jesus not only deigns to speak to him but desires to stay at his home. That is how Jesus sees friendships. He is not aloof, but ready for sincere personal focus on you.

Yet this serves only to further irritate His detractors who can only see a case of associating with sinners. As for condoning his lifestyle, the very next verses make this question clear -

"Behold, Lord, half of my possessions I will give to the poor, and if I have defrauded anyone of anything, I will give back four times as much."

Here we see that in fact the man has come to his senses about how he makes his living, and the very presence of Jesus has convicted him to make his errors right. That is what coming to Jesus does to the sincere. We immediately perceive our incredible inadequacy in the light of His complete righteousness. We come into agreement between ourselves and Heaven as to who we are.

Note that he admits to having defrauded, meaning he has demanded more than was levied and perhaps even more than a normal livelihood would have demanded. That he can give back as much as four times tells us just how much he was used to extorting.

Note here also, that Jesus does not absolve his necessity to do as he promises.

"Today salvation has come to this house, because he, too, is a son of Abraham. "For the Son of Man has come to seek and to save that which was lost."

It's not a matter of merely seeing the man's faith and desire to repent. By not correcting him or revising the man's promises He agrees that restoration is appropriate. He focuses rather on the spiritual awakening evidenced by the man's new attitude.

"son of Abraham" means that He has traversed the Law and come all the way back to the simple saving faith born out of a right conscience, as what characterized Abraham's faith.

He has been found, having been all this time lost. We puzzle at this term because people today certainly know where they are and where they wish to go. They would not characterize it as being lost. But lost in the world view of Jesus means lost to the Kingdom. When we say, "We lost Uncle Fred last year" we mean he is lost to the world of the living, no longer present to enjoy life and the family. Mankind is lost with respect to the joys and blessings of the Kingdom and that lost state is all the more vivid as people grope in the darkness for spiritual meaning and purpose.

To be found is to come to the end of that groping and searching, and to be gained once again into the family of God.

Today salvation has come . . " This should set aside any notions that salvation is a "wait and see" proposition. Jesus declared that salvation was at hand for Zaccheus, not something that waited for its assurance on how Zaccheus' life played out. It means that despite the works which James connects as an essential part of being saved[51], something immediate is at hand that Jesus could say without any such works in the case of Zaccheus – *"today salvation has come to you."*

Then they came to Jericho. And as He was leaving Jericho

Thought to be one of the classic discrepancies of the Bible, the critic questions how He could be coming to Jericho and leaving it after having done so with respect to Zaccheus? It cannot be that respecting Zaccheus He was merely approaching the borders of the city, then later came to it proper here, since the former account says He was passing through.

This is resolved by our later knowledge of twin cities named Jericho, one ancient and one new. The ancient site had become a wary place and virtually a ruin by the time of Jesus, since the incident with Joshua and the falling down of its walls. By Jesus day it was largely ruins, but some people lived there. But a new town, Herodian Jericho, had sprung up a short distance south from the old, and on the way toward Jerusalem, such that one could be said to be leaving Jericho and approaching Jericho at almost the same moment.[52]

Another concern is that Matthew mentions two men (20:29-34) while Mark and Luke mention only the one, and it seems hard to believe they would have left out this detail. But we see in many other places that in the East there is no obligation like there is in the West to tell exacting accounts of all details. We do this also today. If I say I have a son in Baltimore, that doesn't mean I've precluded having a daughter also.

---

[51] James 2:14-20

[52] A. T. Robertson, Word Pictures in the New Testament, Broadman, Nashville (1931)

Here in Mark, the man is actually named, Bartimaeus (and even his father is known) which may account for why the other is ignored in deference to him.

"Jesus, Son of David, have mercy on me!"

Son of David, would ordinarily not be much more than identifying someone in David's line, but the context here is all important. It is a very public appeal and for healing. Combined with 'Son of Man', it would be taken by everyone in earshot as a declaration of Him being Messiah, who was to give sight to the blind.

The man is scolded to keep quite, no doubt because his calling out was unrefined, perhaps awkward and blurtish. We see such people today in towns and cities and might be tempted to see them as eye-sores who are better not seen, even more, not to be heard.

"Call him here."

We might attribute this in part to the fact that the man recognized Him as Son of David. It is inconceivable that anyone coming to that conclusion on seeing Jesus would have his appeal brushed aside.

By stopping, Jesus was not only dispensing compassionate healing, but acknowledging the incredible exercise of faith it would have taken to recognize Him as such.

"Rabboni, I want to regain my sight!"

Rabbi meant great teacher, which many agreed was appropriate for Him, including some of the Pharisees. 'Rabbon' meant great master, meaning someone with exceptional wisdom and insight, enough to have disciples who would look to Him as Master. Socrates would have been the equivalent in the secular world.

To add 'i' – rabboni - is to add the personal pronoun 'my' – My Great Master.

His request is simple. He doesn't want riches and servants and position. Simply to regain the sight he once had.

"Go; your faith has made you well."

If someone were to accuse Jesus of magic or some kind of supernatural craft, He would be able to point over and over to instances where He made it clear that the faith of the patient is what made them well. And everything in the NT tells us that healing and the faith to be healed go hand in hand. You cannot have healing without the faith to be healed.

But we must caution against the idea that the right quantity or quality of faith is the key, as do the prosperity preachers who promulgate that the reason you are not healed or rich is that you lack the specific measure of faith needed - gain that and the rest is assumed.

Faith is relatively simple. It is the belief that you can be healed of God accompanied by the belief that to receive healing will glorify God. It may be seen also as going a step further and believing God wishes to heal you, now.

Those who merely touched the hem of His garment had no time to ponder the science of applied faith, no preparation in the presence of new generation faith healers who would help them learn the agony of prayer for just the right faith. They simply believed and touched and were healed.

Why everyone is not healed who prays is beyond man's discernment to tell (though many claim to know all about why.) It is between the Healer and the believer, it is also about the mitigating effects of sin and doubt, such that it becomes something other than faith. It is also about the will of God, which may, contrary to some preaching, desire to make us strong in infirmity rather than removing it.

Luke 19:11-28, John 11:55-57, John 12:1, Matthew 26:3, John 12:2-3, Matthew 26:8, John 12:4-8, Matthew 26:13, John 12:9-11

11 While they were listening to these things, Jesus went on to tell a parable, because He was near Jerusalem, and they supposed that the kingdom of God was going to appear immediately. 12 So He said, "A nobleman went to a distant country to receive a kingdom for himself, and then return. 13 "And he called ten of his slaves, and gave them ten minas and said to them, `Do business with this until I come back.' 14 "But his citizens hated him and sent a delegation after him, saying, `We do not want this man to reign over us.' 15 "When he returned, after receiving the kingdom, he ordered that these slaves, to whom he had given the money, be called to him so that he might know what business they had done.

16 "The first appeared, saying, `Master, your mina has made ten minas more.' 17 "And he said to him, `Well done, good slave, because you have been faithful in a very little thing, you are to be in authority over ten cities.' 18 "The second came, saying, `Your mina, master, has made five minas.' 19 "And he said to him also, `And you are to be over five cities.' 20 "Another came, saying, `Master, here is your mina, which I kept put away in a handkerchief; 21 for I was afraid of you, because you are an exacting man; you take up what you did not lay down and reap what you did not sow.'

22 "He said to him, `By your own words I will judge you, you worthless slave. Did you know that I am an exacting man, taking up what I did not lay down and reaping what I did not sow? 23 `Then why did you not put my money in the bank, and having come, I would have collected it with interest?' 24 "Then he said to the bystanders, `Take the mina away from him and give it to the one who has the ten minas.' 25 "And they said to him, `Master, he has ten minas already.' 26 "I tell you that to everyone who has, more shall be given, but from the one who does not have, even what he does have shall be taken away. 27 "But these enemies of mine, who did not want me to reign over them, bring them here and slay them in my presence." 28 After He had said these things, He was going on ahead, going up to Jerusalem. (Luke 19:11-28)

55 Now the Passover of the Jews was near, and many went up to Jerusalem out of the country before the Passover to purify themselves. 56 So they were seeking for Jesus, and were saying to one another as they stood in the temple, "What do you think; that He will not come to the feast at all?" 57 Now the chief priests and the Pharisees had given orders that if anyone knew where He was, he was to report it, so that they might seize Him. (John 11:55-57)

1 Jesus, therefore, six days before the Passover, came to Bethany . . . at the home of Simon the leper . . . where Lazarus was, whom Jesus had raised from the dead. 2 So they made Him a supper there, and Martha was serving; but Lazarus was one of those reclining at the table with Him. 3 Mary then took a pound of very costly perfume of pure nard, and anointed the feet of Jesus and wiped His feet with her hair; and the house was filled with the fragrance of the perfume . . . 8 But the disciples were indignant when they saw this, and said, "Why this waste? . . . 4 But Judas Iscariot, one of His disciples, who was intending to betray Him, said, 5 "Why was this perfume not sold for three hundred denarii and given to poor people?"

6 Now he said this, not because he was concerned about the poor, but because he was a thief, and as he had the money box, he used to pilfer what was put into it. 7 Therefore Jesus said, "Let her alone, so that she may keep it for the day of My burial. 8 "For you always have the poor with you, but you do not always have Me." (John 12:1, Matthew 26:3, John 12:2-3, Matthew 26:8, John 12:4-8)

13 "Truly I say to you, wherever this gospel is preached in the whole world, what this woman has done will also be spoken of in memory of her." (Matthew 26:13) . . .

9 The large crowd of the Jews then learned that He was there; and they came, not for Jesus' sake only, but that they might also see Lazarus, whom He raised from the dead. 10 But the chief priests planned to put Lazarus to death also; 11 because on account of him many of the Jews were going away and were believing in Jesus. (John 12:9-11)

Commentary

and they supposed that the kingdom of God was going to appear immediately.

This is an odd interlude before coming to Jerusalem and the parables spoken on this occasion are going to be paradoxical to the disciples because they are ominous and their outcome in real life will not be readily apparent.

The disciples have concluded by all the foregoing teaching and by Jesus' readiness to go into the city that the Kingdom He had preached about as near at hand, was now about to be manifested.

They have at this point dismissed all talk about Him being delivered into the hands of His enemies and killed. They prefer to believe that He will do something, perhaps spectacularly, to wrest authority and power from the Jewish leaders and perhaps also from the Romans (if a kingdom is to be established.)

But Jesus is seen to have noted this among them and tells a parable that has two noted threads of foreboding -

"A nobleman went to a distant country to receive a kingdom for himself,

It was completely uncommon that a nobleman with a business in one country would receive an entire kingdom elsewhere, even less that he would then return to his former holdings to resume care for his old business and slaves, etc. The nobleman would certainly have moved to his new kingdom to enjoy the benefits of rule there.

Instead, this was a rather special circumstance which had its living examples in the persons of what were called 'client kings.' These were persons of note who were designated by a conquering power to administer a country on their behalf. Herod the Great was just such a client king, and went to Rome to receive his kingship from the Roman Senate on the recommendation of Augustus.

Later, his son Archelaeus went also to Rome in 4 B.C. on the death of his father, to receive his fourth part of that kingdom as tetrarch. And surprisingly, just as the parable states, a delegation of upset citizens was sent ahead to plead their case in Rome that he not be made tetrarch. Archelaus had recently slain some three thousand Jews in a dispute among the Pharisees. Herod Antipas took up their cause (and one for himself as well) and argued that Archelaus not be allowed to rule. The Romans decided in Archelaus' favor, to their detriment, having later to send procurators to administer Archelaus' regions.[53]

Hence, the details would be rather fresh in the minds of Jesus' audience. There would have been a man of noble birth, who was indeed not liked by his own countrymen, who went to a far country to receive his kingdom and then returned.

Here, of course, the story becomes less politically oriented and more practically poignant.

---

[53] F.F. Bruce, New Testament History, Doubleday, New York (1980), p 25

"And he called ten of his slaves, and gave them ten minas and said to them, `Do business with this until I come back.'

A mina was a sixtieth of a talent in ancient times. As earlier noted in the Parable of the Talents (Matthew 18:23), a talent would be about $60.00, were it to simply be converted into our modern coinage, i.e. based on our penny.

Using an equivalent hourly wage of $15.00 for unskilled manual labor, the ancient penny would be $120. In today's money the talent would then be about $720,000, or 6000 times the daily wage. This also depends on whether the silver talent was meant (which would have been less) but the mention of the mina tells us that the gold talent was in view, because the mina was related to the gold talent, not the silver.

At this equivalency, a mina would be $12,000 of equivalent purchasing power in our system today (1/60 of a talent of $720,000. (The inflation amounts to 12,000 times or 1,200,000 percent over two thousand years.)

Each received one mina each, as opposed to a mina spread among the ten. We might wonder why they didn't run and set themselves free, having a significant amount of money to establish themselves elsewhere?

First, slavery in ancient times was not easily escaped by one's own efforts or by simple flight. You could not just slip into society unnoticed given enough money. Money would not erase the tell tale signs of prior slavery, which usually included a mark. Without emancipation papers from the master and not being on any obvious business, the jig would soon be up, and back to the master you would soon be sent for severe punishment.

Second, there are ten, and all ten would need to be in agreement as in a conspiracy, which would be hard to arrange.

Lastly, in many ways for the poor and disadvantaged, slavery with a good master was preferable to the precarious and threatened life one might manage on their own. Here you were at least provided for.

"But his citizens hated him and sent a delegation after him, saying, `We do not want this man to reign over us.'

Here, the secondary theme in the parable in now introduced. The nobleman is not liked much in his current kingdom, and his citizens take the opportunity to express this in his absence.

Nothing more is made of this except the mention of the delegation. We must therefore set this theme aside for the moment while the rest of the parable is told - *"When he returned, . . . he ordered that these slaves. . be called to him, . . . so that he might know what business they had done.*

So, despite the interjection of the hatred of his citizens, the story returns immediately back to the accounting of the slaves with their money.

'Master, your mina has made ten minas more.'

This, and the master's response sets the tone of what "doing business" meant. There was an expectation of making the investment grow or produce - *'because you have been faithful in a very little thing, you are to be in authority over ten cities.'*

We wonder how a slave could be given this much independent authority, but again, the parallel to real life is not essential. The idea is that good results from smaller responsibilities yield greater responsibilities as a reward.

So also with the second who has done half as well and receives rewards proportionally. But these are not really the points on which the parable turns -

"Another came, saying, `Master, here is your mina, which I kept put away in a handkerchief;

This is the person on whom the parable focuses. He has not done as the others, to invest, but has hidden the mina on the basis of fear. That fear was not that he might lose the mina and have to account for it. He does not say that he worried if he lost the mina that the master would be harsh. Instead he says, *'for I was afraid of you, because you take up what you did not lay down and reap what you did not sow.'*

This slave worries over the loss of the increase. He knows if he gains something from investment, it will be his own doing and work, but the master will take it as his own.

The emphasis is on taking up what he *did not sow*, not on getting back the amount invested. That he did in fact sow. The increase would have been the thing not sowed but gained.

What the slave was effectively telling his master is that for fear and spite, he purposely did not invest so that the master would be disabled from taking what the slave had wrought by his own efforts.

Now we might expect Jesus to take up the slave's cause, since he would have been "cheated" out of an increase based on his own efforts. But Jesus does not take up his case, but rather that of the master.

"I tell you that to everyone who has, more shall be given, but from the one who does not have, even what he does have shall be taken away.

This is the first lesson from this parable – that faithfulness in a little brings opportunities to be responsible and faithful in more. That our concern should be less for self and more for making our master successful.

First, we must recognize, as Jesus does, that the seed money was the master's, not that of the slaves. He is entitled to the increase because he put his money at risk.

Their context and ours is about investing and business, not about personal agendas and fears. Note that Jesus has the master say, "You should at least have gotten basic interest in the bank."

So it is about performing one's duties and being responsible.

Second, the slaves will not be without reward for their efforts. They will get significant blessings in authority and responsibility. This, the third slave sacrificed to ensure his own pride of management would not be lost if expended.

In terms of modern application, there are few identical situations of slave and master. But we are given talents and gifts, and perhaps even money by our Great Master, and these to invest in the Kingdom.

If we take the attitude of the good slaves, we will invest our talents without care for our own remuneration, but for the joy of the increase it brings to God and His Kingdom.

If we should take the attitude of the bad slave, we will always be thinking in terms of ours and His and making sure ours is acknowledged. We will be embittered if what we have done of ourselves goes to His glory and not ours. (There are some people who retreat from service if it is perceived ahead of time that they will get no personal credit or aggrandizement.)

Now He returns to the secondary theme -

"But these enemies of mine, who did not want me to reign over them, bring them here and slay them in my presence."

This seems harsh, since we infer that Jesus is stating this as a lesson. He is not condemning the master for his harshness against his enemies. In fact, He makes no follow-up comments about the meaning at all. He lets the weight of it stand raw and unaided, as He then gets up to leave for the city.

In this parable, the master, though hard-nosed, is righteous and industrious. He is also just by rewarding good work and punishing bad attitudes. In these things the nobleman represents Christ Himself. Thus the enemies of the nobleman are the enemies of Jesus as rightful king.

There are other parallels. The nobleman goes away to receive a kingdom and then return. Christ comes in His first advent to seek and to save. He has invested gifts and talents among the sons of light and even among those of darkness (Mozart was gifted but not known as a religious man.)

At His death and resurrection, He goes to receive the kingdom of His Father and the preparation for His return. There at that time, the men who exemplify and foreshadow the men who will be living at His return, revile Him and spew hatred against Him. They too say they will not have Him to rule over them.

While He is gone, others in the world, including the many of His chosen people, come to also hate Him, and many say, "We will not have Him to rule over us."

He will come again, after receiving His Kingdom, and He will find those same – the ones who reject Him. And we see in the pictures of the Revelation that all such are gathered and slain.

Now the Passover of the Jews was near

This will be the last Passover of Jesus' ministry and life. It will be the one around which His crucifixion is hastily arranged. So the time of year is late March, early April. The Passion week will begin on Sunday as Jesus enters the city on a donkey and will end the following Sunday with His Resurrection and Ascension.

As a brush-up, the Passover was the first feast of the new year. After the new year was determined by observation of the new moon (between March and April), the evening of the 14th day (as it turned to the 15th) was the celebration of that meal that commemorated the angel of death passing over the houses bearing the seal of blood from the sacrifices, and the going out of Egypt the next day.

So did it symbolize the covering of Christ's blood that we be spared the judgment of death, and that we be freed thereby to newness of life.

How the Passover of this year in Jesus life plays out will be told in its proper place as this accounting unfolds.

Despite their charge that He departs from the traditions of the elders, we are told that the Jews expect Jesus to at least be faithful to come to the feast. So they see this as their opportunity to take Him.

Jesus, therefore, six days before the Passover, came to Bethany . .

This would be the weekly Sabbath – a Saturday. This is somewhat counterintuitive because of the way we calculate time spans in the western tradition compared to the east. Normally, we would say that six days before an event begins counting the day before it. So if an event occurred on Thursday, we would begin counting Wednesday back to Friday to get to the sixth day prior.

But the Jews counted the same day of the event when counting backwards, which in our example above would make the sixth day Saturday not Friday.

As for the sixth day here in the gospel, all depends on which day the Passover fell for this year. In the Gospels we are told that the disciples celebrated the Passover the night before His Crucifixion which was on Friday, making the Passover on Thursday. If so, then six days before the Passover would make the visit to Bethany occur on the Sabbath, which accounts for why He had stopped there instead of going on into the city. He is seen taking His Sabbath rest in Bethany.

And if tradition has some validity in these affairs, we also find that the next day when He rode into Jerusalem became Palm Sunday in the Church calendar, hence the previous day at Bethany would have been the weekly Sabbath.

at the home of Simon the leper

Here, more authentication that the day was a Sabbath. If Jesus had come to visit Lazarus' family on just any day, He would have come to Lazarus' home. Why Lazarus and his sisters are at another man's home is easily explained by people seldom celebrating the Sabbath in isolation but rather with friends, taking turns in each other's homes.

So they made Him a supper there, and Martha was serving;

These duties were permissible on the Sabbath.

Mary then took a pound of very costly perfume of pure nard, and anointed the feet of Jesus

In this accounting, only John tells us that it was Mary. Matthew and Mark mention 'a woman,' which has created much distress over the authenticity of the gospels in allowing such a discrepancy. Surely they knew her name, so it would be disrespectful to her to merely call her a woman.

This is not resolved by an appeal to the place of women in these times. Mary was commended by Jesus in the earlier visit, so it would be out of keeping for His biographers to call her merely a woman.

Perhaps there was some need to protect Mary from the authorities and since Mark and Matthew were circulating much earlier than John, it may very well have been a move on their part to keep her name disassociated with this act of anointing, whereas Martha had merely served them a Sabbath's repast.

As for the disciples present, their human souls still lack the spirituality of their later years.

But the disciples were indignant when they saw this, and said, "Why this waste?

We must remember that these were much more desperate times materially than the average person is in today. Something like the ointment she used would have been very hard to come by in those days. And they say it right out – it was costly. As such, it clearly could have been put to better use if it was to be given at all.

"Why was this perfume not sold for three hundred denarii and given to poor people?"

Judas picks up on this indignation to mask his general impiety. He mirrors their concerns by expanding on why it was a waste – it could have been used for the poor. Surely this would catch the ear of Jesus, who was keen on helping them, especially in telling the rich man to sell what he had and give the proceeds for their benefit. Fits right in with a recent teaching, says Judas in his mind.

But the writer tells us his truer motive -

Now he said this, not because he was concerned about the poor, but because he was a thief, and as he had the money box, he used to pilfer what was put into it.

Meaning that Judas was grieving over the resources it would have turned at market, and the additional coins over which his pilfering fingers might fly.

Now it is interesting that Jesus must have known this was going on, yet He has made no move to curtail it or discipline Judas. Perhaps this was due to the patent fact that despite such behavior, the Son of God was not going to be without money on any account. And the actions of Judas were to be handled much like He deals with personal freedom today.

The Lord certainly knows our sins through and through, yet He does not part the clouds with lightning bolts of discipline. This is to say that there are some things He leaves to be governed by our free will in the hopes that we will curtail these on our own, by having our wills conform steadily to His.

"Let her alone, so that she may keep it for the day of My burial.

He upbraids them in contradiction to all their expectations in regard to what could have been done for the poor. And it was out of character to His teaching about them. But we must observe the setting itself. He was not allowing that it be used for self – that would be a contradiction. But rather He was allowing it to be used for this special purpose – to anoint Him for burial, which happened to be a powerful theme He very much needed to continue discussing and demonstrating as they neared the moments that would bring it on.

Note the capper that secures this meaning – *"For you always have the poor with you, but you do not always have Me."*

There would be plenty of other opportunities to serve the needs of the poor. They were certainly not going anywhere quickly, then or in any age. However, He was to be with them but a week more.

"Truly I say to you, wherever this gospel is preached in the whole world, what this woman has done will also be spoken of in memory of her."

We are now living two millennia since then and the name of this Mary has been heard in the ears of every generation in the western world since then. The person living in Europe in the 900's A.D. heard it, those living at the time of the great explorers to the new world heard it, and we are alive to hear it still today.

When we think about it, she was just an ordinary person who would otherwise have been completely forgotten as all of her neighbors most certainly have been. Yet, because of her connection with Jesus in this one act and her former desire to sit at His feet, she has become known to millions of people.

It is as though her reason for having lived is now summed up in her relationship to Jesus. Not a bad concept for any of us to embrace.

The large crowd of the Jews then learned that He was there

Jesus is now of such notoriety that He cannot have privacy for long anywhere He goes. Even as He is teaching in this small interlude of time, crowds are ferreting His whereabouts and beginning to gather at Bethany. It must have been a constant plague in some of His disciples eyes, always taking the edge off whatever private time they could manage with Him.

And we learn that the people come there also to now see Lazarus as well, being the subject of such a great miracle just recently done – *that they might also see Lazarus, whom He raised from the dead.*

But the chief priests planned to put Lazarus to death also;

Here is a little verse tucked away in the gospel accounts that we seldom hear read or take much notice of ordinarily. But it tells us that our dear and rather innocent Lazarus has now become a target of the Pharisees also, that in fact his very life is now in jeopardy.

Now the Pharisees surely knew where Lazarus lived, so it would hardly be a case of trying to find him. It would more likely have been a problem of how to arrange things without angering the people. What charges could have been levied? What charges worthy of death could have been advanced?

What is of note here, is the absolute degree of wickedness taking hold of these men. We sometimes too naively plead the case of the Pharisees by noting that they were simply trying to be faithful to the faith of their fathers and to God's Word. And over-zealousness is not necessarily abject evil.

But here we see that evil has in fact really taken hold in their hearts – an evil that Jesus earlier warned His disciples to avoid wherever possible – *"beware the leaven of the Pharisees."*

And this is not overstated in the least. Consider that Lazarus was merely a man who received the benefit of Jesus' power and the miracle of God in his life, that he was used to demonstrate that a man can be raised from the dead. He had no axe to grind against the Pharisees. He was not a malcontent or a seditionist. He simply received the effect of that miracle, having no decision in the matter at all. He was clearly dead at the time.

Yet the Pharisees wish to kill him. And is it for his part in the miracle – that he was in fact raised? No. It was for the self-centered reason that the news of this was causing masses of the people to come over to Jesus – *on account of him many of the Jews were going away and were believing in Jesus.*

They had paid no heed to the miracle itself and the tremendous import it conveyed, but focused rather on the disaffection this was creating against them. Clearly in this, one can see hearts of abject evil, filled so much with self as to measure the works of God against one's own motives and greed.

This is the audience to which Jesus will soon willingly submit, and the one from which understandably His disciples hide when the time comes for making themselves known.

Few scenes are the picture of such hatred and vitriol as we will soon see when we enter the last week of Jesus life.

John 12:12-19, Luke 19:29-44, Matthew 21:3-4, Mark 11:4, Matthew 21:7, Mark 11:10-11, Matthew 21:10-11
12 On the next day the large crowd who had come to the feast, when they heard that Jesus was coming to Jerusalem, 13 took the branches of the palm trees and went out to meet Him, and began to shout, "Hosanna! BLESSED IS HE WHO COMES IN THE NAME OF THE LORD, even the King of Israel." (John 12:12-13)

29 When He approached Bethphage and Bethany, near the mount that is called Olivet, He sent two of the disciples, 30 saying, "Go into the village ahead of you; there, as you enter, you will find a colt tied on which no one yet has ever sat; untie it and bring it here. 31 "If anyone asks you, `Why are you untying it?' you shall say, `The Lord has need of it.' " . . and immediately he will send them." 4 This took place to fulfill what was spoken through the prophet: 5 "SAY TO THE DAUGHTER OF ZION, `BEHOLD YOUR KING IS COMING TO YOU, GENTLE, AND MOUNTED ON A DONKEY, EVEN ON A COLT, THE FOAL OF A BEAST OF BURDEN.' " . .

32 So those who were sent went away and found it just as He had told them. . . a colt tied at the door, outside in the street; . . 33 As they were untying the colt, its owners said to them, "Why are you untying the colt?" 34 They said, "The Lord has need of it." . . 7 and brought the donkey and the colt, and laid their coats on them; and He sat on the coats. . . as it is written, 15 "FEAR NOT, DAUGHTER OF ZION; BEHOLD, YOUR KING IS COMING, SEATED ON A DONKEY'S COLT." 16 These things His disciples did not understand at the first; but when Jesus was glorified, then they remembered that these things were written of Him, and that they had done these things to Him. (Luke 19:29-31, Matthew 21:3-4, Luke 19:32, Mark 11:4, Luke 19:33-34, Matthew 21:7, John 12:14-16)

36 As He was going, they were spreading their coats on the road. 37 As soon as He was approaching, near the descent of the Mount of Olives, the whole crowd of the disciples began to praise God joyfully with a loud voice for all the miracles which they had seen, 38 shouting: "BLESSED IS THE KING WHO COMES IN THE NAME OF THE LORD; . . 10 Blessed is the coming kingdom of our father David; Hosanna in the highest!" . . Peace in heaven and glory in the highest!" 39 Some of the Pharisees in the crowd said to Him, "Teacher, rebuke Your disciples." 40 But Jesus answered, "I tell you, if these become silent, the stones will cry out!" (Luke 19:36-38, Mark 11:10, Luke 19:39-40)

41 When He approached Jerusalem, He saw the city and wept over it, 42 saying, "If you had known in this day, even you, the things which make for peace! But now they have been hidden from your eyes. 43 "For the days will come upon you when your enemies will throw up a barricade against you, and surround you and hem you in on every side, 44 and they will level you to the ground and your children within you, and they will not leave in you one stone upon another, because you did not recognize the time of your visitation." (Luke 19:41-44)

10 When He had entered Jerusalem, all the city was stirred, saying, "Who is this?" 11 And the crowds were saying, "This is the prophet Jesus, from Nazareth in Galilee." (Matthew 21:10-11)

17 So the people, who were with Him when He called Lazarus out of the tomb and raised him from the dead, continued to testify about Him. 18 For this reason also the people went and met Him, because they heard that He had performed this sign. 19 So the Pharisees said to one another, "You see that you are not doing any good; look, the world has gone after Him." (John 12:17-19)

11 Jesus . . came into the temple; and after looking around at everything, He left for Bethany with the twelve, since it was already late. (Mark 11:11)

Commentary

On the next day the large crowd . . . took the branches of the palm trees and went out to meet Him,

The next day is now Sunday following the Sabbath He spent in Bethany where the anointing by the young Mary had taken place. The feast which the Jews are anticipating is the Passover – a week away, and the last of Jesus ministry and life.

That the crowd noticed His approach and began to treat Him as a coming king tells us how many had actually now embraced who He was, and with enough courage to publicly declare it in the sight of the authorities. The waving of the palm branches and Hosannahs date back to the time of the Maccabees and the revolt against Macedonian rule over Palestine. The victory accomplished in the 2nd century B.C. was spontaneously celebrated by people picking these branches and singing Hosannah ("save us now") and the custom continued in use since then for victory parades.

It should be noted that from that time until the time of Jesus there were few such occasions in practice because there were no national conflicts to speak of. There occurred a very brief period of less than a hundred years of independence, followed by Roman rule in which "victories" of this kind would hardly have occurred. So the occasion here is perhaps the first in a very long time where such symbolism was recalled and heaped on an individual of prominence.

The meaning is clear that the people were expecting Jesus to fulfill the remaining aspects of Messiah – in returning the land to independence from foreign rule and the inauguration of the Kingdom promised of old (Dan 2:44.)

BLESSED IS HE WHO COMES IN THE NAME OF THE LORD

The New American Standard and other NT editions highlight this as an application of an OT declaration (Psalms 118:26.) But from our perspective, this seems hard to see as a unique fulfillment, since it could be applied to virtually anyone who came preaching or prophesying.

The reason it is seen as significant has to do with what accompanies this statement in the psalm – " *19 Open to me the gates of righteousness; I shall enter through them, I shall give thanks to the LORD. 20 This is the gate of the LORD; The righteous will enter through it. 21 I shall give thanks to You, for You have answered me, And You have become my salvation. 22 The stone which the builders rejected has become the chief corner stone.*"

Again, we might wonder how this is being made so significant as to be applied to Jesus, since it could easily apply to David, and after all, he was the author. David was speaking about himself and how the nations may be gathered around him but he will trust in the Lord rather than men. He can indeed be seen as entering the gates and honoring the Lord as his salvation.

What suggests that this should be applied also to Jesus is the principle in Scripture of "double fulfillment." Proclamations in an OT context are seen to be foreshadowings of a later application in the New. The sign that this is happening is usually in some enigmatic phrase or statement that can't be completely or thoroughly explained in the first context.

Which brings us to v.22 in the psalm – *"The stone which the builders rejected has become the chief corner stone."*

There is certainly apt application to David in that he was initially considered unsuitable for king, but was found to be the best of the nation's kings. But we don't find the Jews using this terminology with respect to David – the idea of him being a cornerstone seems to have fallen into obscurity almost as soon as the psalm was written. It is as though it was all along intended for someone else.

David's building was of his own house. When we compare that to how Christ fit so criticality into a number of major themes – the building of God's Kingdom, the key to salvation and eternal life, the resolution of man's dilemma of sin – one can see the concept of cornerstone being so much more completely fulfilled in Him as to question that David alone was ever meant.

When He approached Bethphage and Bethany, near the mount that is called Olivet,

Some confusion here, in that Bethany is mentioned, since He seems to have left Bethany. In the east, things were less definite and exactingly described as in the Greek tradition. When one looks at a map of the area, Bethany is furthest east with Bethphage on the way toward Jerusalem which could easily be seen in the distance.

The home of Lazarus may very well have been on the outskirts of the main dwellings that comprised Bethany proper. So, leaving Lazarus' home, He could easily be said to approach Bethany's main cluster of homes on His way also to Bethphage.

Bethany means 'house of dates' (the fruit); Bethphage – 'house of figs.'

These are both on the eastern side of Jerusalem across the Kidron Valley, hence near the Mount of Olives.

The French word 'Olivet' is not specifically in the Greek text as such, but is a sort of anachronism folded back into the text at the time of translation. The word is 'elaion' which simply means olives. How the mount came to be called by its French equivalent - 'Olivet' – is very obscure.

He sent two of the disciples,

The village ahead must mean Bethphage. He describes that it has been "arranged" that a colt will be made available to them. We have no indication that He Himself pre-arranged this as one would normally make such arrangements, but that this is a case of divine intervention with the animal's owners.

"on which no one has ever sat" would only be known by the owner. It is rather a mark of the miraculous affair being arranged. Not only was the colt to be made available by means of a simple answer (that would never have sufficed otherwise) but Jesus' ability to sit on it without the normal difficulties expected would be exceptional.

`BEHOLD YOUR KING IS COMING TO YOU, GENTLE, AND MOUNTED ON A DONKEY, EVEN ON A COLT, THE FOAL OF A BEAST OF BURDEN.' "

Recited from Zechariah 9:9, we see that two beasts are in view, both of which we later see being brought to Jesus (Matthew 21:7.) There was no pre-fulfillment of this in prior OT times. It was clearly seen as being purely messianic and future by the Jews. It was considered extraordinary because such a noted person as Israel's rightful king would not be expected to come on a mere colt.

Some might ask that if this was messianic, why didn't the Jewish leaders make the connection and see Jesus as their Messiah. The answer is simply that knowing the indicator in the OT, one who aspired to be seen as Messiah could simply make this arrangement to authenticate themselves. Since the leaders already rejected Him for other reasons, they saw this as a flagrant attempt to misappropriate the sign to gain followers.

To be technically accurate, Jesus is said here and in the prophecy to sit on the foal of the donkey, the donkey being its mother. Error in the account has been charged since the prophecy states he would come riding on a donkey. Also, "even on a colt" is often understood as "and on a colt" which would suggest riding on both the donkey and the colt, another contradiction.

But this is a case of customary wording both in the original and in English. The words "even a colt" is a literary means of further qualifying a general statement. 'Even' here means "specifically.' And technically, a foal or a colt is a donkey, so it could be said He rode a donkey without error, the point being to say it was not the mother.

.. and laid their coats on them; and He sat on the coats

This gives further moment to the charge of inconsistency, in that by sitting on the coats it implies He sat on both animals. But this is not demanded from the verses, since more than one coat could easily have been placed on each animal and sitting on any one of them would constitute sitting on coats.

Also, this is followed up by a repeat of Zechariah – *"BEHOLD, YOUR KING IS COMING, SEATED ON A DONKEY'S COLT."* which would settle that it was one animal. (Note that this second citation is not a separate reference but a paraphrase of the first. The writer specifically adds this to allay the implications that 'coats" might imply both animals.)

These things His disciples did not understand at the first;

This is a little tough to understand clearly because we later hear His disciples re-stating Psalm 118:26 with the addition of the word "king" which they would need to have gotten by recalling Zechariah 9:9, mentioned below.

This statement may refer to the deeper understanding of the connection between these prophecies, but did not preclude applying the 'king' of Zechariah to the "he" of the psalm. They would certainly spend much more time later pondering their mission with Him and to take more seriously the task of researching all the OT references He had fulfilled. Such a task would be paramount to any further preaching to the Jews because they would be keenly interested in the proofs of His messiahship.

As soon as He was approaching, near the descent of the Mount of Olives, ...

The location indicates that He was intent on entering through the East Gate, which we now see walled up today in the Byzantine walls around the Temple compound. The East Gate was aligned directly with the entry path to the Holy Place, and was the customary route of a victorious king into the city proper and directly to the Temple.

"BLESSED IS THE KING WHO COMES IN THE NAME OF THE LORD;"

This is not a separate reference that uses the word "king." It is really just a paraphrase of the verse from Psalm 118:26 in which king is added on the strength of combining Zechariah 9:9 with Psalm 118. But it does demonstrate the ability to relate key features from the various prophecies in those following Him.

Hosanna in the highest!" .. Peace in heaven and glory in the highest!"

The use of the highest was routinely a clarification and a proclamation that one was talking about the pinnacle of spiritual origins. The highest Heaven was not merely a place among many, but the ultimate place above all others. The God being asked to save is the one above all others, the highest court of appeal.

"Teacher, rebuke Your disciples."

The things said were obviously troublesome to the authorities. One couldn't have what they regarded as a mere man accepting praise as king. It is clear that the Pharisees were close at hand to observe this event, in no way joining the crowd in their rejoicing, but to be ready to detect any inappropriate or illegal proceedings.

The Pharisees were well aware that Jesus had made claims tantamount to being Messiah, so the call to quiet His disciples would have been to some degree without serious expectation. But the Pharisees had an obligation to go on record for rebuking Him and charging that He discipline His followers in what they perceived as formal indiscretion.

The answer is among the most far reaching and poignant in the New Testament. -

"I tell you, if these become silent, the stones will cry out!"

There is more here than just poetic energy. In Daniel's prophecy of the Seventy Weeks, we have a formula for calculating the arrival of Messiah from a specific point prior in the ancient past. The angelic prophecy stated that seventy weeks were determined on Daniel's people and this period was broken down into three periods: 62 weeks and 7 weeks to Messiah the prince, then a final week after which the Kingdom would be established forever. (Dan 9:24ff)

As to the beginning of the period - and also of the first 69 weeks - the angel explained that the beginning would be marked by the decree to rebuild Jerusalem (being that at the time of Daniel it lay in ruins.)

There are several schemes that set the date of that decree, each with a varying point of reference. Of these, only one can be seen as coming true precisely as predicted – the decree of Artaxerxes in Nehemiah chapter two. Sir Robert Anderson ("The Coming Prince", Kregel re-print)[54] has successfully calculated the period to come true to the very day, i.e the period from the decree to an event that would represent the coming of Messiah comprises the exact number of days required.

The formula depends on an understanding that the weeks are not literal weeks but weeks of years, based on the fact that Jacob worked for Laban one week to acquire his wife and this turned out to be seven years not merely one week.

---

[54] Kregel, Grand Rapids, (1957) p. 127

The period thus is calculated as being 173,880 days, using the Jewish lunar calendar of the times. When the Jewish calendar is then calibrated against the Julian-Gregorian calendar, the period ends with a date in the life of Jesus.

As it happens, that date is the very day of His triumphal entry into Jerusalem here before us.

One can now understand the statement, *"if these become silent, even the stones will cry out!"* It is as though all nature knew what day it was. If man was to be silenced, nature itself would declare the day for all to hear.

Please be aware that the excursus of this explanation is very complicated and many aspects require careful research into the sciences involved and the history of the calendar in general. Without the patience to do that, a great deal of confusion and numerous miscalculations by novice students can result.

"If you had known in this day, even you, the things which make for peace!

Jesus is said to weep here and we can understand why. If we are caught up in the incredible irony of the Jews killing their own Messiah, we can have immense compassion for all the opportunities ready to be embraced, all the prophecies ready to be fulfilled if only they were ready to hear.

Coupled with this is the love the Son and Father had for the people of God and the foreknowledge of the pain and suffering that will ensue because of this rejection. The account of Josephus of the fall of Jerusalem to the Romans is bone chilling in terms of human suffering. People swallowing down their life savings in coins and running to the Romans were subsequently hacked to death to retrieve the ingested money. Those not with the rebellious factions were mercilessly slaughtered by their own countrymen, such that the terror inside the city was more dreadful than that outside.

Jesus knows what is ahead in light of this rejection. Not merely a few years of suffering, but centuries of it were now waiting for them. And the tragic tone in all of that was that it could have been alleviated were they to accept His love and that of His Father. So, yes, tears were appropriate.

But now they have been hidden from your eyes.

This will be the case for the next two millennia at least. Paul states that blindness in part has happened to Israel until the fullness of the Gentiles has come in (Rom 11:25.) Here also is reiterated the indictment of Isaiah – "having ears they hear not .. that they should turn and I heal them." (Isaiah 6:10.)

"For the days will come upon you when your enemies will throw up a barricade against you, . . . and they will not leave in you one stone upon another, because you did not recognize the time of your visitation."

All of these predictions were fulfilled in the destruction of Jerusalem some forty years away. Barricades were thrown up to hem them in that none could escape the city without running into the Romans. The city was leveled to the ground, except for a section of the temple wall on the west, today known as the Western Wall. Even Antonia, the Roman garrison, was torn down. With few exceptions, every living person inside was put to the sword or died by fire.

With respect to the Temple, it was torn down stone by stone to level ground, as were the adjoining walls. Some of those stones are still seen today in the exact place they came to rest down the slopes.

The Temple had caught fire contrary to Titus' orders against it. The gold overlaying the ceiling and upper appointments melted and drizzled down into the cracks of the stones, such that the Romans dismantled every piece of masonry to scrape off the metal. (See discussion also at Mark 13:1-4.)

Some scholars deny this was a punishment for their rejection of Messiah and that this was merely the result of inciteful actions against the Romans that had an inevitable outcome anyway.

But Jesus makes it clear, *" because you did not recognize the time of your visitation."*

When He had entered Jerusalem, all the city was stirred, saying, "Who is this?" . . So the people, who were with Him when He called Lazarus out of the tomb and raised him from the dead, continued to testify about Him.

The timing was right for bringing everything to a head. The recent raising of Lazarus added considerable numbers to his followers (such that Lazarus was sought for punishment), and this produced more acute testimonies that would unnerve the authorities. It also increased by significant magnitude the eagerness and anticipation to see Him in the city.

This is said to account for the size of the crowd greeting Him with Hosannahs.

"You see that you are not doing any good; look, the world has gone after Him."

Hyperbole typical of eastern modes of expression is employed here. As they looked about them, the tumult was undeniable. This was an event sociologique in purely visual terms. The milder days of simply wondering where He was and what the people in Galilee were doing had now come home as a gathering storm.

Jesus . . came into the temple; and after looking around at everything, He left for Bethany with the twelve, since it was already late.

Almost unimpressed, Jesus leaves barely as soon as He has arrived. He, of course, had seen it all before. The retreat to Bethany was not on account of any feast days or ceremonial rest, but merely to spend the night out of the city in peace.

Mark 11:12-18, Luke 19:47,48, Matthew 21:14-16, John 12:20-26

12 On the next day, when they had left Bethany, He became hungry. 13 Seeing at a distance a fig tree in leaf, He went to see if perhaps He would find anything on it; and when He came to it, He found nothing but leaves, for it was not the season for figs. 14 He said to it, "May no one ever eat fruit from you again!" And His disciples were listening.

15 Then they came to Jerusalem. And He entered the temple and began to drive out those who were buying and selling in the temple, and overturned the tables of the money changers and the seats of those who were selling doves; 16 and He would not permit anyone to carry merchandise through the temple. 17 And He began to teach and say to them, "Is it not written, `MY HOUSE SHALL BE CALLED A HOUSE OF PRAYER FOR ALL THE NATIONS'? But you have made it a ROBBERS' DEN." 18 The chief priests and the scribes heard this, and began seeking how to destroy Him; for they were afraid of Him, for the whole crowd was astonished at His teaching. (Mark 11:12-18)

47 And He was teaching daily in the temple; but the chief priests and the scribes and the leading men among the people were trying to destroy Him, 48 and they could not find anything that they might do, for all the people were hanging on to every word He said. (Luke 19:47,48)

14 And the blind and the lame came to Him in the temple, and He healed them. 15 But when the chief priests and the scribes saw the wonderful things that He had done, and the children who were shouting in the temple, "Hosanna to the Son of David," they became indignant 16 and said to Him, "Do You hear what these children are saying?" And Jesus said to them, "Yes; have you never read, `OUT OF THE MOUTH OF INFANTS AND NURSING BABIES YOU HAVE PREPARED PRAISE FOR YOURSELF'?" (Matthew 21:14-16)

20 Now there were some Greeks among those who were going up to worship at the feast; 21 these then came to Philip, who was from Bethsaida of Galilee, and began to ask him, saying, "Sir, we wish to see Jesus." 22 Philip came and told Andrew; Andrew and Philip came and told Jesus. 23 And Jesus answered them, saying, "The hour has come for the Son of Man to be glorified. 24 "Truly, truly, I say to you, unless a grain of wheat falls into the earth and dies, it remains alone; but if it dies, it bears much fruit. 25 "He who loves his life loses it, and he who hates his life in this world will keep it to life eternal. 26 "If anyone serves Me, he must follow Me; and where I am, there My servant will be also; if anyone serves Me, the Father will honor him. (John 12:20-26)

Commentary

Seeing at a distance a fig tree in leaf, He went to see if perhaps He would find anything on it; . . . He said to it, "May no one ever eat fruit from you again!" And His disciples were listening.

This is rather enigmatic because of the phrase *it was not the season for figs*, which surely He would have known.

This is not a lesson that needs to engage the seasons correctly to be effective. The fact that the season was not yet for figs simply served to permit the tree to be an object lesson about things in general that bear no fruit. Remember that the conditional clause beginning this section was that Jesus was hungry and came to the tree for nourishment. So the lesson is really about expectations of fruit and not finding any. The issue of the season is irrelevant with respect to the lesson itself.

His disciples are said to be listening, which is another way of saying they were intent on the meaning of His words. Curiously, He does not explain any extended meaning for the curse, yet we will not be satisfied that this was merely a tantrum about finding nothing to eat.

We will see later that Jesus provides an explanation dealing with the disciples' wonder at the response of nature to the curse of Jesus. He uses the incident to instruct them on what they can expect from the use of faith.

But that later instruction is not the import of why Jesus cursed the tree in the first place. There is a grand convergence of two ideas in the same event – the condition of needing physical nourishment and this then being the stage on which a more subtle message to Israel could be set.

The curse is related to Israel's dirth of good fruit in the Kingdom of God. In every way, the Son of God came to His people expecting to find good works, especially among those leading the nation. They ought to have had the heart of God more than any others, hence the expectation was greater. But He found no such works, not even a faith worthy of mention. They were found virtually barren.

Hence the curse, *"May no one ever eat fruit from you again."* This is, again, a form of hyperbole, because we read elsewhere in Paul that, in fact, fruit will once again come from Israel. The context here is that no fruit will be had from them *as they remain in their unfaithfulness.*

Hyperbole is used to amplify the intensity of the condition being described, not to declare some final indictment or immutable decree. In the case of the actual tree this was final and effective. In the case of Israel, it was dependent on where they went next.

And He entered the temple and began to drive out those who were buying and selling in the temple,

We saw this recounted earlier (John 2:14-17), so this is a second occurrence. As one might expect after the first incident, the dealers had no intention of actually closing down. We can readily imagine the confused looks on that first occasion - What was the big deal? They had no clue that what they were about was inappropriate. Hence, we see them back in place just as before.

This is an important analogy about the secular enterprises of man. We take initial thought to plan what we will do with our lives to make a living. Having no real guidance, we fly by the seat of our pants and consult whomever happens to be ready at hand, and we take off on recommendations that are actually ill-conceived. Then when someone presents the tension or even outright conflict such things present in the Christian life, we wax puzzled and stunned that we are so wholly on the other side of the fence.

'MY HOUSE SHALL BE CALLED A HOUSE OF PRAYER FOR ALL THE NATIONS'? *But you have made it a ROBBERS' DEN."*

The life with God is meant to be contemplative not ritualistic. We are to take time to discern God's will and purpose that we may be obedient and ready to effect them. Jesus virtually shouts that this is the real purpose of the Temple – to fellowship with God.

Now we can't minimize into oblivion the necessities of the sacrificial system – they were after all commanded. But they were to place thoughts in the mind of the worshiper regarding his sin and his need to restore his relationship with God. The ritual was not to become the main event, yet that is precisely what the Jews made of it, such that arrangements for merchants selling "authorized" and acceptable victims was tolerated as just a logical part of what the Temple was now about.

Elsewhere it was said that the zeal for His house has consumed Him (John 2:17.) It was a passion that the house of God was for one purpose and this was being stolen away and in fact hidden from the people by the institutions of the temple. Being "consumed" is an almost anti-climactic expression.

The chief priests and the scribes heard this, and began seeking how to destroy Him;

You would think that this recitation of the OT exhortation (Isaiah 56:7) would have brought the men to some sense of shame and repentance. But their evil hearts can think of only one thing – this man is embarrassing us and showing us to have missed the intent of our God. This is what comes from an entrenched system of thinking that dismisses any further need to review the basis for one's actions.

for they were afraid of Him,

Notice it was not mere hatred alone. The mention now of fear indicates that they perceived the legitimacy of the truths He was speaking, yet they were now irretrievably on the opposite side of those truths, hence fear now comes to the fore. He must be done away with – that is the only solution.

and they could not find anything that they might do, for all the people were hanging on to every word He said.

This, of course, is their chief dilemma. So many aspects of His character and teaching were unassailable. Were He thoroughly and consistently contrary to Moses, it would be a done deal on how to handle Him in full view of the people. But they could not deny the insight and wisdom He possessed from above, nor His power to deliver from disease and even death. They could not deny that such things would be impossible in a malefactor or a charlatan, despite their feeble public charge that He thus operated.

They were clearly stuck with the problem of the people and their recognition that their own case had little prospects of succeeding against the dynamic of the crowd itself. And despite the legitimacy of Jesus' teaching, this practical side could not be avoided. You just can't easily sway a crowd bent rightly or wrongly the opposite direction from your own wishes.

"Do You hear what these children are saying?"

Their only present scope of action was to quell whatever indiscretions might occur among the people and try as best they could to keep outright offenses minimized. It says that the people, including children, were proclaiming Him Son of David (which we have seen earlier is a technical term for Messiah, not merely the innocuous acknowledgement of simple facts - that He was in the lineage of David.)

"Yes; have you never read, 'OUT OF THE MOUTH OF INFANTS AND NURSING BABIES YOU HAVE PREPARED PRAISE FOR YOURSELF'?"

This could be seen as a convenient use of Scripture (Psalms 8:2) to authenticate oneself – children are praising so let's quote the prediction.

But, of course, if it is a true fulfillment, the posing of a contrived usage has no moment. And the test of that is in all the other things that authenticated Jesus.

The quote is more a paraphrase since the psalm does not include "*you have prepared praise for yourself.*" This is being added in this recitation. But we are dealing with the Lord of Glory, the Son of God, who was there when the verse was inspired into the mind of David. Where then is the legitimacy in criticizing any impropriety?

As a retort to the Pharisees, this would have been basically lost on them, but nonetheless fulfilling the need to connect all the dots from Old Testament to New.

Now there were some Greeks among those who were going up to worship . . . "Sir, we wish to see Jesus."

These sought out Philip because he was from Bethsaida. The reason they did this is that the Galilee was Gentile territory and Bethsaida was a noted town there, perhaps a place they frequently themselves. Their hopes were that by contacting Philip, their request would be all the more understood and helped.

"The hour has come for the Son of Man to be glorified.

It is almost as though Jesus cares nothing about their background or the vantage point of their approach to Him. He does not launch into a discussion about the difference between Jew and Gentile. Instead He speaks on the presumption that all men are equal in their approach to Him – all men essentially want the same thing.

This statement about the Son of Man being glorified would have been enigmatic in the ears of those who had not been adequately prepared all along the way with Him. They would likely not know that Son of Man was a key word for Messiah. Still, these were words that would help to authenticate that they were in the presence of the genuine article.

And being glorified was a concept they might relate to in their own heritage of mythologies. Visitations of the gods in mortal flesh was common for the Greeks and such events often concluded in the god being seen as returning to divine attributes – glorification.

Now this is not to say in any way that the Greek men here thought of Jesus this way, but only to say that the idea was not foreign to them – they could embrace this concept with some ease.

From Jesus' perspective, He was offering them rather logical expectations about a man sent from God and claiming to be the Son of God. To talk about soon being glorified would make sense.

"Truly, truly, I say to you, unless a grain of wheat falls into the earth and dies, it remains alone; but if it dies, it bears much fruit.

This is meant not just for the Greeks, but for all in attendance, and for us as distant extensions of His disciples. There was a principle in nature that a seed must die in the earth in order that a new sprout come of it and then bear fruit. It is as if the design of nature has already prepared us for this idea.

Of course, Jesus meant that He will necessarily have to die that the fruit intended for the Kingdom may come from Him. And we must also remember that this whole notion of dying was being resisted in His disciples, so reiteration in any form was helpful.

"He who loves his life loses it, and he who hates his life in this world will keep it to life eternal.

This has of late become wholly unpopular to the degree that some people abandon Christianity ideologically on this concept alone. We have been trained now for several decades that we are to accept ourselves as we are, and all such talk of denouncing ourselves is simply wrong.

But Jesus is reiterating the idea that all men are born in sin and that life will manifest itself in wrong actions with wrong motives. Even the supposedly philanthropic things we may do that genuinely help society have the stain of selfishness and self-promotion. We do such things to be noticed and praised (or paid well), which is proven whenever those things are not delivered.

To love our life purely as it is, will end up with the loss of that life and life eternal. To acknowledge that our natural life, in and of ourselves, is wrong and that we ought to seek that life that is pleasing to God is the key to "keeping life" in the sense that it will go on eternally for us.

"If anyone serves Me, he must follow Me; and where I am, there My servant will be also; if anyone serves Me, the Father will honor him.

In this vein, the subject then moves to one about sacrifice, the giving up and abandonment of the old allegiances and purely horizontal commitments, and the contemplation of "following" Him and taking on the role of servant, where our will is in the background and His will is foremost.

CHAPTER 11
Conflict with the Pharisees

John 12:27-36, Mark 11:19-33, Matthew 21:20-32, Luke 20:1-8

27 "Now My soul has become troubled; and what shall I say, `Father, save Me from this hour'? But for this purpose I came to this hour. 28 "Father, glorify Your name." Then a voice came out of heaven: "I have both glorified it, and will glorify it again." 29 So the crowd of people who stood by and heard it were saying that it had thundered; others were saying, "An angel has spoken to Him."

30 Jesus answered and said, "This voice has not come for My sake, but for your sakes. 31 "Now judgment is upon this world; now the ruler of this world will be cast out. 32 "And I, if I am lifted up from the earth, will draw all men to Myself." 33 But He was saying this to indicate the kind of death by which He was to die. 34 The crowd then answered Him, "We have heard out of the Law that the Christ is to remain forever; and how can You say, `The Son of Man must be lifted up'? Who is this Son of Man?" 35 So Jesus said to them, "For a little while longer the Light is among you. Walk while you have the Light, so that darkness will not overtake you; he who walks in the darkness does not know where he goes. 36 "While you have the Light, believe in the Light, so that you may become sons of Light." These things Jesus spoke, and He went away and hid Himself from them. (John 12:27-36)

19 When evening came, they would go out of the city. 20 As they were passing by in the morning, they saw the fig tree withered from the roots up. 21 Being reminded, Peter said to Him, "Rabbi, look, the fig tree which You cursed has withered." 22 And Jesus answered saying to them, "Have faith in God. 23 "Truly I say to you, whoever says to this mountain, `Be taken up and cast into the sea,' and does not doubt in his heart, but believes that what he says is going to happen, it will be granted him. 24 "Therefore I say to you, all things for which you pray and ask, believe that you have received them, and they will be granted you. 25 "Whenever you stand praying, forgive, if you have anything against anyone, so that your Father who is in heaven will also forgive you your transgressions. 26 But if you do not forgive, neither will your Father who is in heaven forgive your transgressions."

27 They came again to Jerusalem. And as He was walking in the temple, the chief priests and the scribes and the elders came to Him, 28 and began saying to Him, "By what authority are You doing these things, or who gave You this authority to do these things?" 29 And Jesus said to them, "I will ask you one question, and you answer Me, and then I will tell you by what authority I do these things. 30 "Was the baptism of John from heaven, or from men? Answer Me." 31 They began reasoning among themselves, saying, "If we say, `From heaven,' He will say, `Then why did you not believe him?' 32 "But shall we say, `From men'?"--they were afraid of the people, for everyone considered John to have been a real prophet. 33 Answering Jesus, they said, "We do not know." And Jesus said to them, "Nor will I tell you by what authority I do these things." (Mark 11:19-33)

28 "But what do you think? A man had two sons, and he came to the first and said, `Son, go work today in the vineyard.' 29 "And he answered, `I will not'; but afterward he regretted it and went. 30 "The man came to the second and said the same thing; and he answered, `I will, sir'; but he did not go. 31 "Which of the two did the will of his father?" They said, "The first." Jesus said to them, "Truly I say to you that the tax collectors and prostitutes will get into the kingdom of God before you. 32 "For John came to you in the way of righteousness and you did not believe him; but the tax collectors and prostitutes did believe him; and you, seeing this, did not even feel remorse afterward so as to believe him. (Matthew 21:28-32)

Commentary

"Now My soul has become troubled;

We are still among the things said immediately after the Greeks had been brought to Jesus. His immediate response to their coming was to speak of Him soon being glorified.

Having said that, He then changes the tone to that of his troubled soul. This is enigmatic for us because we all along have seen Jesus fearless about consequences to Him personally, but only in relation to upsetting the divine timetable of events.

To cry out to be saved from this hour, seems out of sorts. First, it is not the hour in which He now speaks, but that hour, which is an idiomatic phrase for the many hours of His punishment soon at hand.

In terms of His spirit, there is really no source of such troubling because spiritually He is one with the Father and He committed long ago to the business of the Cross. But in the curious and enigmatic convergence of humanity and divinity (fully God, fully man) there is room for some anguish over the physical ordeal ahead of Him.

We must bear in mind that this is not to be a petty flogging, whose wounds one could get over in a few days. He clearly knows it will be an excessively brutal affair. Couple this with the fact that this is being done willingly, not by the mishaps of some unfortunate turn of events. The will that says I'll do it can just as easily say, "I've changed my mind." Christ above all men has the mixed blessing of knowing ahead of time what is in store.

This should not be characterized in any way as a breach of courage. But courageous men still hate and dread the prospects of horror to which they have nevertheless wholly committed.

and what shall I say, `Father, save Me from this hour'?

Yet it is not an actual request. That will come later in the garden before He is arrested. Here it is a question – "what shall I say?" He is exposing the incredulity of asking against the commitment of doing.

But for this purpose I came to this hour.

This is the rejoinder to the possibility of the question. He was born to this purpose.

Now we certainly see that in the garden He doesn't speak of the propriety of the question but asks it outright – *"Father let this cup pass from Me."* But the closer we get to the moment of suffering the more it comes into focus and the farther away seems the rejoinder. And He has a very real human nature in His incarnation.

As to Him stating His purpose, it is important to acknowledge that while He came preaching the Kingdom, and bringing healing to the lame and sight to the blind, His whole kingship and the opening out of the Kingdom is wrapped up in the one sacrifice waiting to be offered that will pay once and for all the debt for all sin. He came most importantly to die, because the whole sacrificial system of the Old Covenant was a postponement and a temporary substitute, awaiting the one and only pure sacrifice that could resolve the dilemma of man's sin. To come and not die would be to continue the interim arrangement and resume waiting for its denouement.

So the Cross was a critical part of His coming, hence His words, *"for this purpose I came to this hour."*

"Father, glorify Your name."

Not "glorify thy son." He is completely in the background in this expression. This arrangement and all He had come to do was to point toward the Father, not toward the Son, that He not supplant but serve.

Then a voice came out of heaven: "I have both glorified it, and will glorify it again."

This is a commendation that the work of the Son has already glorified the Father's name to overflowing, such that the former cannot be said to be inadequate and waiting yet for the hallowed trumpets yet to come. He makes it clear that His name has already been glorified, but it is not a one-time event. He will yet glorify it again at the Cross.

We learn next that not everyone heard this as discernable speech -

So the crowd of people who stood by and heard it were saying that it had thundered; others were saying, "An angel has spoken to Him."

One might suppose that there were different effects accounting for different appreciations. But more likely the voice was heard by Jesus directly, but all others heard what sounded like thunder. Yet among the faithful, the thunder was understood as God having spoken to Jesus.

There is really no science that would dictate that the speaking of God will effect itself on raw nature as thundering by the sheer physics of things. This is not nature responding to the voice. It is rather a deliberate effect caused by the Speaker on those whom He so chooses to perceive it.

"This voice has not come for My sake, but for your sakes.

He makes it clear that this is not for His own glorification – to impress. But rather, to signify the significance of the events about to unfold. The salvation of all mankind is now just off stage awaiting its signal. It is now attended by an annunciating trumpet.

Now judgment is upon this world; now the ruler of this world will be cast out.

We understand this not to be the final judgment we see in the Revelation, but judgment of the sin principle, judgment of all men in that their destiny is now conditional to the Cross and their relationship to it. And in a very real sense, Satan's rule of the world is now judged in that His end is fixed, his suzeraincy and free hand in human affairs has now changed.

To say that he is cast out is to some degree more poetic than literal, because he is certainly active in the world today, which would not be the case were he literally barred from the present world. It is to say that going forward, wherever he may exercise his evil designs, these may be overturned and annulled. When Satan fell from Heaven, the earth was assigned as his realm (John 14:30, Isa 14:12-17, Ezek 28:12-13) , and even here, God was ultimately sovereign. If men became his subjects having no faith with which to combat him, such became their state and such became the way of heathen nations, who demonstrated their allegiances to him,

But now, he will not have such expectations, but rather will find the Spirit of God resisting him and undoing his evil work.

"And I, if I am lifted up from the earth, will draw all men to Myself."

This is reminiscent of the thing said to Nicodemus – *"As Moses lifted up the serpent in the wilderness, even so must the Son of Man be lifted up;"* (John 3:14)

The serpent was a type of the lifting up that will also apply to Christ. This is not a lifting up as in exaltation. It refers to the Cross, because of the physical similarities in the analogy – the serpent was put on a wooden fixture and lifted up in view of the people. So Christ will be put up high on a wooden fixture that all men may see Him.

It is that event that will draw all men, because it is rigorously sympathetic that a righteous man was made to die. That quandary will cause men to ponder the circumstances and learn of the One who was crucified and why that had to be. This would not be accomplished nearly as well by simply exalting Christ among unbelievers.

And of course the gospel writer tells us this is the meaning – *"But He was saying this to indicate the kind of death by which He was to die."*

It would not be stoning, but crucifixion, which meant that the Roman civil authority would be involved, meaning a crime respected also by them would be part of the case against him. We will learn later that this charge was sedition.

how can You say, `The Son of Man must be lifted up'? Who is this Son of Man?"

The crowd now expresses its more extensive ignorance by inferring that by "lifted up" Jesus means He will ascend to Heaven, and in their understanding, Messiah was to remain permanently once having arrived.

The next step in logic was to infer that Jesus must not therefore be the Son of Man, Messiah, hence the question, "Who is this Son of Man?"

"For a little while longer the Light is among you. Walk while you have the Light, so that darkness will not overtake you;

Jesus does not engage their technical argument, but instead resorts to the subject of Light among them. That will ultimately be the key that Messiah is with them, they will be enlightened as to the truths of God. They are exhorted to walk in them because Light is Light and the technical issues of messiahship can easily be cases of misunderstanding.

It is becoming the sons of Light that is more important than testing the credentials of Messiah. Were they to focus on the former, what matter would it be if they understood less the real nature of His messiahship? They would now have life.

These things Jesus spoke, and He went away and hid Himself from them.

His resolve was to let everything now come to a head among the leaders. That was the reason for now making His journey to Jerusalem. But even in this, we sense a timetable of events, and nothing is to be done out of the will of His Father.

One has the marvelous sense of a God in complete control. His arrest, trial and crucifixion may appear as the inevitable collision with evil men and being subject to their evil plans, but it is God in control all the way. He will not be arrested until the moment God has ordained. The very hour of His crucifixion was to be timed with the sacrifices of the Feast of Unleavened Bread following the Passover.

Thus, we see Him removing Himself from premature interference with that plan.

When evening came, they would go out of the city.

It is not said that the disciples hid with Him, but we see them soon together again so as to make plans to leave the city. As they leave, they come by the fig tree that was cursed and see that nature obeyed His command -

21 "Rabbi, look, the fig tree which You cursed has withered." 22 . . "Have faith in God. 23 "Truly I say to you, whoever says to this mountain, `Be taken up and cast into the sea,' . . it will be granted him.

The query by the disciples is now past the point about its application – the dead fruit of Israel. It is more a case of amazement that nature has obeyed His command.

So Jesus uses the incident for yet another lesson – to explain the kind of power at their disposal as children of the Kingdom.

Many have criticized this as a pointless example, since no one attempted to move a mountain or succeeded at doing it, so why use it as an example?

It was used to illustrate what was available, not that moving mountains was to be part of their repertoire. Some go too far in dismissing this as never intended at all. But Jesus was in fact saying that should the moving of a mountain pertain to the will of God in our work, there is enough power at our disposal to do that very thing. The grand question is that in the case of mountains, would they ever be themselves obstacles?

And in this, we err in not appreciating the eastern mind. Often it is helpful to use an extreme example not so much to convey the point but to convey the importance and power of the point.

As for mountains, we do see the prediction that the Mount of Olives will in fact be unsuitable as it is when Christ descends, and it will be made to split such that a river proceeds from it (Zechariah 14:4.) So mountains moving is not totally dismissable as hyperbole.

24 "Therefore I say to you, all things for which you pray and ask, believe that you have received them, and they will be granted you.

In the example of the mountain above, Jesus did qualify having a faith that did not waver or doubt. This implies a very intimate and clear knowledge of the will of God by means of a powerful faith. Faith is said to bring real knowledge, a knowledge that is beyond what science and reason can supply. This, the humanistic rationalist denies because it is irrational and escapes detection by his purely natural powers of perception.

That said, the knowledge faith brings cannot be marched into a court of law or a science convention and proposed as facts. It is personal and inwardly subjective, which baffles the rationalistic mind, but comforts the faithful soul.

Now as to the formula here – that believing one has received the thing desired ensures the receiving of it – this is not meant to open the door to abuse. It is not a mechanism. It is an exercise of faith and faith always has an object in God as Father, or the Holy Spirit or the Son. We cannot have faith apart from these, so the whole question of believing that we will receive a fortune in stock options or win the lottery is misplaced, because having these has nothing to do with faith, which is to serve God and His purposes.

So what does the believing exhortation then mean?

People pray in all kinds of emotional and willful states, many of which are hesitant or lack any real confidence. They often see God as rather miserly in dishing out requests, or brooding over the imperfection of our human frames that we would ask for things pertaining to our simple livelihood, like bread on the table. So they often pray merely hoping He will condescend to hear and perhaps begrudgingly grant their requests.

Certainly the above might apply to purely selfish requests based on greed and self-aggrandizement. But with respect to our daily needs for sustenance and raiment, for health and safety, for the work of the ministry, He is ready to bestow these. Yet He also encourages us to not see these as remote possibilities but bestowals of grace waiting in the wings to be grasped firmly by a faith that expects to receive them because we already know Him to be a God of love and blessing.

We are to believe that we will receive them despite human doubts or the lies of Satan that such things are beyond our feeble and pitiful expectations.

But we must emulate the disciples and be about the divine mission of the Kingdom, else God is our butler or Santa Claus or servant, from whom we seek good things to spend it on ourselves. *You have not because you ask amiss, that you may spend it on your lusts.* (James 4:3.)

25 "Whenever you stand praying, forgive, if you have anything against anyone, so that your Father who is in heaven will also forgive you your transgressions.

Here, Jesus takes the opportunity to not let slip an essential ingredient in our prayers – that confession of enmity against others, the promise to forgive and the desire to be forgiven be included. It is a keeping of short accounts with the Lord, which means that every opportunity of prayer ought to include this because we so easily slip into things that need to be forgiven. We are not then to let these soak and sour, being piled up for some future time when we will clear our slate en masse.

Now forgiving others is not actually engaged here in patent action because we are praying, not talking with our brother or sister. But it begins with the attitude that will result in forgiveness in reality, because the beginning of forgiveness occurs in the heart, and that we can certainly muster as we pray.

"So that your heavenly Father will forgive . ."

We wince that this is a conditional. We want to rely on the unconditional forgiveness of God which matches His unconditional love. But He declares it does not work that way. Our forgiveness of others is the conditional to opening His forgiveness to us. This is not about the forgiveness that accompanies salvation and our first confession of all our past sins. Many of those we may not have the opportunity any longer to make right, yet salvation can occur with the heart that forgives.

But it is clear that our cooperation in forgiveness is essential to God releasing His, as in the parable of the talents, where the forgiven servant has his master's forgiveness revoked because he did not reciprocate in kind with those indebted to him (Matthew 18:24.)

Notice also the warning -

26 But if you do not forgive, neither will your Father who is in heaven forgive your transgressions."

So in essence we have two conditions of unforgivableness – the blasphemy against the Holy Spirit and the refusal to forgive others. And we should be careful to distinguish between refusal and simple neglect. Refusal and hardness of heart is the case to be worried about. As for neglect, we are obliged to pray that God reveal what we have forgotten.

"By what authority are You doing these things, or who gave You this authority to do these things?"

Authority is a principle that rules across all human existence. Seldom is man his own authority. We are born under the authority of parents, we leave home and come under the authority of employers. Barring this we live under civil and federal authorities. Top executives are under the authority of the stockholders. Even Jesus claimed no self-based authority but that of His Father.

With respect to the Pharisees, it came indirectly from the high priest. The Sanhedrin was not a body called out in the OT, nor were the parties of Pharisees and Sadducees. They existed on the formal authority of the high priest to permit them, who exceeded to the need for such a legislative body and system, but did so from necessity not from biblical precedent. Moses had no such council. But these were no longer the days of Moses.

And even in their exercise of this, they held to the rabbins, not to themselves. They quoted the famous schools, which created the noted contrast with Jesus' approach – to speak as one having authority independent of the schools.

So their question seems somewhat contradictory because they have already been given the equivalent of this answer though it was not asked directly until now. As above, they were certainly in earshot when the people expressed amazement at His teaching, distinguishing it from the manner of the Scribes.

They had also heard Him explain by demonstration – *"But, so that you may know that the Son of Man has authority on earth to forgive sins,"* (Luke 5:24)

The question has a mixed purpose. There is no doubt that some curiosity exists among them. But more than this, they are laying a trap for the gathering of evidence at trial. If He can admit divinity or self-originated authority He can be vilified as a blasphemer.

29 "I will ask you one question, and you answer Me, and then I will tell you by what authority I do these things.

In purely reasonable senses of fair play, one is expected to answer, not ask a question. It is considered evasive and ultimately disrespectful of the questioner. In Jesus' case here, He does not say He won't answer, or that He chooses to substitute a question for the expected answer. But He poses a question to qualify whether He will answer or not.

This is often used in philosophical discussions to weed out the jesters from the serious students. One might ask for a demonstration of serious engagement, like an upfront commitment to abandon one's position if it can be shown to be false. If the questioner says he can't ever be made to abandon it, the opponent has ample cause to decline an answer on the basis of intellectual dishonesty. One is posing a question whose answer will be disregarded on all accounts.

Here then is the deciding question -

30 "Was the baptism of John from heaven, or from men? Answer Me."

They soon discover they have been trapped by their own "trappee." The tables have been turned on them and they now face the dilemma they hoped would be His.

The reason for the question about John becomes readily apparent in the ensuing text – *31 "If we say, `From heaven,' He will say, `Then why did you not believe him?' 32 "But shall we say, `From men'?"--they were afraid of the people, for everyone considered John to have been a real prophet."*

Now we have to ask why, apart from setting them into a trap, this particular question would pave the way for not having to answer them?

Any answer about His authority would ultimately have to include a perception of divine will, and they would have to be capable of that kind of intimacy in order to appreciate the answer. In this they were clearly deficient, hence, the first question to be asked ahead of theirs was, "Are you in a frame of mind and heart to see and value the answer for what it is?"

The question about John accomplished this perfectly, because it revolved around the ability to see John as from God, which was clearly evident on all counts. As such they could not give in to admitting it and they could not deny it, regardless of their own opinions, meaning fear of the people ruled out simple honesty, which, in terms of options, was not much better – *33 they said, "We do not know."*

Under such conditions, Jesus saw no point in answering them – *33 " "Nor will I tell you by what authority I do these things."*

28 . . ."a man had two sons,"

Jesus doesn't leave the foregoing hanging in the air, but offers a parable that could be an exhortation to repentance, but is also an indictment about their present hearts.

The two men are distinguished not by their initial hearts but by their final actions. It is not those with merely the intent to do the will of God, but those who end up doing it who please Him. The Pharisees had all the promissory notes on hand about purposing to do God's will, but let their dispositions interfere with the doing of it.

The prostitutes and tax collectors already had a disposition against doing the will of God, yet changed it and did it in the end. Such will enter the Kingdom before those who merely promise.

Now this does not mean the prostitutes and tax collectors as they are, unchanged. It is not an endorsement of their life style, as liberal Christians would have us believe – "Jesus accepts us just as we are without conditions." It is certainly an acceptance as we are, but not a magnanimity that lets us remain as we are.

The Pharisees cannot lean on their promissory notes if they end up not doing. The dregs of society canceled all bad accounts and attitudes when they change into people desiring to do the will of God and end up also doing it. Blessed are the doers of His Word, not merely the hearers.

Then He reminds them of how they treated John -

32 "For John came to you in the way of righteousness and you did not believe him; but the tax collectors and prostitutes did believe him; and you, seeing this, did not even feel remorse afterward so as to believe him."

This is what institutionalizing faith begets. It becomes a machine unto itself and we along with it. It is like the man in church who takes on the project of making name tags for everyone. He works hard to get materials and coordinate printing and organize distribution. He owns the project, so much that it now has a life of its own.

Then someone declines their name tag, and the man acts as if a law has been broken – "We have a trouble maker in our midst." When all along it has never been really asked where name tags fit into the worship of believers?

The Pharisees were so caught up in their schtick, that real revelation was unrecognizable. Ordinarily, when the light turns on and one realizes he's been on the wrong side all along, remorse and regret come to the surface to enable a change. But here, the entrenchment is so deep and pervading that they feel no natural remorse as to be turned to the right.

This, of course, is intolerable speech in their ears, and only furthers their commitment to do away with Him.

Mark 12:1-9, Luke 20:16, Matthew 21:33-46, Matthew 22:1-15, Luke 20:20-26

1 And He began to speak to them in parables: "A man PLANTED A VINEYARD AND PUT A WALL AROUND IT, AND DUG A VAT UNDER THE WINE PRESS AND BUILT A TOWER, and rented it out to vine-growers and went on a journey. 2 "At the harvest time he sent a slave to the vine-growers, in order to receive some of the produce of the vineyard from the vine-growers. 3 "They took him, and beat him and sent him away empty-handed. 4 "Again he sent them another slave, and they wounded him in the head, and treated him shamefully. 5 "And he sent another, and that one they killed; and so with many others, beating some and killing others. 6 "He had one more to send, a beloved son; he sent him last of all to them, saying, `They will respect my son.'

7 "But those vine-growers said to one another, `This is the heir; come, let us kill him, and the inheritance will be ours!' 8 "They took him, and killed him and threw him out of the vineyard. 9 "What will the owner of the vineyard do? He will come and destroy the vine-growers, and will give the vineyard to others" . . . When they heard it, they said, "May it never be!" (Mark 12:1-9, Luke 20:16)

42 Jesus said to them, "Did you never read in the Scriptures, `THE STONE WHICH THE BUILDERS REJECTED, THIS BECAME THE CHIEF CORNER stone; THIS CAME ABOUT FROM THE LORD, AND IT IS MARVELOUS IN OUR EYES'? 43 "Therefore I say to you, the kingdom of God will be taken away from you and given to a people, producing the fruit of it. 44 "And he who falls on this stone will be broken to pieces; but on whomever it falls, it will scatter him like dust." 45 When the chief priests and the Pharisees heard His parables, they understood that He was speaking about them. 46 When they sought to seize Him, they feared the people, because they considered Him to be a prophet. (Matthew 21:42-46)

1 Jesus spoke to them again in parables, saying, 2 "The kingdom of heaven may be compared to a king who gave a wedding feast for his son. 3 "And he sent out his slaves to call those who had been invited to the wedding feast, and they were unwilling to come. 4 "Again he sent out other slaves saying, `Tell those who have been invited, "Behold, I have prepared my dinner; my oxen and my fattened livestock are all butchered and everything is ready; come to the wedding feast."' 5 "But they paid no attention and went their way, one to his own farm, another to his business, 6 and the rest seized his slaves and mistreated them and killed them. 7 "But the king was enraged, and he sent his armies and destroyed those murderers and set their city on fire.

8 "Then he said to his slaves, `The wedding is ready, but those who were invited were not worthy. 9 `Go therefore to the main highways, and as many as you find there, invite to the wedding feast.' 10 "Those slaves went out into the streets and gathered together all they found, both evil and good; and the wedding hall was filled with dinner guests.

11 "But when the king came in to look over the dinner guests, he saw a man there who was not dressed in wedding clothes, 12 and he said to him, `Friend, how did you come in here without wedding clothes?' And the man was speechless. 13 "Then the king said to the servants, `Bind him hand and foot, and throw him into the outer darkness; in that place there will be weeping and gnashing of teeth.' 14 "For many are called, but few are chosen."

15 Then the Pharisees went and plotted together how they might trap Him in what He said. 16 And they sent their disciples to Him, along with the Herodians, . . . and sent spies who pretended to be righteous, in order that they might catch Him in some statement, so that they could deliver Him to the rule and the authority of the governor. 21 They questioned Him, saying, "Teacher, we know that You speak and teach correctly, and You are not partial to any, but teach the way of God in truth. 22 "Is it lawful for us to pay taxes to Caesar, or not?" 23 But He detected their trickery and said to them, 24 "Show Me a denarius. Whose likeness and inscription does it have?" They said, "Caesar's." 25 And He said to them, "Then render to Caesar the things that are Caesar's, and to God the things that are God's." 26 And they were unable to catch Him in a saying in the presence of the people; and being amazed at His answer, they became silent. (Matthew 22:1-15, Luke 20:20-26)

Commentary

1 "A man PLANTED A VINEYARD AND PUT A WALL AROUND IT, . . . and rented it out to vine-growers and went on a journey.

We have here a parable that sums up in one story the entire plan of God respecting man. In it we find the sheer fact of God's ownership of the world, His trust of it to His creatures, His repeated revelation of His will to men, His patience in man's relation to it, and His enduring love in finally sending His own Son to ensure the outcome – a genuine and valued fruit.

In the parable we have an owner of the vineyard who placed it in the custody of growers. Likewise, God created the world in which we live and entrusted it to man's care.

The owner then sent representatives to assess the fruits gained – *" 2 At the harvest time he sent a slave . . 4 Again he sent them another slave . . 5 And he sent another . ."* These, the growers mistreated and some were killed.

God likewise has sent prophets along the path of man's history, seeking to find faith and calling men to it. These were routinely mistreated, ridiculed and in some cases slain.

Then the owner sends his son – *6 "'They will respect my son.'"* But they see him as the heir and kill him – *7 " `This is the heir; come, let us kill him, and the inheritance will be ours!'"*

Likewise, God sent His Son to set things straight according to His Kingdom, but He most especially was mistreated, spat upon and killed.

Notice also the parallel of throwing the body out of the vineyard and the that of Messiah's death and humble burial, whose grave had to be borrowed from another, and that outside the walls.

This is a testimony that will be made to ring in the ear of every man who rejects God – that His love has worked all along the way to reveal and encourage man to faith. He has not neglected that revelation nor expected man to get it by osmosis, but sent men with voices so as to speak in the ears of His audience. Despite mistreatment and even murder, God continued to send His messengers.

Finally, He fulfilled His commitment to send His only Son, that despite unfaithfulness and hatred, the Son would die for their sins.

Here is a testimony, exemplified in the patience and forbearance of the vineyard owner, of a love that suffers long and endures in providing opportunities for salvation.

Notice now how we are then prepared to evaluate those who, despite all this, prefer to disrespect God and His free gift -

9 "What will the owner of the vineyard do? He will come and destroy the vine-growers, and will give the vineyard to others"

This is almost identical to the message of Nathan before David in the story of the man who slew his neighbors ewe lamb, taking no thought about his neighbor's love for it. David did not wait for the question, but rose in indignation and stated, *"As the LORD lives, surely the man who has done this deserves to die."* (2 Sam 12:5)

Here also, the indignation is anticipated – that the owner will give these men their just punishment and turn the vineyard over to men who will respect and care for it.

The point is all too plain. The people were by now quite used to seeing the deeper meaning behind such stories. It was clear that the vineyard owner was an analogy to His Father and the slaves were the prophets and the Son was the very man in front of them, whose life the authorities now sought.

16 When they heard it, they said, "May it never be!"

This is not repugnance at the ire of the owner – that he would destroy them. It was repugnance at the analogy – that somewhere in all of this there were real counterparts who would be therefore destroyed in reality. The indictment was clearly indicated, but they shuddered at the thought of its reality. Hence, their response. "May such things never come about concerning us."

42 .. `THE STONE WHICH THE BUILDERS REJECTED, THIS BECAME THE CHIEF CORNER stone;

He caps off this analogy by reminding them of a Scripture that indicts them for the very thing they now shudder at in horror. Their fear of its reality is made justifiable by citing Ps 118: 22 which anticipated the very thing now happening in their midst – the stone summarily dismissed as unacceptable has become the critical stone necessary for the building. As the son was rejected and cast away in the parable, so now the Son of Man is about to be killed and cast away.

42 .. AND IT IS MARVELOUS IN OUR EYES'

The marvel is not at what we now see as the gateway to salvation, but is the irony in rejecting that which was essential to salvation. It remains a marvel in our minds today that Israel long awaited their Messiah, amid innumerable trials that prompted prayers for victory and deliverance through Him. Yet now He comes and is rejected and killed by those seeking Him. That is indeed marvelous in our eyes! It is marvelous in its incredulity.

43 "Therefore I say to you, the kingdom of God will be taken away from you and given to a people, producing the fruit of it.

Not counting on the people's discernment, especially in the emotionally charged events about them, Jesus lays the concluding application right out on the table for all to see – the promised Kingdom will be taken from them and given to others,

This is certainly a prediction about the Gentiles coming to saving faith and their better care over the affairs of the Kingdom than what has now been evidenced by the Jews. Paul describes this as bringing the Jews to jealousy (Romans 10:19, 11:11.)

44 "And he who falls on this stone will be broken to pieces; but on whomever it falls, it will scatter him like dust."

This is clearly enigmatic, since He predicts calamity regardless of one's encounter with the stone. Yet, the meaning is different depending on one's position in faith.

The analogies mean to apply the one falling on the stone as the faithful and the one on whom the stone falls as the unfaithful.

To the recalcitrant, should it fall on them, the force will break them into pieces which will be scattered by the dust of sheer impact, meaning they will be finally and completely judged as to faith and destroyed thereby.

To the faithful, the stone is seen as that upon which they willingly fall for support with the full intent of abandoning their former life – a life that must be first broken in pieces by the force of moral and spiritual will, being seen as unsatisfying and unrewarding.

In each case, Jesus as the stone is the critical factor of one's destiny. The faithful abandon their former life to accept His life and the eternity it promises. To the unfaithful He is the key to the destiny of those who keep a firm hold on their former life, which will ultimately be judged by Him.

45 When the chief priests and the Pharisees heard His parables, they understood that He was speaking about them. 46 When they sought to seize Him,

The leaders, being used to this form of teaching, were quick to see the analogy, primarily because they were of above-average learning compared to the simple folk Jesus addressed outside the city.

Again, they have reason for anger because of such attacks, but are stopped by the obvious adoration of the people around them. Which is to say that all those now come to Jerusalem were not universally against Him, but in fact, those who were seemed now in the minority.

One might question how men of learning, ability and authority couldn't simply act on that authority without fear of the people? This was not, after all, a case of democratic elections. There was no such thing as a constituency, or running for office.

But to a large extent, being unpopular with the people was not a mode the leaders were willing to risk. Ordinarily, they could not be booted from office, but a tumult of the masses could at least consign them to some ineffective position within the hierarchy. It's somewhat like the Catholic policy toward priests and bishops who misbehave. They are hardly ever defrocked and asked to resign, but often are shifted around to lesser positions of influence or even consigned to lame duties of no consequence, as a sort of lifetime penance.

"The kingdom of heaven may be compared to a king who gave a wedding feast for his son.

Jesus has talked already at length about analogies to the Kingdom, but always in remote areas. Here He takes the opportunity to bring the urban leaders into contact with it, yet now in a more foreboding manner. Before, the Kingdom was pictured as a thing desired and treasured. Here, it is the means of an indictment against those no longer suitable for it.

The wedding feast is an apt example because it includes the ideas of necessary participants and invited guests; the element of accepting or declining invitations. A fitting vehicle for letting these men see themselves as they are.

3 "And he sent out his slaves to call those who had been invited to the wedding feast, and they were unwilling to come.

We know through hindsight that this will be about the Pharisees because the key condition is the invited guests who are unwilling to come, which would not be an expected point to highlight. Most would have died for a royal invitation.

Different from customary expectations also is the patience of the king to give them another chance, especially to include enticements – "' "Behold, I have prepared my dinner; my oxen and my fattened livestock are all butchered and everything is ready;'"

Uncommon to the analogy is the mistreatment of the heralds – " 6 and . . seized his slaves and mistreated them and killed them."

We learn something here about the use of parables. There were no strict rules that all features must be true in reality. Everyone knew in the case of such devices that the speaker was performing illustration, hence the purpose was to devise and employ a fitting story. So the extreme rarity that a real king's heralds would be murdered in real life did not undermine the effectiveness or usefulness of the parable.

This also forestalls the ideas of some that Jesus would never make up a story or engage pure fiction. Always, Jesus used situations that could be easily imagined and were fully rational, whether the situations had actually occurred or not.

7 "But the king was enraged, and he sent his armies and destroyed those murderers and set their city on fire.

Such was the clear history of Israel's past. When Judah's sins had risen to the point of unavoidable punishment, Nebuchadnezzar came with his army and killed huge numbers of God's people, and destroyed both city and Temple. Any learned man familiar with this history would get the analogy being crafted.

9 `Go therefore to the main highways, and as many as you find there, invite to the wedding feast.'

The Kingdom is ironically appreciated most by the unsophisticated and humble, and rejected more so by the learned and influential. In the analogy of the wedding feast, those ordinarily spurned and rejected are now royal guests. We picture them with their unrefined manners and speech sitting amid royal furnishings to enjoy what was of scarce expectation before.

10 and gathered together all they found, both evil and good; and the wedding hall was filled with dinner guests.

We might expect in an analogy of the Kingdom to find only the good so gathered. But the immediate context is the invitation, and in relation to God's Kingdom, God is not partial but calls all – the good and the bad – to it. What men do with that calling determines who remains to become its citizens. It is not a calling to remain as one is, but to come and be changed.

11 "But when the king . . . saw a man there who was not dressed in wedding clothes, . . . 12 . . `Friend, how did you come in here without wedding clothes?'

Some puzzlement is normal here. Has not the king invited the poor and rejected? Is it likely these would have wedding clothes worthy of a royal affair?

But this is resolved by better knowledge of the customs. In the ancient east, it was customary for the host to provide special gowns and clothes for guests to change into before entering the banquet hall of the feast. This ameliorated the problem of class distinctions which otherwise would demarcate the less fortunate, less wealthy from the rich. Everyone changed and for the small space of an evening, everyone became at least visually equal.

So how did a man come to be in the hall without wedding clothes? He must have refused the garments out of indignation, or perhaps slipped in uninvited. Either way, we have some trouble seeing this as applicable to the Kingdom, since God will then be impeccably discerning about His invited guests.

If we insist that the analogy must be only about the final state of the Kingdom, then this dilemma will remain problematic. But if we see the wedding feast as embracing the whole concept of Kingdom from its preaching in the Gospels, to the institution of His Church and beyond to the eternal state, then the analogy here to the man without proper clothes is to portray the condition of the church in this overall plan. Both the good and the bad will come through its doors, some of the bad will even join, particularly in those churches where scrutiny of character and genuine faith are repugnant.

As such, it is less critical to see the man tied to the formal conduct of the feast, but more to the preliminaries that occur prior, therefore, the time of the church where *"many are called but few chosen."*

And the man was speechless.

A seemingly innocuous observation, but interesting in this day and age, where so much confidence is placed in other paths to salvation. Those who travel them almost in defiance of the exclusivity of Christ and His Church will be speechless at the revelation of the truth and the call to account for themselves.

13 ". . `Bind him hand and foot, and throw him into the outer darkness;'"

We wince at this because all the man seems to be guilty of is not having the right attire. But as explained above, he would have to have been stubborn and indignant, meaning he was not willing to abide by the rules of the feast. Men who decide they will make their own rules respecting salvation and the Kingdom will find the same outcome.

So, in the case of the feast, it would be over the top, but in the case of the Kingdom, the stakes are much higher and the indignation more actionable. Since the man is to represent the seriousness of the latter, the action of the king against him at the feast is necessary, though excessive in appearance.

13 .. " outer darkness; in that place there will be weeping and gnashing of teeth.' "

There are many who approach Christianity, ready to reject this aspect of it. This is primarily due to an over-emphasis on love and peace among all human beings non-judgmentally, and the attractive nature of fair play made a normal expectation nowadays in the atmosphere of democracy. Combine this with the recent notion now in vogue that everyone gets a reward irrespective of earning one, so that we not wound the spirits of underachievers and one gets an ideology and world view out of sorts with NT messages and themes.

And there are those who simply cannot accept this kind of suffering handed out by a supposedly loving and just God. Certainly, there will always be extenuating circumstances and the recognition that all people do some good in their lives.

But we are dealing with Jesus as Son of God, who knows all such approaches in all the minds of all God's creatures, and all the seemingly contradictory pictures this generates, yet still, without a syllable of qualification, warns us of the horrifying nature of such a destiny.

Men are clearly going to make up any number of strategies to get around the truth and in essence make up a truth to their own liking, but reality teaches us that this is folly. Better to face reality, especially if there are escapes provided to avoid its unpleasantries.

Jesus as Son of God warns us that there is such a place and in it people weep and gnash their teeth. Will we pit our feeble wisdom and knowledge against someone who has been there to see the patent truth?

14 "For many are called, but few are chosen."

This need not obligate one to a Calvinist interpretation – that God calls but sovereignly chooses only so many. It is equally applicable, if standing separately, to a case where all are called but some reject the calling. If therefore God rejects those who do not themselves choose, he cannot be said to choose as many as are called, which is the same as saying many are called but few are chosen.

The main point of either view is that the way of righteousness is not broad nor are there many among humanity's roll call who find it and live by it. The call is simple and generous, but man chooses to be complicated and selfish.

16 And they sent their disciples to Him, along with the Herodians,

The Pharisees on hearing these subtle forms of condemnation, make plans to trap Him. "Their disciples" means those who follow the party of the Pharisees. The Herodians are those who ingratiate themselves to Herod for personal ambition and gain. Monarchs or their equivalents always attract the obsequious, some of whom end up being successors, making monarchies a rather terrible and fearsome lineage wherever they operate in human affairs.

The addition of the Herodians is for evidentiary needs – they wish for a charge that will catch the eye of Antipas or Pilate, thereby passing the odium of death over to them – *20. . so that they could deliver Him to the rule and the authority of the governor.*

So now, quite expectedly, comes a question that involves the civil authorities -

22 "Is it lawful for us to pay taxes to Caesar, or not?"

They think this an effective trap because to say yes will sow disaffection among the people for siding with their Roman overlords, and to say no will place Him in the very jeopardy they desire – sedition against Roman law.

24 "Show Me a denarius. Whose likeness and inscription does it have?" They said, "Caesar's."

Unlike modern times, empire nations did not mint their own coins out of a national treasury, since the treasure was the king's or emperor's own. In the Republic, Rome did mint coins that belonged to the commonwealth of the nation and enabled the operation of commerce. In the empire, the emperors effectively claimed the coinage as their own stash, and the minting of coins was the creation of property belonging to the emperor. In other words, with the coming of imperial rule, the line became very thin as to what the state owned distinct from what the emperor owned. His image on coinage declared it was his coin on loan to the citizens for the conduct of business, but ownership of money was an illusion.

In the United States, when gold was the standard, there was something of intrinsic value behind the issue of all money. Paper money only "represented" the equivalent gold owned by the federal government. So an individual dollar was not technically owned by the holder but on loan from the people as a whole. Today, in place of gold, the U.S. poses its gross national product, the value of its property, land and materials, as the essential backing of its bills.

This is the reason Jesus asks about the image on the coin, to point out who the legal owner is. If Caesar owns the coinage, it is not unlawful to render back to him what he already owns – " *"25 Then render to Caesar the things that are Caesar's, . . "*

Now it might be argued that Caesar owns the money by ungodly acquisition, and that ultimately God owns all monies because they are made or backed by material only God owns as creator. And this is technically true. But for commerce to take place, the idea of ownership, debt and repayment is necessary, and it is inevitable that the idea of mere stewardship of God's money would fade in man's collective awareness.

Jesus certainly knows that Caesar does not own the coinage and that taxation by Rome is excessive. But it is also one of those systems God has allowed in the course of permitting government to share in the rule of law and authority begun at the table of nations in Genesis, following the Tower of Babel (Gen 11:7.) Such is reiterated in Paul's address about obeying the ruling powers (Romans Ch 13.)

25 and to God the things that are God's.

The requirements of human society are necessary evils. To fight against them is foolhardy. Hence, it is all the more important that one not neglect the rendering to God of those things belonging to Him, which are not monetary but spiritual.

This was an answer that technically sided with the Romans, but because the question of ownership was alluded to, rendering to Caesar what was his served to weaken the effect of commending ongoing payment. The addition of care for God's things in essence saved the moment from catastrophe by re-affirming that He honored God, who in the end was the only path by which they could expect deliverance effectively from their oppressors.

26 . . and being amazed at His answer, they became silent.

This is the immediate, almost built-in, reaction of people when they have been trumped in their plans and designs. Men are usually too black and white in their formulations about controversial issues, and when the truth turns out to be somewhere in the middle, they are ill-prepared for it. Silence becomes the only reaction.

Matthew 22:23-33, Mark 12:28-34

23 On that day some Sadducees (who say there is no resurrection) came to Jesus and questioned Him, 24 asking, "Teacher, Moses said, `IF A MAN DIES HAVING NO CHILDREN, HIS BROTHER AS NEXT OF KIN SHALL MARRY HIS WIFE, AND RAISE UP CHILDREN FOR HIS BROTHER.' 25 "Now there were seven brothers with us; and the first married and died, and having no children left his wife to his brother; 26 so also the second, and the third, down to the seventh. 27 "Last of all, the woman died. 28 "In the resurrection, therefore, whose wife of the seven will she be? For they all had married her."

29 But Jesus answered and said to them, "You are mistaken, not understanding the Scriptures nor the power of God. 30 "For in the resurrection they neither marry nor are given in marriage, but are like angels in heaven. 31 "But regarding the resurrection of the dead, have you not read what was spoken to you by God: 32 `I AM THE GOD OF ABRAHAM, AND THE GOD OF ISAAC, AND THE GOD OF JACOB'? He is not the God of the dead but of the living." 33 When the crowds heard this, they were astonished at His teaching. (Matthew 22:23-33)

28 One of the scribes came and heard them arguing, and recognizing that He had answered them well, asked Him, "What commandment is the foremost of all?" 29 Jesus answered, "The foremost is, `HEAR, O ISRAEL ! THE LORD OUR GOD IS ONE LORD; 30 AND YOU SHALL LOVE THE LORD YOUR GOD WITH ALL YOUR HEART, AND WITH ALL YOUR SOUL, AND WITH ALL YOUR MIND, AND WITH ALL YOUR STRENGTH.' 31 "The second is this, `YOU SHALL LOVE YOUR NEIGHBOR AS YOURSELF.' There is no other commandment greater than these."

32 The scribe said to Him, "Right, Teacher; You have truly stated that HE IS ONE, AND THERE IS NO ONE ELSE BESIDES HIM; 33 AND TO LOVE HIM WITH ALL THE HEART AND WITH ALL THE UNDERSTANDING AND WITH ALL THE STRENGTH, AND TO LOVE ONE'S NEIGHBOR AS HIMSELF, is much more than all burnt offerings and sacrifices." 34 When Jesus saw that he had answered intelligently, He said to him, "You are not far from the kingdom of God." (Mark 12:28-34)

Commentary

23 On that day some Sadducees (who say there is no resurrection) came to Jesus

The Pharisees and Sadducees were the two controlling religious parties in Jerusalem. They alternated back and forth in supremacy and the period in which we find Jesus is the time of the Pharisees.

Their existence came about during the inter-testimental period – between Persian rule and the coming of the Romans into Palestine. The Pharisees were what we would call the conservative party today. They adopted a stricter policy and practice respecting the Mosaic Law, and were thereby rigorously legalistic – hence Jesus' statement, *"unless your righteousness exceed that of the Pharisees, you can not enter the Kingdom of Heaven."*

The Sadducees (their name is taken from a priest named Zadok – hence Saduc or Sadducees) were what we would call the liberal party, who often took exception with the literality of Scripture, more readily appropriating foreign ideas (hellenization) into their teaching and practice.

Don't be fooled that in their opposition to the Pharisees they were closer to Jesus. They were even farther away from Him in spiritualizing and allegorizing teachings and commandments. They were in fact more like modern liberal Christians, who enjoy trapping conservatives in sophistries and conundrums because they believe what to them are fables.

The mention of them not believing in the resurrection shows that they are here to trick Jesus into a contradiction by posing the case of multiple marriages and the dilemma this creates if there is a resurrection.

24 .. "Teacher, Moses said, 'IF A MAN DIES HAVING NO CHILDREN, HIS BROTHER AS NEXT OF KIN SHALL MARRY HIS WIFE .. 25 "Now there were seven brothers with us; .. whose wife of the seven will she be? For they all had married her

The OT precept is Deut 25:5 and is sometimes called the law of the "kinsman redeemer." (This was exercised in the case of Boaz respecting Ruth. (Ruth 2:1.)

This is an extreme scenario. But liberals enjoy ferreting out the one counterexample that might upset a whole doctrine. In fact, liberals do this regularly and extensively to avoid taking any of such precepts and commands to heart.

While quite rare, it might feasibly come about that all brothers were sequentially obligated to marry their brother's wife to continue the legitimacy of his children.

And the reason for this scenario is obvious – if there is a resurrection, all seven will be seen as the husband of the one woman, and in Heaven such unrighteousness would not be allowed. If monogamy was the rule on earth, how could it be abandoned in Heaven?

But Jesus would not be trapped by such machinations, because He knew the truth about what happens in Heaven ..

29 ... "You are mistaken, not understanding the Scriptures nor the power of God.

We may search extensively and find no OT verse discussing how marriage is to relate to spouses in Heaven. So it isn't a charge of being ignorant of some particular Scripture about this, but of being ignorant of Scripture about the nature of the resurrection. Job discloses knowledge of it (Job 19:26), Ezekiel presents a vision of it (Eze. 37), and Daniel prophesied about it in Dan. 12:2.

This is a beautiful illustration of what is called the analogy of faith. We are not to interpret one area of Scriptural teaching such that it nullifies the effect of another. They must all be taken together as the whole counsel of God, and our duty is to seek harmony not contradiction.

In this case, it is about Deut 25:5 being pitted against the other verses on the resurrection. Classic to liberal thinking is the rejection of the veracity of the Word to act in this manner. The reason liberals do not take heed of the correlating verses is their general mistrust of the Bible as a whole. Hence, they are generally not impressed with a cross reference.

Here the Jews are at least obligated to heed other teaching in Scripture, since it forms the basis for their existence as God's people. It is more likely that they have little working knowledge of the entire Scripture to know beforehand the correlations that would prevent their error. This was the business of the Scribes, who maintained the Scriptures and studied their texts. (It was a scribe who informed Herod that Messiah was to come from Bethlehem.)

30 "For in the resurrection they neither marry nor are given in marriage, but are like angels in heaven."

What a marvelous window into what Jesus has seen. He not only knows that angels exist but He knows of their state concerning marriage simply because He was actually there in past millennia to see firsthand. They would be so common a sight in the Heavenly surroundings that we see Him here speaking in almost subdued matter-of-fact fashion. Were we to be given a glimpse of them, we would be talking non-stop about nothing else.

Now as to their being no past or future marriage in Heaven, some approach this revelation with despair, wishing the joys of a blissful marriage on earth could extend into eternity. Others are rather thankful they don't.

But it isn't for fear of bringing the unpleasantries of some marriages into the eternal state that caused this state of affairs to be established (no such conflicts and enmities would be allowed on any account), but rather that marriage simply has no moment or purpose in our new state as redeemed servants of God.

Heaven is the place where we become what we were meant to be – the true children of God. Marriage was both a means and blessing of earthly life that provided companionship, pleasure and the procreation of succeeding generations. The need for such things, aimed at human conditions, is no longer required in the Heavenly estate. We are not in need of companionship, we have no need to reproduce offspring, and temporal physical pleasure is no longer a need.

The golden aspect of marriage – relationship – will in fact be retained in Heaven, in that we will certainly know our spouses, family members and friends, but now in a new way and in another context.

31 "But regarding the resurrection of the dead, have you not read . . . 32 `I AM THE GOD OF ABRAHAM, AND THE GOD OF ISAAC, AND THE GOD OF JACOB'? He is not the God of the dead but of the living."

Without a resurrection, the Sadducees were obliged to regard death as the doorway to oblivion. Nor was it for them merely the spirit living on without the body, as Jesus shows next. No one actually exists after death in this frame of mind, therefore the verse just quoted would be tantamount to saying God was the God of the dead. And regardless of liberal or conservative bent, no one was willing to admit that.

Therefore, Jesus had successfully turned the table round, making them the ones now trapped for an answer. They certainly could not in the full hearing of the people propose that Abraham, Isaac and Jacob were but the mere dust of the dead. Their embarrassment was now rampant.

No wonder the writer adds – *33 When the crowds heard this, they were astonished at His teaching.*

28 One of the scribes came and heard them arguing,

Now arrives one of the bigger guns – a scribe – who would be armed with detailed recollections of the Scriptures, much more than either Pharisees or Sadducees would have acquired.

28 . . "What commandment is the foremost of all?"

Ordinarily, this would be an improper question because to break one commandment was to break them all, which precludes the idea that a commandment would be better than another. All precepts could kill by bringing a divine sentence of death.

But both the scribe here and Jesus knew that there was a commandment that "summed up" the totality of the Law -

29 . . "The foremost is, `HEAR, O ISRAEL ! THE LORD OUR GOD IS ONE LORD; 30 AND YOU SHALL LOVE THE LORD YOUR GOD WITH ALL YOUR HEART, AND WITH ALL YOUR SOUL, AND WITH ALL YOUR MIND, AND WITH ALL YOUR STRENGTH.'

Were man to do this, he would fulfill the intent of all the commandments. But it meant that one would have to love the Lord so powerfully that He would know the Lord intimately enough to avoid sins of commission and those of omission as well. And that is a tall order.

But that this is nigh impossible does not erode its truth. It is true that if an ant could lift me out of the way, he would not have to go around my shoe. The fact that he can't does not make the statement false.

31 "The second is this, `YOU SHALL LOVE YOUR NEIGHBOR AS YOURSELF.' There is no other commandment greater than these."

The reason these are the greatest is because they summarize the specific precepts and commandments in themselves. To practice these conscientiously, not carelessly or casually, would cause one to do all the others.

The expanded version of this is, *"Therefore all things whatsoever ye would that men should do to you, do ye even so to them: for this is the law and the prophets."* – the golden rule (Matthew 7:12.)

The idea is that we have a built-in register that tells us how we prefer to be treated by others, and that will also be common in our fellow man. So we can consult our own desires to know how to behave toward others. If we appreciate being loved and affirmed, we ought to love and affirm others (on the proviso that others do value that also, which we find they in fact do.)

We sometimes misunderstand this when it comes to gift-giving. Some folks feel that to honor this verse they should give gifts that they themselves value. But it is the opposite. If we wish to be blessed by gifts we appreciate, then we should bless others with gifts they appreciate, because it is not the gifts but the experience of joy that is to be given to others.

The reason this commandment sums up all the Law is that if we anticipate the good things our neighbor needs and desires, doing all we can to so bless him will include the things written out in detail in the Law. We will not defraud our brother because we would not wish to be defrauded. We will not covet because we would not want our neighbors eyeing our possessions. We will help him in distress because that's what we would want were we in his same difficulty. We will not bear false witness because we do not wish to be lied to.

32 The scribe said to Him, "Right, Teacher; You have truly stated that HE IS ONE, AND THERE IS NO ONE ELSE BESIDES HIM;"

This is rare among the Scribes. Here we have a man who is willing to let the truth of the Word constrain him, rather than having his own life constrain the Word. He recognizes truth and sound teaching when he hears it.

He adds then a quotation to his commendation of Jesus – that there is but One God. This is from Deut 4:35, and is a paraphrase rather than an exact quote. The OT reference says, . . *that you might know that the Lord is God; besides him there is no other.*

This has been provided in the OT and reiterated in the New to forestall any notion that the God of Israel is but one of many. His is not only the One God, but He is alone by Himself, ergo, all others are false.

It is popular today to reject this idea, proposing instead that there are many paths to the truth and one therefore has options. But whatever path avoids or un-authenticates the exclusivity of God in Christ is false, because there is no god besides Him.

33 ". . is much more than all burnt offerings and sacrifices."

The reason he can say this in conclusion is that the sacrifices dealt with individual sins and none satisfied a compliance with the whole of the Law. The precept being quoted however has the expectation of doing so, where the sacrifices did not.

34 ". . . "You are not far from the kingdom of God." After that, no one would venture to ask Him any more questions.

Jesus is not one to be affected by flattery. His commendation is not because the scribe happens to be supporting Him. Neither is Jesus among the crowd of people who hold grudges by group association. He is well aware that in many cases the Scribes join the evil programs of the Pharisees and are skilled at making the Scripture a tool for those ends. Here, he recognizes a heart that acknowledges both the truth of the Scriptures and its proper application.

To say he is "not far" is to also deliberately say he is not quite there. It is to recognize the gap but to encourage him that the gap is not imposing.

When He saw that he answered intelligently . .

Christians are sometimes accused of leaving their brains at the door when entering their church. The recognition here of "intelligence" is to speak of the good use of those faculties given to man by God at the Creation. We have a brain and we are expected to put it to good use.

This is becoming unpopular today because it is so quickly associated with the studiousness of theology or intense philosophizing. Often theologians demonstrate that in themselves and their work good theology and good communication have never met.

But what is being commended here is the exercise of the mind to embrace the larger picture above the details; to perceive what is at stake and not get lost in the minutia. That is really what intelligence was meant to do, but our weakness as human beings often sends us off on rabbit trails that test the patience of others.

Also, with the advent of the dumbed-down education, many Christians are understandably intimidated by the results of intelligent study, and prefer to label it as "man's wisdom" not God's, not realizing that this does disservice to the God who gave it in His provident grace.

"no one would venture . . "

One of the reactions to excellent wisdom is to exercise considerable caution about silly questions or especially those formed for entrapment. To pursue these would be to risk exposure and vilification. So they are observed to quit their questions on the observation that they are not dealing with a person of ordinary expectations.

Matthew 22:41-45, Mark 12:37, Matthew 22:46, Matthew 23:1-22

41 Now while the Pharisees were gathered together, Jesus asked them a question: 42 "What do you think about the Christ, whose son is He?" They said to Him, "The son of David." 43 He said to them, "Then how does David in the Spirit call Him `Lord,' saying, 44 `THE LORD SAID TO MY LORD, "SIT AT MY RIGHT HAND, UNTIL I PUT YOUR ENEMIES BENEATH YOUR FEET"'? 45 "If David then calls Him `Lord,' how is He his son?" 46 No one was able to answer Him a word, nor did anyone dare from that day on to ask Him another question. . . And the large crowd enjoyed listening to Him. . . 46 No one was able to answer Him a word, nor did anyone dare from that day on to ask Him another question. (Matthew 22:41-45, Mark 12:37, Matthew 22:46)

1 Then Jesus spoke to the crowds and to His disciples, 2 saying: "The scribes and the Pharisees have seated themselves in the chair of Moses; 3 therefore all that they tell you, do and observe, but do not do according to their deeds; for they say things and do not do them. 4 "They tie up heavy burdens and lay them on men's shoulders, but they themselves are unwilling to move them with so much as a finger.

5 "But they do all their deeds to be noticed by men; for they broaden their phylacteries and lengthen the tassels of their garments. 6 "They love the place of honor at banquets and the chief seats in the synagogues, 7 and respectful greetings in the market places, and being called Rabbi by men.

8 "But do not be called Rabbi; for One is your Teacher, and you are all brothers. 9 "Do not call anyone on earth your father; for One is your Father, He who is in heaven. 10 "Do not be called leaders; for One is your Leader, that is, Christ. 11 "But the greatest among you shall be your servant. 12 "Whoever exalts himself shall be humbled; and whoever humbles himself shall be exalted. 13 "But woe to you, scribes and Pharisees, hypocrites, because you shut off the kingdom of heaven from people; for you do not enter in yourselves, nor do you allow those who are entering to go in.

14 Woe to you, scribes and Pharisees, hypocrites, because you devour widows' houses, and for a pretense you make long prayers; therefore you will receive greater condemnation.] 15 "Woe to you, scribes and Pharisees, hypocrites, because you travel around on sea and land to make one proselyte; and when he becomes one, you make him twice as much a son of hell as yourselves. 16 "Woe to you, blind guides, who say, `Whoever swears by the temple, that is nothing; but whoever swears by the gold of the temple is obligated.' 17 "You fools and blind men! Which is more important, the gold or the temple that sanctified the gold?

18 "And, `Whoever swears by the altar, that is nothing, but whoever swears by the offering on it, he is obligated.' 19 "You blind men, which is more important, the offering, or the altar that sanctifies the offering? 20 "Therefore, whoever swears by the altar, swears both by the altar and by everything on it. 21 "And whoever swears by the temple, swears both by the temple and by Him who dwells within it. 22 "And whoever swears by heaven, swears both by the throne of God and by Him who sits upon it. (Matthew 23:1-22)

Commentary

41 Now while the Pharisees were gathered together, Jesus asked them a question:

This seems hardly worth commenting on, but it is actually very significant. Jesus is about to switch roles and ask a question of them. He already knows the question and their answer, but He doesn't take one or two aside to stump them with it, but takes advantage of the fact that a large number of them are now seated together in a crowd, listening to Him, but also counseling with one another on their strategy to get rid of Him.

He has been careful to wait for this moment so as to silence them once and for all, in terms of these silly tests. They won't be able to mischaracterize Him to their cohorts as playing unfair. Everyone important will have been here to see for themselves.

42 "What do you think about the Christ, whose son is He?" They said to Him, "The son of David."

The thrust of this question is to focus light on the misunderstanding of their expectations about Messiah. This question will reveal that there was an apparently diminished view about Messiah, in that he would be under David in authority, He being David's descendant. This acknowledgment would open an opportunity for them that Jesus ought to at least do what David His father did, which was to be obedient to the Law.

'the Christ.' He is not asking them what they think about *Him*, but about Messiah, which in Greek is *christos*. Specifically though, He is asking them to consider who's son they think Messiah to be, God's or merely David's?

Missing this entirely, they reply as expected - "David's son."

43 . . "Then how does David in the Spirit call Him `Lord,' saying, `THE LORD SAID TO MY LORD, . . '"

Now we need to be clear that the word Lord here is 'adonai' not the tetragrammaton YHWH for God's name. David is not calling him God, but a Lord whose authority he is under. The question is about the apparent contradiction this proposes that a man's son could be his Lord – " 45 "*If David then calls Him `Lord,' how is He his son?"*

This verse establishes that a greater than David is in view, not merely a descendant. And if so, Messiah is not obligated merely to those things a son would do. It is to gift them with the insight to take a second look at Jesus and the role of Messiah and see if they truly do have merit in their accusations against His actions and teaching.

"SIT AT MY RIGHT HAND, UNTIL I PUT YOUR ENEMIES BENEATH YOUR FEET"'

To which of David's descendant was this ever fulfilled – to sit at the right hand of Majesty on High? Which of David's descendents ever expected such a fulfillment?

And the large crowd enjoyed listening to Him

These are certainly not the Pharisees themselves, but the crowd of others on the sidelines and periphery, thoroughly enjoying the trouncing these august leaders are getting.

46 No one was able to answer Him a word, nor did anyone dare from that day on to ask Him another question.

This meant questions of trickery and subterfuge. It does not mean that no one asked Him any question of any type ever again. It means that this put an end to the entrapment sessions contrived by his enemies – until the trial of course, where we find intimidating and polemical questions posed in great furor.

2 . . "The scribes and the Pharisees have seated themselves in the chair of Moses; 3 therefore all that they tell you, do and observe

Jesus is not one to hold a prejudice that nullifies the good even if spoken by evil men. Men are responsible for how they apply good things and for the sincerity of their hearts, but we are not to discount truth if it happens to be spoken by someone ordinarily of an evil mind. Taking this proclamation of truth as a signal to follow them is another matter -

3 ". . but do not do according to their deeds; for they say things and do not do them.

When it comes to an exemplar, we are to be very careful to find someone who demonstrates the Word in their actions, thoughts and attitudes. This, Jesus warns them to avoid concerning the Pharisees. It was not a case of misstating the Law. It was a case of drawing improper and even dangerous conclusions from observing their behavior.

This is the delicate precariousness of this whole scene. It was not a case of righteous good against abject evil. It was not Gandalf against the Balrog.[55] It was Christ against men who were upholding express commands of God, and that conundrum can confuse and complicate people's understanding of the issues.

Religious truth is about the heart more than about individual precepts, and that makes it possible to be against one who proclaims the letter but lives not according to the Spirit. This had to be enraging speech, because Jesus was in essence telling everyone that these men had been terrible failures as examples.

4 "They tie up heavy burdens and lay them on men's shoulders, but they themselves are unwilling to move them with so much as a finger.

That this is not just a partisan accusation, Jesus provides some examples. To comply with certain precepts of the Law, there had to be some accompanying instruction. The Sabbath was a good example. How much could a person work or expend energy on the Sabbath and not break the intent of the Law?

A Sabbath day's journey is an example of what resulted, as was how much a man could carry in his arms, or how much preparation of food was allowed, etc.

Clever laws that permitted people to put things in their clothing so as not to be in the act of carrying them also came to be. The result was a significant corpus of explanatory ordinances outside the Law by which the Pharisees "bound" people to certain modes of obedience.

Jesus was noting that they were diligent to contrive these while finding clever ways not to abide by them themselves.

The adage to tie up burdens and not move them with their finger is not to say they moved no finger to relieve them but rather to say that they had no intention of making even the slightest effort to "engage" these same burdens for themselves.

5 "But they do all their deeds to be noticed by men; for they broaden their phylacteries and lengthen the tassels of their garments.

A phylactery was a little box containing a copy of the Mosaic Law[56], usually meaning the Ten Commandments. So the bigger it was, the more was the inference that the person had more of the Law beyond the decalogue stored therein, hence was more spiritual and obedient.

The lengthening of tassels is akin to chevrons on military dress – the more stripes down the arm, the more authority - although it is difficult to know whether these carried any hierarchy of ranking authority.

As we mentioned earlier in the ministry among the villages, the times were very different from our own in that a man's position among his fellows was extremely important as to his treatment in society. Any and all opportunities to flaunt those privileges before others were sought and arranged as often as possible – *" they do all their deeds to be noticed by men"*

6 "They love the place of honor . . the chief seats . . 7 . . respectful greetings in the market places, and being called Rabbi by men.

It was traditional among kings and princes that in processions they would look to one side and the other, taking note of who was present and who was properly emulating obeisance or not. It was a moment to enlarge (or at least re-check) one's appreciation by the crowd.

---

[55] Lord of the Rings - The Fellowship of the Ring, New Line Cinema, (2001)
[56] Deut 6:8

The Pharisees came to emulate this by seeking out places of honor and chief seats so that they would not only be seen but might see how others respected them.

8 "But do not be called Rabbi; for One is your Teacher, and you are all brothers.

In a contrast that couldn't be more opposite, He exhorts them to not seek to be called Rabbi. This is not to say they were not to teach or instruct. Rather, it is an exhortation to not seek the title. The reason is simple humility. If one was blessed of God to teach, it was not of their own doing, hence there is no claim to a title.

9 "Do not call anyone on earth your father; for One is your Father, He who is in heaven.

Some common sense applies here. He does not mean for children to stop calling their dads 'fathers.' It was in reference to what the Jews practiced in terms of the patriarchs. These were fathers of note[57] over the faith of Israel, fathers as to rank and importance, and this Jesus exhorts them not to do.

This bears on the practice in Catholicism of calling one's priest 'Father' and the pope – 'Holy Father.' Catholics are obliged to justify this by their sacred tradition – that this practice arose in the early church by those who knew Jesus more intimately than others or were the associates of those that had. This tradition is a source of authority in the Church and, with respect to what Jesus teaches here, reserves the divine right to interpret it correctly.

Some Protestant churches have retained this designation for those organizations that operate a priesthood. Others, violently oppose this on the grounds of Jesus' admonition here, calling such persons pastors or the term 'reverend.'

To show respect on a purely horizontal plane is not ruled out, but there is a thin line over which we are not to cross in calling someone father as a light of knowledge, wisdom and truth which is here seen to be reserved jealously by our Heavenly Father.

10 "Do not be called leaders; for One is your Leader, that is, Christ.

The intent, as above, is to avoid a shift of focus from God to man where spiritual matters are concerned. God desires a real relationship with us, not one mediated by someone else. This was permitted in more primitive times, but with the advent of Christ as Son, this idea of mediation is not to be enjoined going forward. This therefore runs into difficulty in church polities where the priest is seen as mediator between congregant and Christ. If there is to be a mediator, it will be Christ and no other man. (Witness the tearing of the curtain in the Holy of Holies at Christ's death – taking away the mediatorial barrier between priest and worshipper.)

11 "But the greatest among you shall be your servant.

Completely contrary to the way of men then as now. The pattern has always been that greatness is not related to the servants role, but rather, great men are marked by having servants. The reason is that human greatness is seldom without its side effects of dominance, power and subjugation.

Man has become great in the past by the use of power and influence and that usually meant stepping on someone to get things done. In the wake of many great people there are almost always those who are still stinging from the dis-acknowledgment or side-stepping that great people must inevitably do to get things done.

---

[57] In ancient Rome, the Senate was formally addressed as 'Fathers of Rome.' See Meier, Caesar, Basic Books, New York (1982) p. 36

To be great is to not let every issue ensnare you and many times the lesser people become over-stepped in the path to greatness.

But God counts things differently. Greatness in His eyes is not material or secular achievement, but heavenly achievement whose chief aim is aid and help to others in need. That is a servant's role – to serve needs, not indifferently through programs, but personally through involvement and contact.

The disciples are not to set up shop and hire people to do the menial duties. Jesus never had "headquarters" for His ministry office. His place was out among the people, serving their needs.

12 "Whoever exalts himself shall be humbled;

It's not that exaltation is now forbidden altogether, but that it is not to come from our having arranged it. Our exaltation is to come from others, from God.

There is nothing more detestable than the person who angles for compliments or pats himself on the back. It is a sign of not being willing to wait until such compliments can come from others genuinely and unsolicited. And in many cases, it is precisely because one knows he is unlikely to get such compliments to start with (hence the wait will be endless) that he short-circuits the process for immediate gratification.

But there is more here. The one who exalts will be humbled. Inevitably, the self-exalter is soon avoided or paid back for his self-centeredness by having no friends. Life becomes all the more sad. It is a sort of forced humility and some turn this into bitterness or even hatred; others to a form of self-loathing.

From God's viewpoint it is more a matter of acquainting us with our true selves that we can more honestly reach out to God for His affirmation. He cannot be blamed for the way people react to the principle. We are the ones who are plagued with sin. He is righteous in all His motives and purposes.

12 . . " and whoever humbles himself shall be exalted."

So the corollary is the real truth to be sought – he who humbles himself will be exalted. But this does not mean he who is humble per se. Many are humbled by circumstances but they are in no frame of mind to be exalted by God. The operative word is "himself." It is a deliberate act of the will; an attitude of mind that says, "I am second, not first. I am willing to be last that others may be blessed."

In this day and age, we are told just the opposite. Not only are we just as good as everyone else, but we must "take" what we deserve because no one else is going to give it to us, being that they too are grasping for what they think they deserve. We have learned to be the captains of our own futures and all other people are objects around which we must navigate to get where and what we want for ourselves. Witness the attitudes and behavior of motorists in traffic.

Today, we see people running to grasp what they desire for themselves, to not let opportunity slip over the best in life. In the Gospels we see Jesus running nowhere for any urgent thing. He is completely content in letting what we might see as better opportunities fall by the wayside, because He is fully confident and at peace with who He is and how His needs will be met.

That is the peace and humility He desires for us.

Woes Against the Pharisees

13 "But woe to you, scribes and Pharisees, hypocrites, because you shut off the kingdom of heaven from people;

Now a series of indictments against the Pharisees. They are first hypocrites because they preach but do not practice. And it is not to enjoin perfection as the only way to avoid hypocrisy. We are all fallen and will all fail to live up to what we teach others to do. But here, hypocrisy is an attitude, a contract we make with ourselves ahead of time – that we will not abide by such and such teaching, or we will find some clever way to avoid it. This is the frame of mind that operates in the Pharisee – abject legalism for others, utter contempt for it within oneself.

"shut off the kingdom of heaven from others."

This was happening not only from their hypocrisy but from their legalism. People seeing their hypocrisy deduced that the truth of the kingdom was a myth, at least in these men. And whether they sought it elsewhere or not presented the precarious opportunity to neglect it altogether, which is a form of barring one from the truth.

In terms of legalism, the letter of the Law is later described as having no power to cure the illness - *"Accordingly both gifts and sacrifices are offered which cannot make the worshiper perfect in conscience,* (Hebrews 9:9) . . . *For the Law, since it has only a shadow of the good things to come and not the very form of things, can never, by the same sacrifices which they offer continually year by year, make perfect those who draw near.* (Hebrews 10:1.)

So it was an enormous mistake to emphasize the letter without reference to the principle of bankruptcy and the appeal to mercy before the Law. The whole concept of a perfect mediator, a perfect sacrifice is bound up in the inadequacy of the intermediate system –that it was temporary. To then cause the believer to base his view of the Kingdom on legalism within the labyrinth of the Law was to bar one from its truth and thereby from entering it.

13 . . "nor do you allow those who are entering to go in."

And here is the insidiousness of their error. They attempt even to block those who have found the Kingdom and its entrance. It is a certain sour grapes in them – those who have found the door are pouring salt on their wounds by enlarging the magnitude of their own error. And this at the hands of the simplest of people, the poor and dejected.

Now we might ask how the Pharisees could "prevent" people from embracing the salvation offered by Jesus, if it is a heavenly operation? We must keep in mind that salvation is an ideological process of faith and it is enabled by the influence and persuasive effect of ideas. The Pharisees had created a system which threatened the believer if abandoned. It also had an effective means of re-explaining truths to their advantage, especially to those who were largely illiterate or unstudied and depended on those who were.

So it was an effectively communicated fear of setting aside the traditions of the elders and a more articulate ability to out-maneuver the still somewhat gullible that kept many in legalism or brought them back to it from the freedom taught by Jesus.

14 Woe to you, . . . because you devour widows' houses,

The plight of the widow was quite different than today. People did not have annuities and investments, or life insurance to ward off the condition of having no provider. Widows were very vulnerable to someone coming in and managing their affairs. What better candidate than a righteous man like a Pharisee? But it was a design impassioned by greed, and soon explanations would arise as to why the home must be sold to make ends meet.

Their houses were in this sense devoured by soon becoming the additional holdings of a Pharisee.

14 . . "and for a pretense you make long prayers; therefore you will receive greater condemnation.

It is not on account of prayers but because prayers are made a companion to evil actions. And the prayers themselves were of no merit, since they were offered only for show.

15 "Woe to you, . . . [you] make one proselyte; . . you make him twice as much a son of hell as yourselves.

The indictment is not in seeking candidates for the faith of God, but in how this is undone by what they made of him. They disciple such people into copies of themselves, following their own traditions which led them to the same wooden, faithlessness that blinded them from the truth. As to sons of hell, this refers to apprentices in the same deceits and conniving that have been condemned above.

16 "Woe to you, . . . `Whoever swears by the temple, that is nothing; but whoever swears by the gold of the temple is obligated.'

Jesus elsewhere upbraids swearing by anything, therefore it seems out of sorts to be complaining about distinctions among oaths. But it is to show the depths of deception and unprofitability in this practice. In their swearing, they had come to disregard the Temple in favor of its gold, the altar in favor of its offering, all of which increased the desperate nature of these meanderings.

Hence – *17 "You fools and blind men! Which is more important, the gold or the temple that sanctified the gold?"*

22 "And whoever swears by heaven, swears both by the throne of God and by Him who sits upon it.

This is not an admonition to improve the manner in which one swears. Jesus counters this elsewhere - *"But I say to you, make no oath at all, either by heaven, for it is the throne of God,"*
(Matthew 5:34)

The admonition applies to their lost sense of value. Were it useful to swear by these things, how could one take a lesser view of the greater essence and He who ensures it?

Thus, we find in this indictment an exposure of the problems of micro-managing the affairs of God. We sometimes call this "getting wrapped around the axle." We become buried in the details of a process or a thing, and we lose sight of what was originally more important.

Matthew 23:23-39, Mark 12:41-44

23 "Woe to you, scribes and Pharisees, hypocrites! For you tithe mint and dill and cummin, and have neglected the weightier provisions of the law: justice and mercy and faithfulness; but these are the things you should have done without neglecting the others. 24 "You blind guides, who strain out a gnat and swallow a camel!

25 "Woe to you, scribes and Pharisees, hypocrites! For you clean the outside of the cup and of the dish, but inside they are full of robbery and self-indulgence. 26 "You blind Pharisee, first clean the inside of the cup and of the dish, so that the outside of it may become clean also.

27 "Woe to you, scribes and Pharisees, hypocrites! For you are like whitewashed tombs which on the outside appear beautiful, but inside they are full of dead men's bones and all uncleanness. 28 "So you, too, outwardly appear righteous to men, but inwardly you are full of hypocrisy and lawlessness.

29 "Woe to you, scribes and Pharisees, hypocrites! For you build the tombs of the prophets and adorn the monuments of the righteous, 30 and say, `If we had been living in the days of our fathers, we would not have been partners with them in shedding the blood of the prophets.' 31 "So you testify against yourselves, that you are sons of those who murdered the prophets. 32 "Fill up, then, the measure of the guilt of your fathers.

33 "You serpents, you brood of vipers, how will you escape the sentence of hell? 34 "Therefore, behold, I am sending you prophets and wise men and scribes; some of them you will kill and crucify, and some of them you will scourge in your synagogues, and persecute from city to city, 35 so that upon you may fall the guilt of all the righteous blood shed on earth, from the blood of righteous Abel to the blood of Zechariah, the son of Berechiah, whom you murdered between the temple and the altar. 36 "Truly I say to you, all these things will come upon this generation. 37 "Jerusalem, Jerusalem, who kills the prophets and stones those who are sent to her! How often I wanted to gather your children together, the way a hen gathers her chicks under her wings, and you were unwilling. 38 "Behold, your house is being left to you desolate! 39 "For I say to you, from now on you will not see Me until you say, `BLESSED IS HE WHO COMES IN THE NAME OF THE LORD !' " (Matthew 23:23-39)

41 And He sat down opposite the treasury, and began observing how the people were putting money into the treasury; and many rich people were putting in large sums. 42 A poor widow came and put in two small copper coins, which amount to a cent. 43 Calling His disciples to Him, He said to them, "Truly I say to you, this poor widow put in more than all the contributors to the treasury; 44 for they all put in out of their surplus, but she, out of her poverty, put in all she owned, all she had to live on." (Mark 12:41-44)

Commentary

23 "Woe to you, scribes and Pharisees, hypocrites! For you tithe mint and dill and cummin, . . 24 "You blind guides, who strain out a gnat and swallow a camel!

The setting aside of a tenth of the produce of one's crops was called for in the Law (Lev 27:28,32.) While every law was assessed in terms of sin, Jesus here indicates that there were "weightier" laws of greater importance because of their consequences. Certainly a man was regarded more seriously who killed than a man who neglected a tenth part of his grain. All were sin, but all were not of equal weight.

Here the Pharisees are judicious to tithe of the most insignificant herbs, while neglecting the weightier matters like caring for the needy even if it meant work that might be questioned on the sabbath – the works of *"justice, mercy, faithfulness."*

He does not accuse them of doing irrelevant things (tithing cummin and dill) – *" these you should have done"* but of neglecting the weightier for them – *"[you] strain out a gnat and swallow a camel!"*

Were they to inadvertently take in a gnat (an unclean food), they would strain on it to get it back up from their throats, so as not to take it into the stomach, yet in other items of neglect, they had in effect swallowed another unclean food – a whole camel (Lev 11:4) – without a flinch.

25 "Woe to you, . . . For you clean the outside of the cup and of the dish, but inside they are full of robbery and self-indulgence.

Here, a rather silly exercise is pictured – the care for the appearance of the outward view of the cup or dish, while neglecting the filthiness in the cup, the very thing that would be taken in. *" . . first clean the inside of the cup and of the dish, so that the outside of it may become clean also."*

27 "Woe to you, . . . For you are like whitewashed tombs which on the outside appear beautiful, but inside they are full of dead men's bones and all uncleanness.

Tombs were traditionally whitewashed if standing out in the open, as evidenced by many of those placed outside the East Gate. There was no doubt in anyone's mind that the inside of such a tomb would be uncleanness. Jesus was not teaching it was expected to be otherwise.

The point is that the Pharisees are being likened to this arrangement, for their inner righteousness was being compared to the most obnoxious of unclean conditions. They were full of insincerity and acts that disrespected the Law they levied on others. Their very manner in seeking means to do away with Him despite finding adequacy in the Law was a perfect example. They would arrange for the needs of the Law if the facts could not suffice of themselves.

29 "Woe to you, . . . For you build the tombs of the prophets and adorn the monuments of the righteous,

This is somewhat subtle in thrust and meaning. He noted that they professed to *not* be partners with those who killed the prophets, but they were in fact acting just like them at that very hour. They sought to kill Him for the righteousness He proclaimed. By saying that they have admitted being descendents, He picks up on the idea "the sins of the father are repeated in the son", and this is a subtle way of condemning them by using their own words – *32 "Fill up, then, the measure of the guilt of your fathers."*

33 "You serpents, you brood of vipers, how will you escape the sentence of hell?

For those who prefer Jesus as loving and never saying an unkind word, there is here cause to rethink this as more a case of naivite than historic fact. His words are accusatory in the maximum degree. It is exceedingly negative and critical, which will set ill with those who see all negativity as a sin against humanity. His likening of them to whited tombs is even ingeniously critical, by using a rather vivid figure. Many believe this kind of thing should not be part of Christian behavior toward others. And in one sense this is correct and true – we ought to prefer love to criticism and negativity. Similarly, just because Jesus did this does not necessarily open the door for us as His followers to be free with this form of address.

On the other hand, the conditions were such that hard words were necessary in order to provide no quarter, no sense of accommodation for their evil thoughts and actions. There is a point when Christian love will just be walked over and used for further evils. Jesus advised His disciples to know when to shake the dust from their feet. Like it or not, that is negative and condemnatory action.

So love in the hands of Jesus was not devoid of all unpleasantness and rebuke. Here, it is time to call things what they are, and these men had determined for themselves a destiny that needed to be made known. It is not without an opening for mercy and forgiveness, but it would be certain should they persist without repentance.

34 "Therefore, behold, I am sending you prophets and wise men and scribes;

Herein is the unbounded love of God yet displayed. Mercy and longsuffering are still being extended to them. He will yet send them prophets, men of Godly wisdom, and men of the Scriptures, that they may have yet more opportunities to turn and be saved. This longsuffering was seen centuries earlier in Jeremiah's words to a stubborn people, with the Babylonians virtually upon them. *" Call unto me, and I will answer thee, and shew thee great and mighty things, which thou knowest not."* (Jeremiah 33:3)

Yet He knows the outcome – *34 " and some of them you will scourge in your synagogues, and persecute from city to city,"*

He then connects this anticipated end to the corporate guilt they all share in killing the prophets sent to them of old -

35 so that upon you may fall the guilt of all the righteous blood shed on earth, from the blood of righteous Abel to the blood of Zechariah, the son of Berechiah, whom you murdered between the temple and the altar.

They are repeating the sin of Abel who despised the righteousness of his brother. Similarly down through the ages, men continually persecuted messengers of righteousness because they shined unwanted light on their evil deeds. Jesus ably summarizes this condition by sweeping across the times from Able to Zechariah, who was the most recent of their crimes, being done to death in the very act of his service.

He does not accommodate any notion that this was a slaying from altruistic motives – to preserve the heritage of the faith of their fathers. He clearly calls it murder. Hence, upon them falls the guilt of all that righteous blood because they are of the same insidious mind and evil heart. Were they to have been present at those events, they would have joined league with the murderers.

What is marvelous here is that God sees all the details. He not only knew of the murder of Zechariah but the exact location the crime was committed. This is ready testimony to those who think God is too transcendent to be concerned about the details.

36 "Truly I say to you, all these things will come upon this generation.

Meaning judgment for those acts. The cup of iniquity was filling again for all of Israel. They had suffered at the hands of the Assyrians for disobedience and spiritual harlotry. They had suffered the exile of the Babylonians for the same reason some 150 years later. Now time had managed to fill the cup once again – *"Fill up, then, the measure of the guilt of your fathers."* . John, they rejected and assented to his death. Now, Jesus is the malefactor worthy of death in their eyes.

The judgment Jesus alludes to is of course the destruction of Jerusalem in 70 A.D. at the hands of the Roman authority. Historians enjoy dispelling this idea by pointing out that it was due to the insurrections and sorties against local Roman centers of control that brought down the inevitable hammer of retribution. But Jesus makes it clear that there were higher principles in play for which the Romans were merely tools in His hand to effect His divine will.

Now some may object to the idea of inflicting punishment for the nation's historic sins on a particular generation. And this is based on the reasoning that men ought to pay for their own errors in their own times, not those of their ancestors.

But it is a case that the generation punished exemplifies in their own free will actions and evil hearts the hearts of their ancestors in rejecting their God and His emissaries. They were not committing the sins of idolatry. That had been effectively dealt with by Babylon. But they still had the evil mind that slew the righteous of past ages.

And to highlight the percipient evil of the present generation to whom Jesus spoke, they were in the awful place of rejecting their own Messiah and putting Him to death. Can they be seen other than the sheer epitome of all those former crimes?

With Sodom, the judgment fell on that generation that had excelled in the most vile and detestable forms of evil. The sins of their ancestors had not been ameliorated or reformed over time, but had been perfected and embellished by the time the angels visited the city. To coin a phrase from the NT, *"it was the fullness of time."*

37 "Jerusalem, Jerusalem, . . . How often I wanted to gather your children together, the way a hen gathers her chicks under her wings, and you were unwilling.

Herein is the longsuffering of God expressed. Despite their errors and abuse of God's love toward them, He extended his wings that they might yet gather under them. The indictment wasn't as much that they relished in sin, but that when repentance and forgiveness were yet offered, they spurned it.

Here, Jerusalem is figurative for the nation and its corporate mind, but especially in the wickedness of its leaders. All the greatness that Jerusalem meant to the world was about to be thrown down and made a rubbish heap – *38 "Behold, your house is being left to you desolate!*

Desolation was a term that meant abandoned of both God and man. It was likened to a wasteland where nothing worthwhile could be expected from the ground, hence no one found reason to dwell there.

In terms of history, this was aimed more at the religious significance for Judaism. That greatness was to become desolate, although physical desolation also lasted some sixty years. (The Romans refurbished part of the city under Hadrian, naming it Aelia Capitolina - A.D. 131.)

39 "For I say to you, from now on you will not see Me until you say, `BLESSED IS HE WHO COMES IN THE NAME OF THE LORD !' "

To the Jews, this was good news. They wished to be rid of Him forever, so such a conditional would virtually guarantee its success. But from a purely messianic point of view, Jesus was telling them that they would not see their Blessed Messiah until they could say of Him, *"Blessed is He who comes in the Name of the Lord."*

Ordinarily, we might think this to be rather vague in reference to Jesus and Messiah. Could they not say this about anyone? But this is a quotation from Psalms 118:26, which was regarded as messianic. This is the same Psalm from which we get, *"Open to me the gates of righteousness; I shall enter through them, . . This is the gate of the LORD; . . . The stone which the builders rejected Has become the chief cornerstone. "*

So it is not a mere phrase, but a specifically messianic adulation which would herald the entry of Messiah into the city at the very gate appointed for that purpose.

Next, we will see an interlude from the woes and then a discourse on end times.

41 And He sat down opposite the treasury, and began observing how the people were putting money into the treasury;

This is a little vignette, as it were. between two great narratives of powerful moment – Jesus' condemnation of the Pharisees and His discourse on end times. It seems almost misplaced somehow and might easily be forgotten were it not for the thing we learn from it.

This was not the Roman tax, but a corporate duty Israel observed to support the Temple. It has been translated down into our tithes and offerings in the Christian Church. God has always placed on the hearts of His people the need to contribute to the practical needs of religious service. Many people today resent this from a God who does not need anything.

While it is quite true that God could have miraculously supported the human institutions He ordered into being, He made it such that man would participate, especially in terms of some level of personal sacrifice. In this way, man has a part, a contribution also.

But much has to do with the heart. Those who truly desire to give, do not do so begrudgingly, nor do they consider it a necessary evil. They are eager with both money and time. Those who always consider it a burden will never see the joy in this kind of giving, that which is willing to bless from what one has, but will always be focused on the giving up or relinquishing of what they regard as deserved.

In Jesus' day, the giving also operated with yet another kind of behavior – self-aggrandizement. To be seen as giving large sums enlarged one's respect and honor among others. By such, the rich and influential were seen regularly to give.

*"began observing **how"*** Notice it was not the procedure of the giving, but how people engaged in the giving. We can be sure this included the inner hearts as well as the body language. We can imagine Him reading each man's heart as he tossed in his offering.

42 A poor widow came and put in two small copper coins, which amount to a cent.

We need to be careful of the English words used here. The "two copper coins" are the Gk. *'lepton*, and the word 'cent' is the word *'quadrans'* – a fourth of a Roman 'as.'

(Note: the lepton was the coin placed on the eyelids of the dead. It's expendability in this function tells you how much value this woman's coins had.)

In terms of equivalency, this was about $1.85 in today's purchasing power. The Roman *as* was 1/16th of a soldier's daily wage – the denarius. The quadrans was one quarter of that. So the quardans would have been 1/64th of a day's wage or about $1.85 in today's money.

Having noted the foregoing of the rich and influential, this amount is virtually insignificant. It's absence in the total would not have been felt in the least, were it not to have been given. It is somewhat like the young child putting in a nickel toward an offering for world hunger. It would be winked at and considered more an experience for the child than of any monetary usefulness.

But Jesus specifically calls attention of this offering to His disciples - *43 . . "Truly I say to you, this poor widow put in more than all the contributors to the treasury;"*

This had to create immediate dismay because it was in practical terms so contrary to reason. Yet His disciples were now rather used to the complete opposite of expectations from Him.

44 for they all put in out of their surplus, but she, out of her poverty, put in all she owned, all she had to live on."

Other translations say, "her whole living." To give out of abundance is painless, because one knows his living is still assured. He can return to his house, his servants still there waiting with a change of clothes, food ready to eat and his bath before bed. Were they to toss in their whole living, the house sold, servants dismissed, food gone, it would be another story; one in which they would not likely be giving at all.

Yet this grim prospect did not stop the old woman from her duty to God's house.

Today, we consider this a fabulous tale with no continuity for us whatsoever. We would be arguing what a $1.85 could possible mean in criticality to the Church that we become completely destitute in giving it? We would be asking if this is the God we are to envision in our faith – one that callously takes a widow's last meal that the Church be provided for?

Yet we hear of no such attitude in her by our Lord. Were she to have had such an attitude as moderns do today, she would not have been singled out by Jesus so as to now live in exemplary posterity.

So what message does this convey to us in modern times? Are we to then give all that we own to the Church?

We are to emulate her heart, not her act. If it be that we are asked to repeat her act, God will make that known. But before that, we must have her heart for that to succeed. Without it, we would be merely going through the motions, and that is not what is happening here in the gospel.

We must be honing ourselves in prayer and devotion, that were it to be asked of us, we would be ready. That is a very tall order and everything in our present world screams just the opposite, as if to train us hurriedly away from such a heart. As we look at this dear woman, we see that her desperate poverty is misleading. She is of greater courage, devotion and faith than any one person we might know today, especially our own selves. And that is why Jesus pointed us to her.

CHAPTER 12
The Olivet Discourse and End Times

Mark 13:1-4, Matthew 24:8, 12, 14, Mark 13:9-13, Luke 21:20-24

1 As He was going out of the temple, one of His disciples said to Him, "Teacher, behold what wonderful stones and what wonderful buildings!" 2 And Jesus said to him, "Do you see these great buildings? Not one stone will be left upon another which will not be torn down."

3 As He was sitting on the Mount of Olives opposite the temple, Peter and James and John and Andrew were questioning Him privately, 4 "Tell us, when will these things be, and what will be the sign when all these things are going to be fulfilled? . . what will be the sign of Your coming, and of the end of the age?" (Mark 13:3-4, Matthew 24:3)

4 And Jesus answered and said to them, "See to it that no one misleads you. 5 "For many will come in My name, saying, `I am the Christ,' and will mislead many. 6 "You will be hearing of wars and rumors of wars. See that you are not frightened, for those things must take place, but that is not yet the end. 7 "For nation will rise against nation, and kingdom against kingdom, and in various places there will be famines and earthquakes. 8 "But all these things are merely the beginning of birth pangs. (Matthew 24:4-8)

9 "But be on your guard; for they will deliver you to the courts, and you will be flogged in the synagogues, and you will stand before governors and kings for My sake, as a testimony to them. 10 "The gospel must first be preached to all the nations. 11 "When they arrest you and hand you over, do not worry beforehand about what you are to say, but say whatever is given you in that hour; for it is not you who speak, but it is the Holy Spirit. 12 "Brother will betray brother to death, and a father his child; and children will rise up against parents and have them put to death. . . . 12 "Because lawlessness is increased, most people's love will grow cold. . . . 13 "You will be hated by all because of My name, but the one who endures to the end, he will be saved. . . 14 "This gospel of the kingdom shall be preached in the whole world as a testimony to all the nations, and then the end will come. (Mark 13:9-12, Matthew 24:12, Mark 13:13, Matthew 24:14)

20 "But when you see Jerusalem surrounded by armies, then recognize that her desolation is near. 21 "Then those who are in Judea must flee to the mountains, and those who are in the midst of the city must leave, and those who are in the country must not enter the city; 22 because these are days of vengeance, so that all things which are written will be fulfilled. 23 "Woe to those who are pregnant and to those who are nursing babies in those days, for there will be great distress upon the land and wrath to this people; 24 and they will fall by the edge of the sword, and will be led captive into all the nations; and Jerusalem will be trampled under foot by the Gentiles until the times of the Gentiles are fulfilled (Luke 21:20-24)

Commentary

1 . . "Teacher, behold what wonderful stones and what wonderful buildings!"

His disciples were men who were proud of their nation. The Temple was an edifice known throughout the world as well nigh a wonder. When Herod's renovations were completed, the temple and compound would have been the largest religious building complex in the world. The Temple of Jupiter Capitolinus in Rome was a much larger single edifice, but Jerusalem's surrounding compound surpassed it, larger also than that of Thebes (Karnak) in Egypt.

We are now aware of the magnitude of this feat in materials used and engineering skill required. The platform of the Temple compound was hardly anywhere supported directly on the ground, but it straddled the pinnacle of a mount and necessitated a lateral expanse of flooring which literally suspended out above the tapering mountainsides. Thus, it was largely supported by tiers of arched substructures which joined the level platform to the ever receding ground. This was what made the construction a marvel of the ancient world; not only for its size but that it was made to hang without direct earthly foundation.

Certain key stones are known to weigh upwards of 500 tons in the lower courses. There are no modern cranes in existence today that could lift or move these into place. How the ancients quarried them and moved them remains a complete mystery.

As for the construction, no mortar was used to secure them but they were placed merely on top of one another. The joints were so finely planed that many refuse the entry of a thin dollar bill between them.

It is completely understandable that as Jesus walked with them along its walls, they would be curious of His opinion of them.

2 And Jesus said to him, "Do you see these great buildings? Not one stone will be left upon another which will not be torn down."

At first, we might take this as a denigration for all human efforts to express physically the worship of God. We flag in more recent times at the incredible cost and labor to produce cathedrals and monuments, when people starve for lack of monetary relief. But Jesus was not denigrating the idea of the Temple, per se. (It was ordained by God in David's time to be built.) Were He to be dissing the whole idea of buildings in man's worship, He would not have railed *only* against its misuse as a house of prayer (Matt 21:13.)

Instead, Jesus is providing realistic insight into what is about to take place for both Temple, city and people. When these things were asked, the temple complex was still under construction. It would continue as such until A.D. 64, after which a mere six years later, it would be leveled to the ground by the Roman legions.

History and archaeology record the fulfillment of this prediction. Today we see virtually no single stone of the Temple itself in its original place and scarce any original stones in place for the complex.

Titus, the Roman commander of the siege, had ordered that the Temple building itself not be destroyed. This command was frustrated when a fire broke out in the building and sheer greed sealed its fate. The ceiling and column capitals had been gilded over with gold. The fire was so intense that this soon melted and drizzled down into the cracks and joints of the construction. The greed of the soldiers (who had rights to the spoils of war) occasioned the dismantling of the building. With so many soldiers involved in this event, each was desperate to get some of it. As pickings grew thinner, even the small amount that could be scraped from crevices was sought, hence each stone was dislodged.

Titus had also given word that one section of the outer wall on the west should remain standing. This has remained today as the Western Wall. It has the greatest number of original Herodian courses of all the visible construction today.

4 "Tell us, when will these things be, and what will be the sign when all these things are going to be fulfilled?"

The scene is now at the Mount of Olives in full view of the Temple. The walls and appearance would be much different than what we see today. Certainly, there would be the view of the valley between, descending down and then sharply up again to the foot of the walls. But the walls would not be topped with the typical Byzantine designs we see today in smaller stones. Instead, the Herodian stones would have risen consistently all the way to the tops of the walls. The Temple would have protruded up differently than the Dome of the Rock, being rather offset from center so as to align with the East Gate. At the S wall, the red-tiled roof of the inner, three-tiered colonnade would have jutted up above its walls in contrast to the adjoining colonnades.

Its permanency would seem unquestioned. So the disciples were intensely curious when these predictions should come to pass. They further wished to know what sign might be looked for. The reason is simple - a general answer like "the cup of iniquity being filled" or "until the times of the Gentiles is full" might be just as perplexing.

The Chronological Gospel Commentary – The Four Gospels

The intrigue is two-fold. The prediction not only involves the incredible demise of the most sacred of their buildings, but its manner of demolition implies war, in the midst of which no person would wish to be.

4 .. *"what will be the sign of Your coming, and of the end of the age?"*

Matthew preserves two additional questions – the sign of His coming again, and the end of the age. These, they connected in that Messiah would put an end to the current state of affairs wherby Israel was subject to foreign rule and would inaugurate the physical-political kingdom promised of old. This would effectively end the current age and begin the next.

As to a sign, the disciples are expressing in customary terms that they wish not to be left out due to ignorance of the exact time. If the signs will be enigmatic or mystical, they do not wish to be found dull of sight and sensibility. And in the presence of someone like Jesus, we would feel exactly the same.

4 "See to it that no one misleads you. 5 "For many will come in My name, saying, `I am the Christ,' and will mislead many.

First, an appropriate warning. If times are perilous or otherwise close in description to what is expected, gullible people will be ready to follow a trickster. So they are to be on the lookout for such as say they are He.

This tells us that Christ, the genuine article, will *not* come announcing Himself as here again, or saying "I am the Christ." We are not to expect this, hence anyone doing so will be false. It is as though God knows the infantile logic of imperfect men, who in taking advantage of the situation, will feebly reason that Christ would come with a big announcement. They reason in their small minds that He will see the need, as they would, to announce, "I am the Christ." It is a form of logic produced by the mind that does not know Him.

For those who know Him, He will not need to announce He is here. That, of course, *would* be needed by those who are not of His fold. Hence, it becomes a very real demarcation line between the false and the true.

. . and will mislead many.

We might ask how many could be misled if those calling are false? There will always be an unfortunately large contingent of people who are always on the verge of believing anything, because belief suspends the need for the hard work of actually finding out. To be diligent, cautious and careful in what one chooses to follow interferes with the free-flowing mind and smacks all too much like debunking the magic. Some will prefer to be wowed by the magic. So to scrutinize is to not believe.

We sometimes ponder how so many could have been led away by Jim Jones in the Guyana mass suicide? It is simply the preference for easy belief over diligent faith. Some wish earnestly to simply be led. They question their ability to scrutinize, so following becomes a lazy man's faith.

6 "You will be hearing of wars and rumors of wars. See that you are not frightened, for those things must take place, but that is not yet the end.

War is a frightening prospect, so it is difficult to contemplate having the will to not be afraid. There is assurance here that one will be given the peace needed, but it is not clear that all will be spared the effects. Certainly the command to not be afraid will need the special enabling of the Spirit, what the church has come to call grace.

More in focus seems to be the idea that this is not to catch them in desperation or without hope. These things *are to be expected,* so when they come, they are not to be alarmed as if the world has fallen off its kilter and God has abandoned them.

Such rumors would not signal the end in and of themselves - *"that is not yet the end"* - since the Romans provided such an atmosphere as virtually a defining feature of their warlike culture. But the times were now at the beginning of the Roman Peace, so the revisiting of frequent wars would be a sign.

7 "For nation will rise against nation, and kingdom against kingdom,

Nothing remarkably outstanding about this if taken piecemeal. Such has been the history of their remote and recent times. But the tone of this indicator is that this is wide-spread such that the times are characterized by nation against nation. Such was not the case at the present time.

7 ".. and in various places there will be famines and earthquakes.

Again, famines and earthquakes presently occurred in different places, but the tone is again of a feature that *characterizes* the times.

It will not be the notice of an occasional conflict or earthquake, but people will be sitting up and taking notice that conflicts are abounding and earthquakes uncommonly frequent.

8 "But all these things are merely the beginning of birth pangs.

'Birth pangs' is used to indicate that a process is in play – one that involves preliminary events that culminate in something major. Stresses and troubles will signal the approaching time of something quite painful, requiring a firm grip on oneself.

In using this term, He is preparing them for a description whose magnitude and seriousness deserves the preparation.

9 "But be on your guard; for they will deliver you to the courts,

Persecution will be part of this period of the end. It makes sense that if the world is soon to be judged and Satan is soon to be bound, these would raise a ruckus in rebellion of the anticipated defeat. It would be a time to rip away as many as might come to faith and attempt even to dislodge the faithful.

The world will raise up its hackles to question the reasonability of the Godly cause, to identify the righteous as non-team players, to judge and cut short those who would disrupt the desires of common society.

That the courts will be involved discloses that the legal systems will have been corrupted away from their biblical origins into something purely man-made, full of fair play and the reasoning of imperfect humanity. Gone will be the appeal to absolutes. In fact, all such things will be despised as sectarian imposition over the will of the people. Hence, the righteous will have no haven in the courts.

To be flogged in the synagogues will signal the punishment of righteousness by those who are supposed to represent and protect it. So desperate will be these times.

While Paul encourages us to submit to the governing powers, governors and kings will themselves come to the state where they no longer respect, even if only formally, the biblical basis for their authority.

Kings and emperors were hardly ever God-fearing men, but they seldom messed with the standards and precepts of their society. In other words, they may have developed loopholes or exemptions for their own evil actions, but they maintained the legitimacy of the courts to judge and control crime and injustice for the common person. Contracts were held as binding, and torts against personal injury continued to operate despite the reprehensible character of the monarch.

In modern times, while modern governments may not have personally respected the Bible among all its public servants, they have upheld the high standards of law, many of which came from religious sources.

But in end times, such persons will be no protector of the old righteousness. The Bible may not de facto be citable as a defense of right action in an appeal to a president, a prime minister, or a king.

The purpose of the believer before kings and governors will not be to gain protection, but to provide witness – *"for My sake, as a testimony to them."*

10 *"The gospel must first be preached to all the nations.*

Some like to taunt that it will be impossible to discern if every living human being has been reached with the Gospel. But the verse doesn't necessitate this degree of literality. It merely states that all nations in general will have heard. Some might argue that it would then have merely said "in all nations," but "to all nations" implies all the people in those nations.

But we have seen hyperbole used many times to give force to something that will be general in scope and not literally all-inclusive. In Mark 1:5 it was said that all of Judea was going out to Him. We are certainly to understand that an immense number of its citizens were doing so. But we could not push this to mean every living human being in the entire province, that not a single person was still in their home or tending to some other business. Consider that this is also said for Jerusalem, but we have no evidence that Herod Antipas was among those going out to Him.

In terms of technology, reaching all nations was not feasible until just recently. Now quite feasible. Witness the recent innovations in internet phone technology.

11 *".. do not worry beforehand about what you are to say, but say whatever is given you in that hour; "*

Being hauled before kings and governors, or any antagonistic inquisitor would be reason to worry about the right things to say. Were we to meet with the President of the United States to promote something important to us, we would plan for weeks on the material we would need to present and how it should be presented. We would be understandably nervous that we not flinch in the moment and say all the things we wished to avoid.

Surprisingly, we are not to make such preparatory plans when in the dock for our faith before magistrates and monarchs. We are not to worry over the right words, because the right words (the very ones we could not have planned beforehand) will be given us at the very moment needed.

And He tells us Who will be giving them – the Holy Spirit of God.

12 *"Brother will betray brother to death, and a father his child; and children will rise up against parents and have them put to death.*

Some find fulfillment of this in the terror of the Roman persecutions, where children betrayed their own parents, and vice-versa, in order to be spared the horrors of the arena. It was not enough to offer sacrifice to the person of the emperor, but being associated with the proscribed practice of Christianity made you an equal suspect or useful informer. And you could not get away with a feigned offering. Your sincerity would be tested by your willingness to join the emperor in ferreting out those in hiding.

These were terrible times and we can understand how many concluded the end was near and Jesus was on the brink of appearing again. But history now tells us that He did not come even with such signs as these so vividly mimicked. In hindsight we learn that such were the foreshadowings of more fearsome times yet to come.

12 "Because lawlessness is increased, most people's love will grow cold.

Desperate times can have the adverse effect of driving people away from their God. Lawlessness is especially insidious because God has always ensured that law either preserves or heals from the wickedness of the times. Thus, the loss of the rule of law is to some a sign that God has abandoned us, and if so, He is not worthy of love. In the holocaust, laws were abrogated to achieve evil ends, but it was law common to the victors that put an end to that regime and reliably judged and disposed of its henchmen.

Lawlessness will increase because the enforcers of the law will be increasingly ineffective and compromised by their own wickedness. The right way will be expressible, but no longer enforceable. It will be the rule of the most clever, not the rule of the most morally upright.

In such conditions, people's love for God and for each other will turn to self-preservation. Whatever love is expressed will be self-serving and therefore cold and meaningless.

13 "You will be hated by all because of My name, but the one who endures to the end, he will be saved.

This is opposite to the conditions we expect and sincerely wish for. We present the best news available, the remedy that will bring people out of darkness into light, out of bondage into freedom, so we expect it to be praiseworthy and endorsed as of the highest character. (That was the general attitude about priests and ministers for centuries in the Christian world of the West.)

But Jesus is predicting that this will turn to hatred for the work and the worker, not because of some personal issue with individuals, but because they are called by that Name.

Today, some have come to call our present time the "post-Christian era." This is primarily because they see the church and Christianity as increasingly unpopular. It is not that it has lifted the veil from a previously hidden agenda of evil. But that the world has increasingly incorporated an agenda for evil while the Church has stood firmly in place. Combine this with the increasing attitude that what is popular is right and you have a formula for persecution against firm-standing absolutes that will be seen as intransigent and callous.

<u>Note</u>: the Romans called Christians "haters of mankind" because they didn't participate in pagan festivities or neighborhood reveling.) Tacitus, <u>Annals,</u> Oxford Press

13 .. "but the one who endures to the end, he will be saved."

This promotes challenges to two key doctrines – the perseverance of the saints (ala Calvinism) and the independent NT teaching of salvation by grace as opposed to works righteousness. The Calvinist claims that the believer is assured of their salvation, hence this cannot suggest that some believers will not endure to the end. They are forced to offer that all elected believers will endure and this is merely a statement of that assurance as guaranteed.

Others see that the statement only has meaning against the backdrop of those who will not endure, hence some will fall from the faith, else why the warning about enduring? This is countered with the necessity of exhortations if the means of enduring is also predestined.

As such, interpretations cannot be pressed exclusively one way or the other without liability elsewhere. Regardless, we are to take seriously the exhortation to endure. Whether ordained that we will succeed or not, we must enter the process and gain the encouraged end.

As to works righteousness, the emphasis on grace must be balanced with James' exhortation[58] to works as the sine qua non for testing the faith that counts before God. So it need not be a death knell to the idea of sovereign grace. The true believer saved by grace will not be found without vindicating works.

---

[58] James 2:14-20

14 "This gospel of the kingdom shall be preached in the whole world .. then the end will come.

Here, a reiteration of v.10, but more conditionally connected to the coming of the end. Here, the preaching is the condition that signals the end. And very nearly due to the need for a technology that evaded earlier accomplishment and by necessity would arrive near the very end.

What is surprising in its frankness about reality is that an end is in the offing. We have hear our Lord of glory telling us for a fact that there is coming an end to our present world. For those who are convinced that such things are just a persistent fable, these are sobering thoughts.

20 "But when you see Jerusalem surrounded by armies, then recognize that her desolation is near.

Were it not for this section in Luke, we would be free to consistently apply all these circumstances (and those coming up about the Abomination of Desolation) to some future commencement of end times events, i.e. nothing would compel them to be historically fulfilled in the lifetimes of the disciples.

But here we have an event that can very easily be seen as applying to the siege and destruction of Jerusalem in 70 A.D. But we also see mention of the commencement of the times of the Gentiles, which cannot be commencing in end times. We also see historically that this period of Gentile rule in relation to Jerusalem did in fact begin within the disciples lifetime.

For some, this doesn't mitigate too strongly. The address to the present disciples by "you" is offered as equivalent to what we see in Luke 21:28 where it is clear the future is meant, but the present "you" is used. And we do see the nations warring against Jerusalem in end times:

3 "Behold, I am against you, O Gog, prince of Rosh, Meshech and Tubal. . . 8 "After many days you will be summoned; in the latter years you will come into the land that is restored from the sword, . . 9 "You will go up, you will come like a storm; you will be like a cloud covering the land, you and all your troops, and many peoples with you." . . 11 and you will say, 'I will go up against the land of unwalled villages. I will go against those who are at rest, that live securely, all of them living without walls and having no bars or gates, (Ezekiel 38:3-11.)

Others see the parallels with the antichrist and the abomination, next to be described, as critical to a future fulfillment.

But among the problems of the historical fulfillment scenario is the inability to connect the dots on all other aspects of the end times prophesy. If 70 A.D. is the fulfillment, then all the other predictions from the prophesy of Daniel will need to have been fulfilled also. This will be discussed further in the warning about the Abomination of Desolation of Daniel. But essentially, Titus, who conducts the siege cannot be seen as the prince of Daniel who commits the abomination described there.

Hence, one of the better interpretations is to separate Luke's narrative here from the other end times dialog, making it a discussion with its own context, while the warning about the abomination of Daniel will have another. The main issue with this is that it breaks the context in an abnormal way. Abnormal or not will be better assessed by studying the following.

22 because these are days of vengeance,

One characteristic that seems to be missing from the end times siege of the city is the note of vengeance. It is certainly a time of hatred for the people and city of God, but the nations that gather then are not paying back Israel for an injustice.

Contrarily, the Romans are in fact paying back in vengeance for Judea's unrelenting attacks on local Roman governing bases – albeit in response to the bitter persecutions and treatment by Florus. This is merely to say, that in the case of 70 A.D., the issue was indeed vengeance.

and Jerusalem will be trampled under foot by the Gentiles until the times of the Gentiles are fulfilled

This is a prediction that does not appear in Matthew and Mark. It relates specifically to the events after 70 A.D., where Jerusalem will become the property of Gentiles. First, the Romans continued to govern the region and in the reign of Hadrian established a refurbished section of the city called Aelia Capitolina.

Along with the later dissolution of the Roman Empire to the barbarians kingdoms, the land of Palestine and Jerusalem were of little interest to European hordes, and they became the scene of local and small-time skirmishes, but also the subject of more and more Arab infiltration. The Jews, proper, were considered scattered abroad among the nations, which to a very large extent was true.

The Muslim invasions and the subsequent failure of the Crusades placed the land in Muslim hands for over a millennium, until the British Mandate of the early 20th century, brought on primarily because of the influx of Jews returning to the land where the issue of rights and ownership turned to bloodshed.

Surprisingly, the final outcome of the UN accords that recognized Israel in 1948 and gave them a partition of the land did not give them Jerusalem. Even since the acquisition of the city into Jewish control, there is a forced recognition of Muslim holdings and sites that cannot be violated. Hence, the city and specifically the Temple area are still *"trodden down by the foot of the Gentile"* to this day.

The single sign of the Dome of the Rock – a Muslim shrine over a Jewish sacred site, is a vivid picture of the continued applicability of Jesus' words here.

When will the times of the Gentiles be fulfilled? No signs or predicted details were provided. The consensus is the coming of the Son again, as we shall see in the remainder of the Olivet Discourse here.

Matthew 24:15-21
15 "Therefore when you see the ABOMINATION OF DESOLATION which was spoken of through Daniel the prophet, standing in the holy place (let the reader understand), 16 then those who are in Judea must flee to the mountains. 17 "Whoever is on the housetop must not go down to get the things out that are in his house. 18 "Whoever is in the field must not turn back to get his cloak. 19 "But woe to those who are pregnant and to those who are nursing babies in those days! 20 "But pray that your flight will not be in the winter, or on a Sabbath. 21 "For then there will be a great tribulation, such as has not occurred since the beginning of the world until now, nor ever will (Matthew 24:15-21)

Commentary

15 "Therefore when you see the ABOMINATION OF DESOLATION which was spoken of through Daniel the prophet,

The first thing that strikes the mind is that Jesus believed this to be a real event, not a figurative description of something else. Daniel has been characterized as completely allegorical, full of figure and imagery, that we are bereft of knowing how to apply it to modern life. Many understand how some figures were fulfilled historically (Daniel tells us of the progress of world empires) and how those are now ancient history. What of the future? Who is to make heads or tails out of those mysterious things?

But Jesus had every expectation that the narrative about future things was just as real. There was to be an abomination that would make desolate and the disciples are asked to be on the look out for it.

The pertinent passage is Daniel 9:27 . .

*27 "And he will make a firm covenant with the many for one week, but in the middle of the week he will put a stop to sacrifice and grain offering; and on the **wing of abominations will come one who makes desolate**, even until a complete destruction, one that is decreed, is poured out on the one who makes desolate."*

The *he* in this passage is the "prince that shall come", namely the antichrist, the one who boldly speaks against the Most High.

Daniel's prophecies deal with the future of the world from Daniel's time forward to the coming of Messiah and beyond to the resolution of man and God. A very broad, far-reaching scope, perhaps the largest in all prophecy. A key feature is the coming of a terrible kingdom after the fourth empire from Daniel's time and its leader who seduces the entire world under his control. Such a person is pictured as a kingdom of ten toes on a great image, a little horn on a beast with ten horns who speaks boastful things against the saints and their God.

He is interposed between the present order and the age to come, as a great nemesis to the program of God, one who needs to be destroyed in order to make way for the coming Kingdom. He represents the great final thrust against God by man and Satan – to have their own way.

The mention of the Abomination of Desolation concerns an event in this person's career that will signal a turn for the worst to those who serve God. Before this, the prince will beguile the people into a covenant - *he will confirm a covenant with the many for one week.* This necessarily involves the Jews, because we will see later that he has enough access and control over sacrifices and offerings as to make new laws concerning them – *he will put a stop to sacrifice and grain offering;*

The scheme in Daniel's prophecy of the Seventy Weeks is that weeks are weeks of years, not literal weeks, hence a covenant of one week is a covenant of seven years. This corresponds to the last of the seventy weeks of the prophecy, the first sixty-nine weeks being the subject of other events. Hence, this seven-year covenant is identical to the last or seventieth week of Daniel.

Since the first sixty-nine weeks close with the coming of Messiah and His death, and no historical events since then can be seen as fulfilling the last and final week of years, most accept that this last week is yet future.

Now there are other schemes of interpretation that make all these events matters of history fulfilled, but they do so at the expense of completeness and consistency. More will be said on those theories when we discuss the relationship of this warning to that of the siege of Jerusalem.

But with the warning about the abomination, if this is to be future, one must wonder what meaning this could have for those He was addressing.

Some offer that the manner of the fulfillment does not nullify the need for warning, so the events of 70 A.D. work just as well. Still, Jesus would certainly have known that an event some forty years away would look for all the world like the very thing being described, and if this was in fact not the event from which they were to flee, He was obligated to clarify.

A closer look at the details will help.

As to the abomination itself, Daniel states, *"and on the wing of abominations will come one who makes desolate."* So the term Abomination of Desolation is not used precisely by Daniel. But since Jesus is using it to speak of the abomination mentioned here in Daniel, it is understood that these are one and the same.

Daniel does not describe what constitutes the abomination, only that it will come and be administered by one who makes desolate by doing so. What is made desolate? It is assumed to be the Temple and its functions, since the land is still very populated with citizens and activity after this point. And Jesus identifies the location of the desolation – *"standing in the Holy Place . ."* Mark has, *"standing where it ought not,"* (13:14.) This makes it clear that something will be set up in the Temple that offends God and spoils it for future service. We later learn that it is antichrist himself, sitting in the Temple to be worshipped (2 Thess 2:4.)

Christ's warning revolves around them seeing this arrangement take place.

(let the reader understand),

These are the words of the writer, not our Lord. Matthew is helping the reader with a parenthetical inside his narrative of Jesus' words. It is there to let the reader know that some additional understanding will be needed to make better sense of this statement. And we can understand why.

'Abomination of Desolation' is not the precise term Daniel used. Furthermore, the reader may not be familiar with what Daniel said on the subject at all. So Matthew is indicating that a correlated study in Daniel may be helpful to understanding the context and meaning. It's very much like saying, "Be prepared to go to Daniel to see what Jesus means here."

Fulfillment

As earlier, Luke has conveyed Jesus' teaching on the imminent siege of Jerusalem, and the events are very similar with the same kinds of warnings. Some cannot resist the urge to have all these events fulfilled historically in the destruction of Jerusalem under Titus in 70 A.D.

But then we must ask who was the antichrist? Since Titus was the perpetrator of the destruction, he is the only local candidate. But Titus was no antichrist according to the biblical criteria. He made no seven year covenant or treaty known to history, he did not break such a treaty mid-stream. He did not set himself up to be worshiped in the temple (there was no temple when he got through.) Titus did not cause all to have a mark, as in the Revelation.

But most importantly, he was not destroyed by the arrival of Christ in the Second Coming, which would obligate us to believe that Christ has in fact now come – *"Then that lawless one will be revealed whom the Lord will slay with the breath of His mouth and bring to an end by the appearance of His coming;"* (2 Thess 2:8.)

When considering these criteria, Titus cannot be the antichrist. This effectively removes 70 A.D. as the fulfillment of the Abomination of Desolation spoken of by Daniel and Jesus. We are left to then understand the abomination Jesus mentions as applicable to the time of the end, and the mention of the siege of Jerusalem as a foreshadowing event of very similar nature, which will occur within their lifetimes.

And since the end times antichrist is related to Rome, it is fitting that the near term destruction of the city by then-present Rome be folded in to the warning, as it is in Luke.

As for the applicability of the disciples to Jesus' warning about the abomination, the disciples are often the recipients of warnings and teaching applicable to the whole church in any age. They would thus represent those who will in fact be on the scene in those days, and to them the warning will be precisely the same – flee.

16 then those who are in Judea must flee to the mountains.

The 'those' intended are those of His followers, or those who worship God in general, because the times are about to change for the faithful of God. Traditional worship whether Judaistic or Christian is on the verge of being supplanted by something Satan has conceived as a counterfeit against God.

The warning is to those in Judea, which causes us to wonder about the locale and applicability. If this is a picture for the whole world and for all believers everywhere in it, why warn only those in Judea and why are only those to flee?

This has caused many to interpret that this is not an end times warning, but one that has been historically fulfilled. But Judeans are mentioned because they are in direct proximity. If the effect is to be worldwide, there is nothing barring the applicability of the warning if the conditions imposed are valid elsewhere in the world. Wherever compulsory worship of a false deity is imposed, the call to flee is appropriate.

17 "Whoever is on the housetop must not go down to get the things out that are in his house. 18 "Whoever is in the field must not turn back to get his cloak.

Now the urgency of the situation is described. The turnover from world benefactor to evil dictator is to be so swift that those who are not alert may get caught in the immediate effects if they don't leave in haste. Some have questioned the effectiveness of fleeing if the whole world is to be thus affected. Where would one go? But the exhortation is "to the mountains" meaning despite universal rule, there is only so much that soldiers and men can do in locating people. There may very well be refuge in remote places considered not worth the bother.

Despite this, we do read the Revelation that many are caught and made to suffer - that the image of the beast should both speak, and cause that as many as would not worship the image of the beast should be killed. (Rev 13:15.)

The urgency is characterized as not even having enough time to go in and get belongings after getting down off one's roof.

19 "But woe to those who are pregnant and to those who are nursing babies in those days!

Similarly as to the siege of Jerusalem, the need to move in haste will not be sensitive to those with impairments. Women carrying or nursing will not be able to move in haste.

The same would apply to having to travel long distances in the cold of winter, having scarcely gathered enough to keep warm. The stress of the Sabbath is that one will be torn between complying with the Law and going a mere Sabbath-day's journey and breaking the law to get a decent distance away from trouble.

21 "For then there will be a great tribulation, such as has not occurred since the beginning of the world until now, nor ever will

In coordinated interpretations of these dialogs, scholars often try to integrate Luke chapter 21 with Matthew and Mark and the result is that this verse gets interposed near or after the discussion of the siege of Jerusalem. The attempt to harmonize these as talking only about one set of events feeds the interpretive scheme that all such predictions are now fulfilled historically. But as we saw earlier in Luke, the events of 70 A.D. cannot serve all the needs of the prophesies and other NT information on the subject.

As for how Luke's material is then to relate to what we have here, there is an interesting observation in Daniel, in the midst of this great prophecy. *"Then . . Messiah will be cut off and have nothing, and the people of the prince who is to come will destroy the city and the sanctuary. And its end will come with a flood; even to the end there will be war; desolations are determined. "* (Daniel 9:26.)

Here, the city is seen to be destroyed directly following the cutting off of Messiah. There is no other event but 70 A.D. to fulfill this. Also, note that it is not the "prince" who destroys the city, but the "people" of the prince. But v.27 does not then continue with the activity of the people but returns to the that of the prince – *" 27 "And **he** will make a firm covenant with the many for one week,"*

This signals us that the events of 70 A.D. are being telescoped into a detail of the events of the future prince. It tells us that they are thematically related but this does not obligate them to be temporally related.

The prince will act, and as a side note, the people of this prince will also have acted as a foreshadowing of him (a previous event that destroyed the city), but not in the same time frame or context.

If the prince that shall come will be related in modern times to a re-appearance of imperial Rome, then the people of that future prince can always be seen in some way as the Roman people, whether ancient or modern. And it is a matter of history that they destroyed Jerusalem in 70 A.D.

In summary, Jesus has given them a real and imminent warning of events soon coming to them – the war with the Romans and the resultant siege of the city. The conditions of warning and fleeing are going to be very similar and the people involved will fulfill an interesting detail within Daniel's great prophecy.

Then Jesus warned the disciples of the abomination of Daniel, not as men who would in fact see it personally, but as types of those disciples who would see it. Hence, it is a warning to all believers in the person of the disciples to whom Jesus spoke.

Jesus then caps the discussion by mention of the Great Tribulation to follow, which is to be tied to the events after the abomination of Daniel not those following the fall of Jerusalem, since no such event succeeded its destruction in 70 A.D.

(Some offer that the devastation of the land and the enslavement of the Jews was certainly tribulation, which we could not deny. But Jesus' words are that it will be greater than any before or ever again, and this could not be assigned to that persecution of the Jews. Certainly, the holocaust was many times more severe in total suffering and involved considerably more people than the Romans abused and murdered. Thus, Jesus words would be misspoken, not encountering the events of the 20th century.)

Matthew 24:22-35, Luke 21:25-28

22 "Unless those days had been cut short, no life would have been saved; but for the sake of the elect those days will be cut short. 23 "Then if anyone says to you, `Behold, here is the Christ,' or `There He is,' do not believe him. 24 "For false Christs and false prophets will arise and will show great signs and wonders, so as to mislead, if possible, even the elect. 25 "Behold, I have told you in advance. 26 "So if they say to you, `Behold, He is in the wilderness,' do not go out, or, `Behold, He is in the inner rooms,' do not believe them. 27 "For just as the lightning comes from the east and flashes even to the west, so will the coming of the Son of Man be. 28 "Wherever the corpse is, there the vultures will gather.

29 "But immediately after the tribulation of those days THE SUN WILL BE DARKENED, AND THE MOON WILL NOT GIVE ITS LIGHT, AND THE STARS WILL FALL from the sky, and the powers of the heavens will be shaken. 30 "And then the sign of the Son of Man will appear in the sky, and then all the tribes of the earth will mourn, and they will see the SON OF MAN COMING ON THE CLOUDS OF THE SKY with power and great glory. 31 "And He will send forth His angels with A GREAT TRUMPET and THEY WILL GATHER TOGETHER His elect from the four winds, from one end of the sky to the other. (Matthew 24:22-31)

25 There will be signs in sun and moon, and on the earth dismay among the nations, in the perplexity of the roaring of the sea and the waves, men fainting from fear and the expectation of the things which are coming upon the world; for the powers of the heavens will be shaken . . But when these things begin to take place, straighten up and lift up your heads, because your salvation is drawing near. (Luke 21:25-28)

32 "Now learn the parable from the fig tree: when its branch has already become tender and puts forth its leaves, you know that summer is near; 33 so, you too, when you see all these things, recognize that He is near, right at the door. 34 "Truly I say to you, this generation will not pass away until all these things take place. 35 "Heaven and earth will pass away, but My words will not pass away. (Matthew 24:32-35)

Commentary

22 "Unless those days had been cut short, no life would have been saved; but for the sake of the elect those days will be cut short.

In Matthew and Mark's context, this applies to the end of days, to the time of the end, when God will begin the judgment of nations and peoples by the appearing of Christ again. Here, there is a statement concerning grace, not for the guilty but on behalf of the elect.

The elect are all the saved who are living during this period of tribulation. Some interpretations offer that all the saved will be raptured away from this scene and will not suffer the wrath of God in these times. But we see clearly people coming to the faith of God and being thus martyred – *"And he had power to give life unto the image of the beast, that the image of the beast should both speak, and cause that as many as would not worship the image of the beast should be killed."* (Rev 13:15.)

So it is clear that believers will be living to suffer these things. They may not be members of the historic church prior to the commencement of these horrors – the rapture may well have taken the faithful of the Church as Christ's Body – but there are clearly believers after that event who suffer at the hands of the beast.

One distinction is that the wrath of God is not poured out on His saints *"We are not appointed unto wrath."* (I Thess 5:9.) Still, the kinds of things happening to the world are hard to avoid in their indiscriminant effects on man generally.

This is what is meant here in this verse. The things God will do to the wicked in the world will have spill-over effects on the people of God, including natural effects and persecutorial effects from the antichrist. These days are to be shortened for the sake of believers caught in their effects.

23 "Then if anyone says to you, `Behold, here is the Christ,'

A reprise of v.4 is reiterated. It is very essential that His followers not be misled by false Christs and charlatans taking advantage of the crisis. If anyone is announcing themselves as such, it will be a dead ringer for deception and even spiritual destruction. Christians need to heed this quite seriously, since it is mentioned more than once. When the time comes, people may be in various states of understanding, some very poor in their exposure to the pertinent Scripture. As such, they will be operating on very basic, summary knowledge and will be easy prey for confidence men.

27 "For just as the lightning comes from the east and flashes even to the west, so will the coming of the Son of Man be.

The figure here is meant to convey the idea of unmistakability. Where the Son of Man actually is, will be as clear to believers as the lightning in the sky. No one will need to heed mystical heralds who offer to reveal His secret place.

The figure also conveys the idea of suddenness. In I Thessalonians Chapter 4, we have the idea of believers caught in the midst of their daily activities, then hearing the trump of God (I Thess 4:16.)

28 "Wherever the corpse is, there the vultures will gather.

Here, a more ominous figure – one we hesitate to associate with the Body of Christ and the prospect of believers in these times. The host of believers are not generally associated with the carrion around which vultures will gather, nor vultures who feed on it. Some believe it is merely a metaphor – that vultures are uniquely apt at spotting potential food, so Christians will have the keen insight to know the location of Christ at His appearing. This coordinates with the basic idea that believers will be very aware of Christ's return, as in I Thess 4:16ff.

But some see it as conveying too much the idea of a search, or Christians being on the lookout in various places and this is precluded by Paul's discussion in I Thessalonians.

Others interpret this as a contrasting figure. The believers will know where Christ is just as lightning is known. Similarly, those who are judged and slain by His coming will also be known just as a corpse is known by its scavengers.

29 "But immediately after the tribulation of those days THE SUN WILL BE DARKENED, AND THE MOON WILL NOT GIVE ITS LIGHT,

In coordinating this with Luke, some interpreters force the idea that the tribulation has occurred (the things that attended the events of Jerusalem's destruction in 70 A.D.) and as promised here, the Son of Man has come in the form of the conquering Church. But as elsewhere noted, this has a number of non sequiturs and misalignments in terms of all the prophesies governing these events.

This verse does give some endorsement to those who reject the idea of a rapture separate from the second coming. If the coming of the Son of man in the clouds here is that pictured in I Thessalonians, then there is no rapture before the tribulation, and the Church is destined to go into it.

In this scheme, it does show the appearing *"immediately after the tribulation of those days . ."*

For rapture enthusiasts, this is rather the Second Coming distinct from a rapture that occurred secretly as in I Thessalonians.

***THE SUN WILL BE DARKENED, AND THE MOON WILL NOT GIVE ITS LIGHT, AND THE STARS WILL FALL** from the sky*

Generally, teachers note this as a quote from Joel 2:10 and 2:31. But this quotation is a redaction of many OT passages that contribute details. The sun and moon being darkened is found in Isaiah 13:10 and Ezekiel 32:7 as well as Joel. But the stars falling is found in Isaiah, while this detail is missing from Joel.

These events all mirror the scenes in the Revelation – *" The fourth angel sounded, and a third of the sun and a third of the moon and a third of the stars were struck, so that a third of them would be darkened and the day would not shine for a third of it, and the night in the same way."* (Rev 8:12.)

In terms of planetary physics, we need to clarify what falling stars could *not* mean if taken completely literal. We know with all certainty that stars are really suns elsewhere in the universe and if a large meteor or small asteroid were to fall from space onto the earth, there would be no need to talk about future events beyond this, which clearly the Bible continues to do. An entire sun would be a magnitude of planetary destruction hardly conceivable.

So stars falling cannot mean from our local sky nor to the earth in any meaningful astronomical sense.

As of their appearing to fall, many are millions of light years away from the earth. For them to "fall" would mean they would be caused to move many billions of light years in actual distances so as to be no longer visible from the earth. This is not beyond the Lord's power to do, but students need to be aware that this is less trivial then the simple language of Scripture implies.

Some see this as a marked increase in the more benign meteoric showers in which debris enters the atmosphere and disintegrates before hitting the surface.

On the other hand, these could very well be specially arranged visual effects made to accompany the events, that only "appear" as stars falling.

The important thing for us is to not mitigate the reality of the appearance of the phenomenon. Something will definitely be seen and it will be describable if only in visual terms as stars falling.

and the powers of the heavens will be shaken.

This is ancient phenomenological language – the language of appearances. It is not scientific, nor was it meant to be. Shaken need not mean vibrated. It can certainly mean upset or abnormally operating. Nothing more is described as to what specific effects are to be seen. It could be a summary statement for all the things just described in more detail, or it could mean sounds and visual effects of a universe out of sorts.

The purpose in these things is the upset of normalcy. People will not be able to return to life as it was. When we suffer calamities, our constant, abiding desire, even our hope, is the return to normalcy – *"this too shall pass."* We comfort ourselves that eventually things will get back to normal.

But here, all the things people count on for that normalcy will be out of whack. It will signal that nothing will be the same again and that will be extremely unsettling and despairing for many. The way back to how things were will be forever gone and the only way left will be one filled with foreboding.

30 "And then the sign of the Son of Man will appear in the sky, and then all the tribes of the earth will mourn,

Many contrast this with the appearing in I Thessalonians in which the appearing there first affects the dead who are raised, then the living in Christ, but nothing whatsoever is mentioned as to the tribes of the earth who will mourn at this appearing. This tends to endorse the idea that there are two comings, one for the Church and one for judgment.

The sign is not as in some symbol. It will not be, as in Daniel's day, a hand writing on a wall. Rather, it is the Son Himself, coming in the clouds. The reason this is described as a sign is because it will be completely extraordinary, supernatural and contrary to reason.

At the Ascension, the angel instructed the disciples that Christ would come again *as He has left* – in the air. He ascended into the air and will descend from it again (Acts 1:11.)

This is said to be the occasion of the tribes of the earth mourning, in other words, the appearing will cause them to mourn. This is not a mourning as for a loved one now dead, but for their own lives now on the verge of being lost.

So many today live lives of acquisition and enjoyment. They are busy grasping in a purely horizontal plane, having dismissed any semblance of the vertical plane from their lives. What a complete shock when the Son of Man appears! "All those silly, myth-believing Christians were right!" And then will come the immediate awareness that their past and present lives will not stand up to the judgment now descending in full glory and power.

In the film *Independence Day* (Twentieth Century Fox, 1996), the arrival of the alien ship over downtown Manhattan caused untold havoc and all normal activity, talk and facial expressions turned to the same common, jaw-dropping posture of disbelief. All past dismissals of the existence of aliens was over. Reality was breaking through in unmitigating terms. Such will be the appearing of our Lord. All questions about His existence and centrality to man's own existence will be at an end.

31 "And He will send forth His angels with A GREAT TRUMPET and THEY WILL GATHER TOGETHER His elect from the four winds, from one end of the sky to the other.

For many, this is a quintessential proof against the Rapture being a separate coming. We have here the gathering of the elect from all over the earth. If the rapture is a coming for the saints as described in I Thessalonians chapter 4, is this not one and the same with it? And if so, then the Rapture is not before but after the tribulation, being one and the same with the Second Coming.

For rapture theorists, this is explained as the gathering of those saints who come to the Lord after the Rapture, during the tribulation (most Rapture students freely acknowledge that there will be such, described in Revelation as those under the altar of sacrifice (Rev 7:14.))

The importance for us is that all the saints prior to this coming in whatever accompanying conditions, will be gathered to Him and made separate from the rest of humanity.

25 "There will be signs in sun and moon and stars, and on the earth dismay among nations, in perplexity at the roaring of the sea and the waves,

Luke, surprisingly, turns his attention again to the events of the more far-reaching tribulation – that of Matthew and Mark – the day of wrath and vengeance. We know this simply because the descriptions given did not take place subsequent to 70 A.D. – there were no noted signs respecting the moon, sun and stars; men did not faint away at the sight of what was happening in both the earth and the heavens.

Most especially, men did not thereafter see the sign of the Son of Man in the clouds. We are obliged instead to see this as Luke returning to the same context as the other synoptics – that of end times.

Luke joins up with the accounts of Matthew and Mark almost verbatim (v.25ff) in describing the appearing. He has cleverly combined the witness of those who heard Jesus' discuss Jerusalem's siege and fall with those who wrote of His words concerning the fulfillment of Daniel's predictions. (Luke was not an eyewitness at the Olivet Discourse.)

28 "But when these things begin to take place, straighten up and lift up your heads, because your redemption is drawing near."

This is a very real expectation that such signs are not allegorical, not figurative of something else, not metaphorical. They are real enough to serve as a visible signal. Those on the alert are to know that their redemption is at hand.

For the believer, what redemption can this mean? Most today are taught that redemption is a fact patent at salvation, when the believer is converted through confession and faith. We stand today as the redeemed. It is not generally thought of as something held in abeyance, something we yet wait to have applied.

But the present belief that attends salvation faith is based on the truth of what will take place at the end of our lives when we go to meet the Savior. We are redeemed in position, we are counted as the redeemed. But the reality of that redemption is when we are captured out of the world and out of the grasping arms of death into life. To be redeemed is to be bought back into life from an impending death.

And while we are no longer dead as we live for Him, there is that final moment at the end of life, when real death is pushed away forever and we enter eternal life, patently and actually redeemed.

It is much like the man who buys a ticket for a cruise. He has in his hands the right to the cruise. His expectation that he will be allowed to go is as assured as it can be before actually going.

But once he walks up the gangway and onto the ship, his right to be on the cruise with full benefits is realized. The thing the tickets held in promise is now patent fact. He now has something the mere tickets did not.

until the times of the Gentiles are fulfilled. [Please see the additional note added for this section in Luke in the previous commentary section that begins the Olivet Discourse above. p. 564]

32 "Now learn the parable from the fig tree:

This is not the lesson of the cursed fig tree from the prior visit. We see readily from the discourse that the tree is a lesson as to expectations and signs of the seasons. It is not mentioned to highlight the failure in meeting expectations for fruit, but this is about the normal tree that serves within its growth and appearance to provide indicators of the seasons.

This was the very basis for the curse in the other example. The normal expectation was that the tree by its behavior helped determine seasons and held the expectation of growth and fruit. It was cursed because it had failed in this regard, as Israel has failed in her expectations.

But here, the tree is living up to expectations, and is an apt analogy for seeing the signs of the end of the age.

34 "Truly I say to you, this generation will not pass away until all these things take place.

Many false ideas have sprung from this verse, due to the degree of literality and applicability placed on it. The two chief views are that the generation refers to that of the disciples themselves or, alternatively, to the generation that sees these signs.

There is no doubt that the most ready understanding would be that this refers to those to whom He is talking (and this is augmented by Luke's reference to the siege which really did take place in their lifetimes.) But there simply isn't anything from subsequent history after this discourse we could attach to these fulfillments. Christ did not come again in their lifetimes, Satan was by no means bound as described in the Revelation, attending Christ's reappearing.

The Chronological Gospel Commentary – The Four Gospels

As the words can be easily meant to apply to any generation that sees all these signs, not merely and only to the generation listening to Him, the verse presents no historical problems, except for the rigidly dogmatic.

35 "Heaven and earth will pass away, but My words will not pass away.

Here is the staying principle on which all Christian hope resides. Let man and men come and go. Let their deeds and wars and philosophies have their sway in world affairs. The truths of Christ, no matter how "out of it", old fashioned and out of touch they will be made out to be, will continue just as valid and true beyond even the time permitted for the earth and heaven to remain. We can take comfort in the permanency of that – to know that the salvation that is in Christ will not pass away, that we will not some day find that it's effectiveness has run its course and we are in jeopardy once again for our souls.

Therein is confidence that none of the other religions can offer.

Matthew 24:36-51, Luke 21:34-36, Mark 13:34-37, Matthew 25:1-13
36 "But of that day and hour no one knows, not even the angels of heaven, nor the Son, but the Father alone. 37 "For the coming of the Son of Man will be just like the days of Noah. 38 "For as in those days before the flood they were eating and drinking, marrying and giving in marriage, until the day that Noah entered the ark, 39 and they did not understand until the flood came and took them all away; so will the coming of the Son of Man be.

40 "Then there will be two men in the field; one will be taken and one will be left. 41 "Two women will be grinding at the mill; one will be taken and one will be left. 42 "Therefore be on the alert, for you do not know which day your Lord is coming. 43 "But be sure of this, that if the head of the house had known at what time of the night the thief was coming, he would have been on the alert and would not have allowed his house to be broken into. 44 "For this reason you also must be ready; for the Son of Man is coming at an hour when you do not think He will. (Matthew 24:36-44.)

"Be on guard, so that your hearts will not be weighted down with dissipation and drunkenness and the worries of life, and that day will not come on you suddenly like a trap; 35 for it will come upon all those who dwell on the face of all the earth. 36 "But keep on the alert at all times, praying that you may have strength to escape all these things that are about to take place, and to stand before the Son of Man." (Luke 21:34-36.)

Commentary

36 "But of that day and hour no one knows, not even the angels of heaven, nor the Son, but the Father alone.

We find it difficult to entertain that some things were not known by the Son of God, if we believe Him to be God in the flesh. An ancient theory called the *kenosis* taught that Christ divested Himself of His divinity to become a man (kenosis means an emptying.) This theory ran into theological conflicts with the divinity of Christ – He was, was not, then was again – and divinity does not come and go (except in the movies.)

The orthodox belief is that the Son retained all His attributes, but willingly chose not to avail Himself of them. In the interest of identifying with man, his human frailties and temptations, He would be best able to demonstrate the power of the Spirit to overcome those limitations, which is among the chief reasons for the incarnation. Man was to have spiritual power shown to him in the midst of human limitation, that he might emulate it and avail himself of it. It is the greatest testimony of God in the life of man – that God makes the difference between living as designed and mere survival.

That this is a more cogent treatment of the problem in the incarnation is seen by the infrequent and special use of His powers at key points (mysteriously disappearing from the midst of angry crowds, the Transfiguration, appearing on the opposite side of the lake when no time for travel could be accounted for, the falling back of the soldiers who came to arrest Him.) So while Christ chose not to employ His powers, there were exceptions; but the exceptions do not nullify His example for us; since in most aspects He lived and operated within human limitations – the trial, scourging and crucifixion were all submittals to human limitation that avoided divine power for deliverance.

Now as to the "hour", this is the hour (or period) when the things just mentioned and warned about will take place. But we see in the next verses that the hour does focus more specifically on His coming.

However, as to the timing of these events and His coming, we have a formula in the book of Daniel for calculating this coming. I Thessalonians chapter 4 tells us that the coming of Christ will coincide with the termination of antichrist, and that the career of that evil prince is specifically set down within Daniel in very exacting terms of duration – time, times and half a time, three and one-half years (Dan 7:25, 12:7.) We further find this period described as forty-two months (Rev 11:2, 13:5) and 1260 days (11:3, 12:6.)

Daniel prophesies that antichrist will break the covenant of seven years "in the midst", so it is no surprise to see a relationship of the three and one half years as the mid-point of the seven year covenant; hence a mid-point in the last and seventieth week of the prophecy.

Now some find this exact degree of literality unenlightened, wooden and never intended by God in the first place. To some it is all highly figurative and with numerological insight, these durations might mean all sorts of different things, which then take away the obligation to see them literally. But the proven rule of interpretation is that if the plain sense makes sense, seek no other. Because we are in a highly figurative text filled with images that are clearly thematic representations of real things, does not mean everything we meet is up for grabs – so speculate freely as we wish.

The seventy weeks do work out when applying plain sense understandings of durations in real history and time. Three and a half somethings are exactly half of seven somethings, and unless some other candidate is better indicated, there is just no warrant to depart from the normal understanding of years. Those that take this immediate tack, do so because of other presuppositions before beginning, many of which are less well-founded than the plain sense. In other words, if we are to depart from plain meanings, let it be for cause, not because its fun.

Either by reference to the seven year covenant-treaty or to the last three and one half years of that period, one can calculate the exact day of its end – from the day of the Abomination of Desolation to the coming of Christ will be 1260 days, according to Scripture. If any man who has the facts will be able to calculate that day, how can it be that the Son of God does not know it?

Some offer that Christ was speaking in that present, which did not preclude the possibility of Him knowing later by the above arrangement. But this would mean that there are historical events future that Christ must wait to be apprised of, and this is contrary to His attributes, of which certainly now He has no self-imposed hindrances. Meaning that He must surely be able to see ahead to that specific and momentous day on the calendar when antichrist will effect the seven-year covenant (or more specifically, the day of the Abomination.) If so, it is a simple calculation to get to the day of His appearing.

This prompts many to speculate that the coming He is referring to as not being known by Him, but only the Father, is the Rapture – the secret coming for the Church before the great tribulation. That event is not subject to prophetic calculation.

However, the "hour" mentioned embraces by natural context the events warned about, not just His coming, so this is not an iron-clad resolution.

37 "For the coming of the Son of Man will be just like the days of Noah.

If this is the Rapture and the day will take everyone by surprise, the context does not match that in I Thessalonians, one of the up-gathering of the elect to be forever with the Lord. It is here instead a scene of impending judgment, more in keeping with the theme and context of the Second Coming. As such, this would re-introduce the problems of Christ's omniscience ahead to that very day.

Still, rapturists would offer that the relation to Noah concerns more the theme of being spared and saved, hence the Noahic account is a picture of the rapture rather than of judgment. However, it is the judgment that is actually in focus – *"they did not understand until the flood came and took them all away"*

Regardless of how we resolve that associated issue, the teaching here concerns the precarious suddenness of that appearing for those in the world. The example from Noah is one certainly of judgment. There was a promise to not judge the world again in the same fashion (total annihilation by a flood), which implies that there will be another judgment but not of the same magnitude and type.

Here, this later implied judgment is pictured and related back to the "conditions" that preceded the Noahic event. As things prevailed in Noah's day, so will things be in the end times. It is both a signal to the suddenness of the coming and the oblivious conditions of the people about to be judged – *" . . they were eating and drinking, marrying and giving in marriage, . . and they did not understand until the flood came and took them all away; so will the coming of the Son of Man be."*

Certainly, this must be with respect to the unbelieving world of future days. Believers who have studied these warnings (who have taken Jesus' teaching here to heart in every age) will know the times and not be taken by surprise, neither will they be oblivious in self-reveling.

40 "Then there will be two men in the field; one will be taken and one will be left."

From a rapture model of interpretation, this is understood as meaning that the one taken is taken in the rapture, leaving the unbeliever behind. But again, the rapture interpretation is undermined by the relationship to Noah and the first great global judgment. In that context, the one taken would be taken in judgment, the other left as a citizen in the new kingdom.

The primary issue with this interpretation is that the one left to be a citizen would not seem to be in these circumstances – working side-by-side with a person set for judgment. When Christ comes for the Church and His believers, even if it be only and singularly at the Second Coming, they will then be transformed so as to be *"forever with the Lord"* (I Thess 4:17), so this arrangement would not obtain. All unbelievers would be essentially left to themselves, vacant the presence of believers at that very moment of appearing.

All of which is to say that the intended meaning remains ambiguous. No one interpretation leaps out ahead of its alternate.

One possible resolution is that the business of taking and leaving behind is not meant to picture the actual reality of action, but merely conceptualizes judgment vs. salvation, like a parable. The one taken is a "picture" of the one destined for judgment, the other is a picture of the believer, i.e. between two people in a field, one is set for judgment and one will escape it, whether one is physically and actually arrested next to a believer or not.

The important idea is that of suddenness, in the midst of ordinary life where no expectations of such conditions will occupy man's attention -*" 42 "Therefore be on the alert, for you do not know which day your Lord is coming."*

The other important idea is that there will certainly be the two classes of people. This does not cooperate well with the idea that all will be saved and none go to judgment. The existence of the two classes is very real and very ominous.

43 " if the head of the house had known at what time of the night the thief was coming, . ."

The analogy to common sense brings this teaching home to every man. They are being told ahead of time about signs and signals, just as if a man were to be told when a thief would enter his house. Common sense is now counted on to do the rest. No man would choose to sleep or be going about his affairs normally at that hour. Neither should those in the know be found slumbering or off the alert.

44 ". . . for the Son of Man is coming at an hour when you do not think He will.

Initially, this seems contradictory. He has just advised them of the times. He has just encouraged them to follow common sense and be on the alert as one who has been informed of the hour of the thief, yet he says the Son of Man will come at an hour ***not*** expected.

And this is meant from the perspective of the believer - "an hour when **you** do not think" - but it can't refer to wholesale ignorance of the times, since He has just explained the indicators. It means rather that they may know the approximate time, but not the very hour.

34 "Be on guard, not . . weighted down with dissipation and drunkenness and the worries of life, and that day will not come on you suddenly like a trap;

The worries of life will have the effect of making that coming too sudden – like a trap. As we strive and work to achieve and acquire, we set goals for the future (and place our hearts desires in those future plans and goals.) Should we worry and micro-manage those plans, we all the more count on the payoff of their coming to fruition.

The sudden and abrupt coming of the Son of Man will upset those plans and we will sense that coming as a trap – one that asks us to re-assess our allegiances. We will be split between the worries of getting things accomplished and engaging the utter planetary shift of world order about to take place – *"for it will come upon all those who dwell on the face of all the earth."*

Picture the individual who has lived with moderate financial resources his whole life. He has the opportunity of a lifetime to realize a billion-dollar windfall in a sound and secure venture. He works extremely hard and commits all his current resources to getting there. The Second Coming appears. It will of course mean that the entire world as he knows it will change. The opportunity he's been waiting for may in fact vanish into thin air. He will be caught by it, as in a trap - pitting his earthly desires for wealth against his spiritual values.

The warning is to not be so entangled in earthly affairs and allegiances that that day not take us as if in a trap. It means saying no when the appeal of opportunities is overwhelming, but the enmeshment with the world will be intensified. We must at all times be easily "detachable" and that is a hard thing to arrange in this day and age.

36 "But keep on the alert at all times, praying that you may have strength to escape all these things that are about to take place, and to stand before the Son of Man."

Here we have support for either a rapture model or a Second-Coming-only model. The escape is irrelevant to when. It may be before the events (which is more the idea of an escape) or in the midst of these events, which cannot be ruled out as an escape any more than the Israelites could be ruled out as escaping the plagues in Egypt.

Again, much depends on the completeness of the escape and the word "all." Some of the judgments and raging evil of the times will be hard to avoid for believers, if living in the midst of it. (Today, believers do not all live in Goshen.) Both "all" and "escape" connote that none of the events or their effects will touch them at all, which leans in the direction of having been taken out before they commence.

Combining this with the extension – *"to stand before the Son of Man"* while not mandatory, conveys the idea that the escape effects the new posture of standing in His presence. One escapes to the place of standing in it, hence no longer in the world.

Mark 13:34-35, Matthew 24:45-51, Mark 13:35-47, Matthew 25:1-13

34 "It is like a man away on a journey, who upon leaving his house and putting his slaves in charge, assigning to each one his task, also commanded the doorkeeper to stay on the alert. 35 "Therefore, be on the alert— . . . 45 "Who then is the faithful and sensible slave whom his master put in charge of his household to give them their food at the proper time? 46 "Blessed is that slave whom his master finds so doing when he comes. 47 "Truly I say to you that he will put him in charge of all his possessions. 48 "But if that evil slave says in his heart, `My master is not coming for a long time,' 49 and begins to beat his fellow slaves and eat and drink with drunkards; 50 the master of that slave will come on a day when he does not expect him and at an hour which he does not know, 51 and will cut him in pieces and assign him a place with the hypocrites; in that place there will be weeping and gnashing of teeth. (Mark 13:34-35, Matthew 24:45-51.)

. . for you do not know when the master of the house is coming, whether in the evening, at midnight, or when the rooster crows, or in the morning-- 36 in case he should come suddenly and find you asleep. 37 "What I say to you I say to all, `Be on the alert!' " (Mark 13:35-47)

1 "Then the kingdom of heaven will be comparable to ten virgins, who took their lamps and went out to meet the bridegroom. 2 "Five of them were foolish, and five were prudent. 3 "For when the foolish took their lamps, they took no oil with them, 4 but the prudent took oil in flasks along with their lamps. 5 "Now while the bridegroom was delaying, they all got drowsy and began to sleep.

6 "But at midnight there was a shout, `Behold, the bridegroom! Come out to meet him.' 7 "Then all those virgins rose and trimmed their lamps. 8 "The foolish said to the prudent, `Give us some of your oil, for our lamps are going out.' 9 "But the prudent answered, `No, there will not be enough for us and you too; go instead to the dealers and buy some for yourselves.' 10 "And while they were going away to make the purchase, the bridegroom came, and those who were ready went in with him to the wedding feast; and the door was shut.

11 "Later the other virgins also came, saying, `Lord, lord, open up for us.' 12 "But he answered, `Truly I say to you, I do not know you.' 13 "Be on the alert then, for you do not know the day nor the hour. (Matthew 25:1-13.)

Commentary

34 "It is like a man away on a journey, who upon leaving his house and putting his slaves in charge,

This is a reprise of the early teaching (Luke 12:41ff) about the worthiness of the watchful slave compared to the unworthiness of the careless one, who lets the delay of his master relax his diligence and watchfulness.

Again, the idea expressed is man's propensity to give occasion to his evil intentions when the threat of getting caught is distant and remote. While there is time, we think we have license to indulge our desires. The slave in charge takes advantage that no one greater is around to curtail him, and indulges his desire to lord it over the others. He is trying out his new authority without the restraint that responsibility requires. He is then surprised when his master comes unexpectedly, and his deeds are disclosed.

Jesus is warning us concerning the time of the end that we will fall prey to this same temptation, yet we will be deceived as to how much time we have to make amends and repent. Like the master in the parable, the Lord of the Last Day will come when we least expect it, especially if we are busy taking advantage of the indefiniteness.

If we seek blessing and approval from Him at His coming, we should ensure we are found doing His will. To do that in the midst of ignorance about the timing means that we are obligated to be always faithful to it. The slothful servant is the one who believes he only has to be diligent and faithful when the master is near or at hand.

35 ". . for you do not know when the master of the house is coming, . . . 36 . . in case he should come suddenly and find you asleep. 37 "What I say to you I say to all, `Be on the alert!' "

There can be no doubt that the message is watchfulness as to His coming again. Watchfulness to stave off the temptations to do evil, watchfulness to read the times, that we not be ensnared by them, watchfulness to discern the things God may call us to do as the days grow short, watchfulness as to moral and spiritual purity at His appearing.

1 "Then the kingdom of heaven will be comparable to ten virgins,

An analogy from Jewish culture is now given to highlight the conditions of His coming again. There will be classes of people, at the very least the wise and the foolish. The details of the Jewish wedding need some background in order to see the application.

When the wedding day approaches, the bridegroom is away and separate from the bride with his selected friends – today called the groomsmen, but back then, the friends of the bridegroom (John 3:29). The bride is usually in her parents' home where guests will partake of the wedding feast after the solemnizing of the marriage. In many cases, a dwelling extension has now been attached to the parents home, in which the couple will live until they are financially able to provide a home of their own.

Traditionally, the coming of the bridegroom, the wedding and then the feast were set to occur in the evening hours. The exact time was intentionally to be a mystery in the hands of the bridegroom. His approach was to be heralded by one of his friends.

The bride's attendant girlfriends (the bridesmaids) had the duty to take lamps out to light the path for the bridegroom's party.

This parable highlights the period of waiting, in which the maids in the house are waiting to hear the shout of his approach. It is here that some may grow sleepy while waiting for the call. The parable is not about their having been asleep, but on the condition of their preparedness when woken by the call.

the foolish took their lamps, they took no oil with them,

We later find that these who so acted were counting on others to help them if they ran out. They in essence considered the extra preparedness too much effort or of little concern. It was also a failure to think ahead that the time might be longer than expected and what they might need if it was.

Today, it is popular to believe that someone else will always bail us out of any potential dilemma, so that we may spend our time and resources on enjoying the now with little concern for the next day. Some parents raise their children this way, always there to rescue them (certainly out of love), but failing to teach them how to avoid the sting of dilemmas by being prepared on their own. The child raised this way never thinks about consequences, because his parents have always bailed him out.

Contrast the prudent. They saw the eventuality ahead and prepared accordingly, *" but the prudent took oil in flasks along with their lamps."* They were cruel enough to themselves to at least say no to the laziness that would have avoided additional time and work.

5 "Now while the bridegroom was delaying, they all got drowsy and began to sleep.

So, as it happened, the eventuality believed to be most unlikely, did occur. The bridegroom delayed his coming considerably – it would not occur until midnight. And quite naturally, the wait brought on uncontrollable sleep.

"But at midnight there was a shout, `Behold, the bridegroom! Come out to meet him.'" – the traditional announcement according to custom. The wisdom of the decisions made would now be put to the test.

7 "Then all those virgins rose and trimmed their lamps. . . . 8 `Give us some of your oil, for our lamps are going out.'

The ancient lamp of the Middle-East was a covered bowl (reservoir) with a refilling hole and a protruding spout in which was placed a twisted cloth wick. The purpose of trimming them was to cut off the burned portion by pulling out clear wick and cutting off the charred end. This was necessary to avoid the lamp going out entirely but also to avoid smoke from the charred end still burning. The pulling out of fresh wick, trimming the burnt portion and refilling the lamp all came to be called trimming.

There were two times routinely that you trimmed a lamp – when relighting it each day at evening, and every so many hours thereafter when the wick had burned down.

In the case of the virgins waiting and falling asleep, the trimming was not to relight the lamp for evening, but to adjust the wick after having already burned that evening. As still burning, the lamp had to be blown out, then trimmed and re-lit from an alternate. In the case of the foolish, their lamps needed not only to be trimmed but refilled. We see this from the statement *"our lamps are going out."*

Predictably, the foolish virgins thought they could avoid the inconvenience of poor planning and expect now a rescue from the wise. To them it is all an emergency, the urgency of which will cause others to help them. It is a classic case of how failure to prepare and an emergency become no liability for the foolish, but rather for the very ones who prepared. The foolish have no difficulty asking those who planned ahead to sacrifice the benefits of doing so, that they be unhampered by their indolence.

But shouldn't the wise expect to benefit from their prudent preparations? That expectation has no respect among the foolish. The others' prudence merely provides an available resource in the eyes of the foolish.

9 "But the prudent answered, `No, there will not be enough for us and you too; go instead to the dealers and buy some for yourselves.'

We need not try to re-think how the oil available might in fact have been enough, if lighting the path for the short walk to the house was the purpose. The point is that in any situation, one lamp is not intended to suffice for two, and instead of depriving those who prepared of their supply, it is appropriate to go get oil for oneself.

10 "And while they were going away . . the bridegroom came, and those who were ready went in with him . . and the door was shut.

In all practical terms, the foolish could not have gone and come back in time. The shout and the commencement of the walk to the home were very close upon each other. We are not to assume that the foolish went away on the proviso that all would wait for their return. It was a foregone conclusion that they were going to miss the procession.

But the lamps would be needed for other aspects of the evening feast, so going and returning with more oil would not be considered a waste. They would simply return to the home with their oil for the remainder of the evening's activities.

However, the parable turns on the ominous mention that *"the door was shut."* It is a preparation of the audience that the expectation of returning to the festivities in general was not assured.

11 "Later the other virgins also came, saying, `Lord, lord, open up for us.'

We should not worry the issue of who might have been open to sell them oil at this late hour. In parables, generally, this kind of detail was never traced to ground in order to make the teaching effective. People expected this mode of speech to skip or even disrespect normal expectations of detail in the interest of the teaching objective.

The use of "Lord , lord" is outside our expectation, because the person in charge would be the bride's father, in most likelihood a friend of the several families involved. Friends do not ordinarily address each other as Lord, nor did children address their friends' parents as 'Lord.'

But in the case of the wedding feast, the host was called the lord of the feast. So, in terms of pure custom, this appellation was perfectly in order.

But now the response -

12 "But he answered, `Truly I say to you, I do not know you.'

Ordinarily, the host would not have said this, even if there was dismay at their indolence and laziness. He might scold them as silly geese and foolish empty heads, but he would not have told them he did not know them.

This is a case of Jesus deliberately revising the analogy to fit the lesson at hand. This was by no means a mere recounting of the customs of the wedding feast, things with which they would all be completely familiar.

Many aspects not only must have some import to the relationship of Christ to His disciples, but must inform us vividly about end times as well.

Earlier, we remember Jesus talking about those who would come to Him in the judgment, proclaiming their deeds done in His name. He would say to them, "Depart from me ye workers of iniquity. I never knew you."

So we are now quite prepared to relate this indictment – "I never knew you" – to topics about the judgment. The lord of the feast is now suddenly at the end, a stand-in for the Lord of Glory, who will judge the living and the dead. All who are foolish with respect to the things of God will be told they are not known of Him and the door is now shut. All the special pleading will be of no consequence, as will be the case in the end. We will not be able to marshal excuses about unfair conditions or being disadvantaged, or the like.

Hence the warning, *13 "Be on the alert then, for you do not know the day nor the hour."*

Parable Analogies

Some complications result in trying to make certain identifications between the maidens, the bride, the bridegroom and the Church.

We can relate the bridegroom and the shout to Christ and the Second Coming and that it will be at an hour unexpected. But then the one pronouncing judgment on the foolish maidens is not clear. Is he the bridegroom or the bridegroom's father or the lord of the feast, the father of the bride?
The bride is often a figure for the Church – *"the marriage of the Lamb has come and His bride has made herself ready."* (Rev 19:7) Stressing this would remove the virgins as analogous to the Church if the bride is the Church.

But there is no indication that all these identifications are intended in the parable, nor that keeping who's who straight is critical to its understanding. It is clear that the virgins are analogous to Christ's followers, because the exhortation is to us that we be alert, as the five were. This necessitates that we put in the background any ready identifications that might be based on other figures and metaphors in Scripture.

We are instead, to enjoy and appreciate the case of the figures in the foreground and how they apply to us and Him.

And to that end, the point is about being on the alert, being prepared for a delay, and because we want earnestly and sincerely to participate in His great feast, that constrains us to act diligently and wisely. We are also to learn that there will be those in the midst of His Church who are foolish and careless in regard to what He has prepared. Thus, there are some to whom it will be said, "I do not know you."

Sobering words for all of us, that we not be found among them.

Matthew 25:14-46, Matthew 26:1-5, Luke 22:3-6, Matthew 26:15

14 "For it is just like a man about to go on a journey, who called his own slaves and entrusted his possessions to them. 15 "To one he gave five talents, to another, two, and to another, one, each according to his own ability; and he went on his journey. 16 "Immediately the one who had received the five talents went and traded with them, and gained five more talents. 17 "In the same manner the one who had received the two talents gained two more. 18 "But he who received the one talent went away, and dug a hole in the ground and hid his master's money.

19 "Now after a long time the master of those slaves came and settled accounts with them. 20 "The one who had received the five talents came up and brought five more talents, saying, `Master, you entrusted five talents to me. See, I have gained five more talents.' 21 "His master said to him, `Well done, good and faithful slave. You were faithful with a few things, I will put you in charge of many things; enter into the joy of your master.'

22 "Also the one who had received the two talents came up and said, `Master, you entrusted two talents to me. See, I have gained two more talents.' 23 "His master said to him, `Well done, good and faithful slave. You were faithful with a few things, I will put you in charge of many things; enter into the joy of your master.' 24 "And the one also who had received the one talent came up and said, `Master, I knew you to be a hard man, reaping where you did not sow and gathering where you scattered no seed. 25 `And I was afraid, and went away and hid your talent in the ground. See, you have what is yours.'

26 "But his master answered and said to him, `You wicked, lazy slave, you knew that I reap where I did not sow and gather where I scattered no seed. 27 `Then you ought to have put my money in the bank, and on my arrival I would have received my money back with interest. 28 `Therefore take away the talent from him, and give it to the one who has the ten talents.' 29 "For to everyone who has, more shall be given, and he will have an abundance; but from the one who does not have, even what he does have shall be taken away. 30 "Throw out the worthless slave into the outer darkness; in that place there will be weeping and gnashing of teeth.

31 "But when the Son of Man comes in His glory, and all the angels with Him, then He will sit on His glorious throne. 32 "All the nations will be gathered before Him; and He will separate them from one another, as the shepherd separates the sheep from the goats; 33 and He will put the sheep on His right, and the goats on the left. 34 "Then the King will say to those on His right, `Come, you who are blessed of My Father, inherit the kingdom prepared for you from the foundation of the world. 35 `For I was hungry, and you gave Me something to eat; I was thirsty, and you gave Me something to drink; I was a stranger, and you invited Me in; 36 naked, and you clothed Me; I was sick, and you visited Me; I was in prison, and you came to Me.'

37 "Then the righteous will answer Him, `Lord, when did we see You hungry, and feed You, or thirsty, and give You something to drink? 38 `And when did we see You a stranger, and invite You in, or naked, and clothe You? 39 `When did we see You sick, or in prison, and come to You?' 40 "The King will answer and say to them, `Truly I say to you, to the extent that you did it to one of these brothers of Mine, even the least of them, you did it to Me.'

41 "Then He will also say to those on His left, `Depart from Me, accursed ones, into the eternal fire which has been prepared for the devil and his angels; 42 for I was hungry, and you gave Me nothing to eat; I was thirsty, and you gave Me nothing to drink; 43 I was a stranger, and you did not invite Me in; naked, and you did not clothe Me; sick, and in prison, and you did not visit Me.' 44 "Then they themselves also will answer, `Lord, when did we see You hungry, or thirsty, or a stranger, or naked, or sick, or in prison, and did not take care of You?' 45 "Then He will answer them, `Truly I say to you, to the extent that you did not do it to one of the least of these, you did not do it to Me.' 46 "These will go away into eternal punishment, but the righteous into eternal life." (Matthew 25:14-46)

1 When Jesus had finished all these words, He said to His disciples, 2 "You know that after two days the Passover is coming, and the Son of Man is to be handed over for crucifixion." 3 Then the chief priests and the elders of the people were gathered together in the court of the high priest, named Caiaphas; 4 and they

plotted together to seize Jesus by stealth and kill Him. 5 But they were saying, "Not during the festival, otherwise a riot might occur among the people." (Matthew 26:1-5.)

3 And Satan entered into Judas who was called Iscariot, belonging to the number of the twelve. 4 And he went away and discussed with the chief priests and officers how he might betray Him to them . . 15 and said, "What are you willing to give me to betray Him to you?" And they weighed out thirty pieces of silver to him. . . . 5 They were glad and agreed to give him money. 6 So he consented, and began seeking a good opportunity to betray Him to them apart from the crowd. (Luke 22:3-4, Matthew 26:15, Luke 22:5-6)

Commentary

14 "For it is just like a man about to go on a journey, who called his own slaves and entrusted his possessions to them.

The *For* is there to refer us to the previous dialog about being alert and watchful when our Lord comes, meaning that the following will amplify or further explain its import.

We halt a bit at the idea of putting one's possessions in the charge of slaves. They surely would be looking for any opportunity to escape misery and hardship, and having their master's wealth to themselves would be an occasion too good to pass up.

But slavery in ancient times was not wholly as we have come to know it in more recent times - the last three centuries in Europe and America. To be sure, there were forms of punitive slavery in ancient Rome and other kingdoms that were worse and extremely cruel, but there were also many beneficial slave arrangements that resembled more the concept of hired hands and stewards than de-humanizing abuses that characterize so much of slavery.

A person could come into slavery from financial troubles or social indebtedness. Courts could award a person as slave to one's creditor if the sum of the debtor's possessions could never resolve the debt. In Jewish life, this was temporary until the debt was discharged by benefit of labor. In Rome, it was seldom temporary.

Still, there were many masters who treated well those who were penitent and showed promise in industry, talent and ability.

We must also bear in mind that to take an opportunity to pilfer and run, placed the perpetrator in much greater jeopardy with society at large, since their identity would be hard to evade, irregardless of a simple change of clothes.

And there were many benefits to doing well while the master was away – improvement of one's conditions as a reward for meeting the expectations of trust and responsibility. True, one was not free, but in terms of daily life, possessions, a certain dignity over one's abilities and accomplishments, it could easily be not much different than working as a free person for a proprietor or business owner.

This is the situation Jesus' is using for the parable.

15 "To one he gave five talents, to another, two, and to another, one, each according to his own ability; and he went on his journey.

This is a reprise of the teaching we find in Luke (19:14-28) where the amounts are in minas rather than talents. The principle is exactly the same – the slothful servant did not understand that the money entrusted was assumed to be for investment, not simple storage. The master's purpose was to make money grow by its use, not merely keep it.

Similarly, in terms of end times, we are to consider the blessings given to us are opportunities of spiritual and monetary investment, entrusted to us by God as His stewards. To value them as merely keepsakes or possessions is against the nature of the gifts.

(For the value of the talent, see at Matthew 18:23-35, above.)

29 "For to everyone who has, more shall be given, . . . from the one who does not have, even what he does have shall be taken away. 30 "Throw out the worthless slave into the outer darkness; in that place there will be weeping and gnashing of teeth.

Again, we recoil from the harshness of taking away even the money at least preserved, so that the slave had nothing. But it is the master's money not that of the slave.

In terms of application, we recoil because we see then a God who will strip us of our possessions and give them away to someone else, if we fail to measure up to His assessment. In today's valuation of things this would be unfair and harsh. Certainly an over-reaction we ourselves would not countenance.

But in terms of end times, the issue of who has what is basically over. That it is end times and not earthly affairs is signaled by the statement – " *"Throw out the worthless slave into the outer darkness;"* The subject has changed subtly outside the realm of normal affairs.

It is a matter of what these accrue to us in our assessment before God. The parable is saying He will not credit slothfulness to our account so our poor efforts will be taken from us in terms of accounting, such that we have nothing really to show for ourselves, were we to try to claim it.

31 "But when the Son of Man comes in His glory, and all the angels with Him, then He will sit on His glorious throne.

Focus now turns to that assessment, the moment when souls will be made to appear before Him. From the idea of democracies and people's states where thrones and subjects are modes of rule away from which progress is supposed to have been made, we see a return to the idea of a throne, and a ruler sitting on it, and subjects standing before him. It is the old idea of absolute monarchy returning; kings instead of democracies.

32 "All the nations will be gathered before Him; and He will separate them from one another, as the shepherd separates the sheep from the goats;

Goats are not male sheep, as some uninformed persons understand. They are a different species from sheep, though they have the same habits of herding and rumination. Sheep are pasturing animals (genus: Ovis, family: Bovidae) while goats are mountain and cliff dwellers (genus: Capra, family: Bovidae.)

Thus, the goat is not a version of sheep, but a related species, singled out in biblical application as the opposite figure from sheep. Sheep are the easily led ones who follow and depend on their shepherd. Goats are typically figured in spiritual terms as the ones on whom offerings for sin are personified (the scapegoat.)

Thus, in this picture by Jesus, the sheep are the righteous, the goats are those worthy of punishment.

In the end, Jesus tells us, there will be a need to finally separate the righteous from the wicked, to judge and assess each to their own destinies. They are no longer to remain mixed.

This bears witness with another earlier teaching about the tares and the wheat where the Planter states, "'Allow both to grow together until the harvest; and in the time of the harvest I will say to the reapers, "First gather up the tares and bind them in bundles to burn them up; but gather the wheat into my barn."'" (Matt 13:30.)

Our social and philosophical proclivities must give way to the rather strong idea that in reality there will be this separation and the destinies will be as they are portrayed. It is an ominous outcome that many today reject.

Interestingly, the test is the same for both – a case of works proceeding from faith.

35 `For I was hungry, and you gave Me something to eat; I was thirsty, and you gave Me something to drink; I was a stranger, and you invited Me in; 36 naked, and you clothed Me; I was sick, and you visited Me; I was in prison, and you came to Me.'

Here, faith was not held in the abstract, but worked its way into everyday affairs among the needy and poor. There are people today who are arm-chair Christians – they love the literature of Christianity but shrink from the work of it. Jesus is telling such people that the mere love of the Word and books about the Word will not be enough. This is not, however, works righteousness. It is a testing of the faith that counts by its natural outworking. If we have such a faith, we cannot be an arm-chair Christian for long. We will be compelled to do something for others.

It is also a commentary on the view of the state to meet those needs. Government can be counted on to further its own interests which can very easily mean that benevolence will come and go. In God's view, the needs of the poor are to be better met by those who have stability and reliability in the Lord, fostered by a true and sincere compassion.

But notice. The righteous are puzzled . . .

37 ". . `Lord, when did we see You hungry, and feed You, . . or give You something to drink? . . . 40 "The King will answer and say to them, `Truly I say to you, to the extent that you did it to one of these brothers of Mine, even the least of them, you did it to Me.'

Ironically, those doing the good deeds are unaware of them, contrasted with the wicked who are calculating and tallying them up for vain glory.

That they are told they were doing them unto Him all along, does not mean such recipients were phantoms or Jesus masquerading as the poor and needy. It means, rather, that Jesus was with the poor in the downtrodden despair of their own poverty and need. We picture the needy being held in the lap of Jesus unseen. As they came and helped and comforted, He was as much a recipient was the visible person because He was so identifying with their hurt and suffering. To relieve them could not be separated from relieving Him also. But even still, it is His regard that it was done unto Him irrespective of how it is explained.

41 "Then He will also say to those on His left, . . . 42 for I was hungry, and you gave Me nothing to eat; I was thirsty, and you gave Me nothing to drink;"

Here is applied the same test, which the wicked and selfish failed. He was there embracing the poor, hungry and needy and these indicted had walked by uncaring or unwilling. These were sins of omission, yet it is clear also that sins of commission (avarice, greed, selfishness, laziness and indolence) were the cause, and moved them away from such duties.

44 "Then they themselves also will answer, `Lord, when did we see You hungry, or thirsty, . .

In contrast, some good deeds are known (and ready to be cited), but they are not known to have been done unto Him. This is because they were done to others at the expense of the truly needy - "We helped society, and let society help these poor wretches."

They were, of course, clueless that He was being likewise neglected. Those who use their pocketbooks to soothe their civic and religious consciences often show their disdain for the poor and hungry. It will break their stride and cast unwanted aspersions on their image, so donations and giving from afar is the safe and respectable offering that can be appealed to when the time comes.

41 . . `Depart from Me, accursed ones, into the eternal fire which has been prepared for the devil and his angels; . . . 46 "These will go away into eternal punishment, but the righteous into eternal life."

This is quite serious. It is not a mere play to make a point and prick our consciences. Jesus is describing a scene that will play out in abject reality. There are those to whom this will really be said and decreed.

We can rationalize to our hearts content about what kinds of service will count in the end, but we have here at least been adequately warned that our service to Him is as personal as our service to an individual person in need.

2 "You know that after two days the Passover is coming, and the Son of Man is to be handed over for crucifixion."

It is the Tuesday before the Thursday Passover which will be the scene of the Last Supper, before His arrest. Jesus closes the foregoing subject and begins preparation of His disciples for the events of the current week – His last on earth as God in the flesh.

They are to get and grasp that this is the end of their blessed time with Him in the body. He announced the approaching Passover, innocuous at first, but then adds that it will be the occasion of His arrest and death, not by natural means, not by being taken into Heaven, but death as a criminal of the worst sort – one that is not punished by the slight penalties of a court, but by death in the most offensive manner.

For those who find this time reference confusing (because the Jews will refer to the Passover on Friday), more explanation will be given at the point of Christ's trial. Suffice it to say, that Jesus celebrated the Passover at the correct time according to the Jews, else His disciples could not have acquired the provisions needed. Nor was Jesus' Passover "magical", being arranged sovereignly despite what the Jews were doing.

3 Then the chief priests and the elders of the people were gathered together in the court of the high priest, named Caiaphas;

The scene changes for the gospel writer, to inform us what is happening at the same moment among the elders of the Sanhedrin. Caiaphas' tenure of office was from 18 A.D. to the Passover of A.D. 36. His father and previous high priest, Annas, was still living in the city at the time of Jesus' arrest and trial.

The court of the high priest would mean at his home. Meetings in the precincts of the Council were too public and sympathizers on the council could not be avoided.

4 and they plotted together to seize Jesus by stealth and kill Him. 5 But . . "Not during the festival, otherwise a riot might occur among the people."

The word "plotted" is used because they had a difficult case, and if plotting was now invoked, they knew it might not succeed. They are caught between the correctness and authority of His teaching and their hatred for His indictments against them. They could rationalize away His teaching, but as for which crime He could be found worthy of death, they had great difficulty, because the Roman authority had little care for doctrinal squabbles. It had to be something that offended Roman provincial law or something local the Romans respected equally well – like judgments involving the Temple, which was protected.

But there was the additional problem of how to handle His demise outside public view. We see clearly the gap between their own concerns and those of the people they were by implication charged to serve. We must remember that these men were not appointed to public office as in public governmental service today. There was no oath of office to represent the people or even serve their needs as their servants.

The priests and elders held their duties as unto God and to the Temple service, but it was indirectly implied that they served "between" God and the people and there was a duty to properly represent God to them and them to God.

So to be out of sorts with the people was always an unwise course for which despotism would never do as a solution.

3 And Satan entered into Judas who was called Iscariot, belonging to the number of the twelve. 4 And he went away and discussed with the chief priests and officers how he might betray Him to them

The scene changes again to the company of the disciples, but after the session of teaching. Judas goes away to meet with the authorities to betray Jesus.

We are aware through commentary and external treatises that Judas was not a team player along the way in Jesus' discipleship of these men, but there is little in the Gospels that spells out his discontent or enough of a rejection of Jesus to be secretly thinking about betraying Him. This conclusion is something authors have surmised to have been his state of mind at earlier points.

We know that Jesus knew and even proclaimed that He had chosen one of them as the one who would betray Him – *"Did I Myself not choose you, the twelve, and yet one of you is a devil?"* (John 6:70.) But we have no indication by his behavior that he began living the part until now.

We have record that Judas acted with obvious worldly motives and reasoning (the perfume from the woman.) But certainly, to be available to Satan's use implies reticence at the acknowledgments the others were making. He may have felt Jesus was too radical for his sense of duty to the old way. There has to be disenchantment for him if he is to live out his feelings in the direction of Jesus' enemies.

"Satan entered into Judas" Here we have the statement proposed as fact that beings outside the human plane can "enter" a person. We of course saw this in the many exorcisms Jesus performed earlier. We see here the very act, which cannot now be rationalized away as just having the propensity to evil while Satan stands aloof. Rather, we have the active intermingling of supernatural evil into human flesh and mind. It's the stuff of movies which many take as fantasy. Here is the genuine article, very real indeed.

The move played elegantly into His enemies hands, since Judas would have inside knowledge about where Jesus was and how He could be taken outside public gaze.

We ponder how Jesus would allow this to continue, but we must remember that He knows this is all needful to the plan of His Father.

"What are you willing to give me to betray Him to you?"

Fitting in with his attitude toward the disciples' purse, we see Judas desiring to be enriched by this move. We cannot give Judas credit that he was desiring to preserve the Mosaic traditions by parting company with what Jesus represented. He could have done that by simply leaving, as many former disciples did at the hard teaching about eating flesh and drinking blood (John 6:66.)

But Judas had to know that going to the authorities meant Jesus' death and that takes an evil mind to have no care for such things. Further deepening his evil mind and heart is this desire to be enriched by the deed. To do so, one must be especially callous to not mind profiting at the horrid death of another.

And they weighed out thirty pieces of silver to him

The silver shekel was worth considerably less than the gold. If he had been paid in gold it would have amounted to over $7,000 in equivalent money today. As it is, six gold shekels equaled fifty silver. That would make the silver worth about $28.00 and the payment a little over $800.00

Both parties being satisfied at the arrangement, he consented, and began seeking a good opportunity to betray Him to them apart from the crowd.

CHAPTER 13
Last Passover and Passion Week

Luke 21:37-38, John 12:37-50, Luke 22:7-13
37 Now during the day He was teaching in the temple, but at evening He would go out and spend the night on the mount that is called Olivet. 38 And all the people would get up early in the morning to come to Him in the temple to listen to Him. (Luke 21:37-38.)

37 But though He had performed so many signs before them, yet they were not believing in Him. 38 This was to fulfill the word of Isaiah the prophet which he spoke: "LORD, WHO HAS BELIEVED OUR REPORT ? AND TO WHOM HAS THE ARM OF THE LORD BEEN REVEALED ?" 39 For this reason they could not believe, for Isaiah said again, 40 "HE HAS BLINDED THEIR EYES AND HE HARDENED THEIR HEART, SO THAT THEY WOULD NOT SEE WITH THEIR EYES AND PERCEIVE WITH THEIR HEART, AND BE CONVERTED AND I HEAL THEM."
41 These things Isaiah said because he saw His glory, and he spoke of Him.

42 Nevertheless many even of the rulers believed in Him, but because of the Pharisees they were not confessing Him, for fear that they would be put out of the synagogue; 43 for they loved the approval of men rather than the approval of God. 44 And Jesus cried out and said, "He who believes in Me, does not believe in Me but in Him who sent Me. 45 "He who sees Me sees the One who sent Me.

46 "I have come as Light into the world, so that everyone who believes in Me will not remain in darkness. 47 "If anyone hears My sayings and does not keep them, I do not judge him; for I did not come to judge the world, but to save the world. 48 "He who rejects Me and does not receive My sayings, has one who judges him; the word I spoke is what will judge him at the last day. 49 "For I did not speak on My own initiative, but the Father Himself who sent Me has given Me a commandment as to what to say and what to speak. 50 "I know that His commandment is eternal life; therefore the things I speak, I speak just as the Father has told Me." (John 12:37-50.)

7 Then came the first day of Unleavened Bread on which the Passover lamb had to be sacrificed. 8 And Jesus sent Peter and John, saying, "Go and prepare the Passover for us, so that we may eat it." 9 They said to Him, "Where do You want us to prepare it?" 10 And He said to them, "When you have entered the city, a man will meet you carrying a pitcher of water; follow him into the house that he enters. 11 "And you shall say to the owner of the house, `The Teacher says to you, "Where is the guest room in which I may eat the Passover with My disciples?"' 12 "And he will show you a large, furnished upper room; prepare it there." (Luke 22:7-13.)

Commentary

37 Now during the day He was teaching in the temple, but at evening He would go out . . 38 And all the people would . . to come to Him in the temple to listen to Him.

This arrangement was partly to avoid the stealth of those who sought to do away with Him secretly and would use the cover of night to effect such plans; but also to retire from the press of the crowds and have time for more intimate talk and fellowship among those who loved Him.

To the chagrin of the Pharisees, the people flock to Him and actually come early to anticipate His arrival. The scene of so many coming with eager hearts to hear Him had to paint a confusing picture at best for the leaders. They were conspiring to kill one whom, right in front of their eyes, was thronged not with rebel-rousers and seditionists, but seekers of God's great blessings. They would be constantly attending the need in virtually every second thereafter to re-convince themselves of His malevolence and acts worthy of death;

and that despite everything they were witnessing in front of them – *. . though He had performed so many signs before them, yet they were not believing in Him.*

38 This was to fulfill the word of Isaiah the prophet which he spoke: "LORD, WHO HAS BELIEVED OUR REPORT ? AND TO WHOM HAS THE ARM OF THE LORD BEEN REVEALED ?"

The author is reaching back into the OT to mark the fulfillment of passages that would ordinarily be somewhat obscure as to connections. That he is under the marvelous leading of the Holy Spirit, assures us that such connections are both valid and clearly intended by God.

The words are from Isaiah chapter 53. To understand why they are employed here as a fulfillment, we need to look at the last verses of chapter 52.

Isaiah has just revealed a very harrowing aspect to Israel's expected Messiah – the servant of these passages. *"Just as there were many who were appalled at him-- his appearance was so disfigured beyond that of any man and his form marred beyond human likeness -- so will he sprinkle many nations . ."* It is in Isaiah's time an anticipation that Messiah will be accepted by some while rejected by others to the degree that there will be suffering on that account, rendering Him hard to look at or recognize.

Ironically, these are Scriptures the Jews had available to them when Jesus stepped on the scene. But the hardness of their hearts prevented them from making the connection – that they were effecting the very assaults they found so perplexing concerning the One they eagerly expected.

v.15 *"For what they were not told, they will see, and what they have not heard, they will understand."*

This refers to those who will accept Him. The nations on whom He is said to "sprinkle" are those who were not told, yet will see, those who had not heard, yet will understand. The corollary is ominously dreadful – those who *were* told will not see Him, those who *did* hear will not understand.

We are now ready for 53:1 – *Who has heard our report and to whom has the arm of the Lord been revealed?* The answer is: not those who heard or were told, but those who in fact lacked such revelations. Both the people of Judaism, whom the Pharisees neglected in sound and honest teaching, and the Gentiles, who certainly were well outside the specific revelation of God among the Jews. These are those who will respond and accept Him. They will hear the report and see the arm of the Lord revealed.

40 "HE HAS BLINDED THEIR EYES . . . SO THAT THEY WOULD NOT SEE WITH THEIR EYES AND PERCEIVE WITH THEIR HEART, AND BE CONVERTED AND I HEAL THEM."

This is a profound statement of what is called judicial blindness. Some have attempted to make this into a case of the Jews refusing to see on their own account, but the verse clearly states that the blindness is imposed by God – *He has blinded their eyes*, not *they have blinded their own eyes*. Linguistically, this cannot be reset into a frame which makes them blind themselves – at least at this particular point.

On the other hand, we cannot force this to the extent that God summarily blinded those who wished to see. In essence, the resolution *is* in their own willful choice to reject and not see, but that preceded this indictment by many centuries – days which over and over prepared their hearts to be cold toward the truth of God in Christ and wholly recalcitrant to His revelation among them.

So in essence, the conditions that precipitated their judicial blindness were self-imposed by their own corporate and individual wills. God's indictment and summary blindness was an outcome, not an arbitrary, pre-emptive decree.

The writer is hauling in the very OT prediction that perfectly applies, because all along it was known in the counsels of God that they would fulfill it.

41 These things Isaiah said because he saw His glory, and he spoke of Him.

We have no explicit statements that Isaiah saw, visually, the Christ. But his prophecies are so specific that whether in words revealed or in a vision unmentioned, Isaiah can be said to have seen Him as is now later spoken.

For the great prophets, we must understand that their great words came from an overwhelming impression of some thing, revealed of God. That vision or realization so consumed them that it produced the fervor and fire of their writings. It compelled them to do what they could not avoid; God filling in the details with words immortal and unforgettable.

42 Nevertheless many even of the rulers believed in Him, but because of the Pharisees they were not confessing Him, for fear that they would be put out of the synagogue;

We are not to infer that the Herodians or the Roman authorities came to believe, though we hear that a few did. Rulers here means those of the Jews, because the fear in their confession has to do with the synagogue, which the Herodians seldom if ever frequented, certainly scant few Romans ever did.

But it tells us that there was a remnant of the faithful among the rulers of the Jews, who were largely at a disadvantage among the prominent Pharisees (the humble and caring seldom rise to the top.)

The fear respecting the synagogue seems trite in our day and age, because to be tossed out of one church does not restrict one from worship altogether. There are plenty of other churches in town.

But in ancient times, there were no such luxuries. The synagogue in your vicinity was all there was and though one could endure the inconvenience of traveling to a neighboring assembly some distance away, the authorities would have made certain that all synagogues in traveling distance were notified.

To be cast out of the synagogue was to be denied the routine means of spiritual sustenance, to be divorced from the only commonwealth of faith. There, the Word was read and heard, there would be elders to whom questions and advice could be sought. There would be fellowship one could not get in the business of everyday life. It is unclear how much this judgment also affected their obedience at the feasts in the great Temple.

In all respects, this was a serious outcome and one to be genuinely dreaded.

This is what is so touching about the man born blind (John 9:1ff), whom Jesus healed and who was then put out of the synagogue. He was in the very midst of contemplating the reality of his judgment when He was made to know of the very presence of the Messiah, seated with him and comforting him. What need was there then for synagogues and temples?

44 And Jesus cried out and said, "He who believes in Me, does not believe in Me but in Him who sent Me. 45 "He who sees Me sees the One who sent Me.

Hebrews 3:1 calls Christ the Apostle. The reason is here in the above verse. He is one "sent" among whom there is none greater. And a characteristic of God's sent ones is that they point not to themselves but to the One who sent them. Jesus takes no personal credit for belief toward Him as Son, but credits the belief as in His own Father, who is the object of their belief if they believed Him and His words.

It is like the mirror that directs sunlight into a dark cave. The thing reflected is the sun. The mirror generates nothing on its own, but passes along the radiance of the thing desired. Though we have much to praise God concerning Jesus Himself, He would turn it all toward the Father as the ultimate object of praise. To praise Jesus is to praise His Father.

The Son revealed nothing independent from the Father as His own, but it was as if the Father were to part the clouds and speak directly to man.

46 "I have come as Light into the world, so that everyone who believes in Me will not remain in darkness.

Here, the awful condition of man is reiterated and brought forward from the ancient, primitive past. Man is consigned to darkness in his self will and in what he shares in Adam. Without God, he is left to grope about as best he can to make sense of his world. It is no wonder the world and man in it are as bizarre as they are.

This is exclusivity of Christ above all other claimants and light bearers. In Him man finds the light that relieves his darkness.

Interestingly for the sons of evil, their condemnation will be that they loved the darkness rather than the light (John 3:19.)

47 "If anyone hears My sayings and does not keep them, I do not judge him;

A careless reading of this section will yield a contradiction – first He says He does not judge, but then it will be by His words that men are judged.

But there is a key element of time in the middle. The judging that will take place according to His words is at the end, meaning that while there is time and opportunity for salvation, He does not judge in terms of final judgments. Our works may temporarily accuse us according to the Law, but Jesus is here to convert us from them that we may not pay the price that our deeds will beget us – *"for I did not come . . but to save the world."*

On the other hand, we are not to take that grace for granted. If we slack and let time expire, it will be His words that condemn us in the end. We will have wasted His grace in the interim.

49 "For I did not speak on My own initiative, but the Father Himself who sent Me has given Me a commandment as to what to say and what to speak.

And we find precisely as above in v.44 that it is not His own independent words, but all which the Father gave Him to speak. So while His words will condemn the wicked, it will end up being the same words as of the Father – *50 " . . His commandment is eternal life; . . I speak just as the Father has told Me."*

7 Then came the first day of Unleavened Bread . . 8 And Jesus sent Peter and John, saying, "Go and prepare the Passover for us, so that we may eat it."

The Feast of Unleavened Bread was not a single feast day but one of many days, as indicated by the phrase, "the first day of Unleavened Bread." It commemorated the new year, which had begun some 13 days earlier at the sighting of the new moon, on which day the priests declared the first day of the new year. As for feasts and religious convocations, Unleavened Bread was the first to be celebrated in the year – *"This month shall be the beginning of months for you; it is to be the first month of the year to you."* (Exodus 12:2.)

The feast was a full seven days, the Passover being the first celebration on the evening that began the first day, followed by six days of the feast in which the Jews ate unleavened bread.

There are differences in understanding whether this Passover preparation of Jesus and its eating were separate or simultaneous with that of the Jews in Jerusalem. Some offer that the disciples were asked to go get provisions for the following evening, not the evening about to commence. This they propose because the Pharisees do not enter the praetorium of Pilate for fear of being defiled from eating the Passover and that meeting occurred on the day Christ was crucified. If so, Jesus could not have celebrated the Passover along with the rest of Judaism the night before. Some support is appealed to in the words we will encounter later in which Jesus seems to express His concern that He will not be able to share it at the normal time, since the crucifixion will occupy that day for Him.

However, that interpretation presents other problems it cannot solve. First, the text clearly states that the order to go and prepare was *on the day* when the lamb had to be sacrificed (v.7), not the day prior. The interposition of time for getting provisions is not a problem, since the daylight hours prior to the evening of the same day that began Passover were not only free but understood to be for that purpose by the Jews.

Second, the disciples would not have been able to acquire provisions and a place for celebrating it on a day not authorized. Anyone permitting a room to be used for an illegal celebration would have been suspect by the authorities, which would have made their cooperation highly unlikely.

Against these concerns, we have the fear of defilement by the Pharisees the next day and the command to Judas at the supper to go and get provisions for the feast (which wouldn't be necessary if the supper was underway.)

These two anomalies will be discussed when we enter the details of the supper.

9 "Where do You want us to prepare it?" 10 . . "When you have entered the city, a man will meet you carrying a pitcher of water;

Similar to the arrangement for the colt, there was a divine preparation of the person and the room. This ameliorates the concern for someone offering a room on the wrong day, but it doesn't deal with how provisions were acquired ahead of the appointed time, especially the lamb, which had to be slaughtered by a priest.

But the strongest point controlling the timing is the statement that it was the same day as that appointed for the sacrifices, which rules out any option for a different day.

`The Teacher says to you, "Where is the guest room in which I may eat the Passover with My disciples?"'

This public declaration makes an authorized celebration less likely because it is begging for exposure and destroys the secrecy that would be needed according to simple common sense. If you are making unauthorized arrangements for which considerable jeopardy might result, you don't make a bold announcement about your plans. Jesus followed this mode of operation many times by warning people to not make His actions known.

a large, furnished upper room; prepare it there."

This would mean an owner of above average possessions and wealth. Very few ordinary homes had enclosed upper rooms – many had places of comfort on the roof but not enclosed as a second story. We have nothing but legend and unverified traditions for speculating who this benefactor may have been. For him to have been compliant to God's purposes, to the degree that the words spoken by the disciples were recognized as a sort of password for access, implies someone already in service to God.

As for the church designated as the scene of the supper, its authenticity to the site is unverifiable and the product of local traditions. Certainly, the interior masonry and architecture have no continuity to the place itself, except to perhaps stand over the site, which is impossible to know historically.

Luke 22:14-18, John 13:1-20

1 Now before the Feast of the Passover, Jesus knowing that His hour had come that He would depart out of this world to the Father, having loved His own who were in the world, He loved them to the end. (John 13:1.)

14 When the hour had come, He reclined at the table, and the apostles with Him. 15 And He said to them, "I have earnestly desired to eat this Passover with you before I suffer; 16 for I say to you, I shall never again eat it until it is fulfilled in the kingdom of God." 17 And when He had taken a cup and given thanks, He said, "Take this and share it among yourselves; 18 for I say to you, I will not drink of the fruit of the vine from now on until the kingdom of God comes." (Luke 22:14-18.)

2 During supper, the devil having already put into the heart of Judas Iscariot, the son of Simon, to betray Him, 3 Jesus, knowing that the Father had given all things into His hands, and that He had come forth from God and was going back to God, 4 got up from supper, and laid aside His garments; and taking a towel, He girded Himself.

5 Then He poured water into the basin, and began to wash the disciples' feet and to wipe them with the towel with which He was girded. 6 So He came to Simon Peter. He said to Him, "Lord, do You wash my feet?" 7 Jesus answered and said to him, "What I do you do not realize now, but you will understand hereafter." 8 Peter said to Him, "Never shall You wash my feet!" Jesus answered him, "If I do not wash you, you have no part with Me." 9 Simon Peter said to Him, "Lord, then wash not only my feet, but also my hands and my head." 10 Jesus said to him, "He who has bathed needs only to wash his feet, but is completely clean; and you are clean, but not all of you." 11 For He knew the one who was betraying Him; for this reason He said, "Not all of you are clean."

12 So when He had washed their feet, and taken His garments and reclined at the table again, He said to them, "Do you know what I have done to you? 13 "You call Me Teacher and Lord; and you are right, for so I am. 14 "If I then, the Lord and the Teacher, washed your feet, you also ought to wash one another's feet. 15 "For I gave you an example that you also should do as I did to you. 16 "Truly, truly, I say to you, a slave is not greater than his master, nor is one who is sent greater than the one who sent him. 17 "If you know these things, you are blessed if you do them.

18 "I do not speak of all of you. I know the ones I have chosen; but it is that the Scripture may be fulfilled, 'HE WHO EATS MY BREAD HAS LIFTED UP HIS HEEL AGAINST ME.' 19 "From now on I am telling you before it comes to pass, so that when it does occur, you may believe that I am He. 20 "Truly, truly, I say to you, he who receives whomever I send receives Me; and he who receives Me receives Him who sent Me." (John 13:2-20)

Commentary

1 Now before the Feast of the Passover, Jesus knowing that His hour had come . . . having loved His own who were in the world, He loved them to the end. (John 13:1.)

This is a rather long sentence and because of the insertion of two extended phrases, we may lose sight of the sentence itself. The short version is: "He loved them to the end."

This is extended up front by "knowing that His hour had come" and "that He would depart out of this world to the Father" and "having loved His own who were in the world." But the main point of the sentence is that He loved them to the end.

The purpose is to show the frame of mind of the Savior as His key jumping off point approaches. We might see it as a finality but He saw it as a transition back to the Father. For us, we are to realize that through all His earthly life, despite the difficulties of training and molding the team to be left behind, He has loved them up to and through the end of His life among them.

to the end also signifies duration through the events of the end, meaning He loved them even into the events that brought about the end, namely the Crucifixion. In that very act that precipitated the end, He showed the quintessential love for them and the world.

PROBLEMS OF HARMONY IN THE LAST SUPPER

We now begin a rare section of the gospels in which there is some disconcordant material of note between the four evangelists. Of the synoptics, Luke departs in terms of the order of events from Matthew and Mark (he places the institution of communion – Eucharist – near the beginning of the supper, the others nearer the end.) Only John records the washing of the disciples feet. Only Luke records the dispute over who was the greatest, but he leaves out the giving of the sop to Judas and his subsequent departure.

Ordinarily, there is no issue with one writer leaving out what another includes. In many cases, certain of the gospel writers are known for preferring a thematic account rather than a chronological one (John.) But in this section, we have the difficulty of several verses being tied together consecutively with words like "having said this, He . ." This makes it very difficult to break up narrative so as to align it with similar words in the other accounts.

What follows is the best attempt to put all the statements and actions in the Supper into a chronological sequence and not do violence to the accounts themselves as they are, i.e. to not cast unwarranted aspersions on the form chosen for those accounts as being inadequate or lacking. Each was written to emphasize elements thematically, with lesser concern for exact chronology.

"I have earnestly desired to eat this Passover with you before I suffer;

We are told that this was said "when the hour had come." This was not after the Passover meal, called the Paschal supper, but as it was beginning. Jesus is seen taking up the inaugurating position of reclining at table with the disciples, which was done to formally begin the supper.

Originally, the Mosaic prescription in Exodus was that they eat standing, with shoes on their feet and staff in their hand, ready to leave Egypt (Ex 12:11.) Later the Talmud records the traditional change to reclining as a sign of freedom where the need for haste no longer existed.

The procedure of this meal, called the Seder, involved several steps prior to the serving and eating of the dinner itself (the lamb.) Today, there are fifteen steps, ten of which precede the actual meal, and are commemorative and accompanied by the account of the Exodus and other explanations by the host.

These steps also involved what we see later – the offering of the First Cup and later still, Jesus dipping the unleavened bread in the *charoseth* and giving it to Judas. Just before this was the eating of the *maror* – bitter herbs and the charoseth was to take the sting out it, and also represented the sweetness of freedom after the bitterness of slavery. This dipping was the ninth step, followed by a tenth, then followed by the dinner itself.

"before I suffer." Some see in this a hint that Jesus was conducting the supper before the appointed time, since He knew He could not have it with them at the official time. But this phrase does not obligate us to that conclusion, since it can easily mean it is the last He will be able to enjoy with them before ascending. And there are a number of issues in having this supper occur before the appointed time or as another meal altogether.

16 for I say to you, I shall never again eat it until it is fulfilled in the kingdom of God."

We know clearly why He will not eat it again with them in mortality, because He will not be available in the flesh, having risen to the Father. But we also find Him speaking of eating it again in the Kingdom, i.e. it is not finished but rather to be resumed and repeated under other conditions. There are two meanings: a) the time is reserved for the Marriage Supper of the Lamb pictured in the Revelation, hence, He will not be actively an eating participant until then; b) the time is after the ascension when He enters mystically as the Presence in the Eucharist.

The latter is not specifically taught in Catholic doctrine – that the Mass is this fulfillment of Christ resuming His participation because the kingdom is fulfilled. The Mass is not a Passover meal, but a repetition of the receiving of bread and wine as body and blood, something He did specially and uniquely outside the procedure for the Paschal meal on that occasion. Nor in the Mass, is Christ seen as eating the Eucharist with His disciples.

The former then remains the only meaning that succeeds – that He is referring to resuming its celebration with them in the Kingdom gained at the resurrection of the saints – at the Marriage Supper of the Lamb.

There is some hesitancy as to whether it will then be identical or in some sense modified to reflect as Paul tells us, that He has become our Passover lamb (I Cor 5:7.) To be sure, there will be eating of some kind involved.

17 And when He had taken a cup and given thanks, He said, "Take this and share it among yourselves;

This is *not* the cup of the communion, because Luke will later mention that cup and the bread in the traditional manner we recite it in the church today. Instead, this is the first of The Four Cups of the Paschal celebration, offered, prayed over and shared at the beginning of the ceremony.[59]

Jesus also reiterates in specific what was said in general about the Passover – *for I say to you, I will not drink of the fruit of the vine from now on until the kingdom of God comes."*

3 Jesus, . . . 4 got up from supper, and laid aside His garments; and taking a towel, He girded Himself.

Before this act Judas is described as having become the agent of Satan in Jesus' betrayal, which at first seems unconnected to the context of washing the disciples feet. What has Judas' heart being given to Satan have to do with this act?

But this is provided to contrast what Jesus will do in love and humility for all of them. While Judas is ready to betray, Jesus is ready to serve, making the need to betray all the more antithetically out of place. Who betrays a man who is wholly given to the well being of these men?

We are further reminded that this act comes at the juncture of His return to where He came from – *He had come forth from God and was going back to God.*

"He got up from the supper" - to wash their feet.

This is not part of the Seder, nor is this the customary washing at the arrival for a meal. There was a washing of the hands by the host, followed by a similar washing by the guests at a later step, but never was the host seen washing the guests feet.

This is an addition for special reasons in the midst the formal celebration, as later also will be the presentation of the bread and the wine.

He laid aside His outer, more formal cloak, normally done when doing labor. The cloak was bulky for getting up and down or moving along in a squatting position, and was set aside. In poorer people who had only one long outer garment, it was folded up and tied to free the legs.

Jesus girded a towel, which means He wrapped it around His waist in a manner that allowed the larger portion to hang in front, so that He could dry their feet without dragging along the towel.

---

[59] Edersheim, Life and Times of Jesus the Messiah, Eerdmans, 1971, p.496.

"Lord, do You wash my feet?"

Not a question of curiosity but of abhorrence. It's equivalent to "You don't think you're going to wash *my* feet do you?"

"What I do you do not realize now, but you will understand hereafter."

The understanding would come very soon, but at the moment, no one could comprehend why their Lord would do such a thing for them. For all, it should be the reverse. (The Baptist stated this – *"it is I who should be baptized by you."* He realized the place of Jesus and his place below Him.)

"Never shall You wash my feet!"

This is not pride talking, but supreme embarrassment over the unworthiness to have this done to him. Peter knew himself very well, that he was not the most spiritual or patient of men. What bothered him is what bothers us at the thought of this service in modern times – that our sheer position sitting above someone bending low to wash our feet conveys superiority on our part – a sort of master-servant relationship we would never wish to vaunt publicly. That the person is the Lord Jesus was indeed too much to picture in Peter's mind.

But this is precisely the picture and the imagery intended. It is to "permit the humility of service from another."

As for understanding later, none were to let the act done only to them stand, but were to adopt the same role and position for others, hence, the superior impression would be done to death by the reciprocal act.

"If I do not wash you, you have no part with Me."

Why so harsh? Why does this particular conditional have such importance? It is because service is the essence of their ministry. Where human planning would envision and arrange for the perks of management, their ministry will be one of self-deprecation, dis-allegiance to possessions, and suffering at the hands of those being helped. No room for haughty or arrogant spirits.

"Lord, then wash not only my feet, but also my hands and my head."

This is a great credit to Peter's flexibility in the presence of spiritual truth. For the average person today, the response would be one of pause as one weighs the options before them. The sophistication of today's citizen would hesitate the leap we see in Peter – "then do it all and more besides!" Peter has not merely acquiesced to some necessary unpleasantry, but is now fully on board in an instant of time.

"He who has bathed needs only to wash his feet, but is completely clean; and you are clean, but not all of you."

The point is to contrast the person who needs more than a foot washing, because he is elsewhere not clean. One can have recently bathed, yet need the dust of the streets washed away when coming to eat. He is made completely clean because the former bathing has taken care of all but the feet, now completed in the washing.

For the disciples, they are clean from their baptism by our Lord and their work for the Kingdom, therefore the washing of their feet also serves here to symbolize the "lack" of necessity for any further washing.

To contrast this, He now states that someone among them is not thus clean, but needful of the inner cleansing which they all share – *For He knew the one who was betraying Him; for this reason He said, "Not all of you are clean."*

12 [He] reclined at the table again, He said to them, "Do you know what I have done to you?"

There is still need to drive the lesson of the act home. He cannot rely on their getting the picture by mere observation, so He asks them to consider the object in mind for having done this. This is perhaps the primary reason why churches generally do not practice this service today. It levels the playing field among all men and makes all into servants, when many are building mini-empires of notoriety and influence in the Church.

14 .. "If I then, the Lord and the Teacher, washed your feet, you also ought to wash one another's feet."
15 "For I gave you an example that you also should do as I did to you."

It is to be reciprocal among them, that no one person assume a position above servant. The argument against which none could succeed is that if Jesus is Lord and has done this, there remains no excuse for them who are not divine Lords. And Jesus had the best reasons on the planet for exempting Himself from such an act. If He set aside such legitimate claims, we have no standing to avoid it with illegitimate ones.

17 "If you know these things, you are blessed if you do them."

The blessing is not in doing so through ignorance, but in doing so with full knowledge of the humiliating action such duty does to one's pride. To do so in that knowledge is the secret to the blessing it will bring because one is deliberately putting self under for the greater glory of God.

18 "I do not speak of all of you. I know the ones I have chosen; but it is that the Scripture may be fulfilled, `HE WHO EATS MY BREAD HAS LIFTED UP HIS HEEL AGAINST ME.'"

He now turns to the subject of His betrayer. What He has done and what He has commended in them does not apply to the one who is in their midst but no longer of them.

To know the ones chosen is not about knowledge per se. He knows all things. He is rather speaking of that knowing that is intimate with Him, therefore also with His Father. He knows all, including the betrayer. He chose all, including the betrayer, which is reiterated by the OT quote that predicts the irony that such a one will sharing His bread.

This of course tells us that the betrayal was planned as a necessary to the Cross and the work of salvation. Yet Judas will not be able to claim that he served the needs of God, hence, could be found at fault. Judas as a person was not predetermined by the prophecy. His own decisions moved him into the place of fulfilling it.

As for the plan of God, it is a case of God seeing the picture across all time and for all persons and all actions. The plan of the incarnation came first. That necessitated all the issues of invading man's world for good or ill. Logic acknowledged the risk of rejection. Foreknowledge saw that rejection patently so. The prophecy proclaimed the facts including betrayal and the irony of it. But this does not exonerate anyone who played into the role. All persons are still held accountable for their own decisions.

For us as disciples, we often get the impression that we came to Him, that we made the choice. But as He chose His disciples, so He chooses us also - *"No one can come to Me unless the Father who sent Me draws him; and I will raise him up on the last day."* (John 6:44.)

19 "From now on I am telling you before it comes to pass, so that when it does occur, you may believe that I am He.

He surely is telling them ahead of time that they be not overwhelmed at the irony of one among them being the betrayer. But He focuses on the effect being to secure ever more their belief in who He is.

There are two aspects of this. First, purely the effect of prediction and fulfillment to bolster faith, especially in a person. His ability to know this kind of detail ahead of time will assure them again, and to a greater degree, that He is the one He claims to be.

Second – the prediction ahead of time will work against any doubts about His nature and person. The act of Judas could, for the weak in faith, work evil in terms of doubt, by bolstering the Pharisees' case that He is against the true religion by violating Mosaic tradition. It is to forestall any who might reconsider that perhaps Judas has finally done the one right thing – committing Jesus' revolutionary ideas to its long overdue judgment among those who were duty-bound to protect the faith.

He then reiterates His earlier encouragement that those who receive Him are receiving the One who sent Him – a connection to the will of the Father above, who is over all and in whom all things have their being

John 13:21-22, Matthew 26:22, John 13:23-26a, Matthew 26:23-25, John 13:26b-30
21 When Jesus had said this, He became troubled in spirit, and testified and said, "Truly, truly, I say to you, that one of you will betray Me."

22 The disciples began looking at one another, at a loss to know of which one He was speaking. . . . 22 Being deeply grieved, they each one began to say to Him, "Surely not I, Lord?" . . 23 There was reclining on Jesus' bosom one of His disciples, whom Jesus loved. 24 So Simon Peter gestured to him, and said to him, "Tell us who it is of whom He is speaking." 25 He, leaning back thus on Jesus' bosom, said to Him, "Lord, who is it?" 26 Jesus then answered, "That is the one for whom I shall dip the morsel and give it to him." (John 13:21-22, Matthew 26:22, John 13:23-26a.)

24 "The Son of Man is to go, just as it is written of Him; but woe to that man by whom the Son of Man is betrayed! It would have been good for that man if he had not been born." 25 And Judas, who was betraying Him, said, "Surely it is not I, Rabbi?" Jesus said to him, "You have said it yourself." (Matthew 26:23-25.)

26 So when He had dipped the morsel, He took and gave it to Judas, the son of Simon Iscariot. 27 After the morsel, Satan then entered into him. Therefore Jesus said to him, "What you do, do quickly." 28 Now no one of those reclining at the table knew for what purpose He had said this to him. 29 For some were supposing, because Judas had the money box, that Jesus was saying to him, "Buy the things we have need of for the feast"; or else, that he should give something to the poor. 30 So after receiving the morsel he went out immediately; and it was night. (John 13:26b-30.)

Commentary

He became troubled in spirit, . . "Truly, truly, I say to you, that one of you will betray Me."

This follows His encouragement that those who receive Him receive the Father. The change in mood is not from becoming aware of the fact of the betrayal – He has known this from the beginning. And since this is a necessary part of the redemption plan, we find it hard to understand what would be troubling about something known so far in advance.

Rather, this is more about the person of Judas himself. There will be a betrayer according to prophecy, but woe to him by whom it comes. Jesus had invested Himself in all of them, including Judas, and we can't really assume that in his case, Jesus did so tongue in cheek. His purity in spirit would have offered Judas as much sincere nurture and appeal to righteousness as the others.

Hence, that Judas rejected this and was bent on the execution of his evil mission is troubling, not in its facticity, but in what it means to Jesus' relationship with the man.

Another source of this troubling is the sheer magnitude of what is about to happen. Knowing the outcome in advance does not assuage the impact of that truth when time comes to effect it in reality. It means the engines that will precipitate so arduous an end are on the verge of ignition and spin up.

one of you will betray me. This has to be reiterated several times because it is frankly an irony too bizarre to imagine. It is almost painfully exemplary of the human condition. Man cannot manage the affairs of righteousness cleanly and purely, but seems inevitably destined to tarnish its purity with his imperfections and propensities toward evil. So it is, even among those He has chosen – one among them will betray Him; will play into the hands of His enemies with a mind thinking to be doing right but upsetting the work of God. Man will always be to some extent reticent, conflicted, hesitant to relinquish control over self to the Master of the Universe. And in that reticence, in that divided heart lies all his troubles.

It is quite natural that because He is so specific that it is one among them at that very moment, they begin the query as to who it could be – *looking at one another, at a loss to know of which one He was speaking.* Hence, come the many individual questions, "Is it I?", "Surely not I, Lord."

23 There was reclining on Jesus' bosom one of His disciples, whom Jesus loved.

From this we have some idea of who sat where at the table. The one whom Jesus loved has been traditionally identified as John. This makes sense since he would have been named if this were another writer, as Peter is named in just a moment. This is John's own account, so humility is appropriate in talking about himself as merely a certain person. That he is close enough to lean on Jesus' chest, John is obviously immediately next to Him in the seating arrangement.

Since Jesus will later state that the betrayer is one with whom He dips at the table, Judas would be immediately to the other side of Jesus.

24 So Simon Peter gestured to him, and said to him, "Tell us who it is of whom He is speaking."

We learn here of Peter's position in relation to the others. In the arrangement of the supper, the table was not a long surface where all lined up along one side, nor did some sit on its opposite side, since the arrangement of the table for the Seder is now well known – a triclinium.

Rather, the table consisted of a set of tables formed into a U-shape, open at one end. The center was for serving and removing dishes, while guests sat around the outside edge facing in.

That Peter does not ask Jesus directly but asked John, reveals that he was either too far away to ask Jesus in a normal tone, or Jesus was now distracted by the others, and John was appealed to in the hopes he had heard. But John is not more privy to the identification - *He, leaning back thus on Jesus' bosom, said to Him, "Lord, who is it?"*

26 Jesus then answered, "That is the one for whom I shall dip the morsel and give it to him."

John, Matthew and Mark differ as to the time of the dipping. Here in John, the dipping is said to be about to happen in a future moment – shall dip = *'bapso'* – future active indicative.

In Matthew, it is definitely past – having dipped = *'embapsas'* aorist participle.

In Mark it is present – is dipping *'embapsomenos'* present middle participle.

Suffice it to say that each of the writers saw this condition differently. People in proximity dipped the matzah into the mixture often, so it could be said either way – "the one who has been dipping with me" or "the one who dips with me", meaning has dipped and continues to dip.

But John uses future, perhaps because he will also recount how Jesus actually gives the sop to Judas, and since this is future, he understands the identification to be more a prediction tied to that act, hence future.

But just before revealing the betrayer using the sop, He takes a moment to share its poignancy first -

24 "The Son of Man is to go, just as it is written of Him; but woe to that man by whom the Son of Man is betrayed!"

It is decreed that Christ must "go" (as in go to His death), but no man can justify his act in enabling that death by appealing to divine purposes. Again, each man is responsible for his actions. That God has willed the death does not exonerate those who effect it. (God used Babylon to judge Judah, but then judged Babylon for being of the mind to be so used.)

In terms of responsibility and predestined will, were it a case that God knew no Jew would in fact be as bold as to betray or arrest and kill Messiah, Christ's sacrifice would have come about some other way. In other words, the necessity that He should die did not make necessary that Judas or the Pharisees must sin to effect it.

24 .. "It would have been good for that man if he had not been born."

To call the alternative that a man be not born a good thing is to emphasize the grave magnitude of the crime. No matter how much our modern culture promotes the mindset of the second chance, no matter how much we are conditioned to believe that all men have some good in them and harsh judgment eliminates all opportunity for restoration, the act of complicity in Christ's death is too large, of too great a magnitude to be rationalized in this manner.

When we realize that the history of creation past and the future yet to come centers on the Person and nature of Christ and what He accomplished among men, His betrayal cannot be assuaged by the generosity of liberal minds. It's affront to Heaven and all that is holy calls for just accountability. Its severity and the eternal anguish of knowing what one has done easily and appropriately rise to the level of wishing one's life had never even happened.

25 And Judas, who was betraying Him, said, "Surely it is not I, Rabbi?" Jesus said to him, "You have said it yourself."

On the heels of hearing what awaits such a betrayer, we find Judas actually asking if it is he. Some have attributed the question to the clever move of covering his intentions – to be seen as among all the others equally puzzled. This certainly goes along with the insidious nature of what Satan is doing in him. A mock question would be clever and elusive.

But with the rather devastating indictments just spoken, we cannot fail to appreciate the enormous weight of conviction this had to have imposed. To the recalcitrant agent of Satan, there would be a sort of cynical dismissal in the mind. But hardly this question, in the light of such sure words of one's doom. He now knows himself to be precisely the very man.

It is almost as if there is suddenly a brief window of disbelief that he has entered into these arrangements to his own jeopardy. It is like asking, "Have I really done this to my master or is there some hope remaining that He is talking about someone else." Hence, the feeble, yet much too late – "Surely it is not I?"

Jesus said to him, "You have said it yourself."

Were it a cynical question with ulterior motives, we would expect Jesus to be ominously silent. We might expect that Jesus would disrespect the question by turning rather to the group at large with more statements like the previous.

That he says this to Judas personally, indicates some level of compassion at Judas' plight. All that comprises the circumstances in which he finds himself are the result of his own words, and even here now, his question is turned into an affirmative admission, but sadly so, and without anger.

26 So when He had dipped the morsel, He took and gave it to Judas, the son of Simon Iscariot.

Now comes the signaling action. Now that the expectation is out in the open, now that Judas has been made to know that Jesus knows, he his given the sop and told to do his deed in haste.

The morsel is in other translations called the 'sop.' It is most frequently understood to mean a piece of matso (unleavened bread) dipped in the charoseth (a mixture of crushed nuts, apples, cinnamon, and honey.) Because the cracker easily soaks up the moisture, it becomes sop-like, but not to the degree that it falls apart. Much like sticking a cookie in hot chocolate, just the right amount of time produces a result that can be taken safely to the mouth. Too long and it falls apart.

Others more familiar with the Jewish tradition and the tractate on Pesach (Passover) in the Talmud, understand that by the time of Jesus, the unleavened bread was combined with the herbs and wrapped in a small piece of the lamb to make a sort of sandwich, which was then dipped. This makes more sense since the accounts use the phrase "while they were eating" which seems more applicable if the pieces were not just matso and sauce.

The reason also for specifying Iscariot is to not confuse Jesus' gesture as condemning the other Judas, whom we know as Jude, the brother of James who was the brother of the Lord, making Judas also the brother of Jesus (Matthew 13:55.)

27 After the morsel, Satan then entered into him.

We learned of this possession earlier (luke 22:3) in relation to the first meeting with the Pharisees. It is assumed that these "take overs" were transitory and were repeated when needed.

As to being possessed of the devil, the effect is not always to take on the dark and craven appearances we associate with it. Here, Judas is still rational to continue to conduct the business at hand with the Pharisees and lead them later to the place of prayer in the garden.

But to be sure, those who so yield their lives to Satan will become such persons of altered states, principally because his aim is to destroy. Judas simply did not live long enough to become the raving madman Jesus healed near the Mount of Transfiguration. (Matthew 17:15.)

Jesus said to him, "What you do, do quickly."

We might ask why Jesus would encourage speed in arranging for such a physically horrifying experience as His scourging and Crucifixion. We would be encouraging as much delay as possible. Nor does there seem to be a concern that if he delays he might not succeed.

What does seem more to account for the need for haste is the divine time table according to which all the next day must operate. There is the weekly Sabbath that will close the activity of the next day earlier than planned, although provisions were made for executions that ran into or even began on the Sabbath. Such concerns might influence the authorities to hold Jesus until Sunday.

The important thing is that the exact timing for Jesus' being on the Cross and dying was of great importance to the Father. We have every assurance that the very hour was appointed in Heaven, therefore the encouragement to haste ensured it all the more.

As for timing, Jesus dying at the ninth hour (3:00 PM) would have coincided with the feast offerings of the 15th of Nisan, called the second Chagigah according to the Jerusalem Talmud (Pes. 6.3, 6.4.)

28 Now no one of those reclining at the table knew for what purpose He had said this to him.

The statement to Judas was overheard but not understood. But also this confusion reveals that they did not notice the sop given to Judas, else they would certainly have made the connection of the announcement that the betrayer was dipping with Him, followed by the giving of the sop, followed by Jesus' exhortation to do his deed quickly.

The sheer fact of confusion about what Judas was being asked to do in haste or that it concerned the provisions for the feast, makes it clear that the conjoining steps respecting an identification had escaped their immediate notice.

We should note that the giving of the sop did not immediately follow the prediction that it was someone with whom He dipped. There was the intervening speech about the fate of the one who betrays Him. Then the sop was given. The routine plenitude of hands at bowls would make this particular distinction inconclusive if observation were the key means.

because Judas had the money box, that Jesus was saying to him, "Buy the things we have need of for the feast";

This is a supposition of theirs, but it gives us a very important piece of information about whether this was a true Passover meal or not. If Judas could be supposed as needing to buy provisions for a feast yet to come, that feast could not have been the regular Passover, despite the appeal that this would then coincide with the Jews' fear of being defiled concerning it.

If the feast meant the Passover dinner, Judas would have had the entire next day to purchase provisions, there was no need for haste. But if the feast was the first day of the following Passover evening, it was a holy day with needs for participation beginning early, making the need to buy last minute provisions more likely.[60]

30 So after receiving the morsel he went out immediately; and it was night.

Exeunt Judas. There is of course no other reason for him to stay. Any longer would be a sham and Jesus had in essence dismissed him. Important also is the need to exclude Judas from the communion ceremony about to take place. If Paul cautioned believers from taking of the elements unworthily, could Jesus have allowed an agent of Satan to participate in its inaugurating moment?

---

[60] Mishna Sabbath, 23,2; Edersheim, ibid, p. 508.

Matthew 26:26-29, Luke 22:21-40, John 13:31-36, 38

26 While they were eating, Jesus took some bread, and after a blessing, He broke it and gave it to the disciples, and said, "Take, eat; this is My body." 27 And when He had taken a cup and given thanks, He gave it to them, saying, "Drink from it, all of you; 28 for this is My blood of the covenant, which is poured out for many for forgiveness of sins. 29 "But I say to you, I will not drink of this fruit of the vine from now on until that day when I drink it new with you in My Father's kingdom." . . But behold, the hand of the one betraying Me is with Mine on the table.(Matthew 26:26-29, Luke 22:21.)

And they began to discuss among themselves which one of them it might be who was going to do this thing (Luke 22:23)

24 And there arose also a dispute among them as to which one of them was regarded to be greatest. 25 And He said to them, "The kings of the Gentiles lord it over them; and those who have authority over them are called `Benefactors.' 26 "But it is not this way with you, but the one who is the greatest among you must become like the youngest, and the leader like the servant. 27 "For who is greater, the one who reclines at the table or the one who serves? Is it not the one who reclines at the table? But I am among you as the one who serves. 28 "You are those who have stood by Me in My trials; 29 and just as My Father has granted Me a kingdom, I grant you 30 that you may eat and drink at My table in My kingdom, and you will sit on thrones judging the twelve tribes of Israel. (Luke 22:24-30.)

31 . . . "Now is the Son of Man glorified, and God is glorified in Him; 32 if God is glorified in Him, God will also glorify Him in Himself, and will glorify Him immediately. 33 "Little children, I am with you a little while longer. You will seek Me; and as I said to the Jews, now I also say to you, `Where I am going, you cannot come.' 34 "A new commandment I give to you, that you love one another, even as I have loved you, that you also love one another. 35 "By this all men will know that you are My disciples, if you have love for one another."

36 Simon Peter said to Him, "Lord, where are You going?" Jesus answered, "Where I go, you cannot follow Me now; but you will follow later." 37 Peter said to Him, "Lord, why can I not follow You right now? I will lay down my life for You." (John 13:31-36.)

31 "Simon, Simon, behold, Satan has demanded permission to sift you like wheat; 32 but I have prayed for you, that your faith may not fail; and you, when once you have turned again, strengthen your brothers." 33 But he said to Him, "Lord, with You I am ready to go both to prison and to death!" 34 And He said, "I say to you, Peter, the rooster will not crow today until you have denied three times that you know Me." . . But Peter kept saying insistently, "Even if I have to die with You, I will not deny You!" (Luke 22:31-34, Mark 14:31.)

38 Jesus answered, "Will you lay down your life for Me? Truly, truly, I say to you, a rooster will not crow until you deny Me three times. (John 13:38.)

Commentary

26 While they were eating, Jesus took some bread,

As stated earlier, this is not a step in the normal Paschal meal. There are cups of wine taken at certain steps and there are pieces of unleavened bread taken at other steps. There may even be moments where the taking of the matzah is followed by wine for digestive reasons rather than for ceremonial ones.

But one is hard-pressed to find these ceremonially conjoined quite the same way in Pesach or in resemblance of what Jesus now demonstrates.

and after a blessing, He broke it and gave it to the disciples, and said, "Take, eat; this is My body."

First of note is that this bread is to be shared among them. It is meant to be taken in as opposed to consecrated and left as a symbolic offering.

We must not neglect the intrinsic connection to John 6:53ff, where Jesus made it clear that all must eat His flesh and drink His blood, else have no part in Him. So enigmatic was this, that some drew back and *'walked with Him no more.'* The Pharisees who heard this thought he actually meant cannibalism or literally partaking of His flesh and blood. So exceedingly rigorous was His meaning (which was not re-stated when He saw that the Jews understood it literally) that we are obliged to correct the opposite extreme – that these were purely symbolic injunctions never meant to be taken farther than that.

Thus, there must be a way in which we would incorporate as much literality as we can without venturing the insane or irrational.

That He did not intend the extreme literalism which the Pharisees mistakenly concluded is evident in the fact that when it came to demonstrating His meaning from John 6:53, He chose bread and wine as elements. He did not extend His arms to the group that they partake literally of His flesh, nor did He open His veins when exhorting them to drink. Hence, we are at least one step removed from an absolute literality in the direction of substitutionary symbols.

I Cor 11:24 adds, *"which is broken for you,"* the addition of which is bolstered by the fact that Jesus here breaks the bread in giving it to them.

But this flies in the face of Psalms 34:20, predicting no bones of Him be broken, fulfilled when the soldiers neglected the breaking of His legs on the cross; and Exodus 12:46 – the law respecting the Passover lamb, that no bones of it be broken in the preparation, roasting and eating.

The breaking of His body therefore must refer to the damage done to it from the scourging, nails, and effects of crucifixion. In Psalms 22:14 we have the testimony of Messiah, *"I am poured out like water, And all my bones are out of joint; My heart is like wax; It is melted within me"* which is not the breaking of bones, but certainly what we might recognize as the breaking of the body.

The exhortation of remembrance concerns our frequent recollection that He gave His body to suffer, that such suffering is what effected the death so necessary for our salvation.

27 And when He had taken a cup . . . "Drink from it, all of you; 28 for this is My blood of the covenant, which is poured out for many for forgiveness of sins.

Again, we have a theme that these are given for remembrance – remembering that His blood was poured out" and its purpose, for the forgiveness of sins. We are to be certain in our minds that without the shedding of blood there can be no forgiveness of sins (Heb 9:22.) This is to say that God has established in His economy of balancing the scales between sin and restoration, that blood be shed. The explanation of which is not given in detailed excursus. We have in Moses the statement that the life is in the blood (Gen 9:4, Lev 17:11) therefore we can marry this with the strong statement that the soul that sins shall forfeit his life. In this, a life is to be given for payment, but it appears that the principle accommodates equally as efficacious a substitutionary sacrifice for that of the perpetrator.

Thus the offer of His body to be brutalized and damaged for us and His blood to be shed should be regular points of remembrance and appropriation for us as we live for Him. They are the fundamental means by which we have any approach to God as sinners.

But also there is more in observing the words, "this is My body . . . this is my blood." In them we have a doctrine being presented. His disciples are to regard them as His body and blood, not as mere unleavened bread or mere wine. This means they are to regard themselves as eating His body and drinking His blood as they partake, not merely remembering His sacrifice as they eat the approved symbols established for it.

This, the Protestant churches often miss in communion, compared to the Catholic Eucharist. They portray the elements as remembrances, but seldom teach the actual eating of Christ in the ordinance. In some marvelous way we do not understand, Jesus is establishing a procedure and elements by which we eat His flesh and drink His blood. The implication is that He then inhabits the elements or that they become His flesh and blood in some way unexplainable.

For the Catholic, it is a small jump to the notion that the bread and wine are necessarily transformed by our Lord, signaled by the tinkling of the bells at every Mass.

Protestants resist this degree of extension by lack of the mechanics of this described in Scripture, except for the more vague words, "This is My body" which can be meant spiritually just as powerfully as it can be meant physically. But from a purely thematic point of view, Catholics can be seen as living closer to the import of John 6 than Protestants, but one must also face the issue of how far the literality of transformation of actual substance can be taken, given the bare facts in the NT itself.

The Holy Church presents that this has been the teaching of the Church since the apostles, yet the specific details of a transubstantiation that bear on the physics involved are missing, being similarly ambiguous in employing words like "they are His Body and Blood." In other words, the farther away one gets in time from the apostles, the more one hears of the physical change in substance for the elements in Church teaching. The closer one gets to the apostles, the more this teaching resembles Jesus' simple words – "This is My body" – which really doesn't inform us about literal transubstantiation any more than a purely spiritual, representative transformation. And honesty might serve us to conclude that such vagueness was intentional on our Lord's part.

Where Protestants err (or do some disservice to the importance at hand) is in making these purely symbolic, for remembrance-sake only, and leaving out, without much comment at all, the eating of flesh and blood, which all believers are commanded to embrace and affirm according to John chapter 6.

A better Protestant view is that we become one with the Christ of the communion table by partaking of the elements that represent partaking of Him. Where there is no physical union as food assimilated into our body, there is Christ taken within by means of His indwelling Spirit, which is to devour Jesus and take Him down into our lives that His presence assimilate to every inch of our being. We become unified with Him in giving up ourselves to Him.

29 "But I say to you, I will not drink of this fruit of the vine from now on until that day when I drink it new with you in My Father's kingdom."

A reiteration of the preamble He gave at the beginning of the supper. Some infer that this forever closes the earthly practice of the Passover in favor of Christian communion as its replacement, but the words cannot be pressed that far. There may be other reasons for ending Passover as historically and mosaically obligatory, but as for these particular words, we must remember that Jesus is talking about "His" participation as partaker of the wine, not every Jew's participation. He is telling them "He" will not share it with them again until an appointed time. This is not the equivalent of ending Passover, since it was never conditional on Him being co-partaker with them.

There is, however, the clear notion that Christ is now our Passover lamb, for which none need to be offered in the future. Thus, we see in Church practice a clear supplanting of Passover with the Eucharist and Protestant communion. And this may be the real import of His words here – that something intermediate it now to be instituted until the appointed time.

24 And there arose also a dispute among them as to which one of them was regarded to be greatest.

This had come up before (Luke 9:46, Mark 9:34.) It is a weakness of our human nature to appreciate advancement in learning and abilities and to begin to make assessments of ranking and value compared to others. This was furthered in them by Jesus' hint that there were levels of estimation in servants of God (John the Baptist was greatest among those born of woman yet a different assessment would be made for any citizen of the Kingdom - Matt 11:11.)

As for the error in assuming assessments at all, Jesus does not rebuke them, as if this whole idea would have been foreign to the Kingdom. (With the mother of James and John, Jesus affirms that there are in fact places reserved at His right hand and left, but to whom these will be given is not be known in the present age - John 20:23.)

Instead of outright rebuke, He teaches them kindly and poignantly -

"The kings of the Gentiles lord it over them; and those who have authority over them are called `Benefactors.'

This is likewise a reprise of the discussion presented earlier in which Jesus declares Himself a ransom for many (Matt 20:28.) It's point and reiteration is to drive home the strong notion that they are to be different than the strong men of the world, the benefactors to society. In every culture and nation around them, men who were influential and possessed ruling prowess have been given charge of affairs from businesses to governments. But such men are marked by arrogance about their abilities, a haughty nature that follows the logic: if there are lords then there are servants.

They are called benefactors in that this has been the chosen means by which God preserves order and well being in society. He has willed that human governments be instituted to punish and deter evil and reward the good and the righteous. We may complain that this has not worked out very well, but that is ultimately more a matter between God and individual responsibility than some malady with the principle itself. In general, He has embued goodness and ability into men with respect to the affairs of society, and to a large extent this works, and has worked for the history of man. That there will be exceptions making some grief for those ruled is the inevitability that comes with fallen man. But we must recognize that this does not move Him to have angels govern the affairs of men.

27 "For who is greater, the one who reclines at the table or the one who serves? Is it not the one who reclines at the table?

Here, He appeals to common sense, i.e. it is the one who reclines at table who is greater. Those serving are of a lower station in life, evidenced by the patent fact that they are not among those reclining at the table. They were not invited to the event to partake. They were brought there to serve, and that difference cannot be avoided in the reality of human affairs. They are not inferior as persons, but their station – the function they serve in society – is not equal to others, in that some are more important by virtue of what they can contribute.

You cannot for the sake of equality and equal opportunity take the average person in society and set him or her down in a corporate CEO's desk and expect equality of contribution. Nor is it just a matter of education. It is not a matter of just providing the opportunity. There are those who have been given the capacity to lead and manage affairs of great magnitude and others who haven't, no matter how much education they receive.

Jesus is merely appealing to the normal expectation in society.

But I am among you as the one who serves.

Having legitimized the common sense of the above, He tells them plainly that this is *not* to be their mode of operation – they are to operate counter-intuitively to what has just been affirmed. And He teaches this by telling them that He Himself is among them as one who serves (He being the greatest above all men would certainly be inferred as exempt.) Yet if He is not exempt, then neither are they.

And the service to which He refers respecting Himself is that which they have just recently observed – the washing of their feet. Not that this constitutes the service being now discussed, but the *attitude* of service being discussed. Thus He clarifies and reinforces with " *"But it is not this way with you, but the one who is the greatest among you must become like the youngest, and the leader like the servant."*

28 "You are those who have stood by Me in My trials;

As for privilege and rank, He affirms their place in relation to Him – it is they compared to others who have not disassociated themselves from His trials and reviling. That is to be rewarded, but not in terms of position and hierarchy in earthly terms – *" I grant you that you may eat and drink at My table in My kingdom,"*

That is where the reward and recognition is to be given. And it is based on the unassailable truth that the Father has given the Son a Kingdom. Similarly then shall He have authority to grant them to partake at His table.

There are some who might venture that this then applies to the Twelve above all other believers and we as subsequent followers should not expect such a partaking. But if we come to be governed by what governed them, as we come to serve as they served, there is every expectation that all who emulate His chosen disciples would share places with them. But as to how far this can be pressed to serve as doctrine will not concern those who take Him at His word about being servants, since those with that attitude will be thankful merely to be in the Kingdom. To be concerned about our equal place at tables and such is the very thing being rebuked in this lesson. Hence, those who choose to incorporate such things into the pantheon of necessary doctrines are unwittingly revealing their failure to grasp its message.

and you will sit on thrones judging the twelve tribes of Israel.

This is a profound extension, considering the lack of excursus of its meaning here or elsewhere. It is profound because in the disciples' minds the universality of the twelve tribes of Israel throughout their history has been virtually sacrosanct. No mortal person would have entertained the authority to judge them, yet this is part of the new order for which Jesus has been vilified by the authorities.

It fits with all the overturned attitudes and approaches that have held sway in the past. It is an essential part of a legitimate concept of dispensational history. While some teachers have made more of this principle than could be borne out in Scripture, there is no doubt that the changes Jesus has taught about can only be adequately explained in terms of a change in dispensation – the way God will now deal with man.

There is no question that the laws of the Sabbath were meant to be followed, not merely reasoned in the heart. The man who so reasoned in the days of Moses was stoned to death for picking up sticks. He did not get away with letting his heart be his guide about the Law.

Jesus has now asked that man consider the dictates of a heart of righteousness in respect to the Law – that compassion to heal a man on the Sabbath supplants the letter of the Law. But they would not have been able to get that from the Law itself. It made no provision to do what one's heart told them was best.

That is why this change can only be explained in terms of a changing dispensation. The Law served its purpose until the revelation of Christ. Now the curtain has been eternally rent concerning that mode of operation, that mode of approach. That is why the disciples could violate the letter of the Sabbath without impunity. The role of the exact letter of the Law was changing. And this accounts for the whole problem between Jesus and the Pharisees. Things were changing and they could not countenance it. They were not being abolished, but were being fulfilled into a new order going forward.

As for the judging, we see thrones in the Revelation and crowns of judgment, but not a clear picture of who judges whom. There are now twenty-four thrones, presumably twelve for the tribes and twelve for the apostles. But it is this verse that establishes that the new work of the apostles in Christ will grant them the higher authority to judge the acts and works of the old dispensation, because, frankly, the Scripture teaches that all was accomplished there pointed to Christ *"the Law was our schoolmaster to point us to Christ"* (Gal 3:24.)

31 . . . "Now is the Son of Man glorified, and God is glorified in Him; 32 . . . God will also glorify Him in Himself, and will glorify Him immediately.

Jesus is describing the extensive nature of reciprocation between Father and Son. As the Father is glorified by what the Son does, He will also glorify the Son in His own power and will. That this is "immediate" does not point to some event just about to happen that very minute, but to the Heavenly estate in which all things are happening at that very moment, outside the sight of man but in full view of God and its inhabitants.

It is to say that the reciprocal glorification is instantaneously effected because of the union between them. And that this is seen immediately in Heaven and will be seen also at the proper time to those on the earth.

33 "Little children, I am with you a little while longer. You will seek Me; and as I said to the Jews, now I also say to you, `Where I am going, you cannot come.'

In this vein He begins the reminder that He is departing to the Father and the time is but short until then. But He masks the exactitude of this transition in more vague terms. Rather than specifically describing where, He tells them He is going where they cannot come. This will prompt some to ask where and can they come also.

We get the "just visiting this planet" connotation from His words. We are brought back into the reality that He pre-existed elsewhere in the counsels of God and is now returning. As such, we are amazed that none of what has happened or will happen the next day will manage to effect His return.

What is ironically horrifying is that He was born into the world in beauty and loving care. But He will not be able to leave it until the world has exacted its penalty for having come. It is as though all the world's ugliness and evil is wreaking the fullness of its hatred as His foot is out the door. Certainly, a bitter testimony of man's hospitality to the Son of God.

34 "A new commandment I give to you, that you love one another, . . . 35 "By this all men will know that you are My disciples, if you have love for one another."

It is not new in the sense of never having been heard before. But new in terms of the next thing now commanded. We find this reiterated and appropriated best in John the Apostle as he writes his epistles. He was so well known for having this as his theme in all his sermons and addresses.

Jesus conditions their love for one another on Himself – *"as I have loved you, also love one another."* The expectation of supernatural love as He possessed is a tall order. But there is also another aspect we can appreciate immediately.

He encountered and engaged them being the Perfect from Heaven. Every imperfection would have been unnervingly obvious. To know all that He knew and accept them anyway sets Him apart in the depth and nature of His love. But He asks that since He can do it knowing what He knows, we are less excusable from doing it, lacking what He knows. We have less reasons in terms of sheer knowledge to be critical.

Hence, the command is not as arduous as He must love, but is do-able, and so is reasonably commanded.

They are further to be known by their love for one another. It will be so very opposite to the way the world operates. The reason they are to be known by this is that they are being chosen to demonstrate what God is like before men, and He accepts all men in all their weaknesses and foibles. By showing love for each other, people will see a glimpse of the God being preached and will long for that love also.

36 Simon Peter said to Him, "Lord, where are You going?"

Jesus has been vague about the details, so we expect Peter and the others wanting to know more. But there is a real heart's plea here as well. He has become beloved of them and we cannot embrace easily the idea that one so dearly loved must depart, especially when it is unclear when and where they will see Him again.

They are realizing they are coming to the end, and it has been far too brief. We can imagine it almost being tearful, as a child might crack his small voice in wanting to know where daddy is going and why he can't come.

We see this in Peter's, *"Lord, why can I not follow You right now?*

Remembering now that the place to which His master must go is into the hands of His enemies, Peter adds that he will lay down his life for Him. And Jesus must remind him of the serious things his boldness entails.

31 "Simon, Simon, behold, Satan has demanded permission to sift you like wheat;

A very interesting verse because it speaks of Satan's relationship to believers and how much permission vs. protection Christ allows.

Satan esteems Christians in terms of their potential affect on his work. Concerning many, Satan might likely say: 'No problem. Take no thought about them.' Then there are those about whom he might say: 'Big trouble. We need to deal with them.'

Peter was of the latter group – big trouble – and Jesus was in fact apprised that Satan had specifically requested to sift him like wheat. We recall the negotiations in Heaven concerning Job (1:1ff.) Such trifling and testing of God's servants is by permission, which tells us that Satan cannot cross certain lines on his own. (This gives us insight into the strength behind Paul's encouragement that we are not tempted beyond that which we are able – according to God's command of our very lives – I Cor 10:13.)

The image or sifting wheat is not especially picturesque of trials and persecution, nor does it seem to be apt to temptations. Sifting wheat ordinarily ferrets out impurities gathered in the harvesting process It results in the finer, purer material being left behind. This is hardly Satan's motive.

Rather, Satan is sifting to discover the bad, that it be used for his purposes. His ferreting out is to use the bad, not cast it away. To sift a man is to separate him from himself in ways that expose his propensity for evil and exploit it.

As we apply this picture to our own lives, we should be asking ourselves whether we are in the group about whom Satan says, "No problem" or are we in the other group about whom he is gravely concerned because we greatly threaten the success of his efforts.

32 but I have prayed for you, that your faith may not fail; and you, "

Notice, that Jesus doesn't indicate that Satan's request was denied. Satan has asked to do something whose purpose is the downfall and despoiling of a believer, and the Father has permitted it. The response of Jesus is that He will pray that Peter's faith not fail.

We often pray for deliverance, when God is more interested in endurance by faith. There are exceptions and we should not become fatalistic in assuming there is no remedy in God at all – that we will merely suffer all things with little advantage. He heals and delivers, but according to His will.

32 . . "when once you have turned again, strengthen your brothers.

The Greek has *'epistrepsas'* from epistrepho, which means to turn back again to one's former state. It gives here the hint that there will be a turning away in the course of Satan's affects, but it will not be successful since there is the clear prediction that he will turn back again and that position is characterized as being ready for the strengthening of the brethren.

Some might offer that no failing is to be seen in this and that *epistrepsas* describes Peter's turning away from Satan's taunts and temptations, but the word implies in its meaning a return from the latter to the former, meaning one has not simply emboldened one's current state. It is a turning again to one's original state, implying that the immediate state is away from that to which one now turns back.

The prayer is not that Peter never stumble ever in this testing, but that his faith not fail, which is that his faith not give out.

"Lord, with You I am ready to go both to prison and to death!"

Peter is obviously bolstered in this confidence that principalities and powers are contending for him, so much so that he ventures a boldness about which he is still largely ignorant. Again, his faithfulness is in the long scope of his life as an apostle, not in every singular event he will encounter. Ironically, he mentions prison and death respecting which the very next evening he will be seen to fail. Jesus knows the truth about his promise -

"I say to you, Peter, the rooster will not crow today until you have denied three times that you know Me."

This is, of course, the proof text that Jesus' words about Peter's unfailing faith did not mean never failing in any respect ever. Jesus not only knows the fact of the denials but the signaling condition by which time they will have all occurred. It is an unassailable prediction to be that precise. It has every semblance of being completely true. There is solid expectation in testing the outcome because the expectation follows so rigidly from the conditions stated – the third crowing of the day.

Despite this, Peter insists in his loyalty, as the parallel in Mark states, *But Peter kept saying insistently, "Even if I have to die with You, I will not deny You!"* (14:31.)

We need to be compassionate with Peter's later denials despite his courage here. As he later stands by the fire while Jesus entertains serious trouble at the hands of the high priest within, he is certainly reminded that association with Jesus would mean the same punishment. He is not facing a merely unpleasant incarceration and the deprivations of prison. Roman scourging was merciless and brutal, often meted out by soldiers who delighted in the suffering they were causing. There was often a certain lack of care and control from superiors that left criminals at the discretion of their tormenters. Abuses might be handled merely by harsh words, but not before the damage had been suffered.

This had to play on Peter's mind as a more severe consequence than he had realized, and standing at the fire, he was at the very demarcation line between peace and well-being and indescribable suffering. The reality of that causes one to think long and hard about their decisions and whether they have the courage to cross the line and change everything.

To bolster their confidence that they will be provided all that they need, including the faith to endure, Jesus reminds them of His provision in their ministry -

John 14:1-15

1 "Do not let your heart be troubled; believe in God, believe also in Me. 2 "In My Father's house are many dwelling places; if it were not so, I would have told you; for I go to prepare a place for you. 3 "If I go and prepare a place for you, I will come again and receive you to Myself, that where I am, there you may be also. 4 "And you know the way where I am going."

5 Thomas said to Him, "Lord, we do not know where You are going, how do we know the way?" 6 Jesus said to him, "I am the way, and the truth, and the life; no one comes to the Father but through Me. 7 "If you had known Me, you would have known My Father also; from now on you know Him, and have seen Him." 8 Philip said to Him, "Lord, show us the Father, and it is enough for us." 9 Jesus said to him, "Have I been so long with you, and yet you have not come to know Me, Philip? He who has seen Me has seen the Father; how can you say, `Show us the Father'? 10 "Do you not believe that I am in the Father, and the Father is in Me? The words that I say to you I do not speak on My own initiative, but the Father abiding in Me does His works.

11 "Believe Me that I am in the Father and the Father is in Me; otherwise believe because of the works themselves. 12 "Truly, truly, I say to you, he who believes in Me, the works that I do, he will do also; and greater works than these he will do; because I go to the Father. 13 "Whatever you ask in My name, that will I do, so that the Father may be glorified in the Son. 14 "If you ask Me anything in My name, I will do it.

Commentary

1 "Do not let your heart be troubled; believe in God, believe also in Me.

This whole line of discussion is quite naturally making them all uneasy and carries much foreboding. Jesus takes a moment to reassure them that they are not to let these things weigh down their hearts. To succeed in this He exhorts them to believe in God, and also in Him. This may seem too obvious, but we will see why He says this in a moment.

'pisteuete' is both the 2nd person plural indicative (you believe) and the 2nd person plural imperative (believe!), depending on context. When accompanied by other commands, it is to be taken as an imperative, as it is in Mark 1:15 – *"repent and believe."*

This command is important at this very juncture because they are being asked to believe in one who is about to be arrested and treated as a criminal against the nation. It is a word that says, "My Father is in control of the situation and I in the middle of it. Don't let these things worry you."

2 "In My Father's house are many dwelling places; if it were not so, I would have told you; for I go to prepare a place for you.

Among the most comforting and hopeful statements in the NT. By dwelling places they are to understand that these are for them – places of abode. As they had earthly homes before beginning with Him, there is a parallel plane in which dwellings and homes also exist in the heavenly state, waiting for them to continue life there in some semblance of similarity to here.

This hints that death is not an ending but merely a transition. The concept is one of a continuum of consciousness in which death merely changes the scenery and place - "we shall all be changed in the twinkling of an eye." Scripture does speak of the dead as those who sleep (I Cor 15:6) but this is seen as from the external point of view – the repose of the dead as their bodies are buried. Paul also clearly states that to be absent out of the body is to be present with Christ (2 Cor 5:8.)

"for I go to prepare a place for you."

Adding to the comfort that such places are there waiting for us is the knowledge now that it is He who actually prepares them. This is a bit counterintuitive as we see Him on earth in rather austere and bleak circumstances. There are no royal appointments in His here and now, but stark and minimalistic surroundings – "the Son of Man has nowhere to lay His head."

But this is the Creator speaking, who is soon to return to scenes of indescribable glory. If He prepares these dwellings for us, what wonders, beauty and comfort await us? He, above all, will know how to furnish and fit rooms in the grandest style, not according to man's decadent tastes, but to that glory which once innately inspired them.

We will have a place of our own that gives every evidence of His personal touch in all its aspects.

3 "If I go and prepare a place for you, I will come again and receive you to Myself, that where I am, there you may be also.

The "if" here is all important. The chief comforting idea expressed is that there are places prepared. Preparations and places obligate that we are destined to go, that we may join Him. The "if" serves to set up a validating condition that assures us He will indeed call for us.

4 "And you know the way where I am going."

We find out shortly that not all know – *"Thomas said to Him, "Lord, we do not know where You are going, how do we know the way?"* But this does not undermine the statement. The way is not known in practical, earthly terms, but spiritual ones. They need only consult His teaching and foreshadowings – He came from above and will return. As for the mechanics of their going, has there been any discussion or instruction on how one ascends into Heaven? It is all wrapped up in His Person, to do and accomplish all that man cannot begin to fathom.

He and they are destined for Heaven. In this, they know the destination. As for the way, the need not worry for maps and instructions. The One standing in front of them *is* the Way.

"I am the way, and the truth, and the life; no one comes to the Father but through Me.

For Thomas, all must be boiled down into practical terms. He did not excel in the metaphor department. The subtleties of analogy and figure were lost on him. Nor does Jesus take time to train him in looking beyond the pragmatic to how the spiritual undergirds the temporal. He merely states that He is the Way. It will now be up to Thomas to figure out how His complete command over Life and Truth eliminates any and all worry about the practical concerns for the way.

Interestingly, this is a variation on what was spoken also at the raising of Lazarus – "your brother will rise again." (John 11:23.) For Martha, the concern was life and the meaning of the rising He mentions. Jesus, there also, pointed to His mastery over Life as the key to all that was happening and predicted.

For the witness of the gospel in our modern world, these are the most profound words that can be spoken in Christian witness. In NT times, there was less local legitimizing of false religions until the gospel began to reach into the Gentile world. Judaism was the *lingua franca* of religious truth in their land. The question of other paths was certainly there but not as influential as it is today.

In Jesus' time, this question revolved more around accepting Him as key to salvation compared to the traditions of Moses and the historic faith of Israel.

Today, this declaration finds itself standing amid a new pantheon of religious claims for truth. Modern man is democratized into the belief that there are many paths, not just one. That is, after all, what fair play and equal opportunity dictate. Today we have Islam, the eastern religions, the New Age and a host of "light bearers" all calling for our allegiance. The Christian must now take the hugely unpopular stand that Christ alone is the only truth to be had and all others are false. Many go weak at the knees before such a prospect.

Liberalism retreats from this declaration, and to that degree ceases to be Christian. It is more concerned about its marriage to the world – science, philosophy, politics – and so this kind of exclusivity must not be allowed to wound diverse, individual needs for authentication. Let the Bible suffer, not man's right to diversity.

But Jesus' words were not intended for another world now long since gone to dust. They must be spoken all the more in this one, because the lie is on the move to rob Him of that exclusivity – to make Him merely an "also ran." And real truth about Life cannot be had until one embraces that exclusivity.

There is a real world beyond the physical stuff of our world, in which "principalities and powers" wage conflict and righteousness emanates from one Source. It is inescapably true that man was created and has fallen, and there is one remedy only for this state of affairs. Men are all destined for Hell (which is the clear warning of Jesus) and unless we do something about it, we are surely going to go there.

The fact that the world is unhappy with that message doesn't alter its reality or inevitability one iota.

For Thomas, Jesus assists Him toward the kind of thinking and believing that will resolve this for him -

7 "If you had known Me, you would have known My Father also; from now on you know Him, and have seen Him."

This comprises all the excursus Jesus intends to give Thomas on how to find the way. He must see the all-embracing fact of the Father, as evidenced in the Son. That will answer all concerns. He is to be Heavenly-minded that he may be of earthly good, meaning the spiritual will always explain the earthly. This Thomas must learn, whether it be difficult or easy. We too, because it is necessary.

"and you have seen Him." Jesus is so united with the Father that He can say with complete confidence that they have seen the Father already (in Him.) But this takes eyes moved by the Spirit in order to see in that way. Such, the Pharisees did not have, to their misfortune.

8 Philip said to Him, "Lord, show us the Father, and it is enough for us."

They are not getting it, even as Jesus is speaking such truths.

We need to be compassionate on our apostolic pioneers. Would we fair as well trying to comprehend a complete change in thinking, especially from a mindset so rooted in longstanding traditions?

It is clear that they do not all yet understand the reciprocal relationship in Persons between Father and Son. To see the Son is to see the Father. But this is very hard to grasp because God has been forever the unseen One – *"no one shall see My face and live."* Getting used to this idea of seeing the Father by looking at Jesus would require all the historic legacy of teaching and understanding which we've become accustomed to, but which they presently lack.

All that most can do is join with Philip in mustering the only desires of faith that seem to make sense – "if we are to see Him, it is enough that you show us the Father."

"Have I been so long with you, and yet you have not come to know Me,

This is somewhat like saying, "Haven't you been paying attention all along the way?" It highlights the mode of appreciation in some of these men - there is still the mystery of how this Father-Son thing is working. Much of this is still wrapped up in not having any man represent physically the Person of God. The "knowing" part of their encounter is still seen very much as empirical, rather than a knowing that is wholly in Spirit.

And this invades our whole understanding of God. He is proclaimed to be a Spirit, and those worshiping Him must do so in Spirit (John 4:24.) This takes some getting used to. For many, worship is very much an empirical thing. We attend a place of worship where we see with our eyes the surroundings of the place. We sing by direction from ministers, where the words have been printed for us, we partake of communion elements which are very physically present things.

But to perceive Him in our spirits is rigorously subjective, more so to come to "know" Him.

But that is precisely why Jesus points Philip and Thomas (and the rest) to His ministry among them. God has come down in human form and lived among them. There has been a knowing that has nothing to do with His physical appearance. That is the Father. He can be known as we know a friend independent of his physical appearance. Thus, *"how can you say, `Show us the Father'?"* We are to learn of this and follow.

For us, we are obliged to deal with what is left to us - His testimony and teaching in Scripture. But because His physical appearance made no difference for them, its absence from the Scripture will make no difference for us today. We too can come to know Him as they did because it wasn't about being physically present.

The words that I say to you I do not speak on My own initiative, but the Father abiding in Me does His works.

Our chronological approach to the gospels reveals how many times He has had to make this point. It is a very difficult hump to get over, but He is determined that they embrace it. The identity issue is all important if one is to jettison any and all ideas that Jesus is in some way still just a man on whom God has bestowed special power and insight. They know that that notion is somehow wrong (they are not as Judas in perceiving Him purely on a secular level.) But they have not come into it so positively that they now own it.

He declares that nothing He says is beyond what His Father bids Him do. He takes no subject or action farther on His own authority than that which is happening with His Father. For this reason, Jesus can say if you have seen Him you have seen the Father. This is a completely invasive identity and one we cannot afford to let slip. If we do, Jesus merely lines up with all other claimants of insight and truths about God. That He is to be identified with and in union with the Father makes Him stand above all others, and to the rejection of all others as false.

11. . otherwise believe because of the works themselves.

For some, this new concept of divine identity will be so difficult to embrace that Jesus appeals to the testimony of His works.

This is not a contradiction of His earlier condemnation of the generation that seeks a sign (Matt 12:39.) There, it was said of people who insist on a sign to believe and will inevitably rationalize the sign into practical explanations because they are predisposed to skepticism from the start. Against this meaning in all cases, are Jesus' repeated occasions where miracles are performed and faith is made strong.

Here, He can count on the works having the right effect in them. No one can explain them by side-stepping the endorsement of God. And not miracles alone, but the teaching that accompanied them.

For us, that is why they are portrayed in the NT, that we may follow this exhortation and come to the same conclusion.

12 ". . he who believes in Me, the works that I do, he will do also; and greater works than these he will do; because I go to the Father.

Seldom taught in the churches today is the idea that we will excel above the works of Jesus. Yet here it is in black and white. We simply have not seen this in most of our own personal experiences. Jesus' miracles in the Bible still stand out as unsurpassed, so we often question what this must have meant, or more importantly, why it is not happening today?

Certainly, much has to do with the church's relationship to the power of the Holy Spirit. We learn in Paul that the enabling to do these very things will be effected by the gifts of the Spirit. But we are commanded to seek them, they are not bestowed deterministically. The history of Christ's church reveals a waning in this respect as men appealed less to the Holy Spirit and more to their own wits and abilities to solve the problems and difficulties they encountered.

The Church became a scene of administrative affairs and political entanglements while the kinds of works mentioned here faded into the background. Evangelism and ministry were going on, but other affairs were often more center stage.

Today it is popular (some feel even necessary) to refer all such exhortations to the past, where authentication of the fledgling church was needed. Now, being established and set in its place in human society, time has changed our priorities. Until, of course, we read these words again, and our minds and hearts are pricked with some sense of real failure in its fulfillment.

He says it is because He goes to the Father. The need for similar and greater works is expressly because we are going to be left behind by Him, but not alone from Him. We will be stepping in where He once walked and has yet to walk. It is completely reasonable that we will need as much or more of the miraculous in doing that.

The average believer is certainly going to ask how they can effect the miraculous in their paltry lives and connections? Grace is the enabling of us to do what we cannot do of ourselves. We are placed where we are in life to do just that – to do what we and others cannot do by ourselves. And in demonstrating that, we reveal God and His Son.

So each of us must ask ourselves in what way do we see opportunities to appeal to that marvelous grace and do what we could not otherwise accomplish? Here's a hint: the easiest form of these "grace opportunities" is almost always in front of us at every moment – to love when our carnal, selfish nature is crying out that we cannot and will not. Succeeding in that alone is always a testimony of doing the works Jesus did daily in His work among us.

13 "Whatever you ask in My name, that will I do, so that the Father may be glorified in the Son. 14 "If you ask Me anything in My name, I will do it.

Now the promise of success. As anyone contemplates doing even what Jesus did, much less greater than He did, we see the immediate need for help. We know ourselves too well to be haughty and arrogant to believe we have it by nature.

So He readily lets them know that they need only ask. And with a promise that whatever they ask in His name will be done for them.

We see also now in this context how ridiculous is the idea that this could ever be used for personal gain. The context is clearly the doing of His works and greater. For this, one needs power. Ask for that, and one will receive it. Ask for wealth, fame and personal power and you will hear nothing but silence. Hence, the silly and foolish are quick to proclaim that it doesn't work.

Not only the context above, but the qualifier – *"in My name . . .that the Father be glorified."* should caution us that asking for a Lear Jet or to be the next American Idol is a bit out of place. To ask in Christ's Name is not a magic word but a condition of mind that places us in His world of values and needs. We see the needs and things to be done and we agree. Then the call for power naturally follows because it cannot be spoken for the satisfaction of our lusts and desires.

But let us renew for ourselves this one confidence – He guarantees and warrants unambiguous success in getting the answer to what we ask. Read it again. He says, "I will do it." We must believe this to see it happen, because happen it will if we are full of faith.

John 14:15-31, Luke 22:35-38, Matthew 26:30.

15 "If you love Me, you will keep My commandments. 16 "I will ask the Father, and He will give you another Helper, that He may be with you forever; 17 that is the Spirit of truth, whom the world cannot receive, because it does not see Him or know Him, but you know Him because He abides with you and will be in you.
18 "I will not leave you as orphans; I will come to you. 19 "After a little while the world will no longer see Me, but you will see Me; because I live, you will live also. 20 "In that day you will know that I am in My Father, and you in Me, and I in you. 21 "He who has My commandments and keeps them is the one who loves Me; and he who loves Me will be loved by My Father, and I will love him and will disclose Myself to him."

22 Judas (not Iscariot) said to Him, "Lord, what then has happened that You are going to disclose Yourself to us and not to the world?" 23 Jesus answered and said to him, "If anyone loves Me, he will keep My word; and My Father will love him, and We will come to him and make Our abode with him. 24 "He who does not love Me does not keep My words; and the word which you hear is not Mine, but the Father's who sent Me.

25 "These things I have spoken to you while abiding with you. 26 "But the Helper, the Holy Spirit, whom the Father will send in My name, He will teach you all things, and bring to your remembrance all that I said to you. 27 "Peace I leave with you; My peace I give to you; not as the world gives do I give to you. Do not let your heart be troubled, nor let it be fearful. 28 "You heard that I said to you, `I go away, and I will come to you.' If you loved Me, you would have rejoiced because I go to the Father, for the Father is greater than I.

29 "Now I have told you before it happens, so that when it happens, you may believe. 30 "I will not speak much more with you, for the ruler of the world is coming, and he has nothing in Me; 31 but so that the world may know that I love the Father, I do exactly as the Father commanded Me. (John 14:15-31a.)

35 And He said to them, "When I sent you out without money belt and bag and sandals, you did not lack anything, did you?" They said, "No, nothing." 36 And He said to them, "But now, whoever has a money belt is to take it along, likewise also a bag, and whoever has no sword is to sell his coat and buy one. 37 "For I tell you that this which is written must be fulfilled in Me, `AND HE WAS NUMBERED WITH TRANSGRESSORS'; for that which refers to Me has its fulfillment." 38 They said, "Lord, look, here are two swords." And He said to them, "It is enough." (Luke 22:35-38.)

31 . . "Get up, let us go from here." . . 30 After singing a hymn, they went out to the Mount of Olives. (John 14:31b, Matthew 26:30.)

Commentary

15 "If you love Me, you will keep My commandments.

This was a tall order even for the disciples. In modern times, many cry out for more applicational sermons that tell us how to apply Jesus' teaching in everyday life. Many are weary of sermons and lessons that analyze words and the history of interpretations or the theological positions pro and con. Certainly, Jesus spoke plainly about the use of His teaching in life. It is interesting that we find no scholarly dissertations or theologizing in any of His teaching.

On the other hand, those who cry out for applicational teaching are often not prepared for what ought to come next. Having been clearly apprised of how a teaching should be applied, it suddenly dawns on them that what is being asked is far from their inclination to do, and in some cases they are downright recalcitrant against it. One can see why this kind of teaching ceased to be a front-running feature of the church as more self-aggrandizing men came to the fore in its leadership and administration.

The widow's mite has a practical application – give in faith and don't let worries about how you are going to live hinder you from acting in faith. However, many today will not take that application home with them because, having little to live on, they have all kinds of other beliefs about why God will understand if they set this one aside.

Man has learned in his corporate history since then to cleverly rationalize a great deal of Jesus' teaching as inapplicable, or such as can be begged off because conditions are now quite different. Times have changed.

We often don't relate loving someone else to obeying them, usually because instruction and conformity are not the fundamental basis for loving relationships on the human plane. Usually we complete the sentence with, "we will do things that make them happy and fulfilled." But in Jesus' case, His happiness is that we obey, because that will please the Father, and we must face the reality that our relationship with Father and Son is about becoming someone rather than mutually meeting needs.

We have then an adage and a rule by which we can measure our love for Him – the degree to which we obey His commandments and yearn to do so out of love, rather than obligation. Our desire is to be based on the desire to fulfill the needs of righteousness. Begrudging service is of no value to anyone.

Some may ask, what are the commandments of Christ? They are not catalogued in the NT, so we are always obliged to read the gospels through in order to refresh our memories.

Here is a list as best can be gleaned from doing just that:

- You must be born again
- Live by the truth and come to the light
- Repent for the Kingdom of Heaven is at hand
- Be fishers of men
- Put new wine into new wineskins
- Hear Christ's word and believe the One who sent Him
- Desire mercy more than sacrifice
- Consider the Sabbath as made for man, not man made for the Sabbath
- Prefer meekness, mercy and compassion
- Hunger and thirst after righteousness
- Be pure in heart
- Be peacemakers
- Accept persecution for righteousness' sake
- Let your light shine – don't hide it under a bushel
- Do not hate, it is the same as murder
- Call no one a fool
- Reconciliation with your brother is higher than sacrifice and worship
- Do not lust, it is the same as adultery
- Root out and cast away whatever causes you to sin
- Do not divorce, except for unfaithfulness
- Make no oaths
- Let your yes be yes, your no be no
- Don't retaliate in kind but in love
- Give more to the man who steals out of his need
- Go an extra mile in helping others
- Love your enemies
- Pray for those who persecute you
- Don't do acts of righteousness to be seen of men
- Acknowledge the Father's holiness
- Pray that His Kingdom come on earth
- Ask the Father for your daily needs
- Ask for forgiveness as you also are forgiving others
- Pray to not be led into temptation, but delivered from evil
- Fast with joy not sadness
- Store up treasures in Heaven
- Don't be divided between the world and God
- Don't be anxious about your life, food, clothing
- Trust God to provide

Christ's Commandments (cont.)

- Don't judge lest you be also judged
- Give with liberality and generosity
- First judge and correct yourself before criticizing others' faults
- Don't throw your pearls before swine
- Knock, expecting doors to be opened for you
- Enter through the narrow gate, avoid the wide path and wide gate
- Watch out for false prophets
- Speak not against the Holy Spirit
- Let signs bolster faith but don't make them a criteria for faith
- Don't be superficially clean, but inwardly clean
- Prefer justice and love above offerings and legal obedience
- Avoid hypocrisy
- Fear God more than man
- Acknowledge Christ publicly before men
- Watch out for all kinds of greed
- Avoid storing up treasures on earth
- Be ready for service, not slothful
- Expect division among family and friends because of Christ
- Bear fruit in season and out of season
- Let the Word fall on good soil and yield many fold
- Protect the Word from being stolen by the devil
- Don't let the cares of the world choke the Word in you
- Exercise our faith, no matter how small
- Ask to be sent into the harvest of souls
- Pray for authority over evil
- Don't seek to be above your Master
- Seek the Bread of Life that comes down from Heaven
- Eat the flesh and blood of the Son of Man
- Avoid traditions of men supplanting the Word of God
- Deny yourself and take up your cross
- Lose your life to gain it
- Obey government and laws of obligation – taxes
- Become children in faith and trust
- Don't be the means by which temptation comes
- Confront a brother in error, first privately, then publicly
- Forgive seventy times seven – or unendingly
- Extend mercy to others that has been shown to you
- Go and sin no more
- Know the truth so that it sets you free
- Follow the shepherd of the sheep not the thief who sneaks in
- Don't wrangle with enemies of God, shake the dust off and move on
- Take His yoke upon you, it is easy
- Love God with all your heart, soul and strength, and your neighbor as yourself
- Consider all men your neighbor without partiality
- Be persistent in prayer and petition
- Don't seek places of honor but be humble
- Be kind and charitable to the poor
- Consider the cost of discipleship
- Don't let your saltiness become worthless
- Value the finding and saving of one lost over the many who are saved
- Be forgiving in the presence of repentance
- Excel in practical matters, make your master successful
- Consider the Law valid and not abolished
- Let your righteousness exceed that of the Pharisees

Christ's Commandments (cont.)

- Watch out for false Christs and false Second Comings
- Be willing to give up possessions to serve
- Avoid self-righteousness, false religion and legalism
- Go and preach the gospel to all nations, making disciples of all men

Of immediate concern will be how we can succeed at such a set of commandments and avoid the temptation to fall back into OT legalism.

16 "I will ask the Father, and He will give you another Helper, that He may be with you forever;

Having been challenged to do all that He has commanded, He realizes that men are fallen and in themselves exists no sufficient capacity. Here, His compassion and understanding, even in the above command, is expressed in His desire to pray that we receive a Helper.

We know in the next verse that this is the Holy Spirit, and what is interesting here is that this is to be an unending divine service. Not only will the Spirit be with us in this life, but we will find our relationship will extend into eternity.

This is the aspect of grace that is not so much unmerited favor as supernatural enabling. We will need it desperately to succeed, and regrettably, the church has in many places and times lost touch with this appeal for power, making the Christian life as difficult to live out as can be imagined. Many historically gave up, naively neglecting this key, or compromised to merely doing their best.

17 that is the Spirit of truth, whom the world cannot receive, because it does not see Him or know Him,

He then makes it clear to them who the Helper is. He will be called elsewhere the Comforter and His role will be to not only bring to remembrance things taught but to convict of sin. It will be as though we will have a built in thermometer or regulator to keep things in check.

We learn later in Paul that the Holy Spirit will be the key to the bestowal of gifts for the service of Christ among men and in the Church.

This the world cannot understand because all of this awareness and relationship comes through belief. It is knowledge one cannot acquire until belief is engaged. The unbeliever wants it the other way around – to have the knowledge before the belief, thus, they and the world are forever fruitless in this regard.

but you know Him because He abides with you and will be in you.

Here is the promise to all who believe. The Spirit in the OT abided or dwelt upon men, but there is no indication of an indwelling. Men were said to be filled with the Spirit, which is certainly an inner condition, but this was not a dwelling, as in taking up residence. The Spirit came and went but did not permanently abide.

Now, Jesus is introducing change in this relationship. Unlike any other dispensation of God, we receive an indwelling presence of God right within our being. There, fellowship with the Father and His Son can take place without intermediaries. We become our own temple before God without need for a priest between God and us.

He speaks future – *"will be in you"* and we see this fulfilled on the Day of Pentecost, scheduled to occur at the end of fifty days from the Passover (or first harvest.)

For the modern believer, we do not have to wait the fifty days. Being filled with the Spirit can happen at conversion.

18 "I will not leave you as orphans; I will come to you. 19 "After a little while the world will no longer see Me, but you will see Me; because I live, you will live also.

The concept of being orphaned is very much more in view with them concerning Him than we might think, since it seems like an abandonment is about to take place, one which leaves them adrift in the world to remember all He has taught. They must begin to stretch their wings as a bird thrown out of the nest in terms of the works they must now accomplish without Him.

They have relied so very much on Him being around to answer a million questions and correct all their missteps. Now it seems too early entirely to be sending them off on their own.

This is confirmed by the fact that the disappearance will be real – He will be absent from the real world if they will no longer be able to see Him. His immediate qualification that they will see Him is confusing at best. How will they see Him if He is invisible to the world? They can only speculate in their minds, since the mechanics of it all has not been discussed or disclosed.

We know the rest of the story from Acts, that He does in fact appear to them after death – they do see Him at a time when the rest of their world thinks Him dead and buried. But we also know that He ascends, leaving them at long last to their same concerns about being on their own.

His statement about them seeing Him again is directly tied to His post-resurrection appearances more as an assurance to them of their own resurrection, not to assuage their misgivings about going it on their own without Him.

All Christians take comfort and hope in that Christ is the first of the Resurrection, and His success in it assures us that ours will be successful also – *"as I live, you shall live also."*

20 "In that day you will know that I am in My Father, and you in Me, and I in you.

The purely vindicated truth will then be made manifest. How will they know He is in the Father? There will be no visible indication of that unity. It will be the deduction of patent effects – they are in Heaven, hence all that He stated about the Father, His will for them and the Father's purposes in the Son, will be self-evident because they will then be patently true. It will be a profound, overwhelming recognition that what they were told before is in fact true, no longer simply by faith, but now by sight.

The truth of being in Him and He in us will be something perceived in the mind and soul, which cannot be described until then. But it will be a knowing that His presence with us will convey.

21 "He who has My commandments and keeps them is the one who loves Me; and he who loves Me will be loved by My Father, and I will love him and will disclose Myself to him."

Here is something for the present world and time. As they and we also strive to keep His commandments, we will be loved by the Father and the Son, and this especially - He will "disclose" Himself to us. This is something the world cannot grasp because it cannot be comprehended outside faith. It is an inside thing, meaning a thing whose privileges come from being on the inside of the household of faith. It is much like the uninvited peering in the windows of the ball, not able to know what it is like to be at the ball unless inside and experiencing it.

Here is the promise of awareness of Him and knowledge of that disclosure to every believer. Yet can all believers claim that recognition? Some draw a blank when asked this question. Yet here is the promise. Shouldn't we then expect the result?

For everyone this is a matter of cultivation. The conveyance of truth and knowledge in the Holy Spirit does not come as an audible voice ala Charlton Heston. It comes in among our own thoughts and needs to be discerned from them. That takes a learning experience that few engage. The result is the all too frequent question – "What is the will of God for my life?" It is a question that comes from a life that has not cultivated a listening for His voice within, distinguished from our own thoughts.

22 Judas (not Iscariot) said to Him, "Lord, what then has happened that You are going to disclose Yourself to us and not to the world?"

Here is the question of all who are plagued to one degree or another with the need for practical and natural explanations. Judas is thought here to be the same as was also called Thaddeus – the brother of that James who was the Lord's brother, meaning this Judas who was also the Lord's brother.

His question is framed as one who is still confused about the spirituality of so much of what is going on and about to happen. He is asking more about the mechanics, the logistics, of this arrangement where the world will not see Him but they will.

There are some who traditionally believe that Judas was slow to accept his brother completely as Son of God, and this may have retarded his advancement to the deeper understandings of how He has come from above and will return there, yet be seen of them.

23 . . . "If anyone loves Me, he will keep My word; and My Father will love him, and We will come to him and make Our abode with him.

Here is the key to all of our Christian life in the living and knowing of it. We will have His presence and that of the Father within us. This is completely new from an OT standpoint. Former believers did not have the concept of God taking up residence within. This implies intimate contact with the emotions, mind and will, such that we are able to actually perceive directly, where before man was left with indirect means – mediators, miracles, Scripture.

Now man has a built in interpreter and revealer who will disclose meaning and significance, and the unction to act. It is like having God as house guest, but more here a member of the family.

We will find later that He is neither merely a member but has asked to become the new head of the family, that we relinquish our former roles to Him.

24 "He who does not love Me does not keep My words;

We should be careful that we don't try to apply this in the corollary – those who don't keep His words simply don't love Him. It is certainly true in the forward direction that those who do love Him will naturally desire to do what He said. This is a valid test of our love for Him, in assessing within ourselves any presence of that desire. If we love Him, it will be there that we can recognize it.

But a failure to do particular things or our willfulness to leave some things undone while doing others with a sincere desire is not an indicator that we have no love for Him at all. Life is a process of sanctification and as such we will perpetuate our efforts to root out disobedience and self-centeredness, which means we will have moments when we say, "I don't want to." As with Jesus' other teachings and especially reiterated in John's epistles, it must be asked: do we continually sin as a habit or is our aim to please Him? What characterizes the desires of our heart - love and obedience or disaffection and getting away with as much as we can? These are the things that signal if we love Him.

25 "These things I have spoken to you while abiding with you. 26 "But the Helper, . . . He will teach you all things, and bring to your remembrance all that I said to you.

He differentiates between what has been taught to them in His presence and how they will not only recall what has been already revealed but gain more after He leaves.

We see here every parallel to a well-thought-out plan for success. He has instructed them, given them authority and power, but in recognition that they are weak in their human capacities, He will provide a Helper who will ensure their success while taking things on their own.

It is like a trainee in a company who has been given charge of a project, and after training, the company provides an expert to accompany the employee, who will rehearse for him all the training provided and give new, ongoing guidance in every step needed.

The Father wants this enterprise to succeed. He leaves nothing out in overcoming the limitations of His servants.

This activity seems especially needful for the twelve as they established the early church but we later learn in Paul that this was not intended just for them. All believers are expected to avail themselves of this Helper as they also become His disciples and live for Him in the same callings that extend from the Twelve – *"But earnestly desire the greater gifts."* (I Cor 12:31)

Of special need is His capacity to bring to our remembrance things we have read in His word. We might think that this was meant for the disciples only because there was no written word at first for them – all had to be remembered from their three years with Him. But our study of the Word serves in very much the same role as did their hearing His teaching verbally. We go our way with our reading in our minds, and when we come upon a situation where we must recall it, we are often without a Bible just as they would have been. We've had things explained. But often we are alone to recall them.

We then rely on the faithfulness of the Holy Spirit to *"bring to remembrance"* all He has said whether spoken or written.

27 "Peace I leave with you; My peace I give to you; not as the world gives do I give to you.

"not as the world gives." How does the world give peace? Conditionally and without any guarantee of longevity. It does not do well in ensuring peace when conditions change. In fact, peace is often the first thing sacrificed when principles and wills are in conflict. The private goals of dictators take no heed to the devastation of peace their plans and hatreds wreak on the people who are caught in the middle.

But the peace Christ gives is eternally enduring. We are sometimes misled by momentary interruptions that cause strife, pain or heartache. But when the dust settles we come to recognize that His peace is still there for the taking, and it is we who have left it aside for the urgencies of our own making.

Paul will later discuss this peace as an end to the enmity (or war) between us and God. We are at peace with God. But the peace Jesus is describing is His own peace, the peace of Christ, the peace of God, which can only come when a peace with God has been declared. The latter opens the door to the former.

28 "You heard that I said to you, 'I go away, and I will come to you.' If you loved Me, you would have rejoiced because I go to the Father, for the Father is greater than I.

This is not a stern correction – *"you would have rejoiced"* but another teaching that is meant to hone their motives and help them separate the carnal from the spiritual. They heard Him respecting his departure. Were they more Heavenly-minded, were they closer to Him in His desires in the Father, they would be rejoicing for the blessing it will mean to Him.

That's a hard one when focused on our own issues, as they were now at the announcement of His leaving. They were as yet not that spiritual as to set aside their own concerns and be glad at the announcement.

29 "Now I have told you before it happens, so that when it happens, you may believe.

As before, He explains that He is preparing them with predictions, that when things happen they are not dismayed by despondency, unexpected outcomes, but will be ever more believing.

the ruler of the world is coming, and he has nothing in Me;

This is in reference to Satan, not the local ruling authorities, who could not be spoken of in the singular. Satan is called the ruler of this world subsequent to his casting out from Heaven and being given the earth as his domain (Isaiah 14:12.) Man's dominion has been forfeited at the Fall and given to Satan who has been busy claiming its territory to his will and control – as the *"prince of the power of the air"* (Eph 2:2.) Such conditions have been highlighted even in the titles of great works and great writers - Milton's poetic series *Paradise Lost*. God is now in the business of reclaiming lost ground, and He is choosing to do that in us.

That he is coming, in Jesus' words here, indicates that he is coming to have his victory over the Son and the plan of God. But it is fleeting and completely counterproductive to his aims, because he is unwittingly unleashing the power that will spell out His eventual downfall and annihilation. The prophecy to Satan in Genesis is about to be engaged – *"you shall bruise His heel but He shall bruise thy head"* (Gen 3:15.)

The statement that he has nothing in Him, is to declare that none of Satan's efforts are from Him nor will they constrain Him. Nothing this ruler will do can undermine the plan of God – he has no part in the positive aspects of that plan, nor can his negative role upset it.

31 but so that the world may know that I love the Father, I do exactly as the Father commanded Me

One might ask that if the end is known, why are the characters going through the motions? Jesus knows that Satan will be defeated, so why let him have his little victory? Why not cut to the chase and make way for the Kingdom?

An obligation of planning the future is to let the future play out. If you know the war is to be won, there must be a war to win. Jesus knows that Satan can make no lasting difference and his fate is sealed. Yet He continues in the will of the Father that the Father be all the more loved by mortal men who cannot see the end from the beginning and must live out their days in the confines of space and time.

35 "When I sent you out without money belt and bag and sandals, you did not lack anything, did you?"

Their experience had been one of no preparation as men count preparedness. Individual money belts were not necessary even though one would be away from their own food at home and would need to buy. Yet they found no lack of food among those whom God had prepared to take care of them.

In terms of provision, they readily answer, "No, nothing."

Having no sandals did not mean barefooted. It meant no extra pair in terms of preparedness, when the first pair wore out. In all these things, they had learned that God authenticated their work by providing for them and assuaging any concerns that with every step they were moving farther away from security and provisions at home.

This is intended to tell them that with respect to faith needed, they will not be lacking in able supply than they were concerning money, food and sandals.

36 "But now, whoever has a money belt is to take it along, likewise also a bag,

But with respect to the money belt and clothes, things have now changed. It is not that God cannot continue to do as before, but that He desires that they appear as men taken care of instead of men in need. There is also a matter of their reputation. To begin on the basis of having helping hands in every town is one thing.

To be continually dependent on charity wherever they go will become tiresome in people's minds. Too long in this mode will end up being counterproductive. People will regard them as indolent beggars who have abandoned their homes and trade in order to live off others who are poor and needy themselves. There is now to be none of that, with some exceptions.

36 .. and whoever has no sword is to sell his coat and buy one.

Ordinarily, we expect Christians, certainly the apostles, to be men of peace, not answering evil with evil. So it is very difficult for us to comprehend our Lord in this command. But it is precisely because of the fickle nature of unregenerate people that these changes are now invoked. Satan can be counted on to sow disaffection and hatred against the work of God. There will now be men in every place poisoned by resentment, disappointment, revenge and envy to the extent of doing serious violence.

If there is to be martyrdom, they are to endure it in peace, not in kind. But there are simply going to be occasions when it will be necessary to protect oneself from violence that is merely precarious, and as such will serve no purpose to suffer, especially if their time of death is not presently appointed. Jesus demonstrated this by escaping the mob so as not to suffer prematurely their violence. He used a tool for self defense. It is evident that they are not to be gifted routinely with that same kind of tool. And if not, a sword for self-defense is the meaning intended.

Whether the use of the sword to kill or to scare was intended is hard to discern. Certainly, it will signal for bullies and ruffians that they are not to be trifled with. But the call here is not to be aggressive with the sword, but defensive, to protect oneself from untimely evil. Certain not all will be run off by the mere presence of swords.

We do know from the Law that men who killed in defense of themselves and family were not liable to punishment. It is difficult to imagine that one was all along intended to be weaponless.

37 "For I tell you that this which is written must be fulfilled in Me, `AND HE WAS NUMBERED WITH TRANSGRESSORS';

We find here the reason for this change in approach and preparedness. He is to be killed as a criminal against the nation. This changes their assessment from itinerant preachers to seditionists and subverters of the faith. To be identified with Him, they too will be numbered among transgressors.

38 They said, "Lord, look, here are two swords." And He said to them, "It is enough."

This is among the strangest verses in the NT because it flies in the face of so much we embrace about Christ and the nature of our transformed lives. We are to be about love. We are to assess peacemakers more blessed than those who cannot turn the other cheek.

So the exhortation above to purchase a sword is odd in this section on preparation. Now, we also encounter the disciples' observation and Christ's reply.

They happen to have two swords, which if completely forbidden would be expected already to have been abandoned via His corrective. But here they are, still in tow.

Jesus' reply that these are enough is equally puzzling if they are to be men of peace. We reel from any hint that Jesus would authenticate their use for violent response, which we must agree is their sole purpose.

Some have offered that "it is enough" is equivalent to Jesus' saying, "enough of this," as if the manner in which the disciples have taken His words is too bizarre to address. But the Greek does not support this translation, since that phrase would be constructed differently enough to forestall this translation (i.e. it would be spotted for what it is and translated accordingly.) But more, we would still have to explain His exhortation to go and buy swords.

As for how we can reason that two swords among eleven men would be enough, we can only speculate. It is very possible that in their company as they are, two swords is sufficient among those accustomed to preferring peace. This would not be mitigated by His command that they each buy one in the future, because then they would be in smaller groups where two swords might be the normal count.

Another reason may very well be the anticipated fracas with the temple guard by Peter, in which Jesus may be simply saying, "You have enough to satisfy the inevitability of predestined events about to happen a few hours from now."

30 After singing a hymn, they went out to the Mount of Olives.

All of this discussion is of course still taking place in the upper room at the conclusion of the Paschal meal. Usually sung at the end of the meal is the Hallel which is six Psalms completely recited (113-118.) This would not be considered a *'humne'*, encompassing all, but a series of hymns sung.

Thus, it is difficult to be dogmatic that they sang the traditional full Hallel, a portion of it, or something else on Jesus' direction. Only that the signing corresponded to that step where the Jews traditionally sang the Hallel.

Matthew 26:31-33, 35, John 15:1-26

31 Then Jesus said to them, "You will all fall away because of Me this night, for it is written, 'I WILL STRIKE DOWN THE SHEPHERD, AND THE SHEEP OF THE FLOCK SHALL BE SCATTERED.' 32 "But after I have been raised, I will go ahead of you to Galilee." 33 But Peter said to Him, "Even though all may fall away because of You, I will never fall away." . . All the disciples said the same thing too. (Matthew 26:31-35.)

1 "I am the true vine, and My Father is the vinedresser. 2 "Every branch in Me that does not bear fruit, He takes away; and every branch that bears fruit, He prunes it so that it may bear more fruit. 3 "You are already clean because of the word which I have spoken to you.

4 "Abide in Me, and I in you. As the branch cannot bear fruit of itself unless it abides in the vine, so neither can you unless you abide in Me. 5 "I am the vine, you are the branches; he who abides in Me and I in him, he bears much fruit, for apart from Me you can do nothing. 6 "If anyone does not abide in Me, he is thrown away as a branch and dries up; and they gather them, and cast them into the fire and they are burned. 7 "If you abide in Me, and My words abide in you, ask whatever you wish, and it will be done for you.

8 "My Father is glorified by this, that you bear much fruit, and so prove to be My disciples. 9 "Just as the Father has loved Me, I have also loved you; abide in My love. 10 "If you keep My commandments, you will abide in My love; just as I have kept My Father's commandments and abide in His love. 11 "These things I have spoken to you so that My joy may be in you, and that your joy may be made full. 12 "This is My commandment, that you love one another, just as I have loved you. 13 "Greater love has no one than this, that one lay down his life for his friends. 14 "You are My friends if you do what I command you.

15 "No longer do I call you slaves, for the slave does not know what his master is doing; but I have called you friends, for all things that I have heard from My Father I have made known to you. 16 "You did not choose Me but I chose you, and appointed you that you would go and bear fruit, and that your fruit would remain, so that whatever you ask of the Father in My name He may give to you. 17 "This I command you, that you love one another.

18 "If the world hates you, you know that it has hated Me before it hated you. 19 If you were of the world, the world would love its own; but because you are not of the world, but I chose you out of the world, because of this the world hates you. 20 Remember the word that I said to you, 'A slave is not above his master.' If they persecute me, they will also persecute you.; if they kept my word, they will keep yours also.

21 But all these things they will do to you for my name's sake, because they do not know the One who sent me. 22 If I had not come and spoken to them, they would not have sin, but now they have no excuse for their sin.

23 He who hates me hates my Father also. 24 If I had not done among them the works which no one else did, they would not have sin; but now they have both seen and hated me and my Father as well. 25 But they have done this to fufill the word that is written, THEY HATED ME WITHOUT A CAUSE.

26 When the Helper comes whom I will send to your from the Father, that is the Spirit of truth who proceeds from the Father, He will testify about me 27 And you will testify also because you have been with me from the beginning. (John 15:1-26.)

Commentary

"You will all fall away because of Me this night, for it is written, `I WILL STRIKE DOWN THE SHEPHERD, AND THE SHEEP OF THE FLOCK SHALL BE SCATTERED.'

It is curious that at the Cross we do not find them present except John, and no explanation as to where they are. John is there with Jesus' mother and the other women, but the absence of the others is too curious to be merely an oversight of the writer.

The OT citation (Zech 13:7) is difficult because it is often seen as a judgment of those to whom the Shepherd came. The rest of the verse reads, "and I will turn my hand on the little ones." This is most often read as applying to the Jews of the city, whom after the Crucifixion will suffer the effects of the siege and fall of Jerusalem. The next verse describes the division in thirds, where two-thirds will perish and one-third will survive.

As applied to the disciples, this is puzzling. For certain, the Messiah is going to be struck, and while it is His enemies doing the deed, we understand from prophecy that this is the chosen means by which God will enable salvation, therefore He has ordained the striking. In fact, it is absolutely necessary. Isaiah records the purpose of God, *"But the LORD was pleased to crush Him,.."* (53:10), and Jesus will highlight this to Pilate, *" "You would have no authority over Me, unless it had been given you from above;"*

But we fail to see the Lord turning His hand on the little ones in reference to the disciples.

For starters, the added line from Zechariah is after all deliberately left out by Jesus, as was the "day of vengeance" in the reading from the scroll in Nazareth (Luke 4:21). So we are hardly warranted to force an application.

But when looking at the Hebrew, the word for turn is *'shuwb'*, which can also mean *to restore*. Thus, it would read that He would strike the Shepherd and restore His hand to the little ones. (See this usage in Isaiah 1:25.)

From the NT history that progresses from here, their absence in hiding at the Crucifixion and the despondency that follows is not debilitating to their calling. This does not, in the end, interfere with the work they inevitably accomplish. So whether they scatter in relation to faith or fear, they are seen to be restored and regathered.

But here, Jesus' main point is to warn them beforehand that they are going to react this way and He knows all about it. He also adds a note of hope – *" "But after I have been raised, I will go ahead of you to Galilee."*

They of course react.

33 ... *"Even though all may fall away because of You, I will never fall away."*

Notice that none ask about the appearance in Galilee. This is completely glossed over in favor of the point of the moment which is the falling away. We can see here why there was need for the angel at the tomb to remind them respecting his appearance in Galilee.

v.33 is a reprise of the same conversation in Mark 14:31. This time the others join Peter – *All the disciples said the same thing too.*

Peter repeats his promise despite Jesus' reminding Him that He knows the very conditions of the denial – the crowing of the morning rooster. We cannot fault Peter for showing a naïve bravura despite what he must know to be Jesus' impeccable knowledge of the real future. No matter how certainly someone might affirm to us that we will fail or stumble in some deficiency, we would protest it by nature.

1 *"I am the true vine, and My Father is the vinedresser.*

The figure of the vine is given where we might expect a tree and branches instead. But the vine is more appropriate because of the fruit so readily associated with it (a vine is solely for its grapes, where a tree has more use than its fruit, many of which have none.)

The branches on which the fruit is born are also more readily seen as being wholly dependent on the stock of the vine. And more ready also is the idea of regular pruning, because the yield of the crop is all important, hence pruning gets more attention than with other plants, hence – *2 "Every branch in Me that does not bear fruit, He takes away; and every branch that bears fruit, He prunes it so that it may bear more fruit.*

3 "You are already clean because of the word which I have spoken to you.

Some infer by this that the disciples are considered saved. Others see this as a preparatory cleansing while waiting for the events of the Cross.

Salvation is both a state of grace and a restoration of relationship with God. We are converted from our former lives of sin through confession and repentance and the receiving of enabling grace to now live according to righteousness. We are regenerated in the receiving of the Holy Spirit who causes our spirit to be alive unto God. And we are forgiven on the basis of a sacrifice that meets the needs of justice against our sins and their penalty.

While the conversion, and the partnership with the Holy Spirit in the work of Christ's ministry were certainly present, the Sacrifice was yet to be made at this point. We have learned since that in the sacrifice man gains the right to approach God in the present and in the Heavenly estate. So theologically, there is here prior to the event of the Cross a piece missing that completes the theological picture.

Still, we are dealing with the Son of God who is certainly entitled with divine authority to declare who are saved. Despite our concern about timing, He does call them clean, and we would have a difficult time explaining that this cleanness was as yet ineffective in their approach to God.

Some see this as a case in which their salvation is so sure a thing, but a few hours away, that this is just an issue of timing than functional operation.

4 "Abide in Me, and I in you.

The word abide means to take up residence, to live with a person or circumstances. When Jesus says He is the vine and we are the branches, we are to apply this to our living – we are to take up our living in Him and He in us. But what does this really mean?

Very often, the modern Christian today sees the Christian life as an "activity" they add to their lives, rather than a radical renovation of their former lives. This can be difficult to understand because we see ourselves as having to go on living in the same world, the same family, the same job. And since those things don't change, we rethink what it must mean to "abide" in Him such that all things are made new.

But Jesus did not mean primarily a change in the outward things. To abide in Him is to take on His world view, His attitude toward that same world, same family, same job. Instead of wrailing against all those folks who comprise what's wrong with society, we are to find a heart of compassion and apply love where there once was strife. Instead of wishing to be disassociated with our families, Christ will renew a desire to be a better member of those families. Instead of complaining about our jobs and our bosses, He will inspire us to find ways to make the company and the boss successful from our contribution.

It's a world view that changes as we come to dwell in Him and He in us. It's a forsaking of the old and a putting on of the new. But too often, Christians are content to have Christ as merely one of the activities we incorporate into our otherwise unchanged life.

4 .. As the branch cannot bear fruit of itself unless it abides in the vine, so neither can you unless you abide in Me.

We see here what the abiding is purposed to do – to bear heavenly fruit. They are to get rid of the idea that they can do this now on their own, even though He is making it painfully clear they will be physically on their own. Their connection to Him, as the branch must be to the vine, is critical to their success.

For the modern church, there are many who do not get this connection. It is too mystical, too spiritualistic. We are practical people, so we must be resigned to do what our mind and body can manage. The result is a fruit that is humanistic, off-white and largely ineffective. No wonder some look at the church and see no palpable difference.

But the born again brother or sister of Christ, as servant of the living God, must be moved by the vine itself, must seek the enabling and nourishing power in the vine to be successful; and if we are failing, it may be that we are on our own steam - *"neither can ye unless ye abide in Me."*

6 *"If anyone does not abide in Me, he is thrown away as a branch and dries up . . and they are burned.*

Regrettably, there are many discarded branches in the church today. God is going to have His will manifested in the world one way or the other. If we will not make ourselves available, He will simply side-step us for someone who will. The more we set our members aside for our own desires and will, the more we are cast off from His, and are merely in the mode of waiting to be gathered and burned. We should join with the disciples and Paul in saying, "May it never be."

8 . . . *and so prove to be My disciples.*

We have here then a test of true discipleship. We are to bear fruit, which marginalizes those who believe they can take Christ in to assure their salvation, but speak to no one nor lift a hand to the work of His ministry. We have cultivated the lazy man's Christianity in which folks sit and soak and their exhilaration is in looking forward to the lunch bunch after church. So many say, "I've had my day. Now it's time to enjoy retirement."

But discipleship is about winning the battles, advancing the front of the gospel message and making the kind of difference in other peoples lives that no one else can do quite as well. It is getting our marching orders from the Master and bearing His yoke in the advancement of the Kingdom.

We are to regard the Kingdom as a work in progress, whose building stones are the souls of men. The harvest is plentiful, so there really is no room for the notion that one can go out to pasture.

If we are puzzled about where we are bearing fruit, we have to that degree ceased being His disciple. Time for re-evaluation and change.

9 *"Just as the Father has loved Me, I have also loved you;*

"Just as the Father has loved" means unconditional love that is eternally present, eternally powerful. Man has learned to love conditionally (we only love the lovable.) As such, those truly in need of love are left out in the cold. We are more educated about that today, but our attempts to remedy this are still full of human failings. We recognize the need to love an unlovable person and we even make decisions and efforts to do so, but we want these episodes to be short, quick fixes – nothing long term. But people are often messy in their troubles and down-heartedness.

Man is forever enlarging the quantity and quality of his enjoyments, so doing the hard work of loving the difficult and trying people in life is no fun. It is relegated to certain corners of our life that will not interfere with the maximization of fun. Surprisingly, the messy situations we are asked to love don't go away with a hug here and there.

God sees all of this on a regular basis. And if we're accustomed to thinking that we at least have our act together with respect to the difficulties of being loved, think again. He is absolute perfection. Virtually everything we do is going to be sub-standard compared to His way of things; He will always see the better way we should have acted or done such-and-such. To a perfect person, this is well-nigh intolerable (just ask a perfectionist and see.) So God has a very real challenge in every human being to accept them in their weakness and shortcomings, yet loves us sincerely and more completely than we can imagine.

As the Father loves us, we must practice the same for others. That is something that won't improve if we don't take action, and it will always come down to deliberate decision. If we wait for the feelings, we will be waiting a very long time.

10 "If you keep My commandments, you will abide in My love;

We seldom relate living in love to the obedience of rules. It usually engenders bitterness and frustration. But in Christ's commands, we see that they are all about having a proper love toward our fellow man and toward the Father. It is all about putting self in the background and preferring others, which is often seen as the quintessential definition of love. In God's case, we believe He desires the best for us, the greatest happiness and joy - *"I have come that you might have life and that abundantly"* (John 3:29.) We will see shortly in vs. 11 that this includes joy.

This breaks the old mold on obedience by causing us to learn about love the more we do them.

11 "These things I have spoken to you so that My joy may be in you, and that your joy may be made full.

Some see the Christian life as hard and arduous and as such find little joy in it. But something must be true about Jesus' words here. He certainly places heavier burdens on us than the Law ever did – *"if a man lusts, he has committed adultery."* Yet He talks about joy.

The joy is in the delight of His righteousness and being privileged to be chosen as His disciple. When we are made right with the world, when our burdens are laid down and His are taken up, there is joy in the renovation of our souls and the newness of life He brings. The Christian life is going to have its hard moments and difficulties, but imagine the unsaved who must face them without remedy. We have the confidence that He will not leave us destitute or in want of His touch in all things.

12 "This is My commandment, that you love one another,

It must be a command because good intentions are easily spoiled by a bad bowl of soup. We can so easily become disenchanted, the magic dissipates and we are stuck trying to live off of an emotional high rather than the grace we will need. (Notice in Moses – the veil was used over his face to hide the dissipating glory, that the people not be discouraged by its waning.) We are prone to this, and that is why there is need for command from Him, not just good intentions. We cannot be depended upon in and of ourselves.

13 "Greater love has no one than this, that one lay down his life for his friends.

Our commitment to our friends seldom extends ahead of time to our willingness to die for them. We are too busy enjoying life and to die takes us promptly out of the midst of that enjoyment. Many today have lost the altruistic sense of dying for one's country. When the death toll gets high, we begin saying, "Patriotism is OK, but this is more than I bargained for."

The heroes and heroines usually become so in the heat of the moment, but less so of late by premeditation or commitment to be sacrificial. Our current generation is too busy asking "What's in it for me?"

To be willing to lay down our lives so that our friends are benefited or saved is ultimate love because it is a willingness to forsake all future times with them, in fact, all future per se. We can't do that and then expect to go on enjoying the fruits of friendship. We are done; out of the picture entirely. It may work out in the flash of a moment, but few today think about such a commitment as part of their love for their friends.

14 "You are My friends if you do what I command you.

Many consider it too flip to declare Christ as friend. This comes from the manner of holiness and position that has been typical in the development of the organized church. If we are reticent to be too liberal in calling our priest our friend, we are less likely to do so with Christ.

Yet He regarded us as such. He is not aloof, but rather like the companion with whom we can share our dreams and our hurts.

What disables us in this regard is that He is not physically present as friend, so we must re-think the meaning and it often comes down to Him working in and through our Christian friends in expressing His role in this regard. But we must never conclude that that is the sum total of what He meant. He is in glory and He regards us as friends in His Heavenly estate. That He uses intermediaries to effect the physicality of His friendship does not nullify His inner attitude of mind as He is and where He abides.

This is new for many people raised in the formal liturgies. But we and they must embrace the idea that He is directly approachable in prayer and spiritual fellowship. He is present with us, though we find that hard to understand.

15 "No longer do I call you slaves, . . . but I have called you friends, for all things that I have heard from My Father I have made known to you.

The figure of slaves is easy to slip into because servants are very close to that idea – we have tasks over which we feel obligated and the focus is often narrow and specific. But here, He is distinguishing between the competency in mind of the slave compared to the friend. The slave does not have the mind of his master to know what he is up to in his plans. He is assigned a piece to perform but seldom knows how his piece fits in with the rest.

In the case of the disciples, they are now privy to the plans of the Kingdom, they see the over-arching principles and initiatives in play that control and dictate where and why they are doing the work of ministry. They are let in on the mind of the Master.

If we are to follow as His disciples also, we too must embrace the larger picture, as opposed to the microcosm of life in such and such a church, in such and such a town. The field is said to be ready for harvest, the Kingdom is in the building process. And unless specifically told otherwise, that field is considerably large as to embrace the whole world. That is what God is doing. He is gathering citizens from all corners of the world. We are to be His helpers, His friends in that. We need only then ask: How? Where? And be ready for an answer.

16 "You did not choose Me but I chose you, and appointed you that you would go and bear fruit, and that your fruit would remain,

Today, we think the opposite - we are asked to make a decision after the sermon has ended, and that's very much us making a choice. But we find that He has chosen us beforehand. (His statement that we did not choose is hyperbole to emphasize that He really made the more significant choice before we made ours.)

This bears on the subject of how everyone can be chosen yet all do not come? In the Calvinist frame this is answered by only the elect being chosen by Him. In the Arminian camp, all of humanity is chosen but individuals can unchoose themselves. Each have their appeals and weaknesses.

But regardless of how we work out election in our mind, there is a fact still cogent and real in which we must affirm we are chosen by Christ to be His disciple, and that should constrain us to not treat it lightly. There is a grave responsibility that comes with Him having chosen us, an accountability that hangs in the balance, against which we will be assessed in the end.

What is equally "appointed" is that their fruit will have long lasting effect. This is part of the assurance of divine participation. When we witness, or teach or counsel, we can often wonder if our help has gotten through much less will it last to have some modicum of permanent fruit?

That which is initiated in Him and with Whom we partner in the work is promised to bear fruit. The burdens and tasks we take on for ourselves, albeit with good intentions, are implied as not having such assurances. They may or may not bear fruit because the key enabling principle is that they be "appointed."

This is more applicable to specific ministry callings and unctions. The Great Commission is certainly appointed, so doing its work is going to bear lasting fruit. But in respect to many other things, where we find ourselves failing we might be surprised to learn how vague we are about having been appointed to such-and-such, and how much we may have run out on our own.

so that whatever you ask of the Father in My name He may give to you.

We learned the last time this was spoken that it applies to the context of doing His work. Where He has appointed us to work, He will not leave us destitute of the means. If we need to build an orphanage, the physical and monetary resources are going to be there as we pray for them. This teaches us that His tasks for us do not run away out from under Him, nor is He caught by unforeseen circumstances where all best-laid plans are now off.

18 "If the world hates you, you know that it has hated Me before it hated you.

Not a terrific advertisement for the Christian life. Again, it is a matter of one's world view about Christianity. It will be an abundant life, and a life full of joy. But it will be one that is routinely opposed to the world as a system. We will be the fly in the ointment in so many areas of life around us, and that will spawn any number of troubles and persecutions.

The ancient Romans called early Christians "haters of mankind." This sounds quite strange since Christianity is all about love, both for the brethren and for man in general. The reason for the epithet is that the Romans had a quite different idea about what a good citizen and friend entailed. The obligations of Roman sociability involved activities Christians could not indulge. They were thus the quintessential party poopers or "downers" of the times, not because they were morose and dour, but because they cast moral aspersions on the Roman sense of fun.

What is important here is that if we are to be hated, it should be for the right reasons. If we ourselves have caused that hatred because of insensitivity, prejudice, or sectarianism, we can't claim persecution for righteousness' sake. The hatred we receive is our own doing. But where we are truly persecuted for His teaching, for presenting His Way in the world, we are not to take it so personally as to lose heart that we have failed. We are to recognize that were He here doing those very things, they would spurn Him also.

This is because the war on that level is not about personalities, people against people. It is about principalities and powers who wage these battles in high places (Eph 6:12.)

19 If you were of the world, the world would love its own; . . . 'A slave is not above his master.' If they persecute me, they will also persecute you.;

Jesus' understanding of the world incorporates all its facts no matter how fine or how ugly. To gain the love of the world, one must show he has thrown in his lot with it. Go along and you will be accepted. Set yourself apart from it and it will turn on you, not for mere lack of conformity but for shining a light on the sins of others.

We think of Jesus as having the perfect approach, the best model of sharing the truth, the best way to get His points across. Would that we could have that ability and insight when we witness. Yet even with that magnitude of perfection in speech and delivery, men rejected Him. Because one cannot leave the words of Jesus at the lectern. They demand change. Such men persecuted our Lord with all His ability and perfection. And if it is about the bottom line, then we can understand how little it mattered how well spoken He was, nor what measure of that we employ. We too will be persecuted once the bottom line is comprehended.

21 But all these things they will do to you for my name's sake, because they do not know the One who sent me.

It is important for us to count the cost of being associated with His Name. There are some Christians today who wish to take on the activities of church life, but wish in other circles not to be known as of His Name. This, of course, is precisely what Jesus meant when warning us that to be ashamed of Him begets a similar response from Him.

22 If I had not come and spoken to them, they would not have sin, but now they have no excuse for their sin.

Would they not have sin? In the specifics mentioned yes. Not in life in general. They would not have sinned against the greater, much clearer light shed upon their lives and in their hearing.

23 He who hates me hates my Father also. 24 If I had not done among them the works which no one else did, they would not have sin; but now they have both seen and hated me and my Father as well. 25 But they have done this to fulfill the word that is written, THEY HATED ME WITHOUT A CAUSE.

There is no clever maneuvering allowed here – *I'll cast my lot in with God but I can't do the Jesus thing.* Here it is made clear that they are inextricably joined, so that they cannot be separated. And we understand this even from human nature. We resent a friend who likes us but bad-mouths our parents. With Jesus and the Father it was more powerfully and essentially a unison. While we might think of cases where children welcome disparagement of their overbearing parents, nothing of this pertained in the union of Son and Father.

THEY HATED ME WITHOUT A CAUSE

When we contemplate the goodness of God and that of His Son, we can easily understand that any hatred is without cause. But ironically, while it is bold to hate the God of our Creation where there might be reasoned some cause (the tyrannical gods of the Greeks and Romans), it is hard to venturing such danger without cause.

Why do men take such a course anyway? Because there are those for whom the righteousness of God is not a thing of virtue and desire. It annihilates our own willful desires because they are so regularly contrary to God's. So it becomes popular to ridicule God and His Christ to more firmly establish our right to our own wills.

26 When the Helper comes whom I will send to your from the Father, that is the Spirit of truth who proceeds from the Father, He will testify about me 27 And you will testify also because you have been with me from the beginning. (John 15:1-26.)

Jesus here promises a help from the Father in contemplation of His announcement that He cannot remain with them. We know Him to be referring to the Holy Spirit as the verse continues, hence editions of the Bible capitalize *Helper.*

And we learn that His role will be to further testify in the human heart of the truth concerning the Son. That is the marvelous gift given as He is leaving to return to the Father. That for all who believe from this point forward, an inner witness, indwelling the believer, will help, inspire and teach the individual as they walk in faith. No other religion can make such a claim that is this interpersonal.

But we must take seriously the challenge – that if the Spirit will be about witnessing to the Son, we also must emulate this in testifying to that same truth.

John 16:1-33

1 "These things I have spoken to you so that you may be kept from stumbling. 2 "They will make you outcasts from the synagogue, but an hour is coming for everyone who kills you to think that he is offering service to God. 3 "These things they will do because they have not known the Father or Me. 4 "But these things I have spoken to you, so that when their hour comes, you may remember that I told you of them. These things I did not say to you at the beginning, because I was with you. (John 16:1-4.)

5 "But now I am going to Him who sent Me; and none of you asks Me, `Where are You going?' 6 "But because I have said these things to you, sorrow has filled your heart. 7 "But I tell you the truth, it is to your advantage that I go away; for if I do not go away, the Helper will not come to you; but if I go, I will send Him to you. 8 "And He, when He comes, will convict the world concerning sin and righteousness and judgment; 9 concerning sin, because they do not believe in Me; 10 and concerning righteousness, because I go to the Father and you no longer see Me; 11 and concerning judgment, because the ruler of this world has been judged.

12 "I have many more things to say to you, but you cannot bear them now. 13 "But when He, the Spirit of truth, comes, He will guide you into all the truth; for He will not speak on His own initiative, but whatever He hears, He will speak; and He will disclose to you what is to come. 14 "He will glorify Me, for He will take of Mine and will disclose it to you. 15 "All things that the Father has are Mine; therefore I said that He takes of Mine and will disclose it to you.

16 "A little while, and you will no longer see Me; and again a little while, and you will see Me." 17 Some of His disciples then said to one another, "What is this thing He is telling us, `A little while, and you will not see Me; and again a little while, and you will see Me'; and, `because I go to the Father'?" 18 So they were saying, "What is this that He says, `A little while'? We do not know what He is talking about." (John 16:5-18.)

19 Jesus knew that they wished to question Him, and He said to them, "Are you deliberating together about this, that I said, `A little while, and you will not see Me, and again a little while, and yo will see Me'? 20 "Truly, truly, I say to you, that you will weep and lament, but the world will rejoice; you will grieve, but your grief will be turned into joy.

21 "Whenever a woman is in labor she has pain, because her hour has come; but when she gives birth to the child, she no longer remembers the anguish because of the joy that a child has been born into the world. 22 "Therefore you too have grief now; but I will see you again, and your heart will rejoice, and no one will take your joy away from you. 23 "In that day you will not question Me about anything. Truly, truly, I say to you, if you ask the Father for anything in My name, He will give it to you.

24 "Until now you have asked for nothing in My name; ask and you will receive, so that your joy may be made full. 25 "These things I have spoken to you in figurative language; an hour is coming when I will no longer speak to you in figurative language, but will tell you plainly of the Father. 26 "In that day you will ask in My name, and I do not say to you that I will request of the Father on your behalf; 27 for the Father Himself loves you, because you have loved Me and have believed that I came forth from the Father.

28 "I came forth from the Father and have come into the world; I am leaving the world again and going to the Father." 29 His disciples said, "Lo, now You are speaking plainly and are not using a figure of speech. 30 "Now we know that You know all things, and have no need for anyone to question You; by this we believe that You came from God." 31 Jesus answered them, "Do you now believe? 32 "Behold, an hour is coming, and has already come, for you to be scattered, each to his own home, and to leave Me alone; and yet I am not alone, because the Father is with Me. 33 "These things I have spoken to you, so that in Me you may have peace. In the world you have tribulation, but take courage; I have overcome the world."
(John 16:19-33.)

Commentary

1 "These things I have spoken to you so that you may be kept from stumbling."

Stumbling conveys the imagery of tripping over a stone. If we are looking around or at our friend, we may not see the stone in the way. This connection pictures stumbling as a failure or a misstep, or in Paul's use –

a sin. We fall to our embarrassment. In Paul, we are hindered from progressing further, being sidetracked by sin.

For the disciples, there are many things ahead that may tempt them to lose faith or slip in terms of human reactions, whose sin or missteps may undo the work of God. He has just highlighted the proper attitude toward the hatred they will receive, which without teaching may have resulted in retaliation on their part, thus undermining their mission and ministry.

2 "They will make you outcasts from the synagogue,

As with the case of the man born blind (John 9:1), this was serious in any Jew's life. The entire temporal substance of their corporate worship would be taken from them, and this extended into public life. For Jews, their faith was not merely an aspect of being a citizen. Judaism was a race, faith and national identify, which could not be disassociated from the religious component (unless you cared little for reputation and standing.)

For the disciples, it was no longer critical in terms of ultimate state before God. They could be assured that no matter how the nation treated them, their place in the Kingdom was assured. They are being asked to forsake any expectations about their place in Jewish society. Being shunned from the synagogue placed them in the category of harlots and highwaymen, who might live among them but without hope of position or help from the commonwealth of citizens.

This, God could easily overcome in special provision. But we will find that not long after the ascension, most of the Twelve have begun missions away from the city where the probations of the Jews would be of little consequence.

but an hour is coming for everyone who kills you to think that he is offering service to God.

This is the insidious nature of dealing with unbelief in an atmosphere of orthodox faith. When witnessing to the unbeliever, the stakes are known and acknowledged. A clear case of unbelief vs. belief. But reaching people who already believe they are exercising a correct and orthodox faith is extremely difficult.

We wince at how the Jews could say some of the things they did to Jesus and go through with their plans for his scourging and death. They certainly knew the horrors of it, which were easily justified when dealing with a murderer or the instigator of a rebellion. But dealing with a man who authenticated His teaching and wisdom with miracles required a more rigorous rationalization respecting the service of God. This is an intricacy the average person often finds ethereal to discern. It is very subtle and takes an insight and awareness like that of Jesus to assess with confidence.

What is amazing in this statement is that Jesus does take this clever subtlety into account, He sees it ahead in all its delicacy, how thin the line can appear between genuine service and actual evil. He discerns it rightly because He can read the heart which jettisons all need to weigh sides and philosophize about motives, good or bad.

The Pharisees will be on the wrong side of this thin line, clothed in the noble declaration of serving God. The disciples are not to be fooled or taken in by it.

(You see here at this final hour so much special instruction to prepare them for the ramping up of Pharisaic rage and conflict ahead. It is much like the commander on a sortie who advises his men of the most critical cautions and procedures as they are just over the wall from their first assault. Gone are the formal, more casual lessons and training. What is needed now are instructions that respect the imminent danger and caution.)

3 "These things they will do because they have not known the Father or Me.

What evils have managed to proceed out into the world because of this failing? It is because men do not know the truth that they resort to false and half truths they have acquired for coping with the world's circumstances. The comfort of the Pharisees in serving God is not an internal witness, but a formal deduction from mere paperwork and tradition. It is much like legislating the codes of a municipality, technical expertise and not much need for operations of the heart. God's work requires the heart, not mere technical training. Hence His indictment - *"they have not known the Father or Me."*

4 .. "These things I did not say to you at the beginning, because I was with you.

Here then is the key distinction. Much preparation is being given knowing He will not be available for a follow-up huddle. While He was with them with plenty of time before His passion, the urgency of last minute instructions was not present. He was clearly in the middle of their efforts and in control of all things.

5 "But now I am going to Him who sent Me; and none of you asks Me, `Where are You going?'

At first, a complete contradiction since both Peter and Thomas had done this very thing (John 13:36.) Our Lord knew this perfectly well, so He must be referring to the nature of their former question. They did not ask and then pursue with keen interest.

We see this today in modern life. Someone asks us a question and midway through our answer we see they've lost interest or aren't getting it, and there are no follow-up questions. We might then characterize that as having not really asked with an interest in knowing. In the midst of a difference of opinion, we might offer that they had yet to really ask.

7 ". . . it is to your advantage that I go away; for if I do not go away, the Helper will not come to you; but if I go, I will send Him to you.

He prefaces this with "I tell you a truth." This is more than a phrase to get their attention. It means He is exposing a principle by which Heaven has been decreed to operate. A covenant has been made between Father, Son and Holy Spirit, similar to the covenant the Son made with the Father to give His life as a ransom. The Holy Spirit must wait until the Son has ascended, therefore it is needful if He is to come that Christ ascend.

All of that stricture and command is being put in place to serve the plan concerning these men. What a position of privilege that the things concerning these mere mortal men can cause orders in Heaven to be this specific and contingent. It gives us a glimpse at how very important this enterprise is in all the universe. And everyone of us who enter into their faith and work have a similar privilege that gains the clear attention of all in Heaven.

8 "And He, when He comes, will convict the world concerning sin and righteousness and judgment;

Here we find another definitive role of the Holy Spirit. He is to be Helper and Comforter, but He will also be the means by which men sense conviction about sin and the same about what is right. This is not merely for believers – *"[He] will convict the world . ."*

For the unbeliever, this means that the Spirit will act on the natural moral conscience that was bundled with creation to give every man the sense of what they ought to do and what violates that righteousness. Paul says that God has made Himself known to every person (Rom 1:18-20) and the Spirit will make an appeal to that knowing in all men, such that Paul can say none will have an excuse. As we also know, men will harden their hearts to that witness that their consciences become seared.

For believers, this is the regulator within us, the moral and spiritual compass that informs us of that which bears witness and that which offends, would we consult it. He is imparted to us because man has failed in the previous two dispensations – conscience and law. Man was allowed to live by his conscience, to do what was right in his heart. But his ability to deceive his own heart caused an increase in sin, and that increase occasioned the need for the Law. But here also, the Law was incomplete in that it did not live with the man, but depended on his memory to recall in one situation or another.

Now man has been given that witness to abide within himself, that he may appeal to Him wherever he goes.

9 concerning sin, . . . 10 and concerning righteousness,

Notice the demarcation of convictions. The conviction of sin is primarily for the world, the conviction of righteousness primarily for the believer. The world will only be able to comprehend the general revelation and that which comes through moral conscience. The deep things of the Spirit – those things taught them by Christ – are not comprehensible in unregenerate people. This level of reminding and recall, along with an ongoing intimacy in terms of the Spirit are only available to the believer.

11 and concerning judgment, because the ruler of this world has been judged.

The convicting efficacy of this role is enabled by the fact of Satan's judgment. Were his judgment to remain open there would be a wavering as to what of him is condemnatory and what might be otherwise. It is the finality of the judgment that frees the Spirit to convict concerning judgment.

We might ask how he is judged (past tense) yet still works and has yet to work. It is of course wrapped up in God's knowledge of the end from the beginning. He sees the judgment of Satan. Some formulations of our idea of the future incorporate the notion that it is comprised of what God has willed, whether including what creatures of free will do, and what He has decreed will be done in the judgment and resolution of all things.

This meant to give confidence to them and to us, that the one who plagues us is judged. Many believe there is power in reminding him of this when rebuking him.

12 "I have many more things to say to you, but you cannot bear them now.

There are two senses in which this can be seen. A) insights into the future that they would be able to comprehend – amazing and wonderful things yet to unfold for the Church and the world. B) trials and difficulties ahead that we might likely praise Him for His wisdom in sparing us.

Certainly, we can appreciate the experiential collision we have here between Christ who eternally sees the real future of actions and outcomes, and man, who can only see the present and must imagine the future. Christ is here making the appropriate adjustment to their condition, something we would rightly expect from a divine person.

13 "But when He, the Spirit of truth, comes, He will guide you into all the truth;

The "all" here is accommodating to their needs and purposes. It is not meant to be taken absolutely. They were not to receive knowledge of our modern world, medicine, technology, etc. But most assuredly, all that they needed to do the work of ministry in their sphere of influence among those whom they would come into contact was going to be provided. *" it will be given you in that hour what you are to say."* (Matt 10:19.)

We would do well to appeal to the Holy Spirit just in the areas of our own callings, yet so many proceed on their own steam and their own wits.

He is called the Spirit of Truth because He is apprised of the truth about reality, and that is something we desire if we are honest and courageous. We normally wish to have the real facts at our disposal to avoid missteps that will have to be corrected or will work against our objectives. On the other hand we can see times when we would rather not know. The use is largely up to us, but the important thing is that we are to be given access to One who has that knowledge.

It may not come in detail, but rather in firm unmistakable conviction. We may get the sense that we ought not to be where we are, and have nothing rational to go on except the amazing sense of being uncomfortable. Likewise, we may be given the awareness of how perfectly right we are in a situation and the sense that we know exactly what needs to be done.

This is truth coming our way, and it is more immediate than the analysis of rational descriptions could be because, if we learn to cultivate it, our feelings are the end results of rational analysis and we are already there.

In more rational terms, certainly the Spirit is going to enable our understanding of Scripture, preaching and the interaction of ideas. In those experiences, feelings are often largely out of place because the material is meant to be rationally taken in and understood. In these cases, the Spirit can actually convey the content to our minds, by His intimate connection with our thoughts, or provide someone in our path who can convey it.

13 ". . for He will not speak on His own initiative, but whatever He hears, He will speak; and He will disclose to you what is to come.

As with the Son, the Spirit seems to be in subjection to the Father, not because of inferiority, but according to agreed upon roles. Christ said continually that He did nothing except what He saw the Father doing, nor spoke anything except what was given Him from above. Here we see the Holy Spirit adopting this same role, which takes away any fuel for the confusion over Persons of the Trinity.

We are not to worry the issue of listening to three Persons, on the expectation that they can have unique and potentially conflicting commands or revelation to us. They speak in unity, each saying what the other has or will say. It is a model of unity to which man ought to aspire, were He to cultivate the insight into discerning the Spirit reliably.

Important in this statement is the expectation that He will disclose such things to them, which means there is going to be outright comprehension. The disclosure implies awareness, recognition and understanding. God is not one who revels in obfuscation and delights in promising clarity and then making things vague. He instead delights in making things known to us. *"If with all your hearts you truly seek Me, Ye shall ever truly find Me."* (Jer 29:13.) *" He is a rewarder of those who seek Him"* (Heb 11:6.)

14 "He will glorify Me, for He will take of Mine and will disclose it to you. 15 "All things that the Father has are Mine; therefore I said that He takes of Mine and will disclose it to you.

This tells us that we have already had an encounter with the Holy Spirit if we have come to know and understand what Jesus said and taught. We don't have Christ present today that we can go and hear His teaching directly. There is no presidential library where we can listen to His tapes. His playback facility is the Holy Spirit and Scripture. And He promises "disclosure."

16 "A little while, and you will no longer see Me; and again a little while, and you will see Me." . . . 17 "What is this thing He is telling us, `A little while, and you will not see Me; and again a little while, and you will see Me'

Jesus is speaking quite plainly, no hidden imagery or metaphors in play. The dilemma with the disciples is not the words but that they are not privy to the action that He will execute in relation to His death, burial and resurrection. (One action of finality at a time with them.)

Of course, in hindsight we see it clearly. Very soon He will be down off the Cross and in the tomb. Then again, shortly, He will be seen of them as resurrected. And there is yet another disappearance when He is taken up into Heaven.

As it is, they can only consider this so much double-talk.

"Are you deliberating together about this, . . 20 "Truly, truly, I say to you, that you will weep and lament, but the world will rejoice; you will grieve, but your grief will be turned into joy.

One can weigh the advantages and disadvantages of being naïve or privy to the facts ahead, but it is clear that Jesus wishes for His own reasons to spare them the stark details. Instead, He re-asserts that the understanding will come as they experience what is ahead.

We know the meaning of these things in hindsight. The world here means the world that will be changed by His death, not specifically the world in the next few hours. While His disciples will be grieving at His death, the immediate world about them, the Jews, will not be rejoicing. The world outside Judea will not know to rejoice.

Yet, it is as though the world to come is looking in on these events and rejoicing in anticipation of what will be made available to it. It will be the world that receives the message of good news and salvation.

In this, the disciples' grief will be turned into joy also, partly because they will see that death could not hold Him, but also that the world is so greatly benefited by Him.

23 "In that day you will not question Me about anything. Truly, truly, I say to you, if you ask the Father for anything in My name, He will give it to you.

We have "built in," this marvelous quality that assuages grief and pain when they have ceased and the joys of life replace them. In many cases, this is the hope that gets many of us through difficult trials – the knowledge that all things come to their end and we are soon to be out on the other side, with all of it behind us.

Here, He promises that they will see Him again. It is the greatest authentication that nothing will be lost in what appears as the victory of wicked men. It is, instead, part of the path that leads to the Kingdom and because of it, they will be able to ask anything in His name and receive it.

As before, these are not magic words. To ask "in His Name" is to ask respecting His Name and all it stands for. Since He is living, we cannot ask in His Name in error and expect anything from it. He is alive to discern whether we have His Name properly before us in the asking. This precludes asking that we may indulge our lusts and greed.

His Name will embody more than His Person - all that He taught and came to do. The name will be the icon that in one word represents the change in both world and universe, that which can never be put back the way it was. Men and women, great and small, will be asked one question: "What have you done respecting Jesus?" That will be the name upon which all eternal destiny turns.

This bears also on our attitude in prayer. We are unfortunately building the wrong case before God - so many prayers prayed, so many seemingly unanswered. James has a comment on this, "Ye ask and do not receive because ye ask amiss." (4:3.) Our response to Jesus' words here is to begin building a legacy of answered prayer, of supply in the face of need, of success in the course of accomplishment. That is what He promises. It is now up to us to claim it and see it lived out in reality.

24 "Until now you have asked for nothing in My name; ask and you will receive, so that your joy may be made full.

Not that they have never asked for anything, but that this principle of asking in His Name for the services of the Kingdom is yet to be inaugurated. While He was with them, they asked Him directly as a son asks his father. The son does not ask his father for help or knowledge "in his father's name." He simply asks directly. Now, a new petitionary procedure is being made ready. Beyond asking in the name of God, they are told that petition will now come to God in the Name of the Son. It is a change instituted in Heaven, the new play book for the coming age.

Some folks obsess on the exact formulation of prayers – that if we do not specifically pray to the Father in the name of the Son, we will be ineffective, that we are to leave off praying to Jesus or to the Holy Spirit.

It seems clear that Jesus is establishing a proper attitude about the direction of prayer. It is to be to His Father, and we don't find prescriptions to pray to Jesus. In modern life, we will find folks doing both, in some cases even interchangeably. As in all things, we must have confidence that God reads the heart and it is hard to believe that He refuses to hear on occasion of the wrong formula. Still, Jesus is giving us direction which, except for cases of ignorance, ought to be practiced as taught.

It is less a case of being penalized for ignoring it and more a case, like so often in Paul, that if a man prays, he will do well; but if he prays like Jesus taught, he will do better.

25 "These things I have spoken to you in figurative language; . . . but will tell you plainly of the Father."

This is difficult in light of their most recent puzzlement over what He meant by "in a little while." How is He now speaking plainly? And how do they recognize this at v.29? He is not directly answering their question about going away and then coming again. He has further spoken vaguely about the world rejoicing while they grieve. We have difficulty seeing plain speech here.

But something is happening to them as He unfolds the certainty about their access to the Father and the sure success they can expect from their prayers. They perceive a change in contrast to His characteristic use of parables and metaphor, which He had explained earlier (Matt 13:13, Mark 4:11.)

26 ". . and I do not say to you that I will request of the Father on your behalf;"

This seems strange, almost alienating. But He is not declaring that He is done asking on their behalf. Rather, He is declaring that they will be able to ask the Father on their own – *" Therefore let us draw near with confidence to the throne of grace,"* (Heb 4:16.) It is the Father's love that chose them, it will be His love that will hear them directly. This is virtually an end to the mediatorial idea respecting one's approach to God, even including to some extent Jesus. He is quite clearly saying that with respect to prayer, they and we are not to think of Him in this way. We have direct access to the Father. Our prayers are not stopped at the door for credentials.

But we must not take this so far as to undermine Christ as mediator altogether - *"For there is one God, and one mediator also between God and men, the man Christ Jesus."* (I Tim 2:5.)
He is talking here about our confidence in prayer.

29 . . . "Lo, now You are speaking plainly and are not using a figure of speech. 30 "Now we know that You know all things, . . . by this we believe that You came from God."

We don't see the transition vividly, but it is the disclosure He has made about access to the Father, not having to depend on Him to intervene for them, and their confidence that anything they ask will be granted, that moves them to this acknowledgment. But what is functionally taking place is Lesson 101 in their discernment of the Holy Spirit. They are putting the pieces together in the Spirit that could not be properly assembled by unaided reason. They are getting it.

In fact, we might go so far as to conclude that the whole resolution of "in a little while" and "the world will rejoice while you yourselves will be grieving" is coming clear. The plan of God is unfolding in their cognition, they see why He must go, that they be enabled. They perceive that they are on the very cusp of power and great glory for the work of the Kingdom, and all these things formerly said are falling into place.

We have therefore captured in this Scripture the very moment these men get divine assistance, the moment when it jels.

This is characterized by the statement, *""and have no need that anyone question you."* It's like saying, *"We get it now, we're on our way."*

And what do we see hereafter? An amazing maturity in taking on the mantle of church affairs and ministry, a closeness to the Holy Spirit that can discern such things as the case of Ananias and Sapphira according to the very will of God. We see the knowledge of the Father being ever more fully and clearly disclosed to them because Jesus has ascended. This is counter to our reasoning. The spiritual is always harder to discern than the patently factual. But in their case, the spiritual conduit of knowledge surpasses that of His presence with them on earth. He has revealed the Father plainly to them through the person of the Holy Spirit.

30 . . " by this we believe that You came from God." They own it for the first time, truly and genuinely.

"Do you now believe?"

This is not a check against their naivite. It is not meant as a correction ("You say you get it but do you really?") It is a reminder that this entails much that will still be difficult to experience. *" an hour is coming, . . . for you to be scattered, each to his own home, and to leave Me alone;"*

This is what getting it entails. Commitment means enduring the ugliness the world will sling at righteous. Their humanity will even fail them from time to time, but this will not upset the plan of God.

His mention that they will leave Him "alone" and by Himself would seem to undo all the positive achievements of the last few moments, but He adds the tag of hopefulness and salvation – *"yet I am not alone."* He will not be alone because of the presence of the Father, hence, neither will we be alone in our darkest hours.

33 "These things I have spoken to you, so that in Me you may have peace.

These words tell us He is not correcting naïve exuberance, but has reminded them "that they have peace in Him." He is coupling the wariness of the next few hours with the peace and confidence they will be given in the Holy Spirit. It will not overcome their initial dread and need to hide, but that is viewed as momentary, because they will very soon thereafter have the fulfillment of this whole scene made manifest. He will appear to them again and they will have the glorious privilege of watching Him ascend into the heavens.

33 .. "In the world you have tribulation, but take courage; I have overcome the world."

A tribulation that is not expected nor explained is a source of doubt and change of heart. It signals that something is wrong and we must surely be on the wrong track. He has fully anticipated this and assures them that this is planned, necessary and not a plan gone wrong.

In modern Christian life, the average Christian in peaceful areas of the world knows little of this kind of persecution and trouble. We certainly get buffeting from the world and ridicule from pleasure seeking, hedonistic elements of our society who often try to knock us down a peg in an ideological contest. But in very few areas of the world is the modern Christian asked to put their life and well-being on the line. Still, persecution is persecution, in the sense of suffering and taking abuse for one's stand for Christ.

The statement that He has overcome the world is not to promise exemption from trials and persecution, but that the world will not succeed in its designs. James will be beheaded not too long from now. That might seem a poor instance of overcoming the world, but this statement is meant to apply to the final outcome. Battles may be lost here and there. There will certainly be casualties. But the great war is already won.

John 17:1-12

1 Jesus spoke these things; and lifting up His eyes to heaven, He said, "Father, the hour has come; glorify Your Son, that the Son may glorify You, 2 even as You gave Him authority over all flesh, that to all whom You have given Him, He may give eternal life. 3 "This is eternal life, that they may know You, the only true God, and Jesus Christ whom You have sent. 4 "I glorified You on the earth, having accomplished the work which You have given Me to do. 5 "Now, Father, glorify Me together with Yourself, with the glory which I had with You before the world was. 6 "I have manifested Your name to the men whom You gave Me out of the world; they were Yours and You gave them to Me, and they have kept Your word.

7 "Now they have come to know that everything You have given Me is from You; 8 for the words which You gave Me I have given to them; and they received them and truly understood that I came forth from You, and they believed that You sent Me. 9 "I ask on their behalf; I do not ask on behalf of the world, but of those whom You have given Me; for they are Yours; 10 and all things that are Mine are Yours, and Yours are Mine; and I have been glorified in them. 11 "I am no longer in the world; and yet they themselves are in the world, and I come to You. Holy Father, keep them in Your name, the name which You have given Me, that they may be one even as We are. 12 "While I was with them, I was keeping them in Your name which You have given Me; and I guarded them and not one of them perished but the son of perdition, so that the Scripture would be fulfilled. (John 17:1-12.)

Commentary

THE GREAT PRIESTLY PRAYER

1 Jesus spoke these things; and lifting up His eyes to heaven,

We are without much indication of exactly where Jesus and the disciples are in relation to the Mount of Olives. They are not yet in the garden scene in which the disciples fall asleep and Jesus prays privately about His impending ordeal. We have then the notion that all the forgoing has been spoken while they are on the way. But at this juncture, Jesus takes time to pray this now famous prayer. There is no indication He has gone apart from them, but we would assume He has stopped somewhere, and now in their midst turns his eyes toward Heaven and prays.

The prayer has three distinct themes:

Prayer for Himself

"Father, the hour has come; glorify Your Son,

The point of glorification is yet many hours off. *"The hour"* is a metaphor, meaning the time for the unfolding of these events has come. The purpose of that time is the glorifying of the Son. We have recollections of other temporal and physical alignments. Those of the planets and eclipses have been pointed to as signaling great events.

Unknown to the world but seen of Heaven and the Father is the whole of the universe revolving around this one place in space and time. All of prior human history points to Jerusalem and this next day, because all of human history has been fundamentally about sin and man's redemption; all of history since points back to it.

And what is that glorifying of the Son about to take place? The gruesome picture of His scourging and crucifixion, followed by His resurrection where He is now made clean, with unstained garments, unhurt, and most notably alive and free from the corruption of the grave.

To call this a glorification is to point to the zenith of what He was about. He stated clearly that He came to die (John 12:47, Mark 10:45.) He came also to offer Himself as King. (John 18:37.) The latter is cause for glory enough, but when we realize that concomitant with this was the giving of His life to pay the rightful penalty due all men for their sins - an act of unimaginable scope - we cannot help but add glory upon glory.

Not only does His death reach back to rectify the condition of man over the ages, but it reaches forward, forever changing the state of affairs for mankind, and further still to the end of all human history, where all the nations of the world will not only be judged but the world wholly transformed because of Him. He will finally be King in patent fact.

that the Son may glorify You,

We are not to get the idea that the Father is stepping aside to make room for His replacement by the Son. Christ makes it clear that His own glorification is purposed to send more radiance toward the Father, that He be found and declared all the more loving, righteous and full of majesty than the past has ever proclaimed.

This is unshakable dedication, devotion and love between Father and Son. It is an enviable thing, and meant in every way to be so. Our earthly relationships are often imperfect enough that virtually everyone wishes they could be greater, closer, more purely loving and fulfilling, so much so that we look curiously at those rare moments when we see it in someone else's family. And blessed are those who see it in theirs and know its value.

So the Son and the Father continue to emulate what is meant to be desired and experienced in us.

2 *"even as You gave Him authority over all flesh, "*

He speaks this as an authenticating mark – "You have given Me authority over all flesh." It is a mark that authenticates that He and the Father are to be glorified.

How was Christ given such authority and so extensively if those who hate Him are now about to kill Him? This can *only* be seen if it is part of the intended plan. The horrible affairs of the next several hours are not events that have caught God by surprise – a plan with an unexpected and deleterious wrinkle. He says this clearly to Pilate – *"You would have no authority over Me, unless it had been given you from above;"* (John 19:11.)

What is so needful for mankind to realize and engage is that all human affairs are now under that authority. Slave and toil as we may for our own gains, in the end it will all come before the Son who will judge the living and the dead. And many will be devastated to find that life has all along hinged on this one relationship.

What is your world view? All will be found as misplaced and misguided that did not include the glorification of the Father in the Son.

2 *". . . that to all whom You have given Him, He may give eternal life."*

This sounds selective, but the language was intentional. It is not to all but to those whom the Father has given Him. This is not to restrict or limit the call to everyone respecting faith. "Many are called but few are chosen." (Matt 22:14.) Still, this is not a private club whom God has assembled amongst His "in crowd." It is the host of the faithful who responded to the call of faith.

There are some who are not happy with eternal life being restricted like this. "If you're not part of God's chosen, you get Hell and damnation."

But it's much like the man who gives a party at his home and invites all whom he loves and who love him. A neighbor who has hated him ever since he moved into the neighborhood comes to the door, asking why he was not invited? Does the host need to explain or account for himself in any way? Not that any reasonable person would insist. There is no expectation of favor from those whom we have chosen to hate or ignore or disrespect.

This is not the same as the command that we love our enemies. We are to do that sincerely, as God does. But when it comes to final rewards and outcomes - who is invited to eternal rest - God is not obligated on the basis of His love to treat His enemies equally as those who love Him. If they received His love and yet continue in hatred and disaffection, they have no claims to blessing and reward. His love extended them "opportunities" to participate. The outcome is based on their choices.

"eternal life" This is the great question of Job – "If a man die, shall he live on?" - and the question of every circumspect man who has ever lived. Here, Jesus is now seen as the one and only Answer to that question. He has the authority to extend this feature of existence to mankind, and that given Him by the Author and Source of life.

When we perceive within ourselves our life, the awareness of being alive, few are without any expectation or desire that it simply go on unending. We innately perceive life as a continuum despite the reality of death. Certainly, in old age, we have no desire to spend an eternity with the infirmities of a worn out body. But we do desire earnestly that the act of living not simply end, as a carnival ride comes to an end and its time to get off. Everything about our lives - perception, awareness of self, intelligence, emotion, the love of beauty, exhilarations and pleasures tell us this can't just end arbitrarily, and we become senseless dissipations into utter oblivion.

The desire for an ongoing continuity is answered in Jesus Christ.

3 "This is eternal life, that they may know You, the only true God,

This is the entire purpose in the event called life. To miss this is to be as the man in Michelangelo's <u>Last Judgment</u>, who, coming away from the assessment of his life, sits with his head in his hands and a dull, stark stare at how meaningless his life has been.

Eternal life is not about fulfilling a bill of requirements. It's not about trying really, really hard to be good. It's all about knowing the Father as the only true God.

Today, this is being fought with subtle fury by Satan and his forces. He is busy in millions of supposedly modern people's lives, planting the seeds of multiple options, multiple paths, so that as many as possible be deflected from the one true path. Jesus is telling us clearly that there is no one else out there listening. We may choose to invent or create in our minds all sorts of "others" to whom we might give our allegiance and worship, but only one is truly there. This was the impetus for the aptly titled chapter *The God Who is There* from Francis Schaeffer's, *How Shall We Then Live?* It is a dissertation on the truth about reality – there is only one God out there to be reckoned with.

and Jesus Christ whom You have sent.

A unique view to how Jesus regards Himself. He is the one using this designation instead of others. He had become very used to hearing what others called Him. Any who talked to Him or talked about Him, referred to Him as the son of Joseph and Mary or that man from Galilee, or Jesus of Nazareth. He had called Himself the Son of Man. Here, we see Him acknowledging that designation that will characterize the epistles to follow and all of Christendom.

These are not His first and last names, but His given name (Yeshua) and His title – the anointed One – the Christ. He is affirming Himself as Jesus, born into the family of man, but mysteriously also the Anointed One of prophecy, the Son of God.

In the union of Father, Son and Holy Spirit, the Father sent "the Son." Yeshua and Christos were pertinent to the human scene in space and time, the names by which mortal men would know Him. He came as a child born to real parents, and as Messiah, the Christ, the one expected of all prophecy.

5 "Now, Father, glorify Me together with Yourself, with the glory which I had with You before the world was.

He prefaces this with a summary accounting of his accomplished work. All that was assigned has been fulfilled, and in this we postulate that no single thing was left undone. In this, He proclaims to have glorified the Father. But in those things that glorification is not self-contained. They are part of the glorification program, but its fulfillment is not yet complete in them alone. There is something yet to be done that will cap the glorification for all future generations of man.

In full accord with our expectations about someone coming from another realm, He speaks of returning to the glory He had before the world was created. He is called the Beloved in Heaven (Song of Solomon 6:3, Isa 5:1, Luke 3:22) and we have the idea that the angels referred to Him in this way – that He was precious and beloved in all of Heaven. His words spell out His desire to return to that pre-incarnate existence.

6 "I have manifested Your name to the men whom You gave Me out of the world;

Out of the world – should quicken us toward the reality that when we come to Christ, our orientation to the world has forever changed. This is to condition every motive, desire, plan, aspiration, achievement, outlook and world view. That we are in the world is now a mere necessity, no longer that which defines our existence. Before this, everything was tacitly based on our being in world. Our parents, our wives and husbands, our children, our homes are all predicated on the fact that we must live in the world. Our schooling, our jobs, our careers, our goals imply the necessity that life must engage the world.

Now, we join with the old gospel song, "This world is not my home, I'm just a passin' through." We are not to be taken out of the world, but it no longer defines who we are and what we do. We are souls just visiting this planet because our new home, our new country is elsewhere (Heb 11:16, Eph 2:19, Phil 3:20.)

Those given to Jesus were spiritually gathered "out" of the world, to be disassociated with its ways and purposes. Every believer must likewise consider themselves chosen out of it and must kill that heart and desire that slew Lot's wife, as she longed for the world being destroyed.

6 ". . . they were Yours and You gave them to Me, and they have kept Your word.

In the immediate sense, this refers to the disciples. We find that they were already the Father's and He gave them to the Son for His purposes. In the extended sense, all believers in Christ have belonged to the Father and are given to Christ in every age to do the work of His ministry. The point of this distinction is to make it clear that Christ gathered no one whom the Father had not already chosen. We find this reiterated in Paul, "Ye were chosen before the foundation of the world." (Eph 1:4.)

Now a commendation, and one we would not at this point expect. They have kept the Father's word. Certainly the totality of all God had said and would say is beyond their lifetimes and their capacities. But Jesus is speaking in general terms. They were called and they responded. They were taught and accepted it (questions and puzzlements do not mitigate against their coming to accept it.) They asked and received.

7 "Now they have come to know . .

Much reiteration here of the chain of knowledge and gifts. They have come to know that all is from the Father. They have come to acknowledge that Jesus is not just a blessed man but truly from the Father, as seen in the previous section, above, and their revelation from the Spirit.

Prayer for His Disciples

9 "I ask on their behalf; I do not ask on behalf of the world, but of those whom You have given Me; for they are Yours;

What He asks on their behalf is the request that still remains in context – that He be glorified and thereby glorify the Father. He asks this not on behalf of the world – for the world's benefit – because the world is not yet prepared for these events. The crucifixion will mean nothing more to the world than a malefactor being punished, e.g. Christ is one who "suffered the extreme penalty during the reign of Tiberius." [61]

It will take the ministry of preaching to bring its importance to them. So, He asks on their behalf, that they will be emboldened by what they will witness, how they will come to see the Son and Father glorified in such things. As powerful as the Transfiguration was to authenticating Jesus, so much more the Resurrection, when they see Him cheat the grave and stand alive in their midst.

11 "I am no longer in the world; and yet they themselves are in the world, and I come to You.

A summary description of the mechanics of the exchange. He is to leave this world and hand off ministry to them, as they remain in it. Could Jesus have remained and reached the entire world by extraordinary means? Yes. That He and His Father chose to use men tells us of the quality and character of the work. It is to be interpersonal, not mass processing. Nor is it to be the supernatural personal appearance of the Son of God everywhere throughout time. Men are to be gathered through a one-on-one dialog between evangelist and unbeliever. It is to be the witness of a transformed life. The supernatural life of Jesus, for which no transformation from sin was meaningful, despite its power and clarity, was now less directly applicable as those who had been changed by Him. A certain aspect of our being creatures was needed for this communication, which made them mysteriously more useful than the eternal presence of the Creator.

11 ". . . Holy Father, keep them in Your name, the name which You have given Me, that they may be one even as We are.

At first, we might wonder about the specific Name, since Jesus is not the Name of God, nor were they called Jesusites. As for a name, they are to be known as Christians, which again is not the Name of God.

Here, Jesus is not referring to His Name as a label, but what His name means. Ye-shua is made up of *Ye* (from Yahweh) and *shua*, meaning salvation – *God is salvation.* "Ye" for Yahweh is explained by the practice in later Hebrew of shortening certain highly repeated syllables and parts of words. Yeshua is a shortened form of Yehoshua, and *Yeho* is a revised form of *'Yahu'*, which is itself an abbreviated form that stood for the tetragrammaton of the sacred name YHWH (Yahweh.) So the path is: Yahweh === Yahu === Yeho === Ye.

But Christians are still not called Yeshuans or Jesusites in a titular sense. Still, it would be an undisputed fact in the world that the use of "Christian" meant a direct path to the name Jesus, and in truth cannot be separated from that name, of which Yahweh is now seen to be a component part.

So contrary to the function of a mere label, Christians are kept in Yahweh by being in the Person by whom they are saved for Yahweh.

12 ". . and I guarded them and not one of them perished but the son of perdition, so that the Scripture would be fulfilled.

The security of the disciples has been repeated many times and is based on the principle that those given to Christ were chosen by the Father. It is hard to inculcate the idea what the Father begins can be hindered from fruition.

---

[61] Tacitus, Annals, Bk XV

The Father entrusted them to Him, now He turns their care back to the Father who will manifest it in the Holy Spirit.

As for the exception – the son of perdition - it might be said that he upsets the claim, since he was lost, were it not for the additional phrase – *that the Scripture be fulfilled.* So it is not a loss of those intended to be kept, but of the one who was already accounted for as lost by necessity. This is not to exonerate Judas as a person. It is to avoid counting as failure the necessity planned ahead of time for betrayal by someone. Christ was to die by purpose and plan, and that by betrayal. So he who chose to fill that role was never chosen to be kept, and therefore cannot be lost from that company.

John 17:13-26
13 "But now I come to You; and these things I speak in the world so that they may have My joy made full in themselves. 14 "I have given them Your word; and the world has hated them, because they are not of the world, even as I am not of the world. 15 "I do not ask You to take them out of the world, but to keep them from the evil one. 16 "They are not of the world, even as I am not of the world. 17 "Sanctify them in the truth; Your word is truth. 18 "As You sent Me into the world, I also have sent them into the world. 19 "For their sakes I sanctify Myself, that they themselves also may be sanctified in truth.

20 "I do not ask on behalf of these alone, but for those also who believe in Me through their word; 21 that they may all be one; even as You, Father, are in Me and I in You, that they also may be in Us, so that the world may believe that You sent Me. 22 "The glory which You have given Me I have given to them, that they may be one, just as We are one; 23 I in them and You in Me, that they may be perfected in unity, so that the world may know that You sent Me, and loved them, even as You have loved Me. 24 "Father, I desire that they also, whom You have given Me, be with Me where I am, so that they may see My glory which You have given Me, for You loved Me before the foundation of the world. 25 "O righteous Father, although the world has not known You, yet I have known You; and these have known that You sent Me; 26 and I have made Your name known to them, and will make it known, so that the love with which You loved Me may be in them, and I in them." (John 17:13-26.)

Commentary

THE GREAT PRIESTLY PRAYER *(cont.)*

Prayer for His Disciples cont.

13 ". . . and these things I speak in the world so that they may have My joy made full in themselves.

We do not generally see Jesus in the gospels as especially joyful. He is routinely serious and very focused, but we wouldn't characterize that image of Him as noticeably joyful. We are, of course, completely without the usual visual sense of His speech, facial expressions and tone of voice.

Yet He speaks of His joy as a matter of fact, something that would not have puzzled His writers. One doesn't need to be perennially giddy and gleeful to be joyful. Joy is an inner happiness, peace and contentment that is notably free from worry and despondency.

For us, it is transitory and often noticeably felt when things are going especially well – when we are having the best and most meaningful time with our wife or husband, our children are especially well-behaved or on the path to achieving our hopes for them, we are financially more secure than any time before, etc.

The joy of Jesus was not temporal but spiritual, not earthly but other worldly, Kingdom and Father related. For Him, His joy was in being rightly and successfully found within the Father's will, making known to men the blessings of a life rightly related and restored to God, seeing the purposes of the coming Kingdom being fulfilled. It was joy about the world that was always meant to be, now invading and converting the world that had gone wrong. This is the joy He wishes His disciples to have and He has spoken all that has gone before to that end.

For us today, we need to be asking if we have that same joy? Are we caught up in what God is doing in our world? Are we as full of joy to be part of it as were the disciples? Sadly, many Christians and many churches today have been talked out of this kind of joy. The proof of the pudding is in the reaction many churches have to an especially exuberant and joyful visitor. (Soon he will be taken aside and instructed "more wisely.")

This is not just an option we might consider. But here, Jesus is telling us that it is an expected outcome of His sojourn among us, something to be fulfilled in every generation.

14 "I have given them Your word; and the world has hated them, because they are not of the world, even as I am not of the world.

Hatred from the world is going to be a sign of effectiveness in the Spirit. We fight this and church programs have gone to great lengths to avoid this outcome, partly through fear and partly through an unhealthy alliance with the world. Whether from modern philosophy, science, changing social mores and values, many a modern-day church has stepped back to rethink how confrontative it should be against the world, and whether tolerance and accommodation are more apropos for today's unique problems?

But the NT consistently proclaims that the agenda of the world in every generation goes back to the arch-enemy of God. Satan will be ready in every generation to woo both believers and unbelievers toward the delights and practicality of the world, and make true righteousness painful to defend and live.

In the next several hours, the world is going to express its opinion of true righteousness, whether in the hatred of the leaders and elders who have been beguiled into mixing the world with their religion, or in the Roman soldiers who savagely scourge, laugh and taunt Jesus.

The chief problem in modern Christians is the dilemma of wanting a decent and pleasurable life by having some of what the world offers, and being one set apart from those things to stand for righteousness. Many a modern Christian has become adept at juggling both in a sort of self-imposed naivite that is reinforced by the observation that it can and often does seem to work. Standing on principles, especially biblical ones, is becoming less reasonable as time marches on.

15 "I do not ask You to take them out of the world, but to keep them from the evil one.

To say they are not of the world introduces the question: to what degree, since they obviously remain in it?

Jesus, therefore, follows up this comment with a clarification – "I do not ask You to take them out [it]." But they are to stand apart from it, to disassociate themselves from its world view and values. Hence, the principle prayer is that they be kept from the evil one, since standing apart from it will come under immediate attack and temptation by the devil.

even as I am not of the world.

This is the new identity – that we join Christ in being not of the world any longer but of the world to come. We are to share in the citizenship of that Kingdom as Christ has always enjoyed that citizenship. It is a whole change of attitude toward those allegiances we formerly found so necessary. It will mean giving up the aspirations to greatness in the world's eye (something we were trained at home and in school to aspire) and rather accept what greatness means in God's eyes.

As we live our Christian lives, we must have ever before us the distinction that we are fundamentally no longer a friend of the world, but are citizens of another country.

17 "Sanctify them in the truth; Your word is truth.

To be sanctified is to be made holy, but holiness essentially means "set apart." The idea of spiritual cleanliness and purity has been associated with holiness and has taken over its definition because those who are set apart for God's service are clean, upright and virtuous. But being clean and pure in thought and deed are the outcomes of having been set apart, which is its primary meaning. ('Holy Bible' means the book that is set apart from all other literature.)

Sanctification is spoken of in Scripture as a process, whereas salvation is immediate and assured – *that each of you know how to possess his own vessel in sanctification and honor* (I Thess 4:4, 2 Tim 2:21); *by grace you **have been** saved, and that not of yourselves* Eph 2:8.)

The tool and means of our sanctification is the Word of truth. Sanctification is the slower process of rooting out the world and replacing it with godliness. The encouragement and exhortation to do will come from exposure to His Word, because it will take something with authority to move us. Preaching can do so for a moment, but we can so easily rationalize it as just someone's opinion. The Word of God stands objectively apart from that. No matter what man may come to espouse, rationalize or philosophize, he can always turn back to the Bible which will continue to speak its message, the same yesterday and today.

The primary reason why many Christians do not appear much different from the unbeliever is their lack of frequent and regular exposure to the Word. They are living the Christian life as an activity and according to their own wits, which is always fruitless and to some degree dangerous.

His Word does not contain all truths. $E=MC^2$ is not in the Bible but is nevertheless an absolute truth. The Bible's truths are those most important to living by the instruction manual - who we are, why we are here and where we should be going. Try as men might to get along without it, the Bible continues to be the only place which so comprehensively accounts for secular man's condition and remedy. It is the source for understanding the life every person knows he must live.

18 ". . . I also have sent them into the world.

We must make no mistake about becoming a Christian. It will eventually come down to being sent, to making a dent, to witnessing the truth to the world. The purpose in establishing His Church in the world is to invade it with the truth.

Today, the world loves to vilify evangelism as just a case of imposing our ideas on everyone else. In democracies, this is intolerable because in a democracy everything is about fair play for the majority. The least popular thing is the notion that most everyone else is wrong and we are right. Yet in Jesus, this is the reason for being sent, to convert the world to right thinking and right belief, which must have the premise that others are wrong.

However, evangelism incorporates the idea of an invitation, rather than legislation. Yes, there is a tacit assumption of the other man being wrong and Jesus being right, but it is up to the individual to assess and choose. In Roman Catholicism, the Holy Church came nigh to what might be called legislated faith, through its very close association to the state, especially in terms of punishments and national decrees.

Throughout most of Europe for centuries it was socially necessary to be a member of the church whether one was a Christian inwardly or not. The politics and wars of many nations often revolved around a relationship to the "true faith." The transition of England from a Protestant Henry VIII to a Catholic Mary Tudor to a Protestant Elizabeth I is an example. Heads rolled, the careers of counselors were ruined, and wars were waged over which would win - Catholicism or Protestantism.

that they themselves also may be sanctified in truth.

Truth, by its very nature is set apart. It is always that thing out there that represents reality as it really is, and is always somehow not what we possess or have acquired. To the degree that we miss it or fail to acquire it, we live among the masses. When we find truth and embrace it, we see ourselves as set apart from what the world values and believes because it is what comprises reality and everything else is an illusion, deception or distortion. Therefore, truth does sanctify in that it sets us apart from naivite and deception toward what is real and authentic.

Prayer for All Believers

20 ".. but for those also who believe in Me through their word;

One can focus too heavily upon the Twelve and come away with the question, "Where then do we fit in?"

In many ways, the Twelve are unique. To them were given the keys to the Kingdom of Heaven, the power to bind and to loose. To them was given an apostolic authority we are hard-pressed to see replicated today as it was in them. Certainly Protestants have no extant instance of apostleship, except in the missionary. Catholicism proclaims to have kept not the office but the authority alive in its succession of bishops. But it is difficult to assess if that longevity and continuity accrues from the force of human tradition or divine.

But in many other things, the disciples are forerunners and exemplars of all who will have Christian faith. Surely the washing of each other's feet was meant to extend to others besides the Twelve. The call to evangelize the world was not to them only, but to us in every age.

*"through **their** word."* Notice it is their word (i.e. that of the apostles.) There is a handing off taking place. The words of Christ are imparted and entrusted to the apostles, to whom the rest of the world will now relate, as Christ has ascended.

To some extent then, Christians are to have deference to the apostles in terms of the content and meaning of Christ's teaching. He does say it will be "their word." We find this in Paul, *" remember me in everything and hold firmly to the traditions, just as I delivered them to you . . . stand firm and hold to the traditions which you were taught,"* (I Cor 11:2, II Thess 2:15.)

However, we need to understand the "forms" in which that word would be maintained. We hereafter see a deliberate program to write Scripture which became the NT. That body of material contained the very things being discussed here – those things Christ passed along for them to maintain and teach. But there remains today a difference of opinion between Protestant and Catholic as to what was bequeathed and remains intact today: their Scriptures, or their Scriptures and their unwritten tradition.

21 ".. that they also may be in Us, so that the world may believe that You sent Me.

We need as modern believers to embrace the idea that unity in Christ and the Father was not intended for just the first disciples. Here, He proclaims the purpose that this unity be extended to all who believe, which means we have a real expectation to live up to.

What is critical here is that it is to be a signal to the world that Jesus was sent of God. Our unity in Him and among ourselves will convey that. We can certainly see what the opposite has done. Our disunity among ourselves has become a sore spot with those outside, and the press is ready to advertise every instance it can find.

But, contrary to our thinking, unity with Christ and the Father are also expectations the world has. Most intelligent people know what Christ stood for, that He called for faith and obedience to righteousness. While they may not have the spiritual insight about what it all means, they do have the expectation that Christians ought to act like the Christ about whom they've read. We are to be unconditionally loving, forgiving, slow to anger, positive and uncritical, humble not grasping, not greedy for gain, wealth and power. When the world sees the opposite characters in Christians, it has an excuse to denounce the efficacy and significance of Jesus. "If Christians can't live it, what difference does Christ make?"

Hence, from this opposite example, we derive the corollary – that if more Christians acted like Him, more would have greater confidence that He came to make a difference, one that they themselves can experience. They will believe *"that You have sent Me."*

22 "The glory which You have given Me I have given to them,

To a large extent, this was still waiting in the wings. The majority were to live out uneventful lives in terms of what the world recognized at the time. The glory given here is in how they would come to be remembered. Their names would be as well known as Caesar, Napoleon, Aristotle, Alexander. Twentieth century people know newer names like Hitler, Einstein, and Mozart; but most will also acknowledge names like Peter, Paul, and the four evangelists, (without necessarily mentioning the NT.) One can say something simple like, "Paul wrote . . " and most will know you are talking about the apostle. Many also know that these are not just ancient names but that their lives and work have had far-reaching effects on Western civilization since.

23 I in them and You in Me, that they may be perfected in unity

We see here the key to unity, being in Christ as He is in us. He is in us de facto, by the indwelling of the Holy Spirit in every believer. But we nevertheless find disunity. If being in Christ is the key, then to some extent or the other, men practice or perceive this imperfectly. Thus, in this prayer the unity asked for is not axiomatic, but something to be cultivated, striven for and acquired over time. It is a prayer that prays for the end goal, but recognizes it to be a process in which some may succeed and others may fail.

24 "Father, I desire that they also, whom You have given Me, be with Me where I am

Again, we have to temper the meaning of this with other things He has just prayed – that they not be taken out of the world. So, this cannot mean that He wishes them to accompany Him to Heaven at His resurrection. This is rather a prayer of that desire knowing that its fulfillment will come when their work is done. He is adding to the prayer for unity that they be rewarded also with coming to be with Him where He will be.

24 ". . for You loved Me before the foundation of the world.

Christ's eternality is here disclosed as befits Him being Creator and one with the Father, who Jew and Christian agreed preceded the material creation of the world. It is to take us back in time to see that the love between them existed before all we know and see came into being. It is a continuity that augments our expectations about a creator-god. He would precede His creation, and that is precisely what we see Jesus saying.

Paul says that *we* too were chosen, certainly therefore loved, before the foundation of the world, (Eph 1:4.) So we find that the time before the Creation was filled with relationships within the deity, with decrees, agreements and plans, which included the plan to create, the will to permit the Fall of man, the covenant with the Son to offer Him as a sacrifice, and the choosing of the faithful who would believe in Him. In this we find God caught by no means off guard in any aspect of human consequences.

The impact of this for our own lives is the assurance that if we were known this way so far back in time, our salvation is no less assured, but carries the power and efficacy of One who sees the future, the end from the beginning.

25 "O righteous Father, although the world has not known You, . . . these have known that You sent Me;

This is the profound claim of Christians – that they have gained knowledge of what the world has not known. Yet this cannot be demonstrated back to the world that it may see the proof patently as a scientific fact. Its verification comes only by faith.

If stated as an act of knowing then it is expected to be perceivable, as opposed to those who claim it is unknowable and man can do no better than to merely infer or suppose. That is the defensive explanation of those who do not know Him yet need to still justify their place in the church and religious life. It's not, "Ye shall guess the truth . ." but "Ye shall *know* the truth."

26 and I have made Your name known to them, and will make it known,

This sounds at first like double-talk – "have made known, and will make it known." A person might ask, "Which is it?" One can make known by announcement and declaration, "I come from the Father," and one can make known by revealing intimate meaning, "Ask anything in My name . ."

The former can be done at the beginning. The latter can be a processing that continues into the future.

As for the Father's name, the disciples are launching into a world outside Judea that will speak the names of many other gods. Pilate will ask Jesus, "What is the truth?" despite having in every niche and wall images of his gods. The disciples will be declaring the name of the only God who is there, compared to which all the rest are mere counterfeits.

Next, the arrival at Gethsemane, more prayer for the coming ordeal, the arrest and trial of Jesus.

CHAPTER 14
His Arrest and Trial

Mark 14:32-34, Luke 22:41-45, 47-48, 49,51, Matthew 26:40-46,50-54, John 18:2-3, Mark 14:43-44, 46-47, John 18:4-9,11

1 When Jesus had spoken these words, He went forth with His disciples over the ravine of the Kidron, where there was a garden, in which He entered with His disciples. (John 18:1.)

32 They came to a place named Gethsemane; and He said to His disciples, "Sit here until I have prayed." 33 And He took with Him Peter and James and John, and began to be very distressed and troubled. 34 And He said to them, "My soul is deeply grieved to the point of death; remain here and keep watch." (Mark 14:32-34.)

41 And He withdrew from them about a stone's throw, and He knelt down and began to pray, 42 saying, "Father, if You are willing, remove this cup from Me; yet not My will, but Yours be done." 43 Now an angel from heaven appeared to Him, strengthening Him. 44 And being in agony He was praying very fervently; and His sweat became like drops of blood, falling down upon the ground. 45 When He rose from prayer, He came to the disciples and found them sleeping from sorrow, . . . 40 . . and said to Peter, "So, you men could not keep watch with Me for one hour? 41 "Keep watching and praying that you may not enter into temptation; the spirit is willing, but the flesh is weak." 42 He went away again a second time and prayed, saying, "My Father, if this cannot pass away unless I drink it, Your will be done." 43 Again He came and found them sleeping, for their eyes were heavy. 44 And He left them again, and went away and prayed a third time, saying the same thing once more. 45 Then He came to the disciples and said to them, "Are you still sleeping and resting? Behold, the hour is at hand and the Son of Man is being betrayed into the hands of sinners. 46 "Get up, let us be going; behold, the one who betrays Me is at hand!" (Luke 22:41-45, Matthew 26:40-46.)

2 Now Judas also, who was betraying Him, knew the place, for Jesus had often met there with His disciples. 3 Judas then, having received the Roman cohort and officers from the chief priests and the Pharisees, came there with lanterns and torches and weapons. (John 18:2-3.)

43 Immediately while He was still speaking, Judas, one of the twelve, came up accompanied by a crowd with swords and clubs, who were from the chief priests and the scribes and the elders. 44 Now he who was betraying Him had given them a signal, saying, "Whomever I kiss, He is the one; seize Him and lead Him away under guard." . . . 48 But Jesus said to him, "Judas, are you betraying the Son of Man with a kiss?" (Mark 14:43-44, Luke 22:47-48.)

4 So Jesus, knowing all the things that were coming upon Him, went forth and said to them, "Whom do you seek?" 5 They answered Him, "Jesus the Nazarene." He said to them, "I am [He]." And Judas also, who was betraying Him, was standing with them. 6 So when He said to them, "I am [He]," they drew back and fell to the ground. 7 Therefore He again asked them, "Whom do you seek?" And they said, "Jesus the Nazarene." 8 Jesus answered, "I told you that I am He; so if you seek Me, let these go their way," 9 to fulfill the word which He spoke, "Of those whom You have given Me I lost not one." . . . 46 They laid hands on Him and seized Him. (John 18:4-9, Mark 14:46-47.)

49 When those who were around Him saw what was going to happen, they said, "Lord, shall we strike with the sword?" (Luke 22:49.) . . . 10 Simon Peter then, having a sword, drew it and struck the high priest's slave, and cut off his right ear; and the slave's name was Malchus. (John 18:10.) . . . 11 So Jesus said to Peter, "Put the sword into the sheath; the cup which the Father has given Me, shall I not drink it?" (John 18:11.)

52 "Put your sword back into its place; for all those who take up the sword shall perish by the sword. 53 "Or do you think that I cannot appeal to My Father, and He will at once put at My disposal more than twelve legions of angels? 54 "How then will the Scriptures be fulfilled, which say that it must happen this way?" . . . 51 But Jesus answered and said, "Stop! No more of this." And He touched his ear and healed him. (Matthew 26:50-51 John 18:11, Matthew 26:52-54, Luke 22:51.)

52 Then Jesus said to the chief priests and officers of the temple and elders who had come against Him, "Have you come out with swords and clubs as you would against a robber? 53 "While I was with you daily in the temple, you did not lay hands on Me; but this hour and the power of darkness are yours." . . . 12 So the Roman cohort and the commander and the officers of the Jews, arrested Jesus and bound Him, . . . 56 "But all this has taken place to fulfill the Scriptures of the prophets." Then all the disciples left Him and fled. (Luke 22:52-53, John 18:12a, Matthew 26:56b.)

51 A young man was following Him, wearing nothing but a linen sheet over his naked body; and they seized him. 52 But he pulled free of the linen sheet and escaped naked. (Mark 14:51-52.)

Commentary

THE ARREST

1 When Jesus had spoken these words, He went forth with His disciples over the ravine of the Kidron, where there was a garden,

Immediately east of the eastern wall of the Temple compound the ground recedes very steeply into a ravine (many recall of the modern tombs and crypts now placed up on this slope near the wall.) Soon the ground descends quite deep and then ascends up to the Mount of Olives. This is the Kidron Valley. On the way up this slope on a sort of plateau is the traditional site for Gethsemane.

There has been little intense and extended prayer in the preceding hours of the supper and the teaching along the path. Now the object is fervent prayer both of Jesus and His disciples. The hour is very near for His arrest. As they gather to pray, the authorities have not been idle. They are presently gathering Temple police and troops from the city garrison for the arrest.

32 They came to a place named Gethsemane; and He said to His disciples, "Sit here until I have prayed."

It is not a command to merely sit, but to also pray while on watch, as we see from Jesus' upbraiding later. It isn't clear why they are to be on watch, since the arrest is necessary and will not be resisted by Him with any force. Perhaps it is for their safety in not being taken advantage of by the soldiers, or to be generally on watch for criminals and thieves. They may very well have wondered how to pray and about what specifically. Jesus has only given them general comments on what is next, but the immediate moments have not been spelled out toward which they might pray specifically.

He will separate with Himself Peter James and John and go a bit further away. To them He announces His inner grief. There are those who like to make hay of the favoritism being demonstrated here, but we have nothing historically or otherwise to indicate the others were bothered by this separation. It was the Lord's doing and we must believe they gave Him the benefit of the doubt as to His reasons.

". . deeply grieved to the point of death . ."

Having seen the film *Passion of the Christ* (Icon Productions © 2004), we are now brutally acquainted with the ordeal before Him. There is no doubt about His ultimate survival beyond those moments, but He is a man and He will feel the pain, and no matter how much we might know the ultimate outcome, getting to the end by way of extreme suffering and pain is not glibly entertained.

As we contemplate great suffering, or painful illness, our hearts can faint to such a degree that the depression can seem like the onset of death. A blanket of dread and depression can effectively simulate what we might take as dying or feeling life and well being draining away from us.

We cannot begin to relate to what Jesus was now suffering. All the more aptly described as grief unto death.

"Father, if You are willing, remove this cup from Me; yet not My will, but Yours be done."

This is the plea of a son to his father, and certainly based on the ordeal of agony just about to take place. We can be confused here in our imperfect understanding by oversimplifying how His motives and will ought to nullify any anguish and dread. Conversely, we might wish to attribute this to some weakness of faith – that He wished to be let off.

It is not weakness in faith but weakness in body. As above, we cannot divorce Him from all the feelings and repugnance of pain. As we see Him in His passion, He is not one standing stoically, letting men do what they will, (it doesn't matter, it doesn't actually hurt.) Rather, His was called suffering because it was painful and grievously so. If He was man (and we cannot deny this) then with His humanity comes the dread of suffering.

Yet he did not insist on begging the easy way out or to have the Father find some other means. He quickly qualifies that He is here to do the Father's will.

43 Now an angel from heaven appeared to Him, strengthening Him.

How the eyewitness of Luke's material knew this detail is not disclosed. Did one of them see this appearance or something that moved them to that conclusion? Did Jesus tell them afterwards? Did God reveal it to Luke in the course of composition? We don't really need it explained since we know the record to be inspired and that God was capable of getting this detail into Luke's hands.

The point is that Heaven came to His aid, which tells us that things greater than mere human events are now taking place. One cannot trivialize and liberalize these events into all that sort of thing one can readily predict about men and troublemakers. Angelic intercessions do not accompany the ordinary discord and strife men wage in their selfish and picayune attacks.

44 . . . and His sweat became like drops of blood, falling down upon the ground.

Believers in past ages have gone further in saying they *were* drops of blood. The phenomenon is not imaginary. The clinical term is hematohidrosis, whereby blood vessels very near the sweat glands constrict with the pressure of stress, followed by a release in which the blood swells into the vessels causing extreme dilation. The blood can seep such that it mixes with sweat and is sent out through the pores. That this is rare is simply because this kind of stress is rare.

As for why Luke did not simply say He sweated blood, we can certainly understand. He is a physician and this is a very rare, perhaps unheard of phenomenon for him. He is caught between the testimony of the unskilled eyewitness and his own medical background. He dares not dismiss it as ecstatic emotion getting the best of the observer, nor can he put the phenomenon into medical perspective. The best path is to speak in the language of appearances – it appeared like drops of blood, which doesn't deny that is was but remains one step removed from affirming it biologically. It is perhaps a bit of humanity left in the record from its author which does no disservice to the divine record or its inspiration.

45 When He rose from prayer, He came to the disciples and found them sleeping from sorrow,

Luke is the only evangelist to tell us their sleep was from sorrow. We can certainly understand how all the events, from the preparations to a long supper to teaching and walking would cause any man to doze once settled into a watchful posture late into the evening. But Luke places sorrow in an important enough position as to be mentioned.

We should not minimize the effects of sorrow in helping to induce sleep. We say, "She cried herself to sleep" so we have in our experience that sleep can easily follow from sorrow.

But the Lord is less accommodating than we might be. He upbraids them.

40 .. "So, you men could not keep watch with Me for one hour?"

There is both an observation and a command said here. When stated as a question, it is an observation turned into an indictment. He is not only observing that they did not, but voicing what they ought but failed to have done. Some might offer that Jesus is being unrealistic and perhaps draconian in expecting men to deny their sleep for the work of the Kingdom. There is no penalty levied, He is not wroth. But He is letting them know that the subjugation of the body for higher work is an expectation. They will need to work towards it and shun the temptation to make excuses for it.

41 "Keep watching and praying that you may not enter into temptation; the spirit is willing, but the flesh is weak."

Here is the command. Despite the difficulty in bending the flesh to our wills, we are to make up our minds to succeed, not excuse and cave in. He reiterates His command to watch and pray. And the reason is that the need is not over. He must return again to pray more and He needs them to support Him still.

But He adds that this will keep them from temptation. In the immediate scene, the temptation is to let despondency give birth to utter discouragement. To let worry beget cowardice or hesitancy in courage. Being alone with the night and their thoughts, Satan was ready to move in and undo all that the night had wrought. Praying while being alert enough to be on watch meant refusing to give the mind over to what Satan would wish and work.

In the modern scene, many centuries and many miles away from Gethsemane, we too are to fight off those episodes of temptation by prayer. We are to recognize them early and take appropriate defensive action, by occupying ourselves with prayer.

Our constant battle will be just as it was for them, having a willing spirit ready to do all for Him, but a body that will not cooperate for lack of strength and endurance.

42 He went away again a second time and prayed, saying, "My Father, if this cannot pass away unless I drink it, Your will be done."

Strangely, the content of this second prayer is summarized in a repeat of His plea that the cup pass from Him. We have no doubt that more was prayed, but God wished that this repetition characterize this second session with the Father. It is to make all the more vivid His humanity. This subject was obviously very heavy on His mind, to be mentioned as being prayed for here and yet a third time – *and went away and prayed a third time, saying the same thing once more.*

45 ... "Behold, the hour is at hand and the Son of Man is being betrayed into the hands of sinners."

The time has arrived. Before the evidence is at hand, He knows the nearness of it and rousts them to wakefulness. He knows his enemies are almost within earshot, their hardware and weapons giving testimony of their approach amid the quite of night.

He doesn't announce it as one might rouse the company to a sneak attack by the enemy. It is not proclaimed as an emergency come upon them, but a well ordered step in an unfolding plan – *"the Son of Man is betrayed into the hands of sinners."* The betrayal is the step in the plan, not the appearance of men armed to the teeth.

Again, a reference to the "hour" as representing the commencement of His ordeal.

46 "Get up, let us be going; behold, the one who betrays Me is at hand!"

Not "let us get out of here" but "let us prepare to go with these men." "Behold" seems a very distant word that we wish to imbue with some sense more serious than simply saying "See." But that is really what is being said, "See, the one who betrays me is here."

2 Now Judas also, who was betraying Him, knew the place, for Jesus had often met there with His disciples.

This seems like Judas had merely guessed, based on past experiences. This would be pretty risky if only a guess. One doesn't get permission to take charge of provincial soldiers and Temple police on a hunch. You had better have intelligence that knows where the arrestees are.

What is meant here is that Judas was privy to the plans for the evening that all must have known as the supper was ordered and conducted. That he knew the location merely means that the path to it would be familiar as opposed to some place secret.

One might wonder why this was being done at night? Certainly the factor of Jesus' popularity constrained their actions. It would be impossible to keep the news of His arrest secret, but to do it at night at least avoided the issues anticipated from action in the light of day.

Also, the time would help exclude certain members and facilitate the sort of "kangaroo" court they had in mind. And one must not forget the need they had to wrap up this affair before the first offerings pertaining to the week of Unleavened Bread, following the Passover meal.

3 Judas then, having received the Roman cohort and officers

Some common sense is needed here in reference to cohort. A cohort was a tenth of a legion, which meant between 300 and 600 men (the legion varied between 3,000 and 6,000 men.) Secondly, Jerusalem did not station legionary troops in the city under the procurators, but rather the base for the Tenth Legion was at Caesarea with reinforcements available also from Syria. According to F.F. Bruce, Jerusalem had a force of 720 infantry and 240 cavalry, raised to more during periods that anticipated unrest. [62]

It is difficult for us to believe, that over three hundred seasoned troops plus Temple guards were mustered at night to arrest just twelve men, irrespective of any supposition they might be armed. That it could have been the seventy of Jesus' followers would be precluded, since Judas knew who would be there, and three hundred men is still overkill, since we're not talking about an insurrection but an arrest.

The use of "cohort" is simply to say that the men who were arranged for were from the city cohort, much as we might say the National Guard was sent in to control an emergency. We don't mean every infantryman, all armored vehicles and every tactical aircraft in the region.

We learn later that the contingent was sizeable enough to require the presence of their commander (John 18:12), hence more reason to call them the cohort when in actuality something less.

43 .. by a crowd with swords and clubs, who were from the chief priests and the scribes

The chief aim here was intimidation to forestall any thought of resistance or trouble. It must have been questioned what twelve men could do, and common sense told any reasonable person that merely double that amount in Roman-trained soldiers would easily subdue anything these men might attempt. But the Romans were adept at intimidation, and overwhelming forces (within reason) were routine in the interest of

---

[62] Bruce, New Testament History, Doubleday, 1969, p.195.

an easy surrender. The added presence of clubs would tell the party involved that resistance would be significantly painful.

44 . . "Whomever I kiss, He is the one; seize Him and lead Him away under guard."

Judas is now fully under Satan's power if able to utter such words without blinking an eye. Any benefit or edification he may have received from Jesus, which ought to have scrutinized his bent of mind, had no influence here. He is sold to the human commonwealth who were wittingly or unwittingly the agents of Satan.

48 . . . "Judas, are you betraying the Son of Man with a kiss?"

This is not a question from naïve incredulity, but again an observation formed as a question. It was something whose irony Judas was being asked to consider. He was betraying the Master with a sign of endearment and affection, a supreme contradiction. The purpose was to let Judas know how far he had gone in his zeal – that hypocrisy and empty gestures were now his tools.

For us in modern times, Christians often ignore the effect of their sin on their relationship with God and glibly participate in worship and church services as though the two are miles apart. It is plainly repugnant to the Spirit of grace to willfully sin and a few hours later be singing "How Great Thou Art." How can we consider seriously uttering those words while we sweep under the carpet some sin against the One we are prompted to call Great? Nor are things made better by reminding ourselves that we are such-and-such in the church and being about the King's business obligates God to wink at our weaknesses.

4 . . "Whom do you seek?" 5 They answered Him, "Jesus the Nazarene." He said to them, "I am [He]."

Jesus immediately shows His captors that He is not one to be wary of. He asks in the tone and parlance of normal discourse, much the same as if the police had come to one's door.

Notice the reaction visited upon them: *they drew back and fell to the ground (v.6.)* This is often explained as a sort of "show of stuff" by our Lord, to let them know with Whom they are dealing. That this did not dissuade them is hard to imagine, but carnal man is capable of every manner of rationalization, and they were duty-bound.

An interesting observation is in what Jesus actually says. The Greek has *ego eimi* – "I am." The "he" is not actually present in the text and many translations show "[he]" in brackets, indicating it is being supplied to make sense.

Some have attempted to connect this to the I AM of Scripture (Ex 3:14) and Jesus' statement to the Pharisees – "before Abraham was I am." But this is really a case where the rule of context is critical. The construction *ego eimi* is used elsewhere without "he" and is understood to mean "I am he" without jumping to a conclusion from the literally short "I am" (Mark 13:6, Luke 21:8.) The context in these passages necessitates that the listener supply "he" to make sense.

In the case of John 8:58 and Abraham, supplying "he" does not make sense, since this would mean that Jesus was saying He was Abraham, so supplying it would introduce nonsense. But He neither said *I was.* Hence, the Jews knew in this context Jesus was in fact appropriating the divine connection, as in Exodus 3:14 – *"tell them I AM hath sent thee,"* and their reaction was predictable.

Here in John 18, there is no obstacle to contextually supplying "he" because it is a straightforward reply to their question. Still, one has to wonder why they fell back at this particular set of words? What is also interesting is that in the repeat of this question and answer we have precisely the same Greek words for "I am" yet nothing happens and the men are able to take Him.

God is doing something in response to the words, if simply to show them whom they are dealing with.

"I told you that I am He; so if you seek Me, let these go their way," 9 to fulfill the word which He spoke, "Of those whom You have given Me I lost not one."

What is noteworthy here is that the fulfillment of the prophecy is controlling their actions. It is a request, but one they could not refuse, and that because God was in charge of these affairs. It is likely, had they acted on their own, that some or all of His disciples would suffer with Him. The controlling influence of the prophecy ensured this would not happen, and men secular or otherwise were made to obey it.

And this despite what follows next.

49 When those who were around Him saw what was going to happen, they said, "Lord, shall we strike with the sword?"

We see clearly how they had misunderstood His exhortation about carrying swords. Were this the time, He would have reacted differently.

10 Simon Peter then, having a sword, drew it and struck the high priest's slave, and cut off his right ear; and the slave's name was Malchus.

John is the only evangelist to tell us the name. The presence of the high priest's agent was to ensure that Jesus was taken to the intended places as decided in the Sanhedrin. There were to be interviews and interrogations somewhat out of the norm, and this man was undoubtedly there to effect these decisions.

11 .. "Put the sword into the sheath; the cup which the Father has given Me, shall I not drink it?"

Definitely not the fulfillment of Jesus talking to them earlier about carrying a sword. Resistance at this juncture was in fact against the will of the Father.

Hard as it was to understand, Jesus was preserving the engines that would effect the will of God, that He must suffer and die.

52 .. "Put your sword back into its place; for all those who take up the sword shall perish by the sword."

The reason for this exhortation despite His earlier instruction to carry a sword is that this is an aggressive not a defensive act. Peter is on the offense, and this is not to be the way with them. Those who pursue this means to settle difficulties will come face to face with the principle in the world that all who do so will be caught by this same method. Sooner or later someone bigger and better will defeat them.

53 "Or do you think that I cannot appeal to My Father, and He will at once put at My disposal more than twelve legions of angels?

If it was thought that some aggressive or defensive action could save the day, He reminds them that He has the resources quite readily without Peter's intervention. If such a host is ready at hand and they have not been called, is it not plain that this is not the moment for escape?

Twelve legions is 72,000 angels. This is hyperbole for effect. It is certainly true He could ask for that exact number. But it is more likely He is making a point about how many He could ask for, and the number mentioned is simply enough to make His point.

We are not to infer that angels have legions, since this is not only a human term but a uniquely Roman term. It is simply a term with which they could easily relate.

But the point is that Heaven also must obey the dictates of the prophecy – "How then will the Scriptures be fulfilled, which say that it must happen this way?"

Jesus then ends this fracas with "Stop! No more of this."

And He touched his ear and healed him.

This is done not only to avoid having it added to those charges already compiled, but to have the opposite effect concerning them. In the very midst of His arrest, He takes the time to correct a rash act and restore a man to his unmutilated self. How ironic that such an account would cry out against the crimes they were ready to levy against Him. "He is a malefactor, and Oh, by the way, He restored the ear of Malchus."

We marvel at the command of the elements made available in just a touch. In it, the man's flesh was reconstituted and the places sliced were brought into union with it. The vessels severed were joined once again, without sutures or the time needed to grow into union with one another. Nerves were restored so as to connect with the trunks and bundles left behind, cartilage is mended and joined. A procedure that would take hours to perform in a hospital and weeks from which to recover was completed in but a moment.

52 .. "Have you come out with swords and clubs as you would against a robber? 53 "While I was with you daily in the temple . . . but this hour and the power of darkness are yours."

The show of force for a robber would primarily be for intimidation, since robbers are among the more clever and resourceful and might outsmart a smaller band. He is asking them to consider seriously whether He is such a person. And there is proof in simple reason, were they to think about it. Would a thief make himself available in public where he could be taken any time?

While we have stated that the hour is fulfilling prophecy and the intent of the Father, it cannot nevertheless be disassociated with them and their motives. It is their hour for the wrong reasons, even if it is the Lord's hour for the right ones.

The "power of darkness" describes the sheer advantage the cover of night is providing them in many more ways than one.

12 So the Roman cohort and the commander and the officers of the Jews, arrested Jesus and bound Him,

The mention of the commander being present tells us that despite the haste of their move, the Jews had planned well. To ensure the death penalty, they had to formulate a case that would be taken seriously by the Roman authority. The reason is that in non-free provinces, the Romans proscribed the exercise of the death penalty from local officials. There were abuses that the Romans winked at, but this would be a very public thing concerning a very public figure. They needed Pilate's cooperation.

The charge at present was speaking against the preservation and sanctity of the Temple, which seems like merely a provincial, religious ordinance, but the Romans respected it to the degree that they made violations punishable, even for Roman citizens. This will not be the charge for which Jesus is crucified, but this will be explained as His interviews and "trials" ensue.

Then all the disciples left Him and fled.

Part of this behavior is so that the prophecy of losing none of them be fulfilled, but part is also due to what Jesus predicted in addition – "as the Shepherd is struck, the sheep will scatter." Jesus is left alone to face is accusers. We later find that Peter follows from a distance, so as to be seen outside the residence of Caiaphas as He is interviewed there.

Then we have this curious anecdotal ending to the section -

51 A young man was following Him, wearing nothing but a linen sheet over his naked body; and they seized him. 52 But he pulled free of the linen sheet and escaped naked.

The tumult of the cohort and guards surely woke those in nearby homes. It is reasonable a small crowd gathered at a distance and that the man here came out in haste, taking no time to even dress. But there is more to suggest he was not just a bystander, but among Jesus' other more remote disciples.

The failure to name the man is thought by some to indicate the modesty of Mark, being the man himself, as others would have named him. Whoever he is, he was not one of the Twelve, given his condition. Mark would not be one of those disciples coming from the supper, nor do we know if he was among the seventy. But the fact that he fled indicates he was in the same fear as the disciples, which would not have been the case with a simple bystander.

As for the man being Mark, this is pure speculation since it is not necessary that the other writers would have mentioned his name.

John 18:12-16,18, 19-24; Luke 22:54-58, Matthew 26:69-74, John 18:26, Luke 22:61-68, Mark 14:60-64, Luke 22:71, Matthew 27:1-10

12 So the Roman cohort and the commander and the officers of the Jews, arrested Jesus and bound Him, 13 and led Him to Annas first; for he was father-in-law of Caiaphas, who was high priest that year. 14 Now Caiaphas was the one who had advised the Jews that it was expedient for one man to die on behalf of the people. 15 Simon Peter was following Jesus, and so was another disciple. Now that disciple was known to the high priest, and entered with Jesus into the court of the high priest, 16 but Peter was standing at the door outside. So the other disciple, who was known to the high priest, went out and spoke to the doorkeeper, and brought Peter in.

19 The high priest then questioned Jesus about His disciples, and about His teaching. 20 Jesus answered him, "I have spoken openly to the world; I always taught in synagogues and in the temple, where all the Jews come together; and I spoke nothing in secret. 21 "Why do you question Me? Question those who have heard what I spoke to them; they know what I said." 22 When He had said this, one of the officers standing nearby struck Jesus, saying, "Is that the way You answer the high priest?" 23 Jesus answered him, "If I have spoken wrongly, testify of the wrong; but if rightly, why do you strike Me?" . . 24 So Annas sent Him bound to Caiaphas the high priest. . . 54 Having arrested Him, they led Him away and brought Him to the house of the high priest; but Peter was following at a distance. (John 18:12-16, 19-24; Luke 22:54.)

18 Now the slaves and the officers were standing there, having made a charcoal fire, for it was cold and they were warming themselves; and Peter was also with them, standing and warming himself. . . 56 And a servant-girl, seeing him as he sat in the firelight and looking intently at him, said, . . 69 "You too were with Jesus the Galilean. . . This man was with Him too." . . 57 But he denied it, saying, "Woman, I do not know Him." (John 18:18., Luke 22:55-56, Matthew 26:69, Luke 22:57.)

71 When he had gone out to the gateway, another servant-girl saw him and said to those who were there, "This man was with Jesus of Nazareth." 72 And again he denied it with an oath, "I do not know the man." (Matthew 26:71-72.)

58 A little later, another saw him and said, "You are one of them too!" . . 73 . . the bystanders came up and said to Peter, "Surely you too are one of them; for even the way you talk gives you away." . . 26 One of the slaves of the high priest, being a relative of the one whose ear Peter cut off, said, "Did I not see you in the garden with Him?" . . 74 Then he began to curse and swear, "I do not know the man!" And immediately a rooster crowed. (Luke 22:58, Matthew 26:73, John 18:26, Matthew 26:74.)

61 The Lord turned and looked at Peter. And Peter remembered the word of the Lord, how He had told him, "Before a rooster crows today, you will deny Me three times." 62 And he went out and wept bitterly. (Luke 22:61-62.)

63 Now the men who were holding Jesus in custody were mocking Him and beating Him, 64 and they blindfolded Him and were asking Him, saying, "Prophesy, who is the one who hit You?" 65 And they were saying many other things against Him, blaspheming.

66 When it was day, the Council of elders of the people assembled, both chief priests and scribes, and they led Him away to their council chamber (Luke 22:63-66.)

55 Now the chief priests and the whole Council kept trying to obtain testimony against Jesus to put Him to death, and they were not finding any. 56 For many were giving false testimony against Him, but their testimony was not consistent. 57 Some stood up and began to give false testimony against Him, saying, 58 "We heard Him say, `I will destroy this temple made with hands, and in three days I will build another made without hands.' " 59 Not even in this respect was their testimony consistent.

60 The high priest stood up and came forward and questioned Jesus, saying, "Do You not answer? What is it that these men are testifying against You?" 61 But He kept silent and did not answer.

Again the high priest was questioning Him, . . saying, 67 "If You are the Christ, tell us." But He said to them, "If I tell you, you will not believe; 68 and if I ask a question, you will not answer. . . 61 "Are You the Christ, the Son of the Blessed One?" 62 And Jesus said, "I am; and you shall see THE SON OF MAN SITTING AT THE RIGHT HAND OF POWER, and COMING WITH THE CLOUDS OF HEAVEN." 63 Tearing his clothes, the high priest said, "What further need do we have of witnesses? 64 "You have heard the blasphemy; . . For we have heard it ourselves from His own mouth. . . how does it seem to you? " And they all condemned Him to be deserving of death. (Mark 14:60, Luke 22:67-68, Mark 14:61-64, Luke 22:71, Mark 14:64.)

1 Now when morning came, all the chief priests and the elders of the people conferred together against Jesus to put Him to death; 2 and they bound Him, and led Him away and delivered Him to Pilate the governor. 3 Then when Judas, who had betrayed Him, saw that He had been condemned, he felt remorse and returned the thirty pieces of silver to the chief priests and elders, 4 saying, "I have sinned by betraying innocent blood." But they said, "What is that to us? See to that yourself!" 5 And he threw the pieces of silver into the temple sanctuary and departed; and he went away and hanged himself. 6 The chief priests took the pieces of silver and said, "It is not lawful to put them into the temple treasury, since it is the price of blood." 7 And they conferred together and with the money bought the Potter's Field as a burial place for strangers. 8 For this reason that field has been called the Field of Blood to this day. 9 Then that which was spoken through Jeremiah the prophet was fulfilled: "AND THEY TOOK THE THIRTY PIECES OF SILVER, THE PRICE OF THE ONE WHOSE PRICE HAD BEEN SET by the sons of Israel; 10 AND THEY GAVE THEM FOR THE POTTER'S FIELD, AS THE LORD DIRECTED ME." (Matthew 27:1-10.)

Commentary

THE TRIAL - Preliminaries

We must keep in mind that the Pharisees were from first to last constrained by one contingent factor in their case against Jesus – keeping the interest of the Roman authority so that Jesus could be put to death. It was paramount that their charges not devolve into mere provincial squabbles or religious differences, since these would result in a lesser punishment or dismissal entirely (which in fact actually happens with Pilate.)

Of additional concern was the legitimacy and cogency of charges in the eyes of the general Jewish public because the leaders must not be seen as unjustly condemning a man in Judaistic terms either. This furthers their resolve to this a judgment by Rome than from themselves.

The charges that would move Pilate to capital punishment were sedition, or instigation of an uprising against the peace or against the authority of Rome, and speaking against the Temple. The charges that would influence the Jewish citizenry would be blasphemy, teachings and actions contrary to Moses, and speaking against the Temple.

12 . . and the officers of the Jews, arrested Jesus and bound Him, 13 and led Him to Annas first;

A case presented to Pilate would have more weight were it to carry the endorsement of the high priest. In this case, there were technically two: Caiaphas and his father Annas, who was deposed by Gratus, yet maintained considerable respect in the Sanhedrin.[63] (In Jewish practice, the high priest served for life and did not retire, but in these circumstances some exception must have been allowed for Annas, perhaps due to very ill health.) Annas also appears to have retained his superior influence over his son, despite being in retirement, since he is deferred to first.

We must be careful to not get confused by "high priest" in this section. Until Jesus is sent to Caiaphas, high priest refers to Annas during this interview.

---

[63] The Jewish Encyclopedia, Funk & Wagnalls, 1906, Vol vii, p.166

14 Now Caiaphas was the one who had advised the Jews that it was expedient for one man to die on behalf of the people.

This is a parenthetic, informing us of the rationale behind Caiaphas' desire to have Jesus put to death. This is not to be understood as a tradition or a ritualistic appeasement, as sacrifices in pagan cultures offered human beings to satisfy judgment or wrath.

Caiaphas was arguing that it is better that one man die than let the whole nation come under persecution from their oppressors, provoked by the civil unrest that would result if Jesus were allowed to go unchecked - *"If we let Him go on like this, all men will believe in Him, and the Romans will come and take away both our place and our nation."* (John 11:48-50.)

15 Simon Peter was following Jesus, and so was another disciple.

We are not told who the other disciple was, making all else a matter of speculation. It is usual for the author to keep himself out of the narrative or mentioned in the third person, which would mean that John was the one accompanying Jesus and subsequently inviting Peter inside as well. But this is pure conjecture, and we must consider that since the opportunity to name the man was deliberately neglected, his obscurity was intentional.

"I have spoken openly to the world;.. and I spoke nothing in secret. 21 "Why do you question Me? Question those who have heard what I spoke to them;.. "

The questions from Annas about His teaching could be seen as straightforward in which case Jesus would be seen as being unnecessarily difficult in suggesting Annas get his information from others. He answered others whenever they asked, why not the high priest?

But Jesus is also aware there is an ulterior motive in this questioning, hence His suggestion to interrogate witnesses. He knows they will be inconsistent. But He also sees the need to let Annas know that His teaching has not been secretive or hidden; that He routinely made His views known in the most public way – in the very Temple itself under the noses of the authorities and no actions had been taken.

This proves offensive to those holding Him.

22 . . . one of the officers standing nearby struck Jesus, saying, "Is that the way You answer the high priest?"

The truth can be seen as insolent when evil men have a scheme in play. Again, the high priest here means Annas not Caiaphas.

Jesus defends His remarks in relation to law and truth. It is certainly clear that according to custom, the high priest deserved respect. But respect for the truth trumps social mores and must not be set aside for the latter. He had not told the priest to go to Hades or that he served the prince of darkness. These would be justifiable cases of disrespect. But lacking these, to be struck otherwise must have some basis against truth or law, and this Jesus points to in His reply - "If I have spoken wrongly, testify of the wrong;"

The proof is in the inability to proceed further. There is no law or ordinance that can be pinned on Jesus from this interrogation and Annas is personally ill-prepared for the process of interrogating others as recommended by Jesus. He is obliged to send Him "bound to Caiaphas the high priest." (v.24)

and brought Him to the house of the high priest;

The house of Caiaphas will be the scene of Peter's denials, Jesus' mistreatment by the guards, and of the hurried gathering of selected leaders in a hasty quorum of the Sanhedrin before the official inquest.

At present, there are multiple sites for this house in Jerusalem. The one that is most traditional is under the Armenian St. Saviour's Church on Mt. Zion, around which archaeologist Magen Broshi did research in the seventies. There is yet no consensus as to one definitive site.

At this location, Peter remains at a distance, but is able to see Jesus within, as we later learn in relation to his denials.

56 And a servant-girl, seeing him as he sat in the firelight and looking intently at him, said, . . 69 "You too were with Jesus the Galilean.

56 And a servant-girl, seeing him . . . 69 "You too were with Jesus the Galilean. . . This man was with Him too."

Care must be taken in understanding the harmony of these accounts in the various gospels. Unless one has a very good memory, reading the accounts in isolation from one another may not reveal the issues that affect harmonizing these into one account. And the visual assist one gets in a Harmony of the Gospels (texts laid side by side) may induce the conclusion that there were more than three denials by Peter. Furthering the tenacity of discrepancies is the fact that the writers do not consistently position the observations and denials in the same place in the order of events.

But if one leaves the unwarranted necessity that all authors were somehow committed to presenting all the details in the exact same order as each other, harmony can be had by choosing to simply align statements wherever they are found in the other gospels, and one will find that there are no violations of conflicting contexts.

In some cases, more than one question or observation was made to Peter at a time before a particular denial, and when comparing accounts superficially this can give the impression that more instances were asked and answered than the three predicted by Jesus. (Matt 26:34.)

Peter is now among those who arrested Jesus who are also joined by bystanders now gathered at the commotion. He is recognized by several as either the Galilean, or the one with the Nazarene, or the one who struck off the ear of the servant.

Luke 22:56 quotes the girl saying, "This man was with Him too." But this is not a contradiction against Matthew's quote: "You too were with Jesus the Galilean." It is likely she said both as is represented in the combined Scripture text for this section above.

57 But he denied it, saying, "Woman, I do not know Him."

Here then is Peter's first denial. All the promises of faithfulness and loyalty have drained out the bottom of his feet as he sees the reality of the soldiers weapons, the seriousness of the leaders inside who have their malefactor in their hands, and the expectation that real pain and punishment are only moments away. To be associated with the indictment end of these proceedings means sharing that pain and suffering. It is sobering and intimidating.

71 When he had gone out to the gateway, another servant-girl saw him . . "This man was with Jesus of Nazareth." . . . "I do not know the man."

Peter now attempts to remove himself from the piercing scrutiny of those around the fire who have begun to look at him intently. But there are others out at the gateway, ready to keep this now unwanted scrutiny visible.

This then is Peter's second denial.

58 A little later, another saw him

The safety of the passage of time is illusory, for soon others speak up about his identity, and even note his accent - "even the way you talk gives you away."

And here, finally, someone who was in the garden scene notices him and remembers the incident of the ear. As we read the combined text, there are three comments made all at once that serve to mount up a volcano of tension and fear. So we see Peter's reaction culminate in an outburst –

74 Then he began to curse and swear, "I do not know the man!" And immediately a rooster crowed.

We reel from the idea that a converted man would curse and deny, especially with Jesus but a few yards away. We are all somewhat duplicitous in letting our deportment slip when no one of the church is around. But in the presence of our pastor, we watch our words carefully, if not for the simple fear of embarrassment. Ironically, we forget that the risen Lord hears every word.

In Peter's case, Jesus is certainly in earshot of this outburst, which tells us the pressure and strain of conflict Peter was suffering.

As we see from the crowing of the rooster and the harmonization employed above, there were in fact three denials as Jesus predicted.

61 The Lord turned and looked at Peter. . . 62 And he went out and wept bitterly.

Despite the railing and high pitch of the dialog within, Jesus is fully aware of what is taking place out in the courtyard. As the sign occurs, He takes His attention off His enemies and looks knowingly at Peter. It is the fatality of perfect knowledge, how it devastates and seals reality at the same time.

We don't see Peter again until the events of Resurrection Sunday and beyond. His grief is understandable as is his desire to be by himself. To promise bravery and boldness, to be told the opposite thing one fears will in fact happen, and to then realize that it has just happened is a revelation about oneself too bitter and painful to endure. It is not just an unfortunate eventuality, a mishap or a setback. It is deeply rooted in the revelation that one has preferred self over devotion and loyalty, and the knowledge that the very opposite is what one was chosen to be about.

63 Now the men who were holding Jesus in custody were mocking Him and beating Him,

We now have the reaction of the brutish world where churlish men live their lives horizontally with little or no sense of the vertical. To them, Jesus is merely misguided and deserves the lesson He's about to get. Why not add ridicule to highlight the wrong-mindedness that brought Him to the place He is in now?

They know Him to be proclaimed as a prophet, so why not give Him a real test? To cover His head and ask Him to name the one striking Him would certainly prove His prophetic abilities. That is how carnal, unregenerate man engages the spiritual, in silly distortions of heavenly things in order to have them conform in some semblance of understanding to their limited minds.

This is perhaps the best demonstration of what it means to cast pearls before swine. One hopes for the light of remediation and conversion, but one finds it being turned into worldly jest for the hysterical entertainment of friends. Jesus is for them a side show whose opportunity is not to be missed for the sake of pure entertainment. This is why Jesus does not do as He did with the men who caught the woman in adultery, to write in the sand things that dissembled them out of personal embarrassment. He could have named the men with some personal details to boot, and so proved He was the genuine article. But it is what they are about that would make this an empty exercise.

66 When it was day, the Council of elders of the people assembled, both chief priests and scribes, and they led Him away to their council chamber

For those who explain that the whole interrogation by the Sanhedrin took place in the house of Caiaphas, this verse corrects that misapprehension. Jesus and the elders remove to their usual place of business.

"When it was day" does not mean full daylight. Matthew and Mark clarify that it was very early, which we should understand as the dawning of the day. The reason this is warranted is that Pilate conducted business early in the day and their affairs in the Sanhedrin and the formulation of the charges to be brought needed to be concluded much before that.

55 Now the chief priests and the whole Council kept trying to obtain testimony against Jesus to put Him to death, and they were not finding any.

The first charge at issue – that would weigh in with Pilate – was speaking against the Temple. It was an easy way to get the death sentence, since Roman respect for the safety and sanctity of the Temple need only have testimony of its violation, and Jesus was remembered to have spoken out publicly in this case.

But as is the way with eyewitness testimony from people of an eastern mind, getting consistence remembrance of exact words was a doubtful expectation. In the western world people were more analytical and detail-oriented. In the east, people sufficed it to have merely the gist of things. The thematic and figurative value of things was more important than exact words, and it was exact words that were desperately needed now.

Thus, we have mention that the leaders attempted to secure false testimony to mitigate this eventuality. But their haste and lack of quality control produced an ironically similar result. The preparation of their testimonies had forgotten to include harmony or perhaps the fear of so august an interrogation muddled the witnesses' minds, as is evident in the misrepresentation of what Jesus said, "We heard Him say,`I will destroy this temple made with hands, and in three days I will build another made without hands.'"

He had not said anything respecting with or without hands. This is recorded as a conclusion in the minds of the observers.

60 The high priest stood up and came forward and questioned Jesus, saying, "Do You not answer?

The rule in ancient times was that silence conveyed consent. The high priest is reminding Jesus that unless He speaks up to clarify His version of the charges, He will be seen as agreeing with their claims, regardless of the inconsistencies. With respect to speaking against the Temple, Jesus remains silent.

Considering the rule, this would sound like Jesus was enabling them to conclude consent, but we must remember that this charge would have to stand up in the process before Pilate, and there the inconsistencies of witnesses would end the matter. Jesus was simply letting this point die its natural death.

But as to the next question, Jesus is not silent.

60 . . Again the high priest was questioning Him, . . saying, 67 "If You are the Christ, tell us." . . "If I tell you, you will not believe;

This is the serious question which Jesus does not ignore. This is the question to satisfy the Jews – that He would be guilty of blasphemy. It is not, however, an issue that Pilate would respect as to the death penalty.

But their hopes are in the expectation that if they protest how grievous this charge is in Jewish eyes and that it would promote unrest and violence among the people, Pilate might indulge their provincial mores and precepts. (Notice that among the first charges before Pilate will be that of misleading the nation, which some understood as "sowing disaffection.") There is here also a rather self-serving move to pass the odium of capital punishment away from themselves as spiritual leaders and onto the Romans.

As for Jesus, He first chides them in being intellectually dishonest. They don't want to know the answer for the right reasons, to follow Him – *"If I tell you, you will not believe;"* . They merely wish to use it as a tool to condemn Him. This is proven by His observation that they would not answer any of the questions He might ask in due course - *" . . if I ask a question, you will not answer."*

Insistent that this claim be answered directly by Jesus, the high priest asks it again – *61 "Are You the Christ, the Son of the Blessed One?"*

The title 'Christ' is used by Caiaphas to mean Messiah, as the specially Anointed One of Scripture. As for Son of the Blessed One, Caiaphas is not revealing a Trinitarian view of God in Judaism, but is employing exemplars from the OT wherein messengers and Messiah are often called sons of God, meaning a separate agent who is especially blessed with this role (Gen 6:2, Job 1:6, Dan 3:25.)

62 And Jesus said, "I am; and you shall see THE SON OF MAN SITTING AT THE RIGHT HAND OF POWER, and COMING WITH THE CLOUDS OF HEAVEN."

The simplicity of admitting, "I am" was all that was necessary for them to take action. But Jesus gave them more by going to the very limit of daring. He removed all doubt that He might have misunderstood what His claims meant. He attributed the OT messianic quote to Himself – "Sit at my right hand" (Psalms 110:1.), "coming in the clouds of heaven" (Daniel 7:13.)

63 Tearing his clothes, the high priest said, "What further need do we have of witnesses? 64 "You have heard the blasphemy; . . For we have heard it ourselves from His own mouth.

This was by design, as the high priest has learned in the proceedings that basing their case on witnesses remembering His speech was doomed. And he says as much here – "What further need have we of witnesses." His attempt to get fresh evidence in the very hearing of the Sanhedrin now trumped all other approaches.

The tearing of his garments comes from no express commandment, but was traditional. David commands it of Joab as part of the recompense for killing Abner - "Rend your clothes, and gird you with sackcloth, and mourn before Abner." (2 Sam 3:31.) It thus became a sign of grievous offense.

In response, all members responded with a unified sentence, *64 . . And they all condemned Him to be deserving of death.*

2 and they bound Him, and led Him away and delivered Him to Pilate the governor.

Pilate was now in Jerusalem, not in Caesarea, primarily due to the impending feast of Passover. Heightened security was reasonable considering the swelling of the city with pilgrims and travelers, choosing to celebrate in the city instead of their places of residence. (We find this same mixed, international crowd laying over until Pentecost, still largely present to witness the miracle of tongues in the disciples.)

Before rendering the account of the business with Pilate, Matthew closes the subject concerning the end of Judas.

3 Then when Judas, . . felt remorse and returned the thirty pieces of silver to the chief priests and elders, 4 saying, "I have sinned by betraying innocent blood."

Judas at long last comes to reckon with his sin. Hours before, He had no problems of conscience leading soldiers to take Him, nor betraying Jesus with a kiss. Now time has passed and Judas sees events actually unfolding toward such a terrible end and he becomes conscious of his sin. Perhaps it was the manner and deportment of Jesus before His accusers that portrayed this was not merely a deranged leader or someone misguided. Whatever the path, he had come to realize that he had betrayed the genuine article and there was in all likelihood no remedy remaining for him.

We are not to think that Judas did it for the money. There were patriotic, altruistic motives to be sure – protecting the nation from error, being of palpable service to Israel's most illustrious leaders. But now the money was a symbol of his folly, hence the attempt to be rid of it. He could not undo the deed, but he could lessen the weight of it by refusing to be paid for it.

"What is that to us? See to that yourself!"

There really was no other response from the priests. They certainly could not minister to him in his sins, because they were also their own and deliberately so. Nor was there a remedy in sacrifices. To acknowledge it would obligate them to do the same.

All they could do was reply that his perception of his sin was his own and one they did not share or likewise perceive – "What is that to us?" Which is to say it had no meaning in their world view. This prompted their recommendation, since they were under no obligation to do anything about it – "See to it yourself."

This was not a recommendation to commit suicide, but simply to say it was his business to resolve a sin they deemed to be purely the result of his own tortured mind.

5 And he threw the pieces of silver into the temple sanctuary and departed;

He was in immediate proximity to the door of the Temple sanctuary, being in the court of Israel just outside. The priests would have had their offices in the colonnades surrounding this courtyard. If they would not take back his money, he would force its re-contribution back to the Temple by throwing it onto the floor of the Holy Place, whose doorway must have been open.

and he went away and hanged himself.

Thought to be a genuine contradiction with Acts 1:18 where his death is attributed to a mishappened fall, this is simply a matter of Matthew electing to summarize his death in terms of hanging himself without the need to explain the resultant outcome. The intent was to hang himself and he attempted it in earnest. This is what Matthew is stating. It is not a case where he decided otherwise and threw himself contradictorily down the cliff.

The mishap was no doubt due to him choosing the wrong branch, to which in his anguish he may have paid little attention. The location may very well have been at the edge of a ravine of sharp rocks upon which his momentum alone would have caused such injuries.

"It is not lawful to put them into the temple treasury, since it is the price of blood."

Blood money did not refer to Judas' death in relation to their contract with him, but to their having paid to secure Jesus' death. It was money that paid for the shedding of blood, and as such it was offensive to have it associated with the benevolence of the Temple.

This concern epitomizes the problem with the Pharisees and priests. They feared contamination of ritual and tradition more than the contamination of their hearts and souls. They could worry that the floor of the sanctuary could be corrupted by blood money (which in purely practical terms it could not) but had no worry whatsoever about sin, which in every real sense respecting their souls, could.

and with the money bought the Potter's Field

This was not for Judas as some might surmise, but for the indigent dead. There are the equivalent of Potter's Fields in most cemeteries in major cities and towns. They are set aside for the disposition of persons who have died without family to claim them and make proper arrangements. Generally, the county or city has funds for the preparation costs, and has purchased areas of ground for burials.

The name here in the gospels refers to the prior existing name – a place where men discarded broken or defective pottery. Interesting, is the analogy to the picture of human beings as pots made by the Creator as potter and their use and outcome varying as life unfolds for the individual.

Paul discusses this in Romans, that the potter has the right to make each pot according to his wishes, for noble or ignoble use (9:21.) We see other lessons in which clay that resists the potter's work may be smashed or in other cases smoothed into a smaller lump to be made into something lesser.

Here, the broken pots are symbols of wasted lives, whose usefulness has expired or disappointed their owners, now to be thrown out on the pile. It is ironic that the money for the quintessential act by which Judas will be known down through history will be used to pay for the disposition of other wasted lives.

The prophecy being quoted is from the post-exilic prophet Zechariah (11:12,13.) Chapter 11 is a look to restored Israel after the exile, in which she prospers for a time. Yet the day comes when she is visited by her Messiah, and while the remnant accept Him, the larger portion reject Him. Chapter 11 chronicles the ultimate end of her state, which includes this section in which the Shepherd pays thirty pieces of silver for the field in which the residue of the nation is to be disposed.

But we find it was written to do double duty in foretelling in exact detail of the amount of money paid to Messiah's betrayer.

Next, we come to the trial before Pilate ..

Matthew 27:2., John 18:28-38, Luke 23:2, Matthew 27:11-14, Luke 23:5-7
2 and they bound Him, and led Him away and delivered Him to Pilate the governor. (Matthew 27:2.)

28 Then they led Jesus from Caiaphas into the Praetorium, and it was early; and they themselves did not enter into the Praetorium so that they would not be defiled, but might eat the Passover. 29 Therefore Pilate went out to them and said, "What accusation do you bring against this Man?" 30 They answered and said to him, "If this Man were not an evildoer, we would not have delivered Him to you." 31 So Pilate said to them, "Take Him yourselves, and judge Him according to your law." The Jews said to him, "We are not permitted to put anyone to death," 32 to fulfill the word of Jesus which He spoke, signifying by what kind of death He was about to die. (John 18:28-32.)

2 And they began to accuse Him, saying, "We found this man misleading our nation and forbidding to pay taxes to Caesar, and saying that He Himself is Christ, a King." (Luke 23:2.)

33 Therefore Pilate entered again into the Praetorium, and summoned Jesus and said to Him, "Are You the King of the Jews?" 34 Jesus answered, "Are you saying this on your own initiative, or did others tell you about Me?" 35 Pilate answered, "I am not a Jew, am I? Your own nation and the chief priests delivered You to me; what have You done?" 36 Jesus answered, . . 11 "It is as you say." . . "My kingdom is not of this world. If My kingdom were of this world, then My servants would be fighting so that I would not be handed over to the Jews; but as it is, My kingdom is not of this realm." 37 Therefore Pilate said to Him, "So You are a king?" Jesus answered, "You say correctly that I am a king. For this I have been born, and for this I have come into the world, to testify to the truth. Everyone who is of the truth hears My voice." 38 Pilate said to Him, "What is truth?" And when he had said this, he went out again to the Jews and said to them, "I find no guilt in Him." (John 18:33-36, Matthew 27:11, John 18:36-38.)

12 And while He was being accused by the chief priests and elders, He did not answer. 13 Then Pilate said to Him, "Do You not hear how many things they testify against You?" 14 And He did not answer him with regard to even a single charge, so the governor was quite amazed. (Matthew 27:12-14.)

5 But they kept on insisting, saying, "He stirs up the people, teaching all over Judea, starting from Galilee even as far as this place." 6 When Pilate heard it, he asked whether the man was a Galilean. 7 And when he learned that He belonged to Herod's jurisdiction, he sent Him to Herod, who himself also was in Jerusalem at that time. (Luke 23:5-7)

Commentary

SCENE FOUR - THE TRIAL BEFORE PILATE

28 Then they led Jesus from Caiaphas into the Praetorium, and it was early; and they themselves did not enter into the Praetorium so that they would not be defiled, but might eat the Passover.

The Praetorium was originally the commander's tent in the field and since the room for official business often adjoined his living space, praetorium came to be the official headquarters or meeting hall where the emperor or a general heard cases and transacted business. Praetorium comes from the Latin *praetor*, which was the highest civil rank in the Roman Republic. In the empire it was subjugated below consul.

The Jews use the term here to mean the place the governor conducted official business. In this case, there are two views - Antonia, a Roman fortress adjoining the Temple compound at its NW corner, or the Palace of Herod on what is today the Western Wall. The palace has advantages because Pilate, having his wife with him, would have benefited on her account with more luxurious surroundings than the spartan and austere Antonia. But conversely, there was never a reference to a praetorium at Herod's palace.

However, modern archaeology has not located anything in the palace ruins that might represent an outdoor tribunal. Conversely, a pavement that would correspond to the lithostratos of John 19:13 has been located under the Church of the Sisters of Sion, over the ruins of Antonia.

Having room for an outdoor tribunal, the crowd of people attending the proceedings, a place for the scourging and ready access out to the western hillside is harder to picture among the confines of the Herodian remains we see today. In addition, the Praetorium was a known place of Roman authority and would not have been understood as in the palace of Herod.

And we have Pilate having to send Jesus to Herod, which is an odd way of speaking about a man who is in the same building. Furthering this inequity is the knowledge that Pilate and Herod were not conciliatory, but became so only after these events.

eat the Passover

Since we observed Jesus eating the Passover just the preceding evening, many will find it odd that the Jews are in fear of not being able to eat it the following evening on account of defilement.

Passover was often applied to the entire Feast of Unleavened Bread, and to the meals had during the six days following the traditional Passover Seder. [64] Can this then be a fear, not about eating the Pesach at the Seder, but about eating the meal associated with the first day of unleavened bread (15th of Nisan) and the offering in the Temple?

Some observations. First, if this were the morning before the evening of Pesach – the Passover supper – the Jews would not have been defiled against eating it that evening for the simple reason that the daylight hours were still allowed for business and preparing for the evening meal. The Sabbath of the Passover did not begin until 6:00 PM. And we have the earlier stated problem of Jesus trying to celebrate Passover on an unauthorized evening.

Should they become actually defiled, there was an ordinance that they could wash ceremonially, so as to be considered "washed of the day," [65] allowing them to partake of Passover.

However, such rules did not apply to the first day of Unleavened Bread. In fact, there was a holy convocation that occurred during the morning hours, for which defilement would be serious. While the Passover lamb could be offered in the Temple on behalf of others, the offering of the first of Unleavened Bread – the Chagigah - had to be offered in person, not by someone else. It was offered and had to be eaten before evening.

Hence, worries about all these affairs and the functions of the first day of Unleavened Bread would quite easily mount up to the fear we see clearly evident here, but would be of no concern were it the day prior.

29 Therefore Pilate went out to them and said, "What accusation do you bring against this Man?"

His need to go out to them follows from the preceding. Obviously, an outdoor tribunal was set up in a location that afforded Pilate the ability to go inside and come out again to the crowd.

As with all tribunals, the first order of business is to get the charges clearly stated up front.

---

[64] Pesach 92a, 36b; Edersheim, Life and Times of Jesus the Messiah, Eerdmans, 1953, Ch 14.
[65] *Ibid*

30 "If this Man were not an evildoer, we would not have delivered Him to you."

From the Jewish side, they are informing Pilate that this is a capital case, needing his ratification – that is why they are there. But before they can get the charges stated, Pilate gives them the jibe that pretends this is a petty case which they can handle themselves. *"Take Him yourselves, and judge Him according to your law."* It is a jibe because he knows from experience and by Roman decree that if they are coming to him it is a capital case.

31 .. The Jews said to him, "We are not permitted to put anyone to death,"

As earlier explained, this was by Roman decree in non-free provinces [66] The Jews had to get endorsement whether executed by them (stonings) or the Romans. Many have cited the stoning of Stephen and the beheading of James as contradicting this, undermining the emphasis on Roman permission. This is effectively answered by F.F. Bruce.

Up to the stoning of Stephen there are no challenges of record, and the decree was rather fresh at the time of this trial, having been decreed barely three years earlier. But by the time of Stephen's and James' deaths, Pilate had fallen from favor with Tiberius for not only his own actions but his association with the prefect Sejanus (to be explained later during the details of the trial.)

These were not a case of taking advantage of an interregnum (between governors), but it was a case of taking liberties they could count on a governor ignoring for personal and political reasons. [67] But not so with Jesus, at this earlier stage.

32 to fulfill the word of Jesus which He spoke, signifying by what kind of death He was about to die.

How did their cautionary remark fulfill the prediction of Jesus? By forcing Pilate into the position of not only judging it to be capital but to being the agent of the execution, they were ensuring the usual death sentence for this kind of crime – crucifixion - which would fulfill Jesus' early comments (Mt. 20:19, 26:2, John 12:32 - lifted up.)

2 .. "We found this man misleading our nation and forbidding to pay taxes to Caesar, and saying that He Himself is Christ, a King."

Here then are the formal charges, framed in words that would catch Pilate's attention. Notice that speaking against the Temple has been completely dropped. Misleading the nation sounds tame, but it meant that He was "stirring up the people" in a divisive way that would affect the forceful peace imposed by the Romans (Luke 23:5.)

We also see a new charge – forbidding to pay tribute – added by lawyers and doctors in the interest of piling on charges Pilate would be foolish to dismiss. This was based on the incidents of Jesus' being questioned about why His disciples did not pay the Temple tax (Matt 17:24.) and the trick question from the Pharisees about the tribute money (Luke 20:22.)

In the case of the Temple tax, it was subsequently paid, but the collectors had gotten the impression that He showed no care for such business.

33 Therefore Pilate entered again into the Praetorium, and summoned Jesus and said to Him, "Are You the King of the Jews?"

This private interview to better gather facts tells us he had both sized up the accused on first looks and was also suspicious in taking the Jews word for it. The question had to have been asked sarcastically because it

---

[66] Jerusalem Talmud, Sanhedrin 1:1, 7:2; Bruce, New Testament History, Doubleday, 1969, p. 200.

[67] ibid pp. 200-201, note 18.

could not have been taken seriously by Pilate. Not only did the Herodians have formal precident from Rome as the new royal house, despite procurators now in Judea, but Caesar was now master and lord over the region, and the man before him gave no signs of being politically or militarily formidable.

34 Jesus answered, "Are you saying this on your own initiative, or did others tell you about Me?"

Jesus takes advantage of this bit of sarcasm to make it personal – "Is this your confession?"

Ironically, every man great and small would ever hence be required to answer this question, and more than this - is He Son of God? It is a secularly based question being turned into a religious one.

Pilate gets the inference, and immediately stands apart from it -

35 . . "I am not a Jew, am I? Your own nation and the chief priests delivered You to me; what have You done?"

The rhetorical question here is to signify that he is being asked to take the question as religious, which would mean he would have found it important to answer as a Jew, which he clearly is not.

Instead, Pilate cleverly puts the issue back into Jesus' court – this is a Jewish matter and Jesus is a Jew. He, not Pilate, should be concerned about what His countrymen are saying. To this Jesus replies, "It is as you say." (v.11.)

Would not Pilate then be prepared to agree with the Jewish charges? He has here a confession. But he is not hasty in this, as seen by him giving Jesus space to add comment –

36 . . "My kingdom is not of this world. . . then My servants would be fighting . . but as it is, My kingdom is not of this realm."

In so many words Jesus has diffused the political interest Pilate would have had in this confession. Pilate may have no idea which world Jesus is referring to, but he can safely conclude it is not this one, nor specifically, this provincial realm over which he and Rome have suzeraincy.

But let us be clear, violence to secure His realm would be called for if the time were right, meaning there is coming a time yet future when His servants will be expected to fight.

Pilate needs one more reassurance. Jesus has answered somewhat enigmatically. He is no king of the moment, but He is not denying He is a king in fact – 37 "So You are a king?"

37 . . . "You say correctly that I am a king. For this I have been born, and for this I have come into the world, to testify to the truth. Everyone who is of the truth hears My voice."

The continued affirmation of this claim would ordinarily be subject to punishment, but Pilate is faced with the reality that there is no substance to the insurrectionary needs of that claim. All he sees is an itinerant prophet and a band of similarly harmless followers. Nothing in this threatens anyone at his level of authority.

He does not stop listening, at least enough to have heard Jesus' mention of the truth. Here then is a monumental convergence of two world views, each having their own cut on the nature of what comprises truth. Pilate's world view is rigorously practical. He is not known to have been philosophical, particularly academic, or contemplative. His world had no time for such things. He had been drawn from the equestrian order, which was often less noble, more practical and pragmatic, and seldom patrician.

Still, Pilate was insightful enough to perceive that the answers to life were by no means complete in the gods or traditions of his own nation. He is intrigued by the confident mention of truth, and from a completely foreign world view.

38 Pilate said to Him, "What is truth?"

Some have offered that this was never phrased as a question, but the presence of the Gk *'tis'* makes it a question grammatically. 'Tis' is a *who, which, what* word, so by its very nature it obligates a question.

But questions can be asked more as statements in the rhetorical, "Who knows what the truth is?" which is not meant to be answered, merely observed.

Pilate is not in any frame of mind to have asked this sincerely. He is in the middle of an incident and there is no time for philosophical dialog. It's a bit like seeing a fire start in your home, you need to get moving to put it in check, and your neighbor asks, "Ever wonder if light is a particle or a wave?" Interesting question but badly timed.

He returns to the crowd outside, bringing Jesus out with him again - *"I find no guilt in Him."*

The crowd raises its accusations to Pilate. He observes that, contrary to the norm, Jesus is not wrailing back at his accusers with accusations of His own.

12 ... "Do You not hear how many things they testify against You?" 14 And He did not answer him

Pilate is caught between what he knows to conclude about Jesus and the vehemence of the crowd. Something is amiss or at least unexplained. Jesus is not a malefactor, yet the people are not here on a lark. The question is now put to Jesus to reconcile. It is like asking, "You tell me A, but how do you explain B?"

Jesus remains silent because this will just come down to a case of technicalities over religion and Pilate is in no position, expertise or authority to decide between them. Jesus could certainly have defended His case better than any lawyer known to man, but how would Pilate appreciate the arguments? It would be mere minutia in his equestrian mind.

Never the less, he as was "quite amazed."

5 But they kept on insisting, saying, "He stirs up the people, teaching all over Judea, starting from Galilee even as far as this place."

This is a signal to get this business out of his own hair and into someone else's. The mention of Galilee only provided opportunity, not necessity. He was accused of the same all over Judea, so technically he could hear the case as properly as Herod. The mention of Galilee was an opportunity too good to pass up.

Pilate and Herod were at odds on several prior grounds, many of which involved Pilate's manhandling and violence. Delegations to Rome had in fact accused him before the emperor. Sending Jesus to Herod was a back-handed gesture that pretended to defer to the other's jurisdiction, but was merely putting the hot potato in Herod's hands.

he sent Him to Herod, who himself also was in Jerusalem at that time.

This undermines the suggestion that Pilate was staying at Herod's palace. It could have meant sending Jesus to that place in the same palace where Herod was in residence, but the addition of "also in Jerusalem at that time" does not ordinarily suggest, "the very same building."

Nor can one surmise that Pilate was in the palace and Herod was in one of his other palaces. The record makes it clear he was in Jerusalem, and there was only one palace for him in the city.

Luke 23:5-18, Matthew 27:19, Mark 15:6-11, John 18:39-40, Matthew 27:22-30, Luke 23:20-23, John 19:1, John 19:4-15

8 Now Herod was very glad when he saw Jesus; for he had wanted to see Him for a long time, because he had been hearing about Him and was hoping to see some sign performed by Him. 9 And he questioned Him at some length; but He answered him nothing. 10 And the chief priests and the scribes were standing there, accusing Him vehemently. 11 And Herod with his soldiers, after treating Him with contempt and mocking Him, dressed Him in a gorgeous robe and sent Him back to Pilate. 12 Now Herod and Pilate became friends with one another that very day; for before they had been enemies with each other. (Luke 23:5-12.)

19 While he was sitting on the judgment seat, his wife sent him a message, saying, "Have nothing to do with that righteous Man; for last night I suffered greatly in a dream because of Him." (Matthew 27:19.)

13 Pilate summoned the chief priests and the rulers and the people, 14 and said to them, "You brought this man to me as one who incites the people to rebellion, and behold, having examined Him before you, I have found no guilt in this man regarding the charges which you make against Him. 15 "No, nor has Herod, for he sent Him back to us; and behold, nothing deserving death has been done by Him. 16 "Therefore I will punish Him and release Him." (Luke 23:13-16.)

6 Now at the feast he used to release for them any one prisoner whom they requested. 7 The man named Barabbas had been imprisoned with the insurrectionists who had committed murder in the insurrection. 8 The crowd went up and began asking him to do as he had been accustomed to do for them. 9 Pilate answered them, saying, . . "But you have a custom that I release someone for you at the Passover . . "Do you want me to release for you the King of the Jews?" 10 For he was aware that the chief priests had handed Him over because of envy. 11 But the chief priests stirred up the crowd to ask him to release Barabbas for them instead. (Mark 15:6-9, John 18:39, Mark 15:9-11.)

18 But they cried out all together, saying, "Away with this man, and release for us Barabbas!" (Luke 23:18.)

22 Pilate said to them, "Then what shall I do with Jesus who is called Christ?" They all said, "Crucify Him!" 23 And he said, "Why, what evil has He done?" But they kept shouting all the more, saying, "Crucify Him!" (Matthew 27:22-23.)

22 And he said to them the third time, "Why, what evil has this man done? I have found in Him no guilt demanding death; therefore I will punish Him and release Him." 23 But they were insistent, with loud voices asking that He be crucified. And their voices began to prevail. (Luke 23:22-23.)

Pilate then took Jesus and scourged Him. (John 19:1.)

27 Then the soldiers of the governor took Jesus into the Praetorium and gathered the whole Roman cohort around Him. 28 They stripped Him and put a scarlet robe on Him. 29 And after twisting together a crown of thorns, they put it on His head, and a reed in His right hand; and they knelt down before Him and mocked Him, saying, "Hail, King of the Jews!" 30 They spat on Him, and took the reed and began to beat Him on the head. (Matthew 27:27-30.)

4 Pilate came out again and said to them, "Behold, I am bringing Him out to you so that you may know that I find no guilt in Him." 5 Jesus then came out, wearing the crown of thorns and the purple robe. Pilate said to them, "Behold, the Man!" 6 So when the chief priests and the officers saw Him, they cried out saying, "Crucify, crucify!" Pilate said to them, "Take Him yourselves and crucify Him, for I find no guilt in Him." 7 The Jews answered him, "We have a law, and by that law He ought to die because He made Himself out to be the Son of God."

8 Therefore when Pilate heard this statement, he was even more afraid; 9 and he entered into the Praetorium again and said to Jesus, "Where are You from?" But Jesus gave him no answer. 10 So Pilate said to Him, "You do not speak to me? Do You not know that I have authority to release You, and I have authority to crucify You?" 11 Jesus answered, "You would have no authority over Me, unless it had been given you from above; for this reason he who delivered Me to you has the greater sin."

12 As a result of this Pilate made efforts to release Him, but the Jews cried out saying, "If you release this Man, you are no friend of Caesar; everyone who makes himself out to be a king opposes Caesar." 13 Therefore when Pilate heard these words, he brought Jesus out, and sat down on the judgment seat at a place called The Pavement, but in Hebrew, Gabbatha. 14 Now it was the day of preparation for the

Passover; it was about the sixth hour. And he said to the Jews, "Behold, your King!" 15 So they cried out, "Away with Him, away with Him, crucify Him!" Pilate said to them, "Shall I crucify your King?" The chief priests answered, "We have no king but Caesar." (John 19:4-15.)

24 When Pilate saw that he was accomplishing nothing, but rather that a riot was starting, he took water and washed his hands in front of the crowd, saying, "I am innocent of this Man's blood; see to that yourselves." 25 And all the people said, "His blood shall be on us and on our children!" (Matthew 27:24-25.)

Commentary

SCENE FIVE – BEFORE HEROD ANTIPAS

8 Now Herod was very glad when he saw Jesus; for he had wanted to see Him for a long time, because he had been hearing about Him and was hoping to see some sign performed by Him.

What we know of Antipas should tell us that his gladness was hardly for righteous reasons. Like John the Baptist, Jesus is a curiosity, a flight into philosophico-religious dialogue, much like dinner conversation. We have no indication that Antipas was ever inclined to take heed of it. He listened to John because John spoke with such definiteness and spirit. In one sense he reckoned it to be perhaps more possibly true than all the rest he'd been told. But the cost he would have to pay to embrace it was always too high for his aspiring tastes. His infatuation with John didn't stop him from giving up the man's head for a dance.

Jesus was actually more notorious than John, but as a miracle worker, less than for His teaching, because less of His teaching was noised abroad, compared to His miracles – *[he] was hoping to see some sign performed by Him.*

9 And he questioned Him at some length; but He answered him nothing.

We have no text of the interview but Jesus' silence indicates there was no point in answering such a man (contrasted with Pilate whom Jesus did answer.)

We can imagine the scene. Herod arranging his court with all his sycophants present and snickering, his countenance dominated by that amused grin of a spoiled ruler, and a series of demoralizing questions that ridiculed the claim to be Son of God.

The presence of the priests and their accusations seem mere stage dressing since we see little that resembles an inquest about the charges.

11 And Herod with his soldiers, after treating Him with contempt and mocking Him, dressed Him in a gorgeous robe and sent Him back to Pilate.

Jesus has yet to be scourged and suffers only the effects of being roughed up by the guards at Caiaphas' house. In Antipas' world view, this is no claimant to his kingdom. He has no noble retinue, no cohort of guards, police or infantry, no palaces or prisons. His kingdom could be ended in a matter of minutes by the sword that ended John's life. He is too pitiful to punish. The only response is to mock Him and pretend to exalt Him as king.

This brings up the question as to why Herod sent Jesus back to Pilate? By sending Him to Herod, he might let Him go and Pilate would be no one to complain. Jesus would be both out of his hair and potentially set free, which was the finding of Pilate anyway.

Herod had likewise found nothing punishable, merely pitiable. But the accusations being made by the Jews indicated that alleged crimes were still valid for Judea. While Herod was not necessarily apprised of

Pilate's assessment of innocence and a desire to release Him, some spirit of reconciliation with Pilate moved Herod to respect the charges pertaining to Judea, and thus sent Him back to Pilate for disposition.

While Pilate did not expect to have Jesus back in his lap again, the record states that this gesture on Herod's part mended their differences.

for before they had been enemies with each other.

Much of this had to do with the kingdom Herod felt he deserved at his father's death passing instead to Roman authority. No doubt the trump was rubbed in whenever the occasion permitted.

Herod suffered the permanent indignity of having the very city of his own residence ruled by a foreign power. Jerusalem and Judea were the pinnacle of his father's realm and he was now begrudged the rule of Galilee, a considerably less-populated rural region several leagues to the north.

We have also the recent case of Pilate deliberately inciting displeasure by attempting to force the storage of religiously offensive votive shields in Herod's palace – a move resulting in complaints to Tiberius that led him to order their removal to Caesarea. [68]

We can attribute this unexpected change of heart to divine superintendence. The outcome against logic moved to ensure that Jesus was not to be let off His destiny at the Cross.

SCENE SIX – BACK BEFORE PILATE

19 While he was sitting on the judgment seat, his wife sent him a message, saying, "Have nothing to do with that righteous Man; for last night I suffered greatly in a dream because of Him."

The move by the Jews to transfer the odium of capital punishment to the Romans was not to be tolerated by the Almighty. This was an act of Jewish faithlessness, a sign of their bankruptcy in true righteousness and love of the Father. They will be made to bear that indictment, hence, divine means are employed to assist in getting Pilate out of the picture. Here is one such move.

Having Pilate's wife troubled by a dream and the superstitious dread she attributes to it may not have clinched Pilate's decision, but it had its effect in his continued effort to free Jesus. As to why his personal findings did not result in a categorical end of the matter we shall see shortly.

Theologically, let us be clear that the sins of all of us put Jesus on the Cross. But there can be more in this by also being iniquitously responsible for effecting His death in space and time. This is a proper conclusion because there must be meaning in Jesus' additional words, "They that delivered Me unto you have the greater sin."

13 Pilate summoned the chief priests and the rulers and the people, . . . "I have found no guilt in this man" . . 15 "No, nor has Herod," . . . 16 "Therefore I will punish Him and release Him."

Despite the new gesture from Herod, Pilate was again stuck with the dilemma of judging an innocent man. Having repeated his judgment and the concurrence of Herod, he perceived the crowd was determined to have blood. He reasoned that this might very well be ameliorated with a flogging.

We must be careful to understand that Pilate does not order the scourging to actually punish (he is convinced Jesus is innocent.) The scourging is for the crowd – in the hopes it will dispel and appease.

---

[68] Philo, Embassy to Gaius, p. 299-305.

6 Now at the feast he used to release for them any one prisoner whom they requested.

We must be clear that the introduction of this detail is in relation to Pilate's effort to have Jesus released according to the custom, since we will soon see Pilate suggesting Jesus as the candidate not Barabbas. It is the crowd that rejects Jesus and asks for Barabbas.

The man named Barabbas had been imprisoned..

The details of the insurrection mentioned by Mark are not recorded in Scripture. Some attribute Barabbas to the band of rebels called Sicarii, but their organization and part in the rebellion was not until the war against Rome in which Masada fell (A.D. 66-73.)

Suffice it to say that bands of insurrectionists (of whom the Zealots have ideological identity) created incidents in protest of Roman rule, which culminated into those actions that precipitated the siege and destruction of Jerusalem.

Barabbas' Name

For Barabbas, virtually all versions of the Greek text have *'Iesoun ton Barabban'* – Jesus the son of Abbas in Matthew 27:17. However, the words *'Iesoun ton'* (Jesus the) are presented in brackets (there were no brackets in the manuscripts.) The reason for their presence is to indicate that they are not universally supported by all manuscripts, thus their inclusion in the text is not beyond question, warning against any dogmatic reference to them. There are also suppositions that more manuscripts carried the full name but were expunged of the first name by Origen (on grounds of offense to the sacred name) and continued to be absent in the manuscript tradition that continued from him.

However, the text we use today is more the work of rigorous textual research which has now largely side-stepped the influence of ancient church superstitions and fears, and resembles the discipline of a defensible linguistic science. Today the bracketed words show some respect for the manuscripts that carry the variant, while telling translators which reading is the more sound in relation to all texts considered.

This explains why in English translations, we only have "Barabbas" not "Jesus the son of Abbas." Still, there is a certain appealing irony in that bar Abbas means "son of the Father" which lends itself to having Jesus a son of the Father set free by human will, while Jesus the true Son of the Father is left to die for the sins of the world.

"But you have a custom that I release someone for you at the Passover; Do you want me to release for you the King of the Jews?"

Here is Pilate's renewed attempt to release Jesus as innocent. We must not get the idea that Pilate was becoming a believer or that Jesus had affected him to the degree that he sought this out of admiration. No doubt Pilate was impressed with our Lord (Mark 15:5), but his was purely a political set of reactions and counter-reactions. He was aware of his unpopularity in Rome, and to be further accused of condemning an innocent man was an indictment he did not wish to add. He is caught between keeping to the straight and narrow and doing the right thing before the law, and the anger of the people.

Yet we will see that this is turned around to the Jews' advantage a bit later.

10 For he was aware that the chief priests had handed Him over because of envy.

Amid his conflict over doing the right thing or caving in to public pressure, Pilate has time for sarcasm. In calling Jesus "King of the Jews," he was highlighting that he was well aware that this whole scene was based in envy – that Jesus was more rightfully the head of their religion than their hypocritical leaders – and they knew it. They knew Him to be right but desired His death – for envy.

That a pagan could see this and use it as a jibe was significant. The crowd would have none of it –

18 But they cried out all together, saying, "Away with this man, and release for us Barabbas!"

22 . . "Crucify Him!"

Pilate makes yet two more appeals – the one to force them to speak outright the disposition of Jesus "what shall I do with Jesus?", the other to reiterate the question, "What evil has he done?"

There is now unison in their answers – "Crucify Him." Ironically, the city that was characterized by Hosannahs at His entrance a week before, was now shouting for His death. No doubt there were sympathizers with the Pharisees who helped the din of voices by initiating these cries. It was now the age-old problem of mob dynamics.

I will punish Him and release Him."

After a third time of reticence and reluctance – "I have found no guilt demanding death" – he offers a second time to merely punish and release Him; and taking charge of matters, he orders Jesus to be scourged.

The flagrum was a short leather whip with a laced-up handle ending in strands of leather originally just knotted at the ends, but later tied so as to entrap small bits of bone or pieces of stone. The effect was more savage than being whipped, since the flesh was torn, as were the muscles underneath.

In the film *The Passion of the Christ* (Icon Productions © 2004), the brutality of this scene was portrayed as to its savagery but less accurately as to severity. We must remember that Jesus is subsequently taken back into the Praetorium, shown standing again with Pilate before the people, and interviewed again by Pilate inside before finally being given over to the people's demands. In the film, there are thirty-two strokes with rods, then twenty-eight with the flagrum. The NT does not state the number given, but Paul tells us the custom was thirty-nine (II Cor 11:34 .) Jesus is portrayed as near dead after the scourging and barely able to speak. We need to recall that Paul received the same but appears to have survived much better than we see of Jesus in the film.

Of note in the film was the counting in Latin. Were we to have been there, we would have heard the sequences:

one, two, three . .
unus
duo
tres

ten, eleven, twelve . .
decem
undecem
duodecem

twenty, twenty-one, twenty-two . .
viginti
viginti unus
viginti duo

thirty, thirty-one, thirty-two . .
triginta
triginta unus
triginta duo

Pilate did not desire to kill Jesus with the scourging. Were forty lashes ordinarily delivered with the severity seen in the film, Pilate would have easily risked having this lighter punishment end in an execution. If Pilate had no insight that Jesus was extraordinarily capable of surviving it, this tells us that it was ordinarily not this severe, and that most men survived to take in its message.

This is not to minimize the suffering dealt to our Lord by any means. It was brutal and horrifying. But we should let the remaining details of His passion temper our zeal to embellish by engaging the fact that it did leave Him capable of standing and of speaking further with the governor.

27 Then the soldiers of the governor took Jesus into the Praetorium

The scourging, however brutal, was insufficient to prevent Him this further indignity. These are Roman troops, not local police. Being "condemned" by orders and duty to such an inhospitable place as Judea often expressed itself in despicable treatment, excess and brutality when the occasion arose.

Being Romans did not mean cultured members of that society. While every high-born citizen spent time in the army as a right of passage to public office, such were among the officers. The larger bulk of the army was comprised of men from the poorer ranks, obligated to service with meager pay and tours of duty at ten years routinely. Often, they welcomed service and pay over poverty, but many knew they would be returning to houses and property sold out from under them, and a wife now married to someone else. Bitterness and anger were common.

As with the brutish guards at Caiaphas' house, a similar bent of mind mocks Jesus, less physically, but with greater indignity. Imagine the irony when such men who knelt in mockery will kneel in judgment before the same Jesus of Nazareth – *"every knee shall bow and every tongue confess . ."* (Rom 14:11.)

29 And after twisting together a crown of thorns, they put it on His head

The thorns from the bushes of the region were considerably larger than we are used to in other areas of the world. They were easily two inches or longer, and as such had plenty of length for refining their points. They were extremely sharp and their wounds were not trivial. And blood from head wounds is often profuse.

4 Pilate came out again and said to them, "Behold, I am bringing Him out to you so that you may know that I find no guilt in Him."

The picture a scourged Jesus composed for Pilate must have been halting at best. He allowed its awfulness in the interest of assuaging the violence of the people. If they were to see Him now, they will certainly feel "Enough for a deluded prophet." Such was the meaning of "ecce homo" *Behold the man.*

They renew their cry that He be crucified.

"Take Him yourselves and crucify Him, for I find no guilt in Him."

Here is where the terms of the trial evolve to their final form. Pilate is now intent on absolving himself of Jesus guilt and punishment, and recommends that they take Him themselves and do as they are demanding. Note – he is not giving permission that Jesus be crucified by Roman soldiers, i.e. a Roman endorsement for the death penalty. He is telling them to do what he knows they cannot do without Roman assistance. It is like saying, "Take Him and crucify Him (which by the way you can't do)."

7 . . "We have a law, and by that law He ought to die because He made Himself out to be the Son of God."

Note that the Jews do not take this nor do they accept this as carte blanche to put Him to death themselves. On the one hand, they need Roman cooperation for crucifixion (they are not a people practiced in this). They are secondly not interested in taking back to themselves the odium of death.

They are thus eager to recite the Roman decree forbidding them to inflict capital punishment. But to be sure, they add more. Jesus is charged with being Son of God. To this, Pilate is said to respond in fear.

Did Pilate fear Jesus being such a person? His interviews had left him leaning to the negative, but still to some degree undecided. What then could be the basis for him being even more afraid? "Son of God", real or imaginary, meant that this problem was not going to go away. Jesus was now more than a king.

Whether to stall for time or to get one last bit of insight on how to handle the dilemma, he returns to the interior of the Praetorium and orders that Jesus be brought in.

9 .. "Where are You from?"

We would be hard-pressed to infer that Pilate was asking about His heavenly origin. It is not a question about this new charge – Son of God. It is more a question about where in the world of human affairs has Jesus come from that He has managed to arrive in his jurisdiction and cause such an uproar?

Jesus' silence is understandable. It is not a time for defense in the interest of release, even if the governor seems ready to do so. Nor is it time to explain His origins. Pilate is not of the frame of mind nor the readiness of comprehension to understand the answer. It would only be characterized as a sort of delusional madness. (*"For the word of the cross is foolishness to those who are perishing"; "a natural man does not accept the things of the Spirit of God, for they are foolishness to him; and he cannot understand them, because they are spiritually appraised"* I Cor 1:18, 2:14 .)

No matter how practically disposed to justice Pilate may be, he is beyond this kind of understanding.

10 .. "Do You not know that I have authority to release You, and I have authority to crucify You?"

This, rather, is a question Jesus can answer because it deals with the practical, and with a principle Pilate understands – authority.

"You would have no authority over Me, unless it had been given you from above; for this reason he who delivered Me to you has the greater sin."

Jesus is in essence telling Pilate that he is doing the will of the Father by having been granted such authority over Him, while those who are accusing Him are the ones insidiously culpable. They are culpable, even though effecting the Cross, because their guilt is in their deliberate decision. Jesus had taught that temptation was inevitable in the world, but woe to him by whom it comes (Luke 17:1.) The ancient nations had been used to punish Israel, but then were not off the hook for that willingness to punish.

Judas effected the arrest and death of Jesus, but he always had the choice to not be the one by whom it came.

but the Jews cried out saying, "If you release this Man, you are no friend of Caesar; everyone who makes himself out to be a king opposes Caesar."

This is the final turning point in the trial. We find that Pilate immediately effects the indictment and punishment forthwith. It is this statement that sealed the outcome.

How is it that such a statement from so disrespected a people could move Pilate to action? Consider also that the Jews were not as privy to Pilate's relationship with Caesar than he himself was. He would know the truth of such a taunt. Second, he was not ordinarily the kind of person who would listen to this kind of logic – that an act such as this in an out of the way province would make him persona non grata with Caesar.

All of this is reasonable, were it not for seemingly unrelated affairs thousands of miles away, in the city of Rome.

We learn from Roman historians that Tiberius was reclusive as emperor, seldom living in the capital, but preferring a sort of working retirement in Capri. As for Rome, he left its management to his trusted prefect, Lucius Aelius Sejanus. Sejanus had, however, taken advantage of his unscrutinized power and conceived of a plot to seize power for himself.

Tiberius was soon apprised of this and arranged for a meeting of the Senate on the pretext of bestowing further honors on Sejanus. He was subsequently charged, arrested and executed. The date: October 18th, 31 A.D. [69]

What does this have to do with our man Pilate? There is convincing evidence that Sejanus was Pilate's benefactor in that Sejanus had recommended him for his current position. There is also evidence that Sejanus was a Jew-baiter and that Pilate's notorious nettling of the Jews was at the instigation of Sejanus.

After the fall of Sejanus, everyone related to him was suspect. It was part and parcel with what came to be called "The Terror" that prevailed during Tiberius' overtly paranoid reign.

The scene before us with Pilate is but a mere two years later. *Caesari amici* – Caesar's friend – was an important distinction for any governor. Equally respected and feared was the opposite.

Pilate did know one thing despite the Jews lesser knowledge of politics at Rome: they were not fearful of mounting deputations to the emperor to plead their cases.

Here they had managed to use the right terminology at last. Pilate will now acquiesce to the people's will and on the charge of sedition. It is this charge that will keep him from scrutiny by Tiberius. To do otherwise was to invite unrest and even revolution, which is what sedition means.

13 Therefore . . Pilate . . . brought Jesus out, and sat down on the judgment seat at a place called The Pavement, but in Hebrew, Gabbatha.

This appears to be the tribunal proper, from which the judgment was intended to be pronounced according to form. Gabbatha was the Aramaic name for the place of judgment which included the pavement, whereas the Pavement (lithostratos) had become a proper name for the floor in this area outside the Praetorium.

As above, this would tend to rule out the palace of Herod, because Gabbatha and its Pavement were related to Pilate's praetorium, not Herod's place of judgment. This distinction is furthered by the existence of such a pavement under the church that overlays Antonia, and the lack of any such structure in the palace ruins. [70]

14 Now it was the day of preparation for the Passover; it was about the sixth hour.

This would again seem to dictate that the Passover of the Jews was about to take place that evening, and that the Passover celebrated by Jesus was otherwise.

The day of preparation for the Passover can be incorrectly understood to mean the day they prepared the Passover. But the day before any Passover was never called the "day of preparation." And as earlier, there would have been no fear in the Jews for entering the praetorium if such a day were at hand.

In practice, this term was always used to designate the day before the weekly Sabbath, Friday. That it is used in close association with the Passover, yet called "day of preparation," simply means that the regular Friday before Sabbath has coincided with the daylight hours following the Seder and the beginning day of the Feast of Passover. In other words, this phrase means, "the Friday before the Sabbath in the feast of Passover."

---

[69] Maier, <u>Church History</u> "Sejanus, Pilate and the Date of the Crucifixion", 1968, p. 3ff
[70] Thompson, <u>The Bible and Archaeology</u> Eerdmans, 1962

"the sixth hour" – ordinarily between 11:00 AM and 12 Noon. Night and day were divided into two periods of twelve hours beginning at the 6:00 hour. The first hour was between 6:00 and 7:00 AM. The sixth hour would be between 11:00 AM and 12 Noon.

(Note: there is reason to adjust this period to 9:00 AM - 12 Noon as a reference point, due to Mark's statement later respecting the third hour. See the next chapter at Mark 15:25)

14 .. "Behold, your King!" .. 15 "We have no king but Caesar."

In a final taunt, Pilate jabs the Jews with the suggestion that they are ordering him to crucify their "king." It is a bit of sarcastic irony aimed at the ludicrous nature of their collective will. Equally ironic is the pose taken up by the Jews – "We have no king but Caesar!" Have they forgotten why Judea is a hostile province? Why their priestly vestments are locked up with the governor, from whom permission to wear them must be formally appealed?

We see the lengths such evil men will go to have Jesus put out of the way. They will feign the most repugnant allegiance imaginable.

24 .. he took water and washed his hands in front of the crowd, saying, "I am innocent of this Man's blood;

It was a formal act for show and legal distinction, but it had no ultimate effective power in itself. Men who were insidiously guilty invoke such public displays. It was a more dramatic form of public verbal statement, for whatever that might be worth.

25 And all the people said, "His blood shall be on us and on our children!"

This is an unexpected statement in the midst of such vitriol and determined hatred – if we read it as genuine. It is in all likelihood a statement of pragmatic pride which is boldly willing to risk blood upon their heads and their offspring. It is like saying, "Let His blood be on our heads, and we'll go even further in our confidence – let it be on our childrens' heads too."

The supreme irony is in how true this would come to be.

CHAPTER 15
His Crucifixion

Luke 23:24-34, Mark 15:20-21, Mark 15:21-25, 27, 28, John 19:17-24

24 And Pilate pronounced sentence that their demand be granted. 25 And he released the man they were asking for who had been thrown into prison for insurrection and murder, but he delivered Jesus to their will. . . 20 After they had mocked Him, they took the purple robe off Him and put His own garments on Him. And they led Him out to crucify Him. . . 17 They took Jesus, therefore, and He went out, bearing His own cross, to the place called the Place of a Skull, which is called in Hebrew, Golgotha. (Luke 23:24-25, Mark 15:20, John 19:17.)

21 They pressed into service a passer-by coming from the country, Simon of Cyrene (the father of Alexander and Rufus), to bear His cross. (Mark 15:21.)

27 And following Him was a large crowd of the people, and of women who were mourning and lamenting Him. 28 But Jesus turning to them said, "Daughters of Jerusalem, stop weeping for Me, but weep for yourselves and for your children. 29 "For behold, the days are coming when they will say, `Blessed are the barren, and the wombs that never bore, and the breasts that never nursed.' 30 "Then they will begin TO SAY TO THE MOUNTAINS, `FALL ON US,' AND TO THE HILLS, `COVER US.' 31 "For if they do these things when the tree is green, what will happen when it is dry?" (Luke 23:27-31.)

32 Two others also, who were criminals, were being led away to be put to death with Him. 33 When they came to the place called The Skull, there they crucified Him . . 34 But Jesus was saying, "Father, forgive them; for they do not know what they are doing." (Luke 23:32-34a.)

23 They tried to give Him wine mixed with myrrh; but He did not take it. . . . 25 It was the third hour when they crucified Him. . . 27 They crucified two robbers with Him, one on His right and one on His left. 28 And the Scripture was fulfilled which says, "And He was numbered with transgressors." (Mark 15:23, 25, 27, 28.)

19 Pilate also wrote an inscription and put it on the cross. It was written, "JESUS THE NAZARENE, THE KING OF THE JEWS." 20 Therefore many of the Jews read this inscription, for the place where Jesus was crucified was near the city; and it was written in Hebrew, Latin and in Greek. 21 So the chief priests of the Jews were saying to Pilate, "Do not write, `The King of the Jews'; but that He said, `I am King of the Jews.'" 22 Pilate answered, "What I have written I have written." 23 Then the soldiers, when they had crucified Jesus, took His outer garments and made four parts, a part to every soldier and also the tunic; now the tunic was seamless, woven in one piece. 24 So they said to one another, "Let us not tear it, but cast lots for it, to decide whose it shall be"; this was to fulfill the Scripture: "THEY DIVIDED MY OUTER GARMENTS AMONG THEM, AND FOR MY CLOTHING THEY CAST LOTS." (John 19:19-24.)

Commentary

24 And Pilate pronounced sentence that their demand be granted. 25 And he released the man they were asking for

As we learned in the preceding verses, Pilate was made to be compliant by the mention of Caesar – his relationship now precarious, as mentioned above. His transformation from deliverer to coalescent executioner with the mob is striking. He pronounced a sentence he knew was not just or true because he feared men more than he feared God.

It is at this point that Barabbas is released to satisfy the custom at Passover – a move he had hoped would have effected the release of Jesus.

24 .. but he delivered Jesus to their will

This is not to be understood as letting the Jews crucify Him themselves, as most know that Roman soldiers effected the procedure. It is a statement that puts the culpability upon the Jews.

In recent times, following the release of *The Passion of the Christ*, (Icon Productions, ©2004) modern Jews have objected to renewed prejudicial defamation in being blamed for the death of Christ, made fresh by such portrayals in the film. It is a replay of the scene we find here in the gospels – the Jews trying to shift the stain of capital punishment to the Romans.

Christians will simply point to the NT as historical proof, which falls on deaf ears since the Jews do not accept it as authoritative. Hence, modern Jews have the luxury of hiding behind the controversy over its historicity and can easily offer that things were not as they have been portrayed through the centuries.

But what documents do they put forward of equal historicity for these accounts? The Jewish Encyclopedia merely comments that Jesus was punished according to the Law. There are no eyewitness records independently theirs that are preserved from those times; nothing that counts as heavily in terms of historical reporting as the gospels.

What was often said in the heat of complaints is that modern Jews were being defamed for crimes they did not commit, which was a tacit admission that at least their ancestors did. But it is convenient to complain about attribution of attitude when one lives in the safety of not having to face its proving ground. What was not said was how readily they might join their ancestors' vitriol and hatred were those same circumstances to arise in modern times.

17.. bearing His own cross,

The cross was customarily employed unassembled. The condemned was made to carry just the patibulum (cross beam), not because it was compassionately lighter, but because the main upright beam was impossible due to its weight. The upright was usually taken separately by soldiers as part of the preparations at the place of execution.

The cross has been pictured variously from rough hewn members of tree trunks and limbs to finished and dressed lumber. The truth is somewhere in between. The anticipated purpose of the instrument would make finely finished wood less likely considering its ignoble intention. Neither did haste and economy necessarily dictate the use of hacked tree limbs.

Rather, the Romans were known for being prepared and resourceful, to the degree that they went to the additional trouble and nuisance of digging trenches and putting up fortifications around their camps each night before resting from their march. In the famous episode of Spartacus in Italy (73 B.C.), Crassus crucified six thousand slaves along the Appian Way. While he certainly did not have this number of manufactured crosses on hand in his campaign, it illustrates how resourceful the Romans could be when the need arose. It is therefore reasonable that fully stationed troops such as those in Jerusalem had sufficient time and resources to prepare for the eventualities of capital punishment.

Of note here, is that this beam was carried over the shoulder, and the shoulders of our Lord were already swollen with the pain of scourging. Technical analysis of the dorsal view of the now famous image on the Shroud of Turin shows abrasions on both shoulders. It is reasonable that the beam was shifted between sides or carried laterally over both shoulders. These additional injuries beyond the visible effects of scourging are hard to see without assistance, and the import of such findings must also be considered in relation to the general questions of authenticity concerning the Shroud.

17... to the Place of a Skull, which is called in Hebrew, Golgotha.

Some have offered that this was not a skull-like formation but a place where the skulls and bones of criminals lay out on the ground. This is hardly likely since in Judaism it was unlawful to leave a dead body unburied, even if the Romans made no effort to dispose of those crucified.

The location is not universally accepted. Candidates are the Church of the Holy Sepulcher just west of Antonia, and Gordon's Calvary discovered in 1842 (Thenius) considerably further NW. Neither is conclusive and each has its dubious factors.

The Church of the Holy Sepulcher is said to enclose both the site of Calvary and the garden tomb. But much of its condition in ancient times is known, principally that the area was barren and desolate, which contradicts the gospel of John which states the tomb was in a garden, had the expectation of a gardener and that fresh tombs were still being constructed (John 19:41, 20:15.) The latest tombs presently known date from years B.C., which would preclude the fresh tomb described for Jesus. [71]

The other problem with Holy Sepulcher is its location. The old city wall is variously understood. It was augmented in stages – first, second and third walls. The third wall, which clearly encloses Holy Sepulcher, is removed as a disqualifying factor, because it is attributed after this period to Herod Agrippa I (41-44 B.C.).

The second wall was certainly present at the time of Jesus. Some conjectural tracings of the 2nd wall have it enclosing the Church of the Holy Sepulcher, which would eliminate the church as a candidate location. (While the gospels do not state that the tomb was outside the city, we have the statement that Jesus was crucified outside the gate - Heb 13:12. Also, Jewish law prevented both executions and burials within the city.)

But more widely accepted tracings of the 2nd wall place Holy Sepulcher outside, but just barely.

This, however, doesn't remove its difficulties as the site of Calvary. There were laws preventing burial sites to the west within so many cubits of the city for reasons of defilement (winds would blow across the city, carrying defiling odors.) Still, tombs are unquestionably at this site. However, these are of 2nd century origin and were cleared of human remains before Herod's refurbishment and expansion of the Temple[72]. While this handles the difficulty of the tombs at Holy Sepulcher, it would have precluded any new tombs, of which Jesus' grave was one (John 19:41.)

Gordon's Calvary farther NW of the 2nd wall would have been at a lawful distance for both crucifixions and burials, and has more of what could be considered a garden in association with a nearby tomb attributed to Joseph of Arimathea.

However, this alternate for the tomb commemorated as that of Jesus is claimed by some scholars to not have been a new tomb but an OT tomb at the time of Jesus [73]. Compounding this is the subsequent reworking of the interior benches in a manner that notably altered the tomb, something that scholars find hard to reconcile with a place the Church would have venerated. [74] Conversely, Holy Sepulcher has the advantage of being kept sacred with a traditional history back to Constantine (4th century.)

What attracts many to Gordon's Calvary is the visible formation that resembles a skull and that its elevation would have been more conducive to public demonstration. The features actually show what could be seen as two skulls side-by-side. Some contend that these features were not visible in Jesus' day, but the result of later excavation and surface work in the area.

As for the name Calvary, no one in Jesus' day called the place by that name. Calvary comes from the Latin *calva* meaning bald.

---

[71] Chadwick, Revisiting Golgotha and the Garden Tomb, Meridian Magazine, 2003

[72] Chadwick, ibid.

[73] Murphy-O'Conner, The Holy Land: An Oxford Archaeological Guide from Earliest Times to 1700, Oxford Press, 1998, pp.45-57

[74] ibid.

The Chronological Gospel Commentary – The Four Gospels

21 They pressed into service a passer-by coming from the country, Simon of Cyrene . . to bear His cross.

A sense of the duration of time is lost during these accounts, but Jesus has obviously been carrying the cross beam for sometime and has fallen a number of times to prompt the soldiers to "press into service" someone on the sidelines. Nothing beyond this is mentioned of him. His sons are seemingly of more notoriety, him being mentioned as the father of Alexander and Rufus. This designation without further qualification carries the assumption that they are well known at the time of the writing.

Acts 19:33-34 mentions an Alexander who attempted to defend St. Paul in his Ephesian difficulty. Some take this as referring to the son of Simon.

A Rufus is mentioned by Paul (Romans 16:13) as a disciple of the Apostles, who lived at Rome and to whom St. Paul sent a greeting [75]

"Daughters of Jerusalem, stop weeping for Me, but weep for yourselves and for your children.

The group of women mentioned here were weeping for obvious reasons. They had no doubt followed Him and adored Him as Messiah. Now they had seen Him strikingly disfigured, His hands shaking as He tried to hold onto the beam, His knees weak and often collapsing. Looks here and there filled with the shock of unimaginable pain. He was so different now to look upon, like watching one's own child being beaten and abused. Tears flowed in visible recognition that something so wrong was unfolding before their eyes.

But amid this, Jesus diverts their tears for Him to the appropriate place – to their nation and kindred. That is the greater tragedy of this moment and of those to come. His suffering was horrifying, but it was effecting salvation. The future suffering would be likewise horrifying but for sin.

The judgment coming is such that it will be hard to be a Jew in those days. It will be preferred that one was barren, hence – *"behold, the days are coming when they will say, `Blessed are the barren, and the wombs that never bore, and the breasts that never nursed.'"*

Ahead of them was the destruction of the city. Not only would there be terror without but terrors within as their own people would take advantage of the situation to wrest control and power from each other, killing, stealing and abusing their own citizens.

Josephus records that people escaping to the Romans swallowed down their savings that they might avoid notice from robbers and thieves, only to be hacked to pieces by Arab and Syrian mercenaries who had been informed of the treasures hidden in their bowels. [76]

30 "Then they will begin TO SAY TO THE MOUNTAINS, `FALL ON US,' AND TO THE HILLS, `COVER US.'

He quotes Hosea 10:8, a prophecy historically against Ephraim and its capital Samaria of an 8th century Israel, rebellious and split from her sister Judah. In the mouth of our Lord we find it having a double fulfillment in the impending doom of post-Resurrection Jerusalem. Further still will it be fulfilled in the days when nations shall mourn at the judgments which they will attribute to the "wrath of the Lamb who sits on the throne" (Rev 6:16.)

---

[75] Cornely, <u>Commentary in the Epistle to the Romans</u> (Latin) Paris, 1896, 778 sq.
[76] Josephus, Wars Book v, ch x, sect 1, ch xiii, sect 3

"For if they do these things when the tree is green, what will happen when it is dry?"

The comparison is against times when nature is cooperating and fervent in the newness of life and those times that are arduous and trying, when nature and the seasons are opposite.

If those wreaking this kind of suffering can do so at the time of their visitation (when the tree is green) what will they be capable of in times of stress and anguish (when it is dry)?

"Father, forgive them; for they do not know what they are doing."

Here is the ultimate exemplar for loving one's enemies. This is said at the express point when their rage has reached the extreme of inflicting pain and incomparable suffering without remorse. Yet He can pray that this be not held to their account.

Were the Jewish leaders not glad to see Him get what was coming to Him? Nor was it a case of reluctantly obeying orders while holding a sympathetic view. Soldiers laughed and priests showed faces of smug satisfaction.

Our human reaction would be to let condemnation and just recompense be their reward if they are of such a determined mind to resist God. We would easily relegate them as the chaff of human existence, fit only for the fire. They made their bed, let them lie in it.

Not so with Jesus. He taught us to love our enemies, and at the hardest point imaginable, He succeeds in living up to His own exhortation.

This is not contradictory to His statement to Pilate – that those delivering Him had the greater sin. They were sinning, but He prays on account of their not knowing the magnitude of their crimes.

The earlier perception of envy on their part made it clear that some knew they were killing an innocent man, but nothing suggests that they consciously conspired to kill someone they knew to be their Messiah. It was a deliberate act based on deception, not on perfect knowledge.

23 They tried to give Him wine mixed with myrrh; but He did not take it.

The point of this act was to dull the senses. Most spent considerable time on the cross, even a few days, before dying. Some respite was extended to victims who lingered. Jesus had not been on the Cross long, but the sight of His wounds and scourging hastened this gesture earlier than usual.

As it is, He refused it for reasons most likely related to His need to finish the great work of God as to salvation, making its prolongation counterproductive.

25 It was the third hour when they crucified Him.

This appears to be in direct contradiction to our reading from John that it was the sixth hour (19:14.) What contributes to our immediate sense of contradiction is the implied idea that when an author mentions things like "the third hour .. the sixth hour" he is used to identifying events accurate to the hour. Hence, we might elsewhere expect "second hour .. fourth hour."

But this is hardly a real expectation about ancient times, primarily because the ancients simply didn't possess portable instruments of technology that would tell them the hour when the need arose. The water clock, the hour glass, and the sun dial were roughly accurate to the hour but few had them and one didn't carry such instruments everywhere they went.

By necessity, people had to resort to a more approximated reference to time, using instead the major divisions of the day, which happened to be named according to the hour they commenced. Thus we have early morning: 6:00 – 9:00 AM, the third hour: 9:00 – 12 Noon, the sixth hour: 12 Noon – 3:00 PM, and the ninth hour: 3:00 – 6:00 PM, skipping use of second, fourth and fifth hours. [77]

Still, how they knew even these hours without instruments is puzzling. Sunrise and sunset were a cinch. All that remained was to calibrate one's memory of the sun's position at 9:00 AM, Noon and 3:00 PM. Obviously, there was imprecision, which actually helps us resolve our difficulty here.

The conflict, however, with the time markers was originally thought to be a copyist error, where the letters used to represent *third* and *sixth* were easily subject to being misread. But this would not have resolved the problem, because John and Mark are not talking about the same time point (event) in the day. Mark mentions the time He was crucified, John the time the trial was still in progress.

The other problem in this particular case is that the crucifixion happened to take place near the demarcation point between two divisions of the day – those hours designated by 'third hour' and those designated by 'sixth.' Thus, a writer had the option of personal preference, much like the discrepancy in two views of a glass of water – half full or half empty.

If the crucifixion began at 10:30 or 11:00 AM, Mark may have regarded this as nearer the third hour, which began at 9:00 and extended to 12 Noon. John may have regarded it as nearer the sixth hour, beginning at 12 Noon. [78] (John did say "about the sixth hour", which allows for actual times before and after.) And we have the three synoptics consistently reporting later: "when the sixth hour came, darkness . . " indicating the crucifixion began sometime before not at the sixth hour (Matt 27:45, Mark 15:33, Luke 23:44.)

The problem with this explanation is that the 10:30 - 11:00 AM suggestion does not allow enough time for all the intervening arrangements in getting Jesus to Golgotha and up on the Cross with enough time to spare that the other gospel writers could then say subsequenlty, "when the sixth hour came, darkness . ." Also, John does not use sixth hour in reference to the crucifixion but to the last moments of the trial before Pilate (19:14.) We have to accommodate time for leaving the tribunal, the brief moments of mockery by the guards, the sluggish journey to Calvary along Via Dolorosa, nailing His body to the cross, the placing and securing of the cross in the ground. And some time needs to transpire on the cross for the synoptics to first report that the crucifixion took place at the third hour.

A resolution of this involves an appeal to different time reference systems between Mark and John, Mark using the Jewish reference and John using the Roman. In this difference, the Jews counted the hours from the demarcation point above – day hours being counted from 6:00 AM; the Romans counting a day's hours from midnight, as we have in modern times. In this case, according to Jewish reckoning, Jesus trial overlaped the nighttime hours into the day at the 6:00 AM hour, so that the crucifixion would have followed at the third hour (9:00 AM). But for the Romans, the trial being still in progress at the 6:00 AM hour would be the sixth hour of their day, as John has it. Hence, we have Jewish – 6:00 AM, 9:00 AM: *first* and *third* hours; Roman – 6:00 AM, 9:00 AM: *sixth* and *ninth* hours.

.. they crucified Him ..

The perversion of mind that would conceive of, no less commit to action, the idea of nailing a human being to a piece of wood elucidates the degree of degenerate thinking the human mind can sink to in the indulgence of evil. And bear in mind that the perpetrators of such actions did so not with repugnance, but with relish.

---

[77] Tenney, Pictorial Encyclopedia of the Bible, Zondervan, Vol 2, 1976 pp 217,
Gleason Archer, Encyclopedia of Bible Difficulties, Zondervan, 1982, pp. 363-364,
Ramsay, Hasting's Dictionary of the Bible Suppl Vol., Hendrickson, 1909, pp. 475 to 479
[78] Ewald, Life of Christ, p 325

Experiments with living persons tied in the same positions as crucifixion have revealed that the process was one that alternated between keeping oneself raised enough to breathe and slumping into asphyxiation to relieve the pain of doing so. In cases where the feet were nailed, the pain would induce the need to slump rather than stand which put pressure on the wounds in the feet. This caused asphyxiation since the positions of the arms would restrict the chest from normal breathing movements. Similarly, the pain from wounds in the wrists would be most intense, holding the full weight of the slumped body. As soon as the effects of asphyxiation were intolerable, the victim would need to again raise himself to breathe, repeating the awful cycle of pain and asphyxiation over and over again.

From the details learned from the Shroud of Turin, we now have much more information on the physical aspects of crucifixion in ancient times. Despite paintings consistently portraying nails in the palms, researchers have determined that this was anatomically and mechanically inadequate for bearing the weight. However, many paintings also show cords binding the arms which would preclude the problem of nails alone having to be sufficient. [79]

But the definitive evidence is from the Shroud which shows nails in the wrists not the palms. This makes sense anatomically because the hollow at the wrist would hold the weight irrespective of cords being applied or not.

27 They crucified two robbers with Him, one on His right and one on His left. 28

Adding to the sting of criminality respecting Jesus, He was crucified with two other criminals. For us in modern times, the Cross is a symbol of our religion and the saving work of Christ for us. To those of the times, it was an instrument of punishment. Were we to wear a cross on a chain, the people of those times would equate it to wearing the image of a noose and gallows. In the 18th century it would be like wearing an image of the guillotine.

To be hung among other criminals was to associate Him with those whom society disposes of as malefactors. Jesus was not positioned on one end, but in the middle, so as to be deliberately among them – *28 "And He was numbered with transgressors."*

19 Pilate also wrote an inscription . . . "JESUS THE NAZARENE, THE KING OF THE JEWS."

Pilate exercised one last jab at the Jews with the titulus (sign) placed above the head of Jesus on the cross. It was not merely to anger the Jews but to also make a statement from the Roman perspective. Rome was master of the world, and in respect to the Jews, the only sovereign power over them. To make known in a public way that Rome was crucifying the Jewish claimant to be King was a further sign of that absolute power, even if done tongue in cheek (Pilate knew Jesus not to be politically such a person.)

The Jewish leaders complained immediately. This is somewhat confusing since they were present at Golgotha but this complaint is lodged with Pilate who was not present. As we have learned from John, he is not one to spend time elucidating the logistics between scenes and events. No doubt they saw the titulus at Golgotha, then went to Pilate at Antonia to complain, and an expression of the time involved was not considered necessary.

Their request was that it not be declared as fact that Jesus was king. Since Pilate had personal investment in the jibe, we can understand his reply, "What I have written I have written" v.22.

John states that because of the international character of Jerusalem at Passover, the title was written in Latin and Greek as well. Of some archaeological interest, is the discovery and preservation of what is

---

[79] Zugibe, The Cross and the Shroud , A Medical Inquiry into the Crucifixion, New York, Paragon Press, 1988 pp 30-33, Barbet, Doctor at Calvary, New York: P. J. Kennedy & Sons, 1953; New York: Image Books, 1963.

claimed to be the titulus of the True Cross, housed in the Church of Santa Croce in Gerusalemme, Rome. While not conclusively so, the manner of its discovery, its history and the unique manner in which it is inscribed have caused many to conclude that it may be genuine. [80]

23 Then the soldiers, when they had crucified Jesus, took His outer garments and made four parts,

The implication is that they tore these into their parts (concluded from the decision not to tear the tunic or cloak, v.24) As to why torn garments would be of value, we can only speculate. They would hardly be of value as clothing. Perhaps the regular need for pieces of cloth for other purposes made this a routine act.

It is a commentary on the utter bankruptcy Jesus had (even in death) with respect to worldly possessions. He left mortal life with virtually the same possessions He had at His birth, a cloth about his loins.

The decision not to rend the cloak was more momentous than would seem. It was to fulfill the great prophecy, *"THEY DIVIDED MY OUTER GARMENTS AMONG THEM, AND FOR MY CLOTHING THEY CAST LOTS."* (Psalms 22:18.) Whether the prophecy obligated the actions of the guards or the prophecy foresaw the real future in which those actions occurred, the prediction and fulfillment are equally amazing, considering it was written some one thousand years prior.

There is no legitimate tradition as to the history of this cloak after the Crucifixion. Speculation as to its outcome was fictionalized in the famous novel, <u>The Robe</u>, by Lloyd C. Douglas, later immortalized in film in Henry Koster's *The Robe*, (20th Century Fox, 1954).

Matthew 27:39-56, Luke 23: 35-37, 39-43, John 19:25-30, Luke 23:46-49, Mark 15:39-41
39 And those passing by were hurling abuse at Him, wagging their heads 40 and saying, "You who are going to destroy the temple and rebuild it in three days, save Yourself! If You are the Son of God, come down from the cross." 41 In the same way the chief priests also, along with the scribes and elders, were mocking Him and saying, 42 "He saved others; He cannot save Himself. He is the King of Israel; let Him now come down from the cross, and we will believe in Him. 43 "HE TRUSTS IN GOD; LET GOD RESCUE Him now, IF HE DELIGHTS IN HIM; for He said, 'I am the Son of God.' " 44 The robbers who had been crucified with Him were also insulting Him with the same words. (Matthew 27:39-44.)

35 Soldiers also came up and mocked him. offering him wine and vinegar and saying, 'If you are the king of the Jews, save yourself." (Luke 23: 35-37)

39 One of the criminals who were hanged there was hurling abuse at Him, saying, "Are You not the Christ? Save Yourself and us!" 40 But the other answered, and rebuking him said, "Do you not even fear God, since you are under the same sentence of condemnation? 41 "And we indeed are suffering justly, for we are receiving what we deserve for our deeds; but this man has done nothing wrong." 42 And he was saying, "Jesus, remember me when You come in Your kingdom!" 43 And He said to him, "Truly I say to you, today you shall be with Me in Paradise." (Luke 23:39-43.)

25 . . . But standing by the cross of Jesus were His mother, and His mother's sister, Mary the wife of Clopas, and Mary Magdalene. 26 When Jesus then saw His mother, and the disciple whom He loved standing nearby, He said to His mother, "Woman, behold, your son!" 27 Then He said to the disciple, "Behold, your mother!" From that hour the disciple took her into his own household. (John 19:25-27.)

45 Now from the sixth hour darkness fell upon all the land until the ninth hour. 46 About the ninth hour Jesus cried out with a loud voice, saying, "ELI, ELI, LAMA SABACHTHANI ?" that is, "MY GOD, MY GOD, WHY HAVE YOU FORSAKEN ME ?" 47 And some of those who were standing there, when they heard it, began saying, "This man is calling for Elijah." (Matthew 27:45-47.)

---

[80] Franchi, <u>Santa Croce: An historical and artistic guide to the Church, the Cloisters, and the Museum</u> Becocci, 1976.

28 After this, Jesus, knowing that all things had already been accomplished, to fulfill the Scripture, said, "I thirst." 29 A jar full of sour wine was standing there; so they put a sponge full of the sour wine upon a branch of hyssop and brought it up to His mouth. (John 19:28-29.)

48 Immediately one of them ran, and taking a sponge, he filled it with sour wine and put it on a reed, and gave Him a drink. 49 But the rest of them said, "Let us see whether Elijah will come to save Him ." (Matthew 27:48-49.)

30 Therefore when Jesus had received the sour wine, He said, "It is finished!" . .
46 And Jesus, crying out with a loud voice, said, "Father, INTO YOUR HANDS I COMMIT MY SPIRIT." Having said this, He breathed His last . . And He bowed His head and gave up His spirit. (John 19:30a, Luke 23:46, John 19:30b.)

51 And behold, the veil of the temple was torn in two from top to bottom; and the earth shook and the rocks were split. 52 The tombs were opened, and many bodies of the saints who had fallen asleep were raised; 53 and coming out of the tombs after His resurrection they entered the holy city and appeared to many. . . 39 When the centurion, who was standing right in front of Him, saw the way He breathed His last, he said, "Truly this man was the Son of God!" . . 54 . . those who were with him keeping guard over Jesus, when they saw the earthquake and the things that were happening, became very frightened . . (Matthew 27:51-53, Mark 15:39, Matthew 27:54.)

40 There were also some women looking on from a distance, among whom were Mary Magdalene, and Mary the mother of James the Less and Joses, and Salome . . and the mother of the sons of Zebedee. . . 41 When He was in Galilee, they used to follow Him and minister to Him; and there were many other women who came up with Him to Jerusalem. (Mark 15:39-40, Matthew 27:56, Mark 15:41.)

48 And all the crowds who came together for this spectacle, when they observed what had happened, began to return, beating their breasts. 49 And all His acquaintances and the women who accompanied Him from Galilee were standing at a distance, seeing these things. (Luke 23:48-49.)

Commentary

39 And those passing by were hurling abuse at Him, wagging their heads 40 and saying, "You who are going to destroy the temple and rebuild it in three days, save Yourself!

The contradiction of a claimant to so many aspects of power now crucified as a criminal was irresistible for His enemies. He had claimed to be Son of God, Israel's Messiah, and a man to whom all authority had been given. Now He had ironically been delivered into their hands to become subject to mere men on a criminal's cross, disgraced and defeated in their eyes. They further justified their evil deeds from Deuteronomy – that no Messiah of Israel's God would hang from a tree (Deut 21:23.)

All those who had an axe to grind against Him were delighted to rub this in. And in many ways, men in every age have looked for opportunities to similarly deride the One who lays such callings upon men against their selfish desires. He embarrasses their self-centeredness, nullifies the worth of all that is purely humanistic, all that is done without respect for God. He makes all men thoroughly wrong and Himself thoroughly right, and that is intolerable to prideful men.

So when He is fallen, men cannot resist the opportunity to kick Him when He is down. It justifies their rejection and authenticates the continued pursuit of their own way.

The jibes take up the form of insidious reminders about bold claims of power, yet being unable to do the simplest thing – to free oneself of one's bonds and come down from agony and certain death.

It is a complete misunderstanding of this kind of power. It is not a case of ability, but of will. They cannot conceive that any person, anointed or not, would wish to remain on a cross. His strength was in His will to remain there, not in His ability to free Himself. This was seen as weakness, but it exceeded the ability and strength of any man who had lived or would ever live. Who could exercise their will to such a degree that it could overcome the desire to reach for that power that would free them from unimaginable agony?

In the Steven Spielberg film, *Schindler's List* (Amblin Entertainment 1993), Schindler suggests to the camp commandant (Fiennes) that real strength is not in having the power to kill but in being able to decide not to kill. The commandant is intrigued, but his evil heart is not up to the strength needed and he reverts to his former, murderous self. This is where Jesus proved how strong He could be and how possessed of power He truly was. The world sees His death as weak-kneed and helpless, not what a superhero would have done. But he proved his strength in staying on the Cross to securing that precious work that would benefit all mankind.

wagging their heads

This observation describes more than shaking one's head in disgust. It is a movement of the head that mirrors a bold swaggering born of self-righteous indignation, a sort of cocky arrogance at having gotten the upper hand.

One can only imagine the supreme embarrassment when such behavior is played back for them at the Judgment.

42 *"He saved others; He cannot save Himself.*

Added to this is the irony in the word "salvation." To save oneself from crucifixion would seem like peanuts compared to saving others from hellfire. The latter involves a power beyond the physical realm, authority over the principalities of Heaven and the law of righteousness and judgment. Surely someone possessed of the latter would not be denied the former.

Yet again it is a mistake about classes of things. Salvation is theological, spiritual, incorporeal. Rescue is merely about the temporal and the physical. The principles that govern each are wholly unrelated and of different orders. But this distinction is lost on the carnally minded.

43 *"HE TRUSTS IN GOD; LET GOD RESCUE Him now, IF HE DELIGHTS IN HIM;*

It is difficult to know if these quotations from Psalms 22 are intentionally applied from the OT by the Jews themselves or the foreknowledge of God placed such words in the mouth of David as applying to his own despair while serving the needs of a future picture here at the Cross - what these men were foreseen to say.

For the Jews to deliberately and cognitively use them from the Psalms, they would have to consciously turn them around to be legitimate vilifications compared to their illegitimate use against David. In David's case they were taunts against a wholly righteous man. Such persons had been guilty of ridiculing David, God's anointed King. Here, without some adjustment in thinking, they would be taking up the same posture with its attendant condemnation. So to use it against Jesus, they would have to convert these statements to legitimate insults, which would seem to be a deliberate contortion of Scripture they were publicly obligated to revere.

In truth, our evangelist is tying them to the reprehensible taunts against David. He is divinely inspired to make the connection for his audience. These Jews are in the same boat with David's accusers, for before them is One greater than David.

44 *The robbers who had been crucified with Him were also insulting Him*

This is a difficult observation to coordinate with the later fact that one of them appealed to Jesus to save Himself and them also.

We might wish to attribute this to Matthew's imprecision, including both thieves in the taunts of just the one – "One of the criminals . . was hurling abuse at Him." (Luke 23:39.)

But if this does violence to one's sense of divine anointing and the grace of inerrancy, we must conclude that perhaps both thieves did join the chorus of insults from below, but Dysmas later saw in our Lord's suffering something that convicted his heart, and he made his appeal in the moment of a newly imbued faith. And we must remember that agonizing suffering can make any man say things they later come to regret.

40 But the other answered, and rebuking him said, "Do you not even fear God, since you are under the same sentence of condemnation?

The NT does not name him, but tradition identifies him with the later beatified Saint Dysmas. What he says is striking. They are both about to meet their Maker. Why exacerbate their case further before God? Now is the time to be making amends with a righteous Judge, not adding to one's indictments.

But more than this, the crime is all the more enlarged because it is against an innocent man – "but this man has done nothing wrong."

It is also an amazing anomaly in relation to our modern world view. The man is acknowledging that they are getting just recompense for their actions in life. Today, the mode of operation is to deny everything to the very last and hope that cleverness and perfection in that expertise common to the dramatic arts will convince everyone that the truly guilty are innocent on some exceptional ground yet overlooked. If you can fool the right people, perhaps one can escape the consequences.

Here, in ancient times now long gone, there is still some vestige alive in man that can confess sin and the just nature of one's punishment.

This, Jesus sees as redeemable.

"Jesus, remember me when You come in Your kingdom!" 43 And He said to him, "Truly I say to you, today you shall be with Me in Paradise."

The man remembers enough about Jesus to know that He taught men about the coming Kingdom. Whether here now or waiting in the wings, the man knows in some way this Jesus is connected with such a realm and that death will not interfere with His return to it. Notice, he does not venture the daring to be gathered into it, but merely to be remembered there.

To this Jesus assures him he will not only be remembered but will come to be with Him there. For all who wish to stress the arduousness of a life of good works, Dysmas has little time to mount them up for the day of salvation. He has certainly performed a good work at his moment of faith, bearing evidence that he had the faith that counts before God. For those who stress that quantity will mean something in the eternal assessment, this is a case to the contrary.

With this verse, we have the issue of immediacy vs. delay in enjoying the blessings of Heaven. Some have qualified their understanding on the word *'paradeiso'* to not mean the Heaven of salvation but the holding place of the righteous prior to a judgment that would grant them access. In Catholic terms this would be Purgatory, but even if so, the man would be seen as part of the host of those saved. The question would be whether the rigors of Purgatory could ever be seen as paradise, and further, is the risen Christ there among those who are being purged of temporal effects?

Protestants, not bound by a doctrine of purification conditional on entrance into Heaven see this as immediate enjoyment of the blessed state. Much bears on our understanding of when the assessment of works for rewards will occur in the progression of end state resolutions, but some justification is found in the souls of the martyrs seen under the altar during the events of the Revelation, with the Second Coming yet future (Rev 6:9.), also in Paul's statement that to be absent from the body is to be present with the Lord (2 Cor 5:8.)

25 . . . But standing by the cross of Jesus were His mother, and His mother's sister, Mary the wife of Clopas, and Mary Magdalene.

As for more clarification of all the people present at the Cross, see on at Mk 15:40. The subject of Jesus' aunt (Mary's sister) is variously understood. If the comma in English and the phrase "Mary the wife of Clopas" are meant parenthetically "His mother's sister (Mary wife of Clopas)" then this Mary and her husband Clopas would have been Jesus' aunt and uncle, and their children His cousins. If the comma is not parenthetic then "His mother's sister" stands on its own as a person not named, followed by another person who is named. (There are no commas in Greek. One must get parenthetic allusions from context or observation.)

The Greek may give us some help but not conclusively so. In the list of names later presented in Mark chapter 15, the word *'kai'* ("and") separates each person mentioned – Person 1 *and* Person 2 *and* Person 3. (Mark's rendition names other people present, so this does not inform us directly on those mentioned in John, but sets a pattern of usage that is important.)

In John, we don't have *kai* between "His mother's sister" and "Mary of Clopas," which would lend itself to the idea that this subsequent Mary is meant to be parenthetic, a qualification which identifies the sister herself.

The raw Greek reads: *"of Jesus the mother of him and the sister of the mother of him Mary of the Clopas and Mary the Magdalene."* As you can see, there is no "and" separating Mary of Clopas into a consecutive person named in the list as is the case with Mary Magdalene.

Against this is Broadus' observation that having two daughters in the same family named Mary would be extraordinary and a commitment to a life of confusion. [81]

Ultimately, there is nothing else in Scripture about Mary of Clopas that would preclude this identification, but neither is there something stronger to make it firm. The Greek above is offered as an observation, not a definitive argument.

The presence of Mary, His mother, cannot escape our compassion. She was not entirely without preparation of this eventuality, but it was couched in vague and obscure speech. And even if forewarned, the fulfillment is none the easier when it and us are brought together in its stark reality.

She may very well have remembered here the prophesy of Simeon, *"A sword shall pierce through your own soul,"* (Luke 2:35.)

26 . . . "Woman, behold, your son!" . . .27 ""Behold, your mother!"

As earlier mentioned, we do not find the other disciples present at the Cross. But the charge respecting His mother was hardly a case of choosing the only one there. John is called the disciple whom the Lord loved (John 13:23), not to the exclusion of the others, but especially so that it be made to stand out as extraordinary. It in fact accounts for John's presence at the Cross and for him being in truth the best choice for caring after Jesus' mother.

The words are far from our modern sense of speech. We would say it more plainly, "Woman take this one as your son" . . . "Son, take my mother has your own." But the modes of expression are of days long ago when it was more poetic and picturesque to say, "Look upon your son . . .Look upon your mother." It was less direct and hence more meaningful as the intention jelled in the mind.

27 . . From that hour the disciple took her into his own household.

---

[81] Broadus, <u>Commentary of Matthew</u>, Kregel, (1990) p.578

John clearly had parents still very much alive. He is among the "sons of thunder" – the sons of Zebedee, whose wife (John's mother) will be seen shortly to also be very present in these affairs. This was clearly not a command for disaffection from his own mother in favor of that of our Lord, but a command to care for her in addition to his duties to his own parents.

Whether "household" means that of his own parents or one now independent of them isn't said. John may very well have had separate quarters than his parents by this time in his life. He was independent enough to take up with the apostles, which would be less likely were he young enough to still need permission from his parents.

We have here some insight into the senior and convalescent care of elders. There were no private or government funded rest homes for the aged. Families were expected to take care of their own, making for a frequent scene of having parents and grandparents living with their offspring until death. It is the advancement of self and the disconnected style of modern families that finds children moving hundreds of miles away without much concern for how their parents will be cared for. The result has been the necessary rise of rest homes and convalescent facilities for largely abandoned parents.

In ancient times, you knew your obligations. So your relationships had to be nurtured among the generations simply because they were going to be permanent members of the household for a significant part of your life. Life was less me by myself, and more me in an ongoing relationship to "them."

45 Now from the sixth hour darkness fell upon all the land until the ninth hour.

We are not told that this was supernatural, but the darkness of a building storm would have been anticipated and reported perhaps more innocuously. No doubt it was caused by the use of nature, since lightning attended it later, but its sudden occurrence caught observers in ominous fear of its portents.

As above, the explanation that Jesus' crucifixion began at 9:00 AM rather than closer to 12:00 Noon would allow time for all the above to transpire so as to arrive at this observation over time. The other explanation, following John's mention of Jesus still before Pilate "about the sixth hour," would cause this observation to happen almost immediately. There is also import from the later notation that the soldiers had come to break the legs and found Him already dead, meaning that this action in response to orders that this be concluded quickly plays less well if Jesus was on the cross for nearly six hours.

46 About the ninth hour . . "ELI, ELI, LAMA SABACHTHANI ?". . . "MY GOD, MY GOD, WHY HAVE YOU FORSAKEN ME ?"

The ninth hour would be the fourth division of the day, which commenced at 3:00 P.M. Discerning the hour for eyewitnesses would have been difficult if the clouds were now obscuring the sun. But in the Temple not far from these proceedings the priests were accustomed to blow their trumpets at key hours of the day marking the times for sacrifice. 3:00 PM was such a time, thus, Jesus may very well have cried out just after such a trumpet was sounded in the Temple.

The Hebrew and Aramaic for God is "El." The addition of "i" adds a personal possessive – God of me." Why Matthew found it necessary to include the Hebrew words in the Greek text ahead of their translation is not clear, except that to his Jewish audience such words could not then be attributed to some maladaption between languages. The words were important and having the original speech removed all doubt.

They are more from the previous citation from Psalm 22 and attribute David's cry to Jesus Himself. Because it is a direct quote, the importance of having the original would ensure the Jews understood He was not parroting David, but claiming David's words.

In Mark we have 'Eloi' compared to Eli in Matthew. Matthew quotes the Scripture directly, hence the Hebrew spelling. Mark quotes Jesus directly, hence the Aramaic spelling – Eloi.

Of more importance is why Jesus quoted this, thus attributing the forsaking of the Father to His own condition. Had not all of these affairs been in perfect accord with the Father's will and the covenant between Son and Father established since time immemorial?

The most cogent and effective explanation is that we are in fact witnessing in the text the very moment when Jesus was taking on the sins of the world – the efficacy of the sacrificial lamb taking hold. As such, the Father would be repulsed by the presence of sin now made to come upon the Son, upon which He could not look. Jesus then sensed that revulsion and in His state as God but also man, perceived it as abandonment.

Paul later describes this in more theological detail, pointing out that Jesus became sin for us, that it might die with Him at the Cross - "For he hath made him [to be] sin for us, who knew no sin; that we might be made the righteousness of God in him." (2 Cor 5:21.) "The death he died, he died to sin once for all; but the life he lives, he lives to God." (Rom 6:10.)

47 And some of those who were standing there, when they heard it, began saying, "This man is calling for Elijah."

On the scene, those hearing Him did not hear clearly or supposed the wrong things from His use of 'Eli.' The first two syllables of the name Elijah are pronounced exactly the same – *el-eee*. Eli is short for Elijah (el-eee-yah.) Thus, some bystanders mistook Him for calling out to the prophet.

28 . . knowing that all things had already been accomplished . . "I thirst." 29 . . they put a sponge full of the sour wine upon a branch of hyssop

His statement, "I thirst" was not said to fulfill all Scripture, but was said having now known that all Scripture had been fulfilled. This was attempted earlier with the vinegar but refused. Now he receives it from the soldiers below, a sponge being filled with virtually the same drink – sour wine.

Those misunderstanding His call to Eli now watch to see if Elijah will appear to save Him. This was not a completely unsubstantiated desire. Malachi had prophesied that Elijah would come before the "great and terrible day" (Mal 4:5.) In no way did they believe the time had come for this fulfillment and this is said tongue-in-cheek, waiting for the disappointment to further ridicule Jesus – *49 . . "Let us see whether Elijah will come to save Him ."*

30 . . . "It is finished!" . . "Father, INTO YOUR HANDS I COMMIT MY SPIRIT."

What was finished was not His life but His work; and not merely His deeds, but the effecting of salvation. It was the completion of the plan, not the end of the Worker's part in it. Salvation was now complete, the Sacrifice to end all sacrifices made.

We sometimes think of His statement committing His spirit to His Father as being made as easily as the actors have portrayed it in films. Rather, it was at the very moment His biological life was ebbing away. It was said loudly, but exhaustedly. The breath rushed out of Him at this statement and He slumped into that final position of absolute stillness that marks the dead. His body is but molecules and atoms, tissue and bone. He is as still and un-animated as the wood to which He has been nailed, but so much more precious than any creation of God. Where He would have thrown the locks of His hair back to see clearly, the wind now moves them according to the dictates of simple nature.

That His death is described as the giving up of His spirit is to let us in on the nature of all men, who do house for a brief time the sacred spirit from God, giving life to mere flesh, and conversely turning life into mere matter as it leaves. We too will leave our vessels to meet the destiny our lives and decisions have dictated for it.

Life and awareness are then not tied ultimately to the body, but to the continuity of the spirit. As Paul states, to be absent from the body is not the end, but the continuation of the spirit's journey. For some back to God, for others to a place made ready for the unrighteous.

51 And behold, the veil of the temple was torn in two from top to bottom; and the earth shook and the rocks were split.

The immediate response to 'It is finished' respecting the plan of God is the dissolution of the old order. God signaled this unmistakably by the tearing of the Temple curtain that guarded the Holy of Holies, Israel's most sacred and intimate location for the very Presence of Almighty God. For it to be torn was to announce that such Presence was at an end. God, as in the day when the prophet saw the train of God's glory lifted up and vacating the former Temple, was forever changing both the conditions and the means by which He would now be approached.

We have only the Scripture to state that it was torn from top to bottom. After the fact, this would be difficult to assess by merely looking at the remnants, unless it was left partially together at the bottom to guarantee this observation. Or perhaps the Levites attending the Temple saw it from the Holy Place.

No such facts would remain in Judaism's history. You will not find mention of it in their accounts of this period. The curtain was no doubt repaired with the same aplomb that ignored every other aspect of the momentous events of their visitation. The sacrifices continued, the Levitical procedures progressed until the Romans made them impossible in 70 A.D. But from God's perpective, this was merely going through the motions, devoid of substance and recognition.

52 The tombs were opened, . . saints . . were raised; 53 . . they entered the holy city and appeared to many

That such things accompanied His death should have shaken our Lord's enemies into repentance. And some who were fence-sitters did indeed come over to faith in Him, but mostly of the people themselves. Of the leaders, we have few testimonies, due primarily to the risks publicly and professionally this would entail.

"asleep" was a term that described the repose of the dead, and slumber implied a future waking, which for all believers was part of the theology of the resurrection. Said to have occurred after His resurrection, we have no difficulty maintaining that He was the first fruit of the Resurrection, these mentioned having not preceding Him.

Their appearance to many does not mean they were recognized, since many would not have a clue what the saints of old looked like. Again, this is NT witness informing us by inspiration that the saints did appear.

What a wonderful testimony and vindication of the promise of resurrection – that saints whose lives had been captured by the grave and whose security in the resurrection was only a hope, be now called upon to demonstrate its reality in relation to the Cross and His Resurrection.

This is as we might expect on general principles. If the genuine article from God was done to death and raised to victory over the grave, we would expect all of nature to declare the day and the deeds for what they were. Lightning and darkness, hills and rocks rent asunder, manifestations in the Temple and the very dead giving witness.

"Truly this man was the Son of God!"

Such events caused even the heathen soul to admit the clear truth of what was happening. Here is a man of no regard for the superstitions of a desert nation. Yet seeing all nature declare what day it was for both world and universe, even the hardened soldier who was long past being phased by crucifixions uttered words of changing faith.

So also his band with him, perhaps short of his confession, but frightened by the reaction of nature about them. The Romans were not without their superstitions either. They consulted the entrails of animals for omens or blessing of the gods. Long before Augustus' birth, lightning struck part of a wall related to his birth place at Velitrae, which was taken as a good portent that a native of that town would come to the supreme power. He erected a temple to Apollo when part of his house was hit by lightning on the Palatine. An omen was perceived when lightning struck out the first letter of his name in an inscription. [82]

It is in perfect accord that soldiers from a culture that valued the portents of the heavens would consider the ominous aspect of its present effects.

40 There were also some women looking on from a distance, among whom were Mary Magdalene, and Mary the mother of James the Less and Joses, and Salome . . and the mother of the sons of Zebedee.

Here again the Magdalene is mentioned with his dearest followers, but with a different group than in John. This is not a contradiction, but a change in authors who noticed different groups of the same assembly. Of interest is the mention of another Mary making four women present with the same name - Mary Magdalene, Mary the mother of Jesus, Mary wife of Clopas and Mary the mother of James and Joses.

Some have supposed that the Mary of James and Joses is another way of identifying the mother of Jesus, since He too had brothers named James and Joses (Mark 6:3.) But this would be a strange way of referring to someone so revered as the Lord's mother.

Also, James the Less is a designation that has consistently applied to James son of Alphaeus. It is not out of the ordinary that he had a brother also named Joses (an alternate for Joseph.) Salome is best concluded as another independent person, not a sister with James and Joses. There is no comma as in the English but the formation of the Greek prevents her from being part of that family. The raw Greek has: *and Mary of James the little and of Joses mother and Salome*, . . Were Salome to be seen as sister, she would have been presented ". . and of Salome mother."

41 When He was in Galilee, they used to follow Him and minister to Him; and there were many other women who came up with Him to Jerusalem.

The care and ministry of these women brought them to Jerusalem where against their naïve hopes they became witnesses to His suffering and death. Here is God's wonderful plan and sovereignty over the affairs of those who give themselves to Him. We note that Jesus had no infrastructure, no formally organized support as missionaries today often candidate to acquire. We see no central office to which He returns, stocked with provisions for each leg of His various journeys. He walked out into the world and the world of the faithful took care of Him and His disciples. As He taught that not a single sparrow falls from its nest without the Father knowing it, we can be abundantly sure that no need of the Son would go uncared for. Here are those who lent themselves to the Father's hands.

When people question what the will of God is for their lives, what ministry is in store for them, it is not particularly enigmatic or hidden as we suppose. We need only be yielded and ready to do His bidding in all things and He will fill our lives with service that is delightful and full of His good pleasure. These women did not become Amy Simple McPhersons or Katherine Kuhlmans. They did not start great movements for Jesus that we know of. They are famous down through history for being available, steadfast and obedient in the simplest of things – food, clothing, prayers, hospitality. And their names have become more renown than those who have blessed whole stadiums in modern times.

---

[82] Suetonius, Lives of the Twelve Caesars, Loeb Classics, chs 10, 30, 97

48 And all the crowds who came together for this spectacle, when they observed what had happened, began to return, beating their breasts.

Now comes the remorse and anguish of what has been done to One so innocent and full of the Lord's righteousness. But it is in the people, the throngs, who have come to see the spectacle - those who have ever been so easily led by their leaders down barren paths in an empty faith.

Now they have ringing in their ears the indictment of Scripture – "they shall look on Him whom they have pierced and they will mourn for Him, as one mourns for an only son, and they will weep bitterly over Him like the bitter weeping over a firstborn" (Zechariah 12:10.)

Although John includes the citation a bit later and somewhat disconnected, it is in reference to this reaction by the people. Could any other response be more directly related to its fulfillment?

We often ask how the people of God to whom such specific oracles were given concerning their own Messiah could then ironically kill Him at His visitation? These among the people are realizing the very weight of that sin and how they have fulfilled Jesus characterization – "shall the blind lead the blind? Will they not both fall into the ditch?" (Luke 6:39.)

CHAPTER 16
His Resurrection

John 19:31-42, Mark 15:42-45, Matthew 27:38, Matthew 27:59-66, Luke 23:55-56, Matthew 28:1-4, Mark 16:1-4
31 Then the Jews, because it was the day of preparation, so that the bodies would not remain on the cross on the Sabbath (for that Sabbath was a high day), asked Pilate that their legs might be broken, and that they might be taken away. 32 So the soldiers came, and broke the legs of the first man and of the other who was crucified with Him; 33 but coming to Jesus, when they saw that He was already dead, they did not break His legs.

34 But one of the soldiers pierced His side with a spear, and immediately blood and water came out. 35 And he who has seen has testified, and his testimony is true; and he knows that he is telling the truth, so that you also may believe. 36 For these things came to pass to fulfill the Scripture, "NOT A BONE OF HIM SHALL BE BROKEN." 37 And again another Scripture says, "THEY SHALL LOOK ON HIM WHOM THEY PIERCED."
(John 19:31-37.)

42 When evening had already come, because it was the preparation day, that is, the day before the Sabbath, 43 Joseph of Arimathea came, . . 38 being a disciple of Jesus, but a secret one for fear of the Jews . . a prominent member of the Council, who himself was waiting for the kingdom of God; and he gathered up courage and went in before Pilate, and asked for the body of Jesus. 44 Pilate wondered if He was dead by this time, and summoning the centurion, he questioned him as to whether He was already dead. 45 And ascertaining this from the centurion, he granted the body to Joseph.
(Mark 15:42-43, Matthew 27:38, Mark 15:43-45.)

38 . . So he came and took away His body. 39 Nicodemus, who had first come to Him by night, also came, bringing a mixture of myrrh and aloes, about a hundred pounds weight. 40 So they took the body of Jesus and bound it in linen wrappings with the spices, as is the burial custom of the Jews. 41 Now in the place where He was crucified there was a garden, . . . 59 And Joseph took the body . . 60 and laid it in his own new tomb, which he had hewn out in the rock; . . in which no one had yet been laid. 42 Therefore because of the Jewish day of preparation, since the tomb was nearby, they laid Jesus there . . and he rolled a large stone against the entrance of the tomb and went away.
(John 19:38b-41, Matthew 27:59-60a, John 19:41-42, Matthew 27:60b.)

55 Now the women who had come with Him out of Galilee followed, and saw the tomb and how His body was laid. 56 Then they returned and prepared spices and perfumes. And on the Sabbath they rested according to the commandment. (Luke 23:55-56.)

62 Now on the next day, the day after the preparation, the chief priests and the Pharisees gathered together with Pilate, 63 and said, "Sir, we remember that when He was still alive that deceiver said, `After three days I am to rise again.'

64 "Therefore, give orders for the grave to be made secure until the third day, otherwise His disciples may come and steal Him away and say to the people, `He has risen from the dead,' and the last deception will be worse than the first." 65 Pilate said to them, "You have a guard; go, make it as secure as you know how." 66 And they went and made the grave secure, and along with the guard they set a seal on the stone.
(Matthew 27:62-66.)

2 And, behold, there was a great earthquake: for the angel of the Lord descended from heaven, and came and rolled back the stone from the door, and sat upon it. 3 His countenance was like lightning, and his raiment white as snow: 4 And for fear of him the keepers did shake, and became as dead [men].
(Matthew 28:2-4.)

1 In the end of the sabbath, as it began to dawn toward the first [day] of the week, . . Mary Magdalene, and Mary the [mother] of James, and Salome, had bought sweet spices, that they might come and anoint him. 2 And very early in the morning the first [day] of the week, they came unto the sepulchre at the rising of the sun. 3 And they said among themselves, Who shall roll us away the stone from the door of the sepulchre? 4 And when they looked, they saw that the stone was rolled away: for it was very great.
(Matthew 28:1, Mark 16:1-4)

Commentary

31 Then the Jews, because it was the day of preparation, so that the bodies would not remain on the cross on the Sabbath (for that Sabbath was a high day),

We see now clearly here that this was the day before the weekly Sabbath (Mark 15:42), not the day before the Passover Seder. Concern for the Law would not leave the bodies exposed. But it was now some time after 3:00 PM with just a few hours remaining before commencement of the Sabbath.

Despite the Law, we see none of them making arrangements for His burial. The principal matter was concluded - His death. Considering the time of day, the approaching Sabbath was more important than His likewise constrained burial. Perhaps their knowledge of Joseph's offer relieved them of any further concern. As for the Romans, criminals were left on their crosses unburied for citizens or family to dispose of if they had the means.

Joseph's offer relieved both the Pharisees of the fudging they were doing respecting the Law, and Mary and her relatives, considering the shock and stress of the day.

"a high day"

That this Sabbath was a high day gives force to our understanding that it was not the evening of the Seder, because the Jews had incorporated methods for making sure the Passover meal did not fall on the weekly Sabbath, but there were no such concerns about it coinciding with the feast days. This designation is telling us that the weekly Sabbath was high because it was falling on one of the days comprising Unleavened Bread.

asked Pilate that their legs might be broken, and that they might be taken away.

The reason for this procedure is now obvious as we understand the physical cycle of torment on the cross. Breaking the legs would render the victim unable to lift himself up to breathe, thus hastening his death by asphyxiation.

32 So the soldiers came, and broke the legs . . 33 but coming to Jesus, when they saw that He was already dead, they did not break His legs.

We can understand their survival for several reasons. They no doubt did not suffer scourging prior to their crucifixion (this was not automatic, but depended on circumstances). Jesus' suffered it principally because Pilate had wished to substitute scourging as an appeasement. Jesus' stamina to endure also the cross would have been seriously diminished compared to the other men.

But we must also incorporate the plan of the Father. There is a marvelous convergence of imagery and prophesy from the past revelations of God. Jesus was the final and complete Passover lamb , sacrificed for the world, marking us for freedom and covering us by His blood against the angel of death.

At the first commandment of the Passover, God specified that the bones of the Paschal lamb were not to be broken in the roasting and eating of it – "nor are you to break any bone of it" (Ex 12:46.) Many believe that contrary to having the conditions of Passover controlling what happened at the Cross, the foreknowledge and anticipation of the Cross reached back to constrain the very manner of how its prototype – the lamb of sacrifice – was first inaugurated.

34 But one of the soldiers pierced His side with a spear, and immediately blood and water came out.

Medically, this is understood very well. For most everyone else, it is puzzling. At death the blood ceases to circulate and red blood cells easily separate from serum. Serum is clear, and would appear like water to the ancients. Ordinarily, blood in the vessels begins to settle to the lowest point of the body (lividity) but the heart can retain blood in its chambers, since it is not pumping.

John saw the puncture of the heart, releasing what was now held there, the blood having separated into its two visible components. Some question the heart as the target since the wound was in the side. But it is just as likely that a soldier would aim at the heart from the side through the space between ribs (i.e. it is not necessary that a thrust from in front under the sternum is the only path).

The two quotes are from Exodus 12:40, Zech 12:10 - *"not a bone of Him shall be broken"* . . *"They shall look on Him whom they have pierced."* In Zechariah we seek in vain to know what case God cites wherein He was pierced. There were no prior manifestations or visitations who were thus treated. But the wounding refers to the matters of heart and spirit not flesh. Isaiah was at this point on record saying that Messiah would be *"wounded for our transgressions"* (Is 53:5), therefore more than the spear in the hand of the soldier, it was our own sins that caused Him to be pierced at the Cross. In this sense then, the sins of God's people would be the cause, and aptly remembered when Judah and the house of David were protected from their enemies.

However, in Zechariah the scene is being spoken post-exilically (after the exile of Judah and her return). She has already paid for her forsaken Sabbaths in seventy years of captivity. This must then refer to the future restoration of Israel, especially to those armies who will encompass Jerusalem, whose horses He will frighten. In that day, the Jews will corporately be reminded of their sins, specifically the killing of their Messiah – the One whom they caused to be pierced. It is here being precursored in the anguish of those Jews at the Cross who beat their breasts, but will be fully measured in the end of days.

We too as Gentiles are brought to grief as we realize that our sins caused Him also to be pierced. All men will be brought to realize this, thus the verse has fulfillments that extend continuously into the future.

43 Joseph of Arimathea came, . . 38 being a disciple of Jesus, but a secret one for fear of the Jews . . a prominent member of the Council, who himself was waiting for the kingdom of God;

The secrecy can be understood in human terms. He had much at stake, like the rich young ruler with many possessions. Thus he was resigned to believe in secret out of fear. In this case, it was more than the prospect of persecution and being ostracized. The Jews had shown the limits they were capable of transgressing to break their adversaries.

In modern terms, all men must count the cost of discipleship, and for this reason few come. Jesus will change one's entire future from what we had planned to what accords with His needs and purposes. It is a real forsaking and when one has put his eggs in a certain basket with years of hopeful expectation, the thought of letting go of it is repugnant, as all giving up of self is repugnant.

Yet in Joseph there is some semblance of perseverance in his new belief and admiration. He will do what he can with what he has.

The Scripture states that he was also waiting for the kingdom of God. All literate Jews got this expectation from places like Daniel – " " *. . the God of heaven will set up a kingdom which will never be destroyed, . . it will crush and put an end to all these kingdoms,"* (2:44.)

This is the backdrop against which Jesus had preached the approach of that Kingdom. This was not new to His hearers. They were expecting it and He came preaching that it was now at hand.

Ironically, it did not come in patent fact, not because it was an empty proclamation, but because they rejected its King. Instead, another type of that Kingdom was inaugurated - the one that would reign in people's hearts. This interim sovereignty was not a last minute substitution for an offer gone bad, but was an interim "occupation" (Luke 19:13) until the days of its real fulfillment would come.

43 .. and he gathered up courage and went in before Pilate, and asked for the body of Jesus.

The gathering of courage related to the wariness of coming into direct personal contact with a man like Pilate. Men have often naively assumed that an audience with those in power will ensure justice, only to find that their wishes in the hands of a corrupt official can go horribly awry.

In the notorious audience with Gaius Caligula, the Jews hoped for some lenient relief by mentioning that they had daily offered sacrifices in their Temple for him, to which he replied, "You offered them for me, but none to me." [83]

While Pilate had shown some compassion for Jesus, he had not changed in his general attitude toward the Jews, much of which may have been due to his relationship with Sejanus, a notorious Jew-baiter. [84]

Though the Romans ordinarily relished the idea of leaving the bodies of crucified criminals conspicuous as a warning, the time would come for disposition and burial. Family members were expected to ask for the body.

The only conditional was that they be in fact dead, since ordinarily the punishment could last days on the cross. The affairs of finishing them off in this case had been out of Pilate's immediate purview, having delegated the team of soldiers and their centurion to manage it. Pilate therefore entertained the normal expectation that one so crucified might not be dead this early – "summoning the centurion, he questioned him as to whether He was already dead."

39 Nicodemus, who had first come to Him by night, also came, bringing a mixture of myrrh and aloes, about a hundred pounds weight.

There was no embalming done on remains among the Jews (it was still a largely Egyptian specialty). This is generally due to the Jewish attitude toward the body, regarded as a shell or container for the spirit. Its veneration and preservation were unnecessary.

The spices were for the comfort of those who were to come and formally prepare His body in burial. These men risked ceremonial uncleanness in handling Jesus' body and this may not have been avoided by using sheets in which the body might be taken down and in which it may have been placed, since touching things that had been in contact with a corpse was just as defiling (Numbers 19:11-19). Also, it is impossible to imagine them not having to touch Him even if employing sheets.

The defilement would ordinarily be somewhat innocuous, since there was a Mosaic procedure for becoming clean again, which was at the very most merely inconvenient (Numbers, *ibid*). In this case, the defilement of seven days would prevent them from any and all participation in Unleavened Bread. This is therefore a great sacrificial gift on their part.

---

[83] Philo, Embassy to Gaius, p. 299-305
[84] Philo, In Flaccum 1, Embassy to Gaius, p. 150-160

41 Now in the place where He was crucified there was a garden, .

This is one of the critical pieces of information for locating the site of both Calvary and the tomb. These were in close proximity to one another and the tomb was in a garden. A further reason for Joseph's involvement was his intention to offer his own freshly carved tomb for Jesus' burial. We may have some assurance that Mary remained relatively poor in terms of her ability to have a family tomb, and even if she did, it would not be as far away as Jerusalem. That it was a new tomb is also important in the location of Calvary since archaeological discoveries would need to be associated with the 1st century, i.e. they must not be limited to periods B.C.

and he rolled a large stone against the entrance of the tomb and went away.

Not for preservation purposes but to keep away thieves or those who might desecrate the deceased person.

By "he rolled" the stone, we might be tempted to infer that this had to mean "they" since one man rolling it into place implies the ease of another man rolling it away. But the same would be true of two men. More likely the trench for this stone was inclined and it was kept back by a wedge at its base. With a little help, this wedge might be dislodged allowing the stone to roll by sheer weight into position.

Luke further tells us that the women followed to note the location so they would be apprised when coming later (v.55). Much of this tells us that the place became easily known among His followers, which would bolster the case for Holy Sepulcher being the authentic location, since it is largely by tradition that a Church came later to occupy the location. Also, Hadrian built a pagan temple over the spot, no doubt discovered by inquiry into that tradition which could very easily have been handed down from the individuals whom we see here. They knew, therefore others came to know it also. Still there is the problem of no newer tombs than the 2nd century B.C.

56 Then they returned and prepared spices and perfumes.

The women returned to their homes to prepare what would be needed after the Sabbath. Some see this as a confusion in the Gospels - why did the women need to come if the men had already prepared the body and to the tune of a hundred pounds of spices?

Of first note is that the women did not come back until after the Sabbath, making it necessary to do some preparation that would last through the interim. Second, the gospels do not say that the men used all the hundred pound supply. Much could have been left for the women.

Custom established that the family did the preparations, which included washings, anointing and wrapping with spices. This also ordinarily meant the women of the family. We are not told the names here but that they were among those who had followed Jesus up from Galilee. But the Sunday visit to the tomb subsequently names them (Mark 16:1-4) and these align rightly with those given at the scene of crucifixion – Mary Magdalene, Mary the wife of Alphaeus and mother of James and Joses, and Salome.

None of these were earlier named as relatives of Mary (Mark 15:40), but it may be that Mary welcomed this help, being in no position to do this herself, and having few women family members to do it either. (There is no evidence that Mary took this action as interference by others or as an affront to her own duties.)

63 . . "Sir, we remember that when He was still alive that deceiver said, `After three days I am to rise again.'"

The Jewish leaders had come again to Pilate for some added security. They were by then aware that Jesus had been taken down and laid in a tomb, and they were knowledgeable of where, since they ask that the tomb now be sealed and guarded.

They did not fear that unless measures were taken He would in fact rise. Rather, they were very fearful that His followers would concoct a deception that He had risen. The seal and the guard would frustrate such plans, since the tomb would have to be accessed in order to effect a deception.

We can understand why this was regarded as a greater deception than that which comprised Jesus' teaching. It would vindicate His claims and bolster adherents to the new faith. This is precisely the argument Paul later makes in his epistles (I Cor 15:17-19).

So we can see all the more its effectual power if it can be voiced as efficacious in the mouths of His enemies.

64 "Therefore, give orders for the grave to be made secure until the third day,

Mention of the third day here and in the teaching of Jesus Himself raises the apparent contradiction that there are only two days following Friday to Sunday, not three. But the Jews did not count elapsed time as does the modern Western world. They included the starting day in the count of elapsed days. Thus, three days from Friday would include Friday, making Sunday the third day. Also, "until the third day" did not mean until the beginning of that day but until its close. The guard was then intended to remain until Sunday evening.

The seal requested was not a hermetic seal, but an official seal, the breaking of which would betray a deception, just as official seals on the entrances of Egyptian tombs are not sufficient as locks, but whose disturbed state would be a sign that someone has entered unauthorized.

"You have a guard; go, make it as secure as you know how."

This did not mean permission to arrange for their own guards and security. It is merely a form of speech that they had the men necessary from him.

2 And, behold, there was a great earthquake: for the angel of the Lord descended from heaven, and came and rolled back the stone from the door, and sat upon it. 3 His countenance was like lightning, and his raiment white as snow:

We are not told the necessity of the earthquake, so we are to infer it was an attendant sign. It did not have a functional purpose, since the angel is then described as moving the stone. The arrival of the angel and the opening of the tomb was not to effect the Resurrection. We aren't given an account of the Resurrection from inside the tomb as it occurred, but rather, it will be described as having occurred to those visiting the tomb.

Countenances as lightning and raiment as white as snow are consistent descriptions of persons in Heaven. This is directly related to John's description of Jesus as the Light, it being the purest light of the universe, uncolored, untinted, unrefracted by human means. As such, heavenly light is as purely white as can be conceived. This is approached in the laboratory and in some machines (the carbon arc searchlight) in which the light emitted is remarkably white compared to other sources. We can only infer that they mirror the qualities of light seen by the privileged few of the Bible (Dan 7:9, Matt 17:2, Rev 1:14).

4 And for fear of him the keepers did shake, and became as dead [men].

"Keepers" means the guards, not those who normally tended the garden, of whom Mary mistook Jesus to be. It is not clear whether the fear caused them to collapse or they were sovereignly put to sleep. The latter seems preferable considering that much is yet to transpire at the tomb and men soon come to their senses in purely natural circumstances. This is understandably necessary because such men would have interfered with these affairs, being on guard expressly to prevent them.

We have to wonder what fate awaited them when they returned to their commander. How could they have explained the real reason for failing to be at their posts, and mitigating any such explanation and heightening their failure would be the fact that the very thing they had been sent to prevent had in fact occurred.

1 In the end of the sabbath, as it began to dawn toward the first [day] of the week, . .

This section of the narrative in these accounts has become one of the most complex harmony issues between the gospels. Harmony would never have been much of an issue were John to have never written his version of these events, since the synoptics are in accord as to the time of day and who came to the tomb – it was dawn and three women came. In John, it is still dark and only Mary Magdalene is said to have come.

As for who did or did not come, we must first take into account that the gospel writers were not themselves eyewitnesses of these particular details of the visit. Each had to rely on an interview with the women involved. In the case of the synoptic writers, they may have interviewed one or more of the women, thus gaining from them clearer references to the group. John, on the other hand, may have interviewed only Mary Magdalene, and she may have conveyed the story in the first person, "When I came to the tomb, I saw . ." If her version was intensely first person, John may have kept this consistent by a reference equivalent to, "Mary Magdalene (the one who told me what happened) came to the tomb . . "

This understanding also helps us in the area of the confusion over details of the angels and their interaction with the women.

they came unto the sepulchre at the rising of the sun.

Ordinarily, people incorporate variously what others mean by things like 'dawn.' Some might mean the moment the sun is seen above the horizon. Others might accept dawn as the first glimmer of light below the horizon – "dawn's early light." As for it being still dark, much depends on one's specific location at the early glow of dawning light. Where others might see considerable light on the horizon, you might still be in darkness, depending on what buildings intervene.

However we seem to have here a piece of information from Mark - "at the rising of the sun" – that clearly contradicts John's "came early to the tomb, while it was still dark." Much however depends on whether Mark is referring to the general state of the sun, or necessarily the effect of the sun at the tomb itself. The sun may have been considered rising from the perspective of the whole land and the city, but the tomb being sunken into a valley below the hill of crucifixion would still be in darkness. Thus, Mark might be referring to the time the sun was rising in general, while John was describing the light conditions still remaining at the tomb itself.

3 . . "Who shall roll us away the stone from the door of the sepulchre?" 4 And when they looked, they saw that the stone was rolled away . .

Helping us with the imprecision common to folks in the East and the appearance of contradictions above, we have an example in this verse of this less precise mode of speech. The women are said to have arrived at the tomb, but they are clearly not close enough to see that the stone has been moved, meaning they are clearly some ways off. They have time to ponder how they will negotiate its massive weight. Yet strangely this is still described as having come to the tomb. They subsequently come close enough to see that it has been moved.

Clearly the men writing these accounts were aware of the imprecision of having come but not really. Yet this bothers none of them, meaning that it was accepted, leaving the context and the unveiling of the whole picture to clarify meanings.

Mark 16:5-9, Luke 24:4-12, John 20:2-17

5 Entering the tomb, they saw a young man sitting at the right, wearing a white robe; and they were amazed. 6 And he said to them, "Do not be amazed; you are looking for Jesus the Nazarene, who has been crucified. He has risen; He is not here; behold, here is the place where they laid Him. 7 "But go, tell His disciples and Peter, `He is going ahead of you to Galilee; there you will see Him, just as He told you.' " (Mark 16:5-7.)

4 While they were perplexed about this, behold, two men suddenly stood near them in dazzling clothing; 5 and as the women were terrified and bowed their faces to the ground, the men said to them, "Why do you seek the living One among the dead? 6 "He is not here, but He has risen. Remember how He spoke to you while He was still in Galilee, 7 saying that the Son of Man must be delivered into the hands of sinful men, and be crucified, and the third day rise again." 8 And they remembered His words, (Luke 24:4-8)

8 They went out and fled from the tomb, for trembling and astonishment had gripped them; and they said nothing to anyone, for they were afraid . . . 2 So [Mary] ran and came to Simon Peter and to the other disciple whom Jesus loved, and said to them, "They have taken away the Lord out of the tomb, and we do not know where they have laid Him." 9 . . and [they] reported all these things to the eleven and to all the rest. 10 Now they were Mary Magdalene and Joanna and Mary the mother of James; also the other women with them were telling these things to the apostles. 11 But these words appeared to them as nonsense, and they would not believe them. (Mark 16:8, John 20:2, Luke 24:9-11)

12 But Peter got up and ran to the tomb; . . 3 . . and the other disciple went forth, and they were going to the tomb. 4 The two were running together; and the other disciple ran ahead faster than Peter and came to the tomb first; 5 and stooping and looking in, he saw the linen wrappings lying there; but he did not go in.

6 And so Simon Peter also came, following him, and entered the tomb; and he saw the linen wrappings lying there, 7 and the face-cloth which had been on His head, not lying with the linen wrappings, but rolled up in a place by itself. 8 So the other disciple who had first come to the tomb then also entered, and he saw and believed. 9 For as yet they did not understand the Scripture, that He must rise again from the dead. 10 So the disciples went away again to their own homes. (Luke 24:12, John 20:3-10.)

9 Now after He had risen early on the first day of the week, He first appeared to Mary Magdalene, from whom He had cast out seven demons. . . 11 Mary was standing outside the tomb weeping; and so, as she wept, she stooped and looked into the tomb; 12 and she saw two angels in white sitting, one at the head and one at the feet, where the body of Jesus had been lying. 13 And they said to her, "Woman, why are you weeping?" She said to them, "Because they have taken away my Lord, and I do not know where they have laid Him." 14 When she had said this, she turned around and saw Jesus standing there, and did not know that it was Jesus.

15 Jesus said to her, "Woman, why are you weeping? Whom are you seeking?" Supposing Him to be the gardener, she said to Him, "Sir, if you have carried Him away, tell me where you have laid Him, and I will take Him away." 16 Jesus said to her, "Mary!" She turned and said to Him in Hebrew, "Rabboni!" (which means, Teacher). 17 Jesus said to her, "Stop clinging to Me, for I have not yet ascended to the Father; but go to My brethren and say to them, `I ascend to My Father and your Father, and My God and your God.' " (Mark 16:9, John 20:11-17.)

Commentary

5 Entering the tomb, they saw a young man sitting at the right, wearing a white robe; and they were amazed.

The mention by Mark of a young man when Matthew clearly names the personage as an angel has created endless ammunition for Bible debunkers in every generation who question its historical reliability. But this is clearly a matter of how much insight the observer had in making the designation: angel vs. man. Those quoting the assessment at the moment of seeing, like Mark, would relate whatever the observer concluded at the time – a young man. Matthew, who may very well have incorporated later reflection and insight, would have clarified that what was seen was in truth an angel.

This helps us also understand that the appearance respecting this angel was not as in the movies – a spectacle of glory and light – but this angel was made to appear very much like an ordinary person, enough at least to be mistaken for such. (The others will be different in this respect.)

Their amazement was that someone unknown and unexpected was in the tomb at all. The immediate questions would then have been where was Jesus and who is this man?

6 And he said to them, "Do not be amazed; you are looking for Jesus the Nazarene, who has been crucified. He has risen; He is not here;

The first thing to offer in the midst of astonishment and fear is the speaking of recognizable facts. This he does immediately. He discloses his knowledge that they seek Jesus of Nazareth. He adds for assurance sake that this is the same Jesus just crucified. The immediate statement, *"He is not here."* acknowledges that He is missing, but not by accident or mishap. He even points to the place where they laid Him to indicate his complete familiarity with all they seek. It is an effort to let them know that everything is happening as divinely ordained.

7 "But go, tell His disciples and Peter, `He is going ahead of you to Galilee; there you will see Him, just as He told you.' "

Adding forthwith to the sense of authority and command, the angel begins to urgently instruct them and in complete accord with what Jesus had explained earlier (Matt 26:32.) The gospels do not relate instructions about where specifically in Galilee they would see Him, but this does not mean that instructions of this detail were not given. They may all have understood a place frequently used for coming back together in their ministry journeys, or some other place may have been specifically told to them. (This is simply common sense since they have no problem finding it and Him.)

4 . . behold, two men suddenly stood near them in dazzling clothing; 5 and as the women were terrified and bowed their faces to the ground,

It is clear these personages are not mere men by what attends their appearance. In other heavenly descriptions, the observer has been able to describe the colors and textures of things seen. Here, while women are known for paying close attention to what people are wearing, too much is happening and so unexpectedly that they are disabled from taking any more fashionable interest than "dazzling clothing."

The bowing of the face to the ground is more than just staring at the ground in embarrassment. They may very well have sunken to their knees with their faces turned away and to the ground. We see this in many paintings of such appearances, the observers with an outstretched arm toward the vision, while looking away from the sight in fear and worry.

4 . . the men said to them, "Why do you seek the living One among the dead? 6 "He is not here, but He has risen. Remember how He spoke to you while He was still in Galilee,

The speech of the angels mirrors that of the first angel, and for that reason some have supposed a contradiction in the record. But it is obvious that amazement and shock have overwhelmed the observers. Repetition of the assessment of the situation is indeed called for. They reiterate that Jesus is no longer in the tomb and is now risen from the dead as He explained before.

Seeking the living among the dead is a poignant question for all ages. All must make the clear deduction that if Jesus rose, He will not have simply gone the way of all flesh. He has not long ago gone to dust in some unknown grave. If men seek Him, He will not be an object of veneration, as deceased saints, but He will be found among the living. This is not to say He is there to be discovered on some street in modern times, but never the less fully alive as mortal men are alive to ponder it, yet in His Heavenly abode, directing the affairs of His Church.

The further words of the angels serve a very important purpose here – to help connect the dots respecting the prediction and fulfillment, that it was a deliberate intention that He die and rise again the third day. This is key because He had revealed this mystery in moments of training and discipleship, at a time when they were not so keen to understand its import. In human weakness, they could not be depended on to recall these present affairs as fulfilling those predictions. It was critical that this connection be made so as to see the unfolding plan of God at work – " *8 And they remembered His words,"*. These affairs were not the regrettable mishaps of mere men throwing an unexpected monkey wrench into the plans of God

8 They went out and fled from the tomb, for trembling and astonishment had gripped them; and they said nothing to anyone, for they were afraid

Nonetheless, they flee in fear and astonishment. We are left to wonder if they will do as the angels have said. *"they said nothing to anyone"* is contradicted almost immediately by the record of them telling the disciples and Mary telling Peter and John. What is meant is that they told no one along the way or outside the company of disciples, for fear that they would be accused of violating the order protecting the tomb or worse, that they had fiddled with the evidence such that they would be complicit in that deception the Jews feared most.

2 "They have taken away the Lord out of the tomb, and we do not know where they have laid Him."

John brings us back to his own unique focus which perplexingly does not coordinate well with Mark. In Mark the women enter the tomb, they hear the announcements and exhortations, they flee. In John, this whole set of events is left out and Mary is said to run to Peter and John at the sight of the stone rolled away.

Again. much of this is entirely dependent on the testimony of the eyewitness, which in John's case is assumed to be Mary Magdalene alone. She may have split off from the other women and gone to where she knew Peter presently was staying. John then follows the story from Mary's experience. The other women may have then gone to an assembly of the rest of the disciples to whom Peter and John may also have soon gathered.

With Peter, Mary blurts out that the Lord is missing and is assumed stolen away by unknown agents. This is difficult to reconcile with the twice mentioned message of the angels, that He has risen as predicted and is going to a known place; and further that they are said to have "remembered these words."

We can only conclude that every aspect of these moments has been overwhelming, and in the run back into the city many thoughts human and otherwise may have easily blurred the details of what transpired (note that she completely ignores what most would think the most astounding - the appearance of angels.) Her most urgent message returns to the basic fact observed when coming to the tomb – Jesus was missing and His whereabouts are unknown. She sees Peter as the remedy, the man in charge, who can do the most toward finding the answers. So to Him she relays the principal crisis at hand – He is missing.

Luke then continues respecting the other women.

9 .. and [they] reported all these things to the eleven and to all the rest.

The context of Luke has been the women, not Mary alone. Due to the reaction of these men, the women must have conveyed considerably more about the events at the tomb, for they entertained that what was being told them was nonsense (v.11.)

10 Now they were Mary Magdalene and Joanna and Mary the mother of James; also the other women with them were telling these things to the apostles.

John having separated Mary from the others, we find Luke including her in the group that informed the eleven, which would have included Peter (Judas being no longer among them.) It is obvious that Peter, John and Mary Magdalene soon joined the others such that Luke reports the whole company as he does.

Exemplifying the Eastern method of handling details intentionally different than our Western mentalities, we note that while there was the impression that certain women came to the tomb, we find in Luke that more were actually there – *"also the other women with them were telling these things"* We also have the first mention of Joanna being included.

12 But Peter got up and ran to the tomb;

Despite the astounding news, Peter has a mind to straighten this out for himself, especially if it might involve mischief. We don't know for a fact that John was the one who ran also and overtook him, but the custom of avoiding mention of the author in first person and the generic use of "the other disciple" in place of a real name indicate the man was the author, John.

John is said to notice the nature and appearance of the wrappings, but does not enter (v.5.) It takes the boldness of Peter to transgress the threshold and check things out inside.

and he saw the linen wrappings lying there, 7 and the face-cloth which had been on His head, not lying with the linen wrappings, but rolled up in a place by itself.

Much is made of the character of the wrappings. This is primarily because the expectation was that of disarray. Were a person to awaken in their tomb, not having been really dead, they would certainly care little about the wrappings - let them fall where they may. The same would be true of robbers as was their initial expectation.

The neatness found served to demonstrate deliberateness according to plan. A man who could take the time to fold his funerary linens was not desperate but calm and collected, fully possessed of His health and mind. This had to be a curiosity that could not avoid mention.

9 For as yet they did not understand the Scripture, . . 10 So the disciples went away again to their own homes.

In hindsight we routinely find ourselves amazed at the dullness of not getting the Lord's instruction. They had been with Him for three years, a privilege every Christian longs to have enjoyed firsthand. They heard the testimony of the women – in complete accord with those predictions. Yet they are said to have not yet understood.

But note that they did not yet understand the ***Scripture***. They had heard His words, but there was that unsettled territory of how much of it all was confirmed and substantiated in OT Scripture. Not that they doubted until so confirmed, but that such confirmation might help their understanding. That would take study. And the materials and opportunities were not readily at hand. They were resolved to return home where they could silo themselves in quite and solitude, to rehearse things said and try to put the pieces together.

9 Now after He had risen early on the first day of the week, He first appeared to Mary Magdalene, from whom He had cast out seven demons.

We come now to the actual appearances. Up to now the facts were tainted by the absence of evidence. But notice the kindness of our Lord in not leaving things that way. He did not intend that His Church be founded on the forceful maintenance of a supposition – "we assume He arose."

We find Mary back at the tomb. The assumption is that on the swift departure of Peter, she followed them back to the tomb, but remained outside. Despite the annunciations provided before, she cannot shake her despondency that someone has absconded with the body. This contributes to the notion that Mary was more intimately involved with Jesus, since her reactions are more irrational and seem more in keeping with someone involved romantically, as has become recently fashionable among the more liberal students of these affairs.

We may certainly conclude rightly that Mary was deeply affected and committed to Jesus to such a degree that her emotions were ruling her reactions. But none of that forms a basis for the kind of intimacy purported by revisionist liberals. Lacking any substance to confirm, such theories rely on the inability to factually disprove, which has always been a specious argument.

Thus, we find Mary outside the tomb, weeping. She is intractably focused on His disappearance.

13 . . . "Woman, why are you weeping?"

Interestingly, the angels only appear to the women (none appeared to Peter and John). As she weeps, she looks inside, perhaps again for the unnumbered time. It would be a gesture that physically matched her inner feelings of loss – the bench inside the tomb was the last place His body had been. It's emptiness reinforces her inner grief. "I am justified in my weeping. There, His grave still declares Him stolen away."

On this occasion, she again sees two angels. They certainly know why she is weeping. The question was meant to elicit her response because something related to its answer was about to appear. She repeats the one thing that justifies our analysis above of her current state of mind – *" they have taken away my Lord, and I do not know where they have laid Him."*

14 When she had said this, she turned around and saw Jesus standing there, and did not know that it was Jesus.

As in the scene yet to come at Emmaus, Jesus has been transformed bodily in such a way that He is not immediately recognizable. Many have suggested that this was mere incredulity – they did not expect to see Him so they did not recognize Him. But were His appearance to be that of His mortal life with them, it would take a lot of incredulity to overcome visible fact. Certainly for Mary, His face and features would not have escaped her.

Hence, He was notably different such that incredulity could play a role, but not so thoroughly as to prevent her from embracing Him soon after.

15 . . "Sir, if you have carried Him away, tell me where you have laid Him, and I will take Him away."

That she mistakes Him for the gardener highlights the otherness of His appearance and also the further legitimacy of emphasizing her state of mind as controlling all that we see of her here. She is bent on finding out where He has been taken.

16 Jesus said to her, "Mary!"

Here then is the power and promise of the Resurrection in patent fact. It is the real Jesus, the genuine article. Nothing has been stolen away. He is no longer missing. All that He promised about Himself is standing right in front of her. He has been victorious over the grave, it could not hold Him. And He is not so divinely and supremely exalted that the intimacy that characterized His sojourn with them is now too mundane. He knows and speaks her name.

So intimately spoken is this that she can recognize Him through and beyond His transformation.

She turned and said to Him in Hebrew, "Rabboni!" (which means, Teacher).

While there is continued disagreement about the precise meaning and its theological implications, the most reliable import from Hebrew is that the addition of *'i'* makes the noun personal – meaning "my dear Teacher." As to why John did not elucidate this in his translation for his audience is a mystery. There has to be more to this term than that used earlier - "Rabbi" is also translated 'teacher' in 1:38 – simply because the form is notably revised. We would rightly infer an introduction of at least some change in meaning.

17.. "Stop clinging to Me, for I have not yet ascended to the Father;

The English translation makes this appear rather abrupt and petulant. It is meant as a caution, not an irritation. The rendering in the KJV - "Touch me not;" gave rise to the understanding that it was His resurrected nature that could not be touched by mortals. But *'hapto'* in the Greek conveys fastening, adhering, clinging. In the negative present imperative it means to stop doing what is presently being done, meaning that she was already touching Him. He is saying that both He and she cannot be detained, rather than He cannot be touched. (He later invites the disciples to touch Him as with Thomas, Matt 28:9, John 20:27.)

The condition is attributed to not having yet ascended which has caused the side trails that propose some substantive or anatomical reason connected to His unascended body. But all the theorizations about what was deficient in His pre-Ascension state are thoroughly speculative and are obliged to reach beyond reason without any hint from Scripture.

It is hard to conclude that her affection would cause some functional defilement against the Ascension being accomplished. Weaker still is the idea that time was of such essence that her show of affection was upsetting a timetable measured in actual minutes. What would a few minutes really do in delaying an Ascension still set back by several intervening events yet future?

When we look at His command to her, it is clear that there is urgency in getting His message to the disciples. She is not to indulge her natural wishes to enjoy His fellowship and love, but help to effect the completion of those things necessary before He ascends – " . . *but go to My brethren"*

and say to them, `I ascend to My Father and your Father, and My God and your God.' "

The message was that He is about to ascend to the Father. There are things He needs to impart to them (the receiving of the indwelling Spirit, the Great Commission), hence, they need to hasten to their meeting with Him in Galilee.

Many who denounce Christ's deity point to His reference here to "my God." One who is God does not call God His God. But this is simply the human mind trying to make sense of a concept and constitution beyond its capacity to comprehend. Bringing things incomprehensible down into the confines of a limited mental frame of reference is a folly beguiled of too much confidence in self and reason.

The mystery of the Incarnation is that God became man, and in so doing became separate from God, while being equal with God in ways we are bereft of fully comprehending. The veracity of the Trinity over our feeble minds is not in finding at last some way to understand it anyway, but in the veracity of Jesus and His authority to declare the truth about reality. We believe it to be so because He was there to know and He is the One who was raised from the dead.

Matthew 28:9-15, Luke 24:9-35

9 And behold, Jesus met them and greeted them. And they came up and took hold of His feet and worshiped Him. 10 Then Jesus said to them, "Do not be afraid; go and take word to My brethren to leave for Galilee, and there they will see Me."

11 Now while they were on their way, some of the guard came into the city and reported to the chief priests all that had happened. 12 And when they had assembled with the elders and consulted together, they gave a large sum of money to the soldiers, 13 and said, "You are to say, `His disciples came by night and stole him away while we were asleep.' 14 "And if this should come to the governor's ears, we will win him over and keep you out of trouble." 15 And they took the money and did as they had been instructed; and this story was widely spread among the Jews, and is to this day. (Matthew 28:9-15.)

13 And behold, two of [the disciples] were going that very day to a village named Emmaus, which was about seven miles from Jerusalem. 14 And they were talking with each other about all these things which had taken place. 15 While they were talking and discussing, Jesus Himself approached and began traveling with them. 16 But their eyes were prevented from recognizing Him. 17 And He said to them, "What are these words that you are exchanging with one another as you are walking?" And they stood still, looking sad. 18 One of them, named Cleopas, answered and said to Him, "Are You the only one visiting Jerusalem and unaware of the things which have happened here in these days?" 19 And He said to them, "What things?" And they said to Him, "The things about Jesus the Nazarene, who was a prophet mighty in deed and word in the sight of God and all the people, 20 and how the chief priests and our rulers delivered Him to the sentence of death, and crucified Him.

21 "But we were hoping that it was He who was going to redeem Israel. Indeed, besides all this, it is the third day since these things happened. 22 "But also some women among us amazed us. When they were at the tomb early in the morning, 23 and did not find His body, they came, saying that they had also seen a vision of angels who said that He was alive. 24 "Some of those who were with us went to the tomb and found it just exactly as the women also had said; but Him they did not see." 25 And He said to them, "O foolish men and slow of heart to believe in all that the prophets have spoken! 26 "Was it not necessary for the Christ to suffer these things and to enter into His glory?" 27 Then beginning with Moses and with all the prophets, He explained to them the things concerning Himself in all the Scriptures.

28 And they approached the village where they were going, and He acted as though He were going farther. 29 But they urged Him, saying, "Stay with us, for it is getting toward evening, and the day is now nearly over." So He went in to stay with them. 30 When He had reclined at the table with them, He took the bread and blessed it, and breaking it, He began giving it to them. 31 Then their eyes were opened and they recognized Him; and He vanished from their sight. 32 They said to one another, "Were not our hearts burning within us while He was speaking to us on the road, while He was explaining the Scriptures to us?" 33 And they got up that very hour and returned to Jerusalem, and found gathered together the eleven and those who were with them, 34 saying, "The Lord has really risen and has appeared to Simon." 35 They began to relate their experiences on the road and how He was recognized by them in the breaking of the bread. (Luke 24:9-35.)

Commentary

9 And behold, Jesus met them and greeted them. And they came up and took hold of His feet and worshiped Him. . . . "Do not be afraid; . . leave for Galilee, and there they will see Me."

Despite the expectation that the meeting was to take place in Galilee, Jesus meets with the disciples where they are. That they take hold of His feet further explains that the warning to Mary was not physiologically based, unless as some do, we wish to propose that Jesus ascended to the Father in the intervening moments.

Suffice it to say that many ascensions are without mention in the NT and they only come into necessity when one theorizes that there was something physiological that required an aloof posture, equally unsubstantiated.

Conversely, here He does not say to the disciples, "Stop clinging to Me" but accepts their worship moving directly to His exhortation that they begin the journey to the Galilee. This has been chosen as the scene of His public Ascension.

11 .. some of the guard came into the city and reported to the chief priests all that had happened. 12 .. the elders and consulted together, they gave a large sum of money to the soldiers, 13 .. "You are to say, `His disciples came by night and stole Him away while we were asleep.' 14 "And if this should come to the governor's ears, we will win him over and keep you out of trouble."

We can conclude that these were soldiers of the Roman cohort, not those of the Temple police, since the Jews sought men from Pilate's cadre, and we see them being offered protection when they return to the governor.

What is noteworthy is that they come to the priests, not back to their commander. It is clear that they know all too well the ruthless manner of Roman discipline – the penalty throughout the empire was an ignominious summary execution. They perceived the Sanhedrin as a formidable influence with Pilate, irrespective of his demeanor. Surely they would have some remedy to spare them the pain of their assured punishment.

Some have questioned that the jeopardy for the guards would not have been typically worrisome because they were not in combat nor on normally recognized Roman state business, but had gotten duty from a rather reluctant Pilate over a petty provincial squabble. Leniency might be reasonably expected.

But this whole affair had become a great deal more than could be dismissed as a minor case in a no account province. The Jews had pulled their trump card of tacitly suggesting an embassy to Rome was in the offing. It had been made very clear that security of the tomb was inextricably related to a proper resolution and an avoidance of further unpleasantries. The role of the guard might easily become a feature in such a case. Suffice it to say that the guard had regular reasons to be in dread about the manner of their duty.

Given the above, it is hard to conceive how the explanation contrived would hold much water with the governor, since the reason for an armed guard was to prevent confiscation of evidence, the very thing being offered as an excuse.

This is precisely why the Sanhedrin offered to also defend them before the governor, should he seek discipline against them. There would be need for more than a prepared excuse. The money was offered as a surety that the guards would cooperate, rather than taking the option of fending for themselves in clearing their names with Pilate.

and this story was widely spread among the Jews, and is to this day.

This seems the only alternative available to His malefactors. They could not affirm the Resurrection, nor could they produce the body. The idea that it was stolen shows the desperation of their position. How is this to be explained by the presence of the guards? Certainly guards have fallen asleep despite the severity of Roman punishment. Were it so here, His disciples might very well have handled the extraction of the body in exceptional silence, but the business and noise of first moving the stone cannot be squared with guards merely asleep.

Nevertheless, this is the strategy agreed on in the hopes that few would ask probing questions. That this is maintained still in modern times can be readily seen in treatments of the life of Jesus in Jewish scholarly literature. [85]

---

[85] The Jewish Encyclopedia, Vol VII, p. 170

13 And behold, two of [the disciples] were going that very day to a village named Emmaus, which was about seven miles from Jerusalem.

We hear for the first time an account involving disciples other than the Twelve. Of these two, the only one mentioned is Cleopas, who is new to our known list of His followers. It will be made known shortly that these are of that company (described by "to all the rest.") to whom the women recounted the events at the tomb.

As to why they were on their way to Emmaus is not explained. The Feast was not over, since it was Sunday, the third day of Unleavened Bread. It is not clear if they had concluded that the remaining sacrifices were now unnecessary, especially at the report of the Temple curtain being torn, or that their troubled minds dictated home, rest and reflection above the dictates of the feast.

We can affirm at least part of the latter, since we are told those things they were discussing - *14 And they were talking with each other about all these things which had taken place.*

15 . . Jesus Himself approached and began traveling with them. 16 But their eyes were prevented from recognizing Him.

Again, we have insight that His corporeal nature was not so unrecognizable that intervention would not be needed. Mary did not double-take the Lord, recognizing His voice but encountering the puzzlement of a wholly different appearance. Yet it was different enough to allow her to mistake Him for the gardener.

Here, there is additional reason for Him not being recognized, primarily because there will be extended dialog which must be had anonymously and recognition might come too soon.

17 . . "What are these words that you are exchanging with one another . . and said to Him, "Are You the only one visiting Jerusalem and unaware of the things which have happened here in these days?"

The rejoinder from Cleopas assumes that Jesus had walked along enough to have gotten the gist of their discussion. (It would not make sense had Jesus just now stepped up and asked. In their minds, He would seem to have known the topic.)

We find here how incredibly public the event of the crucifixion was.

19 And He said to them, "What things?"

It is clear that Jesus is setting a stage, since He knows perfectly well what things. For them, despite His having walked a short space and certainly gotten the gist, they may very well have concluded He was visiting from elsewhere and such events were not readily understood, since they do not further upbraid Him, but begin an honest accounting for His benefit.

All this is to elicit their more formal accounting of these events, in preparation for His interpretation for them. Vagaries and speculations must be swept away and the freshness of the recollection must be recounted.

19 . . "The things about Jesus the Nazarene, who was a prophet mighty in deed and word . . 20 and how the chief priests and our rulers delivered Him to the sentence of death, and crucified Him.

We note that they do not say He was the Son of God or the Messiah. What they are therefore intent on understanding by discussion along the way is what the meaning of the empty tomb might be. They themselves are not quite as far along in their acknowledgement of His nature as were the eleven.

They recount the testimony of the women and how perplexing this discovery is. Jesus immediately intervenes with words that tie the facts together.

25 And He said to them, "O foolish men and slow of heart to believe in all that the prophets have spoken!

This was said also of the Twelve – (Matt 15:16.) We can sympathize to some degree because the whole corpus of OT revelation was formidable to have fresh in the mind in all respects. But this doesn't ameliorate the "fact" that the keys to understanding these things were there. The man with passion will search them out. Others, in varying degrees, less diligently.

It is to say that they have not been left bereft by the Lord, but He has been diligent to provide the connective tissue for explaining all these affairs, were they to look. And we cannot ignore that Jesus gave them sufficient hints by constantly quoting OT references that were being fulfilled.

In today's Church, we have only ourselves to blame for not understanding the plan of God in Christ. We are replete with resources for gleaning the knowledge of the oracles of God. Despite this, many choose a Christian life that seems to spurn the discipline of the library, the practice of diligent study to prove to oneself that what one is being preached is true. We are ready to take the word of others who can spend the time and have the skills.

For these men and for all of us, Jesus is exhorting that we find out for our own selves and prove the Word of God for what it is.

26 "Was it not necessary for the Christ to suffer these things and to enter into His glory?"

Necessary. This conveys plan and purpose, not mishap and accident. To be despondent about how things concerning their master had fallen out is to miss the reason He came, the reason they were chosen. The word necessary immediately told them that they were missing this connection to all that had gone before, extending back into the OT itself.

27 Then beginning with Moses and with all the prophets, He explained to them the things concerning Himself in all the Scriptures.

Would that we could have that teaching from His lips on file. We find also Paul conveying the truths of the Gospel with the only tool he had at the time – the Old Testament (Acts 17:2, 18:28.)

Beginning with Moses, we find the full expression of acceptable righteousness in the Law and the sacrifices – the high standard that compliance with a righteous God demands. We see in Moses the deliberately intended desperation of fulfilling the Law and the yearning for that grace that would enable its fulfillment. We learn also that the rock in the wilderness with Moses was related to the Rock that is Christ (I Cor 10:4.)

We also find in Moses the expectation of One who will come – the prophet (Deut 18:18) – who is Christ the Messiah.

The kingdom prophets foretold of Him with expectations that were never completely fulfilled in their historic settings.

Isaiah 53:3-4 - *"He was despised and forsaken of men, A man of sorrows and acquainted with grief; And like one from whom men hide their face He was despised, and we did not esteem Him. 4 Surely our griefs He Himself bore, And our sorrows He carried; Yet we ourselves esteemed Him stricken, Smitten of God, and afflicted."*

Jeremiah 23:5 – *"I will raise up for David a righteous Branch; And He will reign as king and act wisely And do justice and righteousness in the land."*

Jeremiah in Lamentations 4:20 – *"Under his shadow We shall live among the nations."*

Daniel 9:26 - *"Then after the sixty-two weeks the Messiah will be cut off and have nothing,"*

Zechariah 14:4 - *"In that day His feet will stand on the Mount of Olives"*

28 And they approached the village . . and He acted as though He were going farther. 29 But they urged Him, saying, "Stay with us,

The revelation of Himself was held in abeyance until intimate disclosure could be had. His pretense to be going further was rightly timed with that marvelous weaving together of the "old, old story" from Old Testament to the present. They were amazed and wanted more, hence, they could not bear His leaving them so soon – "Were not our hearts burning within us," (v.32.)

So with all men, the revelation and disclosure of the truths of God come on the heels of a deliberate concentration and quiet reflection, seldom amid raucous distractions. The listener must be intent on hearing, focused on the subject at hand and seeking what can be gained from the Spirit. God speaks in the still small voice (I Kings 19:12), which is hard to hear when everywhere we have the busy work of "doing church."

28 . . He took the bread and blessed it, and . . began giving it to them. 31 Then their eyes were opened and they recognized Him; and He vanished from their sight.

His action at the table mirrors that of the upper room Supper where He first revealed the procedure of Holy Communion. It was appropriately reminiscent of the sacrifice promised and now completed, and of the taking in of Him as food and drink – *"For My flesh is true food, and My blood is true drink"* (John 6:53.)

This is the moment chosen for the scales to fall from their eyes and to see Him as the risen Lord. He is no longer the One crucified, but the One living and in whom union was exhorted – the union witnessed by the imagery of the bread and wine. He was that which came down from Heaven. The sustaining power was not at an end, but now in perpetua.

This now fulfills all of their need for Him presently among them. As soon as they see, but more importantly understand, the more free He is now to depart. He does not stay the night, as if He needed rest. No longer bound by human flesh, He is free to be where He is needed without inconvenient delays. But this disappearance also fulfills the expectations commensurate with a divine person. He can vanish, having complete command over nature and His own form. His going is as to be expected and simply confirms they have been with the risen Lord.

32 They said to one another, "Were not our hearts burning within us while He was speaking to us on the road, while He was explaining the Scriptures to us?"

There is a heart within the righteous seeker that wishes for the arrangement of all things in their rightful place, the explanation that satisfies the yearnings of the heart. The false seeker is ready to find fault and contradiction. This is because he is overlaying a template of his own making into which all explanations must fit. He is not asking so as to be changed, but seeking to justify not being changed.

The true seeker is ready for the truth. There is something within that is able to affirm, "This is so right. These are the truths of God. This makes sense." It is not purely intellectual, philosophical and rational, but also emotional and spiritual. Something rings true within and this cannot be analyzed as can other forms of knowledge. It is an awareness, just as that gained by these men going to Emmaus.

The secret to us having that awareness made manifest is a disposition to receive, being ready and desirous of the truths of God. It is much like the dictum of psychologists, "You must want to change before any therapy can have its benefit."

"The Lord has really risen and has appeared to Simon."

We now see the extended purpose in this meeting with Jesus on the road. The disciples in Jerusalem are about to hear an independent confirmation that will bolster their faith in these affairs all the more. Here are men on the path away from this scene, receiving confirmation of the risen Lord, matching the import of what the others have experienced. As questions must have continued to arise among the Jerusalem disciples, in comes an unexpected testimony bearing the remarkable signs of concord with all that has happened that day. It is grace to the effecting of their faith. These things are the way they are supposed to be. This is the beginning of His Church in them. It is not to be a slow and recalcitrant start, but is attended rather with miracles and confirmations that loosen the brake and begin that momentum needed toward a new work in the Kingdom of God.

Next, another appearance to them all before that planned in Galilee . .

CHAPTER 17
Final Commission and Ascension

Luke 24:36-44, John 20:21-29, John 21:1-24

36 While they were telling these things, He Himself stood in their midst and said to them, "Peace be to you." 37 But they were startled and frightened and thought that they were seeing a spirit. 38 And He said to them, "Why are you troubled, and why do doubts arise in your hearts? 39 "See My hands and My feet, that it is I Myself; touch Me and see, for a spirit does not have flesh and bones as you see that I have." 40 And when He had said this, He showed them His hands and His feet.

41 While they still could not believe it because of their joy and amazement, He said to them, "Have you anything here to eat?" 42 They gave Him a piece of a broiled fish; 43 and He took it and ate it before them. 44 Now He said to them, "These are My words which I spoke to you while I was still with you, that all things which are written about Me in the Law of Moses and the Prophets and the Psalms must be fulfilled." (Luke 24:36-44.)

21 So Jesus said to them again, "Peace be with you; as the Father has sent Me, I also send you." 22 And when He had said this, He breathed on them and said to them, "Receive the Holy Spirit. 23 "If you forgive the sins of any, their sins have been forgiven them; if you retain the sins of any, they have been retained." 24 But Thomas, one of the twelve, called Didymus, was not with them when Jesus came. 25 So the other disciples were saying to him, "We have seen the Lord!" But he said to them, "Unless I see in His hands the imprint of the nails, and put my finger into the place of the nails, and put my hand into His side, I will not believe."

26 After eight days His disciples were again inside, and Thomas with them. Jesus came, the doors having been shut, and stood in their midst and said, "Peace be with you." 27 Then He said to Thomas, "Reach here with your finger, and see My hands; and reach here your hand and put it into My side; and do not be unbelieving, but believing." 28 Thomas answered and said to Him, "My Lord and my God!" 29 Jesus said to him, "Because you have seen Me, have you believed? Blessed are they who did not see, and yet believed." (John 20:21-29.)

1 After these things Jesus manifested Himself again to the disciples at the Sea of Tiberias, and He manifested Himself in this way. 2 Simon Peter, and Thomas called Didymus, and Nathanael of Cana in Galilee, and the sons of Zebedee, and two others of His disciples were together. 3 Simon Peter said to them, "I am going fishing." They said to him, "We will also come with you." They went out and got into the boat; and that night they caught nothing. 4 But when the day was now breaking, Jesus stood on the beach; yet the disciples did not know that it was Jesus.

5 So Jesus said to them, "Children, you do not have any fish, do you?" They answered Him, "No." 6 And He said to them, "Cast the net on the right-hand side of the boat and you will find a catch." So they cast, and then they were not able to haul it in because of the great number of fish. 7 Therefore that disciple whom Jesus loved said to Peter, "It is the Lord." So when Simon Peter heard that it was the Lord, he put his outer garment on (for he was stripped for work), and threw himself into the sea. 8 But the other disciples came in the little boat, for they were not far from the land, but about one hundred yards away, dragging the net full of fish. 9 So when they got out on the land, they saw a charcoal fire already laid and fish placed on it, and bread.

10 Jesus said to them, "Bring some of the fish which you have now caught." 11 Simon Peter went up and drew the net to land, full of large fish, a hundred and fifty-three; and although there were so many, the net was not torn. 12 Jesus said to them, "Come and have breakfast." None of the disciples ventured to question Him, "Who are You?" knowing that it was the Lord. 13 Jesus came and took the bread and gave it to them, and the fish likewise. 14 This is now the third time that Jesus was manifested to the disciples, after He was raised from the dead.

15 So when they had finished breakfast, Jesus said to Simon Peter, "Simon, son of John, do you love Me more than these?" He said to Him, "Yes, Lord; You know that I love You." He said to him, "Tend My lambs." 16 He said to him again a second time, "Simon, son of John, do you love Me?" He said to Him, "Yes, Lord; You know that I love You." He said to him, "Shepherd My sheep." 17 He said to him the third time, "Simon, son of John, do you love Me?" Peter was grieved because He said to him the third time, "Do you love Me?" And he said to Him, "Lord, You know all things; You know that I love You." Jesus said to him, "Tend My sheep.

18 "Truly, truly, I say to you, when you were younger, you used to gird yourself and walk wherever you wished; but when you grow old, you will stretch out your hands and someone else will gird you, and bring you where you do not wish to go." 19 Now this He said, signifying by what kind of death he would glorify God. And when He had spoken this, He said to him, "Follow Me!" 20 Peter, turning around, saw the disciple whom Jesus loved following them; the one who also had leaned back on His bosom at the supper and said, "Lord, who is the one who betrays You?" 21 So Peter seeing him said to Jesus, "Lord, and what about this man?" 22 Jesus said to him, "If I want him to remain until I come, what is that to you? You follow Me!" 23 Therefore this saying went out among the brethren that that disciple would not die; yet Jesus did not say to him that he would not die, but only, "If I want him to remain until I come, what is that to you?" 24 This is the disciple who is testifying to these things and wrote these things, and we know that his testimony is true. (John 21:1-24.)

Commentary

36 While they were telling these things, He Himself stood in their midst . . . "Peace be to you." 37 But they were startled and frightened . . . "Why are you troubled, and why do doubts arise in your hearts? 39 "See My hands and My feet, . . touch Me and see, for a spirit does not have flesh and bones" . . 40 He showed them His hands and His feet.

The things being discussed were the events at Emmaus from the previous section. As it happens, Jesus appears here in addition to His command that they go to Galilee to see Him. The urgency of the command to meet in Galilee seems lessened, though we cannot attribute a change of mind to our Lord. We will see there the receiving of the Great Commission, but the Ascension will take place back in the "vicinity of Bethany."

Perhaps these appearances were to avoid partiality, in that only some had already seen Him earlier. But these had not been accidents either.

His first words are "Peace be to you," which would be appropriate since we find them immediately startled and in fear. They are as yet unused to such appearances and have little to tell them apart from those of ghosts and spirits. There was and remains a natural dread of the spirit world because it was unknown what power they wielded, and they were in touch with the finality of things which were deemed as coming too soon into the mortal life of the beholder. Contact with them carried an expectation that they might contaminate the blessings of life with the gloom and uncertain miseries of death. Not much has changed in all these centuries. Despite the modernity of man, his reason and science, he anticipates the same fear of such things.

"Why are you troubled, and why do doubts arise in your hearts?

Meant somewhat rhetorically (He certainly understands their fear), He is nevertheless telling them they are to get over such fears by testing the new horizons of reality – He is not a ghost but a living person. They understandably doubted but there is now no cause for further doubting.

39 "See My hands and My feet, that it is I Myself

Inspection is needed and He invites it. This is indicated because He is enough unlike His former appearance that mere visual recognition will not combine with His words to get them over their fears - "See that it is Myself."

His hands and feet are pointed to because they bear the marks of His suffering. An imposter would not have them. His mere spirit would not be assumed to have them either – eternal life was presumed to provide other vessels, not the ones lived in life. Wounds would be erased.

So to see these very wounds served to authenticate Him beyond all doubt. It also assured them that to some unknown degree, resurrection was corporeal, not in the sense of its limitations, but of its form. We are not to become disembodied spirits, but the body has a role in the eternal state, meaning hands, legs, ears, feet. The human package, at least in form, is more than earthly, but intended for eternity.

.. bones ..

This qualification anticipates that they were to inspect Him to that degree, to feel that He had real bones not being a mere apparition. John later describes this as having "handled of the Word of Life." (I John 1:1, KJV.)

"Have you anything here to eat?"

This is said following the comment that they still were having difficulty believing what they were seeing. To bring the corporeal reality into even sharper clarity, He asks to eat, something their meager comprehension of spirits would not conceive of them ever doing. He is every bit as real and bodily-oriented as they are, yet He clearly died.

This is the great hope and query of every man since the foundation of the world – "if a man die, shall he live again?" (Job 14:14.) That has been emphatically answered, "Yes." The grave could not hold Him, it will not hold us. We are living and we are designed for life. We see that very real life appearing again, unstained by death.

This sort of thing makes sense to any careful thinking person. The very character and nature of life suggests that it is meant to go on, not come to an abrupt end with no explanations. The sheer depth to which we become aware of our lives, all its interactions and the world around us, cannot be without meaning, a meaning that includes continuity. In opposition, that is what the existentialists and atheists wish to pose as the bald truth about reality - until they come to it at last and face the oblivion they have contrived. Some face the barrier courageously, hoping that bravery in the light of truth will secure the annihilation of all unpleasantries beyond by vacating perception and being altogether. One cannot experience if one does not even exist.

Those who anticipate what God has incorporated into His creation - the expectation of eternity - find tremendous hope in seeing Jesus appearing with bones and flesh to feel and an appetite that wishes to eat.

44 ... "These are My words which I spoke to you ... that all things which are written about Me in the Law of Moses and the Prophets and the Psalms must be fulfilled."

It is still very important to not let the amazement of the moment distract them from the realization that this was all according to plan. He must reiterate the tie up of these things to what He taught them, and more importantly, that they were voiced in the saints and prophets of old. These are to be tied together because the unfolding plan of God cannot be set aside in favor of something new. There is a marvelous continuity with all that has gone before. God has been active in the plan of salvation since the very beginning. "I know that my Redeemer lives" is among the earliest expectations in the Bible (Job 19:25.)

In later years, the disciples will be busy proving this in Holy Writ, as Matthew cites more OT fulfillments than any other gospel account. They will be spurred on to tie up the connections by study, recollection and inspiration.

The End of John's Gospel Narrative

21 "... as the Father has sent Me, I also send you."

His repetition of "Peace be with you" is certainly due to Him seeing as yet some fear and amazement in them. It is like a reiteration that says, "Please, all of you, be at peace." Earlier theorizations and predictions were things entertained in more academic surroundings, they had no immediate moment when taught. But reality is unfolding for them in the now and it is hard to take in.

It is important for Jesus to reiterate their "sentness" which is the meaning behind 'apostle.' The world awaits conversion. It is the thing that has gone bad, gone off track, needing remedy. He came to effect the functional pieces that will make the conversion possible and a process that actually works. They are the means, the legs and mouths that will go to the lost and make it known.

God has done the heavy lifting. Man's task is to do what is remarkably easier in constrast – to simply announce, declare, and disciple.

22 And when He had said this, He breathed on them and said to them, "Receive the Holy Spirit.

This verse is almost lost in the excitement with which preachers emphasize all that has gone before it. In isolation from Acts, it can be seen as the gift of the indwelling Spirit that will characterize the Church age. But in conjunction with the descent of the Spirit in Acts, it provides a conundrum. If the disciples didn't receive the Spirit until Acts 2:4, what is it they receive here?

This becomes a regrettable demarcation line between evangelicals and charismatic believers. (It is equally regrettable that a term like 'evangelical' has come to be used as a negative description of someone who denies the continuity of the gifts of the Spirit. Evangelicals are so described because such churches characteristically minimize the charismatic spiritual gifts in the life of the modern day church in the interest of emphasizing evangelism. However, 'evangelical' is a much broader term than distinguishing itself around the issue of the gifts.)

The best explanation that preserves the plain sense of both John and Acts, it that the Holy Spirit was received in John 20, and the same Spirit filled the disciples for empowering in Acts. Those who wish to have both the infilling and empowering restricted to Acts, must make John 20 a sort of perfunctory exercise that did not really effect anything of substance. It would be a sort of promissory note, hinting at what would take place at Pentecost.

But we have to put ourselves in the place of the disciples. He breathed on them and said "Receive." They would have every expectation of experiencing the commensurate effect. To experience nothing would invite confused looks and begging Jesus to further explain, which we find He does not do. It is a straightforward command to them, hence, a straightforward result would be expected.

For charismatics, this is posed as proof that believers receive the Spirit in two blessings, the latter which bestows the gifts, the former which inaugurated the believer into the Body of Christ. The first is connected with salvation, the latter with empowerment to works. Understandably, the evangelical community resists this separation because for anyone who has not participated in the second experience – that comparable to Pentecost – there will be a feeling of having missed something essential; and that is going to rub Christians wrong by suggesting defectiveness or inadequacy.

The inadequacy may not in fact be something related to the believer but to how the believer has been taught. If the church for ecclesiastical reasons neglected part of the teaching, the student of church history will conclude that the now vacant experience must have been meant for bygone ages, when in truth it is not being sought because it has not been taught.

Complicating this is the import one can apply from the lordship of Christ over the Church. How could something essential fall by the wayside by mere neglect? Yet, the history of the medieval church bears witness to the longsuffering of God in the presence of inadequate, unfaithful and even unregenerate administrators. Faith came through it all, despite what men did, and for some, the revival of the gifts in sectors of Christian experience seems to call for revisiting any final assessments.

We are, after all, compelled by our attitude toward the Word of God and the actions of Jesus to retain meaning both here and in Acts. And if so, something rigorously legitimate and helpful occurred in both places.

23 "If you forgive the sins of any, their sins have been forgiven them; if you retain the sins of any, they have been retained."

This was originally said to Peter in the hearing of the others (Matt 16:19, 18:18.), but here now the pronouns are notably plural – "If you all forgive the sins of any . . If you all retain. . " (apheite, krateite.) Clearly, this power to bind and loose was in the hands of all His apostles. Today, Catholics see this in the exclusive operation of the office of St. Peter, namely the Pope and the college of bishops, believing them to have succeeded to the apostolic office, not the individual apostles.)

And we can see the commission to forgive or retain in the confessional, where more than St. John's claim that each believer has an advocate in Christ is seen. If the apostles are truly being set up with these powers, confession to them is being established as well, else we are bereft of explaining how their forgiving powers were to operate at all, posing that I John 1:9 is the whole of the subject. (What do powers to forgive offer if the believer can get forgiveness alone with Christ?)

Protestants tend to view this as powers applied to special cases rather than that of every individual believer's action, else 1 John is set off balance by the speciality of this apostolic power. We see this in effect in the case of Ananias and Sapphira (Acts 5:1.) Here the apostles exercise a completely external assessment of their sins where no exercise of I John 1:9 is given time or opportunity.

Furthermore, it was impracticable for the sins of all members of the churches to be heard by the apostles, which has begotten the idea of delegation to local priests. But Protestants see no Scriptural authority for extending a strictly apostolic power to ordinaries among the priesthood. It is clearly seen in the NT as identifying the unique position of the apostles, which in Catholic eyes, is not fulfilled in the priest. On the other hand, Protestants have no present means or office that expresses the apostolic authority given in these verses. In most Protestant thinking, it died with the apostles, meant only for the formative years of the early church.

24 But Thomas, one of the twelve, called Didymus, was not with them when Jesus came

The scene is now later, after this appearance with the disciples at which Thomas was absent. He represents for all future believers those who prefer to walk by sight. We cannot attribute to him no faith at all, but as yet a preference for what is familiar, that which can be seen and touched – the empirical method of validation. He is not close what we might call a scientist, but the rationalism he prefers is akin to that mindset. Show me and I will affirm it. The idea of believing where there is an absence of facts is slow to jel for Thomas. But that is what faith is, otherwise it is science and reason. (One does not need to "believe" in what has just been demonstrated as fact.)

As for Thomas, we cannot forget that he has been present to witness many "facts" concerning the nature and person of Jesus. This is not about belief that Jesus is Lord or Son of God. This is about whether He has risen or whether his friends are merely gullible or impressionable.

To be sure, there is a place for being certain and using the reasoning abilities God gave us for that purpose. But there is also a place for exercising proper faith. As followers it is not A or B. It is both in their appropriate place. We are not waiting for a word of faith to begin brushing our teeth. Faith will not change the mathematics that calculates our tax bill, but receiving extraordinary means to pay them can be.

26 After eight days .. 27 .. He said to Thomas, "Reach here with your finger,"

Notice that Jesus does not deny Thomas the validation. While He will have something to say about his approach to faith, He recognizes that faith is not meant to be blind faith, but that which has a basis in fact. The authentication by touch and sight will become an exhortation to exercise his faith when there are no facts at hand, in other words, he will be building a legacy of faith experiences confirmed by their outcomes.

It is not improper to expect faith to address things in the real world. Jesus did not come to galaxy far far away where we are expected to believe all the things about him from afar. He came to a real world, our own, full of magistrates, towns, fig trees and human institutions. The expectation that these cross-validate is not improper.

Jesus came, the doors having been shut,

What is often overlooked in this account is that Jesus appeared while the doors were shut. We emphasize the marvelous and deliberate corporality of his body, yet it is not bound by the material universe either. It is a validation sign that He has returned to that state that is within nature but beyond it, having flesh and bone, making human speech according to natural language, but fully free to move and work as He wills.

27 .. and do not be unbelieving, but believing."

Here is where Jesus does not leave Thomas where he is, but exhorts him to go further. He must move to the new position that adds faith as the chief dimension of his life not the occasional one. While Jesus did not upbraid him for requiring validation and willingly gave it to him, He moves to what comes next. "OK, Thomas, now you've seen. Where do we go from here? What will you do with it?" This is why walking by sight is not enough. If we are to operate by faith, then we must get on with it, which means we must see gracious accommodations of sight as helping that transition rather than defining it.

"My Lord and my God!"

Among the proof texts of Jesus divinity, this is not blasphemy, since Jesus does not correct Him. It is one of the few times when a man calls Jesus God directly. Other references record the inference that He was making Himself out to be God or attributing this to Himself, but we have here an outright address. As to a charge that this was merely one man's opinion, there is no objection from the others, and another person had to concur, namely John, for it to be recorded.

29 .. "Because you have seen Me, have you believed? Blessed are they who did not see, and yet believed."

Jesus highlights the nature of faith that for many is repugnant. He comments in the form of a question to Thomas – you have seen so that is why you now believe? Again, Jesus was willing to accommodate this if it leads Thomas to exercise faith.

But Jesus moves to that intractable condition of faith that asks to believe without seeing. And He describes this as more blessed. We would describe it as more arduous.

The reason it is more blessed is in the results gained. Faith is described as an assurance and further as the evidence of things not seen (Heb 11:1), meaning that in the process, something like evidence is made known to us. Faith then conveys knowledge, which is antithetical to the rationalistic philosopher and the scientist. What is being said is that there is greater joy in exercising faith where no evidence is present, only to find its truth made evident – that it worked. The exhilaration is in knowing that something has united God and us in the operation. We have come into knowledge from above, not from below, and that is substantially more exciting than seeing a predicted reaction from known facts.

1 After these things Jesus manifested Himself again to the disciples at the Sea of Tiberias,

We now have the meeting which Jesus and the angels announced was to take place after the Resurrection. We find seven mentioned in this company, which included Peter, James and John. But we don't see Matthew or the others here by name. Of the Eleven, four unnamed disciples are not present.

This does not hint at some supposed disunity commencing immediately after the Crucifixion. Our Lord accepts the company as assembled, which implies understanding of the absence of the others, and it is the oneness of communication and fellowship that will supply all with knowledge, not a mandatory attendance at all places and times.

Of interest is the impression that they are here merely occupying time – Peter has said, "I'm going fishing," which some have characterized as a sort of despondency over what to do next. We are not to infer that he has decided to return to his former life, but in the absence of instructions and a plan of action, he will fill the time with an activity he knows very well.

It would seem that even their former trade has become lackluster compared to the new life they have had with Jesus. The fishing is not productive, as if to say "without Him, we merely exist."

4 . . . Jesus stood on the beach; . . . 5 . . "Children, you do not have any fish, do you?"

John tells us that they did not recognize Jesus as the man on the shore. We aren't told why and the obvious explanations are less than satisfactory. Again, many offer that this is merely because they did not expect Him. But after two appearances and instructions to meet in Galilee, this is less cogent. Nor is it due to a difference of appearance, for they are now apprised of this after the earlier meetings. It may likely be due to not having expected Him at the shore or in the midst of fishing. Perhaps their idea was a meeting in a house or a room, as before.

He does not ask them if they have any fish, but asks a question that is a comment on their state of affairs – *"You haven't caught any fish, have you?"*

6 . . "Cast the net on the right-hand side of the boat and you will find a catch."

Anyone who has fished knows that if the fish aren't biting on one side of the boat, dropping lines on the other side will make no practical difference. But in the hands of our Lord, all nature is available and ready to command. Whether the fish were created on the spot or summoned from distant places, they become available for the Lord's use.

This is the Jesus they have followed, who attends His work and teaching with the unexpected, the miraculous, the enigmatic. His arrangements are always seemingly against practicality or the commonly expected; and are thus made to stand out as all the more memorably.

In the business of doing what we have been called to do, we can yield to the weight of practicality and begin thinking that the burden is all on us. It is we who must make it happen. And in that comes the fear of failure as the world is incredibly larger than we ourselves and we are forced to ask if we are workers or mere dreamers?

But faith expects the extraordinary despite the practical, because all of nature is His. What unleashes this kind of power is faith, and we are too often too practical for His purposes.

Here, He does not simply meet with them on the shore, but accompanies His appearance with something extraordinary. This prompts John to make the recognition.

7 .. "It is the Lord."

In this case, it was the miracle, but we are not to hold out for the miracle to make the recognition. He would have us know His presence by that cultivation of Spirit that senses when God is near and working. If we are mindful of His intentions for us, we will know the way. We will not be in the midst of our own way, then to be surprised at His appearance. To cultivate the Spirit of God is to be able to say without miracle or wonder, "He is here working."

7 .. *So when Simon Peter heard that it was the Lord, he put his outer garment on .. and threw himself into the sea.*

For most Jews, men had two items of clothing for routine activities – a cloth tied about the loins and an outer garment which we might see as a dress, or a long garment going from shoulder to ankles. In cold weather or for formal dress, a third item – a cloak – was needed.

For work, the outer garment was cast off leaving the man free at the legs and arms. In cases where work was notably in the public gaze, the outer garment would have been kept on but pulled up and tied to free the legs (just the undergarment would have appeared much like a man working in his underwear today.) For fishermen, practicality and remoteness from land dictated that the outer garment could be removed.

Here, Peter puts this garment on to make the swim to the shore (which we would consider very inconvenient, like swimming in one's bathrobe), but it was socially the appropriate thing to do. Coming to shore in his skivvies may not have mattered much to Jesus, but to Peter it would have shown less respect.

It is now a trend in churches of late to wear casual attire to the degree that some people come in tee shirts and sneakers. It is part of the shaking down of traditions and the reinvention of church in what some characterize as postmodern times, where alternatives and creative reconstruction are the mode of day.

The argument goes that God is no respecter of persons, He sees the inside not the outside, so it shouldn't matter what we wear. But God is also One who is to be respected, and when we dress for church not much different than when making a ham sandwich at the refrigerator, we are outwardly saying to others that He is of the same approximate importance (or that we are incredibly lazy to expend the extra effort.)

Does this mean we should all be decked to the nines for church? Not as a fashion contest. But we should give God the best of what we have rather than the ordinary. And if we can afford a little better in the interest of giving Him better, we should do so.

9 *So when they got out on the land, they saw a charcoal fire already laid and fish placed on it, and bread.*

"already laid" - another extraordinary aspect to appreciate. Jesus has acquired fish and coals and fire quite without their help nor having fished with them. It is a comforting scene by all accounts. Peter is dripping from the swim, the weight of his soaked garment adding to the chill now seeping into every pore. The pungent smell of the coals and fish and the anticipated warmth by the fire are inviting even before Jesus makes it formal. But first, he has the work of the nets, which Jesus encourages with, "Bring some of the fish which you have now caught."

He invites them all to a breakfast which for anyone would be a welcome rest after a morning of work. Of interest is the exact number caught, 153, considering that most story tellers use round numbers. Facts like these add to the general historicity of the NT accounts, making them exceptional among texts of the ancient past.

None of the disciples ventured to question Him, "Who are You?" knowing that it was the Lord.

We shouldn't make too much of the unspoken question, "Who are You?" This is not a statement that they had retained some doubt, but a mode of speech that contrasts the mere facts of initially wondering who the man on the shore was and their subsequent acknowledgement. It is a way of saying, "They set aside their question of who He was, knowing it was the Lord."

Again, *He* serves them. He delights in sharing with them what He has prepared (including some bread) and what they have caught also.

14 This is now the third time that Jesus was manifested to the disciples, after He was raised from the dead.

There can be no question as to the importance of highlighting how many times Jesus appeared in post-resurrection events. Certainly the test of the validity of the Resurrection is the expectation that He should be seen alive by credible people, and not just once in private, but several times and outside the confines of a secret meeting place.

The addition of specific details, how many fish in the net, the process of the catch and the drag to shore, what was on the fire, what they ate, all help the reader conclude that a real event was taking place not a phantasm or a dream.

15 . . . "Simon, son of John, do you love Me more than these?" . . . "Yes, Lord; You know that I love You." . . "Tend My lambs."

We come now to an encounter between Peter and Jesus that in our mind is long overdue. We cannot forget that Peter denied the Lord three times and there has been nothing more than his own remorse expressed in Scripture. With the many meetings with the risen Jesus, we might expect some moment of reconciliation and that moment has now come.

Of interest is that Jesus asks this three times, as if to match one-for-one the three denials. Peter certainly gets the message at the third repetition, as he is said to be grieved. It has become clear that Jesus is referring to the denials. The failure Peter has ever felt since is coming crashing in.

Of interest also, and seen only in the Greek, are the Aramiac verbs used by Jesus vs. Peter. Jesus consistently asks, "Do you *agapas*.?" Do you love Me with God's love, unconditionally? Peter replies, "You know that I am fond of you" - *'philo'*.

The difference between agapao and phileo is striking. Phileo can be quite endearing, but it is not of the same depth and character as agapao. Jesus has consistently used agapao in His teaching on love, we are encouraged to go beyond phileo and approach the love God exhibits.

The contrast does show the reticence in Peter to match the expression Jesus is using. Much can be attributed to his own humility and the clear knowledge that this exchange is in the context of his earlier denials about which he has to feel inadequate toward so positive a love as is mentioned by Jesus.

17 He said to him the third time, "Simon, son of John, do you love Me?" . . Peter was grieved

John substitutes a translation of 'Barjona', which merely means son of Ioannes, son of John. In this third repetition, Jesus changes to use Peter's verb – phileo – saying in effect, "Are you fond of Me, Peter?" It is a way of telling Peter He's noted his choice of words.

We might expect Peter to make the transition to agapao, but surprisingly we find that he repeats *philo* back without change. Peter is being rigorously honest – he can at this moment truthfully muster an endearing fondness, not knowing in himself if he truly does love *en agape*. To be false at this moment is not only unlike the Peter we have come to know, but would certainly be seen as less than sincere by one such as Jesus. Philo is what he can say with honesty. In his grief and sorrow, he chooses honesty rather than another episode of false bravado.

"Tend My lambs." . . ***"Shepherd My sheep."*** . . ***"Tend My sheep.***

At each renewal of love, Peter is charged with this task. Many believe this substantiates Peter's role as head of the Church, since this is said nowhere as powerfully or personally to the others. It cannot be denied that the role of caring for and feeding the rest lies with him as of this meeting. And while other charges could have accompanied the other responses, that the same is repeated makes this all the more certain and deliberate. Nor can we deny that this is precisely the role to which the Church came to regard him with significance.

But we cannot either ignore that others came to fulfill this role in practice, if not more visibly than Peter. Paul certainly contributed more than Peter in this regard, and Paul's writing was notably that of edification, education, and dissertation concerning not only the theology of the NT but its application in the churches.

For these reasons, some offer that Jesus' charge to Peter was restorative in direct relation to his denials, but is not meant to be more than this. He is restored to the trust of feeding and caring for Christ's disciples, as was common to the Twelve in relation to the other disciples. And we see this confirmed in the added role of Paul as thirteenth apostle, and in John, whose visits to the churches were cherished and valued being as he was, such long lasting vestige of that holy company of originals.

Of importance to us is the role of the church shepherd. They are to care for and feed the flock. More than performing miracles and evangelizing, they are to disciple, which means to teach, nurture and raise up new saints for the work of the advancing Kingdom. To feed means to have the sustenance attained in oneself, which necessitates study and mastery of the teachings of Jesus.

Hence, we find in Paul the restrictive qualifications of elder as one who is apt to teach (I Tim 3:2.) Let every one aspiring to lead in the church consider this charge. To teach is to benefit the church in the greatest way possible, because it places the tenets and precepts of Christian life in the hands of others, and straightens the path on which others must tread for themselves.

18 *"Truly, truly, . . when you grow old, you will stretch out your hands and someone else will gird you, and bring you where you do not wish to go."*

Jesus is being graciously kind to Peter in presaging the manner of his death. He is not being horrifyingly honest with antiseptic clarity. He cares for Peter and this is not the time to be brutally frank, so He describes Peter's death in softened terms which will not frighten him back into a corner.

The stretching out of his hands and girding him unwillingly refers to his martyrdom at the hands of a pagan ruler – "this He said, signifying by what kind of death he would glorify God." As he ministers in Rome, it will not take long for the authorities to recognize that the new sect of the Jews is a religion, diametrically opposed to the social fabric of Roman worship and social life. A violent collision will be inevitable. It will be delayed only by the time necessary for it to gain the attention of the highest authority.

Peter was crucified in the Circus of Nero, formerly the circus of Caligula, the site of which was just south of what has become the present day Saint Peter's basilica at the ancient Vatican Hill. Anecdotal testimonies of this execution describe it as occurring near the obelisk of the circus, a monument which has been preserved into modern times and now stands in the center of St. Peter's square. (It was moved by Pope Julius II at the completion of St. Peter's from its original position of some fifteen hundred years in the ruins of the circus.)

19 . . *"Follow Me!"* 20 . . *Peter, . . saw the disciple whom Jesus loved following them; . . 21 So Peter seeing him said to Jesus, "Lord, and what about this man?"*

Despite the softening approach, Peter has been given the surety that he will be martyred. He has to be wondering what lies in the future for the others. John stood out because John would have been seen as especially affectionate with Jesus, and Peter would have been keen to know what Jesus saw concerning him.

Peter's question might seem to betray a resentment, that he has been singled out for the short straw, the raw end of the deal. He seems to have supposed a fairer outcome for John, and he is now checking with Jesus to see if parity exists among all the men, or has he been singled out?

"If I want him to remain until I come, what is that to you?

Jesus does not satisfy this check for equity, but actually establishes that such an equity is not in the purposes of God. This is not about being fair, but about the plan of God. Each has their unique destiny in the ministry of the Cross, each must take its unique course.

When we surmise that we are being treated to some disadvantage, the whole notion of what is fair comes to the fore. That would be democracy, but that is not a principle that necessarily binds to plans of God. He is obligated to fulfill His righteousness, not maintain a surety that all things are fair.

All acts and destinies of the righteous will meet in the glorified Kingdom. It is a case of many different paths of service being rewarded in the same glory of His eternal presence. So how any particular man gets there at the bidding of God is less important than the fact that he will get there in the end, and enjoy eternity in the rewards of service.

This is almost identical to Christ's teaching about the workers in the vineyard, each of whom come to work for an agreed wage. It is not until some are apprised that others are getting the equivalent of higher wages (the same pay for less work) that complaints arise. But the truth is that all agreed for the wage presented (Matt 20:13.)

23 Therefore this saying went out among the brethren that that disciple would not die;

As can be expected, the propensity to embellish or extend meaning beyond its intent begins early, as here the church takes this statement to mean John will not die. Since John is writing and knows the truth, he takes this moment to correct it. (John did not write until the 90's so there was time for this embellishment to circulate.)

In hindsight, we are puzzled about the qualification. To be sure, it is made clear Jesus did not state that John would not die. But it is also equally clear that Jesus did not come back before John's death. And since Jesus is yet to come back, "remaining until I come again" would imply longevity into the modern age, which clearly has not occurred.

The only sense in which the words can be understood without forcing some sort of contradiction, is that John is slated to live a natural life not terminated by martyrdom in the course of waiting for the Lord's return. All such believers can be said to be living in anticipation of the Lord's return, and the fact that He does not return in any particular person's lifetime past does not nullify their having lived in that expectation.

It is taken simply as an alternate way of saying, "John will live in the expectation of my return," period.

Of historical interest is the testimony that despite being lowered into a vat of boiling oil, he came out unscathed, the result of which sent him to Patmos in exile. [86] Certainly an event that would have been in accordance with the proclamation of Jesus.

---

[86] Tertullian, De praeScript., xxxvi,

24 *This is the disciple who is testifying to these things and wrote these things, and we know that his testimony is true.*

We now have John authenticating his work as an eyewitness account. It clarifies that the references to the disciple whom Jesus loved is he himself, since the disciple just mentioned who concerned Peter is now one and the same as the author. It is important historically that this note be present, as it undermines later criticisms that such accounts were fabrications or the works of those coming much later.

As to "we know that his testimony is true," this is not something to which all men in all ages could concur as easily as John could at the time. By "we," he is referring to those of this company, to the unified witness of Jesus' followers, whose commendation would be validated by the inner witness of the Holy Spirit. Of equal value, though not mentioned, is the corroborative power of opportunity at the time to cross-validate the account with others still living from these times. If you doubted the accuracy, one still had access to people who had been there.

Of similar weight is the presentation and dissemination of these accounts in a notably hostile environment, where hostile parties are mentioned in the accounts, namely the Jewish authorities. Were these to be historically and factually inaccurate, there were parties with a vested interest in blowing the whistle and exposing what would be a fraud. The lack of such attacks on the facts and historical details vindicates their authenticity more than most other assertions.

John will close off his wonderful gospel with more words which will be presented in their appropriate place chronologically, but this constitutes the end of his own account.

The Close of the Synoptic Accounts with Contributions from Acts

Matthew 28:16-20
16 But the eleven disciples proceeded to Galilee, to the mountain which Jesus had designated. 17 When they saw Him, they worshiped Him; but some were doubtful. 18 And Jesus came up and spoke to them, saying, "All authority has been given to Me in heaven and on earth. 19 "Go therefore and make disciples of all the nations, baptizing them in the name of the Father and the Son and the Holy Spirit, 20 teaching them to observe all that I commanded you; and lo, I am with you always, even to the end of the age." (Matthew 28:16-20.)

Commentary

16 *But the eleven disciples proceeded to Galilee, to the mountain which Jesus had designated. 17 When they saw Him, they worshiped Him; but some were doubtful.*

Apart from John's account, Matthew discloses the events in Galilee respecting a meeting on a mountain in the region. He therefore skips over the events at the shore recounted by John, primarily because he wishes to convey the Great Commission against which all other events were secondary. As explained earlier, the authors of the four gospels were each impressed with a peculiar emphasis and this controlled what they included and neglected in their accounts. That God was gracious to give us four views ensures that we will see all the facts and themes necessary and in contexts and styles appropriate to them.

Matthew tells us the disciples proceeded and Jesus then appeared. This is somewhat out of sorts with John's account, since there we see Jesus with them and beckoning them to follow Him (John 20:19). This would indicate that some time after their meeting at the shore, Jesus left their midst and they conducted themselves to the mountain. An indeterminate amount of time has transpired between the scene on the shore and the mountain.

The mountain is said to be known to them, but this instruction from Jesus was nowhere recorded.

17 When they saw Him, they worshiped Him; but some were doubtful.

Their worship most likely consisted of kneeling to the ground or uttering words of praise and joy at seeing Him. Today, our worship involves singing, responsive readings, or in charismatic congregations, ecstatic utterances of praise and adoration. Some regard the giving of tithes and offerings as acts of worship.

Worship is adoration, the declaration of His majesty and glory, the expression of our devotion and love to Him. We rehearse His attributes and the wonder of His ways and grace among us.

. . but some were doubtful.

It is hard to imagine for us that any of this company would be doubtful having seen the appearances recounted thus far. But we must understand the completely extraordinary and overwhelming nature of this phenomenon. No one was prepared for the patent reality of someone rising from the dead, even if adequately forewarned. It was all abstract prediction much of which they could barely make sense. They could not picture it in reality and now reality was crashing in on them right in front of their eyes. It caused the more pragmatic minds to question whether they were living some sort of extended fantastic dream, like Daniel, or had perhaps gone slightly out of their normal minds.

At all accounts, this was not a doubting about their mission, that He was the Christ or that what He had taught was truth mingled with doubtful eventualities. The doubtful posture of some here is in strict relation to their taking in what they were seeing – that they were looking at a very real, very alive resurrected person. This is particularly why Jesus, seeing their astonishment, asked for food (Luke 24:41).

18 And Jesus came up and spoke to them, saying, "All authority has been given to Me in heaven and on earth.

The very first thing one needs to move their doubts toward faith is a declaration that these things are occurring with the blessing and concurrence of Heaven. Jesus therefore immediately offers that His appearing is in accord with having been given all authority in Heaven and on earth. It is to say that what they are seeing is a direct result to His command over the forces of nature, including the destiny of those who die.

His resurrection was His own work affecting Himself, meaning that His Spirit, separate fundamentally from the flesh in which He had resided, was continual - beyond His physical death - and was endowed with all power to cause that body to be raised, according to the will of the Father. We find this separate existence apart from His body in the epistles of Peter where He is said to have descended while in the grave to the place of the dead and there to preach to the souls in captivity (I Pet 3:19.)

THE GREAT COMMISSION

19 "Go therefore and make disciples of all the nations, baptizing them in the name of the Father and the Son and the Holy Spirit, 20 teaching them to observe all that I commanded you;

Here is the purpose of the first advent revealed. There is to be a "society" of the redeemed, those who have been reclaimed from the bondage of the devil's realm. It is a new work, unlike that done in the house of Israel. They are to be transformed in relation to sin and indwelt by the presence of the Holy Spirit.

The inauguration of this society, which the NT calls the Church, is first to be made possible by dealing once and for all with man's sin. The society cannot be merely a second run of Judaism, whereby men lived according to a list of do's and don'ts, and attempted obedience largely by the ineffective exercise of purely human will. That whole dispensation had failed because men were stained by spiritual weakness, lacking the kind of spiritual power to fulfill it.

The purpose of that dispensation was to prove the inadequacy of man's own efforts apart from the Spirit – *"not by might, not by power, but by My Spirit, saith the Lord"* (Zech 4:6.) The new covenant with the new society of the faithful was to be marked by a power to succeed unlike anything in the past. Christ was to be present in every believer, enabling him to fulfill the requirements of righteousness.

The command here is that they go and make disciples, as He had made of them. All the foregoing was just a beginning, so any thought that things were coming to an end would be wrongheaded. His death did not signal a winding down, but a winding up.

Notice that He does not asking them to go and merely preach the good news. He asks them to do something intensely personal to their hearers – to make disciples. This meant that they must invest the time not only to preach but to teach, instruct and guide all men to the same Way in which they now lived. In every real sense, this was the formation of a new society, whereby one is apprised and trained in its manner and customs.

"baptizing them . ."

Whatever one's view about the efficacy of baptism to salvation, there is no doubt that it was a command of the Lord. All believers must undergo its operation on them in relation to their saving faith. Nor can groups that minimize the efficacious nature of the ordinance take too casual a view of it. For here we see Jesus commanding it in close proximity to the discipling process; as they are discipled they are to be baptized.

We see later in I Peter that baptism conveys a public message of conversion from the carnal life to the spiritual. It is a visible declaration that one's life has been transformed and it sets before the public an expectation that the believer will show evidences henceforth – "baptism doth also now save us (not the putting away of the filth of the flesh, but the answer of a good conscience toward God,) (3:21). The conscience toward God is the commitment to live up to the vow given, which will be tested by one's actions in public within both the secular and church communities.

". . of all the nations"

We further learn that this mission is not to the Jews alone, as if to fulfill the limited prophecies respecting the chosen people of God. But the whole of the Gentile world around them was included in the call. Some might offer that this is a strictly NT invention and contrary to the covenants with Israel. Yet as we read Isaiah 9:2, there was an exhortation to Judaism to preach to the Gentiles – "The people that walked in darkness have seen a great light: they that dwell in the land of the shadow of death, upon them hath the light shined."

This was spoken in relation to those who dwell in Naphtali and Galilee, which were notably Gentile areas. The prophecy was to the Jews, but would have its fulfillment in Jesus, who walked chiefly in these areas, doing at long last what Israel had neglected.

For some, this is the "pushy" aspect to Christianity that many shrink back from. There are some who believe that Christians have no business butting into other people's way of life, or worse their religions. We are often irritated when Jehovah's Witnesses or Mormons come to our door to convince us we are in the wrong faith and must profess theirs to be truly saved.

But truth in its essence justifies its propagation and those judgments that identify falsehood from truth. To be caught on the wrong side and to not have been warned is at the very least irresponsible.

An anecdote will serve to bring this concept home. A man and his family were travelling on a mountain road in a hard rain. They could barely see ahead of them with wipers smacking at full tilt. Ahead of them they see a figure in a rain suit waving frantically. They ponder whether it is a ruse concealing some evil mischief or a real warning. They mused about the subtle traps clever men can perpetrate to accomplish their evil ends. As they approached, not slowing much, the man became more erratic in his movements, confirming in every gesture their worse fears. As they passed him, he had the most horrified look, his shouts being drowned out by the incessant drumming of the rain on the roof. Finally, they think it prudent to stop and see, being ready at the first sign of trouble to speed away. The man, out of breath, exclaims, "I'm so glad you stopped. The bridge is out ahead, and you would have gone right into the river."

This is the mission of the righteous – to warn others of the impending fate awaiting them. It will be seen as brazen, crazy, fanatical, and self-righteous to assume everyone else is on the wrong path. But if the bridge is truly out ahead, the risk to reputation is worth the bother.

"teaching them to observe all . ."

It becomes clear that the teaching of our Lord was not just information for the curious, but meant to be a way of life, a guidebook for righteous living. It was paramount that they pass along this teaching intact to others, it was not to be the private reserve of the disciples alone.

The history of Christianity and the advance of the Church into the modern age (and our very salvation within it) is the direct, linear result of their obedience to these commands and their faithfulness in preserving that teaching for all generations. By linear is meant that each redeemed soul that lives today is directly related to another soul who shared with them the gospel, who in turn was affected by yet a prior soul doing the same; all the way back in a linear, spiritual genealogy of faith; each man and woman touching the next life forward.

We can therefore understand the great emphasis historically as to what the most right and complete version of Christ's teaching was, hence the rise of denominations, each with a proclamation and proofs that their version is the most faithful.

In the midst of this morass one can easily become conflicted and confused, since it is a patent fact that not all denominations teach the same things. How then does one fulfill the command to teach all that Jesus taught, seeing that one is committed to be part of some body of believers to be a member of the church at all, and this entails exposure to sectarian beliefs.

The command of Jesus was not to find the denomination with the right faith and teach likewise, but to teach His words, the assumption being "as recorded." Which means that the source of that teaching is not a denomination but the New Testament record. The rightness of teaching is not in the evaluation of the virtues of a denomination, but in how close they represent the NT record. That record is the test against which all professions of faith are to be measured. It scrutinizes, cautions and validates human expressions of that teaching. Therefore, knowledge of that Word independent of affiliations is implied. Church history, however, took a notably different course.

The historical extension of the church of the apostles (the Roman Catholic Church) entertained considerable doubt that the independent believer had the intellectual and spiritual capacity to understand God's Word aright. This is understandable from a purely practical point of view. (Look at the disciples and how often they misread Jesus and had to be corrected.) This inevitably led to the establishment of the teaching authority of the Church – the magisterium – by which the witness of the apostles and the interpretation of Scripture was stringently guided; and as events would have it, the rise of a doctrine on how to deal with heretical beliefs and interpretations. It explains why Catholicism developed the notion of the One True Church, by virtue of holding and preserving the sacred Tradition of the apostles and all opinions Scriptural.

But the test of this process was again and always Scripture itself. The means of preservation cannot evolve so as to supplant or compete with the source by which it is authenticated. This is simply because the Word is eternal, righteous and good, and men are not so endowed with the same inerrant reliability. It is often seen as a Catch-22 – the Scripture is pure and holy, but to understand the Word it must come through human interpretation. Thus, to speak of the Word as independently understood apart from human understanding is in some sense to speak nonsense.

What is often forgotten (or neglected) is that the understanding is not purely human. We are promised that the Holy Spirit will guide us to all knowledge of His words (John 14:26.) This means that we are to be aided in a way that offsets the limitations of human understanding. Why then not unity? Why the numerous denominations?

To one extent or the other, the lack of unity betrays some measure of inability in discerning the understanding of the Holy Spirit. There will be some measure of human import that sets a people apart from the understanding of others. The existence of this condition, seemingly unchecked by Christ as Lord of His Church, does not nullify the precept that we are all to be one in our understanding. The precept is still a valid exhortation that we must strive to fulfill. But it is His grace toward us that He is patient and longsuffering in our weaknesses and failings. It is also a testimony that enough of His work among us is being accomplished to preclude summary judgment that might correct our errors.

The Church is a dynamism, a living work in progress, primarily because people are not programmable machines, but are independent souls, whose independent wills must be permitted in the act of supreme love toward them. So the precept and exhortation stand sacrosanct – we are to strive for unity in faith and teaching - but there is immeasurable grace in the meantime.

For every modern believer, there is here an implicit obligation to take unto oneself the tools and skills for understanding God's Word as a cognition between the believer and God alone. Thanks be to God that we live in an age where such tools are readily and reasonably available. We not only have the means to translate and derive meaning by proven interpretive processes, but we have a rich legacy in our forebearers, those who have done this very thing in times prior to ours, and serve as guides in helping us do the same.

In the early periods of the Church, there was an understandable concern about independent interpretation among the laity and for that reason it jealously restricted lay access directly to the Scriptures. For centuries the average layperson was wholly unequal to the task, and in the hands of an ignorant populace, error was not inevitable but certain. But in modern times, methods, processes and tools are now available to those with the desire for independent study. And what discerns between good study and that poorly or lazily done is once again the independence of the NT writings, to which all scrutiny and critique can be referred.

20 ". . and lo, I am with you always, even to the end of the age."

In the film series, *Lord of the Rings* (New Line Cinema, 2001-2003) the character Gandalf explains near the end of the story that the time of elves and dwarfs is ending and the age of man is dawning. This is a theme lifted directly from Scripture, especially considering that the author (Tolkien) based his thematic conceptions on the belief that heroic tales were vestiges of biblical themes. In Jesus, we have a clear declaration that the age of secular man will come to a close and the age of the Kingdom will supplant it. It is as old as the Bible and expressed in books like Daniel and the Revelation.

So, this idea is not foreign to the disciples, who knew very well this expectation before meeting Jesus – they asked Him "will you at this time establish the Kingdom of old?" (Acts 1:6.)

The comfort is that in leaving them, He is promising to yet be with them and that presence will last until the next age commences. It is to assure them that at no time will He have abandoned them for seemingly weightier matters. Since the end of the age will usher in the Kingdom and their physical presence with Him eternally, this promise for the interim (considering its extent) is the same as saying "always."

Mark 16:15-18, Luke 24:45-53, Acts 1:6-26, Mark 16:20, John 20:30-31, 21:25

[16 "He who has believed and has been baptized shall be saved; but he who has disbelieved shall be condemned. 17 "These signs will accompany those who have believed: in My name they will cast out demons, they will speak with new tongues; 18 they will pick up serpents, and if they drink any deadly poison, it will not hurt them; they will lay hands on the sick, and they will recover." (Mark 16:15-18.)]

45 Then He opened their minds to understand the Scriptures, 46 and He said to them, "Thus it is written, that the Christ would suffer and rise again from the dead the third day, 47 and that repentance for forgiveness of sins would be proclaimed in His name to all the nations, beginning from Jerusalem. 48 "You are witnesses of these things. 49 "And behold, I am sending forth the promise of My Father upon you; but you are to stay in the city until you are clothed with power from on high." 50 And He led them out as far as Bethany, (Luke 24:45-50.)

6 So when they had come together, they were asking Him, saying, "Lord, is it at this time You are restoring the kingdom to Israel?" 7 He said to them, "It is not for you to know times or epochs which the Father has fixed by His own authority; 8 but you will receive power when the Holy Spirit has come upon you; and you shall be My witnesses both in Jerusalem, and in all Judea and Samaria, and even to the remotest part of the earth." 9 And after He had said these things, He was lifted up while they were looking on, and a cloud received Him out of their sight. 10 And as they were gazing intently into the sky while He was going, behold, two men in white clothing stood beside them. 11 They also said, "Men of Galilee, why do you stand looking into the sky? This Jesus, who has been taken up from you into heaven, will come in just the same way as you have watched Him go into heaven." . . 52 And they, . . returned to Jerusalem with great joy, 53 and were continually in the temple praising God.
(Acts 1:6-11, Luke 24:52-53.)

13 When they had entered the city, they went up to the upper room where they were staying; that is, Peter and John and James and Andrew, Philip and Thomas, Bartholomew and Matthew, James the son of Alphaeus, and Simon the Zealot, and Judas the son of James. 14 These all with one mind were continually devoting themselves to prayer, along with the women, and Mary the mother of Jesus, and with His brothers.

15 At this time Peter stood up in the midst of the brethren (a gathering of about one hundred and twenty persons was there together), and said, 16 "Brethren, the Scripture had to be fulfilled, which the Holy Spirit foretold by the mouth of David concerning Judas, who became a guide to those who arrested Jesus. 17 "For he was counted among us and received his share in this ministry." 18 (Now this man acquired a field with the price of his wickedness, and falling headlong, he burst open in the middle and all his intestines gushed out. 19 And it became known to all who were living in Jerusalem; so that in their own language that field was called Hakeldama, that is, Field of Blood.) 20 "For it is written in the book of Psalms, `LET HIS HOMESTEAD BE MADE DESOLATE, AND LET NO ONE DWELL IN IT'; and, `LET ANOTHER MAN TAKE HIS OFFICE.'

21 "Therefore it is necessary that of the men who have accompanied us all the time that the Lord Jesus went in and out among us-- 22 beginning with the baptism of John until the day that He was taken up from us--one of these must become a witness with us of His resurrection." 23 So they put forward two men, Joseph called Barsabbas (who was also called Justus), and Matthias. 24 And they prayed and said, "You, Lord, who know the hearts of all men, show which one of these two You have chosen 25 to occupy this ministry and apostleship from which Judas turned aside to go to his own place." 26 And they drew lots for them, and the lot fell to Matthias; and he was added to the eleven apostles. (Acts 1:13-26.)

[20 And they went out and preached everywhere, while the Lord worked with them, and confirmed the word by the signs that followed. (Mark 16:20.)]

30 Therefore many other signs Jesus also performed in the presence of the disciples, which are not written in this book; 31 but these have been written so that you may believe that Jesus is the Christ, the Son of God; and that believing you may have life in His name. . . 25 And there are also many other things which Jesus did, which if they were written in detail, I suppose that even the world itself would not contain the books that would be written. (John 20:30-31, 21:25.)

Commentary

16 "He who has believed and has been baptized shall be saved; but he who has disbelieved shall be condemned.

Some controversy continues over whether Mark 16:9-20 was part of Mark's original gospel, or was added later. Most of what is contained in this section can be found elsewhere as corroborative endorsement for the ideas, but some statements are unique to this section and because of their extraordinary nature have spawned issues between denominations.

The primary reason for not including them in some of the latest editions of the Bible (e.g. NIV) is their absence from such bastions of reliability as the uncial codices Sinaiticus and Vaticanus. These are two of the oldest complete NT manuscripts and their use as standards for assessing the original text of the NT has been critical. Notable scholars who question the authenticity of the verses are Hort (Westcott and Hort) and Bruce Metzger (foremost authority on the NT text.) Scholars who accept the verses as genuine include such men as R.C.H. Lenski, respected for his NT commentary.

One controversial issue introduced by accepting these verses is that of the efficacy of baptism to salvation. Mark 16 is the only place in the NT that provides a functional connection between baptism and the effecting of salvation – "and has been baptized shall be saved." Yet, of contrasting interest is the corollary which leaves out baptism, the lack of which is not included in what condemns.

In essence, the church which wishes to make baptism mandatory before salvation can be made effective will rely on Mark 16 being genuine. Those churches that consider it a command of the Lord but not a sine qua non to salvation stress the question of authenticity for the verses.

Perhaps the safest approach is to adopt the following explanation, "It is not the lack of baptism that condemns but the despising of baptism that condemns," [87] meaning that the reasonable time span between believing faith and the event of being baptized does not undermine the effect of salvation, but neglecting it, avoiding it or disbelieving its importance betrays a defect in faith that might be judged as affecting salvation.

18 they will pick up serpents, and if they drink any deadly poison, it will not hurt them; they will lay hands on the sick, and they will recover."

While we find a living example of this with Paul at Malta (Acts 28:3-5), in which he shook off a viper that had bitten him with no ill effect, many question that this would be a general admonition - "they will pick up serpents" – since we are forewarned not to test the Lord by our actions. This moves some to question the authenticity of such verses because they seem out of keeping with the tenor of Scripture and add an element of the magic show to the humility characterizing Christian ministry.

It is therefore not an admonition to arrange for show, but that such things would occur on occasion and serve as testimony to the glory of God.

---

[87] Baptism Saves, <u>Doctrinal Issues</u> Copyright 2003 - 2007 The Lutheran Church--Missouri Synod.

45 Then He opened their minds to understand the Scriptures,

This is a sovereign act that begins the transformation from disciples still in training to that mature body of apostles we find in the early church age. As we see clearly, their independent understanding had to be enabled by Jesus. It was not something their secular minds would eventually grasp. This is echoed in Paul's great epistle to the Corinthians – *" But a natural man does not accept the things of the Spirit of God, for they are foolishness to him; and he cannot understand them, because they are spiritually appraised."* (I Cor 2:14.)

The same is true in the modern church age. We are wholly dependent on a relationship in God through the Holy Spirit, whose purpose is to enlighten us as well as bring to remembrance the things spoken in His Word. This is chiefly why discussions with unbelievers or people of other religious beliefs (even if they claim they seek truth from the Bible) can be largely unfruitful if attempted purely in the flesh. There must be an enabling for truth to be seen as truth. This is not to say that human common sense is wholly unprofitable (the Bible is written in plain sense language), but without the insight of the Holy Spirit, one can take things read to distant harbors unintended and make applications quite different from what God had in mind.

46 .. "Thus it is written, that the Christ would suffer and rise again from the dead the third day, 47 and that repentance for forgiveness of sins would be proclaimed .. "

Directly following this "opening of their minds," Jesus reiterates the most essential things, meant to complete their knowledge in an over-arching explanation of all the has happened. In their unenlightened minds, they are still unclear how the transition from old to new is to be understood. They are obviously still reeling from the sheer events of Calvary and why He had to die.

In a 21st century world we now understand much of the theology behind God's plan of salvation. But for the apostles, they had no legacy of explanations and understandings to which they had become accustomed. All was new and smacking headlong against the backdrop of so long a tradition of the old faith.

Of first mention is that the suffering of Christ had been "written" of old. This does not mean that all the OT verses demonstrating this suddenly came to their minds. But it does mean that much of what Jesus had shared from OT quotations now jelled as a collective affirmation. Their spirits agreed inwardly with this acknowledgment, the OT picture began to make more sense in lieu of being discrete verses from times past.

Another key acknowledgment was that a truly effective repentance from sins could now be made and was now being proclaimed. That repentance was made available in the power of the Holy Spirit " specifically in His Name," meaning in relation to His work on the Cross. Before this point, continual, repeated sacrifices implied ineffective repentance, or a repentance without the power to change one's inner disposition and ability to resist future offenses. The new covenant and new dispensation was making that power available to the believer.

47 ".. beginning from Jerusalem."

The proclamation is to go further, in keeping with His commission that they go to the uttermost parts of the world. The key in emphasizing this is that they are not to ignore Jerusalem for the sake of the rest of the world mission, but rather their mission begins in Jerusalem. This we see in the pattern unfolded in the Acts.

48 "You are witnesses of these things.

One of the most important aspects of the new faith is that it was not to be purely theoretical and mystical, but patently factual, capable of being witnessed and seen. The Resurrection was not a hopeful expectation. They were not left to wonder or hope that Jesus had risen. They saw with their own eyes.

For modern Christians to share a faith worth believing, there has to have been a discernable event related to what is being proclaimed. Christian faith has to have been actually experienced and the effects perceived before one can witness, else one is dealing with an abstract philosophy, nothing more. The power of the testimony of the Gospel message is that it was born to us through eyewitnesses who actually saw the events occur in fact.

49 "And behold, I am sending forth the promise of My Father upon you; but you are to stay in the city until you are clothed with power from on high."

The sending cannot be purely pragmatic and humanly practical. It requires empowering, more than the insight now given them, to understand the Scriptures, they need functional power to conjoin Heaven with earthly affairs, that they bring down strongholds and break the hold of evil powers to free souls to be saved. That they must wait for power implies that they do not have the capacity for these things in their own strength. This is a powerful element in the concept of "Grace."

This aspect of ministry is often lost in modern times. So much of the church is operated very much like all other human organizations, with boards of trustees, budgets that must be underwritten with pledges, and initiatives very much constrained by the same things that constrain secular business – the limitations and capacities of the church in terms of finances and people.

But the pattern in the NT is that an enterprise of God is accompanied by the power and resources to accomplish it, but the worker must wait for that provision. So often, over-zealous workers step out ahead of the Lord and find that they are not ready, nor are the provisions adequate, and the result is doubt and skepticism that God still works as He did in days of old. A mentality develops that it's up to us or not at all. Hence, the church is less miraculous and more mundane and humanistic.

Transition to Jerusalem, Bethany and Mt. of Olives

50 And He led them out as far as Bethany,

A subtle transition of scene and place. The area of the Mt of Olives will be the scene of the Ascension. While the words do not convey the real sense of time, it is clear that after the former dialog, Jesus led the group from the Galilee all the way down to Bethany.

6 So when they had come together, they were asking Him, saying, "Lord, is it at this time You are restoring the kingdom to Israel?"

This information from Acts helps us to complete the remaining dialogues with the disciples before closing the gospel accounts. *When they had come together* is the natural expectation from having left Galilee and arriving near Bethany.

We see here the still somewhat confused picture in their minds as to how these events and the coming Kingdom are to work in concert. With a resurrected Messiah, the natural expectation is that the King is now ready to bring in that Kingdom, deliver Israel from her oppressors and establish the Kingdom that would rule all kingdoms, as pictured in Daniel (2:44, 7:27.)

7. . "It is not for you to know times or epochs which the Father has fixed by His own authority;

Of first importance is that this answer essentially translates to no. To say that the time is not to be known precludes that it is on the very heels of occurring. This of course agrees with His statement to Pilate, "My Kingdom is not of this world" (John 18:36.) By this juncture in His ministry, the Kingdom is not to be made physically manifest because the citizens invited to it have refused its citizenship and its King.

This will be a point of theological distinction that will occupy the centuries yet to unfold – in what sense did the Kingdom announced by John and Jesus come and yet not come?

Answering this is the single verse from Luke in the analogy of the king who went away and left his affairs to his servants with the words, "Occupy until I come" (Luke 19:13.) Since this is an analogy to Christ and His first and second advents, the church age is seen as an occupation in the spirit of the Kingdom until He comes again to establish it in the earth – *"Thy kingdom come, Thy will be done on earth as it is in Heaven."*

The implication in telling them it is not for them to know the times and epochs is to further the notion that they are to concentrate on the other aspects of the Gospel, for which a concern about end times will be considered misplaced. The history of the Church is a testimony to how much needed to be done.

8 but you will receive power when the Holy Spirit has come upon you; and you shall be My witnesses both in Jerusalem, and in all Judea and Samaria, and even to the remotest part of the earth."

We have here the promise of an operation of the Holy Spirit, described very much like that in the OT, of coming upon them. We find this later described by Paul and others as being filled with the Holy Spirit, which many associate with the receiving of the Spirit at salvation. Yet we have the earlier account of John wherein Jesus breathed on them and commanded that they receive the Holy Spirit.

The better explanation is that the indwelling took place as an abiding presence at John 20:21, but when the Spirit then purposes to work a great thing in them, He fills them in a manner which would have appeared very similar in power and behavior to those upon whom the Spirit descended in OT times. The western analytical mind tends to make hay out of minute distinctions ('upon' vs. 'filled') but for the ancient eastern mind, these could be variable descriptions of the same experience. What precludes us from going the other direction and inferring that OT saints were therefore indwelt is the express statements that this was a new thing – ""I will put my law in their minds and write it on their hearts." (Jer 31:33.)

And we learn what the power and anointing will be for – *and you shall be My witnesses both in Jerusalem, and in all Judea and Samaria, and even to the remotest part of the earth."*

The pattern is the city of Jerusalem, then the land of Judea, then Samaria, then the Gentile world. This is not meant exhaustively, but in order of general ministry emphasis. Certainly all of Judea and Samaria were not witnessed to when Paul struck out for his Gentile ministry. It is to direct that the ministry must be set up in this order, i.e. they are not to sail to distant parts of the world with things at home left neglected.

We see this reiterated in Paul's frequent phrase – "to the Jew first then also to the Greek." This is to emphasize that Judaism is to remain key to the advancement of the Gospel. It is their story, whether they recognize its fulfillment or not. God's covenant with His people obligated Him to preach first to them before reaching out to the world. We see this almost rudely said in Jesus' treatment of the Canaanite woman and the analogy of the dog getting the crumbs from the master's table (Matt 15:22.) There was a clear preference for Israel in the witness of the coming light, though this runs against our notions of impartiality with God.

THE ASCENSION

9 And after He had said these things, He was lifted up while they were looking on, and a cloud received Him out of their sight.

They were actually witness to Him being lifted up, it happened as they watched. We have to imagine them seeing at one moment His body firmly on the ground, then beginning to rise purely by himself with no mechanism or angels pulling His flesh and bone aloft.

For people in the modern age of superheroes and fantasy cinema, this is often perceived as the supreme demonstration of power over nature and energy. It is the thing we have all often experienced in dreams (usually aided by our extremities as if swimming). Yet to lift and move while being still, by mere thought and will, is to command unimaginable power.

Faith in who He was cannot have lacked anything after witnessing this scene. It does not say that He dematerialized, as we envision ghosts in films, but that He ascended intact and visible until taken into a cloud and out of their sight. The reason for this distinction is the later statement that He sits at the right hand of the Father and that the glorified body is deliberately intended to inherit eternal life, not merely a disembodied spirit, His being the first of that resurrection (Rev 1:5.)

10 .. while He was going, behold, two men in white clothing stood beside them.

Now, to further authenticate that Heaven is participating in His ascension, two messengers appear and by their message indicate that they are in full knowledge of what is taking place. There message is almost detached from the reality that constrains humanity, since they wonder why the men are gazing yet into the sky. For those in Heaven it is part and parcel with what occurs there all the time, but we wonder how they could expect mere men to take it as equally normal?

However, when we take the complete message, we can see a way of understanding this – "Why are you gazing into the sky .. He will come again, just as you saw Him leave."

Their message addresses the sorrow that He is being taken finally and completely away. He is not leaving them destitute, nor will He never be seen by them again. He will return again and in the same manner as He left.

That message of comfort seems to have worked, as we see below ..

52 And they, . . . returned to Jerusalem with great joy, 53 and were continually in the temple praising God.

For the authorities who thought they had finally rid themselves of the "Jesus" problem, their troubles are only beginning. They will find not one man working and teaching but twelve, and eventually hundreds more. It's as if the truth long suppressed has finally broken its bonds and is leaking from every nook and cranny. It cannot be stopped or suppressed. Every effort to do so frees more of it to the light.

They are beginning on the path that is to be the steady state of the Church – believers at large in the world filled with the Holy Spirit – to which we in these times are now their distant progeny. We are in precisely the same atmosphere as they were following the Ascension. We are at large in the world, but not alone. We have the marvelous gift of the indwelling Spirit.

13 When they had entered the city, they went up to the upper room where they were staying; .. 14 These all with one mind were continually devoting themselves to prayer, along with the women, and Mary the mother of Jesus, and with His brothers.

In human projects, the first order of business is to develop a plan, acquire resources and begin organizing work. In heavenly projects, the first order of business is prayer. What occasions the need is that contrary to human projects where a breakdown of objectives are known, the disciples know that to step out before the Holy Spirit has made opportunity would be foolish or even deleterious. They have the great commission, but they must do as Jesus did – to walk where and how they see the Father working.

It is surprising in both churches and individual Christian lives how seldom this is tried. We are an enterprising people and all around us seems to be the horsepower to get things accomplished if we only know the goal. So men do not bathe their plans in prayer, but step out thinking that given the general mandate, whatever their hands fall upon must be His will in it all. We are not prone to patient waiting, nor to discerning instruction from spiritual sources. It is so much easier to dive right in, and because there is a certain measure of success, we come away thinking we have discovered the formula.

But very much like the young fool who is too much in love to seek God about marriage, we get engaged and married to many things in life, only to later see the folly of our decisions.

Our society is very used to the efficiency model for business and action. When we need an answer, we set a deadline on a schedule then we go down to an office where another manager's staff works to meet that timeline and we get our answer. But God is not just another manager down the hall who will be helping us with "our" project.

Prayer is not getting God to do what we want or need, but Him getting us to agree with His plans and His way. We conform to Him, not vice versa. That takes patience and time, time enough to discern and know. And if one doesn't know, the answer isn't 'go anyway,' but wait and keep praying. So much of prayer is getting ourselves out of the way that we may see His way in things.

. . and with His brothers.

In the statement "his brothers" we are to understand that James and Jude are among His followers but it's unclear if this is because their mother is present or because they are becoming His followers. That they become His followers is beyond doubt (as the epistles of James and Jude bear witness.)

We find here the full eleven in attendance among a company of others numbering considerably large. The replacement for Judas will be chosen shortly.

15 At this time Peter stood up in the midst of the brethren

The result of their prayers has revealed the divinely appointed need to replace Judas to make them the Twelve once again. Peter is in the lead and takes the initiative to explain the purposes God foretold concerning Judas and the need to fulfill what the Psalms also depict - that another must take his place (Ps 69:25, 109:8.)

Judas, amazingly, was not shunned, and we are further in wonder that he was chosen knowing his future deed – *"For he was counted among us and received his share in this ministry."*

Peter demonstrates respecting Judas what would be later voiced in Peter and Paul – "He was willing that none should perish" (2 Pet 3:9), "Many are called but few chosen." (Matt 22:14.) Judas had the same opportunity to do what was right as the others. His end was not pre-determined for him, merely the role to be played. But he alone made his choices to play it.

We are reminded of what Jesus taught earlier - *" The Son of man goeth as it is written of him: but woe unto that man by whom the Son of man is betrayed!"* and *" Woe unto the world because of offences! for it must needs be that offences come; but woe to that man by whom the offence cometh!"* ((Matt 26:24,18:7.)

18 (Now this man acquired a field with the price of his wickedness,

We have here another account of Judas' end which has been seen to contradict the earlier account of him hanging himself. First, we are not to conclude that Judas purchased the field himself ahead of time, but that the money he received (technically then his) was used to buy the place for his grave.

As explained earlier, the fall is not inconsistent with him hanging himself, since the fall was caused by his efforts to do just that, i.e. in both accounts he does hang himself. Acts recounts what took place next, whereas the gospels leave this out.

As to how a fall from a tree could cause so much damage, see more at Matthew 27:5.

that field was called Hakeldama, that is, Field of Blood

This is the Greek transliteration of the Aramaic *hegel dema*, which meant field of blood. Originally, the field was called the Potter's field due to its source of intensely red clay used by potters. The figure of Judas' blood being added to the red clay caused locals to change its name accordingly.

Peter now addresses the need to fill Judas' empty slot.

21 "Therefore it is necessary that of the men who have accompanied us . . . one of these must become a witness with us of His resurrection."

This informs us (as skipped in the gospels) that there were others accompanying the Twelve from the very beginning – *" all the time . . beginning with the baptism of John until the day that He was taken up from us"* As to why these were not mentioned we must defer to God's wisdom in superintending those accounts.

So we find two new names mentioned of that company - Joseph Barsabbas and Matthias. Barsabbas meant Son of the Sabbath, or son of rest, not to be confused with Barabbas, son of the Father. Some connect him with the Justus mentioned by Paul in Colossians 4:11 (Henry), but the name could easily be that of another man. Also, we have the Judas Barsabbas mentioned in Acts 15, but we are unable to make this identification firmly, since he would have to have had yet a third name other than Justus.

26 And they drew lots for them, and the lot fell to Matthias;

Some question the procedure of lots as being not of faith. It seems a rather arbitrary procedure, since it depended on mere chance. But we have biblical precedence in the use of lots or other devices (the Urim and Thummim) for determining very specific answers.

There is no doubt these men have been recently blessed with the gift of the Holy Spirit, so the expectation is that they would be freshly imbued with the spiritual discernment as to which man was indicated. But having been given the gift does not imply seasoned experience in discerning His influence, especially something so specific as one man's name over another.

Nor is there any hindrance in God working in the drawing of the lots to effect His will. This worked in times past. The Urim and Thummim were stones with effectively Yes and No on opposing sides. They were cast and the answer read out, equally subject to the chance of the throw. But if God was in the throw, His will could be effected as easily as writing it in the sky.

As for spiritual insight routinely being this specific, we find this rarely occurring even in the Bible. God spoke directly to Abraham and showed him the specific mountain on which the sacrifice was to be made. But not every ancient father had such direct and specific revelation. The pattern was often more general – a sort of "unfolding" in which God made manifest His will in steps and the progress of events.

We find this today in Christian experience. We get a premonition, and in following it, we discover more that either confirms or dissuades us. Often the conviction is in the form of extreme excitement at the incredible rightness of the opportunity before us. Other times it is in the intense feeling of disappointing God in failing to take up an opportunity. But seldom and rarely do Christians hear the conviction of the Holy Spirit telling them, "Go to Sixth Avenue and turn right." For such reasons, men in ancient times turned to divinely honored means like the lot.

And we have Peter's prayer, setting up the conditions that God would use this very means to reveal His choice – ""You, Lord, who know the hearts of all men, show which one of these two You have chosen." We further see that God honored it in the choice that was made.

In later ministry, Paul would ask that the elders lay hands on men chosen by God. It is understood that more discernment in the Spirit evolved over time precluding the need for devices. Men were able to see the hand of God on men in their midst and upon these they were directed to lay hands and raise to ministry. This was not a case of hearing a voice out of Heaven naming the man, but of the discerning the results of having lived with members of the assemblies and making spiritually guided observations.

In the modern church, we have gone back to a procedure comparable to the lot and other external devices. Seldom in a church is a man chosen to pastoral office among the congregation. Rather, churches often appeal to a convention or an organization who sends candidates, or in some cases simply appoints new men to the churches. It is a sign that cultivating our hearing of the Holy Spirit is a thing of the past, and we would rather let the decision be made by that means common to secular appointments. We invite men who have never darkened the door of our church, who don't really know us from Adam. We conduct interviews, listen to one or two sermons, and vote.

In contrast, Paul asked that the elders look among themselves to see whom God was raising up to ministry. Despite the use of the lot, Peter and the others were doing this very thing with men they had known in their company for a good while. It was not a case of not having a clue, but of not knowing which specific man of two excellent disciples was divinely intended. (I Tim 5:22.) Paul's list of qualifications for elders and deacons (I Tim 3:2, 2 Tim 2:24) is a template which implies that the discernment is to be applied to men "in their midst" about whom they have intimate knowledge. Hardly possible with a candidate sent from across the country.

20 And they went out and preached everywhere, while the Lord worked with them, and confirmed the word by the signs that followed.

Again, some question the inclusion of this verse in the original of Mark, but its testimony agrees with the rest of the NT as to not discount it as promoting something foreign or unsubstantiated. Certainly the test of authenticating work in Christ is in the results. And these were readily and regularly confirmed in the work of disciples.

As to signs, there was in their work always something that could not be explained except to appeal to the miraculous presence of God. This was Jesus' pattern also, such that men were heard to say, "No man works like this. God is surely with Him."

With the election of Matthias, the signal has been given to begin ministry, and we next see them going out and "preaching everywhere." Their ministry and work have begun in full swing.

We move finally to John's Postamble.

John's Postamble

30 Therefore many other signs Jesus also performed in the presence of the disciples, which are not written in this book;

Against the charge that the Bible denies us access to all things said and done, and therefore is not a reliable historical account, John's makes a clear admission that this was intended. Enough has been written that we may believe. We have been taken over the hurdle of faith and being now on the path, the unfolding of knowledge will take the rest of our lives.

All that is in Scripture is true and trustworthy for our instruction. But the living of our Christian lives will add chapters which could not be written in books. We are not to make the mistake of canonizing these experiences as Scripture, but we will not be able to say that the Lord has not added to our instruction in the things we live, suffer and accomplish.

As pertaining to John's statement, there are in fact many things Jesus did say that are left out. But all the essentials are there for us to partake with confidence. The object is that we can successfully come to profess amidst all the other allegiances being advertised that "Jesus is the Christ, the Son of God." And that by believing we may have life in His name and no other. The answer to the question, "If a man die, shall he live on?" has at last been answered.

even the world itself would not contain the books that would be written.

The lack of books and the feasibility in writing them is met by that unending supply of living servants in every age, who have ever told the "old, old story." For each generation places new lives into the world at large as new books, guided and stayed by that eternal, written Word that has remained constant and present, surviving all the ages and those to come. It has survived to be ever present because the Word is a Person who is living, the Person of Jesus Christ, eternal Savior, Lord of Heaven and earth.

Michael Hagerty holds a Bachelor of Arts in Philosophy from the University of California, Irvine, and is an alumnus of Talbot Seminary, La Mirada, California (1975-1978)

The Chronological Gospel Commentary – The Four Gospels

INDEX OF TOPICS AND SCRIPTURE

(Note: some Scripture verses indexed here may have page references to the text in another Gospel used to represent verses of parallel usage, e.g. Matthew 20:24-28 will point to a page for Mark 10:41 because Mark represents the parallel content.)

A

Abomination of Desolation, 564
Acts 1:6-26, 737
Agrippa, and Herod, 44
Andrew, and Peter, 75
Andrew, as disciple, 112
Angels, at tomb of Jesus, 702, 709
Anna, Jesus birth, 43
Annunciation to Mary, 19
Annunciation, to Joseph, 31
Annunciation, to shepherds, 36
Antipas, son of Herod, 52
Antipater, father of Herod, 44
Apostles, calling of the twelve, 134
Archelaus, son of Herod, 52
Ascension, 732, 737
Augustus Caesar, the census, 33

B

Baptism with the Holy Spirit, 61
Barabbas, released instead of Jesus, 676
Beatitudes, 138
Bethlehem, Joseph's return to, 35
Blasphemy of the Holy Spirit, 200
Born again, Jesus' teaching, 86
Bridegroom, Jesus' teaching, 94, 127

C

Caiaphas, as high priest, 482
Caiaphas, high priest, 582
Calendar, origin of Christian dating, 34
Calendar, use of Roman years, 55
Calvary, location of, 687
Cana, healing at, 106
Cana, wedding at, 80
Canaanite woman of Tyre and Sidon, 329
Capernaum, Jesus teaching in, 116
Census, problems with, 34
Centurion, his slave healed, 184
Circumcision, of Jesus, 39
Cleansing the Temple, 83
Corban, teaching on, 323
Crucifixion, abuse from passers by, 692
Crucifixion, burial of Jesus, 702

Index Help - *some Scripture verses indexed here may have page references to another Gospel used to represent identical verses with parallel usage, e.g. Matthew 20:24-28 will point to a page for Mark 10:41 because Mark represents the parallel content.*

Crucifixion, centurion confesses Jesus is son of God, 693
Crucifixion, day of preparation, 702
Crucifixion, did not break Jesus' legs, 702
Crucifixion, earthquake at, 702
Crucifixion, I thirst, 693
Crucifixion, save yourself and us, 692
Crucifixion, temple curtain torn, 693
Crucifixion, tomb secured unto the third day, 702
Crucifixion, two thieves, 685
Crucifixion, women at the cross, 692
Crucifixion, women at the tomb, 702
Crucifixion, you shall be with me in Paradise, 692
Crucifixion,.of Jesus, 685

D

David and the Showbread, working on the Sabbath, 130
Day of preparation, meaning, 702
Demon possession, 196
Demons, authority over, 283
Demons, casting out at Capernaum, 117
Demons, satanic oppression, 232
Demons,. 'Legion – for we are many', 254
Disciple, meaning of, 104
Disciples
 argue over who will greatest, 603
 baptized with Jesus baptism, 498
 could not cast out demons, 352
 go fishing after Resurrection, 721
 here are two swords, 616
 Lord is it I?, 598
 misuse of power, 421
 named, 279
 not walking with the twelve, 91
 power to bind and loose, 365
 power to forgive sins, 721
 receive the Holy Spirit before Pentecost, 721
 replacement of Judas, 737
 send forth to ministry, 279
 shake the dust off your feet, 279
 shall see the kingdom coming with power, 343
 some offended and depart, 319
 to take no money, 279
 who will be the greatest, 358
 will you at this time restore, 737
 worker not following the disciples, 365
Discipleship, deny yourself and follow me, 343
Divorce, and Deuteronomy, 157
Divorce, Jesus' teaching, 154

E

Egypt, flight to, 48
Elizabeth and Mary, 23
Emmaus, Jesus appears, 715
Eternal life, Jesus' teaching, 90

Index Help - *some Scripture verses indexed here may have page references to another Gospel used to represent identical verses with parallel usage, e.g. Matthew 20:24-28 will point to a page for Mark 10:41 because Mark represents the parallel content.*

F

Faith, as a mustard seed, 352
Faith, help my unbelief, 352
Fasting on the Sabbath, 126
Feast of Unleavened Bread, 52

G

Gabbatha, 677
Galilean ministry, 96, 112, 113, 116, 120, 134
Genealogies, of Jesus, 13
Golgotha, 685
Gospel, unpopular aspects of, 269
Gospel, will be devisive, 289
Great Commision, 732
Great Commission, 737
Greeks, 'we would see Jesus', 520

H

Healing, Bartemaeus, 503
Herod
  death of, 50
  eclipse at death, 52
  heirs to kingdom, 52
  in relation to Rome, 44
  king of Judaea, 16
  king of the Jews, 44
  slaughter of infants, 48
Temple of, 85
Herod Antipas, and John the Baptist, 295
Herod Antipas, hears of Jesus work, 295
Herod Antipas, John the Baptist, 112
Herod Antipas, son of Herod, 52
Herod, became friends with Pilate, 676
Herod, desires to see Jesus, 676
Herod, I find no fault in him, 676
Herod, punishes Jesus, 676
Herod, warning from wife, 676
Herodians, 132, 532
Herodias, 112
Holy Spirit, a help in public defense, 219
Holy Spirit, given to disciples before Pentecost, 721

I

Isaiah Chapter 42:1-25, 132
Isaiah, scroll read by Jesus, 109
Isaiah, picture of Messiah (Ch 42), 132
Israel, house if now left desolate, 551

J

James and John, mother requesting preference, 498
James, call of, 112
Jerusalem, surrounded by armies, 557

Index Help - *some Scripture verses indexed here may have page references to another Gospel used to represent identical verses with parallel usage, e.g. Matthew 20:24-28 will point to a page for Mark 10:41 because Mark represents the parallel content.*

Jesus
- about thirty years of age, 65
- Abraham rejoiced to see His day, 400
- abused of Pilates soldiers, 676
- accused of blasphemy, 662
- accused of sedition, 671
- and John's disciples, 73
- and the Father, 270, 400
- and the Kingdom of God, 114
- and the Law, 152
- and the paralytic, 120
- and the Pharisees, 126
- and the Sadducees, 539
- and the tax collectors, 458
- and Zaccheus, 503
- anointed by Mary at Bethany, 506
- anointing at the Pharisee's house, 192
- appears at Sea of Tiberius, 721
- appears to disciples after resurrection, 721
- appoints the seventy, 425
- are you the Christ?, 441
- arrest in the garden, 653
- asked about inheriting the kingdom, 490
- asked if he is the Christ, 662
- at Bethany, 435
- at Caesarea Philippi, 338
- at Capernaum, 116, 184
- at the feast of the Jews, 265
- at trial – he makes himself as son of God, 676
- authority in judgment, 270
- baptism by John, 63
- be not offended, 189
- before Abraham was I am, 400
- before Annas, 662
- before Caiaphas, 662
- before Pilate, 671
- before Pilate - crucify him, 676
- before the cock crows you will have denied me, 603
- before the Sanhedrin, 662
- behold the man, 676
- behold your son, behold your mother, 692
- birth in December, 36
- birth of, 29
- burial by Joseph and Nicodemus, 702
- calls himself the light, 588
- children praise Him with Hosannah, 520
- circumcision and dedication, 39
- cleanses the Temple, 83, 520
- commandments – (a listing), 616
- compared to John the Baptist, 270
- conflict with the Jews, 374
- conflict with the Pharisees, 274, 394, 441, 458, 524
- conflicts in accepting Jesus as the Christ, 380
- Cross and faith related, 271
- crown of thorns, 676
- curses the fig tree, 520
- dates for birth, 34

Index Help - *some Scripture verses indexed here may have page references to another Gospel used to represent identical verses with parallel usage, e.g. Matthew 20:24-28 will point to a page for Mark 10:41 because Mark represents the parallel content.*

Jesus *(cont.)*
  daughters of Jerusalem, 685
  eats with sinners, 124
  entering and leaving Jericho, 503
  equated with God, 265
  eternal life, 441
  evidences of Messiahship, 189
  exclusiveness of, 269
  false witnesses at his trial, 662
  Feast of Tabernacles, 374
  first interview with Pilate, 671
  flight to Egypt, 48
  foretells his crucifixion, 582
  foretells His death, 498
  foretells his departure, 603
  foretells Peter's manner of death, 722
  forewarns of his death, 352
  forgiveness of Peter, 721
  forgives sins, 120
  garden of Gethsemane, 653
  Gerasene demoniac, 254
  get behind me Satan, 338
  go, make disciples, 732
  good shepherd, 416
  Great Commission, 737
  harvest is plentiful, 425
  having siblings, 280
  healing of the man with dropsy, 452
  healing on the Sabbath, 232, 265, 374, 452
  heals on the Sabbath, 129
  heals the centurion's slave, 184
  hints at betrayer, 598
  his ascension, 732, 737
  I am not of this world, 394
  I am the Resurrection and the life, 481
  I and the Father are one, 441
  I come not to judge but to save, 588
  identifies with the Father, 388
  in Bethsaida, 332
  in Galilee, 329
  in Nazareth, 106, 279
  in the home of the Pharisee, 209
  in the temple, 441
  in the Temple as a child, 52
  instituting communion, 603
  is crucified, 685
  Israel to be desolate, 446
  issues the great commission, 732
  last Passover, 506
  Last Supper, 603
  making of wine, 81
  meaning of His Name, 31
  meeting on the road to Emmaus, 715
  mocked and beaten by the guards, 662
  mocked by Herod's guards, 676
  more conflict with the Pharisees, 400
  my kingdom not of this world, 671

Index Help - *some Scripture verses indexed here may have page references to another Gospel used to represent identical verses with parallel usage, e.g. Matthew 20:24-28 will point to a page for Mark 10:41 because Mark represents the parallel content.*

Jesus *(cont.)*
  my sheep hear my voice, 441
  near Bethsaida, 300
  not welcome in his home town, 106
  officers of the priests affected by Jesus, 385
  Oh Jerusalem, 446
  on adultery, 490
  on Herod, 446
  on John the Baptist, 441
  on the baptism of John, 524
  on the Law of the Sabbath, 323
  Passion week, 513
  Passover week, 506
  Passovers of, 83
  paying taxes, 352
  Pharisees guilty of the blood of the righteous, 551
  Pharisees of their father the devil, 400
  polemic against the Pharisees, 551
  prayer in Gethsemane, 653
  preaching in the disciples' cities, 295
  prepares for last Passover meal, 588
  priestly prayer, 642
  priestly prayer, 647
  professed as the Son of God, 481
  promise of the Holy Spirit, 737
  promises the Holy Spirt, 616
  pronounces judgment on Jerusalem, 514
  raises Lazarus, 481
  recognized as Messiah, 503
  resurrection appearances, 715
  reveals the betrayer, 603
  save me from this hour, 524
  saw Satan fall from Heaven, 425
  scroll of Isaiah, 106
  second interview by Pilate, 676
  sent to Herod, 671
  sent to Pilate, 663
  Simeon at birth, 41
  some believers among the rulers, 588
  some Jews proclaim him the Christ, 385
  Son of Man coming in the clouds, 569
  statements at the tomb, 709
  stills the sea, 250
  storm at sea, 250
  struck by an officer of the priest, 662
  supported through charity, 196
  take this cup from me, 653
  teaching in the temple, 374
  teaching in the Temple, 520, 588
  teaching not as the scribes, 117
  temptation, 66
  testimony of his miracles, 380
  the hour has come, 520, 642
  thundering, 'an angel has spoken to him', 524
  to be numbered with transgressors, 616
  to go to Jerusalem, 421
  to Pilate – you have no authority over me, 676

Index Help - *some Scripture verses indexed here may have page references to another Gospel used to represent identical verses with parallel usage, e.g. Matthew 20:24-28 will point to a page for Mark 10:41 because Mark represents the parallel content.*

Jesus *(cont.)*
- to the Greeks with Philip, 520
- to the Pharisees, those who killed the prophets, 551
- today you shall be with me in Paradise, 692
- tomb secured unto the third day, 702
- Transfiguration, 348
- trial of, 662
- trial, the Pavement, 677
- triumphal entry, 513
- troubled in soul, 524
- twelve apostles, 134
- unbelievers have been blinded, hardened, 588
- washes disciples feet, 593
- wedding at Cana, 80
- weeps over Jerusalem, 514
- who do men say that I am?, 338
- who touched me?, 258
- who will sit at my righthand, 498
- why have you forsaken me, 693
- with the disciples in the garden, 653
- woe to his betrayer, 598
- woe to you Scribes and Pharisees, 544
- women associated with, 196
- words at the Ascension, 737
- you are gods, 441
- your house is left desolate, 551

John 1:1 and Jehovah's Witnesses, 9
John 1:1-13, 9
John 1:14-18, 13
John 1:19-34, 70
John 1:35-44, 73
John 1:45-51, 78
John 1:49, 10
John 2:1-12, 78
John 2:13-25, 83
John 3:1-16, 86
John 3:17-36, 91
John 4:1-16, 96
John 4:17-38, 100
John 4:39-54, 106
John 5:1-23, 265
John 5:24-36, 270
John 5:37-47, 274
John 6:1-4, 300
John 6:3-14, 300
John 6:17a, 304
John 6:21, 304
John 6:41-59, 313
John 6:60-71, 319
John 7:1, 329
John 7:2-24, 374
John 7:25-39, 380
John 7:40-53, 385
John 8:1-21, 388
John 8:22-38, 394
John 8:40-59, 400

Index Help - *some Scripture verses indexed here may have page references to another Gospel used to represent identical verses with parallel usage, e.g. Matthew 20:24-28 will point to a page for Mark 10:41 because Mark represents the parallel content.*

John 8:56, 276
John 9:1-41, 408
John 10:1-21, 416
John 10:22-42, 441
John 11:1-54, 481
John 11:55-57, 506
John 12:1-11, 506
John 12:12-19, 513
John 12:20-26, 520
John 12:27-36, 524
John 12:37-50, 588
John 13:1-20, 593
John 13:21-22, 598
John 13:22-35, 446
John 13:23-30, 598
John 13:31-36, 603
John 13:38, 603
John 14:1-15, 611
John 14:15-31, 616
John 15:1-26, 626
John 16:1-33, 634
John 17:1-12, 642
John 17:13-26, 647
John 18:1-12, 653
John 18:12-16, 662
John 18:18, 662
John 18:26, 662
John 18:28-38, 671
John 18:39-40, 676
John 19:1-15, 676
John 19:16-24, 685
John 19:25-30, 692
John 19:31-42, 702
John 20:1, 702
John 20:18, 715
John 20:20-29, 721
John 20:21-25, 737
John 20:2-17, 709
John 20:30-31, 737
John 21:1-24, 721

John the Baptist
  and Elijah, 71, 348
  and Herod Antipas, 295
  arrested by Antipas, 112
  baptism of Jesus, 63
  baptism with the Holy Spirit, 61
  beheading by Herod, 295
  behold the Lamb of God, 73
  birth of, 16, 26
  commencement of ministry, 56
  conflict with Jewish authorities, 58
  his message, 11, 62, 70
  inquiry about Jesus, 187
  lesser than Jesus, 94
  seeking truth about Jesus, 188
  tribute by Jesus, 187

Index Help - *some Scripture verses indexed here may have page references to another Gospel used to represent identical verses with parallel usage, e.g. Matthew 20:24-28 will point to a page for Mark 10:41 because Mark represents the parallel content.*

John, call of, 112
John, selected to live longest, 721
John's disciples and Jesus, 73
Joseph of Arimathea, 702
Joseph, annunciation of the angel, 31
Joseph, Mary's pregnancy, 29
Joseph, return from Egypt, 50
Joseph, return to Bethlehem, 35
Judas Iscariot, as disciple, 137
Judas, as betrayer, 593
Judas, betrays Jesus with a kiss, 653
Judas, chosen as betrayer, 319
Judas, concern for Jesus anointing, 506
Judas, fate of (Acts), field of blood, 737
Judas, leaves the supper, 598
Judas, paid thirty pieces of silver, 663
Judas, Satan enters, 582
Judas, thirty pieces of silver, 582

L

Law, applies more strictly in Jesus, 153, 154
Law, Jesus' teaching on, 152
Lazarus, Pharisees desire to kill him, 507
Leaven of the Pharisees, 215
Levi, called as disciple, 124
Lord's prayer, 160, 435

Luke 1:1-4, 13
Luke 1:5-25, 16
Luke 1:26-38, 19
Luke 1:39-56, 23
Luke 1:57-80, 26
Luke 2:1-7, 33
Luke 2:8-20, 36
Luke 2:21-35, 39
Luke 2:36-38, 43
Luke 2:40-52, 51
Luke 3:1-6, 55
Luke 3:8, 55
Luke 3:9-18, 59
Luke 3:19,20, 112
Luke 3:23, 13
Luke 3:23, 62
Luke 4:1-13, 66
Luke 4:5-7, 66
Luke 4:14-30, 106
Luke 4:14-20, 106
Luke 4:31-41, 116
Luke 4:44, 120
Luke 5:1-11, 112
Luke 5:12-26, 120
Luke 5:17, 120
Luke 5:27-39, 124
Luke 6:1-11, 129
Luke 6:12-19, 134
Luke 6:20-23, 138, 141

Index Help - *some Scripture verses indexed here may have page references to another Gospel used to represent identical verses with parallel usage, e.g. Matthew 20:24-28 will point to a page for Mark 10:41 because Mark represents the parallel content.*

Luke 6:24-29, 145
Luke 6:30-36, 145
Luke 6:37-42, 175
Luke 7:1-9, 184
Luke 7:10, 184
Luke 7:11-28, 187
Luke 7:29-30, 187
Luke 7:31-50, 192
Luke 8:1-3, 196
Luke 8:4-15, 236
Luke 8:16-18, 241
Luke 8:19-21, 205
Luke 8:22-25, 250
Luke 8:26-39, 254
Luke 8:40-56, 258
Luke 9:1-5, 279
Luke 9:6-9, 295
Luke 9:10-17, 300
Luke 9:18-22, 338
Luke 9:23-27, 343
Luke 9:28-36, 348
Luke 9:37-45, 352
Luke 9:47-48, 358
Luke 9:49-50, 365
Luke 9:51-56, 421
Luke 9:60-62, 250
Luke 10:1-24, 425
Luke 10:25-37, 431
Luke 10:38-42, 435
Luke 11:1-13, 435
Luke 11:14-23, 196
Luke 11:27-28, 205
Luke 11:29-32, 200
Luke 11:33-36, 205
Luke 11:37-54, 209
Luke 12:1-8, 215
Luke 12:8-23, 219
Luke 12:24-40, 222
Luke 12:25, 173
Luke 12:41-59, 227
Luke 13:1-17, 232
Luke 13:18-21, 241
Luke 14:1-33, 452
Luke 14:33-35, 458
Luke 15:1-32, 458
Luke 16:1-31, 463
Luke 17:1, 361
Luke 17:2-3, 358
Luke 17:3,4, 365
Luke 17:5-6, 352
Luke 17:7-10, 361
Luke 17:11-19, 421
Luke 17:20-37, 471
Luke 18:1-14, 476
Luke 18:15-30, 490
Luke 18:31-34, 498
Luke 18:35-43, 503

Index Help - *some Scripture verses indexed here may have page references to another Gospel used to represent identical verses with parallel usage, e.g. Matthew 20:24-28 will point to a page for Mark 10:41 because Mark represents the parallel content.*

Luke 19:1-10, 503
Luke 19:11-28, 506
Luke 19:29-44, 513
Luke 19:45-48, 520
Luke 20:1-8, 524
Luke 20:9-19, 532
Luke 20:20-26, 532
Luke 20:27-28, 539
Luke 20:39,40, 539
Luke 20:41-47, 544
Luke 21: 5-24, 557
Luke 21:1-4, 551
Luke 22:7-13, 588
Luke 21:25-28, 569
Luke 21:25-33, 564
Luke 21:34-36, 574, 578
Luke 21:37-38, 588
Luke 22:1-6, 582
Luke 22:14-20, 593
Luke 22:21-40, 603
Luke 22:22, 598
Luke 22:35-38, 616
Luke 22:40-53, 653
Luke 22:54-58, 662
Luke 22:61-68, 662
Luke 22:71, 662
Luke 24:1-3, 702
Luke 23:1-7, 671
Luke 23:5-7, 671
Luke 23:5-18, 676
Luke 23:18-19, 676
Luke 23:20-23, 676
Luke 23:23-34, 685
Luke 23:35-37, 692
Luke 23:39-45, 692
Luke 23:46-49, 692
Luke 23:50-54, 702
Luke 23:55-56, 702
Luke 24:4-12, 709
Luke 24:9-35, 715
Luke 24:36-44, 721
Luke 24:45-53, 737

M

Magdalene, Mary, 196
Magi, and Jesus birth, 45
Magi, legendary names, 45
Magnificat of Mary, 24
Mammon, meaning of, 171

Mark 1:2-6, 55
Mark 1:7,8, 59
Mark 1:9-11, 62
Mark 1:12-13, 66
Mark 1:14-20, 112

Index Help - *some Scripture verses indexed here may have page references to another Gospel used to represent identical verses with parallel usage, e.g. Matthew 20:24-28 will point to a page for Mark 10:41 because Mark represents the parallel content.*

Mark 1:21-38, 116
Mark 1:39-45, 120
Mark 2:2-12, 120
Mark 2:13-14, 124
Mark 2:15-22, 124
Mark 2:27, 129
Mark 3:3-19, 134
Mark 3:4, 129
Mark 3:5-6, 129
Mark 3:21, 200
Mark 3:28-30, 200
Mark 3:31-35, 205
Mark 4:1-20, 236
Mark 4:21-32, 241
Mark 4:35-41, 250
Mark 5:1-20, 254
Mark 5:21-43, 258
Mark 6:1-11, 279
Mark 6:12-16, 295
Mark 6:17-29, 295
Mark 6:30-31, 300
Mark 6:33-35,37, 300
Mark 6:45-52, 304
Mark 6:51, 308
Mark 7:1-13, 323
Mark 7:16, 323
Mark 7:19, 323
Mark 7:24, 329
Mark 8:1-13, 332
Mark 8:13, 14, 332
Mark 8:17-21, 332
Mark 8:22-26, 332
Mark 8:27-33, 338
Mark 8:34-38, 343
Mark 9:1, 343
Mark 9:2-13, 348
Mark 9:14-28, 352
Mark 9:30-32, 352
Mark 9:33-42, 358
Mark 9:38-41, 365
Mark 9:43-50, 361
Mark 10:2-27, 490
Mark 10:32-34, 498
Mark 10:35-40, 498
Mark 10:35-45, 498
Mark 10:46-52, 503
Mark 11:1-11, 513
Mark 11:12-18, 520
Mark 11:19-33, 524
Mark 12:1-17, 532
Mark 12:18-27, 539
Mark 12:28-34, 539
Mark 12:35-40, 544
Mark 12:41-44, 551
Mark 13:1-13, 557
Mark 13:5-31, 569
Mark 13:14-31, 564

Index Help - *some Scripture verses indexed here may have page references to another Gospel used to represent identical verses with parallel usage, e.g. Matthew 20:24-28 will point to a page for Mark 10:41 because Mark represents the parallel content.*

Mark 13:32-37, 574
Mark 13:34-47, 578
Mark 14:1,2, 582
Mark 14:3-9, 506
Mark 14:10,11, 582
Mark 14:12-16, 588
Mark 14:19-21, 598
Mark 14:22-25, 603
Mark 14:27-31, 626
Mark 14:32-52, 653
Mark 14:60-64, 662
Mark 15:1-5, 671
Mark 15:6-19, 676
Mark 15:15, 685
Mark 15:20-21, 685
Mark 15:21-28, 685
Mark 15:29-32, 692
Mark 15:33-38, 692
Mark 15:39-41, 692
Mark 15:42-47, 702
Mark 16:1-4, 702
Mark 16:5-9, 709
Mark 16:10-13, 715
Mark 16:14, 721
Mark 16:15-20, 737

Mark, questionable ending, 737
Mark, these signs shall accompany, 737
Mary and Martha of Bethany, 435
Mary anoints the feet of Jesus, 506
Mary Magdalene, Jesus at the tomb, 709
Mary, annunciation to, 19
Mary, betrothal and pregnancy, 29
Mary, visit to Elizabeth, 23

Matthew 1:18-25, 29
Matthew 1:24-25, 30
Matthew 2:1-23, 43
Matthew 2:13-16, 48
Matthew 2:19-23, 51
Matthew 3:1-3, 55
Matthew 3:2, 62
Matthew 3:4-6, 55
Matthew 3:7, 55
Matthew 3:9-12, 59
Matthew 3:13-17, 62
Matthew 4:2-7, 66
Matthew 4:10, 66
Matthew 4:11, 66
Matthew 4:12-22, 112
Matthew 4:23-25, 120
Matthew 5:1-8, 138
Matthew 5:9-12, 141
Matthew 5:13-20, 150
Matthew 5:21-48, 154
Matthew 5:38-39, 145
Matthew 5:41, 145

Index Help - *some Scripture verses indexed here may have page references to another Gospel used to represent identical verses with parallel usage, e.g. Matthew 20:24-28 will point to a page for Mark 10:41 because Mark represents the parallel content.*

Matthew 6:1-13, 160
Matthew 6:14-23, 166
Matthew 6:24-34, 170
Matthew 7:1-6, 175
Matthew 7:7-29, 179
Matthew 8:1-14, 120
Matthew 8:14-17, 116
Matthew 8:18-34, 250
Matthew 8:28-34, 254
Matthew 8:5-13, 184
Matthew 9:11-17, 124
Matthew 9:1-8, 120
Matthew 9:18-26, 258
Matthew 9:27-34, 262
Matthew 9:35-38, 279
Matthew 10:1-4, 279
Matthew 10:5-14, 279
Matthew 10:16-23, 285
Matthew 10:24-39, 289
Matthew 10:40-42, 295
Matthew 11:1, 295
Matthew 11:12-15, 187
Matthew 11:16-19, 192
Matthew 11:20-27, 425
Matthew 11:28-30, 431
Matthew 12:1-8, 129
Matthew 12:9-10, 129
Matthew 12:11-12, 129
Matthew 12:15-21, 129
Matthew 12:22-30, 196
Matthew 12:31-32, 200
Matthew 12:33-37, 200
Matthew 12:38-42, 200
Matthew 12:43-45, 205
Matthew 12:46-50, 205
Matthew 13:1-23, 236
Matthew 13:24-43, 241
Matthew 13:44-52, 241
Matthew 13:53-58, 279
Matthew 14:1-2, 295
Matthew 14:12-21, 300
Matthew 14:22-27, 304
Matthew 14:28-31,33, 304
Matthew 15:1-9, 323
Matthew 15:10-20, 323
Matthew 15:21, 329
Matthew 15:22-28, 329
Matthew 15:29-31, 332
Matthew 16:1-4, 332
Matthew 16:6-7, 332
Matthew 16:13-23, 338
Matthew 16:24-28, 343
Matthew 17:1-13, 348
Matthew 17:20-27, 352
Matthew 18:1-6, 10-14, 358
Matthew 18:21,22, 365
Matthew 18:23-35, 371

Index Help - *some Scripture verses indexed here may have page references to another Gospel used to represent identical verses with parallel usage, e.g. Matthew 20:24-28 will point to a page for Mark 10:41 because Mark represents the parallel content.*

Matthew 18:7,12-14, 361
Matthew 19:3-12, 490
Matthew 19:13-15, 490
Matthew 19:16-26, 490
Matthew 19:27-30, 490
Matthew 20:1-16, 476
Matthew 20:17-19, 498
Matthew 20:20-23, 498
Matthew 20:24-28, 498
Matthew 20:29-34, 503
Matthew 21:1-11, 513
Matthew 21:12-19, 520
Matthew 21:17, 513
Matthew 21:20-32, 524
Matthew 21:42-46, 532
Matthew 22:1-22, 532
Matthew 22:23-40, 539
Matthew 22:41-46, 544
Matthew 23:1-22, 544
Matthew 23:23-39, 551
Matthew 24:1-21, 557
Matthew 24:15-21, 564
Matthew 24:22-35, 569
Matthew 24:36-51, 574
Matthew 24:45-51, 578
Matthew 25:1-13, 574, 578
Matthew 25:14-46, 582
Matthew 26:1-5, 582
Matthew 26:3, 506
Matthew 26:6-13, 506
Matthew 26:15, 582
Matthew 26:17-19, 588
Matthew 26:22, 598
Matthew 26:23-25, 598
Matthew 26:26-29, 603
Matthew 26:30, 616
Matthew 26:31-35, 626
Matthew 26:34-35, 603
Matthew 26:36-56, 653
Matthew 26:69-74, 662
Matthew 27:1-10, 662
Matthew 27:2, 671
Matthew 27:11-14, 671
Matthew 27:15-30, 676
Matthew 27:26, 685
Matthew 27:31-32, 685
Matthew 27:33-34, 685
Matthew 27:35-38, 685
Matthew 27:38, 702
Matthew 27:39-56, 692
Matthew 27:57-66, 702
Matthew 28:1-4, 702
Matthew 28:5-7, 709
Matthew 28:9-15, 715
Matthew 28:16-20, 732

Index Help - *some Scripture verses indexed here may have page references to another Gospel used to represent identical verses with parallel usage, e.g. Matthew 20:24-28 will point to a page for Mark 10:41 because Mark represents the parallel content.*

Matthew, called as disciple, 124
Miracles
   blind Bartemaeus, 503
   casting out demons, 262, 352
   coin in the fish's mouth, 352
   demon possessed man, 196
   draught of fish, 721
   feeding of the five thousand, 300
   feeding the four thousand, 332
   Gerasene demoniac, 254
   healing the blind, 332
   healing the daughter of Jairus, 258
   healing the ten lepers, 421
   healing the two blind men, 262
   healing the woman stricken by a spirit, 232
   heals on the Sabbath, 129
   heals the blind in the Temple, 520
   man born blind, 408
   only by prayer and fasting, 352
   pool of Bethesda, 265
   raising Lazarus, 481
   testify that he is the Christ, 380
   walking on the sea, 304
   woman bleeding for twelve years, 258
Miraculous draught of fishes, 112
Money, value of the mina, 506
Money, value of the talent, 371, 506
Mount of Olives, teaching at, 138
Mount of Olives, woes (exhortations), 145

N

Nathanael, called as disciple, 78
Nazarene, 52
Nicodemus, and Jesus, 86

O

Olivet discourse, 557
Olivet Discourse, 138

P

Parables
   a house built on sand, 179
   dishonest manager, 463
   fig tree, 232, 569
   murderous tenants, 532
   mustard seed, 241
   nobleman who received a kingdom, 506
   Pharisee and the tax collector, 476
   prodigal son, 458
   rich man and Lazarus, 463
   sower, 236
   talents, 582
   tares and wheat, 241
   ten minas, 506

Index Help - *some Scripture verses indexed here may have page references to another Gospel used to represent identical verses with parallel usage, e.g. Matthew 20:24-28 will point to a page for Mark 10:41 because Mark represents the parallel content.*

Parables *(cont.)*
   ten virgins, 578
   vineyard, 476, 532
   wedding banquet, 532
   widow, persistent, 476
   wineskins, 127
Passover, explained, 52
Passover, Jesus' last, 513
Peter
   and Catholics, 75
   called as disciple, 112
   great confession, 338
   names of, 75
   petros and rock, 75
   primacy of, 75
   walks on the water, 304
Peter, at tomb of Jesus, 709
Peter, denies Jesus, 662
Peter, his address after the Ascension, 737
Peter, his commission to care for the flock, 721
Peter, I will lay down my life for you, 603
Peter, manner of death foretold, 722
Peter, questions John selected to remain, 721
Peter, reconciles with Jesus, 721
Peter, Satan desires to sift him life wheat, 603
Peter, strikes off the ear of Malchus, 653
Peter's mother, healed, 118
Petros, issue in Peter's name, 75
Pharisees
   ask for a sign, 332
   by what authority, 524
   conflict with Jesus, 400
   early attempts to seize him, 385
   entertaining Jesus, 209
   guilty of the blood of the righteous, 551
   invite Jesus to dine, 192
   origin of, 86
   their plans after the raising of Lazarus, 482
   tithing mint and cummin, 551
Pharisees, fearful of entering the Praetorium, 671
Philip, brings Greeks to meet Jesus, 520
Philip, called as disciple, 76
Pilate, became friends with Herod, 676
Pilate, finds no fault in Jesus, 671
Pilate, governor of Judea, 55
Pilate, offers Barabbas, 676
Pilate, sends Jesus to Herod, 671
Pilate, what is truth, 671
Pilate, you are no friend of Caesar, 676
Pontius Pilate, harrassment of Jews, 232

Index Help - *some Scripture verses indexed here may have page references to another Gospel used to represent identical verses with parallel usage, e.g. Matthew 20:24-28 will point to a page for Mark 10:41 because Mark represents the parallel content.*

Q

Quirinius, census issues, 34

R

Rachel, Ramah, slaughter, 48
Ramah, weeping, 48
Resurrection, angels at tomb, 709
Resurrection, conspiracy with the guards and priests, 715
Resurrection, disciples at tomb, 715
Resurrection, events on the road to Emmaus, 715
Resurrection, Jesus appears after, 715
Resurrection, Jesus at the Sea of Tiberius, 721
Resurrection, Jesus eats food after being raised, 721
Resurrection. Jesus appears to his disciples, 721
Roman military service, 185

S

Sabbath, gleaning on, 129
Sabbath, healing on, 129
Sabbath, made for man, 131
Sadducees, origin of, 87
Salome, asks for the head of John, 295
Samaritan woman, and Jesus, 96
Samaritan woman, testimony of, 106
Satan , Jesus saw him fall from Heaven, 425
Satan, and Jesus, 66
Shepherds, annunciation to, 36
Shepherds, issues with December, 36
Simeon, and Jesus Birth, 41
Similitudes, 138
Simon of Cyrene, 685
Slavery, benefits and abuses, 185
Sychar, woman and Jesus, 96
Sychar, woman, testimony of, 106

T

Teaching
    a house built on sand, 183
    a little while and you see me no more, 634
    about demons, 196
    accounting at the judgment, 200
    acquiring eternal life, 270
    acts with true rewards, 160
    against worry, 219
    as in the days of Noah, 574
    ask anything in my name and I will do it, 611, 634
    authority, 186
    barrenness of the fig tree, 520
    be not a stumbling block to faith, 361
    become great as the servant of all, 498
    become sons of the light, 524
    blasphemy of the Holy Spirit, 200, 219

Index Help - *some Scripture verses indexed here may have page references to another Gospel used to represent identical verses with parallel usage, e.g. Matthew 20:24-28 will point to a page for Mark 10:41 because Mark represents the parallel content.*

Teaching *(cont.)*
   bless the poor, 452
   blind guides, 323
   bread out of heaven, 308
   brother will betray brother, 285
   charity and giving, 148
   charity and possessions, 222
   children – to such belongs the kingdom, 490
   children and their angels, 358
   Christ as David's son, 544
   Christ's coming, peace and division, 227
   come to save the lost, 358
   coming of the Son of Man – end times, 471
   compassion vs. Sabbath law, 323
   cost of discipleship, 250
   demonic oppression, 232
   demons, demon possession, 205
   deny yourself and follow me, 343
   depart from me, I do not know you, 446
   destruction of the temple, 557
   disciple not above his teacher, 289
   disciples shall judge the twelve tribes of Israel, 603
   do not hide our light, 205
   do not judge by appearance, 374
   doing the will of God is the one who obeys, 524
   easier for a camel, 491
   eating the flesh of the Son of Man, 313
   end times - be alert at all times, 574
   end times, abomination of desolation, 564
   end times, false Christs, 569
   eunuchs for the kingdom's sake, 490
   evil of asking a sign, 200
   example from Jonah, 200
   expect persecution from the Jews, 634
   extra mile, 148
   eye is the lamp of the body, 169, 205
   eyes that do not see, 332
   faithful and wise servant, 578
   faithful in little is faithful in much, 463
   false prophets, 179
   Father and the Son, 265
   fear God more than men, 215
   fishers of men, 114
   for I was hungry and you have me to eat, 582
   forgiveness and mercy, 371
   forgiveness, proper fasting, 166
   forsake all to follow Him, 452
   fulfillment of the Law, 152
   generosity, 179
   God does not forgive those who forgive not, 524
   Golden Rule, 149, 179
   good and bad fruit, 200
   good and slothful servants, 227
   good Samaritan, 431
   good servant, 222
   great tribulation, 564, 569
   greatest commandment, 539

Index Help - *some Scripture verses indexed here may have page references to another Gospel used to represent identical verses with parallel usage, e.g. Matthew 20:24-28 will point to a page for Mark 10:41 because Mark represents the parallel content.*

Teaching *(cont.)*
  greatest is to be the servant of all, 358
  hairs on your head are numbered, 289
  hating father and mother to follow Him, 452
  hatred against Christ's followers, 285
  hatred of the world for the truth, 374
  He is the God of the living, 539
  he who confesses, I will confess, 289
  he who endures to the end will be saved, 288
  he who hates his life will keep it, 520
  he who loses his life will find it, 289
  he who receives a prophet, a righteous man, 295
  He with more is given more, 241
  how God gives, 179
  how many times shall we forgive, 365
  how the kingdom shall come, 471
  I am the Bread of Life, 313
  I am the light of the world, 388
  I am the Resurrection and the life, 481
  I have overcome the world, 634
  I prepare a place for you, 611
  I will draw all men unto myself, 524
  if I be lifted up from the earth, 524
  If you love me keep my commandments – (a listing), 616
  insecurity of riches, 219
  instruction in witnessing, 289
  instructions on going into cities, 425
  Jerusalem trodden down by the Gentiles, 557
  judgment at the end of the age, 582
  judgment of eternal fire, 582
  kingdom entered forcefully, 463
  Kingdom is like a mustard seed, 241
  Kingdom like a feast and invited guests, 452
  Kingdom of God, 114
  Kingdom of God is within you, 471
  Kingdom taken from Israel, 532
  last shall be first, 476
  Law, 152
  law of the Sabbath, 323
  Law, the smallest detail upheld, 463
  lead us not into temptation, 164
  leaven of the Pharisees, 215
  lest they hear and I should heal them, 236
  let not your heart be troubled, 611
  light and lampstand, 241
  lilies of the field, 172, 222
  Lord's prayer, 160, 435
  losing one's life to save it, 343
  lost coin, 458
  lost sheep, 458
  love neighbor as oneself, 539
  love your enemies, 146
  making vows, 154
  man who wished to bury his father, 250
  marriage – shall be one flesh, 490
  marriage in Heaven, 539
  meaning of Mammon, 171

Index Help - *some Scripture verses indexed here may have page references to another Gospel used to represent identical verses with parallel usage, e.g. Matthew 20:24-28 will point to a page for Mark 10:41 because Mark represents the parallel content.*

Teaching *(cont.)*
   millstone, cast into the sea, 358
   misuse of God's power, 421
   more on his departure, 634
   more the Comforter, what He will teach them, 634
   more valuable than sparrows, 289
   murder, adultery, lying, divorce, 154
   narrow is the way, 446
   need for a sword, 616
   no one knows the day or hour, 574
   not as the scribes, 117
   not one jot or tittle shall pass from the Law, 463
   on adultery, 490
   on authority as disciples minister, 603
   on charity and proper giving, 176
   on condemnation and mercy, 388
   on Corban, 323
   on defilement, 323
   on divorce, 490
   on Hell, 446
   on humility, 452, 476
   on hyprocrisy, 209
   on Isaiah 6:10, 236
   on judging, 227
   on paying taxes to Caesar, 532
   on prayer, 162
   on retaliation, 147
   on seeking praise, 146
   on the Holy Spirit, purpose and role, 616
   on the judgment, 290
   on this rock, 338
   on vows, swearing, 158
   on worry, 172
   one taken, the other left, 471
   one will be taken, the other left, 574
   other food, 104
   parable of tares and wheat, 241
   parable of the debt of 10,000 talents, 371
   parable of the fig tree, 232
   parable of the sower, 236
   pearl of great price, 241
   pearls before swine, 175
   persistence a sign of faith, 476
   Pharisees - blind guides, 544
   Pharisees – do what they teach, not what they do, 544
   Philip – he who has seen me has seen the Father, 611
   power to bind and loose, 365
   predestination, vessels of wrath, 236
   promise of a Comforter, 616
   promise of his coming again, 616
   proper fasting, 167
   receive this child, 358
   regarding judging, 175
   render to Ceasar, 532
   requirements to inherit the kingdom, of God, 491
   response to the ungrateful, 150
   Resurrection, question of, 539

Index Help - *some Scripture verses indexed here may have page references to another Gospel used to represent identical verses with parallel usage, e.g. Matthew 20:24-28 will point to a page for Mark 10:41 because Mark represents the parallel content.*

Teaching *(cont.)*
    you cannot serve God and mammon (wealth), 463
    you did it unto the least of these, 582
    works and faith, 288
Temple, Herod's and Zerubbabel's, 85
Temptation, of Jesus, 66
Thomas, doubts the Lord's rising, 721
Thomas, questions Jesus about the where he is going and the way, 611
Tiberius Caesar, fifteenth year of, 55
Tiberius Caesar, Roman emperor, 56
Times of the Gentiles, 557
Tomb of Jesus, angels at, 702, 709
Tomb of Jesus, differing accounts, 709
Tomb of Jesus, Jesus reveals himself to Mary, 709
Tomb of Jesus, linen wrappings, 709
Tomb of Jesus, Peter at, 709
Tomb of Jesus, stone rolled away, 702
Transfiguration, 348
Trial of Jesus, false witnesses, 662
Tribulation, the Great, 564, 569
Tyre and Sidon, 329

U

Unleaved Bread, Feast of, 52

W

Widow of Nain, healing, 187
Wineskins, Jesus' teaching, 127
Woman caught in adultery, 388

Z

Zaccheus, 503
Zacharias, 16
Zacharias, speaks again, 26

Index Help - *some Scripture verses indexed here may have page references to another Gospel used to represent identical verses with parallel usage, e.g. Matthew 20:24-28 will point to a page for Mark 10:41 because Mark represents the parallel content.*

www.ingramcontent.com/pod-product-compliance
Lightning Source LLC
Chambersburg PA
CBHW081413160426
42811CB00096B/826